THE FUNDAMENTALS
OF
PSYCHOANALYTIC TECHNIQUE

photograph by Filiberto Mugnani

R. Horacio Etchegoyen

THE FUNDAMENTALS
OF
PSYCHOANALYTIC TECHNIQUE

REVISED EDITION

R. Horacio Etchegoyen

Foreword by
Robert S. Wallerstein

with a chapter by
Gregorio Klimovsky

Translated by
Patricia Pitchon

London
KARNAC BOOKS

First published in Great Britain in 1991 by
H. Karnac (Books) Ltd.
6 Pembroke Buildings
London NW10 6RE

This revised edition published in 1999
Paperback edition 2005

British Library Cataloguing in Publication Data
Etchegoyen, Horacio
      Fundamentals of psychoanalytic technique
           1. Psychoanalysis
           I. Title
    150.195
    ISBN 1 85575 455 X

10 9 8 7 6 5 4 3 2 1

Edited, designed, and produced by Communication Crafts

Printed in Great Britain by Hobbs the Printers Limited, Southampton, Hampshire

www.karnacbooks.com

To Élida

CONTENTS

PART TWO
On transference and countertransference

PART THREE
On interpretation and other instruments

PART FOUR
On the nature of the psychoanalytic process

Partly for its merits and to a great extent through the workings of Lady Luck—*grela* in the tango parlance of that art's great Argentinian exponent Discépolo—my book was well received. Analysts praised it as compulsory reading, and some actually read it.

In my view, much of its popularity had to do with the generous notices by Nasim Yampey in *Revista de Psicoanálisis* [1986] and *Acta Psiquiátrica y Psicológica de América Latina* [1987], León Grinberg in the *International Journal of Psycho-Analysis* [1988], whose authoritative voice is heard throughout the psychoanalytic world, Terencio Gioia in *Psicoanálisis* [1987], Jorge Olagaray in the Mendoza daily *Los Andes* [1987], Ángel Costantino in *Correo de la Salud Mental* [1987], Max Hernández in Peru, Jaime P. Nos in the *Journal of the American Psychoanalytic Association* [1990], Joan Coderch in *Revista Catalana de Psicoanálisis* [1988], Jorge Ahumada in *Clarín* [1987], Eduardo Müller in *La Nación* [1987], Omar Lazarte in the Mendoza daily *Hoy* [1988], as well as some others I no longer recall. *La Razón* reproduced one of the chapters on the therapeutic alliance in two successive instalments in 1986. Klaus P. Fink, when he was in London, wrote a careful review for the Book Club of 1992, pointing out the enthusiastic interest that reading the book awoke in him.

Fresh comments ensued when the Karnac version appeared in 1991. Otto Kernberg penned a thorough and attentive study, again for the *Journal of the American Psychoanalytic Association* [1995]. The indefatigable Joseph Reppen presented a long and detailed review, in *Volume 5* [1994] of *Psychoanalytic Books*, ably written by Robert Caper. Volume 10 of *Melanie Klein and Object Relations*, produced under the skilled direction of Otto

Weininger, contained a review by Edward Emery [1992] entitled "Horacio Etchegoyen and the historical eye", by which I was greatly moved. When I read the notice by Richard D. Chessick in the November 1992 issue of the *American Journal of Psychiatry*, my gratification at his praise was tempered by the food for thought afforded by his criticisms. The *International Journal of Psycho-Analysis* printed a further review in 1993, written by Patrick Casement, a celebrated analyst from the Independent Group.

* * *

I fondly recall the dauntless efforts of the late Mario Leff on the first Amorrortu edition, produced under the wise direction of my namesake Horacio and the learned and tireless José Luis Etcheverry. At almost the same time, in 1987, thanks to the enthusiasm of my disciple Newton Aronis, the first Portuguese edition was published by Artes Médicas, whose director, Henrique Kiperman, was an admirer of the book from the beginning. The Brazilian edition includes an intelligent "Apresentação" by David Zimmerman, which truly enhances it.

The enthusiasm and erudition of Roberto Speziale-Bagliacca and the advice of Jorge Canestri led to the publication in 1990 by Astrolabio in Rome of *I Fondamenti della Tecnica Psicoanalitica*, under the patient and able guidance of Francesco Gana. Roberto's "Prefazione" salutes the book as a classic—no mean prophecy coming from a man thoroughly versed in the psychoanalytic literature. The Italian edition contains a few additions (paragraphs, not chapters) that complement certain topics and bring them up to date. This applies in particular to part 2, "Transference and counter-transference", in which I include ideas from Kohut, Kernberg, Joseph, and Anne-Marie Sandler, and Meltzer's later work, as well as some remarks on empathy and a new section on transference addiction. I was also able to accommodate in the first Astrolabio edition some material on the ideas of Joyce McDougall and on the excellent book by Thomä and Kächele, which deserve more attention than I had hitherto been able to devote to them.

These additions were also included in the English edition, which, after a long period of gestation, finally saw the light of day in 1991 and contained an addendum to chapter 11, "Signifier, repetition and transference", which does not appear in the Italian edition. Harry Karnac thought from the beginning that the book ought to be translated into English, and Cesare Sacerdoti made this enterprise possible with a patience and skill in no way inferior to those of Amorrortu, Kiperman, and Gana. Sacerdoti felt from the outset that he was publishing a work that was destined to last— and let us hope that he is right. Robert S. Wallerstein's generous and considered Foreword surely contributed to the book's success among the English-speaking psychoanalysts of the Old and New Worlds. Patricia Pitchon's careful translation, revised by Christine Trollope, yielded a perfectly satisfactory text, which was elevated by Klara King to a high standard of excellence by virtue of her profound knowledge of English. The additions for the new edition were translated by Slotkin with his known expertise. The work was further enriched by Cesare's zeal in personally undertaking the meticulous revision of every single item in nearly forty pages of references and an author and subject index amounting to another twenty. Sacerdoti's edition has since 1991 been the most complete of all.

* * *

The second Amorrortu edition includes, of course, the new sections from the Italian and English editions, while some minor amendments, which will also be made to the English, Italian, and Portuguese versions and will feature in the first German and Romanian editions, are also being introduced. I should have liked to develop certain topics at greater length, but I have been able to do this only to a limited extent. The commentary on Lorenzer's interpretative hermeneutics could have been longer and more penetrating; I have my doubts about hermeneutics in general and about the narrativistic stream that has been gaining currency in the last few years. Using Margaret Little's book, I have been able to discuss Winnicott's technical ideas more amply. I have added a few comments on Joan Coderch's recent volume and taken account of the work of Fabio Herrmann and Bernardo Álvarez Lince. These three authors have made a profound study of psychoanalytic interpretation, and their contributions are of genuine interest.

By the time the second Amorrortu and Karnac editions are published, the German and Romanian translations will no doubt be ready. Whereas I am very proud of the former because German is the psychoanalytic language par excellence, the latter moves me deeply because it exemplifies what can be achieved by the enthusiasm of a small psychoanalytic community seeking sources of information. The second Artes Médicas edition will most probably make its appearance in 1999.

The production of the second edition, which was in no way a simple matter, would not have been possible without the tenacious and intelligent labours of my secretary, Estela Korol.

* * *

From the beginning, the book was intended to serve as a comprehensive manual of technique, but not an exhaustive one. With all its shortcomings and merits, it is fine as it is. If I had more time, I would try to abridge it— but that would be tantamount to writing it anew.

I wish to thank everyone involved.

Buenos Aires, 28 August 1998

PREFACE

It is not easy to write a book, and even less so, I can assure you, to write a book on psychoanalytic technique. When I was preparing this one I realized why there are many articles on technique but few books.

Freud published his immortal works at the beginning of the 1910s, but he never got round to writing the text he had promised so often. *The Interpretation of Dreams* speaks at length of technique, and so do the works of Anna Freud and Melanie Klein on the psychoanalysis of children, but no one considers them—and with reason—books on technique. Nor are *Character Analysis* and *The Ego and the Mechanisms of Defence*, despite the fact that they had a decisive influence on the practice of psychoanalysis, similar to that ten years earlier of *The Development of Psycho-Analysis*, in which Ferenczi and Rank spoke out militantly for a practice in which emotion and libido would have their proper place.

The only book by Smith Ely Jelliffe, *The Technique of Psycho-Analysis*, published in 1914, is undoubtedly the first book on this material; but it has been forgotten, and no one takes any account of it. I read it in 1949 (more than four decades ago!), and recently I went through it again, with the planned intention of quoting from it, but I could not work out how to do this.

With the exception of this abandoned monument, the first technical book is Edward Glover's *The Technique of Psycho-Analysis*, which was published in 1928. Glover gave a course of six lectures on the subject at the Institute of Psycho-Analysis in London, which appeared in the *International Journal of Psycho-Analysis* for 1927 and 1928 and immediately afterwards as a book. It is true that earlier, in 1922, David Forsyth had published *The Technique of Psychoanalysis*, but this did not have any greater impact. When I was finally able to read it, I found it well-written and well-thought-out, and very good for its time and place.

A course similar to that of Glover was given by Ella Freeman Sharpe for candidates of the British Society in February and March of 1930, published in the *International Journal of Psycho-Analysis* (Volumes 11 and 12) under the title "The Technique of Psychoanalysis". These excellent lectures were later included in her *Collected Papers*.

In 1941 Fenichel published his *Problems of Psychoanalytic Technique*, which developed and expanded his valuable essay of 1935, in which he had acknowledged the contributions of Reich and Reik, subjecting them to searching criticism. Fenichel's is a true technical book, as it is clearly located in that field, tackles a wide spectrum of questions and registers the first problems of his era.

Five years later there appeared Sandor Lorand's *Technique of Psychoanalytic Therapy* (1946), a clear, concise work, which briefly discusses general problems and is especially concerned with technique in different psychopathological conditions.

After a long interval, in 1955 Glover decided to publish a second edition of his work, which keeps to the general lines of the first one but is amplified and reconciled with the advances in Freud's structural theory. It can be said that this edition is Glover's technical book by antonomasia—a classic that, like that of Fenichel, has had a lasting influence on all scholars.

After Glover came Karl Menninger, with his *Theory of Psychoanalytic Technique* (1958), which lucidly studies the analytical process in the coordination of contract and regression.

Argentinian psychoanalysts contributed throughout the years with important technical articles, but with only one book, Heinrich Racker's *Estudios sobre técnica psicoanalítica*, which was published in Buenos Aires in 1960. Among other subjects, this work develops the author's original ideas on countertransference. More than thirty years after its publication, we can affirm today that the *Estudios* are a lasting contribution, and the years have shown the book's growing influence—not always recognized—on contemporary psychoanalytic thought. In their type of research, the studies do not form a technical book, a complete text; in spite of this, doubtless because of their excellence, they have been used as such in many psychoanalytic centres. (Recognizing the book's merits, Karl had invited Heinrich to the Menninger Clinic as Sloan Visiting Professor; but Racker declined the invitation because by that time the cancer that eventually led to his death had been diagnosed.) The valuable work *Lenguaje y técnica psicoanalítica* (1976a) by our well-remembered David Liberman shows the author's original ideas, and especially his theory of styles, without being, or being considered, a technical book.

There was an interval of more than five years after the *Estudios* before the publication of *The Technique and Practice of Psychoanalysis* (1967) in which, with his well-known erudition, Ralph R. Greenson deals with a group of basic themes such as transference, resistance and the analytical process in the promising first volume. It is surely a pity that this endeavour stopped in mid-stream, since the great analyst from Los Angeles died before finishing it.

While Greenson, with this text, was becoming the authorized spokesman for ego psychology, in London there appeared *The Psychoanalytic Process*, in which Donald Meltzer put together in an original and disciplined way the thought of Melanie Klein and her school. Although this little masterpiece does not tackle all the problems of technique, it gives us important explanations about the development of the analytical process from the point of view of the positions theory and of projective identification.

Like the Argentinians, the French analysts have contributed important technical articles but few books. There is Sacha Nacht's *Guérir avec Freud* (1971), in which this influential analyst expounds his main ideas, without going so far as to write a treatise, nor intending to do so. Another contribution is Jacques Lacan's Seminar I, entitled *Les Écrits techniques de Freud*, presented in 1953 and 1954 and published in 1975, in which this original thinker brings forward a profound reflection on the concept of the ego. Taking the contrary view to Nacht, the leader of l'école freudien challenges Anna Freud's and Hartmann's conception of the ego and sets it against his own concept of the subject; but to discuss the technique of psychoanalysis was not at all his intention.

A concise manual dealing with the great majority of problems of technique is that of Sandler, Dare and Holder, *The Patient and the Analyst* (1973). It is polished and clear, based on a wide bibliography in which all psychoanalytic schools have their place; and it certainly reflects the personal opinions of Sandler, an outstanding pupil of Anna Freud, a forceful theoretician and an indefatigable reader. Shortly before the appearance of the Spanish edition of my book, Thomä and Kächele's *Lehrbuch der psychoanalytischen Therapie* was published in Germany. It is a comprehensive and timely book, which is similar to mine in its intentions but is based on different theoretical principles.

* * *

This survey of the few published texts was certainly intended to justify the appearance of this book; but I also mean it as an attempt to tackle, if not all, at least a large part of the problems of psychoanalytic technique, dealing with them thoroughly and impartially.

I propose to offer the reader a complete panorama of the problems as they exist at present, with the lines of theory from the past to the present and from the present to the future as we can imagine it now. In general, I am following a historical method of explaining the themes, watching how concepts rise and develop and how ideas come into focus and become specific, and also how they sometimes become vague and confused. Psychoanalytic knowledge does not always follow an ascending course, and it is not only the fruit of the genius of a few, but also of the efforts of many.

The more I read and re-read, the more I think and observe the analysand on my couch, the less I tend towards extreme and dichotomous positions and the more I avoid both complacent eclecticism and the uncompromising defence of scholastic positions. Finally, I have managed to convince myself that to defend ideas at all costs stems from ignorance rather than from enthusiasm, and as unfortunately I have the former in abundance and am not short of the latter, I use it to read more and reduce my shortcomings. I sometimes like to say that I am a fanatical Kleinian so that people will not get me wrong; but the truth is that Klein does not need anyone to defend her, nor does Anna Freud. When I read the polemical texts from the 1920s, I can identify with the two great pioneers and appreciate both their lofty thought and their human anxieties, without feeling any need to take sides.

Like most authors, I think the union of theory and technique is indissoluble in our discipline, so that no matter how involved we become in one, we pass to the other without realizing it. I have tried to show in every chapter in what way the two are linked, and in the same way I have done my best throughout the book to make people realize how the problems are grouped and how they influence each other. This has been simpler, I believe, because the book was written as such, and it was only exceptionally that any previous work formed an integral part of it.

* * *

Perhaps it is worth explaining briefly to the reader how this work took shape. From the beginning of my analytical career in the 1950s I felt attracted by technical problems. When anyone enjoys a task, he is interested in the way it should be done. I was lucky enough to have my training analysis with Racker, who in those years was forming the theory of countertransference, and I was analysed again after that with Meltzer, when he was writing *The Psychoanalytical Process*. I believe that these propitious circumstances strengthened my vague initial enthusiasm, as did also the hours of supervision with Betty Joseph, Money-Kyrle, Grinberg, Herbert Rosenfeld, Resnik, Hanna Segal, Marie Langer, Liberman, Esther Bick and Pichon Rivière over the years.

In 1970 I began to lecture on theory of technique to fourth-year students of the Argentinian Psychoanalytic Association; later I performed the same task for the Buenos Aires Psychoanalytic Association. I was lucky, because the students were always interested in my teaching, and as time went on, I learned with them and from them to discover the problems and face the difficulties. The Institute of Psychoanalytical Training of my Association understood this effort and gave more space to the subject, which now occupies a seminar in the final two years. The generous stimulation of pupils and students, friends and colleagues made me think of writing a book summarizing this experience, which might help the analyst to reflect on the fascinating and complex problems that form the backbone of our discipline.

As time passed, my teaching became stripped of all urge towards cate-chesis, in so far as I was capable of distinguishing between the science and the politics of psychoanalysis—that is, between the unalterable demands of psychoanalytic research and the always contingent (though not neces-sarily negligible) compromises of the psychoanalytic movement. If this book attains any merit, it will be by helping the analyst to find his own road, to be true to his own self, even though he may not think as I do. I have more than once changed my way of thinking, and I do not exclude the possibility that my analysands, from whom I am always learning, may still make me do so more than once in the future. My one aspiration is that this book may help my colleagues to discover in themselves the analysts that they really are.

* * *

Once I had decided upon my task, I thought carefully whether it might be more convenient to seek collaborators and put together a treatise with them. I had no lack of friends to help me, and in this way I might achieve a stricter specialization and a depth to which a single person could not aspire. I finally decided, however, to sacrifice these attractive aims to the conceptual unity of the book. I proposed to show how the problems could be coherently understood without the help of eclecticism or dissociation. I am not, on the other hand, unaware that various treatises of this type (and very good ones) have been written recently under the direction of Jean Bergeret, León Grinberg, Peter L. Giovacchini, Benjamin B. Wolman and others. I did make an exception to my rule in the case of an outstanding man, Gregorio Klimovsky, who contributed Chapter 35, "Epistemological Aspects of Psychoanalytic Interpretation", which is without doubt the best essay I know on this subject.

When I began to write, I certainly (and fortunately!) did not think that the project was going to take me more than five years; and it is only today that I realize how necessary were the strength and confidence of my chil-dren Alicia, Laura and Alberto. I also appreciated the exchange of ideas with my friends Benito and Sheila López, Elena Evelson, Leon and Rebe Grinberg, Rabih, Polito, Cvik, Guiard, Reggy Serebriany, Elizabeth Bianchedi, Painceira, Zac, Guillermo Maci, Sor, Matte Blanco, Wender, Berenstein, Maria Isabel Siquier, Yampey, Gioia and the unforgotten David Liberman, and many others. From a distance I had the encourage-ment of Weinshel, Maria Carmen and Ernesto Liendo, Zimmermann, Pearl King, Limentani, Lebovici, Janine Chasseguet-Smirgel, Blum, Green, Yorke, Grunberger, Vollmer, Virginia Bicudo, Rangell and many more. In recent years I have benefited from my intellectual and friendly contact with Riccardo Steiner, Robert Wallerstein, Peter Cutter, Roberto Speziale-Bagliacca, Max Hernandez, Jorge Canester, Otto Kernberg and Joe and Anne-Marie Sandler.

I should have liked to name my pupils one by one, because I remem-ber them at this moment and I owe them much. There is nothing, however, to compare with the continual presence of my wife Elida, who never tired of encouraging me and stayed with me through the long hours when I was drafting and redrafting, and through the difficult moments when I was struggling in vain to think what I wanted to write and to write what I had succeeded in thinking. More than dedicating the book to her, I should have recognized her as my co-author. Reina Brum Arevelo, my secretary, carried out her difficult task efficiently and affectionately—without anxiety and without anger, as Strachey would have said.

The publication of this book in English represents for me a supremely important accomplishment, and I would like to thank especially my friend and publisher, Cesare Sacerdoti, who, like Harry Karnac, has always had great confidence in the book and has taken great pains to achieve this admirable edition. These good intentions could not have been brought to fruition without the devotion with which Patricia Pitchon applied herself to the translation, without Christine Trollope's revision and without the meticulously attentive eye of Klara King. Between them they have succeeded in rendering into English both the content and the spirit of the Spanish edition. Many thanks to everyone!

Buenos Aires, 2 February 1991

FOREWORD

Robert S. Wallerstein, M.D.

The century-long history of psychoanalysis, as both science and profession, has been simultaneously marked by two contradictory trends to this point. The one has been the universalist thrust of a psychology constructed to encompass an understanding of human mental functioning, both normal and abnormal, as expressed and lived out by all people everywhere, regardless of the wide varieties of historic, social, economic, and cultural circumstance that may imprint particular characteristic forms of behavioural and dispositional expression in the varieties of ways and places that people live in the world. The other has been the particularist thrust in different regional, national, and language settings that has given, in each instance, a particular and distinct form to the psychoanalysis of that area—the British Kleinian as well as object relational theoretical perspectives or schools, the Franco–German philosophical and hermeneutic cast, the (French) Lacanian linguistic formulation, the American (natural science) ego-psychological paradigm, the Latin-American first Kleinian and then Bionian emphasis, the more recent American self psychology, to name the more prominent.

A consequence of these divergent historical trends in analysis has been the tension created within the psychoanalytic discipline overall, of all of us being simultaneously adherents of a putatively universally applicable psychoanalytic theory and therapy, while each individually pursuing our theoretical psychoanalytic understandings and clinical psychoanalytic work within the particular framework dominant within our distinct national and language area and our special place in historic time. One manifestation of the particularist emphasis, that more-or-less guides (almost) all of us, has been a restriction in our reading and writing, for the most part, to the literature of our own dominant theoretical perspective and our own language group—often primarily the books and journals published in our own country. This tendency has marked the small number of previous books on psychoanalytic technique as well—and Etchegoyen in the very first paragraphs of his preface remarks on this paucity of books in this area, while briefly describing the provenance of each, albeit he acknowledges that there are indeed a great many articles that deal with matters of technique and the theory of technique.

This newest book on psychoanalytic technique by Horacio Etchegoyen of Buenos Aires—perhaps the most influential figure, as clinician and as teacher, in Latin American psychoanalysis today—may well be the harbinger as well as benchmark of a new era in psychoanalytic scholarship. It is an impressively comprehensive effort to truly encompass the *world-wide* literature in his chosen topic area, that is, to compare and contrast at least the literature written in the four major psychoanalytic languages (also the four official languages of the International Psychoanalytical Association)— English, German, French, and Spanish—thus of course bringing the major developments in relation to technique and the theory of technique that have arisen within the diverse theoretical perspectives of psychoanalysis into conjunction with each other. It has taken him nearly a thousand (wellworth-reading) pages of heroic labour to manage this virtuoso feat, but the reward to all of us is enormous. The most significant writings in each of these languages and within each of the theoretical paradigms that have flourished in each of these language areas, from the earliest to the most recent—literally to 1989—are presented to us, juxtaposed as similar or differing comprehensions and/or renderings of all the many issues central to the understanding of technique for us all.

For the English-language readers to whom this translation is addressed, we are given intensive introductions to the work of a whole host of Latin-American authors who have been only spottily translated into English—and Etchegoyen singles out for special presentation and explication Liberman's very detailed development of linguistic or communicative styles and their linkages to personality styles, Baranger's and Liberman's conceptions of the "analytic couple", Bleger's (and also Liberman's) understandings of the psychiatric (diagnostic) interview, and the developments from Melanie Klein of Racker's writings on the transference neurosis and the countertransference neurosis (this latter *has* been translated into English), and of Grinberg's writings on projective counteridentification. He also, incidentally, helps build the bridges of cross-cultural and crosslanguage consequence by tracing the influence of Jurgen Ruesch from San Francisco upon Liberman's linguistic–communicational emphasis and the relationship of Harry Stack Sullivan's writings on psychiatric interviewing to Bleger's. Etchegoyen does the same for us with the French-language literature, not just the Lacanian (and Lacan has been only partly translated into English), but also the very important contributions of the Anzieus and again many others. With the German-language literature, Etchegoyen brings us less of the heretofore inaccessible, because Freud and Ferenczi and Abraham and all those who came subsequently who are drawn upon have been much more comprehensively translated into English—Freud, of course, totally.

And to help us fully appreciate the kaleidoscopic sweep of Etchegoyen's ecumenical survey, we will note his—for the most part—very discerning and very appreciative assessment of the contributions of almost all the very many familiar American and British psychoanalytic writers (and here Erikson stands out surprisingly as almost the only seriously neglected exception), but also such stunningly knowledgeable forays as his appropriately placed drawing upon the writings of the non-analyst Leo Kanner on infantile autism, the early psychiatric–philosophical writings on insight by Reid and Finesinger and by Richfield, the once highly influential but by now obscure and almost forgotten teachings of Blitzsten, and the quintessentially American psychiatric–psychoanalytic writings of Robert Knight.

A paradigm instance of how all of this many-sided ecumenical approach—theoretically and linguistically—to psychoanalytic issues can afford striking and novel illuminations is in the important Chapter 26, entitled, "Interpretation in Psychoanalysis", where the viewpoints of Freud, of Karl Jaspers (with his distinctions between understanding and explaining psychologies), of Bernfeld (with his demarcation of final, of functional, and of genetic interpretations), of Anzieu, of Lacan, of Racker, of Reik, of Löwenstein, and of Eissler—indeed, writing amongst them in all the four languages—are all developed sequentially and also comparatively. This to me is the essence of Etchegoyen's method, and this chapter is a particularly felicitous expression of it. And perhaps it should be added, though it could also be said that it should go without saying, that within each topic area Etchegoyen starts with a detailed study of the writings of Freud, in all their own (at times complicated) evolution over Freud's lifetime, with then the additions of Ferenczi and Abraham and Jones, and then Melanie Klein (Etchegoyen's own theoretical allegiance), and then beyond that the fanning-out in divergent directions world-wide, although expectably with a heavy weighting on the influence of the British Kleinians, particularly Bion, Rosenfeld, Money-Kyrle, Segal, Joseph, and Esther Bick, and the British independent or object relations school, particularly Winnicott and Balint.

All of this—and here the wary American reader might wonder—is presented to us, I feel, in an unpretentiously well-tempered and even-handed and quite undogmatic way, surprising only to those of us still insulated by old-fashioned stereotypes about Kleinians. Etchegoyen believes that one should state one's positions forthrightly and says of himself in the Preface that "I sometimes like to say that I am a fanatical Kleinian so that people will not get me wrong"—and then goes on to add that "the truth is that Klein does not need anyone to defend her, nor does Anna Freud". But what becomes more than crystal-clear throughout the text is that Etchegoyen is far from being a fanatical Kleinian.

xxxivFOREWORD

Which is not to say that his Kleinian persuasion does not come through in this book: it certainly does. It is very much there in his extended discussion of the concept of the therapeutic alliance, which he presents in detail as clearly an American ego-psychological creation, but at the same time very critically (but not more critically than such mainstream American writers as Brenner, Curtis, and Martin Stein). It is also there in the rather short shrift he gives in the one chapter devoted to psychoanalytic psychotherapy as a technical offshoot of psychoanalysis as therapy, though he does manage to cover the contributions of Knight, Gill, and Bibring in this delineation, as well as their struggle against the deviating views of Alexander and French in the fierce debates that marked this issue during the decade of the 1950s.

Or again, Etchegoyen enters the lists on the old Freudian–Kleinian argument on the reach backward in time of the analytic instrument, challenging again the traditional ego-psychological position that the traumatic and/or conflictual happenings of earliest infancy are beyond verbal analytic recovery, by presenting an extended clinical vignette from his own experience where the breast-feeding problems of a two-month-old were presumed to be embedded in the adult character formation and dispositions in such a way as to be amenable to activation in the transference and therefore ultimately analysable. And in many places throughout the book, whether quoting his own views or that of a wide array of other Latin-American or British Kleinians, issues of separations (whether the traumatic separations of unhappy life experience or the regular weekend and holiday separations of everyday analysis), of separation anxiety and the defences against it, of depression and mourning and the effort at reparation, are presented as the primary dynamic in much of psychopathology, rather than what would be more expectable and familiar to an (American) ego-psychological audience, the vicissitudes of the oedipal triangulation and the varieties of castration anxiety and the defences against it.

Having said all that, Etchegoyen is surprisingly objective in his several and extended discussions of the very controversial and polemical confrontations on issues both of theory and of technique, and in work with both adults and children, between the adherents of Anna Freud and Melanie Klein, and he is not averse to indicating the places where he feels the Freudian position to be more in accord with the data of our consulting-rooms. And he is able both to avoid proclaiming Melanie Klein as always the most direct inheritor of the Freudian legacy and to point out the instances where he feels Freud's own views to have been shown to be mistaken or inadequate and to have been subsequently modified or replaced altogether by clinically and theoretically better explanation. In all of this, it should be added, Etchegoyen is modest in the assertion of his own views, though his sympathies are usually clear; and, incidentally, he is also modest in his appraisal of psychoanalysis as an instrument for human betterment. In one of his more felicitous lines, he states that after a good analysis we are indeed better than previously, but not necessarily better than others. And—for a Kleinian—he does take some very surprising positions, much more to be expected among that often beleaguered minority of empirical psychoanalytic therapy researchers in America, like his spirited defence (as he says, despite Melanie Klein) of the use of tape-recording as an acceptable memory device for the analyst, or his espousal of systematic and planned follow-up inquiry in order to learn more about how and how much psychoanalysis has enduringly helped. And he is quite willing to differ with even his most admired and revered Latin-American colleagues and mentors, like his specific disagreement with Liberman's emphasis on the importance of the properly selected "analytic couple" (in America we speak of the issue of analyst–patient "match"), to which Etchegoyen counterposes the view that in most instances the best analyst makes for the best couple.

Having said all this about the form and structure of Etchegoyen's book—the panoramic and virtuoso sweep of his encompassing literally almost the entire world's literature in his topic area—together with the sober and unpolemical and undogmatic comparing and contrasting of differing regional and theoretical perspectives—what can be said about Etchegoyen's vision, as it emerges in the way he marks out his topic areas and builds his argument within them, about the nature and the essence of psychoanalytic technique, and how, properly deployed, it works to effect enduring change in personality organization? As probably should be clear from what I have said to this point, Etchegoyen's explanatory edifice emerges as a complex fabric of many, not always clearly articulating, components. Certainly, expectably, the analysis of the transference is the central element. And yet, Etchegoyen points out repeatedly—and this is a major example of just how un-stereotypically Kleinian he is—that not everything is transference, though transference exists in everything, which, he emphasizes, is not the same thing. And transference is spelled out in many—and at times (to Americans) unfamiliar—ways, like the following of the implications of the distinction between transference as memory and transference as desire; or the many form variants of the transference neurosis, like the transference psychosis, where he follows the English more sweeping usage rather than the American more restricted focus, or the transference perversion, where the drives function not as desire but as ideology (he explains this quite lucidly), or the transference addiction, with its genetic roots in masturbation, called the "primal addiction" (and reflecting the primal scene); or the various permutations of the locus of transference, including the reverse Lacanian view, which Etchegoyen characterizes as the emergence of transference only when the dialectical process of analysis fails due to the *analyst's* resistance or countertransference (called transference by entrapment).

From this focus on transference (and countertransference) Etchegoyen passes, in an updated version and restatement of the classical position in both the Freudian and the Kleinian metapsychologies, to interpretation of the transference—leading ineluctably to insight (with extended working through), and onto enduring change and cure (he does not shrink from this word). In this sense, Etchegoyen advocates a firm return to the early fundamental change dynamic—and the word "fundamentals" is in the title of his book—while giving far less pride of place and importance to the growing world-wide focus on the nature and structure of the analytic relationship as a vital component of the ameliorative or the change process, whether in the ego-psychological idiom of Loewald and Stone, or the language of the therapeutic or working alliance as with Zetzel and Greenson, or of the "new beginning" of Balint, or of the holding environment of Winnicott, or the container/contained imagery of Bion, though Etchegoyen finds places to discuss each of these, and for the most part very approvingly as significant conceptual expansions.

As against this focus on the mechanisms that make for change in desired directions, Etchegoyen arrays—and here he presents views that are undoubtedly unfamiliar to American audiences—the forces opposed to analytic treatment progress, and he adumbrates these under three main rubrics: (1) acting out, or the substitution of action for memory and insight (though he wavers here on the issue of how much the action can nonetheless be taken as the embodiment of the blocked memory); (2) the negative therapeutic reaction (NTR), or the undermining and wiping out of achieved insight; and (3) the "reversible perspective", the Bion and Money-Kyrle conceptions of the anti-insight, or the patient's playing the analytic game by rules different from those of the analyst. Phenomena under all of these rubrics can then coalesce into the psychoanalytic "impasse", which is to be distinguished from both the uncoercible resistance of the *patient* and the technical (and countertransference) errors of the *analyst*, which can of course also block the unfolding analytic process. The true impasse is declared to be neither of these last two but, rather, a reflection of a fully developed analytic process brought to a halt by the converging forces of acting out, NTR, and reversible perspective, unless each of these can be systematically analytically diagnosed and undone.

The spelling out of all of this is, however, the task of the author of this book, not of the Foreword. I trust that my task is complete enough if I have spelled out for the English-speaking audience the importance and the excitement of this book, for the enlarged understanding it brings to its topic area, for the nature or the theory of psychoanalytic technique, as well as for its role as initiator and exemplar of a new and necessary genre of psychoanalytic literature, the truly comprehensive survey and juxtaposition of world-wide psychoanalytic theoretical and clinical views and trends, necessary if psychoanalysis is to maximize its capacity to integrate its conceptions and to evolve better, more encompassing, and more scientifically intelligible theory, and then a clinical practice more logically related to the theory via empirically testable inferential links, in accord with established canons of science. It is very much too bad that there are so few of us who have Horacio Etchegoyen's capacity to begin to take us on that next journey.

PART ONE

INTRODUCTION
TO THE PROBLEMS OF TECHNIQUE

CHAPTER ONE

Psychoanalytic technique

1.1 Demarcation of the concept of psychotherapy

Psychoanalysis is a special form of psychotherapy, which itself first began to be a scientific discipline in nineteenth-century France, at which time two great schools of suggestion were developing—in Nancy with Liébeault and Bernheim and in the Salpetrière with Jean-Martin Charcot.

By what I have just said—and without wanting to review its history—I have located the birth of psychotherapy in the hypnotism of the nineteenth century. This assertion is open to discussion, but we will see that it also has important points of support. It is often claimed, and with good reason, that psychotherapy is an old art and a new science; it is this new science of psychotherapy that I place in the second half of the nineteenth century. The art of psychotherapy, on the other hand, has illustrious and very ancient antecedents, from Hippocrates to the Renaissance. Vives [1492–1540], Paracelsus [1493–1541] and Agrippa [1486–1535] initiated a great renewal, culminating with Johann Weyer [1515–1588]. These great thinkers, promoters of a *first psychiatric revolution* according to Zilboorg and Henry (1941), offer a natural explanation of the causes of mental illness but no concrete psychological treatment. Frieda Fromm-Reichmann (1950) sees Paracelsus as the father of psychotherapy, based at the same time—she says—on common sense and on an understanding of human nature. But, if this were the case, then we would be confronted with an isolated fact in the historical process; because of this I prefer to place Paracelsus among the precursors and not among the creators of scientific psychotherapy.

Reasoning as Frieda Fromm-Reichmann does, we could cast Vives, Agrippa and Weyer as fathers of psychotherapy.

Three centuries had to pass before these innovators were followed by other men who can, indeed, be found at the dawning of psychotherapy—the great psychiatrists who issued forth from the French Revolution. The major figure among them is Pinel, and at his side, although in another category, we can place Messmer: these are precursors, but not yet psychotherapists.

In the final years of the eighteenth century, when he brought about his heroic *hospital reform*, Pinel [1745–1826] introduced a human focus that was both dignified and rational, and of great therapeutic value in treating the sick. His brilliant disciple Esquirol [1772–1840] went on to create a regular and systematic treatment in which diverse environmental and psychic factors commingle; this has since become known as "moral treatment".

This *moral treatment* of Pinel and Esquirol, which Claudio Bermann studied critically long ago in the *Jornadas de Psicoterapia* [Córdoba] (1962), still maintains its importance and its freshness. It is the sum of *non-physical* measures that preserves and raises the morale of the patient, especially of one who is hospitalized, thus avoiding the serious iatrogenic creations of the institutional milieu. Nevertheless, because of its impersonal and anonymous character, moral treatment is not yet psychotherapy; it pertains to another class of tools.

The audacious conceptions of Mesmer [1734–1815] spread rapidly, especially with the works of James Braid [1795–1860] towards 1840. When Liébeault [1823–1904] converted his humble rural consulting-rooms into the most important investigating centre for hypnotism in the world, the new technique—which twenty years earlier had received from Braid, an English surgeon, not only his name but also his backing—was applied as a tool both of investigation and of assistance. Liébeault used it to show "the influence of morale on the body" and to cure the patient. Such is the importance of his works that Zilboorg and Henry, in their work already quoted, do not hesitate to place the beginnings of psychotherapy in Nancy.

We will accept this assertion with a proviso. The hypnotic treatment Liébeault inaugurated is personal and direct, and directed to the patient; but it still lacks something for it to be psychotherapy: the patient receives the doctor's curative influence in a totally passive attitude. From the most demanding point of view, Liébeault's treatment is personal, but not *interpersonal*.

It was when Hyppolyte Bernheim [1837–1919], following the investigation in Nancy, began to emphasize increasingly that *suggestion* is the source of the hypnotic effect and the motor force of human conduct that the doctor–patient interaction surfaced, which, in my judgement, is one of the defining characteristics of psychotherapy. In his *New Studies* Bernheim concerns himself in effect with hysteria, suggestion and psychotherapy.

1 PSYCHOANALYTIC TECHNIQUE

A little later, in the works of Janet in Paris and of Breuer and Freud in Vienna, where the interpersonal relationship is visible, the first melody of psychotherapy begins to sound. As we shall shortly see, Sigmund Freud [1856–1939] can be credited with taking psychotherapy to the scientific level with the introduction of psychoanalysis. From that moment on, *psychotherapy* will be a treatment directed to the psyche, within the framework of an interpersonal relation, and with the backing of a scientific theory of personality.

Let us sum up the characteristic features that mark psychotherapy in its historical development. Through its *method,* psychotherapy addresses the psyche via the only practicable path: communication. Its *instrument* of communication is the word—or, better still, verbal and pre-verbal language—both "medication" and message at the same time; its *framework is* the interpersonal doctor–patient relationship. Lastly, the aim of psychotherapy is to cure, and any process of communication that does not have this purpose (teaching, indoctrination, catechesis) will never be psychotherapy.

As the scientific methods of suggestive and hypnotic psychotherapy were reaching their maximum development, there began a new investigation, which would cause a Copernican revolution in the theory and praxis of psychotherapy. Towards 1880, Joseph Breuer [1842–1925], in applying the technique of hypnosis to a patient known since then in our annals as Anna O (whose real name was Bertha Pappenheim), found himself practising a radically different form of psychotherapy. (Strachey—see his introduction to Freud and Breuer's *Studies on Hysteria,* 1955—informs us that Anna O's treatment lasted from 1880 to 1882.)

1.2   The cathartic method and the beginnings of psychoanalysis

The evolution in a few short years from Breuer's method to psychoanalysis is due to the genius and effort of Freud. In the first decade of this century, psychoanalysis already presents itself as a corpus of coherent doctrine and extensive development. In those years Freud produced two articles on the nature and methods of psychotherapy: "Freud's Psychoanalytic Procedure" (1904a) and "On Psychotherapy" (1905a). These two works are important from the historical point of view and, if read with attention, reveal here and there seeds of technical ideas that Freud would develop in his writings in the second decade of the century.

It is worth mentioning here an interesting change in our knowledge about a third article by Freud, entitled "Psychical (or Mental) Treatment", which for a long time was dated 1905 and included in the *Gesammelte Werke* and in the *Standard Edition* as having been published in 1905. In 1966, Professor Saul Rosenzweig of Washington University, St. Louis, Missouri, found that the article had actually been published in 1890, in the first edition of *Die Gesundheit* [Health]—a medical manual containing

articles by various authors. It was only the third edition of this encyclopaedia which was published in 1905 (see Strachey, 1955). Now that we know
the real date of the original publication, the great difference between this
article and the two we are going to discuss is not surprising.

The 1904 work, appearing without the author's signature in a book
by Löwenfeld on obsessive neurosis, detaches psychoanalysis clearly and
decisively from the cathartic method, and this last from all the other procedures of psychotherapy.

From the moment of the great discovery of suggestion in Nancy and at
La Salpetrière, three stages are etched out in the treatment of neurosis. In
the first, suggestion is utilized, and then other procedures are derived
from it, to induce healthy behaviour in the patient. Breuer renounces this
technique and uses hypnotism, not in order that the patient should forget,
but in order for him to expose his thoughts. Anna O, Breuer's famous
patient, called this the "talking cure". Breuer took a decisive step in using
hypnosis (or hypnotic suggestion), not so that the patient would abandon
his symptoms or direct himself towards healthier modes of behaviour, but
to give him the opportunity of speaking and remembering, the basis of the
cathartic method. The third step would be taken by Freud himself, when he
abandoned hypnotism.

In Breuer's and Freud's *Studies on Hysteria* (Freud, 1895d), the beautiful unfolding of psychoanalysis can be followed from the case of Emmy
von N, where Freud uses hypnosis, electrotherapy and massage, to that of
Elisabeth von R, whom he already treats without hypnosis and with
whom he establishes a real dialogue, from which he learns so much. The
clinical history of Elisabeth shows Freud utilizing a procedure half-way
between Breuer's method and psychoanalysis proper, which consists in
stimulating and putting pressure on the patient to remember.

When the clinical history of Elisabeth ends, the *method of associative
coercion* is also ended as a transition to psychoanalysis, that singular dialogue between two people who are, Freud says, equally masters of themselves.

In "On Psychotherapy" (1905a), a lecture given at the Vienna Medical
School on 12 December 1904 and published in the *Wiener Medicale Presse*
the following January, Freud establishes a convincing difference between
psychoanalysis (and the cathartic method) and the other forms of psychotherapy that had existed until then. That difference introduces a cleavage
that provokes, according to Zilboorg and Henry (1941), the *second revolution* in the history of psychiatry. To explain it, Freud relies on Leonardo's
beautiful model differentiating the plastic arts that operate *per via di porre*
from those operating *per via di levare*. Painting covers the empty canvas
with colours, and, in the same way, suggestion, persuasion and the other
methods that *add* something to modify the image of the personality; on the
other hand, psychoanalysis, like sculpture, takes out what is superfluous
to allow the statue that slept in the marble to surface. This is the substantial difference between the methods used prior to and after Freud. Of

course, after Freud and through his influence, there appear methods such as neopsychoanalysis and ontoanalysis, which also act *per via di levare*— that is, which try to liberate the personality from that which prevents it from taking its pure form, its authentic form; but this is a subsequent evolution we need not discuss now. What does interest us is to differentiate psychoanalytic method from other psychotherapies of suggestive inspiration, which are repressive and act *per via di porre*.

From the preceding arises the fact of a substantial relationship between the theory and the technique of psychoanalysis, a point Freud himself makes in his 1904 article and which Heinz Hartmann studied throughout his work, for example at the beginning of his "Technical Implications of Ego Psychology" (1951). In psychoanalysis this is a fundamental point: there is always a technique that gives form to the theory, and a theory that sustains the technique. This permanent interaction of theory and technique is peculiar to psychoanalysis, because, as Hartmann says, the technique determines the method of observation of psychoanalysis. In some areas of the social sciences there is a similar phenomenon; but it is not unavoidable, as it is in psychoanalysis and psychotherapy. Only in psychoanalysis can we see that a particular technical approach leads inexorably to a theory (of cure, of illness, of personality, and so forth), which, in turn, reacts on the technique and modifies it to make it coherent with the new findings; and so on indefinitely. On this is based, perhaps, the somewhat pretentious term *theory of the technique*, which tries not only to give theoretical backing to the technique but also to point out the inextricable union of both theory and technique. We will see throughout this book that each time an attempt is made to understand a problem of technique in depth, one moves imperceptibly into the theoretical terrain.

1.3   *The theories of the cathartic method*

What Breuer introduces is a technical modification that leads to new theories of illness and cure. Not only can these theories be verified through the technique but, in the measure in which they are refuted or sustained, they can modify the technique.

The cathartic technique reveals a surprising fact, the *dissociation of consciousness*, which this method makes visible because it produces an *amplification of consciousness*. The dissociation of consciousness crystallizes in two fundamental theories—in three, if Janet's is added. Breuer postulates that the cause of the phenomenon of dissociation of consciousness is the *hypnoid state*, whereas Freud tends to attribute it to a trauma. (For greater detail, see the first chapter of Freud and Breuer's "Preliminary Communication" in *Studies on Hysteria*—1895d.)

Janet's explanation refers to the *lability of psychic synthesis* [*insuffisance psychologique*], a neurophysiological, constitutional factor, which rests on Morel's theory of mental degeneration. Thus, if, for psychotherapy to be scientific, harmony is required between its theory and its technique, Janet's method does not achieve it. In maintaining that the dissociation of consciousness is due to a constitutional lability in synthesizing the phenomena of consciousness, and in ascribing this dissociation to Morel's doctrine of mental degeneration—that is, to a biological, organic cause—Janet's explanation does not open the way to any scientific, psychological procedure but, at most, to an inspirational psychotherapy (which in the long run will act *per via di porre*), never for a psychotherapy that is coherent with its theory, and therefore etiological.

Breuer's and, above all, Freud's theories, on the other hand, are psychological. The *theory of hypnoid states* postulates that the dissociation of consciousness is due to the fact that a certain happening finds the individual in a special state, the hypnoid state, and because of this it remains segregated from consciousness. The hypnoid state can have a neuro-physiological cause (fatigue, for example, so that the cortex remains in a refractory state), and it can also arise from an emotive, psychological happening. According to this theory, which oscillates between the psychological and the biological, what the cathartic method achieves is to bring the individual back to the point where the dissociation of consciousness (because of the hypnoid state) had occurred, so that the event can enter into the normal associative course and therefore be "used up" and integrated into consciousness.

Freud's hypothesis, the *theory of trauma*, was by then purely psychological, and the one definitely supported by empirical facts. Freud defended the traumatic origin of the dissociation of consciousness: it was the event itself that, because of its nature, was capable of being ejected from, and rejected by, consciousness. The hypnoid state had not intervened, or had intervened in a subsidiary fashion; it was the traumatic event that the individual had segregated from his consciousness which was decisive.

In any case, without entering into a discussion of these theories (Gregorio Klimovsky has utilized the theories of the *Studies on Hysteria* to analyse the structure of psychoanalytic theories), what matters for our present reasoning is that a *technique*—cathartic hypnosis—led to a discovery, the dissociation of consciousness, and to certain theories (of trauma, of hypnoid states), which, in turn, led to a modification of the technique. According to the traumatic theory, what hypnosis did was to widen the field of consciousness so that the segregated fact might return and become incorporated, but this could also be achieved by other methods and another technique.

1.4   *Freud's new technique: psychoanalysis*

Freud always declared himself to be a poor hypnotizer, perhaps because this method did not satisfy his scientific curiosity; he therefore decided to abandon hypnosis and to develop a new technique to reach the trauma—a technique that was more in keeping with his idea of the psychological reason for wishing to forget the traumatic event. He took this daring step on remembering Bernheim's famous experiment of *post-hypnotic suggestion* (when Bernheim gave a person in a hypnotic trance the command to do something upon awakening, the command was carried out exactly, and the author could not explain the reason for his actions, appealing to trivial explanations; nevertheless, if Bernheim refused to accept these *rationalizations*—as Jones would call them much later—the subject ended up remembering the command received while in the trance.) On this basis, Freud changed his technique: instead of hypnotizing his patients, he began to stimulate them, to provoke them to remember. Freud worked in this way with Miss Lucy and above all with Elisabeth von R, and this new technique, *associative coercion*, confronted him with new facts that would again modify his theories.

Associative coercion confirmed for Freud that things are forgotten if one does not wish to remember them, because they are painful, ugly and disagreeable, contrary to ethics and/or aesthetics. This process, this forgetting, was reproduced before his eyes during treatment; he would find that Elisabeth *did not want* to remember, that there existed a force opposed to memory. In this way Freud discovered *resistance*, a foundation stone of psychoanalysis. What had at the time of the trauma conditioned forgetting is what was at this moment conditioning resistance: there was a play of forces, a conflict between the desire to remember and the desire to forget. Then, if this was so, coercion was no longer justified, because it would always meet with resistance. It would be better for the patient to speak, and to speak freely. Thus a new theory, the theory of resistance, lead to a new technique, *free association*, which was proper to psychoanalysis and introduced as a technical precept, the *fundamental rule*.

With a recently created technical instrument—free association—new factors would be discovered; as a consequence, the theory of trauma and that of remembering gradually cede their place to the theory of sexuality. The conflict is no longer only between remembering and forgetting, but also between instinctive and repressive forces.

From this point on, discoveries multiply: infantile sexuality and the Oedipus complex, the unconscious with its laws and contents, the theory of transference and so on. In this new context of discoveries, *interpretation* appears as a fundamental technical instrument and in complete agreement with the new hypotheses. With the aim only of recovering a memory, neither the cathartic method nor associative coercion had needed interpretation. Now it was different; it was now necessary to give the individual precise information on himself and on what was happening to him, and what he was ignoring, so that he would be able to understand his psychological reality; we call this interpretation.

In other words, during the first decade of this century, the theory of resistance was being vigorously extended in two directions: on the one hand, the unconscious (that which is resisted) was discovered, with its laws (condensation, displacement) and its contents (the theory of libido); on the other hand, the theory of transference arose, a precise way of defining the doctor–patient relationship, as resistance always occurs in terms of the relationship with the doctor.

The first indications of the discovery of transference, as we will see in chapter 7, are found in the *Studies on Hysteria* (Freud, 1895d); and in the epilogue of "Dora", written in January 1901 and published in 1905 as the "Fragment of an Analysis of a Case of Hysteria", Freud already understands the phenomenon of transference almost in its totality. It is precisely from this moment on that the new theory begins to affect the technique and it leaves its mark on the "Recommendations to Physicians Practising Psychoanalysis" (1912e) and "On Beginning the Treatment" (1913c), works that are contemporary with "The Dynamics of Transference" (1912b).

The immediate repercussion on technique of the theory of transference is a reformulation of the analytic relationship, which is now defined in rigorous and precise terms. As we shall see later, the setting is no more than the technical response to what Freud had already understood in the clinic on the peculiar relationship between the analyst and his analysand. So that the transference can manifest itself clearly and be analysed, Freud had said in 1912 that the doctor should be like a mirror, reflecting only what is shown (today we would say what the patient projects). When Freud formulated his "Recommendations", the *belle époque* of the technique—during which he invited the "Rat Man" to kippers and tea (Freud, 1909d)—was definitely over.

The coherence on this point between theory and technique can be understood; the doctor should not show anything of himself. Without allowing himself to become enmeshed in the transference, he will limit himself to returning to the patient that which the latter has placed on the smooth mirror of his technique. This is why in studying transference-love Freud (1915a) says that the analysis should develop in abstinence, and this sanctions the substantial change of technique in the second decade of the century. Without the existence of the theory of transference, there would be no reason for these recommendations, which are totally unnecessary in the cathartic method or in the primitive psychoanalysis of associative coercion. Here we see again that singular interaction between theory and technique specific to psychoanalysis.

We have dealt with the theory of transference in some detail because it illustrates clearly the thesis we are developing. As Freud became aware of the transference, of its intensity, of its complexity and of its spontaneity (although this can be disputed), a radical change is imposed on the setting. The lax setting of the "Rat Man" could include tea, sandwiches and kippers, as Freud did not yet know the extent of the rebellion and rivalry in the paternal transference (see David Rosenfeld, 1980; Mahony, 1986, treats this subject in detail).

The modification of the setting, which becomes more rigorous by virtue of the theory of transference, permits in turn a greater precision in appreciating this phenomenon, as a stricter and more stable setting avoids its contamination and makes it clearer and more transparent. This was a slow process, and it continued after Freud. It is enough to re-read the story of Richard, analysed in 1941, to see Melanie Klein purifying her technique, and the technique of all of us, when she arrives with a package for her grandson and realizes that her patient reacts with envy, jealousy and feelings of persecution (Session 76, *Narrative of a Child Analysis*, 1961). She realizes that she has made a mistake, that one should not do this. Only a long process of interaction between practice and theory led the setting to become stricter and therefore more competent and reliable.

We have considered the interaction between theory and technique because it helps us to understand the importance of studying both fields simultaneously and to affirm that a good psychoanalytic training should respect this valuable quality in our discipline, whereby speculation and praxis are harmoniously integrated.

1.5   Theory, technique and ethics

Freud often said that psychoanalysis was a theory of personality, a method of psychotherapy and an instrument of scientific investigation, wanting to point out that due to a special condition intrinsic to that discipline the method of investigation coincides with the curative procedure, because in the measure in which one knows oneself one can modify one's personality—that is, cure oneself. This circumstance is not only valid as a philosophical principle, but it is also an empirical fact of Freudian investigation. It need not have been so, but in fact Freud's great finding—that by discovering certain situations (traumas, memories or conflicts), the symptoms of the illness are modified and the personality becomes enriched—broadens and reorganizes itself. This curious circumstance unifies in one single activity the cure and the investigation, as shown in Hanna Segal's lucid exposition (1962) in the Symposium of Curative Factors at the Edinburgh Congress. Bleger (1971) also dealt with this point in discussing the psychological interview.

Just as there is a strict correlation between psychoanalytic theory and technique and investigation, so the relation between ethics and technique also arises in a singular manner in psychoanalysis. It can even be said that ethics are a part of the technique, or, in another way, that what gives sense and coherence to the technical norms of psychoanalysis are its ethical roots. Ethics are integrated into the scientific theory of psychoanalysis not as a simple moral aspiration but as a necessity of its praxis.

A failure of ethics in psychoanalysis leads inexorably to technical failure, as its basic principles, especially those that structure the setting, are founded on the ethical concepts of equality, respect and search for truth. A dissociation between theory and praxis, always lamentable, is doubly so in psychoanalysis, because it ruins our instrument of work. In other disciplines it is feasible, up to a certain point, to maintain a dissociation between the profession and private life, but this is impossible for the analyst.

No one is going to pretend that the analyst has no failings, weaknesses, duplicities or dissociations, but he should be able to accept them deep down inside in consideration of the method, of truth and of the patient. The analyst has his own unconscious, his own personality as his working tool; this is why the relation between the ethics and the technique becomes so urgent and indissoluble.

One of the principles Freud proposed, one that is simultaneously technical, theoretical and ethical, is that we should not give in to the *furor curandis*; and today we know without doubt that *furor curandis* is a problem of countertransference. Nevertheless this principle does not affect what I have just said, because we should not lose sight of Freud's warning, which is different from the desire to cure when it means fulfilling our task. (Further on I will have something to say about Bion's 1967 proposal that the analyst work "without memory and without desire", and also about Lacan's "desire of the analyst", 1958a.)

The *furor curandis* theme leads us back to ethics, because Freud's warning is no more than the application of a more general principle, the *rule of abstinence*. Analysis, Freud affirms at the Nuremberg Congress (1910d) and reiterates many times (1915a, 1919a, etc.), has to proceed in privation, in frustration, in abstinence. This rule can be understood in many ways, but in any case no one will doubt that Freud means that the analyst cannot give the patient direct satisfactions, because should the latter achieve these, the process comes to a halt, takes a wrong turn, is perverted. In another way it can be said that direct satisfaction takes away from the patient the capacity to symbolize. Now the rule of abstinence, which is a technical device for the analysis, is an ethical norm for the analyst. This is clearly because the technical principle of not giving the analysand direct satisfaction has its corollary in the ethical principle of not accepting those he can offer us. Just as we cannot satisfy the patient's curiosity, for example, neither can we satisfy our own. From the analyst's point of view, what the analysand says comprises only associations, fulfilling the fundamental rule; and what he associates can be considered only as information pertinent to his case.

What we have just said covers the problem of professional confidentiality and redefines it in a stricter, more rigorous way, whereby it becomes for the analyst an aspect of the rule of abstinence. To the extent that the analyst can take what the analysand says only as material, the analysand never informs him of anything; nothing the patient says can the analyst say that he had said, because the analysand has only given his material. And material is, by definition, what informs us about the patient's internal world.

Free-floating attention implies receiving in the same manner all the patient's associations; to the extent that the analyst tries to obtain from them information that is not pertinent to the analytic situation, he is functioning badly, he has become a (perhaps perverse) scoptophiliac child. Furthermore, experience shows that when floating attention is perturbed, there operates, usually, the analysand's projection. Therefore, the analyst's disturbance should be considered a problem of countertransference or projective counter-identification, if we follow Grinberg (e.g. 1963).

What I have just set out is not only a technical and an ethical principle, but also a healthy mental hygiene measure of protection for the analyst. As Freud says in "'Wild' Psychoanalysis" (1910k), we have no right to judge our colleagues and third parties in general through the affirmations of the patients, which we should always hear with a benevolent, critical doubt. In other words—and this is stringently logical—everything the patient says is opinion and not fact. It is clear how difficult it is to establish and maintain this attitude in practice, but I think in the measure in which we understand it, it will be easier to achieve it. The fundamental norm is, once again, the rule of abstinence: to the extent that information does not violate the rule of abstinence, it is pertinent and it is simply material; if not, the rule of abstinence has been transgressed. At times, it is only the feeling of the analyst, and in the last instance his countertransference, that can help him in this difficult discrimination.

The principle just given should not be taken rigidly, without flexibility. Some general information the patient could give us collaterally can be accepted as such without violating the norms of our work (for example, if the analysand tells us that the lift is not working). Similarly, there can be deviations that do not add up to a fault, to the extent that they are within cultural usage, and this give and take does not lose sight of the general movement of the process. But the basic rule remains: no intervention of the analyst is valid if it violates the rule of abstinence.

CHAPTER TWO

Indications and contraindications according to the diagnosis and other particulars

The therapeutic indications for psychoanalysis constitute a theme worth discussing, not only because of its practical importance, but because as soon as it is studied it reveals a theoretical background of real complexity.

2.1   Freud's opinions

Indications and contraindications were lucidly established by Freud in the aforementioned conference of the Medical College in Vienna on 12 December 1904. There Freud began by presenting psychotherapy as a medical–scientific procedure; he then delineated its two fundamental modalities, the expressive and the repressive, on the basis of Leonardo's beautiful model of the plastic arts.

In the course of his lecture Freud emphasized the contraindications for psychoanalysis, in order to limit it finally to its specific field, the neuroses (what we today call neurosis).

In this conference, and also in the earlier work commissioned by Löwenfeld, Freud affirmed—and it is a very original thought—that an indication for psychoanalytic therapy should arise not only from the subject's illness but also from his personality. This difference continues to be valid: an indication for psychoanalysis must consider the person no less than the diagnosis.

In considering the *individual*, Freud says frankly (and also with a certain ingenuousness) that "patients who do not possess a reasonable degree of education and a fairly reliable character should be refused" (see "On Psychotherapy", 1905a, p. 263). This idea had already been expressed in the work for Löwenfeld's book, where he says that the patient should possess a normal psychic state, a sufficient degree of intelligence and a certain ethical level, because without these the doctor would soon lose interest and would consider his effort as not being justified. This point of view would nevertheless be revisable today from the angle of the theory of countertransference, because if the analyst loses interest, one can suppose that something is happening to him. It can also be refuted, even with Freud's own arguments: he often asserted that no one knows the potentialities that lie hidden in an individual who is ill.

Yet, from another angle, the (social) value of the individual is a factor influencing priorities in the analyst's time, in such a way that it can perhaps justify some type of selection. When candidates took nearly or completely non-fee-paying patients in the Racker Clinic in Buenos Aires, there was a selection, but one carried out by the Clinic, not by the therapist, and it gave preference to teachers, professors, nurses and others whose activity put them in contact with the community and who, therefore, had a particular effect on the mental health of the population. The analyst's own selection, on the other hand, is always risky, because a countertransference factor can always complicate it, and in extreme cases it can border on megalomania and narcissism.

Still within the indications that depend on the individual and not on the illness, Freud considers that *age* places a limit upon analysis, and that people nearing fifty lack sufficient flexibility; moreover, the mass of material to be worked through is so great that analysis would be prolonged indefinitely. Freud had already made these same reservations in "Sexuality in the Aetiology of the Neuroses" (1898a), where he asserts that psychoanalysis is applicable neither to children nor to people who are very advanced in years (p. 282).

These two factors are considered with greater optimism today. No doubt the passage of years makes us less flexible, but a young person can also be rigid, as this depends to a great extent on character, or on character armour, as Wilhelm Reich (1933) would say. Age is a factor to be taken into account, without being in itself decisive. In their detailed study of indications and contraindications, Nacht and Lebovici (1958) accept in principle that age places a limit upon analysis, but they emphasize that the indication always depends on the particular case. And it must be borne in mind that life expectancy has altered considerably in recent years.

Even less do we consider as an obstacle now the amount of material, as Freud himself taught us that the decisive happenings cover a limited number of years—infantile amnesia—and, on the other hand, these events repeat themselves ceaselessly through the years and concretely in that singular life history that is transference.

Although Freud's warnings do not compel us today as much as previously, advanced age does always pose a delicate problem, which the analyst should face with equilibrium and conscience. In deciding whether to dedicate his time to an older person or to reserve it for another with a greater life expectancy, the analyst faces a human and social problem. As is the case with the rule in analysis, so here, likewise, we cannot provide a fixed norm. The indication will depend on the patient and on the analyst's criterion, because life expectancy is a determining factor for the demographer but not for the analyst, who should look only at the concrete person. Is there a moment when socially analysis is no longer justifiable for an elderly person? Here also we cannot make any definitive inference, because some people die young and others live to a great age. Kant published his *Critique of Pure Reason* when he was 57 years old and had already retired as professor in Königsberg, so if this modest, retired professor of philosophy had come to analyse an inhibition about writing, perhaps, very sure of myself, I might have rejected him due to his advanced age!

Luckily, our criterion has gone on being modified and has become more elastic. Hanna Segal (1958) relates the analysis of a man aged 74, which proceeded excellently, and Pearl King (1980) treats this theme in her account of the New York Congress with a depth that leaves no doubt about the efficacy of analysis for older people. King emphasizes above all that the problems of the life cycle of these patients appear clearly in the transference, where they can be apprehended and resolved through strictly psychoanalytic methods.

This theme was considered many years ago by Abraham (1919b). In contrast to Freud and to the majority of analysts of his time, Abraham maintained that "the age of neurosis is more important than the age of the patient" (1973, p. 316), and he presented various case histories of people over fifty who responded well to psychoanalytic treatment.

2.2   Indications according to diagnosis in Freud's view

In relation to indications for analysis *according to clinical diagnosis*, the caution with which Freud discusses these is admirable. Concretely, he considers psychoanalysis as the chosen method in chronic and serious cases of hysteria, phobias and aboulias—that is to say, the neuroses. In the cases where there are ostensible psychotic factors, the indication for analysis is not pertinent for him, although he leaves the possibility open in the future for a special approach to psychosis. Nor does he recommend it in acute cases of hysteria and nervous exhaustion. And of course he sets aside mental degeneration and confusional states.

To cut a long story short, only the nosographically reduced but epidemiologically extended nucleus of neurosis is accessible to analysis: Freud was adamant about this and did not change his position from these earlier works up to *An Outline of Psycho-Analysis* (1940a [1938], p. 173), where he again says in chapter 6 that the ego of a psychotic cannot offer itself to analytic work, at least until we find a plan better adapted for him.

However, it is undeniable that something has changed in the course of this century, and that certain important paths have opened up with the psychoanalysis of children (made possible by his daughter, Anna, among others) and with the new theories of personality that deal with the first year of life and allow access to illnesses that, from the time of Freud and Abraham (1924), were known to have their fixation-point within that period.

Although Freud always insisted that only neurotics should be treated, it seems his own cases did not always conform. We have a basis for diagnosing "Dora" as a case of psychopathic hysteria, and the "Wolf Man" as borderline; he later developed a clear paranoid psychosis, which Ruth Mack Brunswick had to treat for a few months towards the end of 1926, as she related in her paper, "A Supplement to Freud's 'History of an Infantile Neurosis'" (1928a). This analysis, which lasted from October 1926 to February 1927, was not the only one: As Speziale-Bagliacca tells us, Pankejeff returned to analysis with Ruth in 1929. As we all know, Freud himself made the diagnosis and indicated the treatment, which he remarked on with satisfaction in *Analysis Terminable and Interminable* (1937c). Freud's opinions should therefore be considered critically, as Leo Stone (1954) does. We can find proof of Freud's broad criterion for indication of treatment, without going further, in the same conference of 12 December 1904, when he offers the example of a (serious) manic-depressive psychosis that he himself treated (or tried to treat).

Finally, let us say that Freud's indications are sensible in any case; clear cases of psychosis, perversion, addiction and psychopathy are always difficult, and it is necessary to think carefully before taking them on. These patients put the analyst on the line, and they can only be rescued in very favourable circumstances. (We will return to the topic of criteria for analysability in chapter 3.)

In his two articles at the beginning of the century, Freud points out that in acute cases or emergencies psychoanalysis is inappropriate—for example, he mentions anorexia nervosa as a contraindication. (By extension, we could also say the same of a patient with suicidal tendencies, principally the melancholic.)

In his lecture of 1904 Freud asserts that analysis is not a dangerous method if practised adequately, which merits a moment's reflection. I think Freud wants to say here something that held true for the cautious doctors of the Vienna Medical College who heard him: analysis is not dangerous because it does not lead anyone astray, it is not going to turn anyone into a madman, a pervert or an immoral being; and it is necessary to emphasize that Freud says that analysis cannot damage the patient *if adequately practised*. However, it is undeniable that psychoanalysis badly practised does harm—much harm at times, unfortunately. (Liberman, throughout his work, offers accurate reflections on the iatrogenic theme in analysis.)

2.3   *The Arden House Symposium of 1954*

Arranged by the New York Psychoanalytic Society, the Arden House Symposium on the Widening Scope of Indications for Psychoanalysis took place in May 1954. Anna Freud, Edith Jacobson and the main exponent, Leo Stone, took part.

Without doubt Stone's paper is of enduring value. He is a realist rather than an optimist, as he does not widen the limits for indications but shows how legitimate efforts were always made to surpass those limits. He remembers that in the 1920s and earlier, Abraham began to treat manic-depressive patients, with Freud's decisive support. (As I have just pointed out, Freud did not hesitate to try his method with a severe cyclical psychosis. It is sometimes forgotten that Freud analysed a young homosexual woman who had made a serious suicidal attempt, a case he published in 1920; and that when he decided to break off treatment because of the intense negative paternal transference, he suggested to the girl's parents that they should look for a woman analyst if they wished to continue treatment—1920a, p. 164.) Stone also mentions Ernest Simmel's attempts to treat alcoholic addicts and hospitalized psychotics and, during the same period, Aichhorn's treatment of deviant young people in Vienna. Abraham also wrote the story of a foot and corset fetishist for the Nuremberg Congress of 1910. Ferenczi studied the tic in depth in 1921, as did Melanie Klein in 1925.

Before reviewing the indications that fall outside the framework of neurosis, Stone points to the limits of psychoanalysis itself as a method. He says, with reason, that a psychotherapy that is psychoanalytically oriented but does not propose to resolve the problems of the patient in the transference and via interpretations should not be thought of as psychoanalysis, whereas if these objectives are maintained, in spite of (and thanks to) having recourse to Eissler's parameters (1953), we will not be working outside our method. Both for Stone and for Eissler, the parameter is valid if it does not impede progress and if ultimately, once stirred up, the transference can be fully analysed.

Leo Stone considers that the nosographic criteria of psychiatry are necessary but not sufficient, because they have to be completed by a whole series of dynamic elements of the personality of the potential patient, such as narcissism, rigidity, dereistic thinking, emotional alienation and emptiness, euphoria, megalomania and many more.

An important assertion of Stone's—with which I am in full agreement—is that the indication for psychoanalytic treatment rests in certain cases on the concept of *transference psychosis:* "One may speak with justification of a transference psychosis, in the sense of a still viable variant of transference neurosis, in the extreme forms" (1954, p. 585). What is widened, then, and on theoretical bases that I consider to be firm, is the concept of transference neurosis, which we will discuss in chapter 12.

Stone concludes that transference neuroses and the characteropathies associated with them continue to be the first and best indication for psychoanalysis, but that the objectives have widened and broach practically all nosological categories of a psychogenic character (1954, p. 593), a point of view that coincidentally informs all of Fenichel's book (1945a).

So we see that Leo Stone considered the indications in breadth and, paradoxically, affirmed that neurotic disturbances of moderate gravity that can be resolved by way of brief psychotherapy do not constitute an indication for psychoanalysis, which should be reserved for more serious neurotic cases and for those that cannot be resolved through other, simpler techniques or via the pharmacological methods of modern psychiatry. This point of view is also shared by Nacht and Lebovici (1958). And we shall see that only on this point did Anna Freud differ from Stone.

Edith Jacobson (1954a) also spoke at Arden House, on the psychoanalytic treatment of severe depression. She considers cases that can vary from the most intense reactive depressions to cyclical psychosis in the strict sense, via borderline cases, which are the most frequent. In all of these the author finds that the difficulties in the development and analysis of the transference are very great, but not impossible. She believes the most satisfactory results are obtained if the more archaic pregenital fantasies can be recovered and analysed in the transference (p. 605).

Anna Freud's commentary (1954) coincides basically with Stone and rests on her own experience with serious characteropathies, perversions, alcoholism, and so forth; but, as a lay analyst, she had not treated severe psychotic or depressive cases. She believes that it is valid and interesting to treat all these cases and agreed with Stone on the use of parameters to make them accessible to the method, although she warns that the excessive effort and prolonged duration demanded by difficult cases should be weighed when considering indications. With a criterion we have already called social, Anna Freud (1954, p. 610) considers that neurotic cases particularly should be borne in mind.

Significantly, when Anna Freud again discussed indications for analysis in chapter 6 of *Normality and Pathology in Childhood* (1965), she reaffirmed her views of the Arden House Symposium.

In conclusion, at the Arden House conference, no one questioned the theoretical validity of applying the psychoanalytic method to psychogenic disturbances that transcend the limits of neurosis, although everyone agreed that this is a particularly difficult task.

2.4   The Nacht and Lebovici Report

In *La psychanalyse d'aujourd'hui* (Nacht et al., 1958), Nacht and Lebovici separate the indications and contraindications of psychoanalysis in virtue of the clinical diagnosis and the patient, following Freud (1904a) and Fenichel (1945a).

With reference to the indications *through the diagnosis*, these authors single out three groups, as did Glover (1955): the accessible cases, the moderately accessible ones and the least accessible ones. Nacht and Lebovici consider psychoanalysis as being applicable to neurotic states—that is, to the symptomatic neuroses—but much less to character neuroses; disturbances pertaining to sexuality, such as male impotence or female frigidity, are frequent and acceptable indications, whereas in the case of perversions, indications are more fragile and difficult to establish.

Although Nacht and Lebovici rely on the (surely very Freudian) principle that there is no absolute opposition between neurosis and psychosis, they are inclined to think that in clear cases of psychosis analytic treatment is difficult to apply, whereas less serious cases encourage this attempt.

As for the indications *through the personality*, Nacht and Lebovici accept Freud's criterion on age, on which they place an even stricter limit, as they consider that only an adult under forty should be analysed (p. 70), although they admit exceptions.

These authors consider that the secondary gain of the illness, if deeply rooted, constitutes a contraindication, or at least a factor considered as a serious obstacle. They also hold ego strength to be a factor of primary importance, as narcissism, masochism in its more primitive forms, latent homosexual tendencies that set their seal on the functioning of the ego, and cases prone to acting-out are negative factors that must be considered, as should mental weakness, which impedes full understanding of the interpretations.

2.5 The Copenhagen Symposium of 1967

At the XXV International Congress, a symposium entitled "Indications and Contraindications for Psychoanalytic Treatment" was presented by Samuel A. Guttman (1968), with the participation of Elizabeth R. Zetzel, P. C. Kuiper, Arthur Valenstein, René Diatkine and Alfred Namnum.

If we contrast this with the 1954 symposium, it becomes evident that the tendency to widen the indications for psychoanalysis takes a backward step and narrows. As Limentani (1972) says, there is first a process of expansion and then of contraction, beginning with Freud's circumspect affirmations at the start of the century. Limentani considers that the tendency to return to restricted guidelines depends at least partially on the more selective criteria of admission of candidates to psychoanalytic institutes, which began to gain ground around the world from the time of the Second World War. Limentani concludes that it is evident that in these more rigorous models there is an implicit acknowledgement that psychoanalytic treatment cannot resolve all psychological problems.

Together with a greater prudence about the scope of the method, the Copenhagen Symposium singled out an important factor, the motivation for analysis, which appears explicitly in Kuiper's work (1968) but also informs the other papers.

The central theme at Copenhagen is, without doubt, analysability, which Elizabeth R. Zetzel developed with rigour. We will be dealing with this concept, because of its importance, in chapter 3.

When Guttman opened the symposium, he put forward a restrictive criterion in relation to the applicability of psychoanalysis, using what seems to me somewhat circular reasoning. He said that psychoanalysis as a method consists in the analysis of the transference neurosis, so that if the latter does not develop fully, it cannot be resolved by analytic methods, and psychoanalysis is therefore not applicable. Given that the only illnesses in which *by definition* a transference neurosis takes hold are precisely the neuroses of transference—that is, hysteria in its two forms of conversion and anxiety and obsessive neurosis, with the corresponding characterological disturbances—then these are the only valid indications. To my mind this begs the question, because what is being discussed is whether the other patients can fully develop transference phenomena according to the nature of their illness and their symptoms, and whether these can be resolved in the analytic setting.

Psychotic, borderline, perverse and addicted patients can only be analysed, Guttman says, if the course of treatment permits the development of a transference neurosis or if neurotic conflicts concealed in the conduct of the patient are discovered.

As we will later see, the transference neurosis should be understood as a technical concept, which does not necessarily imply that other psychopathological presentations cannot develop analogous phenomena. We have just seen that Stone admits for severe cases a psychotic transference; and much earlier, in her brilliant paper, "Analysis of a Case of Paranoia", Ruth Mack Brunswick (1928b) speaks concretely of a transference psychosis and the manner of analysing and resolving it. Clinical experience seems to show that each patient develops a transference according to his suffering and his personality. In this sense, it is convenient to reserve the term "transference neurosis" for the neuroses themselves and not to extend it to other situations.

2.6   *Some special indications*

A more current theme concerns the use of psychoanalysis in organic illnesses where psychic factors play a notorious part, and which have become known, with reason, as *psychosomatic* illnesses. Theoretical and technical problems that should be critically studied converge here. Although it is true that from the doctrinaire point of view it is a valid concept that all illness is both psychic and somatic (or psychic, somatic and social), the empirical facts show that the weight of these factors can be very unequal.

The indication for psychoanalysis will vary, first, according to the greater prominence of psychological factors; second, according to the response to medical treatments effected previously; and, third, according to the type of illness. Ulcerative colitis, for example, even in its most serious forms, is an illness that almost always responds satisfactorily to psychoanalysis, whereas essential obesity, diabetes and coronary illnesses do not usually offer a favourable response. Bronchial asthma and hypertension benefit at times (not always) from analysis, gastroduodenal ulcer somewhat less. In the last few years I have seen the regularization of arterial pressure in patients who sought help not for hypertension but for neurotic problems, and the clinicians who attended them discharged them in view of the favourable evolution of their condition.

It is always necessary to note that not all psychosomatic patients respond similarly to psychoanalysis, and neither do neurotics. And there are illnesses in which the psychogenesis can be relevant; but once the pathological process is under way, it can no longer be halted by psychic means. As an example, there are many studies that prove convincingly that the psychological factor is important in the appearance of cancer, but it is highly improbable that, once produced, it can be made to recede by stirring up psychological factors that had played a part in its appearance. It is possible, nevertheless, that analytic treatment can to some extent assist in a better evolution of this disease.

In any case, all the factors cited—and perhaps others—must be collated before deciding in favour of psychoanalysis; and, in doing so, it will be made clear to the patient that he should continue the pertinent medical treatments. In no case is this more obvious than in obesity, in which psychological help is plausible and often efficient but can never go beyond what the calorie count dictates. It is also evident that if the psychosomatic illness can be cured through medical or surgical means that are simpler than a lengthy and always difficult psychoanalytic treatment, then the patient should opt for those, if his specifically mental symptoms are not too relevant. Here the theme of motivation presents itself again.

In chapter 6, when we consider the contract, we will discuss the technical problem medical or surgical treatment presents for a patient in analysis; but let us say at this point that if the roles are well defined and each one fulfils his function without stepping out of his field, the analytic process has no reason to be disturbed.

It is well known that feminine sterility and masculine infertility, if not due to organic causes, respond at times to analysis. Well before these types of patients were analysed, Dr Rodolfo Rossi pointed out in his medical clinic lectures that sterile couples sometimes conceived their first child after the adoption of another child.

* * *

We have said that, up to a point, the significance of a person for society can have weight in the indication for analysis. This takes us to another problem of theoretical importance and social consequence, the analysis of the *normal person*. In other words, up to what point is it legitimate to indicate analysis as a prophylactic method, as a method to improve productivity and fullness of life in an otherwise normal person? Whereas it is true that, in principle, no one openly supports this type of indication, certain distinctions can be made.

Thus far the normal man is an abstraction; and clinical experience shows convincingly that he almost always presents disturbances and problems that are important. Whoever is analysed without being formally ill, as is the case of many future analysts, does not usually regret it: during the analysis he is able to visualize, sometimes in amazement, the grave defects of his personality linked to conflicts, and to resolve these if the cure proceeds favourably.

It is undeniable that the most elemental common sense advises us to think deeply before indicating prophylactically a long and difficult therapy such as psychoanalysis, which demands a great investment of effort, affect and anguish, of time and money. The person who is in analysis has embarked on a path, taken a decision; analysis is almost a life choice for many years. But this vital choice also includes the desire to analyse oneself and to search for the truth, which, if genuine, will justify the enterprise in the long run.

Where this type of indication presents itself most in practice is in the psychoanalysis of children, because here life expectancy is ample and the problems of normal development are barely distinguishable from infantile neurosis.

2.7 Something more about personal factors

We have already emphasized that the indication for psychoanalysis should not be based only on the type and grade of illness of the patient but also on other factors that always carry weight and are sometimes decisive. Some of them depend on the person, others (which are almost never considered) on his environment.

We have already considered the social value of the person as a criterion of indication. Anyone who occupies a significant place in society justifies—if he is ill—the great effort of analysis. We have also said that this factor does not imply a value judgement; and in including it among his selection criteria, the analyst should be sure he does not allow himself to be persuaded through prejudice or an affective factor (countertransference) but by an objective evaluation of the importance of the treatment for that individual and of that individual for society.

Among the factors we are now considering is the psychological attitude of the patient in view of the indication for analysis. This is something Freud's work of 1904 already takes into account and which the present authors also point out as being of basic importance.

Nunberg (1926) discovered many years ago that every patient brings to the treatment both neurotic and rational desires for a cure, and certainly the consequences of both will show the healthy and ill aspects, which will develop as transference neurosis and therapeutic alliance. Sometimes the neurotic (or psychotic) desires to be cured can constitute from the beginning a very difficult situation and even lead to what Bion described in 1963 as a reversible perspective.

Yet what we are considering here goes beyond the desires for cure a person may have, and which an analysis can finally modify; this is something previously existing and proper to each one, the desire to embark on a venture that offers only the search for truth. Because, whatever the form of analysis proposed, the patient always realizes that we are offering a lengthy and difficult treatment—as Freud (1905a, p. 262) said—the basic premise being that of knowing oneself; this is not attractive to everyone and is pleasant for no one. From this point of view I would dare to say that there is a *vocation* for psychoanalysis, as there is for other tasks in life.

Freud preferred spontaneous cases (of self-referral) because no one can be treated on the basis of the wish of another. Although the manifest expressions of the patient are always equivocal and can be evaluated only during the analysis itself, a profound mental attitude in the face of truth and self-knowledge notably influences the development of psychoanalytic treatment. Doubtless Bion (1962b) refers to this when he speaks of the psychoanalytic function of the personality.

The factor we are studying is difficult to detect and evaluate at the start, because a patient who seems to have come for treatment spontaneously and very resolutely can later reveal to us that it was not so; and, vice versa, someone can approach us under the pretext of family advice or demands, and yet he may have a genuine desire for treatment. At times, finally, the lack of spontaneity, of authenticity, is enmeshed in the very pathology of the patient, as in the case of the *as if* personality of Helene Deutsch (1942), and then it is part of our task to analyse it and resolve it if possible. This problem can also be viewed from the angle of the altruistic surrender of Anna Freud (1936), in which these individuals can have access to analysis only as a function of others and not of themselves, a theme to which Joan Riviere (1936) also refers in her article on negative therapeutic reaction. In any case, the indication is always more fragile and the prognosis worse in these cases. When Bion was at the Argentine Psychoanalytic Association in 1968, he supervised a case where the man had been sent by his wife. "And does this man always do what his wife tells him?", Bion asked wisely.

At the Copenhagen Symposium, Kuiper (1968) asserts accurately that the motivation for analysis and the desire to know oneself are decisive, rather than the type of illness and other circumstances, although he declares himself to be decisively in favour of not extending the reaches of psychoanalysis but of confining them to the classic neuroses. To widen the limits for indications, Kuiper says, leads to dangerous variations of the technique, which is damaging to the experienced analyst and even more to the candidate.

Perhaps the one who has posed this problem most accurately is Janine Chasseguet-Smirgel (1975) in her studies on the ego ideal. She says that, beyond the diagnosis, there are two types of patients with regard to their behaviour during psychoanalytic treatment. There are patients with a spontaneous and intuitive knowledge of the psychoanalytic method, with a genuine desire to know themselves and to get to the bottom of their problems, who look for *la voie longue* in a complete and rigorous analysis. Others, on the other hand, always search for the resolution of their problems through *la voie courte*, because they are incapable of understanding the great human proposition that analysis formulates, and they lack the insight that would allow them contact with their conflicts. We can see that this is about an attitude towards analysis (and I would say towards life) that weighs deeply and definitively in the process and, because of its nature, cannot always be modified by our method.

We must not confuse motivation for analysis with the search for concrete relief from a symptom or from a particular situation of conflict. The latter attitude, as Elizabeth R. Zetzel (1968) pointed out in Copenhagen, implies a very lax motivation, which is lost with the dissolution of the symptom and leads immediately to a lack of interest in the continuity of the process, if not to a flight into health.

At times these problems can present themselves very subtly. A training analyst worked with a candidate who was very interested in his training and barely concerned about his serious neurotic symptoms. After a brief period of analysis in which the candidate made sure the treatment offered a certain cure, the desire to be considered a patient and not a colleague began to appear in his dreams, together with an acute fear that, if he changed his objective, analysis would be broken off. In this case, the true motivation in the search for oneself was covered by a less valid one, which could be abandoned thanks to the analysis itself. As might be supposed, that candidate is an excellent analyst today. Unfortunately, the reverse situation, of the treatment being only a pretext to achieve the status of psychoanalyst, is much more frequent.

A factor of the social or family environment that influences the possibility and development of analysis is that the future patient be adequately sustained in the absence of the analyst—that is, between sessions, over the weekend and during holidays. A person who is completely alone is always difficult to analyse. Naturally, this varies with the psychopathology of the patient and with the means each one has of finding company, within himself or without. In the neurotic, by definition, this internal support exists; but even so a minimum of family support is necessary too, which the patient obtains for himself precisely because of his internal conditions.

With children, and much more with psychotics, psychopaths, addicts or perverts, if the family milieu does not offer concrete help, even if only of a formal and rational nature, the analytic enterprise becomes almost impossible. If the future patient depends on a family environment hostile to analysis, the task will be more difficult, and it will be worse if that dependence is concrete and real—an economic one, for example. In our culture, a husband who maintains his family and wants to be analysed, in opposition to his wife's wishes, will be an easier patient than a woman economically dependent on her husband, considering as equal for both the extent of projection of the resistance on to the spouse. These factors, although they do not touch the essence of analysis, should be weighed at the time of indication.

2.8 The indications for the analysis of children

The fervent controversies over indications and contraindications for the analysis of children and adolescents were modified and attenuated in time, no less than the disagreements about technique.

Freud (1909b) was the first to apply the psychoanalytic method to children, in treating Little Hans, a child of five years with a phobia about horses. We know that Freud carried out this treatment through the child's father; but he employed the basic principles of the analytic technique of the time—that is, interpreting to the boy his oedipal desires and his castration anxiety. Commenting on the case at the end of his paper, Freud emphasizes that the analysis of a child in early infancy has corroborated his theories of infantile sexuality and of the Oedipus complex and, what is more important for our theme, that analysis is applicable to children without risks for their cultural adaptation.

Freud did not continue with these early thoughts throughout his work. Only at the end of his life did he return to the theme of infantile analysis in the *New Introductory Lectures on Psychoanalysis,* where he says again that the analysis of children not only confirmed in a lively and direct way the theories elaborated in the analysis of adults, but also demonstrated that the child responds very well to psychoanalytic treatment, so that gratifying and lasting results are obtained (1933a, "Explanations, Applications and Orientations", p. 148).

The first analysts of the 1920s differed on many points of technique in analysing children and on the age from which treatment was applicable. Hug-Hellmuth (1921) maintained in her pioneering presentation at the Hague Congress that a "proper analysis according to psycho-analytical principles can only be carried out after the seventh or eighth year". In her *Einführung in die Technik der Kinderanalyse,* published in 1927 on the basis of four conferences she had given a year earlier at the Vienna Society, Anna Freud also considers that analysis is applicable to children from latency onwards and not before. In the second edition of her book (1946), the author nevertheless extends this limit considerably and holds that children in early infancy are analysable from the age of two years (p. viii).

Melanie Klein, on the other hand, was always of the opinion that children could be analysed in early infancy, and in fact she treated Rita when she was 2 years, 9 months old.

If we leave aside the impassioned polemic that reaches one of its peaks at the Symposium on Child Analysis, at the British Society in 1927 (on 4 and 18 May—see *International Journal of Psycho-Analysis, 8,* 1927, pp. 339– 391; Melanie Klein, Joan Riviere, M. N. Searl, Ella F. Sharpe, Edward Glover and Ernest Jones participated), we can conclude that the majority of the analysts who follow Anna Freud and Melanie Klein think that analysis is applicable to children in early infancy and that all children, normal or disturbed, could benefit from analysis. Yet Anna Freud (1965, p. 218) says wisely that the analysis of a normal child is a task that belongs by right to the child himself and to his parents. As for the age limit, Anna Freud points out with reason in chapter 6 (already cited) that if the child has developed neurotic symptoms, it is because his ego has opposed the id impulses, and this allows one to suppose that he would be disposed to accept help to triumph in his fight.

In the literature one of the most remarkable attempts at early analysis is shown by Arminda Aberastury (1950), who studied a girl of 19 months with a balloon phobia. The phobia, which emerged at the time of the mother's new pregnancy, developed significantly, until it transformed itself into a phobia of noises made by things that burst or explode, in the measure in which the mother's gestation was reaching full term. At that moment the girl had a session with the analyst, who was able to interpret the main contents of the phobia, with a good reception, it seems, on the part of the patient, who did not return for treatment after this one session. The polemic about the scope of the psychoanalysis of children also seems to have ended. It seems applicable both to infantile neuroses and to non-neurotic disturbances (of character and behaviour, borderline and psychotic children).

CHAPTER THREE

Analysability

W e saw in chapter 2 that determining the indications for psychoanalysis if there are no specific and undeniable contraindications always involves a complex process in which a series of factors must be considered. None of these is in itself a determining factor, although some carry more weight than others. An indication arises only as a result of a careful evaluation of all the elements. We will see now that there are even greater complexities, because the concepts of analysability and accessibility go beyond indications.

3.1 The concept of analysability

The Copenhagen Symposium showed, as we have said, a general tendency to narrow the indications for psychoanalytic treatment, and this attempt took definitive shape in the concept of *analysability*, introduced by Elizabeth R. Zetzel, one of the most authoritative representatives of ego psychology. This work is the culmination of the author's long investigation on transference and therapeutic alliance, which begins with her work in 1956 (presented a year earlier at the Geneva Congress) and which unfolds in her accounts at the three Pan-American psychoanalytic conferences in Mexico (1964), Buenos Aires (1966) and New York (1969). At the latter, which was unfortunately the last of the series, I was able to discuss with her the first psychoanalytic session (Etchegoyen, 1969). Although Dr Zetzel's work in Copenhagen refers exclusively to feminine hysteria, it is based on criteria that mark the limits of analysability in general (Zetzel, 1968).

Zetzel's starting-point is that object relations are established *before* the oedipal situation and are of a diadic type. In the pre-oedipal stage of development, then, the child establishes a bipersonal object relation with the mother and with the father independently. It is indispensable for the child to consolidate this type of link in order to face the triangular relation of the Oedipus complex afterwards. What fails by definition in the neurotic is precisely the oedipal relation, which is reached via regression in analysis as a transference neurosis. Thus for Zetzel (as for Goodman) the transference neurosis reproduces the Oedipus complex, whereas the therapeutic alliance is pregenital and diadic (1966, p. 79).

The establishment of firm diadic relations with the mother and the father independently creates the conditions necessary for presenting, and in the best cases resolving, the oedipal situation, on the basis of Erikson's "basic trust", because it is equivalent to the possibility of distinguishing between external and internal reality. Understandably, distinguishing internal from external reality matters as much in psychoanalytic treatment as does demarcating the transference neurosis from the therapeutic alliance. This capacity for discrimination goes together with a sufficient tolerance in the face of anxiety and the depression of the Oedipus complex, which opens up the means of renouncing it and of overcoming it. In this sense Zetzel (1966, p. 77) establishes a link between her ideas and Erikson's "basic trust" (1950) and also with Melanie Klein's concept of the depressive position (1935, 1940).

Those who could not complete these decisive steps in development will be unanalysable, because they will continually tend to confuse the analyst as a real person with the imagos transferred on to him.

At the first two Pan-American congresses Zetzel (1964) presented her criteria for analysability with great clarity. Her work, "The Analytic Situation", presented in Mexico in 1964 and published two years later, identifies the basic functions for the development of the therapeutic alliance:

1. the capacity to maintain basic trust in the absence of immediate gratification;
2. the capacity to maintain the discrimination between the object and the self in the absence of the needed object; and
3. the potential capacity to admit the limitations of reality (p. 92).

3.2   The good hysteric

On this basis, Elizabeth R. Zetzel maintains that, despite the fact that hysteria is the neurosis *par excellence* of the genital—or in other words the phallic—stage, genitality is often only a façade behind which the analyst will discover strong pregenital fixations that will make his work very difficult, if not completely fruitless.

Zetzel recalls an English children's rhyme about the girl who "when she was good, . . . was very very good, but when she was bad, she was horrid", to differentiate hysterical women precisely in these two categories, good (analysable) and bad (unanalysable)

Actually Zetzel specifies *four* clinical forms of feminine hysteria with reference to analysability.

Group 1 corresponds to the good hysteric, the real hysteric who presents herself ready for analysis. Generally this is a young woman who has clearly gone through her adolescence and has completed her studies. She is a virgin or has had an unsatisfactory sexual life, without being frigid. If she has married, she has not been able to respond completely in her marital life, whereas in other spheres, such as academic ones, she can demonstrate positive achievements. These women decide in favour of analysis when they suddenly understand that their difficulties lie within and not outside themselves. Analysis shows that the oedipal situation was presented but could not be resolved, often due to real external obstacles, such as the loss of separation of the parents at the height of the oedipal situation.

Group 2 is that of the potential good hysteric. This is a more diverse clinical group than the previous one, with disparate symptoms. These are generally younger women than those of the first group and always more immature. The ego-syntonic obsessive defences that lend unity and fortitude to the women of Group 1 are not satisfactorily structured in these, so that there are passive traits in the personality and fewer academic or professional achievements. The major problem in this group with reference to analysis is the beginning phase, where intense regressions may occur, preventing the establishment of the working alliance, or a flight towards health, which leads to a sudden interruption. If these risks can be handled, the analytic process will develop without major difficulties, and the termination phase can be resolved in a satisfactory manner.

Group 3, the *so-called good hysteric* group, is analysable only by way of a long and difficult treatment. These are depressive characteropathies where resources or reserves were never mobilized against each life crisis that had to be faced. To a low self-esteem is added the rejection of femininity, passivity and devaluing. Despite these difficulties, these are attractive women, and of undeniable merit, who conceal a depressive structure with hysterical defences organized around seduction and personal charm. They seek consultation generally later than the previous groups, already defeated, and with a considerable impairment of major ego functions. If these patients go into analysis, they soon reveal a depressive structure, with strong dependence and passivity vis-à-vis the analyst. The analytic process becomes difficult to manage because of the patient's inability to discriminate between the therapeutic alliance and the transference neurosis. The final stage of analysis leads to serious problems; in consequence, the analysis becomes interminable.

Group 4 comprises the most typical and unredeemable so-called *good hysteric* group. Florid presentations with marked traits that seem to be genital nevertheless show, in the course of the treatment, a notorious incapacity to recognize and tolerate a genuine triangular situation. A precocious transference takes on, quite often, a tone of intense sexualization, which rests on a tenacious desire to obtain *real* satisfaction. (This singular pattern will be studied in detail in chapter 12.) Incapable of distinguishing internal from external reality, these hysterics make impossible the therapeutic alliance, the basis for an analysable transference neurosis. Despite appearances, despite a manifest eroticism, the structure is pseudo-oedipal and pseudogenital. These are patients who tend to develop prematurely an intense, eroticized transference, from the stage of face-to-face interviews— an observation we will have to consider when discussing the concept of therapeutic regression in chapter 40. Their history reveals important changes during the years of childhood, such as the absence or loss of one parent or both in the first four years of life, severely ill parents with an unfortunate marriage, a prolonged physical illness in childhood or the absence of significant object relations with adults of both sexes.

3.3   The analysable obsessive

The theme of analysability is again discussed in Elizabeth R. Zetzel's posthumous book, published in collaboration with Meissner in 1974 (Dr Zetzel died towards the end of 1970, aged 63), and in it her previous points of view are confirmed and clarified. In chapter 14 of that book, Zetzel again discusses her theory of the analysability of hysteria, but she adds interesting considerations on the analysability of obsessional neurosis.

In the first place, she maintains that the analysable obsessive neurotic does not present difficulties upon entering into the analytic situation, but he does do so in the development of a frank and analysable transference neurosis during the first phase of analysis. Hysterical patients, on the other hand, develop a frank transference neurosis with ease and speed, but establishing the analytic situation (therapeutic alliance) is difficult for them. In other words, obsessional neurosis causes difficulties in the analytic process and hysteria causes difficulties in the analytic situation.

What is decisive in determining the analysability of obsessive patients is their capacity to tolerate instinctive regression, in order to constitute the transference neurosis without the latter disturbing the therapeutic alliance. In other words, the obsessive has to tolerate the recurrent conflict between love and hate in the transference neurosis, distinguishing it from the analytic relation.

Hysterical symptoms are not sufficient proof of analysability; similarly, an indication for therapy cannot be based on the presence of obsessional symptoms. The analysable obsessive patient always shows that he managed to establish a genuine, independent (diadic) relation with each parent, and that his problems derive from the unresolved triangular oedipal conflict. If reactive formations and obsessive defences in general appeared *before* the genital oedipal situation, then the patient will be obsessive, but not analysable. If these defences were prematurely established, "it may be impossible to establish a therapeutic alliance which is sufficiently secure and which would facilitate the annihilation of relatively rigid defences which are maintained with an intense charge" (Zetzel & Meissner, 1974).

3.4   Comments and criticisms of the analysability concept

The criterion of analysability attempts precision in indications and counterindications for analysis that go beyond diagnostic categories. The concentric movement that limits the indications for psychoanalysis strictly to the neuroses—as Guttman proclaimed upon opening the Symposium of Copenhagen—now goes a step further and affirms that although all neurotics are potentially capable of establishing a transference neurosis, not all can achieve it. Only in some cases are conditions right for psychoanalytic treatment to develop normally. In studying feminine hysteria, Elizabeth R. Zetzel defines four groups, as we have seen, and she concludes that only the first two are really analysable.

The criterion of analysability expounded by Zetzel is based on the theory of autonomous functions of the ego; it is not surprising that other authors do not accept it. Nor is the view fully shared by authors who follow the same line of thinking, such as Leo Stone, Edith Jacobson and Anna Freud herself. Furthermore, authors of other schools in France, England and South America consider the psychoanalytic method to be applicable to types of patients other than those who establish a transference neurosis; although it is more difficult, it is also possible to analyse the psychotic, pharmacothymic, perverse or psychopathic aspects of the transference. With a different theoretical base, those who admit the object relation from the beginning of life feel able to analyse pre-oedipal development and are of the opinion that analytic work can gradually demarcate the two areas claimed by ego psychologists, which, in effect, always exist, even in the most disturbed cases.

The analysability concept of ego psychology is then arguable from the theoretical point of view. Although it is prudent and legitimate in measuring the difficulties in cases that do not meet the major exigencies of the method, it should not limit us operationally.

The major drawback of the analysability concept is, in my view, rooted in its inflexibility. We cannot ignore the fact that there are no pure cases. Were we to apply Zetzel's criteria with rigour, we would soon be left without patients, because even the best of her hysterics will go through psychotic situations at some point. Furthermore, the capacity to differentiate external from psychic reality, for example, is not achieved in absolute terms and once and for all; it varies in each person, in each moment of life, in the face of each anxiety situation. In fact, it increases with development, with mental growth; and it is a prime function of analysis to promote it. As it is never completely absent, even in the most disturbed patient, the analyst will always have the right to think that with his method he can reinforce and enrich it. If this confidence in his working tool and in the patient's capacity to develop can lead him more than once along the dangerous path of therapeutic omnipotence, it is no less true that the inflexible criteria of analysability already mentioned can operate artificially in the interviews that form the basis for an indication. As soon as the patient perceives that he is being examined to determine whether he will be accepted or rejected (with all that this means for the unconscious), it is probable that he will try to adapt to what is expected of him, which can vitiate the relationship from the beginning. The danger of an implicit contract in which the patient and the analyst agree that psychotic aspects are not going to be considered is a certain possibility, especially for an inexperienced analyst. And even the most experienced analyst can never escape the reality of a test that will, in effect, play a part in his countertransference and in the attitude of the patient, who in some way must perceive this. The analysability concept denies the patient the benefit of the doubt, and this is certainly its Achilles' heel.

In short, I use the criteria of analysability of the great analyst from Boston to establish a prognosis, but not to select my patients.

3.5   The concept of accessibility

The concept of analysability illustrates the way in which some—though not all—ego psychologists understand the analytic praxis. It is a clinical stance based on the classic theories of psychoanalysis. We can now compare it with the concept of *accessibility*, which stems from a very representative figure of the Kleinian School. This concept comes from Betty Joseph, who proposed it in an article in 1975. Although her intention is not to offer an alternative to analysability, I think that in studying these simultaneously and in comparing them I am responding to the broad theoretical lines that lie beneath the ideas we are discussing. What Betty Joseph first points out is that accessibility does not depend on nosographic type but on the deep-level personality of the patient. She does not distinguish two types of patients, accessible and inaccessible, but considers some patients more difficult to reach than others; and she tries to study what constitutes this difficulty. It follows from this that accessibility can be established only in the course of analysis; analysability, on the other hand, aspires to the prior detection of the situation, effecting a classification of future analysands.

"The patient who is difficult to reach" described by Betty Joseph does not correspond to a peculiar diagnostic category, although the author links her investigation with the *as if* personality of Helene Deutsch (1942), the false self of Winnicott (1960a), the pseudo-maturity of Meltzer (1966) and the narcissistic patients of Rosenfeld (1964b). This is, rather, a special type of dissociation whereby a part of the patient—the "patient" part of the patient, as the author says—remains mediated by another, which presents itself as a collaborator of the analyst. Nevertheless, this part, which apparently collaborates, does not really form a therapeutic alliance with the analyst but, on the contrary, operates as a factor hostile to the true alliance. (Compare this with the therapeutic pseudoalliance of Rabih, 1981.)

The patient seems to collaborate, he speaks and discusses in an adult manner, but he forms a link as a false ally who talks with the analyst about the patient he himself is. The technical problem consists in *reaching* that needy part that remains blocked by the other, the pseudocollaborator.

What appears in these cases as free association is simply an acting out that attempts to guide the analyst, when it does not push him to "interpret" what the patient wants; at other times, a true interpretation is used for other ends, to find out the analyst's opinions, to receive his advice or to learn from him. The analysand misunderstands the analyst's interpretations, taking them out of context or with his own bias.

On other occasions, the part of the ego with which we should establish contact makes itself inaccessible because it is projected into an object, which could be the analyst himself. The result is that the analysand remains extremely passive, and the analyst, if he gives in to the pressure of what has been projected into him, assumes an active role and feels a desire to achieve something, which is no more than a countertransferential acting out.

Throughout her paper, Joseph insists on the need to treat the material more from the point of view of the manner in which it arises than of the content, to clarify which parts of the ego disappeared and where they must be sought. Content interpretations are most subject to misunderstanding by the patient, often because in them there is a technical error of the analyst—that is, an acting out of what the patient projected into him and which the analyst could not contain within himself. In this way, the analyst remains identified with, instead of analysing, a part of the self of the patient.

The concept of accessibility, in conclusion, arises out of the analytic work and attempts to discover the reasons why a patient makes himself inaccessible—or almost inaccessible—to psychoanalytic treatment, the idea being that the phenomenon should be explained in terms of narcissism and special types of dissociation; but it is not useful for predicting what is going to happen in the course of the cure—nor does it attempt to do this—which distinguishes it from the criteria of analysability.

3.6   The analytic couple

The last theme we are going to discuss is very absorbing: it is the problem of *the analytic couple*. Analysts of various schools believe firmly that the analytic situation, as an encounter of two personalities, remains somehow determined by that encounter, by the couple. Others—and I am among them—find this concept unconvincing.

We have seen that the analysability concept refers specifically to the patient; nevertheless, in the last instance it can also include the analyst. The concept of accessibility is a more linking one; it would be difficult to say that a patient *per se is* not accessible; it is more logical to say that in practice the patient has not been accessible to me, and I am therefore involved in his failure. Nevertheless, at least as I understand it, with regard to indication the concept of the analytic couple goes much further than this shared responsibility, because no one can deny that in an enterprise such as analysis success or failure belongs to both parties. The same is said, equally correctly, of marriage.

Yet what we are discussing now is something more specific: whether a particular patient will respond better to one analyst than to another or—which is the same thing—whether an analyst can treat some patients better than others. Only if this is true can the concept of the analytic couple be maintained.

Among us, Liberman and the Barangers favour the concept of the analytic couple, although with diverse theoretical bases, and in the United States Maxwell Gitelson (1952) backed it resolutely.

Liberman starts from his ideas on *complementary linguistic styles*. Psychopathy is to obsessional neurosis, for example, what the language of action—the epic style—is to reflective language—the narrative style— (Liberman, 1970–72, Vol. 2., chapter 6: "Los datos iniciales de la base empírica" [The Initial Data of the Empirical Base], and chapter 7: "Pacientes con perturbaciones de predominio pragmático. Psicopatías, perversiones, adicciones, psicosis maníaco-depresivas y esquizofrenias" [Patients with Predominantly Pragmatic Disturbances: Psychopathies, Perversions, Addictions, Manic-depressive Psychoses and Schizophrenias]).

The treatment of an obsessional neurosis begins to succeed when the individual can resort more to the language of action; and vice-versa, a psychopathy begins to modify itself when the patient can reflect, when he begins to realize, suddenly, that he now has "inhibitions" and has to think. (I was able to follow this fascinating process step by step in a psychopath whom I treated years ago—Etchegoyen, 1960.)

I understand that Liberman speaks not so much of the psychopathological as of the instrumental aspect of complementary styles: in order to interpret an obsessional neurosis, it is necessary to employ the language of action—a language of achievements, as Bion would say; vice versa, a good interpretation for a psychopath is simply to detail for him, in orderly fashion, what he has done, showing him the sequences and consequences of his action; this, which seems not to be an interpretation at all, is the most thorough interpretation for this case.

Liberman's theory of complementary styles is a valuable addition to the technique and to psychopathology; but to make the various qualities of the ego instrumentally operational does not mean, without further ado, that the couple exists. What the thoroughly competent analyst does is to form the couple that is required; and for this, according to Liberman et al. (1969), the analyst should have an ideally plastic ego. Along this path, in my view, the idea of the couple is refuted rather than confirmed, because the greater the tonal riches of the analyst's personality, the better an analyst he will be.

The greater one's flexibility, the better one will be able to form the couple that is required, supplying the notes the patient lacks. In consequence, in this sense, the good couple is always formed by the best analyst.

The Barangers' (1961–62, 1964) view is different. They start from the theory of the field and the bulwark. The field is basically a new, ahistorical situation, traversed by lines of force that proceed now from one, now from the other component of the couple. In a given moment, the field crystallizes around a *bulwark*, and this implies that the analyst is more sensitive to certain situations. The theory of the bulwark supposes that the analyst always contributes to its creation, because the bulwark is a field phenomenon. Although the patient constructs it, the bulwark is always linked to the limitations of the analyst. The couple fail because of what one has done and the other has been unable to resolve.

In "La situación analítica como campo dinámico" [The Analytic Situation as a Dynamic Field], the Barangers (1961–62) define clearly what they mean by the bipersonal field of the analytic situation and affirm that it is a couple-field structured on the basis of an unconscious fantasy which belongs not to the analysand alone but to both parties. The analyst cannot be a mirror, if only because a mirror does not interpret (Baranger and Baranger, 1969, p. 140).

The task consists not only of understanding the basic fantasy of the analysand, but also of acceding to something that is constructed in a couple-relationship. This implies, naturally, a position of considerable renunciation of omnipotence on the part of the analyst, that is to say, a greater or lesser limitation of the people we can analyse. Needless to say, this is not about the possible "sympathy" or "antipathy" we can feel at first sight towards an analysand, but of much more complicated process (Baranger and Baranger, 1969, p. 141.)

This position is very clear, yet it is not accompanied by a satisfactory explanation of these "much more complicated processes", because the complexity may have to do with the subtleties of analysis, which always put the analyst to the test, and not specifically with the interaction. It would be necessary to demonstrate this, and while we await this demonstration we can continue to think that the best analyst is the one who best avoids the continual and unforeseeable traps of the analytic process, the one who best dismantles the bulwarks.

Proceeding from different theoretical suppositions, Gitelson also decidedly confirms the importance of the analytic couple, as can be seen in his memorable 1952 work. This essay is, above all, a study of countertransference, with many reflections on the concordance between patient and analyst, especially at the beginning of analysis. Following the inspiration of Blitzsten, as did Rappaport (1956), Gitelson studies the possible significance for the analytic process of the appearance of the analyst in person in the first dream of the analysand and one of its consequences—that at times it could determine a change of analyst. In this case, then, the concept of the analytic couple is based on a peculiar configuration of the phenomenon of transference and countertransference. (I will return to these ideas of Gitelson in speaking of transference love and in the chapters on countertransference.)

It is possible to think that Bion's idea of *reverie* (1962b) supports the concept of the analytic couple. What Bion postulates is a capacity for resonance with what the patient projects; but this does not have to depend on certain registers, but on a global capacity of the personality. The more *reverie* he has, the greater the degree to which the analyst is able to receive the patient and therefore the better an analyst he is. What limits our task is the capacity for understanding; but this capacity is not necessarily specific; it is not proven that it refers to a specific type of patient. It may be valid to think that it is, rather, a general way of functioning of the analyst. These arguments are still more appropriate to Winnicott's idea of *holding* (1955), which is clearly a condition that does not depend on the patient. In my view, the concept of *holding* suggests the idea of a couple less than does that of *reverie*.

There are other reasons for doubting the validity of the concept of the couple. The analytic function is very complex; sooner or later the analysand always finds the analyst's Achilles heel. In the end the analyst will have to do battle in the worst places, because it is there that the analysand will wage it; and the analyst will emerge successfully in the measure to which he can overcome his personal difficulties and his technical and theoretical limitations. As Liberman says (1972), the patient feeds back not only the analyst's findings but also his errors, so that sooner or later the difficulty will appear. If I dislike treating obsessive neurotics because I find them boring or lacking in imagination, agreeableness or spontaneity, then all my patients will manifest obsessive traits at some time, precisely because I could not resolve them. Or, worse still, all my patients will be seductive hysterics or amusing psychopaths who repress the obsessive neurosis present in each one of them. Not only does my patient repress or reinforce these features; I believe that a certain "natural selection" takes place: If I analyse hysterical, schizoid and perverse traits well but I neglect the obsessive ones, then these symptoms are increasingly going to prevail. I remember a distinguished colleague who consulted me once because many of his patients had suicidal fantasies. Studying the material of his patients I reached the conclusion that, in acute contrast with his good level of work generally, he did not analyse them well on this point. He then told me that he tried to avoid patients with suicidal tendencies, because his elder brother had committed suicide when he was an adolescent. When I began my practice, I lived in fear of transference love—and all the female patients fell in love with me.

Experience tends to demonstrate that patients who encounter failure with one analyst present the same problems again with another, and the resolution of these problems depends on the ability of the new analyst. There are certainly cases where the analysis of a patient, having failed (in the same way) with one or several analysts, evolves favourably with a new one. Leaving competence aside, several elements must be considered. First, the previous analysis or analyses may have promoted certain positive changes; and, second, some specific new situation may be present. In the case of a fourth child, perhaps only in the fourth analysis will a better functioning come to the fore. So the patient is not the same, nor is the situation.

3.7   Preferences in relation to the analytic couple

One must not confuse the problem of the analytic couple with the *preferences* one may have for certain cases or illnesses. This disposition is sane and reasonable and has nothing to do with countertransference. That an analyst selects a case of the illness he is studying is unremarkable. If the opportunity were offered to treat a fetishist, I would probably take him with a view to investigation; but I do not think that would carry weight specifically in my countertransference, nor that I would form a better couple with him than with another analysand. Quite simply, there are conditions that present a legitimate conscious interest; and I speak of conscious interest to underline that this type of choice is rational. The interest, and even enthusiasm, that a case can arouse exist in fact in the course of an analysis, but in a more rational and less specific way than the theory of the analytic couple supposes. Some time ago a young colleague expressed her wish to have her training analysis with me. Among the reasons she gave was that I am, like her, a Basque. This seemed to me an agreeable and sympathetic reason, and in fact I was sorry not to have the time available to meet her request. I do not believe, despite this, that for this reason we would have formed a better couple.

The idea of the analytic couple leads at times to a singular selection. A latent or manifest homosexual may prefer an analyst of his own or the opposite sex; an envious man may refuse treatment with a prestigious analyst. These are problems that should be resolved within the analysis, and not through searching for an analyst who "plays ball". The theory we are discussing is based on seeking an analyst who is adequate to the personality of the patient.

We have discussed this theoretically; but there is still an important practical objection to add: namely, that it is not easy to fathom, in one or two interviews, the deep-level personality of the future patient. As Hamlet said and Freud reminds us, it is not easy to play upon the instrument of the spirit. I am inclined to think that many of these selections are made on weak and unscientific bases, and at times on too simplified ones.

The situation is different if the specific request comes from a patient. If a patient expresses the wish to have analysis with a young or an old analyst, with a man or a woman, an Argentine or a European, I try to please him in order not to add another resistance in the opening phase of his analysis by going against his wishes, but I do not think this will necessarily lead to the constituting of a better couple. That will happen only if the unconscious fantasy that motivates that preference is analysed. One must not forget that analysis is a deep and singular experience, which is not at all conventional. An eminent colleague, a brilliant psychiatrist, once sent me a homosexual young woman, convinced that she needed a male analyst. The epicentre of my relation with the patient was, nevertheless, the maternal transference. The father appeared strongly only at the end of the treatment when the positive Oedipus complex reached its full intensity; the perversion had abated long before.

What is certain is that the more exigencies the patient has in choosing an analyst, the more difficult will his analysis be; but this is something that depends on his psychopathology, not on the couple. A woman who found herself somewhat beyond the middle-age crisis in life asked me to analyse her because mutual friends had spoken well of me to her. I told her I had no time available, but that I could refer her on. She accepted in principle, but warned me that she wanted an analysis with a male, non-Jewish analyst. I referred her to a top colleague of Italian origin, but she did not want to know. She could not understand how I could have sent her to that analyst, who was a disaster, who was not aware of anything. She added that she had thought about it again and decided not to go into analysis. Some time later she came to tell me that she had again decided to have an analysis; but it would be with me, and she would wait as long as necessary. I understood the seriousness of her condition and decided to take charge. Contrary to my presuppositions (or prejudices), this woman had an excellent beginning to her analysis, which refuted all my hypotheses. There had been a serious attempted suicide in her history, and she was really gravely ill; and yet, the fact that she had chosen her analyst and that he responded seemed to have facilitated the task. Nevertheless, in the end, when I thought the situation had definitely stabilized, she broke her treatment off from one day to the next and therefore made me err not once but twice!

In taking a patient, one takes many patients, and these "many patients" who constitute, in reality, the one patient will demand that we be all possible analysts; this is, perhaps, my major objection to the idea of the analytic couple.

* * *

To sum up: Having studied the idea of the analytic couple, we have offered a critique and considered another aspect that, in the manner of Goethe's elective affinities, must be borne in mind—that of the patient's and the analyst's preferences. This is, however, something that has to do not with the analytic dialogue, but with the conventional situation that analysis begins by being but soon ceases to be.

CHAPTER FOUR

The psychoanalytic interview: structure and objectives

We have been following a natural course in the development of our themes: we began by defining psychoanalysis, we then looked at indications for it and now we have consider the instrument that establishes them—the *interview*. We are going to follow the work of Bleger (1971) closely—it is clear and precise, a real model of investigation. (Bleger's work was published in 1964 by the Psychology Department of the Faculty of Philosophy and Letters of the University of Buenos Aires, where Bleger was an eminent professor; in 1971 it formed part of his book, *Temas de psicología*, shortly before his much-regretted death.)

4.1 Definition of the concept

The term "interview" is very wide: everything that is a "vision" between two (or more) people can be called an interview. (In order to simplify the exposition, we will refer to the simplest interview, the one that takes place between *one* interviewer and *one* interviewee, without ignoring that the number at either pole can vary.) Nevertheless, it seems that this term is reserved for an encounter of a special type, not for regular contacts. Dictionary definitions include: "oral examination of an applicant for employment, a college place, etc."; "conversation between a reporter etc. and a person of public interest, used as a basis of a broadcast or publication"; "meeting of persons face to face, esp. for consultation". This face-to-face meeting has as its aim the discussion or elucidation of some task by particular persons who obey certain constants of time and place. A newspaper interview, for example, is one in which a reporter goes to see someone—let us say a politician—in order to sound him out with regard to some current topic. So it is necessary to delimit the type of interview to which we will be referring in this section of the book.

As the title says, we are concerned with the *psychoanalytic interview* carried out prior to undertaking psychoanalytic treatment. Its objective is to decide whether the person who consults us should undertake psychoanalytic treatment, which depends on the indications and contraindications already studied.

However, this definition, while being strictly accurate, has precisely this fault: it is rather narrow. For this reason many authors, following Harry Stack Sullivan, prefer to speak of the *psychiatric interview*, which has a wider meaning. (Harry Stack Sullivan, undoubtedly one of the greatest psychiatrists of our century, developed the neopsychoanalysis of the 1930s, together with Karen Horney and Eric Fromm. His enduring book, *The Psychiatric Interview*, based on his lectures in 1944 and 1945, with some additions from his 1946 and 1947 classes, was published posthumously in 1954, with the sponsorship of the William Alanson White Psychiatric Foundation.) In any case, the adjective creates problems, because the interview can conclude with the advice that psychoanalytic or psychiatric treatment should not be undertaken. Because of this, Bleger prefers *psychological* interview, emphasizing that the objective is to carry out a psychological diagnosis and to evaluate the psyche (or personality) of the interviewee, going beyond an assessment of whether he is ill or well.

Although it is true that we understand the psychoanalytic interview as one whose prime objective is to decide whether or not to proceed with psychoanalytic treatment, we allow ourselves a wider range of choice. Thus we are not going to limit ourselves to telling the interviewee whether he should be analysed; if he should not, we will probably offer him an alternative, such as another type of psychotherapy or pharmacological treatment, and the interview that began by being analytic becomes psychiatric.

From the particular point of view we are considering, the best title for this section might be, simply, "The interview", without adjectives.

These points are pertinent; but it must be pointed out that they classify the interview through its objectives, and not through its technique or the person who carries it out. With the latter focus we can say validly that an interview is psychoanalytic if it is carried out using psychoanalytic methods and (if we wish to be more formal) if it is carried out by a psychoanalyst.

4.2   Defining characteristics

We have just seen that the interview is a *task* that can be understood through its objectives or through its method.

As with any other human relationship, the interview can be defined through the task it sets itself, through its *objectives*. These are always present, and even if they are neither made explicit nor formally recognized, they direct or determine the course of the relationship.

The objectives, in turn, obey guidelines that always exist, even if unrecognized. It is therefore *always* necessary to define the guidelines explicitly at the beginning of the interview, going beyond the possible perception of a doubt on the part of the interviewee.

It is no less important to define the interview at the beginning of our study, to clear up problems that might be confusing. Let us say to begin with that the objectives of the interview are radically different from those of psychotherapeutic treatment, a point many authors, such as Bleger (1971) and Liberman (1972) are right to insist on. In the case of the former, the objective is to orient the patient towards a particular therapeutic activity; in the latter, to carry out what was first indicated. So the first condition is to delimit precisely the objectives of the interview. We can then say that only what will contribute to those objectives is legitimate.

A basic rule of the interview, which largely conditions its technique, is to facilitate the interviewee's free expression of his mental processes, which is never achieved with a formal framework of questions and answers. As Bleger says, the relation one tries to establish in the interview is one that gives the subject the greatest liberty to expound, to show himself as he is. It follows that Bleger underlines the great difference between anamnesis, interrogation and interview. Interrogation has a simpler objective: to get information. But the interview aspires to see how an individual functions, not how he *says* he functions. What we have learned from Freud is, precisely, that no one can give *bona fide* information about himself. If he could, the interview would be superfluous. Interrogation is based on the supposition that the interviewee knows, and its aim is to find out what it is that the interviewee knows, what he is conscious of. The psychological interview, on the other hand, is based on a different supposition; it seeks information the interviewee *does not* know, so that, without disqualifying what he may tell us, it will illustrate, rather, what we will be able to observe in the course of the interaction engendered by the interview.

The psychological interview is, then, a task with a particular technique and set of objectives, which proposes to orient the interviewee with regard to his mental health and the best treatment for him, should he need it.

Delimited in this way, the psychological interview follows objectives that refer to the one who consults; but it can also broach other objectives if the results aim elsewhere. We are considering the patient as the beneficiary; there are alternatives, such as the interview that benefits the interviewer, who is carrying out a scientific investigation, or third parties, such as when a selection is made of the personnel of a company or the candidates of an institute of psychoanalysis. Although these objectives can be combined and are not mutually exclusive, what qualifies an interview is its prime objective.

Another defining characteristic of the interview for Bleger is investigation: the interview is a tool that both applies psychological knowledge and is also used to test it (Bleger, 1971, p. 9).

In centring his interest on the *psychological* interview, Bleger also proposes to study the psychology of the interview itself. "In this way we limit our objective to the study of the psychological interview, but not only to point out some of the practical rules that make possible its correct and efficacious use, but also to develop in some measure the psychological study of the psychological interview" (Bleger, 1971, p. 9). The rules with which the (technical) interview is carried out are one thing; the theories on which these rules are founded (theory of the technique) are another.

4.3   The field of the interview

The interview configures a *field*, which for Bleger signifies that "between the participants is structured a relation on which everything which occurs depends" (Bleger, 1971, p. 14). The first rule—Bleger continues—consists in trying to give shape to that field, particularly through the variables that depend on the interviewee. In order to fulfil this condition, the interview should be supported by a setting where are conjoined the constants of time and place, the role both of the participants and of the objectives they follow. (We will later see how these ideas can be applied to psychoanalytic treatment.)

So far we have studied, following Bleger, the objectives (or aims) of the interview, its framework and setting; we come now to the field where the interaction leading to these aims develops.

"Field" has a precise sense for Bleger—that of an adequate compass within which the interviewee can play. To achieve this, the interviewer tries to participate as little as possible, such that the less he participates, the better will be the field. This certainly does not mean that he does not participate at all or that he remains outside, but that he leaves the initiative to the other, to the interviewee. He is—to use an apt expression of Sullivan's (who is also the creator of the theory of the interview) so well liked by the *maestro* Pichon Rivière—a *participant observer*. I understand by this one who maintains an attitude whereby he is recognizably in the field as an interlocutor who neither proposes themes nor makes suggestions, and to whom the interviewee has to react without a stimulus other than his presence, without an intention other than that of furthering the task.

In short, the interviewer participates in and conditions the phenomenon he observes and, as Bleger says with characteristic precision, "the maximum objectivity we can achieve is reached only if the observer is incorporated as one of the variables of the field" (Bleger, 1971, p. 19).

This is the most expedient attitude for achieving the aims proposed, the one that best allows us to fulfil our task, which is none other than that of seeing whether the person should be analysed, or, in a wider sense, whether he requires psychiatric or psychological help. If we involve ourselves beyond what our position of participant observer dictates, whether by asking too much (interrogation), giving support or reassurance, expressing open sympathy, giving opinions or speaking about ourselves, we are going to undermine the sense of the interview, converting it into a formal dialogue or a common conversation. In trying to consolidate the relation through these methods, we may end up by paying a very high price—higher than we thought. Analysts who are beginners have to be warned, rather, of the converse attitude—too professional and hermetic—which causes confusion, anxiety and anger in the disoriented interviewee.

The alternatives posed by interrogation or interview should not be considered an inevitable dilemma; it is part of our art to amalgamate and complement them. There are no fixed rules for this; all depends on the circumstances and the field. At times a question can help the interviewee to speak of something important, but it must not be forgotten that it is more important still to consider why that question was necessary in order for the subject to speak.

Sullivan underlined the processes of anxiety that arise in the interview both for the interviewer and the interviewee. The anxiety of the interviewee certainly informs us at first hand about his problems; but at times it is necessary, as Meltzer (1967, p. xii) would say, to modulate anxiety when it reaches a critical point. During the interview this can be very relevant, because the interviewer's task is *not* to analyse the anxiety, and then sometimes we may need to lessen it in order to achieve the aims of the interview.

Regarding the initial anxiety of the interview, it is better to accept it without interference, but not if it is the result of the interviewer's excessively reserved attitude. As Menninger (1952) said, the interviewee took the first step in coming, and it is logical (and humane) for the interviewer to take the next step with a (neutral and conventional) question about the motives for the consultation, in order to break the ice.

4.4   *The setting of the interview*

As we will see in the fourth section of this book, the psychoanalytic process can take place only in a particular setting. The interview also has its setting, which can be no other than the one marked out by its aim: to

gather information from the interviewee to decide whether he needs treatment and of what type. The setting is constituted if some variables are
(arbitrarily) fixed as constants. From that decision and from that moment
on the field takes shape and the task becomes possible.

We have said that both the interviewer and the interviewee are engaged in the interview; we now have to study the rules that regulate the
functioning of both. We must indicate how the interviewer should conduct
himself, while *participating* in the interview, to study his interviewee objectively. The idea of objectivity is essential for psychology no less than for
the physical or natural sciences, but from within its own guidelines. The
"instrument" of the psychoanalyst is his mind, so that in the interview we
investigate how the interviewee behaves with others, without losing sight
of the fact that we ourselves are that other to whom that person has to
relate.

The setting of the interview demands that the variables of time and
place be fixed as constants and that certain rules be stipulated to delimit
the roles of interviewer and interviewee with regard to the task to be
fulfilled. The analysand should know that the aim of the interview is to
respond to the analysand's consultation about his mental health and his
problems, to see whether he needs special treatment and what that possible treatment should be. This defines a difference in the attitudes of the
participants, as one will have to reveal what is happening to him, what he
thinks and feels, whereas the other will have to facilitate that task and
evaluate it.

The situation therefore is asymmetrical, and as this arises necessarily
from the function of each one, it is not necessary to indicate it systematically. A reserved but cordial attitude, contained and continent but not
distant, forms part of the role of the interviewer, which he will preserve
afterwards throughout the psychoanalytic treatment if he carries it out.

The interview is always carried out face to face; the use of the couch is
formally proscribed. Therefore it is preferable for the two participants to sit
facing a desk or, better still, in two armchairs placed at an angle that will
allow both persons to look at each other or turn away comfortably and
naturally. If no other facilities are available, the interviewee can sit on the
couch and the interviewer in his analytic chair, but this is inconvenient in
that it suggests the arrangement of a session and not that of an interview.

The meeting can be initiated by a request for details of the interviewee's identity, after which he will be told how long the interview will last
and that it may not be the only one, and he will be invited to speak. The
interview certainly does not obey the rule of free association, as does the
psychoanalytic session.

I am not in favour personally of an ambiguous opening in opposition
to cultural usage, in which the interviewer remains silent, gazing expres-
sionlessly at the interviewee, who does not know what to do. I recall an
experience that a candidate (today a prestigious analyst) related about his

first interview for admission. He greeted the training analyst who was interviewing him and, being nervous in that situation, asked permission to smoke and lit a cigarette. Mute and poker-faced, the interviewer looked at him fixedly while he looked about the room in vain for an ashtray. Finally he had to get up, discreetly open a window, and throw the cigarette into the street. This type of attitude is much too exaggerated and operates simply as a contrivance, not as a stimulus to expression. It reminds me of the anecdote of the professor of psychiatry who, to demonstrate to his students at the psychiatric hospital the characteristic affective coldness of schizophrenics, told a catatonic that his mother had died, and the boy fainted.

4.5   The technique of the interview

In fixing the parameters of the setting of the interview, we have established implicitly the bases of its technique.

Most authors maintain that the interview technique is singular and proper to itself, and different from that of the psychoanalytic or psychotherapeutic session.

Not only are the objectives of each different, which will necessarily affect the technique, but so are the instruments, as free association is not proposed and interpretation is reserved for special situations.

Without having recourse to free association, which, in fact, requires a setting other than that of the interview and is justified only if it has interpretation as its counterpart, we can obtain the necessary information with a non-directive technique, which leaves the initiative to the interviewee and helps him discreetly during difficult moments.

A simple pre-verbal message, such as a light nod of the head, a friendly look or a neutral comment, is usually sufficient for the interviewee to re-establish communication previously interrupted. Rolla (1972) looks at the interviewee who has remained silent and stimulates him by moving his head and saying "yes" gently.

Ian Stevenson (1959), who wrote about the interview in Arieti's book, stimulates the interviewee with light gestures, words or neutral comments, or even with some conventional question arising from the client's material.

A very interesting experiment by Mandler and Kaplan (1956), cited by Stevenson, shows to what extent the interviewee is sensitive to the interviewer's messages. The subjects of the experiment were asked to pronounce freely all the words that came into their minds, with the experimenter listening and offering a grunt of approval every time the subject pronounced, for example, a word in plural form. This stimulus was sufficient to increase significantly the number of plural words. We can imagine, then, how much our implicit or explicit interest will influence the interviewee's choice of topics.

The Mandler and Kaplan experiment justifies convincingly what we all know: the importance in the interview of a gesture of approval, a look or the slightest smile, and, equally, of the "hmm!" or similar interjection. The same is achieved with the old technique of repeating in a neutral or slightly interrogative form the last words of the interviewee:

"The difficulties, it seems to me, began there" [*brief silence*].
"There. . . ."
"Yes, there, doctor. Because it was then that. . . ."

(All these techniques make up the theoretical corpus of Roger's non-directive psychotherapy).

4.6   On interpretation in the interview

It is necessary and convenient to discriminate between the interview and the psychotherapy session, as we have repeatedly said. A noticeable difference between them is that we do not operate with interpretation in the interview. There are those who are very strict on this point, and they have their reasons; there are also others who are not so strict and who interpret under certain circumstances. Liberman is very strict on this point because he holds that the setting of the interview does not authorize the use of the interpretation and also because he wants to single out the interview as what he calls a *contrasting experience*, which will ultimately enable the subject to understand the difference between the interview and the session. Liberman fears that if the contrast is not achieved, the first interpretations of the negative transference will be decodified as the analyst's value judgements. I suppose Liberman wants to indicate that the difference between what happened before and what happens now, in the session, enables the analysand to understand the sense of the analysis as an unconventional experience, where the analyst does not give opinions and interprets instead.

According to Liberman, "having carried out interviews prior to the initiation of psychoanalytic treatment makes it possible, once the latter has started, for the patient to have incorporated another type of interactive communication, which functions as a 'contrasting experience' of inestimable value for the first transference interpretations we will be able to offer" (1972, p. 463).

Whereas Liberman is very strict in proscribing the use of interpretation in the interview, Bleger considers that there are particular and precise cases in which interpretation is pertinent and necessary, "particularly each time communication tends to be interrupted or distorted" (Bleger, 1971, p. 38 [translated for this edition]). This idea continues Pichon Rivière's line of thought, when he conjoined clarification with the interpretation of resistance to the task in his *grupos operativos* ["operative groups"] (Pichon

Rivière et al., 1960). This is why Bleger says that the optimum goal is the *operative interview*, where the problem brought by the interviewee can be elucidated in the form in which it manifests concretely in the interview.

It is worth indicating here that all our ideas on this point stem from Pichon Rivière, and more from his permanent verbal mastery than from his writings. Among these is the work he published in 1960, in collaboration with Bleger, Liberman and Rolla, in *Acta*. His theory in this brief essay has as its starting-point *anguish in the face of change*, which for Pichon is of two types, *depressive* due to the abandonment of a previous link, and *paranoid* due to the new link and the ensuing insecurity (Pichon Rivière et al., 1960, p. 37).

The aim of the *operative group* (p. 38) is the clarification of basic anxieties that arise in relation to the task. The technique of operative groups (and, let us add, of the interview as a special type of these) is summed up in these words: "The technique of these groups is centred on the task, where theory and practice are resolved in a permanent and concrete praxis of the 'here and now' of each indicated field" (Pichon Rivière et al., 1960).

For my part, I believe, with Bleger, that interpretation in the interview is legitimate if it aims at removing a concrete obstacle to the task at hand. But I never use it to modify the structure of the interviewee (that is, to give him insight), simply because the latter, however laudable, is not the purpose of the interview, nor is it what the interviewee needs at this time. The subject has come not to acquire insight into his conflicts, but to carry out a task that informs him about a concrete and circumscribed theme, namely, whether he should undergo treatment, and if so, of what type.

At times I use interpretation as a test to see how the interviewee reacts. The interpretation I use in this case is always simple and superficial, almost always genetic, joining the statements of the subject in a causal-type relationship, in the manner of, "Don't you think that what you've just remembered could have some relation to . . .?" This is a type of test that informs at times about the interviewee's capacity for insight.

* * *

To sum up: the famous and controversial problem of interpreting during the interview should be resolved bearing in mind our objectives and the material within our reach. The resolution should not be a simple yes or no.

CHAPTER FIVE

The psychoanalytic interview: development

We have said in chapter 4 that in the interview a *field is* formed, because both interviewer and interviewee participate, both being part of the same structure: what belongs to one cannot be understood if the other is set aside. Equally, we could say that the interview is a *group*, where the protagonists are interrelated and depend on and influence each other reciprocally.

The group of the interview and the field of that group can only be studied through the processes of *communication* that every human relationship entails; and communication means here not only *verbal* in which words are exchanged and used, but also *non-verbal* communication through gestures and signals, as well as *para-verbal* communication channelled through the phonological elements of language, such as tone and timbre, their intensity, and so forth. We will return to this shortly when we consider styles of communication.

5.1 The anxiety of the interview

A new and unknown situation, in which he will be evaluated and on which a good part of his future may depend, will necessarily provoke anxiety in the interviewee. For similar but surely less pressing reasons, the interviewer also arrives at the meeting with a considerable measure of anxiety. Although he might have held many interviews in his professional career, he knows that the situation is different and therefore new each time, not only because a professional's future is tested each time he operates, and more so in this case, where he may commit himself for many years to the treatment of a person, but also because he knows that the interview is a challenge no analyst can be sure of meeting with success. In other words, a responsible interviewer must be concerned about his interviewee, about his task and about himself. To all these understandable and rational motives are added other more important ones, which derive from the significance each of the actors unconsciously attaches to the meeting.

As we have already said, Sullivan was the first to develop the theory of the interview, and he did so on the basis of the operations realized to dominate anxiety.

The maintaining of anxiety in the interview within acceptable limits depends in great measure on the ability of the interviewer. If anxiety is too low or absent altogether, the interviewee will lack the most authentic incentive and the most effective vehicle through which to express his problems; if it is too high, the process of communication will suffer, and the interview will tend to become disorganized.

A special problem with anxiety in the interview is that the interviewer must not have recourse to procedures that prevent it, such as reassurance or suggestion, nor can he resolve it with the specific instrument of interpretation.

In general, rather than being increased by the silence and reserve of the interviewer, the anxiety of the interviewee rises, rather, in direct proportion to the ambiguity of the interviewer's signals. Hence the importance of explaining at the beginning the objectives and duration of the interview, before inviting the interviewee to speak about what he will. The interviewer must be explicit, clear and precise on this point, without an abundance of details and signals that can perturb the free expression of his client. The abundance of signals usually is an obsessive defence of the interviewer, just as his excessive ambiguity is a schizoid way of making the other uneasy. A dignified and moderate participation that responds to the amount of anxiety the interviewee has will be the best way of motivating him and modulating his anxiety. At the same time, as Sullivan said, the interviewer will have to confront his client with anxiety situations, as a meeting where the interviewee is always comfortable and tranquil can be called a psychiatric interview only with difficulty.

As we have said, Sullivan's entire conception of the interview stems from his idea of *anxiety*. Anxiety always arises from that human relationship the interview necessarily constitutes; and in the face of anxiety, the *ego system* of the person responds with its *security operations*. Therefore, for Sullivan, anxiety opposes, in the *social* situation that is the interview, the establishment of a free and reciprocal process of communication. (On these bases Sullivan built his conception of modern psychiatry.)

Rolla (1972) describes different modalities of anxiety in the development of the interview. First, there is anxiety at the beginning (which this author calls "of approach"), and this has to do with exploratory strategies and with curiosity. At the other extreme, at the end of the interview, "separation anxiety" dominates. During the development of the interview, moments of anxiety—a crisis of anxiety—can inform us specifically about perturbed areas in the mental structure of the interviewee. Rolla calls that critical anxiety "confusional"—a term I do not find convenient because of its possible theoretical overtones.

5.2   Problems of transference and countertransference

The theme of anxiety leads us to the phenomena of transference/countertransference that take place in the interview.

The interviewee reproduces in the interview conflicts and guiding patterns relating to his past, which assume actuality, an immediate and concrete psychological reality where the interviewer is invested with a role that strictly does not correspond to him. Through these "transferences" we can obtain valuable information about the mental structure of the subject and the type of relationship he has with others.

The interviewer, for his part, responds to all these phenomena not only in an absolutely logical way, but also in an irrational and unconscious way, which constitutes his countertransference. This type of reaction, because of its nature, can, of course, disturb his much desired objectivity; but, at the same time, if the interviewer registers it and is able to link it with the effect the interviewee has on him, then he will succeed not only in recouping his objectivity, momentarily lost, but also in reaching deep and certain information about his interviewee. The countertransference is a very useful technical instrument in the interview, although Bleger warns us with good reason that its use is not easy and requires preparation, experience and balance (1971, p. 25).

López and Rabih, in an as yet unpublished work, deal with the theme of countertransference in the first interview. They point out that because of its structure and technique and the objectives it pursues, the initial interview is radically different from the analytic treatment. It is important in itself and also because it exerts a profound influence on the psychoanalytic treatment that may follow from it.

For López and Rabih, a peculiarity of the interview is the amount of anxiety it mobilizes, which they study in the light of the theory of projective identification (Klein, 1946) and of the countertransference. The initial interview, because of its characteristics, leaves the analyst particularly vulnerable and often defenceless in the face of the projective identifications of his client. This may occur for various reasons, among which the authors single out the intense extraverbal communication the interviewee employs, precisely to evacuate his anxiety in a particularly tense situation. In the face of this strong impact, the interviewer cannot use the legitimate device of interpretation, which would under other circumstances help the analysand while resolving the excess charge of countertransferential anxiety. And he cannot do so, as we have said, because the objectives do not authorize it, nor has a setting been established where interpretation can operate. As Bleger says, "Any interpretation outside the context and timing is an aggression" (1971, p. 39). Or, let us add, a seduction.

The greater the anxiety of the interviewee, the greater will be his tendency to "discharge" in the interview, transforming it, as López and Rabih say, into a very brief therapy, with a deceptive relief that can mobilize a typical flight into health. In these cases, the excess countertransference charge can only be intense; but from it the interviewer can obtain information that will allow him to operate with maximum precision.

According to López and Rabih, there are three moments when an interviewer is particularly exposed to projective identification: the opening, the closing and the formulation of the contract. The third does not, in fact, belong formally to the interview, but to that no-man's land where the interview has ended and the treatment has not begun. It is also at that point that all types of magic fantasy cures stand in contrast to the reality of a long and uncertain task.

5.3   The evolution of the interview

An original and important point in Liberman's (1972) paper is that the interview has an *evolution* and that from it we can derive valuable predictions. Being an experience prior to psychoanalytic treatment, the interview informs about basic facts. To begin with the analyst will fix the criterion of analysability of that person with regard to himself; the future patient, for his part, will leave the interview with an experience that he will, in due course, be able to compare with the session, and thus obtain an initial understanding of psychoanalytic method. Thus the interview allows us to evaluate what we can expect of the potential analysand and, reciprocally, what he will need from us.

If a problem presented at the beginning evolves favourably, we have the right to think that the interviewee has resources to overcome critical or traumatic situations—the vital crises, as Liberman says. If the converse occurs and the problem is worse at the end than it was at the beginning, then we have the right to establish a less favourable prognosis.

This evolution may occur in just one interview, but it is more possible and detectable in two. This is why Liberman insists that the functional unity is that of two interviews and not just one. I am fully in agreement with him on this point, for various reasons: The favourable or unfavourable evolution of a particular conflict or crisis can be discerned at times. In addition, it is necessary to bear in mind that the interviewee usually changes from one interview to the next, and the interviewer himself can change and may even recover from the impact the first meeting might have had on him. Lastly, I find it advisable to give the interviewee time to think over his experience before bringing it to an end. In his commentary on Liberman's work, Héctor Garbarino (1972) expresses the view that a second interview is not always necessary, but in my opinion this may be so only in very special cases. Berenstein (1972), in his commentary on Liberman's work, also declares himself in favour of several interviews: "Carrying out two or three interviews allows one to see how that patient and that analyst register the separation and the encounter" (p. 487). I agree with Berenstein about the importance, in the evaluation, of the way in which the interviewee responds to the separation and new encounter.

When we speak of *the* interview, then, we are referring to a functional unity. In general there should never be just one interview, but as many as will be necessary to fulfil the task undertaken. To sum up, it is advisable, then, to say at the outset that the initial interview will not be the only one and to underline eventually that interviews are not treatment (nor should we transform them into treatment by prolonging them too much).

During the interview we have the opportunity of studying some of the vital crises that the interviewee has undergone in the course of his life, and in particular the one that most interests us—the current one, which the subject necessarily undergoes during the time he consults us. If we are unable to detect that vital crisis with its unconscious and infantile elements, Liberman asserts, we run the risk of beginning an analysis blindly.

To detect the evolution that occurs in the series of interviews, Liberman makes use of the ego functions he described and also of his theory that those functions correspond to particular styles: the reflective style, with the search for the unknown and without suspense; the lyric style; the epic style; the narrative style; the dramatic style with suspense and the dramatic style with aesthetic impact. Through the changes of style during the course of the interviews, Liberman can reach the unconscious conflict, the anxiety and the defences, detecting how they modify themselves, now diversifying and widening if the evolution is favourable, now becoming stereotyped and restricted if the course is negative.

5.4   Prospective indicators of the analytic couple

We have already said that between an interviewee and an interviewer (just as between an analysand and an analyst), there exists an interaction that constitutes a field. So it is evident that psychopathological problems cannot even be thought of except through a linking theory, a theory of object relations, which in psychoanalytic theory is called theory of transference and countertransference. The process does not occur exclusively in the patient but in the *relation*.

When we discussed the indications for psychoanalysis, we considered the *analytic couple*; we must now return to this theme within the framework of the interview. If the analytic couple does exist, is it possible to predict it in the interview? Liberman thinks it possible, if the indicators he proposes are used.

Decidedly in favour of the analytic couple, Liberman utilizes interviews to evaluate to what extent the interaction established between interviewer and interviewee will be curative or iatrogenic. In the former case we will take on the task proposed—that is, we will select our patient; in the latter we will know how to disqualify ourselves in time, to give the interviewee "a new opportunity, referring him to another person with whom we believe there can be a conjunction of factors that will favour conditions for the psychoanalytic process to develop" (Liberman, 1972, p. 466).

The indicators Liberman offers for the diagnosis of the prospective compatibility of the couple rely on what we have just seen about the evolution of the interview. If during the interviews a vital crisis is reproduced, and it is, paradigmatically, the one that the interviewee is in the process of undergoing, the one that has in some way led him to the interview, and if this crisis is resolved well, then we can expect that the course of that analysis will follow this favourable model. The isomorphism between the motives for the consultation and the conflicts the patient really has also establishes an auspicious prognosis. In the same way, the greater the analyst's capacity to discern the defence mechanisms mobilized by the patient, the better his situation will be in treating him, the more so if in the course of the interviews these mechanisms change. We have just mentioned the stylistic register as a fine and precise guideline to measure the evolution of the process.

The instruments Liberman lists measure without doubt the analysability of the subject and/or the capacity of the analyst; but do they really measure what Liberman proposes to discover? If there is no isomorphism between the motives the subject offers and his real conflicts (as the analyst sees them, let us suppose correctly), the only thing one can infer is that the patient is very disturbed. Vice versa, if the analyst quickly and penetratingly discerns his potential patient's defence mechanisms, one can infer that he is a competent analyst; but one would still have to prove that the competence derives from a specific system of communication between both of them, because otherwise we would again be faced with the trivial fact that the best couple is achieved if the patient distorts little and the analyst understands much.

Grave pathology on the part of the patient, according to Liberman, can cause him (Liberman) to disqualify himself in order to preserve himself and not damage his instrument of work. It would be nice to ask him to whom he would send this patient, who could damage even *him*, no less! It is clear that here Liberman is simply speaking of indications and analysability, which has nothing to do with the couple, especially when he affirms that "generally the analysts who are just starting their practice are those who will take charge of the more difficult patients which have been discarded by others" (Liberman, 1972, p. 470). The fact that the most capable analysts will have, in general, the most analysable patients is one of the great and painful paradoxes of our practice.

I find the converse case legitimate and plausible—that is, that an analyst who is a beginner and conscious of his limitations should step aside in the face of a difficult case and refer it to a very experienced analyst such as Liberman was. Nevertheless, it is obvious that in this case the criterion of an analytic couple has not been used but simply the one I propose, namely that if other variables are constant the best analyst always forms the best couple. I personally think that an analyst has every right not to take on a particular case, simply because he does not like it or because he considers it difficult; but he should do so without taking refuge in the comforting idea of the couple.

There are other analysts who, without employing Liberman's sophisticated armoury, allow themselves to be led simply by the feeling that the interviewee awakens in them; but I very much mistrust this type of feeling, as it is more applicable to marriage or to sport than to analysis. If after an interview has ended I tell myself I would or would not like to analyse that person, I think a problem of countertransference has been posed, which I have to resolve. No doubt if he seems disagreeable to me, to refer him offers this unfortunate character the means of finding an analyst more sympathetic to him at the outset; but it does not resolve the problem of the feelings he awakens in others. The theme will arise fatally in the analysis and can be resolved only there. Certainly no one proposes that a woman who has fallen in transference love should change her analyst and be treated by a woman.

Finally, I think that the problem of the analytic couple is always based on the error of thinking that the relationship between the analysand and the analyst is symmetrical. One forgets that, however many problems the analyst may have and however much his insalubrious profession may affect him, he is also protected by the setting. If we underline the psychopathology of the analyst, we are going to believe in the importance of the couple; and if we accentuate his abilities, we will believe that the better the analyst, the better he analyses. In my view, this methodological difference can explain, perhaps, the context in which the problem arises, although it does not solve it. The difference between the analyst's ability and his psychopathology does not stem simply from the emphasis with which this dilemma of options is posed, as a good capacity for analysis that is radically linked to the analyst's psychopathology would be worthless. The fate of the analytic relation is defined by the psychopathology of the patient and the qualities of the analyst.

Lastly, one must not confuse some conventional aspects of the beginning of the analysis with its substantial problems. Beyond what is conjunctural, once the process has been established, all this will disappear, and only the psychopathology of the patient and the capacity of the analyst will carry any weight.

In abandoning the idea of the couple, I renounce the chance of making predictions about how the specific link between a particular analyst and a particular analysand will influence the process; but I do so because I consider that the variable studied is illusory or so complex that it cannot be validly considered.

5.5   A thorny clinical case

There are cases that do pose a very unusual situation. Very disturbed by the suicide of his wife, a man decided to consult a woman analyst, who had the same name as the deceased. The analyst consulted faced an acute problem. She wondered whether it would be better for the patient if he were referred to a colleague who would not "really" replicate such unfortunate circumstances. On the other hand, she was aware that the choice was strongly determined by the tragic homonym.

In fact, she had several alternatives: to refer the patient, or to take him on without touching on this delicate matter at all, prudently delegating it to the process that would be initiated. Nevertheless, the analyst felt that both possibilities postponed to an uncertain future what was happening here and now. She decided to pose the problem in the second interview and did so as if it were a contingent and casual subject. The interviewee reacted vividly and averred that, when he had decided to consult her, he had not noticed this circumstance. Yet he understood that the analyst's name could have had something to do with his choice. When this brief moment of insight had passed, he again denied the conflict and affirmed that the circumstance noted would not carry weight in the course of his analysis. The analyst told him that it was a fact that had to be considered and did not hesitate in taking him on, realizing that she was facing a difficult task. She thought that to insist on a change of analyst, going against the patient's (strong) denial, would reinforce that man's omnipotent destructiveness and would have been as if she had given herself up for dead.

To conclude the comment on this interesting case and to elucidate my way of thinking, I can add that I would have done what this analyst did (and I would not have sent the patient to an analyst with a different name, as Gitelson or Rappaport might have done). My conduct would be different, of course, if the patient had opted for a different analyst. In that case, I would have met his request without the least hesitation, abstaining from the use of interpretation in order to convince him. The "interpretation" in that case would be, for me, no more than a countertransferential acting out, as the patient could never receive it in these circumstances as impartial information that would give him better criteria for a decision.

There is still another alternative to consider. Although the analyst in my example (a very experienced technician) decided to take the patient on, she could have excused herself on the basis of a lack of capability. If this is the case, the analyst should recognize his limitations and recommend another who is more experienced. In this way he would give the future analysand proof of his honesty and would inform him, implicitly but formally, about the degree of his illness. None of this would be achieved, however, by saying in this case that the difficulty resided in the homonymy, in the "couple". In the first instance, I inform the patient about my limitations and his; in the second, both are evaded.

5.6   The referral interview

The referral interview covers a very restricted thematic set, which seems simple, but is not so. In reality, it poses complex problems, which can create difficulties in practical management, although they do contribute to a better understanding of the theory of the interview in general.

The referral interview is, in any case, more complex than the other type, as we must obtain from it sufficient information to establish an indication, at the same time preventing the interviewee from forming too close a link with us, thereby endangering our purpose of sending him to a colleague. There is also a third difficulty in this type of interview, and this is the prudence with which we should receive information (if not confessions) and gather data from one who, by definition, is not going to be our analysand.

Liberman insists in his work that in these cases the interviewer should give the name of only one analyst, in order not to reinforce in the interviewee the idea that he is the one who is doing the interviewing. I remember vividly and not without a certain bitterness some people I interviewed when I settled in Buenos Aires in 1967, on my return from London. They were all sent by generous colleagues and friends who had recommended me. Some of these interviewees had my name only; in other cases, I was included in a list of possible analysts. Those who came with their list treated me at times as if they were carrying out a selection of personnel (and, even worse, they did so confident of their great psychological ability!). There are many analysts who do, in good faith, give several names, so as to offer the future analysand a chance to choose, to decide which analyst suits him; but I believe, with Liberman, that they are mistaken.

On the other hand, I remember a middle-aged man referred by a colleague who had given him my name only. The first interview was rough and difficult, and we arranged to meet again a week later. He said then very sincerely that I had seemed to him at first—and still did—unpleasant, rigid and arrogant, so he thought he would not come again and would ask Dr. R. (the colleague who had sent him to me) for the name of another, more cordial and congenial analyst. Then he thought things over again and decided he needed a doctor able to treat him (as Dr. R. without doubt had told him I was), and not a pleasant and attractive friend. This was a patient able to satisfy even Dr. Zetzel!

So I am in complete agreement with Liberman's warnings on this point, and I always give a prospective patient whom I refer just one name. At the same time, I usually ask him to let me know how the pending interview had gone, and I tell him that I am at his disposal, should any difficulties arise. With this I leave open the possibility of his ringing me again if he does not like the analyst to whom I sent him, without reinforcing his manic mechanisms, nor fomenting a reversible perspective.

But I do not feel that the analysand chooses his future analyst, just as the latter chooses the former. I think Liberman conflates two problems here, probably because of his declared adherence to the theory of the analytic couple: the fact that the analysand should never carry out an "interview" of his future analyst does not mean he does not choose him.

I believe that in fact and by right the future analysand does choose his analyst, although I know well that mostly he does so for not very rational reasons; and I know how little we can do to prevent this. The reasons we were chosen, together with the neurotic fantasies of healing that Nunberg studied in his classic essay of 1926, generally appear only long after analysis has begun.

However much it may hurt us, the truth is that we offer our services to the future patient, and he will always have the right to accept or reject them. The idea that I also have the right to choose my patients is unacceptable to me, because I always see my feeling of rejection as a problem of my countertransference. I am not referring here, of course, to the considerations that are decisive in taking on a patient or not, in terms of predilections and conscious convenience, as we saw in chapter 3.

5.7   The feedback

All analysts agree that at the end of the cycle of interviews we have to say something to the interviewee as a basis for our indication. There are analysts (and I am among them) who prefer to give brief reasons, because they believe a very detailed report lends itself more to misunderstanding and facilitates rationalization. Others such as the Liendos (Gear & Liendo, 1972), on the other hand, are more explicit.

In my opinion, feedback should go no further than regarding the basic objective of the realized task—that is, to advise the interviewee, always very succinctly, on the treatment best suited to him, the indication and the basis for it.

In reality, and without considering normal or pathological curiosity, the reasons that establish the indication in principle are not within the area the patient needs to know about.

CHAPTER SIX

The psychoanalytic contract

Just as there is a natural continuity from the theme of indications and contraindications to that of the interview, so there is also continuity from the interview to the contract. Placed between the indications and the contract, the interview should, therefore, be the instrument that on the one hand allows us to establish the indication for treatment and on the other hand leads us to formulate the contract. Thus one of the strategies of the interview will be to prepare the future analysand to subscribe to the metaphoric *psychoanalytic* contract.

6.1 General considerations

Perhaps the word "contract", which is in common use in Spanish- and Portuguese-speaking countries, is not the best because it suggests something legal, something very prescriptive. It might be better to speak of the agreement or the initial accord; but in any case the word "contract" has its strength and is the one in current usage in the above-mentioned countries. In the second part of *Outline of Psychoanalysis*, Freud (1940a [1938]) used the German word *Vertrag*, which means "contract", but it was translated as "pact", which in our discipline strongly suggests a psychopathic action. Strachey also translates *Vertrag* as "pact". Nevertheless, because of the initial objection indicated, one does not speak to the patient about the contract when formulating it; one tells him, rather, that it would be convenient to agree on the bases or conditions for treatment. A friend who was formerly a student of mine in Mendoza told me what happened to him with one of his first patients, to whom he proposed "the drawing up of the contract". The patient, a lawyer with a florid obsessive neurosis, came to the next interview with a rough copy of the contract for the doctor's approval. Thus the word should remain in the domain of the analysts' jargon, not in the patients' domain. We can add briefly that my former student, today a distinguished analyst, made not one but two mistakes. He used the word unadvisedly, and he also created an anticipation of anxiety for the next interview. If the theme of the contract is introduced, it should be resolved immediately and not left to the next interview. In the face of that anxious wait, an obsessive lawyer can react as that man did.

The purpose of the contract is to define concretely the bases for the work to be carried out, such that both parties have a clear idea of the objectives, the expectations and also the difficulties analytic treatment engages them in, in order to avoid ambiguities, errors or misunderstandings that may arise subsequently in the course of the therapy. I would rather say, to avoid the label of being optimistic, that the agreement will serve its purpose when ambiguity surfaces, so it can be analysed using as a base what was said initially—because misunderstandings will unavoidably arise during treatment. From this point of view it could be said that the analytic process consists in some way of fulfilling the contract, and clearing up misunderstandings so that it remains in force.

It is implied here that what is worth most is the spirit of the agreement, whereas the letter can vary in accordance with the situation, with each patient and at each moment. Precisely by attending to the spirit we hold some stipulations to be inescapable and not others. This comes from the reading of two essays that Freud wrote in 1912 and 1913, where he formulated precisely the clauses of the analytic pact.

In the "Recommendations to Physicians Practising Psycho-Analysis" (1912e) and in "On Beginning the Treatment" (1913c), Freud formulates the basic theories of the contract—that is, its spirit—at the same time as he establishes the fundamental rules that compose it, in other words, its clauses.

Freud had a singular talent for discovering phenomena and at the same time explaining them theoretically. Each time we reflect upon it, we are again surprised by the precision and the exactitude with which he defined the terms of the analytic pact and established the bases for fixing the setting. To understand the contract, it must be thought of with reference to the setting; vice versa, the setting can only be studied with reference to the contract because, clearly, it is after concluding certain agreements, which can only be called contractual, that certain variables are fixed as constants of the setting.

These two papers define the strategies that must be used to start the treatment and, prior to these strategies, the agreements that must be reached with the patient to realize the singular task that analysis consists of. Included in the idea of the contract is that the treatment should be ended by common agreement; for this reason, if only one of the two decide to do so, it is called not termination, but interruption of the analysis. Of course, the analysand has the right to rescind the contract at any time, and in very special circumstances so does the analyst.

As Menninger says, every transaction in which there is some type of interchange is based on a contract ("The situation of psychoanalytic treatment as a negotiation between two contracting parties"—Menninger, 1958, chapter 2, "The Contract"). At times this is a brief or an implicit one, but it always exists, and both parties refer to it to carry out the task agreed on, especially if difficulties arise. Although the psychoanalytic contract has its particularities, Menninger continues, in the last instance it is not substantially different from one that can be established when one goes shopping or commissions work from a professional or a worker.

Once the clauses of a contract, of whatever type, have been made explicit, a type of interaction, a task, has been defined; it is for this reason that it is important to expound them clearly. Difficulties that arise later on can only be overcome if the rules by means of which a particular kind of work will develop have been correctly stipulated.

It is also worth noting that the psychoanalytic contract implies not only rights and obligations, but also risks—the risks inherent in any human enterprise. Although the contract is based on the intention of offering the future analysand the greatest security, one must not lose sight of the fact that the risk can never be completely eliminated; to pretend it can would be a mistake considered as over-protection, omnipotent control, mania or idealization, according to the case. I once heard that one of the best woman analysts in the world, at an already advanced age, warned the candidate she was taking on of the risk he ran in the circumstances.

6.2 Freud's recommendations

In the two papers mentioned, Freud says concretely that he is going to make recommendations to the doctor, the analyst. These recommendations, which proved useful for him, may nevertheless vary and not be the same for everyone, he prudently affirms. Although it is true that Freud does not set down fixed rules but, rather, suggestions, the recommendations he makes are in fact universally accepted, and they are the rules we propose to the patients in some measure, implicitly or explicitly, because they are the basis of the task.

When Freud says these recommendations suit his individuality but can vary, he opens up an interesting discussion—that of the difference between style and technique. Although not all analysts make this distinction, I am inclined to think that the technique is universal, and the style changes. It is true that there is a certain ambiguity, because readers may ask what I mean by style and by technique. They may also argue that to classify something as technique or style depends on my personal predilections, at my discretion. All this is entirely true; the more I say that certain rules form part of my style, the more I circumscribe the field of technique as a universal heritage of all analysts and vice versa; but, in any case, I think there is a difference between things that are personal, proper to the style of each analyst and others that are universal, which correspond to a field in which all of us somehow have to concur. I believe this to be a valid difference, always remembering that there will be rules whose location in one field or another is imprecise. I think this imprecision should be accepted as part of the intrinsic difficulty of our task.

Some of Freud's recommendations, which he considers as being eminently personal—such as asking patients to lie down so he does not have to endure being stared at—have become indispensable to our techniques. Clearly what Freud introduces here as something that is part of his style is entirely a universal technical rule. A few analysts discuss this: Fairbairn (1958) is one.

In general, all those who cease to be psychoanalysts because they question the basic principles of our discipline begin by removing the couch from their consulting-room, as did Adler, seeking to lessen his patient's feeling of inferiority. This can be fundamental for an individual psychologist, but never for a psychoanalyst who recognizes in the feeling of inferiority something more than a simple social position between analyst and analysand.

This is why I do not think Fairbairn's (1958) reflections in "On the Nature and Aims of Psychoanalytic Treatment" are convincing. Fairbairn warns analysts about the danger that too strict an adherence to scientific method may make them forget the human factor, which is indispensable and not subtractable from the analytic situation. This leads the great analyst from Edinburgh to mistrust the validity of certain restrictions of the analytic technique, such as the fixed time of the sessions and the use of the couch. He doubts whether it is suitable for the patient to lie on the couch and for the analyst to place himself out of the patient's sight (Fairbairn, 1958, p. 378), a fortuitous inheritance of the hypnotic technique and of some of Freud's peculiarities. In this way Fairbairn finally abandoned the couch, although not without a certain conflict, it seems, because he explains that he is not in favour of the face-to-face technique used by Sullivan (who carried out his famous psychiatric interviews in this way), but, rather, he sits at a desk and places his patient in a comfortable chair, not in front of him but to the side . . . and so forth, and so forth. For someone like me, who likes and respects Fairbairn, these specifications evoke a slight smile.

If I stress the difference between the general and the particular, between the style and the technique, it is because they are sometimes confused, leading to heated and useless discussions. In other words, we can elect our style, but the technical rules come to us from the analytic community, and we cannot vary them.

The way I receive my patients, for example, and the way I ask them to enter the consulting-room, are entirely part of my style. Another analyst will have his own method; unless it is too dissonant with current cultural usage, no method can be considered inferior. Consequently, no one can give a technical rule on this point. When one moves to another consulting-room, it is probable that some of these forms change.

In any case—and it is important to indicate this—once I have adopted my own style, it becomes part of my setting and *my* technique.

In the discussion of the interview technique we pointed out that Rolla (1972) is inclined to stipulate very strictly how to greet the patient, how to sit down, how to seat the patient, and so on. I consider these rules as part of a personal style, not standard elements of the interview. It is proposed, for example, that the interviewer and the interviewee sit in armchairs at a certain angle to each other, in order not to face each other. In my judgement this prescription is part of a style, and no one can say that a person who has a revolving armchair is making a technical mistake.

Returning to Freud's recommendations—they make up the fundamental clauses of the analytic contract, to the extent that they point to the fundamental rule, the use of the couch and the interchange of time and money—that is, the frequency and duration of the sessions, weekly rhythm and holidays.

6.3   Formulation of the contract

The contract should be formulated on the basis of the premises established by Freud that we have just enumerated. It is preferable to centre attention on what is fundamental, and it is neither prudent nor elegant to be too fussy or to issue too many directives. The fundamental rule can be introduced with few words, and with it the use of the couch. Then come the agreements about timetable and fees, days off and holidays, and method of payment. Nothing more.

When we emphasized that what is essential is the spirit and not the letter of the contract, we had in mind that not even the essential clauses have to be introduced at the outset; vice versa, others can be included according to the circumstances.

The rule of free association can be introduced in diverse ways, and even not be made explicit at the outset. As Racker said in a footnote in his third study, the fundamental rule might not be set out at the beginning. It will, in any case, soon be made known to the analysand, for example when he is asked to associate or to say everything that occurs to him about a particular element of the manifest content of a dream (Racker, 1968, p. 71, n. 2).

No one doubts that it is best to communicate the fundamental rule without delay, but there can be exceptions. It must be presented with care to a patient beset by obsessive thoughts so as not to create too great a problem of conscience right at the start. On the other hand, a hypomanic patient—and certainly a manic one—will not need a special stimulus in order to say everything he thinks. In the same way, to emphasize to a psychopath that he has the freedom to say what he will can simply give him the green light for his verbal acting out.

I want to emphasize that even with the agreement we called funda-mental—the rule of free association—special circumstances can arise in which it is advisable to follow a path other than the usual one, without this meaning in any way that we can depart from the rule.

The fundamental clauses of the contract answer an inevitable question in the mind of the interviewee when the indication for analysis is given to him: what does the treatment consist of? Whether or not it is formulated, this question offers us the opportunity to propose what is most important in the contract. We can say, for example: "The treatment consists in your lying on this couch, in the most comfortable and calm attitude possible, and in your trying to say everything that comes to mind, with the greatest freedom and least reserve, trying to be as spontaneous, as free and as sincere as you can." In this way we introduce the fundamental rule and the use of the couch, after which we can speak of timetables and fees.

It is advisable to introduce at the outset the rule about the patient paying for a missed session, but if the interviewee appears to be very anxious or suspicious, it can be left aside and brought up after the first missed session. This postponement, however, sometimes causes problems, because the patient can believe it to be a concrete response to his absence, not a general rule.

On the other hand, other rules should not be proposed at the begin-ning—that is, in the interview—but when they arise in the course of treatment. A typical example could be that of changes of times, or gifts. These are contingent rules, which have to do more with the style of the analyst than with the technique; it is justifiable to discuss them only when the occasion arises. If a patient thinks of making the analyst a gift, or dreams of it, the latter can explain his point of view in such a case.

6.4   Authoritarian contract and democratic contract

Insofar as it will regulate the real aspect of the relationship between ana-lysand and analyst, the accord must necessarily be just and rational, egali-tarian and equitable. Here lies the utility of differentiating the democratic contract from the authoritarian or the demagogic contract. The *democratic* contract is one that takes note of the needs of the treatment and harmo-nizes them with the interest and comfort of both parties.

I have repeatedly observed that young analysts tend to think in good faith that the contract places a greater obligation on the future analysand than it does on them, but in this they are entirely mistaken. Certainly most patients think this way, which is no more than a part of their conflicts. In reality, the analysand only commits himself to fulfil certain agreements that make up the task—and not even actually to fulfil them, but to have the intention of doing so. It is not authoritarian for the analyst to be vigilant and to insist on these agreements, because he should be the custodian of the agreed task as is any worker responsible for his work. And to each obligation of the analysand corresponds symmetrically an obligation of the analyst. At times patients complain that the analyst fixes the holiday period, for example, but there is nothing unilateral or authoritarian in this: every professional fixes his period of rest; furthermore, if this constant remains at the patient's discretion, the work of the analyst becomes disordered.

The contract is rational where agreements are adjusted to what has been decided as being most favourable to the best possible development of the analytic process, in accordance with the art. The regularity and stability of the meetings are justified not only because of a mutual respect between the parties, but because they are necessary for the development of the cure.

From these points of view, it is not difficult to define the *authoritarian* contract as one that puts the convenience of the analyst before the carrying out of the task. If the contract seeks to please or pacify the patient in detriment to the task, it should be called *demagogic*.

If the interviews have developed satisfactorily and have culminated in an indication for analysis, then in founding this indication the analyst will formulate the objectives of the treatment. He will explain to the interviewee that psychoanalysis is a method that enables the analysand to know himself better, which must give him better opportunities for managing his mind and his life. From this arises the question of what the treatment consists in and, consequently, the rules about how, when and where this work, which analysis is, will be effected.

In this way the fundamental analytic rule arises naturally—that is, how the analysand should behave during treatment, how he has to inform us, how he should give us the material with which we are going to work and what our work comprises: feeding back information, interpreting. In this manner we introduce the rule of free association, which can be formulated in diverse ways, and then the constants of time and place, frequency, duration, interchange of money and time, and so forth. Everything, then, occurs naturally, because if I tell someone he is going to work with me, he will immediately ask me how often he has to come, at what time, how long we are going to work for, and so forth. In this context it is expected that the future analysand will ask about the length of the treatment, to which one will reply that analysis is long, it takes years, and its duration cannot be decided beforehand. One can also add that to the extent that one can see the analysis progressing, one worries less about its duration.

We must not lose sight of the fact that, due to their singular nature, the clauses of the psychoanalytic contract are not inviolable, nor do they require of the patient that he adhere to more than knowing them and trying to fulfil them. The analytic contract is not a *contract of adherence*—legal parlance to characterize a contract in which one party imposes and the other must comply: the two parties subscribe (metaphorically) to this agreement, because they consider it convenient.

This is why we said earlier that the contract is important as a reference-point for the subsequent conduct of the patient. We discount at the outset that the analysand will not comply with it; he will not be able to comply with it. The rule is formulated not to seek compliance, but to see how the analysand behaves in the face of it. What has often been called the "permissive attitude" of the analyst consists precisely in that the rule is expounded but not imposed. When an impediment to compliance arises, what matters is for the analyst to see what it is about: the analyst will confront a lack of compliance not with a normative (and even less, a punitive) attitude, but with the specific quality of his understanding.

If I tell the patient to lie on the couch, this is different from my telling him he *has* to lie down, and also from not telling him anything. Only in the first instance is the way open for analysis. In the third, I would never be able to make an interpretation about *voyeurism*, for example. The patient would say, with reason, that it is not due to *voyeurism* that he does not lie down, but because I did not tell him he had to. If I leave it up to him and he decides to remain seated, there is nothing more to say. On the other hand, if I have asked him to lie down and to speak, and the patient tells me he does not like to lie down because he feels anxiety or because it does not seem natural to him to speak lying down to someone who is seated, or whatever, then he is presenting a problem that can and should be analysed. This means that only once the analyst has formulated the rule can he analyse it if the patient does not comply with it. I developed this theme at some length in a paper presented at the Pan-American Congress in New York in 1969.

Tolerance in the face of a lack of compliance with the rule has, in my opinion, nothing to do with ambiguity. I avoid being ambiguous; I prefer to say things in a definite way and not to leave it to the patient to suppose them. If, for example, the patient asks me in the first session whether he may smoke, I say yes, he may, and there is the ashtray. (It belongs entirely to the analyst's style whether or not he allows his patients to smoke.) Some analysts prefer to say nothing, or to interpret the meaning of the question. I think this is an error because interpretation is possible only if the terms of the relation were fixed beforehand. The patient does not understand it as an interpretation, but as my way of saying he can or cannot smoke. If I tell him, for example, "You want to dirty me", he will understand that I do not allow it; if I tell him, "You need me to give you permission", he will understand that I am not opposed to it. In neither case will he have received an interpretation. This is why I prefer not to be ambiguous. If after that clear reply the patient again poses the problem, the analyst has no course other than to interpret. Precisely because he was clear at the beginning, he can be stricter later.

The same is applicable to free association. The fundamental rule should be given to the patient clearly: the idea that in the first place he has the freedom to associate, that he can associate, that he can say everything he thinks; at the same time, he should know that the analyst hopes that he will not keep things to himself, that he will speak without reserve. I do not tell him he has the obligation to say everything he thinks, because I know this is impossible; no one says everything he thinks, not even in the last session of the most fulfilled analysis, because resistance and repression are always there. I therefore try to make the patient see that he has the freedom to say what he thinks but also that he should say it even if it is difficult for him, in such a way that he can know the rule exists and that a lack of compliance with it will be material for my work.

When I began my practice, I did not introduce the rule about lying down on the couch sufficiently clearly; the majority of my patients remained seated, and I did not know what to do. A more pleasing example is one where a student of mine consulted me because *all* his patients remained silent. Although he had already read *Character Analysis* and interpreted their silence, he achieved nothing. His difficult and enigmatic situation could be resolved only when he explained how he had formulated the fundamental rule: "You can say everything you think, and you also have the right to remain silent." With this agreement, the patients opted for the simplest course. This formulation, by the way, is a typical example of the demagogic contract.

This takes us back to the starting-point. We said the contract should be just and equitable. In the case just cited, the contract was demagogic, as it gave the patient more freedom than he in fact has. The fundamental rule is certainly a generous invitation to speak freely, but it is also a severe requirement where it asks that resistance be overcome. This is why I do not think the analytic atmosphere is permissive, as it is often said. The analytic contract implies responsibility, a great and shared responsibility.

6.5   *The contract and cultural usage*

The agreements in a contract, as rules that establish a relationship between two parties, have to adjust to cultural usage. Psychoanalysis should never place itself outside the general norms that rule relationships between people in our society. The analyst should try to respect cultural usage where it is valid. If it is not, and if this can affect him, then he can denounce it and discuss it. Let us take, for example, the question of the payment of fees by cheque. In our country it is cultural usage to pay in this way, and in this sense it would be inappropriate to refuse an analysand's cheque, as long as it came from his account and not, of course, from third parties, because this already implies an abuse of confidence if not a psychopathic act. If an analyst asks his patients to pay him in cash because this is more convenient for him, it is part of his style and his right to do so. I do not do it, because it seems to me that it does not accord with custom and with my personal style. If an analyst were to tell me that he does not receive cheques because the cheque negates the libidinous link with money, I would say that he is mistaken. If a patient thinks that in paying by cheque he does not pay, or he does not dirty the relationship, or whatever, one must analyse these fantasies and the implicit failure to symbolize without taking a precaution that would be appropriate for the active technique. A European analyst once said that he requires payment by cheque so that the patient will not think that he avoids paying his taxes, but in my view this procedure corresponds also to the active technique. It would be better to analyse why this patient thinks thus (or why he *does not* think thus, if this were to occur in Buenos Aires!). A young man, an executive with an important firm, who managed money badly often came with his salary cheque and wanted to transfer it to me. At times he wanted me to function as his bank and return to him the remainder, having deducted my fee. I never accepted this type of arrangement and always preferred to wait for him to set aside the amount and pay me then, even while knowing the risk that he would spend it in the meantime. When he became a partner in the firm, I did accept a company cheque if it was for the exact amount of my fee, although it was signed by the firm's accountant and not by him.

I never accept payment in foreign money, nor on account, but this rule can vary in certain circumstances. An analysand came to the final session before the holidays worried because he had miscalculated the amount to be paid and he no longer had enough money available to pay me. He asked me if he could complete the amount owed in dollars or whether I preferred payment in pesos on his return. I told him to do as he wished and centred my attention on the separation anxiety—of which the patient was conscious for the first time, having denied it invariably for many years. Variations such as these are not, in my view, a change of technique and cannot compromise in any way the course of the treatment.

If an analysand becomes ill and misses sessions for a time one can modify at this juncture the rule of charging for the missed sessions. It will depend on the circumstances, on what the patient proposes and also on what is possible for him. A man of means is not the same as one of scant means; one who asks that his situation be considered is not similar to one who does not pose the problem. The rule can vary within certain limits. There is always a point in every human relationship when it is necessary to know how to listen to the other person, to know what he desires and expects from us, without our being obliged to please him. To accept the opinion of the patient does not always mean gratifying him or conforming to his wishes; similarly, not to accept it does not always have to be a snub or a frustration.

Journeys pose an interesting problem. A Solomonic solution, which I learned from Hanna Segal when she came to Buenos Aires in 1958, is to charge half the fee. This implies, on the one hand, a commitment for the patient, because he continues to take responsibility for his treatment even if he does not come; on the other hand, it covers to some extent the analyst's loss of fees, as "it is not bad business" to charge half the amount for hours one can freely dispose of. A wealthy prospective patient was unsure whether to begin analysis before or after the summer holidays. This person had told me that she was going to Europe and asked me whether I would charge for missed sessions if she should begin treatment beforehand. I told her that if she started treatment before the trip, I would charge her half the value of the missed sessions. This remained a rule for the future; but on one occasion she suddenly went away to a resort for a few days, despite my interpretation of the meaning of this absence. This time I did not exempt her from full payment, so that her unilateral decision would be clearly evident, as would my disagreement with it.

One must not lose sight of the fact that money is not the only thing that counts in these cases—not even the most important thing. For the above-mentioned person, who had money to travel whenever she wished and who limited her journeys to indispensable ones during her prolonged treatment, the reduction of fees had, rather, the character of recognition on my part that her journeys were justified. In the same way, a person can ask that a session be cancelled, or for a change in the time, in order not to feel at fault, not because of the cost of the session or in order to manipulate the analyst psychopathically.

An interesting aspect is that of the influence of inflation upon fees. Among us, the paper presented in 1960 by Liberman, Ferschtut and Sor at the Third Latin-American Psychoanalytic Congress in Santiago, Chile, has become a classic. This work is important because it shows that the psychoanalytic contract seals the destiny of the process and is, in turn, subordinate to cultural factors—in this case, inflation. Santiago Dubcovsky (1979) returned to this theme recently, showing convincingly the effect that inflation has on analytic practice, and the possibilities of neutralizing it, not so much through measures that pretend stability, but with flexible and reasonable agreements, which respect the principles of the method and take account of the necessities and possibilities of both contracting parties.

It is necessary to take great care in these matters and not to slide into a superegoic, irrational attitude. I was taught this by my first patient, today a distinguished lawyer in La Plata, whom I treated for an episodic impotence that worried him very much and that he attributed, not without some reason, to a very strict father. At that time, long ago, my setting was much more lax than it is now, and I had no idea what its stability meant. My patient always asked to change or make up lost sessions when he had to take examinations or to study, and I always conceded to these requests, without ever questioning or analysing them; the "rule" was simply, in these cases, to reach agreement on the time of the session. After he had completed his studies and was very pleased to have overcome his impotence, he went off for a couple of days with a girl to enjoy himself. As always, he asked for a change of time, and I told him I would not grant it, because this was a different situation. He then told me, categorically, that I was the same as or worse than his father: that when he had asked me to change the session time in order to study, I always conceded this; but not if he wanted to go out with a girl. He was right, at least from his point of view. I should have analysed with greater care his previous changes and also this one before giving him a reply. This example shows the importance of the rule, because in this case the rule was that I "had to" change the time. With the patient who went on journeys, on the other hand, the rule was that she was responsible for the session, although I could consider a particular case.

It is always necessary to bear in mind that the contract is a rational act, between adults. Therefore the equanimity with which it is made establishes the basis for mutual respect between analyst and analysand, which is also called the working alliance.

6.6   *The limits of the contract*

The contract establishes a list of conditions with the obligations of analyst and analysand. These relations are reciprocal and, more than this, they have to do with the treatment itself as a legal entity (if I am allowed to use this legal expression). Nevertheless there are rights and obligations that the analyst and the analysand have as people that do not pertain to the contract. It is not always easy to discriminate on this point, and I often see my students hesitate and, to be frank, my colleagues also.

An analyst can supervise one of his patients. It is a right all analysts have, and it is even an obligation if he is a candidate; but in no way can this be included in the contract. Analysts I had occasion to treat have expressed the wish that I should or should not supervise their cases, but I have never replied; I have never felt in any way the need to do so. If the patient refers to something that has to do with the contract, on the other hand, it should be replied to. If he asks me whether I will keep in confidence what he tells me, I say yes, I am obliged to keep professional secrets, even though he should know this and his question may be determined by other factors. But I do not feel obliged to answer questions on points that are at my discretion and for me to choose. If a colleague were to ask me to supervise the spouse or a close relative of a patient of mine, I would not do so; but I do not consider this decision as part of my contract with the patient. If he were to pose this question, I would not feel obliged to explain. I also do not like to supervise patients linked to me through ties of friendship. I discovered once, in supervising a case of homosexuality, that the partner of that man was someone I had known since my youth, and thus I unintentionally found out about his perversion. I think most analysts accept this type of limitation, but they should not be considered in any way as clauses of the contract. An analysand found that I was the supervisor of a candidate who treated his spouse and asked me whether I would supervise that case. I decided to reply that I would not, but I did not consider the posing of this issue as part of the contract.

One of my first patients in Mendoza asked me whether I was a member of the Association, and I answered in the affirmative. He explained then that he had been in treatment with a doctor who had told him he would psychoanalyse him, even though he was not an analyst. When he then asked me whether I was a member or a candidate, I did not feel obliged to reply. Neither in this nor in the former question did I miss the paranoid components (suspicion) and the manic ones (denigration) that were in play, but I did not guide myself by them but by the rational aspect of the contract (naturally according to my best understanding at that moment). In other words, one must separate—where possible—paranoid suspicion from rational mistrust and see where the former ends and the latter begins. And we should not forget that the patient's initial trust is not always very rational.

It is therefore important to demarcate clearly what can be part of the contract and what is part of the internal domain, the individual freedom of each one. That I take notes during or after the session, or that I record, are my way of carrying out my work; I do not have to justify this to the patient. With respect to the tape recorder, there is much heated discussion. Melanie Klein declared herself totally against its use, in the preface to her *Narrative of a Child Analysis* (1961). If one considers that the tape recorder is a device of the analyst for registering his work and studying it, I do not think it violates any technical or ethical precept. No one would think he proceeds wrongly by taking notes after the session. This is precisely what Melanie Klein did with Richard. In my view there is no substantial difference between these procedures; they are two ways of registering a session. If we imagine a character with total recall (such as Borges's *Funes el Memorioso*) who became an analyst, he would not use a tape recorder, but he would be able to reproduce the sessions as if he used one. As a mechanical memory for the analyst, I consider the tape recorder a completely valid device.

6.7   The trial treatment

Among the many problems the contract poses, it is worth mentioning the famous and by now quite forgotten trial treatment. Freud used it to make a diagnosis, according to what he says in "On Beginning the Treatment" (1913c). At the present time most analysts prefer to leave this problem for the interviews. The trial treatment without doubt creates uncertainty in the patient, which muddies the field, because it is undeniable that when one is put to the test, one does everything possible to avoid being rejected.

It seems better, therefore, to entrust the problem of the indication to the interviews and not to include it in the treatment itself as a trial analysis. In any case, in the difficult cases, it is not certain that the interviews can resolve the problem, and one must also bear in mind that it is not prudent to prolong them too much, because they can create unnecessary anxiety in the interviewee and complicate the future analytic relation through the ties that are developing, and even more so where the setting of the interviews makes it inadvisable to interpret the transference that is developing.

This difficulty was mentioned specifically by Freud, who did not wish to favour the establishment of a transference relation before initiating treatment, and probably made use of the trial treatment for this reason. Doubtless this reason carries weight; but the risk can be lessened if the interviews are carried out taking account of their objectives clearly and respecting their own setting.

PART TWO

ON TRANSFERENCE
AND COUNTERTRANSFERENCE

CHAPTER SEVEN

History and concept of the transference

The theory of transference, one of Freud's major contributions to science, is also the pillar of psychoanalytic treatment. In reviewing the works in which the concept makes its appearance and those covering its total development, one is struck by the brevity of this time period—as though the theory of transference had arisen all at once and in its entirety in Freud's mind, although the opposite has always been claimed, namely, that he elaborated on it bit by bit. Nevertheless, it is possible that these two assertions are not contradictory, if the former refers to what is central in the theory and the latter to its details.

7.1 The context of discovery

A recent re-reading of "The Concept of Transference" by Thomas Szasz (1963) made me reconsider this little dilemma, which is surely interesting from the point of view of the history of psychoanalytic ideas. As we all know thanks to Jones (1953–57, Vol. 2) and to Strachey's "Introduction" (1955) to Freud and Breuer's great work, *Studies on Hysteria* (1895d, pp. ix–xxviii), Anna O's treatment took place between 1880 and 1882 and ended with an intense transference and countertransference love—and, one might even say, para-transference, due to the jealousy of Breuer's wife. The three protagonists in this little sentimental drama registered it as a human episode similar to any other. Towards the end of 1882 (the treatment had ended in June of that year), Breuer commented to Freud on this traumatic outcome; but it seems that Freud also did not at first associate the state of falling in love with the therapy. When, a little later, Freud commented on this situation in a letter to Martha Bernays, then his fiancée, he reassured her, saying that this would never happen to him because "for that to happen one has to be a Breuer" (Szasz, 1963, p. 439).

At the beginning of the 1890s, as Jones points out, Freud urged Breuer to communicate his findings on hysteria and observed that Breuer's reticence was founded on his sentimental episode with Anna O. Freud managed to reassure Breuer by relating that something similar had also happened to him, and he therefore considered the phenomenon to be inherent in hysteria.

These details allow us to assert now that in the period of just over ten years between the end of the treatment of that famous patient and the "Preliminary Communication" of 1893, Freud was in the process of developing the basis of his theory of transference.

7.2   Transference and false connection

In the clinical histories of the *Studies on Hysteria* (1895d) there are repeated observations on the singular characteristics of the relationship that is established between the psychotherapist and his patient—in the case of Elisabeth von R, these comments become very clear. In chapter 4 of Freud's "The Psychotherapy of Hysteria", the idea of the *transference* is definitely categorized as a singular human relationship between the doctor and the patient through a *false connection*.

Freud's reasoning on discovering the transference is based on an evaluation of the dependability of the pressure technique (associative coercion). Although he lists three circumstances in which the method fails, he feels that they only validate it.

The *first* occurs when there is no more material to investigate in a particular area; obviously the method cannot be said to fail where there is nothing more to investigate. (You will remember that at this point Freud observes the attitude of the patient, his facial expression, his serenity, his authenticity, in order to appreciate what is really happening.)

The *second* circumstance, described by Freud as *internal resistance*, is doubtless the most characteristic of this method and precisely the one that led to an understanding of the battle of tendencies—that is, the dynamic point of view, the value of conflict in mental life. Freud asserts correctly that in these cases the method continues to be valid, since the pressure technique fails only to the extent that it meets with a resistance; but it is precisely by means of this resistance that one will manage to reach, via association, the material sought.

Lastly, the *third* case, that of an *external obstacle*, marks another apparent failure of the method, and its explanation should be sought in the particular relation of the patient with his psychotherapist; this is why it is external—neither intrinsic nor inherent in the material. Freud distinguishes three cases here, which we can call offence, dependence and false connection.

If the doctor has offended the patient through some small injustice, inattention or lack of interest, or if the patient has overheard some adverse comment about himself or his method, his capacity for co-operation becomes dulled. While the situation persists, the pressure technique fails; but once the point of controversy has been cleared up, co-operation is reestablished, and the procedure functions efficiently once more. It does not matter, Freud points out, whether the offence is real or only felt by the patient; either case presents an obstacle to the pressure technique as a way of working for patient and doctor; and co-operation is reestablished only through the necessary explanation. Here Freud already incorporates in his theories, albeit implicitly, the idea of internal reality, *felt* by the patient, which will be of great importance for the future theory of transference.

The second form of extrinsic resistance comes from a special fear the patient has: that of *dependence*, of losing his autonomy, even of remaining sexually attached to the doctor. Let us say en passant that it is unusual for Freud not to see a false connection here, based on the theory of seduction he held at the time. In this case, the patient refuses to cooperate and rebels, to avoid becoming prey to a feared and dangerous situation; and here also the pertinent explanation (in the last instance the *analysis* of that fear) resolves the problem.

The third type of extrinsic resistance is the false connection, where the patient ascribes to the doctor (unpleasant) representations that arise during the work. Freud calls this "transference" [*Übertragung*] and points out that it occurs by means of a false, erroneous connection. Freud gives a convincing example, which is worth quoting: "In one of my patients the origin of a particular hysterical symptom lay in a wish, which she had had many years earlier and had at once relegated to the unconscious, that the man she was talking to at the time might boldly take the initiative and give her a kiss. On one occasion, at the end of a session, a similar wish came up in her about me. She was horrified at it, spent a sleepless night, and at the next session, though she did not refuse to be treated, was quite useless for work" ("The Psychotherapy of Hysteria", 1890d, pp. 302–303). And Freud adds: "Since I have discovered this, I have been able, whenever I have been similarly involved personally, to presume that a transference and a false connection have once more taken place" (p. 303).

It should be pointed out that Freud notices here in removing the obstacle that the transferred wish that had frightened the patient so much appeared as her next pathological recollection, as the one demanded by the logical context; that is, instead of being remembered, the wish appeared with direct reference to him, to Freud, in the present. In this way, despite the nascent theory of transference being explained as the (mechanical) result of associationism, Freud already locates it in the dialectic of past and present, in the context of repetition and resistance.

It is worth emphasizing that Freud notes already in this text that these false connections of the transference constitute a regular and constant phenomenon of therapy and that, while increasing the work, they do not constitute an extra task; the work for the patient is the same—that is, to conquer displeasure at remembering a particular wish made at a certain moment. We should observe that Freud speaks here specifically about *desire* and *memory*, but he does not yet note the relationship between the two, which will engage his attention in "The Dynamics of Transference" (1912b).

On rereading these two admirable pages in "The Psychotherapy of Hysteria", one is gripped by the idea that already in 1895 the entire theory of transference was potentially in Freud's mind, and with it the whole of psychoanalysis—the idea of conflict and resistance, the prevalence of psychic reality, and of sexuality. We will see presently that, in fact, in the "Postscript" to the case of "Dora" ("Fragment of an Analysis of a Case of Hysteria", 1905e [1901], pp. 112–122), the theory is expounded in its complete form.

7.3   Transference of the wish

In section C on "Wish-Fulfilment", chapter 7 of *The Interpretation of Dreams* (1900a), Freud uses the word "transference" to give an account of the process of dream-work. The unconscious wish could never reach consciousness nor evade the effects of censorship unless it assigned its charge to the day's residues in the preconscious. Freud also calls this mental process "transference" [*Übertragung*]. Although he never says he employs the same word because it is the same phenomenon, many authors are certain of the conceptual identity. In Argentina, Avenburg (1969) and Cesio (1976) are of this opinion. Avenburg says, for example, that transference is nothing other than the utilization of the analyst as the day's residues, indifferent in themselves, as a support for the unconscious wish and its infantile object. Cesio, for his part, bases his reasoning on the two ways in which Freud uses the word transference; applying to the transference the mechanisms of dream-work, he concludes that the identity is evident.

According to Jacques-Alain Miller (1979), a distinguished exponent of the Lacan school, the term transference appears in *The Interpretation of Dreams*, but only later does it acquire its more specialized—that is, clinical—meaning. This author goes a bit further, because he barely takes into account the theory of the false connection in the *Studies on Hysteria* (1895d). This undoubtedly somewhat partial point of view is understandable because what interests Miller is to support Lacan's idea of the signifier—the dream takes over the day's residues, empties them of meaning and assigns to them a different value, a new significance. "That is where Freud speaks for the first time of the transference of meaning, of displacement, of utilization by the wish of forms very strange to it, but which it takes over, charges, infiltrates and endows with a new significance" (Miller, 1979, p. 83). With a similar attitude, Michel Silvestre (1987b), the young and ill-fated exponent of the same trend, asserts that transference is in the first place a transference of the signifier, a "representation" (*Demain la psychanalyse* ["Tomorrow Psychoanalysis"]); and Guillermo A. Maci (1983) says expressively that the subject in analysis is always transferred, swept along by the signifier.

It is notable, however, that other authors study and expound the theory of transference without in any way taking into account section C, which we are considering. I point out this difference because I believe it is relevant to basic theoretical problems on the nature of the transference phenomenon.

Personally, I feel that the utilization of the same word in the two contexts mentioned does not necessarily imply a conceptual identity between them for Freud. However, applying the ideas of Guntrip (1961), we can think that in the *Studies on Hysteria* and in the "Postscript" to "Dora" Freud expounds a *personalist* theory of transference, and in chapter 7 he gives an account of the same phenomenon through a focus on process—mental *process*. I agree with Strachey on this point. He explains in a footnote (1900a, p. 562) that Freud used the same word to describe two different but not unrelated psychological processes.

7.4 *The transference in "Dora"*

In the "Postscript" to the analysis of "Dora" (published in 1905 but undoubtedly written in January 1901), Freud develops a wide and comprehensive theory of transference, including all the ideas that crystallized in the work of 1912, which we discuss in chapter 8.

During psychoanalytic treatment, according to Freud, the neurosis ceases to produce new symptoms; but its power, which has not been extinguished, is applied to the creation of a special class of mental structures, almost always unconscious, to which should be given the name of *transferences*. ("It may be safely said that during psycho-analytic treatment the formation of new symptoms is invariably stopped. But the productive powers of the neurosis are by no means extinguished; they are occupied in the creation of a special class of mental structures, for the most part unconscious, to which the name of 'transference' may be given"—1905e [1901], p. 116.)

These *transferences* are impulses or fantasies that become conscious in the course of treatment, and they have the peculiarity that past characters now become incarnate in the doctor. Thus psychological experiences are relived as if they belonged not to past but to the present and now related to the psychoanalyst. Some of these transferences are almost identical to the original experience, and, applying a metaphor borrowed from printing, Freud calls them *reimpressions*; others, on the other hand, have a more ingenious construction whereby they undergo the modelling influence of some real event (related to the doctor or to his circumstances), and they are then *new editions* rather than reimpressions—products of sublimation.

Experience consistently shows—Freud continues—that transference is an inevitable phenomenon of psychoanalytic treatment; a new creation of the illness, it should be fought as were the earlier creations. If the transference cannot be avoided, it is because the patient uses it as a device to ensure that pathological material remains inaccessible; but, he adds, it is only after it has been resolved that the patient is able to become convinced of the validity of the constructions realized during the analysis. We see, then, that transference already makes its appearance here with its two aspects—as obstacle and as agent of cure—thus posing a great dilemma for Freudian reflection.

Freud does not doubt that the phenomenon of transference complicates the course of the cure and the work of the doctor; but it is also clear that, for him, it adds nothing essentially to the pathological process, nor to the development of the analysis. In the last instance, the work of the doctor and the patient does not differ substantially, whether the impulse to be dominated is referred to the person of the analyst or to any other.

Freud asserts in the "Postscript" (in 1905e [1901])—and, indeed, throughout his works—that psychoanalytic treatment does not create the transference but discovers it, makes it visible, just as with other occult psychic processes. Transference exists outside and within analysis; the only difference is that in the latter it is detected and made conscious. In this way, the transference is developing and being discovered continually; and Freud concludes with these enduring words: "Transference, which seems ordained to be the greatest obstacle to psychoanalysis, becomes its most powerful ally, if its presence can be detected each time and explained to the patient" (Freud, 1905e [1901], p. 117).

7.5   Defining characteristics

With what Freud said in the "Postscript" to "Dora" we can now characterize the transference. It is a general phenomenon, universal and spontaneous, which consists in joining the past with the present through a false connection, which superimposes the original object on the present one. This superimposition of past on present is linked to objects and desires from the past that are not conscious for the subject and that give his conduct an irrational seal, where the affect does not seem appropriate either in quality or in quantity to the real, actual situation.

Although in the "Postscript" to "Dora" Freud does not consign this phenomenon to infancy, since he says, for example, that at a certain moment Dora makes a transference from Herr K. to him, at every moment in his reasoning there is evidence of the existence and importance of the paternal transference—that is, a reference to the father, although not necessarily to the father of her childhood.

An accurate resumé of Freud's ideas on transference appears in the five lectures he gave at the invitation of G. Stanley Hall at Clark University, Massachusetts, in September 1909, and published in the following year. In his fifth lecture Freud speaks of the transference, underlines its function as an ally in the analytic process and defines it rigorously along three parameters: reality and fantasy, conscious and unconscious, present and past. The emotional life the patient cannot remember is relived in the transference, he concludes, and there is where it should be resolved.

At this point, then, the Freudian theory of transference should be considered as worked out and complete. Transference is a peculiar object relation with an infantile root, of an unconscious nature (primary process) and therefore irrational, which confuses the past with the present, which gives it its character of inadequate, maladjusted, inappropriate response. Transference, as a phenomenon of the *Ucs* system, belongs to psychic reality, to fantasy and not to factual reality. This means that the feelings, impulses and desires that appear in the present moment and in relation to a particular person (object) cannot be explained in terms of the real aspects of that relation, but only if they are referred to the past. This is why Greenson (1967) says that the two fundamental traits of a transference reaction are that it is repetitive and inappropriate (p. 155)—that is, irrational.

In light of this Freudian characterization, most authors try to understand the transference in the dialectic of fantasy and reality. As indicated by Freud in diverse contexts, by Ferenczi in 1909, later by Fenichel (1941, 1945a) and more recently by Greenson (1967), the psychic event is always the result of this dialectic—a mixture of fantasy and reality.

A reaction is never one hundred percent transferential, nor an action entirely just and balanced. The greater the influence of repressed impulses seeking discharge through derivatives, the more warped will be the correct evaluation of differences between past and present, and the greater, too, will be the transferential component in the conduct of the person in question, as Fenichel (1945a) says. We should consider, therefore, the transference as the irrational, the unconscious, the infantile in human conduct, co-existing with the rational, the conscious and the adult in a complementary series. Certainly as analysts we should not think that everything is transference; we should discover the portion of it that exists in every mental act. Not everything is transference, but transference exists in everything, which is not the same thing.

Later on we will return to this extremely complex theme to try to elucidate the relation between fantasy and reality in the transference, as well as the interplay between transference and experience, which seems to me fundamental for a more precise definition of the phenomenon.

7.6   The contributions of Abraham and Ferenczi

The theory of transference expounded by Freud in the "Postscript" (in 1905e [1901]) evoked the interest of his first disciples. Freud himself, in his 1912 article, comments on a work by Stekel in 1911; and Abraham and Ferenczi had also published by this time two important works that complete and broaden Freud's ideas.

Abraham's work, "The Psycho-sexual Differences between Hysteria and Dementia Praecox", dates from 1908. Abraham, having taken up Jung's ideas on the psychology of dementia praecox of a year earlier, centres the difference between hysteria and dementia praecox on the disposability of the libido. Dementia praecox destroys the individual's capacity for sexual transference—that is, for object love. This withdrawal of the libido from an object to which it had been transferred at one time with particular intensity is typical, because dementia praecox implies precisely a ceasing of object love, the withdrawal of libido from the object and the return to auto-erotism. The presenting symptoms of dementia praecox, as studied by Jung, are for Abraham a form of auto-erotic sexual activity.

Abraham's work emphasizes the capacity to transfer the libido, but it neglects the fixation on the past. Thus the difference between "real" love and transference is not made clear. It is because of his interest in differentiating two types of processes, neurosis and psychosis, that Abraham sacrifices the difference between present and past in the object relation, which is transparent in the epicrisis of "Dora". It is important to note that Abraham practically delimits here the two great groups of neuroses that Freud was to describe in 1914 in "On Narcissism: An Introduction".

I believe that Abraham's contribution in this work is relevant for the psychology of psychosis, but not for the theory of transference.

* * *

Jung's and Abraham's investigation was continued, a year later, by Sandor Ferenczi. He emphasizes the importance and the ubiquity of the transference and explains it as the mechanism through which the typical forgotten experience is placed in contact with an actual event through unconscious fantasy. The transference, as a general tendency of neurotics, finds in the course of analytic treatment the most favourable conditions for its appearance, where repressed impulses, which, thanks to the treatment, are becoming conscious, are directed *in statu nascendi* to the person of the doctor, who acts as a type of catalyst.

Ferenczi understands clearly that the tendency to transfer is the basic trait of neurosis—or, as he says, that neurosis is the passion for transference: the person flees from his complexes and, in a total submission to the pleasure principle, distorts reality according to his desires.

This characteristic of neurotics allows a clear distinction between neurosis, dementia praecox and paranoia. According to the ideas of Jung

(1907) and Abraham (1908a), in dementia praecox the person withdraws his libido (interest) completely from the external world and becomes autoerotic. The paranoid person cannot tolerate the instinctive impulses within himself and liberates himself from them by projecting them on to the external world. Neurosis, at the opposite pole to paranoia, on the other hand, instead of expelling unpleasant impulses, seeks objects in the external world to charge them with impulses and fantasies. To this process, the opposite of projection, Ferenczi gives the enduring name of *introjection*. Through introjection, the neurotic incorporates objects in his ego so as to transfer his feelings to them. Thus his ego is widened, whereas the paranoid ego is narrowed.

Whereas Abraham's work is a decisive yardstick in differentiating neurosis from psychosis and in distinguishing two classes of libido (auto- and allo-erotic) in terms of object relations, Ferenczi's work deals specifically with the theory of the transference, making it clear that its extent measures the degree of illness. Thus he clearly establishes the dialectic of the transference between fantasy and reality and is able to base the phenomenon on the mechanisms of projection and introjection, a theme that will be central to the investigation by Melanie Klein, his analysand and disciple. Ferenczi's two contributions are without doubt fundamental.

CHAPTER EIGHT

The dynamics of transference

In this chapter we deal with "The Dynamics of Transference", which Freud wrote in 1912 and included in his technical works. In fact it is essentially a high-level, theoretical work (Strachey noted this—see Freud, 1912b, p. 98). Freud attempts to solve two problems: the origin and the function of the transference in psychoanalytic treatment. It must be noted that transference, in this study, is an essentially erotic phenomenon for Freud, although the development of his thought leads him to classify transference as positive (erotic) and negative (hostile).

8.1 *The nature and origin of transference*

The *origin* of transference must be sought in certain models, stereotypes or clichés, which we all have and which arise as the result of the innate disposition and the experiences of our early years. These models of erotic behaviour are repeated continually throughout life, although they can change in the face of new experiences. In fact, only a portion of the impulses that feed these stereotypes reaches full psychic development— the conscious part, which directs itself to reality and is at one's disposition. Other impulses, arrested in the course of development, set aside from consciousness and from reality, prevented from any expansion outside fantasy, remain in the unconscious.

Freud distinguishes here two phenomena that arise from the past: one that has reached full psychic development and remains at the disposition of consciousness (of the ego, in terms of the second or structural model), and one set aside from consciousness and from reality. In this Freudian reflection I base my idea of transference as contrasting with *experience*. I mean that stereotypes are composed of two classes of impulses: conscious impulses, which help the ego to understand present circumstances using models from the past and within the reality principle (*experience*), and unconscious ones, which, subjected to the pleasure principle, take the present for the past in search of satisfaction, of discharge (*transference*). The stereotypes of behaviour, then, are *always* models from the past in which these two factors, experience and transference, are present in a complemental series. Although Freud does not establish this difference, it is necessarily entailed if one wishes to define transference precisely.

To return now to Freud's exposition: if an individual's need for love is not entirely satisfied in real life, his attitude will always be one of search, of awaiting, in relation to everyone he meets or finds; and it is very likely that both parts of the libido, conscious and unconscious, will apply themselves to this search. In accordance with the previous definition, the conscious part of the libido will apply itself to this search in a rational and realistic manner, whereas the unconscious will do so with the sole logic of the primary process seeking a discharge.

There is no reason why the analyst should be an exception in such circumstances, and so the patient's unsatisfied libido will direct itself to him as it would to any other person, as Ferenczi stated in his essay of 1909. If what could be justified rationally is exceeded in quantity and in nature, this is because this transference relies more on what has been repressed than on conscious, anticipatory ideas. In my view, if transference is to be distinguished from the totality of behaviour, we should consider that the "conscious, anticipatory ideas" do not belong to it. I even think that the absence of this distinction leads Freud into theoretical difficulties.

With respect to its nature and intensity, then, Freud is clear and definite, and throughout his writings he maintains the identical opinion: transference is the same both within and outside analysis; it should not be attributed to the method, but to the illness, the neurosis. Note what he says, for example, about the sanatoria for nervous illnesses.

8.2   Transference and resistance

The other problem Freud poses is more complex: why does transference appear during psychoanalytic treatment as *resistance*? At the beginning of his paper, he finds a clear and satisfactory answer to this problem, but things become more complicated later on.

Freud's explanation is based on the idea that a necessary condition for neurosis to arise is the process described by Jung (in "Über Konflikte der kindlichen Seele", 1910) as *introversion*, according to which the libido that is capable of consciousness and is directed towards reality is diminished, distances itself from reality and feeds the subject's fantasies, reviving the subject's infantile imagos. The pathological process develops from the moment of that introversion (or regression) of the libido, and two factors contribute to its realization: (1) the absence of satisfaction in the real and actual world, which initiates the introversion (current conflict and regression), and (2) the attraction of unconscious complexes or, better still, the unconscious elements of those complexes (infantile conflict and fixation).

Where psychoanalytic treatment consists in following the libido in this regressive process in order to make it accessible again to consciousness and serviceable for reality, the analyst becomes in fact the enemy of the forces of regression and repression, which operate now as *resistance*. Here the relation between resistance and transference could not be clearer: the forces that set the pathological process in motion are now directed against the analyst as an agent of change who wishes to reverse the process. Ferenczi (1909) noticed this, saying that the impulses liberated by the treatment were directed towards the analyst, who acts as a catalytic agent.

This reflection, which transforms an explanation of process into the personalistic one that corresponds to it, is the same as that always used by Freud to establish the analogy between repression and resistance. Moreover, Freud relies on the linking (personalistic) phenomenon of resistance to justify his (process-type) theory of repression. I think that this reflection suffices to give an account of the relation between transference and resistance. Nevertheless, Freud is dissatisfied and asks another question: why does the libido withdrawn from repression during the curative process become linked to the doctor so as to operate as a resistance? In other words, why does resistance utilize the transference as its best instrument?

Analytic treatment, Freud continues, has to overcome the introversion (regression) of the libido, which is motivated by the frustration of satisfaction (external factor) on the one hand, and by the attraction of unconscious complexes (internal factor) on the other. Thus each act of the analysand counts on this factor of resistance and represents a compromise between the forces that gravitate towards health and those that oppose it (Freud, 1912b, p. 103). When we follow a pathogenic complex into the unconscious, we soon enter a region where resistance makes itself clearly felt, so that each association must carry its seal: and at this point transference enters the scene (ibid.). As soon as any element in the subject matter of the complex is suitable for being transferred onto the figure of the doctor, this transference takes place and produces the next association, which announces itself as a resistance: a stoppage of the associative flow, for example. It is inferred from this experience that the element in the subject matter of the complex suitable for being transferred has penetrated into consciousness with priority over any other possible one *because* it satisfies the resistance. Again and again "when we come near to a pathogenic complex, the portion of that complex which is capable of transference is first pushed forward into consciousness and defended with the greatest obstinacy" (Freud, 1912b, p. 104).

There is a point here in Freud's reasoning that I have always found difficult to understand. If the portion of the complex capable of transference is mobilized because it satisfied the resistance, then it cannot be, at the same time, that which awakens the strongest resistance. Along the same line of reasoning, it is claimed that the resistance causes the transference (the transference idea reaches consciousness because it satisfied the resistance) and the opposite—that the transference idea reaches consciousness so as to mobilize the resistance (and it is defended with the greatest tenacity).

Freud does not seem to notice his ambiguity (or what I call his ambiguity) and gives the impression of favouring the second alternative—that is, that transference is utilized to promote the resistance. Freud notes that the transferential link, in transforming a wishful impulse into something related to the very person to whom the impulse is directed, makes it more difficult to admit. This is incompatible with what he had said before— that for the patient the work is the same. In this way, it seems that Freud wants to say that the impulse (or the desire) becomes a transference in order to be able to be ultimately resisted. What Freud actually says is that "it is evident that it becomes particularly hard to admit to any proscribed wishful impulse if it has to be revealed in front of the very person to whom the impulse relates" (Freud, 1912b, p. 104).

In short, Freud's point of view in this paper could be expressed by saying that the transference is serviceable for resistance because: (1) the transference is the most effective distortion, and (2) because it leads to the strongest resistance. In accordance with Point 2, transference is only a tactic the patient employs so as to resist and, if this is so, it can no longer be said that the cure does not create it.

In any case, if we wish to clear up this difficult problem with the means Freud gives us in *Inhibitions, Symptoms and Anxiety* (1926d), we can say that the emergence of an (anxious) memory sets up a *resistance of repression*, which transforms it into a linking phenomenon that coalesces immediately in the *resistance of transference*. Perhaps this is what Freud meant in 1912 if he asserted, first, that there is no better way to avoid remembrance than transferring and, immediately afterwards, that transference is what conditions the strongest resistance, because what is present at the moment is more difficult to recognize. However, this explanation is as valid as its converse—namely, that the impulse that arises in the transference revives the memory, as Freud himself said in 1895.

The contradiction I believe I have noticed derives from Freud's reference to transference at times as a function of *memory* and at others as a function of *desire*. With regard to remembering, the best resistance will be transference, because it transforms a memory into something present—"live and direct", as the television people say. From the point of view of desire, on the other hand, its actuality will be what awakens the strongest resistance. At no time does Freud distinguish between resistance to memory and resistance to desire, and, therefore, in my view, he allows a contradiction to remain; but he certainly never loses sight of the complexity of the phenomenon. He cannot rid himself completely of the mechanistic idea of the false connection, yet in his early example in "The Psychotherapy of Hysteria" he clearly perceives the interplay between these two factors and points out that stirring up the resistance to the transference leads straight to the pathogenic memory (1895d).

To repeat: that which most adjusts itself to the resistance to memory is transference, without doubt, where by means of it the patient does not remember. What could be better for not remembering than exchanging the memory for actuality, the present? For this to happen, it is obvious that the subject matter of the pathogenic complex most adjusted to the present situation will penetrate into consciousness, thereby allowing the complex to repeat itself instead of being remembered. To avoid the memory, there is nothing better than the occurrence of transference: as an example, just when I was about to remember my rivalry with my father, I began to feel rivalry with my analyst, and this transference served me marvellously well in eluding the memory. This is what Freud (1909d) observes in connection with the "Rat Man", and he says so specifically.

When we assert, instead, that it is the transferential event that conditions the strongest resistance, this is because we are no longer thinking about memory but about wishful impulses. What situation could be more embarrassing for us than recognizing a desire if its object is present?

8.3 The transference resistance

To resolve the complex relation between resistance and transference with which Freud deals in 1912, I propose to view it from two different angles, which, while they are in some way irreconcilable, yet operate in unison, each serving as a resistance to the other. This is why Ferenczi says—wisely—that if the patient speaks of the past, we should speak of the present; if he speaks to us of the present, we should speak to him of the past.

If what we seek is to recover the pathogenic memory, then the transference operates as the best distortion, in such a way that as resistance to

the memory increases, so the analysand will try to establish a transference to avoid remembering. But if we consider the desire, the impulse
itself, then the reverse will be the case. It will always be more difficult to
confess to a present desire, a desire directed to an interlocutor, than to
remember what had been experienced with another person in the past.
The problem is linked, then, to the antinomy between memory and desire.
It is worth pointing out that this antinomy traverses the entire praxis of
analysis from beginning to end. I have considered this point at length
because I believe it encloses a great theoretical problem. What I have
considered as a contradiction in Freud's thought derives in the last
instance from his doubts on the ultimate nature of the transference phenomenon. This doubt is not only Freud's; it appears continually in many
discussions on the theory of the technique. As Racker (1952) points out in
"Considerations on the Theory of Transference", there are analysts who
consider the transference only as resistance (to remembering) and those
for whom memories serve only to explain it. In other words, there are
analysts who utilize the transference to recover the past and others who
have recourse to the past in order to explain the transference. However,
this antinomy is inconsistent, because the transference is *at the same time*
past and present, and its resolution brings with it the solution to *both*, not
just one. The unconscious is atemporal, and the cure consists in giving it
temporality, in redefining a past and a present. In this sense, if it is successful, analysis resolves dialectically Heidegger's three stases of time.
Memory, transference and history are, in reality, inseparable. The analyst
should enable the past and the present to converge in the mind of the
analysand, overcoming repressions and dissociations that try to separate
them.

It may be advisable to remember that the concept of the transference
resistance does not belong to the Freud of 1912, but rather to the Freud of
1926. In chapter 11, section A of *Inhibitions, Symptoms and Anxiety*, particularly on p. 160, where he classifies three kinds of resistance of the
ego, Freud defines the transference resistance with precision (1926d, pp.
157–164). He believes the transference resistance to be of the same nature
as the repression resistance, but with special effects in the analytic process
since it succeeds in "re-animating a repression which should only have
been recollected" (1926d, p. 160). This phrase, again, is ambiguous. It
could be understood to mean that the transference resistance is the same
thing as the repression resistance, only that it is referred to the analyst
and to the analytic situation; or, conversely, that the (resistance of) transference re-animates a repression that should only have been remembered.
In the first case Freud would say that the repression resistance is the
same as the transference resistance, only viewed from another perspective; in the second, the obliteration of the memory provokes the transference.

8.4   The enigma of the positive transference

Perhaps the major problem Freud poses in 1912 is why transference, basically an erotic phenomenon, is so well suited to be a means of resistance in analysis, which does not seem to happen in other therapies. We should not forget that, to resolve this enigma (if it is one), Freud classified the transference as positive and negative, just as he divides the former into erotic and sublimated. Only the negative and positive transferences of erotic impulses act as a resistance; and these two components, Freud continues, are the ones we eliminate, making them conscious; while the third factor, "which is admissible to consciousness and unobjectionable, persists and is the vehicle of success in psychoanalysis exactly as it is in other methods of treatment" (1912b, p. 105). The German original (*Studienausgabe, Ergänzungsband*, p. 165) has *unanstössige Komponente*, where "*anstössig*" means what is socially inadmissible and "*unanstössig*" the opposite—that which is unobjectionable and acceptable. Racker (1952) translated more freely, "sublimated positive transference" (*Transference and Countertransference*, passim, especially p. 74). From this point of view, Freud accepts straight away, without hesitation, that psychoanalysis operates ultimately through suggestion, if by suggestion is meant the influence of one human being on another by means of the transference.

It is perhaps worth remembering here the postulates of Ferenczi's essay of 1909, especially the second part, where he studies the role of the transference in hypnosis and suggestion. Without according great importance to the differences between these two phenomena, Ferenczi supports Bernheim's view that hypnosis is only a form of suggestion. (As we know, in 1921 Freud finally declared himself against Bernheim—or in favour of Charcot, which is the same thing—asserting that suggestion is a form of hypnosis; the hypnotizer takes the place of the ego ideal—the superego— of the hypnotized and thus exerts his influence.) Remember the woman whom the great Hungarian treated first with hypnotism and then with psychoanalysis. In the second treatment the transference love arose, and then the patient confessed to having had similar feelings during the previous cure, and that it was due to love that she had obeyed the hypnotic suggestions. Ferenczi then concludes that hypnosis can operate because the hypnotizer awakens in the hypnotized subject the same feelings of love and fear he had for the (sexual) parents of his childhood. Suggestion is, for Ferenczi, a form of transference. The medium feels for the hypnotizer the same unconscious love he had felt as a child for his parents. Ferenczi's paper concludes: "*According to this conception, the application of suggestion and hypnosis consists in the deliberate establishment of conditions under which the tendency to blind belief and uncritical obedience present in everyone, but usually kept repressed by the censor (remains of the infantile-erotic loving and fearing of the parents) may unconsciously be transferred to the person hypnotising or suggesting"* (Ferenczi, 1916, pp. 92–93. Ferenczi's italics in original).

Leaving for later on the arresting theoretical problem of the relation between transference and suggestion, everything leads one to suppose that, on this point, the unusual intensity of the transference phenomenon, which neither Freud nor his disciples had as yet realized, shakes for a moment the solid theoretical frame that could be built in the "Postscript" to "Dora".

In this case, in fact, Freud uses a psychotherapeutic rather than a psychoanalytic criterion. It is true that the positive transference of erotic impulses (submission, seduction, hetero- and homosexual attraction, and so forth), which is not touched in psychotherapy, operates favourably for the cure, if by cure we mean a better repression of the conflicts; in psychoanalysis, instead, insofar as it is analysed, it is transformed into resistance. There is no need to explain why transference is so suitable as a means of resistance in analysis and not when other methods are used, because this is not the case; but only in analysis is it revealed, as Freud himself taught us. If I practice a psychotherapy that utilizes the homosexual submission of my (masculine) patients to make them progress and improve, I can certainly say that no problems of transference resistance arise; but the truth is that I establish a perverse link with my patients and nothing more.

The need Freud feels to explain why the transference operates in analysis as an obstacle, as a very strong resistance, is based on a premise Freud himself rejects and which is, in fact, not sustainable: the transference is not stronger within the analysis than outside it. Racker (1952) makes this same mistake, in my view, in trying to explain why the transference is so strong in analysis, availing himself of what he calls the abolition of rejection.

Analysis does not create these phenomena, as Freud said on many occasions; they are in human nature, and they are the essence of the illness. Ferenczi (1909) said that the *quantum* of transference is the *quantum* of illness, of neurosis. Let us take a very simple and true example—a patient of passive–feminine character who avails himself of homosexuality as a defence in the face of castration anxiety. In reality, what do I as an analyst add to this when I mobilize the defence? I give the analysand access to something that was always present, because his homosexuality avoids the castration anxiety while at the same time realizing it, as, in fact, a passive homosexual does not use his penis, or at least uses it badly. Only from the economical point of view is it true that, in stirring up his defence (homosexuality), his castration anxiety is increased. More exactly, his anguish does not increase; it becomes evident where analysis has stirred up a specific way of managing it. (I set aside here the problem of whether anxiety or feelings in general can be unconscious, because it is not pertinent to my line of reasoning.)

8.5   *Function of the transference*

Another way of understanding what we are saying is to ask to what extent the functional explanation of particular phenomena is pertinent, to what extent functionalism is useful in psychoanalysis. We know that *functionalism* attempts to explain social and, particularly, anthropological events through their *function*—that is, through their role in the social system to which they belong. (Malinowski and Radcliffe-Brown are the principal interpreters of this orientation, which Nagel [1961, section 2, chapter 14] discusses thoroughly.)

Without entering upon a discussion of its epistemological foundations, functionalism does not seem to be applicable to psychoanalysis, because of the type of events our discipline deals with. Freud taught us that the symptom always expresses all the terms of the conflict; it is never simple, it is complex. Wälder (1936) bases the principle of multiple function on this teaching, as it tells us that functionalism is always equivocal in psychoanalysis, where there is no linear and simple causality, where the function varies with the perspective of the observer. According to the functionalist "theory" of our hypothetical analysand, homosexuality fulfils the function of protecting him from castration anxiety; but for me, being his analyst, it fulfils the "function" of making him ill.

The idea of explaining transference *as a function* of resistance leads, perhaps, to an excessively simple position. Not only is the functional criterion insufficient in psychoanalysis; it can, at times, mislead us. In the development of the cure, for example, one must discriminate between expectations of how it should be carried out and the real fact of how it is developing. These are two different things. At the end of his essay, Freud says that the analysand wants to act [*agieren*] his unconscious impulses, instead of remembering them, "in the way the treatment desires them to be". Nevertheless, the truth is that the cure—or, in this case, the analyst—has no cause to wish for anything. The psychoanalytic process develops with reference to its own dynamics, which we as analysts should respect and, as far as possible, understand.

In this sense one could say that much depends on the emphasis placed on phenomena, on the perspective with which the problem is viewed. On the one hand it is true that transference-love sets itself against the development of the cure, to convert it into an *affaire*, into a pure satisfaction of desires; it really does become an obstacle. On the other hand, one must not forget that this obstacle is the illness itself, which consists precisely in that this patient cannot apply his libido to real situations, to real objects; so that transference-love, in this sense, is not an obstacle, but the very material of the cure.

I have reasoned thus to understand Freud's determination to explain transference as a function of resistance, and this reasoning leads me further on to object to the classification of transference proposed by Lagache in his valuable report of 1951. At this stage let us say that the classification of the transference into positive and negative should be phenomenological—that is, by means of the *affect* (as with Freud in 1912) and not by means of the *effect*, the utility, as Lagache proposes—precisely in order to avoid the functional connotation, which, as we have just seen, is quite misleading.

8.6 *Transference and repetition*

At the end of this arresting article, Freud gives a vivid description of psychoanalytic treatment and shows us the direction his investigation will take. He points out that, to the extent the treatment enters into the unconscious, the patient's reactions reveal the characteristics of the primary process, which lead him to evaluate his impulses (or desires) as actual and real, whereas the doctor tries to locate them in the context of the treatment, which is that of the vital history of the patient. On the result of this battle, Freud concludes, depends the success of the analysis; and, although it is true that this battle develops fully in the field of the transference and presents the psychoanalyst with his greatest difficulties, it also gives him the opportunity of showing the patient his forgotten erotic impulses, in the most immediate and conclusive way, as it is impossible to destroy an enemy *in absentia* or *in effigie*.

Thus Freud opens the new theme of his investigation, the transference as a repetitive phenomenon, which will engage him for many years. In fact, two years later he studied the transference through the concept of *repetition*, which he distinguishes from the concept of *memory*.

In Lecture 27 in the *Introductory Lectures on Psycho-Analysis* (1916–17), when he again expounds his ideas on transference, he also emphasizes that neurosis is a consequence of repetition. The analysis of the transference allows the transformation of repetition into memory, and thus the transference, constituting at first an obstacle, becomes the best instrument of the cure.

CHAPTER NINE

Transference and repetition

9.1 Resumé of chapters 7 and 8

It is worth reiterating that when he wrote the postscript to the analysis of "Dora" (1905e [1901]), probably in January of 1901, Freud had a concrete idea of the nature of transference and of its importance, even though subsequently the development of this theory arrived at obscure and/or debatable points. The transference should be continually analysed, he says, and adds that only when the transference has been resolved does the patient acquire real conviction about the constructions that were offered to him. This is very clear, and today we all subscribe to it fully. For my part, I think the patient not only acquires conviction once the transference has been analysed but also that he has the right that this should be so, because only the transference can show him that in reality he is *repeating* the patterns of his past: all the rest does not go beyond a mere intellectual comprehension, which is unable to convince anyone.

Let us also remember, briefly, the article (Freud, 1912b) in which Freud gives a theoretical explanation of the phenomenon of transference, placing it in relation to the treatment and to resistance.

With respect to the treatment, Freud reaffirms what he said in 1905, that the treatment does not create the transference but *discovers* it. This is a very Freudian (and very important) concept, which is sometimes forgotten when the spontaneity of the phenomenon is discussed, as we shall see in discussing the psychoanalytic process. In this sense, Freud is categorical: transference is not an effect of analysis, rather, analysis is the method that concerns itself with discovering and analysing the transference. In this sense it can be plainly and simply said that the transference is, in itself, the illness: the more we transfer the past to the present, the more we mistake the present for the past and the more ill we are, the more disturbed is our reality principle.

The other problem Freud poses in 1912 is the relation of transference to *resistance*. This theme certainly merits an attentive effort. In terms of his concept of the cure at that time, Freud is of the opinion, and will reiterate this two years later in "Remembering, Repeating and Working Through" (1914g), that whereas the treatment aims at discovering past pathogenic situations, evoking and retrieving memories, the transference operates as resistance because it reactivates the memory, making it current and actual, at which point it ceases to be a memory. However, Freud also says in this article, and many times elsewhere, that an enemy cannot be conquered *in absentia* or *in effigie;* and with this he in fact signals a change, up to a point, in his then current concept of treatment; and it will change precisely on understanding the significance of the transference.

Freud is interested in explaining the intensity the transference acquires in the psychoanalytic cure and why it serves the aims of resistance, in open contrast to what (apparently) occurs in the other treatments of nervous illness—a very debatable point of view, as we have already said.

Freud begins from the fact that in our modalities of the love relation certain patterns, stereotypes or clichés occur that repeat themselves continually throughout life; in other words, each one faces the amorous situation with all the baggage from his past, with models that, once reproduced, make up a situation where past and present are in contact.

Freud also points out clearly that there are two levels or two components in this phenomenon, because a part of the libido has developed fully and is within reach of consciousness, whereas another part has been repressed. Although it contributes to the mode of reaction of the individual, the conscious libido will never be an obstacle for development; it is, on the contrary, the best instrument to apply to the present situation what has been learned in the past.

On the other hand, the other, not fully developed part of the libido is the victim of repression and, at the same time, the one attracted by the unconscious complexes. Through this double mechanism, this libido suffers a process of *introversion*—using Jung's term, which Freud supported at the time. It is this unconscious libido, withdrawn from reality, that basically (and, in my view, exclusively) provokes the transference phenomenon.

Through this theoretical model, Freud explains convincingly the relation of the transference to resistance. To the extent that the doctor's action is directed towards liberating this libido, which had been withdrawn from consciousness and removed from reality, the same factors that produced its introversion will now act as a (transference) resistance. In this sense one can say that the *mental* conflict the patient brings is transformed into a *personalistic* conflict, as soon as the analyst intervenes to mobilize it.

These ideas are fully extant in current psychoanalytic practice. The only modification could be in their range, since they should apply to all types of relation and not just to the love life. Without detracting in any way from the importance of the libido in the theory of object relations, we would say now that the other type of impulse, aggression, is also subject to this same process.

Freud is not satisfied with this in explaining the relation between transference and resistance. He adds that the transference begins to operate the moment the process of evoking memories is arrested (through resistance), and that it does so precisely at the service of this process of resistance: instead of remembering, the patient begins to transfer, and for this purpose chooses out of the whole complex the most suitable element for transference. In other words, as he does not wish to remember, the patient utilizes as resistance the element that best fits the present situation, out of various possibilities his complex offers. From the whole complex, then, the element that first mobilizes as resistance is the one most suitable for transference, because the best distortion is the transferential one.

We have already pointed out that Freud seems to struggle with a contradiction here—which also overtakes him in the chapter 3 of *Beyond the Pleasure Principle* (1920g)—between whether the transference is the element of resistance itself or the element that is resisted, whether resistance causes the transference or, conversely, the transference causes resistance.

To combine Freud's two assertions, we said in chapter 8 that the element of the complex that is employed first as resistance (to the memory) is the transferential element and that this element, once employed, sets off a stronger resistance (in the analytic dialogue). (Freud has substituted the idea of memory for that of the complex, which is wider and which he takes from Jung.)

9.2   Remembering and repeating

The concept of transference neurosis introduced in "Remembering, Repeating and Working-Through" (1914g) has a dual importance. Freud indicates, first, that when analysis begins, in the first stage sometimes called the analytic honeymoon, a calm is produced, leading to a diminution and even a disappearance of the symptoms, but this certainly does not constitute a cure. What has happened, in reality, is a sort of transposition of the pathological phenomenon, which has begun to express itself at the level of the treatment itself. The neurosis that had previously been a part of the daily life of the individual now has as its starting-point (and goal) the analysis and the analyst. Freud calls this process, which occurs spontaneously at the beginning of the treatment, *transference neurosis*, and he ascribes it to a mechanism he had already mentioned in 1905, and especially in 1912—repetition.

Establishing the concept of *transference neurosis*, Freud indicates a clinical fact—that the pathological phenomena that had occurred in the life of the patient now begin to operate in that intermediate zone between the illness and life which is the transference, thereby founding a technical concept. It is important to emphasize this because we have already seen how the concept of transference neurosis leads some analysts to a restrictive position in the field of indications (or analysability), when they utilize it in a nosographic and not a technical sense, basing themselves on another concurrent work of Freud's—"On Narcissism: An Introduction" (1914c)— in which he contrasts transference neurosis with *narcissistic neurosis*.

The concept of *repetition is* not new, since it is implicit in that of transference, to the extent that something returns from the past and operates in the present. However, we should note that Freud's 1895 idea of false connections does not necessarily imply repetition, as does the stereotype or the cliché.

In this article Freud contrasts remembering and repeating, and one should not forget that if repetition occurs, it is because the memory is not there, as the latter is the antidote to the former. Let us note then, that in 1914 Freud utilizes the concept of repetition with a precise criterion, because he contrasts it with remembering. Up to 1912 this conceptual difference had not been so definite. In the work of that year, the dynamics of the transference are understood by means of resistance to remembering; but in 1914 the repressed memory is repeated in the transference. In this way, the concept of remembering is linked more clearly to that of experience, because it is precisely when one can make use of the mass of memories that one possesses experience.

In 1914 the concept of repeating had not altered substantially from that of 1912 or 1905, although it was more formal and contrasted with remembering. But in 1920 the idea of repetition changed: what had until then been a descriptive concept and entirely subordinate to the pleasure principle became a genetic and explanatory concept *beyond* the pleasure principle. This was to be the great change in Freud's thinking at the beginning of the 1920s.

9.3 Repetition as an explanatory principle

Freud's change vis-à-vis the theory of transference, in *Beyond the Pleasure Principle* (1920g), arises in the context of a deep reflection on pleasure and human nature. The question Freud asks himself is whether there is something beyond the pleasure principle; and after reviewing three clinical examples—children's play, the dreams of traumatic neurosis and the transference—he replies in the affirmative.

What Freud asserts specifically in chapter 3 of *Beyond the Pleasure Principle* is that the transference is motivated by the compulsion to repeat and that the ego represses it to serve the pleasure principle.

The transference now appears to be thoroughly serving the death instinct, that elemental and blind force that seeks a state of immobility, a constant situation, and which does not create new links or new relationships, leading ultimately to a state of stagnation. It suffices to conjoin these two ideas to take note of something that often goes unnoticed: The transference (which is, by definition, a link) serves the death instinct (which by definition does not create links but destroys them).

Repetition now becomes the explanatory principle of the transference. Ruled by the compulsion to repeat and the death instinct, the transference then becomes what is resisted (and not the resistance); and the ego, which opposes the compulsion to repeat, represses the transference, because for the ego repetition is what threatens, what destroys and annihilates.

Transferential repetition, mostly blind and always painful, shows and demonstrates that there exists an impulse (which Freud often called "daemonic"), which tends to repeat situations from the past beyond the pleasure principle. It is precisely the degree of unpleasure occurring in these conditions that leads Freud to postulate the compulsion to repeat as a principle and the death instinct as an instinctive factor of the same type as Eros. Repetition, as a principle, redefines the transference as a *need to repeat*.

If the transference implies a tendency to repeat ascribed to the death instinct, the only thing an individual can do is to oppose this through a resistance *to* the transference that will in this case be mobilized by the pleasure principle, by the libido. The libido explains not the transference but, rather, the resistance to the transference. If we compare this theory with that of 1912 and 1914, we see it as diametrically opposed, because earlier on the transference was what is resisted, a libidinous impulse, and the ego defence opposed it as a resistance *of* transference. The theory of transference has turned about-face.

To evaluate this change adequately it is essential to remember that Freud takes the theme of the transference as a clinical example that supports his theory that there exists a death instinct whose principal attribute is repetition; but he does not in fact revise his theory of the transference. And when Freud's writings after 1920 are reviewed, none seems to imply this modification. For example, when he speaks of psychoanalytic treatment in the *New Introductory Lectures on Psychoanalysis* (1933a), he says that in regard to the theory of the cure he has nothing to add to what he had said in 1916 (1933a, p. 151). Nor does he modify the idea of the transference as something within the pleasure principle in *An Outline of Psychoanalysis* (1940a [1938]). Freud's attitude is different in other areas he investigates—masochism, for example. In "A Child Is Being Beaten" (1919e) masochism is secondary; in "The Economic Problem of Masochism" (1924c) it is primary (the death instinct).

If we really accept the hypothesis that the transference is ascribed to the death instinct, then the whole theory of analytic treatment requires a profound revision.

However, this revision has not been effected because, as I understand it, with the passage of time neither Freud nor his followers ever placed the transference under the aegis of the death instinct.

9.4 Transference of impulses and defences: Anna Freud's solution

In "The Dynamics of Transference" (1912b) Freud establishes the important link between transference and resistance that we have already studied, according to which transference serves resistance. We have said that the relation between the two is not always clear, and we tried to resolve that enigma via memory and desire. As we have just seen, these dynamics change substantially in *Beyond the Pleasure Principle* (1920g), when the transference is conceived as a death impulse against which the ego, serving pleasure, mobilizes the life instinct to repress it. Many, if not all, analysts since then have been concerned to resolve this dilemma of whether it is the transference that is resisted or the resistance.

I believe this alternative was wisely resolved years ago by Anna Freud in chapter 2 of *The Ego and the Mechanisms of Defence* (1936), where she says, in the manner of Solomon, that the transference is both—that is, that there is transference of impulses and transference of defences. (Anna Freud distinguishes a third type of transference, *acting out* in the transference, which will engage us further on.)

Thus Anna Freud studies the transference with the structural method, thanks to which it is made clear at the outset that both the id and the ego can intervene in the transferential phenomenon. The theoretical change Anna Freud proposes is, in my view, substantial and resolves the problem so naturally and with such precision that at times it goes unnoticed. Anna Freud's conception is more comprehensive and coherent than the previous ones; it tells us there is transference not only of positive and negative impulses, of love and hate, of instincts and affects, but also of defences. Whereas the transference of impulses or tendencies corresponds to invasions of the id and is felt by the analysand as extraneous to his/her (adult) personality, the transference of defences repeats in the actuality of the analysis the old infantile models of ego functioning. Here sane analytic practice advises us to go from the ego to the id, from the defence to the content. It is perhaps this work, Anna Freud continues, that is the most difficult and at the same time the most fruitful in analysis, because the analysand does not perceive this second type of transference as an extraneous body. It is not easy to convince the analysand of the repetitive and extemporaneous character of these reactions, precisely because they are ego-syntonic.

9.5   Lagache's contribution

The other problem raised by Freud in 1920 is the nature of the transferential repetition. Before 1920 (and probably also later), repetition is for Freud only a *descriptive* principle, whereas the dynamics of the transference are explained through instinctive needs that seek permanent discharge and satisfaction, according to the principle of pleasure/unpleasure. In 1920 repetition is elevated to an *explanatory* principle of the transference, which now becomes an instance of the compulsion to repeat, which expresses the enigmatic, mute death instinct. The lucid reflection of Lagache (1951, 1953) is based on these two—actually antithetical—Freudian theses.

Lagache sums up and contrasts these two postulates of Freud's in an elegant aphorism: *the need for repetition and the repetition of the need.* Lagache does not accept that repetition can stand as an explanatory principle, as a cause of the transference; he thinks, on the contrary, that one repeats due to need and that need (desire) is checked by the ego. The conflict is, then, between the pleasure principle and the reality principle.

Transference is a phenomenon where the pleasure principle tends to satisfy the impulse that repeats; but the ego, serving reality, tries to inhibit this process to avoid anguish, not to relapse into the traumatic situation. However, it is proper to the ego function to seek both the discharge of the impulse and pleasure, such that in each repetition there is a new search; a need is repeated in order to find an outlet that will satisfy the pleasure principle, without ignoring thereby the reality principle.

This point of view is the one Anna Freud implicitly supports in 1936 and which in my view Freud adopts when he returns to the theme in *Inhibitions, Symptoms and Anxiety* (1926d). His concept of the transference is the earlier one, that needs repeat themselves. The transference conditions one of the resistances of the ego, analogous to the resistance of repression, whereas the principle of the compulsion to repeat remains integrated into the theory as the resistance of the id. The id opposes a resistance to change, which is independent of the transference, of the transference resistance.

9.6   The Zeigarnik effect

Lagache takes as a supporting point for his reasoning the psychology of learning (or habit); and he has recourse to an experiment to explain the transference, the *Zeigarnik effect.*

In 1927 Zeigarnik made a very interesting experiment: he gave individuals a task and interrupted it before it had been completed. He found that these persons were left with a tendency to try to complete the task. Two other psychologists, Maslow and Mittelman, applied these results not only to experimental psychology but also to general psychology, and Lagache bases his explanation of the origin of transference on this. The theoretical support Lagache finds in learning theory he also finds in structural theory, since the Zeigarnik effect is, in the last instance, an application of the law of good form of Gestalt psychology.

The principle Lagache bases himself on is clear and shows neatly what he wants to say when he asserts that a need is repeated and not that there is a primary need to repeat; the need to complete the task, to close the structure, is repeated. In transferential repetition there is always a desire to complete something that had remained incomplete, to close a structure that had remained open, to achieve a solution for what was inconclusive. Taking the simplest example, a man who repeats his direct oedipal situation does so not only from the desire to possess his mother, but also with the intention of finding an outlet for his dilemma, between the incestuous desire and castration anxiety, not to mention the impulse for reparation, and so on.

Supported by structuralist and gestaltic concepts, Lagache works with the supposition that the mind operates in search of certain integrations, of certain experiences it lacks, which need to be completed and assumed. These ideas are clearly included in the great psychoanalytic theories. It becomes obvious that maturity, from this point of view, consists of being able to tolerate frustration. As he matures, man acquires the means to accept frustration if a task remains incomplete and to finalize it when reality makes this possible.

Inconclusive problems that will appear in the transference are precisely those that, because of their nature, because of their importance, by definition remained inconclusive in the decisive stages of development and need an object relation for their solution.

Basing himself on the Zeigarnik effect, Lagache manages to understand the transference beyond its content, impulses and manifestations, with a theory of motivation and of the operations an individual carries out to satisfy motivation and need. Thus he lucidly resolves the dilemma of transferential repetition—a decisive contribution to the theory of transference, and hence to psychoanalysis.

9.7   *Transference and habit*

In the new phase of his thinking, Lagache brings in the idea of *habit* to give an account of the objectives of transferential repetition. Transference should form part of a more comprehensive psychological theory, that of habit: what is transferential repetition but the exercise of a habit that comes to us of old, from our past?

The transference is linked to certain habits, and we always face a new experience with the baggage of our old habits, with our previous experiences. Everything consists in our instrumental use of those habits to find— or not to find—the solution to the problem posed.

To reformulate the theory of transference based on habits, Lagache finds himself obliged to abandon, apparently without regrets, the classification of the transference into positive and negative according to its content of instincts or affects; and, availing himself of learning theory, he tells us that *positive* transference presupposes the effective or positive utilization of old habits in order to learn, and that *negative* transference consists in the interference of an old habit with the learning process.

It should not be thought that what Lagache proposes is a mere change of nomenclature in the classification of the transference. What he offers us is a conceptual change, a change in our way of thinking, and he is well aware of this. I want to make it clear in advance that in what follows I disagree totally with Lagache.

The classification of the transference into positive and negative, according to Lagache, should be abandoned, for various reasons. In the first place, the transference is never positive or negative, but always mixed, ambivalent; on the other hand, we know today that the feelings that are transferred are not only those of love and hate, but also those of envy, admiration and gratitude, curiosity, contempt and appreciation—the whole scale of human emotions. Thus it becomes somewhat Manichaean and schematic to speak of positive and negative transference. Nevertheless, this objection is not decisive, since beyond ambivalence and the variety of feelings, the theory of instincts recognizes only two instincts: love and hate, *Eros* and *Thanatos*.

Another of Lagache's objections is that classifying the transference as negative or positive always implies a slide towards axiology. Apart from the inadvisability of making value judgements on what occurs in the treatment, in fact this value is always debatable, because negative transference is not negative, nor is positive transference positive with regard to the aims of the cure. This criticism by Lagache does not seem consistent to me either. It is true that the terms "positive" and "negative" (which in the end he does not replace) lend themselves for use as value judgements; but this is only a deviation of the theory, and we know that any theory can be undermined through ideological aims. To avoid this risk, Lagache's classification takes the problem of value to the theory itself: it is now the analyst who qualifies the patient's response as positive or negative, according to how it meets his expectations.

The classification of the transference as positive or negative according to the content is doubtless very schematic, because the instincts or affects transferred are never pure. Freud himself indicates this in "The Dynamics of Transference" (1912b) and asserts that the transference applies narrowly to the term *ambivalence* which had recently been created by Bleuler. Moreover, this classification is purely observational, not dynamic—although it is in any case useful in that it orientates us—and, further, it refers to the patient. Lagache's refers instead to the analyst; and this is precisely the problem. It is obvious that, as Lagache says, the patient's negative transference—that is, his hostility—can be very useful to the aims of the treatment, in the same way that an intense, erotic, positive transference is always pernicious. Here Lagache's criticism, however, begs the question: if a positive transference is spoken of, no reference is made to its value for the treatment. It is Lagache who makes it.

Lagache proposes, therefore, that instead of a classification in terms of emotions, of *affects*, the transference be classified in terms of *effects* and that, as in learning theory, one should speak of positive transference if an old habit favours learning and of negative transference if it interferes. In learning theory, the terms "facilitation" and "interference" are also used.

With his theory secured, Lagache can assimilate the negative transference to resistance, whereas the positive transference is the one that facilitates the development of the analysis.

What analysis offers the patient, Lagache continues, is the habit of free association. In the last instance, what the patient has to learn in analysis is to free-associate, and this capacity ultimately implies the cure. Lagache proposes that positive transference should be the one with those past habits that facilitate free association, such as trust; and negative transference the one with habits that interfere.

Lagache's proposal is, then, to classify the transference in terms of its result and not its content. Thus Lagache does manage to include the transference in learning theory, but he does not resolve, it seems to me, the problems psychoanalytic theory faces on this point.

To the extent that we explain the positive transference as past learning that allows us to carry out free association, we are speaking of a process that adjusts itself to the real situation and is, therefore, no longer transference. So the concept of positive transference remains in the air, is annulled, is completely superimposed on the rational attitude of the patient facing analysis as a task.

The concept of negative transference also suffers where it remains completely tied to that of resistance—although resistance, as we all know, also has a legitimate place in the treatment. The value judgement that was avoided where the instincts were concerned is now applied to the operations of the ego. There is a return to Freud's criterion (1912b) that resistance feeds the transference. Lagache says, specifically, that the negative transference implies an associative interference in the learning process, inasmuch as it is an inadequate behaviour that is not compatible with free association. This is equivalent to saying simply that the patient has resistances.

Moreover, as we have said, the repetition of old habits that adjust themselves to the real and current situation is by definition no longer transference, and it is preferable to call it *experience*. An old habit that allows us to be well adjusted to reality is a new development where patterns from the past are not repeated but applied; something interrupted is not retaken so to say, from the point of view of the Zeigarnik effect. If we wish to continue explaining the transference via the Zeigarnik effect, as Lagache taught us, then we will see that it is not applicable to what

Lagache calls positive transference, as by definition there is no task that has remained incomplete there.

Lagache's classification fails, therefore, in my opinion, because it does not distinguish between transference and experience. This is why when I defined the transference, I contrasted it with experience, where the past promotes an understanding of the situation, not a misunderstanding of it. By definition, we call transference only an experience from the past that is interfering with the understanding of the present. Memories are our treasure; far from interfering, they help us, they make us richer in experience and wiser. Experience implies having memories and knowing how to use them.

* * *

To sum up: from a classification that attempts to integrate the transference into learning theory, Lagache has to modify the concept of transference, incorporating with it that of rational adaptation to new experience, and with this he incurs a new contradiction and even detracts from his most valuable contributions.

9.8   Transference, reality and experience

We have begun this chapter with the concept of repetition to explain the transference; it is time now to study it through reality and experience. Of course these relations are complex, but we can try to explain them, taking as a starting point Freud's idea of clichés and complemental series.

Freud divides the libido into two parts: the conscious part, which is at the ego's disposal, to be satisfied in reality, and the one that is not conscious because it is fixated on archaic objects. On the balance of these two factors depends the first complemental series, the (pre)disposition through fixation of the libido, which makes up the *infantile conflict*. The second complementary series depends on the first, in terms of disposition, and on privation [*Versagung*], which makes up the *current conflict*. When the current conflict, which can always be reduced in this scheme to a deprivation, occurs, a part of the libido that was applied to an object in reality (be this the spouse, work or study) has to apply to another object, and, if this fails, it takes the regressive path. This is the phenomenon Jung (1910) called introversion of the libido.

On this basis, my belief is that the portion of the libido that seeks channels of satisfaction in reality has to do with experience and not with transference. This idea is applied to all human events no less than to the erotic encounter, where elements from experience always intervene. How will one inspire love and how will one relate to one's partner if not on the basis of past experiences? To the extent that these experiences operate as memories at the disposal of the ego and are conscious, our ability to operate realistically will be greater. The other part of the libido, that linked to unconscious imagos, is always by definition dissatisfied and seeks discharge without taking the elements of reality into account.

Where the present situation creates a deprivation, that libido which remains floating, dissatisfied, tends to introversion, to charging the unconscious imagos to obtain a satisfaction that reality does not offer. This is what is called "current conflict", and it is always linked to a situation of deprivation, which, in turn, depends on the infantile conflict, because the more the libido is fixed on archaic objects, the more exposed one will be to frustration. In other words, the more intense the process of introversion of the libido, the more disposed is the individual to transference and, conversely, the greater the part of the libido that does not suffer this process, the greater will be the possibility for real adaptation in erotic relationships.

* * *

The libido at the disposal of the ego is the one that allows one to face the present situation with a baggage of experience that makes adaptation to reality possible. Decisive in this, in my view, is the reality of the task, which arises from the contract—the *Vertrag*, as Freud said. What reason (and reality) dictates is that the woman seated behind me tries to solve my problems and to help me; therefore I have to cooperate with her in every way I can. My relation with my analyst, if I am within the framework of reality, cannot be other than the reality of the treatment. Insofar as my infantile libido attempts to attach itself to this woman, I am already erring. Here my reality judgement fails. The *task* then is, in my view, what guides us to apprehend reality, the anchor that ties us to it; and everything that is not linked to the task can be considered, by definition, transference, since it occurs in an inadequate context.

In this way, once a link has been established between the task (or the contract) and the goals, the relation between transference, reality and experience can be understood. What gives sense and reality to my objectives and to my feelings is that they are shaped for the fulfilment of the proposed task. The adjustment to reality indicated here belongs to the individual, to the subject. Reality is, then, subjective; it belongs to the analysand and cannot be defined from the outside—that is, via the analyst—without an abuse of authority, as Szasz explains so well (1963).

9.9 Transference *WITHOUT* repetition

We have seen that Freud discovered transference when working in his consulting-room, where it was imposed on him as an undeniable, unexpected and an almost inconvenient clinical fact; we have also seen that he explained it in various theoretical ways. Although at first he had recourse to the simplistic hypothesis of a false link, he saw at the same time that it did not appear for no reason at all; and with the perspicacity of genius he realized that this link was not conjunctural but was, rather, a testimony to the same events as those he was investigating. This understanding led him to explain transference as an effect of repetition. This concept was clearly enunciated in 1905 through the model of new editions and re-editions, became the stereotype plates of "The Dynamics of Transference" (1912b), and was formalized in the remembering/repeating dialectic of 1914. We have already indicated that in 1920 a crisis occurred in the dynamics of transference which ceased to be closely linked with resistance and became the thing resisted; but the effect of repetition was not by any means questioned. On the contrary, it was accentuated, insofar as transference became a tributary of the death instinct and repetition compulsion was set up as its explanatory principle.

For many years no one doubted that transference had its roots in repetition, until in his Seminar XI, *Les quatre concepts fondamentaux de la psychanalyse*, Lacan (1964a) determinedly questioned this hypothesis and, as we shall see in chapter 11, broke the connection between repetition and transference.

In more recent years other excellent scholars such as Meltzer, the Sandlers and Merton M. Gill also came to question the link between repetition and transference.

* * *

In *The Kleinian Development* (1978), Meltzer follows, from a very original point of view, the great arc that goes from Freud to Melanie Klein, and from her to Bion. Meltzer clearly expresses these ideas in his article "The Kleinian Expansion of Freud's Metapsychology" (1981), which was incorporated as chapter 3 in *Dream Life* (1983). Freud always works on neurophysiological lines in accordance with the spirit of his times, which sought to place psychoanalysis among the sciences capable of *explaining* facts of nature—as Meltzer says. In this context the great discovery of transference can only be understood as a repetition of the past.

Melanie Klein's model rests basically on the existence of an *internal world* of objects in which the individual lives as fully as in the external world, and where transference appears as the externalization of the immediate present of the internal situation, not as a relic of the past.

Bion's model, finally, considers the mind as a thinking apparatus in which the basic dilemma is between truth and lies, starting from the emotional experience of life in which emotion is placed at the very heart of meaning. In this epistemological model, relations in the internal world engender meaning, and consequently "all of our external relationships have a certain transference quality that they derive meaning from what exists in our internal world" (Meltzer, 1981, p. 183). I suppose that with this sentence Meltzer is indicating that our external relationships take their meaning from what happens in the internal world, and not simply—for that would be obvious—that they are always infiltrated by transference elements.

As can be seen in the outline given, Meltzer asserts that psychoanalysis has been transformed from an explanatory into a phenomenological and descriptive science connected with meaning and emotion, and therefore transference has to be understood more as an updating of the present internal world than as the repetition of the past. Thus transference becomes the seal that stamps psychic reality and phantasy on the outside world without involving the repetition of past models. Moreover, what Meltzer is telling us is that, far from misleading us, transference is our compass, guiding us in the external world.

* * *

Although it starts from different premises and deals with a different set of problems, the penetrating research of Joseph and Anne-Marie Sandler has points of contact with Meltzer and, as we shall see later, with Lacan also. In "The 'Second Censorship', the 'Three Box Model' and Some Technical Implications" (1983), the Sandlers suggest a type of psychic apparatus that endeavours to reflect the relevant aspects of the inter-phase between the topographical and structural theories. The idea that there exists a second censorship between the preconscious and the conscious systems, often considered by Freud but never incorporated in the topographical theory, facilitates the relationship between psychoanalytical theory and clinical experience. It delimits three areas of the mind, so that we have the model of the three boxes—that is, the three systems: unconscious, preconscious, and conscious. However, in the Sandlers' view the two censorships delimit three psychological compartments that are not identical with either the three strata of the first theory or the three instances of the second. The *first system* comprises infantile reactions and the most primitive desires, peremptory urges that may originate from instinctive needs, but also unpleasant feelings and anxiety, the total experiences that remain hidden by infantile amnesia behind the first censorship—"the child inside the adult", to use the authors' metaphor. It is the equivalent of the id or the system unconscious, but much more than that—the reactions, phantasies, and wishes that develop early in the child's life, together with the defensive transformations belonging to this stage, whose essential aim is to avoid unpleasure.

The *second system*, which is separated from consciousness by the second censorship, was classically called preconscious, but it also represented the unconscious parts of the ego and the superego of the structural theory. The contents of this second system may be considered as *derivatives* of the infantile desires of the other system, which passed the barriers of the first censorship. Unlike the earlier one, the second system ("present unconscious") is directed towards the present, not the past, and is attuned to reality even though it is unconscious. In psychoanalytical clinical practice the main example "is the unconscious transference phantasies that arise in analysis, which do not express themselves directly" (ibid., p. 421).

The second censorship also has special characteristics; its chief mission is to avoid feelings of shame, embarrassment and humiliation. The transference situation presupposes the externalization of this second censorship on to the analyst, and consequently the analyst's main task, in the Sandlers' view, is to help the patient eventually to accept the infantile wishful aspects of himself that have aroused painful conflict and have become threatening during the course of his development (ibid., p. 423).

All these ideas acquire more precision in "The Past Unconscious, the Present Unconscious, and Interpretation of the Transference", in which the Sandlers (1984) discuss the book by Merton M. Gill and Irwin Z. Hoffman, *Analysis of the Transference* (1983), which we shall consider when we speak of interpretation.

In this work the Sandlers reaffirm what they said in 1983, but they define more precisely the past and the present unconscious, which emerged from the model of the three boxes. The *past* (or infantile) *unconscious* is made up of the immediate and peremptory impulses, responses, and wishes formed in the first years of life, constituted by what the authors call *the child within the adult* with its object relations and its internal world ruled by primitive defence mechanisms such as projection and denial. The past unconscious lurks behind the first censorship, which coincides with the crystallization of the superego, the close of the oedipal period and the entry into the latency period—that is to say, up to the fifth or sixth year. The *present unconscious,* on the other hand, is influenced above all by reality, and its main function is to maintain a balance in the present.

Faced with the impulses from the past unconscious, the present unconscious has two types of adaptive processes. The *first* is when "the past is updated to the present" (Sandler & Sandler, 1984, p. 372). Thus the past is repeated in the present, and it is at that point that we can begin to speak of transference. In the Sandlers' example, when the analyst's comment is felt as derogatory, the patient reacts, for example, with a grandiose and reassuring oedipal phantasy produced by the past unconscious, which must in its turn adapt itself to the present and become syntonic. If this updated form of the infantile impulse does not cause conflict, it will reach consciousness unimpeded. This, however, is rare, and what happens most often is that the infantile impulse reaching the present unconscious causes conflict and sets in motion a *second* type of adaptive process in which defence will operate, converting it into a derivative that will then have to pass through the second censorship.

Immediately after making these points, the Sandlers move towards a flexible definition of transference that will reach the full sense of *relationship* (ibid., p. 378). Within their own frame of reference, they maintain that "transference occurs when the person of the analyst is represented *in any way* in wishful fantasies and thoughts in the present unconscious, or in conscious ideation" (ibid., p. 378—italics in the original). Though the manifest transference material may be the repetition of a past in the present consciousness, as was explained earlier, it may also be a resistance against the unconscious transference material; and the authors therefore emphasize the need not to jump to the conclusion that all the manifest transference content is a repetition of the past.

In the Sandlers' view it is very important to establish *"the major distinction between transference as any content which includes a reference to the interpersonal relationship between the patient and the analyst, on the one hand, and transference as an unconscious re-experiencing or repetition of an important past relationship, on the other"* (ibid., p. 388, italics in the original). In this distinction, I believe, the Sandlers are maintaining the theoretical need to discriminate between a present unconscious and a past unconscious. The interpretive work must be directed in the first place towards the contents of the present unconscious and the first censorship, so that the analysand may acquire a better tolerance of the infantile aspects of his personality; and it is only by reconstructions that we can in some cases arrive at the past unconscious.

In "The Past Unconscious, the Present Unconscious and the Vicissitudes of Guilt", the Sandlers (1987) introduce a methodological distinction between what is conceived and what is perceived: we can *conceive* the content of the past unconscious but not *perceive* it, since it is something we can only reconstruct from our theories, but which we never see and which is never accessible to consciousness. Moreover, the past unconscious is essentially unalterable: *"What is changeable, we believe, is the way in which the reflections of the past unconscious are accommodated to and dealt with in the adult psyche"* (ibid., p. 335—italics in the original).

The present unconscious, on the other hand, is accessible to us, since, as a functional organization, it adapts phantasies so that they can enter consciousness as derivatives through the use of defence mechanisms including projective identification (ibid., p. 336). In other words, the contents of the present unconscious are perceived; those of the past unconscious are reached only through reconstruction—that is, they are only conceived.

The role of interpretation in achieving insight into the contents of the present unconscious and the internal world is central to the analytical process; but the concurrent analysand's identification "with the analyst's tolerant attitude towards the existing child-like, 'silly' or perverse aspects of the patient is also crucial" (ibid., p. 338).

In distinguishing two types of unconscious, the Sandlers' theory implies not only a redefinition of transference, the subject with which we are now concerned, but also a conception of how it should be interpreted, and, already in the epistemological field, the data on which the psychoanalytical theory is founded.

On this latter axis turns Wallerstein's well-balanced reflection (1988) on opening the Montreal Congress of 1987. There is a theory on which all of us analysts can agree, one that arises from our interaction with the analysand in the consulting-room. This theory operates on the data provided by the Sandlers' present unconscious, which in Wallerstein's view coincides with the *clinical theory* of George S. Klein (1966). The other theories, those on a higher level, which attempt to account for the past unconscious (or what Klein, with a certain contempt, calls metapsychology) cover a wide range, which, in Wallerstein's view, comprises only the *metaphors* that divide us into schools.

* * *

If the ideas we have just explained are understood as a healthy reaction to an ingenuous concept of transference in which the past is repeated word for word, we can welcome them unrestrainedly into the theoretical field of psychoanalysis. The Sandlers were right to say (personal communication, 1988) that the past and the present are not isomorphic. Certainly we sometimes seek the past to such an extent that we do not see the present at all.

However, the ideas of all these authors go beyond this legitimate warning. Meltzer, for example, advances the idea of linking transference with repetition as a (delayed) result of Brücke's assistant, who tries to locate the psychological fact in the explanatory framework of the natural sciences. Perhaps the theory of the false link may be considered an ideological relic of the Freud who studied the *Petromyzon Planeri* or the effects of cocaine, but not the theory of repetition, which establishes the dialectic of past and present and offers us the instruments for solving it cleanly. Transference is not a relic of the past but the living struggle of a past to become present, to occupy a space that is no longer its own. From this point of view I defined psychoanalysis as "the method which recognizes the past in the present (transference) and seeks to discriminate it, basically thanks to the interpretation" (Etchegoyen, 1988, p. 82).

The Sandlers propose to extend the concept of transference to become synonymous with the relationship between patient and analyst and respond to the functioning of the present unconscious—that is, the system that is turned towards the present and not towards the past. Thus, transference is restricted to the present unconscious, to what is *perceived*, and has nothing to do with repetition, which is confined to the past unconscious, is never accessible and is always *conceived* or reconstructed.

In order to support this conception of transference we have to keep a sharp division between the Sandlers' two types of unconscious; and yet they themselves say that the transference phantasies of the present unconscious are rooted in those peremptory urgencies of the past unconscious—which are, in my opinion, precisely those that are repeated. The fact that we cannot always justify this repetition, and that sometimes we have recourse to genetic interpretations so as not to see what is really happening with the analysand, must not lead us to throw out the baby with the bathwater.

As Popper (1953) rightly says, science consists of conjectures and refutations. The major aim of our science is, precisely, to reach and reveal the

Sandlers' past unconscious—that is, the deep unconscious, the systematic unconscious. We may make many mistakes in the attempt; but that must not make us abandon so high an undertaking, however difficult it may be. And when all is said and done, was that not what Freud claimed when he sought to cut through infantile amnesia?

CHAPTER TEN

The dialectics of the transference according to Lacan

10.1   Summary

To synthesize what has been studied so far, it could be said that, considered at a theoretical level, the theme of transference poses two fundamental questions, on which all studies focus: (1) the spontaneity of the transferential phenomenon or, as is also said, the degree to which the analytic situation determines it, and (2) the nature of transferential repetition. These are without doubt two essential points, among others. Miller (1979) asserts that the transference remains connected to three fundamental themes: repetition, resistance and suggestion, a point of view that coincides with the foregoing.

We have spoken at length about the *spontaneity* of the transferential phenomenon, and we indicated that Freud has a clear position on this point: he never tires of insisting that transference does not depend on analysis, that analysis detects it but does not create it, and so on. This theme runs from the "Postscript" to "Dora" through *An Outline of Psychoanalysis* (1940a).

Some authors have pointed out, not without some justification, that when in 1915 Freud speaks of the transference love, he considers it a phenomenon provoked by the treatment, and he tries to demonstrate this to the analysand; but I believe this does not contradict the previous position, because what Freud means is that the conditions of the treatment make this process (which belongs to the illness) possible: the treatment sets it in motion, although it does not create it—so much so, that the participation of the analyst is clearly called *countertransferential seduction*, in recognition of his negligence.

As for the converse position, the most lucid work is undoubtedly Ida Macalpine's (1950). It is also the most extreme, in that it maintains that the transferential phenomenon is a response to the constants of the setting, and she defines it as a special form of adaptation, via regression, to the conditions of sensory deprivation, frustration and asymmetry of the analytic situation. This is not the moment to discuss this point of view, which will engage us further on; but I will say that the elements Ida Macalpine proposes are, for me, very debatable, as I try to show in my work "Regresión y encuadre" ["Regression and the Setting"] (1979a), which has been incorporated in this book as chapter 40.

Lagache and other authors—for example Liberman (1976a)—adopt an accommodating and eclectic position, saying that there is a predisposition to transference at the same time as a possibility of realization—both elements are a part of the process. However, this solution avoids rather than resolves the problem. There is no doubt that there is a complemental series between the situation offered by the analytic setting and the predisposition brought by the patient; but the real problem is to see which is the decisive element. For example, it is my opinion that if the Oedipus complex did not exist, the analytic setting would stir up not the transference love but a love like any other: what tilts the balance is the patient's Oedipus complex. Moreover, the setting is planned so that the transference can arise without being disturbed, not the reverse. (I do not take account of the countertransference for reasons of simplicity and method. That the analyst may participate with his own oedipal conflicts does not change the nature of the phenomenon, although it complicates it.)

As for the second theme, the nature of *repetition*, we owe to Lagache the most judicious study, a real model of clinical investigation.

No one doubted that transference is a repetitive phenomenon until Lacan's Seminar XI, *Les quatre concepts fondamentaux de la psychanalyse* (1964a), in which its symbolic value is considered and is distinguished from repetition. After Lacan, though apparently not through his influence, other authors questioned that relationship, as we saw in the last part of chapter 9. We recall that Freud, at any rate, saw this relationship as undeniable, without altering the ambiguity of his position, since he shifts and shifts again from "The Dynamics of Transference" (1912b) to the third chapter of *Beyond the Pleasure Principle* (1920g); and, it can be added, with good reason, that he also shifts his position in 1926, when in *Inhibitions, Symptoms and Anxiety* (1926d) he refers the idea of repetition to an impulse of the id, which he conceives as resistance, whereas the transference operates as a factor that stirs up a specific defence of the ego, the resistance of transference, which remains equivalent to the resistance of repression. It is difficult to decide whether this position of Freud's returns to the previous idea or implies a third phase in the course of his investigation, as I am inclined to think. The so-called resistances of the ego in the 1926 classification agree with the first explanation in 1912—that is, with the theory that the transference appears as a response to the activity of the analyst who opposes the introversion of the libido; the resistance of the id includes, at the same time as it circumscribes, the principle of repetition as conceived in 1920. Whatever our position may be in this regard, Freud's two alternatives still stand: one, that the transference serves the pleasure principle, and consequently the reality principle; the other, that the transference expresses the impulse of repetition of the id, which the ego tries to impede insofar as it is always a painful phenomenon.

We have already discussed this thoroughly, and we can only say, not to conclude the discussion but to recall the discriminatory elements at our disposal, that the idea in *Beyond the Pleasure Principle* is not the one Freud utilizes in general after 1920 when he refers to the transference. Thus, for example, after that year Freud changes drastically his concept of masochism, but he does not do the same with transference. There is an important point of controversy here, as best expressed by Lagache (1951), with his concise aphorism of *the need for repetition versus the repetition of the need* (see chapter 9). Lagache is decidedly in favour of the repetition of the need, insofar as he bases his whole explanation on the Zeigarnik effect—namely, that if there is a need, it tends to repeat. If what is understood instead is that the transference serves the death instinct, then it must be concluded that there is a need to repeat.

To evaluate Freud's view on this aspect of the transference, it is worth bearing in mind that the concepts of 1920 do not properly refer to the transference. Freud uses them, as he does the dreams of traumatic neurosis and children's play, as a clinical support for his idea of a death instinct; but he does not propose at any time to revise his theory of the transference.

In any case, Lagache is decidedly in favour of Freud's earlier thesis (the earlier and the final one, I would say), wherein he theorizes that the transference, under the aegis of the pleasure principle, tries to repeat a situation to find a better outcome. On this attempt is based, in the end, the possibility of psychoanalytic treatment.

10.2   *The dialectic of the analytic process*

Lagache presented his valuable work at the Psychoanalytic Congress of Romance Languages in 1951, and there Lacan expounded his ideas on the transference. Having confirmed Lagache's account, he then developed his own points of view. (Another Lacan work on this theme, which is also in the *Écrits*, is "La direction de la cure et les principes de son pouvoir" [The Direction of the Cure and the Principles of Its Power], presented at Royaumont in 1958; in this his 1951 theme is restated.)

The idea Lacan starts from is that the analytic process is essentially *dialectical* (and I want to make it clear that he refers to Hegelian dialectics). Analysis should be understood as a process in which thesis and antithesis lead to a synthesis, which reopens the process.

The patient offers the thesis with his material, and faced with that material we have to accomplish a dialectical inversion, proposing an antithesis that confronts the analysand with the truth he is rejecting—which would be the latent material. This takes the process to a new development of the truth and the patient to a new thesis.

As this process unfolds, the transference neither appears, nor is it necessary for it to appear. This is the key point and, in my view, Lacan's fundamental thesis: the transferential phenomenon arises if, for some reason, the dialectical process is interrupted.

To illustrate this theory, Lacan takes the analysis of "Dora", where this movement is clearly seen. Lacan says that no one has pointed out (and it is remarkable) that Freud (1905e) expounds the "Dora" case really as a dialectical development in which certain theses and antitheses occur; and he asserts that this fact is neither casual nor a product of methodological necessity; it answers to the very structure of the case (and of all cases).

The *first thesis* Dora presents, as we all know, is the serious problem that the unlawful relationship of her father with Frau K means for her. This relationship exists, it is visible, incontrovertible; and what most worries Dora, because it affects her directly, is that in order to cover up that relationship, her father ignores the advances with which Herr K besieges her. Dora thus feels manipulated by a situation that is extraneous to her. Freud accomplishes here the *first dialectical inversion*, when he asks Dora to see what part she plays in these events, with which he reverses the process: Dora proposes a thesis ("I am a plaything of circumstance"), and Freud proposes to her the antithesis that she is not as passive as she pretends. This first dialectical inversion confronts Dora with a new truth.

Dora, then, has to recognize that she participates in all this and benefits, for example, from Herr K's gifts and those of her father and from her situation with Herr K not being denounced for the same reasons, and so forth. She appears now as actor rather than as victim.

At this moment Dora has a sudden attack of jealousy with regard to her father, and this is the second situation she brings about, her *second thesis*: How can I fail to be jealous in such circumstances? What daughter who loves her mother would not be jealous? Freud, however, does not allow himself to be deceived and again reverses the argument, accomplishing the *second dialectical inversion*. He tells her he does not believe her reasons are sufficient to justify her jealousy, because the situation was already known to her. Her jealousy must have other causes: her conflict of rivalry with Frau K, not so much as mistress of her father as wife of Herr K, who is the one who interests her. Here is *the second dialectical inversion*, says Lacan, which Freud carries out with the observation that here the pretended object of her jealousy does not reveal the real motive—rather, it masks an interest in the person of the subject-rival, an interest whose nature, which is much less acceptable in common discourse, cannot express itself other than in an inverted manner (see Lacan, 1951, *Écrits*, p. 220). From this arises, once again, a new version of the truth—Dora's attraction to Frau K.

For this second development of the truth, which arises from Dora's jealousy of her father's relations with Frau K, Freud proposes two explanations: (1) oedipal love for the father, and (2) love for Herr K. Dora manifests her jealousy by pretending she is jealous of her father as a daughter; but Freud's second dialectical inversion contains in fact the two antitheses I have just enumerated. Freud shows Dora, in the first place, that her jealousy of the father is erotic and that she is identified with her father's two women (Dora's mother and Frau K), and, in the second place, that she is in love with Herr K, and if she has to strengthen the filial link with her father, it is to repress her love for Herr K, her fear of not resisting his flirtation. Infantile love for the father had been reactivated to repress love for Herr K, as is clearly seen from the interpretation of the first dream and from what Freud says in the first chapter (1905e [1901]), p. 70).

Freud failed to carry out a *third dialectical inversion*, which would have led Dora from love of Herr K to a homosexual link with Frau K.

It is clear that Lacan seeks a rectification of the subject in favour of the real, which occurs as a dialectical inversion. This procedure shows that the patient, Dora in this case, was not maladapted, as Hartmann (1939) would say but, on the contrary, too well adapted to a reality she herself contrives to falsify.

10.3 Transference and countertransference

For Lacan, if Freud could not accomplish this third step, it is because his countertransference betrayed him.

It is certainly true that in the "Postscript", in a footnote (1905e [1901], p. 120), Freud says specifically that he failed because he was unable to understand the homosexual situation between Dora and Frau K, and he even adds that, before he had discovered the importance of homosexuality in the psychoneuroses, he was unable to understand them thoroughly. For whatever reason, Freud in fact did not manage to carry out this third dialectical inversion; he should have told Dora that beneath her jealousy of Herr K lay her love for Frau K. Had he done so, Dora would have found herself confronted with the truth of her homosexuality, and the case would have been resolved, according to Lacan. Instead, however, Freud tried to make Dora conscious of her love for Herr K while also insisting that Herr K could be in love with her. There Freud is *hooked into* the transference and does not reverse the process.

If Freud puts himself in Herr K's place, Lacan continues, it is because a countertransference phenomenon prevents him from accepting that Dora does not love him, as identified with Herr K; she loves Frau K. Lacan says that as a result of his countertransference, Freud insists too often on the love Herr K inspires in Dora, and he then comments that it is surprising how Freud always takes Dora's varied replies as confirmation of what he interprets to her (Lacan, 1951, *Écrits*, p. 224).

Lacan subsequently points out that the fact of having placed himself as a substitute for Herr K would have saved Freud from insisting too much on the value of the proposals of marriage of the former (ibid., p. 225). In this way, Lacan opens up the problem of the value of the transferential interpretation in the analytic process. It is evident that, for Lacan, the transferential interpretation fulfils a function that we could call hygienic, inasmuch as it preserves the analyst but "... *ne ressortit à aucune propriété mystérieuse de l'affectivité* ..." [it does not refer to any mysterious property of the affect]. The transference takes on meaning in the dialectical moment in which it is produced, which usually expresses an error on the part of the analyst. Freud thinks, instead, that he should have given Dora a specific transferential interpretation—that is, that she imputed the same intentions to him as Herr K had. This transferential interpretation is not agreeable to Lacan, since Dora would have received it with her habitual scepticism (disavowal, *Verleugnung*); but "the very opposition it would have engendered would probably have orientated Dora, in spite of Freud, in the right direction: a direction that would have led her to the object of her real interest" (ibid., p. 225). It is not, then, a "transferential" interpretation that sets the analysis in motion, but the dialectical reversal of the process, which, on this specific point, would lead Dora to make contact with her love for Frau K.

Freud's blindness is linked to his countertransference, which does not allow him to accept that Dora does not love him as a man. Identifying himself with Herr K, he tries to convince Dora that Herr K (who is himself) loves her; at the same time, he tries to awaken Dora's love for Herr K (= Freud), when in fact at that moment Dora's libido is basically homosexual. The entrapment arises then, due to a problem of countertransference: Freud's unwillingness to accept himself as being excluded. Insofar as the countertransferential problem blinds him, Freud remains entrapped, and the process is cut off.

As this situation has universal validity for Lacan, it follows that transference is the correlate of countertransference. If Freud had not been blinded on this point by his countertransference, he could have remained extrinsic to these difficulties, confronting Dora with her homosexual feelings. The analyst himself is, then, the cause of the stagnation of the process, and the transference *appears* as an entrapment through which the analyst remains involved in the situation. For this not to happen, the analyst should return to the analysand his feelings through a dialectic reversal. Or, it might be better to say, conversely, that if the analyst does not succumb to his countertransference, he can offer the appropriate antithesis.

Lacan describes the transference as the moment of failure in the context of the dialectical relations of the cure; if the dialectical process fails, the transference appears as an entrapment, an obstacle.

In the case of Dora this is obvious, because Freud himself recognizes his error in not telling Dora that the most powerful unconscious instinct of her mental life was her homosexual love for Frau K. Freud managed to point out to her that her lack of rancour towards one who had accused her was surprising; but he did not go any further.

10.4   The omitted dialectical inversion

The third dialectical inversion, says Lacan, should have confronted Dora with the mystery of her own being, of her sex, of her femininity. She had remained orally fixated to the mother and in this sense expresses the mirror stage, where the subject recognizes his ego in the other (Lacan, 1949, 1953a). Dora cannot accept herself as the object of desire of a man.

The dialectical inversion Freud did not carry out would have led Dora to recognize what Frau K meant for her. Lacan insists that when Herr K tells Dora at the lake that his wife means nothing to him: "You know I get nothing out of my wife" (Freud, 1905e [1901], p. 98), he clumsily breaks the spell of what he meant for Dora, the link with the woman. Hence that slap, which has passed into psychoanalytic history. Lacan makes the subtle point here that Dora's brusque reaction has a cause other than the almost manifest jealousy of the governess of the K's children, inasmuch as it expresses the rupture of the imaginary relationship Dora had maintained with Frau K through her husband. Nevertheless, the lakeside scene and the slap Dora gives her seducer cannot be explained, in my view, without taking account of the heterosexual jealousy of the Oedipus complex. Dora's "childbirth" nine months after this scene constrains Lacan's reasoning, and he has to say that the latent phantom pregnancy that will follow this scene is not an obstacle to his interpretation: it is notoriously produced in hysterics precisely in virtue of their male identification (Lacan, 1951, Écrits, p. 224). I make this comment here because I believe that the Lacanian technique of dialectical reversal of the material to "unhook" from the transference can only be supported by the idea that there is always only one problem—not several—to resolve. Freud, on the other hand, does not doubt that the slap by the lake was an impulse of jealous revenge (Freud, 1905e [1901], p. 106).

Had Freud confronted Dora with her homosexual link to Frau K, thus carrying out the third dialectical inversion Lacan expects, he would not have put himself in the place of Herr K, a victim of his countertransference, nor would he have felt the need to make Dora recognize her love for Herr K, with whom he identified.

Nevertheless, I think there is a new simplification by Lacan here: nothing contradicts the fact that had Freud proceeded as is suggested, Dora could have felt rejected, identifying her analyst with a weak father, for example, who yields her to her mother. It is not clear why Lacan, who is sceptical about the interpretation of the transference, which Dora would have received with her habitual disavowal, believes that his third dialectical reversal would have fared better.

10.5   Brief review of some of Lacan's ideas

In Lacanian theory, the mirror stage is a germinal moment of the structure of the ego. It should not be understood as a genetic step, although it is clearly a phase prior to the oedipal one, but as an attempt to give an account of primary narcissism in structural terms. The mirror stage implies a dyadic situation between the mother and the child, where the latter discovers his ego mirrored in her: the subject discovers his ego in his reflection in the mother, because the first notion of the ego comes from the other (Lacan, 1949, 1953a).

The ego is in substance eccentric, it is an otherness: the child acquires the first notion of his ego upon seeing himself reflected in the mother, that is to say in the *other*, and this other is in lower-case letters; afterwards will appear the *Other*, with a capital letter, who is the father of the triangular situation.

In the relationship with the mother, which is always dyadic, there occurs a new development of the mirror stage when brothers appear, and with them primitive jealousy and aggression. In this situation, although there are phenomenologically three, in reality there continue to be two, because the relation of the child with his brother is defined in virtue of the desire he has to occupy the place he has near the mother, insofar as he is wanted or loved by her.

A fundamental rupture of the dyadic relation occurs only after this second moment of the mirror stage, when the father appears. The father enters the scene and cuts that imaginary and narcissistic link, forcing the child to locate himself in a third place, the classic configuration of the Oedipus complex, which *subjects* the child to the symbolic order—it makes him subject, tearing him away from his imaginary world, making him accept the phallus as a signifier that orders the relation and the difference between the sexes.

Lacan understands Dora's relationship with Herr K as being imaginary—that is, dyadic: Herr K is a brother with whom she has a problem of rivalry (and aggression) over the mother, represented by Frau K. In this context, Dora's father also serves as a rival brother (Dora's father is weak and does not know how to impose himself as such).

In the mirror stage the child, who obtains his primary identity reflected in the mother, identifies with her desire in order to maintain that
dyadic structure and to be loved in a narcissistic way. Now in Freudian
theory the desire of the mother, as that of all women, is to have a penis;
and the child imagines (and this word is employed in its most literal
sense) himself as the penis the mother wishes to have. It is in this sense
that the child is the *desire of desire*, because his only desire is to be desired
by the mother. In the mirror stage, then, there is an *imaginary* relation in
which object and subject mirror each other and are essentially the same.

The imaginary relation of the child with the mother is consolidated,
then, in a (narcissistic) situation in which the child becomes the part lacking in the mother, the penis she always wanted to have and always loved,
also in a narcissistic manner. The child is her desire, desire of desire,
where the imaginary situation occurs in which the child can satisfy the
desire (of having a penis) of the mother. It is precisely at this point that the
father appears on the scene, and the triangular situation takes shape.

10.6   *The symbolic order*

Lacan distinguishes three stages in the Oedipus complex: In the *first*, the
father is located in the condition of a brother, with all the problems of
rivalry proper to the mirror stage—that is, for the child he is one more
rival who tries to occupy the place of the mother's desire. Until this moment the child had lived in an imaginary world of identification with the
mother, where the father does not count.

In the *second* oedipal phase, the father carries out the castration: he
separates the child from the mother and makes him feel he is not the
mother's penis (and makes the mother feel the child is not her penis). Here
the father appears basically as a (superego) castrator. This castration is
absolutely necessary for development, according to Lacan (and according
to all analysts).

Once the father has completed the castration and has established his
Law, once he has put things in their place, separating the child from the
mother and breaking the specular fascination that had united them, the
third phase occurs, in which the father is permissive and giving and facilitates for the child an identification that is no longer linked to the superego
but to the ego ideal: it is the moment when the child wishes to be like the
father. When the child recognizes that the father has the phallus and understands that he himself is not the phallus, he wants to be like the father
(who is not the phallus desired by the mother either, because the father *has*
the phallus, but *is not* the phallus). This allows the child to pass from a
situation where his dilemma was whether or not to be the phallus (second
phase) to another, a third phase, where he wishes to have a phallus but no
longer to be one. (Isidoro Berenstein, 1976, has often indicated that the
outcome of the Oedipus complex implies that the son renounces being the

father but not being *like* the father, who has renounced his mother instead of marrying her.)

This passage implies access to the symbolic order, because Lacan admits, as does Freud (1923e, 1924d, 1925j), a phallic stage, where the phallic-castrated alternative—that is, the presence or absence of the phallus—is what will determine the difference of the sexes. The moment the castration is carried out, the child painfully recognizes this difference: he is not the phallus, the mother has no phallus, and on this axis are established all the differences with the phallus as a symbol, as an expression of a singularity that makes it the first signifier.

This substantive and substantial change, which orders the relation between the sexes, between father and son (and between all men), arises from the replacement of an empirical fact by a *signifier*: the penis as anatomical organ is substituted by the phallus as a symbol. Lacan calls this, appropriately, the *paternal metaphor*: when it appears as a symbol of the differences, the phallus is a metaphor, and this metaphor is the *Law of the Father*, the law that subjects the individual to the symbolic order, forcing him to accept the castration and the value of the phallus as a symbol: the individual becomes subject, he *subjects himself* to the culture.

10.7   Mirage of the transference

I undertook this brief review of some of Lacan's ideas in order to clarify the basis on which he discusses Freud's technique with Dora. Lacan thinks Freud could have resolved Dora's neurosis, and adds with a fine irony that Freud would have gained a great deal of prestige had he resolved this third dialectical situation Dora presented! Through an error of countertransference, Freud makes a mistake and, instead of confronting Dora with her homosexual conflict with Frau K, tries to push her along the heterosexual path towards Herr K, with whom he had obviously identified himself.

One of Lacan's theoretical suppositions, which emerges from the review of his theories, is that the relation of Dora with Frau K is signed by the mirror stage: oral fixation and homosexuality, linked to wishing to be the mother's penis. Herr K is Dora's rival, in the position of an equal, a brother, and when Freud identifies with Herr K he places himself in a situation that is imaginary in the fullest sense, because it is something Freud imagines but which is not true; and it is imaginary, also, in that Freud begins to reverberate in a dyadic relation—that is, of equal images, without operating the symbolic cut that he should have effected from the position of a father. What Freud should have done at that moment was to impose the Law of the Father and separate Dora from Frau K.

As conceived just now, the transference phenomenon is always a failure of the analyst, who gets hooked into an imaginary situation. The transference situation in terms of you and I is something devoid of significance, which only reproduces indefinitely the imaginary fascination. Hence Lacan deplores the excessive emphasis in current psychoanalytic practice on the *hic et nunc* (here and now).

To conclude: the transference is not real (in the sense of symbolic reality); it is something that appears when the analytic dialectic stagnates. The analyst's art and science consists in re-establishing the symbolic order, without allowing himself to be captured by the specular situation. To interpret the transference, Lacan says poetically, "is nothing other than filling with a mirage the emptiness of that *point mort*" (Lacan, 1951, *Écrits*, p. 225). In his opinion, and according to Lacan's entire line of reasoning, the transference interpretation does not operate of itself; it is a mirage, something that deceives us twice because it keeps us on the imaginary plane of the mirror stage and because it does not allow us to operate the dialectical inversion the moment demands.

This opinion, as original as it is extreme, is attenuated, I would say, by the effect of contrivance the transference interpretation has for Lacan. He asks (quoting again from p. 225): "What is it, then, to interpret the transference? Nothing other than filling with a mirage the emptiness of that *point mort*. But this mirage is useful, because although deceptive, it fires the process again." Compare this with what I said earlier about the transference interpretation Freud would have wished to give Dora (1905e [1901], p. 120), which could (only) have orientated her in the right direction through opposition.

It is necessary to remember on this point that, for Lacan, the imaginary is always deceptive, and, moreover, reality is a structure different from empirical or factual reality. Lacan calls reality, following Hegel, the reality we see through our own structured perception. As the machine or the factory produce a transformation of energy, Hegel said, so also we never see factual or empirical reality but a structured reality. Lacan refers here to this reality—to the reality that is rational.

10.8   Transference and historicity

Let us repeat that analysis is a dialectical process, which investigates the history of the patient and where the transference arises the moment the analyst ceases to offer the corresponding antithesis. The transference is thus defined as resistance and more precisely as the analyst's resistance. Lacan imagines an analytic process in which, ideally, the transference could not exist: if the analyst were to understand *everything*, then the process would follow its course, and the transference would have no reason to appear.

Lacan asks what, finally, is that transference of which Freud says that its work is pursued *invisibly* behind the progress of the treatment, and whose effects in any case "escape demonstration"? Could it not be considered as an entity totally relative to the countertransference defined as the sum of prejudices, passions, perplexities—even insufficient information on the part of the analyst at a given moment of the dialectical process (Lacan, 1951, *Écrits*, p. 225)?

Weakening somewhat this incisive opinion, his "intervention" ends with these words: "We believe, however, that the transference always has the same intended meaning, indicating the moments of error and also the analyst's orientation, the same value, to call us back to our role: a positive inaction, to facilitate the 'correct dramatization' of the patient's subjectivity".

Lacan insists again and again on this theme. In his 1958 article, for example, Lacan (1958a) says that resistance stems from the analyst, inasmuch as he is always the one who obstructs the dialectical process. What interests Lacan is to reconstruct the life of the patient historically; and this process is interfered with each time the transference changes the past for the present. The technical consequence is that in this dialectical process of reconstruction, the analyst should unhook himself from that dual or imaginary situation, and to do this he operates always specifically as a father. In his paper on the Oedipus complex Willy Baranger (1976) points out that "the specific function of the analyst seems to us to be located in an essentially *paternal* register (whether the analyst is male or female), as it is situated on the very border that separates and defines the imaginary order and the symbolic order" (p. 311). And he adds immediately that to confront the subject with castration is specifically a paternal function—that is, the analyst always intervenes to break the mirage of the mother–child dyad.

10.9   *Lacanian management of the transference*

Lacan's ideas, which we have just expounded, are projected in his technique, which seems tough and severe to me. Let us say to begin with that just as Lacan uses the case of "Dora" to illustrate his thesis of the transference as a failure on the part of the analyst, so it can also be taken to show that Lacan's dialectical focus is insufficient. It should be borne in mind that Freud *constructs* with Dora his theory of the transference, so that it is not precisely this case that best lends itself to a study of how this theory operates in the treatment. What Freud himself thinks is that he failed because he did not pay enough attention to the first note of warning, and the transference took him by surprise (1905e [1901], p. 119), not that he allowed himself to become hooked into it, as Lacan asserts. The only way of disengaging from the transference is to interpret it from the place of the object assigned to the analyst at that moment. The Dora Lacan imagines possesses, it seems to me, too high a degree of rationality to keep to the line of reasoning he proposes.

Lacan's theory of the transference is, without doubt, technically supported in the difference between the imaginary and the symbolic. Inasmuch as the transference is always an imaginary phenomenon, what the analyst must do is to break it, to transform the imaginary relation into a symbolic one. It is noteworthy that this "surgical, cure, of a cut, a rupture, depends not on the level the process has reached, but entirely on the analyst, to the point that its neglect is always a phenomenon of countertransference. From this point of view the concept of *holding* (Winnicott, 1958) does not count, nor does Freud's voice seem to be heard, which advises us again and again not to interpret before having created a sufficient rapport.

Lacan insists on the idea of rupture, and this idea (this signifier, he would say) should be recognized as a plastic image of his technical conception. Baranger also puts this forward in the work cited, one of whose conclusions is that the early Oedipus of Melanie Klein has led to "considering the analytic situation as the maternally oriented framework in which dual and not triadic relations unfold" (Baranger, 1976, p. 314). The container–contained theory of Bion (1962b), however, is introduced as a thinking factor and so has no specular reference.

In his Rome lecture, Lacan (1953b) distinguishes the *empty* word from the *full* word. Where the resistance is maximal in the face of the possible access of the revealing word, the discourse turns and deviates towards the empty word—the word as mediation, to entrap the interlocutor. This coupling with the *other* (lower-case letter) impedes the access of the *Other* (capital letter). This is why Lacan says resistance is always something projected in the I–you system, the imaginary system. The moment that change is produced, the basis for the transference is built up.

If the resistance crystallizes in the specular system called I–other (lower-case letter) inasmuch as the analyst considers the patient's ego as an ally (in the sense of the therapeutic alliance), he falls into the specular trap in which the patient finds himself; he remains locked into that dual and imaginary relation. Lacan thinks the current focus of the technique loses sight of resistance as resistance to something the patient does not want to face, and not resistance to the other. Therefore Lacan criticizes the preferred interpretation of the *hic et nunc* of the transference. The analytic relation should not be conceived as dual, as dyadic, but as integrated by a third term, the Other (capital letter) which determines the symbolic historicity. Finally, the transference is a mirage the analyst must disengage from.

Let us say, to conclude this point, that the technique Lacan proposes seems applicable only in the case of neurotics, in that it implies that access to the symbolic order is always possible—that is, that the analysand can abandon from the beginning the imaginary order and differentiate himself from the object.

CHAPTER ELEVEN

The theory of the *sujet supposé savoir*— the subject supposed to know

L acan's thought is complex, and it has vitality. Therefore it is not strange that it changes—especially with respect to a theme such as transference, which engaged him often throughout his extensive work.

Up to this point the transference had remained located in the domain of the imaginary, where analyst and patient mirror each other and remain prisoners of their narcissistic fascination. From this perspective the psychoanalytic process is only going to take shape once the analyst has transformed that dual relation into a symbolic one, for which it is necessary for him to break the dyadic relation and to occupy a third place, the place of the code, the place of the Great Other.

11.1 The "sujet supposé savoir" (the subject supposed to know)

In *Les quatres concepts fondamentaux de la psychanalyse* (1964a), in Book XI of his seminars, Lacan offers a new hypothesis, which assigns to the transference a place in the symbolic order. This proposal, which is known as the theory of the *sujet supposé savoir* (S.s.S.)—or the "subject (who is) supposed to know"—has as its starting point a reflection on knowledge and the symbolic order.

The starting point of Lacan's argument is a study on the function of the analyst. It is one thing for the analyst to be included in the dual relation of the mirror stage and quite another for him to occupy the third place the symbolic order demands.

Basing himself on this difference, Lacan questions the position of the analyst in the analytic situation no less than the position of analysis in science.

The function of the analyst is to disappear as an "I" (ego, *moi*), says Miller (1979, p. 23), and not to allow the imaginary relation to dominate the analytic situation. The analyst should be in the place of the Other. Miller expresses this conception of the analytic process with a simple graph, along one of whose axes is inscribed the imaginary and reciprocal relation of the *I* and the *a* (the other, *autre*, lower-case letter) and along the other the *subject* and the great *Other* (ibid., p. 23). Michel Silvestre uses the same schema in "El saber del psicoanalista [The Knowledge of the Psychoanalyst] (1987a).

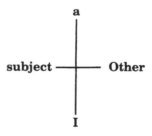

Science proposes to separate the symbolic from the imaginary, the signifier from the image. The signifier, Miller says on p. 60 of his third lecture, can exist independently of a subject that expresses itself through it. (Compare this with Bion's, 1962b, idea of the apparatus for thinking thoughts.) However, each time scientific progress creates a signifier as a new invention, we are led to think it was always there, and then we project it in a *subject supposed to know*. Descartes made science possible because he placed God as the guarantor of truth, and he was able therefore to separate him from scientific knowledge. Science presents itself, then, as a discourse without a subject, as an impersonal discourse—the discourse of the subject (who is) supposed to know, in person (Miller, 1979, p. 66).

For Lacan, "something of God persists in the discourse of science from the function of the S.s.S.", says Miller (ibid., p. 70), "because it is very difficult to defend oneself from the illusion that the knowledge invented by the signifier has always existed", that it was always there.

11.2   The subject supposed to know in the transference

On the basis of these ideas Lacan articulates the new theory of transference. When he introduces the rule of free association, the analyst tells the patient that everything he says will have value, will have meaning; and in this way, with the mechanism of the treatment in place, the analyst becomes for the patient the subject (who is) supposed to know.

Although the analyst thus becomes, in the cure, the subject (who is) supposed to know, what Lacan asserts is that the psychoanalytic experience consists precisely in evacuating it. Structurally, the S.s.S. appears, then, with the opening phase of analysis; but the issue is the ending and not the beginning. The ending of analysis means ejecting the S.s.S., understanding that it does not exist. For this reason analysis occupies a special place in science, because only in analysis can the S.s.S. remain included in the process and be ejected at the end. If there is a truly atheistic science, Miller states, it is psychoanalysis (1979, p. 68).

The analysis of the transference consists in discovering—Miller asserts—that there is no S.s.S. in the real sense (ibid., p. 125), and he emphasizes, then, that this process, in which the S.s.S. is evacuated at the end of the treatment, coincides with the loss of the object, the mourning for the object, precisely as Melanie Klein proposes (1935, 1940).

In other words, according to the theory of the S.s.S., the analysand tries at the outset to establish an imaginary relation with the analyst, since in attributing to the analyst knowledge about what is happening to him he is assuming that he and the analyst are one. When the analyst does not allow himself to be placed in that role and makes the analysand understand that the only one who understands what is happening to him (what is his desire) is the analysand himself, the symbolic level is reached.

This idea is true and we all accept it. The analysand attributes to us a knowledge of him that we do not have, and our task is to correct this judgement, which stems from a narcissistic fascination. Winnicott (1945, 1952) would say that we have to disillusion the patient progressively, until we make him understand that the all-knowing object exists only in his imagination.

As a first approximation to this theory we can say that, at the start of the cure, the analysand supposes that the analyst possesses the knowledge that concerns him, and that in due course he will gradually come to abandon this supposition. We have already said that the S.s.S. is the immediate consequence of the analyst's introduction of the fundamental rule when treatment begins. It should not be deduced from this, however, without going any further, that the S.s.S. arises from the patient attributing omniscience to the analyst, an all-embracing knowledge that covers and reaches everything. When this phenomenon occurs in its pure state, we are already facing psychosis; the patient believes the analyst knows his thoughts (paranoia) and even provokes them, as in the transitivistic delusion of schizophrenics. In these extreme cases the transference functions at its maximum and the S.s.S. emerges in all its magnitude; and in this form, intentionally or not, Lacan elegantly defines the transference psychosis.

In other more common and less serious cases, when the analyst introduces the fundamental rule and with it gives the patient a guarantee that everything he says can be interpreted, the analysand generally shows himself to be sceptical and fears, rather, his ability to deceive the analyst. Lacan offers a simple example: that of a patient who conceals his syphilis because he fears this will lead the analyst to an organic explanation and will make him deviate from the psychological (1964a, *Écrits*, p. 212). The patient may think, then, not only that the analyst knows everything but, conversely, that the analyst will be deceived if he offers him certain data.

It is necessary to point out that inasmuch as it attributes the transference to the very constitution of the analytic situation, to its structure— which Lacan likes to call the *analytic discourse*—the theory of the S.s.S. accords the transference a place of its own and can no longer denounce it, it seems to me, as the analyst's moment of error. The transference arises from the patient at the very moment the analyst introduces the fundamental rule; and the more ill the patient is, the more he will see the analyst as the S.s.S. in person, as, for example, in the case of the paranoiac. Ferenczi had already said in his essay of 1909 that the amount of transference is directly proportional to the degree of illness.

In this way, I believe the theory of the S.s.S. implies that each time we enunciate an antithesis and operate a dialectical reversal, we are implicitly supporting our analysand's belief that we are the S.s.S., which compels us to interpret this belief—that is, to integrate to the antithesis we have proposed the transferential element with which the patient receives it. If this is so, then the technique should vary and approach one that uses the transference interpretation as an indispensable and daily instrument. For this reason, I doubt that Lacan's two theories are easily reconcilable.

11.3   The transference and the symbolic order

This great change in Lacan's thinking can be noticed in *Les quatre concepts* prior to his proposing the theory of the S.s.S., when he says in chapter 11 that "the transference is the *mise-en-scène* of the reality of the unconscious" (1964a, p. 133). With this assertion Lacan approaches the opinion of all analysts generally—that is, that the transference is a universal phenomenon and that it derives basically from the functioning of the unconscious, from the primary process. According to what Freud has taught us, Lacan continues, the reality of the unconscious is sexual, it is desire. And this desire, which sets in motion the transference, Lacan concludes, is the desire of the other—that is, the desire of the analyst. For this reason the presence of the analyst is very important for Lacan, and he devotes chapter 10 of the book to this topic. The Freudian field—Lacan says here—is a field that is elusive by its very nature; and for that reason the analyst's presence as witness is indispensable (ibid., p. 116). Although Miller takes care to state specifically that the analyst's wish—certainly a very singular one—is not to identify with the other, respecting the patient's individuality (Miller, 1979, p. 125), I have the impression that Lacan is not optimistic, and what he calls "wish, is an exclusively sexual desire, to such an extent that he asserts that the entry of sexuality into the analysis of Anna O was the work of Breuer (Lacan, 1964a, p. 144), as we shall see in a moment.

This brings us to the other expression of Lacan's thought. If asking the patient to talk and to say everything that comes into his head installs on the one hand the S.s.S. as the backbone of the transference, on the other hand it confers on the analyst a power over the meaning of what the analysand says. His position as interpreter converts the analyst into a master of the truth, Lacan asserts, to the extent that he decides retroactively the significance of what is directed to him. At this moment, and as a subject who is supposed to know the meaning, the analyst is already the Other. Here, then, a difference between the Other who really knows and the subject (who is) supposed to know is clearly established; and everything leads me to suppose that this difference is the same as that between the imaginary order and the symbolic order. As guarantor of the analytic experience, the analyst is the great Other, and this is the point at which the transference becomes symbolic.

The symbolic level of the transference evidently appears, then, when the analyst, rather than occupying the place of the S.s.S. that the patient assigns him, occupies instead the place of the Other. How this path is to be traversed without falling into authoritarianism nor falling into ideological affirmations, if one abstains from transferential interpretation, is, I think, easier to conceive than to execute in the actual practice of the consulting-room.

It is necessary to indicate here that, for Lacan, it is always the listener who decides on the meaning; in any dialogue, he who is silent holds the power to the extent that he confers significance on what the other says; but when the listener becomes a speaker, this power is, in fact, shared. Analytic dialogue, on the other hand, is completely asymmetrical, because the analyst is silent, or, if he speaks, it is to sanction the significance of what the analysand has said. In this manner, only the analyst holds the power. From this point of view, the analytic discourse (situation) is constitutively a *pact* between the analyst and the patient where the latter accords the former the place of the Great Other.

11.4   *Constituting effect and constituted effects*

The pivot of the transference, that which is its foundation, is, then, the singular manner in which the analytic discourse is established by the invitation to free associate, which constitutes an asymmetrical dialogue. This level is constitutive, transphenomenal and structural. This is not an experience but a structure. Therefore Lacan insists on not confusing the *constituting effect* of the transference (structure) with the *constituted effects* (phenomena), which derive from the former. The structure goes beyond the phenomena and consists in the analyst putting himself in the place of the Other, the Great Other. On the phenomenological plane, this structural situation can originate diverse feelings (experiences)—contempt, credulity, admiration, mistrust, and so on.

I want to insist at this point—because it seems to me a Lacanian concept of real value—that in formulating the theory of transference one must not confuse the phenomenal with the structural dimension. The axis of the S.s.S. does not refer to an experience of the analysand but to a supposition that arises from the very structure of the situation. Therefore, as we have just seen, the phenomenon can be precisely the converse: that the analysand believes that the analyst does not know, that he can be deceived.

This difference between the structural and the phenomenal in the analytic discourse is undoubtedly basic to an understanding not only of Lacan's new theory on the transference but of the theory of transference in general. The phenomena Freud outlined, discovered and studied in the transference, and which, for Miller, are repetition, resistance and suggestion, turn on the structural and *transphenomenal* structure of the S.s.S. This is why Lacan distinguishes the constituting effect of the transference from the consequent constituted effects already in his 1953 Rome lecture, the starting point of his investigation; incorporating this work in his *Écrits* of 1966, he declares in a footnote that with the difference between constituting and constituted effects that which he will later designate as the support for the transference—that is, the S.s.S.—is defined.

The symbolic theory of the transference is based on what Lacan called at the beginning of his investigation the *analytic pact*—Freud's *Vertrag*. In his lecture in Rome, Lacan speaks, in effect, of the patient believing that his truth is in us, that we know it from the moment he concludes the initial pact with us. In this way the constituting effects of the transference with their mark of reality take shape for Lacan (1953b, *Écrits*, p. 308).

The constituting effect of the transference, to the extent that it depends on the structure of the analytic discourse, has a relation to the real and the symbolic and is not linked to repetition, whereas the constituted effects that follow from that structure are repetitive. In this way, on its symbolic level, the transference remains unlinked to repetition, a point on which Oscar Masotta (1977) insists particularly in his prologue to *Los Cuatro Conceptos* (Spanish edition of *Les quatre concepts*).

Lacan says that in fact this illusion, which impels us to search for the reality of the subject beyond the wall of language, is the same as that through which the subject believes his truth to be in us, already given, that we know it in advance; and that, for the same reason, it is open to our objectivizing intervention.

He continues, saying that the patient surely does not have to take responsibility for that subjective error which, whether confessed to or not in his discourse, is immanent in the fact that he entered analysis, and in his having concluded his initial pact. And the subjectivity of this moment cannot be neglected—especially if we find in him the cause for what we could call the constituting effect of the transference, in that they are distinguished by an indication of reality from the constituted effects that follow from them (see *Écrits*, p. 308). In the footnote already cited, Lacan notes that he defined there what he was later to designate as the support for the transference, the subject (who is) supposed to know.

In his next paragraph he adds, to clarify the above, that Freud insisted that a reality factor should be distinguished in the feelings brought to the transference, and that Freud concluded that it would be an abuse of the subject's docility to wish to persuade him in all cases that these feelings are a simple transferential repetition of the neurosis (see ibid., p. 308).

It seems to me that in this way, by introducing reality in the transference, Lacan approaches, albeit along a very different path, the concept of the therapeutic alliance of the ego psychologists. Where it is based on the analytic pact that the patient seals when he accepts the fundamental rule, the symbolic theory of the transference corresponds to the plane of reality, not to the repetitive one. Nevertheless it is appropriate to ask oneself here whether we can still go on calling this "transference", or whether it would be better to call it simply "therapeutic alliance, or "psychoanalytic pact". In other words, the constituting effect of the transference, where it is distinguished by its indication of reality, belongs to the symbolic order; but it is no longer transference, at least not in the strict form in which we had originally defined it. In my view, from that point only the constituted effects deserve that name.

11.5   *Final comment*

We could say, in summary, that the theme of the transference occupies a very important place in Lacan's thought, and in his written work it crystallizes, at two points at least, into two theories that unite the transference with the imaginary and the symbolic order.

The *imaginary theory of the transference*, enunciated in 1951, is conceived by Lacan as a dyadic process, specular and narcissistic in that a third person is lacking, the Other who refers to the code and redistributes the roles in the mother–child couple, imposing the Law of the Father. If the analyst does not locate himself as the third person who has to effect the cut (castration), he enters an imaginary field where he reverberates indefinitely in the I–you situation. This is what happened to Freud with Dora: identifying himself with Herr K, Freud wished to be loved by Dora instead of indicating to her the homosexual link with Frau K.

Many years later, in 1964, Lacan proposed a series of ideas that articulate the *symbolic theory of the transference*. According to this theory, the analytic discourse is a structure that is defined when the relationship begins, when the analyst introduces the fundamental rule. From that moment the analyst occupies a particular place in that recently formed structure, and it is the place of the S.s.S.

It is evident that where he assigns the analyst the position of the S.s.S., the analysand tries to establish an imaginary and narcissistic relation: if the patient asserts that the analyst knows what is happening to him, to the patient, it is because the analyst and the patient are one; but if the analyst does not allow himself to be placed in this position and denounces it as a mere supposition of the patient, then the symbolic level is attained. In this way, as we all know, the function of the analyst is to remain finally excluded from the life and the mind of the analysand.

ADDENDUM *Signifier, repetition and transference*

Before closing these two chapters, I shall try to describe Lacan's ideas on transference according to his own guidelines. Although this is not easy, it is the only way to understand this great thinker, who in many ways keeps firmly apart from other lines of doctrine in present-day psychoanalysis.

Lacan goes back to Freud in his proposal to formalize his theories on structural linguistics and combinatorial mathematics. He does it with his original notion of the *signifier*, which points like a compass, directing the whole of *Le champ Freudien*. I have no intention of developing fully Lacan's theory of the signifier, as it would be outside the scope of this commentary, but I shall try to explain it insofar as it applies to transference in psychoanalytic practice.

Throughout his work, Lacan tirelessly stresses that the unconscious is structured like a language, and it is no mere chance that the *Écrits* begin with "Le séminaire sur 'La lettre volée'" [The Seminar on "The Purloined Letter"] (1955), in which he takes Poe's story to illustrate his theory of the signifier. Lacan maintains that the characters in the story are defined in relation to the letter as signifier, which determines the fate of whoever has it. In the relationship between the king, the queen, and the minister, the position of the latter changes when he appropriates the letter and at the same time remains caught in it. Further on in the story, when the relationship takes shape between the chief of police, the minister and Dupin, the latter, too, as the possessor of the letter, becomes something different from what he was up to that moment. "It can be said that when the characters take possession of the letter, they are caught and carried along by something which increasingly predominates over their individual peculiarities" (1954–55, "The Ego in the Theory of Freud and in Psychoanalytical Technique", p. 295) The characters are defined by their position in relation to a single protagonist, the letter. The content (*signified*) of the letter has thus—and this is undeniable—no importance in the plot of the story.

Lacan comes to think that whoever has the letter suffers through its influence a process of feminization based on some contingencies in the plot, and it is obvious that in this way he wants to convince us that the power of the letter as a signifier is to catch the subject and make him feminine. That the thief, by appropriating "the queen's letter" (because it was stolen from her), identifies with the damaged object and acquires some feature of his victim's personality, is something that does not enter into Lacan's reasoning in any way; and it could not do so without seriously impairing his theory, because then the letter would be not only a signifier but the symbol of an "empirical" object such as the breast, the penis or the mother, for example. I mean that there are many ways in which Poe's story can be psychoanalytically understood, and not just a single one, as Lacan claims. Thus Freud would see the queen as the woman with a penis, the phallic mother, and Melanie Klein would have no doubt that the queen with the letter is the mother who contains within herself the father's penis, the babies, and the faeces that the son–minister attacks with envy and jealously.

The notion of the signifier appears continually throughout Lacan's work; thus we read, for example, at the beginning of section 2 of chapter 11 of *Les quatre concepts* (1964a) that: "*Vous saisissez pourquoi la relation du sujet au signifiant est le repère que nous avons voulu mettre au premier plan d'une rectification générale de la théorie analytique, car il est aussi premier et constituant dans l'instauration de l'expérience analytique, que premier et constituant dans la fonction radicale de l'inconscient*" ["the relation of the subject with the signifier is the reference-point which I wished to place at the forefront of a general rectification of analytic theory, for it is as primary and constitutive in the establishment of analytic experience, as it is primary and constitutive in the radical function of the unconscious"] (*The Four Concepts*, p. 138). The signifier is primary, then, in the theory and practice of psychoanalysis, and also primary in the functioning of the unconscious.

Lacan's signifier is without a doubt heir to Ferdinand de Saussure's theory of the linguistic sign (1916); this is defined as the combination of a concept (signified) and an acoustic image (signifier) and is expressed in a diagram that has become famous:

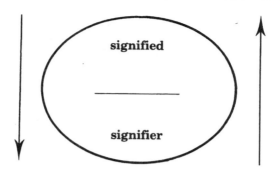

This diagram shows us the two inseparable faces of the sign as a closed system (ellipse), in which the horizontal line expresses the link between the two elements, the arrows its going and coming relation, while the ellipse itself implies the univocal connection of the two terms.

Lacan reverses this relationship to indicate the preeminence of the signifier, and he thickens the dividing line so that the signifier remains above (not to say in the air), alone and deprived of all relationship with the signified, because the barrier separating them is impenetrable. With ellipses and arrows removed, Lacan's famous algorithm finally looks like this:

$$\frac{S}{s}$$

where the capital S is the signifier and the small s is the signified.

Once the relationship between the signifier and the signified is broken, meaning can come only from the relations of combination (syntagma) and substitution (paradigm), which are established in the links of the symbolic signifier chain. This is thus set up, as Ríos (1984) points out, in a closed axiomatic system, which is surprisingly analogous to Hilbert's mathematical formalism (ibid., p. 120), in which a signifier is bound only to another signifier, split off from any empirical (or objectal) reference: the sign is "for someone", but the signifier is such only for another signifier. It is no wonder then that Oscar Masotta, in his painstaking study "Psychoanalysis and Structuralism" (1969), says that when psychoanalytic theory starts from object relations, it falls into a kind of wild empiricism, which appears to forget that Freud speaks (more frequently, but not always—may I add) of object finding [*Objektfindung*] or object choice [*Objektwahl*], and not of object relation [*Objektbeziehung*], so that the object begins by not existing. It is certain that the theory of object relations comes rather from Berlin, Budapest and London than from Vienna, and that in Freud's view the object is contingent on the impulse and must be found. It is no less certain, on the other hand, that Freud distinguishes the object of the impulse from the love object of the ego. That the object does not exist at the beginning is explained on the basis of the theory of primary narcissism, which Freud accepts most of the time. Freud also says that the finding of the object is in reality a re-discovery, and while many writers see it as a return to the first object, Lacan considers it as proof that desire can by definition never find its object. Like an inverted Parmenides, Lacan tells us that "non-being" exists (Ríos, personal communication).

This brief digression may perhaps help us to understand in what strict (and also extreme) sense Lacan tells us unceasingly that "A signifier is significant only for other signifiers" and also that "a signifier is what represents the subject for other signifiers", from which it follows that the analyst must put himself in the place of the subject, who lets a signifier represent him for another signifier. That is why Maci can say, in *La repetición significante* (1983), a valuable book devoted to this subject, "The subject of analysis is always *in transference*; he is always *transferred*" (chapter 6, p. 203, italics in the original), which must be understood strictly as "the subject is carried along by the trend of the signifier" (ibid., p. 207). Another outstanding pupil of Lacan, the Argentinian Juan David Nasio (1984), affirms that insofar as it is structured like a language, the "unconscious consists of this formal relationship between a recognisable signifier and other unrecognisable and virtual signifiers" (ibid., p. 23).

Insofar as they place transference in the field of signification, the followers of Lacan take as the birth certificate of the concept paragraph C of chapter 7 (Freud, 1900a), in which the name "*Übertragung*" is given to the process by which the unconscious desire is transferred to the preconscious in order to open the way to consciousness. According to these authors the theory of transference begins in 1900 and not in 1895. Here there is a distinct watershed between those (including myself) who understand transference as *transference of objects* and those who think of it as *transference of signifiers*. It could not be otherwise, since Lacan, as we have just seen, thinks of the object as an absence. It is nevertheless very clear that in the view of the Freud of "The Psychotherapy of Hysteria", the *person* of the doctor has its place in the phenomenon just described, so that "transference on to the physician takes place through a *false connection*" (1895d, p. 302). We remember Freud's example of the patient who wanted him to kiss her as she had had the same wish many years before with another man. And Freud concludes that as soon as he could understand this phenomenon, every similar demand upon his person had to be reduced to a transference by false connection.

With his usual precision, Maci (1983) says that transference is a cycle; he reminds us that the word *Übertragung* means something that is supported and transported, that circulates. Transference, however, does not carry with it anything substantial and concrete, but the subject of a discourse (ibid., p. 203). The subject is swept along by the significant trend, and Lacan's famous aphorism with which we began must be understood, according to Maci, not as meaning that the signifier represents the subject, but simply that it puts it in its place, attaches it to the network of significance, which is a desiderative chain (ibid., p. 207). From the same point of view, Masotta says that "it is necessary to situate the subject in the interstices of the relationships of substitution and combination which unite one signifier to another signifier . . ." (1969, p. 43). The same is expressed by Jacques-Alain Miller (1969) with the concept of *suture*, insofar as it is the point at which the subject is attached to the symbolic chain of significance. The suture designates the subject's attachment to the chain of discourse in which it figures as an element that breaks down under the idea of being the possessor of a place (ibid., p. 41).

At the beginning of "The Seminar on 'The Purloined Letter'", Lacan (1955) maintains that repetition compulsion [*Wiederholungszwang*] begins with what he calls the *insistence* of the chain of signification; and he exemplifies it by the structure that is repeated in the story between the scene in which the king does not see the letter, the queen sees that the king does not see it, and the minister sees it, and the other scene, in which the one who does not see it is the chief of police (who is now taking the place of the king), while the minister is in the place of the queen and Dupin in that of the minister. That is to say, the characters change, but the places do not, and the theft is repeated. This is how Lacan understands repetition compulsion and the function of the psychoanalyst (Dupin), insofar as the movements are determined by the place that the signifier (the letter) occupies in the trio. The second scene repeats the first, but thanks to this repetition the analyst–Dupin is able to understand the first, not by his personal merits but because he occupies the place of the subject of the unconscious.

When, later, he stresses the material nature of the signifier, which cannot bear to be cut, he asserts that the signifier is the symbol of absence and death, and he gives us his explanation of what Freud placed beyond the pleasure principle in 1920: the subject follows the line of the symbolic, and his own being is modelled on the moment when he reaches it in the signifier chain (Lacan, 1955, *Écrits*, p. 30) so that it is determined by formal language. There is an element that governs human experience beyond life, which Freud calls death instinct (or drive), and which in Lacan's view is symbolic repetition, in which we see that "*L'ordre du symbole ne peut plus être conçu comme constitué par l'homme, mais comme le constituant*" ["the symbolic order can no longer be conceived as constituted by man, but as constituting him"] (ibid., p. 46). The autonomy of the symbolic, he said later (ibid., p. 52), is the only one that can free from its mistakes the theory and practice of free association in psychoanalysis.

Heidegger's recognized influence in Lacan's thought is obvious here and leads him to a very unusual vision of the 1920 dualist theory of the instincts, with a Freud who is denuded of every empirical reference, and a man who exists only for death. Lacan believes that in this way he liberates Freud from his limitations and penetrates into the essence of his thought, although it is possible that he may be wrong, and further from the master than he believes.

* * *

Lacan's algorithm, which sanctions the autonomy of the symbolic, is, without a doubt, a legitimate attempt to apply the formal axiomatic method of the mathematicians, and structural linguistics, to Freud's discoveries. In this, Lacan's merit is great and unquestionable.

There are, nevertheless, many ways of understanding this theory, and it is one thing to propose it as a methodological model that can in fact give us an explanation of the combination of free association and the subtle relationships that Freud was capable of working out from a parapraxis, a symptom or a dream (and which, thanks to him, we can all bring out in our everyday work), and a very different thing to set up syntactic combinations as the only source of meaning, making the signifier independent of any reference to things. In this way semantics (including pragmatics) are subordinated to syntactics. As a model, the theory of the signifier will be acceptable to all (or almost all) analysts; but many will find it difficult to follow when it is proposed as a closed system of interconnected elements that do not admit any relationship with extralinguistic entities.

In its strictest version, Lacan's theory plainly asserts that the syntactic relationship between signifiers exactly accounts for the meaning, without any semantic reference to things. This is what Hilbert thought in mathematics, with his famous theory of implicit definition, according to which mathematical concepts depend on the syntactic system in which they are placed by convention. Within this system, the significance of each term varies in relation to the other signifiers, and thus the user of the system— the "subject", as Lacan would say—cannot in any way interfere with this combination. As Gregorio Klimovsky (1984) says, "the majority of formal mathematical languages admit non-isomorphic interpretations or models" (ibid., p. 50). In other words, if we attach to an axiomatic system a dictionary that assigns a fixed meaning to its terms (excluding logical terms), we get what is called an *interpretation* of the system; and we can say that this interpretation provides an *adequate model* if the axioms are true. This model is obviously not a syntactic but a semantic system. According to this point of view, present-day mathematics tend to recover the semantic value of their systems and to seek their application in something external.[1]

Even while admitting mathematical formalism as a method, we have to say that we have a very long way to go before we arrive at the factual sciences, because the factual sciences do not consist simply of a formal set of signs (or signifiers) but of something in which there is designation and definite conditions of truth. Scientific language has semantic references, and on them depend its conditions of truth and its informative qualities. As for Freud, as Klimovsky has shown (1989) in his outstanding paper read at the International Congress in Rome, there is no doubt that he was convinced that he had discovered *things* and that his theory of the unconscious is semantic. It is certain that Freud paid great attention to the combination of significant elements, and for some reason he constantly stresses the importance of condensation and especially displacement mechanisms; but he never doubts that the meaning comes from the relationship of the signifier with things that are not signifiers.

The forgetting of Signorelli's name, of which Freud makes a masterly analysis in the first chapter of *The Psychopathology of Everyday Life* (1901b), illustrates what we have been saying. There it is obvious that the associations can be considered as a signifier symbolic chain in which Freud, as the subject, is caught. He does not doubt for a moment, however, that the suicide of a patient who was very important to him, and whom he had received in Trafoi, was a semantic reference to the contents "death and sexuality" and an effective factor in the appearance of the signifiers Botticelli and Boltraffio (for Signorelli). To Freud, who always understood psychoanalysis as a natural science, the meaning is something more than the relationship between signifiers.

* * *

A brave attempt to develop the logic of the signifier in a strict form is made by Jacques-Alain Miller (1969), based on Frege's ideas on number. Frege starts with Leibniz's concept of truth—that is, that truth is that everything is identical with itself. It follows from this that there is a class of things that are not identical with themselves, which, in fact is an empty class, since there cannot be an object subsumed into the class of things not identical to themselves. This empty class is the number zero. In this way the concept of non-identity with itself is represented by zero, which sutures the logical discourse ["C'est l'énoncé décisif que *le concept de la non-identité-à-soi est assigné par le nombre zéro* qui suture le discours logique"—p. 46, italics in the original]. In this way logic can maintain itself, as Frege wishes, without any reference to reality.

In this way, Miller goes on, zero appears in a place indicated by subsumption in which the object is lacking; zero is a blank that makes the lack visible; and, at the same time, zero is counted as one (although the concept of zero has no more part in reality than a blank), and thus it is converted into the general support of the succession of numbers (ibid., p. 47). It is necessary that zero should be a number, that zero should occupy the suturing place of what is missing, so that the discourse of logic may close.

Starting from this complex mathematical statement, Miller concludes that if zero is nothing more than the possessor of the suturing place of absence, if zero has had to be returned to the succession of numbers, then there can be no obstacle to recognizing the relationship that the chain of signifiers maintains with the subject. Then the subject, to conclude, is that object of the impossible which logic knows as non-identity with itself.

Miller's explanation is doubtless ingenious in identifying zero with absence and the logic of arithmetic with that of the signifier; but when these ideas are applied to clinical psychoanalysis, we immediately realize the enormous distance that separates the logic of the signifier from what happens in the session.

* * *

In "La signification du phallus" [The Meaning of the Phallus] (1958b), which he read in German at the Max Planck Institute in Munich on 9 May 1958, Lacan explains his theory of the signifier in relation to the castration complex. The relationship of the subject with the phallus is established independently of the anatomical difference between the sexes, since the phallus is not an object, still less an organ, but a signifier destined to show the effects of meaning by its presence. Unlike all other signifiers, the phallus has no counterpart but its absence, and this absence—let us make this clear—refers not only to the woman's sexual equipment but also to death. At this point it is fair to say that Lacan faithfully follows Freud, in whose view the unconscious does not record either the female genitals or death. Freud came to think that the female is constituted on the basis of castration (penis envy), but Lacan goes a step further, affirming that the man, too, does not derive his sex from his biological shape. For both men and women the phallus establishes the absence on which desire is based and sets going the signifier's chain of desire.

The man's need deviates through the fact that he speaks, as then he remains subject to the demand that returns to him estranged, alienated. This, in Lacan's view, is not the effect of the child's dependence, but of the conformation of the signifier and the fact that the spoken message comes from the place of the Other (1958b, p. 690). In this way desire is distinguished from necessity and from demand.

The demand, in Lacan's view, refers to something other than the satisfaction claimed; it is above all the demand for presence or absence, the demand for love. Everything that can be conceded is transmuted by demand into a proof of love; and between need and demand there is a split [*Spaltung*] in which desire appears. As Jinkis says (1974), the signifier must be considered in relation to the absence in the Other, which is the basis of the symbolic chain (ibid., p. 82). The signifier is present in the subject, which is the typical place where it operates. In this way, as Lacan reiterates, the subject is inhabited by the signifier.

That is why the phallus is the signifier by autonomasia, the *bar* that falls over the meaning and thanks to which the unconscious is language. Both men and women desire from the other that which they lack, and this essential lack is the phallus. The man wants to find the phallus in the woman to overcome his fear of losing it, and the woman longs to receive from the man the phallus which she lacks. We can only desire that which we lack, and in the act of love each one gives to the other that which he does not possess. Lacan, we must not forget, maintains throughout his work an entirely narcissistic conception of love, and nothing infuriates him more than the concept of genital oblativity (*oblation*: according to the *Shorter Oxford Dictionary*, "that which is offered to God or to a deity; an offering sacrifice"), which—he deplores—introduced a Frenchman (Laforgue) to the theoretical body of psychoanalysis. This entirely narcissistic conception of love, according to which sexual desire seeks its complement in the other, compels Lacan to maintain that the sexual relation does not exist—a strange but inescapable corollary of his conception of erotic life.

As we said above, Lacan closely follows Freud's view of the phallic phase (1923e) and female sexuality (1931b, 1933a, Lecture 33). According to Freud, in the infantile phallic phase there is only one sexual organ, which the little boy is afraid of losing and the little girl wants to have. But the distance from the phallic phase to the theory of the phallus as a signifier is without a doubt very long, and as far as I can see insurmountable. Freud uses the noun "phallus, to indicate the leading organ of the infantile genital stage, which in his opinion (but not in that of Jones, Karen Horney, or Melanie Klein) is common to girl and boy, because both imagine themselves endowed with an identical organ, which is the penis in the male and the clitoris in the female, to both of which that name can be applied. Whereas Freud refers this condition to the anatomical differences between men and women (Freud, 1925j), Lacan emphatically affirms at the beginning of "Die Bedeutung des Phallus" (1958b) that the sequelae of the castration complex in the man's unconscious and *Penisneid* in the woman's are insoluble by any reduction to biological data.

The leap from Freud's phallic phase to the genital sexuality of the adolescent can be understood within his (phallocentric) theory, even if it is not shared. The theory advanced by Lacan, breaking any connection between human sexuality and biology, is much bolder, more abrupt, and, in my view, without sufficient foundation. Apart from his insistence on presenting the phallus as a signifier, Lacan never explains in what this step from zoology to culture consists. Sometimes he has recourse to mythological references to account for this function, reminding us of palaeolithic myths in which monuments glorify a phallus that does not appear to have any relationship with man, whose member it was, and then the phallus is a symbol like any other; sometimes he surprises us with concrete references such as *"ce signifiant est choisi comme le plus saillant de ce qu'on peut attraper dans le réel de la copulation sexuelle*" ["This signifier is chosen as the most outstanding of what can be grasped in the reality of sexual copulation"] (1958b, p. 692). In this case the "phallus" is simply the penis; on the same page he has recourse to turgidity to support his arguments, with the result that the phallic signifier is no more than the penis surrounded by the phantasies that are inherent in every human being. The transformations that Lacan offers us in the last pages of the work that he presented at the Max Planck Institute illustrate how some psychological and psychopathological characteristics of men and women can be explained from the point of view of the theory of the phallic phase, but add nothing, in my opinion, to the value of the phallus as a signifier. On the contrary, when Lacan tries to account for male impotence and female frigidity with his theory of the phallus as a signifier, his explanations are poor and vividly reminiscent of Adler's masculine protest (1912); the same can be said for homosexuality.

Thinking as I do that Lacan's efforts to justify his theory of the phallus as the first signifier fail, it might then be contrasted with others, but this is not relevant to my commentary; and I have only to point out, if but briefly, its ideological components. This subject has been discussed by Roberto Speziale-Bagliacca in his well-documented book *Sulle spalle di Freud* [On Freud's Shoulders] (1982). This author considers that Lacan's theory forms the phallic ideology peculiar to the authoritarian personality. Speziale-Bagliacca affirms that the phallus is plainly and absolutely the erect penis, and he refers to what Lacan himself says and also to the ancient myths of phallic cults; and he maintains that this conception (which from the social point of view is *machismo*) is in the service of manic defences in an attempt to escape dependence and avoid depression. In this author's view Lacan's technique (and especially the sessions of free time) is strongly influenced by a difficulty in understanding the containing aspects of the setting, which have to do with the mother and the maternal function of the analyst, which Freud's genius was capable of moulding into the norms of the cure. Following Fornari (1981), Speziale-Bagliacca considers that there is a paternal code and a maternal code, and not only the Law of the Father, as Lacan says. (Ahumada, 1992, has also written about the active constituents of Lacan's technique.)

* * *

We have seen that in Lacan's view the unconscious is the territory of the signifier (1964a, *The Four Concepts*, p. 152), and we remember now that: "*Le transfert est la mise en acte de la réalité de l'inconscient*" (*Les quatre concepts*, p. 133) ["the transference is the enactment of the reality of the unconscious", *The Four Concepts*, p. 146]. As Freud taught us, the reality of the unconscious is sexual, so that transference must contain the weight of sexual reality, which runs beneath what happens at the level of the analytic discourse (*Les quatres concepts*, p. 155) and this sexual reality is nothing more nor less than desire.

At this point in his thought, Lacan roundly affirms that the desire that comes into play in transference is the analyst's desire; this assertion coincides with another indispensable articulator of his theory: *desire is the desire of the other.* That is to say, if desire expresses that sexual reality which is the putting into action of the reality of the unconscious, then the analyst's desire *signifies* the patient's.

We shall consider the analyst's desire in greater detail in the chapters on countertransference; but let us say for now that Lacan goes back to the paradigmatic experience of Breuer with Anna O (Bertha Pappenheim) as the basis of a statement that he himself fears might leave his audience stupefied. He affirms, then, that the *chimney-sweeping* went smoothly while Anna O provided more signifiers, and in her chatter there was not a trace of sexuality until Breuer introduced it. In Lacan's view even the pseudocyesis of that hysteric and historic patient is no more than Breuer's desire. It was he who wanted to have a child; and Lacan (1964a, chapter 12, section 3) gives us the beginning of a proof that seems to him fully to confirm this: in Italy with his wife on a sort of second honeymoon, Breuer made her pregnant. To make his thought clearer, he immediately asserts that Freud—who in Lacan's view is the one who really knows about analytical experience!—gives Breuer an easy get-out by assuring him that the transference rises spontaneously from Bertha's unconscious, that the desire is not his, Breuer's, but hers. It is from this great mistake in which Freud denies Breuer's desire that the *Studies on Hysteria* and psychoanalysis itself arose. I must confess that though he does no more here than carry to its extreme what he said in his "Intervention on Transference" and in other writings, Lacan's originality and audacity do in fact leave me stupefied.

It is worth mentioning, on the other hand, that this forthright assertion on "Breuer's desire" does not stand up to the proof of facts. Lacan uses the version given by Jones (1953–57, Vol. 2) of Breuer's journey with his wife in June 1882, when he interrupted Anna O's treatment (chapter 11, "The Breuer Period,). However, Ellenberger's careful investigation has succeeded in showing conclusively that Dora Breuer, the last child of the marriage, was born on 11 March 1882—thus, before her parents' famous second honeymoon in June (Ellenberger, 1970, p. 483; Sulloway, 1979, pp. 79–80). Apart from this "empirical" refutation, which comes from the register of births, Lacan's assertion does not appear consistent with his own way of thinking, since, as Ríos says (personal communication), it could only be maintained by demonstrating that Anna O did not have that desire, which is difficult to prove, especially for someone who maintains that desire is the desire of the other. Lacan completely rules out the possibility that it was Anna O who made Breuer feel the desire to make her pregnant (and, by displacement, his wife).

If we have followed Lacan's thought correctly, we may conclude that according to his theory transference is to be understood basically as a transference of signifiers in search of a desire that, as such, will never be satisfied. Desire is not the same as need; and it is impossible to satisfy it because it runs constantly from one point to another. The chain of signifiers consists of this; with its metonymic displacement, it confers meaning. That is why Lacan says in "L'instance de la lettre dans l'inconscient ou la raison depuis Freud" [The Instance of the Letter in the Unconscious or Reason Since Freud] (1957) that "the signifier establishes the absence of being in the object-relation" (*Écrits*, p. 515); and he also states in the same article that in the chain of signifiers the sense *insists* (holds its ground, persists, urges, addresses the subject) but does not *consist*, since none of the elements of the chain carries the meaning (p. 502). It is right here to leave out of account the beauty and precision with which Lacan is capable of expressing himself.

With the displacement of desire, with the metonymic slide of the signifier in search of significance, Lacan can establish a new relationship between transference and repetition. Repetition is not based on need (compare with Lagache) but on the search for something new, and in this sense transference at its symbolic level is not a repetition of things of the past nor a shadow of early loves (1964a, chapter 19, section 2) but, on the contrary, the action of the symbolic, an instrument of access to unconscious material. Lacan states categorically in section 2 of chapter 3 of Seminar XI that the concept of repetition has nothing to do with transference, even though it was when studying the latter that Freud discovered it.

Where I believe I understand Lacan's thought on this subject with greater certainty is in what he says in chapter 5, "Tyché and automaton", of *Les quatre concepts*, in which, juggling with these Aristotelian terms, he reminds us of Freud's effort to find the real background of the trauma, to be sure there and then that repetition [*Wiederholung*] does not refer to the return of need but is demanding something new.

Here Lacan takes up again the famous game of the wooden reel, which Freud describes in chapter 2 of *Beyond the Pleasure Principle* (1920g). As we all remember, this 1½-year-old boy, Freud's grandson, threw the reel, saying "*fort*" [gone], and pulled it back again by the thread, exclaiming "*da*" [there]. Interpreting this game, Freud tends to think that the child is trying to overcome the trauma of his mother's disappearance by changing the passive into the active; but Lacan maintains that this phenomenon is secondary. In Lacan's view the game of the reel is rather the response of the subject to the effect of the mother's absence, in which the reel does not represent the mother but a small thing of the subject. The object is what Lacan calls *objet à*. In other words, the child's game symbolizes repetition, but not of a need that would call for the mother's return, but the repetition of her part as the cause of a *Spaltung* in the subject, "overcome by the alternating game of *fort–da*, which is here or there, and whose aim, by its alternation, is simply that of being the *fort* of a *da* and the *da* of a *fort*" (*The Four Concepts*, p. 65). If I do not misunderstand, Lacan means that the reel as *objet à*, the remains of the subject in reality, is what represents the signifier *fort* for the signifier *da*. The game of the reel does not express the need for the mother's return but repeats her part in order to symbolize it. In the same way the analyst as *objet à* must allow the signifier to circulate (significant metonymy); he must put himself in the place of the subject who is allowing a signifier to represent him (or relating him) with another signifier. Lacan's emphasis on *listening* is because he understands it as the reception of the flow of signifiers (Max Hernández, personal communication). Lacan optimistically believes that the repetition is solely to symbolize, when the reality is that repetition occurs also so as not to symbolize, not to think, not to remember. Transference must not be confused with working through. Personally I believe—I say this in passing—that Lacan's thought suffers in general because it is too intense and tends to see problems in a narrow and unilateral way.

In his interesting essay "La transference", Michel Silvestre (1987b) states that the signifier has a curative force insofar as it can represent the subject for another signifier (p. 39) and adds that the "repetition is the resort of the symbolic order and of the logic of the signifier" (p. 41). What the psychoanalyst has to do is to let the symbolic record take the place of the motive power of treatment, and in this way the curative effect of the signifier is exerted (p. 42). Silvestre's inescapable conclusion is that there is no other resistance to analysis than that of the analyst himself (as Lacan repeats throughout his work) "in the measure in which he opposes the action of the symbolic order" (p. 42).

As can be seen, these ideas do not refer to a conflict between the S.s.S. and the (capital) Other, or between the imaginary order and the symbolic order; rather, they suggest to us complete, not to say blind, confidence in the deployment of the signifier and its curative potential. Thus the signifier is endowed with an almost human and personal quality. To it is delegated the analyst's own task, that of overcoming resistances, supposing that, in the short or in the long term, the signifier will be capable of triumphing over them. This is the price—a high one, in my opinion—that the school of Lacan finally pays for taking as the reference-point of psychoanalytical theory and practice the relationship of the subject with the signifier.

Note

1. I am especially grateful to Professor Klimovsky for his indispensable and generous help in this part of my study.

CHAPTER TWELVE

The forms of transference

*T*ransference neurosis is a dual-aspect term introduced by Freud in 1914 in two enduring works. In "Remembering, Repeating and Working-Through" (1914g), he defines it as a *technical* concept, in that he indicates a special modality of development of psychoanalytic treatment, according to which the original illness is transformed into a new one orientated towards the therapist and the therapy. In "On Narcissism: An Introduction" (1914c), on the other hand, transference neurosis is instead contrasted with narcissistic neurosis and is, therefore, a *psychopathological* (or nosographic) concept.

12.1   Transference neurosis:
some specifications

The two above-mentioned meanings of the term are not generally differentiated, partly because Freud himself always thought that the narcissistic neuroses lacked the capacity for transference and remained, therefore, beyond the reach of his method.

Paper presented at the Twelfth Latin American Congress of Mexico on 21 February 1978. First published in *Psicoanálisis*, 2, no. 2; reproduced here with minimal modifications.

If we try to be precise, however, what Freud affirmed in "Remember-ing, Repeating and Working-Through" (1914g) is that, at the onset of treat-ment, the illness suffers a notable shift, which makes it crystallize in the cure. Freud says, in his beautiful essay, "We have only made it clear to ourselves that the patient's state of being ill cannot cease with the begin-ning of his analysis and that we must treat his illness, not as an event of the past, but as a present-day force. This state of illness is brought, piece by piece, within the field and range of operation of the treatment, and while the patient experiences it as something real and contemporary, we have to do our therapeutic work on it, which consists in a large measure in tracing it back to the past" (1914g, pp. 151–152).

Developing the same concept, as early as 1905 Freud had said in the "Postscript" to "Dora": "It may be safely said that during psycho-analytic treatment the formation of new symptoms is invariably stopped. But the productive powers of the neurosis are by no means extinguished; they are occupied in the creation of a special class of mental structures, for the most part unconscious, to which the name of *transferences* may be given" (1905e [1901], p. 116).

These quotes make it clear, in my view, that Freud conceives transfer-ence-neurosis to be a special effect of the initiation of the psychoanalytic cure in that the production of new symptoms ceases and other new ones arise, which converge on the analyst and his setting.

I think it was Melanie Klein, in the Symposium of 1927, who best defined the transference-neurosis from the technical angle. She indicated there with particular emphasis that if the Freudian method of respecting the analytic setting is followed and one responds to the child's material with interpretations, leaving out any pedagogic measures, the analytic situation is established equally well or better than in the adult, and the transference neurosis, which constitutes the natural milieu of our work, develops fully. Of course Klein spoke of transference neurosis then be-cause she did not yet know that in the following years—and largely thanks to her own efforts—the psychotic phenomenon in particular, and narcissism in general, were to become incorporated in the operative field of the psychoanalytic method.

It is worth quoting here Melanie Klein's definitive statements: "In my experience a full transference-neurosis does occur in children, in a manner analogous to that in which it arises with adults. When analysing children I observe that their symptoms change, are accentuated or lessened in ac-cordance with the analytic situation. I observe in them the abreaction of affects in close connection with the progress of the work and in relation to myself. I observe that anxiety arises and that the children's reactions work themselves out on this analytic ground. Parents who watch their children carefully have often told me that they have been surprised to see habits, and so forth, which had long disappeared, come back again. I have not found that children work off their reactions when they are at home as well as when with me: for the most part they are reserved for abreaction in the analytic hour. Of course it does happen that at times, when very powerful affects are violently emerging, something of the disturbance becomes noticeable to those with whom the children are associated, but this is only temporary and it cannot be avoided in the analysis of adults either" (1975, Vol. 1, p. 152).

Thus the symptoms change (increase or decrease) in relation to the analytic situation; the affects, and anxiety in particular, are directed towards the analyst, old symptoms and habits come to the fore, affective reactions tend to be channelled in the analysis (and not outside). Transference neurosis, finally, is defined as the recognition of the presence of the analyst and the effect of analysis.

If I may suggest a concise definition of transference neurosis in its technical sense, I would say that it is the psychopathological correlate of the analytical situation. I mean that the analytical situation is established when transference neurosis appears, and, vice versa, when transference neurosis is divided from the therapeutic alliance, the analytical situation takes shape.

12.2 Transference neurosis and the healthy part of the ego

With this we arrive at another point in our line of thought. At times it is maintained that for the analytic situation to be set up (and for the process to begin), the basic existence of the neurotic phenomenon, as a primary fact, is necessary—a screen onto which psychotic, perverse, drug-induced, psychopathic, and similar situations are projected. The transference neurosis cannot be absent; if a pure psychosis were to exist, there could be no analysis; a neurosis that contains it must exist in some way.

In "On Beginning the Treatment" (1913c) Freud pointed out that the opening phase of analysis is characterized by the patient establishing a link with the doctor. And it is the ego psychologists' great merit to have developed a coherent and systematic theory of the indispensable presence of a healthy part of the ego in order for the analytic process to develop. This line of investigation, which begins with Freud, with Sterba (1934) and with Fenichel (1941), continues with Elizabeth R. Zetzel (1956a), Leo Stone (1961), Maxwell Gitelson (1962) and Ralph R. Greenson (1965a), just to cite the main contributors. For these authors, a healthy part of the ego, which for many is similar to Hartmann's (1939) conflict-free ego sphere, is inherently present in neurosis as a clinical entity, and in it the *therapeutic alliance* (Zetzel) or the *working alliance* (Greenson) is established. With another theoretical focus, Salomon Resnik (1969) prefers to speak of *infantile transference*, which expresses the patient's capacity to relate on a level of play. The child that inhabits the adult—says Resnik—is an essential source of communication in every human being (1969, p. 167).

There are, however, two criteria for analysability: (1) only the person who develops a transference neurosis—in the strict sense—is analysable, and (2) every person with a healthy ego nucleus that enables him to form a therapeutic alliance is analysable. These two are distinct: the mere fact that the healthy part of the ego is stronger and more transparent in the neurotic does not imply that it does not exist in others. We should therefore not confuse transference neurosis with the healthy part of the ego.

This is another reason why so much emphasis has been placed on transference-neurosis and why this concept has not been corrected in the light of facts.

12.3   Narcissism and transference

Whether or not the narcissistic neuroses as understood by Freud (1914c) are capable of transference is a problem that refers to the empirical base, not one of definition, as some ego psychologists would have it—for example, Samuel A. Guttman in the Symposium on Indications at the 1967 Copenhagen Congress.

If we contemplate retrospectively the many fertile years of work that separate us from 1914, the conclusion that the so-called narcissistic neuroses present indubitable transference phenomena is vigorously convincing.

It is not pertinent here to trace the laborious development of all these investigations. It is enough to say that, arising from different sources, they converge, first, in agreeing on the existence of transference phenomena in psychosis, visualizing later the peculiar form of transference "neurosis", in perverts, psychopaths, addicts, and so forth. In all these cases, clinical psychoanalytic practice makes self-evident that the transference "neurosis" of a psychopath is psychopathic, that of a pervert is perverse, and so on. This is why the title of this chapter alludes to the *forms* of transference.

To be more precise, I should say that the great theoretical debate has always pertained to psychosis; the other clinical entities—that is, psychopathy, drug addiction and perversion—are always considered, in practice, as forms of neurosis. (Today, however, there is a steadily growing tendency to approximate them to psychosis.)

Joseph Sandler et al. (1973) speak of "special forms" of transference in referring to the varieties that do not fit the *norm*—that is, transference-neurosis; and they are inclined to the opinion that the psychotic phenomenon lends colour to the transference but does not shape it. Nevertheless, only if we take transference neurosis as the norm can we speak of special types.

I have said that it was first in the field of psychosis that it was possible to study the narcissistic transference. (Freud's beautiful study on Leonardo inaugurates work on the narcissistic object relation in 1910, and it does so in the field of perversion.) Let us also say that this discovery did not occur all at once. Aside from Jung's advanced contributions to the psychology of *dementia praecox* at the beginning of the century, and of the work in the 1940s by Harry Stack Sullivan and his followers, such as Frieda Fromm-

Reichmann, much time had to elapse for H. Rosenfeld (1952a, 1952b) and Searles (1963) to speak openly of transference psychosis, albeit in 1928 Ruth Mack Brunswick had used the term appropriately and expounded clearly her way of confronting and resolving transference-psychosis through analytic means. In his essay on indications for psychoanalysis, Leo Stone (1964) also introduces the term specifically. More recently, Painceira (1979) indicates the inevitable passage through transference psychosis in schizoid patients.

If the works cited above, and others by the same authors, are reviewed, along with the no less pioneering works of Hanna Segal (1950, 1954, 1956) and Bion (1954, 1956, 1957), one is led to conclude that the psychotic phenomenon appears nourished by the transference and radically linked to it, and not—as Sandler construed it—that the psychosis only colours the transference.

Leaving aside the influence of Freud's opinion on all the investigators, if there was a delay in understanding (or seeing) the transferential phenomena of psychosis, this is because they answer to a different, extreme model and, although it may seem paradoxical, a much more immediate and visible one. It is not that the transference does not exist, as Abraham (1908a) or Freud (1911c, 1914c) believed: on the contrary, it is so overwhelming that it enmeshes and envelops us completely. I remember an example given by Frieda Fromm-Reichmann in her beautiful work, "Transference Problems in Schizophrenics" (1939). At the end of a prolonged session during which a spell of stupor had begun to yield, she offered to bring her catatonic patient a glass of milk, which he accepted; she went to fetch it, and when she returned, the patient threw it in her face. One supposes that the patient could not tolerate the end of the session, the distancing of the analyst (breast). Such an extreme dependence is difficult to understand as a transferential and not simply a psychotic phenomenon. Even as fine and wise an analyst as Fromm-Reichmann did not grasp what was happening—the request to be nourished, for the analyst not to go away. (In fact, she could perhaps have given him this interpretation or a similar one, which was the milk he was looking for!)

From the foregoing example there follows a general consequence: if one understands these forms not as special but as the norm of transference itself, one can respond more adequately and strike the correct interpretation. In Fromm-Reichmann's case, the impact on the countertransference of (the patient's) separation anxiety led a very experienced analyst to a type of symbolic realization—the glass of milk—which the analysand, more rigorous than any professor of psychoanalytic technique, angrily refused.

An approach to the phenomena according to this proposal protects us more, I think, from countertransferential acts.

A homosexual patient, to whom I referred in other works (1970, 1977, 1978a), went through a long period during which the analytic situation had a perverse, sadomasochistic slant. In an angry, provocative, polemical tone typical of perversion (the work of Betty Joseph, 1971, Clavreul, 1966, and my works cited above show this characteristic of transference perversion) she complained that I attacked her with my interpretations; I, in turn, would interpret this within the framework of the negative transference with more rigour and severity than was advisable, and thus (as was proved later), I satisfied her masochism. There was a relation of transference and countertransference that can only be conceived as perverse, and it took time for me to realize what was happening; only then could I emerge from the perversion (countertransferential sadism) that mobilized the patient at the time.

Proceeding from this example, I am inclined to think that neither should we conceive countertransference-neurosis (Racker, 1948) as the norm. In each case, the response of the analyst will carry the sign of the transference, a point to which I will return shortly.

A fundamental contribution to the theme we are studying is Bion's work on the characteristics of the psychotic transference: labile, intense, premature and tenacious—if one takes these conditions into account, one can grasp the phenomenon quickly and place oneself in the centre of the transference. To repeat: what is disorientating in the psychotic is that the transference phenomena are so intense, so precipitate, so quick. Remember that dromomanic patient of Freud's who fled after a week, as he tells us in "Remembering, Repeating and Working-Through". Let us listen to Freud once more: "As an extreme example of this, I may cite the case of an elderly lady who had repeatedly fled from her house and her husband in a twilight state and gone no one knew where, without ever having become conscious of her motive for decamping in this way. She came to treatment with a marked affectionate transference which grew in intensity with uncanny rapidity in the first few days; by the end of the week she had decamped from me, too, before I had time to say anything to her which might have prevented this repetition" (1914g, p. 154). (Let us say that this pristine example shows conclusively what transference neurosis consists in for Freud: the production of new symptoms ceases—the patient no longer flees from the home—and there appears a new order of phenomena referred to the analyst and his setting, which is why the patient eventually abandons Freud. Moreover, it can be appreciated here that Freud does not hesitate to place a psychotic symptom as a paradigm of transference neurosis, fulfilling Bion's definition specifications.)

Thus, if the conceptual framework is changed, there is a double advantage. On the one hand, one does not force patients to develop a transference neurosis—one does not put them on that Procrustean bed (the Procrustean couch, I would say); and, on the other hand, what is essential is more easily perceived. Because truly, in a perversion, for example, the neurotic phenomena of transference are always adjectives, almost a way of deflecting our attention.

This opening leads us inevitably to review the modes of interpretation. The content, the form and the opportunity (timing) of interpreting change according to the type of transference, because the interpretation has a great deal to do with the anxieties that fix the point of urgency. According to Benito López (1972), in certain cases (character neurosis), the formulation of the interpretation demands from the analyst a correct correlation between "the verbal signifier and the paraverbal and non-verbal aspects of the patient's communication" (p. 197); he adds that the ways of interpreting vary case by case, ranging from neurosis (where there is a minimal countertransferential participation), through the characterological disturbances, to psychosis.

Whereas the neurotic organization permits the maintenance of interpretations at the level of our habitual model of communication, addictive, psychopathic and perverse structures, and even more the psychotic structure, make a different model necessary—a way of speaking that separates us more each time from the habitual. We touch here on the attractive field of interpretative styles, opened by David Liberman's investigation (1970–72, 1976a).

12.4   On countertransference neurosis

What I have proposed to do in this chapter is to redefine transference neurosis, in order to make the concept more precise and more harmonious with the clinical facts. This being so, Racker's (1948, 1953) prolific concept of countertransference neurosis should be redefined in parallel.

It can be thought that the correlate of the patient's transference is always a countertransference *neurosis* or else that the countertransference assumes a psychotic, addictive, perverse or psychopathic character that is complementary to the transference. For theoretical reasons and particularly drawing on clinical experience, I back the second alternative—as I think Racker would also do. I believe, then, that it is natural for the analyst's response to carry the stamp of the analysand's transference.

In the example previously mentioned, a countertransference perversion developed, which endured for a time and could be resolved only once I had accepted within myself its psychological reality, allowing me to engage in interpretation.

I think this is inevitable if one is to grasp the situation fully—the analyst has to be included in the conflict; and, of course, he has to rescue himself through interpretation. What took me a very long time, I could in fact have accomplished in a minute, if I had noticed my displeasure and hostile impulse the first time the play of angry provocation and latent polemics occurred.

To study this delicate theme in greater depth, one can refer to Racker's concepts of countertransferential position and occurrence (see Racker, 1953, study 6, section 4). Although the countertransferential position implies a greater engagement on the part of the analyst, position and occurrence should not be understood as essentially different phenomena. The more fluid the countertransferential response, naturally the easier it will be for the analyst to understand it and overcome it.

Grinberg's (1956, 1963, 1976a) concept of projective counteridentification also helps to explain this type of relation. This theoretical basis leads us to conclude that the patient puts a part of himself—presumably a perverse part in the pervert, a psychopathic one in the psychopath, and so forth—into the analyst, and that the analyst takes on this projection inevitably, passively.

Otto Kernberg (1965) is right to point out that the countertransferential reaction occurs as a continuum and goes thus from the neurotic pole of the conflict to the psychotic one, such that the more regressive the patient, the greater will be his contribution to the countertransferential reaction of the analyst. And he adds that with borderline patients, and in general with very regressive ones, the analyst tends to experience intense emotions that have more to do with the violent and chaotic transference of the patient than with the specific problems of his personal past.

Betty Joseph's (1971) fetishist also provoked countertransferential phenomena in his eminent analyst. The transference perversion consisted basically in causing excitement in others, and thereby remaining an inert fetish. Joseph says in her work that she had to pay close attention to the tone of her voice and to her composure as an analyst, because the patient exerted great pressure on her to feel excitement while interpreting. Again, the moment of countertransferential perversion is clear here and also the way in which Betty Joseph, with her usual mastery, resolves it. Nevertheless, with the concept of countertransference perversion in mind, her conception could be more precise. Miss Joseph's care in not showing excitement, in fact, already announces in the countertransference the interpretation she herself was to make shortly afterwards, that he puts excitement into her and feels her to be excited. This interpretation arises, evidently, from a moment of (perverse) excitement the analyst feels and transforms into an interpretation. I think it is always logical and prudent to take care not to make mistakes, but I want to emphasize at this point that the care itself already indicates to the analyst what conflict he should interpret. If the analyst simply yields to this carefulness, then he concurs inadvertently with the perversion via the denial [Verleugnung]: he feels and simultaneously rejects (denies) the excitement—a typically perverse mechanism. Instead, by interpreting, as Joseph does quickly and acutely, the analyst comes out of the perversion and in fact no longer needs to be careful.

In a talk presented at the Terceras Jornadas Transandinas de Psicoanálisis (October, 1982), Rapela maintains that, on the contrary, the countertransferential phenomenon depends not so much on the form of the transference as on the disposition of the analyst. Rapela is inclined to think that the proposal I make should be limited to those cases where the countertransferential engagement is very evident and persistent.

12.5 Transference love

The famous transference love—a phenomenon with a long history in the psychoanalytic tradition—can serve to test the ideas in this chapter. By transference love we understand many things. In every analysis there have to exist moments of love, of falling in love, because the cure reproduces the object relations of the oedipal triad, and it is therefore inevitable (and healthy) for this to occur. Guiard has shown this clearly in a series of important works (1974, 1976), and, more recently, so has Juan Carlos Suárez (1977), in whose opinion the strong and persistent erotic counter-transference that arose towards the end of the treatment in the case he presents was not only a useful but also a necessary factor in the process, which culminated in the femininity of his patient.

However, the transference love that most concerned Freud in his essay of 1915, because of its irreducible tenacity, the sudden manner of its appearance, its destructive intention and the intolerance of frustration that accompanied it, seems more linked to a psychotic than a neurotic type of transference. The clinical features Freud pointed out in 1915 almost superimpose themselves on those Bion would describe much later. Thus, for example, in "Development of Schizophrenic Thought", Bion (1956) characterizes the object relation of the psychotic personality as precipitate and premature, and he says that the lability of the transference contrasts markedly with the tenacity with which it is maintained. Bion calls the relation with the analyst premature, precipitate and intensely dependent (1967b, p. 37).

There are, then, various forms of transference love; in a polar sense, there are two: neurotic and psychotic. To distinguish between them, one speaks sometimes of erotic and erotized transference. This differentiation originates with Lionel Blitzsten, who never published it; but his ideas were taken up by other Chicago analysts such as Gitelson and Rappaport.

Ernest A. Rappaport presented an important work at the Latin American Congress of Psychoanalysis in Buenos Aires in August 1956. (That same year, the work was published in the *Revista de Psicoanálisis*, and, three years later, in the *International Journal of Psycho-Analysis*.) His article develops Blitzsten's ideas on the causes and consequences of the erotized transference and on ways of detecting it from the first dream within the analysis onwards.

Blitzsten's basic thesis is that if the analyst appears in person in the first dream, the analysand is going to erotize the transferential link violently, and his analysis will be difficult, if not impossible. That presence in his first dream indicates that the analysand is incapable of discriminating between the analyst and a significant figure from his past, or else that the analyst, due to his appearance and conduct, really is like the said figure. Under these circumstances, the analysis will be erotized from the start. He understands by erotization a surcharge of the erotic components of the transference, which certainly does not signify a great capacity for love but, rather, a libidinal deficiency, accompanied by a great necessity to be loved.

Rappaport quotes Blitzsten as saying: "In a transference the analyst is seen *as if* he were the parent, while in erotization of the transference he is the parent" (see Rappaport, 1956, p. 240).

Blitzsten concludes that in cases where the analyst appears in person in the first dream of the analysand, the situation should be worked through immediately, or the patient should be referred to another analyst.

Although I would not support Blitzsten totally in these technical pre-cautions, the ideas in this chapter coincide in principle with his, where I separate the erotic transference as a neurotic phenomenon from the psychotic phenomenon of the erotized transference. It is a clinical fact, always provable, that in an analysis that evolves normally (and here I take neurosis as the norm), the erotic transference waxes and wanes gradually and tends to reach its climax, as Guiard (1976) says, in the final stage. In the cases Blitzsten studied, on the other hand, the transference love—or, as he called it, the erotized transference—appears at the outset.

In a now classic work on the emotional position of the analyst, Maxwell Gitelson (1952) also confirms Blitzsten's ideas, although his essay poses wider problems, which refer to the theory of transference and countertransference in general.

According to Gitelson, if the analyst appears in person in the first dream of the analysand, one must assume that there is a grave disturbance; and—following Blitzsten—he maintains that this disturbance can originate from the patient having a poor capacity for symbolization, or from the analyst either having made a serious error or having, due to some special quality, a real likeness to the father or the mother of the patient.

Of the three alternatives Blitzsten proposes, the first, a serious disturbance on the part of the patient, raises the question of the indication in terms of analysability; and the second, the analyst's error (unless it was a casual error), raises the question whether a change of analyst—and, eventually, the re-analysis of the analyst—is advisable. (It is evident that Elizabeth R. Zetzel's [1956a, 1968] requirement fails by definition in these cases—that is, that the future analysand be capable of separating reality from fantasy, of delimiting the transference neurosis from the therapeutic alliance.) The third alternative does not seem particularly significant to me, as I do not know whether a manifest likeness of the analyst to the patient's parent is sufficient to condition this type of response. In any case, if it does condition it, I doubt that this is a contraindication of that special analytic couple. The contraindication, and with it the change of analyst, arises, in my judgement, only if the analyst makes a mistake and/or allows himself to become involved so seriously that these elements appear in the first dream. (A very interesting theme reappears here—that of the analytic couple—which it is not pertinent to discuss here.) If we take a clinical example from Rappaport, we can see that what disqualifies the analyst is not a likeness to the patient's mother, but, rather, to a lack in the mother such as if he is, like her, disorderly, disorganized and without any insight about how these conditions can disturb others. (A candidate presented in a seminar a case in which he had appeared in the patient's first dream. When he recounted the dream, with his notes scattered around the table and some of them on the floor, it was obvious to all but the candidate himself that his patient identified him with his disorderly mother.)

Blitzsten's observation is interesting; and I think that the analyst's appearance in the patient's dreams at any time in the analysis and not only at the beginning signifies that a *real event* or *fact* is in play, be this a countertransferential acting-out, great or small, or simply a real and rational action, such as the giving of information on formal aspects of the relationship (change of timetable or fees, for example). In all these cases it is probable that the analyst appears as such. These dreams imply that the patient has a problem with the *real* analyst, not with the symbolic figure of the transference. This type of dream, then, where the patient alludes to us personally, should always be taken as a warning concerning some real participation of ours. [Following this thesis, Manuel Gálvez, Silvia Neborak de Dimant and Sara Zac de Filc presented a careful investigation at the Second Symposium of the Psychoanalytic Association of Buenos Aires, 1979, where they divided the dreams of the analyst into two large groups, according to the patient's capacity for symbolization. If the patient has a deficiency in symbolization, then the appearance of dreams of the analyst, inasmuch as it reveals this deficiency, also implies a reserved prognosis. In patients where symbolization does not fail, the authors confirm and bring into focus the initial thesis in that they distinguish four eventualities: (1) modification and/or alteration of the setting; (2) important countertransferential engagement; (3) information about the analyst as a person; and (4) moments of serious difficulty, which prompt a wish to meet with the analyst.]

In a well-documented clinical work, Bleichmar (1988) was able to follow the evolution of the love transference in a young female adult and to see how it evolved from the pregenital levels, where what was decisive was the relation with part-objects and with the combined parent-figure, to the genital oedipal fantasies, where the parents appear as distinct and the analysand shows herself disposed to face her conflicts, preserving the treatment. There is no contradiction between the two levels, Bleichmar concludes, and the principal task of the analyst consists in distinguishing them and elaborating at each moment a precise strategy to decide which level should be approached.

12.6   *Clinical forms of erotized transference*

In the psychotic transference love—or, to follow Blitzsten, in the erotized transference—it is evident that we can distinguish various forms. The most typical is the one Freud's masterful pen describes as tenacious, extreme and irreducible, ego-syntonic and refusing any substitution—characteristics in which Bion eventually saw years later the mark of the psychotic phenomenon. These are cases, as Freud says, in which falling in love is generally syntonic and appears early on. We could add here that the earlier it appears, the worse the prognosis.

Other cases enter into what Racker (1952) accurately called *transference nymphomania*. There are women who want to seduce the analyst sexually, as they would any other man they know: these cases are larvate or visible forms of nymphomania and must be understood as such.

It is difficult to define nymphomania, and its taxonomic location varies with the accents it may have and even with the point of view from which we see it. At times, nymphomania is fed by an *erotic delusion* (*eroto-mania*), a form of paranoia in Kraepelin's sense similar to persecutory delusions or those of jealousy; at other times it can be the symptomatic expression of a *manic syndrome*; and, finally, if the disturbance is more visible at the level of sexual conduct than in the sphere of thought, nymphomania presents itself as a *perversion* with respect to the sexual object, according to the classification of the *first essay* of 1905. There is also a nymphomania that has all the characteristics of *psychopathy*, in that the fundamental strategy of the patient is to deflect the analyst from his purpose in order to make him act (Zac, 1968).

There can, then, be psychotic (delusional, manic) forms, perverse forms and psychopathic forms of the transferential link with the so-called love transference. I had occasion years ago to witness in my practice a singular clinical picture, which I would retrospectively feel encouraged to classify as a love transference, with all the structural characteristics of *toxicomania*, or *addiction*. This concerned a (female) patient already advanced in years, distinguished, spiritual and cultured, who had never known her father's identity. She consulted me about a dysthymia, which was chronic, intense and resistant to psychopharmalogical drugs. Soon after beginning analysis she developed a very intense love transference, as a consequence of which she needed me as a balm or a sedative, from which she could not be separated for long. The strongly erotized and idealized link with the father's penis as the source of all well-being and tranquillity (and, equally, of all suffering) assumed, through the persistent fantasy of *fellatio*, all the characteristics of an addict's dependence on his drug. Despite my efforts and the patient's (conscious) good disposition, the treatment ended in failure. (We shall return to transference addiction at the end of chapter 13.)

* * *

To sum up: due to its complexity and the subtlety of the mechanisms that animate it, the love transference is an inexhaustible fount of information and equally a hard test for the analyst, for his ability and for his technique. Some of the enigmas that surprised Freud have now been resolved, or, at least, made clearer. This was Racker's (1952) aim when, in commenting on Freud's fine essay of 1915, he said that the great need for love that Freud attributed to these patients—*children of nature* who posed for him the question how love and illness could co-exist—is more apparent than real. They are, on the contrary, women who have a reduced capacity for love (as Blitzsten also said), and it is through the death instinct (or through envy) that they elaborate this entire system of voracity, insatiability, specific demands, lability, and so forth, which often leads the analysis to its breaking point.

We see thus how very dissimilar clinical pictures are grouped within the general nomenclature of transference love (or of erotization of the transferential link).

12.7 Selfobject transferences

In section 12.3 we set out some ideas on narcissism and transference; we are now returning to this topic, and we shall consider the fruitful researches of Heinz Kohut, a Viennese who was trained in Chicago and exerted a growing influence from there.

Kohut was originally an *ego psychologist* in the manner of Hartmann, from whom he took his central idea that narcissism is the cathexis of the self (and not of the ego) and that a distinction is to be made between *self-representation* and *object-representation* (Hartmann, 1950, p. 127).

Starting from this Hartmannian premise, which is also the central axis of the researches of Edith Jacobson (1954b, 1964), who in her turn inspired Kernberg (1975, 1976a, 1980, 1984), Kohut established a new school of *self-psychology*, which partly continues but mainly diverges from ego psychology.

In its classic formulation, the theory of libido leads to a conception of the mind as a tripartite structure (id, ego and superego). Kohut's concept of the self, on the other hand, considers the mind as contents or representations, not instances.

Kohut's first departure from establishment ego psychology can be found in his work on empathy (1959) upon which we shall comment in the chapters on countertransference. With empathy as his method of investigation, Kohut pinpoints a characterological disturbance, which he called *narcissistic personality disorders*. In his view, its difference from the classic neuroses is due, among other things, to the type of transference that develops; Kohut calls it *narcissistic transference*. At the end of his research (he died in Chicago on 8 October 1981, at the age of 68) Kohut (1977, 1984;

Kohut & Wolf, 1978) preferred to call it *selfobject transference*, making a decisive step towards a clearly defined psychology of the self.

In the preface to his first book, *The Analysis of the Self* (1971), Kohut points out that it has always been assumed that the existence of object relations excludes narcissism; but the truth is that many of the most intense narcissistic experiences refer to objects (ibid., p. xiv).

The essential idea of the psychology of the self is that narcissism is not only a stage in the development of the movement of the libido towards the object, but also an independent field that co-exists with object love throughout life. Narcissism is not defined by the target of the instinctive cathexis, but by the nature and quality of the charge (ibid., p. 26). There is a *qualitative* difference between object libido and narcissistic libido, so that the subject can invest narcissistic cathexes in others, and even invest himself with object cathexes. This implies without a doubt an immense change in doctrine, which takes us back to the lively polemics of Freud and Jung in the second decade of the century; but Kohut tends rather to consider this simply a question of terminology, since he is interested in the evolution and dynamics of the more important narcissistic phenomena (ibid., p. 27).

Kohut starts manifestly with the classic conception of primary narcissism, according to which object relations take shape by transferring to another the narcissistic perfection of the early ego, as Freud postulates in his essay on narcissism (1914c); and he maintains that it is the inevitable faults in maternal care that destroy that enviable balance. The child then regains the lost perfection by establishing what are known as "selfobjects". These are the *grandiose self* and the *idealized parent imago* (ibid., p. 25). In other words, the narcissistic libido not only cathects the self; it can also reach out to others, which become *objects of the self*, parts of the same self. As can easily be imagined, to begin with the selfobjects are the parents, and the self is built precisely from that special type of relationship which exists with them as objects felt as parts of the same self. In their recent well-documented book *El psicoanálisis después de Freud* (1989), Norberto and Celia Bleichmar emphasize as a defining characteristic of the selfobjects that they are external objects that the analysand (and the child, in his time) takes as parts of his being. They have, thus, nothing to do with the internal objects of the English authors. This is an important fact (which will make its way into the technique), because Kohut does not work with the mechanisms of introjection and projection. In his earliest work in 1959 he was already saying, referring to transference in the most regressive cases, that "the analyst is not the screen for the projection of internal structure (transference), but the direct continuation of an early reality that was too distant, too rejecting, or too unreliable to be transformed into solid psychological structures" (1959, pp. 470–471).

In his earliest works—for example, the paper he presented in Buenos Aires in 1966—Kohut used the expression "narcissistic self", following

Hartmann, like other authors; but, given that the self is cathected with narcissistic libido, the expression "narcissistic self" is tautological. (It would not be so if we adhered to what was said a moment ago: that the self can be invested with objectal cathexes. This is certainly not a very important contradiction, but I mention it because it shows, as I see it, a basic difficulty of Kohut's reasoning.) For that reason Kohut prefers "grandiose self", which has much more evocative power. In his view this grandiose self coincides up to a certain point with the ego of pure pleasure (Freud, 1915c) which recognizes as good only that which belongs to it. The counterpart of the grandiose self is the *idealized parent imago*, which is finally incorporated into the structure as the superego. It can then be said, and Kohut actually says it, that the grandiose self is the *subject* and the idealized parent imago is the *object* of narcissistic dynamics; but Kohut invariably calls the grandiose self "selfobject", which seems to me to be an important contradiction that he finally resolves in his last works, in which this selfobject is called *"mirroring selfobject"* (Kohut & Wolf, 1978, p. 414). It is perhaps worth pointing out that in his paper to the Pan-American Congress just mentioned, Kohut (1966) gave the name "twin" to what was later "mirror transference". I mention these oscillations because I seem to see in them the Gordian knot of Kohut's postulates on object relations. In other words, there are moments when Kohut the theoretician appears to confuse object with subject, as, according to him, the child and the patient do.

What is certain is that in Kohut's view the self has a bipolar structure derived from the two selfobjects: the object of the grandiose self, from which spring ambitions and aims, and the idealized parent imago, which bears the ideals, with an intermediate zone in which talents and skills are located. What is especially interesting is that this bipolar (or tripolar) structure of the self makes possible the shaping of *two* types of transference, idealizing and mirroring. *The Analysis of the Self* (1971) is basically devoted to studying the special type of relationship of the child's self with the selfobjects and the form in which these phenomena manifest themselves in transference.

Dealing with the narcissistic personality disorders, following a basically clinical course, Kohut maintains that if the analyst keeps the place corresponding to him within the setting, there immediately sets in a therapeutic regression, which is typical of this type of illness, and in which the narcissistic structures of the grandiose self and the idealized parent imago fuse with the analyst's psychic representation, and thus the transference situation takes shape (ibid., p. 29). Simultaneously, the healthy part of the psyche establishes a therapeutic bond with the analyst from which transference will be able to work. A fixed premise of Kohut's, with which I am certainly not going to disagree, is that transference is spontaneously constituted and that the analyst must not encourage or interfere with it.

In this way narcissistic neuroses (in Kohut's sense), together with transference neuroses, move into the realm of analysable disorders, from which borderline states and psychoses are excluded. According to Kohut, in narcissistic disturbances there is already a *cohesive self* that makes analysis possible, because the narcissistic *object* (the idealized parent imago) and the narcissistic *subject* (the grandiose self) are relatively stable elements that can combine with the analyst's psychic representation to constitute the transference phenomenon. We should point out that Kohut understands transference within Freud's schema of 1900 (and not 1895), in which the analyst offers himself as the preconscious support to which the unconscious *object* relation (transference neurosis) or the unconscious *narcissistic* relation (selfobject transference) will be firmly fixed. We have to say at the same time that the essential difference between structural neuroses and narcissistic disorders is the type of libido, objectal or narcissistic, according to cases.

In psychotic and borderline patients, on the other hand, regression has more scope and reaches the stage of the *fragmented self*, corresponding to what Freud called the auto-erotic phase, in which there is no possibility of a therapeutic alliance (or working alliance) that would make analysis feasible. These fragments are pre-psychological and cannot enter into a stable amalgamation with the contents of the preconscious—an indispensable requirement if the transference phenomenon is to be constituted.

It is only on the basis of the theoretical presuppositions that we have given in summary form that we can understand and discuss the two types of narcissistic transference suggested by Kohut: the idealizing and the mirror.

12.7.1 Idealizing transference

This type of narcissistic transference comes from the therapeutic reactivation of the omnipotent object, which is the idealized parent imago, which awakens in analysis a primitive phase of psychic development. *Idealizing transference* is the spontaneous result of the analyst's empathic activity and reproduces the moment at which the psyche, exposed to the disturbance of the psychological balance of primary narcissism, partly recovers the lost experience of perfection, attributing it to a rudimentary selfobject. Kohut calls this object "transitional", following Winnicott (1953), perhaps because it occupies an intermediate position between the external and the internal.

Once the child endows this object with the power of his primary narcissism and converts it into the source of all calm and security, we can understand that his link with it becomes essential: insofar as he lacks this object, he will feel empty and powerless.

Idealizing narcissistic libido plays a significant role in the development of the child and in mature object relations. Combined with object libido, which is also laid at the door of the parents, idealization "... exerts a strong and important influence on the phase-appropriate (re)internal-

ization process and thus on the building up of two permanent core structures of the personality (a) the neutralising basic fabric of the psyche, (b)
the idealized superego—which are invested with narcissistic instinctual
cathexis" (Kohut, 1971, p. 40). It is worth explaining that here Kohut is
again thinking of Hartmann's concept in his famous monograph of 1939
(chapter 5) and *not* of the introjective processes as understood according to
Ferenczi (1909), Freud (1917e), Abraham (1924), and Melanie Klein (1932,
etc.). Hartmann thinks that in higher organisms trial activity is displaced
into the interior of the organism—that is, it is internalizea. In his work,
"Notes on the Superego" (1962), written in collaboration with Loewenstein, he says that we speak of *internalization* when the controls exerted in
interaction with the external world are replaced by internal controls; and
he again points out as a typical example the change from a trial activity in
the external world to thought. Hartmann and Loewenstein assert that in
paradigmatic cases it is easy to see the difference from identification. I
have lingered over this point so that I can explain the way in which Kohut
understands the change caused by the analytical process.

The withdrawal of instinctive cathexes (objectal and narcissistic) from
object imagos plays an important role in the process of formation of the
psychic structure, which Kohut calls *transmuting internalization*, whose
support is the *ego apparatuses* in which primary autonomy is established
(Hartmann, 1939, chapter 9). This process is possible because the child's
idealization of his parents is open to correction, as part of the libido is
withdrawn from the parent imagos to be used in the building of structures
destined for the control of the impulses. The oedipal disappointment that
then takes place leads to the formation of the superego, in which Kohut
also distinguishes the influence of the narcissistic libido (idealized superego) from that of the object libido.

The selfobjects are, then, early objects invested with narcissistic libido
which did not carry out the process of transmuting internalization. In
treatment they come to life with the analyst and form two distinct types of
transference, which can be investigated and worked through systematically (Kohut, 1971, p. 52). Kohut recommends that selfobjects should not
be confused with the incestuous objects of childhood cathected with object
libido, which belong to the field of transference neurosis; but this difference, easier to establish in books than in the consulting-room, is gradually
lost in Kohut's work, as Eagle (1984) and many other authors point out.

Idealizing transference must go back to a specific moment of development in which the relationship with the idealized object suffered a serious
disturbance and interruption, although its genesis must be evaluated
through the phenomena of overlapping ("telescoping") of other analogous
experiences occurring earlier or later. However determined he may be not
to fall into the trap of extreme simplification and to maintain the validity
of the complemental series, the truth is that Kohut thinks that the root of
the pathology of the self is always a failure of empathy on the part of the

parents, which leads him to a position of extreme environmentalism, like that of Winnicott. (See "El problema naturaleza–cultura en psicoanálisis", by Celia Leiberman de Bleichmar, 1989.)

The way in which Kohut deals with idealized transference is interesting, as I believe that here he is making one of his most valuable contributions. The great Chicago analyst insists absolutely rightly that when the idealizing transference takes place, the analyst's neutrality must consist in not repressing it; and he warns that for conventional or theoretical motives the analyst may discourage a process that arises spontaneously. Thus, as we neither stimulate nor suffocate transference love, let us accept with equanimity and—as Kohut would say—with empathy that the analysand idealizes us!

I agree unreservedly with Kohut's attitude when the idealizing transference appears, but I cannot agree with the way he solves it—that is, by interpreting in order to get back to the genetic origin of the disturbance, and invariably deriving the problem from the parents' failure in empathy. What always happens as a result is that the analyst is idealized again, and the patient is absolved from the burden of guilt. This criticism coincides to a great extent with that of Kernberg (1975, 1984), who says that there are various types of idealization and Kohut does not distinguish between them. Sometimes idealization is a defence against aggression; at other times it is a reaction against guilt, and in yet others, finally, it arises from the projection of the grandiose self as Kohut described (Kernberg, 1984, p. 185).

12.7.2 Mirror transference

As sometimes the structure of the self in narcissistic disorders leads to the analytical process being organized around the idealized parent imago, it may also happen that another type of phenomenon, the *mirror transference*, may arise. The analysand then relives his infantile need for an object that fully accepts and supports him. To put it more clearly: in one case the child tries to save his primary narcissism with an idealized object; in the other, he concentrates perfection and power in himself, drawing back with disdain from an external world to which he attributes all imperfections.

The grandiose self holds all good condensed within it, and the rest is only a pretext to deploy his own exhibitionism and power. In this sense the analyst must serve as a mirror, opening to the analysand the road to the unsatisfied needs of his childhood.

In the most mature form of mirror transference, "the analyst is most clearly experienced as a separate person" (Kohut, 1971, pp. 115–116); but he counts only within the context of the grandiose self therapeutically reactivated (by regression). There is a repetition of that phase of childhood in which the gleam in the mother's eye reflects like a mirror the child's showing-off. For this it is fundamental that his mother should participate in his narcissistic enjoyment, since on her depends his future self-esteem. The parallel between what the mother was (or should have been) and what the analyst is now is clear and unmistakable: the analyst acquires importance in his function as mirror, in the measure in which he reflects and confirms the patient's narcissistic pleasure, overcoming his own narcissism, and he agrees not to be credited with any other value.

The analyst has always to be aware of the risks to which his (narcissistic) countertransference can expose him, and he must understand that during the course of the mirror transference the analysand needs him to reflect empathically his idealized image, which will ultimately give coherence to the self.

As the mirror transference is being worked through, the first objective is to mobilize the grandiose self and the formation of derivatives of exhibitionistic impulses and grandiose phantasies. The analysand will finally succeed in openly expressing his wish that the analyst should admire him and praise him, and in his dreams appear magical elements expressing the power of the dreamer, often identification with God. The analyst must integrate into his interpretations the analysand's fear of being rejected because of his grandiose phantasies as he was in childhood by his (nonempathic) parents, and his permissive (empathic) attitude must extend also to acting out, which is inevitable at a certain stage of mirror transference. From this point of view it can be readily understood that interpretations of exhibitionism, omnipotent control, megalomania, or envy, which analysts of other schools might give, lack empathy and serve only to fuel the pathological process.

Perhaps it may be worth while to compare here, for a moment, Kohut's mirror with that of Lacan (1949). These two great researchers go back to the same model, but the underlying theory is not the same, and the technical attitude is very different. Where Lacan (1951) intervenes as the capital Other who breaks the mirroring fascination of Thou and I, Kohut feels that the analysand should develop narcissistic transference in full, giving him the opportunity to make up for the lack of empathy of his parents, who were not capable of putting themselves in the place of a child who needed to be admired. In Lacan's view the relationship of the child with the mother in the mirror stage is imaginary and can cease to be so only when the father imposes the symbolic castration that puts the son in third place. Kohut, on the other hand, considers that the child needs to be admired by the mother, and that there is no need for a third to bring about the transmuting internalization that will constitute the nuclear self.

In order to maintain the internal coherence of his theories, Kohut must of necessity leave aside the immense structuring power of the Oedipus complex and castration anxiety; and, as he certainly knows that phallic exhibitionism exists, he must turn over to the examination of the *pre-phallic* grandiose self to account for his transmuting internalization. It is obvious

that at this point the dividing line between structural neuroses and narcissistic disorder of the personality is conventional and dependent on chance.
As Wallerstein (1985) rightly says, reviewing Kohut's posthumous book,
How Does Analysis Cure? (1984), he has drawn our attention to some valuable clinical and theoretical facts but is mistaken in trying to set them up as
the *only* response that can be offered to the innumerable problems of our
profession. When Wallerstein returns to the subject in his *Forty-Two Lives
in Treatment* (1986), a really outstanding book, he re-affirms that "selfobject
transference" is a valid contribution to the comprehension of the phenomena of transference and countertransference, not only in narcissistic personalities, but in all areas of psychoanalytical clinical practice; but at the
same time he sharply questions "the need for the new theoretical structure
of self psychology, with its dichotomisation between a psychology of conflict and its resolution (the fate of Guilty Man) and a psychology of deficit
and its restoration (the fate of Tragic Man)" (ibid., p. 322).

It is necessary to point out, also, that Kohut includes in the grandiose
self various structures (or concepts) that other authors consider separately.
Thus Rosenfeld (1971) distinguishes an *infantile* self that wants to grow
and is mobilized basically by the libido from a *narcissistic self* that by definition resists every bond of dependence (that is, of love) and whose main
distinctive mark is the death instinct (or envy). Kernberg (1984), for his
part, accuses Kohut of not distinguishing between normal and pathological feelings of grandeur and neglecting the analysis of the negative transference (ibid., p. 186). Kernberg considers that Kohut's grandiose self must
be understood as *pathological*; and it is only through analysis of the positive and negative transference that it can be converted into a *normal* self.
The normal self, in Kernberg's view, is a structure that has integrated
components charged with libido and aggression—that is to say, it includes
good and bad parts.

Kernberg distinguishes normal narcissism from pathological narcissism and maintains that the structural characteristics of the narcissistic
personality must be understood as the consequence of a pathological development of the ego and the superego.

12.7.3 Twinship transference

Kohut distinguishes, however, a third type of narcissistic transference:
twinship or *alter ego transference*. This involves the intermediate area, the
arc of tensions between the grandiose and the idealized poles, which is
where everyone's talents and skills lie.

Initially Kohut considered this twinship transference as a form of mirror transference, but in *How Does Analysis Cure?* (1984) he suggests that it
is a special type of transference with a selfobject that is also special, identical with the analysand, with which company and solitude are shared. As

specific damage to the pole of ambitions leads to mirror transference, and specific damage to the pole of ideals reactivates idealizing transference, when what is strongly affected is the intermediate area of talents and skills, what is sought is an object of the self that can ensure an experience of equality, whose qualities coincide with one's own, in order to feel that the existence of one's being is confirmed.

Twinship transference, which Kohut finally recognized as an autochthonous form, independent of the other two, involves a significant clinical fact that was studied from other points of view by Bion (1950), Hautmann (1983) and Berenstein (1984), and, of course, by Freud and Otto Rank.

Bion (1950) studied the phenomenon of twins and took it as a special form of dissociation and personification, in which the eyes (and especially binocular vision) play a very important part in reality testing and simultaneously in the attainment of insight.

Bion thinks that when the twin relationship in transference is not admitted, it blocks all access to the Oedipus complex. The analyst as twin of the analysand puts him into the state of being an alter ego that has to think for the other. This is a very archaic relationship that implies the denial of any different reality, the impossibility of tolerating an object that is not completely under control.

Based on Bion's work and his suggestion that the relationship with a twin must presumably go back to a very early stage of development, Hautmann (1983) considers that the twin represents the subject's other ego, the self before birth, equating the foetus with the twin—that is, the representation of the self as a dual mother–foetus unit, before the beginning of the capacity to think, which is also the capacity to see and know.

Isidoro Berenstein (1984) follows the same line of thought; in his view twinship is a special form of narcissistic link, which corresponds to a very early organization of the mind in which the object is created as a mirror-image of the ego, or, conversely, the ego becomes the double of the object. Instead of the system of similarities and differences in which the object relation develops, there is here a defence that Berenstein calls "disturbance to the identical"; it consists of systematically divesting the object of the characteristics that distinguish it from the ego. In other words, when faced with the difficult task of accepting its similarities to and differences from the object, the ego establishes an equality.

In agreement with other authors, Berenstein gives importance in such cases to the eyes, and considers that in the origin of this disturbance there are always confusional anxieties that hinder the recognition of differences between ego/non-ego, mouth/breast, etc. Berenstein has two explanations for the twin-structure. On the one hand, there is a constitutive moment that helps to find the object and see it as similar to the ego, and then it has a libidinal sense. On other occasions the death instinct (and a particular type of envy) predominate and tend to wipe out the features that mark the object as different. In any case, Berenstein thinks, like Bion (1950), that the imaginary twin protects the subject from dependence and helplessness; he points out that often such patients accept interpretations saying that they think the same.

All these authors agree with Kohut on the importance of the phenomenon and the need to detect it and solve it in transference; but they do not, as he does, consider it as a halt in development caused by specific faults in the original objects, but, rather, as an expression of the conflict between the child and his environment.

CHAPTER THIRTEEN

Transference psychosis

In chapter 12 we discussed the concept of transference neurosis, and we maintained that it is better to reserve the term for phenomena of a strictly neurotic nature that appear in psychoanalytic treatment, not for every symptom that, one way or another, acquires a new expression in the therapy. This proposal tends to differentiate technique from psychopathology, and with this more than one mistake is avoided, in my opinion.

We now proceed to *transference psychosis*—that is, how psychotic symptoms are reconverted during psychoanalytic treatment to achieve within it their mode of expression.

13.1   *Some historical references*

When we studied the development of the concept of transference, we discussed Abraham's (1908a) effort to establish the psychosexual differences between hysteria and *dementia praecox*. The libido remains linked to the objects in hysteria, whereas it becomes auto-erotic in *dementia praecox*. Incapable of "transference", this libido conditions and explains the patient's inaccessibility, his radical separation from the world. Following the same scheme, a year later Ferenczi proposed a tripartite division of patients: (1) the sufferer of *dementia praecox*, who withdraws his libido from the external world (of objects), (2) the paranoid patient, who projects his libido in the object, and finally (3) the neurotic, who introjects the world of objects. These works were to be reformulated by Freud in 1914, when he intro-

duced the concept of narcissism and proposed the two taxonomic categories of transference neurosis and narcissistic neurosis.

Although this line of investigation maintained that psychosis lacked
the capacity for transference, others thought these phenomena existed, and
among them one of the first was Nunberg (1920), cited by H. Rosenfeld
(1952b), who offered his observations on a catatonic patient, where the
experiences of the illness had a clear transferential colouring.

To my best knowledge, the expression *transference psychosis* first appears in "The Analysis of a Case of Paranoia", which Ruth Mack Brunswick published in 1928. (In that same year she also published the analysis
of a psychotic episode in "The Wolf Man" which Freud had entrusted to
her.) We will discuss this in chapter 15.

From the 1930s onwards, the study of psychosis and of the possibility
of its psychoanalytic treatment developed concurrently in London
(Melanie Klein), in the United States (Sullivan) and in Vienna (Federn).
These thinkers not only undertook the study of psychosis but also maintained that psychosis is accompanied by transference phenomena, however difficult it may be to detect them. In chapter 12 we studied the
contributions of Frieda Fromm-Reichmann and Melanie Klein's disciples
to the development of the concept of transference psychosis, which
achieves its place in the theoretical corpus of psychoanalysis in the middle
of the century. Now we will examine in greater detail the contributions
made by various authors.

A work that deserves to be cited among the forerunners is Enrique
J. Pichon Rivière's, "Some Observations on Transference in Psychotic Patients", which he presented at the Fourteenth Conference of Psychoanalysts of the French Language, in November 1951. Lucidly taking
advantage of Kleinian ideas, Pichon Rivière maintains that transference in
psychotic patients, and particularly in schizophrenics, should be understood in the light of the mechanism of projective identification. The schizophrenic distances himself from the world in a defensive withdrawal of
extreme intensity, but the object relation is preserved, and it is on this
basis that the transference should be understood and interpreted. The tendency to contact others is intense, despite the defensive isolation; and,
because of this, the transference should be interpreted, as should the anxiety that determines the withdrawal from the world of objects.

13.2   The theories of psychosis and the technical approach

All agree that psychosis has to do with pregenital stages of development
and with the first years of life; but they differ in theoretical explanations
and on the practical approach.

At the risk of over-simplifying the problems, I suggest that there are
two major theories and two practical approaches. With regard to the theories, there are, on the one hand, those who, like Melanie Klein, think that

the object relation is established at the outset and that without it there is no mental life; and those, on the other hand, who postulate, as do Searles, Mahler and Winnicott, that development originates from a period where subject and object are not differentiated and that there exists, therefore, a stage of primary narcissism. In the 1920s this discussion took place geographically between Vienna and London—that is to say, between Anna Freud and Melanie Klein—but at the present time the positions are not so definite, and there are some bridges between them.

From these two doctrinaire approaches there follow a variety of methods in the practice; some authors say that the transference psychosis should be interpreted to allow it to be gradually modified through interpretation, others maintain that phenomena that pertain to primary narcissism do not respond to the classic interpretative technique, and it is preferable to allow them to develop in the treatment, arriving at stages that were not reached in early development (see Wallerstein, 1967, for an exhaustive critical study of transference psychosis).

13.3   Transference psychosis and Kleinian theory

The starting point for this investigation was the analysis of Dick, a boy of four with a mental development not exceeding 18 months, who had been diagnosed as a case of *dementia praecox* (today we should surely diagnose it as early infantile autism). Klein used her play technique with Dick, interpreting the child's sadistic fantasies with the mother's body and the primal scene, with no parameter other than giving the names of "father", "mother, and "Dick" to toy cars in order to set the analytic situation in motion. On the basis of this case, Klein proposed a new theory of the symbol and of psychosis, no less than a technique of approach to it with strictly analytic instruments. ("The Importance of Symbol-formation in the Development of the Ego" was presented at the Congress in Oxford in 1929 and published in 1930.)

It was Melanie Klein's disciples, not she herself, who in the final years of the 1940s decided to treat psychotic patients formally, employing the classic technique—that is, allowing the development of a "transference psychosis" and analysing it without parameters. Just as Melanie Klein had maintained that in the child no less than in the neurotic the positive and negative transference should be interpreted impartially, without resorting to any pedagogic or supportive measures, so the same attitude was adopted with the psychotic, without the fear that analysing aggression could obstruct the treatment or damage the patient. Federn had said, instead, in his classic article, "Psychoanalysis of Psychosis" (1943), that the positive transference should be maintained by the analyst and never dissolved if one was not to lose influence over the patient. (According to Federn, the transference is useful in the analysis of conflicts that are at the basis of the psychosis, but psychoanalysis should never undo a positive transference; the analyst would thus lose all his influence, as he cannot continue working with the psychotic in the periods of negative transference as he can with neurotics.) The same philosophy was proposed by Anna Freud in her book on the analysis of children in 1927, and Klein (1927) discussed it vehemently in the Symposium on Child Analysis at the British Psycho-Analytical Society.

When Hanna Segal, Bion and Rosenfeld decided to analyse psychotics, they counted on the theoretical tools forged by Klein in elaborating the theory of the positions and using the valuable concept of projective identification.

One of the first contributions was the case of Edward, which Segal published in 1950, at a time when cases of schizophrenia treated by means of the classic psychoanalytic technique had not yet been recorded. The course of the analysis showed that this technical approach turned out to be operative; and it was this patient who enabled Segal to make her valuable contributions to the theory of symbol formation in 1957. The only technical differences Segal introduced were that the analysis began in hospital and in the home, and the analysand was not asked to lie on the couch and free-associate. The therapist maintained the analytic attitude at all times, without availing herself of supportive or other psychotherapeutic measures, interpreting equally both the defences and the contents, the positive and the negative transference.

Parallel to the contributions mentioned above, we have those of Herbert A. Rosenfeld, who published "Transference-phenomena and Transference-analysis in an Acute Catatonic Schizophrenic Patient" (1952b), where on the basis of very illustrative clinical material he postulates that the psychotic develops phenomena of positive and negative transference, which the analyst can and should interpret and which the patient will understand. The patient will respond to these interpretations, at times confirming them and at times correcting them.

In a paper of that same year, "Notes on the Psycho-analysis of the Superego Conflict in an Acute Schizophrenic Patient" (1952a), Rosenfeld reaffirms: "If we avoid attempts to produce a positive transference by direct reassurance or expressions of love, and simply interpret the positive and negative transference, the psychotic manifestations attach themselves to the transference, and, in the same way as a transference neurosis develops in the neurotic, so, in the analysis of psychotics, there develops what may be called a 'transference psychosis'" (ibid., p. 65). Like Segal and Bion, Rosenfeld thinks that the concept of projective identification opens up a new field for the understanding of psychosis.

Whereas Segal studied the symbolism in psychosis and Rosenfeld refined the technical approach, Bion attended to schizophrenic language and thought, characterizing the transference—as we have seen—as premature, precipitate and intensely dependent. These studies were to lead him to identify two aspects of the personality—psychotic and nonpsychotic—and to develop a theory of thought.

13.4 Symbiosis and transference

While Mahler deepened her rigorous and lucid investigation of child development, the psychosis of childhood and the process of separation–individuation, Harold F. Searles—who is not only a great analyst but also a sagacious observer and a creative and careful theoretician—worked at Chestnut Lodge, in the tradition of Frieda Fromm-Reichmann.

Searles (1963) fully accepts the concept of transference psychosis proposed by Rosenfeld (1952a, 1952b) and that of delusional transference proposed by Margaret Little (1958), and he points out that it is not easy to discover this in the patient's material, for many reasons, one of them being that the daily life of the psychotic consists in fact of that type of reaction. Transference psychosis does not become evident because the psychotic ego suffers a serious deterioration in the capacity to differentiate fantasy from reality and past from present—defining characteristics of the transferential phenomenon. When Searles suggested to a paranoid schizophrenic woman that she found the people in the hospital, including Searles himself, similar to figures from her infancy, she asked impatiently what the difference was. So the psychological distance that enables us to discriminate between the original object and its replica is lacking. (The same concept can be found in Fromm-Reichmann's article "Transference Problems in Schizophrenics", 1939.)

The transference expresses a very primitive ego organization, which goes back to the early months of life, when the feeding infant relates to partial objects he does not manage to discriminate from the self, whereas the neurotic relates to total objects and in a triangular relation. This situation corresponds to schizoid mechanisms—so named by Melanie Klein—and to what Searles prefers to call, as Mahler (1967) does, the *symbiotic phase*. The transference that refers to this phase occurs not only with partial objects but also with parts of the self that relate to them; and, to complicate things further, these two types of transference alternate rapidly.

On the basis of his clinical experience, which confirms Mahler's (1967, etc.) investigation, Searles (1961) distinguishes five phases of evolution in the psychotherapy of chronic schizophrenia: (1) out of contact phase, (2) phase of ambivalent symbiosis, (3) phase of preambivalent symbiosis, (4) phase of resolution of the symbiosis and (5) late phase of individuation.

In Searles, opinion, the aetiology of schizophrenia should be looked for in a failure of the mother–child symbiosis, or even earlier if that symbiosis is not formed as a result of the mother's excessive ambivalence; and he maintains that transference of a symbiotic type is a necessary phase in every analysis, and much more so in the case of a psychotic.

The *out of contact phase* corresponds to Mahler's (1952) autistic stage, in which the homonymous psychosis originates. These are the children who were never able to participate in a symbiotic relation with the mother. The transferential phenomenon exists, nevertheless, in that the analyst is in fact identified, erroneously and bizarrely, with an object from the past. Here is where Little's concept of delusional transference is best applied, and the major problem of the countertransference is that one feels oneself persistently and completely ignored. The counterpart of the delusional transference is that the patient feels himself erroneously identified by other people, and, consequently, that the analyst is not speaking to him but to another.

During this phase, which can last for months or even years, the patient and the therapist do not manage to establish a relation of mutual affection, and it is best for the analyst to maintain a serene and neutral attitude, without wanting to alleviate at once the suffering of the patient, as the inexperienced analyst is wont to do. The more experienced psychoanalyst does not rack his brains trying to understand his patient's silence; instead, he allows his thoughts to follow their own course—if he is not reading a newspaper or an article that interests him.

As the analyst and the patient begin to contact each other, the second stage of the treatment, the *phase of ambivalent symbiosis*, is initiated. The silence and the ambiguity of the communication has gradually weakened the limits of the ego of both patient and analyst, and the mechanisms of projection and introjection on the part of both operate with great intensity, lending a basis of reality to the symbiotic transference, which in this period is characterized by a strong ambivalence. The analyst perceives it in the verbal and non-verbal communication of the patient no less than in his countertransference, which fluctuates rapidly between love and hate, appreciation and rejection.

A characteristic of this stage is that the relationship with the patient acquires an excessive and absorbing importance for the analyst, who feels his relationships within the hospital and even within his family to be in danger. The hostility reaches a very high pitch, and precisely what is decisive in this stage is for analyst and analysand to be able to prove that they can survive the hate of self and other, assuming alternately the role of the bad mother.

Then, gradually, the *phase of full or preambivalent symbiosis* begins to establish itself, in which the analyst begins to accept his role of good mother to the patient and, reciprocally, his infantile dependence on the patient, who is also the good mother to him. The feelings are not now predominantly sexual but rather of a maternal type. It is necessary, Searles says, for analyst and patient to deposit in each other the confidence of the young child that each one is. This phase of the therapy reproduces in a concrete way in the relation with the therapist a happy infantile experience with a good mother. Having reached the stage of preambivalent love, the fear of losing one's individuality ceases to exist, and a state of enjoyable play activity arises between analyst and patient, who change places without fear and playfully explore all the fields of psychological experience.

This is followed by the *phase of resolution of symbiosis*, where the individual needs of both participants arise again. The analyst begins to delegate to the patient the responsibility of either curing himself or making the decision to spend the rest of his life in a psychiatric hospital. Here it is decisive that the countertransference of the analyst should not cause him to fear for the future of the patient and for his own professional prestige; he should understand that the patient really has the last word. At this time relatives and members of the therapeutic team often intervene to prevent the patient from becoming a separate person, lest they lose the gratification of a symbiotic relationship.

The *late phase* of the treatment, *individuation*, is reached when the therapeutic symbiosis has been resolved. This stage is always prolonged, while the patient begins to establish genuine object relations and confronts the problems proper to the analysis of a neurotic.

Searles' clinical acumen, his capacity to capture the most delicate nuances of the relation with the patient and to transmit these to the reader, should not make us forget the distance between his method and the standard treatment—which he certainly does not ignore—and his lack of confidence in interpretation. Searles firmly believes that it is enough to live the symbiosis fully at first and enjoyably later on, so that the patient can evolve and change without words. In effect, he thinks the destiny of the psychotic patient in analysis depends on being able to reproduce in the transference the symbiotic relation, and this is achieved through a nonverbal link, where the moment for transferential interpretations is rarely reached. Searles is inclined to think that the analysts who, like Rosenfeld, tend to give the analysand verbal interpretations of the transference psychosis succumb to an unconscious resistance: they elude confrontation with the period of therapeutic symbiosis. To avail oneself of verbalized interpretations before having successfully passed through the symbiotic phase of the transference is clearly an error: it is equivalent to the analyst employing the transferential interpretation as a shield to protect himself from the degree of psychological intimacy the patient demands from him, in the same way that the patient employs his delusional transference in order not to experience the full reality of the analyst as a person who is present.

The risks Searles indicates are very real, but they are not avoided by abstaining from interpreting; and, on the other hand, the attitude of not doing so can equally be a shield for the conflicts of countertransference.

Searles generously offers us in his works rich clinical illustrations of his way of working, which invariably depict him as a sagacious, profound and committed analyst. If I dare to give an opinion on the basis of what he shows us, I would say Searles is concerned in general more with the patient's well-being, with not hurting him and with showing him his affection, than with interpreting what is happening.

Another great investigator of psychosis, Peter L. Giovacchini, has worked on this theme for many years. Like Searles, he uses the symbiotic transference as his principal instrument; he, however, holds that what is decisive in the destiny of the therapeutic symbiosis is precisely that the analyst interpret it, as he says in all his works, and especially in "The Symbiotic Phase" (1972b).

13.5   Transference in the borderline patient

"Borderline" is a term that can be traced back to nineteenth-century psychiatry. In our own century it is linked with Bleuler's latent schizophrenia (1911) and Kretschmer's schizoid and cycloid states, to mention only the main references. It has always been accepted that there are intermediate cases between neurosis and psychosis, but it is only in recent years, and mainly thanks to psychoanalysts in the United States, that they have been defined as a clinical entity. This singular illness (or syndrome), which is by definition neither one thing nor the other, is certainly not easy to define, and its scope varies with the criteria of whoever is studying it. Authors who claim that the borderline is an independent area point out that the mixture of neurotic and psychotic symptoms produces a particular picture that is stable—stable in its instability—and must not be thought of merely as a transitional state.

Many psychoanalysts have considered cases in which the neurotic façade covers more severe disturbances, but it was apparently Adolph Stern who in 1938 introduced the term that was to become universally accepted. His work is concerned with patients who do not fit into the categories of neurosis and psychosis and exhibit particular clinical characteristics as well as a special form of transference in which narcissism predominates and a relationship of extreme dependence is established, accompanied by marked idealization phenomena, which in themselves suggest a disturbance of the sense of reality. This special type of transference demands a modification of technique, as a supportive attitude becomes unavoidable in the early stages at least. The intensity of the transference dependence, Stern goes on, forces the therapist to be constantly occupied with it and does not leave room for historic and genetic interpretations, a characteristic to which Kernberg returns later.

Stern's work does not clearly distinguish the new entity, and from this point of view Robert P. Knight's contribution is relevant because he studies its clinical features in detail, calling attention to problems of diagnosis, psychopathology, and treatment. It may be said, then, that Knight's conclusive work, "Borderline States", read in Atlantic City, New Jersey, on 12 May 1952 and published in the following year in the *Bulletin of the Menninger Clinic*, is the birth certificate of the new entity.

From the psychodynamic point of view, the borderline state is in Knight's opinion characterized by the weakness of certain functions of the ego such as integration, concept formation and judgement; others, on the other hand, persist, such as (conventional) adaptation to reality, in which these states differ from psychosis.

Knight returned to the subject the following year, but more cautiously or pessimistically, since he speaks of the "borderline schizophrenic patient", by which, in my view, he narrows the field considerably: if the borderline patient is a schizophrenic (mild, pseudoneurotic or whatever), this is not a clinical entity. Perhaps through Knight's influence, analysts in England and the United States link borderline states with schizophrenia and schizoid personalities; but others consider that there are also borderline cases related to manic-depressive psychosis, as Paz says in his updating of the subject in 1964. The author who has devoted most study to this point is undoubtedly Jean Bergeret. In "Les états-limites et leurs aménagements" (1972), Bergeret maintains that the borderline patient does not reach the genital level of the development of the libido but remains at the level of anaclitic dependence, from which, basically, he defends himself against depression. Within this line of thought, Grinberg (1977) distinguishes two types of borderline cases—schizoid and melancholoid—and López (1987) studies in depth the manic mechanisms of this type of patient.

Thanks to the efforts of many authors, among whom Otto F. Kernberg stands out, the borderline state is no longer the dustbin to which cases with a difficult or imprecise diagnosis are consigned, but a clinical entity in its own right. To indicate its individual outline, to emphasize that it is a specific and stable category, Kernberg (1967) prefers to speak in fact of a *borderline personality organization*, and this is the title of his first work on the subject. Carlos Alberto Paz, one of the most outstanding researchers on the subject, speaks of *borderline structures and states* (Paz, Pelento, & Olmos de Paz, 1976–77), to emphasize the structural aspect of the disorder.

The borderline organization of the personality is more easily differentiated from psychosis than from neurosis, and Kernberg lists as important symptoms chronic and diffuse anxiety, polysymptomatic neuroses (multiple phobias), obsessional symptoms tending to become ego-syntonic, twilight states, and paranoid and hypochondriacal tendencies. We must also consider a borderline organization of the personality in individuals with strong paranoid, schizoid, or hypomanic features, and those exhibiting addictive tendencies or impulsive character traits. The authors are unanimous in stating that *rage* is the predominant emotion of borderline patients.

With regard to structural analysis, the lability of the ego is characteristic; it is expressed in intolerance of anxiety, insufficient control over the impulses, and inadequate development of sublimation. To this we may add the predominance of the primary process without any alteration in formal thought, and archaic defence operations centred on the splitting of the ego and including idealization, projective identification, denial and omnipotence. These mechanisms are connected with internalized object relations, which Kernberg discussed in his "Structural Derivatives of Object Relationships" (1966).

The very detailed essay of 1967 ends with a genetic and dynamic analysis of the borderline personality organization, stressing the importance of pregenital aggression, which is closely connected with the early Oedipus conflict (as Melanie Klein pointed out from her very first works).

A year later, Kernberg (1968) considers the treatment of patients with borderline personality organization and surveys a wide spectrum of suggestions. (With some modifications, this work forms chapter 3 of *Borderline Conditions and Pathological Narcissism*, 1975.)

In Knight's papers (1953a, 1953b; Knight & Friedman, 1954) it is stated that the borderline patient does not adapt to psychoanalytic treatment because his very labile ego tends to crumble in the face of the natural and inevitable regression the classic treatment provokes. Knight is therefore inclined to treat these patients by a supportive psychotherapy of an analytic type, seeking to restore the strength the ego has lost. Only when this has been achieved is the way open for conventional psychoanalytic treatment. Paul Federn, in his "Principles of Psycho-therapy in Latent Schizophrenia" (1947), also advises against psychoanalysis and proposes a type of psychotherapy that respects positive transference. He strongly recommends that these patients should not be "cured" of their neurosis so as not to make the latent psychosis manifest.

Some think, more optimistically, that psychoanalysis is possible with the use of parameters, while others, such as Winnicott (1958), Paz (1969), Grinberg (1977a), Rosenfeld (1978, 1987), Painceira (1979, 1987, 1989) and López (1987) consider the borderline patient to be accessible to classic psychoanalytic treatment, although they do not doubt for a moment that he will pose much more difficult problems than does the ordinary neurotic patient. Some of these authors apply the classic technique, while others use parameters to a greater or lesser degree. Margaret Little (1966), for example, considers that there are areas in which words are insufficient and the analysand must be given direct physical contact.

Kernberg, equidistant from all these positions, declares in favour of a special form of modified psychoanalytic psychotherapy. He is of the opinion, as are Knight as well as Frosch (1988a, 1988b), that borderline patients do not tolerate the regression that takes place in analysis because their ego is very weak, and because of their heightened propensity to develop a transference psychosis and to act out; but he does not believe that supportive psychotherapy is useful either, as it generally leads to a dangerous dissociation of the negative transference, which operates with other persons while the relationship with the analyst becomes superficial and empty. The borderline patient should be treated, therefore, by means of a special form of analysis based on diverse technical parameters, or, simply, with a modified psychoanalytic psychotherapy in which, rather than speaking of parameters, it is better to speak simply of technical modifications (Kernberg, 1968, p. 601). Among the technical modifications proposed by Kernberg is a rhythm consisting of three sessions face to face, as well as the systematic working-through of the negative transference without attempting its genetic reconstruction (remember Stern) and the "deflection" of the manifest negative transference away from the therapeutic interaction through its systematic examination in the patient's relations with other people, building up a therapeutic setting that can contain the acting out, establishing strict limits to the non-verbal aggression that will be admitted during sessions, and making use of the environmental factors that may promote a better organization of the patient's life and treatment. On the other hand, Kernberg declares himself in favour of using the positive transference insofar as it can maintain the working alliance without touching on the defences that might destroy it.

At the end of his important 1968 work, Kernberg sums up his therapeutic focus and says: "This particular form of expressive, psychoanalytically oriented psychotherapy is a treatment approach which differs from classical psychoanalysis in that a complete transference neurosis is not permitted to develop, nor is transference resolved through interpretation alone" (p. 616).

What characterizes the borderline patient for Kernberg (1982) is (1) the diffusion of identity, in that the representation of self and object are not clearly delimited; (2) the predominance of primitive defence mechanisms based on dissociation; and (3) the preservation of the proof of reality—precisely what is lacking in psychosis.

This structure basis leads to a special type of transference, which Kernberg (1976b) calls *primitive transference*, in which the object relation is partial. "The transference reflects a multitude of internal object-relations of dissociated (or split-off) aspects of the self and highly distorted and fantastic dissociated (or split-off) object representations" (p. 800).

In his *Object Relations Theory and Clinical Psychoanalysis* (1976a) Kernberg returns to the theme of transference and countertransference in the borderline patient, maintaining and refining his points of view. He insists that the negative transference of borderline patients should be interpreted only in the here and now, as genetic reconstructions cannot be grasped by patients who in effect confuse transference with reality, and that the aspects of the positive transference of a less primitive origin should not be interpreted, in order to facilitate the development of the therapeutic alliance. The most distorted aspects of the transference should be attacked first, leaving until *afterwards* the transferential phenomena that are linked to real childhood experiences.

The strategic aim of Kernberg's therapy consists in transforming the primitive transference into integrated transferential reactions (1976b, p. 800). This is achieved through the systematic analysis of the defensive constellations, which improve the functioning of the ego and allow the transformation and the resolution of the primitive transference, as Kernberg says in his *Internal World and External Reality* (1980, especially chapters 9 and 10).

Kernberg's rules on technique undoubtedly do have a clear coherence with his theoretical position, and yet it is pertinent to question whether he does pay a high price in applying his technique instead of having confidence in the one we all use. It should not be forgotten that the limitations Kernberg imposes on his patient and on himself can in the short or the long run aggravate precisely the difficulties he aspires to avoid.

This is, without a doubt, the most interesting point to consider in a book on technique, and in order to discuss it thoroughly we have to pay attention to the psychotic phenomena that appear in the treatment of the borderline patient.

From his first works Kernberg established the principles that, in his view, should underlie the treatment of these patients. "When psychoanalysis is attempted, these patients may develop a particular loss of reality-testing and even delusional ideas restricted to the transference situation—they develop a transference psychosis rather than a transference neurosis" (1968, p. 600). We should note here that Kernberg employs the term "transference psychosis" to denote an eventuality (or complication) of the psychoanalytic treatment, as does Wallerstein, which is not the meaning given to the term in this book. Transference psychosis occurs when the analyst and the primary object become identical (ibid., p. 607), whereupon the patient loses reality testing.

Despite the fact that in that same work Kernberg points out that a typical characteristic of the patient with a borderline personality organization is that in the face of stress situations or through the effects of alcohol or drugs transient psychotic symptoms develop, he prefers to reserve the term "transference psychosis" for what occurs *within* treatment.

In *Severe Personality Disorders* (1984) Kernberg makes his point of view clear: "I prefer to reserve the term *transference psychosis* to designate the loss of reality testing and the appearance of delusional material within the transference that does not very noticeably affect the patient's functioning outside the treatment setting" (p. 115).

Wallerstein (1967) used the same concept when he reported two cases that showed psychotic symptoms during analysis. Wallerstein takes the term "transference psychosis" from a work by Reider (1957) and applies it to neurotic cases in which a psychotic reaction appears in the course of conventional psychoanalytic treatment, and not to the strictly psychotic cases of which Rosenfeld and Searles speak. In Wallerstein's view these reactions always have to do with the conditions of the setting and are basically reversible—a point of view that he repeats in his enthralling work, *Forty-Two Lives in Treatment* (1986).

The great majority of authors agree that transference psychosis intervenes in such cases for variable lengths of time, and that its contingent presence is one of the defining characteristics of the condition (Rosenfeld, 1978; López, 1987); but whereas some think (Painceira, 1979) that passing through transference psychosis is little short of inevitable, others (Paz, 1969) maintain that the psychoanalytical process can develop without psychotic episodes.

13.6   One of Kernberg's clinical cases

It is worth looking in detail into one of the interesting cases with which
Kernberg illustrates "Transference Management in Expressive Psychotherapy", chapter 7 in his valuable book, *Severe Personality Disorders* (1984).
It concerns Miss M, a graduate student in her late twenties, diagnosed as
infantile personality with borderline features. She exhibited severe depressive reactions, with suicidal ideas and loss of weight, alcoholism and difficulties with study, social life and partnerships—a really serious case.

Kernberg proposed face-to-face treatment (as he uses the couch only
for psychoanalysis) three times a week and laid down certain conditions:
"Miss M had committed herself to stop drinking, not to act on suicidal
impulses but to discuss them openly with me if and when they occurred,
and to maintain a minimum weight by eating sufficiently, regardless of
her mood and appetite" (p. 124). If she could not fulfil these conditions,
the treatment would be carried out in hospital. (It is not clear whether
Kernberg explained to his future patient the differences between the various forms of treatment.) As was logical, the patient promised to fulfil the
doctor's requirements. It was also arranged that she would have the help
of a psychiatric social worker.

This contract does not protect the patient for certain from her self-
destructive and allodestructive tendencies, and in my view it endangers
the psychotherapist more than necessary, which seems to be confirmed by
his countertransference thoughts that arise during the session: Will she be
capable of maintaining the programmed setting? Shall I get any truth from
her? . . . Using the data from his countertransference, Kernberg also draws
the conclusion that the patient sees him as a feared parental figure who is
going to criticize her for not being sincere and reprimand her for bad
behaviour. This conclusion is not only correct; it has a basis in the conditions of the contract. Later Kernberg became aware of a countertransference feeling of impatience, combined with concern for the patient and
irritation because she was spoiling the agreed programme. An aspect that
Kernberg does not mention is that the patient saw him as greedy and
demanding; thus thanks to his contract, Kernberg greatly facilitates the
projective identification of the angry, greedy, infantile part on to the parental figure ". . . because she projected her own angry demands on to it"
(p. 126).

All this happens in a session that took place in the first weeks of treatment. It was raining in torrents, and M arrived distraught, haggard and
wet through; she began to speak of her problems with study, her jealousy
of her boyfriend and Kernberg's fees. Meanwhile he was wondering
whether she had been drinking without daring to admit it, and whether
she would really be able to maintain the outpatient treatment setting.

When Kernberg interpreted her contradictory feelings and pointed out
to her that any interpretation could be misunderstood, either as a police-
type investigation or as evidence of indifference and callousness, Miss M

was able to confess that she had been drinking and was afraid that the therapist would send her to hospital, immediately adding that she was worried that her parents were late in sending the cheque for the fees. (This is where I see the projective identification of greed into the analyst.) Kernberg interpreted that she saw him as more interested in his fees than in her, like a parent-figure who felt annoyed because he had to look after her. This well-aimed interpretation brought immediate relief and opened the way to the analysis of more neurotic, less regressive conflicts.

I really do not doubt the good outcome of the session and Kernberg's impeccable performance. On the other hand, I do not see the use of the conditions with which the treatment began. I am convinced that the problems of transference and countertransference would have been the same, but without the unnecessary touch of reality given to them by Kernberg's initial demands, which are excessive, perhaps naive, and, moreover, unrealistic.

* * *

The main objective of Kernberg's technique is to create the most favourable conditions for the analysis of the conflicts (or some of the conflicts) of the borderline patient, without allowing the regression originated by the setting to bring it to a psychotic level. These objectives, however, are questionable.

As we shall see in chapter 40, in spite of the fact that it is universally accepted, there are many reasons for abandoning the theory that transference neurosis is an effect of the setting, and we can say the same of transference psychosis: the setting contains them but does not cause them; it works only within the limits of the present conflict. I do not believe either that these patients have psychotic symptoms *through* the treatment and *only* in the treatment. I think, rather, that the symptoms appear in fact both inside and outside the treatment, and when they are confined to the analysis it is because it has been capable of containing them without letting them expand. Kernberg thinks, on the contrary, like Knight, Reider and Wallerstein, that the analytical setting causes a localized psychosis.

The clinical entity we are considering does indeed have a short history in psychoanalysis, but in psychiatry it is old. The short and transient psychotic crisis with its remissions and relapses is none other than the *bouffée délirante* studied by the great French psychiatrists of the nineteenth century (Magnan, Lagrain). It occurs when the level of tension in the present conflict increases and always tends towards remission with *restitutio ad integrum*.

Like any other present conflict, that which originates in the analytical setting can trigger off this transient psychosis, and Rosenfeld (1978) has suggested a plausible explanation for its occurrence: transference psychosis is unleashed when the analysand sees the analyst as a cruelly accusing superego. I agree with this opinion, although I do not consider this to be the only cause. There are others, such as, for example, a technical error, an alteration in the setting, and—very important—a crisis of envy in the transference (Etchegoyen, López, & Rabih, 1985). If the primary envy (in the intrinsic and not the reactive sense) is passed over, we run the risk of believing that these difficult analysands always react through their low threshold to frustration, when in reality, on more than one occasion, they are expressing their intolerance of being helped.

Rosenfeld certainly does not favour the appearance of transference psychosis, but neither does he fear it; and he maintains that its detailed investigation opens the possibility of understanding these patients and working out their early conflicts with an archaic and strict superego, which makes demands that are contradictory and therefore confusing. Rosenfeld thinks that this quality of the superego is what differentiates borderline from narcissistic patients (which he described in 1971): in the latter the superego is not so involved, and interpretations of aggression are viable, while in the former there are serious semantic distortions that, by perpetuating conflict and confusion, can lead to psychosis. For the great London analyst whose recent death we all mourn, a distinctive trait of the psychopathology of the borderline organization of the personality is *confusion*, which may be linked with early envy and/or with serious deprivation situations at the beginning of life.

The researches of Carlos Alberto Paz developed simultaneously with those of Kernberg and are no less important. In his "Technical Reflections on the Analytical Process in Borderline Psychotics" (1969), Paz establishes a dialectic between the psychotic and neurotic parts of the personality, following Bion (1957), Katan (1959), and Bleger (1967b) whose meeting-point is the existence of a neurotic transference and a psychotic transference, alternating and interweaving. I fully agree with this point of view and would add that the transition between the two may be very rapid, as can be seen, for example, in Kernberg's material after the interpretation.

Paz advocates a stable setting, with five sessions a week, and clear interpretations that attempt to establish the links between the unconscious and preconscious systems, and between psychic instances, avoiding ambiguity as far as possible, as Melanie Klein (1946) suggested for schizoid states—which were borderline for her. We may add the importance, in such cases, of misunderstanding, which comes not only from disturbances of thought but also from the effect of transferential envy.

Although it will never be wise to have recourse to historical and genetic interpretations to relieve the tension that frequently appears in transference and countertransference, Paz considers that the spontaneous emergence of infantile material is always welcome, because it helps to differentiate the analyst from early objects. The disagreement on this point is more apparent than real, I believe, since Kernberg's reservations were directed against premature historical interpretations. It is worth pointing out that Bryce Boyer (1969), for his part, maintains that interpretations of genetic aspects are more convincing and structural and so encourage the recovery of memories.

An important aspect of the analysis of borderline patients in Paz's view is gradually to correct idealization, which is one of the basic mechanisms of such patients. Idealized objects undergo a process of encapsulation that must be modified step by step. Paz maintains that there exists in the borderline patient a pregenital primal scene with an idealized combined couple, which is encapsulated in the unconscious, and the analysis consists of decapsulating that object. If this process is accomplished, the early Oedipus complex evolves towards its mature forms, and the patient's psychosis recedes.

Bryce Boyer (1969)—who, incidentally, tends to treat the borderline patient by the orthodox psychoanalytic method—also thinks that if the treatment goes well, the transference psychosis gives way to transference neurosis. This is achieved through interpretation and by incorporating new introjects, reducing the severity of the early sadistic superego.

* * *

Two authors who have made an in-depth study of narcissistic (or schizoid) patients are undoubtedly Kohut and Winnicott. There are points of contact between them, as for example the importance they give to the environment; and there are also differences. We have spoken of Kohut when discussing *selfobject transference* in section 12.7. We shall now give an account of some of Winnicott's ideas.

In Winnicott's view, a borderline patient is one in whom the nucleus of the disturbance is psychotic, but whose precarious balance is maintained by the neurotic organization.

The schizoid (narcissistic), the borderline patient, and the schizophrenic belong to the same psychopathological category, although with different degrees of severity, in which the essential feature is the dissociation between the true self and the false self. In all these patients the primitive emotional development (see chapter 16), which is previous to the conflict, is disturbed: the child is born with a (creative) potential for growth, and he will develop spontaneously from the inside outwards until he reaches independence, if he finds a means (the mother) of facilitating this. At the beginning of life it is primary identification that reigns; it is the root of communication and empathy, and in it the child believes himself one with the mother (and the mother one with the child). The baby "has the illusion" that he has created his object, and the function of the mother is in principle to maintain this illusion by presenting herself as the *subjective object* so that the baby may exercise his creative capacity until the necessities of growth cause him to lose that illusion. Winnicott does not believe (as Klein does) that the first moments of life are terrible, since nonintegration is pleasant and the unimaginable anxiety does not arise if the mother neutralizes it.

When this facilitating process does not happen, when the mother fails and is not capable of responding with empathy to the child's demands, he introjects her and forms the pseudo-self. From this moment on, development will be basically a reaction, and the introjection of the maternal role turns the child into his own keeper. The false self, then, is neither more nor less than the introjection of the mother; the baby becomes his own mother, hiding and protecting the true self.

Winnicott distinguishes different degrees of organization of the false self, and Painceira (1989) has specified the differences between the false self of the schizoid and that of the borderline patient. The former has introjected a mother figure with a certain coherence despite its faults. If good intellectual development is added, we have the typical schizoid who achieves well, but has that feeling of internal emptiness, of futility, as Fairbairn says (1941), and who is incapable of forming emotional ties. The maternal environment of the borderline patient, on the other hand, has been more contradictory and capricious, so that its introjection has formed a fragmented false self, which never achieves integration and coherence, but remains the reflection of an erratic and unpredictable introject.

Leaving aside the differences between them, schizoid and borderline patients can be analysed and need to pass in treatment through a profound regression to dependence "which the analyst does not seek, but which the patient needs and the analyst must not hinder" (Painceira, 1987, p. 6).

While this regressive process is operating, the analyst speaks of the true self with the false self, that is, with a mistaken interlocutor; but finally the false self—which brought the patient to treatment—delegates its custodial function to the analyst, and the patient is momentarily destructured to make room for the process of growth of the true self which had been frozen, waiting for more favourable conditions (this topic is covered in chapter 41). When the regressive process of absolute dependence is burnt out, the analyst's capacity to tolerate the experience of fusion is sorely tried. If this is accomplished, the analysand begins to discover his true self and sets foot on the road to independence.

CHAPTER FOURTEEN

Transference perversion

T he thesis of this chapter is that perversion has an individual clinical outline and constitutes a special type of transference.

14.1 Theoretical considerations

It was not easy to grasp the psychopathological unity of the perversions and to indicate their defining characteristics. The phenomenological study is not sufficient, as particular behaviour cannot be defined in itself as perverse, and classifying the perversions according to their form is like categorizing the varieties of delirium according to their content. It was necessary to reach an understanding of the perversions from within their own guidelines, and this has only begun to be realized in recent years.

This paper appeared in its complete version in León Grinberg (ed.), *Prácticas psico-analíticas comparadas en las psicosis* (1977c). The version reprinted here is a summary, which, with minor modifications, was read at the Thirtieth International Congress in Jerusalem and which appeared in the *International Journal of Psycho-Analysis* and in Jean Bergeret et al., *La cure psychanalytique sur le divan* (1980).

The neurosis–psychosis polarity is so clear and definite that the other psychopathological clinical pictures tend finally to fall within its orbit; and the vigorous brushstrokes with which Freud traces the dividing line in his two 1924 (1924b, 1924e) essays inadvertently reinforce this fundamental dualism.

The first attempt to understand perversion concerned neurosis, with the celebrated Freudian aphorism that neurosis is the negative of perversion, and it is still in force, to some extent, as Gillespie (1964) rightly says.

After the *Three Essays on the Theory of Sexuality* (1905d), we find the foundations of Freud's structural point of view in his study on Leonardo da Vinci (1910c), in "A Child Is Being Beaten" (1919e) and in the work of Hans Sachs in 1923. According to this theory, the perverse act has the structure of a symptom, different because it is ego-syntonic and pleasurable but in the final analysis still a symptom, with which the limits between perversion and neurosis are erased. However, to have come this long way only to arrive at the conclusion that the perverse symptom is like any other did not yet touch on the problem of perversion itself.

The irreducible difference in the clinical facts and the difficulty of analysing the pervert finally resulted in an approach to perversion from the opposite pole.

Freud envisioned in 1922 that perversion may have to do with aggressive impulses, not only with libidinous ones; and in his essay on fetishism (1927e) he indicates a peculiar form of access to reality in these patients. Melanie Klein (1932) also emphasized the importance of situations of anxiety and guilt linked to aggressive impulses in the development of perversion.

On these bases Glover (1933) asserts that many perversions are, so to speak, the negative of psychosis—attempts to close the gaps that had remained in the development of the sense of reality.

In studying the psychotic personality (or the psychotic part of the personality), Melanie Klein's followers (Bion, Hanna Segal, Rosenfeld, and others) reached the conclusion that this is very powerful in the pervert.

Thus a new aphorism was coined, according to which perversion is no longer the "positive" of neurosis, but the negative of (a defence against) psychosis, a way of fleeing from madness. (A lucid discussion of the interplay between neurosis, perversion and psychosis can be found in Pichon Rivière, 1946, p. 9.)

It should be accepted without reservation that perversion has much to do with the psychotic part of the personality; but to propose that it is a simple defence against psychosis, a species of lesser evil (to describe it in a way that reveals its ideological root), connotes a value judgement on mental health rather than a psychopathological formula. If we observe the clinical facts without this prejudice, we realize that perversion can be a defence against psychosis as well as one of its causes.

14.2   *The perverse ego*

Only in recent years has perversion begun to reveal its individuality, when the investigation revealed an essential theme, *the division of the perverse ego*.

The starting point is found in "The Infantile Genital Organization" (1923e), where Freud states that, confronted with the first (and deep) impression of the lack of a penis in the woman, the child *verleugnet* [denies, excludes, disavows] the fact and thinks he must have seen a penis. (Strachey uses the verb "disavow" and the noun "disavowal" for *verleugnen* and *Verleugnung*.) In other works of the same period Freud uses the noun *Verleugnung* with reference to castration, the difference between the sexes or a painful reality. (Unlike Elisabeth von R., who is neurotic, a psychotic patient would have *disavowed* the death of her sister—Freud, 1924e, p. 184.)

In applying these concepts to the understanding of fetishism Freud states in 1927 that fetishism represses the affect (that is, the horror of castration) and disavows the representation. The disavowal, in conserving and setting aside the castration, defines for Freud the *splitting of the ego* in the defensive process, which he studies in 1938 in two incomplete works (Freud, 1940a [1938] and 1940e [1938]).

Lacan and his disciples maintain that the explanation of the perversions should be sought in this particular defence mechanism, *Verleugnung*, which essentially differs from repression, *Verdrängung* (proper to neurosis) and from *Verwerfung* [exclusion or foreclosure], which is the structural basis for psychosis. (In "The Neuro-psychoses of Defence", 1894a, p. 58, Freud says: "There is, however, a much more energetic and successful kind of defence. Here, the ego rejects the incompatible idea together with its affect and behaves as if the idea had never occurred to the ego at all." According to Laplanche and Pontalis, Strachey translates the verb *verwerfen* as reject. But in "Neurosis and Psychosis", 1924b, Freud uses *Verleugnung* [disavowal] and not *Verwerfung*.) Lacan (1956) believes that the fetishist passes through the castration but then disavows it. He recognizes the castration, but "presentifying" the imago of the female penis, he imagines what does not exist. The "presentification" is the other side of what is denied. The fetish, Lacan says expressively, presents (incarnates) and at the same time veils the female penis. In the mirror stage, the child is the penis lacking in the mother, the object of the desire (to have a phallus) of the mother. In the culminating moment of the Oedipus complex the father intervenes, relocating the child in a third place: the child is not the mother's phallus and, from then onwards, *the phallus is a symbol* (and not an organ).

The fetish, Rosolato (1966) asserts, is the counterpart of the splitting of the ego. The fetish appears *cut off* from its corporal dependence and at the same time in (metonymic) *continuity* with the body (dresses, etc.). If by this continuity the fetish is a *metonymy*, in that it represents ("presentifies") the penis lacking in the mother, it is also its *metaphor*.

With the theoretical support of ego psychology, Gillespie (1956, 1964), one of the most outstanding exponents of the Independent Group of the British Society, elaborates a clear and broad theory of perversion where the dissociation of the ego also occupies an outstanding place, although it does not specifically recover the *Verleugnung*. Along the same line of thinking, Bychowsky (1966) considers that the homosexual ego suffers a process of dissociation, which he explains as a function of introjects.

For Meltzer (1973), the dissociation of the perverse ego also occupies a major place; it assumes a special form—*dismantling*. This author has made a valuable contribution in distinguishing the sexuality of the adult (having an introjective basis) from infantile and perverse sexuality, both having a projective basis but with different processes of dissociation in the ego structure, linked to anxiety and envy.

* * *

On her return from her first holiday, a homosexual patient expressed vividly the dissociation of the ego (and the basic mechanism of disavowal), saying she felt badly because one of her contact lenses had fallen out and her mother had stepped on it while they were looking for it. Having rejected the possibility of returning to the use of eyeglasses, she had to use only one contact lens and so see things well with one eye and badly with the other. In the following session, she expressed the fear that I had changed during the holidays, transforming myself into a bad analyst.

Exchanging eyeglasses for contact lenses had been one of the first improvements the patient had noticed, and she hid this for a time, fearing I would envy it. Only on returning from her holiday could she come to the consulting-room with her contact lenses (with *one* lens), and she recounted the funny episode.

14.3   Transference perversion

This theoretical detour allows a return to the substance of this chapter—the special type of relation that, perforce, the pervert will develop in the analysis so that the *transference perversion* may be created and resolved. With this denomination I propose to unify the diverse clinical phenomena that are observed in the treatment of this group of patients.

Transference perversion is a technical concept with the same range as transference neurosis, and it allows the study of these patients without making them lie on a Procrustean bed.

The fertile Freudian concept that the originating illness returns within the sphere of the psychoanalytic cure and becomes the object of our labour (Freud, "Remembering, Repeating and Working-Through", 1914g) can extend to other psychopathological groups, with which transference neurosis itself is specified and delimited. This implies accepting that the pathological group Freud contrasted with the transference neuroses in "On Narcissism: An Introduction" (1914c) also has a transferential correlate, as clinical experience seems to imply. (This point of view is not shared by many analysts—Guttman, 1968; Zetzel, 1968.)

My proposal implies delimiting the *technical* concept of transference neurosis from its psychopathological (or nosographic) consequences and is located along the same line of thought that led Rosenfeld (1952a) and Searles (1963) to recognize the individual outline of transference psychosis; and it also gathers up the valuable contributions from current research that have been able to illuminate narcissistic object relations, provide a theoretical basis to gain access to the perversions, and bring into view what is specifically perverse in the transferential link. In an almost diabolical manner, these patients try to pervert the analytic relation and test our tolerance; however, if perversion is what it is, we cannot expect anything else.

Although she does not speak of transference perversion explicitly, Betty Joseph (1971) illustrates its most significant modalities and asserts that the perversion can only be resolved to the extent that the analyst discovers and interprets it *in the transference*. The erotization of the link, the utilization of silence or the word to project excitement into the analyst, the passivity in order to provoke the analyst's impatience and succeed in making the latter act it out with interpretations (or pseudo-interpretations) appear clearly in this fundamental paper. These mechanisms, Betty Joseph continues, are not only *defences* through which the patient tries to relieve himself of his impulses and his (painful) feelings, but also actual *attacks* against the analyst. The nipple having been projectively identified with the tongue, the word is food, just as the nipple–penis itself remains broken and without force, in order to be stimulated by an empty dialogue that tries to excite it and torment it.

After a long holiday, a patient who was a *frotteur* and who usually spoke at length and in an intellectual tone dreamt that *he was returning by ship and engaged in sexual play with a young woman. He gave her a kiss and, on separating, her tongue stretched and stretched in such a way that it always remained in his mouth.*

In her interesting essay on fetishism, Luisa de Urtubey (1971–72) speaks of the "fetishization" of the transferential link and illustrates it convincingly. The subtle effort of the pervert to drag the analyst along appears expressively described in the rigorous work of Ruth Riesenberg (1970) on the mirror fantasy: the analyst's capacity for observing and describing runs the risk of being transformed into scoptophilia.

The persistent impact of the subtle perverse mechanisms on the analyst has been profoundly studied by Meltzer (1973, chapter 19), who emphasizes that the analyst often only realizes that the analytic process has been subverted when it is already too late. The analysis develops, then, within a framework of sterility, and sterility is the *raison d'être* of all perversion. In extreme cases, the analyst acts out his countertransference directly through pseudo-interpretations. Permanent damage to his analytic instrument can begin in this way (Liberman, 1976b). Logically, Meltzer concludes, the decadence of an analytic group continues along this path.

In a brief communication (1973) on the technical problems that the ideology of the patient creates if it is utilized projectively with defensive (and offensive) aims, I was able to illustrate how an instinct is transformed into an ideology and projected. Although this communication referred to vegetarianism, the disturbance described—that is, the transformation of a misunderstanding (Money-Kyrle, 1968) into ideology of the analyst through projective identification (Melanie Klein, 1946)—is essentially perverse (as was the patient in my communication). I arrived then at the conclusion that the pervert does not feel the call of instinct; he has communication with his body only through the intellect. I suppose that it is mainly envy joined to guilt feelings that leads the pervert to feel his instinct not as desire but as ideology. These are reflections that may contribute to clarify the enormous creative potential of the perverse structure. Equally it can be understood why for the pervert, enclosed in a world of ideologies, polemics are so vital.

According to my experience, the erotization of the linking and the "ideological" presentation of sexual life (and of life in general), always accompanied by a rebellious note and a polemical tone, are perverse mechanisms. If these characteristics appear in neurotic patients it is because a perverse aspect of the personality is in play, just as the neurotic transference can be observed in perverse patients, because the clinical pictures are never pure.

With different theoretical support, the French authors reach similar conclusions. Rosolato (1966) maintains that the fetishist perversion always entails an ideology, and specifically a gnostic ideology (gnosticism is based on a consolidated and objective knowing, which considers divinity to be the soul of the world and admits a direct vision of its spirit, an absolute, direct knowledge of God—Guillermo Maci, personal communication): perversion is to gnosticism what obsessive neurosis is to ritual religion. The pervert disavows the Law of the Father in that it imposes access to the symbolic order sanctioning the difference between the sexes, and substitutes for it the law of his desire. Clavreul (1963, 1966), for his part, indicates the peculiar characteristics of the "perverse couple" and considers that the whole of the transference is permeated by a note of challenge. The discourse on love (and on all things) always assumes the character of an argument, a challenge, a rebellion.

These coincidences are interesting because they show that analytic practice, even on different theoretical bases, reveals a group of problems that are the very essence of perversion.

14.4 Clinical material

What I have said is illustrated by the clinical material of the young woman who was analysed for her homosexuality and her tormenting sensation of inner emptiness.

During the first months of analysis the experience that she could change and was changing gradually gained ground: the undifferentiated and entropic world of homosexuality as a way of erasing the differences (of subject and object, of man and woman, of adult and child) began to be more vivid and contrasting, more heterogenous. This renewed her hope and, at the same time, reinforced a pre-existing fear of madness. She asserted that she was not changing but rather than I put things into her head. And, in moments of internal peace never experienced before, there appeared as a categorical imperative the desire to rebel against me by going to bed with a woman (the norm is transformed into an impulse).

The fear of madness emerged in different contexts and the relation between perversion and psychosis was not merely of defence and content. Madness had diverse meanings: the experience of progress led her to manic exaltation or persecutory delusion; at other times the psychosis became linked to the erotization of the transference; or to a massive and indiscriminate regression into infancy (ecmnesia). ("I dreamed that I was travelling on a bus with Américo, Delia's [her younger sister's] ex-boy-friend, sitting on his lap, face to face. Américo had his fly open and was penetrating me; we were talking as if nothing were happening, so the other passengers would not notice." That is how she experienced the analytic dialogue at the time.) "In its most specific form, however, the madness arises from re-contacting reality: discovering the world in its infinite variety and richness is like an error of the senses: *reality must turn out to be madness-making for one who lives in a world of negative hallucinations*. In this sense, perversion is not a defence against psychosis but the psychosis itself" (Etchegoyen, 1970). I quote this paragraph because it accords with Clavreul as to the sense of reality in the perversions and with Meltzer's idea of dismantling. If this special distortion is not taken into account, technical errors are committed which confirm the perverse patient in his belief that psychoanalysis is a subtle form of indoctrination.

By the end of the first year she felt better, this being expressed by the singular process of dissociation we are describing: her confidence in me increased, and she feared I would envy her progress. She asserted she could only feel well provided she had no sexual life in order not to be envied (see the episode of the contact lenses). It was as if she were perfectly acquainted with the concept of aphanisis and the theory of primary envy!

Her definitive and contradictory assertions disconcerted me and made me uneasy. When I wanted to reduce them interpreting their obvious contradictions, I met with a stubborn resistance and with the reproach that I was imposing my ideas on her (and in part she was right).

At the beginning of the second year of analysis she had her first heterosexual relation and felt "mad with happiness". She came confused, dizzy and wanting to vomit: only at the end of the session and with a vivid fear of censure did she communicate this to me.

From that session onwards she had to overcome a strong resistance in order to come to the sessions; she felt humiliated by the progress of the treatment. At times she arrived well-disposed, but as soon as she saw me she would think she should not allow herself to be deceived, that she was coming to do battle and that I only wished to defeat and humiliate her (challenge, argument).

The following session illustrates her polemical and challenging tone. She had come from an examination and thought she had done well. She was still confused and with a tendency to become dizzy. She thought if the exam had been prolonged and she had been unable to attend the session, it would be very difficult to do so on Monday and perhaps she would not come any longer. She remembered that with Dr. X (her previous woman analyst) she began to miss sessions as a consequence of an exam and later abandoned analysis.

A: Perhaps you wish to interrupt treatment and not come any more: you fear that the situation with Dr. X will repeat itself?

P: You put ideas into my head that are completely strange to me. I do not feel in any way that I do not want to come here any more.

A: We will have to see why you feel that these ideas are strange, despite their being simply your own: *you* said that, had you not come today, it would have been more difficult to return on Monday.

P [*emphatically and arrogantly*]: I *tell* you this but I do not feel it, I think it but I do not feel it.

A: But this is a very equivocal argument: inasmuch as you decide that what you say you do not feel, I can no longer interpret anything. (*Precisely because she takes this attitude, this interpretation is not valid.*)

Months later the same polemical attitude appeared in connection with a dream, but I was better able to understand it. It was a period of time in which she alternated between homosexuality and heterosexuality, with a lively fear of madness and of genital penetration. In the dream *she was going to take an exam accompanied by her (female) friend who had slept at her house. Along the way they encountered a popular uprising and returned home frightened.* She remained dissatisfied at having been frightened. I interpreted that the dream seemed to express her conflict between homosexuality (the female friend who sleeps at her house) and heterosexuality (the exam). I suggested that the popular uprising must be the (feared) erection of the penis: she could not face it and took refuge in a secure place, the home, the mother, the girlfriend.

She accepted this with a cordial smile; but . . . another analyst could have interpreted something very different, perhaps that she evades social responsibility. Therefore psychoanalysis always seemed insufficient to her. It is not that my interpretation was incorrect, it was insufficient; it did not cover the whole range of problems.

After hesitating a moment she said that she had, in fact, a great conflict with the penis, a conflict whose principal note was disappointment. After having feared it so long, now she was excited and desired it; but the penis failed her because it never penetrated her well during erection. It was always too small, or her vagina too big; and she remained dissatisfied. (This disturbance is opposed to vaginism, less frequent and less studied. Garma indicated it to me in a personal communication.)

I suggested that she treated my interpretation as a penis that was too small, that left her dissatisfied; but she insisted that I always left the social aspect out.

I replied that, just as she criticized and even had contempt for my interpretation because it was small and insufficient, she also thought I had contempt for her material leaving things out. (I consider this interpretation as correct because it corrects the projection of her peculiar dissociation: *Verleugnung* [dismantling].)

She admitted that she tended to think me sectarian and tendentious. In another tone of voice, she said she thought the girl in the dream must be homosexual and added material confirming her fear of the erect penis.

Four years later she was married and began to consider the possibility of ending treatment, when her husband announced that he wanted to separate from her after almost three years of living together. She reacted with extreme despair, because she thought she could not live without him.

After the separation, she felt everything was crumbling. She feared a relapse into homosexuality, which did occur. During this period, her challenging and polemical tone obliged me to be very cautious in interpreting, and I observed my countertransference carefully in order to avoid projective counteridentification where possible (Grinberg, 1956, 1976a). Any interpretation was felt as disqualifying, with which in turn she would disqualify me. She asserted she was a defined and definite homosexual and that she had married exclusively to conquer my love (paternal love!). Simultaneously she characterized me as an antiquated and selfish mother who only sought to marry off her daughters to be rid of them. And that I should have seen to what extent her relation with Pablo was fictitious and should have interpreted it. I did not do it because I wanted to cure her at all costs. If I had done so—she admitted—she would have experienced me as her eternal "forbidder".

Her conviction about having to please me at all costs was compatible with the no less firm one that I did not accept her return to homosexuality, despite the fact that I always interpreted this new experience—because I felt it to be so—as a desire to decide for herself the destiny of her sexual identity. (Free of the desire to "cure her", at that moment I felt ready for the patient, in effect, to follow her own path. This had been difficult for me because her argument was directed, at heart, to showing me that, just because I had taken her on in analysis, I revealed my prejudice about homosexuality.) I reminded her of dreams in which she had fled from homosexuality as from a jail leaving a brother in her place (Etchegoyen, 1970, pp. 466–471), and I told her she had returned to it to achieve a more honest and authentic outcome.

The analytic dialogue was difficult for her, and an internal voice warned her to tell me only what pleased me. (The only thing that did not fit into her necessity to please me was free associating!)

She began to realize that neither homosexuality nor heterosexuality satisfied her and that, by putting herself in the place of the other to please him (or challenge him), she never found her own place.

When the new homosexual experience had exhausted itself, she again had the sensation of being cured. Her attitude to homosexuality, she said, had changed: it was no longer something bad and abominable but simply something from the past. During those months she had felt that within herself an image of man was restructuring itself which orientated her towards a heterosexual future.

After nine years of analysis her symptoms had abated, her object relations were more mature and she no longer denied her depressive feelings. (At the beginning of the treatment she would brand me as the ideologue of depression, with which she struck the Achilles heel of my scientific ideology.) Her type of transferential relation showed, however, the same characteristics as always, although they were attenuated. She roundly declared that I was not going to let her go or else that I was going to do so in order to get rid of her; and she oscillated between these convictions in an abrupt, changeable manner, without her previous assertions being usable as feedback for her. These characteristics became more ego-dystonic and rectifiable until, in the middle of one month of May, we agreed to terminate analysis at the end of that year, which aroused much anxiety in her.

A month after this agreement she came very late on a Friday and said she did not feel like coming. She recognized that she was angry and felt childish, selfish. She used to believe I was agreeable to everything as long as I could attend to her because she and I were one. Now, instead, she had to make an effort for me to analyse her. When she separated from Pablo that illusion of unity began to be shattered, as she did so following her own impulse and believing I opposed it.

P: When I separated from Pablo, I began to feel that you are not everything to me and I am not everything to you. I do not know how I decide what will please you. I have always been very sure of what would please or displease you about me; but now I realize that this opinion is very subjective. (*I consider that these associations show an important rectification.*)

A: Separating from Pablo was also separating from me, abandoning that idea of absolute accord that unified us. (*One of the reasons for the argument is, precisely, to restore that unity.*)

The following session she arrived late, hostile and anxious, saying it was very difficult for her to speak to me.

P [*with emphasis*]: Today you are not an analyst for me but someone who wishes me to come here all the days of my life, all the years of life left to me. [*Silence.*] Listening to myself, I think I am mad, that it cannot be that I feel this. However, it is what I feel. At the same time I think I am trying to distort everything, because I do not know why I do not want to think that, in reality, you have told me that I can go. (*The disturbance was the same: Verleugnung [dismantling], but now it is ego-dystonic.*)

A: That idea must come from somewhere. (*I preferred to stimulate her association rather than saturate her with an interpretation that was obvious in any case.*)

P: I think I cannot understand that you tell me I can go. Because what meaning is my life going to have when I no longer come here? Then again, something leads me to feel you do not want to help me, you want to keep me locked up here.

A: That seems to be the moment when you attribute to me your own desire always to come here. (*I begin to correct the projection.*)

P: I do not feel my own desire always to come here. That is why I feel you as someone who wants to keep me locked up, instead of feeling like someone who does not want to leave you in peace, which is what I should feel (*depressive anxiety*). I am afraid of feeling unprotected if I am not locked up.

A: When you feel that I want to make you come here all your life, you feel locked up, but more protected than when I tell you to go.

P: When I tell you that you want to keep me locked up I say something crazy; but the truth is that at that moment you become someone else.

A: I become someone else when you get inside me to feel protected and locked up. (*Here I can interpret the projective identification specifically, with the consequent loss of identity and claustrophobia.*)

She could accept this interpretation without conflict and completed it, saying that, in feeling mad, she again placed me in the position of having to keep on taking care of her.

Nevertheless, in the following session, obstinate and anxious, she affirmed that if I agreed to let her go, it was because I wanted to part from her, and I did not love her. She felt childish and silly. (The childishness could now be expressed, but it did not dominate the ego. She feared, at the same time, that I would modify my position, seeing she felt badly. I told her that the idea that I was not ever going to let her go preserved her from the *disillusion* she now felt—Winnicott, 1953.)

P: It is as if I had lived ten years in order to have analysis, and for you. I am afraid that this space will bring back again the emptiness of my previous life, and that everything will lose meaning. I think that in the depths of my heart I always thought you would never let me go.

14.5 Final considerations

I have presented this material with the intention of offering empirical data on the development of the transference perversion, the technical means that permit its resolution and the most frequent errors in its management.

The erotization of the analytic link, a peculiar type of narcissistic object relation that tries to make permanent an illusory subject–object unity, the utilization of speech and of silence to provoke excitement and impatience in the analyst are traits that appear with chronometric regularity in the analysis of these patients, and equally a challenging and polemical attitude, usually latent, which must be discovered and referred to the dissociation of the ego, to the subject–object confusion and to the transformation of the instinct into ideology. For the analyst, this last is a decisive factor.

It is important to indicate that the egoic dissociation, the ideological problems, the argument and the challenge *persist during the entire course of the analysis*. I noticed that right up to the end the patient maintained the perverse characteristics of the transference, although at a level that gradually approached normality. She remained faithful to her own guidelines, while as the cure progressed I waited in vain, dominated by the idea of "transference neurosis", for the transference to pass from the perverse to the neurotic: a very convincing reason, in my view, to maintain the concept of *transference perversion*.

14.6 Transference addiction

Transference addiction has attracted less attention than neurosis, psychosis and perversion, perhaps because few analysts treat addicts (despite the fact that the scourge is so widespread nowadays), and because it is not easy to define a special type of transference link in patients like these, in whom psychological mechanisms are combined with the physiopathological effect of the drug. A peculiar difficulty with the addict is that if the taking of drugs is not checked, analysis becomes difficult, and if it is interfered with, analytical neutrality suffers.

In my opinion a great obstacle to the definition of "transference addiction" lies in the imprecise limits of the psychopathological picture within which it must be located. Firstly both the classic authors (Fenichel 1945a) and those of our day (Dupetit, 1982) consider that addiction exists *with* drugs and *without* drugs. Food, the cinema, reading (unfortunately less than previously!), sport, games of chance, work, television, in fact any human activity can bear the stamp of addiction, and we must not forget that in his letter 79 (22 December 1897), Freud tells Fliess that masturbation is the primal addiction, for which all the others are substitutes. It must be added that it is not the same thing to be addicted to alcohol or morphine as to marijuana, tobacco, coffee, tea, or yerba mate. I am inclined to think that the mental structure is the same in every case but the clinical consequences are different. This is where the quantitative factors of the psychological conflict and the pharmacological action of the drug play a principal role. As Goodman and Gilman (1945) point out in their well-known treatise, in the opinion of many pharmacologists only the phenanthrenic alkaloids of opium create physiological dependence. Although it is certain that psychological dependence on barbiturates, cocaine and amphetamines can be very great, physiological dependence is not as clearly demonstrable as in the case of the phenanthrenic derivatives of opium.

In this context, at any rate, we consider as an addict the patient who turns to alcohol and/or drugs as his main recourse in order to maintain a psychological balance and gain relief from anxiety, and a feeling of pleasure and well-being. When the drug is used to counteract the negative effect that appears as its action ends, a vicious circle is formed, which is very important in the establishment of addiction. The addict's craving is by definition impossible to satisfy insofar as it does not arise from necessity, but from greed.

The great majority of authors consider that the addict's pregenital conflicts (oral and anal) are serious, and that they are invariably amplified by very strong aggressive impulses. Sadism and masochism do not only exist in the unconscious of these patients, but also, quite openly, in their conduct; and they can be triggered not only by frustration but also by envy. At the same time, as Abraham (1908b) and Ferenczi (1914) point out, the addict struggles against very strong and frightening homosexual tendencies. Many authors, such as Fenichel, accord extreme importance to narcissism and to the vulnerability of self-esteem. In the addict, as Fenichel (1945a) says, auto-erotic (preferably oral) satisfaction and narcissistic satisfaction meet.

Beginning with Freud and his immediate collaborators, authors concerned with this subject agree on the importance of oral factors, narcissism and impulses destructive of themselves and others; and almost all of them compare the periods of taking and abstaining from the drug with the cycles of manic–depressive psychosis.

Sándor Radó (1926) maintained that the model and precursor of the genital orgasm of the adult is the baby's satisfaction while suckling (*alimentary orgasm*). It is this early satisfaction that the addict, dominated by his morbid craving, urgently seeks from the drug, which transports him to what Radó calls the *pharmacotoxic orgasm*. In my view, Radó's "morbid craving" is greed or envy, which are basically the same.

In general, authors think that alcohol and drugs are, for the addict, an idealized object and at the same time a bad, persecuting object. On the basis of Melanie Klein's theory of positions, Herbert A. Rosenfeld (1960) maintains that there is in the addict a splitting of the internal object into idealized and persecutory, logically accompanied by a parallel splitting of the self. Though Rosenfeld considers that addicts generally have a structure similar to manic–depressive psychosis, in which the drug acts as a sort of artificial mania, protecting the addict from depressive pain and from persecutory anxieties, he maintains that the addict's basic conflicts have to do with a fixation at the paranoid–schizoid position, in which the object is deeply split.

The addict always takes an extremely contradictory position with respect to his drug and the condition it causes in him, in which exaggerated idealization and the most violent rejection co-exist. The speed with which the drug changes, in the addict's mind, an idealized object that protects from all possible pain into a persecutory object that threatens the most cruel destruction is comparable only with the fluidity of the transference link, which fluctuates rapidly and continuously from love to hate, from tenderness to the most extreme violence. Susana Dupetit (1988) points out the addict's characteristic fear of tender feelings, since they imply dependence and emotional surrender. As soon as they appear they trigger off an immediate defensive reaction of destructive, criminal hate, which not infrequently shows itself in "the gaze of the tiger".

Just as the addict's link with the drug is changeable and extreme, his transference to the analyst rapidly changes its nature, and this is often accompanied by renewed drug-taking and acting out.

By opposite but converging paths transference addiction becomes a bond in which the analyst is both drug and anti-drug; the addict can really relate to his analyst only when he transforms him into the drug (saving and destroying); and, at the same time, the bond of (healthy) analytical dependence is misunderstood (mainly through envy) as a threat of the worst addiction. The transference conflict then leads continually to the drug, and therein lies both the danger and the hope of the psychoanalysis of addiction.

These conflicts often cause a negative therapeutic reaction, which, when severe, becomes very difficult to deal with, all the more so when added to the pharmacological effect of the drug. In the most severe cases, psychoanalytical treatment can be carried out only in hospital, taking a series of precautions (clinico-psychiatric detoxification, adjuvant family therapy, etc.). It goes without saying that addiction to phenanthrenic compounds of *papaver somniferum* requires detoxification treatment with hospitalization; similarly, alcoholism, when it has reached Jellinek's (1953) chronic phase. On the other hand, the heavy drinker and the alcoholic in the prodromic phase (when the palimpsest or blackout appears) can be treated as out-patients. In Jellinek's crucial or basic phase the treatment of the alcoholic in the consulting-room is extremely problematic, if not impossible. Simmel (1948) also thinks that the dipsomaniac must be treated in a clinic, while the other types (the social drinker, the reactive drinker, and up to a point the neurotic drinker, in his classification) can be handled in the consulting-room.

As we shall see further on, the analytical process develops from a mature and reciprocal bond of dependence between patient and analyst, which is called "working alliance", and thanks to which the condition that brings the patient for treatment can be analysed. A distinctive feature of transference addiction is that analytical dependence tends to be converted into an addictive bond, in such a way that the analytical relationship swings like a pendulum between dependence and addiction. It is reasonable to expect that the addict will take the analyst's (good) attitude towards him for an addiction, and in this sense we have to interpret that he believes that the analyst depends on him as on a drug (David Rosenfeld, 1972; Dupetit, 1988). At the same time, as Rosenfeld (1972) points out, if the analysand receives the interpretations like a drug and not like something equivalent to the original object (the breast), the analyst's task will be to discriminate between the two types of relationship.

In an interesting study, Sheila Navarro de López (1980) points out the omnipotent control that the addict maintains over the processes of introjection and projection of the object, the models for which are ingestion and defaecation. The object is reified and converted into a drug (faeces). The analyst follows that course and finally becomes the addict of the drug, which is the analysand. This gives rise to a situation that is particularly painful for the analyst, but which also makes it possible for him to interpret projective identification. In the case reported, the analyst became addicted to her patient to the single end of satisfying her obsession to cure and cleanse her—that is, using her, by reification, as an object-thing for the solution of her own problems. In this way the goodness of the repairing object is replaced (through envy), by the guilty needs to cleanse herself through the patient (ibid., p. 1158).

We have seen earlier (section 12.6) that even transference love can take on an addictive character. We may add now that the analytical situation itself can turn into addiction, which is all the more difficult to resolve when the addictive urge is masked by a manifest desire to be analysed "for as long as necessary".

In an interesting work, Elsa H. Garzoli (1981) warns of the analyst's danger of addiction in face of the dreams that the patient offers him. In the case she presents, the analysand (who exhibited clear symptoms of addiction to milk, coffee and aspirin, as well as alcohol and amphetamines), offered her, in a bright pleasant voice, dreams that were truly fascinating, sometimes horrific in tone, and often coloured, especially in red and blue. The analyst began to notice that with these dreams the analysand had established a stereotyped rhythm in the sessions, into which she herself was drawn, in that she let herself be swept along more by the attraction of the narrative than by the psychotherapeutic process—which, moreover, had stopped. As the author wisely points out, because of our real dependence on the dream as undeniably privileged material, the royal road to the unconscious, there is a very great danger of falling into the trap of countertransference addiction.

We may say in conclusion that the analytical setting lends itself to the insidious formation of an addictive bond, and that we must take care lest it should cause massive interference with the course and termination of the analytical process.

CHAPTER FIFTEEN

Early transference

[1] Pre-oedipal phase or early stages of the Oedipus complex

15.1 Recapitulation

In the previous chapters we reviewed the concept of transference neurosis, attempting to give it a more specific meaning in comparing and contrasting it with other psychopathological forms. As the reader will remember, there are authors, for example Sandler et al. (1973), who prefer to speak of transference neurosis and special forms of transference. For them a transference psychosis proper does not exist, but, rather, a transference neurosis, on which psychosis sets its special seal. We take the opposite position and assert that the transferential phenomenon in psychosis is based on a special and indigenous psychopathology. If we wish to understand the transference in the psychotic and the psychotic himself, we have to discover the corresponding specific form of transference.

It has taken time for this concept to gain ground, and yet, once it is understood, one realizes that it could be no other way. What can be expected of an addict other than that he will try to maintain with the analyst a link proper to his illness, taking him as a drug?

We said, further, that there never exists a pure picture of neurosis but that in each case there are always neurotic aspects and psychotic, psychopathic, addictive and perverse ones; and, consequently, there is always going to be a transference psychosis and a transference psychopathy, and so on, concomitant with the transference neurosis in the strict sense. The ingredients change in each case and also moment to moment, from session to session, minute by minute, and this compels us to be constantly attentive, paying attention first of all to phenomena that dominate the clinical picture and which in fact characterize it in each circumstance. The other methodology, on the other hand, is more dangerous in that it can lead us to impute to the patient the neurotic type of functioning even if it is not the one that fits him. In other words, the more precise we are in describing the facts, the better we can understand our patients.

For tactical reasons, we may try at a given moment to reinforce the neurotic aspects of the transference, which are the most accessible ones. But we will have to be fully aware that we are doing something that has to do with the *management* of the transferential situation, and not strictly with its analysis. On the other hand, as by definition the transference neurosis is the part of the patient closest to reality, everything that can legitimately reinforce it will be to the good, so long as reinforcing is not confused with stimulating.

The theme of this chapter, *early transference*, implies a new widening of the concept of transference (or of transference neurosis). It is another *special form* of transference, which does not refer to the psychopathological configuration but to development, to evolutionary criteria.

To begin with, it is advisable to realize that, through the sole fact of dealing with it, we are already taking a position on this theme—that is, that we think this transference exists and that it can be defined, characterized and studied via psychoanalytic methods. Although this is still a controversial point, I think there is a recognizable tendency to accept it more and more.

15.2   Infantile neurosis

As Freud and later Wilhelm Reich in his *Character Analysis* (1933) said, neurosis in the adult always has its roots in childhood, in the so-called *infantile neurosis*; and this is what appears in analysis as transference neurosis in the strict sense.

The transference neurosis is indissolubly linked to the oedipal situation. The level of neurotic integration is reached when a stage of development—great not so much in time but in effort—is conquered, taking us to the point where the ego can be differentiated from the object, and the objects from each other. We are able to recognize a father and a mother, towards whom we have to establish a relational strategy. This type of link, which, as Freud showed, is linked strongly to instinctive factors, is what we call the *Oedipus complex*. As Elizabeth R. Zetzel (1968) says, only once the dyadic stage of development has been passed is the oedipal situation really able to arise. From this point of view, the Oedipus complex implies a great degree of maturation, in that, having resolved the problems with each parent separately, one is capable of establishing a relation with both simultaneously. The transference neurosis corresponds strictly to this level of development.

Many authors, particularly ego psychologists, think that only if this degree of development has been reached is psychoanalytic treatment feasible, because then the future analysand will be able to distinguish reality from fantasy, the external from the internal, or, in more technical terms, transference neurosis from therapeutic alliance. If this stage of development has not been reached, the individual will be unanalysable, because he is not going to cooperate with us and because the hazards of the analytic situation will certainly lead him, via regression, to the unresolved problems of his early life.

15.3   Pre-oedipal development

Certainly no one doubts that there is a psychological development that extends from birth (or earlier) up until the child enters into the oedipal conflict, just as we have described it. But what happens *before* the oedipal conflict? It is just there that the *pre-oedipal* stage is located. It embraces the first two years of life and corresponds to the pregenital—the oral and the anal—states of development.

The importance of this stage is clear to everyone. Freud concerned himself with it repeatedly, particularly in his works on feminine sexuality (1931b, 1933a, Lecture 33), where he states that in the woman it is particularly important. Ruth Mack Brunswick began the formal study of this stage with her case on delusions of jealousy published in 1928.

The case was that of a married woman of 30, who was referred for treatment because of strong feelings of jealousy and a serious suicide attempt. She was the youngest of five siblings, and her mother had died when she was three years old. Her eldest sister, ten years her senior, had brought her up, acting as substitute mother. This sister, Louise, promiscuous and mentally feeble, was enuretic all her life and died of dementia paralytica, juvenile form, in a psychiatric hospital in Vienna.

The patient married at the age of 28, and shortly afterwards the delusion of jealousy began, with the idea that her husband had had relations with her stepmother. These ideas soon dominated her completely, and she began to feel that people in the street were looking at her.

Shortly after the death of his first wife, the patient's father had remarried, and with the arrival of the stepmother the patient was sent to the country with distant relatives, where she remained from the age of four until she was eleven. However, when she was five, she was brought back from the country to spend some time at home. Three years after her final return home, her sister, then aged 24, entered the psychiatric hospital where she later died.

The analysis was brief—it only lasted two and a half months; but undoubtedly it was intense, and the analyst did not refrain from employing the active technique when she thought it necessary. Based on the dreams and the transference, a period of sexual games with the sister could be reconstructed. They began when the patient was two and were interrupted when she was four and left home. The games, which consisted in reciprocal clitoral masturbation in bed and in the bath, were reproduced in many of the dreams during analysis, similar to the one transcribed as follows:

> A person the patient calls Louise, but who in all other respects is me, puts her on the bed with her. The patient lies with her head on her sister's feet in order to reach the genitals better. Louise is about twelve years old, and the patient is about two and is very small. They masturbate each other simultaneously. Louise teaches her to keep the labia open with one hand and to rub the clitoris with the other. The entire act takes place under the covers. Suddenly she has the most intense orgasm she can remember, a convulsion of her whole body, followed a moment later by the same reaction on her sister's part. Then Louise takes her lovingly into her arms and embraces her. The dream has a sensation of absolute reality. [Mack Brunswick, 1928b]

Later on she remembered that when she returned home at the age of five, the sexual games with her sister had taken on a different character, with vaginal (not only clitoral) stimulation.

In reaching her conclusions on this case, Mack Brunswick considers that the patient's tie with her sister occurred at a very early phase of development, when she was one year old, a period during which, because of the mother's illness, the sister took charge of her upbringing.

The author also points out that the most surprising factor in this case is the total absence of the Oedipus complex. The material is radically pre-oedipal, and the father does not come into it at all. This is not a regression from the Oedipus complex, Mack Brunswick states, but a fixation to a previous state, which can only be explained by the early and profound homosexual trauma that supervened at the pre-oedipal level.

15.4   The pre-oedipal phase
of relation with the mother

Mack Brunswick followed her investigation for a decade in close contact with Freud, and she published it in the same issue of the *Psycho-Analytic Quarterly* (1940) in which the death of the master was commemorated. For the author, the starting point of her investigation is the delusion of jealousy of 1928, which revealed rich and unsuspected information concerning a period hitherto unknown, preceding the Oedipus complex and therefore named pre-oedipal.

In this work, "The Pre-Oedipal Phase of the Libido Development", Mack Brunswick (1940) defines that stage as the period during which there exists an exclusive relation of the mother with the child. The child certainly recognizes other individuals in the external world, and especially the father, but not yet as a rival.

At the beginning, what best defines the object relation is the *active–passive* polarity. The mother's role is active, not feminine; and both boy and girl assume that all people have genitalia like their own. This is the stage Jones called *protophallic* at the Congress of Wiesbaden in 1932 (see Jones, "The Phallic Phase", 1933). With the discovery that there are beings with different genital organs, a second pair of antitheses is established— the *phallic–castrated* (*deuterophallic*, according to Jones) stage. For Mack Brunswick the phallic period begins at the end of the third year, when the child is interested in the difference between the sexes and develops the Oedipus complex, with the peculiarities that Freud establishes for boy and girl.

Although Mack Brunswick closely follows Freud's ideas on the phallic phase (1923e) and feminine sexuality, she proposes significant changes that bring her closer to Klein on certain points—for example, her assertion that the desire for a baby precedes in both sexes the desire (of a woman) to have a penis. ("Contrary to our earlier ideas, the penis wish is not exchanged for the baby wish which, as we have seen, has indeed long preceded it": 1928a, *The Psycho-Analytic Reader*, p. 245.) However, Mack Brunswick explains that this is due to a (primary) identification with the active mother and therefore has nothing to do with the Oedipus complex, nor with the genital instinct. (For a more detailed comparison between Mack Brunswick and Klein, see Etchegoyen et al., 1982b.)

The third, *masculine–feminine*, polarity is only reached for Mack Brunswick with the sexual maturation of adolescence and the discovery by both sexes of the vagina.

15.5   The early stages of the Oedipus complex

Melanie Klein's investigation develops a little earlier than Ruth Mack Brunswick's. In various works she describes the conflicts of the child in the first two years of life. One paper among others written during that decade is salient on this point: "Early Stages of the Oedipus Conflict", presented at the Innsbruck Congress in 1927 and published in the *International Journal of Psycho -Analysis* (1928) .

Klein uses the term *early development* rather than "pre-oedipal development" because in her view the Oedipus complex appears earlier than Freud thought: she describes it at the end of the first year of life (1928), halfway through the first year (1932) and at three months (1945, 1946). To differentiate it from the one Freud describes in the third year of life, it is called *early Oedipus complex*, where the objects are not total, the father and the mother are not differentiated and the entire drama occurs inside the mother's body with the so-called *combined parent figure*—the mother's body, which contains the father's penis. In other words, for Klein the child establishes a very precocious relation with the mother's body and as he begins to discern a special object inside it, which is the father's penis, he already enters into the oedipal situation.

At Innsbruck Melanie Klein proclaimed that the Oedipus complex begins towards the end of the first year, and she described the relation of the child to the mother's body where, together with the anal phase and the cathexis of the faeces, what she calls the *feminine phase* establishes itself—a phase of fundamental value in the development of both sexes.

The concept of early transference is the natural corollary of these hypotheses, although the idea became more refined and precise over the years. (It is important to point out that already in 1929, in "Personification in the Play of Children", Melanie Klein presented an original concept of the transference, which we will deal with shortly; according to this concept, transference has to do with personification, a double mechanism of dissociation and projection, thanks to which the ego is able to lessen the internal conflict with the superego and the id, placing in the analyst the internal imagos that provoke anxiety in the ego.)

15.6   *The origins of the transference*

Klein bases the concept of early transference on what she considers empirical facts, which she discovered in the 1920s with her play technique; but the formalization of her findings came later. The article entitled "The Origins of Transference" was presented at the Amsterdam Congress of 1951 and published in the *International Journal of Psycho-Analysis* (1952a). It is particularly clear and systematic and is the only one on this theme.

This is noteworthy, because, with or without justification, one of the major objections to Klein is that she interprets the transference too much The analysts who, in Buenos Aires or Montevideo, abandoned Kleinian theory to return to Freud or to approach Lacan, took note of the fact that they themselves first began to change by placing less emphasis on the transference. This change in the praxis was supported by various theoretical arguments—for example, that one must attend more to history than to the present, that one must reconstruct more than one must interpret, that one must interpret the *transferences* with the important figures in reality no less than with the analyst, and so forth. This controversy is dealt with further on, when we come to study interpretation; but here we can say that these positions are quite ideological. The truth is, we should never interpret on the basis of suppositions, and it is just as erroneous to interpret the transference where it is absent as to ignore it.

Supported by Freud's classic definition in the postscript to the "Dora" case, Klein maintains that the transference operates throughout life and influences all human relations. In analysis the past is gradually relived and the deeper we go into the unconscious and the further back we can take the analytic process, the greater will be our comprehension of the transference (see Klein, 1975, Vol. 3, p. 48). In this way, Klein gives a universal value to the phenomenon of transference and advocates its study at the most archaic levels of the mind.

The basic assertion in this paper is that the early stages of development appear in the transference, and we can therefore grasp and reconstruct them. This assurance is not new, it implicitly informs the whole Kleinian *oeuvre*; but here it is specifically explained. The transference is a fitting, sensible and trustworthy instrument with which to reconstruct the early past. A few years later, in the first chapter of *Envy and Gratitude* (1957), she calls those first reconstructions "memories in feelings". In that chapter, and supported by Freud's "Constructions in Analysis" (1937d), she states that the reconstructive method of psychoanalysis is valid for elucidating the relation of the child with the breast. Her disputed affirmation that there exists a primary envy of the breast is based precisely on this, because she sees it appear in the transference and from there she reconstructs it. (Without having intended it, I am refuting the arguments of those who say Melanie Klein interprets and does not reconstruct. The truth is that Klein reconstructs a great deal, sometimes too much, but her reconstructions are not always similar to Freud's as he does not take account of early development. When we reconstruct early development we do not recover memories [screen memories] but engrams.)

15.7   Narcissism and object relation

The theoretical basis of this article is that the object relation appears at the outset, with the beginning of life. Klein thus reveals, for the first time, a discrepancy with Freud and Anna Freud that originated much earlier on. Not only does she reject without further ado the theory of primary narcissism, but she goes further in claiming that mental life cannot occur in a vacuum, without object relations. Where there is no object relation, by definition there is no psychology either. There are, then, auto-erotic and narcissistic *states* but not *stages*.

> The hypothesis that a stage extending over several months precedes object-relations implies that—except for the libido attached to the infant's own body—impulses, phantasies, anxieties and defences either are not present in him, or are not related to an object, that is to say, they would operate *in vacuo*. The analysis of very young children has taught me that there is no instinctual urge, no anxiety situation, no mental process which does not involve objects, external or internal; in other words, object-relations are at the *centre* of emotional life. Further-

more, love and hatred, phantasies, anxieties and defences are also operative from the beginning and are *ab initio* indivisibly linked with object relations. This insight showed me many phenomena in a new light. [Klein, 1975, Vol. 3, pp. 52–53]

Klein took this firm position as a result of what she observed in her first years of work with the play technique, and it became, finally, a formal, epistemological position that attempts to give account of the problem by redefining it. Although I am inclined to follow Klein on this point, I consider the problem far from being resolved. The truth is that, as we approach the origins, the difficulties are greater, and the analytic method *par excellence*—that is, the reconstruction of the past through the transference situation—becomes more fallible. On the other hand, one cannot trust that other methods can encompass the problem, precisely because they lack the very essence of psychoanalysis: the transference, the intersubjective phenomenon. This does not mean that the other methods are in any way to be disdained; they are worthwhile in their own right and can be an important aid for psychoanalysis, but we cannot accord to them what is inherent in our discipline.

In her paper Klein states emphatically that she has held this theory for many years, but in fact she makes it explicit only at this point. It is probable that Klein vacillated more than she thought in abandoning the theory of primary narcissism, or at least in announcing this. Halfway through the 1930s, when Joan Riviere travelled to Vienna to read "On the Genesis of Psychical Conflict in Earliest Infancy" on 5 May 1936 (Riviere, 1936b), it is evident that it was going to be difficult for her to abandon the hypothesis of primary narcissism. What is significant is that she was still hesitant when she published this paper in *Developments in Psychoanalysis* (Klein et al., 1952). (The note in which she restates her now weakened adherence to the hypothesis of primary narcissism is on p. 41 of that book and is dated 1950.) If Riviere can be taken as an authorized spokeswoman for the Kleinian school, then this means that these doubts persisted until just before the Amsterdam Congress. When he intervened in the memorable polemic between Joan Riviere and Robert Wälder, Balint (1937) said that the theory of primary narcissism unified Vienna (Anna Freud) and London (Melanie Klein) to some degree. It is the Budapest school (Ferenczi) that is not afraid of rejecting it, with what Balint, following Ferenczi (1924), calls *primary object love*.

Finally, I think (as Balint does) that the decision to abandon primary narcissism as a hypothesis occurs in Budapest before it does in London. Although her work is orientated in this direction, Klein does not easily decide to abandon the Freudian theories. (For greater detail, see Etchegoyen, 1981a.) On the other hand, we should not forget that *Thalassa's* "passive (or primary) object love" is basically an attempt to reconstruct the symbiotic bond with the mother, and is therefore not a complete object relation.

15.8   *Transference and unconscious fantasy*

The field widens considerably if the theory of unconscious fantasy is used to explain the transference. This theory, formalized by Susan Isaacs in the Controversial Discussions of the British Psycho-Analytical Society in 1943 and 1944 (published in the *International Journal of Psycho-Analysis* in 1948), constitutes the backbone of Kleinian investigation. (The famous *Controversial Discussions* have been published—at last—under the expert supervision of Pearl King and Riccardo Steiner.) According to Isaacs, unconscious fantasy is an activity that is always present. If this is the case, then we can interpret each time we grasp how the unconscious fantasy is operating at a given moment. This gives the analyst greater freedom to interpret, without the need for a rupture in the discourse, as Lacan, for example, would say. The Kleinian analyst does not have to await that rupture of the discourse, because the fantasy underlies the most coherent manifest content. Beyond my speaking with faultless logic, beneath what I say my fantasies exist at the level of a primary process.

As a typical expression of the *Ucs* system, unconscious fantasy always operates, at some level, with primary objects and with that portion of the unsatisfied libido that has recharged them via regression (introversion). From this it follows, syllogistically, that the transference is always alluded to and is, to a variable degree, always present. This is why Klein stated in Amsterdam that the transference operates not only if the patient alludes directly or indirectly to the analyst—or, let us add, in the ruptures of the discourse—but *permanently*, and that the issue is to know how to detect it.

15.9   *Instincts and objects in the transference*

From what we have just seen, it is understandable why Kleinian analysts interpret the transference to a greater degree, but in addition they attend more than others do to the negative transference and also cover early development.

Characteristic of Kleinian technique is the emphasis on the negative transference. Its detractors criticize its insistence on it; its defenders say they simply do not reject it. Beyond this controversy, what remains is that the Kleinians interpret the negative transference to a greater extent.

From her early works onwards, Melanie Klein maintained that the negative transference should be interpreted without delay or vacillation. (Wilhelm Reich, with a different theoretical background, said the same thing in his Technical Seminar in the Vienna Society in those years.) Klein's polemic on this point with Anna Freud became more evident. Anna Freud, in her *Einführung in die Technik der Kinderanalyse* (1927), said that the negative transference should be avoided in the analysis of children, and that it is indispensable to reinforce positive sentiments in the child and to guide him with pedagogic measures. Melanie Klein, on the

other hand, held from the beginning—and never changed her opinion—
that the analyst should always interpret impartially both the positive
transference and the negative one, whether the patient is child or adult,
neurotic or psychotic. It is interesting to note that, on this issue, Anna
Freud took a very strict position. When Hermine von Hug-Hellmuth read
her pioneering paper, "On the Technique of Child-analysis" (1921) at the
Sixth International Congress at the Hague in September 1920, she advo-
cated the interpretation of both the positive and the negative transference.
On the other hand, Anna Freud agrees with Hug-Hellmuth on the necessity for pedagogic measures in the analysis of children, which Klein disputed fervently in the Symposium on Child Analysis in May 1927 at the
British Psycho-Analytical Society.

In understanding the transference phenomenon via the theoretical instrument of unconscious fantasy, Klein states, lastly, that aspects linked to
early psychic development can be recovered in the transference. This implies that there are areas of transference that have to do with the breast,
with the penis, with the combined parent figure. The field has thus widened noticeably.

The convergence of these three factors—the continuous action of unconscious fantasy, the interpretation of the negative transference and the
existence of an early transference—explains why we Kleinians interpret
the transference more than others. Certainly these three principles can be
questioned, but we cannot be accused of inconsistency between our principles and our praxis.

In the following section we consider how Klein conceives the so-called
early transference.

15.10 Paranoid and depressive anxieties
in the transference

The central thesis of the Amsterdam paper is that transference stems from
the persecutory and depressive anxieties that initiate development.

At the beginning of life, the child has a dyadic relation with the
mother's breast, in which the mechanisms of dissociation predominate.
These determine the division of the object into two—good and bad—with
the ensuing splitting of the ego and the impulses. The love instincts are
directed and at the same time are projected into the good breast, which is
transformed into the baby's centre of love and source of life, whereas the
hate is projected into the bad breast, which arouses persecutory anxiety
and (logically) aggression. During this period, which forms the *paranoid–
schizoid position* and covers the first three or four months of life, the subject
is basically egocentric, and the preoccupation with the object is absent. (As
we know, Klein attenuated this claim in her 1948 essay on the origins of
anxiety and guilt.)

Melanie Klein's (early) object-relation theory can be summed up in just one phrase: the child feels every experience as the result of the action of objects. From this it follows, logically, that the objects will be classified into good and bad according to whether their actions are experienced as positive or negative, beneficent or maleficent, with their correlate in the subject, the splitting of the ego and the polarization of the life and death instincts. This type of relation, in which persecutory anxiety and splitting predominate, is accompanied by feelings of extreme omnipotence and mechanisms of denial and idealization of the good object (to check the persecution).

This situation changes as the processes of integration take root. The good breast that gives and the bad breast that frustrates begin to approach each other in the baby's mind, and, in consequence, feelings of love for the former begin to be assimilated with feelings of hate for the latter. This brings about a radical change towards the object, which Melanie Klein calls the *depressive position*. What best defines the two Kleinian positions is, without doubt, the nature of the anxiety, centred first in the fear of destruction of the ego and then on the fear that the (good) object will be destroyed, and with it the ego itself.

In Melanie Klein's view the depressive position is basic to development; it forms the psyche and the relations between subject and object and with the world. It implies the capacity to symbolize and to make reparation, to separate itself from the object and allow it autonomy.

Together with the depressive position the (early) Oedipus complex begins, as the integration processes we have just described imply on the one hand the autonomy of the object, and on the other the recognition of the third party.

From another point of view, we can say that for Klein development is based on the processes of projection and introjection, which operate from the beginning of life: the former condition the relation to the external object and external reality, and the latter that to the internal object and psychic reality (fantasy). And both influence each other, as projection and introjection function continuously.

It is precisely under the aegis of these two basic processes that the object relation is constituted and its two areas—the external world (reality) and the internal world (fantasy)—are demarcated. Therefore for Klein the transference has to do with introjective and projective mechanisms, as Ferenczi (1909) and Nunberg (1951) claimed, and therefore she also maintains that the transference originates in the very processes that determine the object relation in the earliest stages of development (see *Writings*, 1975, Vol. 3, p. 53). This is why Klein reaches the conclusion that the transference should be understood not only as comprising direct references to the analyst in the material of the analysand, since the early transference, in that it sinks its roots into the deepest strata of the mind, leads to an appreciation of a much broader and more comprehensive phenomenon (ibid., p. 55).

CHAPTER SIXTEEN

Early transference

[2] Primitive emotional development

16.1 *Introduction*

As we saw in chapter 15, the term *early transference* covers the most primitive, most remote aspects of the transference link. This is a complex and controversial theme because there is no agreement among investigators of early development. Moreover, whatever that development may be, it is still necessary to see whether it can be ascertained and resolved in the analysis.

We followed the course of two great investigations, begun by Melanie Klein and Ruth Mack Brunswick towards the end of the 1920s. I do not think I am being partial in affirming that Klein's work is more far-reaching than is Mack Brunswick's; due to her illness and death, the latter's work did not develop fully.

Thanks to the play technique she developed, Melanie Klein, with her work in the 1920s and 1930s, opened up a path that led in the 1950s to "The Origins of Transference" (1952a). Although she was strenuously opposed, the presence of this theme in psychoanalysis today seems to vindicate her. We must remember that Anna Freud, the other great figure in the psychoanalysis of children, thought that it was in no way possible to gain access to this area, a view shared by many enlightened analysts, such as Robert Wälder (1937) on his trip to London.

Other investigators followed Melanie Klein in dealing with this theme, corroborating some of her points of view, correcting or refuting others. Among the main ones are Winnicott, Meltzer, Margaret Mahler, Bion, Kohut, Bleger, Kernberg, Esther Bick and Balint. Winnicott, whom we will take as the axis of our exposition, came up with an attractive and original development. We will consider the others in relation to some specific problems of psychoanalytic technique.

Without wishing to reopen polemics that now represent closed issues, I will say that at three points in her career Melanie Klein met with strong opposition from the psychoanalytic establishment: (1) when she presented her first works in Berlin at the beginning of the 1920s, (2) some ten years later, when she introduced the concept of the depressive position, and (3) towards the end of her life, when she proposed the theory of primary envy.

The emphasis Klein placed on oral sadism and her way of interpreting sexual fantasies directly to children caused a stir in Berlin, although Klein was only confirming the findings of Abraham, undisputed leader of the German analysts. These tensions, however, were of brief duration, because Klein left Berlin and settled in London in 1926, soon after Abraham's death in December 1925.

In London there was a time, until the mid-1930s, when the entire British Psycho-Analytical Society was grouped around Melanie Klein. But when she wrote "A Contribution to the Psychogenesis of Manic-Depressive States" for the Lucerne Congress of 1934 (published in 1935), many ceased to follow her; Glover declared himself openly in disagreement, considering that she had removed herself completely from Freud and from psychoanalysis.

The third moment of tension occurred in 1955, when Klein presented her work on envy at the Geneva Congress (Klein, 1957). Paula Heimann, who had been Klein's right hand for many years, distanced herself resolutely then. So did Winnicott, who interests us at this point. When the Symposium on Envy and Jealousy, papers from which were never published, took place in March 1969 at the British Psycho-Analytical Society, Winnicott formally declared that from that point onwards there was a major discrepancy between his position and Klein's. He did not want to be unjust and ungrateful, but he felt that with that paper Melanie Klein had embarked on a mistaken path: he considered the idea of primary envy to be unsustainable. (I am quoting from memory but faithfully, I think, as I was able to read the Symposium but was unable to transcribe it, because it is not a public document.) Winnicott, as we know, had never accepted the theory of the death instinct, and it cannot be surprising that he could not admit a primary envy.

In general, Melanie Klein's basic idea was that the child can feel envy of the breast that feeds him and feeds him well. This idea was, and continues to be, combated, perhaps less today than previously. Freud had said something similar in respect of the woman's penis envy, but such strong objections had not been raised. Paula Heimann said at the same Symposium, when she parted from Melanie Klein, that the introduction of the concept of envy of the breast altered the theory of the libido substantially, because the affects come to occupy the place of the instincts. Envy being an affect, an emotion, she could not follow Klein in such a flagrant deviation from the theory of instincts. Paula Heimann, in fact, could have said as much to Freud when he introduced the theory of penis envy to explain female psychology. However, things are never purely scientific. Neither Paula Heimann nor Winnicott felt incompatible with Freud, although they could have, as much or more so than with Klein.

I can say, in conclusion, that Glover ceases to be a Kleinian with the depressive position, and Winnicott with the theory of primary envy. However, what interests us is not to vindicate various positions, but to indicate Winnicott's place and point of departure, as an author who parts from Melanie Klein in a very personal and creative development.

16.2   Primitive emotional development

Winnicott separated clearly primitive (or early) emotional development from the rest of human development. Primitive emotional development comprises the first six months of life, and these first months are very important. For Winnicott the durations are not fixed. Winnicott criticizes Klein's way of dating development as being too fixed and premature; certainly there is nothing obsessive about him.

The first stage, which corresponds to early emotional development, is marked by primary narcissism, and therefore there is no object relation, nor is there any psychic structure. This is a fundamental difference between Winnicott and Klein, who at a given moment in her investigation broke away decisively from the hypothesis of primary narcissism and, further, had always sustained that there exists an ego at the outset.

Winnicott maintains (or returns to) the idea of primary narcissism, and this leads him to maintain decisively that if there is no psychic structure during the first months of life, then the beginning of development cannot be explained in terms of impulses or fantasies. From this derives the theoretically coherent idea that at the beginning of life the child requires an adequate environment and that the outcome of early emotional development is totally linked to maternal care. It is interesting to note the consequences Winnicott draws from this way of understanding development in order to account for phenomena that arise in the transference. Given that this part of development can be said not to be mental, Winnicott arrives at the idea that primitive emotional development is linked to some function of the analyst that is isomorphic with that of maternal care.

Without ignoring the importance of maternal care, Klein thinks, instead, that the child participates from the outset. Winnicott does not think so, as the child has no mind. According to him, the mind appears in order to compensate for the deficiency of maternal care. This dovetails with one of Winnicott's most important ideas, that of the *false self*, which he develops throughout his work and particularly in "Ego Distortion and the True and False Self" (1960a). The false self is always a consequence of the lack of nurture, so much so that when external circumstances allow the individual to abandon that situation, he will do so. If the analyst knows how to conduct the analysis and gives the patient the opportunity to regress, he will go back and begin his journey anew. Winnicott maintains, not without optimism, that we are born with a pure desire to grow and that, if the environment does not interfere too much, this desire takes us forward. Klein, instead, is more sceptical; she thinks everyone both wants to and does not want to grow, or, to use her terms, there is an impulse towards integration and an impulse towards disintegration, in consonance with her declared adherence to the dualist theory of the instincts. It is evident that the conflict between growing and not growing, between advance and retreat, between integration and disintegration appears continually in the consulting-room; but Winnicott may be right in the end in stating that the original impulse to grow exists without conflict at the beginning of life and bad experiences suffocate it. It is understandable that these hypotheses, by their very nature, are difficult to refute. (We will return to this subject in chapter 41, when we discuss regression as a curative process in the analytic setting.)

16.3   *Primary narcissism according to Winnicott*

In chapter 15 we discussed the bases on which Melanie Klein rejected the hypothesis of primary narcissism. We said that, for her, there are narcissistic states—that is, moments in which the relation with the external object is abandoned and the processes of projection and introjection are paralysed—but not a narcissistic stage in which the libido charges the ego before applying itself to the object, as Freud says. Klein points out that Freud hesitates on this point and cites the article from the "Encyclopaedia" (1923a [1922]), to conclude that her disagreement with Anna Freud is more radical than with the father of psychoanalysis.

Closer to Anna Freud on this point than to Melanie Klein, Winnicott states specifically that a stage of primary narcissism exists, which coincides with what he calls primitive emotional development. However, there is one point on which Winnicott is close to Klein, because he recognizes a creative capacity in the child in that state. The child has the capacity to create the object, in the sense of *imagining* that there is something by means of which his hunger can be satisfied. The mother, in turn, is capable of providing the real object (and here real must mean objective, not imagined). If the mother offers the breast and gives him milk, she offers a point of coincidence which leads the child to think he has created that object. In this sense, Winnicott says, that object is part of the child—that is, the narcissistic structure has not been modified. But at the same time something new has been created, which Winnicott calls the *area of illusion*.

Winnicott uses two expressions, taken from psychiatry, to account for this process: hallucination and illusion. Ball defined hallucination as a per ception without an object, whereas in the illusion the object exists but perception of it is distorted. The child first hallucinates the breast, and, when the mother gives it to him, he has the *illusion* that that object has been created by him. In other words, the baby hallucinates the breast as something that has to exist for his hunger and, after the mother has offered the breast to him, as the object that now exists in reality—the hallucination is transformed into illusion, in the psychiatric sense of the word. This is why, in Winnicott's beautiful phrase, the fundamental task of the mother is to disillusion her baby gradually, thus transforming the initially hallucinatory situation into an illusory and then a real one. In this way the object relation is established: when I realize that the breast is not the product of my creation but that it has autonomy, I will have effected the passage from the area of illusion to that of the object relation.

There are some differences on this point between Winnicott's conception and that of Freud. Freud's concept of narcissism seems stricter to me, whereas Winnicott postulates that the idea of the object is within the individual and therefore does not arise from the first experience of satisfaction. For Freud the starting point of development is the mnemic imprint of the first experience of satisfaction. Winnicott does not employ the theory of the mnemic imprint and thinks, moreover, that this concept of illusion is prior to Klein's and Isaacs's concept of unconscious fantasy, which already implies an object. There is more of a psychic apparatus for Susan Isaacs than for Winnicott, but I think the difference is fortuitous here and serves perhaps more to classify analysts according to school than to characterize the facts.

The difference between unconscious fantasy (Isaacs) and hallucination (Winnicott) does not seem great, and may relate more to semantics than to theories. Ethologists would not hesitate to qualify Winnicott's hallucination as a part of *Homo sapiens'* phylogenetic knowledge, and I personally am unable to understand the difference between Winnicott's hallucination and Bion's preconception, except that each belongs to a different school of thought. I think what Winnicott calls hallucination is what is already an idea of the breast; but perhaps here I do no more than profess my own creed. Basing herself on Freud in the *Three Essays* (1905d), Susan Isaacs (1943) maintains that aim and object are defining characteristics of instinct; that instinct, mechanism and object are indissolubly linked. What is distinctive of Kleinian thought is that external reality will only confirm or refute an instinctive genetic predisposition.

Faithful to the hypothesis of primary narcissism, Winnicott says that the idea of the object is not there yet when the child hallucinates the breast as something that has to exist for his hunger. This point of view is disputable, and with it the theory of primary narcissism Winnicott supports. Why does Winnicott say the object is not there yet? If I hallucinate that "there is something that", why not call "*something that*" an object? It is difficult for me to think that when the child hallucinates the breast he does not already have a relation to that object, knowledge of which comes with the genome. In this way the area of illusion, certainly a basic concept in Winnicott's psychology, would be a first contrast with the external object, with reality. Let us leave aside theory for a moment to see how all this is translated in the transference.

16.4   A psychopathological classification

For technical purposes, Winnicott (1945, 1955) divides patients into three types, which, in the final analysis, can be reduced to two. There are, on the one hand, neurotics, who have reached a high degree of maturity. They relate to total objects, they differentiate object from subject, inside from outside, the internal from the external. They are people who suffer at the level of interpersonal relations and from the fantasies that colour those relations. Then there are those patients who were unable to emerge from what Winnicott calls the *stage of concern*—that is, the depressive position; these are depressive, melancholic or hypochondriac patients, in whom what is basically at stake is the internal world of the patient, not strictly speaking the objective interpersonal relations. Although this group is different from the previous one, Freud's classic technique still applies to them. Finally, there are those patients in whom what is disturbed is the primitive emotional development. There exists in them an *early transference* that can in no way be superimposed on the transference neurosis of the other cases. Note that here Winnicott employs the expression "transference neurosis" in a wide sense, as that which crystallizes in the treatment. There are, therefore, two forms of transference: the typical (regular) transference neurosis, in which situations from the past are reproduced in the present, as Freud said in 1914, and early transference, which corresponds to primitive emotional development. In the latter, according to Winnicott, it is not the past that comes to the present (or is reproduced in the present) but the present has become transformed plainly and simply into the past: the transference phenomenon has an immediate reality here, and this compels the analyst to confront it, not with his conventional interpretative equipment, but with *attitudes*.

Although it is true that it is not always clear which are the attitudes Winnicott proclaims, it is evident that he thinks primitive emotional development is inaccessible to interpretation, that it is not a matter of understanding it but of remaking it (or, better still, of allowing it to remake itself spontaneously). We will return to this when we deal with regression in the setting; but Winnicott's position here seems to me to lead to two questions: (1) What does that attitude which replaces interpretation consist in? and (2) When and why will one decide that the conventional (interpretative) technique is no longer operative and that one must prepare to proceed otherwise?

16.5   *The good enough mother*

As we noted above, the key point of Winnicott's entire doctrine is the mother's function. Primitive emotional development is inconceivable without her. Beyond his impulse to grow, to mature, the child depends entirely on the mother to go through the difficult passage from primary narcissism to the object relation. In fact, Winnicott proposes a methodological position here which derives logically from his theories: if a child undergoes a period of primary narcissism in which, by definition, he does not differentiate himself from the mother, then it is logically impossible to study him separately from her. During this first period of his development, the child is not yet what can be called a person, an individual. The child has no impulses or fantasies. Not only does Winnicott reject the idea of the death instinct or of primary envy, but the entire instinctual life of the child is bracketed at that moment. Even oral sadism, while not being ignored, is viewed from another perspective. Winnicott will say that in the *stage of preconcern*, which corresponds to primitive emotional development, the pitiless and cruel attitude of the child, which he calls *ruthlessness*, is not related to sadistic desires but to the needs the child has and which the mother is capable of understanding. Primitive emotional development is completed if and only if the mother gives the child adequately what he needs—the necessary gratification as well as the necessary frustration. An excessively solicitous mother hinders the child's development because she keeps him at the stage of primary narcissism.

The newborn child cannot take charge of his impulses, because in the stage of primary narcissism the impulses come from outside; and the mother has to contemplate that situation. The child does not bring conflicts—the conflict comes to him from outside; and to the extent that the mother fulfils her task well enough, to the extent that she is a *good enough mother* (not a perfect mother), Winnicott says, her child will develop well. If the mother fails, however, then obstacles to development come about. Winnicott calls these obstacles *impingement*—meaning something like disturbance, or making an impact.

A good enough mother is able to place herself at that difficult point where hallucination and reality converge in the child's *illusion* of having created that object. She is also the one who is able gradually to disillusion her baby. This disillusion consists in the baby's gradual realization that the object has not been created by him. The result of this process is the constitution of a link. In other words, the area of illusion is transformed into a link, an object relation.

It is understandable that authors who accept primary narcissism should give more importance to the aggression of the environment than to that of the subject at that point of development. Winnicott believes that, provided he is not disturbed, the child will grow well, as though the impulse to develop were previous to, and independent of, the area of conflict, which is at least debatable. Every gain implies a loss: who would not like to be in the womb, and who would not like to come out of it? The womb is very comfortable but boring; outside it is difficult but more fun.

16.6   *The processes of integration*

In one of his main works, "Primitive Emotional Development" (1945), Winnicott expounds the basic processes of the early ego, which are integration, personalization and realization.

Winnicott postulates a primary state of *unintegration* and differentiates it from *disintegration* as a regressive process. The primary state of unintegration provides a basis for producing the phenomenon of disintegration, especially if the process of primary integration fails or is retarded. The decisive difference between these two processes is that unintegration is accompanied by a state of calm, whereas disintegration produces fear.

The *primary state of integration*, then, is a basic aspect of primitive emotional development in the first months of life, underpinned by two types of experiences: the technique of maternal care and "the acute instinctual experiences which tend to gather the personality together from within" (1945, *Through Paediatrics*, p. 150).

The process of *personalization*, which consists in the person being in his body, runs parallel to that of integration, just as depersonalization does to disintegration. The depersonalization of psychosis is related to the retardation of the early processes of personalization.

Lastly, the process of adaptation to reality—or of *realization*—consists in the encounter of the mother and the baby in that area of illusion already described (ibid., p. 152).

It seems to me that Winnicott assumes infinite possibilities within primary narcissism, which only become organized afterwards. Initially, primary narcissism implies *unintegration*, in the sense that when I feel hunger I am a frantic, angry child, and when I have been given the breast I am a tranquil child. In this sense I do not need to integrate these two aspects, and consequently I can be this or that at a given moment without there being a process of dissociation. Winnicott makes a rigorous distinction between unintegration and dissociation, which Melanie Klein does not do. Winnicott states that the phenomena of unintegration are not necessarily accompanied by anxiety, whereas those of disintegration are, because persecution or loss is already present in the dissociation. On this point Winnicott's ideas are very convincing, whereas Melanie Klein fluctuates between unintegration as a process of development and dissociation as a defence. This point, which Melanie Klein does not manage to resolve, reappears in post-Kleinian thought with Esther Bick's (1968) work on the skin that contains the self. In chapter 9 of *Explorations in Autism* (Meltzer et al., 1975), Meltzer says that Bick's 1968 work opened up the problem of unintegration in contrast with disintegration and related it to a defective containment (p. 234); but the truth is that Winnicott had already raised it in 1945 in "Primitive Emotional Development". To be more exact, the idea stems from Glover with his ego nuclei; Klein refers to the latter's work, undervaluing it in her writing about schizoid mechanisms in 1946.

16.7   Primitive emotional development in the transference

This brief and incomplete sketch of Winnicott's theories serves as a necessary introduction to what really interests us in a book such as this: Winnicott's technique.

In the work he presented at the Symposium on Transference at the Geneva Congress in 1955, Winnicott (1956) maintained that if primitive emotional development has failed, then we as analysts have to give the patient an opportunity to repair those deficiencies. On the other hand, in neurotics and even in depressives—who reached the depressive position in some way—the classic technique can be maintained. As we will see in speaking of regression and the setting, the patient whose primitive emotional development is disturbed requires a concrete experience that allows him to regress and begin his journey again.

To understand Winnicott on this point it is necessary to remember the concept of the *false self*. When the mother does not know how to provide the environment her baby needs, because instead of responding adequately to his needs she interferes with them, she forces the child into a special and aberrant behaviour, leading to the formation of a false self, which replaces her in her deficiencies. The false self, Winnicott (1956) says, is without doubt an aspect of the true self, which it protects and hides as a reaction to the failures in adaptation. Thus the false self develops as a pattern of conduct that corresponds to the environmental failure (p. 387).

If we understand that this is the real situation of the patient, then we can give him the opportunity of returning to the starting point and initiating a new development of his real self. The understanding of the analyst is decisive here, as is his capacity not to interfere with the process of regression. If we are prepared to accompany the patient in this difficult passage towards the sources we should be prepared to make mistakes—warns Winnicott—because there is no analyst, however competent, who does not interfere. When this is the case, the patient will perceive our error and then, for the first time, will become angry. This anger, however, refers not to the error the analyst has just committed but to an error in his upbringing, in the face of which the patient reacted, configuring a false self, because he obviously was not then in a position to protest. The key is that the patient utilizes the error of the analyst to protest about an error in the past, and it is as such that it should be considered (ibid., p. 388).

In this sense, the transference of early states of development paradoxically has a real significance. The analysand is reacting to something that happened in his childhood, becoming angry about a *real* error the analyst made; and what the analyst has to do is to respect that anger, which is real and justified. It is real because it refers to an error I made in my task, and what I have to do is to admit it and, if necessary, study my counter-transference, but never interpret it because, were I to do this, I would be utilizing interpretation defensively, to disqualify my analysand's accurate judgement. (Although there is no opportunity here to discuss this idea, I would like to indicate that neither in this case nor in any other should interpretation disqualify what, for better or for worse, the analysand thinks. The interpretation should not be an opinion but a conjecture on the part of the analyst about what the patient thinks—that is, about his unconscious.) The final part of the paper Winnicott presented in Geneva (1956) differentiates clearly the requirements of clinical work in the two classes of patients he is considering.

The patient who presents deficiencies in his primitive emotional development has to pass through the experience of being disturbed and reacting with (justified) rage. He uses the deficiencies of the analyst for this. In this phase of the analysis, Winnicott (1956) continues, what could be called resistance when one is working with neurotic patients indicates that the analyst has committed an error, and resistance continues until the analyst discovers and takes responsibility for his error (p. 388).

The analyst must be alert and discover his error each time the resistance appears. He also has to know that only by making use of his own errors can he offer the patient a better service in this phase of the analysis—that is, giving him the opportunity of becoming angry for the first time about the issues and failures in adaptation that produced the disturbance of his development.

Winnicott maintains that, in these cases, the negative transference of the neurotic is replaced by objective anger about the deficiencies of the analyst, which implies a significant difference between the two types of work (ibid., p. 388).

Winnicott considers that these two types of analysis are not incompatible, at least in his own clinical work, and that it is not too difficult to change from one to the other, in accordance with the mental process taking place in the analysand's unconscious. ("I have discovered in my clinical work that one kind of analysis does not preclude the other. I find myself slipping over from one to the other and back again, according to the trend of the patient's unconscious process"—ibid., p. 388.)

Winnicott says at the end of his important article that it is a further undertaking to study in detail the criteria by means of which the analyst can identify needs that should be managed through an active adaptation, at least with a sign or show of active adaptation, without ever losing sight of primary identification (ibid., p. 388).

With these final comments Winnicott shows that the two techniques proposed initially as being distinct and distant from each other can alternate, not only in the same analysand, but even in the same session. In this way the classification loses its coherence, and the technique acquires, in my view, an excessively inspirational slant. It is also inevitable that when exceptional measures for more difficult cases are introduced, the desire arises to apply them to simpler cases, on the assumption that he who can do more can also do less.

CHAPTER SEVENTEEN

On the spontaneity
of the transference phenomenon

I want to describe here two brief experiences supporting the idea that the transference appears spontaneously and at the outset. These are two singular cases, partly similar and partly opposite, where the transference establishes itself immediately, seemingly without the influence either of the setting or of my "theories". As two colleagues are involved, I have omitted certain data that would also have supported my thesis.

17.1   Clinical material 1

Several years ago, at the end of October, a colleague consulted me over the telephone. She was very depressed at the death of her only sister. (A brother had died at birth two years before she was born.) She wanted a few interviews before the summer holidays and believed I was the most appropriate person to see. I agreed to see her, despite having little time available, certain that this would be a brief psychotherapy, of limited time due to the holidays three months later and something like a "crisis intervention".

With this plan in mind I agreed to an interview, in which I pointed out to her that I had little time to spare; she agreed to see me once a fortnight, trusting that this would suffice to overcome her state of depression and anxiety. It was made clear that, should she wish to re-analyse herself in the future, there was no possibility of my having any time available. We fixed a time every other week, and I told her I might be able to see her once a week in January. We agreed on the fees, which she decided to pay me each time she saw me. I think that with this she herself accentuated the sporadic character of the meetings.

During November and December I saw her every other Thursday, as agreed. During these sessions, four or five in all, she spoke at length of her deceased sister, of her mother, dead for many years, of her father and an aunt (her father's sister), both of whom lived far from Buenos Aires. She planned to visit them during the holidays in February. She described the character of her father and her aunt, and her fears that they would persuade her to live with them. She spoke of her husband (deceased), of her two children, who were both married (the younger one recently) and also of her previous analysts. There had been several, and all of them had helped her. She spoke of them with respect and gratitude, without excesses, and sincerely.

During these interviews I did nothing other than listen to her attentively and circumspectly offer the occasional question or comment to facilitate the development of her story. Although she placed herself on the couch (and not in the armchair opposite mine which I use for interviews), she remained seated and spoke spontaneously and frankly but without free-associating. Dream material appeared only very tangentially. For my part, I made no interpretation at all, as it was not appropriate to the type of psychotherapy I had proposed to carry out.

After the first interviews, at the end of the first month of treatment, she said she felt much better, and her anxiety and depression had been visibly alleviated. She attributed her improvement to my psychotherapy, which had enabled her to talk about her problems with someone and to be heard. I reminded her this could also be due to the effect of the imipramine she had begun to take before coming to see me, as that drug has a latent period before it takes effect; but she was more inclined to accept her own explanation rather than mine.

Although it is true that I never made an interpretation during the first two months of treatment (if it can be called that), I wish to indicate that my behaviour was completely analytic as to the classic rules of the setting: I attended to her punctually, the interviews lasted fifty minutes, I kept the usual distance and reserve, and so on. For her part, the patient adapted herself without difficulty to this type of relationship and did not try to modify it by virtue of her being a colleague and an ex-student of the Institute.

The first fortnightly session in January was on Thursday 5th, and in it she repeated the development of the previous interviews. She spoke about her anxiety over her impending journey, that her aunt had telephoned long-distance to ask her to come soon because her father was in poor health, and so forth. She asked me if I could give her more sessions in January, as I had promised, and I answered I could, although I did not have a timetable at that moment. I asked her to speak to me that weekend to fix a time for the next session. She also asked me whether there was a possibility I would have times available to analyse her after the holidays or later on, and I answered that, unfortunately, nothing had changed as to the time I had available, and which she was aware of. She had supposed it would be so; but as she really wished to have an analysis with me, she wanted to ask me this specifically. She added that she could wait if I wished it. Her crisis had passed—she commented—and she thought she had no urgent problem that would require analysis immediately. I will say, as an aside, that the way in which she posed the problem at that moment confirmed my first impression that this was a neurotic and not a serious case, one of the good hysterics of Elizabeth R. Zetzel's classification.

She did not speak to me that weekend; she came to the next session at her usual hour, on Thursday 19 January. She apologized for not having telephoned me—she had left it, then she forgot and finally did not do it. Faithful to the technique I had imposed, I interpreted nothing here, and when she asked me for a session for the following week I gave her a convenient time on 23 January. She then began to tell me at length about her father, her conflicts with him and the need she felt for re-analysis to resolve them. While she talked about these subjects, which had come up in the previous interviews, she began to cry copiously. She was surprised by her weeping, more than I was, as I did not know her well. She said Anglo-Saxons such as she rarely cried. She could not explain this weeping and could not remember having cried like this for many years. The subject of her journey and the holidays returned ceaselessly in her material, sprinkled with generous, unrestrained sobs. She could not understand what was happening. She tried to link her strong feelings of sorrow and pain to numerous mourning situations (present, past and future), but she herself did not feel satisfied with these self-interpretations.

As this situation did not improve, I decided to make the first interpretation of this peculiar and very interesting treatment. Very tentatively, as I myself did not wholly believe it, I asked her whether she was crying because the end of the interviews was approaching, and because of the separation the holidays would cause, especially as in the previous session we had returned to the idea that I would have no time available to take her on in case she wanted a re-analysis.

She accepted this interpretation without reservations and noted that she suddenly calmed down. She stopped crying, and her anxiety was replaced by a feeling of astonishment about what had happened. In all her years of analysis there had been no lack of interpretations about separation anxiety, whether over weekends or holidays; but none had seemed as definite as this one. How could it be precisely on this occasion that an interpretation heard so many times (and formulated so many times by her as an analyst) would have this result?

The compliment implicit in her associations—that I could have interpreted better than others—had little relevance here. Mine was a routine interpretation, imposed by the immediacy of the situation and after the most justifiable explanations (the self-interpretations on her diverse losses) had shown themselves to be inapplicable. I assumed then that something else had aroused such a strong reaction in my colleague (and I say colleague because she was that rather than a patient for me at that moment).

In any case, when after this episode she again spoke about my holidays and the separation, she cried again, almost as an experimental proof that this was effectively what was happening to her.

On Monday 23rd she arrived, calm again, as she had been in earlier sessions once she had improved, and she commented again with astonishment on what had occurred. She had never before that Thursday felt that famous separation anxiety so immediately and convincingly. And she still had no explanation. She returned to her usual themes—her father, her aunt, her journey, her friends (many and good), her work. From this she passed on to comments about the institutional crisis. From the first moment she had aligned herself with the independent group, and this did not make her doubt her good relationship with Dr. X, whose assistant she had been in a seminar and whom she appreciated as teacher and colleague. Some time previously, the latter had asked her what her position was. It had been a very tense moment, but she was able to speak with him frankly. The following day she had noticed with sorrow that he had turned his face so as not to greet her. As was to be expected, I made no comment on this theme, and I did not think it was linked to the previous material. (It must be remembered that it was not my intention to interpret what I heard.)

We agreed on another interview on Friday 27th, and I offered her an additional one if she wanted it, to close the cycle.

On Friday 27th she arrived in an enthusiastic mood and again showed herself interested in the intensity of her reaction to the holidays. She repeated that she had never felt it so vividly and sharply. Although she did not doubt that her crying was related specifically and unequivocally to my holidays, she could not explain its quality and intensity. She had never wept like this in all her years of analysis—perhaps even in her whole life. She felt she could only compare this weeping to a memory of when she was five or six years old. Her parents had left for a seaside holiday, and she had been punished and left at home. She had felt then the same pain and resentment she felt with me on Thursday 19th; and she had cried then as copiously and disconsolately as now.

At this point I no longer had any doubt that this was a (transference) repetition of that episode (screen memory) at the age of five or six. To resolve the enigma, it only remained to be seen why she had been punished then and to see whether she had received a similar punishment from me.

She said she could not remember the reason for the punishment, although she could remember her vivid feelings at the time.

She told me then that she would be going out of town to some friends at the beginning of the following week, before leaving for her father's, by which I understood that we were carrying out our last interview. We had agreed that, on her return, she would arrange to meet me again in order to talk about who could analyse her. She had thought of some colleagues, and we would exchange ideas about this.

When we were about to take our leave, she reminded me that I had promised her one more session before the holidays, and I indicated that I was not offering her one because of her journey to Uruguay. She answered that if I had a free hour she would postpone her journey to Montevideo from Saturday to Monday. I proposed she should come the following day, Saturday 28th, so as not to disturb her travel plans.

On Saturday 28th she told me she could not remember the reason for the punishment when her parents had left for the seaside; but, instead, she clearly remembered something that had happened at about that same time. Perhaps, examining it closely, it could have been the reason for the punishment. Or not. She was not sure; but in any case she was going to tell me what she remembered. At that time she had told her aunt (her father's sister) that her mother did not love her and that she always treated her badly and unfairly. Her aunt had not accepted this story and had discussed it with her parents. Her father had told her that these things were not to be discussed "outside the family", and she still recalled vividly her silent mother's look, full of sorrow. Perhaps her parents had punished her by leaving her because of that betrayal and lack of obedience.

She remained silent, and I asked how she might have done something like that to me, something that would reproduce those feelings of infantile rebellion against her parents. And of betrayal, she added.

She remained silent, then said she could not explain this. I asked her to associate freely, and her first association did not now surprise me. She said she sometimes felt uncomfortable with me because she had not joined the new Association; but that could not be the reason. She intended to join it eventually, and so forth. Besides, she knew that could not influence me, knowing me as she did.

I told her that her association was very pertinent and that in fact she felt I was going away on holiday without her to punish her for her "betrayal" in not joining the new Association. I added that this explained why in the session on Monday 23rd she had spoken at length of her awkward encounter with Dr. X. Through these associations, she was telling me she thought I had also turned my face away because of her "betrayal".

She immediately remembered clearly that when she had thought of having these interviews with me, she was afraid I would not agree to them because she did not belong to the new Association.

Upon her return from her journey, we had a final interview. She asked my advice in selecting her new analyst and accepted the one I suggested.

With her new analysis I understand that she resolved her problem with her parents, which she had so spontaneously and openly transferred to me.

17.2   *Clinical material 2*

I will relate now the dream of another colleague whom I treated very informally for a depressive crisis after the death of her husband. This is a very different case from the previous one, because it concerned a friend. When her depression increased, as she did not wish to return to her analyst, she preferred to ask me for help. I accepted her proposal, knowing I was not going to work under the best of conditions because we were friends; but she expected friendly rather than psychotherapeutic help.

We agreed to see each other once a week, on Monday nights, and I refused to charge her a fee, despite the fact that she would have preferred it. The treatment lasted only a few weeks, and we agreed to end it once she noticed that she had overcome the most difficult part of the work of mourning; she thought (rightly, in the light of what happened later) that she was already fit to carry on, on her own.

During the first month of this singular treatment I cancelled one of her interviews. I did it without worrying much because of the lax setting within which we had defined the relation. She accepted this graciously and did not agree to come at a different time, so as not to disturb me. She said she would come the following week at her usual hour.

She arrived very downcast and said her depression had increased. These were the changing states of the work of mourning, she pronounced, while I threw out of my mind the "absurd" idea that the cancellation on the previous Monday could have influenced her mood. I reassured myself, saying her mourning was very recent and that the interviews we were having could not affect her mood in that way.

She returned to her habitual theme—she spoke of her husband, of the illness that led to his death, of memories and anecdotes relating to him in his last years. She also spoke of her (married) children's sorrow over the death of their father. Her sons and daughters-in-law helped her, she added, and this made her feel less lonely. She dreamt again of Ricardo (her husband): *"I dreamt we were crossing the English Channel in a boat, from England to France, from Dover to Calais. Ricardo was following me, wearing a Prince of Wales suit that looked very good on him, and carrying the suitcases. But there were a lot of people between him and me. I sat on a bench, which curiously extended the length of the ship's deck. The part of the bench where I was sitting was a very peculiar bent shape, so that Ricardo and I were almost face to face. I looked, but Ricardo was not there. I began to look around for him and I did not find him."*

As soon as I heard this dream, I had a countertransference thought that I immediately rejected: I wondered whether the Ricardo of the dream was me, as I had not offered her the previous session. Right away I reasoned that only an irritating professional misconstruction could make me think in this way. No sane analyst would think thus, when the analytic situation had not yet been set up, nor was it going to be, according to what had been agreed. Ricardo was her husband's real name. She called me Horacio, as do all my friends; surely she barely remembered that my first name is in fact Ricardo.

I asked her for her associations. She associated then, as was to be expected, with her husband. His death had frustrated a European trip, which had been planned earlier. They had wanted to go to England to visit London once more, and they had intended to go to a town where her father was born. He had died when she was a child. They were to go to Italy, and, of course, to France—how could anyone conceive of a trip to Europe that did not include Paris? Paris enchanted her, it was a city without equal. She also liked London. And Florence. She had been reading French authors of late and noted that she liked them more and more. She would not say Lacan, who is so difficult; but she did like Lebovici and Nacht, Laplanche and Pontalis. Recently she had read a beautiful work by Widlöcher. Imperceptibly, in the last few years she had been growing away from the English school. What would I think! Her supervision with me, despite the intervening years, continued to be, for her, a key moment of her development, she reassured me. Lately she had read a book on creativity, which she thought excellent. She believed the author was Janine Chasseguet-Smirgel.

I dared now to interpret the dream in the transference (!). I said that although undoubtedly this dream was an attempt at working through the mourning for the loss of her husband, which was so much more painful as it put an end to a lovely trip that had already been planned, I thought that the Ricardo of the dream also represented me. Although she called me Horacio, she certainly did not ignore the fact that my first name was that of her husband. She accepted it was so, and that she always identified us to some extent because we were namesakes.

Encouraged by this first response, I continued my interpretation. I told her that in cancelling the previous Monday session I had unwittingly created a new situation of mourning for her. In the state you are in, I added, skipping a session and a week is perhaps not so trivial as we had thought.

She again accepted this suggestion but reminded me this did not amount to much—that I had offered her another hour, and she had not accepted it so as not to burden me. With her usual cordiality she said we should not lose sight of the fact that our encounters were meetings between friends rather than a treatment, and so forth. In other words, she repeated the reasons (or rationalizations) I had thought of myself a moment earlier.

On surer ground, I insisted on my point of view. I said I certainly shared her reasons, and I was not going to consider my absence on the previous Monday as a fault in our friendly setting. (I remembered inwardly at this point that her previous analyst, to whom she had not wished to return, was famous among his friends for the irregularities of his setting.) Nevertheless your dream—I insisted—seems to allude several times to me as the absent one. The position of that singular bench on the ship reminds me of the position of the two armchairs we are sitting on.

And your associations about your growing away from the English school are graphically expressed in the English Channel crossing. So much so, that you had to add that you will always remember your supervision with me, in which you learned the fundamentals of Kleinian technique. And your preference for Paris, without undervaluing London.

There was a moment of tense silence, in which I again thought I had overstepped the mark. I thought my interpretation was too deep and transferential, and inwardly I cursed Melanie Klein, as if everything had been her fault. Then my friend spoke again, with that calm and profound voice that seems to be a trademark of insight. She said the scene of the dream had again arisen in her consciousness—she had seen it clearly for a moment and had noticed a detail that had been absent when she remembered the dream that morning and related it to me in the session. The colour of the seat in the dream was exactly that of the armchairs in my consulting-room. She remembered then vividly that when I had spoken to her on the telephone to cancel the session, she remembered a bad experience with her training analyst. She continued to hold him in esteem, as always, but she preferred not to go back to him precisely because of his lack of punctuality; instead, I was more "English" on this point. She immediately became emotional and remembered that other Englishman, her father, who had died when she was a child and had entered her painful latency phase. Finally she said that yes, the dream did refer to me, and she felt relieved. Immediately she felt spontaneously that she had to make it clear to me that when she had spoken of her father's death during our first talk, she had made an error—a small slip whose meaning was now completely and easily understandable. She had told me her father had died at the age of 50, which was not the case. He had died much younger, at 40. The one who had died at the age of 49 was her husband.

I think that in this material the clarification of the slip relating to her father's death represents a proof, showing, as it does, the moment of insight where father, husband and analyst are conjoined and differentiated. The same applies to lifting the repression about the colour of the dream seat. The way in which this was offered and the context in which it appeared shows conclusively the transference component of the dream. I trust this opinion will be shared by most analysts.

CHAPTER EIGHTEEN

The therapeutic alliance: from Wiesbaden to Geneva

I n the previous chapters we studied transference, as the most important factor in psychoanalytic therapy. We also stated that it can be understood only if it is compared to something that is *not* transference, as Anna Freud maintained at the Arden House Symposium in 1954. So it becomes obvious that the transference occupies only a part of the analytic universe (and the same can be said of any human experience). As I have already said in a previous chapter, on this point I agree with Fenichel (1945a) and Greenson (1967).

When I maintain that not everything that appears in the analytic process is transference, I mean that there is always something more—not that the transference is not there, which means something very different: the transference is there, but not everything that is there is transference. Next to the transference, something that is not transference is always found. Provisionally we will call this something the *therapeutic alliance*. (We prefer the term "therapeutic alliance", which Zetzel, 1956a, introduced, following Sterba, 1934, and which we consider synonymous with rational transference—Fenichel, 1941; with mature transference—Stone, 1961; with working alliance—Greenson, 1965a and others.) I say "provisionally, because we will see in what follows that the concept of therapeutic alliance is more complex than it seems.

18.1   *The therapeutic dissociation of the ego*

Typical of Freud and noticeable throughout his work is the concept that, beyond his resistances, the patient cooperates with the analyst. But unquestionably we owe to Sterba the postulate that the ego is destined to dissociate itself as a consequence of the analytic process. He presented this concept in a paper at the Congress of Wiesbaden in 1932, which was published in the *International Journal of Psycho-Analysis* in 1934, entitled "The Fate of the Ego in Analytic Therapy". This paper deals specifically with the therapeutic alliance ("This capacity of the ego for dissociation gives the analyst the chance, by means of his interpretations, to effect an alliance with the ego against the powerful forces of instinct and repression and, with the help of one part of it, to try to vanquish the opposing forces"— Sterba, 1934, p. 120) and explains it on the basis of a *therapeutic dissociation of the ego* in which two parts stand out—one that cooperates with the analyst, and one that opposes him. The former is directed towards reality; the latter comprises the impulses of the id, the ego defences and the dictates of the superego. (In a 1975 paper Sterba recalls that his presentation pleased neither the Wiesbaden Congress nor the Vienna Society, where he read it again after the Congress, at the end of 1932. His term, *"therapeutische Ich Spaltung"*, thought to be applicable only to psychosis, was fiercely criticized, and only Anna Freud backed Sterba. However, a few weeks after the heated discussion in Vienna, Freud published the *New Introductory Lectures on Psycho-Analysis*, 1933a, where he asserts categorically that the ego can divide and unite itself in the most diverse ways.) The therapeutic dissociation of the ego is due to an identification with the analyst, the prototype of which is the process of formation of the superego. This identification is the fruit of analytic experience in the sense that, faced with the patient's conflicts, the analyst reacts with an attitude of observation and reflection. Identified with that attitude, the patient acquires the capacity to observe and criticize his own functioning, dissociating his ego into two parts.

It is worth indicating where Sterba's and Strachey's essays coincide. Both were published contiguously in the same issue of the *International Journal of Psycho-Analysis* in 1934. While for Sterba what is decisive in the analytic process is the therapeutic dissociation of the ego, for Strachey the key point is that the psychoanalyst assumes the role of an auxiliary superego, differentiating itself from the archaic superego. Despite their differences, these two most excellent works rely on the idea that analytic treatment is founded on a peculiar instrumental distortion of the self; and both lend weight to what was insufficiently understood at the time: the importance of interpreting the (resistance of) transference.

At the beginning of his essay, Sterba defines transference precisely as being dual and comprising both instinct and repression (defence). From the study of the resistance of transference, according to Sterba, we know that the forces of instinct and repression are both included in the transference (1934, p. 118). This idea, which offers a solution to the enigma Freud posed but did not resolve in "The Dynamics of Transference" (1912b), is subsequently developed by Anna Freud (1936) when she speaks of the transference of impulses and the transference of defences. (In this way we can acknowledge Sterba's lucid approach to the problem Anna Freud then resolves.)

In the face of these two aspects of transference which threaten the course of analysis from two opposing flanks, the correcting influence of the analyst gives rise to a third. In interpreting the transference conflict, the analyst contrasts the ego elements in contact with reality and those that have a cathexis of instinctive or defensive energy (Sterba, 1934, p. 119). Thus, the analyst achieves a *dissociation* within the ego of the patient that allows him to establish an *alliance* against the powerful forces of instinct and repression. Therefore, from the very beginning of an analysis that will terminate successfully, *the inevitable fate that awaits the ego is dissociation*.

As we have said, for Sterba the attitude of the analyst who reflects and interprets is fundamental, because it gives the patient a model to enable identification to take place, and the therapeutic dissociation is then sanctioned. The prototype for the therapeutic dissociation of the ego is the process of formation of the superego, but with the difference that it takes place in a mature ego and that its demand is not moral, as it takes up an attitude of serene and objective contemplation. For Sterba, the part of the ego directed towards reality and identified with the analyst is the filter through which must pass all the transference material that the ego, thanks to its synthetic function, will gradually assimilate.

In accordance with these ideas, Sterba can describe the psychoanalytic process as the result of two ego factors: the dissociation that makes possible the conscious taking up of unconscious contents, and the synthetic function that allows them to be incorporated. The analytic process is thus explained by a dialectic of dissociation and synthesis of the ego.

18.2   The resistance of transference

To size up Sterba's contribution in all its magnitude it is necessary to remember here his article "Zur Dynamik der Bewältigung des Übertragungswiderstandes" [The Dynamics of the Dissolution of the Transference Resistance], first published in 1929. In accordance with the 1912 Freudian model on which Sterba relies, the transference is established as resistance to the investigative work of analysis, as the patient acts in order not to remember an infantile experience. This stirs up a defence of the ego in the face of the analyst, who is transformed into a representative of the tendencies the ego of the analysand has to oppose. ("Because the transference serves the resistances, the patient acts out infantile experiences to avoid conscious remembrance of them. This leads on the part of the ego to a defence that is directed against the analysis because the analyst has become, in the transference, the representative of the emotional tendency against which the ego has to defend itself"—Sterba, 1929, pp. 368–369.)

According to Sterba, the work of the analyst consists in overcoming the transference resistance that obstructs the development of the process. "The analyst thereby finds himself in a difficult situation, for he is the object of the emotional repetition operating in the patient in order to hinder the recollections for which the analyst asks" (ibid., p. 369).

"When the analyst interprets the transference resistance he opposes the ego of the patient, as the organ controlling reality, to the instinctual activity re-enacted in the transference" (ibid., pp. 370–371). To assist the ego of the analysand who feels threatened by the id, the analyst offers him the possibility of an identification that satisfies the reality test the ego needs, and this identification is possible because the analyst observes the psychological situation and interprets it to the patient. The analyst's attitude to work and the way he speaks to his analysand—that is, his use of the term "we" and his constant appeal to the task—are a permanent invitation to the patient to identify himself with him. In this way, and availing himself of the interpretation, the analyst offers the analysand the opportunity for identification which is the necessary condition for analytic treatment.

I wanted to reproduce what is essential in this paper—and is not often remembered—because it contains the seeds of the principal theory of ego functioning which Sterba later expounded at Wiesbaden. Together with other contemporaneous papers, such as those presented by Ferenczi and Reich at the Innsbruck Congress and Strachey's paper (cited earlier), Sterba's essay initiates a radical change in the technique, which will centre increasingly on the interpretation of the transference.

18.3   Regression and therapeutic alliance

In July 1955, at the Nineteenth International Congress in Geneva, a Discussion on the Problems of Transference took place. There Elizabeth R. Zetzel read her paper, "Current Concepts of Transference" (published in the *International Journal of Psycho-Analysis* in 1956), where transference is understood as comprising the transference neurosis and the therapeutic alliance. The article poses again an issue that stems from the 1920 controversy between Melanie Klein and Anna Freud on the technique of child analysis and continues to this day.

Whereas Melanie Klein pays special attention to anxiety and unhesitatingly interprets it, ego-psychology emphasizes the functions of the ego as controller and the neutralization of instinctual energy. Here the influence of Hartmann's famous 1939 monograph is decisive in that it recognizes that thanks to secondary autonomy, the original conflict remains totally or partially divorced from unconscious fantasy. The relative unproductiveness of premature interpretations of the transference and also the limits of efficiency of analysis if secondary autonomy has become irreversible are explained in this way. ("Hartmann has suggested that in addition to these primary attributes, other ego characteristics, originally developed for defensive purposes, and the related neutralized instinctual energy at the disposal of the ego, may be relatively or absolutely divorced from unconscious fantasy. This not only explains the relative inefficacy of early transference interpretations, but also hints at possible limitations in the potentialities of analysis attributable to secondary autonomy of the ego which is considered to be relatively irreversible"—Zetzel, 1956a, p. 373.)

According to Sterba (1934) and Bibring (1937), this ego suffers a process of *splitting*, which leads Zetzel to distinguish theoretically between transference as therapeutic alliance and transference neurosis, which she considers as a manifestation of resistance (Zetzel, 1956a, p. 370). The therapeutic alliance is thus defined as part of the transference, although it is made to depend on a sufficiently mature ego, which does not exist in severely disturbed patients nor in children (ibid.). From this we can infer what this author will say in later works as to the origin of that sane part of the ego; it will be prior to the emergence of the oedipal conflict.

For Zetzel, as for the majority of ego psychologists, the analysis of the ego consists in the analysis of the defences; they respect Freud's advice that the analysis should proceed from the superficial to the profound, from defence to impulse. In the first stage of analysis deep interpretation of the contents can be dangerous and inoperative; nor is that of the defences advisable: the instinctual charge at the disposal of the mature ego has been neutralized and divorced from its unconscious sources. The transference neurosis can develop only once the ego defences have been weakened and the hidden instinctual conflicts mobilized (ibid., p. 371).

Transference neurosis is a compromise that serves the purposes of resistance and should be clearly separated from certain premature transference manifestations that appear at the beginning of the analytic process more as a consequence of defensive phenomena than because of a genuine displacement of instinctual contents onto the analyst. Thus the difference proposed by Glover (1955) between floating transference and transference neurosis is maintained.

The key to Zetzel's thinking consists in considering that the transference neurosis is possible only through a process of regression. She believes, as does Ida Macalpine (1950), that the analytic situation foments regression, that indispensable regression which is a necessary condition for analytic work (Zetzel, 1956a, p. 372). According to Zetzel, the therapeutic division of the ego postulated by Sterba and by Bibring can be achieved only once the process of therapeutic regression has taken place, in the first few months of treatment, and as a result of which the areas of transference neurosis and therapeutic alliance are defined. As a manifestation of resistance, regression operates as a primitive defence mechanism employed by the ego in the context of the transference neurosis (ibid.). According to Zetzel, the Kleinian school, on the other hand, considers that the regressive manifestations that appear in the analytic situation imply a deepening of the process; they indicate a diminution rather than a reinforcement of resistance.

According to this theory, regression as a defence mechanism vis-à-vis the analytic setting is what makes possible the reversal of the rigid ego defences, so that they return to the area of conflict.

18.4 From Sterba to Zetzel

Despite her well-known support for Sterba, Dr. Zetzel proposes an original line of thought, which, in my view, distances her perhaps more than she thinks from the essay in Wiesbaden. Sterba maintains that psychoanalytic treatment becomes possible as a result of a dissociation of the ego, one of whose parts—the one directed towards reality—seals an alliance with the analyst in order to observe and understand the other, the instinctual and defensive one. A major point in his reasoning is that this dissociation becomes possible because the analyst interprets. His entire conception relies on the interpretative task of the analyst, who operates on the acting-out of the conflict, transforming it into thought, while it serves as a model of identification for the analysand.

If I have quoted Sterba's 1929 work perhaps rather extensively, it is because I want to underline the importance Sterba accords to interpretation in its dual aspect as language and task.

The clinical material of the Wiesbaden exposition enables us to understand Sterba's ideas and his way of working. There is, for instance, the case of the woman who transferred to her analyst a highly traumatic childhood experience with an ear-, nose- and throat specialist, who had first seduced her with kindly treatment and sweets and then sprung a surprise tonsillectomy on her. The situation confronting Sterba was that the woman identified him with that treacherous doctor, in whom she had concentrated her entire infantile conflict with her father. Logically, the transference resistance consisted literally in not opening her mouth.

The analysis began in obstinate and hostile silence. However, at the end of the second session, the patient gave Sterba a valuable lead. She asked whether he had a changing-room in his consulting-room, where she could change when leaving the session, as she would get up from the couch with her dress wrinkled. In the following session she said that on leaving the previous day, she had had to meet a woman friend, who would surely have noticed her clothes in that state and would have thought she was having sexual relations. Sterba defines this configuration as a clear transference oedipal situation with a sadistic father (the laryngologist, Sterba) and a mother who censured her. I think Sterba's opinion would be shared by all analysts.

Sterba did not hesitate to interpret the significance of the defence here, and he added that with this interpretation they had begun the process he called therapeutic dissociation of the ego (Sterba, 1934, p. 124).

I have offered a fairly detailed account of Sterba's clinical material in order to show the difference between his theory and Zetzel's. For Sterba, the theory of therapeutic regression is unnecessary, and the therapeutic alliance begins to take shape precisely when the analyst interprets. As distinct from Zetzel's "good hysterics", Sterba's patient established a strong erotic transference highly coloured by sadomasochism at the outset, which he was nevertheless able to resolve satisfactorily.

18.5   Two types of regression

As regression occupies a central place in Dr. Zetzel's theory of the thera-peutic alliance, it is worth pausing a moment here, especially if one thinks, as I do, that the subject presents some difficulties. It is not easy to under-stand how the therapeutic regression can be conceived of as a defence mechanism and at the same time invoked as a factor that mobilizes the defences. Would one have to conclude that the regression leads the ego to a situation that antedates his secondary autonomy? If so, it would be diffi-cult to understand the transference neurosis as a manifestation of the re-sistance; and then its distinction from the therapeutic alliance would become more vague. Thus, Winnicott's (1955) concept of regression seems more explanatory and convincing.

Zetzel understands that there is a delicate point here in her theory, and she tries to resolve this issue by distinguishing *two* types of regression in the transference situation.

The concept of regression in the transference can be considered an attempt to work through infantile traumatic experiences or to return to an earlier state of real or fantasied gratification. In the case of the former, the regressive aspect of the transference should be considered a preliminary and necessary step in working through the conflict, whereas in the case of the latter it should be attributed to a desire to return to an earlier state of rest or narcissistic gratification, which seeks a status quo in accordance with the Freudian conception of the death instinct (Zetzel, 1956a, p. 375). Given these two types of regression as opposing aspects of the repetition compulsion studied by Lagache, Zetzel concludes that both are observable in every analysis.

This excessively eclectic solution is, nevertheless, unsatisfactory. As we can see, Zetzel has to conjoin the Freud of 1912 with the Freud of 1920 to account for these two types of regression, even though neither Freud nor Lagache is concerned with regression, but with transference. Nevertheless, the regression in the setting Zetzel conceives of cannot be other than the one that repeats the need in order to resolve it—that is, Lagache's 1951 concept. But what are we to do with the other regression, the one Freud postulates in *Beyond the Pleasure Principle* (1920g)? Confronted with this, the conduct of the analyst should hardly be as Zetzel and Macalpine and the ego psychologists in general propose—that is, to foment the regression. Logically, there is no response to this in Geneva. But there will be further on, and we know of it already from chapter 3: analysability. However much the criteria for analysability can be based on valid clinical facts, it is obvious that they can in no way give account of the problems posed here.

18.6   After the Geneva Congress

Dr. Zetzel's exposition at the Geneva Congress is the point of departure for a penetrating investigation of the role of the therapeutic alliance in the psychoanalytic process. From the comparison and contrast between the therapeutic alliance and the transference neurosis arise the criteria for analysability and the hypothesis of a therapeutic regression in response to the particulars analytic treatment offers the analysand in the beginning. Simultaneously, one notices the attempt to integrate into Hartmann's theories some of Melanie Klein's contributions. This effort is noticeable in "An Approach to the Relation Between Concept and Content in Psychoanalytic Theory" (Zetzel, 1956b), contemporaneous with the Geneva paper, and in "The Theory of Therapy in Relation to a Developmental Model of the Psychic Apparatus" (1965). This article, which appeared in the issue of the *International Journal of Psycho-Analysis* celebrating Hartmann's seventieth year, says expressly: "I have thus tried to narrow the gap between Hartmann's concept of secondary autonomy of the ego and theories emphasizing early object relations by a developmental model which attributes major ego functions to their initiation in the early mother–child relationships" (p. 51). At the beginning of this same article she says unequivocally that in "Concept and Content" she compared the contributions of Hartmann, Kris, Löwenstein and Rapaport with those of Klein and her school (ibid., p. 39).

The results can be found in a book she wrote with Meissner, which appeared after her death (1974). Here psychoanalysis is conceived of both as a structural and a developmental theory, while analytic treatment is understood as a dialectic between the transference neurosis and the therapeutic alliance. The difference between them, however, is less salient and clear-cut.

The therapeutic alliance continues to be understood as being based on the autonomous functions of the ego, and specifically on secondary autonomy; but its origin is to be found in the first object relations of the child with his parents, in particular with the mother. Thus one of the dilemmas posed by the author in 1956 seems to resolve itself if a greater importance is accorded to the early object relation. Zetzel said in Geneva: "Differences in the interpretation of the role of the analyst and the nature of the transference develop from emphasis, on the one hand, on the importance of early object relations, and on the other, from primary attention to the role of the ego and its defences" (1956a, p. 369).

In 1974 the concept that the therapeutic alliance is the indispensable base for analytic treatment was maintained, and it was again defined as a positive and stable relation between analyst and patient, which enables the work of analysis to be carried out (Zetzel & Meissner, 1974, p. 307). As in previous works, the therapeutic alliance is seen as pregenital and dyadic, but its interface with transference neurosis becomes more fluid, conjunctive and functional. In her Geneva paper Zetzel said: "First, as already indicated, those who emphasize the analysis of defence tend to make a definitive differentiation between transference as therapeutic alliance and the transference neurosis as a compromise formation which serves the purpose of resistance" (1956a, p. 371). These assertions are mitigated, it seems to me, in 1974. Zetzel believes that these faculties of the ego are so intimately linked to the resolution of pregenital conflicts experienced in the context of a unilateral relation, that it is not surprising that, when the analyst approaches the level of the pregenital conflicts, the relation that constitutes the basis for the therapeutic alliance is itself included in the analysis of the transference (Zetzel & Meissner, 1974). She asserts that at this level the transference neurosis and the therapeutic alliance tend to become mixed, to the point where it is not possible to distinguish between them. I think these affirmations could be accepted by more than one Kleinian analyst.

18.7   More about analytic regression

I indicated earlier that the concept of analytic regression confronted Zetzel's essay of 1956 with its most serious difficulties. I was only repeating the objections to the theory of regression in the setting formulated in my paper (1979a) which is included in this volume as chapter 40.

Zetzel's 1974 work reaffirms that analytic regression serves to reopen the fundamental conflict that the personality brings to a close at the end of the oedipal period, and thus the means arises of working it through and resolving it. She reiterates what she claimed in 1956, that there are two types of regression. But the types proposed here are not those Lagache discussed in his essay of 1951; therefore Zetzel's classification distinguishes between instinctual regression and the regression of the ego.

She also states that instinctual regression is followed by an increase of energy in the closed system, which in turn mobilizes the signal anxiety. But now an obscure point (at least for me) in the Geneva essay is clearly resolved: Zetzel considers this regressive release of energy as being compatible with the conservation of secondary autonomy, as long as the fundamental functions of the ego remain intact. From this she concludes that instinctual regression is essential in the analytic process and can be considered potentially favourable to adaptation. On the other hand, the regression of the ego impedes the analytic process and should be considered dangerous. Zetzel had already admitted these two types of regression in her work of 1965. She said there, following Hartmann, that the definitive ego characteristics that possess secondary autonomy are more stable than the ego defences, but she made it clear that these qualities can be subject to regression in certain circumstances (1965, p. 41). Later on she returns to this theme and reiterates that even essentially healthy individuals continue to be subject to regressive processes that affect their secondary autonomy in specific situations of tension. She adds that this regression in the analytic situation should be differentiated from instinctual regression, which is an acceptable companion of transference analysis (ibid., p. 46).

With this repeated and categorical assertion that secondary autonomy should remain outside the process of therapeutic regression (which was less evident in 1956), the postulate of therapeutic regression is no longer tied to Hartmann's theories, although Dr. Zetzel might not say so.

Hartmann's theories would be applicable if the process of therapeutic regression were to mobilize the energy linked to secondary autonomy and throw it into the seething cauldron of the primary process, to borrow a vivid metaphor from David Rapaport's classic 1951 essay. But we have just seen that this possibility has been definitely rejected.

Having reached this point, we can foresee that Dr. Zetzel will seek backing from those theories that emphasize the importance of the early object relation, and so it is. "I have suggested as a major premise of this discussion that the first and most significant object relation leading to an ego identification occurs in the early mother–child relationship. The nature and quality of this early achievement has been correlated with the initiation of secondary ego autonomy" (1965, pp. 48–49).

Although regression inevitably accompanies the analytic process, the author concludes, the patient should retain and reinforce his capacity for basic trust and positive identification of the ego. This is an essential prerequisite of the analytic process that depends on regression potentially in the service of the ego (ibid., p. 49).

Having clearly established that the therapeutic alliance depends on secondary ego autonomy and the latter on the (good) object relation with the mother, Zetzel concludes that therapeutic regression is in the service of the ego. With this it becomes difficult to maintain that the transference neurosis is a defence mechanism of the ego and that regression is a manifestation of resistance, as was said at the Geneva Congress (1956a, p. 372). We will return to this absorbing theme in the fourth part of this book.

CHAPTER NINETEEN

The non-transference analytic relationship

19.1   Transference and alliance

In his technical works Freud showed a clear understanding of the highly complex nature of the relation established between analyst and patient, and he was able to formulate it rigorously in his theory of transference. Regarding the course of the cure, he also distinguished two dissimilar and contrasting attitudes in the analysand—cooperation and resistance. Probably because of his firm conviction that even the highest products of the human spirit have their roots in sexuality, Freud included them in the transference. Thus, in his classification in "The Dynamics of Transference" (1912b), he states that the resistances are fed both by the erotic transference if it assumes a sexual character and by the negative (hostile) transference, separating from them the *unanstössige* [unobjectionable] *Komponente*, which are the motor of the cure both in analysis and in other methods of treatment.

Some authors deplore Freud's decision and consider that had he separated these areas more resolutely, subsequent investigation would have been simplified. Freud's position, however, may have something to do with the inherent difficulty of the facts that he was faced with and which we are still discussing.

In any case, no one doubts that the therapeutic alliance often has to do with the positive transference, and even with the negative one (if factors of rivalry, for instance, lead the patient to cooperate), although an attempt to separate the two phenomena conceptually is justified. This enterprise offers a variety of theoretical paths: that of sublimation, which Freud follows; Hartmann's area free of conflicts; and others.

In fact, with few exceptions, the authors follow Freud's criterion and visualize the therapeutic alliance as a special aspect of transference.

19.2 Greenson's ideas

When Greenson, with all the enthusiasm of which he was capable, began to study the problem in the 1960s, he understood his *working alliance* as an aspect of the transference that has not been clearly separated from other forms of transference reaction (1965a, p. 156). Two years later, he stated categorically that the working alliance is a relatively rational desexualized and de-aggressivized phenomenon (1967, p. 207).

In his 1965 work, Greenson defines the working alliance as the relatively rational and non-neurotic *rapport* the patient has with his analyst (1965a, p. 157).

In his book Greenson (1967) describes it similarly: "The working alliance is the relatively non-neurotic, rational relationship between patient and analyst which makes it possible for the patient to work purposefully in the analytic situation" (p. 46). As Sterba had said, the alliance is formed between the rational ego of the patient and the rational ego of the analyst, from a process of identification with the analyst's attitude and work, which the patient experiences at first hand in the session.

For Greenson, the working alliance depends on the patient, the analyst and the setting. The patient cooperates insofar as it is possible for him to establish a relatively rational link based on his neutralized instinctive components, a link he had in the past and which arises now in the relation with the analyst. The analyst, for his part, contributes to the working alliance by his consistent effort in trying to understand and overcome the resistance, by his empathy and his attitude of acceptance towards the patient without judging or dominating him. Finally, the setting facilitates the working alliance through the frequency of the visits, the long duration of the treatment, the use of the couch, and of silence. Greenson, quoting Greenacre (1954), says the elements of the setting promote both the regression and also the working alliance.

The difference between transference neurosis and working alliance is not absolute. The alliance can contain elements of infantile neurosis which eventually will need to be analysed (Greenson, 1967, p. 193). In reality, the relation between the two is multiple and complex. At times an attitude clearly linked to the transference neurosis can reinforce the working alliance, and, conversely, cooperation can be used defensively in order to maintain the repression of the conflict, as sometimes happens with the obsessional neurotic, who always clings to the rational.

The working alliance always contains a mix of rational and irrational elements.

19.3   A tripartite division

As we have seen, in his 1965 paper Greenson proposed that the transference phenomenon (and therefore the analytic treatment) should be understood as a relation between two parallel and antithetical forces—the transference neurosis and the working alliance—which are both of equal importance (1965a, p. 179). In chapter 3 of his book on technique, however, he establishes a different relation when he speaks on the one hand of a working alliance (section 3.5) and on the other of the real relation between patient and analyst (section 3.6).

For Greenson the real signifies two things: that which is not distorted, and that which is genuine. Transference reactions are not real in the first sense of the word, as they are distorted; but they are genuine, they are truly felt. In contrast, the working alliance is real in the first sense of the term—that is, concordant with (objective) reality, appropriate, not distorted—but if it arises as an artefact of the cure, it is not genuine.

I think Greenson's tripartite division adds little to the subject we are discussing. Were we to take it literally, we would have to divide our field of work into three fronts, encouraging whatever is helpful to us in what the analysand says, even if it is not genuine; and accepting his cooperation with us for spurious motives.

Greenson is mistaken on this point, I believe, because he tries to mould into theory the sometimes confusing complexity of the facts.

19.4   Greenson and Wexler at the Rome Congress

At the XXVI International Congress of 1969, accompanied this time by Wexler, Greenson took a decisive step in his investigation: he separated the analytic relation into transference and non-transference. The two familiar parts—transference neurosis and working alliance (or therapeutic alliance)—are upheld; but the latter is conceptually separated from the former. The working alliance is defined at last as a real interaction (at times in quotes and at times without them to show the hesitation of the authors), which can demand of the analyst interventions different from interpretation.

As the authors recall, all this had been specified by Anna Freud with her proverbial clarity in 1954, at the Arden House Symposium; the patient has a healthy part of his personality, which maintains a real relation with the analyst. Leaving aside the respect due to the strict management of the transference situation and its interpretation, one must realize that the analyst and the patient are two real people, of equal rank, with a relationship that is also real. Neglecting this aspect of the relation may result in hostile reactions on the part of patients, which we afterwards qualify as transferred (A. Freud, 1965–71, Vol. 4, p. 373).

As with every human relation, the analytic relation is complex, and in it there is always a mixture of fantasy and reality. Every transference reaction contains a seed of reality, and every real relation has something of transference. The past always influences the present, because there is never a precisely outlined and immediate reality, without support from the past; but this alone does not mean there is transference. ("One can hardly argue the question that the past does influence the present, but this is not identical to transference"—Greenson & Wexler, 1969, p. 28. Greenson's and Wexler's formulation on this point is almost identical to mine when I compared transference and experience.)

If we maintain that the analyst is an impartial observer, equidistant from all psychic instances, then we must assume that the analyst should recognize and work with ego functions that include the test of reality (ibid., p. 38).

I think Greenson's and Wexler's ideas, which I have just summed up, are valid and probably indisputable. It can be asked, of course, what we mean by transference and what we mean by reality. But once we have ceased to discuss this, we will have to recognize that our task consists in contrasting two orders of phenomena, two areas of mental functioning. We can call them, according to our theoretical predilections, material truth and historical truth, fantasy and reality, topic of the imaginary and the symbolic, area of conflict and autonomous ego; but they will always be there.

Before going to Rome, Greenson and Wexler could have found many of their admonitions in the introduction to Meltzer's *The Psychoanalytic Process* (1967), which was already published. Meltzer states that although it is not always accessible, there always exists in each patient—to a greater or lesser degree—a more mature level of the mind, which derives from the introjective identification with adult internal objects and can rightly be called the "adult part". During the analytic task an alliance is formed with this part. An aspect of analytic work that feeds this alliance consists in indicating and explaining the required cooperation, at the same time as stimulating it (Meltzer, 1967, p. xiii). The language and the theoretical assumptions are different, but the ideas are the same.

Objections to Greenson and Wexler's paper in the Rome discussion can be classified as theoretical (and semantic) and technical. I am certain that it is when these two aspects are inadvertently superimposed that the discussion becomes confused and heated. Some analysts seemed afraid that with the key (or hook!) of the therapeutic alliance, dangerous active methods will be reintroduced into their rigorous technique. The risk exists and must be taken account of; but we are not therefore going to throw out the baby with the bath water.

As moderator of the discussion, Paula Heimann (1970) raised certain issues, the most fundamental of which seems to be her opinion that Greenson's definition of transference is too narrow. Freud, Heimann recalls, recognized the mild positive transference as an indispensable factor in the cure. This aspect of the transference is linked to the trust and sympathy that are part of the human condition. Without basic trust, the infant does not survive, and without basic transference the analysand does not undertake analysis.

Heimann's disagreement on this point is categorical yet only semantic: She prefers simply to call basic transference what Greenson and Wexler separate out as the working alliance.

Paula Heimann's technical considerations go deeper into the matter, and we refer to them in the next section.

19.5   How to reinforce the therapeutic alliance

The working alliance not only exists but can be strengthened or inhibited. If it does not exist, then this marks the baseline of unanalysability for Greenson. Taking account of it and strengthening it can transform very disturbed patients into analysable ones.

As we have noted, the analyst's most important contribution to the therapeutic alliance comes from his daily work with the patient, from his behaviour towards the patient and his material, from his interest, his effort and his composure. At the same time the analytic atmosphere—humanitarian and permissive as well as moderate and circumspect—is also decisive.

Each time a new measure is introduced, it must be explained, the more so if it is dissonant with cultural usage, without this preventing careful analysis of the analysand's response.

An element that greatly strengthens the working alliance is the analyst's frank admission of his technical errors, without this implying in any way a type of countertransference confession, a procedure Greenson and Wexler criticize severely.

These are the principal means Greenson and Wexler propose to fortify the working alliance and which, they repeat, have nothing to do with active techniques or a type of role playing.

A playful commentary of Paula Heimann's can serve as the starting point to a discussion of some of the measures Greenson and Wexler propose to strengthen the working alliance.

Greenson states that we must recognize our errors and faults if the analysand perceives them, and Paula Heimann asks him why we do not do the same if the analysand praises us. Greenson side-steps the question by saying that, in general, the patient's praises are exaggerated and unrealistic, but this is not the issue. Would we, then, accept the praise if it were true and justified?

I differ from Greenson in thinking that we should not strengthen or correct the analysand's reality judgement. I continue to think, as did

Strachey (1934), that, even if it sounds paradoxical, the best way of re-establishing the patient's contact with reality is not to offer it to him ourselves.

Let us take the example Greenson (Greenson & Wexler, 1969) proposes, of the patient called Kevin who only dares at the end of a successful analysis to tell his analyst that the latter sometimes talks too much. It was difficult for Kevin to tell him this, precisely because he felt that his judgement was valid. He knew Greenson would tolerate abrupt comments on his part without being disturbed—in fact, anything stemming from his free-associating. But he was afraid of hurting Greenson by telling him this, thinking it was true and assuming Greenson himself would also think so. Greenson replied that he was right, that he had correctly perceived one of his character traits and that he was also right in thinking that this perception was hurtful. In accepting Kevin's correct judgement, Greenson produces what he calls a *non-analytic* measure, which should be distinguished from *anti-analytic* measures, which block the patient's capacity to acquire insight.

To ignore Kevin's critical judgement by evading it or treating it merely as free association or one more datum to be analysed would have confirmed his fear that the analyst could not acknowledge frankly what he was telling him. Or he could have thought that his observations and judgements were only clinical material for the analyst, without intrinsic value or merit. Or, worse still, he might have concluded that what he said and thought was true was nothing more than a transference distortion.

Evading Kevin's observation or responding with an "interpretation" that would devalue it would certainly be, as Greenson says, a grave technical (and ethical) error, all the more lamentable when the analysand was able at last to offer an opinion he believed to be true, which he had withheld for years.

However, these two are not the only possible alternatives. An interpretation might be offered which showed Kevin his fear that the analyst cannot tolerate the pain of something he feels is true, perhaps because the same thing is happening to him at this moment in the analysis, when he is able to see his faults and those of others, and this hurts him. According to my own scheme of reference, an interpretation such as this is aimed at the depressive anxieties of the patient and respects his reality judgement without needing to approve it. To say, instead, that he feels envy of my penis—word (or breast) or that he wants to castrate me would surely disqualify the statement, as Greenson says. But in fact an intervention of this type is not an interpretation, but simply the analyst's verbal acting-out.

I recall a similar situation with a neurotic female patient who was coming out of a long and painful period of confusion. She arrived in a very anxious state and told me she thought she was crazy because she had seen, at the door of an apartment on the same floor as the consulting-room, the doormat I had used in my previous consulting-room. (I had moved to another consulting-room recently, and my wife had placed that doormat at the entrance to the apartment we were now living in.) I barely checked the desire to tell her, I believe in good faith, that her perception was correct, that it was the doormat of the consulting-room. I thought that to withhold that information was neither honest nor good for a patient who already doubted her perception of reality. I immediately associated that, when my wife had placed that doormat in front of our apartment, I was about to tell her not to do it, because a patient might recognize it and find out where I lived. I recalled that I had not done so in order not to take analytic reserve to its extreme. Now I regretted this. I concluded that I had made a mistake—a really mad thing, it seemed to me—something that was incongruent with my technique. I interpreted then that she thought the doormat had come, in fact, from my consulting-room and, seeing it in another place, she thought it was as if I had wanted to tell her where my house was. I added that, knowing my analytic style as she did and having already criticized me once because I seemed rigid to her, she could only think I had gone mad and was telling me so by stating she was mad. The patient's anxiety passed, as if by enchantment, and I felt calm. She replied serenely that she had noticed this on the first day and could not believe it, thinking I would not deviate in that way from my technique. Then she added, kindly, that my wife had probably placed it there without my noticing it. There was only one step from that to the primal scene.

I think, as Greenson does, that to conceal a problem of this type by using the pretext of preserving the setting is completely anti-analytic; so is side-stepping the issue with a defensive interpretation, which disqualifies and does not interpret. Greenson's non-analytic devices, however, are not as innocuous as they seem. Their difficulty lies in making us, as analysts, assume responsibility for the analysand's judgement or perception, which is never a good thing. To however small a degree, they make us abandon our method for a moment. Perhaps this is why Greenson and Wexler reproach Rosenfeld when he says that, if he fails with his interpretation, he thinks in principle that the latter is at fault rather than his method, notwithstanding that, on this point, Rosenfeld does no more than fulfil the expectations of any scientific community.

19.6   The child's therapeutic alliance

It is understandable that the therapeutic alliance has special characteristics in the case of children, due to the special nature of the infant mind. Here we will follow a discussion between Sandler, Hansi Kennedy and Tyson with Anna Freud (1980). Sandler et al. consider that "the treatment alliance is a product of the child's conscious or unconscious wish to cooperate and his readiness to accept the therapist's aid in overcoming internal difficulties and resistances" (1980, p. 45).

This is equivalent to saying that the child accepts that he has problems and is prepared to face them, despite his resistances and those that may come from outside, from the family. Although it is always difficult to draw a neat dividing line between therapeutic alliance and transference, it is always possible to attempt it. At times the child clearly expresses his need to be helped in the face of internal difficulties, at others the alliance is an aspect of the positive transference, and the analyst is only a significant adult by whom the child allows himself to be led and with whom he is prepared to work, or a maternal figure who is going to help him. To this is added the experience of analysis itself, where the child finds himself with a person who understands him and awakens positive feelings in him.

With respect to psychic instances, the therapeutic alliance depends not only on the libidinal and aggressive impulses of the id, but it also arises from the ego and the superego.

There is certainly a difference between the alliance that arises from the acknowledgement of internal difficulties (insight into the illness and a need to be helped) and one that arises from the positive transference. In the past, the successful development of analysis was thought to be centred on positive transference; but today these factors are evaluated with some reservations. Precisely from this arises the idea of differentiating the treatment alliance from the transference. The famous analytic honeymoon is only the result of an analysis that begins with a positive transference.

Just as the superego participates in the treatment alliance, making the child assume responsibility for not missing sessions and working with the analyst, so the parents also form part of that alliance by encouraging him to undertake and continue treatment. In this way, the continuation of the treatment can reside more in the parents than in the child, making an evaluation of the treatment alliance more difficult than in the case of an adult. If the therapeutic alliance fails, the adult ceases to attend, but the child may be forced to continue by his parents.

The treatment alliance can be defined (and conceptualized) in two distinct ways: Descriptively, it is composed of all the factors that maintain the patient in treatment and allow him to continue despite resistance or negative transference. According to a narrower definition, it is based specifically on insight into the illness and on the desire to do something about it, which is linked to the capacity to tolerate effort and pain in facing internal difficulties. The wide definition includes the elements of the id that can support the treatment alliance, while the narrower one takes into account strictly what depends on the ego.

We have already mentioned in speaking of the indications for analysis that Janine Chasseguet-Smirgel (1975) considers that the alliance resides, to a great extent, in the ego ideal, which determines the analysand's objectives.

19.7   Therapeutic pseudo-alliance

Many authors, such as Sandler, Dare, and Holder (1973), Greenson (1967) and others, point out that frequently the therapeutic alliance and the transference are confused, that at times the alliance rests on libidinal elements and, less frequently, on aggressive ones; at other times the alliance itself is in the service of resistance, obstructing the development of the transference neurosis. From these clinical observations, Moisés Rabih (1981) warns that one should always keep the formation of a *therapeutic pseudo-alliance* in mind and pay attention to the clinical indicators that may reveal it.

Rabih considers that the therapeutic pseudo-alliance is an expression of what Bion (1957) calls psychotic personality (or psychotic part of the personality), which assumes at times the form of a reversal of perspective (Bion, 1963). One of the characteristics of a reversible perspective, Rabih recalls, is the apparent cooperation of the analysand.

Where it expresses the psychotic part of the personality, the therapeutic pseudo-alliance conceals, beneath a façade of cooperation, aggressive feelings and narcissistic tendencies, whose aim is precisely to attack the link and obstruct analytic work.

This psychopathological configuration of narcissism and hostility, controlled and at the same time expressed in pseudo-cooperation, with features of hypocrisy and complacency, seriously overburdens the countertransference, as is to be expected. The analyst finds himself in the grip of a difficult situation, as he perceives his work as being seriously threatened by someone who at the same time presents himself as an ally. This is why Rabih maintains that paying attention to the countertransference provides one of the most valuable indicators of the conflict and its correct interpretation. If the countertransference conflict becomes dominant, the analysand's pseudo-cooperation may find its counterpart in the analyst's pseudo-interpretations.

CHAPTER TWENTY

Therapeutic alliance: discussion, controversy and polemics

The idea of the therapeutic alliance is easy to understand intuitively, but it is difficult to conceptualize. Perhaps this is because, in discussing this subject, we all have a certain tendency to justify positions, as polemics are always easier than the calm examination of problems and their complexities. In addition, a theme that touches our praxis so closely and sinks its roots into the history of psychoanalysis lends itself to forthright and intense discussion. At the end of their exposition at the Rome Congress, Greenson and Wexler recalled what Anna Freud had said at the Arden House Symposium to indicate why their presentation might have had a somewhat challenging and polemical tone. I would hope that what I am going to say will be used as food for thought rather than for argument, but, of course, I cannot be certain of my own impartiality.

In previous chapters, when I tried to specify and delimit the concept of transference, opposing it to that of experience on the one hand and that of reality on the other, I indicated explicitly that the behavioural act, the mental process (or whatever one may wish to call it), is the result of these two elements: there is always a bit of unreality (transference) in it and a bit of reality. And the past is always utilized to understand the present (experience) and to misunderstand it (transference).

It will then be a matter of deciding in each case, at each moment, whether to emphasize the one or the other; but in the last instance a good appreciation of the situation (which is called "interpretation" in our work) has to contemplate both things. It is more a question of tactics than of strategy whether to emphasize one or the other, as the situation is always integrated by these two factors.

These two aspects coincide with what we have called transference neurosis and therapeutic (or working) alliance. In my view it is illusory to see one without the other, and it is enough to say that when the analyst contemplates the internal reality, he can only contrast it with the other in order to differentiate it.

The working alliance is established on the basis of a previous experience, where one was able to work with another person, as in the case of the baby at the mother's breast, if we refer to origins. I do not call this phenomenon transference, in that it is an *experience* of the past that serves to locate oneself in the present, and not something that is repeated irrationally from the past, disturbing my appreciation of the present. In this way, I also separate the therapeutic alliance from the transference, as do Greenson and Wexler. But I am in complete agreement with Melanie Klein in seeing both of them as stemming from early object relations, from the relation of the baby to the breast. Zetzel also finally arrived at this, following her own path. Every time the subject utilizes the model of sucking at the breast and the other no less important models of development to understand and fulfil the task presented, he will have realized a working alliance. Every time he tries to utilize the work presented in the present to go back to the breast, he is in a state of flagrant transference. (For the sake of simplicity I use the model of the baby with the breast, but my scheme applies to any object relation—for example, to sphincter training.)

It is usually thought that the therapeutic alliance is more conscious than the transference neurosis, but this is not necessarily so. In most cases the patient emphasizes his cooperation, and then we have to interpret the other part, the resistance. But the opposite situation can occur with a melancholic or a psychopath, where the therapeutic alliance can be repressed, because it is the most unacceptable part, the most feared, the unconscious. In this case it is arguable, of course, whether what was interpreted is the therapeutic alliance or simply the positive transference. But this could be resolved by distinguishing as far as possible the rational component, which is really the therapeutic alliance, where past experiences are in the service of the current task, from the irrational component, which contains the positive transference. More often, the (positive or negative) transference is interpreted, and this strengthens the therapeutic alliance.

It is evident that if we say there are analysts who only see the transference and underestimate reality, we are affirming simply that these analysts are mistaken, if not psychotic—as it is the psychotic who does not see reality. It is enough to read a couple of little Richard's sessions to see to what extent Klein (1961) paid attention to aspects of reality: the mother's illness, the furlough of the brother who was fighting at the front, the invasion of Crete, the blockade of the Mediterranean, and so forth.

In order to be fair, however, we have to acknowledge that neither Melanie Klein nor her disciples, with the sole exception, perhaps, of Meltzer, take account of the working alliance. They take it as implied and obvious, but they do not integrate it into their theory, nor do they believe it is necessary to do so. Despite this theoretical failing—this *fault*, as Lacan would say—all the Kleinian analysts (and no one more, perhaps, than Betty Joseph) analyse continuously and rigorously the patient's fantasies in respect of the analytic task. Bion, whom no one would consider an ego psychologist, had spoken of work groups and basic-assumption groups as early as 1961, as did Enriqué Pichon Rivière in Buenos Aires at that time and earlier. Bion, however, never applied those fertile ideas to the analytic process. I will say, in passing, that in chapter 3 of his book on technique, Sandler (Sandler et al., 1973) courteously recalls Bion on this point. Nevertheless, in the same paragraph he says, more or less, that we Kleinians brush reality aside and only see in the communication and behaviour of the patient a transference of attitudes and feelings postulated as infantile. Does my friend Sandler think, perchance, that if a patient, in the Buenos Aires of today, tells me he cannot pay my fees in full, I will interpret that he wants to castrate me or that he envies my breast? Or does he think, more benevolently, that I will reduce the fees? It would be lovely not to take account of reality. But unfortunately that is impossible.

Paula Heimann said in Rome that some of Greenson's and Wexler's postulates coincided with the most obvious and elementary Freudian teachings; but this can also be unjust, because everything depends on where the emphasis is placed. Neither Greenson, nor Wexler, nor the other authors, beginning with Sterba, who pose the idea of the therapeutic alliance, would ever think they had proposed something that was not part of Freud's thought. What is discussed is whether these authors called attention to something that usually goes unnoticed.

A fundamental difference could be that only the ego psychologists start with Hartmann's idea of the conflict-free ego sphere. But when all these works are studied with care, one sees that the 1939 monograph inspires rather than provides the basis for them. Even in her work in the issue in homage to Hartmann, Elizabeth R. Zetzel bases her concept of the autonomous ego more on the good experience of the dyadic relation with the mother than on the conflict-free ego sphere. It seems to me—although I might be mistaken—that the great analyst from Boston renders homage to Hartmann while taking refuge in Melanie Klein—and, finally, in Freud, in defining the ego as a precipitate of past object relations. The Kleinian school, in any case, does not accept at all that there is something in the mind that is separated from the conflict.

Lacan criticizes the ego psychologist acrimoniously, cruelly, always in a more lacerating manner than he does Klein. He asks indignantly, "who are the ego psychologists, that they give themselves the right to judge reality? And what do they call reality?" Reality for Lacan, as for Hegel, is above all else a symbolic experience: Everything real is rational, everything rational is real. Only reason can give account of the facts; but when it does so, the facts are already transformed through the work of reason. For me, the reality is that I have come together with a group of colleagues to study the therapeutic alliance; but if you ask the maid, she will say that, in fact, there is a group of persons who have met to chat, drink coffee and dirty the living-room. The reality that she sees is very different in that she symbolizes it in another way. Reality changes, the transformations vary. The Lacanian critique of ego psychology starts from our not being able to ascribe to that hypothetical autonomous ego the capacity to judge reality, because we have to agree on what reality is: There is no reality that is not mediated through reason, through the symbolic order. (The Lacanian critique actually goes much further, because it questions the root of the ego in itself: it considers it illusory, imaginary—that is, proper to the mirror stage, which Lacan contrasts with the subject and the symbolic order.)

If we take the work of Susan Isaacs on fantasy or Paula Heimann's paper on transference interpretation at the Geneva Congress of 1955—that is, before she distanced herself from that school—and all the works of Melanie Klein referring to this theme, we see that they constantly indicate that there is an indestructible unity between the internal and the external, that one sees reality through projections that are also perceptions. The process of growth (and equally the one that occurs in the cure) consists in gradually modifying the play of projections and introjections, so that distortion diminishes. From this point of view, then, no psychoanalyst who follows Melanie Klein can interpret without taking reality into account. One must not lose sight of the fact that, by definition, interpretation always marks the contrast between the subjective and the objective, the internal and the external, between fantasy and reality. This is a very clear point in Strachey's work of 1934 and is reaffirmed in Paula Heimann's paper—quoted above—20 years later. It could be no other way. When I tell the patient he sees his father in me, I am implying that I am not this father, that there is another father who is not me. If it were not so, my interpretation would have no meaning.

If we wish to discuss this theme or any other without the intensity to which the theoretical position of each one can lead us, therefore, we should ascertain what each author is really saying and not make him say something with which we are then going to disagree.

The reciprocal critiques of the schools are just only in the sense that each theory carries implicitly the possibility of straying more along one path than another. The theoretical emphasis on adaptive mechanisms can make Hartmann lose the vision of the internal world; but in no way does the risk lie in the theory itself. The breadth of Klein's understanding of the transference exposes her disciples to seeing the transference too much and neglecting reality; but the theory does not say reality does not exist.

Lacan denounces Hartmann because he gives himself the right to decide what reality is—the right to discriminate between transference neurosis and working alliance—without realizing that he runs a similar risk if he decides whether his patient is in the imaginary or in the symbolic order. In my view, Lacan's is the greater risk, because he thinks he has the right to interrupt the session when *it seems to him* that the patient uses what he calls the empty word.

The theory of the working alliance protects Greenson from being arbitrary, accepting what the patient really sees, taking care not to disqualify him. If a patient tells me he sees me more grey-headed and I reply that he confuses me with his father (or, better still, with his grandfather), it is more than likely that I want to disavow a real perception on the part of the patient: I employ a true theory, the theory of transference, to negate reality. Greenson is absolutely right when he points out that there is always a strong temptation, for the analyst, to utilize the theory of transference to negate the facts; we are human, evidently. Wrong use of the theory of transference can lead to this type of disqualifying, and this risk is greater in Melanie Klein's theory of transference in that it is much more encompassing.

It is one thing to utilize the interpretation to understand what is happening to the patient, but another very different one to use it to negate what the patient has seen, what the patient has perceived. Let us say, too, that this is a key point in Paula Heimann's work (1956).

In general, when an interpretation obstructs, it is formulated, as Bleger said, as a negation. It is one thing for me to tell the patient that he sees me as grey-haired because he confuses me with his father, and another for me to tell him that in seeing me grey-haired I remind him of his father. In this last case I do not even judge the patient's perception. I limit myself to saying that if he sees me as grey-headed, he identifies me with his father. I could have no grey hairs, and the interpretation would still be valid.

With this we approach a problem that I believe is fundamental and one that I have already touched upon when I discussed Greenson's way of promoting the therapeutic alliance. I maintain that to accept the patient's judgement or perception as real when it seems so to us does not change things substantially, as Greenson believes. The truth is that an intervention that tends to support the perception of my grey hair is as disturbing as the one that seeks to negate it. Because what we are really attempting is to respect what the patient has perceived (or thinks he has perceived) and make him assume responsibility for that perception.

It is through cracks such as this, a small but undeniable one, that Lacan's criticisms of ego psychologists find justification. Here Lacan could say, with horror, that Greenson imposes his reality judgement on Kevin. Beyond these extreme situations, however, I think the only analysts who impose their criteria for reality on the patient are bad (or very inexperienced) analysts of all schools—and sometimes, also, we must admit, the most experienced analysts during moments when they suffer a great burden in the countertransference. If a patient tells me I greet him in a distant or contemptuous tone, to refute or to confirm this is in reality the same thing: it is as if I think I can dictate the reality of his perception; and this is not so. I remember a patient who, at the end of his analysis, presented me with a problem of this type. He complained that I did not acknowledge what he had perceived in me (and which was very obvious). Instead of supporting his perception, which I have already said seemed true to me, I interpreted that he wanted to depend on me and not on what his judge-ment and his senses told him. In requiring this validation from me, he again delegated to me his own decision on reality. I also pointed out to him the strong idealization this implied: the assumption was that I would tell the truth, that I could deceive neither him nor myself. In the last in-stance, the patient is as capable of perceiving what is happening as the analyst is—and more so, if there is a problem of countertransference. This aspect is important and is often not taken into account. It is inevitable that to the extent we believe that we can appreciate reality better than others, we transform ourselves into moralists or ideologues. As Bion says, the analyst does not deal with the facts but with what the patient *believes* the facts to be.

Typical of many dissident movements in psychoanalysis is the empha-sis on the importance of social reality. This was the case with culturalist psychoanalysis in the 1930s as well as in Buenos Aires in the 1970s. The flag raised by these dissidents was that Kleinian analysis was ideological. Personally, I think that a good analyst, an authentic analyst, always takes account of reality.

Within the Kleinian school, it is Meltzer (1967) who attends most to the idea of therapeutic alliance through what he calls the *adult part*. One does not interpret to the adult part, one speaks to it. We should note that for Meltzer, "adult part" is a metapsychological concept, it is the part of the self that has reached a greater level of integration and, consequently, of contact with the world of external objects. In this way, Meltzer puts for-ward a concept of alliance similar in practice to that of the ego psychol-ogists, although on a different theoretical basis. Meltzer proposes, for example, that the first interpretations be formulated gently and accompa-nied by broad explanations of the way analysis differs from ordinary life situations at home and at school (ibid., p. 6).

It may be that other analysts of the same school think that Meltzer speaks "too much" with the adult part, but it is still the case that, when the situation warrants and given all the care that is required, we should *speak* to our patients. The extent to which we do it and the way we do it will, in fact, vary, because this is a matter of style. The truth is that the analytic dialogue imposes on us, at each moment, a decision about who is speaking in the patient, which is never easy, but neither is it impossible.

According to Meltzer, the analyst's attitude should always depend on what really arises out of the material. If the patient speaks with his adult part, one should respond as an adult; if it is with his infantile part, the correct response is to interpret at the level of the child he is at that mo-ment.

One can criticize Meltzer in that at times one speaks to the adult part, and the one who hears is the child. However, this risk is inherent in any attempt to distinguish the parts of the self. (Bleger used to say that, at times, the patient *rotates*, so that when we speak to his neurotic part, the psychotic part answers us, and vice-versa.) The opposite danger also exists, and, as Meltzer says, not to listen to the adult part can operate negatively as a contrivance of regression. A patient told me once that he "had the fantasy" that so-and-so was a better analyst than I. I told him simply that this was what he really thought, and he became anxious. As Greenson says, it is much easier for the patient to speak from the perspective of his neurosis than from what he feels as reality. He knows, as did Greenson's patient, that the analyst will be serene and equable with his transference neurosis, but that he can become disturbed if he is told facts that may be real.

Another aspect of the theme of the therapeutic alliance is that of the asymmetry of the analytic relation, a point that touches on ethics. It is not always noticed that the type of relation at the level of the transference neurosis is radically different from the working alliance relation. It is important to know that the asymmetry corresponds exclusively to the transference neurosis, while the therapeutic alliance is symmetrical. When the analyst uses the asymmetry of the analytic relation to manage aspects of the real situation (which by definition belong to the therapeutic alliance), he is being authoritarian. This confusion is very frequent, and it must be taken into account. The situation is asymmetrical only if the analyst concerns himself with the patient's transference neurosis; and this asymmetry is nevertheless complementary, double, with which the inherent equality inherent in every human relation is again validated.

A young colleague cancelled a businessman's session the day before it was due. The patient was bothered by this and reproached him because he had not advised him of the cancellation earlier, as he could have used that day for a short business trip. The candidate interpreted the patient's separation anxiety: that he could not tolerate absence, and so forth. This interpretation turned out to be inoperative, and the patient's material showed that it had been experienced—not without justification, I think—as cruel. In other words, if we do not wish to disturb the patient's critical reasoning and capacity for perception, we should take care not to utilize the asymmetry of the transference relation to erase the symmetry of the therapeutic alliance.

I always remember with affection a patient I analysed many years ago when I arrived in Buenos Aires. He was a businessman engaged in modest business pursuits, a neurotic or, rather, a borderline patient, with an envy of the breast such as I have rarely seen, who taught me many things about psychoanalysis. He had been in treatment for a year, when, after the summer holidays, I informed him (as I routinely do) of my work plan for the next twelve months, including the winter holidays and the following summer holidays. He asked me in astonishment how I knew already what the dates of the following winter's school holiday dates would be, as he had not yet read any announcements by the Ministry referring to this. (In Argentina the Ministry of Education fixes the school holiday dates each year.) I answered him casually that I had decided on the date of my winter holiday without taking the school holiday dates into account. Jumping up in fury from the couch, he accused me: "Oh yes! Of course! Naturally! Clearly you, who are so omnipotent and who at your age will not have children of school age, take a vacation whenever you wish. And your patients—they can go to hell!"

Although my North American friends may not believe me, I told him he was right, and that I was going to reconsider what I had done. I could have interpreted many things, all of them true—I certainly did so at the appropriate time!—but first I acknowledged that his claim was justified.

And in the area of transference neurosis, asymmetry is no more than the validation of a reality, a just reality, the difference of roles. It is not true, as the patient thinks, that he is the only one with frustrations. This depends on the viewpoint each one adopts. The patient can complain, for example, that the analyst frustrates him because he only interprets and never speaks of himself. For the analyst, on the other hand, it is always a great frustration to have contact with a person, the patient, for years, and never be able to share an important event in one's life. This is so true that many analysts cannot bear it. The rule of abstinence applies equally to both sides. The asymmetry does not impose supremacy but an acknowledgement of the polarity of the roles necessary to develop any task, not only analysis. The analysand who wants to be her analyst's wife and feels frustrated because her wish cannot be fulfilled forgets that the wife of the analyst cannot be his analysand. It is a mystery which of the two is the winner; but I am convinced that it is much easier to be a good analyst than a good husband.

CHAPTER TWENTY-ONE

Countertransference:
discovery and rediscovery

We have seen in the previous chapters how Freud arrived at an
unconventional idea of the doctor–patient relationship with his
theory of the transference, and we were able to follow the development of the concept from the initial scrutiny of the false connection in
the *Studies on Hysteria* (1895d) to the configuration of the general theory
in the "Postscript" to the clinical history of "Dora" (1905e [1901]). There
Freud defines the repetitive nature of the phenomenon (reprints) and realizes how seriously it disturbs the process of the cure and, at the same time,
its irreplaceable value in that it gives the patient conviction, thus transforming itself from a major obstacle into the most powerful aid for his
method. Lagache (1951) rightly says that Freud's genius consists in transforming obstacles into instruments.

21.1 Origin of the concept

We also owe to Freud the definition of the analytic relation, not only from
the patient's perspective but also from that of the analyst—that is, as a bipersonal, reciprocal relation of transference and *countertransference*. Freud
observed this new and surprising phenomenon early on and conceptualized it precisely.

As we all know, the term "countertransference" is introduced in "The
Future Prospects of Psycho-Analytic Therapy", the beautiful article presented at the Second International Nuremberg Congress in 1910. Freud
probably read it on 30 March at the inaugural discussion.

Freud says in his paper (1910d) that the prospects for psychoanalytic therapy rely on three major factors: internal progress, the growth of authority and the general effect of the work of analysts. By internal progress Freud means the advancement of psychoanalytic theory and practice; by the growth of authority he means that, in time, analysis will deserve a respect and favour on the part of the public that it did not yet have at that time; and, finally, to the extent that psychoanalysis influences the social and cultural milieu, this will also have a general effect on its own progress. Today, more than 80 years later, these three viewpoints have turned out to be true. Although some social currents can discount them at times, the history of our century can never be written without taking Freud and psychoanalysis into account.

As to internal progress, Freud mentions, among the theoretical aspects, symbolism, and, at the technical level, countertransference. He says that in the last few years an understanding had been reached that *countertransference* is also an obstacle to the progress of psychoanalysis. He describes it as the analyst's emotional response to stimuli coming from the patient, resulting in an influence on the part of the analysand on the unconscious feelings of the doctor. Thus he defines it, I think logically, as a function of the analysand.

It has always been claimed that Freud considered countertransference only as an obstacle; but if he introduced it in the context of prospects, this was because he supposed that knowledge of countertransference would mean great progress for psychoanalytic technique.

However, this is not to deny that Freud mentions countertransference as an obstacle that, precisely as an obstacle, should be removed. He says that experience clearly proves that no one can go beyond his blind spots. He adds that we are inclined to demand of the analyst, as a general rule, that he should know about his own countertransference and overcome it; this is an indispensable prerequisite before becoming an analyst. It is interesting that Freud's solution in 1910 for overcoming the blind spots of the countertransference is *self-analysis*. However, two years later, in "Recommendations to Physicians Practising Psycho-Analysis" (1912e), under the influence of Jung and the Zurich group, Freud specifically recommends training analysis.

We see that the subject was on Freud's mind, because he considers it again a few months later. In a letter to Ferenczi on 6 October (see Jones, 1955–57, Vol. 2), he again mentions countertransference—this time, *his* countertransference. That year Ferenczi and Freud had gone to Italy for a holiday, and Ferenczi had been somewhat burdensome, overwhelming Freud with a variety of questions and demands. He was probably jealous; he wanted to be in the position of preferred disciple (which in fact he was, as he was on holiday with the teacher), and he wanted Freud to tell him all about himself. On his return, Ferenczi wrote Freud a long letter of self-analytic nature, expressing fear of having irritated him and regretting that Freud had not reprimanded him, in order to reestablish a good relationship. In his serene reply of 6 October Freud replied that it was true, this had been a weakness on his part. He was not the psychoanalytic super-man Ferenczi had created in his imagination, nor had he overcome the countertransference. He did not treat Ferenczi thus, just as he could not do so with his three children, because he loved them too much and would feel afflicted by them. Thus Freud refers specifically here to the counter-transference, in this case clearly a positive and paternal countertransfer-ence, which prevented a particular course of action, making him weak and liable to err.

From another and perhaps not unconnected point of view, the free-dom with which analytic knowledge was used in personal relations is shocking. Currently we are much more cautious, because we know that these references are generally complicated. Let us remember here that when in *Analysis Terminable and Interminable* (1937c) Freud mentions the patient who reproached him for not having interpreted the negative transference—and to whom Freud replied that if he did not interpret it, it was because it did not appear—he means Ferenczi, as Balint—and Jones himself—assert. (Balint, 1954, says so explicitly in the symposium called "Problems of Psycho-Analytic Training" at the London International Con-gress.) What in 1910 was at play at a cordial and sympathetic level later assumed a different character. (For a more thorough examination of the relation between both pioneers see Etchegoyen & Catri, 1978.)

Aside from these two specific references in 1910 and subsequent sporadic ones, Freud did not return to this theme, and it is evident that he never elaborated a theory of countertransference. Others also did not con-cern themselves with it very much, and so it remained set aside for a long time; with the exception of an occasional contribution, countertransference was not studied until mid-century.

21.2   *Countertransference in the first half of the century*

The 40 years that elapsed between Freud's discovery and the time when this theme was studied again cannot be said to have passed in vain, yet it is certain that nothing substantial was contributed to the study of counter-transference during that time.

There is no doubt that in some of his works, such as "New Ways in Psycho-Analytic Technique" (1933), Theodore Reik sketched out a theory of countertransference based on intuition. But in fact he did not manage to formulate it, nor did he do so in his famous works on silence and surprise (1937). These are, in fact, important studies in the development of the theory of the technique as attempts to systematize the analyst's intuition and to give backing to the idea of free-floating attention, but they cannot be considered as writings on countertransference.

In all his works, Reik indicates that if one has a receptive attitude and trusts intuition more than mere reasoning, suddenly one can grasp better what is happening in the analysand's unconscious, in that there is, in the last instance, an intuitive grasp from unconscious to unconscious, as Freud himself indicated in "The Unconscious" (1915e). We know that during that time Reik developed a theory of analytic insight based on *surprise*, and he affirms that the analyst should allow himself to be surprised by his own unconscious. He does not mention countertransference at all, although his concept implies that of countertransference thoughts (Racker, 1953, study 6, section 4). However, to say that this is a theory of countertransference extends the concepts unduly. Reik maintains that the best way to grasp the analysand's material is through the intuition our unconscious offers us, but he does not specify that this intuition is nourished by a conflict on the part of the analyst, provoked, in its turn, by the transference conflict of the patient. Reik does not say this; it is not within his theory of the process. When he refers specifically to countertransference in "Some Remarks on the Study of Resistances" (1924), Reik considers it a resistance on the part of the analyst (p. 150), and he asserts that it should be overcome by self-analysis. Thus clearly he does not take it to be the source of his intuition.

In some of Fenichel's works, culminating in his 1941 book on technique, there are also contributions to analytic receptivity and to analytic intuition, above all when he engages in the famous polemic between intuition (Reik) and systematization (Reich), but not to countertransference as an instrument with which to understand the analysand.

The theme of countertransference is undoubtedly present in all these works, but none goes so far as to consider it as an instrument of the analyst. What was lacking for a theory of countertransference to be formulated was for someone to combine Freud's idea, which demonstrated the existence of countertransference (and revealed it as an obstacle to the cure), and Reik's idea on intuition as the analyst's major instrument. But this happened only much later and via other routes.

Similarly, some of Wilhelm Reich's references to his own affective reactions as an analyst appear as intuitions, even as sudden intuitions; but it is Racker (1953) rather than Reich (1933) who, in studying them anew, considers them the product of countertransference. Faced with repeated complaints from a passive–feminine patient that analysis did nothing for him, that nothing changed, that he did not improve, and so forth, Reich suddenly had a flash of intuition that in this way the patient was acting his entire conflict of failure and impotence in the transference, castrating the analyst and making him fail. Reich's sudden understanding, says Racker (1953), could not have arisen but for the countertransference experience of failure the patient produced in him. The facts are the same; the theory is different. Reich thinks that his intuition (experience, craft) allows him to understand the analysand's transference, but not that his countertransference is at play—just as he had also not attributed the previous period, during which he could not operate, to being an effect of an inhibition (countertransference impotence). (See "The Meanings and Uses of Countertransference", 1953, section 5. Reich's case is mentioned in his paper presented at the Innsbruck Congress of 1927, "On the Technique of Character Analysis", incorporated as chapter 4 in his book, *Character Analysis*, 1933.)

As long as the theory of intuition resorts to an explanation on the basis of experience, clinical eye or *métier* (craft), it defines itself as being independent of the countertransference—that is, of the conflict the analyst is suffering. The theory of countertransference as formulated by Racker, Paula Heimann and others subsequently specified that the analyst's *métier* consists in listening to and scrutinizing his countertransference—that *that* is his intuition. In establishing a link between the intuition and the countertransference, it is not being affirmed that every interpretation originates in this way, because as far as the analyst may fully retain his capacity for understanding, his countertransference may not intervene. It is possible to maintain, at least phenomenologically, that the intuition arises when we are not decodifying well, because if this is not so, we do not call it intuition. We call intuition a moment of breakthrough in which suddenly something unexpected imposes itself on our understanding. When we come to study the work of López (1972) on the way in which an interpretation is constructed, we will see three levels—the neurotic, the characteropathic and the psychotic—in which the mechanisms of codification vary, and with them the degree to which the countertransference contributes to an interpretation. One can assume, therefore, that the intuition cannot be separated from the countertransference (of the conflict), and that this is also applicable to the other sciences, because the intuition of the physicist or the chemist operates in the same way in the context of discovery.

So, as we have just seen, during the first half of the century the theory of countertransference does not appear in the theory of the technique and is absent from the famous polemic of Reik and Reich.

On the other hand, an early contribution—which, as far as I know, has gone entirely unnoticed—does stand out during that period: namely, that of Ella F. Sharpe to the *Symposium on Child Analysis* in 1927. The author's entire theoretical reasoning turns on her (countertransferential) reactions in treating a 15-year-old girl. But instead of constructing a theory of countertransference as an instrument, Sharpe concerns herself with understanding the analyst's resistances to Melanie Klein's methods, which is natural in the context of the symposium. Sharpe's self-analysis of her reactions to her patient is a model of psychoanalytic investigation of countertransference anxiety and of the analyst's conflicts with his superego, projected into the patient and her parents, and also the management of guilt through mechanisms of negation and projection. The analyst's reaction, this author concludes, is of vital importance in these cases (Sharpe, 1927, p. 384).

I covered Sharpe's investigation in some detail not only because it surfaces at a singular moment in the evolution of psychoanalysis, but also because it is an example of how even the most lucid people can ignore a great problem if the conditions are not right for focusing on it. Before it was possible to discover the countertransference as a problem of the praxis and to formulate it theoretically, it was necessary for the premises of the technique to change, and for the profundity and complexity of the transference phenomenon, the extension and limits of interpretation, the transcendence of the setting and much more to be better understood. And this was achieved thanks to Melanie Klein and Anna Freud, and thanks to Ferenczi, Reich, Reik and Fenichel, Sterba and Strachey, to name a few protagonists.

As analysts, we cannot ignore the unconscious factors that carried weight in that delay. It is not pleasant for anyone to see and to recognize his essential identity with the patient he is treating, abandoning the comfortable, illusory superiority he thought he had. For the pioneers, this was not only inevitable but also convenient, because otherwise the complexity of the factors would have overwhelmed them. As I have just indicated, however, the unconscious factor, although it was important, was not the only one. It was necessary to wait for the technique to progress sufficiently for its shortcomings to be discovered and for that consoling definition, that psychoanalytic work takes place between a neurotic and a sane person, to be revised.

Science, says Kuhn (1962), evolves through crisis. There are moments when the scientific community calmly applies its theories to reinforce and expand knowledge; there are others when a growing unease appears because of increasingly frequent and flagrant anomalies in the application of the theory. Finally, a revolution erupts and changes the paradigm. I really think something like this happened with the recognition of countertransference at the middle of the century.

21.3   The countertransference as instrument

In the 1950s a series of works suddenly appeared in which the idea of countertransference is considered specifically, not only as a technical problem but also as a theoretical problem—that is, re-examining its presence and its significance in analysis.

The most important contributions to the theory of countertransference during those years are, without doubt, those of Heinrich Racker in Buenos Aires and Paula Heimann in London. They were simultaneous contributions, and everything leads us to assume that neither Paula Heimann nor Racker had heard of the investigations of the other. (I remember often having heard Racker comment during those years on the coincidence between his works and Heimann's and on the autonomy of their respective ideas.) Paula Heimann's pioneer work was published in the *International Journal of Psycho-Analysis* in 1950. Three years later Racker published, in that same journal, "A Contribution to the Problem of Countertransference". It appeared in 1955 in the *Revista de Psicoanálisis* under the title, "Aportación al problema de la contratransferencia", but in fact this work, which was included as no. 5 in the *Estudios sobre técnica psicoanalítica* (1960) under the name "La neurosis de contratransferencia", had already been presented at the Argentine Psychoanalytic Association as early as September 1948—that is, prior to the publication of Paula Heimann's paper. The assumption is that she communicated it or prepared it during that same period. If, as seems justified, the discovery (or rediscovery) is attributed in Solomonic fashion to both, it must also be said that Racker's studies are more systematic and complete. Apart from the famous 1950 article and another excellent paper she wrote ten years later, Paula Heimann only returned to the theme in passing. Racker, on the other hand, published a series of works in which he studied important aspects of the countertransference, which he was able to articulate in a broad and coherent theory before his death in January 1961, months after the publication of his *Estudios* (English version: *Transference and Countertransference*, 1968).

If I have credited Paula Heimann and Racker with the discovery, it is because I think they are the ones who emphasize the role of the countertransference as *instrument*—which is properly new—and not because I ignore other work done in those years, which is also valuable. Articles dating from that time that deserve to be considered include that of Winnicott in 1947 and those of Annie Reich and Margaret Little, published in the *International Journal of Psycho-Analysis* in 1951.

Through the contributions of all these authors, and others we will consider, the theme of countertransference was introduced suddenly, and incisively, and it resulted in a sort of revolution, which was not realized without battles. When Racker presented his work at the Argentine Psychoanalytic Association in 1948, he caused unease, and an important analyst said haughtily that the best thing for an analyst to whom "those things" happened was for him to re-analyse himself! As I have just said—and I do not think I am exaggerating—the works on countertransference of those years provoked a change of paradigm: from then on, the analyst's work has been questioned more and has been better criticized. We should also note Lacan's clear statements in his "Intervention sur le transfert", which also dates from that period (1951), where he indicates the importance of the countertransference in the establishment of the transference. Lacan, however, does not consider the countertransference an instrument. To the *École freudienne*, what matters is the *désir du psychanalyste*, and not the theory of countertransference.

What is distinctive in the works of Racker, Paula Heimann and other authors of that period is that countertransference is no longer seen only as a danger but *also* as a sensitive instrument, which can be very useful for the development of the analytic process. To this Racker adds that countertransference also configures, in some way, the field where modification (change) in the patient will take place.

If we compare this with what had been said previously about transference, we see that it had been treated in exactly the same way: transference was a (grave) obstacle, then a (useful) instrument and finally the field in which real change in the patient becomes possible; transference became the theatre of operations. In Lecture 27 in *Introductory Lectures on Psycho-Analysis* (1916–17), which deals with transference, Freud expounded this idea clearly: transference is not only an obstacle to and an instrument of the cure, but it also provides a different outcome for the old object relation, which tends to repeat itself. Freud said then that the moment the transference is resolved, the patient is able to face his problems differently from before, despite the fact that the analyst is again excluded.

On the basis of this Freudian triple model, Racker would say that countertransference also operates in three ways: as an obstacle (danger of scotomas or blind spots), as an *instrument* to detect what is really happening in the patient, and as a *field* in which the analysand can really acquire a live experience and one that is different from the one he originally had—more precisely, "than the one he *thought* he had". I am increasingly inclined to think that the "new" experience always occurs on the basis of another that was positive in its time or, more precisely, of a positive aspect of the entire original experience, which amounts to saying, as did Wälder (1936), that psychic acts are multi-determined.

In the last instance, analysis will do no more (and no less!) than to restore to the patient his past, including also what was good about his past, even though he had previously distorted or misunderstood it. This is a theoretical problem of great density, and I will deal with it later on. (In my Helsinki paper, 1981b, I offer some ideas on this theme—see chapter 28.) At this point let us say that this problem has a technical aspect (when are we going to say that the new *good* experience is original; when are we going to try to refer it to the past), and an epistemological aspect, which, because it includes the problem of universal quantifiers, requires a special focus.

If the three factors studied by Racker are understood, the theory of countertransference can be reformulated as a correlate of that of the transference, wherein the analyst is not only the *interpreter* but also the *object* of the transference. This is obvious, but at times we forget it. The concept of intuition, for example, refers to an interpreting analyst; but when the analyst is only an interpreter, he does not participate in the process, he does not suffer it, he has no passion. But perhaps what is most valuable about the analyst's task is precisely that being an object, he can be the interpreter; this is his merit, as Strachey pointed out in his famous article of 1934.

21.4 The concept of countertransference

Let us try now to specify and define the concept of countertransference. The types we are going to discuss depend considerably on the concept, and vice-versa, so that to the extent to which we distinguish diverse types, we can obtain a wider or more restricted concept.

Joseph Sandler et al. (1973) rightly say that in the word "countertransference" the prefix *"counter-"* can be understood as having two different meanings, which, in speaking of countertransference, are in fact always taken into account: that of "opposed" and that of "parallel". According to the former, "counter" is that which opposes—as in "act and counteract", "attack and counterattack"; by the latter, it is employed in the sense of balance, seeking equilibrium—as in "point and counterpoint" (ibid., chapter 6).

These two meanings operate continuously and sometimes contradictorily in the definitions. When we speak of countertransference in the first sense, we mean that just as the analysand has his transference, so the analyst also has his. The countertransference is defined according to its direction—from here to there—but it also establishes a balance, a counterpoint, which arises from the understanding that one's own reaction is not independent of what comes from the other.

These two ways of conceiving the process gave rise to a great controversy over the definition of countertransference and its differentiation from transference. Most analysts think, as does Freud, that the feelings and instincts of the countertransference arise from the analyst's unconscious as a result of the analysand's transference. Lacan, a rigorous investigator, however, affirms exactly the opposite, as we already have seen in studying his "Intervention sur le transfert" (1951). When he asks himself what transference is, he replies that it could be considered as an entity totally relative to the sum of prejudices, passions, perplexities and even insufficient information on the part of the analyst at a given moment of the dialectic process (1951, *Écrits*, p. 225). We have already criticized this somewhat extreme opinion, modified subsequently by Lacan's new theory of transference, the theory of the subject supposed to know.

The only thing we can do to resolve this dilemma is to fix an arbitrary direction for the process, which Freud, in fact, does (and so does Lacan, in the opposite direction). However, this decision ceases to be arbitrary inasmuch as it is founded entirely on the constants of the setting. The setting and, within it, the analytic reserve justify our defining transference as that which comes from the patient and countertransference as the analyst's response, and not the other way around. If the reverse were the case, the analytic situation would not have been constituted. Lacan is not at variance with this opinion, I believe, in considering that the phenomena of countertransference appear when the dialectic process, which for him is the essence of analysis, is interrupted.

This decision defines the field, the area of analytic work. To call one phenomenon transference and the other countertransference implies that the analytic process begins with the transference—as, in musical counterpoint, there is first a *canto*, to which the *contracanto* responds. Thus the term "countertransference" implies that the starting point is the patient's transference. In addition, it was thought at first, in the early days of psychoanalysis, that only the transference existed, and that the analyst always replied rationally; if not, he was at fault. Later it was seen that this was not the case and could not be the case. An analysis in which the analyst does not participate would be impossible and perhaps an error: there must be a reaction. This definition is operative but not authoritarian, even if it seems so. It is authoritarian to believe that the analyst always reacts rationally, or to forget that in defining the analyst's participation in the process, as we have done, we are only indicating his role without making a judgement on his mental health.

21.5   The countertransference and the setting

What justifies differentiating transference from countertransference is, in the final instance, the setting. The setting determines the phenomena: were it not so, we would speak only of transference or of reciprocal transference, as Luis López Ballesteros y de Torres preferred to translate *Gegenübertragung*.

It is not simply a play on words or a matter of principle to establish the setting as the ordering element—the setting is instituted precisely so that these phenomena can come into being: for the patient to develop his transference and for the analyst to accompany him in the sense of a musical counterpoint, resonating to what comes initially from the patient. If this condition does not come into being, then analytic treatment does not take place. The setting operates as a contextual reference, which allows the play of transference and countertransference; it is the syntactic structure where the signifiers of transference and countertransference will acquire their signification.

The setting determines a different and particular relationship between analyst and patient—a non-conventional and *asymmetric* relation. The patient communicates all his experiences (or at least tries to), and the analyst only responds to what the analysand has told him with what he thinks is pertinent. Only in this way is the type of relationship, with its roles of analysand and analyst, defined. If we consider the countertransference as an autonomous process that is in every respect equal to the transference, then the analytic situation will not be configured. In my view it is not accidental that Lacan's relaxed setting coincides precisely with a theoretical explanation that reverses the terms of the process.

Although the roles of analyst and analysand are defined contractually (as is ultimately any type of human relation), we should bear in mind that this contract, which precedes the task, is also sustained, and to a great extent, by the setting, which helps the analyst to fulfil his role and to maintain an equilibrium greater than that of the patient, while the analyst's training analysis and general training place him in an advantageous position. In this way, the concept of asymmetry comes to depend above all on the setting and only secondarily on the analyst's mental health. As we all know, the analyst who is in analysis functions differently in both circumstances.

The analyst could respond to the patient's transference in an absolutely rational way, maintaining himself always at the level of the working alliance. But the clinical facts prove that the analyst responds at first with irrational phenomena in which infantile conflicts are mobilized. In this sense, this is clearly a transference phenomenon on the part of the analyst. But if we are to preserve the analytic situation, it has to be a *response* to the patient. If it is not, then we would have to say that we are not within the analytic process but are, instead, reproducing what happens in everyday life between two persons in conflict.

21.6   *Concordant and complementary countertransference*

Racker was concerned with the phenomenology of countertransference and its dynamics, and he classified it into various types. Thus, in the first place he distinguished two types of countertransference according to the form of identification (Racker, 1953, study 6, section 2). In the *concordant* countertransference the analyst identifies his ego with the analysand's ego, and similarly with the other parts of the personality, the id and the superego. Alternatively, the ego of the analyst is identified with the analysand's internal objects, and Racker calls this type of phenomenon complementary countertransference, following Helene Deutsch's (1926) nomenclature for identification.

Racker believes that concordant identifications are generally empathetic and express the analyst's understanding, his positive sublimated countertransference. The complementary countertransference, on the other hand, implies a greater level of conflict. To the extent that the analyst fails in the concordant identification, the complementary countertransference intensifies. Racker also indicates that current use of the term countertransference refers to complementary identifications and not to the others, although he maintains that they should not be separated, since in both cases the unconscious processes of the analyst and his past are at play. (Here Racker decides clearly in favour of including the analyst's understanding—empathy, intuition—in the countertransference.)

This classification deserves careful inspection. From a somewhat academic point of view the concordant identification with the analysand's superego is an identification with the internal object. As Racker certainly does not ignore this, the conclusion should be that the analyst's identification with the analysand's superego is concordant when there is coincidence in the appreciation of guilt and complementary when the analyst functions as censor. It is more difficult to maintain Racker's points of view in the case of a patient who reproaches himself, because here the concordant identification could never be the most empathetic one.

Perhaps the model of psychic apparatus Racker uses for his classification (the structural theory) is not the most apt for classifying countertransference. His scheme undoubtedly also suffers because he explains the dynamics of the identifications on the basis of projection and introjection, without reference to projective identification—something Grinberg and Money-Kyrle do take into account, as we shall see in chapter 22.

The concept of projective identification leads us to another important theme, which Racker takes into account only laterally, without conceptualizing it fully: the difference between part objects and whole objects. Racker states: "The greater the conflicts between the parts of the analyst personality, the greater are his difficulties in carrying out the concordant identifications in their entirety" (1968, p. 135). It is evident that the identification Racker has *in mind* is the one concordant with a whole object; but then what counts is integration, rather than concordance.

I think personally that the analyst's understanding or empathy does not depend on his identifying concordantly or in a complementary way, but on the degree of consciousness the process may have, on the plasticity of the identifications and on the object nature of the link.

We arrive here at another point where Racker's classification becomes questionable, since the concordant countertransference lends itself most to a narcissistic type of link. Racker himself recognizes this when he indicates that concordant countertransference annuls, in a certain sense, the object relation, which does not happen with complementary countertransference (ibid., p. 136). In fact, the concordant (narcissistic) identifications are those that imply a greater level of countertransferential participation.

21.7   Empathy

We have just seen that Racker tends to consider *empathy* as a special form of countertransference, and many analysts think as he does. Others, on the other hand, make a firm distinction between the two and assign to empathy its own distinct place. The subject is complex and certainly deserves special study, which we shall attempt now. We have to take into account, meanwhile, that a great part of this controversy depends on what we extend the concept of countertransference to mean. Those who think, like Racker, or in the last analysis like Freud (1915e), that all thought is rooted in the unconscious, naturally maintain that empathy is no exception; however high its yields may be, it can always be referred back to the primary processes of psychic life.

When Wilhelm Dilthey [1833–1911] proposed the classic division between *natural sciences* [*Naturwissenschaften*] and *human* sciences [*Geisteswissenschaften*], saying that nature is explained and the human spirit is *understood*, he opened the way to the philosophical foundations of psychology and psychoanalysis, which thinking people still follow. We should remember that to begin with Dilthey used the concept of *empathy* [*Einfühlung*] as the basic method of the spiritual sciences; but later he preferred *experience* [*Erlebnis*], because he believed that it fitted better into the study of history, which was what basically interested him (Guarigilia, personal communication, 1989).

Following Dilthey's line, the monumental *General Psychopathology* of Karl Jaspers (1913) introduced the difference between explicative [*erklärende*] and comprehensive psychology [*verstehende Psychologie*] and applied this conceptual instrument with great vigour. Jaspers sharply distinguished two types of psychiatric entities: *developments*, which we can achieve with our understanding, and *processes*, which can be explained even though they are not understandable. For example, phenylpyruvic idiocy or phenylketonuria is explained by a genetic error, which fails to transmit the information necessary for the formation of an enzyme, a hydroxylase, which enables phenylalanine to be converted into tyrosine; this seriously affects the development of the central nervous system. Reactive depression, on the other hand, is *understood*, insofar as we can put ourselves in the place of the sufferer.

Within comprehensive psychology, Jaspers distinguishes in turn two types of comprehension: static and genetic. *Static* comprehension is concerned with states of mind that the observer can reach through experience (phenomenology); *genetic* comprehension, on the other hand, describes how one state of mind arises from another, through the connection of motives (*comprehensive psychology*). (We shall return to Jaspers when we speak of interpretation in section 26.2.) Genetic comprehension has, in its turn, two variants. *Rational comprehension* means that we understand according to the rules of logic; we understand the spoken word. *Empathic* (or psychological) *comprehension* enables us to understand the person speaking and takes us into the realm of psychological relationships and into psychology itself (ibid.). Jaspers' conception recognizes empathy as the basic instrument of his comprehensive psychology and hence of psychotherapy.

Starting with these definitions of Jaspers, we shall define *empathy* provisionally as one person's capacity to feel and understand what another feels.

* * *

Freud did not specifically study empathy and was not much concerned with it; but there is no doubt that he recognized its important place in psychoanalytical treatment, as Lerner and Nemirovsky point out (1989). For example, when the question arises in "On Beginning the Treatment" (1913c) at what moment the work of interpretation should begin, he asserts specifically that it must never begin before the analysand has established an operative transference, a regular *rapport*; and he follows up by saying that this bond can be weakened: "It is certainly possible to forfeit this first success if from the start one takes up any stand-point other than one of sympathetic understanding, such as a moralising one . . ." (1912c, p. 140). Strachey preferred "sympathetic understanding"; and although the turn of language does not really alter the concept, it should be pointed out that the *Studienausgabe* gives *"Einfühlung"*— that is, "empathy".

It is worth remembering that it is in *Jokes and Their Relation to the Unconscious* (1905c), that Freud uses the word empathy most often to refer to the understanding that arises between the two persons who interact in the joke. When "wanting to understand", says Freud, the subject puts himself in the place of the person observed, and thus there is a release of psychic energy that is discharged with the laughter.

In the introductory note to this book, Strachey (1960) recalls that Theodor Lipps [1851–1914] is credited with having coined the term *"Einfühlung"*; it is evident, he adds, that Freud was greatly influenced by Lipps' concept of the unconscious and his essay *Komic und Humor* (1898). As we have just seen, however, it was really Dilthey who introduced the concept of empathy, which came to occupy a key position in his philosophical system.

At various points in his book on jokes, Freud points out that the opposition between high spiritual interests and the perturbation produced by some chance circumstance such as the bodily need to relieve oneself is measured by empathy, and this is what produces the comic effect. This comic effect, says Freud (1905c, pp. 181–199), is linked with empathy, insofar as we assess it in the other person, since if it happened to us, there would not be a comic effect, but, on the contrary, a feeling of distress. In this sense Freud appears to use the concept of empathy to measure the difference between one's own ego and the other's, and *not* to understand it and share in it.

In chapter 7, "Identification", of *Group Psychology and the Analysis of the Ego* (1921c), Freud, on the other hand, gives a unique place to empathy, saying that it " . . . plays the largest part in our understanding of what is inherently foreign to our ego in other people" (p. 108).

After Freud, many analysts became interested in empathy, but none have gone into it as deeply as did Ferenczi. His famous essay, "The Elasticity of Psycho-Analytic Technique" (1928) is without a doubt the most original and the most complete work on the subject.

Ferenczi, at the zenith of his genius, shows an admirable balance between the science and the art of psychoanalysis in this article. As Ahumada pointed out to me in a personal communication, it is perhaps because he is in the middle of the road leading from active technique to neo-catharsis, equidistant from two passions that ended by leading him astray. This was the Ferenczi who had just written a definitive article on the problem of terminating analysis (1927), claiming the right of the analyst to be analysed seriously, the Ferenczi who understood and used the technique and method as few knew how, and the Ferenczi who, in Freud's view, had no equal. (See Grubrich-Simitis, 1986, letter of 4 January 1928.)

The starting-point of Ferenczi's essay is a reflection on the scientific nature of psychoanalysis as transmissible knowledge. Anyone who has been thoroughly analysed and has familiarized himself with the principles of the technique can operate efficiently, says Ferenczi, although there will always be a personal residue that he will have to manage with *tact*, which is nothing more nor less than the capacity for empathy. *Empathy* directs us as to what we can and must say to the patient so as not to increase his resistances unnecessarily and to save him from any avoidable suffering, because Ferenczi, as Bion was to say many years later, thinks that psychoanalysis cannot be carried on without pain, and one of his aims is to learn to bear it.

To Ferenczi empathy means taking into account, and up to a point foreseeing, the patient's reaction, so as to be able to speak or be silent at the right moment; but it must never be a naive or sentimental attitude. The analyst must keep his eyes open, while "his mind swings continuously between empathy, self-observation and making judgements" (*Final Contributions*, 1955, p. 96)—an admirable synthesis, which is as valid today as it was then. As he says himself in his letter to Freud of 15 January 1928 (Grubrich-Simitis, 1986), empathy does not mean any concession to the arbitrariness of the subjective factor and requires strict control of personal conflicts—something that some contemporary analysts unfortunately forget.

The relationship between tact and empathy, which Ferenczi established without clearly defining it, was later specified by Poland (1975) and Carloni (1984). Empathy helps us to understand and tact to interpret; the former belongs to the sensory end of the mental apparatus, the latter to the motor one.

Since Ferenczi's work the subject of empathy has been approached only occasionally, until in recent years it once more attracted the attention of analysts, beginning with Kohut's research.

In 1960 Greenson wrote a very comprehensive essay on empathy and its vicissitudes. For this author, empathy is the emotional knowledge of the feelings of another, a preconscious phenomenon that helps us to understand the patient insofar as it enables us to share his feelings.

Empathy implies a delicate balance, the possibility of entering into the other's feelings but without being emotionally involved, playing the part of a participant observer—as Sullivan said. Greenson thus considers that the analyst's empathy may fail through lack or through excess. If empathy is inhibited, the analyst maintains too great a distance through fear of being involved in the patient's feelings; if it is out of control, the analyst's involvement with the patient's feelings is too intense, so that he loses the ideal distance and also his objectivity.

Greenson distinguishes empathy from *sympathy*, in which there is an element of agreement with what the other feels, and therefore a greater degree of emotional involvement. He also differentiates intuition from empathy, because the former belongs to the intellect and the latter to the feelings.

Following the ideas of Melanie Klein, Nora Barugel (1984) distinguishes sympathy and empathy, like Greenson: but she defines them in a different way. In *sympathy* one feels or suffers with the other [*synpathos*] as a result of touching on aspects of oneself that one feels are similar to the object. In *empathy*, on the other hand, one feels or suffers within the object [*em-pathos*], so that identification occurs on the basis of one's own qualities located in the object—that is, from the point of projective identification. Barugel considers both processes as the result of identification and understands them, from the Kleinian point of view, as two modes of identification: introjective and projective.

Yampey (1985) recognizes empathy as a very important condition of psychoanalytical understanding and defines it as the ability to put oneself in another's place and share and experience whatever the other thinks and desires; but he warns against its dangers, when it is dominated by magic, narcissism or infantilism.

In his recent treatise on interpretation, Joan Coderch (1995) assigns empathy a prominent place in the psychoanalytic process and, in particular, in the act of interpretation. Coderch defines empathy as a subject's affective participation in a human reality other than his own, involving the joint operation of the mechanisms of integration and projection. In the former case we allow the other person's feelings and wishes to penetrate us, whereas in the latter it is we who place ourselves in that person's mind in order to understand him. For this author, we attempt by empathy to understand what the analysand is communicating to us "by allowing the emotional experiences he wishes to convey to us to resonate in ourselves" (ibid., p. 311). Coderch holds that empathy is always connected with the countertransference, but is distinct from it.

* * *

In recent years the author who had paid most attention to empathy is without any doubt Heinz Kohut. His scientific trajectory is a great arc of a circle that begins with "Introspection, Empathy and Psychoanalysis" (1959) and closes with "Introspection, Empathy and the Semi-Circle of Mental Health" (1982), passing through the last chapter of *The Analysis of the Self* (1971) before arriving at *How Does Analysis Cure?* (1984), which was published after his death.

Since his inaugural work in 1959, Kohut has categorically asserted that the psychological fact is achieved only by introspection or empathy, which, in his view, is a vicarious form of introspection; and, reciprocally, that what is achieved by these methods is psychological, and the rest is not. In this way Kohut limits psychoanalysis to what happens in the session, what passes between analyst and patient. The rest, that which comes from other fields of observation (such as ethology and the neurosciences, for example), may be useful to us but will never belong to our discipline. Kohut, however, says something more—that empathy must be considered as an essential component of the psychoanalytical method: "We designate phenomena as mental, psychic or psychological if our mode of observation includes introspection and empathy *as an essential constituent*" (1959, p. 462; Kohut's italics). In this lies Kohut's great innovation: empathy ceases to be a necessary condition of the work of analysis (as we have all thought since Ferenczi), to become the very essence of the method, so that it is given a real methodological blank cheque.

The 1959 definition is repeated and perfected in 1971, when empathy is recognized as "a mode of cognition which is specifically attuned to the perception of complex psychological configurations" (1971, p. 300).

In this chapter Kohut reviews the limits of empathy and its wrong use. If empathy is applied to the observation of areas that are outside the field of complex psychological states—that is to say, to non-psychological processes—it leads to an erroneous perception of reality, pre-rational and animistic. If, on the other hand, we do not use empathy when we have to observe complex psychological phenomena, then we fall into an error that is diametrically opposed to the former, which leads to a mechanistic and inert conception of psychological reality.

Up to this moment, since he has built up empathy as a type of specific knowledge—that is, as an essential element of psychological practice—everything would lead us to suppose that Kohut is about to declare himself a partisan of a comprehensive psychology such as that favoured by Dilthey and Jaspers, or that propounded more recently by Alfred Lorenzer (1970) with his theory of scenic comprehension. Kohut, however, strenuously denies this possibility, maintaining that empathy fails when, instead of using it as an instrument for the collection of psychological data or as a mode of observation, claims are made that it can replace the explanatory phases of scientific psychology. In this way—Kohut goes on—we arrive at comprehensive psychology in the sense of Dilthey and Jaspers, but not at explanatory psychology, so that the scientific standards deteriorate, and there begins a sentimental regression to subjectivity (Kohut, 1971, pp. 300–301).

A little further on in the same chapter we find a very clear passage: "The scientific psychologist in general, and the psychoanalyst in particular, not only must have free access to empathic understanding; they must also be able to relinquish the empathic attitude. If they cannot be empathic, they cannot observe and collect the data which they need; if they cannot step beyond empathy, they cannot set up hypotheses and theories, and thus, ultimately, cannot achieve explanations" (ibid., p. 303).

I believe I can detect here a contradiction in Kohut's thought. If empathy serves only to collect data from which an explanation is to be forged, then it cannot be said that empathy is the very essence of the method, but at the very most its starting point. With the development of his research, however, Kohut made his thought clearer.

In his posthumous book, *How Does Analysis Cure?* (1984), Kohut provides us with some arguments to help us to understand this apparent contradiction. In chapter 6 he defines empathy again as vicarious introspection, as the capacity to penetrate by thought and feeling into the inner life of other people, to experience what others experience, be it to a lesser degree.

In chapter 9, "The Role of Empathy in Psychoanalytic Treatment", he tells us clearly that the analyst's empathy consists in unconditionally accepting the patient's narcissistic transference, tolerating mirror transference with its accompanying exhibitionism and control, and idealized transference without limiting it by appeals to reality or interpretations that imply its rejection. Kohut believes that thanks to empathy the analyst genuinely grasps the patient's perception of his psychic reality and accepts it as valid. In order that this key affirmation may be clearly understood, Kohut gives an example that is worth noting. If a patient confesses to him that he has felt wounded because he, Kohut, arrived a minute late, he will not reply that his perception of reality is distorted or that he is confusing him with his mother or father; he will tell him, rather, that we are all sensitive to the actions of those persons who have become as important to us as our parents were in our childhood; and that, in view of the unpredictable character of his mother, and his father's lack of interest in him, it is logical that his perception of the importance of his (Kohut's) actions and omissions should be intensified, and his reactions also.

In this simple but enlightening case I believe I understand, without any fear of being mistaken, that Kohut's empathy consists in accepting without reservations the patient's unease because the analyst was a minute late. In this consists the moment of empathy (although it does not imply, in fact, the collection of data). What Kohut includes in his interpretation on the parents' bad behaviour (as self-objects) should without doubt be understood as the explanatory part of the interpretation, and, it may be said in passing, it comes from Kohut's theories and not from what the patient says; at least, Kohut does not record it nor think it necessary to do so.

With respect to the empathic moment of the interpretation, I believe Kohut is right to accept fully the psychic reality of the patient who felt wounded because the analyst made him wait. The interpretation that Kohut thinks up—and rejects—that the patient is distorting the real facts or that he is confusing the analyst with his mother or father, is not, in my view, strictly an interpretation but a disqualification of the patient's feelings and judgement, and probably an acting out on the part of the analyst who is trying to discharge his aggression and guilt. Only analysts who identify themselves with a very strong superego (and/or those with little experience) would be able to formulate an interpretation like this.

As for the second moment of the interpretation, we must begin by specifying what Kohut is claiming to explain; and this is, without a doubt, that the analysand's transference feelings in face of the (very short) wait he experienced are a logical response to the erratic behaviour of the parental self-objects of his childhood. But what is he really testing with this interpretation? It is certainly not the quality of those long-ago parents, because Kohut has no doubt of this; he knows by empathy that they were not empathic. Nor could he be testing his theory of self-objects, because then he would enter upon a vicious circle; he would be begging the question. What Kohut is testing, and I can see no other possibility, is whether the transference reaction of his patient is explained by what his parents did in his childhood, as deficient self-objects. If this is so, it is obvious that what Kohut is testing is scarcely significant. The analysand cannot but confirm the interpretation, since it is by empathy with what he has said many times that Kohut affirms that the mother was unpredictable and the father uninterested. It is difficult to say how much complicity there may be here between analysand and analyst to convert the present conflict into a past conflict, which would absolve both protagonists; but it is something to be taken into account, which does not enter into the expectations of self-psychology. It could be, for example, that the analysand is displacing on to the very short wait some greater grievance against his analyst, which he does not dare confess.

At any rate, when Kohut judges the parents of his sensitive patient so severely and assertively, he leaves entirely out of consideration what could have been the extremely demanding attitude of this child which conditioned—at least in part—the parents' response. This possibility remains completely outside Kohut's visual field.

A truly explicative psychology would have to test what the patient says and see how he reproduces the conflict of his childhood in the transference, and not attach faith to what he says, which will always be, as Kohut says, very respectable, but not the indisputable historical truth.

Throughout all his work Kohut considers that his basic contribution to psychoanalysis is a new prospect of the phenomenon of empathy, as Brunelleschi's theory on the prospect at the beginning of the Renaissance was new. I, therefore, think that despite what its creator says, the psychology of the self must be envisaged as a comprehensive psychology in which empathy occupies the central place, as the principal method of acquiring knowledge.

Kohut himself says this when he points out that the explicative aspect of the analyst's interventions is based in the last analysis on empathy, and that correct genetic reconstructions do no more than prove to the analysand that he has been understood.

In his posthumous book (1984, chapter 9), Kohut affirms that through the psychology of the self, the analyst succeeds in empathizing with the experience that the analysand has of himself as part of the analyst and of the analyst as part of him. In reality, Kohut thinks that the concept of empathy can be exactly grasped only in the context of self psychology, and to a certain extent he is right, as empathy is redefined starting with the theory of self-objects, and in the same way, self-objects can be defined as that which is achieved by empathy.

In order to preserve the empathic bond, Kohut does not hesitate to avoid interpretations that can "be felt" by the analysand as hostile or admonitory. The analyst will always tend to use tact in interpreting, as Ferenczi taught us; but he should never remain tied to what the analysand is going to feel, because the analysand is free to feel what he pleases, and the analyst's task consists precisely in analysing this experience, not in avoiding it. The care that Kohut takes on this point is in my opinion contrary to the psychoanalytical method and also to the spirit of the search for truth that Freud taught us.

At this point we should also explain Kohut's conceptual change from a theory of conflict to his theory of developmental arrest. Kohut maintains that insofar as his doctrine considers the sexual impulses of object relations as secondary to the organization of the self, it remains under cover from guilt connotations. While the interpretative approach centred on the conflict of impulse and defence lends itself to the analysand *feeling* it as censure, the interpretation of transferences with self-objects will be experienced as the acceptance of development in the normal process of maturation. This decision to maintain the empathic climate *à outrance* seems then to be one of the factors that have influenced Kohut's thought and led him to abandon the theory of conflict and impulse.

If empathy is understood as a way of protecting the analysand from painful truths about himself, then the concept becomes extremely narrow. I agree with Kernberg when he says, "It is very easy for the analyst to consider an intervention 'empathic' when it fits with both his own theory and the patient's conscious expectations or needs" (1984, p. 187).

* * *

At the end of this long discussion, I want to conclude by pointing out that empathy must be considered, as Ferenczi insisted, as a valuable, but not infallible, guide to understanding what the analysand (and other people in general) feels, to understanding and sharing other people's suffering, to reducing it as far as possible, although it may not be in our power to avoid it. I think of empathy as a *necessary* factor of analytical work, since without it we could never be on the same wavelength as our analysand; but it is never *sufficient* for our work, since empathy depends on very many factors that operate more in the context of analogue than digital communication; and in face of this multiplicity of factors and stimuli our own response is never univocal and infallible, since it depends on our own state of mind, our receptivity and our conflicts—in short, on the processes of introjection and projection that shape our countertransference in its widest sense.

As we shall see further on (section 26.2), Jaspers affirms that empathic understanding (which in his view is a form of genetic understanding) gives us a final proof that cannot be further pursued; but later he mitigates this extreme assertion by saying that a comprehensible relationship does not prove *per se* that it is real, and it may be wrong if the objective material on which the understanding of this relationship is based has not been accurately taken. This reference to objective material to which Jaspers himself resorts shows us that even this author has no confidence in his empathy; and to this we have to add, with Lorenzer (1970, chapter 2), that psychoanalysis rejects the possibility of collecting objective data and, for technical and ethical motives, denies itself access to all information that does not come from the analysand.

Lorenzer, on his part, follows Dilthey and Jaspers in suggesting comprehension (and not explanation) as the typical operative form of psychoanalysis; but, more coherent on this point than Kohut, he declares himself partisan of a radical hermeneutic psychoanalysis, in which through *scenic comprehension* the symbolic level of language can be recovered and the destructive process by which symbol has become cliché reversed.

Lorenzer's ideas certainly deserve a separate study; but we may say at once that all his reasoning is based on an *experience of evidence* that is obtained by means of a psychic act accomplished *in* the analyst and is verified in this act (1970, chapter 2, section 1), neglecting, in my view, the infinite snares of countertransference.

Most psychoanalysts concerned with empathy tend to consider it as a complex phenomenon (or affect) connected with processes of identification—a special form of identification, which is generally transitory and preconscious, not regressive, and reversible by nature (Levy, 1985, p. 355; Yampey, 1985, p. 353).

The relationship between empathy and countertransference varies according to the scope we allot to the latter. Annie Reich (1966), and in general all authors who tend to consider countertransference as an obstacle, prefer to separate it from empathy; others, like Racker, consider empathy as a mature or sublimated form of countertransference; but neither side recognizes it as an unequivocal method of collecting data. When Levy (1985) discusses empathy within self psychology, he points out the excessive range that Kohut gives to the term and the contradictory values he assigns to it: sometimes empathy is a reliable instrument for the collection of data, and sometimes it represents the analyst's skill in making the analysand experience his interventions in accord with his desires and needs (ibid., p. 368). Although Kohut does not appear to notice it, these are two very different concepts; and it is precisely the latter that causes many scholars to fear that psychoanalytical neutrality may be compromised in a sort of corrective emotional experience of the type of Alexander and French (1946).

Maldavsky (1986, 1988), in a vigorous attempt to establish a strict metapsychology of the emotions, studies empathy in relation to the specific mechanisms of neurosis (repression [*Verdrängung*]), of perversions and psychopathies as ways of transgressing (denial [*Verleugnung*]) and of psychosis (rejection [*Verwerfung*]) and isolates in each case a special empathic attitude. In accordance with his line of thought, this researcher establishes differences between empathy, countertransference and affective contagion, indicating that the two latter constitute an obstacle to analytic work and the first is valuable in giving direction in clinical practice; the three do not differ either in the affects in play or in their intensity, but in their origin and the way each of them is produced. In Maldavsky's view countertransference arises from a repressed desire on the part of the analyst, the affective contagion of an identification, also repressed; while in empathy the original affect derives from an identification with the patient, which is capable of entering consciousness and serves to accomplish the metaclinical effect of the change of defence.

* * *

In short, we must accord to empathy a distinctive place in our capacity to understand our patient (and our fellow beings in general); but we must realize that it has its limits and can lead us astray. We have the right to believe that psychoanalysis is a natural or hermeneutic science, but we must never think that the road to truth is safe and without bends.

CHAPTER TWENTY-TWO

Countertransference
and object relationship

In chapter 21 we examined the concept of countertransference from its introduction by Freud in 1910 up to the second half of the century, when it was first studied from a different point of view, in another paradigm: as an ineluctable presence, as an instrument no less than an obstacle.

We have seen that Racker studied countertransference from the point of view of the phenomena of identification and described two types: concordant and complementary. We said this classification presents some problems, and we indicated them. Racker's classification is based on a theory of identification which we will now study more thoroughly, following Grinberg and Money-Kyrle particularly.

22.1 Projective counteridentification

With his concept of projective counteridentification León Grinberg made a valuable contribution to the general theory of countertransference or, as he deems it, beyond the theory, as it is concerned with "the real effects produced in the object by the peculiar use of projective identification which comes from regressive personalities" (1974, p. 179).

Grinberg's concept is based on Racker's and follows on from it, and one of its major merits is that, as opposed to Racker, Grinberg takes projective identification into account. He establishes a gradation from concordant and then complementary countertransference to projective counteridentification. What Grinberg specifically postulates is that there is a substantial difference between complementary countertransference, in which, confronted by a particular transferential configuration, the analyst responds by identifying himself with the patient's objects, and the phenomenon he himself describes, in which the analyst finds himself *forced* to play a supervening role. It is the violence of the projective identification that leads him directly, beyond his unconscious conflicts, to assume that role. Grinberg becomes so categorical as to state that the analyst's countertransference is not in play here at all; he even maintains that the same patient with diverse analysts (whom he had the opportunity to supervise) gave rise to the same situation.

Grinberg's contribution singles out a special form of response on the part of the analyst, where projective identification produces maximum effect, and the quality is different. Although it can be located on a scale of increasing disturbance, it is placed beyond the point where a quantitative change becomes qualitative.

Grinberg's ideas are based on easily observable clinical data, clearly registered by the author. The concept of projective counteridentification is useful and operative. However, accepting it does not compel one to share the opinion that in these cases only the analysand is operating (and not the analyst), which can, I believe, be argued and is difficult to demonstrate. The distinction between complementary countertransference and projective counteridentification is not difficult from the clinical point of view if they are quantitatively separated. If we wish to distinguish between them as two different kinds of processes, the distinction becomes more difficult. I do not know whether we have indicators to decide this, despite Grinberg's careful investigation. If the method does not provide us with instruments to make a clinical distinction, then it can also be argued from the theoretical angle that, however strong the patient's projection, the analyst does not necessarily have to succumb to it. If he does, it is because there is something in him that does not allow him to take in the process and feed it back.

22.2   The development of Grinberg's investigation

The concept of projective counteridentification is theoretically as well as technically important, and it poses an open and absorbing question—that of pre- or non-verbal communication. It is therefore worth while to study it in greater depth, following the author's thinking step by step.

Grinberg's first paper on the subject, "Aspectos mágicos en la transferencia y en la contratransferencia" [Magical Aspects in Transference and Countertransference] was presented at the Argentine Psychoanalytic Association on 27 March 1956 and published in 1958. It is a study of magic in the light of mechanisms of identification, where the phenomenon is defined as follows: "Projective counteridentification is produced specifically as a result of an excessive projective identification on the part of the analysand which is not consciously perceived by the analyst who, in consequence, sees himself passively 'led' to enact a role which the analysand actively—although unconsciously—'forced into him'" (1958, pp. 359–360). A month after this presentation, at the Argentine Psychoanalytic Association's *Symposium on Psychoanalytic Technique* in April 1956, over which Heinrich Racker presided, Grinberg presented his paper, "Perturbaciones en la interpretación por la contraidentificación proyectivas" [Disturbances in Interpretation Due to Projective Counteridentification] (1957), in which he makes a special study of the effect of projective counteridentification on interpretation—the essential task of the analyst.

Grinberg had previously published "Sobre algunos problemas de técnica psicoanalítica determinados por la indentificación y contraidentificación proyectivas" [On Some Problems of Psychoanalytic Technique Determined by Projective Identification and Projective Counteridentification] (1956). The second part of this work appeared in 1959 as "Aspectos mágicos en las ansiedades paranoides y depresivas [Magical Aspects in Paranoid and Depressive Anxieties]. Here Grinberg discusses the case of a female patient who, in the first session, made him feel he was analysing a corpse, which coincided with the suicide of the patient's sister when the patient was a child. With this illustrative case Grinberg returns to something he had insisted on from the beginning: the process originates in the analysand and causes a specific reaction in the analyst, by means of which he is led unconsciously and passively to fulfil the roles the patient assigns to him. This is therefore a very special case of countertransference. While in the countertransference response it is characteristic for the analyst to become conscious of his type of response, which he uses as a technical instrument, in the phenomenon of projective counteridentification the analyst reacts as if he had assimilated, really and concretely, the aspects projected into him. It is as if the analyst "ceased to be himself to transform himself, without being able to avoid it, into what the patient unconsciously wished him to become (the id, the ego or another internal object)" (1957, p. 24).

In one of the clinical examples in the Symposium paper, the analysand, who had been very surprised that the analyst's interpretations had halted a bout of diarrhoea, began to speak about music in technical terms and provoked thereby the analyst's admiration and envy, feelings which he had experienced after his diarrhoea had stopped.

On the basis of these papers Grinberg went on to study the effect of projective counteridentification on the technique and development of the analytic process. When he returned to this theme in 1963 in "Psicopatología de la identificación y contraidentificación proyectivas y de la contratransferencia" [Psychopathology of Projective Identification and Projective Counteridentification and of Countertransference], he was particularly interested in the communicative value of projective counteridentification, a process he considers of central importance. In certain situations "projective identification participates in a more active way in the communication of extraverbal messages, exercising a greater influence on the receptor—in our case the analyst" (1963, p. 114).

In an attempt to specify the difference between projective counter-identification and Racker's complementary countertransference, he indicates that in the latter the patient's object with which the analyst identifies is experienced as his own—that is, it represents an analyst's internal object. The situation is, then, that in the case of complementary transference the analyst reacts passively to the analysand's projection, but on the basis of his own anxieties and conflicts. In projective counteridentification, on the other hand, "the analyst's reaction turns out to be largely *independent of his own conflicts and corresponds predominantly or exclusively to the intensity and quality of the analysand's projective identification*" (ibid., p. 117; italics in the original).

The most original (but also, perhaps, the most questionable) aspect of the theory of projective counteridentification is that in these cases the analyst's specific conflicts do not intervene. He is led passively to enact the role the patient assigns to him. Melanie Klein described projective identification (1946) as an omnipotent fantasy in which the subject puts into the object parts of himself with which he is then identified. From then on, progressive investigation has shown the value of projective identification in the process of communication, and thus the idea that projective identification operates in the object gained ground. Grinberg is decidedly in favour of this idea and says so in 1973: "An important part of the theory of pathological projective identification is that it produces real effects on the receptor and therefore, that it is more than an omnipotent fantasy (which is how M. Klein defines projective identification)" (see Grinberg, 1976b, p. 277).

When Bion (1962b) introduced the concept of the beta screen he indicated that due to this screen the psychotic provokes emotions in the analyst (chapter 10), and this assertion coincides clearly with Grinberg's theory. In one of his latest works Grinberg mentions it to characterize the peculiar modality of projective identification he has described (1974). We can assume, then, that these emotions are, up to a point, independent of the analyst's countertransference.

Grinberg's fundamental idea is that in the phenomenon of projective counteridentification the analyst does not participate with his conflicts but remains dominated by the patient's projective process.

From the practical point of view Grinberg's theory helps us in the many cases where the analyst feels invaded rather than engaged in the analytic situation. As for the theory of analytic process, Grinberg offers us a valuable hypothesis to understand the subtle means of communication established between analyst and analysand. As we said earlier, the theoretical delimitation between complementary countertransference and projective counteridentification is not easy to specify. One can always think that the analyst participated in the last instance, despite having felt forced or compelled by the patient's projective identification. However strong the projective identification received, the analyst would have been able to introject it actively and respond adequately. Thus we cannot ignore the possibility that, if he has allowed himself to be dominated by the projective impact, it is due to the countertransference neurosis. In other words, the analyst's passivity can turn out to be an "active" way of not understanding or of preferring to be invaded. On this point, Grinberg's theory is difficult to prove with our clinical methods.

When concrete cases are studied in which the force of impact Grinberg points out is definitely observed (in the supervision material, for example), the analyst's Achilles heel is at times revealed, at times not.

One of Grinberg's cases (1959)—one of the first in which he notices the phenomenon, and a starting point for his whole line of thought—is that of the patient who places in him her dead part, the sister who committed suicide. What Grinberg perceives initially as a countertransferential response of a humorous type is that "she wants to load me with the corpse".

It is demonstrable that on the patient's part there is a definite and total projection into the analyst of what is dead, and that he receives this impact passively. The analyst's countertransference conflict cannot be set aside, however, if only because *every* analyst always feels he is assuming a great responsibility in the first session of a treatment. This heavy responsibility, this load, is referred to in Argentinian slang as "carrying the corpse". With his usual perspicacity, Grinberg noted the patient's cadaverous attitude at the outset and, after his first interpretation, perceived that he had been precise but more superficial than the drama of the moment required. Then he surprised himself with the fantasy of analysing a corpse, and his humorous thought followed immediately. I do not think that, with this excellent material, the analyst's countertransferential participation (in the strict sense) can be cast aside.

22.3   Normal countertransference

Money-Kyrle wrote only one paper on countertransference, in 1956, where he introduced the concept of normal countertransference—that is, something that presents itself regularly and intervenes in its own right in the psychoanalytic process. He calls *normal* countertransference the one where the analyst assumes a parental role, complementary to that of the patient. As countertransference consists in reactivating infantile conflicts, the condition most suited to countertransference is the parental one. Normal means here "the norm" and not that the process is completely sublimated and free from conflict. The analyst assumes a countertransferential attitude on the basis of an unconscious experience in which he feels himself to be the father or the mother of the patient. Let us add that it is again the setting that favours us and safeguards us from developing a *folie à deux*.

The asymmetrical situation which imposes and defines the setting allows us to give an adequate response to what the patient has transferred. But our initial reaction is to feel unconsciously the impact of the transference, which places us in a parental role.

It is obvious that this criterion is opposed to Racker's, since a greater empathy is attributed here to a countertransference of a complementary type.

On the basis of this clear and simple model, Money-Kyrle goes one step further and states that the countertransference can be adequately employed as an instrument on the basis of a double identification, with the subject and his (her) object, because the analyst, in order to fulfil his task well, has to locate himself in the *two* places. This dual mechanism is realized through the projective identification of the analyst's infantile ego into the patient and through the introjective identification of the parent figure. In the normal countertransference, the analyst assumes the role of the parent, projected by the child; on the other hand, he can understand the role of the child not only through that parental position, but also on the basis of a projective identification of his infantile ego into the patient, mobilized by his tendency to effect reparation.

It is clearer now that the Achilles heel in Racker's classification is found in his concept of a process of identification without distinguishing its mechanism, which can be introjective and projective. Money-Kyrle says that in order to function in the best possible way, the analyst needs a dual identification, which I believe includes the two distinguished by Racker: concordant and complementary. If the concordant identification is effected with the analysand's suffering infantile ego without taking into account in any way the parental object, the analyst has probably used projective identification not in order to understand his analysand's infantile ego (empathy) but to get rid of one of his own infantile aspects, which he cannot bear within himself.

Money-Kyrle points out that the analyst's countertransference conflict stems not only from his own unconscious but also from what the patient does to him (or projects into him) in a sort of complemental series. On this point Money-Kyrle agrees with Racker, despite the fact that it is evident he has not read him, as he does not quote him. The subtle interaction between analysand and analyst is studied in Money-Kyrle with all the delicate tracery of musical counterpoint. Following Margaret Little (1951), he indicates that the analysand is not only responsible (in part) for the analyst's countertransference, but that he also suffers its effects. The only solution for the analyst is first to analyse his own conflict, then to see how the patient contributed to creating it and finally to take note of the effects of his conflict on his patient. Only when this process of self-analysis has been completed will the analyst be able to interpret—and then he will not need to speak of his countertransference but basically of what is happening to the analysand. (We will return to this subject at the end of chapter 23.)

When we deal with the dyadic relation of analyst and analysand (in chapter 44), we shall see that Spitz and Gitelson also accept a normal countertransference, which they call diatrophic, and which, for them, appears at the beginning of analysis.

22.4 A clinical case

We have seen throughout this exposition that in order to resolve the problem presented to us by the patient's transference, we must understand what is happening to him (concordant identification), but also what is happening to his object (complementary identification). We have questioned Racker's hypothesis that the analyst's understanding or empathy derives from the concordant identification. Let us add that, in general, it is the beginner who tends to have concordant identifications, because he thinks, like the business employee, that the customer is always right. Real analytic work is quite different from this type of agreement and at times demands that we place ourselves in a perspective different from the patient's, at a point equidistant from him and from his objects.

A woman a little beyond middle age, who had a great conflict with her mother, which began to be resolved near the end of the analysis, presented in a session the problem created by her adolescent daughter, "who was driving her crazy", while her son was ill in bed with mouth ulcers.

Earlier, at the beginning of her last year of analysis, we had reached agreement in principle that her treatment could end that year or the next. Although she was pleased with this agreement, and although I said clearly that in speaking about ending I did not think this could be very soon, a deep rift had opened up between us, and this implied a catastrophe.

Without responding to my (I think prudent) comment that the analysis could end within two years at most, and without having corrected her persistent idea that I was going to analyse her all her life, she came to the aforementioned session with the problem of her two children. On the basis of some significant associations, I told her that the open fissure (rift) between us referred to the birth of her sister while she herself was still being breast-fed. Perhaps the mother might have had cracked nipples in those circumstances. This interpretation seems to have reached her, because she admitted reluctantly that the prospect of ending made her happy but she could not avoid feeling badly when she thought someone would occupy her place on my couch.

She immediately tried to distance herself from her infantile jealousy and returned to the problem of her son's mouth ulcers and her daughter's adolescence, which I interpreted as aspects of her relation to me. The conflict with her adolescent daughter expressed her rebelliousness, and her son's mouth ulcers were, perhaps, the correlate of the supposed cracks in her mother's nipple. I suggested that, perhaps, at the moment of weaning, she had had mouth ulcers, and that one did not know how all that might have been, whether the nipples had cracked or whether her mouth had become wounded. She was again moved and again mentioned a (small) crack in the consulting-room wall which had already appeared in her previous associations (which was for me a valid indication of the climate of transference). But she recovered immediately and said arrogantly that these were only psychoanalytic interpretations, reflections of mine. I again interpreted this judgement at the dual level of her adolescent relation to the mother from the perspective of direct oedipal rivalry and of the oral relation to the breast that withdraws. I pointed out the *biting* tone of her comment, capable of cracking the analytic breast.

Then a very important covering memory arose. What did I know of her mother, she said in a challenging tone; how was I going to resolve for her that insoluble problem; what did I think I was, since she now remembered something she had never told me before, that when she was in her latency (she did not, of course, use this term) and would throw herself on the floor, her mother would lose her self-control completely and would kick her. (The patient employed more vulgar expressions, which denoted the anal-sadistic charge of the conflict.) I would not reply, of course, because I was not going to tell her she was right. Her challenging tone followed two or three interpretations I had made in relation to the adolescent girl she was in the session. They were, I believe, convincing and well-formulated interpretations; but her tone did not change. I experienced a moment of irritation and discouragement and immediately offered the interpretation I think is correct. I then said that at that moment she had thrown herself on the floor with her mouth full of ulcers, of pain and resentment, and that there was no way of speaking to her, of helping her. She was kicking about on the floor, in the hope that I, as a mother, would understand her pain, and trying at the same time to disturb my equanimity so that I would really kick her. The interpretation reached her, and, of course, my countertransference resolved, I was calm.

.   The example shows that, at times, good understanding does come basically from a complementary countertransference. Remember that my previous interpretations, concordant with her pain (mouth ulcers) and her rebelliousness at having to separate from her mother, end the analysis and be herself, had met with a most recalcitrant response. When the tension decreased and it was evident the interpretation had had its effect, I remember I told her, because she is a woman with a sense of humour, "I think Mrs. X (her mother) was right when she kicked you on the floor!" She replied then, with insight, that she herself had told Y (her daughter), just before the session, that "today she felt like kicking her ass".

I believe the material is interesting because the conflict arises at all levels: in the transference, in the present and in childhood; but I am certain that understanding mainly was linked to recognizing and interpreting the patient's action on the object in order to take away his equanimity and capacity to help, and with the hope, too, remote but alive, of being understood.

I do not know whether Grinberg would take this case as an example of projective counteridentification. There are various elements that make one think so: the desire to put into the analyst object the image of the impatient (not to say sadistic) mother is very strong, very violent. It is even worth noting that phenomenologically the situation resembles one he quoted in the paper he presented to the 1956 Symposium. I refer to the case of Dr. Alejo Dellarossa, who was made very tense by a patient who constantly (and masochistically) provoked him so that he would kick the patient out of the consulting-room (Grinberg, 1957, pp. 26–27).

In any case, I think the process is entirely linked to the countertransference: none of these conflicts is alien to my own neurosis and to the possibility of putting myself in the place of the rebellious, adolescent girl, in the place of the lactating infant, in the place of the attacked and cracked nipple, in the place of the girl provoking her mother through resentment and revenge and, finally, in the place of the mother who does not know what to do with her rebellious daughter while understanding that, in the last instance, she is also right. Whatever she does, it cannot be right to kick her. There is a whole series of projective and introjective identifications, made on the basis of countertransference; not from cold reasoning, because my capacity to understand what was happening to her and to resolve it stemmed from a moment of pain, irritation and discouragement.

It is worth noting that, after the interpretation of the maternal negative transference, the material demonstrated that another determinant of the transference conflict was to see how I would behave with my rebellious daughter in the mode of role playing, to learn from me and manage better with her own daughter. On this level, which appeared after the maternal negative transference had been successfully interpreted, the good imago of the mother, the positive transference, was intact—and, I would dare to add, so was the therapeutic alliance.

22.5 The countertransference neurosis

The clinical case just presented to illustrate the contributions of Grinberg and Money-Kyrle also serves to return us to Racker and to one of his concepts—audacious and rigorous at the same time—the *countertransference neurosis*, which is how Racker defines the analytic process as a function of its two participants.

Freud (1914g) indicated that the analysand's transferences crystallize during treatment in the transference neurosis. Racker (1948) applies the same concept to the analyst, without losing sight of the differences between one case and the other: "Just as the whole of the patient's personality, the healthy part and the neurotic part, his present and past, reality and fantasy, are brought into play in his relation with the analyst, so it is with the analyst, although with qualitative and quantitative differences, in his relation with the patient" (1948 [1968, p. 105]).

In his fifth study, just quoted, and in the following one, "The Meanings and Uses of Countertransference" (1953), Racker characterizes the counter-transference neurosis on the basis of three parameters: concordant and complementary countertransference, direct and indirect countertransference, and countertransference thoughts and positions. We have dealt in some detail with concordant and complementary types of countertransference. In chapter 23 we will discuss direct and indirect countertransference, depending on whether the analyst transfers the object of his conflict to the patient or to other figures of particular significance—the patient referred to the analytic candidate by his (admired) supervisor, for example.

Let us look for a moment at Racker's third parameter. At times, when the analyst's countertransference conflict is fluid and versatile, it tends to appear as *countertransference thoughts*. The analyst suddenly finds himself thinking about something that is not rationally justifiable in the context in which it appears or does not seem to relate to the analysand. However, the analysand's associations, a dream or a parapraxis, do show the relation. There are, for example, the countertransference thoughts when Racker left the consulting-room for a moment to look for change, the patient having given him a thousand-peso note and having indicated the change Racker had to give him. Racker left the note on his desk and went out, thinking that on his return the thousand pesos would no longer be there and that the analysand would tell him he had already collected it, whereas the analysand, alone with his beloved thousand-peso note, thought of keeping it or giving it a farewell kiss (1953 [1968, p. 142]).

As in this case, countertransference thoughts do not generally imply a very deep conflict, and just as they surface suddenly in the analyst's con-sciousness, they also appear quite easily in the analysand's material. What is dangerous, Racker says, is to ignore them when they arise, instead of taking them into consideration while awaiting material from the patient which could confirm them. If this is the case, one can interpret with a high degree of certainty. If the analyst's countertransference thoughts are not confirmed by the analysand's material, then one should not employ them to interpret, for two reasons: they may have nothing to do directly with the patient, or they may be remote from his consciousness.

The *countertransference position*—as opposed to thoughts—almost always indicates greater conflict. Here the feelings and fantasies are deeper and more enduring and may go unnoticed. It concerns the analyst who reacts with anger, anxiety or worry towards a particular patient. At times this aspect of the countertransference neurosis is very syntonic and goes completely unnoticed. I remember that, in the beginning, when it did not seem to me to be a great problem to cancel or change the hour of a patient's session, a patient with a passive–feminine character surprised me by saying that, since he was submissive, probably I changed the hour of his session whenever I felt like it, without caring. He was right.

Otto F. Kernberg (1965), agreeing in general with Racker's ideas, describes a special type of countertransference position where the analyst's participation is greater and has to do with the patient's serious pathology. He calls it *chronic countertransference fixation* and believes that it takes shape when the pathology of a very regressive patient reactivates archaic neurotic patterns in the analyst, so that analysand and analyst complement each other in such a way that they seem reciprocally joined. Kernberg attributes this difficulty, which is persistent and difficult to solve, to the strength of pregenital aggression mobilized in both analyst and patient, the mechanism of projective identification, with increasingly vague limits between subject and object. The chronic countertransference fixation appears frequently in the treatment of psychotic and borderline patients, but also during regressive periods in patients whose pathology is less severe.

22.6   Beyond projective counteridentification

I wish to end this chapter with a new consideration related to Grinberg's investigation. In his later works, this author has tried to utilize the concept of projective counteridentification to give a wider vision—Enid Balint calls it "more tri-dimensional"—of the dynamic interaction that is surely the foundation of the analytic relation.

In his introduction to the topic, "The Affects in the Countertransference", at the Fourteenth Latin-American Congress of Psychoanalysis, Grinberg (1982) presented some new thoughts with his customary clarity. He said that at the outset the term "projective counteridentification" was meant to emphasize that the fantasy of projective identification provokes effects in the receptor, in the analyst, who then reacts, incorporating, really and concretely, the aspects projected into him. Grinberg said that he now felt that projective counteridentification does not necessarily have to be the final link in the chain of complex events that occur in the exchange of unconscious communications with patients who, in moments of regression, function with pathological projective identifications (1982, pp. 205–206).

Thus projective counteridentification offers the analyst "the possibility of experiencing a spectrum of emotions which, well understood and sublimated, can become very useful technical instruments in order to come into contact with deepest levels of the analysands' material, in a way which is analogous to that described by Racker and by Paula Heimann for countertransference" (ibid., pp. 205–206). For this to happen, Grinberg adds, the analyst should be prepared to receive and contain the patient's projections.

With these reformulations, projective counteridentification is no longer located outside the countertransference, nor is the analyst's position in relation to it purely passive. Rather, the disposition to receive it and understand it as a message should be recognized as one of the highest offerings of our professional activity.

I think that with the above changes Grinberg clarifies and specifies his earlier thinking, overcoming some mistakes, which I have tried to point out. This marks out the decisive point of his contribution, the communicative factor of the projective identification in the most archaic strata of the human mind.

CHAPTER TWENTY-THREE

Countertransference and psychoanalytic process

We said in a previous chapter that the study of the countertransference really begins when it is no longer perceived through a normative or superegoic attitude, and as an obstacle, and is accepted as an inevitable and ineluctable element of the practice. Racker said that countertransference is homologous to transference; it is at the same time an obstacle, an instrument and a field of interactions.

One of the great themes that always arises in the study of countertransference is the extent to which the process depends on the patient—that is, on the transference—and to what extent on other factors. This problem has often been discussed, and we will study it in what follows on the basis of a classification between two types of countertransference, direct and indirect.

23.1 Direct and indirect countertransference

When the object that mobilizes the analyst's countertransference is not the analysand himself but another, we speak of *indirect* countertransference. When it is the patient who mobilizes it, the countertransference is *direct*. Typical examples of indirect countertransference are: the training analyst, concerned with his first candidate because of what the Association will say, and the analytic candidate concerned with his first case because of what the Institute, his supervisor or his training analyst will say. We all know how our countertransference is influenced by a patient who, for some reason, awakens the interest of friends, colleagues or society in general. This is such an obvious circumstance that often it creates an incompatibility for the analysis from the point of view of the setting.

Racker proposed the distinction between direct and indirect countertransference in his first works on the subject, as in "The Countertransference Neurosis", the fifth of his studies, which he read in 1948. In the sixth study, "The Meanings and Uses of Countertransference" (1953), he noted the most recent contributions and dealt with the work of Annie Reich (1951), who distinguishes two types of countertransference: countertransference in the proper sense, and the utilization of the countertransference in order to act out. "Countertransference in the proper sense" corresponds to Racker's direct countertransference, whereas "the utilization of the countertransference in order to act out" corresponds to the indirect one. If what I want is to be loved by my analysand, my countertransference is direct; but if my relation to the analysand is influenced by my desire to be loved by my supervisor, then my countertransference is indirect, in that I utilize my analysand as an instrument of my relation to my supervisor.

The classification of countertransference as direct and indirect is valid from the phenomenological point of view, but questionable for metapsychology. In the above example, where the candidate is more interested in his supervisor than in his patient, one would have to ask whether there is not, above all, a conflict with the patient himself, displaced on to the supervisor. It could be that the candidate is jealous of his analysand and puts him in the position of the third excluded party, for example. In this way, the candidate would be externalizing his oedipal conflict with his patient, or his sibling rivalry. Even in this last case, in which the analysand is the sibling rival and the supervisor is the parental imago, one can always suppose that if the supervisor occupies the most important place it is because the young analyst displaces his main conflict from one level to another.

In any case, the differences between direct and indirect countertransference, and especially Annie Reich's intelligent reflections, will concern us shortly, when we speak of the relations between the (analyst's) acting out and countertransference.

Not all the cases of indirect transference, however, can be judged as acting out. As we will see further on, the analyst's acting out implies something more than a simple displacement from one object to another; this is a necessary but not a sufficient condition for acting out.

Let us say now that we are going to define counter–acting out—that is, the analyst's acting out—as a special type of countertransference linked to a disturbance of the task. In this sense we should maintain the definition of countertransference we gave at first, indicating that when the countertransference is not a *response* to the analysand's transference, it configures an acting out on the part of the analyst. In this case the patient is only an instrument for the analyst to develop a conflict that does not pertain basically to the patient. We will deal with this further on.

23.2   Gitelson and the analyst's two positions

As we saw in studying the forms of transference in chapter 12, Gitelson (1952) distinguishes two positions of the analyst in the analytic situation and calls only one of them countertransference.

Gitelson says that at times the analyst reacts to the patient as a whole, and this implies a very great involvement, which disqualifies him for this case, while at other times the analyst's reaction has to do with partial aspects of the patient.

23.3   Reactions to the patient as a whole

In some cases, the attitude of neutrality and empathy the analyst should have is lost, and if the analyst cannot overcome this, it means the patient has reactivated a neurotic transferential potential which makes him inadequate for that particular case.

Gitelson quotes a personal example, a young woman who came to analysis due to marital difficulties. From the beginning of the trial analysis she was full of complaints about injustices in her life, which had been very difficult. In the last of her eight weeks of analysis she brought a dream which decided Gitelson's conduct.

In the dream Gitelson appeared in person (see chapter 12: "The Forms of Transference") next to a figure who clearly represented the (female) colleague who had referred the case to him. The patient appeared as a child, but clearly identified. The two adults in the dream were in bed stimulating the child with their feet. Gitelson concludes that his appearance in the dream in person indicated that he, as an analyst, had introduced a factor that was disturbing for the analytic situation, which repeated an interpersonal situation typical of the patient's childhood: the fight for custody between the parents when they were divorced. Gitelson adds that this clinical experience was a direct consequence of a neurotic transferential potential of his own—unresolved at the time—which disturbed his feelings *in toto* towards the patient. Gitelson emphasizes that it was not an episodic response but his reaction to the patient as a person.

Gitelson maintains that this type of reaction cannot be called countertransference, as the patient has become completely, in his entirety, a transferential object for the analyst. Furthermore, the patient realizes this, as his patient demonstrated with her dream. Gitelson adds that the patient was able to have a good analysis with the analyst to whom he referred her.

Gitelson's second example refers to a young analyst and a female analysand who spent her first sessions speaking disparagingly about herself, affirming that no one liked nor could like her. The analyst went out of his way to reassure her: she had made a good impression on him. In the following session the analysand brought a dream in which the analyst appeared exhibiting his limp penis. This patient abandoned analysis during the trial period. (Gitelson is in favour of the trial period during which, in his view, not only the patient's analysability but also the possibilities in the functioning of that particular analytic couple can be tested; on this point, see chapter 6.)

Gitelson concludes, reaffirming his point of view, that these reactions to the patient as a person should be considered *transferences* of the analyst, attributed to the reactivation of an old potential transference. They can refer to a class of patients or a particular patient, and they can be positive or negative. What characterizes them is that they refer to the relation in its totality and always appear early on in the analysis. (Hence the importance Blitzsten assigns to the first dream.)

23.4   Reactions to partial aspects of the patient

Here the analyst's participation is not total. These reactions appear later than the others and arise in the context of an already established analytic relation, while in the previous case the analytic relation had not yet been established. Gitelson considers these reactions as countertransference in the strict sense. They are the analyst's reactions to the patient's transference, to his material or to the patient's attitude towards the analyst as a person.

The analyst's countertransference, thus described and delimited, proves that a non-analysed area of the analyst is always present; but, in that it can be resolved, it does not disqualify the analyst, nor does it make the continuance of the analysis impossible. For Gitelson these are simply the proof that no one has been perfectly analysed, and for this very reason analysis is interminable.

We can see that Gitelson's classification attempts to mark out two areas in the emotional position of the analyst, restricting to only one of them the term countertransference. Let us emphasize that there is no reference, in Gitelson's investigation, to the possibility of using the countertransference as an instrument; there is reference simply to the limits in order to remove it as an obstacle. Gitelson declares himself frankly in favour of the trial analysis and considers it not only a test of the patient's analysability but also of the analytic situation in its entirety, for the patient and for the analyst. Thanks to the trial analysis, the analyst can see whether he is in a condition to include himself in that particular aspect of life the patient offers him.

On page 4 of his essay, Gitelson states that the predominance of some qualities to the detriment of others gives the final picture of the analyst as a person and as a therapist. And he adds that in this totality and according to the predominance of the factors described are to be found the reasons why a particular analyst can have special qualities for one type of patient and fail with another.

The division Gitelson makes between what he calls the transference of the analyst and countertransference has been rightly criticized by Racker and others, who consider that such a sharp division cannot be maintained. No one doubts, on the other hand, that there are two types of reaction here which imply a different involvement by the analyst (and/or the patient) and are of great value in diagnosis and prognosis. We have dealt with this in discussing erotized transference in chapter 12. Although it is true that there are degrees of the countertransference phenomenon, it is also true that the analyst's ability to recognize them and to try to resolve them is what in the final instance defines the outcome of the relation. Everything depends on the analyst's ability and courage to face and resolve the problem. These classifications, Racker says, in that they imply quantitative differences, only show that there is a disposition and an *exposition* in the countertransference phenomenon, similar to Freud's complemental series. In my opinion this scheme also includes Grinberg's projective counteridentification, as a special case in which the disposition tends towards zero and the exposition to infinity.

To indicate the limitations of Gitelson's position, let us say that in his first example he himself recognizes explicitly the part the patient plays in his reaction, as a field where the divorcing parents battle. However "total" Gitelson's reaction was, then, the patient had something to do with its configuration.

23.5 Countertransference according to Lacan

Lacan maintains, in opposition to other writers (as we saw in chapter 10, in his "Intervention sur le transfert", 1951), that the transference begins when the countertransference destroys the development of the dialectic process. It is at the moment when Freud cannot accept the homosexual link that connects Dora to Frau K, because his countertransference makes it intolerable for him to feel excluded (identified with Herr K), that the process is arrested. At that point Freud begins to insist that Dora become conscious of her love for Herr K and even that there are reasons for thinking Herr K loves her. Of course Freud departs from his own method here, since he gives opinions and suggestions; but what is important is to emphasize, rather, that the Lacanian thesis that transference is the correlate of countertransference is articulated via the key points of the Lacanian theory of desire and the constitution of the ego and the subject. Just as the child is the desire of desire, just as the desire of the hysteric is the desire of the other, the father, in the same way the desire of the analyst is what counts for Lacan.

This seems a unilateral conception, and the process is more complex. Freud's countertransference is not something that comes purely from Freud's desire but also from what Dora makes him feel. Knowing what the Oedipus complex is, the love, jealousy, pain and resentment that accompany it, who could maintain that Dora's homosexual link with Frau K has nothing to do with the father? Among many other determinants, Dora's attachment to Frau K has the objective of frustrating the Freud–father, of taking revenge and making him feel jealous. Freud's countertransference conflict arises not only from the prejudices of the turn-of-the-century Viennese man he is, but also as a result of the way Dora, a hysterical (and also psychopathic) girl, operates on him. Freud lacks the understanding needed to operate the third dialectical reversal, which Lacan—with vehemence and not without ingenuity—demands of him. This is not only because of Freud's desire but also because of Dora's desire—and it is not Dora's desire but desires (in the plural). Her desires can be considered independently here. If Freud remains "hooked" and succumbs to his countertransference it is also because Dora has an effect on him, frustrating and rejecting him. Dora's rejection is due not *only* to her pregenital (specular, dyadic, narcissistic) relation to Frau K (mother) but also to her intense jealous feelings in the direct Oedipus complex. Freud never doubts that by interrupting her treatment Dora makes him the object, via acting out, of a revenge that is comparable in every way to the famous slap by the lake.

I would like to discuss this same element on a more modest and immediately accessible plane, in relation to the session I described with my patient. I think that when my patient stated in a challenging way that I should have known that when she used to throw herself on the floor in a tantrum, her mother would kick her, to operate the dialectical inversion, telling her she should see what her part was in those episodes, would not have been sufficient. She was aware that it was her tantrum that had exasperated her mother. I believe the situation can be resolved only if the *hic et nunc* of the transference is fully accepted. It is not enough to refer her to the past; it is also necessary to make her see also what is in the present. I am convinced that if I had limited myself to telling the patient that there was some reason why the mother kicked her when she would throw herself on the floor (and some reason why my patient did this), she would have misunderstood what I was saying. She would have perceived me as a punishing mother or as a father submitting to the mother, for example; but never as an analyst who wants to shatter the fascination of the moment and refer her to her past.

23.6   *On the communication of countertransference*

The best problem with which to end this cycle is one that is always discussed: the confession—or in more neutral terms, the *communication*—of countertransference.

In general, it is thought that one must *not* communicate the countertransference, that the theory of countertransference does not alter the attitude of reserve proper to analysis. When we studied the therapeutic alliance, we said that the analytic process demands a rigorous asymmetry at the level of the transference neurosis, but also a totally equidistant position with regard to the working alliance. The setting requires us to speak only of the patient, but this does not imply that we deny our errors or that we hide our conflicts. To recognize our errors and conflicts, however, does not mean to make them explicit. No one, not even those decidedly in favour of frankness on the analyst's part, advocate that we show the patient the sources of our error and our conflict, because this is equivalent to burdening the patient with something unrelated to him.

If Margaret Little's (1951) work is read attentively, one sees, despite claims to the contrary, that she is not entirely in favour of making the countertransference explicit. She says specifically that it is not a matter of confessing to the countertransference but of recognizing it and integrating it in the interpretation.

Analysis tries to give back to the patient his capacity to think, to restore his confidence in his own thought. This is done by lifting the repressions and correcting the dissociations, not by telling him he is right and that what he thought about us is true. It is a matter of clarifying not what the analyst has felt, but how the patient felt about him, and of respecting what he thought. When in an act of sincerity we endorse what the patient thinks of us, we do him no favour, because in the final instance we will again make him think that we have the last word. The patient should trust his own thought and should also know that his own thought can deceive him, just as the other's thought can.

On this point, the theme of countertransference converges with that of interpretation. The content—and, above all, the form—of the interpretation express the countertransference at times, because most of our countertransferential reactions, when we do not know how to transform them into technical instruments, are channelled through a bad or a badly formulated interpretation. In general, the conflict goes into the formulation.

The problem of the confession or communication of the countertransference touches on the question Winnicott (1947) poses in reference to the *real* feelings in the countertransference. He speaks particularly of the hate the psychotic provokes in the analyst and that it is a real hate. It is a theme that deserves discussion precisely because, by definition, transference and countertransference are not "real".

23.7   Winnicott's ideas on countertransference

Just before Racker's and Paula Heimann's works appeared, Winnicott spoke of the countertransference at the meeting of the British Psycho-Analytical Society on 5 February 1947. Winnicott's contribution is interesting, especially because he offers certain information on his technique with psychotics and psychopaths. However, he does not refer to countertransference, considered in the strict sense, as a technical instrument but rather to certain *real* feelings—particularly hate—that can appear in the analyst.

Winnicott classifies countertransference phenomena into three types: (1) abnormal countertransferential feelings, which should be considered as proof that the analyst needs more analysis; (2) countertransferential feelings, which have to do with the analyst's experience and personal development and on which the work of every analyst depends; (3) the analyst's really objective countertransference—that is, the love and hate of the analyst in response to the real personality and behaviour of the patient, based on objective observation.

According to this classification, Winnicott inclines towards a very wide concept of countertransference, which includes the analyst's unresolved conflicts, his experiences and his personality, and also his rational, objective reactions.

He says, "I suggest that if an analyst is to analyse psychotics or antisocials he must be able to be so thoroughly aware of the countertransference that he can sort out and study his *objective* reactions to the patient" (1947, p. 70).

In the analysis of the psychotic the coincidence of love and hate appears continually, giving rise to problems of management that are so difficult that they can leave the analyst without resources. He says this coincidence of love and hate is different from the aggressive component that complicates the primitive love impulse and implies that in the history of the patient there was an environmental failure at the moment when his instinctive impulses sought their first object (see ibid., p. 70).

Leaving aside for the moment Winnicott's apodictic statements on development, it is notable that the configuration of love and hate just indicated awakens a justified hate in the analyst, who should recognize it in himself and reserve it for the moment when it can be interpreted. Winnicott says that the analyst's main work with any patient is to maintain objectivity towards everything the patient brings, and a special case of this is the necessary ability of the analyst to hate the patient objectively (see ibid.).

The example Winnicott gives is perhaps not the best one for discussing his technique, since it refers to a boy aged nine with serious behavioural problems, who was his guest for three months in his house. In any case, Winnicott affirms that the possibility of his telling the child he hated him every time he provoked these feelings in him allowed him to carry on with the experience.

Just as the mother hates her baby—and for many reasons—so the analyst hates his psychotic patient. And if this is so, it is not logical to think that a psychotic patient in analysis can tolerate his own hate for the analyst unless the analyst can hate him (see ibid., p. 74).

To conclude, Winnicott thinks that if what he maintains is true—that is, that the patient awakens an objective hate in the analyst—then the difficult problem of interpreting it arises. It is a delicate matter requiring the most careful evaluation; but an analysis will always be incomplete if the analyst has never been able to tell the patient he felt hate for him when he was ill. Only after this interpretation has been formulated can the patient cease to be a child—that is, someone who cannot understand what he owes his mother.

23.8 Comments and qualifying statements

Winnicott poses the problem of countertransference in a very original way, and the differences from other writers are evident. In including in the countertransference the objective and justified feeling the analyst may have, we modify the current definition of transference and countertransference; the objective feelings are not included in them other than by extension: when we think that no feeling is absolutely objective, we imply that there must be a non-objective part that comes not from fact but from fantasy and the past. But this is a somewhat academic objection. After all, the commonly accepted definitions are not always the best.

The ideas we are discussing, however, can be questioned also in another way, asking to what extent the judgement of any analyst—even one of Winnicott's stature—is objective with regard to the nature of his feelings. Could it be, perhaps, that the analyst tends to justify his reactions? Who safeguards the analyst from the tendency to rationalize? These are problems we cannot easily solve with our methods, but if we could, another question would arise: how much is there of artefact in Winnicott's technique? If Winnicott's hatred of his rapacious nine-year-old was justified, one would have to ask whether it was rational to take him home. Winnicott himself indicates how generous his wife was in accepting the boy, and one would have to prove that this generosity of the Winnicott couple—laudable as a human expression—was free of any neurotic engagement, which is most improbable. It is not necessary to know a particular couple intimately to suppose that when they decide to introduce a third party into the home, it is because the couple wants problems or because it already has them and thinks to resolve them in this manner. In addition, the Winnicotts' decision to act as the child's hosts arises not only from their generous feelings, which it would be difficult to doubt, but also from a (legitimate) desire to investigate and put the theories to the test. In this case, Winnicott's relation to the child is more selfish (or narcissistic) than it seems, and his hate no longer seems to me to be so objective.

To put this discussion in more stringent terms: the idea of an objective hate in the countertransference meets with three difficulties. The first, which we have just considered, is that of definition, because transference and countertransference are defined precisely by their lack of objectivity. Secondly, Wälder's principle of multiple function should apply here, and one should say, then, that no feeling either is objective or ceases to be so— it always goes both ways. This compels us to take many factors into account, so that when the occasion arises to tell the patient (even at the best possible moment) that we once felt a justified hatred of him, it will always be a simplification and, I fear, also a rationalization, because not even Winnicott is exempt from these faults. Then, if I am going to be truthful, as Winnicott asks me to be, I will have to tell him that I hated him "objectively" three years ago, not only for his insufferable behaviour, but also because I got on badly with my wife at the time, I was worried about my financial situation, the *International Journal of Psycho-Analysis* had rejected one of my articles, the value of the dollar had risen again, Reina continued to be absent, my class on countertransference was not turning out well and this caused conflict with Racker, my analyst, and with my friend León, and . . . God knows what else along these lines, all of it true and objective.

The third objection to Winnicott here is this: I do not think that to feel hatred for a patient—however aggressive, violent, burdensome or bad that person may be—is an objective reaction. It may be entirely justified, but not objective, because what is objective is only that I took the patient on in order to help him to resolve his problems, and I count on my setting to maintain my equilibrium. If I do not maintain it, I lose my objectivity, which is very human and understandable but never objective. Here, as in all cases, objectivity has to be measured in relation to the objectives. If these are lost, objectivity remains suspended. On this point, then, Winnicott has no measure other than his subjectivity.

If I have been clear in my exposition it can be understood that my disagreement with Winnicott's idea of objective countertransference questions, by extension, his management technique, his basic hypothesis that the alterations in primitive emotional development should be resolved via acts (management) and not through words (interpretation). It is precisely because Winnicott thinks he is obliged (and rightly) to attend to real and objective facts that his countertransferential response logically has to end up located also at that level. In saying his feelings are objective, Winnicott correctly perceives something that can be deduced logically from his practice.

Winnicott's theory of development is, as I see it, also connected with this, when he asserts that psychosis is an environmental failure. I think the great English analyst is, on this point, more severe with those who were in charge of that boy than with himself as analyst. Following Melanie Klein, I think that this sad creation that psychosis is comes precisely from the child and his parents jointly (and from many other factors not relevant here, i.e. biological and social ones).

23.9   *Winnicott's new ideas*

In a symposium on countertransference at the British Psycho-Analytical Society on 25 November 1959, Winnicott returned to the theme, revealing that his ideas had changed considerably. He starts by saying that "the use of this word counter-transference should now be brought back to its original use" (1965, p. 158).

Winnicott thinks "professional work is quite different from ordinary life" (ibid., p. 160) and that "the analyst is *under strain in maintaining a professional attitude*" (ibid., p. 160, Winnicott's italics). The psychoanalyst should remain vulnerable, he says, and despite this should maintain his professional attitude during the hours of work (ibid., p. 160). And he adds that what the patient meets with is in all certainty the professional attitude of the analyst, and not the unstable men and women we analysts are in our private lives. Winnicott thus firmly maintains that between the patient and the analyst there lies the latter's "professional attitude, his technique, *the work he does with his mind*" (ibid., p. 161, Winnicott's italics). Thanks to his personal analysis, the analyst can remain professionally engaged without suffering excessive tension.

On this basis, Winnicott favours a clearly delimited and circumscribed idea of countertransference, whose significance "can only be the neurotic features *which spoil the professional attitude* and disturb the course of the analytic process as determined by the patient" (ibid., p. 162; Winnicott's italics).

With this restrictive and stringent concept that again defines countertransference as an obstacle, Winnicott indicates that, in fact, there are two types of patients towards which the analyst's *role* changes substantially.

The immense majority of people who seek treatment, Winnicott continues, can and should be treated in the manner described. However, there is another, smaller, but no less significant group of patients who change the analyst's professional attitude completely. There are the antisocial patients and those who need to regress. The patient with antisocial tendencies is in a permanent state of reaction in the face of deprivation (see ibid., p. 162), so that the therapist finds himself "compelled by the patient's illness, or by the hopeful half of the patient's illness, to correct and to go on correcting the failure of ego-support which altered the course of the patient's life" (ibid., p. 162).

The other type of patient makes regression necessary, because only through a passage through infantile dependency can he recuperate: "If the hidden true self is to come into its own in such a case the patient will break down as part of the treatment, and the analyst will need to be able to play the part of the mother to the patient's infant" (ibid., p. 163).

The primitive need of the patient leads him to traverse the analyst's technique and his professional attitude, which are, for this type of patient, an obstacle, establishing perforce a direct relation of a primitive type with the analyst, even to the extent of merging (ibid., p. 164).

Winnicott separates finally these cases from others in which the ana-lysand breaks through the professional barrier and can provoke a direct response from the analyst. Winnicott believes that to talk of countertrans-ference here is not appropriate; it is simply the analyst's *reaction* to the special circumstance that transgressed his professional environment: to employ the same word for different events merely creates confusion.

To conclude, Winnicott maintains his well-known ideas on the *manage-ment* of regressive patients; but some of his assertions of 1947 (which I have critized here) seem to have changed substantially, in a return to the classic conception of countertransference.

23.10   *Final summary*

Although the presence of the countertransference as an important factor in the analytic process was always borne in mind by analysts, as Ella Sharpe's outstanding example proves, it is undeniable that only from the middle of the century onwards did countertransference become organized in a complete body of doctrine. From that moment, countertransference has made us more responsible for our work and destroyed with valid (and analytic) arguments the idea that an analyst can remain uncontaminated, at the margins of the process. Contrary to what had been thought previ-ously, we now hold that countertransference exists, should exist and has no reason not to exist. We have to bear it in mind, and, as Margaret Little (1951) says, the impersonal analyst is always a myth.

The substantial change that comes from those years is not, however, the one I have just indicated. It is that countertransference is accepted not only as an ineluctable ingredient of the analytic process, but also as an instrument for understanding. This idea, as we have seen, is what Paula Heimann and Racker basically contribute, and this is why we have accorded it a special place in this development.

PART THREE

ON INTERPRETATION
AND OTHER INSTRUMENTS

CHAPTER TWENTY-FOUR

Materials and instruments of psychotherapy

The main part of the studies we are about to begin consists in the study of *interpretation*, the foundation of psychoanalytic therapy. Nevertheless, no one maintains that the analyst's activity is strictly limited to interpretation, and we always do more than this. In a more inclusive sense, then, what we are going to study are the *instruments* of psychotherapy, among which interpretation occupies the central place. At the same time, we should take into account that interpretation is not exclusive to psychoanalysis, as it is used in all the major forms of psychotherapy.

Thus it is necessary to begin by placing interpretation within the context of the complete set of instruments the psychotherapist should work with, and explain why this instrument has a special importance. In addition, we must delimit the concept of interpretation, because depending on whether we adopt a wide or a narrow meaning, we will arrive at different conclusions as to the analyst's task, as to whether he only interprets or does other things. At times this is simply a problem of definition. Logically, if a very wide meaning is assigned to it, everything can be called interpretation; but perhaps this is not the best criterion.

We will begin by studying interpretation as the principal instrument used by all the major (or deep) psychotherapeutic methods. Then, as a second step, we will try to determine the essential characteristics of interpretation in psychoanalysis.

24.1   Psychotherapy and psychoanalysis

To approach this theme, a brief comment on the differences between psychoanalysis and psychotherapy is unavoidable. With the passage of time, Freud's (1904a) poetic idea of dividing psychotherapy as Leonardo had done with the plastic arts has turned out to be the most rigorous of all classifications.

Freud asserted that the method discovered by Breuer—cathartic psychotherapy—and the psychoanalysis developed from it operated *per via di levare*, not *per via di porre*, as did the other methods. This idea appears in almost all the works (in the hundreds), where there is an attempt to differentiate psychoanalysis from psychotherapy.

The reader will doubtless remember the works of Robert P. Knight, among which, from the point of view we are now considering, "An Evaluation of Psychotherapeutic Techniques" (1952) stands out. Here two types of psychotherapy—supportive and exploratory—are recognized. Other writers prefer to speak of repressive and expressive psychotherapy. Merton M. Gill (1954), an outstanding scholar of ego psychology, speaks of supportive and exploratory psychotherapy and says: "*Psychoanalysis is that technique which, employed by a neutral analyst, results in the development of a regressive transference neurosis and the ultimate resolution of this neurosis by techniques of interpretation alone*" (p. 775; italics in original).

Edward Bibring has a similar approach in his classic article of 1954. Bibring distinguishes five types of psychotherapy: suggestive, abreactive, manipulative, clarifying and interpretative. There is no need to explain what Bibring refers to with suggestive or abreactive psychotherapy (abreaction occupies a singular place, as we will see further on); by manipulative he defines that psychotherapy where the doctor tries to provide an image that serves as a model for identification. The clarifying and interpretative psychotherapies operate through insight; the others do not. This point of view is interesting, because only Bibring maintains that clarification (enlightenment) produces insight. The other psychoanalysts think that insight is linked exclusively to interpretation, although there might be a semantic problem here, as Bibring's concept of insight is perhaps descriptive, not ostensive, in Richfield's (1954) sense. When we consider Löwenstein's definition of interpretation in chapter 25, we will see that he does so as a function of insight.

It is interesting that Bibring concludes that psychoanalysis is a psychotherapy that uses these five instruments—that is, suggestion, abreaction, manipulation, clarification and interpretation. However, Bibring thinks there is a difference, which characterizes and also distinguishes psychoanalysis from the other methods: It uses the first three as technical resources and only the last two as *therapeutic* resources. The psychoanalyst is allowed to use suggestion, abreaction and manipulation as resources to mobilize the patient and to facilitate the development of the analytic process. But the only measures he works with as therapeutic factors are those that produce insight. Bibring's idea here seems correct to me, because what differentiates psychoanalysis from the psychotherapies in general (and I refer specifically to the exploratory or expressive psychotherapies) is precisely that in these, suggestion, abreaction and manipulation are used as therapeutic—essential—resources. The paradigm could be the emotional re-education of Alexander and French (1946), where one relies on the manipulation of the transference to give the patient a new experience that will correct the defective experiences of the past. The truth is that if we try to correct the image of the past in this way, we already begin to operate with suggestive or supportive factors. Strictly speaking, the psychoanalyst makes *de facto* use of the resources Bibring identifies as technical, without thereby conceding them an entirely legitimate place in his method.

24.2   Materials and instruments

Bibring's thinking opens up a path towards a second specification, which enables us to approach our theme at last: the difference between materials and instruments of psychotherapy, basically following Knight. It is both a geometric and a Pythagorean difference, according to which what arises from the patient is called *material*, and the analyst operates on this material with his *instruments*.

Both concepts require clarification. As to the *material*, I would say that we should limit it to what the patient brings with the (conscious or unconscious) intention of informing the analyst about his mental state. In this way, we would exclude what the patient does or says not in order to inform, but to influence or dominate the therapist. This part of the discourse should be conceived as *verbal acting out* and not really as material. As we will see in greater detail in dealing with acting out, it is more exact to say that the discourse has two simultaneous parts and therefore includes both. If every communication from the patient includes these two factors, then it will be part of analytic technique to distinguish what the patient offers in order to inform us from what he is *doing* to us with his communication. And this distinction is not changed if what the patient "does" can be transformed by the analyst and understood as material, because the classification is not functional but dynamic—that is, it has to do with the patient's desire, with his unconscious fantasy. In other words, without intending to communicate, the analysand's acting out can inform us.

As to the *instruments*, the same difference should be established, since the analyst's interventions that are not aimed at the development of the therapeutic process have no instrumental character. To be fair, we should call these interventions the analyst's acting out (counter–acting out).

This is not an idle issue, because many discussions on acting out are linked to this distinction. In my opinion, and anticipating this theme, acting out is not material, because the patient does not offer it with the *intention* of informing, of cooperating with the task. It is another matter for the psychotherapist to draw a particular conclusion from it. As Elsa Garzoli says (in a personal communication), acting out does not communicate, although it may inform.

The concept of material should be specified even further, because a third dimension of the discourse must be considered: if the analysand speaks rather than associates.

We referred to this theme indirectly with the therapeutic alliance in studying Greenson's and Meltzer's contributions. The adult part speaks, Meltzer states. And when the patient speaks (or speaks to *us*) we should reply, not interpret.

Greenson and Wexler (1969, 1970) maintain, in my view, the same idea when they distinguish between what is and what is not free association. They maintain that to take as free associations what is expounded as real (which for them has the double meaning of what is not distorted and what is genuine) damages the analysand's perception of reality. (Remember the example of Kevin—section 19.5.)

If we wish to be strict and avoid misunderstandings, therefore, we should restrict the term *material* to what the analysand communicates in obedience to the fundamental rule and leave out as parenthetical what he himself leaves out unconsciously (verbal acting out) or consciously—that is, when he speaks (or thinks he speaks) as an adult, whether or not he thinks this has to do with his treatment.

It should be clear that the specifications just proposed refer entirely to what the analysand feels, to his fantasies, and not to the analyst's judgements. It is part of the analyst's work to indicate to the analysand via what fantasies he is speaking, especially when he notes a discrepancy between what the analysand manifestly assumes and his unconscious fantasies. In other words, the analyst should recognize what the analysand assumes explicitly or implicitly when he speaks, without submitting thereby to those stipulations.

Leaving a more thorough discussion of this fundamental theme for another occasion, let us study now the instruments the psychotherapist employs. For a better development of our exposition we will divide them into four groups: (1) instruments that influence the patient; (2) instruments for gaining information; (3) instruments for offering information and (4) Eissler's parameter (1953).

24.3   *Instruments for influencing the patient*

The psychotherapist has at his disposal various instruments with the use of which he can exercise a direct influence on his patient for the purpose of making him change, of making him improve. This change can consist in an alleviation or disappearance of the symptoms, or a modification of his mental state, or of his conduct which becomes better adapted to the reality he lives in, and so forth. There are many procedures for achieving these ends, such as support, suggestion and persuasion.

All of them propose to achieve a *direct*, immediate change which bears more on conduct than on personality, and they are different from the other methods we are going to study because they are in the service of repressive psychotherapy. Neither suggestion, nor support, nor persuasion aim to open up the field or, in terms of psychoanalytic theory, to lift the repression—on the contrary. They are certainly limited methods, but they can have a curative effect, which is very legitimate in some (minor) forms of psychotherapy.

* * *

By *reassurance (support)* we mean a psychotherapeutic action that tries to give the patient stability or security, something that acts as a backup or a crutch. Here the descriptive expressions of standing on one's feet or continuing to walk are unavoidable, because the concept is intrinsically linked to the idea of something that upholds. There are diverse types of support, such as the measures that alleviate anxiety by trying to distance it from consciousness (repression, negation); those that tend to reinforce the good relation with the other, for which the psychotherapist puts himself in the place of a good object (superego), which Strachey referred to in his 1934 paper; and those that tend to emphasize (tendentiously) certain aspects of reality.

Support is the most common instrument of psychotherapy, the one most available to the general practitioner (or simply to anyone who has to do with interpersonal relations), and the one most freely used. However, although it is the most common, it is not the most adequate one, since it can create a vicious circle by stimulating a dependence that is difficult to resolve and, to the extent that it is not true, can increase insecurity. Logically, this depends on what we call reassurance. I refer to reassurance as something offered to the patient from outside to maintain his equilibrium at all costs. As Glover (1955) indicates, sometimes this support is strongly determined by the countertransference. If, on the other hand, we understand by support or reassurance an attitude of sympathy, of cordiality and of receptivity towards the patient, then, of course, this support is an unavoidable instrument in any psychotherapy. To distinguish between these two alternatives, it is better to speak in these cases of containment (*holding*), following Winnicott (1958, passim), as we will see in studying the analytic process.

As to the influence of countertransferential anxiety in the need to give support, it is worth indicating that the analyst should not confuse the support he gives on occasion with something that is of enduring value.

Meltzer (1967) indicates that adequate maintenance and management of the setting can *modulate* anxiety; but only interpretation can resolve it.

Support or reassurance in psychoanalytic treatment engaged the attention of many writers. Glover deals with it in his book on technique (1955, pp. 285–290). Melitta Schmideberg spoke on this theme at the British Psycho-Analytical Society in February 1934 (her work was published the following year). She considers that support is a method for calming anxiety and is, as such, legitimate in psychoanalysis if used prudently and combined with interpretation. Glover, Ella Sharpe, Paula Heimann and Melitta's mother (Melanie Klein), who supported her (Glover, p. 288), participated among others in a discussion on her work.

* * *

I will deal briefly with another instrument of psychotherapy: *suggestion*. As its name indicates, suggestion (from *sub gerere*) is something that is initiated from below. The basis of the suggestive method is to introduce in the mind of the patient, beneath what he is thinking, some type of judgement or affirmation that can operate thereafter from inside in the direction and with the aim of modifying a particular pathological conduct. Baudoin distinguishes two types of suggestion, passive and active, and he calls the passive *acceptivity* and the active *suggestibility*. In the first case the individual allows himself to be reached by suggestion without any effort to receive and incorporate it. This is the least efficacious and most condemnable type. In suggestibility, on the other hand, the patient participates in the process, which thereby has a more enduring and efficacious result.

For some writers, the psychoanalyst exercises a subtle and indirect form of suggestion, and Freud himself always maintained this idea. He said that, ultimately, the difference between analytic psychotherapy and the others is that the former uses the doctor's influence—that is, suggestion—so that the patient will abandon his resistances and not to induce a particular type of behaviour in him. This provides support for the work of Ida Macalpine (1950) on transference, which for her stems from an underlying phenomenon of suggestion, and even of hypnosis.

If support can be criticized from the point of view that it creates a link that is in a way orthopaedic (we have said that the crutch simile is inevitable), suggestion (even in Baudoin's active form) is also dangerous, because the influence it exercises is very great and can be disturbing. The possibility of leading the patient too much and of exercising demagogy or deceit are the inherent risks of suggestion, albeit without therefore disqualifying it, since all instruments, including interpretation, involve risks. When support and suggestion are directed where they belong, and when the psychotherapist knows the instruments he is using, then they are legitimate and can be useful in some forms of (minor) psychotherapy.

* * *

Dubois's *persuasion* aims at the use of reason and assumes different modalities, involving the exchange of ideas, discussing and even arguing with the patient. (Frankl's *logotherapy*, 1955, is in my opinion a form of persuasive psychotherapy, a more modern and existential one, that nevertheless corresponds in the end with that of Dubois.)

Dubois always tried to differentiate his method from that of support and suggestion, asserting that persuasion is linked to the rational process, to the patient's reason. Although it may appear to have a rational quality, Dubois's method is always charged with affectivity; its arguments are more rationalizations than reasons. The same applies to some psychotherapies of Pavlovian inspiration which arose many years ago and then subsided. Among us one of its practitioners was José A. Itzingsohn, who, however, moved increasingly in the direction of psychoanalysis. In all these methods, the idea of "rational psychotherapy" is linked more to the form than to the content, while psychoanalysis, as Fenichel (1945a) said, is rational, even though it manages irrational phenomena.

24.4 Information-gathering instruments

The instruments in the first category, which we have just studied, seek to influence the patient, to operate directly and concretely on his conduct. They are thus conceptually linked to the repressive methods of psychotherapy, although we have already noted that sometimes the analyst uses them, rightly or not, outside the framework of that debatable Freudian affirmation that suggestion is an indispensable part of analytic procedure, in that we use it to help the patient overcome his resistances.

We will now study two groups of instruments that have opposite aims but a common ground in *information*. We will look at those that gather information first and then at those that offer it to the patient. These two types of resources, because of their nature, are totally compatible with major methods of psychotherapy and of psychoanalysis in the strict sense.

* * *

Among information-gathering instruments the simplest and most direct is the *question*. When we have not heard, have not understood or wish to know data that seem to us pertinent to the analysand's associations, as well as when we think we need to know what meaning the patient gives to what he is saying, we should ask—provided there are no elements that make it advisable for us to interpret or simply to remain silent. To formulate a question and to interpret are not mutually exclusive; to ask in one case, to interpret in another or to do both will depend on analytic art. There are no fixed rules; there cannot be. Everything depends on the patient's material, the context, the information offered by the countertransference. A singular case is mentioned by Ruth Riesenberg (1970) where the transference perversion consisted in wanting to place the analyst in the position of the observer, like people in a fantasy of the patient with the mirror. Fortunately, the able analyst realized this and abstained from asking questions, when to do so would obviously have been a mistake. To be more precise, the analyst put an occasional question at the beginning. But the patient's reply on those occasions was precisely what led her to be cautious, and to think about why the patient behaved in such a singular way in relation to questions that seemed to the analyst quite natural in order to clarify the material. Thus what that article teaches us is that each time we ask, we should pay attention to whether we are really gathering information or whether we have allowed ourselves to be led into a situation that deserves to be analysed.

In the ordinary case, the aim of the question is to obtain precise information, and therefore it is formulated without other purposes or ulterior motives; otherwise we would be doing other things—influencing the analysand, managing him, supporting him and so forth. One of the difficulties of asking is precisely that, without realizing it, we could have ulterior motives—and/or the analysand could attribute them to us. In fact, the latter can be analysed.

The other difficulty in asking is that we disturb free association to a certain extent. Löwenstein (1958) referred to this in the panel on technical variations at the 1957 Paris Congress. Questions have a legitimate place in the technique in order to obtain details and specifications, as Freud did with the "Rat Man"; but only in special cases does the question justify an interruption of the associative flow. I agree with Löwenstein (1958) on this point, since it is not justifiable to interrupt a patient when he is free-associating, although everything depends on the context and the circumstances.

If we ask with a purpose other than to obtain information, we introduce another factor into the situation, and this is always complicated. Olinick (1954) deals with this theme, employing questions specifically as a parameter.

When the patient is anxious or confused, when he cannot speak freely, Olinick considers it legitimate to ask questions, be it to give the ego support or to reinforce the patient's contact with reality, preparing him eventually for interpretation.

This use of questions as a parameter seems dubious to me. Olinick's example, the young woman who begins her analysis by making an effort to show her admiration for her mother and her contempt for her father, and with a great desire to make an impression on her analyst, was resolved with a series of questions on her parental relations. Although the material is too scant for a personal opinion, it has not demonstrated that the acute conflict could not have been resolved by interpreting without parameters.

Here analytic art intervenes, because obviously when the analyst is with a very anxious person or is not right in his interpretation, he can ask a question in order to alleviate the anxiety momentarily. But he has to know that this question is a form of support and its purpose is not to obtain information.

* * *

Another instrument that gathers information is *indication* or *notation*.

Indication, as its name shows, indicates (points out) something, circumscribes an area of observation, calls attention, with the aim of making the patient observe and offer more information. If we wished to place this instrument in Bion's (1963) Grid, we would put it in Column 3 (notation) and Column 4 (attention).

It is true that indication always implies a degree of information the analyst gives to the patient to attract his attention; but I think this is only adjectival: what defines this instrument is that it seeks to receive information.

As in the case of the question, observation can have ulterior motives or can support interpretative elements. There are always meeting-points; they are inevitable; but what matters is to distinguish the different ingredients of the particular case.

The indication (notation) tends to be expressed via a particular form of speech ("note that . . .", etc.); that is, really pointing out or indicating a fact, something the analysand has not noticed and that may or may not be conscious for him. It is not necessary for the patient to be unaware; he may be, and therefore the information the analyst gives him in the indication is incidental. In any case, what is characteristic is that the indication contributes to delimiting a particular area for subsequent investigation. In parapraxes the indication sometimes fulfils the mission of calling the analysand's attention (to them) and of making him aware, of informing him of a lapse he had not noticed.

When Dora offers her associations after telling Freud her first dream, Freud says to her, "Now, I should like you to pay close attention to the exact words you used. We may have to come back to them. You said that '*something might happen in the night so that it might be necessary to leave the room*'" (1905e [1901], p. 65; the italics in the original are a typographical expression of the need for emphasis), and then in a footnote Freud explains why he stressed these words—that is, why he offered Dora this observation.

In making an observation, the analyst does not propose to inform the patient specifically but instead to make him fix his attention on something that has appeared and whose meaning, in principle, the therapist does not know. In the footnote on his observation Freud says that the material is ambiguous and that this ambiguity can lead to the ideas that still lie concealed behind the dream. If the analyst knows with certainty what this is about, then the indication is superfluous and he should interpret. It can be argued that, even knowing the latent content with certainty, the analyst

can prefer at a given moment to make an observation rather than to interpret, thinking, for example, that the analysand is not yet ready to understand or tolerate interpretation. We shall discuss this point in dealing with
deep interpretation; but let us say at this juncture that the analyst's prudence poses a theoretical problem.

* * *

Within the scheme we are developing, the other instrument for gathering
information is *confrontation*. As its name indicates, confrontation shows
the patient two things in counterposition, with the intention of making
him face a dilemma, so that he will notice a contradiction. A patient said
he was fine and therefore approaching the end of his treatment, while
he expressed strong fears of dying of a heart attack. There was certainly a
possibility of variety of interpretations, but the great contradiction he had
not noticed between feeling fine and having a heart attack made me
choose to confront him with this singular fact, safeguarding myself in this
way from his possible misunderstanding of an interpretation in terms of
an opinion on my part, for example, bearing in mind precisely the surprising denial of his fears.

     Another patient who sincerely wished to stop smoking would light a
cigarette every time he began to analyse this very problem. On one of
these occasions I simply confronted him with this fact; I told him that this
was a singular situation: he wanted to analyse his smoking habit in order
to break it, and meanwhile he lit a cigarette. Confrontation, then, reveals
two different aspects—which are contradictory—in the material. This was
really useful to the patient, because it made him understand a whole series
of automatisms, of contradictions in his behaviour, including the function
the cigarette fulfilled for him when he undertook a task, and so forth.

     It is not always easy to differentiate confrontation from making an
observation, since the former can be considered a special case of the latter,
where we call attention to two counterposed elements. Nevertheless there
are some differences, which should not be considered unarguable. We
could say that in general observation has to do with perception, and confrontation has to do with judgement. Perhaps the visual image we used
earlier, that of circumscribing an area, can serve to establish a difference.
Making an observation centres the attention on a particular point in order
to investigate it, while in confrontation the aim is to confront the patient
with a contradiction. To confront is to place face to face two simultaneous
and contrasting elements, which can occur both in the verbal material and
in behaviour. Often, as in the case of the above-mentioned smoker, the
behaviour and the verbal elements are counterposed.

* * *

To avoid misunderstandings, I should indicate that the above distinctions
are dynamic, metapsychological and not phenomenological. The form is

not essential: an observation, a confrontation and even an interpretation can be made formally with a question; conversely, the form of an interpretation is often given to what is only the analyst's comment.

Löwenstein (1951) speaks of these three instruments as preparatory to interpretation, but in my exposition I want to give them more autonomy: being information-gathering instruments, they are not necessarily steps prior to an interpretation. Löwenstein's examples are different from mine, undoubtedly because he is interested in showing some of the fundamentals of his technique. In the first place, Löwenstein distinguishes preparatory and final moments in the interpretative process because he thinks, as do many others—such as Terencio Gioia (personal communication, 1979)—that it is artificial to speak of *the* interpretation, when in fact the analyst's activity is complex and should not be compartmentalized. In addition, Löwenstein considers it essential to graduate the analysand's access to unconscious material, and, in this sense, his determination to distinguish between preliminary and final steps is understandable. This prudent attitude has its difficulties, however, and can even be tendentious, since it is proposed that the analysand should arrive by himself at what the analyst already knows.

I remember one of my first patients, a young man who was intelligent and suspicious. His dreams were not very censored, and I did not dare to interpret them. Instead, I asked questions about the manifest content, which he rejected as being tendentious: "Of course! You ask me that to make me tell you that it is homosexuality [sic] or that that woman is your wife, or my mother." In fact he was right, because that was my intention, and perhaps it would have been better to interpret directly and point out to him that he *wanted* me to interpret "that" so he could then accuse me. It is evident to me now that I feared his paranoid responses (Grinberg would say with greater precision that I had counteridentified myself with his frightened part because of the revelations analysis would have to offer him), and I wished to make him say what *I* had to say. In this case my technical fault is obvious and does not serve, therefore, to refute Löwenstein; but it indicates, in any case, a risk due to prudence. Here we again touch on the theme of deep interpretation.

CHAPTER TWENTY-FIVE

The concept of interpretation

In chapter 24 we dealt with the instruments of psychotherapy, divided into four groups. Of these, we studied those that serve to influence the patient and to obtain information from him. Now we shall study the third group, which includes the instruments that serve to inform, among which is found interpretation. There exists yet a fourth category we mentioned: the parameters.

25.1 Instruments that inform

Of all the instruments that comprise the psychotherapist's armoury, there are three that have distinct forms and uses: information, clarification and interpretation. These three tools are essentially one; but it is advisable to distinguish between them, more on the basis of their range than their characteristics.

* * *

At one end of the spectrum we have *information*, which operates as an authentic instrument of psychotherapy if we offer it to correct an error. If the neurosis stems in some way from mistaken information—and, specifically, mistaken information in terms of interpersonal relations—it is logical to think that any affirmation that perpetuates or deepens those errors perpetuates and deepens the illness; and vice versa, any datum that offers better elements with which to understand reality (or the truth) has to have a therapeutic character.

In its strict sense, information refers to something the patient should know and does not—that is, it attempts to correct an error that stems from the analysand's deficient information. In my opinion it is applied, by definition, to extrinsic knowledge, data pertaining to reality or to the world, not to the patient himself. Thus delineated, information increases the analysand's knowledge; it does not refer specifically to his problems, but to an objective ignorance of the facts, which influences him in some way. In very special (and rare) cases, the analyst can legitimately give that information and correct the error. It is not difficult to find examples in practice—in our own practice—and at first we think, under the influence of the severe psychoanalytic superego, that we have transgressed. However, if we offer this information so that the patient will have data he needs and which he lacks for reasons essentially foreign to him, that information is pertinent and can be useful.

Naturally, I do not ignore the risk involved in giving this type of information. The patient can misunderstand it as support, seduction, a desire to influence or control him, and so forth. But, in any case, if the analysand is unaware of something that affects him and we give him the knowledge he lacks with the sole intent of modifying that situation, I think we are operating legitimately, in accordance with our art.

Certainly it can be said that, in such cases, it is always feasible to offer the information through an interpretation that contains it; but I think this is an artifice that is contrary to the technique and, even more, to the ethics. It means making use of our most noble tool for ends outside its competence and which can only undermine it. We should bear in mind that the analysand will realize, sooner or later, that we are transmitting information to him through an artifice, and then he can suppose that we always operate from ulterior motives, without our being able to give a clear interpretation for his mistrust (paranoia) or his (manic) contempt.

I must point out that I am not referring here to the analysand's ignorance of something to do with the contract or the setting, such as questions about a holiday, vacations, fees, and so forth, because in this case it is clear that the information is unavoidable. I am referring to matters outside the constants of the setting and on which the analyst may not feel obliged to offer information.

Sometimes it is justifiable, for example, to offer medical information to an analysand who does not have it and may not even know he does not have it. The same week that his wife entered the menopause, an analysand who always envied the privileges of the weaker sex had a small rectal haemorrhage. I interpreted this symptom as his desire to be the one who now menstruated, in the double perspective of his acknowledged envy of the woman and his desire for reparation. I was able to place this material at the same time validly along the lines of his homosexual transference and also to his desire to free himself from me, terminating analysis suddenly, as if it were an abortion. I informed him at the same time that blood in the faeces could be a symptom of organic illness and asked him to consult his doctor. Unfortunately my fears were confirmed, and a week later he was operated on for a sigmoid carcinoma.

In special cases—though not always—it is forgivable, if not legitimate, to give a colleague in analysis who wants to become an analyst some general data on certain requirements—for example that there are definite periods when interviews are held—although it is probable that in these cases one will have to interpret the neurotic motives for the aspirant's lack of information.

A patient can have a consultation over what he calls premature ejaculation and the problem can be of another type. Many years ago I took on in analysis a "frigid" woman, and then, when I was able to obtain data on her sexual life during treatment, I learned that her husband ejaculated *ad portas*. It was an error, then, not to ask her in the interviews why she thought she was frigid, what she thought frigidity was. Although it is true this woman needed analysis, it was for other reasons, among them her ignorance of sexual life, her idealization of her husband, and her almost melancholy self-reproaches.

A young colleague once commented enthusiastically that upon leaving the session he would attend the seminar of an eminent analyst who was to visit us. I knew that the visit had been cancelled at the last moment and preferred to give my analysand that information, instead of allowing him to go to the Association and find this out only then. This anecdote, which is seemingly unimportant, nevertheless contains a whole theory of information in the analytic setting. I was evidently not obliged to supply the information that was lacking, but I knew he was not the only one who did not know of the last-minute cancellation of the journey. I myself had asked that members and candidates be advised of the unforeseen circumstance and assumed it had not been possible to alert everyone. Weighing up all the circumstances, I think that not to have informed him would have been excessive on my part.

In many of these cases a delicate situation confronts the analyst, because these "objective" information failures are frequently products of repression, denial on other defence mechanisms. In these cases it is surely more functional (and more analytical) to interpret that he knows something he does not wish to see (repression), whose existence he denies (denial), or that he wants me (or whoever) to know it for him (projection, projective identification).

Again, there is no fixed rule in these cases. Everything depends on the moment, the circumstances, many factors. We are not at fault if what we seek is to inform the analysand, not to ingratiate ourselves, support or influence him, and always provided we think his lack of information should be supplied directly and not interpreted, broadening the analytic dialogue in this way instead of closing it.

It is a lamentable error to think that by giving this type of information we contribute to a change in the patient. We only give him the opportunity of seeing his problems from another perspective, while avoiding his perception of our silence as confirmation of what he had thought.

To conclude, I wish to cite the best example I recall from my reading. In Ruth Mack Brunswick's classic work, "The Analysis of a Case of Paranoia" (1928b), which demonstrates for the first time the pathological fixation of a woman on the pre-oedipal stage, the patient comments, quite freely, that bitches (female dogs) have no vagina, and her analyst gives her the appropriate information.

* * *

Clarification seeks to illumine something the individual knows, but not distinctly. The knowledge exists; but, as opposed to the case of information, the problem here is something more personal. He does not lack information about something extrinsic; rather, there is something he does not perceive clearly about himself. In these cases the therapist's information is meant to clarify what the patient has said. I think clarification does not promote insight but only a re-ordering of information. This is not Bibring's (1954) opinion; for him, the process implies overcoming a resistance—probably in the *Pcs* (preconscious) system.

Clarification refers to some information that pertains to the patient, who cannot apprehend or grasp it.

25.2 Interpretation

At the other end of this spectrum, *interpretation*, in my opinion, always refers to something that belongs to the patient but of which he has no knowledge. I do not use the word consciousness, because I wish to define these three instruments in terms applicable to any school of psychotherapy, not only to metapsychology. The existential psychologists, for example, do not in fact accept differences between conscious, unconscious and preconscious, but they will not object if I say "knowledge" or use the word "consciousness" in the general sense of being aware, of being responsible for or knowing about oneself. The information refers to something the patient is ignorant of about the external world, about reality, something that does not belong to him. Interpretation, on the other hand, always indicates something that properly belongs to the patient, and of which he nevertheless has no knowledge. The difference is very great and will serve to define and study interpretation.

It is sometimes said that interpretation can refer not only to what belongs to the individual, but also to his environment. I do not share this extension of the concept. This is why I insisted on defining and formalizing information itself, so as not to confuse the concept of interpretation.

One interprets only to the patient; "interpretations" to his relatives or friends are always wild interpretations.

Similarly, when Winnicott (1947) says the analyst should interpret to the psychotic the objective hate he once felt for the patient, he is using the idea of interpretation very loosely. With regard to the specifications we are setting up, what we are doing in these circumstances is informing on what we felt at the time, but never interpreting. Interpreting would be to tell him that on those occasions he did something that aroused my hate; but to tell him I hated him is only a piece of information. (We are not discussing here the validity of Winnicott's technique, but only specifying the concept of interpretation.)

Years ago a colleague consulted me about a woman who was in an evident impasse because there was no way of making her conscious of her husband's deceit. The analyst had repeatedly interpreted, on the basis of objective facts, this obvious deception and the defence mechanisms the patient used in order to eschew responsibility. "You do not want to see that your husband is deceiving you. You turn your back on reality, you do not want to see what is obvious. No one can think that a man who goes out every night and returns at dawn with the most varied excuses, who dresses excessively to go out on errands, who ceased to have sexual relations with you months ago . . .", and so forth. To begin with, I told my young colleague that the patient was right not to accept his points of view, which he called interpretations.

These supposed interpretations are no more than opinions (and opinions belong to those who give them, not to the recipient) or, at best, information (in that it belongs to the external world, to objective reality). At most, my young colleague could have told his stubborn patient: "I wish to inform you that there is a high incidence of matrimonial infidelity among men who have business meetings every afternoon or women who go out alone and well-dressed on Saturday nights." It suffices to put it this way for all of us to realize that an intervention of this type is senseless, ridiculous. My colleague's "interpretations" did not sound ridiculous but were completely illogical and lacked method (and ethics), since he could not really know whether this man went out with other women—nor is it the task of analysis to try to find this out.

In any case, my colleague consulted me because the case had stagnated. After these "interpretations", the patient would appeal to her husband; he would deny everything, and she would end up believing him, to her analyst's despair.

When I began this supervision, I pointed out the methodological error to my colleague and, for my part, made no conjecture about whether the husband deceived his wife or not. In fact I have no way of knowing this, and as an analyst (or, in this case, as a supervisor) this is not my task.

The analyst began to pay more attention to the way the patient recounted her husband's outings, which soon gave him a lead. She would wait for him in a state of intense anxiety and excitement, besieged by the image of seeing him in bed with another woman. At the end of this long agony, she would masturbate. That is, all this provoked in her a very intense scopophilic and masochistic pleasure. When this was interpreted to her, there was a dramatic change, in the first place because the woman took responsibility for what was happening *to her* and then because she was able to discuss things differently with her husband. Thus, slowly, the analysis resumed. It is worth indicating here, in passing, the countertransference conflict, in that the patient placed her analyst in the position of the third (other), who imagines the primal scene.

Interpretation can only refer to the patient, and for various reasons— above all, because neither methodologically nor ethically can we know what the other is doing. We know only what happens in the *hic et nunc*, the here and now; we bear witness only to what the patient tells us. This position does not change at all if the analyst were to have access to external (objective) reality, since that reality is not pertinent; only what comes from the analysand is pertinent.

25.3 *Information and interpretation*

We have tried to approach the concept of interpretation on the basis that it is a special way of informing. In that it informs, the information must be, above all, *truthful*. If a piece of information is neither truthful nor objective, it will by definition cease to be information at all. Falling within the range of its definition, the aim must be only to inform, to give knowledge. This is why I insist that interpretation must be *disinterested*. If we have a motive other than that of giving knowledge, then we are no longer strictly interpreting but suggesting or supporting, persuading, manipulating, and so forth. It is worth clarifying two important matters here. First, I am referring to the attitude of the analyst (who formulates the interpretation); what the recipient does has little or no bearing on this. The analysand can give our words another meaning, but this does not change them. If the recipient uses the knowledge I gave him badly, I will have to interpret again, and I will probably aim at the change of meaning effected by my listener. Secondly, I refer to the basic objective of the communication, without assuming that the analyst is "chemically" pure, free of all contamination and in possession of an ideal language free of error or imprecision. At times these inevitable notes added to the interpretation in the strict sense are the only nuances the analysand grasps in order to criticize an interpretation with more or less justification.

Psychoanalytic method, the theory and the ethics, converge in the concept of interpretation (and of information generally), in that we may interpret but not dictate another's conduct. The latter can only be decided by the person himself—in this case, the patient. Lacan is right to protest when the analyst wishes to be the one who defines reality and adaptation (1958a, passim, especially chapters 5, 6 and 7).

The interpretation should, in addition to being truthful and disinterested, be *pertinent* information—that is, offered in a context where it can be operative and usable, although in the end it may not be so used. The interpretation must be opportune, it must provide an acceptable minimum degree of opportunity. I am thereby introducing here another defining feature of interpretation: pertinence (opportunity), which for me is not synonymous with *timing*. The concept of timing is more restricted and precise than that of opportunity, which is more inclusive. An interpretation where timing fails does not therefore cease to be one; an intervention that is not pertinent is not one, by definition. Opportunity refers, then, to contact with the material, to the location of the analyst vis-à-vis the patient.

We have defined interpretation, then, as a truthful, disinterested and pertinent piece of information that refers to the recipient.

25.4   Interpretation and insight

Along a path different from ours, Löwenstein arrived at a definition of interpretation similar to the one just offered (in 1951—that is, a half-century ago). Löwenstein distinguishes the analyst's preparatory interventions aimed at freeing the analysand's associations from interpretation proper, a special intervention that produces the dynamic changes we call insight. Interpretation is an explanation the analyst gives the patient (based on what the latter communicated to him) in order to give him new knowledge about himself. Löwenstein says, in short, that interpretation is information (knowledge) given to the patient, which refers to the patient and provokes changes that lead to insight.

This definition differs from the one we gave in the previous section only in that it includes the *effect* of the interpretation. I concur on this point with Sandler, Dare and Holder (1973), when they say it would be better to define interpretation according to its intention, not its effect. In this sense, Löwenstein's definition would be more acceptable if it said that interpretation aims at producing insight and not that it has to produce it. This is because, in fact, even the most perfect interpretation can be inoperative if the analysand so wishes it. To conclude, it is better to base the definition on the information the analyst gives and not on the patient's response.

In conclusion, Sandler et al. propose, as an alternative, that interpretation is *meant* to produce insight. I therefore agree with their suggestion, since in this case informing is the same as getting the patient to acquire insight.

The relation to insight is important and complex and therefore I prefer not to include it in the definition. Were we to have the *desire* that the analysand respond with insight, we would lose something of our impartial attitude. Insight should be something that arises from our work without

our seeking it directly. Apart from these qualifications and with the specifications of Sandler et al., we can add, as one of its defining features, that
interpretation is meant to produce insight.

Aside from the methodological aspects, which seem decisive to me, the
relation between interpretation and insight is very complex. Perhaps it can
even be maintained that not every interpretation is meant to produce insight, at least ostensible insight. Insight is a very specific process, the culmination of a series of moments of working through by means of lengthy
interpretative work. We will discuss this absorbing theme further on, particularly in chapter 50; it does not relate strictly to the present discussion.
We are seeking defining features of the concept of interpretation, without
pronouncing yet on its relation to insight and working through. This is
again based on the idea that insight can figure among the defining features
without being among the analyst's immediate objectives when he interprets. As we will shortly see, the effect sought by the interpretation is the
decisive element when we define it operationally.

25.5   Interpretation and meaning

In an attempt to define interpretation from another perspective, which
complements the previous one, let us look now at its semantic value.
The analyst—as David Liberman (1970–72) points out—gives the patient's
material a second meaning. The new meaning the interpretation gives to
the material leads me to compare it with the primary delusional experience (*primäres Wahnerlebnis*, Jaspers, 1913).

Jasper's genius defined the primary delusional experience as a new
connection of meaning: suddenly, for the individual, a new relation appears, a new *connection of meaning*, another significance—inexplicably for
Jaspers (but not for Freud)—that is, in a way in which empathy seems
impossible for the phenomenological observer, because, in effect, at the
level of consciousness it would be incomprehensible.

The interpretation is also a new connection of meaning. The analyst
takes diverse elements from the patient's free associations and produces a
synthesis that lends a new meaning to his experience. This new connection
is certainly real, symbolic and, of course, not delusional. (This definition
can fit in perfectly with Bion's, 1963, ideas on the constant conjunction and
the selected fact.)

In contrast to the primary delusional experience, the interpretation
arrives at a pertinent and realistic meaning. Furthermore—and this seems
decisive to me—the interpretation has two features that can never appear
in the primary delusional experience, which always disqualifies and is
never rectifiable.

The interpretation does not disqualify; otherwise it would be a mere
defensive manoeuvre of the analyst (denial, projective identification, etc.),

closer to the primary delusional experience than to information. The interpretation never disqualifies—the primary delusional experience does.

In the midst of a serious marital crisis, the analysand asserts that he
does not seek a divorce, because of his children. On the basis of ample and
convincing material, the analyst interprets that he is projecting into his
children his infantile part that does not wish to separate from his wife,
who represents the mother of his childhood. What does this interpretation
mean; what does the analyst seek through it? He tries to give the analysand new information about his relation to his wife and to his children;
but he does not question the analysand's preoccupations as a father. It
may be that the analysand resolves this conflict by ceasing to project into
his children his infantile part, and that, nevertheless, he decides finally not
to get a divorce, thinking about the fate of his children.

Another difference with regard to the primary delusional experience is
that the interpretation is always a hypothesis, and as such rectifiable. The
delusional idea is not rectified; the hypothesis, on the other hand, if we
follow Popper (1953, 1958, 1963, 1972), is never confirmed and continues
to be valid until it is refuted. The interpretation, then, can be considered as
a scientific proposition, a declarative sentence, a hypothesis that can be
justified or refuted, and this separates it completely from the primary
delusional experience.

In short, therefore, as a new connection of meaning, the interpretation
informs and gives the analysand the means of organizing a new way of
thinking and of changing his point of view (Bion, 1963).

25.6   Operational definition of interpretation

We have defined interpretation in two different and somewhat overlapping ways—as a special type of information and as a new connection of
meaning. From the first point of view the interpretation is a scientific
proposition, a point Bernardo Álvarez (1974) studied some years ago; from
the other perspective the interpretation is characterized by having a semantic value, because it contains a meaning.

We should now consider a third way of defining interpretation, the
operational way. As Gregorio Klimovsky says in chapter 35 of this volume, the interpretation is not only a hypothesis that the analyst builds, but
one to be given, to be communicated. Although in special cases we can
retain the interpretation, the condition of having to communicate it to the
patient is inevitable because, as a hypothesis, the only way of testing it is
to communicate it. That it should be communicated is thus included in the
definition of interpretation. But in communicating it, it is also operative—
that is, it provokes some change, which is what enables us to test it. In this
way the debate is reopened, and Sandler is proved right when he includes
among the defining features of interpretation its intention (more than its
effect, as Löwenstein thought) to produce insight.

These three features, then—information, meaning and operativeness—are the three parameters within which interpretation is defined.

The operational definition of interpretation does not imply that this effect be sought by the analyst directly, as we have already stated. The analyst knows empirically, because his practice has demonstrated it many times, that if the interpretation is correct and the analysand accepts it, it will operate on his mind. However, this does not alter the attitude with which the analyst interprets. His attitude continues to be disinterested, in that what he proposes is to give the analysand elements of judgement so that he may change, without depending on these changes, without exercising any influence other than that of knowledge. The analyst's information is disinterested in the way in which Freud conceived it in the "Recommendations to Physicians" with that surgeon's phrase that says, "*Je le pensai, Dieu le guérit*". The sense in which we give the patient an interpretation is no different: an attitude of freedom for the other—not coercion; of disinterest, not exigency. There is nothing of affective disinterest in this attitude, because the information is given with affection, with the desire that the analysand take charge of this information so as to readjust, re-order or question his conduct by himself later on. The modification of behaviour is not included in our intention when we inform, and this is, perhaps, the essence of analytic work.

25.7 Interpretation and suggestion

In this sense, as I said earlier, what defines psychoanalysis is that it does not use suggestion. Psychoanalysis is the only therapy that does not use placebos. All psychotherapies use communication in some way as a placebo; instead, we renounce it. This renunciation defines psychoanalysis, which is also, for this reason, more difficult. Our intention is to modify not the patient's conduct, but his information. Bion said it with his usual precision: psychoanalysis does not try to resolve conflicts but to promote mental growth.

The patient can take our information as suggestion, support, an order or whatever. I am not saying that the patient may not do this and not even that he should not do it. What defines our work is not the attitude with which the analysand receives our information, but the attitude with which we give it. It is also part of our task to take account of the attitude with which the patient may receive our information and where possible to predict his response, avoiding misunderstandings whenever we can. We can also abstain from interpreting if we think we are not going to be understood, if we foresee that our words are going to be distorted and used towards other ends. When we are proposing an increase in fees, an interpretation about anal-retentive tendencies will be difficult to receive as such. It is probable that the analysand will see it as an attempt to justify ourselves, or something similar, and not as an interpretation.

I think I have made clear, then, that information, clarification and interpretation form a special category of instruments because of the *intention* with which they are offered, a singular intention that can be summed up by saying that it consists in using these instruments not as placebos but as information.

If we wish to utilize the classic scheme of the topographical theory, we can conclude that information, clarification and interpretation correspond to conscious, preconscious and unconscious processes, respectively.

25.8   Final comments

We have tried to define with the utmost rigour the multiple instruments at the analyst's disposal because from this the essence of the practice arises spontaneously. We have managed to show the basic reasons why psychoanalysis has nothing to do with suggestion.

It is advisable to make it clear that in differentiating diverse instruments, we are not suggesting that in practice it is always possible to distinguish between them. In clinical practice things are never simple, and intermediate and imprecise zones appear in which one instrument is imperceptibly exchanged for another. These changes are common; but we are not therefore going to say that the differences do not exist. When an indication is transformed into a confrontation, when a confrontation begins to have interpretative ingredients or vice versa, is something we have to decide each time in every case.

If I have insisted on the existence of various instruments at the analyst's disposal and not only on interpretation, I have done this so as to render its importance fully, to avoid undermining the concept of interpretation by including in it everything the analyst does, or vice versa, thinking that there is no major difference between interpretation and the other instruments.

I think it is artificial to transform into an interpretation what should be a question or an order. In these cases, despite our saying we have interpreted, in fact the patient decodes this for what it is, and I think he is right. To transform something that must be something else into an interpretation is always artificial and, even more, contrary to the spirit of analysis, because interpretation, as we have said, should not provoke a particular type of conduct. (When a patient asks me whether he can smoke during the session, I prefer to tell him he can, instead of "interpreting" that he is asking my permission or trying to see whether I will forbid it.)

There are intermediate zones where one can incline one way or the other—towards confrontation or interpretation, for example. If the patient who enthusiastically analysed his smoking habit while he lit a cigarette had manifested a mocking attitude, I would have made an interpretation rather than confront him.

All this brings up the issue of what the proper place is for indication, confrontation and asking questions in our technique. These steps are preparatory or of less significance than interpretation; but sometimes they respect the rules of the game more, in that they do not introduce elements than can be equivocal.

These differences allow a vindication of the autonomy of these instruments and enable us to respect the basic principles of our work.

CHAPTER TWENTY-SIX

Interpretation in psychoanalysis

In chapter 25 we did two things: we located interpretation in its appropriate place among the various instruments of psychotherapy, and then we tried to approach it through the disparate paths of communication, semiology and operationalism, seeking the defining features at the point of their convergences.

We dealt with this theme deliberately within the broad field of psychotherapy; now we have a different task—the complementary one of the study of interpretation in psychoanalysis.

Psychoanalysis is one among several methods of major psychotherapy. But it has singular guidelines, such as the privileged place it accords to interpretation. Laplanche and Pontalis, in their *Vocabulaire de la psychanalyse* (1968 [*The Language of Psycho-Analysis*, 1973]) are right to say that psychoanalysis can be characterized by interpretation.

26.1   *Interpretation in Freud's writings*

In Freud's work interpretation is defined basically as the path traversed by the analyst's understanding from manifest content to latent ideas. Interpretation is the instrument that makes the unconscious conscious. In *Die Traumdeutung* (*The Interpretation of Dreams*, 1900a) interpretation is equal and contrary to dream work: dream work goes from the latent ideas to the manifest content; interpretation crosses that same path.

For Freud, interpretation is, above all, the act of giving sense to the material. This appears in the very title of his major work, which locates him not among those who studied dreams "scientifically" but among those who assign a sense to them. To interpret a dream is to discover its meaning. Freud's definition is semantic, as can be seen at the beginning of chapter 2 of the above work, where he says that to interpret a dream means to indicate its sense. Interpretation inserts itself as another link in the chain of our mental actions, which thus acquire meaning.

The meaning that interpretation draws out varies in parallel with the different moments profiled by Freudian investigation. As we shall see below, Didier Anzieu (1969) distinguishes three major conceptions of the process of cure and, consequently, three types of interpretation. But for the purposes of our interest at this juncture we will say that interpretation has to do with conflict and desire. Memories are recovered, but they are not interpreted. Interpretation becomes necessary because there are instincts that crystallize as desires, against which defences are erected. As a specific instrument to unravel the conflict, interpretation is linked, as we will see, to the topographic–dynamic–economic tripod of metapsychology.

What Freud thinks of interpretation can be deduced clearly enough by re-reading one of his technical works, "The Handling of Dream-Interpretation in Psycho-Analysis" (1911e). The dream, as in the case of a symptom, is explained by grasping the different fragments of meaning successively, and "one must be content if the attempt at interpretation brings a single pathogenic wishful impulse to light" (1911e, p. 93). This quotation is a hint that, for Freud, in his technical writings, to interpret is to explain the meaning of an unconscious desire, to bring to light a particular instinct, a particular wishful impulse.

Laplanche and Pontalis point out that the word "interpretation" is not interchangeable with *Deutung*, whose meaning is closer to explanation and clarification. The Latin word "interpretation", on the other hand, suggests at times the subjective and the arbitrary. Freud himself, however, uses the word with both these connotations when he compares psychoanalytic interpretation with that of a paranoid person in the *Psychopathology of Everyday Life* (1901b), just as we have seen in defining interpretation as a new connection of meaning.

The authors of the *Vocabulaire*, for their part, quote the way Freud uses it in chapter 7 of "On Dreams" (1901a), where the word acquires that arbitrary connotation. In introducing the concept of secondary revision, Freud says there that it is a process that tends to order the elements of the dream, providing them with a façade that covers the oneiric content at various points, like a provisional interpretation, and when we undertake the analysis of a dream, we first have to rid ourselves of that attempt at interpretation.

As we all know, Freud attributes the secondary revision to the intention of making the dream comprehensible (considerations of representability), and he explains it as an activity whereby the dreamer grasps the material presented to him on the basis of certain anticipatory ideas [*Erwartungsvorstellungen*], which order it to make it intelligible, with which he manages quite often only to falsify it. (The concept of *Erwartungsvorstellungen* is interesting because it sometimes inspires Freud's technique, when he gives the analysand certain information on psychoanalytic theory so that it will operate in this way. Where this *modus operandi* can be observed best is in the clinical history of the "Rat Man".) In these cases, then, the word "interpretation" appears burdened with its less reliable features.

26.2 Comprehension, explanation and interpretation according to Jaspers

In the second part of his *General Psychopathology* (1913), which deals with comprehensive or understanding psychology [*verstehende Psychologie*], Jaspers distinguishes two orders of understandable relations: comprehensive [*verstehende Psychologie*] and explanatory [*erklärende Psychologie*]. *Comprehension* is always genetic; it allows us to see how the psychic arises from what is psychic, how the one who is attacked becomes angry and the one who is deceived mistrusts. *Explanation*, on the other hand, objectively links typical everyday facts or events and is always causal. For Jaspers there is an unbridgeable abyss between understanding and explanation.

In the natural sciences relations are exclusively causal and are expressed through rules and laws. In psychopathology we can explain some phenomena in this way, such as amaurotic idiocy (Tay–Sachs' disease) via recessive inheritance, and similarly in the case of phenylpyruvic oligophrenia. We can establish a justifiable true relation between dementia paralytica and syphilitic leptomeningitis or attribute mongolism to the trisomy of chromosome 21.

In psychology we can know not only causal relations (which are the only knowable ones in the natural sciences) but also a different type of relations when we see how psychic material arises from the psyche in a way that is intelligible to us. We understand the concatenation of psychic events genetically. The evidence of genetic understanding is, for Jaspers, ultimate: we cannot go beyond it. On that experience of ultimate evidence is based the entire psychology of understanding. Recognition of this evidence is the pre-condition for comprehensive psychology, just as the recognition of the reality of perception and causality is the pre-condition for the natural sciences (Jaspers, 1913).

It seems to me that Jaspers tempers his assertions somewhat when he then makes it clear that an understandable relation does not prove conclusively that it is real in a particular case or that it is produced generally. When Nietzsche affirms that from the consciousness of human weakness arise moral exigency and religious feeling because the soul wishes to satisfy in this way its will to power, we immediately have that experience of evidence we cannot transcend. But when Nietzsche applies that understanding to the singular process of the origin of Christianity, he can be mistaken, if the objective material with which the relation is understood has not been well grasped. In this way, Jaspers' comprehensive psychology [*verstehende Psychologie*] rests on inner experience [*Erlebnis*], but it is another matter to apply it to a particular case.

Jaspers then affirms, on these bases, that every act of understanding real particular processes is therefore more or less *interpreting*, which can only in rare cases of a relatively high degree of perfection arrive at convincing objective material (ibid., 1913).

We can find a psychic relation free of any concrete reality comprehensible (experientially), but in the particular case we can only assert the reality of that comprehensible relation provided objective data exist. The fewer the objective data and the less they stimulate comprehension, the more we interpret and the less we understand.

In this way, and in fact with definitions, Jaspers is inclined to disqualify interpretation in general as arbitrary. The greatest difficulty for Jaspers' comprehensive psychology is how to join that evidence of genetic understanding with what he calls objective material. This epistemological difficulty luckily does not arise for Freudian psychoanalysis.

26.3   Bernfeld's classification

Siegfried Bernfeld, one of the great thinkers of psychoanalysis, wrote an extensive essay on interpretation in 1932 ("Der Begriff der 'Deutung' in der Psychoanalyse"). It is one of the few attempts within the psychoanalytic bibliography to specify the concept of interpretation with a methodological criterion.

Beginning from Freud's definitions we have mentioned—that interpreting is unveiling the sense of something, incorporating it into the global context of the person who produced it—Bernfeld proposes three classes of interpretation: final, functional and genetic (reconstruction).

* * *

Final interpretation discovers the purpose or intention of a particular action, lodging it as a link in the chain of events that constitute the intentional context of a person. This intentional context is, of course, unconscious, and the final interpretation is aimed at it. He says the final interpretation refers to the intentional context in which it belongs, an element in question that primarily appears isolated or incorporated in another context.

Bernfeld says the difficulty for final interpretations is that they are easier to accept than to prove, so that it is often assumed that the intention has to be there and that it is finally found. This is what happens, Bernfeld continues, with Adler's individual psychology. In a polemical tone that was surely more justified then than now, Bernfeld maintains that the aim is for psychology to establish a particular link, but to discover what actually exists and is hidden.

Within the Adlerian system, interpretation can do nothing other than discover the intentions that arise teleologically from the final fictitious goal (Adler, 1912, 1918). Freud's theoretical support is completely different, because the unconscious intentions that final interpretation grasps have their starting-point in the instincts, with their corollary of unconscious desire or fantasy. Bernfeld, who certainly knows about this difference, could have brought out precisely the contrast between psychoanalysis and individual psychology, without doubting the right of the former to interpret the final objectives.

* * *

The aim of *functional* interpretation is to discover what role a particular action fulfils, in what way it serves the subject. When we say that a woman refuses to go out into the street so as not to allow herself to be led by her unconscious wish of prostitution, we can say that agoraphobia fulfils in this case the *function* of avoiding that temptation and its dangers.

As Bernfeld indicates, it is not always easy to distinguish between final and functional interpretation, since frequently the function of the act being studied is precisely to fulfil an objective; but at other times the difference is very obvious. When I transform the ring of the alarm clock into birdsong in order to continue sleeping, one can interpret that the dream fulfils the *function* of preserving my repose, and its *objective* or *finality* is to satisfy my desire to go on sleeping.

Bernfeld notes that functional interpretation has two different meanings. (We will return to the theme of functional explanations in psychoanalysis, especially in dealing with acting out. See also chapter 8, where the function of transference is discussed.) In general, it is used to establish a relation between two events or facts, such as when we say we have eyes to see, with a clear teleological connotation. At other times functional interpretation is used to denote a relation between the whole and its parts, such as when we say that x is a function of y. In this case functional interpretation permits characterization of an event or fact in the context in which it belongs.

Bernfeld rightly considers that to the extent that the functional relation requires the delimitation of the domain it applies to, it becomes imprecise and aleatory in psychoanalysis, where there are in fact *many* contexts, and where Wälder's (1936) principle of multiple functions always operates. Bernfeld (1932) says that for the functional formulations of psychoanalysis, the "person" as essence of all personal moments is excessively ambiguous for the constitution of the "totality" to which the said formulations refer.

* * *

Genetic interpretation (reconstruction) is the fundamental method of psychoanalysis for Bernfeld. Psychoanalysis always proposes the reconstruction of psychic processes that really occurred. Bernfeld asserts that this reconstruction is possible because the psychic processes to be reconstructed leave traces, and because a regular relationship exists between psychic events and their traces.

For Bernfeld psychoanalysis is the science of traces, and therefore, he says, the fundamental method of psychoanalytic investigation can be characterized as the reconstruction of past personal events on the basis of the traces they have left behind. Ahead of Freud, he concludes that it is to call the fundamental method of psychoanalysis *reconstruction* rather than interpretation, emphasizing that reconstruction often utilizes final and functional interpretation. Psychoanalytic reconstruction can also be called, in any case, reconstructive or genetic interpretation. (We will see further on that Bernfeld, on the basis of his theory of traces, offers an original version of the methodology of psychoanalysis, utilized by Weinshel and other writers to characterize the analytic process.)

Bernfeld also indicates, accurately, that what is reconstructed is not the process as it was, but only a *model* of the process.

The 1932 essay ends with a very clear synthesis: final interpretation aims at the subject's intentions; functional interpretation refers to the value of a phenomenon in the nexus of a totality, while reconstruction establishes the genetic link of a phenomenon that has remained separated.

26.4 The Anzieus' contributions

Didier and Annie Anzieu deal with interpretation in a series of important works (D. Anzieu, 1969, 1970; A. Anzieu, 1969; Anzieu & Anzieu, 1977), which add valuable elements to the concept of psychoanalytic interpretation.

Didier Anzieu (1969) considers that it is difficult to study interpretation because it reveals the analyst in his totality, both rational and irrational. Anzieu does not, in fact, believe that interpretation arises clearly from the analyst's conflict-free area, directing itself to the analysand's conflict-free area, as seems to be suggested in three articles by Hartmann, Löwenstein and Kris in the *Psycho-Analytic Quarterly* of 1951. And he does not subscribe to Lagache's well-known statement that with free association we ask the patient to rave but with interpretation we invite him to reason together with us. Anzieu believes, on the contrary, that interpretation expresses the analyst's secondary process infiltrated by the primary process, since, he says, interpretation could not reach the unconscious if it were radically extraneous to it (Anzieu, 1972, p. 255).

Following Freud's work on dreams, parapraxes and jokes, Lacan sees the psychoanalyst as the translator of a text, so that psychoanalysis is finally hermeneutics. Disagreeing with this conception, Anzieu thinks the psychoanalyst is a live and human interpreter who translates the "language" of the unconscious for another human being. As the interpreter who translates one language into another, the analyst never operates as a machine or a robot, precisely because all translation is only an equivalence, an approximation.

Beyond hermeneutics and linguistics, interpretation has for Anzieu a meaning that overlaps with artistic interpretation. The analyst interprets in the same sense that the musician interprets his musical score or the actor his role—that is, understanding and expressing the writer's intentions. The interpreter in these cases respects and preserves the text but reproduces it in his way. The analyst, like the musician and the actor, interprets with his personality. He says that psychoanalytic interpretation witnesses the echo found in the analyst, not so much through the patient's words as through his fantasies (ibid., p. 272). Interpretation arises, then, from what the analyst feels, from what, having come from the patient, resonates in him.

In the substantial essay entitled "Elements of a Theory of Interpretation" (1970), Didier Anzieu clothes interpretation with meaning to the measure of the development of Freud's theories, with frequent references to Widlocher's work *Freud and the Problem of Change* (1970), which distinguishes three successive conceptions of the psychic apparatus and, consequently, of change in (analytic) treatment.

The first conception covers Breuer's and Freud's ideas in the *Studies on Hysteria* (Freud, 1895d) and extends to the following period, when Freud established the bases of psychoanalysis. According to Widlocher, the fundamental equation is that the symptom is the equivalent of the unpleasant and forgotten memory; and the symptom is resolved when the (cathartic) cure recovers the memory.

Interpretation becomes necessary in two ways here—from the topographic point of view, to resolve the double inscription between the (two) systems of functioning, as proposed by Breuer, of free and bound energy; and from the dynamic point of view introduced by Freud, to reveal the conflict and lift the repression.

Always within that conception, interpretation directs itself to the primary process, which tends towards perceptual identity displacing energy from the motor to the imaginary pole, with which the discharge fails and the situation repeats itself (Anzieu, 1970, p. 109). In these circumstances, interpretation should promote a process in which that repetitive and automatic tendency subordinate to the pleasure principle can be modified. The secondary process fulfils that function, in that it tends to thought identity, contrasting the pleasurable image with reality, confronting perception and memory.

A singularly important point in Anzieu's thought has to do with a division within the secondary process that characterizes the perception–consciousness system. He says that Freud introduces within the secondary process a subdivision that complements Breuer's distinction between free and bound systems. This subdivision derives from a relatively tardy differentiation of the secondary process. It refers to attention. It characterizes what Freud calls, from 1915 onwards, the perception-consciousness system (ibid., p. 111). So consciousness is the organ that permits the perception of psychic qualities and is the agent of change. According to Anzieu, the psychoanalyst's interpretation is directed to the patient's consciousness, making him "attend" to the functioning of his own psychic reality (ibid., p. 113).

Freud's first conception, which I have just sketched (Anzieu's description is richer and more complex) is basically intellectualist, Anzieu says. He acknowledges that Freud reaffirmed it at the end of his life in "An Outline of Psycho-Analysis" (1940a), where he repeats that the analyst's interpretative activity is an intellectual task.

In Freud's second conception of the cure and the psychic apparatus, "interpretation is conceived of as the producer of displacement of libidinal cathexis" (Anzieu, 1970, p. 128). The symptom is not only the symbol of a lost memory—it also serves the subject's interests, and its resolution demands a displacement of the cathexes that must change their objects and their mode of satisfaction.

Now interpretation is no longer the intellectual act that communicates with consciousness. Anzieu holds that the interpretation brings the patient only a word representation, whereas pathogenic, repressed and unconscious representation is a thing representation (ibid., p. 129). The patient should make both coincide through the difficult work of elaboration (working through). *Deutung* thus cedes its place to *Durcharbeiten*. Psychoanalysis is concerned now not only with the ideational representative, but also with the *quantum* of affect in the transference. Anzieu says that there are in operation here, in addition to interpretation, the psychoanalyst's attitude in the analytic situation, his silence, his interdictions, his interventions in respect of the rules, hours, fees, as equally important and frequently even decisive factors (ibid., p. 130). Here, undoubtedly, first-person interpretation finds its main theoretical support (Anzieu & Anzieu, 1977).

Freud's third conception integrates two main ideas—the repetition compulsion [*Wiederholungszwang*] and the systems of identification that intervene in the structure of the psychic apparatus. In this third stage of Freudian theories, interpretation will operate according to our understanding of its principal postulates. If we follow Bibring and think that in repetition compulsion there is a restitutive tendency, then interpretation has to give account of these two aspects of the automatism of repetition and effect restitution. If we understand instinctive repetition as an attempt to return to a previous state, to recover the lost object, then our interpretation has to direct itself to that archaic level of early object relations, be it the separation between mother and child or, later on, the separation between the subject and his specular image. Anzieu says that in both cases instinctive repetition tends to the return of the previous state, to the repossession of the lost object: the fusion of the feeding infant with the maternal breast, the narcissistic unification of the subject with his imaginary I (Anzieu, 1970, p. 143).

* * *

The three stages of Freudian doctrine Anzieu proposes, following Widlocher, clarify many obscure points in the study of interpretation, showing not only that we interpret from a particular theory but that the very concept of interpretation depends on the framework we place it in.

The Anzieus' rigorous investigation lacks, in my judgement, an articulation between insight and interpretation, with which they could perhaps integrate *Deutung* and *Durcharbeiten* without having to counterpose them.

26.5   Racker: some ideas

Interpretation was a central theme of Racker's investigation, which dealt thoroughly with its content and form, with the resistances to making interpretations, the use of interpretation as a means of avoiding anxiety via acting out, with the analysand's relation to interpretation and many other aspects. We will now study some ideas on how much, what and when to interpret, which Racker offered in his official presentation at the Second Latin American Congress in São Paulo, Brazil, in 1958, when he was at the height of his scientific career.

The theme of the presentation, "Classical Technique and Present Techniques in Psychoanalysis" (1958b), led him to formulate some specifications of interpretation that serve to place it in the general context of the theory and technique of psychoanalysis. The work figures as the second chapter in *Estudios* (1960), and our interest centres on the chapter on interpretation, which discusses the three above-mentioned modal adverbs. Although it may seem paradoxical, where the schools differ most obstinately is in the problem of quantity, because this is where the analyst's activity and the technical value of silence are set against each other.

How much to interpret is a problem that turns particularly on the counterposition of classic and current techniques. A cliché that no one feels able to touch and which Racker discusses, nevertheless, is that the classic analyst is very silent, and his interpretation always arrives as a culmination of a long process of silence. If it were so, Racker says, we would have to conclude that Freud is not among the classic analysts. Freud was very active. With the "Rat Man", for example, he carries on a dialogue, he informs, he explains. Freud really participates considerably. This is evident. In all his case histories Freud reveals himself as an analyst who engages in dialogue, and he probably always worked in this way. In "The Question of Lay Analysis" (1926e), for example, he says the analyst does no more than establish a dialogue with the patient, and in the case histories he reveals how he conceived that dialogue. "Above all, these sessions show with how much freedom Freud unfolded his whole creative personality in his work with the patient, and how actively he participated in each event of the session, giving full expression to his interest. He asked questions, illustrated his assertions by quoting Shakespeare, made comparisons and even undertook an experiment (with Dora)" (Racker, 1958b, 1968, pp. 3–35). Racker refers here especially to the Rat Man (Freud, 1909d, pp. 251–318). Freud wrote nothing, after his case histories, that would lead us to suppose that he modified his attitude later on. One might maintain that he changed later, in the 1920s, as he realized the problems of the setting and the importance of the transference; but Racker finds not one word from Freud to support this assumption.

The fact is that analysts who call themselves Freudian speak little; and it can be said, also, that Melanie Klein's break with classic psychoanalysis meant not being subject to that rule of silence. Taking as a starting point the analysand's anxiety in the session (point of urgency), Klein was led naturally to talk more.

It is evident that those who follow Anna Freud and Hartmann, and who after the diaspora of the Vienna group developed as "Group A" at the Hampstead Clinic in London and as the school of ego psychology in the United States, are very silent analysts. Especially at the beginning of the treatment, the general rule is to interpret absolutely nothing; observations or comments can be made, but not, strictly, interpretations. (There are reasons for thinking that sometimes the key to this technique is not silence but rather not interpreting, waiting for the regressive transference neurosis to be established.)

Analysts of the *Champ Freudien* that inspires Lacan do the same. They do not interpret for months and, without intervening, let the patient speak so that he can develop his discourse and reveal what they call the empty word, until the patient can speak meaningfully. In this long-awaited situation the decisive element in Lacanian technique also excludes an interpretation that responds to the analysand's meaningful words; there is, rather, a punctuation in the discourse, interrupting the session to mark the importance of what has been said, or an approving "hmm!" Just as in poetry, where scansion measures the verse, so, too, Lacanian technique consists in scanning the analysand's discourse to detect the signifier, avoiding the mirage of interpretation, taking care not to respond with it to the speaker's impossible demand.

In "La direction de la cure et les principes de son pouvoir" (1958a), as in other works, Lacan compares the analyst with the dummy in bridge. The patient is the one who bids and plays; the analyst is his companion, who puts the cards on the table. The patient has to move his own cards and those of his analyst, who is silent and passive by definition.

This technical attitude is based on Lacan's basic postulates on symbolism and communication, no less than on his theory of demand and desire. A good analyst always has to be like the dummy, because the desire can never be satisfied. Needs that are biological are satisfied, but not desire, as a psychological act. Wish has to do with the displacement of the chain of signifiers, and it is this metonymic running that gives it meaning, establishing the lack of being in the object relation. With each demand I make of him, my analyst will always respond by "playing dead" (in Argentine slang, "*tirándose a muerto*" [throwing oneself down as dead]) because, in the final instance, all my demands are no more than the discourse I have to pass through step by step until I understand that I have nothing to wait for, that my desire neither will nor can be satisfied. (It would be interesting to scan here the differences and similarities between Lacan and Bion, but it would be a departure from our subject.)

Each theory, then, is consonant with its practice, where it is not accidental that differences appear. Those who practice ego psychology think the analyst should be silent and should interpret prudently, without overwhelming the patient with interpretations, nor try to crack a nut with a sledgehammer; it is necessary to hit the target and be precise. The Lacanians cannot interpret much because they would give the impression that the demand can be answered, which is a mirage. The Kleinians, on the other hand—and in general all those analysts who accept the early object relation—intervene more, in that they attend above all to the development of anxiety during the session, giving the analytic process the character of a dialogue.

To bridge the undeniable gap between Freud's way of analysing and that of those who believe they are his most direct disciples, it is sometimes asserted that the technical writings are directed at the beginner, to whom Freud offers advice he himself does not need to follow. This is certainly arguable; but on the other hand there is no doubt that from the time of Freud's technical writings in the 1910s, the divergences in the practice grew apace. (The contradiction Racker discovers between Freud and the "classic" analysts is, for me, more than anecdotal. It is also found in other areas, and to ignore it leads to controversy at times. On the point we are now discussing, for example, I think it is logical for Melanie Klein to insist that she is the one who follows Freud and not those who propose silence.)

One of these lines of development is exemplified by Theodore Reik in "The Psychological Significance of Silence", where he postulates not only that the analyst should be silent but also that the dynamics of the psychoanalytic situation are based fundamentally on the analyst's silence—that is, more on what the analyst does not say than on what he may say. In the article just quoted and in others in his book, *The Inner Experience of a Psychoanalyst* (1949a), among which "In the Beginning Is Silence" (p. 121) stands out, Reik maintains that the analytic process really begins when the patient realizes not only that the analyst does not speak but that he has become mute, that the analyst does not speak on purpose, that he intends not to speak. That is the moment when the patient most feels the need to do the speaking himself so as to change his analyst's muteness. Racker discusses and criticizes this, because if the establishment of the analytic situation is rooted in this, then what has been created is a strongly persecutory and essentially coercive situation, which has been provoked and operates as a contrivance, not as something spontaneous.

As it is explicitly defined in the above-mentioned articles, the dynamics of the analytic situation for Reik consist in that the analysand experiences the silence of his analyst as a threat that impels him to new confessions. "We get the impression that the analyst's silent attitude is largely determined by the idea that confession as such is a very important or even decisive factor in the cure, which represents a very Christian, but not entirely psycho-analytic idea" (Racker, 1958b [1968, pp. 35–36]). What cures in psychoanalysis, he then says, is to make conscious the unconscious, for which interpretation is required.

In his account Racker then takes up, lucidly and courageously, the issue of the meaning the analyst's interpreting or being silent can have, indicating that either can be an acting out. In fact, both can be either good or bad. Going against classic opinion—although we have seen that this epithet is open to question—he thinks that the analyst's silence is more intrinsically linked to acting out. Since the task of the analyst is to interpret, it could not be said that when he fulfils it, he is acting out. In this way, Racker tends to value interpreting as the analyst's only valid action vis-à-vis all the others, which, in principle, would constitute acting out. On this point Racker's reasoning seems debatable to me, and the general terms are never sufficient to resolve the actual case. Racker says the analyst's essential task is to interpret, and he is right; but listening is also an essential part of our task. In this sense, then, only the concrete case permits us to decide whether silence or interpretation is appropriate and when each is an acting out.

If we contrast interpretation with silence, as Racker does, then implicitly we pronounce in favour of interpretation. But if the alternatives are whether to speak or to listen, then the case is different, because one always speaks when one interprets, but one does not always interpret when one speaks. At times we interpret so as not to listen, with the aim of making the patient cease to speak about something that creates anxiety in us, something we cannot bear, or also with the idea of calming the patient. In these cases, in fact, the so-called interpretation is no more than a neurotic form the analyst employs to cover up the fact that he is unable to contain the patient's anxiety or his own, that he has no instruments with which to tolerate and to interpret it. A similar case occurs when the analyst interprets so that the patient will not think he does not understand him, as Bion (1963, 1970) points out; although he dresses what he says in the garments of interpretation, fundamentally it is an acting out. What should be done here is first to see why I feel that the analysand is thinking that I do not understand him, and then to examine my countertransference to see why I do not want him to think in that way.

The alternatives of interpreting or being silent are, therefore, disposed in four distinct areas: speaking, interpreting, being silent and listening. Neither silence nor words constitute acting out in themselves, nor are they always an instrumental act. In general, we can say that when silence and words are instrumental, both are equally valid; and, vice versa, to the extent that silence and words disturb the development of the session, they constitute acting out. As always in psychoanalytic technique, there are also nuances here. If the patient has an anxiety that overwhelms him, it can be justifiable to speak in order to alleviate this momentarily, while the interpretation that can resolve the problem is sought.

On the whole it can be asserted that the problem of *how much* to interpret is of singular importance because it confronts us with two different, and at times opposed, techniques. The amount of interpretation has more to do with the analyst's theories than with his personal style or the patient's material.

The other two questions Racker asks with reference to opportunity and content are also important.

In respect of *when* to interpret, the problems posed are, of course, linked to the analyst's theories and his personal style; but here the analysand's influence is greater, with his latent or manifest demand weighing on the analyst's countertransference.

Beyond the material and the special nature of the analytic link at any given moment, the analyst's theories constantly influence his decision to interpret. If we follow Klein, attending in preference to the form in which anxiety presents itself during the session, we will think it logical to interpret each time the anxiety level rises critically. In this sense, Klein's technique is linked entirely to the *point of urgency* that marks the *timing* of the interpretation; and, even more, the point of urgency not only authorizes us but also obliges us to interpret without delay. If the anxiety level rises excessively and we do not resolve it in time, we will disturb the analytic situation. Klein's assertions here arise from her practice with the child who ceases to play each time anxiety arises and we do not interpret it. Similarly, in the adult there appears an obstacle in communication that disturbs free association, and the analysand is silent or begins to associate in a trivial way. If he leaves the session in those conditions, he remains predisposed to act out.

In speaking of timing at the Paris Congress, Löwenstein (1958) indicates the importance of the interpretation offered at the right moment, when the patient is ready to receive it; but he acknowledges that it is difficult to define what this moment consists in, and he allows himself to be led by tact, without taking Melanie Klein's specifications on the point of urgency into account and forgetting that tact always sinks its roots, to my mind, into the countertransference. (See section 21.7, "Empathy".)

If we think instead that the moment of interpretation arrives only when a resistance that interrupts the associative flow appears, then we may decide that it is better for the patient to continue speaking and for us to remain silent. (Racker remembers at this point that Freud proceeded in this way with Dora but regretted it.) In this sense, we see that the theory influences the moment of interpretation. Similarly, we may think we have to wait for (and even foment with our silence) the transference neurosis based on a process of regression in the setting.

Finally, and to conclude this theme, we have to consider the content of interpretations—*what* to interpret.

The content of interpretations varies at each moment and in each case. There are many variables, which depend on the material and on the vicissitudes of analytic dialogue, and equally on what we think theoretically of the unconscious. Obviously, as Anna Freud said at the 1967 Copenhagen Congress, certain interpretations that have not been offered before can now be offered because we know more (A. Freud, 1968).

26.6 *The technical parameters*

We divided the instruments used by psychotherapists to carry out their work into four types. Up to now we have studied only three: those that influence the patient, those that are used to gather information and those that give it, among which interpretation stands out. We now have to refer to the fourth type, the *technical parameter*.

This concept was introduced by K. R. Eissler in his essay, "The Effect of the Structure of the Ego on Psychoanalytic Technique", published in 1953. Eissler returned to the theme at the 1957 Paris Congress on the panel entitled "Variations in Classical Psychoanalytic Technique", where Ralph R. Greenson acted as moderator.

According to Eissler, analytic technique depends on three factors: the personality of the patient, real life and the personality of the analyst. His work is exclusively concerned with the first factor.

Just as an ideal analysand can be managed exclusively with interpretation, others require something more. Let us take as an example the phobic who requires, apart from interpretation, the advice if not the command to expose himself to the feared situation. This procedure, this "something more" the patient requires, is what Eissler calls the *technical parameter*.

This parameter is defined as a quantitative or qualitative deviation from the basic model of the technique that rests exclusively on interpretation. And this parameter is founded in Eissler's view on a deficient structure of the analysand's ego.

Eissler has not only defined the parameter, giving a place in the technique to what is sometimes done and not acknowledged, but he has also fixed clearly the conditions in which it can be justifiably introduced: (1) it should be used when the basic technical model has proved insufficient; (2) it should only minimally go beyond the regular technique; and (3) it should be utilized only where it can eventually be dispensed with.

To these three conditions Eissler adds a fourth—that the effect of the parameter on the transferential relation should be such that it can subsequently be abolished with an adequate interpretation. As an example, the parameter could never compromise analytic reserve to the point where it would be impossible to reestablish it in order to continue analysis according to the usual practice.

The four conditions of the parameter need little comment—they are self-explanatory. It is obvious that a measure of this type is justified only when the analyst has exhausted his usual means and introduces it with the greatest circumspection and care. Beyond these strict limits lie the stirrings of acting out. It is also understandable that, as an exceptional measure, the parameter should be dispensed with once it is no longer necessary. If we decide to propose to an analysand who maintains a recalcitrant silence, despite our efforts and his own, that he sit on the couch and try to speak in that way, it is logical that once that resistance has given way to our interpretative activity, the analysand will lie down again. The parameter was introduced, in fact, explicitly, to give him the opportunity of resolving the difficulty of speaking while he was lying down, but not to change the method.

Eissler's third condition, however, is not applicable by definition to one of the most common parameters, the one Freud used with "The Wolf Man": fixing a date for the termination of treatment. This parameter cannot be eliminated before the treatment ends (Freud, 1918b).

Personally, I back Eissler's attitude in introducing the concept of parameter, but not the parameter itself. The attitude is plausible in that it brings sincerity into the technique. It could be good or bad to introduce a parameter; but what is altogether bad is not to realize it has been introduced, or to deny it. This can happen all too easily, and Eissler protects us from this. The honest use of the parameter prevents us from practising a wild analysis covered by false interpretations.

While acknowledging this value in Eissler's technique, I disagree with the introduction of parameters, for various reasons—or perhaps for only one basic reason, that I do not trust the analyst's objectivity when he decides that the basic model of the technique is no longer sufficient. Experience has repeatedly shown me that, in availing oneself of a parameter, it is applied at first only to exceptional cases and then becomes imperceptibly generalized, which is logical. If we found a device that allowed us to resolve a very serious case, what harm would there be in applying it to other, simpler cases?

I remember a conversation years ago with a colleague who was beginning to use lysergic acid. He answered my reservations by informing me that it was an exceptional technique, which he used only with the most hardened cases of pathological character, those that had not been mobilized even after twenty years of analysis. I answered that within not too long a period of time, "a year or two, he would be using LSD with all his analysands". Unfortunately I was right; only my calculations as to the period of time were excessive.

Of course I can perfectly well distinguish the difference between administering hallucinogenic drugs and suggesting a patient sit up on the couch. For the latter case the disturbances that can present themselves are always going to be minor, beyond the way in which a particular patient may react. However, here I am not discussing a matter of degree but laying down the general principle that, as analysts, we have no better way of helping our clients than to remain faithful to the technique.

In discussing this theme it is advisable to clarify an aspect that often goes unnoticed. I think that identifiable parameters are only those the analyst introduces expecting to find in them a legitimate auxiliary to the technique. What the analyst does at the margin of a technical, therapeutic objective will never be a parameter, but an acting out; similarly with what stems from the patient.

As to the analyst's acting out, I remember what I was told by a patient who came to me asking me to recommend an analysis, after having interrupted treatment. He had mentioned in free association that he knew a very efficient plumber, who had resolved a difficult problem with the water-pipes in his house; at that point the analyst, who, it seems, also had serious problems with his water-pipes, interrupted him to ask him the name of that trustworthy plumber. The analysand gave it to him immediately and straight away told him he was not going to continue treatment.

Using the parameter is something the analyst does to overcome a deficiency in the patient's ego structure that cannot be resolved through the regular technique. This parameter is a device *the analyst* employs to sort out an obstacle stemming from the patient. The theory of the parameter assumes that without it the usual analytic process could not continue, and the deduction from this is that the analyst feels obliged to abandon his technique for a moment. This is why I think that what the analysand decides of his own accord is *not* a parameter.

When I tell the silent patient to sit on the couch to see whether in this way he can conquer his muteness, this is because I think that, in this fashion, his so far invincible resistance will be modified. It is completely different for the analysand to decide for himself to sit at a given moment, because he thinks he will speak more easily in this way, or for whatever reason. A parameter here would be to oppose him or to agree with what he has done. To respect my patient's decision without giving up in any way my right to analyse it is to keep entirely within my technique.

In discussing the contract, I said something that tallies fully with what I have just expounded. The analyst has to introduce the rule in the contract. If the analysand cannot or does not wish to comply with it, the analyst will not impose it but then has the right to analyse it.

At the Paris Congress of 1957, the subject of variations in psychoanalytic technique was discussed extensively.

On that occasion Eissler (1958) returned to his theory of the parameter as a device at the margin of the typical instrument of analysis—interpretation. However, I think two restrictions of the theory are noticeable.

On the one hand, Eissler considers that the parameter can often be transformed into an interpretation. In this way, for example, instead of asking a patient to speak of how his parents get along, the interpretation can be offered that he never speaks of this subject, and so forth. Similarly, instead of stimulating the phobic to face the situation that provokes anxiety in him, we can interpret that he resists doing this or something like it.

Eissler also restricts his original theory by introducing the idea of the *pseudo-parameter*. Certain devices that, according to classic definitions, could not be called interpretation operate, nevertheless, as if they were. The pseudo-parameter can be used, for example, in cases where interpretation provokes insuperable resistances and the pseudo-parameter can introduce it imperceptibly. A timely joke can be a device of this type.

It seems to me that, in this way, the theory of the parameter is reduced and even questioned by its own author.

If what Eissler calls pseudo-parameter is no more than a formal device for saying things with tact and respect, it does not deviate in any way from classic technique. If its object is to introduce something on the sly, I would never utilize it, and in such a case I would pay attention to what countertransference conflict had led me to use this uncharitable procedure.

CHAPTER TWENTY-SEVEN

Constructions

27.1 Introduction

In chapters 25 and 26 I tried to specify, in the clearest and most stringent way, the defining characteristics of interpretation in general, and psychoanalytic interpretation in particular. We saw that interpretation can be understood in various ways. From the point of view of communication, it is information with special characteristics; in semiology it is defined by its semantic content, and, lastly, we have understood it also operationally through its effects, which serve to test it.

We also said that when Freud defined it in the book of dreams and in "The Handling of Dream-Interpretation in Psychoanalysis" (1911e), he attended particularly to the sense or meaning. He says, for example, that the *Deutung* [interpretation] of a dream consists in determining its *Bedeutung* [significance].

We also saw in previous chapters that although interpretation is the principal instrument of analysis, there are others that are also employed, even within the strictest technique, which we need not list now.

With that set of tools we did not question at all the preeminence of psychoanalytic interpretation. Now, however, we will do so with *construction*, which, in effect, is equal to interpretation and, in the opinion of some, even more important.

Interpretation and construction are two distinct instruments, but of the same type, the same class. The defining characteristics already studied are applicable to both. Both will give the patient information about himself that is pertinent, belongs entirely to him and of which he is not conscious.

We defined interpretation thus and can define construction in the same way, in principle. If we stay with this definition, then we have to conclude that interpretation and construction belong to the same class. We are then faced with a major problem: how are they distinguishable?

27.2   Construction and interpretation

It is certainly not easy to make the distinction between construction and interpretation, but the difference can be sought from different points of view: in the form or the content, in theory or technique.

It is indubitable that, as its name indicates, construction relies on the joining of various elements to form something, and therefore from a formal point of view we tend to think that constructions are broader and more detailed than interpretations, which can be bare, assertive and even decisive. This distinction is not, however, very satisfactory. A construction can be concise and brief, while there are lengthy interpretations due either to the analyst's style or to the complexity of the theme. The formal aspect, then—the way an interpretation or a construction is formulated—does not seem very useful, despite the fact that Freud takes it into account in giving his example in "Constructions in Analysis" (1937d, p. 261): "Up to your nth year you regarded yourself . . ." and so forth.

The emphasis is usually on the fact that if construction seeks to join various elements in order to form a whole, it is because it always has a historical slant. Construction refers to the past; it tries to unveil a historical situation, something that happened and was decisive in the subject's life. The circumstantial reference to history is always seen as being proper to construction, while the interpretation can omit it. However, this difference is relative and contingent, because exceptions exist in both cases. There are interpretations that do take account of the past and, on the other hand, there is a special type of construction that does not do so. I refer to what Löwenstein (1951, 1954, 1958) calls *reconstruction upwards*, where certain childhood events serve to illumine the present, and not, as is classic, the other way round. Thus a man who felt bothered about the fees began analysis idealizing the analyst and had hostile dreams about a man he himself identified as his deceased father. Löwenstein interpreted that his hostility was directed to the analyst and referred to the fees (1954, p. 191).

At times form and content are confused. "You were weaned with aloe [very bitter] juice" is a construction, although it sounds like an interpretation because it is brief and concise. It would seem to be a construction if we were to say, instead: "It seems to me, since you always find a bitter taste in your mouth at weekends, you smoke too much, are anxious and prefer sweet food, all of which calms down with the Monday morning session, that one could think you were weaned with aloe juice." These two formulations are, however, substantially the same.

If we then set aside the formal aspects so as to establish the difference, we will have to refer to the technical support for interpretation or construction, since construction emphasizes history and interpretation emphasizes the present. But we have seen that this is also quite relative, the only clear difference being that interpretation can lack a reference to the past. However, it can also refer to the past, even to the point where one of the ways of classifying interpretations is into historical and present ones. If we wish to distinguish a historical interpretation from a construction, we might fall into absurdity trying to do so.

Freud tried it in chapter 2 of "Constructions", indicating that interpretation refers to a simple element of the material, such as a parapraxis, a dream or an association, whereas construction covers a complete fragment of the forgotten life of the patient. Sandler et al. disagree with this definition, which seems somewhat strange to them (1973, p. 106n). I agree here with Sandler, and I assume that Freud had to use an ostensive definition of construction because he did not have sufficient conceptual elements to establish the differences ("Up to your nth year you regarded yourself as the sole and unlimited possessor of your mother; then came another baby and brought you . . ."—1937d, p. 261—and so forth).

On the other hand, it is more than debatable that interpretation is partial and construction tends towards the whole. It is enough to re-read some examples of dreams and parapraxes analysed by Freud, such as the dream of the botanical monograph or the forgetting of the name Signorelli, to see to what extent those interpretations reconstruct large fragments of the history, if not the whole life.

What Freud calls construction in chapter 2 could also be called complete interpretation, and then we would be facing a semantic problem, one of definition. Analysts who accept Freud's above-mentioned delineation without reservations are those who believe, in consequence, that it is better to construct than to interpret. However, the technical (and theoretical) differences are better understood if the way in which each analyst uses the past and the present in his clinical work is discussed—a theme to which we shall return.

A delineation that can seem very categorical is that interpretation has to do with desire and construction has to do with history. But in fact this difference fails basically because there are no events without desire and no desires unlinked to events. (We will return to this in dealing with the types of interpretation.)

If the path we have traced until now is the correct one, no clear differences appear between interpretation and construction, either in form or in content. Laplanche and Pontalis think that it is difficult and even inadvisable to keep the term "construction" in the restricted sense Freud gave it in 1937 (1968, *The Language of Psychoanalysis*, p. 88) in that it assumes the somewhat inaccessible ideal goal of complete recollection of all that lies underneath infantile amnesia, since even if memories do not emerge, construction still has a therapeutic effect if accompanied by the confident conviction of the analysand. Instead, they accord importance to construction as an organization of the pathogenic material and quote what Freud says in the *Studies* and the work of reconstruction of a fantasy Freud carries out in "A Child Is Being Beaten" (1919e). The Freudian concept of fantasy assumes it is a method of elaboration that relies partially on the real, as is the case in infantile sexual "theories". In this way the term acquires more a theoretical than a technical sense.

David Maldavsky (1985), who has made a special study of this theme, also gives the concept of construction a particularly theoretical sense, which leads him to a position that is somewhat opposed to that of Laplanche and Pontalis. He asserts that the concept of constructions should be retained because it occupies the centre of all psychoanalytic reflection as the indispensable articulator between theory, clinical practice and technique. For Maldavsky it is the concept of interpretation that is not needed, in that he postulates that any interpretation assumes an underlying construction in the therapist, whether or not he admits it (1985, p. 18). Any attempt to interpret assumes a theory of how the patient's manifestation has been produced, and this is already a construction. For Maldavsky there are two types of construction—those that have to do with inner experiences and those born of purely internal processes such as affects, fantasies and unconscious thoughts. In this way, the concept of construction broadens to cover not only memories but also the entire activity of the primary process, down to what is primordially repressed. It is then logical to maintain that construction is the epicentre of psychoanalytic work, which for this writer has to do with what he calls the primordial masochistic fantasy, where the Oedipus complex, castration and partial instincts (fixations) converge. Construction is aimed in the first place at this heterogenous cluster of psychological events (ibid., p. 20). It also covers the subsequent defensive processes that arise from this cluster which will unfold in time in a subtle and complex combination throughout the whole period of latency.

Having read Freud's article many times, I think the concept of construction is sustainable more in the method than in the theory, the technique or in clinical practice. The characteristic of construction is that it can be compared with the patient's memories, with his history. It is not casual coincidence that Freud begins from methodology in his article. In the first chapter Freud comments ironically that the psychoanalyst is always right: heads, I win; tails, you lose.

Freud answers that what is most interesting is not the patient's explicit response, but that which comes indirectly from the material. Even a change in the symptoms is not conclusive. The worsening of symptoms in a patient in whom we have detected a negative therapeutic reaction at other times can make us assume we were right; and vice-versa, the compliance of the analysand can make him improve after an erroneous construction (or interpretation).

In any case, Freud also accepts willingly that we do not always take the patient's negative reply as proof that we are mistaken. We tend to consider this as resistance, rather than our mistake. Of course this attitude, in which countertransference conflicts can participate, is very dangerous, not only from the methodological point of view but also from the clinical one. Many epistemologists, such as Popper, rely on this point so as to deny psychoanalysis scientific validity.

What Freud takes here as the starting point for the discussion is that the patient's *conventional* reply is not what matters most. It can interest us as an association, as a manifestation of a conduct we should study. But what is really significant as confirming or denying a construction is what arises spontaneously in the material of the analysand. This informs us in general with sufficient certainty on the validity or error of the construction. This assertion by Freud continues to hold true, and today we would complete it only by saying that what our countertransference informs us of also orientates us. We can say, in conclusion, that there is a whole series of indicators that the construction offered to the patient was correct. In what way do these indicators appear?

27.3 The indicators

Let us say to begin with that the issue of indicators is different with regard to interpretation and construction, because there is a precise and valuable indicator in the latter that does not exist in the former, and it is the surfacing of a memory pertinent to the construction that has been proposed. At other times the memory does not appear, but the patient adds details that complement the formulated construction, or he adorns it with elements to which the analyst could never have had access because he does not know them. If I tell a patient that at five years of age he must have thought he was not his parents' child and he replies that now he remembers that precisely at that age his father had left home and his mother had lived with another man for some time, that information, which I really did not have, sufficiently confirms the exactitude of my construction. At times things really do happen in this way, and all analysts treasure this type of direct hit; but we do not always have such luck. Apart from this type of reply, which is offered via memories that surface or details that complement the memory and/or construction, dreams are sometimes confirmatory. What the patient remembered in the hypothetical case I have just mentioned could have been dreamt by him, and that dream would have had practically as great a confirming value as his memory.

As to the patient's reply, then, there is a difference between interpretation and construction. Another difference is that the reply is in general more manifest, more open towards interpretation; the patient will say yes or no. With a construction, on the other hand, if he does not reply with a confirming memory, the analysand will take it as part of his inventory, postponing his judgement. With interpretation, the reply tends in general to be more lively, more immediate. However, this difference is not as substantial as the previous one.

We have said that a construction can be confirmed in various ways: by a memory, by data that complement it, by dreams or parapraxes and also through results. This is because we must not forget that as analysts we work with the theory that a construction (or interpretation) will have results if it is accurate and accepted. As we said in chapter 26, we do not have the intention of modifying behaviour directly, but we trust that results will obtain. Once a construction (or interpretation) has been assimilated as information, it has to operate on the mental life of the patient. Were it not so, analysis would have no purpose.

27.4   Evaluation of the indicators

We have reviewed the principal clinical indicators that inform us on the validity of our constructions and interpretations, indicating the particularities each case presents. Let us evaluate them now briefly.

The indicators we studied go from the most immediate to the most distant replies, and the latter are those that generally have the greatest value as unconventional messages from the unconscious.

The patient's affirmative responses, particularly if they are easy and explicit, should not be valued too much, because they often arise from the desire to please or to appear intelligent. A patient with a serious castration complex displaced to his intelligence intrigued me for a long time with the way he responded to my interpretations. He received them with respect, he showed himself interested and attentive, he asked for clarification at times and always pertinently, and he would end up by commenting on what I had said, sometimes with an added accurate reflection. I perceived something singular in his conduct, but it took me some time to understand it, especially bearing in mind that analysis proceeded regularly. After a long time spent analysing according to Reich's method the attitude with which he received my interpretations, I obtained a convincing reply. He told me he knew I was an eminent [sic] professor, and therefore he tried to understand what I said; he took it for granted that I could not be mistaken; for his part, he did not consider himself very intelligent. Thus, interpretation was not, for this naive analysand, a piece of information and a hypothesis, but the revealed truth, which he had to try to understand, as well as a test to measure his intelligence (as he had measured the size of his penis in his games with his companions during latency). More unconsciously, there existed compliance, seduction and pacification as homosexual defences in the face of his (immense) oedipal rivalry with his father.

When interpretation—or, less frequently, construction—operates at a concrete level, the motor of the response relates to the very act of inter-

preting and not to the informative content of what we have said. This is
the case of the seriously ill hysteric, who, for example, feels the interpretation of her genital anxieties as a penis that really penetrates her. In this
case our only certainty is that the interpretation has been rejected because
it was considered a violating act, as a penis that introduces itself violently.
However, this tells us nothing about the value of the refutation, not only
because verbalization is lacking but because the problem has become displaced and the patient responds not to the informative content of the interpretation but to the *act* of interpreting. Certainly in the case of the example
given here one could validly infer that the interpretation was correct, since
it was rejected just as the feared penis was; but this inference is only an *ad
hoc* hypothesis that would have to be proved.

The appearance or disappearance of a somatic symptom as a response
to an interpretation is always a matter of interest, but the meaning can
vary in each case. I would say that, in general, if the physical response of
the patient implies improvement, I would take this as probable confirmation of the interpretation. But if the patient reacts with a somatic or conversion symptom, I would not say that this is due to an efficient
interpretation but, rather, because it was noxious, except in the special
case of the negative therapeutic reaction.

The *rejection* of a construction or of an interpretation may, therefore,
concern the negative transference or anxiety, rather than the informative
content. *Acceptance* can also be ambiguous if the analysand's desire is to
please us, deceive us or prove to us he understands what we tell him. In
the same way, changes in behaviour and/or modification of the symptoms
are always interesting but not decisive. Glover (1931) wrote about the
therapeutic effect of inexact interpretations.

It must be said that Freud was always cautious and perspicacious in
relation to the analysand's response. He did not back off in the face of a
negative response, nor did he allow himself to be led uncritically by approval. In "Remarks on the Theory and Practice of Dream-Interpretation"
(1923c) he studies dreams that confirm and please. He asserts that one
motive for having a dream that confirms an interpretation is to ingratiate
oneself with the analyst or to please him. And he goes so far in this sense
as to say that even the mechanism of dream formation can be aimed at
pleasing. (See the rather severe way—in my view—in which Freud, 1920a,
evaluates the dreams of his homosexual patient.)

A subtle example of how the analyst can be refuted is the dream of the
butcher's wife with the smoked salmon, in which she renounces the wish
to give a supper-party but satisfies the wish not to satisfy that of her rival,
a woman friend, and refutes at the same time the theory of wish fulfilment
in dreams, which is Freud's wish (1900a, pp. 146–150). Immediately afterwards, Freud quotes the dream of another woman patient—the cleverest
of all his dreamers, he says—who takes a holiday with her hated mother-
in-law only to prove that the theory of wish-fulfilment is erroneous (ibid.,
p. 151).

To conclude, only a very careful analysis of all the elements can lead us to decide with sufficient certainty that what a patient says or does supports or refutes the interpretation. What matters here is to point out that there are indicators, that both the construction and the interpretation can be refuted—even if Popper (1953) offers psychoanalysis as an example of a non-scientific theory because its hypotheses, like those of astrology, cannot be refuted. (In chapter 35, Dr. Klimovsky presents a thorough study of this problem.)

The first two sections of "Constructions in Analysis" (Freud, 1937d) deal with the method, with how a construction can be validated, with what elements we have on the basis of which we can judge whether it is correct and true. Freud indicates that neither acceptance nor formal, conscious rejection can decide its validity. What really matters is what arises out of the associative material or the behaviour, once the construction has been formulated. Nowhere more than here does Freud indicate the truly hypothetical nature of the analyst's communication. The term "construction" strongly suggests the idea of a hypothesis, of something constructed. Nevertheless there is no doubt that the interpretation is also a hypothesis, although it can be formulated in more assertive terms.

27.5   Material truth and historical truth

"Constructions" (Freud, 1937d) is a brief work consisting of three sections, the last of which poses an important problem—that of historical reality and material reality.

If something distinguishes interpretation from construction, it is that the latter tries to recover an event from the past. Construction *seeks out* the past, interpretation finds it.

The influence of the past on the present is a theme that concerned Freud from his earliest works, from the period of his collaboration with Breuer onward. This theme is surely fundamental. Already in 1895, chapter 2 of the third part of "A Project for Scientific Psychology" (1950a [1887–1903], pp. 283–397), Freud speaks of *external reality* and of *thought reality* (p. 373) as two alternatives that must be distinguished from each other, and he says that the external quantity (Q) is maintained always separate from ψ (psi)—that is, from Qn. In *Totem and Taboo* (1912–13) he speaks of *psychic reality* and *factual reality*. In referring to this point Strachey (1966b) indicates that in later writings Freud calls factual reality "material"—as, for example, in *Moses and Monotheism* (1939a) where he speaks of "historical" and "material" truth (p. 127 ff). Earlier (p. 76) he had spoken of *external reality* and *psychic reality*. In "Historical Truth" (Part II, G., p. 128) Freud asks himself why the idea of a single God imposes itself on the mind of mortals and recalls that the response of religion is that this perception is part of the truth, of the eternal truth that there is only one God. Man has been created so that he can grasp the essential truths: if the idea

of monotheism imposes itself firmly on the spirit, it is because man captures the "material" reality that, in effect, there is only one God. Freud,
who in fact is sceptical about man's capacity for discovering the truth,
does not think we are equipped to receive revealed truth naturally. His
experience as a psychoanalyst shows him that man allows himself to be
led more by his desire than by the voice of God. History proves that during the course of time man believed in many things and was mistaken.
The simple fact that men believe something is no guarantee that it corresponds to the truth.

If monotheistic religion has elicited such a strong adherence among
men, this is not because it corresponds to an eternal, material truth, Freud
concludes, but because it responds to a *historical* truth. This historical
truth, which returns from the past and imposes itself on our spirit, is the
fact that, in primitive times, there was certainly a person who appeared as
great and powerful: the father.

This theme had already been developed by Freud twenty years earlier
in *Totem and Taboo* (1912–13), where the father's relation to the primitive
horde is studied. And without going so far, it appears regularly in infancy:
in that we have all had only one father, we are predisposed to accept the
idea of only one God. What leads me to the idea of only one God as true is
the historical reality that I had only one father, and not that the material
facts might be such. (In the case of the myths of humanity, it seems that
Freud prefers the alternative of material truth and historical truth; in individual history, on the other hand, the alternatives are between material
and psychic reality.)

From this Freud concludes that vis-à-vis every human experience
accompanied by a strong conviction, one would have to consider the possibility that it is a response to a historical truth (although not to a material
truth). It is in this sense that he returns to the truth that there is in delusion, saying that perhaps the way to understand it and also to resolve it
analytically would be based, not on its gross distortions (which correspond to material reality), but the part it has of historical truth, which, in
fact, existed and gives it irreducible force. This is the principal theme of a
work by Avenburg and Guiter for the London Congress of 1975.

To Avenburg and Guiter construction "means establishing links between phenomena which have, up to that moment, been apparently separate" (1976, p. 17). The analyst's task is to reconstruct the construction, to
remake it, to rescue it from repression. They consider that Freud plays
with two pairs of concepts: psychic reality and external reality; material
truth and historical truth. They are inclined to think that the concept of
historical truth is more comprehensive than that of internal reality, since if
we try to establish the historical truth with our constructions, we try to see
not only how the individual assimilated particular experiences, but also
the degree of reality of the experiences themselves.

However, Avenburg and Guiter's theory has its limitations, because
the material truth cannot be known by us other than on the basis of the

individual's structure, so it is difficult to counterpose the concept of internal/external reality with that of historical/material truth.

As analysts, we are concerned with internal (psychological) reality. What matters to us is how the individual has assimilated the experience. But, to the extent that we show the analysand how he incorporated a particular experience, we manage gradually to enable him to contrast internal with factual reality.

Analytic work consists in enabling the patient to revise his internal reality (or his historical truth) and gradually to realize that what he considers as facts are only his version of the facts. So the analysand will have to admit that his desire set (and sets) its seal on experience and in this way he has gone on modifying and recreating external reality.

In section 1 of the "Constructions", Freud says that the purpose of analysis is to achieve an image of the forgotten years that is both truthful and complete (1937d, p. 258). I think that this objective is fulfilled if a picture of the past is constructed in which the patient recognizes his own perspective and knows that it is neither the only one nor the best, and that others can have a different version of the same facts.

To obtain a true and complete image of the past, neither memories nor any "objective" data we could gather are sufficient, since we would have to include among them the complex and subtle interaction at a given moment—that is, the nucleus of truth of each version, as Avenburg and Guiter point out. What really matters is the symbolic value of behaviour, the structure of behaviour, since the material truth can be defined only by consensus, or equally if we can see things from diverse perspectives.

The best discrimination of this type has been effected by Lacan. In his seminar on *Les écrits techniques de Freud* (1953–54) he draws a sharp distinction between remembrance and reconstruction. For Lacan memory belongs to the imaginary plane, while the reconstruction of the past aims at re-establishing the historicity of the subject, the symbolic order. What is evoked experientially, then, is no more than a surface level, a manifest content from which the symbolic elements must be reconstructed. The reconstruction concerns the symbolic events that are woven into what has been evoked. (I quote here the teachings of my friend Guillermo A. Maci.)

From this point of view, Freud's article teaches us, then, definitively, that the way the individual distorts the facts can be modified only by recognizing the nucleus of historical truth, not by bringing in objective facts.

The confirmation external facts can offer has only a relative value. At times this is useful. There is no doubt that we are afforded much satisfaction if real facts, which the patient may gather from the family, confirm a construction. Freud warns us, however, that we do not operate on the basis of this type of confirmation, on the basis of facts or events that existed materially. What really matters is the (subjective) conviction of the analysand. In his documented work on constructions, Carpinacci (1975) starts from the concept of historical truth, which "consists in conformity between what is affirmed relative to a historical event and the historical event itself" (1975, p. 269). Carpinacci says that this historical truth can be interpreted scientifically and objectively (material truth) or ideologically and desideratively (eternal truth).

27.6 Construction and historical interpretation

As we will see further on, there are two types of interpretations—historical and actual, from the past and from the present. This classification refers to the content of the interpretation; it is phenomenological, because from the dynamic point of view every interpretation aims in some way at the past. The theory of transference, as we have seen, rests on the superimposition of past and present, in which the past is contained in the present. Through the transference we can have access to the past, and every interpretation of the transference is historical in that it discovers repetition. From this point of view, we can define construction as a type of interpretation in which a special emphasis is given to the historical. Bernfeld established it thus some time prior to Freud. Although for tactical reasons we can limit ourselves to the present or to the past, a complete interpretation takes account of both, since it will always refer to what persists from the past in the present.

Currently there is considerable discussion, stemming from earlier debates, among those who consider construction as the true instrument of analysis on the one hand and those who feel it has no value or do not take it into account, on the other. However, this discussion should be rational and less impassioned.

Above all it is advisable to point out that there are evidently different styles of work and legitimate preferences we should learn to respect. Going now to the crux of the question, I would say that there are without doubt technical divergences among analysts who emphasize the present and those who pay attention in preference to the past. The former interpret (and fundamentally they interpret the transference); the latter construct. In fact two polar types of analysts exist. Racker (1958b) characterized them as those who use the transference to understand the past and those who use the past to understand the transference.

At the round table organized by the Argentine Psychoanalytic Association in 1970 (known as the *Mesa Redonda sobre "Construcciones en el análisis" de S. Freud*, in which Jaime P. Schust—the coordinator—Ricardo Avenburg, Gilberta Royer de Garcia Reinoso, David Liberman and Leonardo Wender participated—*Revista de Psicoanálisis*, 27) Avenburg, decidedly in favour of constructions, said that we were intoxicated by transference. This admonishment may be fair for certain analysts, both then and now, who interpret the transference where it does not exist. The opposite case is nonetheless also true—for example, the candidate who, overwhelmed by the instincts whose expression is directed at him by his patient, tries to make him think about his childhood.

Every method has its virtues and defects. But the difficulties inherent in a method should not be confused with its errors. If the interest is in the transference, the risk is that of not appreciating history; if, in preference, we direct ourselves to the past, we run the risk of not seeing the transference. The analyst should embrace both the present and the past in his work. It is not casual coincidence that Freud indicated in his 1937 work the importance of the analysand's conviction, and it was also Freud who said, in the "Postscript" to "Dora", that conviction arises out of the transference situation.

The alternatives of construction and interpretation can legitimately inspire the style of each analyst. But it is different if the intention is to take the discussion to the technical level, because analytic technique demands that both be integrated and complementary. (For a more detailed discussion, see my work presented at the Helsinki Congress, included as chapter 28 of this book.)

These reflections are also applicable to the problem of interpreting external reality. External reality also has to be integrated into our task, precisely because what gives conviction and what really cures is that I realize that here, with my analyst, with my wife and children at home and with my parents and brothers in childhood I repeat the same *pattern*—I am the same.

There was a time in Buenos Aires, probably due to the experience derived from group psychotherapy, when the present, the here and now, was much emphasized. It was even thought that the analytic situation was ahistorical. As we shall see in a moment, the analytic situation can be explained through the theory of the field, but the analytic process is a transferred and historical situation. When Hanna Segal came to Buenos Aires in 1958 she combated this position, and I remember hearing her say that the insistence on interpreting exclusively in terms of the transference ultimately satisfies the analyst's narcissism and creates a megalomanic situation where the analyst is everything for the patient, when in fact he reflects an object that comes from the past.

In any case, it is true that some analysts think that once the conflict has been resolved here and now, the rest unfolds of itself, the past changes in consequence and ceases to disturb. This thesis is not true, because it ignores that there can be mechanisms of dissociation or repression that break the continuity of the past and the present. There is no dissociation more dangerous in my opinion than that of bad parents in childhood and an idealized analyst in the present.

The difference must be sought, therefore, not between those who interpret and those who construct, but rather in the way these two instruments find expression. There are analysts who reconstruct on the basis of a transference situation and others who propose a construction and then analyse it. The latter is what Freud did at times; but many analysts at present (and I am among them) do not do so because it complicates and at times neglects the transference situation. If at a given moment the analysand recognizes us in our role, if he sees us as analysts, then it becomes possible for us to reconstruct the past; but when the past erupts, occupying the present (transference), this possibility is reduced and even annulled.

The analytic situation is complex and does not lend itself to schematization. Ferenczi said that when the patient speaks of the past, we have to speak of the present, and vice-versa, so that the tendency to dissociate the past from the present will not crystallize. Sometimes the patient speaks of the past or the present to avoid the transference conflict; at other times it is the other way round. A patient comes to me and says he is very worried by what I told him yesterday—a triviality; then it turns out that a little while before the session he had received a communication that had taken him to the brink of bankruptcy or endangered his job. Good analytic work implies correcting this type of repression or dissociation. The only adequate technique is one that contemplates problems in the magnitude of their complexity. (This issue has often been dealt with by the Liendos, who observe how the situation that occurs outside is reproduced in analysis in general with an opposite sign—see, for example, chapter 6 of *Semiologia psicoanalítica*, by Maria Carmen Gear and Ernesto C. Liendo, 1974. In a more recent book, impeccably produced, written in collaboration with Melvyn A. Hill, the Liendos study the sadomasochistic structure of the analytic situation and show how that structure introduces itself and is repeated, indicating at the same time the strategies and the techniques that allow its resolution—Gear, Hill & Liendo, 1981.) Kris gives the same criterion in "The Recovery of Childhood Memories in Psychoanalysis" (1956b), where he says that for the patient, either speaking continually of the past or adhering persistently to the present can function as resistance (p. 56).

I understand the analyst's task as covering two basic functions: making the patient conscious of his *instincts* and making him recover particular *memories*. I know well that both are indissoluble, and therefore I think there can be no sharp difference between interpretations and constructions. I would say, provisionally, that when instincts are emphasized, interpretations are made, and when we place the accent on memories, constructions are made. But since no event is split off from the instincts and no impulse can be expressed without events, it is understandably difficult to establish a dividing line between these two concepts. Perhaps it is not appropriate to do so.

I wish to end this chapter by remembering my teacher, Pichon Rivière, who instilled in us the concept of a *complete* interpretation in which attention centres on what arises in the immediacy of the transference as much as on what happens in external reality and on what comes from the past.

27.7 Construction and delusion

In the last pages of his essay, and on the basis of ultra-clear recollections, Freud offers some reflections on delusions. He asks himself whether the force of conviction of a delusion might be due to its containing a fragment of historical truth rooted in childhood. The task of the analyst should consist, perhaps, in freeing that nucleus of historical truth of all the deformations imposed on it. He concludes with a singular statement: "The delusions of patients appear to me to be the equivalents of constructions which we build up in the course of an analytic treatment—attempts at explanation and cure, though it is true that these, under the conditions of a psychosis, can do no more than replace the fragment of reality that is being disavowed in the present by another fragment that had already been disavowed in the remote past" (1937d, p. 268). He adds that if the construction is effective because it recovers a lost fragment of existence, the delusion also owes its power of conviction to the element of historical truth that occupies the place of the rejected reality (ibid.). ("Just as our construction is only effective because it recovers a fragment of lost experience, so the delusion owes its convincing power to the elements of historical truth which it inserts in the place of the rejected reality"—1937d, p. 268.)

Re-reading *The Psychopathology of Everyday Life* (1901b) not long ago, I noticed that Freud compares the delusional interpretations of paranoid subjects with his own interpretations relating to parapraxes and dreams. He asserts that the paranoid individual has an understanding of unconscious material that is in every way analogous to that of the analyst. The difference is that the paranoic sticks to his interpretation and does not see all the rest (ibid., p. 255). Therefore there is some support in Freud for my idea of defining interpretation by comparing it with Jaspers's primary delusional experience [*primäres Wahnerlebnis*].

27.8 Scenic comprehension

Freud unquestionably always regarded psychoanalysis as a natural science, and it is not for nothing that he likened his work to that of an archaeologist. Yet an implicit hermeneutics can be discerned at many points in his oeuvre. An attentive reading of his testamentary paper of 1937 shows him distancing himself from the archaeological model and stating without hesitation that "for the archaeologist the reconstruction is the aim and end of his endeavours while for analysis the construction is only a preliminary labour" (Freud, 1937d, p. 260). *Reconstruction* makes psychoanalysis a natural science like archaeology, but *construction*, because it confers sense, falls within the sphere of hermeneutics. For a rigorous author like Bernfeld (1932), psychoanalysis is the (natural) science of traces, but for Freud—

who conspicuously does not quote him—psychoanalysis sometimes reconstructs the patient's history and at other times constructs it.

One of the most lucid exponents of the hermeneutic conception of psychoanalysis is surely Alfred Lorenzer. In *Sprachzerstörung und Rekonstruktion* (1970), Lorenzer bases his argument on the two types of comprehension—logical and psychological—proposed by Binswanger (1922), which cover the same field as, or a similar field to, the static and genetic comprehension of Jaspers (1913). Logical comprehension refers to the statement, whereas psychological comprehension, which Lorenzer calls "reliving", is concerned with the speaker.

The cognitive process of psychoanalysis comprises a comprehension that is arrived at by small steps. The first operation performed by the analyst is *logical comprehension*, which seeks to apprehend the analysand's statement in itself—something that is possible because analysand and analyst share a community of language. Hence the analyst can understand the statement—that is, the analysand's material—as an exposition of logically possible facts. A linguistic Gestalt in which the analyst perceives the congruence of the patient's statement then closes. It is precisely the closure of the Gestalt that gives rise to the analyst's conviction, in that it relieves the tension in the gestaltic circuit as the synthetic function of the ego is performed.

The step from logical comprehension to psychological comprehension (reliving) is a key element in Lorenzer's hermeneutics. *Psychological comprehension* (reliving) refers to the person who formulated the statement or, in other words, to what the statement means for the person who uttered it; here, however, immediate and direct evidence of comprehension is not possible, precisely because the analysand and the analyst do not share a community of language, since neurosis by definition entails abandoning the symbolic universe and resorting instead to gesture as an instrument of communication. Psychological comprehension (reliving) is achieved by a series of gestures that have an affective charge and reveal their meaning in the context of a dramatic action. As in the theatre, the analysand's action allows the analyst to apprehend his affective state as a mental Gestalt—that is, to understand it with evidence. Just as, in logical comprehension, evidence arises when a Gestalt is closed and a moment of relief and conviction ensues, so in psychological comprehension (reliving) a Gestalt is closed when we understand a succession of hitherto confused gestures. In other words, logical comprehension is to the statement as psychological comprehension (reliving) is to the dramatic action.

Having made this clear distinction, however, Lorenzer (1970) points out that the practice of psychoanalysis constantly leads us to burst the bounds of both modes of operation, so that an intermediate space is constituted. Logical comprehension in the first instance surely has the aim of considering the patient's communications in themselves, but these are then studied with defined exclusiveness as communications *of the patient*—that is, of *this* patient.

The "gesture" is a fundamental component of the social psychology of George H. Mead (1934), from which Lorenzer takes it. Mead, in turn, borrowed the concept from the psychology of Wundt, but instead of confining it to a mere expression of emotions, as Darwin did, he also invests it with a communicative and social character, so that it becomes a true act of language whereby one animal communicates with another.

When a biological individual regards the actions of others as gestures—that is, as guides to its own action—we have what Mead calls a *social act*. There is a *conversation of gestures*, in which each adapts its behaviour to what the other does, as for example in a dogfight (or in boxing). The gesture implies a type of communication that is in a way symbolic because it has meaning and gives rise to pertinent reactions in the other.

Yet this type of communication is not language proper, insofar as its user is not conscious of what it is doing. The decisive change occurs when the individual is capable of interpreting the meaning of its own gesture— what Mead calls the *significant symbol*. From then on, the biological individual arouses in itself the reaction to which its gesture gives rise and can therefore regulate its behaviour by adopting the other's role (*role play*). This capacity to be an object to oneself characterizes *Homo sapiens*.

Among all the gestures that may become significant symbols, Mead singles out the *vocal gesture*, because it is no longer affected by any other subject: when we speak, *we hear ourselves speak* as others hear us. Pavlov, too, said in 1954 that the word was the signal of signals, characterizing higher nervous activity as second-order conditioned reflexes.

Mead thus conceives the *person*—the self—as the combination of an *I* in which the action and the impulse reside and a *me* resulting from the internalization of the social structure in each of us.

Lorenzer (1970) uses Mead's symbol theory to account for psychological comprehension in the psychoanalytic session and at the same time as a basis for the evidence that arises from the closure of a Gestalt; as he says, gestures have intersubjective meaning because they are rooted in a community of action that is at one and the same time a community of language.

Beres (1970) draws a clear distinction between man and animals in asserting that only man can evoke an image, concept or thought in the absence of an immediate stimulus, because he has the capacity to form *mental representations*—that is, symbols—and not only *mental registrations*, like animals. Following the same line of thought, Lorenzer reserves the name "symbol" for conscious mental representations; unconscious ones he calls *clichés*.

As an unconscious mental representative, Lorenzer's cliché retains a genetic connection with symbols because it originates from them, but it remains excluded from communication within language. By definition, the cliché has the singularity that it is unable to distinguish the object from its representative. Because it lacks autonomy, the cliché needs a scenic structure in order to operate. Hence the drive discharges resulting from the cliché are strictly determined and their dependence on the scenic stimulus constitutes the repetition compulsion, in which the original event that gave rise to the cliché is repeated stereotypically.

Even if cliché-based (that is, neurotic) behaviour resembles that of animals, the two cannot be equated, because human neurotic behaviour (involving clichés) is always mixed with symbol-mediated behaviour and—even more importantly—because it is generated within the latter. Whereas the mechanisms that trigger animal behaviour form part of the gradual accomplishment of an evolutionary plan, according to Lorenzer (1970), cliché-related behaviour in neurosis occurs through the abandonment of an already acquired differentiation, namely operation through symbols. This relapse to the presymbolic level results from a mechanism of disintegration. Hence, Lorenzer concludes, the transformation of symbols into clichés—that is, of symbolic representatives into desymbolized representatives—takes place by repression. At the climax of the Oedipus complex, for example, the mother symbol comes into conflict with the boy's overall system of symbols, so that this representative must necessarily lose its character as such, although it retains its drive cathexis. The object of symbolic love is transformed into the object of the drive: the symbol becomes a cliché.

This process of *desymbolization* always takes place in a relational context that gives rise to a scenic structure corresponding to a concrete point in the subject's personal biography. To continue with the same example, the mother who changes from a symbol to a cliché for the boy in the throes of the oedipal conflict nevertheless retains her relational character for him, because "the cliché has to be considered as the representative of a behaviour *in relation to*" (ibid., p. 107). In other words, the cliché crystallizes a scene in which not only the object but also the self is desymbolized.

Lorenzer (1970) takes the example of Little Hans (Freud, 1909b), in which it is easy to establish the identity of the horse with the father and with Fritzl, Hans's playmate and rival. Hans having been unable to master the conflict (of oedipal rivalry) with the father, the only way out was to modify the representative of the father object by removing its feared aspects: when these are displaced onto the horse, the father symbol is converted into a cliché and remains excluded from linguistic communication. It is not directly evident either to Little Hans or to any observer that Hans actually means *horse + father* when he says "horse". Father and horse thus have false names, so that comprehension cannot be achieved within the framework of a community of language—consequently psychoanalytic comprehension is necessarily revealed as a hermeneutic procedure.

On the basis of the logical and psychological comprehension that make up scenic comprehension, Lorenzer concludes that psychoanalytic work must be performed without any recourse to hypothesis and without the slightest touch of explanation.

As we have seen, in his stipulative definition of logical comprehension and psychological comprehension (reliving) Lorenzer points out that the two are constantly superimposed in the practice of clinical psychoanalysis. Logical comprehension of the patient's words must sooner or later be placed in the context of an understanding of the patient himself; conversely, there can be no psychological comprehension without a logical framework. In this way an intermediate position is reached, yielding a third level of comprehension, which for Lorenzer is precisely the plane of psychoanalytic comprehension. In this sense, *scenic comprehension* implies a model of relationship and thus places particular emphasis on relations between human beings.

Scenic comprehension is governed by the laws of interaction models, coupled with the experience of evidence on which Lorenzer's entire conception is necessarily based. Scenic comprehension, as Lorenzer concludes in the context of one of his main theses, is based on apprehension of the scene (ibid., p. 132).

It should be pointed out that Lorenzer uses one and the same method to take account of logical comprehension, psychological comprehension (reliving) and scenic comprehension; it involves the closure of a Gestalt, accompanied by the relief of tension and the experience of evidence. He applies the same method to analysis: the analyst must proceed by tentatively inserting the interaction models into the hermeneutic circle until the right Gestalt appears. The law of good form is most certainly a valuable contribution to psychology on the part of the Berlin school; we have seen in sections 9.5 and 9.6 how it was used intelligently by Lagache (1951), following Zeigarnik, to explain transference repetition. But Lorenzer's trust in the closure of the Gestalt as the foundation of evidence seems to me to be exaggerated, if only because we might be misled by the pleasure-principle-related search for relief.

In our discussion of interpretation in psychoanalysis, we saw that Jaspers (1913) distinguished two orders of cognitive relations: comprehension and explanation (section 26.2). Comprehensive psychology is based wholly on genetic comprehension, in which we observe how the psychic arises out of the psychic as a form of ultimate, immediate evidence that cannot be pursued further. Lorenzer always invokes this experience of evidence as the fundamental persuasive element in the apprehension of a nexus (Lorenzer, 1970). However, in referring the experience of evidence to the closure of a Gestalt, Lorenzer is beginning to diverge from Jaspers. We know from Kurt Lewin (1935) that relief is felt when a Gestalt is completed because an end is put to a system of tensions. In metapsychological terms, while the Gestalt remains open, the synthetic function of the ego is in a constant state of tension; when it closes, the expenditure of energy ceases and relief arises. In his study of logical comprehension in chapter 2, Lorenzer (1970) says that his feeling of success that comes with the closure of the linguistic Gestalt, which is called "evidence of logical comprehension", is the first certainty attained by the analyst, and he will construct the next steps in his understanding upon it—and he specifies that "certification" of what has been communicated is obtained solely by means of a psychic act that is performed *in* the analyst and by the verification of this act.

Lorenzer (1970) further states that *the experience of evidence in logical comprehension is based on the structural coincidence of the statements of the analyst and of the analysand. The analyst tentatively grafts on meanings, which he substitutes for the patient's in a wide hermeneutic circle. The basis of this procedure is the community of language between analyst and analysand.*

In chapter 5 of the same book, headed "Scenic Comprehension", Lorenzer (1970) gives a number of examples of what is to be understood by scenic comprehension. Case C is a married man of 40 with personal contact difficulties. In a session transcribed in detail, the analysand is seen to be worried by the approaching end of the analysis and by the constant press of ideas flooding in on him. Goethe had the same problem but solved it with Eckermann. The analysand then explains how a new idea occurred to him and comments that what occurs to him so readily does not happen to others. The analyst points out that the analysand is talking about his ideas and not about himself, to which the other responds that *he* is his ideas. The analyst thinks that the patient is right in this respect, and the latter presently says that his ideas die when people do not care for them enough. The word "die" disconcerts the analyst, who then recalls that one of the patient's brothers died shortly after birth and that his mother had had a large number of children. The analyst now sees the patient identified with his mother, producing one son after another with his ideas and putting the analyst in his own place as a son with respect to her.

The analyst's interpretation is in my view correct, and I also understand that the sudden conjunction of various parts of the material constitutes evidence for Lorenzer. However, the fact that this results in a conviction has more to do with Lorenzer's trust in his theories than with the material. This session offers other routes to scenic comprehension, to use Lorenzer's own language. Is the scene with Goethe and Eckermann, with the retinue of associations preceding and following it, not a Gestalt that is more than sufficient for the analyst to interpret this patient's (manic) model of the psychoanalytic dialogue? The analyst did not allow for this possibility—and it is not unreasonable to suppose that this omission gave rise to a somewhat harsh interpretation, which the patient did not find it difficult to refute. The analyst agrees with him internally, while the analysand complains about those who let his ideas die for lack of sufficient care. The analyst is disconcerted by the word "die", presumably because he overlooks the "drama" that is being played out in the session: the patient reproaches him directly for this interpretation, which, by asking him to talk about himself and not about his ideas, does indeed disqualify those ideas. In this way the analyst literally allows the analysand's ideas to die, without noticing how the patient is killing him with his mania and how he is at the same time thinking that this dead analyst—or rather, this killed (= disconcerted) analyst—is of no use to him. Why should we not suppose that this acute countertransference conflict induces the analyst to associate with the analysand's prolific mother and the brother's death instead of thinking about what is happening to himself as a mother in the transference?

I am by no means claiming that my proposed interpretation (or scenic comprehension, if it is preferred) is better than the analyst's, but only that the material presented to us by Lorenzer does not suffice as a basis for the experience of evidence that is so dear and clear to him. What I am sure of is that the experience of evidence is the cornerstone of Lorenzer's hermeneutics, which allows him to construct a psychoanalysis that dispenses with explanation.

Lorenzer believes that the Gestalt we are discussing here—the "mother giving birth to children"—provides the analyst with the strongest evidence; he concludes: "At this point he would have the certainty and also the capacity needed to put the Gestalt into concrete verbal form in the interpretation" (ibid., p. 144).

I have to say that in my opinion the analyst's strong evidence always carries with it a fragment of the countertransference—especially in this session, in which the analyst runs the risk of wanting to conceive an interpretation like a greatly idealized son.

Beyond Lorenzer's rigorous exposition, there can ultimately never be any certainty; if recourse to the test of hypotheses is shunned, it will at any rate be necessary to use interaction models and to put these to the analysand, trusting that the hermeneutic circle will not lead us—as Lorenzer himself warns in his discussion of the "limits and particularities of psychoanalytic hermeneutics" (ibid., p. 208)—into a *folie à deux*. If I am right in detecting an intense mother countertransference conflict in this material, the *folie à deux* is but a step away, via projective counteridentification (Grinberg, 1956, etc.). Helmut Thomä and Horst Kächele (1987) are perfectly clear on this point: unless one proceeds beyond subjective evidence, "hermeneutic understanding would remain exposed to the risk of *folie à deux*" (p. 27). They note that systematic investigation of the analytic situation must include a reference to both comprehension and explanation (p. 27). I am in total agreement with the Ulm researchers on this point.

Lorenzer (1973) maintains that psychoanalysis, like the concept of the symbol itself, has moved from the realm of natural science to that of social science. Since the 1930s and thanks to the important contributions of Cassirer (1923–1929), Susanne Langer (1942) and others, the symbol has come to be seen as a subjective formation mediated by society; this view differs from the psychoanalytic conception.

Lorenzer (1973) considers that "psychoanalysis is an investigative procedure that proceeds almost entirely in the form of understanding through language". In other words, psychoanalysis uses communication by means of symbols in order to gain access to its object. However, this approach is organized in two systems of language, or two hermeneutic circles: the linguistic symbols of the common language and the *private* linguistic symbols of the patient.

This has the corollary that the psychoanalyst's hermeneutic task must be performed on two levels: (1) the level of interpretation of the word-as-symbol mediated by the common language, and (2) the level of the interaction figures, which can be interpreted only in the hermeneutic circle of scenic comprehension. Lorenzer emphasizes that the scenic must be understood fundamentally in the sense of conjunction between human beings, and not as a mere psychosocially oriented function of the ego. The objective of psychoanalytic investigation thus consists of the *"determinate interaction forms that constitute the subject"* (Lorenzer, 1973).

Hence there is no doubt that, for Lorenzer, "clarification of the meaning of the linguistic symbols is but a stopover en route to the interaction forms" (1973).

The separation between the interaction forms and the linguistic symbol is the outcome of the neurotic—or, one might add, psychotic—conflict, and the therapeutic action of psychoanalysis involves re-establishing this communication, which is blocked by the neurosis (Lorenzer, 1973).

Human interaction is predicated on language; human society is a praxis between individuals capable of language and, because linguistic symbols are introduced into children's education as predicates of interaction, social contradictions also slip into language. If a specific interaction form that proves to be incompatible cannot be resolved, the forbidden interaction form must renounce its predicators; the corresponding linguistic symbols are expelled from the realm of language and desymbolized, and "the ex-communicated interaction form of language relapses to the level of prelinguistic interaction forms" (Lorenzer, 1973). These desymbolized interaction forms are the *clichés*, which are manifestations of the repetition compulsion and the transference.

Zur Begründung einer materialistischen Sozialisationstheorie (Lorenzer, 1972) is an attempt to see child development as a natural process that in turn bears the social stamp of its history. Lorenzer is not, of course, making the commonplace point that human beings are moulded from a combination of natural dispositions and cultural influences, but postulating a trial between psychoanalysis and dialectical materialism, based on the process of socialization of the child in its interaction with the mother.

In a fresh attempt at a more rigorous definition of the cliché, Lorenzer writes: "By the concept of the 'cliché', we mean the unconscious interaction forms that are taken back by the combination of desymbolization and fixation to the stage of virulent prelinguistic forms" (Lorenzer, 1972). Three interaction forms are not associated with a predicator and are therefore excluded from language: (1) those not apprehended linguistically; (2) those overcome in the course of normal development; and (3) clichés, which are excluded from language but fixed as interaction forms.

In the prologue of his book, Lorenzer (1973) sets out the principal goals of his research. Psychoanalysis is concerned with specific forms of interaction; it is constructed within the practical dialectic of the socialization process on the basis of the mother–child dyad.

"The specificity of psychoanalytic hermeneutics lies in the fact that, by way of the figures of language, it refers to *interaction forms*" (Lorenzer, 1973). Unlike Lacan (1966) and Habermas (1968), who blur the problems of interaction within communication and language, Lorenzer distinguishes radically between communication and interaction. Lorenzer places *scenic comprehension* beyond the symbolic interaction forms proper to language and adopts a materialistic hermeneutic approach to it.

For Lorenzer, the socialization of the child is *not* connected with language, because it begins with a non-linguistic adjustment on the level of practice and gesture. There is a prelinguistic agreement on interaction forms. Need is prior to the wish and is presymbolic. In other words, the id as a structure is the precipitate of interaction forms determined by society (the mother), which do not attain the symbolic level. The specific interaction forms are prelinguistic but not extralinguistic. They are not symbols, but they are language.

One is immediately struck by the difference between Lorenzer and Lacan: for the former, the unconscious is not structured like a language but is instead the precipitate of socially determined interaction forms in the mother–child dyad, where the prelinguistic agreement is converted into symbolic language when the gesture is transformed by a predicator. In this way Lorenzer protects himself from any kind of subjectivism incompatible with his Freudo-Marxism.

Considering the matter in these terms also makes it clear why Lorenzer never resorts to the empathy that is so dear to Kohut. The *determinate interaction forms* in Lorenzer's system account for the presymbolic communication between baby and mother no less than for the preverbal communication between analyst and patient. Unlike Kohut, Lorenzer does not abandon the theory of drives and always emphasizes that his "cliché" is cathected. Without any empirical and explanatory concession, Lorenzer resorts to a materialistic hermeneutics as a foundation for his ideas. Kohut, on the other hand, trusts in empathy as the appropriate form of revelation of data, which, as discussed in section 21.7, he subsequently subjects to a natural-science explanation. Stripped of their Marxist formulation, Lorenzer's ideas are closer than he thinks to those of Melanie Klein, who would also benefit from the incorporation of some of Lorenzer's contributions into her theoretical structure.

CHAPTER TWENTY-EIGHT

Constructions
of early development

Psychoanalytic treatment proposes to reconstruct the past, erasing the lacunae of early childhood memories, which are the product of repression. It achieves this by lifting the resistances and resolving the transference through the analysis of dreams, parapraxes and screen memories, no less than the analysis of symptoms and of character. The theories Freud formulated, with this method, on human development, infantile sexuality and the Oedipus complex were strongly supported not only by the results of treatment but also by the psychoanalysis of children, where these same phenomena can be seen in *status nascendi*.

In the small child, who lacks verbal instruments of communication, the problems to be investigated cannot be reached directly through language, but there exists the possibility of seeing them reproduced in the transference and of interpreting them, in the hope that the patient's associations will support or refute us.

To meet the aims of this presentation, we will call early development (or conflict) the pre-verbal phase, where there is no preconscious registering of memories, and which covers approximately the pre-oedipal stage described by Freud (1931b, 1933a) and by Ruth Mack Brunswick (1940). We will distinguish it from *infantile* development (or conflict), which corre-

---

At the risk of repetition, I have decided to include at this point the paper I presented at the Helsinki Congress, "Validez de la interpretación transferencial en el 'aquí y ahora' para la reconstrucción del desarollo psíquico temprano", in which I discussed many of the themes in this part of the book. I have added at the end a reconstruction of a dream of Freud, which was inspired by my reading of Max Schur and Harold Blum.

sponds to the Oedipus complex, discovered by Freud, at between 3 and 5 years of age.

Based on clinical material, I maintain the following:

1. Early development is integrated into the personality and can be reconstructed during the analytic process, since it is expressed in the transference and is verifiable through the analysand's response.

2. The early conflict appears in the analytic situation preferentially as preverbal or para-verbal language—that is, not as an articulated language but a language of action. It tends to configure the psychotic aspect of the transference as a function of partial objects and dyadic and early oedipal relations, while infantile conflict is expressed above all in verbal representations and screen memories—that is, as transference neurosis.

3. At times it is possible to perceive the three poles of the conflict (early, infantile and actual) linked into the same structure.

4. The information the analysand offers about his early development should be considered as covering memories, beliefs and family myths, which change, in effect, in the course of treatment.

5. The psychoanalytic method reveals historical truth (psychic reality), the way the individual processes the events and how the events weigh on the individual, but not the material truth, unattainable in its infinite variations.

6. No incompatibility exists between interpretation and construction, given that interpreting the transference implies comparing, as point and counterpoint, the present and the past as members of the same structure.

7. The vital history of the patient is always the *theory* he has of himself, which analysis will reformulate in more precise and flexible terms.

8. The concept of the traumatic situation should be reserved for the economic, since the dynamic conflict always arises between the subject and his environment in a complemental series.

9. The adequate and rigorous management of the transference relation allows the analysis of the early conflict without recourse to any type of active therapy or controlled regression, because analysis does not propose to correct past events but to *reconceptualize* them.

10. If it is accepted that there exists an early transference that can unfold fully in the treatment and is susceptible to being resolved through psychoanalytic methods, the possibility arises of using it as an assumed theory (by assumed theory I mean here an instrument is applied without questioning its validity at the outset—for example, the optical theory of the telescope for the astronomer) to investigate early development and to test the theories that try to explain it, a theme my account does not cover.

I wish to describe a patient, Mr. Brown, whom I analysed for nine and a half years, to illustrate the way a conflict during the early months of life is expressed through the personality and appears in the transference. (The technical aspects were discussed in a seminar directed by Betty Joseph in January 1974 in Buenos Aires. Previously I had discussed this case with León Grinberg.)

When he came to see me, Mr. Brown was 35 years old and had been in analysis for three years, until his analyst died. During the interview he warned me that he was gravely ill and detailed his symptoms: an incapacity for thinking and concentrating, a tendency to drink and to take psycho-stimulants, sexual difficulties (lack of desire, impotence) and anti-Semitic feelings despite being Jewish. He also indicated his blocking of affects and gave as an example his indifference towards his analyst's death.

About the diagnosis, suffice it to say that this is a *borderline* patient with a strong addictive structure and a manifest perversion—a *frotteur*. In order to reach orgasm, he rubbed his genitals against a woman, avoiding coitus. He was not conscious of this perversion, which he sometimes rationalized clumsily.

He said he remembered nothing of his childhood, although he said without emotion that *when he was two months old he had almost died of hunger because his mother's milk had dried up suddenly.*

This event had never been valued by Mr. Brown. It was his previous analyst who deduced that he had probably suffered hunger as a child. The patient responded with the above-mentioned information, and was surprised by the analyst's accuracy. He took him more seriously from then on, although he never did esteem him.

He liked me at the outset, on the other hand, although he considered me a novice. He knew through the colleague who had referred him to me that I had just arrived from London; he was sure he was my first patient, if not the only patient to date in my career. On interpreting his sibling rivalry in the face of this type of material, I received from him only a condescending smile. He did not even listen to me when I told him he was putting his need into me, that he saw me as hungry for patients.

During the first months he was cold and distant; at times he fell asleep suddenly when I interpreted something that might be new to him. He frequently felt hungry before or after the session, and then coprophagic fantasies of extraordinary clarity appeared. He dreamed *he was in a small restaurant where they served him a cat dish. He felt terribly disgusted, but someone told him to eat it, that had it been presented as hare he would not have noticed. The dish smelled of cat excrement.* This dream served to show him his mistrust of his analyst, who presents cat as hare, and his desire of nourishing himself from his own faeces in order not to be dependent.

The boastful tone that Abraham (1920) found originated in the idealization of the emunctory (excretory) functions, and the excreta were the centre of his defensive system, often linked to anal masturbation (Meltzer, 1966).

His rebellious aerophagia, which years later would be an expressive
indicator of his traumatic lactation, appeared as a motive for hilarity and
mocking. He remembered that he used to burp when he was with his
previous analyst. When the latter pointed this out, he replied that he paid
for his burps. When I interpreted that he was proud of his burping and his
money, he remembered that *he began analysis precisely because he suffered
from flatulence and gases,* as well as gastric discomfort and difficulties in
studying. Due to these symptoms, a psychiatrist, Dr. M, had indicated
analysis.

Months later he dreamed *he was in a bar and was served a fizzy soft drink
with a fly caught in the cap of the bottle. He hesitated between drinking it or
complaining to the waiter, and he opted for the complaint.*

Apropos of this dream, he remembered another from his previous
analysis: *I dreamed I was standing in front of Dr. M's clinic, and there was a
group of people eating human flesh. One of them took a half-rotten cranium and
scraped the inside with a piece of bread and ate the brains smeared on the bread.*

He associated to this a moment when he was about to break off analysis for financial reasons, and M proposed that he undertake group
therapy. I told him these dreams explained in part his difficulties in thinking and concentrating. Basing myself on Freud (1917e [1915]) and
Abraham (1924), I added that analysis to him meant actually nourishing
himself with the analyst's thoughts. But as he was incapable of tolerating
them, he expelled them as faeces that he then incorporated again as nourishment. The patient replied that his mouth watered! He added with lively
resistance that this often happened to him with nauseating smells, including his faecal matter.

As an effect of this session he felt anxious, he wanted to cry and inwardly asked me for help. Immediately he was furious because the treatment was not curing him, and he again thought of breaking it off. He
continually affirmed that psychoanalysis was not a human relationship
but a cold commercial transaction.

The coprophagic fantasies and the manic defences, always linked to
thought disturbance, occupied a long period of analysis. Simultaneously,
his oedipal jealousy, his rivalry with his father and his homosexual
impulses were being analysed. His desire to suck the analyst's penis
appeared in dreams and fantasies—a great humiliation for Mr. Brown,
who feared that he was homosexual. The analysis of all these conflicts
succeeded in removing the principal symptoms and made sublimating processes linked to the early conflict appear.

After this evolution, which took about three years, the oral conflict
became evident. He dreamed, for example, *that he took out three thick
threads which emerged from his throat* and associated this with tentacles. This
dream was interpreted as his desire to cling to and to suck from the analytic breast, which seemed to confirm another dream of the same night: *"I
also dreamed that a little girl wanted desperately to 'draw on' my cigarette. I took
it out of her mouth, and she stretched desperately to suck."* Here his orality has

been projected; he is a father who frustrates the need of his infantile feminine part. There were voracious and aggressive feelings for the father's penis inside the mother's body, expressed in a third dream, where *he entered a bank* (the mother's body) *and they wanted him to kill the cashier* (father's penis). *He refused, but others did it, and when he was arrested he denied all connection with the crime, and he managed to escape.* On the occasion of paying arrears of fees, he remembered the time when he was hungry at his mother's breast, *when he almost died because his mother did not realise his need, despite his crying and screaming all day long.*

It is worth comparing this version with that of the interview, because here what is added is that he cried and screamed the whole day long. This modification shows, in my view, that his blocking of affects has been mobilized. This also implies that information referring to early psychic development should be conceptualized as screen memories (Freud, 1899a) despite being narrated as real events, as true stories transmitted by parents and relatives.

Having overcome the blocking of affects, he now cried and screamed the whole day long: my fees were too high, psychoanalysis was pure blah–blah–blah, if he could not pay me it was because of his difficulties, which I was also responsible for. This acute transference conflict culminated in this dream: *"I am in your consulting-room; you are sitting next to me as a medical doctor. Anguished, I tell you I am suffering very much because I have revealed my feelings to other people. You seem identified with my pain and your face, too, shows intense—perhaps a bit excessive—suffering. Then three people burst into the room, a malformed man and a woman; I do not remember the third one. They were friends of yours who came to play cards or to do group psychotherapy. I had changed my clothes, and I looked for my underpants so they would not see they were soiled. I found some, which, perhaps, were yours. You were stroking and touching me to calm my anguish."* He associated the woman of the dream with someone he had seen a few days earlier in the consulting-room, and he had felt jealous. More conscious of his needs, he was now vulnerable to pain: he wanted me to calm him, but he was afraid of coming close and feeling jealousy and/or homosexual attraction. So that his dirty things would not be discovered, he confuses himself with me through projective identification (Melanie Klein, 1946), getting into my underpants.

At times he recognized that analysis was his sole companion, and then he felt a desire to destroy me. His delays in payment had then a nuance of provocation and rivalry; at the same time, he wanted to keep my money so as not to feel alone. When he said that my money stayed with him, his mouth watered. When he obtained a rise in salary, the first thing he thought of was having to pay me, and that made him furious.

When he was about to buy a flat so as to be alone, he dreamed that *I was analysing him sitting on the street beneath a triumphal arch. He spoke in shouts because we were far away from each other. While he was being analysed, he approached with rapid movements, always lying down.* This dream, where his approach is clearly seen, was interpreted in terms of the complete

Oedipus complex: the mother's genitals (arch of triumph) attract him and are guarded by the father's rival penis, which also excites him.

The purchase of a flat, his rise in the firm he worked for, and the improvement in his erotic life made him feel he was progressing, which provoked rage and fear in him. He was afraid of destroying me with his progress, and he was afraid to trust. I interpreted this fear as being based on an initial trust in the breast that then let him down. He replied with a memory I consider basic: *when he was seven or eight years old, a servant had told him a child had starved to death because the mother had given him water when he was hungry, which had kept him quiet without nourishing him.*

This memory is surely a new version of his breast-feeding phase, and it is not by chance that it appeared when he had come closer to the analyst and was beginning to feel Erikson's (1950) basic trust. This material was interpreted not only from the point of view of the early conflict and *in reconstructive terms* ("you must have felt when you were small that your mother gave you water instead of milk") but also *in the here and now*, as a typical resistance of transference: "You think you are progressing because of the analysis and you want to trust me; but something leads you to think that analytic food is nothing but water." I reminded him of his recent desire to see a medical doctor "who will fix everything with two injections", and his repeated affirmations that analysis is pure blah–blah–blah, as well as a fantasy he had recounted a few days previously: "*I am going to a petrol station where they pump air into my backside under pressure, in order to clean me.*"

This material illustrates the principal thesis of my work: early development does not remain cut off from the rest of the personality and can be reconstructed on the basis of subsequent data, which basically have the same meaning or significance. It is not decisive that the pre-verbal be re-signified *afterwards*, as Freud proposes (1918b), or that it have significance at the outset. It suffices that an experience acquire significance *a posteriori* to make it permissible for us to maintain that we can reach it and reconstruct it. There exists support for the suggestion, in the material, that the fantasy of Mr. Brown's latency period (the child nourished by water) is isomorphic with his experience as a lactating infant.

I also consider that interpretation and construction are complementary phases of the same process. Phyllis Greenacre says: "*Any clarifying interpretation generally includes some reference to reconstruction*" (1975, p. 703). If transference implies superimposing the past on the present, then we cannot think that an interpretation of the here and now can be given without the perspective from the past, nor can history be restored without responding to the ever-present transference engagement. In other words, it is not only indispensable to elucidate what happens in the present to uncover the past, but also to utilize memories to illumine the transference. Racker (1958b) said humorously that there are analysts who see the transference only as an obstacle in recovering the past and others who take the past as a mere instrument to analyse the transference. But, as I have just indicated, both things must be done. *"Both the patient dwelling on the past and his persistent adherence to the present can function as resistance"*, Kris says (1956b, p. 56). As Blum (1980a) suggests, one must achieve a synergetic action between the analysis of resistance and reconstruction (p. 40) to restore the continuity and cohesion of the personality (p. 50). Understood in this way, analysis of the transference delimits the past from the present, it distinguishes the objective from the subjective. When this is achieved, the past does not need to repeat itself and remains as a reservoir of experiences that we can apply to understand the present and predict the future, not to misunderstand them.

* * *

From the story of the child nourished by water onwards, Mr. Brown was plagued by flatulence, and his swollen stomach made him think of an undernourished baby. He gained five kilos in a month and had an even greater tendency to fall asleep when he received an interpretation. Envy now occupied an important place; he progressed in order to awaken envy in others and limited his progress in order not to provoke it. With his somnolence he regulated the session so as to control his envy (and also to express it); at the same time he placed into me his hunger and his despair, his undernourished baby.

Then he had this dream: *"I dreamed we were in bed and you checked my stomach, which was painful and full of gases. You were feeling me and making a circular movement to alleviate my pain, while you said, in your grave voice, that I was ill, that it was a 'somatization'."*

He associated this with the other dream in my consulting-room a year and a half earlier. He emphasized that I acted as a doctor, and there were no erotic overtones; once, when he was a child, he had had stomach pains, and his father had told him to massage himself.

I interpreted that he needed me as a father to alleviate his pain. He felt I could, with my hand–penis, take out of his body the bad air his mother's empty breast had placed there—I was myself an empty breast when I spoke in vain. I suggested reconstructively that, when he was on the point of dying of hunger, his father helped him in some way.

Without understanding what was essential in the interpretation, he accepted that a homosexual desire must exist, and he fell asleep. I interpreted that he had now made the dream real: we were sleeping together in bed, and the malnourished baby had been transformed into the pregnant mother. The previous interpretation points to the link of dependency; this one, to its erotization.

The following year, when the patient had had five years of analysis, most of his symptoms had disappeared. His coprophagic fantasies no longer appeared; nauseating smells did not make his mouth water, and he did not expel his thoughts. He could pay attention and study, although with difficulty; his sexual life had become normal and could even be satisfactory. In analysis, on the other hand, the situation was far from easy.

Although his Olympian contempt was no longer in evidence, his resistance to trust was strong, and his demands and rivalry created a continuous stalemate in the analytic setting.

He remembered that at five years of age he used to play "the ballerina and the devil" with a little girl. This game, which coincided with the culminating moment of the Oedipus complex, had to do with masturbation in the face of the primal scene and links up with a screen memory from the same period: *He thought there were devils and witches in his bedroom and in his parents' bedroom.* The devil (or demon) is simultaneously hunger during lactation, the father's penis which calms or excites him and the baby inside the mother who awakens his jealousy. On other occasions the demon was his bottom, Money-Kyrle's (1971) spurious object, the alternative to the breast. The game of the ballerina and the devil was also interpreted, following Herbert Rosenfeld (1971), as two parts of the self: infantile dependent (ballerina) and omnipotent narcissistic (devil).

Halfway through the fifth year of analysis, he brought an important dream, through which his cooperation could be evaluated. It was a moment when the treatment interested him and he wanted to be cured. "*I dreamed I was with Carlos, working enthusiastically on air filters. We had become independent of the firm and were doing well. We had constructed the first absolute filter in the country and were about to manufacture a particle counter, which measures the efficacy of the filters.*" He associated that in the dream he felt as if he had ended analysis, having been cured; his sexual problem was not resolved; the absolute filter sterilizes the air.

I interpreted this dream as a desire to be cured, with my help (Carlos), of the bad air that causes his flatulence (therapeutic alliance) and at the same time as a masturbatory game among brothers, which makes the analysis sterile (pseudo-alliance).

The dream signals important progress: from his new position as a manager he promoted the filtering of air and soon became a well-known specialist. (I referred to this point in dealing with his sublimations.)

After beginning the sixth year of treatment, he entered into a relationship with a woman who gained his trust and attracted him sexually, whom he then married. He experienced this decision as a great achievement of analysis. In a session where he expressed these feelings, flatulence reappeared. I interpreted that he saw me as a mother who was giving birth to him as a healthy infant, and that he wished to imitate me. The flatulence ceased dramatically, and this awoke contradictory feelings of trust and rivalry in him. Shortly afterwards, in a session in which he fell asleep, he dreamed that *he was with an old, bad woman with empty breasts from which only air came out.*

As he progressed, his defensive system became almost impenetrable: he interpreted himself, he slept when I spoke, he repeated my interpretations aloud, making them his own, and so forth. Frequently he interrupted me and completed what I was going to say. He was now a prime example of the patient who is difficult to reach (Betty Joseph, 1975).

As his abdominal symptoms became acute, he consulted a clinician who promised to cure him in a week. He rejoiced because he was going to show me I was wrong; but the clinician was not given the satisfaction of curing him either. In the previous session I had again interpreted his flatulence as pregnancy; he had not listened to me. This time he had to acknowledge, however, that his wife's menstruation was slightly delayed. He thought she was pregnant and felt jealous of the child, as I had interpreted to him a few days before. (This apparent insight often only meant that he—not I—was the one who said it.)

The model of flatulence as identification with the pregnant woman appeared linked now more to envy than to jealousy. I told him he wanted to be the one who would have the child, but without being fertilized by my interpretations. He replied with astonishment that his abdominal tension had diminished and the flatulence had disappeared. (To understand how unconquerable his defensive system was, bear in mind that the *fertile* interpretation of this moment could be transformed later into a blah–blah–blah that again filled the abdomen with gases—imaginary pregnancy.)

At this time he had a very significant dream. He arrived afflicted with flatulence (meteorism) and abdominal troubles, while his wife's amenorrhea continued. *"I dreamed my car had broken down and I took it to the garage. They said the compressor was faulty, and it had to be checked thoroughly to see whether it was serious. This engaged my attention because my car has no compressor. I thought it would be something very serious, like a cancer."*

This dream expresses the conflict at all levels—early, infantile, and current. Mr. Brown's *present conflict* is that he believes he has made his wife pregnant and is going to be a father; this compels him to be more adult and responsible. The *infantile conflict* has to do with the Oedipus conflict and sibling rivalry. This time he remembered the strong feeling of desolation at the age of five, when his (only) sister was born. Lastly, the *early conflict* appears pristinely expressed by the compressor, an introjected breast that pumps air instead of giving nourishment.

His flatulence as airy pregnancy is represented twice: by the compressor and because he thinks his car does not have one. This double representation also applies to his wife's pregnancy, imaginary because unconfirmed and because of his ambivalence. At the same time it symbolizes the pseudocyesis (false pregnancy) of Mr. Brown, with a compressor (uterus) that does not exist in his male body.

As a representation of the analytic process, the dream reveals his position with unadorned precision: we are investigating something that does not exist, which is only air, words borne on the wind, and which, nevertheless, is as serious as a cancer. The analytic process was arrested, had no depth and had been transformed into perverse sexual play [*frotteur*], despite all my efforts. Lacking emotional significance, the interpretations were water or air that swell the baby's abdomen and condemn it to die of hunger. The slang expression "to talk a lot of hot air" [*hablar al cuete*] could never be used with more painful appositeness. During this period he not only identified with the pregnant mother and the malnourished baby: he often projected the baby dying of hunger into the analyst, making me feel devalued and discouraged, and sometimes sleepy.

It is important to indicate that this *impasse* repeated with surprising clarity the suckling conflict, while the oedipal conflict was remembered and relived at another level of communication. Thus two forms of organization, the neurotic and the psychotic (Bion, 1957), could be noted. The neurotic conflict contains the triangular situation of a child of five jealous over the birth of a sister, the intense anxiety vis-à-vis the primal scene through the screen memory of witches and demons, the infantile masturbation (the devil and the ballerina) and the sexual games with maids and little girls—which he now remembered vividly.

The conflict with the breast is expressed in another way, through a language of action, without verbal representations or memories; similarly with the early oedipal conflict (Melanie Klein, 1928, 1945). Analysis reaches them, nevertheless, although the technical problems are different, and the analyst, in the vortex of the repetition, sees himself transformed into the empty breast that pumps flatus into his baby–patient. That this is a very painful process for the analyst does not diminish in any way the beauty of our method, the trustworthiness of our theories.

* * *

To meet the objectives of this chapter, it is relevant that the early conflict finds diverse forms of expression that show its coherent unity with life and history. The adult who consulted me for his aerophagy is the child of the latency period who is moved by the story of the baby nourished with water and hears the story of his unfortunate breast-feeding, just as he is the suckling infant who thought he received air (flatus) instead of food, the man of the coprophagous fantasies who confuses faeces with food and burps with words, and the specialist in air filters.

The unity of this history supports our thesis that early experiences leave their mark and then faithfully express themselves in the latent ideas of the subject's family myths and fantasies, in screen memories and character traits no less than in symptoms and in vocation.

The other thesis is that these early experiences are accessible to classic psychoanalytic technique, although it is extremely difficult to resolve them.

Most ego psychologists think that early conflicts are not analysable. Elizabeth R. Zetzel (1968) affirms that only if the dyadic conflicts with the mother and the father were resolved separately can the transference neurosis be delimited from the therapeutic alliance, a necessary condition for analysability. Although I have just stated that early relations are analysable, I share in practice the reservations of ego psychology, without ceasing to hold that early conflicts and psychotic mechanisms appear in *every* patient.

Others consider early conflicts analysable, with a variation in the technique. If primitive emotional development is affected, says Winnicott (1956), analytic work should be suspended, *"management being the whole thing"* (p. 17). Previously, the Budapest school had maintained similar ideas on the basis of Ferenczi's (1919b, 1920) active technique and of his theory of trauma (1930, 1931, 1932), which inspired the *new beginning* of Balint (1932, 1937, 1952), to give an account of primary object love. Annie and Didier Anzieu (1977) follow this line. For them, grave faults in development require technical changes, because only concrete experiences can mitigate them. As a specifically symbolic act, interpretation can never reach what has not been symbolized.

These arguments have the definite support of common sense; however, the history of the science shows that common sense can lead us astray. In the case presented, a highly traumatic experience during the early months of life was incorporated into the personality of the patient and acquired a symbolic value, which we could reach through interpretation. The suckling two-month-old who "cannot understand our language" is part of a child and an adult who enable us to communicate with him.

The corollary is that I did not need to give this patient the opportunity of regressing. He relived his breast-feeding conflict fully in the classic analytic setting, without any type of active therapy or controlled regression. As an analyst I applied my method rigorously, and when I abandoned it mistakenly, I tried to recover it through the silent analysis of my countertransference, without making concessions to my inaccuracies. (My tolerance towards payment could be considered a parameter—Eissler, 1953 —but it was not something I introduced, and I analysed it like any other symptom.)

* * *

It is appropriate to discuss, lastly, the theoretical evaluation of traumatic experiences in infancy. In the case presented there appears an environmental situation that really endangers the subject's life. However, if we are to continue to use the theory of transference in order to understand the past, we should note that things are not so simple. In the transferential repetition we find a baby–patient who operates continuously on the father and the penis, the mother and the breast, the primal scene. It will be said, with reason, that he does this to transform that catastrophic experience into an active one. But can this exclude a more complex action between the child and his parents? Just as he sleeps in the session so as not to receive the interpretation, he could have slept at the breast, conditioning in part the lack of milk (agalactia). This hypothesis is logical, and there is nothing in the material to refute it. I do not say that this supports Melanie Klein's (1957) theory of primary envy, because other equally valid explanations could be offered. But I do think that the conflict always arises between the subject and the *milieu* with which he interacts, in the manner of Freud's

(1916–17) complemental series. Mirsky et al. (1950, 1952) demonstrated that the high concentration of pepsinogen in some breast-feeding infants bears on their feeling of dissatisfaction and conditions the type of rejecting mother described by Garma (1950, 1954). As Brenman (1980) says, the "Oedipus complex" of Oedipus should be understood as the result of his own oedipal tendencies and of his environment (abandonment by his parents, the vicarious care of the kings of Corinth, and so forth).

Freud's (1937d) warnings notwithstanding, historical and material truth are often confused. *Material truth* consists in the objective facts, which have infinite variables and, consequently, explanations. What is accessible to psychoanalytic method is the *historical truth* (psychic reality), which is the way each of us processes the facts. Therefore I think it is better to speak of psychic reality and factual reality, as Freud does in the "Project" of 1895 (1950a [1887–1902]) and in the fourth essay in *Totem and Taboo* (1912–13)—or of phantasy and reality, following Susan Isaacs (1943) and Hanna Segal (1964a).

* * *

The information a patient gives about his traumatic situations, and in general about his history, is a personal version, a manifest content that must be interpreted, and which in fact changes in the course of analysis.

We have seen that when the blocking of affects lifted, Mr. Brown modified his version of his breast-feeding trauma. Two years after the dream of the compressor, when the *impasse* had given way and analysis was going to end, a new change occurred. During that period the analysand, more conscious of his greed and lack of consideration, was afraid of tiring me. On returning from his holiday, he dreamed of *playing sexual games with a young girl: he gave her a kiss, and the girl's tongue grew enormously and remained in his mouth when they separated.* I interpreted that he erotized the analytic link, denying the holiday separation, and added that the girl's tongue was my pleasing nipple which allowed him always to be at the breast, so that the catastrophic weaning would not be repeated. He worriedly mentioned his new delay in paying the fees and suddenly remembered that *the disturbance during breast-feeding was not that his mother's milk had dried up and he had gone hungry until they began to offer him the bottle, but precisely the opposite: it was with the bottle that he went hungry, because they gave him a smaller ration (of food) than the doctor had ordered.* This new version, in my view, responds to a structural change: there is now a good breast that fed him and a bad bottle: and the father (doctor) is a protective figure, as was suggested in previous material. (Three years after having ended analysis, in a follow-up interview, he changed the memory once more and said that *he had gone hungry with the bottle because the amount indicated by the doctor was insufficient*, a complaint perhaps introducing itself here due to [a premature?] termination of analysis.)

Analysis does not propose to correct the events from the past, which in any case is impossible, but to *reconceptualize* them. If this is achieved and the patient improves, the new version is more equitable and serene, less Manichaean and persecuting. The subject recognizes himself as actor, as agent as well as patient. He perceives better intentions in others, not only negligence and bad faith. Blame is better distributed. A greater role is assigned to life's adversities.

Each one of us keeps a bundle of information, memories and stories which, like family and personal myths, are processed in a series of *theories*, with which we face and order reality, as well as our relation with others and with the world. I use the word "theory" in a strict sense: a scientific hypothesis that attempts to explain reality and can be refuted by the facts Popper (1963) teaches, and which, I believe, corresponds to the psychoanalytic concept of the unconscious fantasy. Neurosis (and mental illness in general) can be defined from this point of view as the attempt to maintain our theories despite the facts that refute them (the link minus K—see Bion, 1962b). What we call in clinical terms *transference* is the attempt to adapt the facts to our theories, instead of testing our theories with the facts.

The psychoanalytic process proposes to revise the patient's theories and make them simultaneously more rigorous and more flexible. This is achieved with interpretation and especially with mutative interpretation (Strachey, 1934) in which past and present are joined for a moment to demonstrate that our theory of considering them identical was wrong.

28.1 The "Non vixit" dream and early psychic development

In recent years, several writers have discovered that one of Freud's dreams in *The Interpretation of Dreams* can serve to illustrate the theme of pre-oedipal reconstructions. It is the one that takes place in Professor Ernst Brücke's laboratory and which in psychoanalytic jargon is known as the "*Non vixit*" dream. Freud analyses it when he speaks of the value of words in the dream in chapter 6 and returns to it further on. The main characters are Ernst Fleischl von Marxow and Josef Paneth, two friends of Freud in the Laboratory, and his great friend Fliess. The text of the dream is as follows:

> I had gone to Brücke's laboratory at night, and, in response to a gentle knock on the door, I opened it to (the late) Professor Fleischl, who came in with a number of strangers and, after exchanging a few words, sat down at his table.

This was followed by a second dream.

> My friend Fl. [Fliess] had come to Vienna unobtrusively in July. I met him in the street in conversation with my (deceased) friend P., and went with them to some place where they sat opposite each other as though they were at a small table. I sat in front at its narrow end. Fl. spoke about his sister and said that in three-quarters of an hour she was dead, and added some such words as "that was the threshold". As P. failed to understand him, Fl. turned to me and

asked how much I had told P. about his affairs. Whereupon, overcome by strange emotions, I tried to explain to Fl. that P. (could not understand anything at all, of course, because he) was not alive. But what I actually said—and I myself noticed the mistake—was, "Non vixit". I then gave P. a piercing look. Under my gaze he turned pale; his form grew indistinct and his eyes a sickly blue—and finally he melted away. I was highly delighted at this and I now realized that Ernst Fleischl, too, had been no more than an apparition, a "revenant" ["ghost"—literally, "one who returns"]; *and it seemed to me quite possible that people of that kind only existed as long as one liked and could be got rid of if someone else wished it.* [Freud, 1900a, p. 421]

Due to various well-established circumstances we need not explain here, this dream certainly took place *circa* 30 October 1898, in the midst of significant events.

The anniversary of Jakob Freud's death two years earlier was on 23 October; a few days earlier, on 16 October, there had been a commemoration of Fleischl in the cloisters of the University, and a bust had been erected in his memory. Freud remembered on that occasion not only his great friend and benefactor but also another who helped him: Joseph Paneth. If Paneth had not died prematurely, he thought, he would also have had his monument in these same precincts.

When Freud resigned from the Laboratory in 1882, Paneth took his place. But his promising scientific career was cut short when he died of tuberculosis in 1890, a year before Fleischl.

Another no less important event was Fliess's operation in Berlin at that time. Freud was really worried because the first reports, which reached him through Fliess's parents-in-law, were not very encouraging. Freud had also been offended by the relatives' request that he keep silent about this news, as if they doubted his discretion. However, Freud acknowledged that he had once been indiscreet in reference to Fleischl and another Josef (probably Breuer) and therefore felt troubled by this request.

Rosa, Freud's sister, gave birth on 18 October; at the end of August, Fliess's daughter was born. She was named Pauline, after his sister, who had died young. Freud told him the new Pauline would soon be the reincarnation of the deceased one. (Freud's niece, his brother Emmanuel's daughter, was also called Pauline. His son was John [Hans].)

Freud remembered that the words *"non vixit"* were to be found on the pedestal of the monument to Kaiser Josef. Freud was then erecting a monument to his friend Josef Paneth, whom he killed at the same time with his look in the dream, as he compared him then to Josef the emperor and to the honoured colleague (Fleischl). Freud remembered that Paneth had once shown signs of impatience, awaiting Fleischl's death so as to occupy his place, but his evil wish was not realized, since he died sooner. Here Freud realizes his contradictory feelings towards his friend, summed up in a phrase such as, "Because he was intelligent I honour him; because he was ambitious I killed him." It is similar in structure to what Brutus says after murdering Julius Caesar.

From these elements Freud can make the first interpretation of the dream: he concludes that those who are "revenants" in the dream, Fleischl and Paneth, were his rivals at the Physiology Laboratory, as his nephew John had been his rival in childhood. (As we know, he was Freud's inseparable companion until the age of three, when Emmanuel Freud and his family left Leipzig for Manchester.)

A coincidence, which Freud immediately remembers, lends support to this interpretation. When Freud was 14, Emmanuel had visited Vienna with his family. Sigmund and Hans appeared as Brutus and Caesar in a Schiller play in a children's theatre. Freud says, "Since that time my nephew John has had many reincarnations which revived now one side and now another of his personality, unalterably fixed as it was in my unconscious memory" (1900a, p. 424). Freud asserts categorically that this relationship had a determining influence on all subsequent relations with contemporaries (see ibid., pp. 424–425).

What Freud does not say in his penetrating interpretation, but what Anzieu (1959), Grinstein (1968), Schur (1972), Julia Grinberg de Ekboir (1976) and Blum (1977) do say, is that Freud had a little brother called Julius. This boy was born towards the end of 1857 and died on 15 April 1858, just before Sigmund's second birthday (on 6 May).

From this fact some enigmas in the dream can be cleared up; likewise some of Freud's biographical data, as well as the scope of pre-oedipal reconstructions, which is what interests us here.

It is singular that in the heroic letters of the summer of 1897 (a year before the "Non vixit" dream), when Freud tells Fliess of his discovery of the Oedipus complex, he mentions Julius, John and Pauline; but a year later Julius is forgotten, completely and forever. In Letter 70 of 3 October 1897, Freud remembers his brother and his nephews without naming them as such:

> . . . that later (between the ages of two and two-and-a-half) my libido was stirred up towards *matrem*, namely on the occasion of a journey with her from Leipzig to Vienna, during which we must have spent the night together and I must have had an opportunity of seeing her *nudam*—you drew the conclusion from this long ago for your own son, as a remark of yours revealed to me—; that I greeted my brother (who was a year my junior and died after a few months) with ill-wishes and genuine childish jealousy, and that his death left the germ of self-reproaches in me. I have also long known the companion in my evil deeds between the ages of one and two. It was my nephew a year older than myself, who is now living in Manchester and who visited us in Vienna when I was fourteen. The two of us seem occasionally to have behaved in a cruel fashion to my niece, who was a year younger. This nephew and this younger brother have determined what is neurotic, but also what is intense, in all my friendships. You yourself have seen my travel-anxiety in full swing. [Freud, 1950a (1877–1902), pp. 261–262]

In this letter Freud describes the Oedipus complex for the first time, and he does so on the basis of his own history, linking it to his infantile jealousy and his guilt about hostile feelings for his newborn brother. The one murdered in the dream, then, is not only John, but also Julius, and *"non vixit"* [he did not live] applies more strictly to him rather than to John or anyone else. We can also deduce, as do all the previously mentioned writers, that Fliess, born in 1858, and Paneth, who was born, like Julius, in 1857, represent the brother more than the nephew. Freud attributes his lapse in the dream, when he says *"non vixit"* rather than *"non vivit"* [he is not alive] to his fear of arriving in Berlin and receiving the unwelcome news that Wilhelm (Fliess) is no longer alive. He associates this with his late arrival at the Physiology Institute, when he had to endure the penetrating and reproving gaze of the great Brücke's blue eyes, which annihilated him.

Max Schur points out precisely that the current conflict in the "Non vixit" dream is Fliess' operation and Freud's growing ambivalence towards his friend, and his joy at outliving him and remaining master of the field, in the face of the fantasy of his death, as really happened when Julius died. Schur maintains that Freud pays attention to infantile material in his interpretation not only thanks to his theoretical interests at the time, but also to avoid the present conflict with Fliess. Schur says, "The dream work can operate genetically in two directions—from the present to the past and vice versa" (1972, p. 167).

Following this line of thought, I want to suggest that Freud's *infantile conflict* with John and Pauline serves, in turn, to avoid the *early conflict* with Julius—using these terms in the way proposed at the beginning of this chapter.

On this point I think one of the theses from my Helsinki paper is confirmed: early conflict and infantile conflict appear joined in the same structure, and the latter can be recovered in the transference.

When Harold Blum took up this theme again in an excellent work, "The Prototype of Pre-Oedipal Reconstruction" (1977), he explained Freud's pre-oedipal conflict, from Margaret Mahler's (1967, 1972a, 1972b) perspective, of the phase of *rapprochement*, as in the third subphase of the separation–individuation process, between 18 months and two years of age. Sigmund Freud underwent this phase precisely during the few months of Julius, life. In this way, on the basis of the theoretical instruments of ego psychology, one can explain not only early development but also the transference phenomena that correspond to this period. Freud himself recognized more than once—and does so precisely in his comments on the dream—that all his adult conflicts with his peers were always linked to his nephew John (and, we can add now, to his brother Julius). Blum's work studies in depth the feelings of the child during this difficult stage of development and underlines the crucial importance of the relationship of the child to the mother—and more so in the special case of

Freud, with a mother mourning her child Julius while expecting Anna, who was born in December 1858.

In underlining the demonstrative value of this dream, Blum affirms that the reconstruction of the pre-oedipal states is possible, and he attributes this to Freud's genius. On this point, however, I think Blum attributes to Freud merit that is strictly speaking Melanie Klein's. She was the one who insisted firmly that the Oedipus complex begins much earlier than the classic theory allows, without ever having been heard by its originator. She also dated drastically earlier the beginnings of the superego, indicating the immense guilt feeling of the small child, because of his sadistic attacks on the body of the mother and its contents: babies, penises and faeces. It is really surprising to note that, on the other hand, the discovery of Freud's Oedipus complex by Freud corresponds strictly to Melanie Klein's early Oedipus complex!

If, as I have just said following Schur's line of thought, the reconstruction of infantile development with John and Pauline serves to repress Freud's early development, where the jealousy conflict with Julius (and shortly afterwards with Anna) occupies a principal place, then it can be validly supposed that Freud's theory of the Oedipus complex suffers for these reasons and is therefore somewhat rigid. Were it not for these personal difficulties, it is probable that the creator would not have needed his complicated theory of the *après-coup* to explain the primal scene of the "Wolf Man", at 18 months.

The "Non vixit" dream, finally, supports (surprisingly) Meltzer's (1968) theory on the terror produced in psychic reality by dead babies who reappear as *revenants*—as phantoms.

CHAPTER TWENTY-NINE

Metapsychology of interpretation

In accordance with the most classic definition, interpretation is the instrument that makes the unconscious conscious, which also corresponds to the theory of the cure. Although in principle we prefer to define interpretation without basing ourselves on the theory of the unconscious—so as to suit all the major schools of psychotherapy—we do not doubt for an instant that the spare Freudian formula is unobjectionable.

Interpretation seeks to make conscious the unconscious. But in accepting this formula we face the problem of seeing in what sense we use the word "unconscious". It has diverse meanings, which find echoes in metapsychology, and metapsychological points of view broaden it.

29.1 Interpretation from the topographic and dynamic points of view

Cathartic therapy, which sought to broaden consciousness via hypnotic sleep, carries as a basic sign the topographical point of view of what would later become metapsychology, although Breuer and Freud noted from the beginning that the discharge of affect (that is, the economical aspect) was fundamental in achieving the results sought.

In abandoning the cathartic method, and through discovery of the *dynamic* conflict of unconscious forces, Freud was able to understand that the topographical passage from one system to another is not sufficient to obtain results. Therefore the dynamic point of view that accounts for the action of resistance appeared. This fundamental step is made explicit by Freud in "On Beginning the Treatment" (1913c). He remembers there that in the early period of analytic technique a mental, intellectualist attitude had guided him, making him believe that it was very important for the patient to regain knowledge of what he had forgotten through repression. The results obtained in this way were completely discouraging. Thus, in transmitting to the patient information about infantile traumas obtained by the anamnesis of relatives, the situation did not change, and the patient behaved as if he were not aware of anything new. Freud relates the case of a hysterical girl whose mother revealed to him a homosexual experience— a certain determining factor in the patient's attacks (1913c, p. 141). The mother had herself surprised the girl in the act, which occurred when she was approaching puberty, but which she had completely forgotten. When Freud repeated the mother's account to the girl, what he obtained was not her recollection but a renewed hysterical attack, to the point of an amentia (Meynert) with a complete loss of memory. And Freud adds here, "After this, there was no choice but to cease attributing to the fact of knowing, in itself, the importance that had previously been given to it and to place the emphasis on the resistances which had in the past brought about the state of not knowing and which were still ready to defend that state. Conscious knowledge, even if it was not subsequently driven out again, was powerless against those resistances" (ibid., p. 142).

In the technical writings Freud insists that the treatment should obtain the expression of what is repressed, through overcoming the resistance. He indicates repeatedly that analysis should always begin from the psychic surface. Thus, for example, in "The Handling of Dream-Interpretation in Psycho-Analysis" (1911e), he says that the interpretation of dreams must be subordinated to the general standards of the method, because "it is of the greatest importance for the treatment that the analyst should always be aware of the surface of the patient's mind at any given moment, that he should know what complexes and resistances are active in him at the time and what conscious reaction to them will govern his behaviour." He says immediately afterwards: "It is scarcely ever right to sacrifice this therapeutic aim to an interest in dream-interpretation" (ibid., p. 92).

29.2 The economic point of view

In the second half of the 1920s Wilhelm Reich, in his Seminar on Psychoanalytic Technique in Vienna, began a revision that was soon to result in significant changes. This great opening was effected with the key of the energetic factor—that is, the economic point of view, one branch of the tripartite system of the 1915 metapsychology.

Reich's investigation is undoubtedly based on the numerous important works on psychoanalytic characterology that had appeared by then, by Abraham, Jones and Ferenczi—in particular Abraham's work "A Particular Form of Neurotic Resistance Against the Psychoanalytic Method" (1919a). (We will return to this work in dealing with the negative therapeutic reaction.) I agree with Robert Fliess (1948) who, in presenting Reich's works and recalling Reich's contributions to psychoanalytic characterology, emphasizes that the premises on which Reich based his character analysis are contained in the 1919 work quoted above (Fliess, 1948, pp. 104–105).

Abraham says that there are patients who will not comply with the fundamental rules nor with other rules of the setting—to the point where they seem not to understand that they have come for treatment, to be cured. This recalcitrance becomes the lever of access to these cases, where marked characterological traits linked to rebellion, envy and omnipotence are discovered. These are patients with a permanent attitude of disobedience and provocation, although at times their resistance hides behind an appearance of good will. They are particularly sensitive to injury to their pride—that is, they are narcissists. This leads them to identify with the analyst on the one hand, and to desire to surpass him on the other, with which they lose sight of the objective of the treatment. In their eager rivalry they often use, among other tactics, a self-analysis that has a clear content of masturbatory rebellion. Abraham ends his work by indicating that the pretended compliance with which these patients hide their resistance makes access to them difficult.

29.3 Latent negative transference

In June 1926, at the Seminar in Vienna, Reich presented the first of a series of seminal works. "Zur Technik der Deutung und der Widerstandsanalyse" ["On the Technique of Interpretation and the Analysis of Resistance"] appeared in the *Internationale Zeitschrift für Psychoanalyse* the following year and forms the third chapter of *Character Analysis* (1933). Reich begins by remembering the difficulties encountered at the beginning of an analysis and indicates that often the negative transference hidden behind conventional positive attitudes is ignored. As a result, almost invariably a chaotic situation is arrived at, where the patient offers material from different strata and ends up going in a vicious circle. (Let us remember that Abraham had insisted on the mask of compliance of the patients he describes.)

The *latent negative transference* is the key to this paper by Reich. It appears frequently and is often ignored. Reich asserts that the negative transference, latent or manifest, is usually not analysed.

Another point of view Reich introduces in this article is that in the beginning deep interpretations—particularly the symbolic ones—should be avoided; he even says that at times it is necessary to suppress deep material that appears too soon.

Latent negative transference requires us to pay maximum attention to the *first transference resistance*. It is at times directly observable when the patient asserts he does not know what to say, as Freud indicated in "On

Beginning the Treatment" (1913c, p. 137). At other times it does not appear manifestly but can be detected in the *manner* in which the patient develops his relation to the analyst.

For real, not neurotic, reasons it is logical for the patient to be mistrustful at first and to find surrender to the analytic task difficult. This attitude, which is rational up to a point, becomes resistance when the treatment begins to disturb the neurotic equilibrium.

An attitude of trust and cooperation at the beginning of an analysis, Reich concludes sceptically, is necessarily conventional. Once we begin to doubt it, our vision of the initial period changes, and the transference resistance becomes clear. (We can think of Freud's attitude in the analysis of "Dora", for example.)

Therefore the first transference resistance constitutes a key, for Reich, since it arises from a real, rational conflict, the natural mistrust of a stranger. It entails the deep conflicts this mistrust is nourished by, in that the analyst is defined as a person who is there to disturb the neurotic equilibrium.

It can be said, then, that the first transference resistance always assumes a character of negative transference (mistrust). Since this negative transference is not usually externalized, is not manifest, Reich says that the first transference resistance configures a *latent negative transference*. On the basis of it there is access to the characterological structure, because it is not given in the contents. In fact, were it manifest in the contents, it would no longer be latent, but patent. It is expressed either as an attitude of obedience and of insincere, pleasant and trusting cooperation, or in a formal and courteous attitude, both of which stick in one's gullet and correspond to the hysterical and the obsessive character, respectively. These two attitudes, and others that may present themselves, are always accompanied by something that reveals them for what they are, and this is a lack of affect, a lack of authenticity.

In this way, Reich describes and discovers the analysand's resistances that are not expressed directly and immediately, those covered up by an attitude of conventional cooperation, behind which stalks the feared latent negative transference. In excessively affable, obedient and trusting patients (who pass for good patients), and in the conventional and correct ones and those who present an emotional block or depersonalization, we can assume there is a latent negative transference.

To discover the first transference resistance, Reich looks at the patient's *behaviour*, and this can soon lead him to a general theory of character.

In analysing these forms of latent negative transference, Reich finds that they are really very complicated. Each of these defences has diverse strata, and it is precisely the systematic analysis of the resistance that allows an ordered access to these strata, with which a chaotic situation is avoided. We should not forget that it is precisely the chaotic situation that leads to Reich's reflection—a concrete and ominous fact of the practice of his time (and, at times, of ours). If we do not respect the stratification of the defence, we are going to produce something like a cataclysm; we are going to have a zone of fractures, of faults, to speak in geological terms.

In this way, Reich changes in this work the concept of the *psychic surface*, since for him it not only comprises the *contents* nearest to consciousness, but also the *way* these contents are offered.

Reich proposes strict rules for interpretation, so as not to ignore the latent negative transference. To begin with, one must always start from an analysis of the resistance, and particularly of transference resistance. Furthermore, in the interpretative task one must have tactics, which should be ordered, systematic and consequent.

Interpretation should be *ordered* because it should not skip strata or jump stages. It should not only begin with the psychic surface, as Freud said so often; it should also attend to the strata that become organized in accordance with the evolution of the neurosis. If in a hysterical patient there appears first an attitude of seduction towards the father in order to repress homosexuality vis-à-vis the mother (as Dora did), it would be an error to interpret the latter before the former. Reich calls this an ordered interpretation of the material.

It is not sufficient to order interpretation: it is also necessary to be *systematic*, to persist in ordering. For Reich, to be systematic means not leaving a stratum before having resolved it.

Finally, Reich considers that the interpretative task should be *consequent* in that we should return to the starting-point with each difficulty and not skip stages. What Reich means is that, in general, when the patient faces a new conflict, he avails himself of his old defensive techniques, and the analyst should refer to these in the first instance. Naturally if one proceeds consequently, the duration of the analysis of the resistance will be shorter on that occasion. But what matters to Reich is that only on this path will we arrive at the conflict we really wish to reach.

29.4 Characterological resistance

At the Tenth International Congress in 1927, in the beautiful town of Innsbruck, Reich presented a new work, "Über Charakter Analyse" ["On the Technique of Character Analysis,]. It was published in the *Internationale Zeitschrift für Psychoanalyse* the following year and constitutes the fourth chapter of his book, *Character Analysis* (1933).

In this article Reich presents a lucid development of the metapsychology of interpretation. He indicates the importance of the topographical point of view, with its unconscious, preconscious and conscious strata. Then he discusses the dynamic point of view, which consists in analysing first the resistance, in order to arrive then at the content. Lastly, he deals with the economical point of view, which is the centre of his reflection. The economical point of view can be defined, in principle, as the order in which the resistance should be analysed. (As I try to show further on,

Reich does not omit the structural point of view, which is proper to the structural theory.)

Reich's point of departure is that the analysand is not accessible at the outset and, in effect, does *not* fulfil the fundamental rule. That is, what Abraham had observed in particular (evident) cases, Reich considers, rightly, to be present in *all* cases to a greater or lesser extent.

There are two methods of helping the patient to fulfil the fundamental rule: the *pedagogic* rule of teaching him what free association is and stimulating him so he will practice it, and the *analytic* method, which consists in interpreting the nonfulfilment of the fundamental rule as if it were a symptom (which it is). If the second method is applied—the one Reich proposes, and which Abraham had suggested ten years earlier—one unexpectedly has access to the analysis of character. This is because the fulfilment of the fundamental rule has to do with character—something that Abraham emphasizes clearly in the work already quoted, and also Freud, to some extent, at the Vienna Medical College Conference of 1904. (It is worth mentioning here that the alternative between analytic or pedagogic methods in the realization of the analytic task, which Reich brought up at the Innsbruck Congress, had been discussed in similar terms, albeit with greater passion, by Melanie Klein, at the Symposium on Child Analysis on 4 and 18 May that same year (*International Journal of Psycho-Analysis, 8,* 1927.)

Different from a symptom, a character trait is syntonic, by reason of its being strongly rationalized, and it serves to link floating anxiety with what Reich calls *charactero-muscular armour*, the expression of narcissistic defence.

Reich holds that it is at the level of characterological structures that the conflicts are congealed, and here the term "congealed" vividly expresses the economical factor. This is because the energy of the conflict has remained linked to the character structure, and our principal task will then be to liberate it. While we are not able to mobilize that energy, things will continue as before, however much the patient acquires knowledge (from the topographical point of view) and grasps the conflict (from the dynamic point of view), since he will lack the motor for the change, and the libidinous impulses will remain absorbed in the character structure.

So what had, until then, been for Reich the study of resistance and its strata now becomes transformed into a richer, more complex situation—the analysis of character. It can be concluded, then, that the difficulty in associating freely expresses the character structure clearly: what had been called the ordered, systematic and consequent analysis of the defensive stratification is now called character analysis. From that moment, Reich distinguishes two types of resistances—ordinary or common resistances and resistances that operate continuously and in the face of *all* conflict, which are the characterological resistances.

One must take account of the fact that by this time, some writers such as Glover and Alexander (supported by Freud's "Some Character-Types

met with in Psycho-Analytic Work"—1916d), had distinguished two types
of neurosis, *symptomatic* and *asymptomatic* or *characterological*.

Reich would now rightly say that character neurosis is *prior* to symptomatic neurosis and that the symptom is only an efflorescence of the character structure; it is always based on the character. What difference is
there, then, between analysing a symptom and a character trait? In other
words, what distinguishes an ordinary type of resistance and a characterological resistance? The fundamental difference, according to Reich, is that
the character trait has a much more complex structure. Originally it was a
symptom incorporated later into the character structure through identifications in the ego and through processes of rationalization that make it
syntonic. This process, which leads from the symptom to the character
trait, implies a greater complexity in the structure of the psychic apparatus. If the symptom is always multidetermined, the character trait will be
more so.

This is the economical focus that Reich offers, to complement the other
two levels at which a process should become conscious. Only if these three
factors are dealt with can interpretation be an efficient weapon in promoting the structural changes analysis aims for.

29.5   Reich's theoretical assumptions

The principal thesis of Reichian interpretative technique is based on two
theoretical supports—libidinous stasis and the theory of character. The
concept of libidinous stasis belongs entirely to the theory of the libido in
terms of an evolutionary process that should lead, through its well-known
stages, to genital primacy, where pregenital sexuality is finally subordinate
to the attainment of orgasm. Reich's theory of character maintains that
each character trait is heir to a conflict situation in childhood. The outcome
of infantile neurosis is the constitution of a phobia during the stage of the
Oedipus complex, and, from there, the ego tries to transform that phobia
into egosyntonic traits that configure the character. This theory of character implies that the symptoms of neurosis in the adult are a consequence of
the neurotic character and appear when the characterological armour begins to crack. On the basis of the work of Glover (1926) and Alexander
(1923, 1927), Reich maintains that symptomatic neurosis is simply a character neurosis that has produced symptoms.

The analysis of character requires, therefore, greater skill and persistence than the analysis of symptoms. The objective is to isolate the character trait so that it becomes ego-dystonic, and for this it is necessary to link
it in all possible ways with the patient's material and with his infantile
history.

The aggregate of character traits forms, for Reich, the *character armour*
(or charactero-muscular armour), which operates as the main defence in
the analysis. This armour has a definite economical function, since it

serves to dominate both external stimuli and internal or instinctive stimuli. Freud demonstrated that symptoms bind free-floating anxiety. Reich applies the same concept to the character trait, which is ultimately a symptom. The charactero-muscular armour establishes a certain equilibrium, which the subject maintains for narcissistic reasons, and from which the transference resistance derives.

Given the persistence and complexity of the characterological resistance, Reich always insists on the importance of order in interpreting and on how to select the material, centring the task on the multiple transference meanings of the character resistances. While characterological resistances persist, deep interpretations should be carefully avoided. From this point of view, what Reich calls selection of the material could be understood as increased attention to the conflict in the transference—i.e., transference resistance.

29.6 Shortcomings of the Reichian technique

The attitude with which Reich analyses the character trait is strictly analytical. Shorn of any attempt to educate or direct the patient, it tries to reach the infantile roots of the character trait on the basis of its meaning in the current conflict. However, the strict division between interpretations of form (character) and of content gives rise to serious theoretical and technical difficulties. Reich even says that, if "deep" material insists on appearing, it will be correct to direct the patient's attention elsewhere. Here is where, in my view, he departs from the sane analytic method he himself has so intelligently defended.

The shortcomings in Reich's technique also appear, more clearly, in his way of attacking the characterological defences that crystallized in the narcissistic or charactero-muscular armour. Thus for example, vis-à-vis a patient with a pronounced emotional block, Reich confronts him continually, for months, with that character trait, until the patient begins to feel annoyed, and then Reich believes that the situation begins to change. The aggression of the patient, however, is linked more to a device of the technique than to a modification of the resistance. Reich recognizes this without realizing it when he says that consistent analysis of the resistance always provokes a negative attitude towards the analyst. There is also something manufactured in the patient's narcissistic indignation in the face of the persistent interpretation of his way of speaking, his affected or mannered language, the use of technical terms to hide his inferiority feelings vis-à-vis the analyst, and so forth. Now we know with certainty that attitudes such as these, always linked to situations of profound conflict, cannot be resolved except by interpretations that reach that level.

Although I believe the above objections to Reich as to the artifice in his procedure to be well founded, they do not lessen his merit in having broadened the reach of interpretation, on the basis of a consistent and enduring metapsychological theory. Thus at the same time he reveals as non-analytic the technique that utilizes suggestion—which is always an aspect of positive transference—to overcome resistances. I think that on this point Reich corrects and also betters Freud.

29.7   The use of positive transference to overcome resistance

Reich's work acquires its greatest significance, as we have seen, when it denounces the use of positive transference to overcome resistance.

In "The Economical Point of View of Analytic Therapy", chapter 2 of *Character Analysis* (1933), Reich offers a very clear vision of his technique, which he considers a logical development to the Freudian method of analysing resistance. What Reich adds is the analysis of character as resistance, which implies going from the analysis of symptoms to the analysis of the total personality.

The economical point of view Reich proposes implies incorporating into the technique the quantitative factor, the amount of libido that should be discharged. This factor has to do with the libidinous economy and the concept of *orgiastic impotence*, which eliminates in the final instance the actual neurosis (or the neurosis of stasis) as the somatic nucleus of the psychoneurosis.

Reich asserts that this objective cannot be reached through education, "synthesis" or suggestion, but exclusively by resolving the sexual inhibitions linked to character.

At the end of the chapter Reich discusses the points at which he disagrees with Nunberg, whose book, *Principles of Psychoanalysis*, was published a year earlier, in 1932. Although Reich shares with Nunberg the idea that the changes promoted by analysis should be explained in terms of the structural theory, he differs radically as to the analyst's activity and in the use of the positive transference to achieve these changes.

Nunberg's position is expounded in chapter 12 of his book, which deals with the theoretical principles of analytical therapy. The analyst should mobilize the positive transference against the resistances. This is something Freud always pointed out, and therefore I think Reich challenges not only Nunberg but also the creator of psychoanalysis. Reich has greater merit than he himself supposes.

To mobilize resistances, Nunberg considers that the analyst should infiltrate the patient's ego and destroy them from that position, thus achieving, finally, a reconciliation between the id and the ego.

Reich criticizes this viewpoint, rightly pointing out that at the beginning of treatment there never exists an authentic positive transference. On the contrary, it is only through the analysis of the negative transference and the narcissistic defences that a real positive transference can be reached. The relation Nunberg conceives, and which he compares to that of the hypnotized and the hypnotizer, only creates an artificial positive transference, fictitious and dangerous for the course of analysis. Reich affirms that when this type of hypnoid transference is established, what must be done is to unmask it as a resistance and eliminate it as quickly as possible.

The course of the cure Nunberg describes shows up to what point he believes that the solution of the conflict is achieved through a reinforcement of the positive transference—which is also, let us add, narcissistic. Nunberg says that as work progresses, the internal conflict is transformed into a transference conflict, and the patient adopts a passive attitude, leaving the analyst with the whole burden of the analysis. Thus the culminating point is reached, because the analysis is in danger of failing, and the analyst begins to lose interest in the case. It is to recover the analyst's love that the patient again takes active part in the analytic work. In total agreement with Reich and in the light of current knowledge, I do not hesitate to affirm that Nunberg's theory of cure is based on an erroneous evaluation of the transference/countertransference conflict, which leaves intact the psychotic aspects of the personality.

29.8 Fenichel's contributions

In an article in the *Internationale Zeitschrift für Psychoanalyse* in 1935, Fenichel published a critique of Reich's contributions on the basis of a commentary on Kaiser's work published in the same journal a year earlier.

Fenichel expresses in this article, as also six years later in his book on technique, his agreements and disagreements with Reich, but more the former than the latter.

It is necessary to point out that from the outset Fenichel declares himself in favour of the existence of a theory of psychoanalytic technique and opposed to Reik's concepts (1924, 1933). As we know, Reik opposes any type of systematization of the technique, stressing the value of intuition and surprise.

Fenichel, therefore, favours Reich, maintaining that Reik confuses the irrational nature of the unconscious with the technique for getting to know it. If the analyst can operate only with his intuition, which is by definition irrational, then his technique can be no more than an art—never a science.

Fenichel considers that Reich's merit has been to warn us against this merely intuitive attitude, basing himself on metapsychological and especially economical principles. From the dynamic point of view Fenichel thinks, as does Reich, that interpretation always begins with what is on the psychic surface: the defensive attitudes of the ego are always more superficial than the instinctive impulses of the id. (Fenichel criticizes, in passing, Melanie Klein's, 1932, technique, which attempts a direct contact with the unconscious.) On this is based the Freudian formula that interpretation of the resistance has to precede interpretation of the content—that is, the dynamic–structural viewpoint. Fenichel agrees with Reich on the characterological resistances and the economical viewpoint. He concludes that Reich's principles in no way depart from the Freudian postulates. But he also acknowledges their originality and innovativeness, in that they are more systematic and consistent than the rules and more general than those proposed by the master.

Fenichel also expresses his theoretical and technical differences with Reich. Firstly, he disagrees with the idea of stratification of the material, which seems somewhat schematic to him because it does not attend to detail. The material is ordered only in a relative way. The chaotic situation is not always the product of an inconsistent and erratic technique: there are also *spontaneous* chaotic situations, simply because the psychological strata have been broken. (Many years later, Bion, 1957, would give theoretical support to this opinion in studying the psychotic part of the personality and the attack on the thinking apparatus.) Fenichel expresses his disagreement by taking up again the geological model of strata. We all know without being geologists that the earth's crust has been structured by sediments deposited in layers. We also know that at times that disposition is altered by tectonic movements, cataclysms that shake the structure. So Reich's confidence in the certain appearance, one by one, of layers of the personality that became organized during development is too optimistic. A later event, a trauma, can modify the strata. Reich could answer, for his part, that these cataclysms could not be studied other than on the basis of what remained, and the psychoanalyst, no less than the geologist, will have to find the destroyed sedimentary strata in the midst of the tectonic disturbances.

Fenichel also criticizes the excessive selection of the material Reich proposes, if for no other reason than that subsequent material could show that what has been left out was in the end the most pertinent. (These problems, unresolved through Reich's technique, are those that Klein also tries to attack with her ideas on the point of urgency and deep interpretation—see chapter 31.)

If dreams can lead us to interpretations of content, neglecting the characterological defence, it is better to ignore them. Fenichel replies that there are, in effect, situations where interpretation of the content is counterindicated because the very act of interpreting the dream has a special significance for the patient. But if this is not the case, nothing can help the patient's understanding more—even of his character defences—than the attentive and careful study of his dreams.

Fenichel disagrees on two other points in the technique of character analysis. First, he questions the amount of the attack on character armour, which can often be very violent. Consistent interpretation of character traits wounds the patient's narcissism more than any other technical measure. We agree here with Fenichel and have already pointed out that this attitude is an artefact of Reichian technique. The management of the character armour is aggressive, and the words Reich uses—attack, dissolution, liquidation, and so forth—are in themselves significant.

Fenichel's other objection goes to the heart of Reich's method, when he affirms that the analysis of the character armour can transform itself, in turn, into a resistance. This depends on the way the patient experiences it. For example, if the patient feels the analyst is trying to break his narcissistic organization in very concrete terms, a perverse anal–sadistic fantasy can be configured in the transference. I remember an anecdote from my own analysis with Racker when I demanded [sic] that he interpret my character resistances. Racker interpreted, of course, my desire to control him omnipotently and to put myself in his place, identified with Reich. Fenichel also gives some examples in which the analysis of the characterological defence is included in the defensive manoeuvres of the analysand, who tries to control the analyst and even induce in him perverse or psychopathic attitudes.

A singular and extreme development of character analysis is found in Kaiser's (1934) study, which Fenichel discusses in the above-mentioned work. Kaiser's reasoning is logical and simple (and also simplistic). The work of the analyst is to remove resistances; therefore, we should do nothing other than interpret resistances. If the interpretation of resistances is correct, then what is repressed will appear spontaneously, without our having to evoke it—that is, to call it up and designate it. If this does not happen, it is because the interpretation has failed, and it needs to be completed or corrected. Without denying that in particular circumstances an interpretation of content can also eliminate repressions, Kaiser feels that from the theoretical point of view this can only be explained by a side effect, in that an interpretation of this type can direct the patient's attention to his resistances and can correct them. Kaiser does not accept, in fact, that an anticipatory idea can be operative in the sense Freud meant—that is, that it is similar to the indication the histology professor gives to the student who is about to examine the preparation under the microscope. A repressed impulse, Kaiser objects, is not in the preconscious system, and therefore no indication can help the subject in the search for something not located in a space accessible to him.

This extreme idea supposes that the unconscious system is impermeable and that we do not in any way have access to the impulse: the only thing we can do is to allow it to appear when the dynamic conditions permit it. Fenichel rejects this argument, indicating that interpretations of content designate not the unconscious impulse, but its preconscious derivative. Freud (1915e) taught us that the unconscious impulse produces substitute formations using the preconscious ideas with which it associates, to emerge thus into consciousness. The defence of the ego operates against the *derivatives* (offspring) of what is repressed. The fate of the derivatives varies according to the dynamic–economic interplay of force at each moment. At times they will reach consciousness; at others they will again be repressed. This is why Fenichel says that analytic treatment can be described as an education of the ego to enable it to tolerate derivatives that are less and less distorted. Fenichel concludes that it is not a question of never interpreting the unconscious, because we cannot even do that. Those in favour of interpreting the contents, Freud among them, attempt to reach, not the repressed instincts but their preconscious derivatives.

Through his interpretative work the analyst shows the patient his ego's errors of perception and judgement of reality, so that the ego divides into an observing part and an experiencing part, which the former begins to consider as irrational. In this way a change is produced in the dynamic of the defence, as Sterba (1929, 1934) has described it.

Fenichel's most important contribution to the theory of technique is, perhaps, to operate with the concept of derivative and not simply of content. The introduction of this concept is of great value, since it contributes to clarifying the difference between primary repression and secondary repression or repression proper. In primary repression [*Verdrängung, Urverdrängung*], the ideational representation of the instinct cannot enter consciousness because of the anticathexis; in secondary repression [*Nachdrängung, Nachverdrängung*], the ego operates by anticathexis and by subtraction.

29.9   Character and the theory of the libido

Reich's works eventually demonstrated the value in Adler's ideas in *The Neurotic Constitution* (1912) as well as their limitations, in that Adler sets the theory of the libido against the theory of character. Following the studies of Freud and his first disciples on this point, Reich confirms that the character is a homeostatic and teleological structure as Adler conceived it, but not, as a result, independent of instinct. On the contrary, it is on the basis of the control of instinct that the character organizes itself. It is finalist, as Adler said, but is constituted on the bases dictated to it by instinct, and this is what Adler could never accept.

In the Adlerian system interpretation always has the objective of discovering the fictitious final goal and undoing the "arrangements" that lead to neurosis, while interpretation in psychoanalysis can be finalistic (teleological) when it discovers the homeostatic devices at the level of character, but in directing itself to the impulses it can never cease to be causal. (We referred more definitively to this theme in chapter 26, when we developed Bernfeld's, 1932, ideas on the final interpretation.)

CHAPTER THIRTY

Interpretation and the ego

30.1 Psychoanalytic technique in crisis

In chapter 29 we studied Reich's works in some detail, culminating with the appearance of *Character Analysis* in 1933. We return to them now, in order to understand them as a response to the debate in which the practice of psychoanalysis found itself embroiled during the 1920s. The crisis reached the two great cities of the time, Vienna and London, since Berlin was no longer in a leadership position after the death of Abraham in 1925. In this chapter we are going to refer to Vienna, leaving the contributions of the British Psycho-Analytical Society for chapter 31.

From 1920 onwards, analysts began to encounter difficulties. They felt that the principles laid down in the technical writings of the second decade were not sufficient, and they sought something new. Among the people in Freud's entourage before Hitler's dark ascent, and long before the diaspora precipitated by the Nazi occupation, a theoretical diaspora had occurred, and two avenues opened up. Some believed that the crisis facing psychoanalytic technique could be resolved only by reviewing its postulates, creating new theoretical supports and, from them, other psychotherapeutic instruments. This was clearly expressed in the group formed in 1934 by Erich Fromm, Harry Stack Sullivan and Karen Horney, who founded neo-psychoanalysis or culturalist psychoanalysis, and also in the development of Ludwig Binswanger's thought. He created existential analysis during that period. On the other hand, those who considered as valid the basic doctrine of psychoanalysis—that is, in the final instance, the

Oedipus complex and the theory of the libido—maintained that to give an account of the problems, it was necessary only to review the principles of the technique; it was technique itself that had to be perfected.

During the 1920s, perhaps the best expression of that moment of crisis was the famous book by Ferenczi and Rank, *The Development of Psycho-analysis*, which appeared in 1923 and was translated into English in 1925. Ferenczi and Rank favoured a technique that would facilitate the expression of affect. At that moment the alternative was between remembering or repeating in the transference, following Freud's essay on the theme. The book, which aroused controversy and made Abraham and Jones suspicious, was an attempt to ensure a more lively development of the analytic process on the basis of instruments that existed at the time.

30.2   Wilhelm Reich's response

When Reich supported the analysis of resistance as preceding the analysis of contents, he was only reaffirming the Freudian postulate that one must always begin with the psychic surface. But on two issues he went further than Freud. First, he emphasized character structure. What was for Freud in his technical writings psychic surface (and later the ego) is character for Reich: not only the ego, but the *operative forms* of the ego that configure character. In *The Neurotic Constitution* (1912), Alfred Adler had made use of character to set aside the libido theory and propose a teleological psychology. Now character was reintegrated in psychoanalytic theory thanks mainly to Reich, without rejecting in any way the causal, instinctual explanation, the theory of the libido.

This is a fundamental element, which is not found formally in Freud, nor even in Ferenczi, Abraham and Jones, who constructed a theory of character but not a theory of character *defences*, as did Reich.

The other element is the systematization of the technique. Reich introduced the idea that technique is not sufficient; it is necessary to have a strategy. This idea derives from the other one because, just as I have been evolving a defensive strategy that crystallizes in a character trait, my analyst has to provide himself with a counterposed strategy.

From his first works in the Vienna seminar, Reich favoured not only an ordered interpretation (the defences before the contents, following Freud's advice), but also a systematic and consequential treatment of the defences (his own contribution).

30.3   In favour of intuition and surprise

If we leave aside those who followed the new paths of culturalism and existential analysis (which are in fact different from psychoanalysis and its technique, which is the material of our study), we find that the other response was given by Theodore Reik. He favoured a non-systematic technique that could be led by intuition.

Reik's principal ideas are found in the paper he presented at the Wiesbaden Congress of 1932 and published in the *International Journal of Psycho-Analysis* the following year. Reik considered it his first technical work after twenty years of practice.

Reik begins by saying that "the essence of the analytic process consists in the series of shocks experienced as the subject takes cognizance of his repressed processes, the effect of which makes itself felt for long afterwards" (1933, p. 322). After emphasizing that to become conscious is an exquisitely experiential phenomenon, he affirms that this shock, specific to psychoanalysis, is the element of *surprise*. For Reik, surprise consists in the encounter, at an unexpected moment or in an unexpected way, with an event or fact whose expectation has become unconscious (ibid.). Surprise is always the expression of our struggle against something that presents itself (to us), and which we knew, but only unconsciously. Regarding analytic experience specifically, the struggle is against the recognition of a part of the ego that we once knew but which is now unconscious. Reik says the most effective insight is one that contains this element of surprise. The metapsychology of interpretation rests on this fundamental fact.

The analyst's reconstruction or interpretation operate not only from the *topographical* point of view, making conscious what is unconscious. There is also an energetic displacement, such as the one Freud studied in the joke (1905c), which has to do with the *economical* aspect. Lastly, there is a *dynamic* effect, in that insight allows the analysand to see how what was repressed corresponds to the material reality of the moment, when the analyst puts into words what had been repressed.

The surprise with which the analysand receives a true interpretation has something magical about it: the analysand sees that what has been expected appears, in effect. Similarly, we are surprised when, after having thought about a friend we have not seen for a long time, we see him in the street. The interpretation produces surprise in this way—it is a specific message that brings something very familiar to the patient's consciousness. He feels the interpretation is a counterpart of something he had thought, although not consciously.

If interpretation operates in this way, the conclusion is that any attempt to systematize the technique is destined to fail. Even more, this is theoretically impossible and radically anti-analytic. Free association is, in fact, meant to create the conditions in which the analyst promotes that moment of surprise with his interpretation—a moment when the analysand recognizes something with which he had always been in contact but which had never appeared to him, and which now reaches him from the outside through the analyst's words.

In this famous article, Theodore Reik maintained that psychoanalytic interpretation had a great deal to do with the technique of the joke. Here, on the basis of a manifest content, there is a structural regression to the primary process which deals with the material through mechanisms of condensation and displacement, so as to emerge again, but differently. This process relies on an economy of psychic expenditure of energy, which produces a libidinal discharge. Similarly, psychoanalytic technique attempts to gather the patient's material, allowing it to become internalized by us and then to appear anew as an interpretation. When we communicate it to the patient, we give him a vision of himself that perforce surprises him.

Reik says, moreover, that the analyst should allow himself to be overtaken by surprise, because he will be able to work truly only through the surprise with which he receives, in his own consciousness, the process of elaboration that has taken place in his unconscious. Obviously Reik warns against any systematization of the technique.

There is no doubt that with his intelligent and impassioned defence of the analyst's intuition, Reik rightly opposed any *a priori* systematization of the material, any attempt (frequent at the time) to intellectualize, to resolve problems through purely rational means. I believe Freud contributed to this, with his anticipatory ideas [*Erwartungsvorstellungen*] .

Reik's justifiable warnings, however, do not necessarily imply that the analyst cannot give particular problems priority, which, in fact, Reich wanted to do. From the perspective of fifty years on, Reik's postulates do not seem to me irreconcilable with those of his opponent.

At the margins of the polemics in Vienna between Reik and Reich, Melanie Klein in London was developing her play technique, which would lead her to new proposals on interpretation and transference, which we will discuss further on.

30.4   *Anna Freud's ideas*

Anna Freud was already a mature analyst and a penetrating investigator in 1936, when she published *The Ego and the Mechanisms of Defence*. She had learned much from her father and her patients, and also, I believe, from her Viennese colleagues, Reich, Sterba and Fenichel among them, and from her polemics with Melanie Klein during the previous decade.

Fenichel's work (1935), which supports and criticizes Reich, as we have seen, is the most immediate antecedent to the new contributions Anna Freud would make.

Her book is, of course, heir to those works of the 1920s in which Freud distinguishes the ego as a psychic instance. As we know, the concept is outlined in *Beyond the Pleasure Principle* (1920g) and acquires its structural outline in *The Ego and the Id* (1923b) three years later. Another three years later Freud again takes up this theme, in *Inhibitions, Symptoms and Anxiety* (1926d), showing us that the ego is at times both patient and agent of anxiety. It suffers traumatic anxiety and uses anxiety as a signal.

We should mention here that, for Lacan and his school, the ego is more passive than "he" thinks, that its activity is a *mirage*, as are its adaptation and perception of reality. This point is dealt with outstandingly in the lucid studies of Guillermo A. Maci (*La otra escena de lo real*, 1979, a clear and rigorous book.)

The Ego and the Mechanisms of Defence (A. Freud, 1936) defines the analyst's task (and therefore the praxis of interpretation) strictly in terms of the structural theory.

Anna Freud's basic interest is in the ego, its functioning, and its way of operating in the face of anxiety. Following the scheme of the three types of servitude of the ego in the last chapter of *The Ego and the Id* (S. Freud, 1923b), Anna Freud distinguishes three types of anxiety: *neurotic* (instinctive), *real* (objective) and *guilt feeling* (in the face of the superego). Real anxiety is objective in that it refers to the world of objects, to reality, with its dangers and inevitable frustrations. The others, on the other hand, are subjective. However, it is obvious, and Anna Freud says it, that there is also a dialectical relation between subjective and objective anxiety, even if only because the anxieties that are now subjective were once objective at a given moment of development. That is, anxiety in the face of instinct has a history, because at some moment in infancy the instinct met with a real repression. There was a moment where this impulse caused an external anxiety, which later became internalized and transformed into neurotic, subjective anxiety.

Anna Freud's book, in my opinion, undoubtedly gathers up Reich's ideas, but it introduces a substantial modification. She does not think the analysis of resistance should be given priority, nor should it be systematic. Rather, she postulates that analysis should oscillate, like a pendulum, between the resistance (ego) and the instinct (id). The analyst's task, then, consists basically in this equilibrium between the analysis of the ego and the analysis of the id. In this way, Anna Freud's technique introduces an important change. The analyst should attend more to the material that appears than to his ideas of how to manage and order it. In general, what arises from the material is first a fraction of the ego (the defence), and when it is interpreted, a portion of the id—the instinct—precisely the instinct that the defence prevented from surfacing.

To conclude, Anna Freud's technique is freer and more versatile than Reich's and attends better to the natural development of the analytic process.

30.5 *Intrasystemic conflict and intersystemic conflict*

Anna Freud's book is followed by Hartmann's famous monograph, *Ego Psychology and the Problem of Adaptation* (1939). Hartmann's work centres on the structure and the functioning of the ego. His scientific credo is adaptation, and his objective is the development of a psychoanalytic psychology. Hartmann distinguishes two different parts in the ego: one that has to do with the conflict (and consequently with the defence mechanisms) and another which constitutes the *conflict-free ego sphere*.

On these bases, Hartmann maintains that the ego has two types of conflict: *intersystemic*, with the id and the superego, and *intrasystemic*, with parts of itself. The intrasystemic conflict, for Hartmann, is by definition the one that occurs between the area of conflict and the area free of conflict. But it is not the only one. There is also the intrasystemic conflict between primary and secondary autonomy. The defensive splitting of the ego that Freud (1940e) studied on the basis of fetishism (1927e), and Sterba's (1934) therapeutic dissociation of the ego, are also intrasystemic conflicts.

Ten years later Hartmann (1951) reviewed the technical consequences of ego psychology, distinguishing two types of interpretations: those that deal with intersystemic conflict, and those that deal with intrasystemic conflict. The interpretations directed to the mechanisms of intersystemic adaptation are predominantly the dynamic–economic type. Those that answer to intrasystemic conflicts are essentially of a structural nature.

This scheme of ego functioning explains a particular effect Hartmann brings out in interpretation. Although generally directed to a specific point, the interpretation branches out in the analysand's mind and can reach other zones. Hartmann calls this the *multiple appeal* of the interpretation. Löwenstein (1957) offers an example of this indirect effect of the interpretation. A patient remembered his strong feeling of inferiority when an older man saw him naked in the pool. He explained it as being due to a mole on his thigh, which embarrassed him. After a period of analysis in which the transference of competitive feelings and his inferiority in the face of the analyst appeared clearly, he again recounted the story of the pool, but now connected his shame directly to the comparison of his penis to that of the big man who was looking at him. The interpretations on castration anxiety and rivalry with the analyst–father operated on another area of the mind.

30.6   The 1951 review

The above-mentioned article by Hartmann was published in the first number of the *Psychoanalytic Quarterly* of 1951, together with papers by Löwenstein and Kris. These three articles represent a thorough review of the theory of interpretation from the viewpoint of ego psychology in the United States.

The three articles owe recognition to *The Ego and the Mechanisms of Defence* (A. Freud, 1936), trying to show that interpretative technique in mid-century is basically the result of Anna Freud's contributions. These writers establish a line of development, beginning with Freud's technical writings, continuing with the theoretical writings that provided the basis for the structural theory in the 1920s, and culminating finally in the book of 1936.

As I said at the beginning of this chapter, I believe Reich occupies an outstanding place in this development, just as Fenichel does, and therefore an outlook that ignores them will always be a partial one. It is good to be able to say that this position finds no support in Anna Freud's great book. On the contrary, chapter 3, "The Ego's Defensive Operations Considered as an Object of Analysis", centres on Reich's concept of the armour-plating of character [*Charakterpanzerung*].

Hartmann says that psychoanalysis is a discipline in which there is a permanent interaction between theory and technique. However, there is an undeniable gap between the technical writings of the 1910s and the structural theory formulated in the 1920s. In the technical articles, Freud's insistence on the concept of *psychic surface* shows that he already had an idea of an ego he had not yet discovered theoretically. The concept of psychic surface implies, in effect, the existence of a defence and an impulse, and that the defence is superficial and the impulse underlies it. In this way the id and the ego are implicitly defined.

Hartmann is surely right to consider Freud's technical writings as forerunners of ego psychology. His technical principles cannot be understood unless they are regarded from the point of view of a psychic institution, the ego, which administers the conflict in some way. That vantage point is obviously the ego. Freud, in the technical writings, advanced in effect what he would formulate theoretically more precisely years later.

To this must be added what I have already mentioned—that the 1920s mark a crisis of the technique. I think some of Freud's theoretical changes are related to this crisis. The ideas about the death instinct, the need for punishment, moral masochism and the negative therapeutic reaction as mechanisms that are almost impossible to solve express, at the level of the context of discovery, the technical difficulties psychoanalysis encountered. Therefore I think it is true not only that the technique had advanced on the (structural) theory, as Hartmann, Löwenstein and Kris maintained, but also that the technique was not evolving in tune with the theory of transference Freud himself had established. The insecurity and the confusion with which Ferenczi and Rank confronted this problem in their essay of 1923, together with the stir they provoked, clearly show the difficulties in applying to clinical practice the rich concept of transference. When Freud speaks of transference in *Beyond the Pleasure Principle* (1920g) he explains it through a demonic impulse to repeat. How is it possible that a patient wishes to repeat experiences that are painful, humiliating, frustrating and disagreeable in every sense, if not because he is moved by a force that goes *beyond* the pleasure principle? At that moment Freud captures the drama, but he does not take on board the intensity of the transference link. The drama is really that the analysand repeats because he is subject to his history, his past. I dare say that in going beyond the pleasure principle what goes unnoticed is that the patient is prepared to make an enormous effort in repeating in the transference the painful but ineluctable experiences from his past. It is the force of desire and the stubborn hope of arriving somehow at a solution that leads to the repetition of the need, which, in the final instance, makes psychoanalytic treatment possible.

Hartmann considers Reich's work in his article, but mostly to undermine it. He affirms that Reich's psychology is pre-structural, that it makes use only of strata nearer or further away from consciousness. On this point, Hartmann establishes an incisive antinomy between strata and structures. Strata correspond to the unconscious, preconscious and conscious divisions of the topographical model. The functional division of id, ego and superego, on the other hand, corresponds to the structural model. In addition, the stratification varies during the course of life, and therefore a correct sequence in interpretation cannot be established, contrary to what Reich suggests.

Hartmann even says that it was Freud and not Reich who proposed the systematic analysis of the resistances (1951, *Essays on Ego Psychology*, p. 143). He asserts at the same time that the decisive opposition Reich proposes between the instinct and the defence is no longer sustainable, that it has lost the clarity it once had. That is, Hartmann criticizes Reich's being systematic as a defect, whereas he acknowledges it as a virtue in Freud.

The difference between instinctual drives and defence, Hartmann continues, has begun to lose its character of absolute opposition, since the instinct can be used as a defence, while the defence can take on an instinctive character (sexualized or "aggressivized" defence). Reich does not ignore this, however. On the contrary, he is the one who, with his psychology of strata, shows us how the ego (and the ego of structural theory) operates strategically, using the instincts as defences, as we have seen. The passive–feminine character, for example, uses homosexual instincts to hide its aggression and rivalry, and so forth. The strata imply, for Reich, an organization that is inescapably egoic.

If we understand by stratum a part of the ego that has become organized throughout the patient's history in the struggle with the environment, as Reich postulates, then the theory of character defences gives an account of approximately the same events Hartmann later considered on the basis of change of function and secondary autonomy. In 1939 Hartmann said that there are sectors of the area of conflict that become autonomous and independent of their instinctual sources and swell the conflict-free area on the authority of a secondary autonomy. This takes place on the basis of what Hartmann calls change of function. Hartmann's ideas here are perhaps broader than those of Reich, since they include normal as well as pathological psychology. But if they are considered dispassionately, without allowing oneself to be led by those scholastic commitments that always influence the psychoanalytic movement, it will be seen that they are similar. Secondary autonomy reformulates Reich's theory of the character trait as a structure uprooted from its instinctual bases. For both theories, the analyst's function seems to be the same: to operate on secondary autonomy (character trait) and bring it back to the area of conflict (to make it ego-dystonic again).

* * *

Kris's article, "Ego Psychology and Interpretation in Psychoanalytic Therapy" (1951), deals particularly with the analysis of the ego defences, understood as activities that participate in the conflict no less than do the instincts of the id. Following his ideas on the preconscious mental process expounded a year earlier, Kris considers that work on the ego defences is an essential part of the analytic task, because it allows a re-ordering, at the level of the preconscious system, of energies previously immobilized by the conflict. Kris does not undervalue Reich's contributions on stratification, but he affirms that Anna Freud takes a step forward when she considers that the resistance of the ego is an essential part of analytic work and not a mere obstacle.

Kris maintains that before reaching the id, an exploration of the ego is required, during which diverse activities (behaviours) of the ego are discovered, which operate as defence mechanisms. The most efficient interpretation is the one that establishes a link between the ego defence and the patient's resistance during analysis, according to Kris (1951, p. 24).

Löwenstein's article, finally, centres in preference on the concept of interpretation, which he distinguishes from the analyst's other interventions, as we have seen in previous chapters, especially chapter 25.

30.7 Löwenstein's contributions

Löwenstein, surely one of the main investigators of interpretation, tries to define it and contrast it with what is not interpretation. I think it is appropriate to explain some of his ideas at this point.

Löwenstein says, and it is obvious, that interpreting is not all we do. He distinguishes (1951) preparatory moments from final moments in the interpretative task. He places among the former indication and confrontation, which I prefer to classify as information-gathering instruments (in chapter 24). Those who maintain that the analyst should only interpret do not ignore the other types of intervention, but they consider them as less important. They do not take them into account from the point of view of the therapeutic process; they regard them as insignificant. Nevertheless, since the psychoanalytic process is subtle and complex, it is better not to leave things out, because they may be decisive in the long run. This is why it is always useful to study the other instruments that shape the analyst's not strictly interpretative interventions, as Perrotta (1974) called them. At the Symposium of the Paris Congress on variations in psychoanalytic technique, Löwenstein (1958) traced a dividing line between interpretations and other interventions, placing the parameter among the latter.

I do not think it advisable to place non-interpretative interventions and the parameter into the same category. It is preferable to distinguish the latter properly, in that it brings in an activity of the analyst who decides to modify his setting occasionally. The former are preparatory interventions or tactics (Löwenstein, 1951), or they can be given autonomy (as information-gathering instruments), as I suggested.

While "preparatory interventions" (1951) or "interventions" (1958) have tactical value for Löwenstein, interpretation shapes the analyst's strategy and is defined as an *explanation* the analyst gives the patient about himself, on the basis of his material.

In distinguishing interpretation from preparatory interventions, Löwenstein indicates that the demarcation between them is imprecise. It is sometimes difficult to decide the passage from one level to another, but the difference nevertheless exists. Preparatory interventions serve to test the analysand's disposition. This is why Löwenstein speaks of an optimum distance where the patient is not too distanced emotionally, nor excessively involved in the situation to be interpreted.

With the concept of optimum distance Löwenstein poses the problem of timing within the theoretical framework of the functioning of the ego and its resistances. This dovetails with the role he assigns to preparatory interventions, which at times assume, I think, the character of tactical interventions that test the degree of the patient's insight and his receptivity. On this point it is understandable that, in defining interpretation through the effect—insight—Löwenstein will define *a fortiori* an interpretation that did not produce insight as preparatory, and that is problematic.

30.8 Confluence of the two Freudian models

Perhaps the most rigorous criticism of the 1951 review, from within its own guidelines, is that it is prone to seek its theoretical foundations in the structural point of view of the second model, neglecting the first. Clifford Yorke's work on the metapsychology of interpretation, published in 1965, attempts to integrate the two aspects.

Yorke starts from the well-known difference Freud establishes, in his metapsychological essays of 1915, between the two phases (or types) of repression. First, there is *primary repression* [*Urverdrängung*], which consists in ejecting from consciousness the representation of the instinctual drive by means of an anticathexis. Then there is *secondary repression* or repression proper [*Verdrängung*], which is exerted on the derivatives of the repressed representation in the preconscious system, formed by a simultaneous process of repulsion and attraction. As we know, in repression proper both anticathexis and the withdrawal of the cathexis of attention (hypercathexis, overinvestment) operate simultaneously. In other words, the process of repression proper begins with a withdrawal of the cathexis of attention from the preconscious derivatives, which are then at the mercy of the anticathexis.

Therefore, Yorke says, the metapsychology of interpretation has to do with a complex chain of metapsychological events. For a derivative to become conscious, the interpretation should remove the anticathexis and restore the cathexis of attention (1965, p. 33). Repression deprives the thing-representation of its connection with the word. The function of the interpretation is precisely to restore it (ibid., p. 34).

In common with many other writers, Yorke maintains that interpretation operates in the two phases (types) of repression—that is, on the demarcation between the two systems: preconscious/conscious, and preconscious/unconscious. The analyst works first on the interface between the preconscious and the conscious, enabling the analysand to make contact with the word-representation, until he can finally approach the instinctual representation that suffered the process of primary repression, once he is sufficiently near the preconscious system. As Fenichel (1935) said, as the analytic process advances, the derivatives suffer less distortion.

Yorke considers the function of verbalization as better understood, on the basis of the idea of a representational world, particularly the representation of the self. As Jacobson (1954b) postulated, the representation of the self can be cathected by instinctual energy no less than can an object representation. The word and the symbol form part of the representative world and can be linked to representations of the self or the object. A part of analytic work consists in modifying through interpretation the distortion of representations that stems from the demands of the ego, of reality and of the introjects. It follows that interpretation imprints changes on the representations of the external world and of the introjects, which can lead to important modifications in the self-representation (Yorke, 1965, p. 36).

In this way, Yorke seeks a synthesis between primary repression and repression proper, which leads to a better integration of the topographical and the structural theories, in order to give an account of the metapsychology of interpretation.

To end this section, it is worth pointing out that Yorke's intelligent research anticipates to some extent the recent studies by the Sandlers (Sandler & Sandler, 1983, 1984, 1987), who also try to establish a bridge between topographical theory and structural theory (as we saw in section 9.9).

CHAPTER THIRTY-ONE

Melanie Klein
and the theory of interpretation

In the previous chapters we studied the metapsychology of interpretation at length, trying to understand it in the light of the topographical and structural theories, beginning with Freud, then Reich and Fenichel, Anna Freud and Hartmann, and up to the most modern ego psychologists in England and in the United States.

At the risk of over-simplifying, I will offer a geographical characterization: this line of investigation was pursued mainly by the Vienna School, which I will now contrast with the English School. By *Vienna School* I mean here the one that formed around Freud between the 1920s and the 1930s and continued in England and in the United States after the diaspora provoked by the *Anschluss* of 1938. The *English School*, on the other hand (as I attempted to define it in a previous work—Etchegoyen, 1981a) was founded and directed by Jones as head of the British Psycho-Analytical Society. Melanie Klein occupied a pre-eminent place in it on her arrival in London in 1926. Towards the end of the Second World War there was a definitive split in the British Society and, under the presidency of Sylvia Payne, Groups A and B were formed. From then on, one cannot speak of the English School, but of three nuclei at the heart of that society: Anna Freud's group, Melanie Klein's group and the independent group (middle group).

In this chapter we will deal mainly with Melanie Klein, in an attempt to understand what is original and proper to her in the use of interpretation.

31.1 *Some antecedents*

It is difficult to study the theory of interpretation in Melanie Klein because she never expounded it formally. It is necessary to examine her writings, but the search is not simple, and gradually it leads to her early work. Careful reading of this early work reveals her as interpreting with that freshness, originality and boldness that would subsequently be the unmistakable mark of her style and her scientific credo, as much as the motive for scandal among her detractors.

Already before her arrival in London, when she practised in Berlin and was in analysis with Abraham, Klein undoubtedly used the instrument of interpretation with a conviction and an audacity rarely found among other analysts. She evoked this attitude herself in 1955, when she described the play technique and compared the cautious procedure of most analysts in the 1920s with her own way of operating: "At the time I began to work it was an established principle that interpretations should be given very sparingly. With few exceptions psychoanalysts had not explored the deeper layers of the unconscious—in children such exploration being considered potentially dangerous. This cautious outlook was reflected in the fact that then, and for years to come, psychoanalysis was held to be suitable only for children from the latency period onwards" (Klein, 1975, Vol. 3, p. 122). Let us remember that Hug-Hellmuth (1921) and Anna Freud (1927), for example, both maintained this.

In the 1955 work just quoted, Klein also recalls that when she decided to analyse Fritz, seeing that enlightenment alone was not enough; she departed from some of the accepted rules, interpreting what seemed most urgent in the material. She therefore soon found that her interest centred on the anxiety and the defences against it.

It can be said, therefore, that almost from the beginning of her practice Klein always recognized interpretation as the essential instrument of psychoanalysis and applied it unhesitatingly whenever she saw fit. It is therefore thought-provoking that she never felt obliged to establish the basis for her theory of interpretation, despite the realization that her way of interpreting differed radically from that of other analysts of her time. It is possible, however, that this recognition came late, and she did not realize it in her early years of work.

Although it is true that Klein never wrote specifically on interpretation, the writings of Strachey (1934, 1937) and Paula Heimann (1956), recognized by all as first-class, were undoubtedly inspired by her.

31.2 *The first works*

Melanie Klein's first interpretations can be found in the second part of "The Development of a Child" (1921), under the heading "The Child's Resistance to Enlightenment". ("The Development of a Child" was published in 1921 in *Imago* and in 1923 in the *International Journal of Psycho-Analysis*; it consists of two parts. The first, "The Influence of Sexual Enlightenment and Relaxation of Authority on the Intellectual Development of Children", belongs to Klein's initial period, which was brief and developed in Budapest. The second part corresponds to a communication to the Berlin Psychoanalytic Society in February 1921, shortly after she had settled in that city.) When she realized that just to enlighten is not sufficient, because the child resists the sexual knowledge offered, she understood that the only valid device to lift repression is interpretation.

When she presented this case at the Hungarian Society in 1919, Anton von Freund argued that Melanie Klein's observations were certainly analytical, but not her interpretations, which only touched conscious aspects of the material. (Klein read her paper, "Notes on the Intellectual Development of a Child", in July 1919 to the Hungarian Psychoanalytic Society. This conference is the basis for the first part of the work we are considering, although she also contributed another, entitled "A Contribution to Early Analysis", in December 1920.) She at first rejected this criticism and maintained that it was sufficient to treat conscious problems if there existed no reasons to the contrary, but not long afterwards she conceded he was right (1975, Vol. 1, p. 30). This anecdote illustrates directly the rapid evolution of her psychoanalytic thought.

If von Freund is right and, at the beginning of her work with Fritz, she enlightened but did not interpret, then the first interpretation that appears in Klein's writings is found in the second part of the work we are considering.

Days after Melanie Klein dared (at last!) to explain the role of the father in procreation, Fritz related his dream-fantasy of the big motor and the little motor that ran into the electric car, and he also said that the little motor was between the big motor and the electric train. Klein explained then that "the big motor is his papa, the electric car his mamma and the little motor himself, and that he has put himself between papa and mamma because he would so much like to put papa away altogether and to remain alone with his mamma and to do with her what only papa is allowed to do" (1975, Vol. 1, p. 35). It is noticeable that this interpretation appears in brackets and Melanie Klein calls it *explanation*. In fact it is very similar to the one the father of little Hans offers him (Freud, 1909b), when he tells him that while he was in bed with his mother in Gmunden, he thought he was the father and was frightened, to which Hans answers movingly, *"You know everything"* (ibid., p. 90; italics in the original). The father offers the same type of interpretation later on, when he tells Hans that he would like to be the papa and be married to the mamma, that he would like to be as big as his father and to have a moustache, and would like mamma to have a baby (ibid., p. 92).

In principle, Klein interprets Fritz's negative Oedipus complex in the same way: "I told him that he had imagined himself in his mamma's place and wished his papa might do with him what he does with her" (1975,

Vol. 1, p. 41). Here, however, Klein continues and calls things by their correct names, because she clearly tells Fritz: "But he is afraid (as he imagines his mamma to be too) that if this stick—papa's wiwi—gets into his wiwi he will be hurt and then inside his belly, in his stomach, everything will be destroyed, too" (ibid., p. 41). I think there is a substantial change here, because Klein dares to name the organs and the functions, translating the symbols instead of alluding to them. This attitude defines a theory, a technique and an ethic: the theory that the child understands the semantic value of the interpretation, the technique that symbols have to be brought back to their origin, and the ethic that it is necessary to tell the child the truth without hiding things.

31.3   Hans, Dora and Fritz

We have just seen how Klein's interpretative technique evolves in her first papers. Her interpretations are at first similar to those of Hans's father— that is, those of Freud—but they soon acquire another character. In that they attend to the functioning of the primary process and its peculiar modes of expression, they become deeper and more engaged because they try to make contact with the unconscious. I think these characteristics are the patrimony of Klein's way of working, of her style, which does not depart, however, from the spirit with which Freud himself interpreted. Freud tells Dora, for example, that she thinks her father is impotent (has no resources) and imagines his relations with Frau K are *per os*, after which he interprets that she identifies with her father's two women (her mother and Frau K) in order to satisfy her incestuous desires. He adds that her jealousy is that of a woman in love. Freud not only interprets Dora's aphonia as an expression of sorrow over the absence of the loved one (Herr K) but also relates it to her unconscious fantasies of *fellatio*, and similarly with her cough and the tickle in her throat.

On this point, Freud in fact meets his detractors, who, he imagines, are horrified, head on. He says the best way of speaking about these things is directly and drily, without malice or timidity, calling a spade a spade— "J'appelle un chat, un chat", Freud says. And Freud certainly did not hesitate to use symbolism when he interpreted to Dora her first dream and her sexual stimulation, comparing her sex to the jewel-case.

31.4   The Salzburg Congress

In the two works Klein published in 1923, "The Role of the School in the Libidinal Development of the Child" (1923a) and "Early Analysis" (1923b), there are no explicit references to her way of interpreting. But it can be seen that the understanding of the fantasies of the child has become more intrepid and profound and already has a decidedly "Kleinian" seal in that it relies on continual reference to the symbolic value of play and the word.

On 22 April 1924, at the Eighth International Psychoanalytic Congress in Salzburg, Melanie Klein read her paper on "The Technique of the Analysis of Young Children". This was never published, and all we know of it is a summary that appeared in the *International Journal of Psycho-Analysis*, 5 (p. 398), but the summary already shows clearly how the play technique operates and the way in which Klein uses interpretation. The play technique consists in applying the rules of dream interpretation to play, testing its validity through the child's response, which, in turn, is contrasted with his fantasies, his drawings and the whole of his behaviour.

By that time Klein had understood that the fundamental mechanism of the child's play is the discharge of masturbatory fantasies (see 1975, Vol. 1, p. 135, n. 2, which outlines some of the ideas of the Salzburg paper). It follows from this that the inhibitions in playing have their origin in the repression of these fantasies, which always refer us to the primal scene. Klein reached the same conclusions in studying the role of the school in the libidinal development of the child in 1923.

Klein (1926) affirms that one can never overestimate the importance of fantasy and its translation into action in the life of the child, at the bidding of the compulsion to repetition. ("In general, in the analysis of children we cannot over-estimate the importance of phantasy and of translation into action at the bidding of the compulsion to repetition"—1975, Vol. 1, p. 136.)

31.5   The experience with Rita

The Salzburg paper must surely have inspired "The Psychological Principles of Early Analysis", in which Klein expands on her play technique and her theory of interpretation. (This article was read at the Berlin Psychoanalytic Society in December 1924—Elsa del Valle, 1979, Vol. 1, p. 55—and published two years later.) As an early indication of what she would expound in "Personification in the Play of Children" (1929), she discovered that the assigning of roles in play permits the child to separate different identifications that tend to form a single whole. It is easy to understand that this conception of play leads naturally to the unhesitating interpretation of the roles that appear, and to increasing attention on transference interpretation. From this point of view, the characteristics that would distinguish Melanie Klein through her way of interpreting already appear in profile.

Petot (1979) rightly points out that the case of Rita, whom Melanie Klein analysed in her home in 1923, effected a substantial change in her thinking and practice. Just as it can be said that Anna O invented the *talking cure*, so it can be asserted that little Rita created the play technique, with her toys and her famous superego teddy-bear.

Not without a certain nostalgia, Klein recalled in 1955 her first session with Rita during the spring of 1923 in Berlin. As soon as they were alone, the girl showed herself to be anxious, remained silent and then asked to go out into the garden. The analyst agreed, and they went outside, while the mother and the aunt watched them sceptically from afar, certain that the attempt would fail. However, the analyst—so inexperienced but so talented—had already decided that the negative transference was dominating the picture. Upon seeing her more tranquil in the garden, and taking certain associations into account, she said she (Rita) feared she would do something to her while they were alone in the room, and she linked that fear to her night terrors, when Rita thought a bad woman would attack her in her bed. Minutes later Rita returned confidently to the room.

This interpretation is historical, for many reasons. We can date it with certainty, and it offers the characteristics proper to Klein's work: it directs itself to the anxiety, takes the transference—including the negative one—into account and links it to the symptoms and the conflict. Petot (1979, p. 121) points out that these interconnected elements reveal the originality of this technique. Melanie Klein refers to this in her 1955 work: her approach to Fritz and Rita is typical of what would later be her technique (1975, Vol. 3, pp. 123–124).

Klein bases her interpretative work on an empirical fact derived from her clinical work, and it is that the child has a greater contact with reality than the adult supposes. Often the alleged deficiency arises not from a lack of capacity for perceiving reality but from the child's disavowal, his repudiation of it. The decisive criterion for the reality-judgement of the child, and therefore his capacity to adapt, depend on his tolerance of frustration, and particularly on oedipal frustration. Thus we are frequently surprised by the facility with which the child accepts the interpretation and even enjoys it. ("We are often surprised at the facility with which on some occasions our interpretations are accepted: sometimes children even express considerable pleasure in them"—Klein, 1975, Vol. 1, p. 134.) In the child communication between the conscious and unconscious systems is easier than in the adult. This is why interpretation produces a rapid effect in him, even a surprising one, although it cannot be taken for granted. His play begins again or changes, his anxiety decreases or increases suddenly, new material appears, the relation with the analyst becomes closer and more lively. In lifting the repressions, interpretation promotes an economical change that reveals itself pristinely in the pleasure with which the child plays.

Here Klein disagrees directly with Freud who, in "The Wolf Man" (1918), affirmed that, contrary to appearances, the material the child offers is in the end inferior to that of the adult, since he lacks words and thoughts, which he has to borrow. This assertion would be shared totally by Anna Freud. She would say that the child's material does not lead us beyond language, when his thought begins to be like ours. ("But so far as my experience goes, and with the technique I have described, it does not take us beyond the boundaries where verbalization begins—that period, in other words, when his thought processes begin to approximate our own"—A. Freud, 1965, Vol. 1, p. 52.) With the child, two methods fail which allow us to reconstruct the past in the adult patient: free association and transference. Klein replies that if play is closely observed and ordered within the context of his entire behaviour, the child offers rich material, especially if we understand it in its symbolic value. The child's fantasies, desires and experiences are represented in the play through symbolism, that archaic and forgotten language which comes to us from phylogeny, as also from the other means of expression Freud discovered in the dreamwork. Symbolism—Klein said at the Symposium—"is the lever we must make use of in child-analysis" (1975, Vol. 1, p. 147).

With this we arrive at one of the basic principles of Kleinian interpretation and perhaps the most controversial one, the utilization of symbols. It is difficult to separate out here properly scientific, theoretical or technical problems from those that arise out of ideology and prejudice, or from legitimate and inevitable personal styles. It is true that a distinctive trait of the Kleinian approach is that she does not hesitate to interpret the symbols directly, but symbolism is only part of the material Klein deals with; she always attends to all the subtle forms of expression of the primary process. Differently from other, more cautious analysts (among whom are included also some post-Kleinian writers), Klein does not eschew symbolism. She avails herself of it as well as of the other modes of unconscious expression. The fact that this procedure exposes her to the error of translating symbols mechanically only proves that Melanie Klein, like any other analyst, can be mistaken. Those who criticize the use of symbols think they are always translated in a stereotyped fashion, never with perspicacity and talent. Beyond the personal predilections and the style of each analyst, I think it is unwise to affirm that Klein's technique consists in a direct translation of the symbols, as Maurice Dayan does (1982). He understands Melanie Klein's technique as a systematic and direct translation of symbols, with a total neglect of everything else. Dayan says that she therefore anchors in the subject the conviction that the manifest content of verbal, graphic and play activities is unimportant, and what counts are only the latent meanings the interpreter finds, unmodified, under the most diverse representations (ibid., p. 272). For Dayan, Melanie Klein interprets with immovable certitude in a discourse of delusional traits (p. 301), which breaks away completely from Freud's methodology and from psychoanalysis. Such extreme opinions serve polemics and rejection more than the comparison of counterposed ideas.

I think Klein had little of the routine and the mechanical in her way of working. In common with all psychoanalysts, she considered that interpretation could be given only on the basis of adequate material. But, as opposed to others, she maintained that children, in fact, often present this material surprisingly quickly and in great variety (1975, Vol. 1, p. 134). The difference should therefore not be sought here, in the theory of interpretation, but rather in what is understood as material—or, in other words, in the scope the concept of unconscious fantasy will be given.

Klein concludes her important work of 1926 comparing the analytic situation in the adult and in the child. Given that the means of expression are different, the analytic situation seems different, but in fact it is in essence the same: "Just as children's means of expression differ from those of adults, so the analytic situation in the analysis of children appears to be entirely different. It is, however, in both cases essentially the same. Consistent interpretations, gradual solving of resistances and persistent tracing of the transference to earlier situations—these constitute in children as in adults the correct analytic situation" (1975, Vol. 1, p. 137).

31.6   The Symposium on Child Analysis

The Symposium on Child Analysis took place on 4 and 18 May 1927, at the British Psycho-Analytical Society. Melanie Klein, Joan Riviere, M. N. Searl, Ella F. Sharpe, Edward Glover and Ernest Jones took part. All the papers have a polemical tone and do not eschew criticisms of Anna Freud and her recently published *Einführung in die Technik der Kinderanalyse*. I am not interested in re-opening this heated discussion, which managed to disturb Freud himself, but in extracting those features that will allow a more realistic sketch of the profile of Kleinian interpretation. Thanks to Riccardo Steiner's exhaustive study, "Some Thoughts about Tradition and Change Arising from an Examination of the British Psycho-Analytical Society's Controversial Discussions (1943–1944)", published in the *International Review of Psychoanalysis*, we now know exactly to what point Freud was emotionally involved in the Symposium, and how much it cost him not to let himself be carried away in the least by his singular position as the father of both Anna and psychoanalysis, by his geographical and theoretical position as a Viennese, faced with the bold propositions of that new arrival who, in spite of herself and with ingenious impertinence, was proposing changes, amplifications and even rectifications to the imposing edifice of psychoanalysis that he had built. Steiner maintains that the changes proposed by Melanie Klein at that moment gave rise to severe anxiety in the scientific milieu, which would have to contain them; he considers that every change of paradigm (Kuhn, 1962) is accompanied at the time by a strong emotional element, which Kuhn himself calls "essential creative tension" (Steiner, 1985, p. 65). To put it in terms of Kleinian theories—Steiner concludes—tolerance of change is maintained at the level of depressive anxiety that the scientific group is capable of reaching at the moment when the change of paradigm occurs.

At the Symposium, not only did two young and creative women pioneers confront each other, not only two schools and two poles of scientific thought—Vienna and London—but also two temperaments. If Anna Freud sees child and adult differently, this is because she considers the ego; Klein sees the similarities, because she sees the unconscious.

When Anna Freud, invited by Kohut, spoke in Chicago in 1966 on "The Ideal Psychoanalytic Institute", she was dissatisfied with the title of her lecture, because she was interested only in the ideal that could be translated into reality. She remembered that as a child she had only been interested in stories that could be true; whenever elements of a supernatural character appeared, her interest decreased. It is not strange that such a child, with so strong an attachment to reality, later studied the ego and its defence mechanisms. I know no corresponding anecdote of Melanie Klein as a small child, but I can imagine her listening, absorbed, to tales of fairies and witches.

In chapter 3 of her book, Anna Freud (1927) presents the theoretical arguments that made her doubt the play technique. Everything the child does in playing does not necessarily have the symbolic value Klein assigns to it. It can also be something innocent, something that has to do with a present and immediate experience, like—I would say—the day's residues of the dream. Klein replies that she does not interpret directly (or wildly), but that she takes the *whole* situation into account. I do not wish to indicate here who is right (and, in fact, I think that this criticism of Anna Freud is sometimes justified, sometimes not), but to demonstrate how Klein defines her interpretative activity here. Once she has understood certain connections, "then I interpret these phenomena and link them up with the Ucs and the analytic situation. The practical and theoretical conditions for the interpretation are precisely the same as in the analysis of adults" (Klein, 1975, Vol. 1, p. 147). Klein's quote matters to me because it supports what I claimed earlier: that the use of interpretation is the same for child and adult; what varies is the concept of material, which has to do, in turn, with the scope of fantasy.

The Ucs system predominates in the child. It can therefore be expected that the mode of symbolic representation will prevail in his mind, and that to make contact with the child we need to have recourse to interpretation.

If we wish to penetrate the child's unconscious, we should attend to his modes of expression, so as to detect anxiety and guilt as soon as possible, because only by interpreting and allaying them will we have access to the unconscious. "Then, if we follow out the symbolism that his phantasies contain, we shall soon see anxiety reappear, and thus we shall ensure the progress of the work" (ibid., p. 148).

31.7   The key points of the controversy

If the presentations at the Symposium are compared with Anna Freud's book, many differences are immediately observable, though not all of them would be sustained in the course of time, and they do not always relate directly to what we are studying here—that is, interpretation. The most notable differences arise in the scope transference is given (and, more widely, the scope fantasy is given), and in how the origin and the structure of the superego are conceived.

Klein (1927) believes firmly that an anxious or hostile attitude on the child's part expresses the negative transference (1975, Vol. 1, p. 145), whereas Anna Freud (1927) feels that a reaction of this sort on the part of a small child may be due to its good link with the mother. ("The more tenderly a little child is attached to his own mother, the fewer friendly impulses he has towards strangers"—A. Freud, 1965, Vol. 1, p. 45.) Conversely, Anna Freud continues, it is precisely those children who have enjoyed little affection in the home who are quick to establish a positive relation with the analyst. ("It is especially with children who are accustomed to little loving treatment at home, and are not used to showing or receiving any strong attention, that a positive relationship is often most quickly established"—A. Freud, 1965, Vol. 1, p. 45.)

Klein replies, in turn, that her experience "has confirmed my belief that if I construe this dislike at once as anxiety and negative transference feeling, and interpret it as such in connection with material which the child at the same time produces and then trace it back to its original object, the mother, I can at once observe that the anxiety diminishes" (Klein, 1975, Vol. 1, p. 145). A little further on, Klein adds that if the child's attitude towards us is friendly and playful, we are justified in assuming a positive transference exists and in making use of it unhesitatingly in our work (ibid., pp. 145–146).

The debate on whether the transference appears early on and whether it should be interpreted at the outset continues almost unabated to this day. This is not the moment to take part in this polemic, but to indicate that the issue is not whether to interpret the transference, but the time of its appearance.

The other great controversial theme is the origin of the superego. Anna Freud, following her father, thinks that the superego is formed when the Oedipus complex declines, whereas Klein postulates that the superego is formed during the period of the Oedipus complex and not suddenly at the end. In this way she thinks that her theory does not constitute a change in Freud's ideas. Klein starts from a fact of observation in her first cases of analysis (Fritz, Felix), and it is that the feeling of guilt appears before the Oedipus complex declines. These first clinical glimmers are further confirmed when she uses the play technique with Rita, Inga or Peter. The night terrors of the second or third year of life are clearly constituted on the basis of the primal scene and persist with no changes in the phallic phase of the Oedipus complex.

On this clinical basis, Klein maintains that the Oedipus complex starts at the beginning of the second year of life ("The Psychological Principles of Early Analysis", 1926) or in the second half of the first year (*The Psycho-*

Analysis of Children, 1932, chapter 1). With the theory of the positions, when the Oedipus complex is finally linked to the depressive position, the date of its beginning is referred to the second trimester of the first year. But then the paranoid–schizoid superego appears *before* the Oedipus complex and determines it, with which Klein's theory says precisely the opposite to what Freud says.

On this precise point, then, Anna Freud is right in the long run, although the classic point of view on the formation of the superego encounters more than one difficulty, as I tried to show in a collaborative paper presented at the Fourteenth Latin-American Congress of Psychoanalysis (1982c).

31.8 Interpretation in "The Psycho-Analysis of Children"

The Psycho-Analysis of Children, which Klein published in 1932, contains a technical and a clinical–theoretical part, which studies the effect of early anxiety situations on the development of the child. The first part, particularly chapter 2, "The Technique of Early Analyses", where interpretation occupies an outstanding place, relates to the objectives of our study. (Chapter 1 is based on the 1926 work already referred to.)

At the beginning of chapter 2, with the case of Peter, aged three years and nine months, Klein shows us how she interprets the primal scene, jealousy due to the birth of a brother and sexual games, based on the boy's play activities and his associations. She asks questions, she measures the boy's response, she probes his receptivity and finally she interprets. She does this with simple words, but she informs at length and in detail, without sparing concrete references to the organs and their functions as well as to the objects (father, mother, siblings, other persons in his environment). Klein insists more than once that interpretation should not be symbolic— that is, allusive. The symbols should be translated literally and without euphemisms. It is not enough to say, as the father of Little Hans said to his child, that he wants to have a moustache like his own, if what one means to say is that the moustache represents the penis. As Klein says in a footnote in this chapter, "If we want to gain access to the child's unconscious in analysis (which, of course, we have to do via the ego and through speech) we shall only succeed if we avoid circumlocution and use plain words" (1975, Vol. 2, p. 32).

Klein indicates in this chapter that as soon as the child offers her material to interpret, she does so *immediately*. The basis for this is that if the child communicates well, this is because he is in a positive transference, and therefore one should interpret before it is too late—before anxiety appears. An interpretation offered at a good moment—and for Klein this means as soon as possible—enables the analyst to regulate the emergence of anxiety: "Thus by making a timely interpretation—that is to say as soon as the material permits—the analyst can cut short the child's anxiety, or rather regulate it" (ibid., p. 25).

Just as it is necessary to interpret when the child is expressing his fantasies, which implies, for Klein, in a moment of positive transference (or, better still, I would say, a moment where the therapeutic alliance is operating adequately), so hesitation might enable anxiety and resistance to arise. The negative transference must in the same way be interpreted without hesitation. It is often expressed through an attitude of timidity, mistrust or embarrassment. On this point Klein coincides with Reich (1927, 1933). Although her strategy is diametrically opposed to his, they both consider the latent negative transference as equally important. Reich proposes a systematic attack on characterological resistance; she seeks contact with the unconscious fantasy.

For Klein, a basic postulate of the effect of interpretation is that only by allaying anxiety at the deep levels of the mind can the child's ego and its relation to reality be analysed validly. "The establishment of the child's relations to reality as well as the stronger emergence of its ego take place in the analysis of children only step by step in connection with progress in ego development. They are a result, not a precondition of the analytic work" (1975, Vol. 2, pp. 25–26). With this definitive assertion I think we can understand what Klein means by direct and deep interpretation, together with her strategy for getting in contact with the unconscious.

Melanie Klein departs here *prima facie* from the Freud of "On Beginning the Treatment" (1913c). There he advises formally that interpretation should not begin before the establishment of an effective transference, of an appropriate *rapport* with the patient (p. 139). However, it can be argued that Klein does not ignore the advice, in that she assumes the rapport exists if the child plays or speaks; but it is undeniable that at this point transference, for Klein, has a different scope from that assigned to it by the creator of psychoanalysis. In addition, she departs from Freud's attitude of confident caution. He thinks that necessary rapport is achieved just by giving the analysand time, provided the doctor exhibits genuine interest, eliminates the initial resistances and avoids committing certain errors, whereas Klein holds exactly the opposite: that rapport is obtained only by interpreting.

31.9   Interpretation in the latency period

Klein's theory of interpretation developed on the basis of her experience of the analysis of young children, where a rich fantasy life and an acute anxiety facilitate access to the unconscious. In the latency period one cannot count on those (favourable) circumstances, and therefore the difficulties in the technical approach increase. In latency the ego has not developed completely, so that the analyst cannot count on the adult's wish for a cure, nor on the development of language that makes free association possible. In other words, the latency child does not play like a young child, nor does he associate like an adult.

The way of approach Klein finds in these difficult circumstances has its point of support in sexual curiosity, where the repression of the epistemic instinct dominates the whole picture. As soon as the material permits, Klein interprets to the latency child that he is preoccupied by the difference in the sexes, the origin of children and the comparison with the adult, taking strict care to make interpretations, rather than explanations. Making interpretations soon leads to the anxiety and guilt feeling in the child with which the analytic situation is established. Intellectual explanations or a pedagogic attitude succeed only in removing the repressed material without resolving it, with which resistance increases.

A case that illustrates very well not only Klein's technique but also her strategy (or ideology) is that of Egon, a child of nine and a half with serious developmental problems and difficulties in establishing contact with people and with reality. (The account appears in Klein, 1975, Vol. 2, as the final part of chapter 4.)

At the beginning of treatment Klein invited Egon to use the couch, which he agreed to with his habitual indifference. But the analytic situation was not established. The analyst understood that the scarcity of the material depended on the difficulties of verbalization that could only be resolved through analytic methods. She then invited him to consider the possibility of playing, and although Egon said, as always, that it was all the same to him, he began a very monotonous and repetitive game with little cars.

She knew that one of the factors that had initiated Egon's difficulties was that, when he was four years old, his father repressed the child's masturbation and demanded a confession about what he had done. Klein tried to differentiate herself from that severe and dominating father by spending several weeks playing with the boy in silence with the little cars and avoiding any interpretation. When at last she decided to interpret in terms of the parents, coitus, of masturbation and oedipal rivalry, the monotonous game began to change, to become richer, to have greater movement, and the boy's behaviour at home was beginning to change.

The case of Egon was almost experimental for Klein. All attempts to establish the analytic situation by trying to achieve a rapport failed, while interpretation of the material succeeded in doing so quickly and clearly. Klein concludes, then, that she wasted time by not interpreting the child's play at the outset and that if she was able to maintain that attitude without endangering the continuity of analysis, it was due only to the intensity with which Egon's anxiety was repressed. In children who are less ill, to delay interpretation leads generally to the appearance of acute anxiety crises, which compel speedy interpretation before it is too late and the child abandons treatment.

In summing up, Klein states that in the latency period it is essential to establish contact with the child's unconscious fantasies, and this is achieved by interpreting the symbolic content of the material as a function of anxiety and guilt. But since repression of the fantasies is more intense at this stage of development than previously, we often have to find access to the unconscious on the basis of representations presented as entirely devoid of fantasies. However, if the analyst is not content to accept this product as a mere expression of resistance and treats it as real material (that is, as *content*), the path to the unconscious can open up. "By paying enough attention to small indications and by taking as our starting-point for interpretation the connection between the symbolism, sense of guilt and anxiety that accompany those representations, I found that there is always an opportunity for beginning and carrying on the work of analysis" (1975, Vol. 2, p. 73).

Following from this, Klein specifies what making contact with the unconscious means. The fact that in analysing children we enter into communication with the unconscious before establishing a fruitful relation with the ego does not mean that it has been eliminated from analytic work. That would be impossible, not only because the ego is closely connected with the id and the superego, but also because we have access to the unconscious only through the ego. What Klein means is that "analysis does not apply itself to the ego as such (as educational methods do) but only seeks to open up a path to the unconscious agencies of the mind those agencies which are decisive for the formation of the ego" (ibid., p. 74). A technical attitude that tries to stimulate the ego interests of the child will not modify the situation substantially, since "it is interpretation alone, in my experience, which starts the analytic process and keeps it going" (ibid., p. 75). Analysis does not direct itself to the ego through educational measures but seeks to open a way to the unconscious.

31.10 *Some characteristics of Kleinian interpretation*

Having reached this point, we can easily understand that Klein interprets in a special way—a way that is different from that of others, although it is not easy to indicate what its peculiarity consists in. Klein interprets more frequently than other analysts, and her tactic consists in interpreting (at least in the child) as soon as possible. If the patient contributes material, she considers that this attitude is born of his positive transference. To delay interpretation will only lead to situations of anxiety and resistance. If anxiety and resistance appear spontaneously, then there is greater reason to interpret in order to allay the former and reduce the latter.

It must be remembered that Melanie Klein's entire general theory of interpretation arises precisely from the vivid response of children to interpretative work. These responses were of such magnitude that they led

Klein to consult Abraham on the approach that should be followed. Abraham replied that, given that the interpretations produced alleviation and analysis was progressing, it seemed logical to him not to modify the method (see Klein, "The Psycho-Analytic Play Technique", 1955a).

From this time on, Klein followed her method, undaunted. It consisted in the end in interpreting the fantasy that was operating (as she saw it) and the anxiety that interpretation could awaken.

This technique has been opposed by very many writers, who consider it brusque and inconsiderate. At times it can be so, as Klein does not take the side-effects of the action of interpreting much into account. The "direct" interpretation can be decoded by the analysand, in effect, as aggressive or seductive, and this can be truer still if the analyst operates with a countertransference conflict. On other occasions, a simple translation of the symbols, omitting the preconscious links in the material, can lead the process to abreaction or intellectualization. All these risks are real and in some measure inevitable in Kleinian interpretation, which should be weighed against the undeniable virtues of this way of operating. It consists in interpreting with no other commitment or goal than that of making conscious the unconscious, without allowing oneself ever to be led by complacency and weakness, without fearing the consequences of saying what the analyst considers is happening in the mind of the analysand, and which he ought to express.

Although it is true that current understanding of the subtleties of the analytic process, of the complexity of the unconscious relation between analyst and analysand derived from the present-day theory of countertransference and from the analysand's concrete response to interpretation (as expounded by Luisa G. Alvarez de Toledo, 1954; Racker, 1958c; Liberman, 1976a, among many others) compel us to be very cautious, the principles laid down by Melanie Klein continue to have, in my opinion, full currency.

CHAPTER THIRTY-TWO

Types of interpretation

32.1   Brief review

We began the study of interpretation on the basis of working measures at the therapist's disposal, measures Knight calls instruments, as opposed to the *material* arising from the patient, which comprises all its modalities of expression. The instruments at the psychotherapist's disposal are many; those available to the analyst are fewer because of his rigorous technique. This is why we said we only count on three basic tools: information, enlightenment and interpretation. Let us remember that, unless interpretation is given a very wide (and imprecise) sense, it should be recognized that, as analysts, we use other elements in order to gather information. The remaining devices that serve to influence the patient, such as support, suggestion and persuasion, on the other hand, are not part of psychoanalytic technique. At most, Bibring (1954) said, they can be used as technical devices but not as therapeutic ones. Even then it must be seen in specific cases whether their use can ever be justified.

We then studied the differences between interpretation and construction, an open theme that was discussed at the international congresses in New York (1979) and Helsinki (1981). Several theoretical points of view are possible here. There are writers who think of them as substantially different instruments. Others think they are essentially the same and only recognize differences of degree in respect of specific technical situations and particular theoretical interests the analysts may have.

In chapter 29 we specifically studied interpretation in its diverse aspects and modalities. Naturally we followed the historical evolution of the technique itself, where the concept of making conscious what is unconscious (through interpretation) became enriched through the diverse metapsychological approaches Freud and some of his disciples had discovered and described.

Thus we distinguished three levels in interpretation: the topographical, which corresponds to the older and simpler formula of making conscious what is unconscious; the dynamic, that of overcoming a particular resistance; and finally the economical, which takes the material at the precise point at which (in the analyst's view, of course) the strongest affects are crystallizing. This economical concept, the axis of Reichian technique, reappeared in another theoretical context and with another terminology—the *timing* of the interpretation and the point of urgency—in Melanie Klein's work. Although it is true that the concept of timing tends, rather, to indicate the importance of the emergent anxiety in that the latter is most relevant to the interpretative task, it implies that the economical factor is in play.

We then studied the structural theory in interpretation, following the path leading from Reich and Fenichel to Anna Freud and her influence on the ego psychologists in the United States and London.

In chapter 31 we attempted to profile interpretation in Melanie Klein. This is not an easy task, in that the theoretical complexities are added to the conflicts of scholastic loyalties. We hope to complete it here and in chapter 33.

32.2   Types of interpretation

Having delineated the concept and studied the metapsychology of interpretation, we will now discuss its *types* (classes). There are really many and various types of interpretation, but we will centre the discussion on four types that encompass the rest: historical and present interpretation, and transference and extratransference interpretation, as illustrated in this synoptic diagram:

$$\text{interpretation}\left\{\begin{array}{l}\text{historical}\\[1em]\text{current}\end{array}\right.\left\{\begin{array}{l}\text{transference}\\[1em]\text{extratransference}\end{array}\right.$$

This diagram covers most interpretative possibilities and is based on two fundamental theories: the theory of the conflict (infantile, actual, current or present) and the theory of the transference—that is, the tendency of human beings to repeat the past in the present. (Further on we will consider other types, such as superficial interpretation and deep interpretation, complete and incomplete interpretation and so forth.) Of course our synoptic diagram can be reversed without varying the concepts: transference interpretation and non-transference interpretation, which is either historical or actual (current).

The interpretation of the patient's history and of his current life, interpretation referring to the past or the present, are not opposed to each other. We are history, and the present is also part of that history, just as the past is also part of the present. Heidegger says that we are time as well as being ourselves. Even without utilizing the theory of transference, we *are* our past: beyond what we do or do not repeat, in each one of our acts, our past can be visualized. Therefore in making this classification no fundamental difference is sanctioned between interpreting the past or the present, because in both cases the individual should be considered in his totality.

32.3   *Historical interpretation*

Despite what we have just said, in practice there are differences between interpreting the historical and the present. To accentuate them leads us again imperceptibly to the problem of constructions versus interpretations, in that the construction always refers to the past. In fact, we call *construction* a special type of historical interpretation, through which we try to recapture a past situation, with its affects, its characters and its anxieties, in the most complete and faithful way possible. Therefore I think that the historical interpretation, in that it accentuates its character as such and attempts a *mise-en-scène* of all the elements that were in play at a given moment, is specifically called construction. (As we saw earlier, the hypothetical character of the construction is in no way specific to it; interpretation is also a hypothesis, and not only due to the decisive reasons of the method but also for reasons of modesty and tact.) As Phyllis Greenacre says, "Any clarifying interpretation generally includes some reference to reconstruction" (1975, p. 703).

If it is difficult to distinguish conceptually interpretation from construction, it is more difficult still to separate construction from historical interpretation. Bernfeld (1932), as we have seen, does not distinguish between them and ends up considering them synonymous. It can be said that construction tries to recover forgotten (repressed) events, and interpretation recovers instincts and desires. This difference, however, is sympathetic and pedagogic rather than rigorous. If the events are forgotten, it is precisely because they were saturated with wishes, and, vice versa, there can be no desires that are split off from the vital experience of the person who has them.

In any case, analysts who utilize construction emphasize the value of the past, convinced that what is fundamental is to reconstruct history, returning to the analysand the place he occupied in the weft of his own life, restoring the moments where that history suffered a cleft.

I am not going to pretend that this great discussion can end here, but I wish to indicate that whatever the theories (and predilections) with which the analyst confronts his singular work, I do not believe there is any analyst who in practice can concern himself solely with the transference and do without historical or present conflict interpretations. And, vice versa, not even the analyst who limits his work to making the most careful reconstruction of the past and who understands transference as an obstacle from which one must free oneself (an imaginary fascination that one must unhook from, as Lacan said in 1951, for example) will think that he can operate without transference interpretations, even if only to remove the obstacle.

32.4 Present (current) interpretation

Our analysands (luckily!) do not, in fact, live in an ivory tower. However stable and powerful the transference neurosis has become, the analysand will have conflicts and anxieties with regard to his environment, which will appear in the session, provided the fundamental rule is observed. At times these conflicts have more to do with the transference than with the surroundings, and then we call them acting out. At other times they refer specifically to the persons who form the social group, and then the problem of interpreting them arises: how and to what extent we have to interpret them—in other words, how the current conflict is interpreted without confusing it with acting out.

A frequent criticism against analysis consists in accusing it of forgetting reality. We also suffer from this criticism from other analysts and likewise accuse others who operate from a different orientation to our own.

However much we are alert to our analysand's relation with his environment, it is not always simple to interpret to him his present conflict. It is debatable whether the interpretation of the present, the real in the life of the patient, can operate as an instrument of transformation. For most psychoanalysts, the interpretation of the present conflict is tactical rather than strategic—it is preparatory. However, let us not forget that the borderline between these two categories is always hazardous, if not ideological. Ultimately the analyst's tactics and strategy change not only with his theoretical orientation but also (rightly) with the infinite fluctuations of the analytic process.

32.5 Interpretative tactics and strategies

Even if we did not note it, our development of the small synoptic diagram dealt not only with the types (or classes) of interpretation but also with interpretative tactics and strategies. If we accept the notion of transference neurosis that "Remembering, Repeating and Working-Through" (Freud, 1914g) proposes, then the interpretation of the present conflict will always be, as we have just said, tactical by definition, while the underlying strategy will be transference. Moreover, when the interpretations of the present conflict are transformed into strategies, we are departing from psychoanalytic method and focusing on the therapeutic situation from a completely different point of view. Perhaps without realizing it, we are engaging in *existential analysis*, since the existential psychoanalyst is interested in the existential encounter, and it is all the same to him whether the encounter takes place within or outside the session. The strategy of existential analysis is to enable the two existents to join; therefore those interpretations are not offered in tactical terms (to arrive at a different situation), but, rather, they are the very foundation of the work. They are strategic interpretations, because the strategy of the endeavour is to find an existential encounter. On the other hand, when I, as an analyst, interpret the present conflict, given that I am operating with the theory of transference, I offer that interpretation tactically, hoping that the link with the past will arise.

In addition, psychoanalysts who think that in our work there is nothing other than the situation of the field, in fact transform the interpretations of the *here and now* into strategies. They think that if the field is modified, the analysand's entire world of objects is necessarily modified. I think this position is erroneous in that it does not take sufficient account of the mechanisms of temporal dissociation. At times the transference conflict is "resolved" by idealizing the analyst and blaming the parents of childhood.

The problem can be resolved only if the analyst makes contact with the analysand in that misty zone where past and present are superimposed, and delineates those two areas through interpretation. Only then does the present become present, enriched by all the notes of the past, and the latter, in turn, is delineated as such—as experience. There are not, then, two distinct areas at the outset; rather, they are defined as a result of analytic work. For the unconscious, Racker said, the analyst is the father and the father is the analyst. Only after adequate interpretation are these two objects differentiated.

32.6 Transference interpretation

The theory of transference is obliged to move between two poles, the non-historical field and the historicity of the subject. We can emphasize either aspect according to our doctrinaire inclinations, but we can never ignore either one. As I have just indicated, the dilemma is not overcome by distinguishing between interpretative tactics and strategies, since these depend less on our theories than on the fluctuations of the analytic process. We have to pass from the non-historical field to history and vice versa in a type of double engagement. Strictly speaking, the dilemma ceases through the straightforward application of the theory of transference, a theory according to which the illness consists in that the past and the present are confused in the mind of the patient.

In her enduring work of 1956, Paula Heimann underlines the importance of the *perceptive function* in the dynamics of transference interpretation. Heimann presented her paper at the Geneva Congress of 1955 (and published it in the *International Journal of Psycho-Analysis* the following year). It is one of the great works on interpretation, as is Strachey's, which we will comment on later on. We will also deal with a postscript by Paula Heimann, which modifies some of the ideas expounded in Geneva. (After writing this article, Heimann distanced herself from the Kleinian school.)

Paula Heimann's starting point is that analytic therapy is directed to the patient's ego, whose primordial function, from which all others are derived, is perception. Perception is to the ego what instinct is to the id, since perception implies that the ego actively cathects the object, through the mechanisms of projection and introjection. In this way, the basic function of the ego, perception, is indissolubly associated with the processes that sanctioned the structure and the development of the ego and the object relation. She says, "Perception initiates contact; and contact involves the main structural mechanisms of introjection and projection, which then build up and shape the ego" (Heimann, 1956, p. 303).

In perception, the life instinct operates in search of union and contact with the object, in the first place the mother's breast; while the aim of the death instinct is to avoid or destroy the contact, the union with the object. It is the life instinct, then, that directs the subject towards the object and engenders perception. On the basis of this major fact we can define the task of treatment as the widening of self-knowledge through the emotional relationship with the analyst. In this way, the transference is really converted into the battlefield where the analysand's conflicts will be resolved, those same conflicts that, in their time, shaped the ego (ibid., p. 304).

The fundamental thesis of this work is, therefore, that the specific instrument of psychoanalytic treatment is transference interpretation (ibid., pp. 304–305), which enables the ego to perceive its emotional experience and make it conscious as it arises and in direct contact with the object.

The other strong thesis of Heimann's work is that unconscious fantasy (as defined by Susan Isaacs) operates at every moment. From this point of view, unconscious fantasy, the cause of the transference, is not something that erupts occasionally in the analysand's relation with the analyst and then interferes with his reason and his desire to cooperate. It is, rather, the fertile womb from which his conscious and unconscious, rational and non-rational motivations are born.

The task of the analyst consists in enabling the analysand's unconscious fantasies to become conscious. This applies both to positive and to negative transference, to his cooperation as much as to his resistance.

There is yet a third thesis in Heimann's work. It refers to the analyst's function. As Freud said, the analyst should be a mirror for the patient; by reflecting him, the analyst gives him the opportunity of perceiving himself in the other: the analyst assumes the role of a supplementary ego for the patient. Heimann concludes that to function in this way, the analyst should let the patient take the initiative; he will always be forbidden to intervene actively with opinions and concepts. At the same time, he will have to analyse his countertransference constantly in order to obtain therefrom indications of what is happening to the analysand, in order to fulfil his difficult task.

If the analyst maintains this equilibrium, Heimann concludes, his interpretative activity can be his reply to an implicit question: what is the analysand doing now, to whom, and why?

32.7   Extratransference interpretation

From the previous discussion, a question repeatedly arises which is always relevant: what is the place of extratransference interpretation in psychoanalysis? Here extratransference interpretation means, according to what has already been studied, that which operates on the present, or on the infantile conflict.

If we wish to pose this problem in Paula Heimann's terms, we could say that everything depends on the perceptual processes at play at a given moment in the analytic situation. As Lacan (1958a, p. 591) says, the interpretation the analyst gives—if he offers it—will be received as coming from the person the transference supposes he is ("*Seulement cette intérpretation, s'il la donne, va être reçue comme venant de la personne que le transfert lui impute d'être*"). In Lacanian technique, this warning surely influences the analyst's attitude of silence, while with the Paula Heimann (1955) of the Geneva Congress, and generally all the Kleinian analysts, it functions as a call to attention so as not to ignore the transference.

Heimann tends to think that only on rare occasions is the analyst fully the analyst for the patient. She points out that those are the moments where the patient becomes conscious of his history and speaks about his objects, his mother or his father, and is really united with them. The analyst becomes a privileged witness of this encounter, in which his persistent labour in the field of the transference crystallizes and bears fruit.

The problem posed, more in relation to the technique, perhaps, than to the strategy, is whether—when a historical or a present interpretation is made—it is the analyst who really makes it or merely the object transferred to him at that moment. If the latter is the case, the patient will perceive the intervention as a threat, a reproach, complicity or seduction: everything except an interpretation, because the centre of dispersion that was in the transference has been omitted.

The risk in extratransference interpretations, then, consists in the patient receiving them with a transference perspective. In Heimann's terms, we will not have modified the perceptual distortion of the patient's ego.

As Money-Kyrle (1968, 1971) says, we will have increased the misunderstanding. However, this risk should not be taken as an insuperable obstacle. The analysand can always misunderstand, and the analyst can always correct this misunderstanding with a new interpretation. And we can also make the opposite mistake by offering a transference interpretation when it would have been appropriate to attend to the infantile or the present conflict. Wishing to be more precise, we will have to say that every interpretation will be well understood by one part of the ego (the observer), and at the same time distorted by the experiencing ego, so that each time we are going to interpret we will have to weigh both possibilities. If the observing ego is sufficient (that is, if we can count on an acceptable therapeutic alliance), the possibility that the interpretation will be operative is naturally greater. It is precisely in these conditions that an extratransference interpretation increases its range.

However, due to its nature, the transference interpretation has better resources to correct the perceptual distortion of the ego (misunderstanding) because it is directed to the immediate, the given. At the same time, the analyst can recover better, as such, in taking the drama back to the real time of its occurrence. These two elements are important, and because they can arise only on the basis of the transference interpretation, they confer on the latter a special value.

If we accept the theory of transference without reservations, we can affirm that, to the extent that we correct the intrusion of the past into the present, we have more opportunities to operate as analysts. Each time I interpret well as an analyst, I extend the sphere within which I can speak as an analyst.

* * *

To sum up: the dilemma of opposition between transference and extratransference opposition is resolved by respecting the complexity of the material without taking refuge in scholastic options. As the great teacher Pichon Rivière said, a good interpretation, a *complete* interpretation, has to take the three spheres and show the essential identity of what happens in the consulting-room with what is happening outside and what happened in the past. If we take only one of these areas, whichever it be, as if the other two did not exist, then we no longer operate with the theory of transference.

32.8   The complete interpretation

As we have just seen, a *complete interpretation* should integrate all the levels the material offers: infantile conflict, present conflict and transference. To the extent that we utilize the theory of transference coherently, basing ourselves on the most classic, most Freudian psychoanalytic postulates, we resolve the contradiction between the diverse levels of operation that converge towards a total situation.

The decisive element in understanding the scholastic differences is to outline in their true hierarchical order the analyst's levels of action. This depends on the theories, but also on clinical practice.

If we postulate, as did Paula Heimann, that reality is perceived on the basis of unconscious fantasy, logically we will think that the immediate reality that is our starting point is the transference. On the other hand, if we maintain that the conflict that is to be analysed is found in a closed circle that we have access to only after a process of regression, we will have to wait in silence for this to occur before intervening. And we will be more silent still if we maintain that the transference is an imaginary phenomenon from which we have to detach ourselves without giving way to the demand.

Some analysts, among whom Ricardo Avenburg (1974, 1983) stands out, say the transference exists both within and outside the session, and therefore there is no difference in interpreting it in one place or another. My maternal transference will be as much with my wife and female friends as with the female analyst who analyses me; and this is true, absolutely true—a fact that illustrates the spontaneity of the transference phenomenon. However, these analysts do not take into account that when my female analyst analyses my maternal transference with my wife or with a female colleague, for me she may not be the analyst. She might be my mother, for example—a mother who does not take responsibility for me and leaves me with the nanny, or a mother who accepts my acting out when I go off with my female neighbour or with the aunt my wife stands for. Or she will be my father, who is going to castrate me because of my incestuous link; or my little brother, jealous when he sees me with mother, and so forth. And, finally, how can my analyst be sure that at that moment my wife is my mother for me? She can be my father, for example. And she can even be, plainly and simply, my wife, without distortions! To be more precise, I should say that, in fact, when my analyst interprets my maternal transference with my wife or with someone outside, she operates on the basis of two theoretical inferences: that my wife—or whoever—is my mother for me, and that she, my analyst, is my analyst for me. These two assumptions can be borne out, certainly. But it is nevertheless paradoxical that, at that precise moment, I distort there, and not here. If, in fact, this were so, one would have to ask in what way the mechanisms of dissociation are operating.

On this point the importance Heimann accords to the perceptual phenomenon is understandable, since it will always be easier for the analyst to notice and for the analysand to correct a perceptual distortion when it occurs in the field. It is more certain to speak of the transference (neurosis) one sees than of the transferences one infers. An error will become inevitable if a countertransference problem leads one to interpret in this way. If the analyst is really being alluded to and still prefers to interpret the present or the infantile conflict, it is logical to suppose that his countertransference is influencing him.

Many of these reflections can apply *mutatis mutandis* to Lacan, or more precisely to the Lacan of the "Intervention sur le transfert" (1951). It is not enough in any way to operate the dialectical inversion of the material, to detach oneself from the transference and to refer the patient to his history, if only because this attitude on the analyst's part can be seen by the patient from the point of view of his transference conflict. Thus, for example, to operate the dialectical inversion (although of course these words are not spoken) will be, for the analysand, homosexuality; to refer him to his history will mean, for him, taking him out of his parents' bed, and so forth. I remember an erythrophobic patient who blushed each time he heard some expression that (at the primary process level) might allude to homosexuality, for example, "to put the car into reverse", to "make a banking investment" (*inversión* in Spanish) and so forth.

All this explains why we have established differences between the tactical and the strategic levels of interpretation, as Löwenstein also does. In schematic form I would like to propose that, in terms of the *analytic situation* (that is, of the field), the transference interpretation is the analyst's strategy, while interpretations of the present conflict are tactical or a consequence of the elaboration that follows the latter: "It is understandable now why you feel that your wife . . ." From the point of view of the *psychoanalytic process*, on the other hand, the transference interpretation is tactical and subordinate to the strategy of establishing its link with the past, with the infantile conflict.

Beyond these general lines, however, we should always begin from what appears manifestly in the material. If what really predominates in the material is the present conflict, to interpret it will be in principle more legitimate, while to locate it in the transference, as the inexperienced analyst sometimes does ("And this also happens to you with me") will be no more than an artefact. This artefact will appear more frequently, of course, in analytic groups for whom it is of fundamental importance to interpret in the transference, generating in consequence an analytic superego that applies pressure in that direction. In any case, it is nevertheless probable that the interpretation of the present conflict only fulfils the tactical function of reactivating the transference conflict, as Strachey said. (We will return to this interesting theme when we study mutative interpretation.)

The extratransference interpretation of the present conflict acquires a different value when it is integrated into the process of working through. As we will see in dealing with insight, the effect of the interpretation should be understood on the basis of the process of working through, which is carried out in large part by showing the analysand to what extent he repeats the same pattern in different contexts (Fenichel, 1941). This is achieved only by attending impartially to the transference, the present conflict and the infantile conflict, as they appear in the material.

A *complete* interpretation is, then, one that covers the three areas of conflict. Here, as in arithmetic, the order of the factors does not alter the product. It is the same for us, whether we follow the path that leads from the transference to the history and from there to the present conflict, or any other. All the combinations are valid, and there is therefore no obligatory route. If we try to apply a strict scheme, we are already erring, because no scheme can cover the infinite variety of experience in the consulting-room. Although it is true that the passage through the transference is unavoidable and privileged, because our enemy can never be conquered *in absentia* or *in effigie*, an analysis where the present conflict is not interpreted is, equally, inconceivable if we are going to be consequent with the concept of working through. This applies even more to the infantile conflict, which is intrinsic to the transference.

The truth is that if we are receptive, the patient's material will lead us continually here and there, turning on these three areas. Analytic objectivity, measured in free-floating attention, implies taking the material as it comes, without prevention—without memory or desire, Bion says with hyperbolic simplicity. The only priority is free association. (See pertinent examples in Etchegoyen, "Instances and Alternatives of the Interpretative Work", 1981c.)

As we have said, both the major difficulty and the risk of extra-transference interpretation are found in that the analyst has generally been assigned a role in the transference. To the extent that this role is strong, every extratransference interpretation is destined to fail, to be misunderstood. When the analyst is the analyst for the patient, and this is measured in the amount of observing ego present in the patient at a given moment, then we can interpret equally within or outside the analytic situation. We do not often have this luck, however, which is not surprising if we adhere to what the theory says—that the libido of the neurotic is linked to archaic figures and is therefore not available for the objects of reality. This is why we can say that the occasion to interpret outside the transference probably does not arise for us frequently. Probability, however, cannot rule specific practice in the consulting-room, and the opposite alternative is valid. Not to interpret the present or the infantile conflict when it is appropriate, offering instead a conventional interpretation in the transference, is an error that reinforces the mechanisms of dissociation and contributes to the idealization of the analyst. As Rangell (1985) says: Attention to the transference neurosis alone, without a relentless establishment of its links to the past, is a technical error of many analysts today" (pp. 87–88).

The mechanisms of dissociation both complicate and enrich the analyst's task. We are accustomed to discovering that the patient dissociates when he speaks of his present conflict or his infantile conflict to avoid the conflict in the transference. But he may do precisely the opposite, artificially reinforcing the conflict with the analyst so as not to see what is happening to him outside or to avoid taking responsibility for his history. And also, of course, to please the analyst, who sees only the transference.

Here we certainly do remain hooked into the transference, in an illusory, imaginary situation, as Lacan says. I remember a rich and very intelligent man who spoke vainly of "his relation with me" on the day he had received the news that one of his main businesses was going bankrupt. No less problematic was another patient who, while he struggled in a transference conflict of unusual intensity, said he was going to speak about me, because that was the only subject *I* was interested in! "My" predilection was a sufficient motive for him straight away to insult me through and through.

Finally, we have to accept perforce the beautiful complexity of the analytic situation and that we can never be sure of anything; we must remain receptive to the material, always attentive to the changes that can occur. The analytic process is very subtle, and we are not going to simplify it with a position taken at the outset.

One of the factors that gives the transference interpretation an irreplaceable value is its immediacy, and, as we shall see shortly, Strachey's theories imply that the analytic setting operates as a testable reality. The setting is the necessary condition for analytic work. The analyst's mental and emotional attitude are part of his setting—necessary conditions for the analytic work, where the sole sufficient condition is interpretation. If the interpretation works, it is precisely because the conditions for the patient to take it as an interpretation are present. Thus if I compete with my patient and I offer him the best interpretation in the world on his oedipal rivalry, that interpretation will never work. And in fact it is not good either; it is a sophisticated way for me to exercise my rivalry, nothing more. If the interpretation is useful, it is because the necessary conditions for its formulation are present.

32.9   *Paula Heimann's correction*

In the *post-scriptum* published in the *Bulletin* of the French Psychoanalytic Association in 1969, Paula Heimann returns to her 1956 article to indicate some changes that had come about during the intervening 15 years.

Now she no longer accepts the Freudian theory of the life and death instincts, which she had enthusiastically embraced from her time as a candidate onwards. There is a primary destructive tendency in the human being side by side with the libidinous one, but the relationship between the hypothetical death instinct and the primary destructive tendency no longer seems convincing to her.

Heimann also thinks that her paper accorded an exaggerated importance to object relations and the mechanisms of introjection and projection that shape the growth of the ego, while ignoring the innate capacities of the ego in respect of potentialities that spur development. Following Hendrick, Heimann feels that the mechanisms of the ego are not only defensive but also executive.

She still thinks interpretation is the only tool specific to analysis, but she now accords greater importance to the analytic situation and to the present conceptions that describe it from the dual angle of the therapeutic alliance and the transference neurosis. The analytic situation as a *milieu* offers the analysand an atmosphere that resembles the familiar milieu of childhood and, at the same time, is exquisitely variable and rich in stimuli.

To the extent that it repeats the original lack of differentiation between the nursing infant and maternal care, the analytic milieu allows the patient to relive the narcissistic illusion of being one with his loving parents and relive the primitive trust a favourable development relies on. It is within the perimeter of this teamwork that the processes of individuation are found, as well as the discovery of the specific capacities of the ego that can correct what has gone wrong.

Changes in the psychic condition of the patient depend on his becoming aware of himself, and this arises from the interpretations of the analyst. But in evaluating the importance of an interpretation we cannot neglect the effect of the psychoanalytic milieu, which, due to its constancy, represents a source of positive transference.

What the analyst offers with an interpretation, and sometimes with a question or a "hmm!", is the perception of a process that should be a point of departure for the ego. It is not appropriate for the analyst to offer the patient the solution to his problems, rather, enlightenment that adds something to what the analysand already knew about himself.

Finally, the analyst should be attentive to the meaning of the transference, but also to the importance of events outside the analytic situation.

The *post-scriptum* of 1969 marks an evident change in Paula Heimann's thinking. Interpretation now shares, with the psychoanalytic milieu, the curative potential of the method, and its range is very limited. It is no longer information that broadens the perceptive capacity of the ego, but an enlightenment that adds something to what the analysand already knew about himself. Without attempting to explain everything, interpretation can be reduced to a "hmm", which can signify understanding as much as doubt.

The transference is no longer the decisive element, and interpretation should also concern itself with external reality.

As to its range and depth, interpretation approaches enlightenment now, and to me it is no mere chance that it is believed to be superimposable on that famous interjection ("hmm"), which can transmit much understanding and affection but little information.

32.10 On the register of unconscious fantasy

Securely based on Susan Isaacs's concept of unconscious fantasy, Heimann's work gives the theoretical reasons that lead Kleinian analysts to interpret the transference with greater breadth and frequency. Melanie

Klein herself explained it in "The Origins of Transference" (1952a): "For many years—and this is up to a point still true today—transference was understood in terms of direct references to the analyst in the patient's material. My conception of transference as rooted in the earliest stages of development and in deep layers of the unconscious is much wider and entails a technique by which from the whole material presented the unconscious elements of the transference are deduced" (p. 55).

Paula Heimann develops these affirmations by Melanie Klein in her essay. López (1972) also bases his work on them when he studies how the unconscious fantasy that feeds the transference in the session can be discovered, and how the interpretation is constructed from there. López bases himself particularly on some elements of the theory of communication and on the information the analyst registers as countertransference. In the typical neurotic patient, López says, the preferred path of communication is verbal; but in characteropathic patients much of the communication occurs along non-verbal or para-verbal channels, which are precisely those that arise most in the countertransference. The understanding thus obtained "is completed through its correlation with the verbal meaning" (López, 1972, p. 196).

When the countertransference engagement is greater still, as in psychosis, the analyst generally has to interpret without attending to the alternative of the verbal signifier.

In the intermediate cases of López's classification, the character disturbances, the analyst can at times correlate the verbal signifier with what is registered in the countertransference, and he then manages to construct an interpretation that includes the verbal signifier (what the patient is saying), the paraverbal component (how he says it) and the non-verbal one (what he does) (ibid., p. 198).

32.11 Merton Gill's revision

An extensive revision of the analysis of transference has taken place among ego psychologists in the United States, starting with Merton M. Gill, who published first an article in 1979 and then a long and erudite monograph in 1982, the first volume of which deals with theory and technique, while the second, written in collaboration with Irwin Z. Hoffman, presents clinical material taken from analytical sessions. As we saw when considering the Sandlers' ideas in section 9.9, this spirit of renewal also reached the Contemporary Freudian Group in London, and one of the articles we studied (Sandler & Sandler, 1984) deals with Gill's monograph and the theory of the two unconsciouses.

Gill returns to the theme of transference concerned because he has the impression that the analysis of the transference is not being carried out in the way he believes it could and should be done. He begins his book by saying that although all analysts consider that the analysis of transference is the heart of our technique, the truth is that it is not carried out in a systematic and detailed way; and he ends by repeating that "the analysis of the transference should play a greater and more central role in analytic technique than I believe it does in prevailing practice" (Gill, 1982, p. 177). He ventures to add boldly that the criticism can be applied to Freud himself, who always thought that "the analysis of the transference is ancillary to the analysis of the neurosis" (ibid., p. 177). On this point Gill and I coincide; and the reader will remember that in chapter 8, "The Dynamics of Transference", I followed Freud's reasoning to show the motives that led him to think of transference (in my view mistakenly) as a tactic of resistance. As I also said in the paper I presented to the First Argentinian Psychoanalytical Congress (Etchegoyen, 1988, p. 97): "thanks to Melanie Klein's genius, transference is at last shaping the strategy of analytic work"; but I am sure that the great researcher from Illinois is not going to admit it yet.

Gill divides the analysis of transference into two steps, two moments. In the first, which is, on the whole, the most neglected, the interpretation is directed towards the resistance to the awareness of transference; in the following step, a consequence of the previous one, the resistance to the resolution of transference should be interpreted (Gill, 1982, chapter 1, especially p. 15 et seq.). In the first case the analysand resists contact with what is transferred; in the second he resists abandoning it. Gill says that interpretation of the resistance to becoming aware of the transference aims to make explicit the implicit transference, while interpretation of the resistance to resolving the transference has the intention of making the patient understand that the already explicit transference must include a determinant from the past, a point with which the Sandlers do not seem to be very much in agreement.

This leads Gill to point out the general neglect of analysing the transference here and now in favour of genetic interpretations that refer the transference conflict to the infantile models that originated it. He realizes at last that, in fleeing from the transference to the past, both analysand and analyst might be relieved of the disturbed affects of the present.

On the basis of these reflections, Gill proposes that the field of the transference should be widened in the analytic situation, attending to the veiled allusions to the transference in the analysand's material, and paying attention to the real circumstances of the analytic situation that determine the transference phenomenon here and now, before employing the genetic transference interpretation. From this it naturally follows that many of the analysand's associations on real facts or events and persons should be interpreted in terms of the transference or as an acting out.

With his usual erudition, Gill (1979) reveals a genuine Freud who, from the autobiography (1925d) to *The Interpretation of Dreams* (1900a) is alerting us to the analytic situation and the analyst himself being permanently alluded to in the analysand's associative material. This would be the source of inspiration, he concludes, for Strachey's notable work on the nature of the therapeutic action of psychoanalysis.

Gill tries to differentiate himself from the Kleinian analysts, assuring us that the latter do not take into account—as he does—the real features of the present analytic situation. But perhaps the talented Illinois investigator could manage to revise this stark affirmation if he were to read Strachey's work, which he so admires, with less passion; if he were to remember what Paula Heimann said about the ego and perception and—last but not least—if he were to reread without prejudice "The Origins of the Transference" (Klein, 1975, Vol. 3).

* * *

To sum up: for its undeniable intrinsic value, for its consistency and clarity, *Analysis of Transference* has been very well received in the international psychoanalytic community. Its author's authoritative voice will doubtless be listened to in North America and most European countries, much more than that of the Kleinian analysts of London and Buenos Aires. The book we are studying will thus help to bring together the positions of two schools that have confronted each other by tradition, perhaps more for historical, geographical and ideological (affective) reasons than for theoretical or technical ones. It is also a good sign that some Lacanian authors such as Nasio (1984) are reading Merton Gill attentively.

CHAPTER THIRTY-THREE

Mutative interpretation

O n 13 June 1933 James Strachey read "The Nature of the Therapeutic Action of Psychoanalysis" to the British Psycho-Analytical Society. This paper was to leave a profound mark on psychoanalytic thought. It is, without doubt, one of the most valuable works in analytical literature, and there are those who say it is the most read, excluding Freud's works, naturally. It appeared in the *International Journal of Psycho-Analysis* in 1934. (It was published again in 1969, when the *Journal* commemorated its fiftieth anniversary; the preceding issue of the same volume had carried obituaries by Anna Freud and Winnicott on the occasion of Strachey's death, at the age of 79, in April 1967. When he read his celebrated paper, Strachey was about 45 years old.)

Shortly afterwards, on 4 August 1936, during the Fourteenth International Congress in Marienbad, Strachey spoke in the Symposium on the Theory of the Therapeutic Results of Psycho-Analysis, together with Glover, Fenichel, Bergler, Nunberg and Bibring—all of them, indeed, first-class analysts. That account reproduced the ideas of the previous work, with some differences I shall point out later.

This chapter is based on Etchegoyen, "A cincuenta años de la interpretación mutativa", published in the *Revista Chilena de Psicoanálisis* of 1982, and "Fifty Years after the Mutative Interpretation", *International Journal of Psycho-Analysis*, 64 (1983): 445–459.

As its title implies, Strachey's work delves into the mechanisms that bring about the therapeutic effects of psychoanalysis, and the result is clear: the therapeutic action of psychoanalysis depends on the dynamic changes that interpretation produces, and particularly on a special type of interpretation he calls *mutative*.

33.1   Background to Strachey's work

Strachey's paper and the Marienbad Symposium have a definite precedent in the Eighth Salzburg Congress in 1924, in which Sachs, Alexander and Radó were presenters. Their papers (published in the *International Journal of Psycho-Analysis* in 1925) reveal, in turn, the direct influence of Freud's structural theory, and particularly the novel concept on suggestion Freud proposed in *Group Psychology and the Analysis of the Ego* (1921c).

Sachs' contribution (1925) suggests that the structural change analysis provokes depends on a modification of the ego ideal (superego). The old conflict between the id and the ego is resolved because the patient's superego conforms to the attitude of the analytic superego and adopts an attitude of sincerity in the face of the impulse that allows the removal of the repression.

Alexander (1925) also considers that the conflict should be resolved on the basis of a modification of the superego. But his assumptions go somewhat further than those of Sachs, since the superego is, for him, an archaic configuration, which the cure should demolish.

Alexander maintains that the superego has no access to reality, nor does the ego have contact with the instincts (1925, p. 22). "The ego is blind to what goes on within and has forgotten the language of the instincts. The super-ego, however, understands this instinctual speech only too well and demands punishment for tendencies of which the ego is quite unaware" (ibid., p. 23). On the basis of these definitions, it is clear why Alexander considers the superego as an anachronistic structure and postulates that the curative process consists in demolishing it, so that the ego can take charge of its functions—which certainly is not achieved without resistances (ibid., p. 25).

This process develops in two stages and deals with the metapsychology of the treatment. On the basis of the transference, the analyst first takes charge of the functions of the superego; then, through the interpretative work and the process of working-through (ibid., p. 26), he reinstalls them in the ego of the patient. The role of the transference in the analytic process consists, then, in transforming the structural conflict between the id and the superego in an external conflict between the patient (id) and the analyst (superego).

It might be worth pausing here for a moment in order to review Alexander's hypotheses and to point out how much they beg the question. Because if one maintains that the superego is totally irrational and that everything rational is deposited in the ego, then it is acceptable to transform the superego into ego, remove it and subsume it in the ego. This criterion finally leads Alexander to his corrective emotional experience. Unlike Alexander, most analysts think the superego has positive aspects, although it is sometimes referred to pejoratively. Freud always underlined this and says it elegantly at the end of his essay on humour (1927d). The superego theory merely indicates the existence of a moral agency within the psychic apparatus, not that the latter is necessarily irrational nor irreversibly cruel.

Lacan (1957–58), who has studied this problem in depth, considers the *superego* as a prohibiting paternalistic structure and the *ego ideal* as the representative of the giving aspects of the father, with whom the child tends to identify at the end of the Oedipus complex. My superego says that I cannot go to bed with my mother, but my ego ideal says I can be like my father and have a woman who is different to my mother. Berenstein (1976) reached the same conclusion, in his own way. Thus one can say, with Lacan, that the superego is a prohibiting agency and that the ego ideal stimulates, without forgetting that both aspects occur in fact simultaneously, and that both are necessary.

In any case, the superego contains a broad, archaic infantile sector, which constitutes a real problem in analysis. No one doubts that the analyst has to confront an immature and irrational superego.

33.2 Radó's parasitic superego

Radó (1925) expounded in Salzburg the economic principles of analytic technique and introduced the concept of parasitic superego.

The point of departure for his thinking is the concept of transference neurosis, which, as Freud described it in 1914, consists in an *artificial* neurosis that appears during psychoanalytic treatment. Our technique directs itself to its resolution. In hypnotic therapy, Radó continues, there is also a transference, to the hypnotist, of the libido of the symptoms, which reproduces exactly the relation of the child with his parents. In hypnosis, then, a hypnotic transference neurosis is formed as an artificial product of the therapy.

For Radó, an artificial neurosis also arises in the cathartic method—one that is more apparent than the former. Here there is the influence of a new factor: the attitude of the hypnotist changes. Instead of operating as a superego that represses the symptoms—that is, the conflict and infantile sexuality—the hypnotist using the cathartic method uses his influence so that the instincts linked to the symptoms are freed from repression. In this way, the symptoms give way and the liberated energy crystallizes in the affective discharge we call abreaction, which is strictly an acute neurotic symptom. For Radó, abreaction is the artificial counterpart of a hysterical symptom. This thought seems to me the most consistent theoretical objection to the value of catharsis in psychotherapy.

There is no essential difference, in Radó's view, between the artificial neurosis of Breuer's cathartic method described above and that of the method Freud subsequently proposed, with a patient who is awake.

The metapsychology of all therapeutic procedures should be sought in Freud's (1921c) explanation of hypnosis: the hypnotist takes the place of the hypnotized patient's ego ideal, usurping its functions through a process of introjection. (The ego ideal of 1921 becomes the superego of 1923.) The hypnotized patient places in his ego an ideal representation of the hypnotist, which is continually modified since sense impressions from the external world and cathexes from the internal world continue to be received. If the introjected object is able to attract the cathexes of the internal world in this way, its sphere of influence increases, reinforced by these. The hypnotist ceases to be simply an introjected object, becoming a real *parasitic* superego. "Should it now succeed in attracting to itself the natural cathexis of the topographically differentiated superego, its sphere of influence is thereby subjected to a new authority and the hypnotist is promoted from being an object of the ego to the position of a *parasitic superego*" (Radó, 1925, p. 40).

This passage of cathexes of the superego onto the introjected object is always only partial and therefore precarious. But, at any rate, the economic change has the consequence of weakening the superego and fortifying the parasitic superego momentarily—that is, while the hypnotist's influence lasts. On the basis of the economic changes just described, Radó concludes, a new superego is formed in hypnosis—a parasitic superego, which is the double of the other one.

This process, Radó says, reproduces the original one, given that the superego was formed initially on the basis of the introjection of the parents, which led to the withdrawal of the incestuous cathexes. In the neurotic this process was not successful, and it is precisely the repressed libido of the Oedipus complex that is invested in the hypnotist, the parasitic superego. This reactivates the feminine masochism of the ego, which provokes an acute modification of the energetic equilibrium of the psychic apparatus. The latter becomes neutralized because the process of identification desexualizes the relation between the ego and the introjected object, which is thus transformed into a parasitic superego through its appropriation of the cathexes of the original superego.

In sum, then, the hypnotist takes the place of an object, which reactivates the masochism of the ego and sets in motion a defensive process of introjection that provokes the idealization of the object and reinforces its authority vis-à-vis the ego, becoming in this way the superego. "The hypnotist first of all takes the place of an object for the ego, turns to the masochistic state of readiness in the ego, is quickly subjected to the defensive process of introjection which brings about his idealization and strengthens his authority over the ego by means of the super-ego" (ibid., p. 44).

We do not know how Radó would have described the function of the superego in the transference neurosis, because the second part of his work was never published. He would probably have established a difference between what he wrote about hypnotic methods and what he did not manage to write about the psychoanalytic method, preserving his line of reasoning. We do know, on the other hand, that Strachey took up the idea of the parasitic superego to initiate his own investigation.

33.3 The auxiliary superego

In opposition to Bernheim, for whom hypnosis was a product of suggestion, Freud (1921c) maintained that suggestion is explicable on the basis of hypnosis—that is, on the basis that the hypnotist is located in the place of the ego ideal of the hypnotized patient, in the same way that the (group) leader is constituted within the ego of the members of the group and operates on them from there. It is therefore this process of introjection, which arises in hypnosis, that conditions suggestibility.

This idea of Freud's—the relation between suggestibility and hypnosis, which provides the backbone for the three Salzburg contributions—also inspires Strachey. It is also the point of departure for many reflections on technical problems. Ida Macalpine (1950), for example, explains transference on the basis of hypnotic suggestion.

Since Freud always thought that, in the final instance, the analyst operates suggestively on the analysand for him to abandon his resistances, then one can say, as a syllogism—Strachey concludes—that the analyst functions because he has located himself in the place of his patient's superego.

Based on Alexander, Strachey thinks there is a moment at the beginning of the process when the analyst takes the place of the analysand's superego. But not, as the Hungarian says, in order to demolish it and return it as a constituent of the ego structure, but in order to operate from an advantageous position. Incidentally, Strachey is not in agreement with the idea that the superego is entirely irrational and unconscious and should be demolished.

What interests Strachey in Alexander's metapsychology is that the analysand's superego is taken over by the analyst, and that this alters in some measure the terms of the conflict. Here, on this point, Strachey accepts Radó's economic principles in that the hypnotized patient introjects the hypnotist as a parasitic superego that absorbs the energy and assumes the functions of the original superego. This process is always transitory and does not last beyond the influence of the hypnotist. But it explains the changes promoted by the hypnotic suggestive treatment and the cathartic cure, and also the always temporary results of these methods.

33.4 The neurotic vicious circle

Now Strachey covers the path that separates the transitory hypnotic methods from the permanent changes that analysis can achieve, and he does so guided by Melanie Klein. The human being functions through continuous processes of introjection and projection, the foundation for the object relation and the structure of the psychic apparatus. The superego appears very early and bears the mark of sadism that the child projects into the object. As Klein (1928) says, if the small child can feel terrorized in the face of a superego that destroys, bites and cuts into pieces, it is because he projected into it his destructive impulses, beyond the aggressive and frustrating characteristics of the parents of his infancy. The object on which the impulses were projected is then introjected with these characteristics, and the new projection depends on them. In this way a vicious circle can be created, where the object becomes dangerous because of the sadism projected into it, which compels a reinforcement of sadism as a defence, or a "virtuous" circle in which the object becomes each time more protective and good, which has to do with the advance of the libido to the genital stage.

The play of projection/introjection enables Strachey to explain simultaneously the mechanism of the illness and its cure. The vicious circle described impedes growth and stultifies the individual in the primary conflicts that impede his access to the genital stage, where the instincts of the id are more tolerable and the superego is more tolerant. If we could break this vicious circle, Strachey concludes, development would be reestablished spontaneously.

When he meets a new object, the neurotic directs to it his impulses, at the same time as he projects into it his archaic objects. In fact this happens with the analyst at the beginning of analysis. The varied objects that form the superego are invested in him. Granted the analyst's real behaviour and assuming the analysand has a minimal contact with reality, the latter incorporates the analyst as an object different from the rest, and Strachey calls this the *auxiliary superego*.

Strachey follows Radó's inspiration on this point; but there is a basic difference. Strachey does not call the superego a "parasite" but an *auxiliary*, and this difference pertains not only to the nomenclature. Radó's supposition is more energetic (the parasite sucks the superego's energies, and this makes the cure possible), while Strachey emphasizes the structural aspect, in that he thinks this location of the analyst as superego opens up the possibility of breaking the neurotic vicious circle that perpetuates and reinforces the mechanisms of introjection and projection, the basis of the object relation. (This is why I do not believe that Strachey marks the apotheosis of an impulse psychology, as Klauber, 1972, p. 386, maintains.)

There are various reasons for differentiating in principle the analyst as introjected object from the archaic superego, among which Strachey mentions the permissive attitude that allows the introduction of the fundamental rule. The auxiliary superego authorizes the patient to say everything that comes into his mind—what Racker called the abolition of rejection (1952 [1968, p. 72]). In this way the new superego ("you may say") functions in a manner opposite to the old one ("you must not say"), although the difference is very fluid and at any moment the rational superego can become transformed, demanding: "If you do not say everything, I shall stop loving you, I shall throw you out of the consulting-room, I shall castrate you, I shall kill you, I shall cut you to pieces", and so forth.

The only way to produce a breach in the vicious circle, Strachey says, is for the projected image not to be totally confused with the real one. The necessary condition for this is the analytic setting; the sufficient condition is interpretation.

The auxiliary superego is distinct not only from the analysand's bad, archaic superego but also from the good one, since its goodness is based consistently on something that is real and actual which depends above all on the setting. "The most important characteristic of the auxiliary superego is that its advice to the ego is consistently based upon *real* and *contemporary* considerations and this in itself serves to differentiate it from the greater part of the original super-ego" (Strachey, 1934, p. 140).

The *setting*, understood here as the analyst's neutral attitude, enables him to remain less involved in the conflict, and in turn allows the analysand to become more conscious of the distortion his projections promote. In effect, the setting gives the patient the really singular opportunity of projecting and seeing that these projections do not correspond to reality, in that the analyst responds with an impartial attitude. But this alone, Strachey continues, is surely not enough, because the pressure of the infantile superego (and in general of the conflict) makes the tendency to misunderstand real experience very great. Since the difference between the archaic and the auxiliary superego is labile and aleatory, it will not be long before the patient finds, in his fantasy or in fact, sufficient motives for narrowing that difference, with which the new superego will be subsumed into the old one.

The analyst, however, has at his disposal a singular instrument to prevent that superimposition, and that is *interpretation*. (I would like to add here that, remembering Pichon Rivière, interpretation not only corrects the misunderstanding, but also "cures" the analyst of his countertransference conflict of the moment, because each time one makes an interpretation one recovers oneself as an analyst, to the extent that one returns to the analysand what really belongs to him.)

Strachey knows full well that the idea of interpretation is ambiguous and charged with affective connotations, if not irrational and magical ones. This is why he tries to specify it with his concept of *mutative interpretation*.

33.5   Mutative interpretation

The economic changes that the presence of the analyst as an auxiliary superego implies allow a particular impulse of the id that will be directed, in principle, to the analyst, to surface in consciousness. This is the critical point, since the analyst does not behave, in fact, like the original object. Therefore the analysand can become aware of the distance between his archaic object and the actual one. "The interpretation has now become a mutative one, since it has produced a breach in the neurotic vicious circle" (Strachey, 1934, p. 143). The analysand now introjects a different object, and with this both the internal world (superego) and the external world change, given that the next projection will also be more realistic, less distorted. The psychoanalyst re-emerges from the interpretative process as a real figure, which is what matters most to Strachey in his article. A correct interpretation always implies an affirmation of the analyst in his function as such. Let us say here that the word "mutative" means, for Strachey, something that changes the psychological structure, just as genetic mutation changes the cellular structure.

Strachey therefore calls interpretation *mutative* when it produces structural changes; he says that it consists of two moments, which he separates didactically in his description to make it more comprehensible. For the theory, however, it is not necessary to give these two phases a temporal demarcation. They can be conceived simultaneously or separately, and frequently the analyst's interpretation covers both in one and the same exposition.

The two phases are never simple and can be very complex. But from the genetic point of view they will always exist. The key to the theory is rooted in the analysand's awareness of *two* things: an instinctive impulse and an object unsuited to that impulse.

33.5.1   First phase

As we have said, the first phase is fulfilled when the analysand becomes conscious of the instinct or, as Strachey says following Freud (1915d, 1915e), of a *derivative* of the *Ucs*. This can be arrived at directly and spontaneously—that is, before interpreting—but it is more usual for the analyst to intervene with successive interpretations so that the analysand can realize there is a state of tension and anxiety. Thus it will be necessary to interpret the ego defence, the censure of the superego and the instinctive impulse in diverse forms and in corresponding order, until the derivative becomes conscious and anxiety is mobilized, in a dose that shall always be moderate. This is because an essential characteristic of the mutative interpretation is that the discharge of anxiety be moderated. If the dose is too low, the first phase will not have been reached. If it is too high, an explosion of anxiety will occur that will make the second phase an impossibility.

33.5.2 Second phase

In this phase the analysand's sense of reality plays an important part in order for him to contrast the real object with the archaic (transferred) one. We have said that this contrast is certainly unstable; the analysand can transform at any moment the real object (analyst) into the archaic one. In other words, the patient is always ready to confuse the analyst with the object of his conflict. The analyst then loses the position of privilege that enables him to effect the mutation. On this point the decisive importance of the setting stands out. If the analyst removes himself from his setting and from his role through unfitting behaviour (acting out), the immediate (and logical) response of the analysand will be to include him in the series of his archaic good and bad objects. In this way the analyst remains incapacitated and the second phase cannot be carried out. Although it is paradoxical—Strachey says in a memorable phrase—"the best way of ensuring that his ego shall be able to distinguish between phantasy and reality is to withhold reality from him as much as possible" (1934, p. 147). Examining it closely, Strachey's paradox is not one: in transgressing the parameters of his setting, the analyst removes himself from reality (which is his work). And now we know with certainty what was not known in Strachey's time, that these transgressions are always rooted in the countertransference neurosis (Racker, 1948; Money-Kyrle, 1956). Studying Strachey's work, Herbert Rosenfeld (1972) indicates that when the analyst concerns himself with a reality external to analysis, the analysand is disturbed and misunderstands him.

33.6 Defining characteristics of mutative interpretation

As described, the two phases of the mutative interpretation have to do with anxiety: the first phase liberates it, the second resolves it. When the anxiety is already manifest, the second phase should be administered. It may be that in this case the analyst prefers to reassure the patient, thinking that the amount of anxiety makes resolving it through interpretation improbable. This conduct can be tactically plausible, although the analyst should then be aware that he has momentarily given up the possibility of confronting the anxiety with specifically analytic methods.

If we wish to describe Strachey's procedure in the language of the structural theory, we can say that the first phase is directed to the id and tries to make the derivative of the instinct conscious. The awareness of the derivative is accompanied by anxiety, and then the second phase is directed to the ego. With this formulation it becomes clear that, on this point, Strachey seems to advance here, in a certain way, Anna Freud's thought, who in 1936 will say that interpretative work has to fluctuate continually between the id and the ego.

Strachey considers that there are certain defining features of the mutative interpretation, which is always immediate, specific and progressive (graduated).

An interpretation is *immediate* when it is applied to an impulse in a state of cathexis. An interpretation that informs the analysand of the existence of an impulse that is not present will never be mutative, although it can be useful in preparing the field. A necessary condition of the mutative interpretation will always be that it relates to an emotion the analysand experiences as something actual. In other words, the interpretation should always bear on the point of urgency, as Klein (1932) repeatedly indicates.

An interpretation is *specific* if it is detailed and concrete, a point Kris (1951) underlines when he recalls the necessity of attending to the preconscious links of the material. Again, there is nothing objectionable in the vagueness, generality or imprecision of an interpretation; in fact, one interprets in this way perforce when approaching a new theme. However, as long as we do not manage to circumscribe the material, as long as we do not manage to focus the interpretation on relevant details, we can never expect a mutative effect. The interpretation should adapt itself exactly to what is happening; it should be delineated and concrete.

Lastly, the mutative interpretation must hold to the principle of an optimum quantity, it must act *progressively*, by well-graded steps, because otherwise either the first phase will not be reached or the second will become impossible. Strachey teaches us to distrust hasty interpretations, which attempt to skip stages. Upheavals are not mutations, and great changes turn out in the end to be short-lived and suggestive in nature.

33.7   Extratransference interpretation

One of the major merits of Strachey's work is the evaluation of the extratransference interpretation, a theme he later considered again in Marienbad. Strachey asks himself whether "no extratransference interpretation can set in motion the chain of events which I have suggested as being the essence of psychoanalytic therapy? That is indeed my opinion, and it is one of my main objects in writing this paper to throw into relief—what has, of course, already been observed, but never, I believe, with enough explicitness—the dynamic distinctions between transference and extratransference interpretations" (1934, p. 154).

The essential difference between these two types of interpretation depends on the fact that only in transference interpretation is the object of the id-impulse present. The effect of this circumstance makes it difficult for the extratransference interpretation to reach the point of urgency (first phase) and, if it does so, it will always be problematic for the analysand to establish the difference between the real absent object and that of his fantasy (second phase). An extratransference interpretation will therefore always be less effective and more risky.

Up to this point Strachey's reasoning aims to demonstrate that it is *factually* impossible for an extratransference interpretation to be mutative, although it may be *logically* possible. However, in a footnote at the end of his paper Strachey offers the theoretical arguments for maintaining that only a transference interpretation can be mutative.

The greatest risk for an extratransference interpretation is that the second phase may become seriously disturbed. It can happen, for instance, that the impulse freed in the first phase is not applied to modify the imago to which it was remitted, but is projected on to the analyst himself. This projection onto the analyst can without doubt also happen in a transference interpretation, but the context is different, because in that case the object of the impulse and the object that mobilized it in the first phase are one and the same person. "It even seems likely", Strachey concludes, "that the whole possibility of effecting mutative interpretations may depend upon this fact that in the analytic situation the giver of interpretation and the object of the id-impulse interpreted are one and the same person" (p. 156n). If the aim of a mutative interpretation is to promote the introjection of the analyst as a real object (meaning not archaic) so that in this way the original superego can gradually begin to change, it follows that the id-impulse that is interpreted must have the analyst as its object. At this point Strachey realizes that all he has said in his paper requires an amendment and that the first criterion of a mutative interpretation is that it must be transferential. The extratransference interpretation can only have a circumstantial, preparatory or tactical value, which opens the road to, or provides feedback for the transference.

With these final reflections Strachey's work achieves its greatest theoretical importance. Transference interpretation is finally rigorously redefined. The mutative effect is ascribed to it not as a factual possibility, but as a logical one—in Reichenbach's (1938) sense. In this way, Strachey provides the theoretical principles for Freud's (1912b) wise reflection that one cannot conquer an enemy *in absentia* or *in effigie*.

33.8   *Some applications of Strachey's scheme*

Having established his theoretical scheme, Strachey can apply it to specify the great problems of psychoanalytic practice. Let us try to study them in ordered fashion.

33.8.1 *Mutative interpretation and reassurance*

Let us begin by discussing the concept of reassurance, as Strachey understands it. Reassurance transforms the analyst into a good object that becomes confused with the good archaic (idealized) object of the patient. Thus characterized, reassurance can therefore never achieve a structural change—that is, a permanent and deep one. In that it fosters the relation with the idealized object, reassurance does not allow the second phase of interpretation, which opens the way to contact with reality.

Ferenczi's (1919b, 1920) active technique operates in the same sense: It facilitates the first phase but then runs into difficulties in resolving the second phase, precisely because the activity transforms the analyst into an idealized object—a seducer, for example.

33.8.2 *Superficial interpretation or deep interpretation*

Where Strachey's specifications become clearest is in discussing the old and always current dilemma of the opposition between deep and superficial interpretation. From his point of view, superficial and deep interpretation are two erroneous ways of interpreting, because only the mutative interpretation is at the correct level. With this theoretical perspective, an interpretation will be superficial if it does not touch the point of urgency and does not free sufficient instinctive energy. It will be deep when it causes too high a discharge of anxiety without resolving it, with which the analyst errs in his function as an auxiliary superego.

It can be said that the superficial interpretation fails in the first place and the deep interpretation fails in the second phase. In one case the impulse does not become conscious, and in the other it cannot be worked through, it cannot be contrasted with reality. The intensity of the anxiety the drive arouses prevents the analysand from having, at that moment, sufficient reality judgement to distinguish the archaic from the real. To express Strachey's vigorous line of thought with greater precision, I will say that, if the analyst makes a deep interpretation in the sense defined above, he does not, in fact, give his patient a good real imago. The patient therefore does not experience confusion, since the therapist has failed in his function as an auxiliary superego, and the analysand perceives correctly that the analyst is, on this point, as irrational as his archaic object.

I believe I follow Strachey's thought faithfully if I assert that we qualify as superficial or deep those interpretations that are simply mistaken, which are based more on the analyst's theories or fears than on what is happening in the session. Thanks to Strachey, the concepts of deep or superficial interpretation reveal, for me, their background as to value and ideology. They are really adjectives employed as a euphemism for correct or inadequate interpretation. If we say an interpretation is deep or superficial, we are acknowledging it does not reach the optimum level and is, therefore, bad.

33.8.3 Mutative interpretation and deep material

The straight application of Strachey's theoretical schemes, as we have just seen, puts us into a better position in that absorbing discussion (a long-standing one) on deep and superficial interpretation. But this reflection also covers another flank of the historical problem, and that is the conduct the analyst should maintain in the face of the spontaneous emergence of deep material.

Although it is true that diverse metapsychological concepts can be applied to define deep material (what is most repressed, most infantile, most regressive, earliest in time and so forth), Klein's influence is also evident here with regard to the way Strachey conceives the point of urgency and the importance of resolving anxiety.

Strachey thinks that if analysis follows a regular course, deep material is arrived at step by step, and consequently there is no reason for unmanageable amounts of anxiety to appear. Only when deep impulses appear prematurely—and this has to do with some peculiarities of the structure of the neurosis—is the analyst confronted with a difficult situation, with a dilemma. If, in this situation, we offer the analysand an interpretation, we can trigger an explosive reaction of anxiety that makes it impossible to operate the second phase of mutative interpretation. However, it is erroneous to believe that the problem is resolved simply by eluding the deep material, interpreting it at a more superficial level or directing oneself to another level of the material. All these options are generally inefficient. This is why Strachey tends to think, finally, that the interpretation of the impulse, however deep, is the safer course. "It is possible therefore, that, of the two alternative procedures which are open to the analyst faced by such a difficulty, the interpretation of the urgent id-impulses, deep though they may be, will actually be the safer" (1934, p. 151).

Thus in this controversial matter Strachey does not agree with Wilhelm Reich's (1927) admonitions when he says that, at the start of an analysis, it is sometimes necessary to ignore deep material and even redirect the patient's attention. Strachey agrees instead with Melanie Klein, who is not afraid to interpret in these cases. However, it is evident that Klein never took Strachey's specifications very much into account as to deep interpretation. And it is a pity, because she would have found there the reasons she lacked in order to explain her way of interpreting.

It is necessary to reiterate that the optimum level is not defined in Strachey's investigation simply in economic terms, as Melanie Klein, in fact, does in referring to the point of urgency. It is also a structural concept, which takes account of the function of the ego, both in tolerating the anxiety and in perceiving the difference between the archaic and the real object. This is consonant with what Paula Heimann (1956) calls perceptive capacity of the ego: up to what point the patient can perceive the difference between the archaic and the real object.

33.8.4   Mutative interpretation and abreaction

Lastly, Strachey studies the effect of abreaction, a theme that was much discussed at the time (and still is, although less so, today). There are those who affirm that abreaction is the essential agent of all the expressive therapies including analysis, while some of us think, as does Radó (1925), that the theory of abreaction is incompatible with the function of analysis. For Strachey, abreaction can calm anxiety but will never produce a real change unless the anxiety corresponds to an external event.

Strachey considers that the term "abreaction" covers two different processes, the discharge of affect and libidinous gratification. Setting aside the latter, abreaction as the discharge of affect can be considered a useful element for analysis, and even an inevitable accompaniment to mutative interpretation. In any case, Strachey concludes, the part it can play in analysis will never have more than an auxiliary nature.

Although it can certainly be maintained, within Strachey's theory, that each mutative interpretation gives the optimum dose of abreaction in that it stirs up the anxiety and resolves it, I think that at present we can definitely settle this issue and say that analysis operates through insight and has nothing to do with abreaction. The theory of abreaction is economical; Strachey's, on the other hand, is basically structural. I think Strachey does not definitely decide to abandon the abreaction theory because he does not work with the concept of insight. He only mentions it contingently (1934, p. 145), but more as a common English word than as a theoretical term. And, nevertheless, I have a basis for affirming that the theory of mutative interpretation offers us—albeit implicitly—a rigorous definition of insight, since the mutation occurs at the precise moment when the ostensive insight breaks the neurotic vicious circle.

I have just indicated as a theoretical limitation for Strachey—the only one I can find—his somewhat complacent position towards abreaction, at least in one of its forms. Herbert Rosenfeld (1972) also deals with this subject. He tries to incorporate into Strachey's thought the concept of working-through. Rosenfeld thinks transference interpretation can set in motion the mutative process, but that this should be followed by a period of working-through so that the mutative development can continue and be reinforced (p. 457). Rosenfeld's opinion does not correspond fully in my understanding with what Strachey postulates. For Strachey, the working-through process is fulfilled in the second phase of the mutative interpretation. Perhaps Rosenfeld seeks to compensate the theoretical deficit just mentioned with regard to working-through. But he sacrifices in this way a fundamental characteristic of mutative interpretation, which by definition includes the process of working-through.

33.9   Strachey in Marienbad

Strachey's circumspect account at the Symposium of the Fourteenth International Congress sounds in principle like a simple summary of his major work. But if it is read carefully, it can be seen to advance along the theoretical line I have emphasized. In his new work, Strachey does not feel the need to mention the mutative interpretation even once. He simply speaks of the transference interpretation from the perspective of the processes of introjection and projection that structure the psyche, in the light of the theory of object relations. And he makes a sharp distinction between interpretations of the transference and the true transference interpretation. From the way he describes it, there is no doubt that the *"true"* transference interpretation is the one he previously called mutative. Every time we interpret an impulse that concerns the analyst, we are making an interpretation *of the transference,* but only if the impulse is active at that moment can a *transference* (that is, mutative) interpretation be made.

Strachey reviews and specifies the factors that make transference interpretation the essential therapeutic instrument of analysis: (1) the patient can establish a comparison between his id impulse and the behaviour of the object, since both are present; and (2) the one who offers the interpretation is at the same time the object towards which the impulse is directed. On the other hand, if the analyst refers a particular id impulse to an object that is not present, there is an increased possibility of an unexpected response towards the one that is present. (For example, the patient may become angry with the analyst who has just interpreted, let us say, his aggression towards his spouse, assuming the analyst to be her ally.)

What is decisive for Strachey is that the object of the impulse be at the same time the one that interprets it, as he pointed out (1934, n. 32), since the phenomenon from the past which repeats itself has a different outcome this time, because the projective/introjective process with the archaic object is modified in the light of present experience. The moment when the transference interpretation is formulated is unique in the life of the patient, in that the target of the impulse does not behave as the original object did, but accepts the situation without anxiety and without anger (1937, p. 144).

Strachey concludes his account, repeating that interpretation, and particularly transference (mutative) interpretation, is the determining factor in the therapeutic results of psychoanalysis, and that the dynamic changes produced can be explained only when sufficient attention is paid to the mechanisms of introjection and projection.

In this way, following and refining his previous work, Strachey arrives at an explanation of the analytic cure in which the effects of suggestion are completely excluded.

33.10   *Strachey at the present time*

Like many other psychoanalysts, I consider Strachey's contribution to be of very great importance, and that his influence continues to be very strong, although the years have not passed in vain and our ideas are not the same as those of 1933.

In the last few years various theorists have been interested in Strachey; Klauber (1972) is one of these. He thinks that in formulating our theories we should take the analyst's personality more into account. We often forget that from the beginning of psychoanalysis it was thought that his therapeutic action is due not only to interpretation, but also to the affective link the patient develops with the analyst: "One of the earliest discoveries of psychoanalysis was that another factor was involved in therapy besides the interpretation of the analyst. This was the development by the patient of strong feelings of attachment" (p. 385). Klauber's interest is directed precisely to this link, which Strachey's theories do not consider. Interpretation is heir to that Freudian psychobiology rooted in Helmholtz via Brücke and has therefore a reductive character that does not include the unavoidable value system present always in that complex human relation that analysis is.

Strachey's essay marks, for Klauber, the apotheosis of the psychobiology of the impulse, in that it proposes to discover and resolve the latent forces that are expressed as "packets of id energy", directed to the psychoanalyst. However, when he affirms that mutation takes place because the patient incorporates in his superego the analyst's attitude towards the impulses, this gives rise to a radical contradiction. It is at last recognized that the analytic situation remains impregnated by the therapist's system of values, transmitted not only through the content of detailed interpretations of the transference but also through unconscious forms of communication.

Sachs in Salzburg, various writers in Marienbad and more than one scholar of our time think that the analytic cure consists in the analysand identifying with a tolerant analyst; but not Strachey. Strachey says something else, as we have seen: that the analyst should operate from the position of superego the analysand assigns him, not to suggest and educate but to interpret his error, to show him the strength of the repetition that always leads him to project his internal object. The analyst does not need to impose his system of values on the analysand; it is enough to show (and demonstrate to him) that he is led too much by his subjectivity.

When the analysand tries to incorporate his system of values, what the analyst should do is expose that attempt as a new form of misunderstanding and repetition.

Klauber accords great importance to what Strachey incidentally called implicit mutative interpretations, and he bases himself on Rycroft (1956), who asserts that interpretation operates not only through the intellectual content the analyst communicates verbally, but also because it bears the analyst's emotional attitude. As a sign of interest and responsibility, it is these implied statements that make the communication real rather than illusory, Rycroft says. (We will return to this in a moment.)

In the same way that the child establishes a link with the mother's *functions* (and not only with the mother herself), with which he shelters himself from changes in the object relation, according to Klauber, so the good result of analysis could be due to the patient establishing a relation with the analytic function. In this way, the effect of the interpretation becomes dependent on the patient's affinity with the analytic method, and up to a point with the analyst's personality, in that it can reinforce the internal coherence of a particular interpretative line. The effectiveness of the interpretation thus becomes more contingent on its (informative) content and approaches the plane of suggestion. Without denying the value of interpretation, Klauber thinks the human mind is satisfied, and in some measure is cured, by what it *feels* as truth.

On this point it is worth remembering Glover's (1931) work on the therapeutic action of inexact interpretations, which can operate in various ways: by reinforcing repression suggestively, by offering better displacements to the forces in conflict and approaching the truth in some way or, finally, in terms of concrete experiences that are a definite obstacle in the path towards objectivity.

It is evident to me that interpretation very often acts through its collateral effect, and what resolves the anxiety of the moment is not the informative content, but that the very fact of interpreting has responded to certain unconscious needs of the patient—for example, for the analyst to speak or to show his interest. Taking this possibility into account, it is understandable that the alleviation of anxiety is not sufficient to prove that an interpretation is correct. When the interpretation operates in this way, we should consider that its effect is only suggestive, that it acts through its *placebo effect*, as Schenquerman (1978) says.

To the extent that he doubts the existence of a direct relationship between the content of the interpretation and the results psychoanalysis achieves, Klauber questions Strachey's fundamental thesis. From Strachey's time until now—Klauber says—the idea has been gaining ground that interpretation operates in that complex and very subtle weave of the transference/countertransference relation. He concludes that if it takes place and acquires its meaning there, we should be extremely cautious in evaluating its effects. "Interpretation thus takes place in the context of a relationship, and we therefore have to be cautious in determining its effects. How much is determined by the content of the interpretations, how much by the subtle understanding of an unconsciously agreed code, how much by the authority lent to the analyst by his convictions?" (1972, p. 388).

Klauber's opinions are wise methodological warnings against validating our interpretations simply by their effects—but not as refutations of Strachey. Strachey's doctrine maintains itself without the need, in any way, for suggestion. On the contrary, each time we are able to reveal the effect of suggestion as something that stems from the analysand's need to meet the demands of a superego projected in us, we achieve by definition a mutative effect, because it is the archaic superego, and not the analyst, who wishes to impose its system of values. That we do not always function at that high level of effectiveness is not the fault of Strachey's theories, but our fault.

When Rycroft asserts that in addition to its informative content every interpretation transmits the implicit communication of an emotional attitude, he indicates the circumstance where that non-verbal communication lends *reality* to the relation in that it shows the analyst is fulfilling his function, which consists in being with the analysand, listening to him and trying to understand him. ("Now this implicit statement is a sign of the analyst's interest in and concern for the patient, of his capacity to maintain an object relationship, at least within the confines of the consulting-room. It tells the patient the one thing that he needs to know about the analyst, and it is the analyst's major contribution to making the relationship between himself and the patient a real and not an illusory relationship"— 1956, p. 472.) The analyst's function is not usually interpreted, it is demonstrated concretely in the task, because facts speak louder than words, although it can and should rightly be interpreted when the analysand questions it or does not perceive it: "You are quiet now because you need to hear my voice, because you wish to see whether I am alive or angry", and so forth. It can be said we are using implicit communication to operate via suggestion only if these interpretations are omitted when there are elements that may make them necessary. Olinick (1954), for example, proceeds in this way when he makes use of questions as a parameter to give the ego momentary support, reinforcing its contact with reality or raising the level of the patient's cooperation.

I will illustrate what I mean with a simple clinical example. The analysand is a psychologist with a marked schizoid personality, which withdraws narcissistically in the face of frustration and jealousy. This strategic defence, not always understood by the analyst, has provoked a rebellious and prolonged *impasse*, resolved later on through more attentive and systematic work on the aforementioned character armour. In the previous session, on a Monday, the analyst had again interpreted the way in which the patient had distanced himself, abandoning the analyst in order not to feel abandoned. He arrived ten minutes late for the following session and commented, in a hopeful tone of voice, that he was talking to two colleagues about the possibility of finding a place for work. He immediately withdrew into himself, and with the memory of previous experiences of failure and misunderstanding, suspicion again arose. and he immediately spoke in a jealous tone of voice about a friend and his wife. Then he said:

P: "Well . . . on Monday . . . something happened on Monday that led me to think it sometimes bothers me when you don't answer me. I do not know how to take it, I do not know if it is approval, disapproval or nothing. But I think it has bothered me. It disorientates me. I had always heard that patients are bothered if the analyst is silent. I do not know if I had realized this, but it makes me feel uncertain." (*Sudden silence. Tension in the countertransference.*)

In this material the patient's basic problems are clearly restated: his desire to work in the analysis and his fear of experiencing failure and frustration again, jealousy towards the couple and so forth. However, what is most noteworthy is that he can now acknowledge that he is a patient like any other, and that the analyst's silence produces uncertainty and unease in him.

When he is suddenly quiet, the analyst has two alternatives, which are both mistaken, in my view: to speak, in order to avoid the same thing happening, as usual, or to remain silent in the hope that the patient will overcome the silence (and the frustration). Neither of these two seems appropriate to me: words will operate suggestively as a corrective emotional experience (Alexander & French, 1946); and silence will act coercively so that the analysand feels obliged to overcome frustration. There is a third possibility, however, and this is to interpret the analysand's silence as a desire to see whether the analyst understands his conflict and can do something to help him. An interpretation such as this tries to avoid any suggestive effect and opens up a new and different avenue, since it is directed precisely towards the conflict that is being raised. It attempts to be a strictly analytical interpretation, while I do not hesitate to qualify the other two as countertransferential acting out, through commission or omission, speaking or remaining silent.

Klauber is surely right to underline the importance of the analyst's presence—as Nacht (1962, 1971) says—but I think both Klauber and Nacht are mistaken when they ascribe to this type of factors the same range as to interpretation. The presence of the analyst (and I give this expression its widest sense here) is a *necessary* condition for analysis to function. The mutative interpretation that carries insight, on the other hand, is a *sufficient* condition: the first types of conditions on their own are not enough: the second works if and only if the first have been fulfilled. To resolve transference rivalry, for example, it is necessary in turn for the analyst not to feel rivalry—that is, that he should not try to score over his patient. This is the same as saying he can tolerate his patient's rivalry "without anxiety and without anger", which is generally achieved only after having analysed the conflict in the countertransference. These are the necessary conditions for effective operation. If they are absent, we can never resolve the conflict, however much we may interpret correctly, precisely because that "interpretation" will be only the fragment of a verbal acting out: for example, we interpret correctly so the analysand can recognize our superiority! The attitude of empathy and objectivity is *necessary*, but not *sufficient*. For the situation to change, we will have to interpret the analysand's rivalry until he sees the objective distance between the archaic and the actual object. Strachey's basic thesis—that is, that only the mutative effect of the interpretation breaks the neurotic vicious circle—is upheld. If the interpretation is not there, the analysand will repeat his conflict, and thus the analyst will remain caught up, in the long or short term.

Jacques-Alain Miller (1979) also maintains that Strachey, following Radó, clings to the Freudian theory of hypnosis to understand how analysis operates, postulating that the analysand is cured when he identifies with the analyst. In my view Strachey does not propose this at all but, rather, the contrary: that the analysand projects his archaic object (superego) into the analyst and tries to reintroject it unchanged, while the situation is reversed precisely if the analyst does not allow himself to be placed as that object and preserves his position.

I think Strachey's theories can be reformulated without doing violence to them in Lacanian language, because none better than Strachey, with his mutative interpretation, knows how to locate himself in the place of the Great Other, and none manages better than he to distinguish himself from the archaic object—the "other" in lower-case letters—that the analysand imagines is reflected in him.

Another writer who concerned himself at length with Strachey's essay is Herbert Rosenfeld (1972), whose ideas correspond in general to those presented in this chapter. For Rosenfeld, Strachey's scheme is enriched by more current concepts being applied to it, without therefore losing its coherence and original force. From what we now know, the analysand identifies projectively not only his internal objects, and particularly his superego, but also parts of his self, making the analyst's task more complex, although the principles of mutative interpretation do not vary in any way.

Since Strachey's time, Rosenfeld rightly says, our knowledge has increased with regard to the processes of splitting, idealization and omnipotence which interfere with the development of the ego and, at the same time, distort object relations, increasing the distance between the idealized object and the persecutory object. These mechanisms operate continuously in the course of the analytic process, influencing the analyst's function considerably. But if the register of his countertransference is adequate, they also give his interpretative work depth and precision.

* * *

Strachey's ideas have lasted so long because they integrate theory and technique in a convincing unit, where the nature of the therapeutic action of psychoanalysis is explained on the basis of concepts that are both clear and precise. Thanks to Strachey, we have come to know why a correct interpretation matters so much in our work, as well as the precise place transference and extratransference interpretation occupy in our practice, and the differences between interpretation, suggestion and reassurance. Let us add that Strachey helps us to distinguish superficial and deep interpretations from the interpretation of deep material.

Finally, last but not least, mutative interpretation laid the foundation at the time for future explanations that would take insight and working-through to the position of principal theoretical instruments of psychoanalysis in our day.

33.11   Strachey once more

When I wrote this work (and this chapter), I did not know for certain that James Strachey was going to appear among us in person once more. Thanks to Pearl King, an outstanding analyst and dedicated archivist of the British Society, there has just come to light a series of lectures and notes written by Strachey in 1941, when England was suffering the Nazi bombings and the English analysts were fervently discussing the great theoretical and technical problems of our science. The first of these writings, which Strachey himself had called "Opening Remarks at a Practical Seminar", was read to candidates on 15 October 1941 and was published in the *Bulletin* of the British Society in July 1989, with a brilliant introductory note by Riccardo Steiner.[1]

In his class Strachey discussed a series of important subjects: the analytical situation as an instrument of observation, the nature of the transference phenomenon, the difference between psychoanalysis and psychotherapy, and again, in depth, interpretation and its types, which takes us back in a direct line to 1934.

As Steiner rightly points out, Strachey's remarks on interpretation "prove to be extremely sharp and pertinent" (Steiner, 1989, p. 14) and throw light on Strachey's thought, showing us in great detail his interest in achieving, by means of the transference interpretation, "the direct emotional experience . . . before any important change can be produced in him [the analysand]" (Strachey, 1989, p. 22). As in 1934, Strachey attempts to explain in what way the interpretation can promote the act of discrimination that separates the past from the present, phantasy from reality, the actual image from that in the transference. At the end of his work, which was unfortunately unfinished, Strachey once more emphasizes what he said in 1934 (p. 156, n. 31): the transference interpretation has one essential characteristic, which is that the object of the analysand's feelings is at the same time that which operates the discrimination. At this point I think I can see an advance in Strachey's thought from 1934 to 1937, in that he now insists that the analyst must take upon himself the feelings of the analysand, who in his turn can take on his own, thus achieving that direct experience that enables him to distinguish past from present, the basis of a fundamental change in his mental equipment (ibid., p. 24). It is not only the introjection of an analyst operating "without anxiety and without anger" (Strachey, 1937, p. 144) that is sought, but the element of reality that is achieved at that moment: taking on the feelings in play without avoiding them, the analyst gives the analysand, not only a model of identification, but also a direct, committed example of the force of psychic reality at the precise moment when it is in operation.

Note

1. I am most grateful to Pearl King, who gave me permission to read Strachey's paper and allows me to quote it; and also to Riccardo Steiner for giving me the opportunity of taking advantage of his valuable comments.

CHAPTER THIRTY-FOUR

Interpretative styles

34.1 Some antecedents

Liberman's original investigation culminates with his proposal concerning interpretative styles. It spanned more than 25 years, starting with the publication of "Identificación proyectiva y conflicto matrimonial" (1956), "Interpretación correlativa entre relato y repetición" (1957) and "Autismo transferencial" (1958). These works, all clinically excellent, already contain the seed of Liberman's future ideas on the singular value of dialogue in the session, laying the foundation for psychoanalytic theory and giving a rigorous account of its practice. In these works, the importance of an interdisciplinary support in communication theory for the interpretative task is already visible. That support will later be sought in semiology.

To place it in its proper context, let us say to begin with that Liberman's research gathers together the preoccupations of the Argentine School about forms of interpretation as an attempt to resolve the dilemma of form and content in interpretation. The latter arises in Wilhelm Reich's character theory and develops in the work of writers such as Luisa G.

This chapter is a translation, with few modifications, of an article I presented in *Psicoanálisis* magazine, in homage to a great psychoanalyst and a dear, departed friend.

Álvarez de Toledo, Geneviève T. de Rodrigué, Racker and others. All these works suggest that the *form* of the interpretation can reach directly certain structures that remained crystallized in the analytic dialogue, where we should go to rescue them. The form in which one interprets, therefore, has to be recognized as an instrument of our work.

Among these works, the one that surely opens up the way is that of Álvarez de Toledo, read at the Argentine Psychoanalytic Association at the end of 1953 and published in 1954. It studies the meaning that the acts of interpreting, of speaking and of associating have in themselves, beyond the contents they can signify. Every act of speech is an action, and in that action are expressed the unconscious desires and the conflicts of the speaker in a direct and concrete manner, so that they become very accessible to interpretation. (Álvarez de Toledo's central idea corresponds noticeably with that of John R. Searle and other philosophers of language, who maintain the importance of *speech acts*—see Searle, 1969.) The word has an intrinsic value as such, and it is necessary to reach the sources of language, to destructure the language in order for the instincts and deep fantasies from which it arose to reappear. All of this is an important part of the material the analysand offers us.

Within the same line of investigation, Racker (1958c) indicates that a good part of the analysand's object relations are present in his relation to interpretation. The interpretation often appears as the object of the instinct, and the unconscious desire of the analysand crystallizes in it, so that we are sometimes allowed direct access to the repressed unconscious material: the analysand's response to what the analyst says is, therefore, always significant.

Geneviève T. de Rodrigué (1966) is also concerned with how the interpretation is formulated. She compares it to the way the mother looks after a child. "The formulation of an interpretation has to be the adequate recipient for the content it expresses" (1966, p. 109). At times the dissociation of the analyst into good mother and bad mother is channelled in the alternative of bad *content* and good (beautiful) *form* of the associations and interpretations, and that is precisely where the decisive battle will be fought.[1]

All these works certainly bear on the beginning of Liberman's investigation. Nevertheless it is also evident that from 1962 onwards, when Liberman published *La comunicación en terapéutica psicoanalítica*, he takes an important theoretical step, because he begins to use a multidisciplinary focus to formulate his points of view, to understand that irreplaceable unit of investigation that the psychoanalytic session is for him. The theoretical support is given, at first, in his 1962 book on communication theory; and then, in the following years, it is semiology, crystallizing in *Lingüística, interacción comunicativa y proceso psicoanalítico*, published between 1970 and 1972.

34.2 Theory of communication

In *La comunicación en terapéutica psicoanalítica* Liberman sets himself a great task—that of pouring the theory of the libido and of the points of fixation—which Freud and Abraham established in the first decades of the century—into the mould of the theory of communication, just as Ruesch proposed in his *Disturbed Communication* (1957). The types or models of communication—and this is the principal thesis—have to do with the points of fixation and, consequently, with transference regression.

Following, then, the path traced by the two great creators of the libido theory, Liberman redefines the clinical pictures of psychopathology according to Ruesch's communicative models. (Ruesch, 1957, proposes, in effect, the following types: demonstrative person; fearful, fleeing person; logical person; action-oriented person; depressive person; infantile person; observing, non-participant person.) The fixation points where Abraham located the principal neuroses and psychoses in his essay of 1924 will now be contemplated from within communication theory. We can say here that the effort is commendable, and, even more important, the result is convincing. Liberman finds a significant relationship between the modes of communication and the points of fixation of the libido. These, on the other hand, also determine the most outstanding moments of the analytic situation. Thus the analytic regression will be to the most significant points of fixation in individual development, according to the dialectic Freud established in the *Introductory Lectures on Psycho-Analysis* of 1916–17, and especially in Lecture 22.

As at other points in his investigation, Liberman here relies on concepts developed by his teacher, Enrique J. Pichon Rivière. Pichon said that there are principal and accessory points of fixation. If the former define the diagnosis, the prognosis relies on the latter, the accessory points. If, for example, an obsessive neurotic has hysterical traits, his prognosis will be better than if he had melancholic or schizoid nuances. (Pichon Rivière's ideas here are similar to those Elizabeth R. Zetzel, 1968, was later to propose about the good hysteric.) I always remember a young patient with a persecutory delusion whom I saw in La Plata. He eventually made a good recovery. I was uncertain about the diagnosis—either a hysterical psychosis or a paranoid schizophrenia—and I consulted Dr. Pichon. He favoured a diagnosis of schizophrenia, but he pointed out the histrionic tone of the delusion ("everything is pre-arranged; everything is a ridiculous farce") as an element that improved the prognosis somewhat, despite the seriousness of the case.

On these bases, Liberman offers six characteristic clinical pictures.

The first of these is the *observing, non-participant person*, fixated at the first oral stage of sucking, who in the psychiatric nomenclature is the schizoid character. These are the people who can observe objectively, grasping the totality, looking at the whole. Liberman indicates here the importance of envy in the disturbance of communication in these patients, in the rupture and disintegration of communication and the relation of this situation to Melanie Klein's theory of the position.

Then there is the *depressive person*, the participant observer, whose point of fixation is at the secondary oral stage and whose process of communication is centred on the transmission of feelings and the regulation of self-esteem.

The third type Liberman proposes is the *action-oriented person*, who corresponds to the psychopath and the perverse person of psychiatric nomenclature, with his point of fixation at the first anal stage (or anal expulsive stage) and an alloplastic model of adaptation. Here Liberman diverges from Abraham, who had attributed this level of fixation to paranoia. For various reasons, I think Liberman's modification is pertinent, since neither Abraham nor Freud ever took account of psychopathy, which was neglected considerably by the classic analysts with the exception of Aichhorn. Paranoia, for its part, began to lose its autonomy from Kraepelin onwards, and was included in what currently constitutes the heterogenous group of schizophrenic illnesses. A person of the third type has, for Liberman, acute difficulties in thinking and refrains from action. He fails in the form of instrumental use of symbols, so that he necessarily perceives tension but cannot decode it in verbal terms. Liberman also includes in this item the perversions, which seems questionable, as I shall show further on.

We then have the fourth group, the *logical person*, fixed at the second anal stage, corresponding to the obsessional neurosis of Abraham's classification, with its classic retentive model of object relation. This type of patient presents a defensive hypertrophy of rational operations, where formal logic is counterposed to the logic of emotions, with a great distance between the secondary and the primary processes. The narrative is orderly, with excessive detail, and the quantity of information transmitted therefore suffers. This type demands a great deal of attention but says very little (Liberman, 1962, p. 179).

The last two clinical pictures Liberman describes have to do with anxiety hysteria and conversion hysteria. The fifth, the *fearful fleeing person*, corresponds to the phobic character of anxiety hysteria. This type finds himself in a permanent state of alert, and the analytic situation is permeated by the anxiety that marks the entire life of these patients. The analyst, in turn, is invested with two contradictory valences, as phobic object and protector.

Liberman's sixth group is represented by the *demonstrative person*, corresponding to the hysterical character and conversion hysteria. The demonstrative person "utilizes as channels of transmission the mind, the body and action" and "to the extent that the positive Oedipus complex finds itself stimulated by the transference regression, he loses the synchronization between the three areas and then transmits in a symbolic code that manifests through symptoms of conversion hysteria and behavioural disturbances in the session, which have been described in the classifications as having a hysterical character" (ibid., pp. 217–218). The demonstrative person is the one who presents the analytic material with the greatest clarity, since thanks to the structure of this type, he manages representational symbols correctly.

To Ruesch's six types, Liberman has correlated in clear terms the stages and sub-stages of Abraham's classification. There is, however, one more type—the *infantile person*, which corresponds to the organo-neuroses—and a special decision is required here. Liberman thinks the infantile person has many features in common with the depressive person. This type localizes his conflict at the level of the autonomous nervous system, and his fantasies are expressed at a visceral level. The infantile person is placed, then, in the same category as the depressive person. Obviously this is an addition to the classification, which presents some difficulties. But let us say here that Liberman's investigation was directing itself to this point in the final years before his death. (Liberman died on 30 October 1983, surrounded by the affection and admiration of innumerable friends and disciples, when he was already acknowledged as a first-class investigator by the international psychoanalytic community.)

Whereas I consider the inclusion of psychopathy in this scheme to be a very important contribution, I have certain doubts as to the advisability of separating the phobic from the demonstrative personality, as do Ruesch and Liberman. In common with Freud and the classic writers, I am inclined to think that there are two hysterias from the phenomenological point of view, but only one for psychodynamics. Reich did not separate the two hysterias in his classification of character, since according to his nomenclature the hysterical character of the woman is superimposed on the passive–feminine character of the man. One could even ask whether what is called the demonstrative person is not simply the normal person, the genital character studied by Abraham (1925) and Reich (1933). When Liberman says that the demonstrative person is one who is able to match the verbal message to the gesture, to mobilize anxiety adequately and everything else, I personally tend to have the impression that he is describing the normal response. Finally, Liberman's position in classing psychopathy and perversion together corresponds with the view of the great majority of classic and present-day writers, but not with the view I expounded in my works on this theme (1973, 1977). There I characterized perversion as an ideological disturbance, at the opposite pole to psychopathy. This is not the place to open a debate that belongs more to psychopathology than to technique, but I wish to point out that the perverse type is generally a man of thought (at times a very creative one) and not a man of action.

34.3 *The ideally plastic ego*

Beyond the works that culminate with his book on communication, Liberman takes another step and tries to define the ego functions as a function of the media of communication and their instruments. This aspect of Liberman's thought, along his general line of investigation, begins by describing "an ideally plastic ego", which displays the six qualities or functions of the models of communication.

The most developed function in the observing non-participant person is the capacity to dissociate himself and observe things as a whole without participating, without allowing himself to become involved by what he observes. He is able to abstract but fails completely in his affective participation.

The depressive person, on the other hand, in acute contrast to the non-participant, can approach the object and see it in detail. But, carried away by this contact, he loses the distance that allows for objectivity.

The major merit of the action-oriented person is that he is able to grasp what his desires are and put them into practice, although his capacity for reflection is always lower than the norm.

At the opposite end of the scale, the logical person counts on the possibility of using thought as trial action; but he tends to remain tied to his reflections without crossing over into action, into operation.

The fearful, evasive person has the virtue of being able to mobilize anxiety to a useful degree in preparing for action, as long as he does not dam it up and paralyse it. If he functions adequately, this personality type is the one that best employs anxiety as a signal.

Finally, the demonstrative person is able to send a message under conditions that make for the highest degree of integration.

34.4 *Models of reparation*

Having tried out his theoretical instruments in the field of psychopathology, Liberman could apply them to distinguish the concept of reparation, assuredly one of the most complex and suggestive concepts of our discipline. (This investigation was carried out mainly by Liberman in a study group that also included J. Achával, N. Espiro, P. Grimaldi, I. Barpal de Katz, S. Lumermann, B. Montevechio and N. Schlossberg, with whom he published it in 1969.) Melanie Klein's work, thoroughly studied by Liberman, certainly exercises on him a measurable and persistent influence, particularly in this sphere.

The nuclear thesis of the work we are studying is that there are different modes of reparation, which imply different outcomes to the therapeutic process. Just as each breakthrough in analytic treatment reveals a different problem pattern that points to a different objective, the ending of analysis can be understood according to the degree to which it reaches that objective.

To classify the different processes of reparation, Liberman studies the ego functions, applying to them the scheme of classification explained above.

Each of the above six personality types demonstrates behavioural tendencies developed excessively, to the detriment of others. The imbalance of the ego consists precisely in this, because the ego displays a series of functions, and its pathology is rooted in the growth of some, to the disadvantage of others.

According to Liberman et al., a normal ego would have to be ideally plastic, so that each of its functions would occupy its proper place without gaining over the others.

In relation to the six types of personality, Liberman distinguishes a variety of capacities of the ego: (1) to dissociate and observe without participating, perceiving the totality of the object; (2) to approach the object and see it in detail; (3) to apprehend its own desires and act on them where the possibility of satisfying them exists; (4) to utilize thought as trial action, which for Liberman implies the ability to adapt oneself to circumstances and to family links of a vertical type—grandparents, parents and children—and a horizontal type, with its diverse degrees of intimacy, which also implies the capacity to be alone; (5) to mobilize a certain amount of useful anxiety preparatory to action; and (6) to send a message where action, idea and affect are adequately combined (see Liberman, 1969, p. 124).

As Liberman et al. rightly claim, this catalogue of ego functions differs from Hartmann's ego psychology, where the ego functions follow the classic path of Wundtian psychology.

An analytic process with a good ending would have corrected the excess of any of these ego functions, attending to deficient ones.

Between these functions, there are certain peculiar polarities, and in detecting them Liberman signals the future direction of his investigation: styles.

One of the clearest polarities is between the man of action (psychopathy) and the logical man (obsessional neurosis). Another convincing one arises between the non-participant (schizoid) person, who has developed excessively the function of abstracting and generalizing at the expense of affective and motor functions, which have become dissociated, and hysterical *autoplastia*.

* * *

To sum up: basing himself on Melanie Klein's (1935, 1940) ideas on reparation as the outcome of the depressive position, Liberman et al. postulate the existence of diverse modes; they distinguish between them with care, establishing "a correspondence between structures and psychopathological processes, and structures and processes of reparation" (1969, p. 137). If the most deficient tendency can be repaired, the vision of the past is modi-

fied and changes occur in the linguistic styles of communication that the
patient employs in the session.

34.5   The patient's styles

Liberman always maintained that Freud discovered two important things:
the unconscious and the analytic session as a unit for investigation.
Liberman's entire inquiry develops within the latter. The study of the
psychoanalytic session led him initially to the reformulation of psychoanalytic psychopathology in terms of Ruesch's communication theory, then to
his original description of ego functioning and models of reparation, and
finally to a classification of communicative styles. Liberman also applied a
sixfold scheme in this case: (1) reflective style, (2) lyric style, (3) epic style,
(4) narrative style, (5) suspense style and (6) aesthetic style. We will try to
characterize them, following mainly Liberman (1976a).

Before beginning with the special treatment of styles, it should be said
that Liberman availed himself of Charles Morris's (1938) theory of signs.
Morris, as we know, distinguishes three areas, in relation to the three factors that constitute the semiotic process: the *sign*, the *designatum* (the thing
the sign refers to) and the *interpreter* or user. Thus, *semantics* studies the
relation of the sign to the object (*designatum*), to which the sign applies;
pragmatics studies the relation of the sign to the interpreter, and *syntax*
studies the way signs are linked to each other.

Supported by the theory of signs, Liberman classified the psychopathological pictures according to the predominance of pragmatics, semantics or
syntax. In general terms we could say that in the great psychoses, psychopathy, perversions and addictions, disturbances of a pragmatic type are
preponderant, whereas the predominant disturbance in schizoid and cyclo-
thymic illnesses, the organoneuroses, hypochondria and traumatic dia-
theses is semantic; synactic disturbance is particularly prominent in the
neuroses.

34.5.1   Style 1 (reflective)

As we have already seen, the observing, non-participant person, the schizoid individual of classic psychopathology, has the capacity for dissociation
developed to a high degree. This allows him to observe without participating—that is, without affect and objectively, in a type of *microscopic perception*—"because the ego is reduced and the objects are enlarged"
(Liberman, 1976a, p. 16).

Everything Fairbairn said in 1941 and Klein in 1946 about the schizoid
personality as to omnipotent control, idealization and dispersion of the
emotions applies here. This is the patient who remains removed, who is
outside; the most silent patient, the one who experiences alterations in his

perception of the 50 minutes of the session, in that at times the session seems too short to him (and interminable to us, because he offered so little material); at times the opposite can occur.

This type of patient always pursues the unknown, the great philosophical problems of life—for example, what is truth, what is intelligence, what is justice, or the origin of the world or of life. For him, to analyse himself is precisely to find an answer to these questions on the basis of a central unknown quantity: what is analysis? But he does so coolly, as one who observes from outside. This patient is able to see things in their totality, but he has a serious problem in speaking, because to speak is to commit himself. These are patients who speak in a low voice, in an inward manner, and the language becomes increasingly cryptic, or neologisms begin to appear. The analyst is always intrigued, everything seems unusual, and at times he ends up with a headache; he tends to idealize the patient, and the patient, in his turn, conceives of the analyst as an individual who thinks. He idealizes him very much, since this type of patient overvalues thought. "With style 1 the patient can be only an optimal receiver, but he finds himself limited as an emitter" (Liberman, 1976a, p. 28). "The reflective style is characterized by the high degree of generality of the emissions" (p. 54), so that vital events are transformed into abstract unknown quantities that are postulated and pursued without suspense. Contemplating his object without affect and without life, the individual loses the limits of his personality, fusing "with a transcendent totality to which the link is predominantly cognitive (in terms of certainty–uncertainty)" (ibid., p. 55).

Liberman remembers a schizoid patient who was very intrigued by the coffee cups that sometimes appeared on his desk (when her session followed a supervision). After a long time, she said, "There are people I have to talk to in notarial language. Those, those, those who come to drink coffee". Her notarial language referred, then, to her having to establish in a (notarial) document, as notaries do, that analysand so-and-so attests to her special interest in knowing what those people who leave the consulting-room when she enters—and with whom she sometimes talks—are doing here. And she attests to her jealous feelings, and that those coffee cups are evidence laid down in that document, and so forth. The degree of distortion is enormous. To speak through a document (or by correspondence) is showing us, in the final instance, that the patient is far away. (I take this example and many of the ideas expounded in this section from a class given by Liberman in seminars on technique by Rabih, Ferschtut and Etchegoyen on 27 November 1980 to the Buenos Aires Psychoanalytic Association [APdeBA].)

In relation to the semiotic levels, the reflective style operates with a certain formal and abstract precision from the syntactic point of view, with a semantic scale of values that varies from observing without participating to being observed participating. As to pragmatics, the reflective style tends to arouse uncertainty, mistrust and indifference in the user.

34.5.2   *Style 2 (lyric)*

The second type, the cycloid individual of classic psychopathology, is discussed clearly in Melanie Klein's two works on the depressive position (1935, 1940) and also in Bleger's (1967a) and Mahler's (1967, etc.) more recent studies on transference symbiosis. These patients adhere to us; they cling. They present communication difficulties because they have no control over their emotions. They are the "impatient" patients who never finish communicating to us. Impatience is invaded by the oral cannibalistic aspect. These are people who, when they speak, say half (of what they wish to say) and "eat" the rest, because there is no demarcation between their verbal and spoken thinking, and their thinking that is verbal but remains thought. The patient hears himself, and the impact of what he is saying makes him eat his words. This forces us to make great efforts to pay attention, to a kind of translation of what we sometimes have not noticed. If we record the session, we do not understand it—as if the tape recorder were not functioning properly. This is because the machine registers exactly what has been said, emitted, without completing what has been omitted. These are patients who demand a great effort on our part, who end up by frustrating us and at times can make us sleepy.

In contrast to Style 1, the self participates affectively, but at the cost of splitting the processes of perception. The affective engagement leads to a partial perception of the object in a type of *telescopic perception*.

The high emotional component that the lyric style transmits is often channelled through a paraverbal code. (Following communication theorists, Liberman distinguishes three codes: verbal, paraverbal and non-verbal. The paraverbal components are all the ingredients of speech not included in the verbal message, such as tone, register, rhythm and intensity—that is, what is phonetic.)

While the theme of Style 1 turns on knowledge, here the themes allude to feelings, to love, guilt and the need to be forgiven. These patients also seek fusion, but not with an abstract entity as do the previous patients, but with the beloved, whose love they desire to possess eternally.

The lyric style is characterized by a profuse inclusion of mood qualifiers in the syntactic area, and by the pragmatic tendency in provoking strong responses in the user.

Addendum: *The lyric style of the infantile (organoneurotic) patient*. The *infantile personality*, which Ruesch described among his basic types, is preserved in Liberman's classification. For various reasons he locates it within the *depressive person* (and consequently as having a lyric style). Perhaps this inclusion could be justified by pointing out that the broad register of the emotions of the lyric style, to the extent that they have a connection with the body, lead us to this type of pathology.

The organoneurotic patient has a formal adaptation to reality, but his emotions are channelled towards the body. He is somewhat similar to the psychopath, in that he does not register his emotions, but he is radically different in not prejudicing third parties, but rather himself, his body.

In his final years Liberman was concerned, as we have said, with psychosomatic illness (Liberman et al., 1982), a theme that has been studied in recent years by Joyce McDougall (1985, 1989) and other researchers. (For a thoughtful exposition on this aspect of Liberman's investigation, see *Del cuerpo al símbolo. Sobre adaptación y enfermedad psicosomática*, which Liberman wrote in collaboration with Elsa Grassano de Piccolo, Silvia Neborak de Dimant, Lia Pistiner de Cortiñas and Pola Roitman de Woscoboinik.)

34.5.3 *Style 3 (epic)*

The epic style, surely one of the best classifications of Liberman's register, corresponds to the man of action (action-oriented person, acting-out character). This is the patient who acts, who resorts to acting out in the session—or acting in, as some call it. For Liberman, acting out is a thought that has not managed to become one and is externalized through an action. The latent content of the acting out is, then, a phrase the subject has not been able to utter.

These patients come to analysis with a secondary motive, which of course they consciously hide from the analyst, and as we shall now see, this is the root of their principal characteristic.

The patient with an epic style demonstrates most convincingly, in my view, the disturbance of the relation of the sign to the interpreter—that is, pragmatics. The pragmatic disturbance implies a marked distortion in the use of signs. The verbal message does not serve the communicative interchange but is, rather, a means of secretly influencing the will of the other. The art of psychopathy consists in inoculation (Zac, 1973).

Liberman has also studied the genetic evolution factors that lead to the pragmatic distortion of the epic style by means of Freud's complemental series and the Kleinian concepts of voracity and envy. "The patients with a pragmatic distortion present a particular difficulty for the psychoanalytic approach, as a consequence of early disturbances which conspire against the need to acquire new forms of codification in the course of the life cycle" (1970–72, Vol. 2, p. 579).

Liberman finds that various factors converge for the pragmatic distortion of the epic style to take shape. In the first place, there is an early envious flight from the breast, with an accelerated muscular maturation because the possibility of depending on the maternal figure has been blocked (ibid., p. 585). Joined to this, as a second complemental series, are a narcissistic and infantile mother and an absent father.

In agreement with Phyllis Greenacre (1950), Liberman says that the tendency to act out has one of its roots in the second year of life, when the child learns to walk and talk, together with sphincter control. In the second year of life, when the process of separation–individuation (see

Margaret Mahler, 1967; Mahler, Pine & Bergman, 1975) is at its height and the child begins to talk to the mother from a distance, she does not respond to him with words, but with gestures. Something fails in these mothers, who are incapable of thinking according to the child's need. They are women who can think only when their own anxiety is in play. While the child cannot speak, there are no problems; she can attend to him without difficulty. But when the child grows, distances himself and speaks, the mother responds with actions and gestures. If the child is hungry, she goes to the kitchen and opens the cupboard, where there are biscuits. The child is led to perfect his techniques of action to get into the openings (or gaps) and becomes a little thief who steals food. Throughout his life this type of person elaborates the theory that he will never be understood. This leads to a delusional *Weltanschauung*. The analyst is someone who has found this "gimmick" of the couch and goes there every day to earn his livelihood at the expense of others and obtains the benefits. This type of patient has the greatest problems with money, with which he also tends to manipulate the analyst.

34.5.4 *Style 4 (narrative)*

The patient with a narrative style corresponds, using a communicative focus, with what has been described as a logical person—that is, the obsessional neurosis of psychopathology. In this patient, formal logic becomes the best instrument with which to counter the logic of the emotions, which the analyst tries to reach through his interpretations. The defensive hypertrophy of the logical operations implies a broad predominance of the secondary process, where the products of unconscious fantasy tend to be completely annulled.

The patient with a narrative style is more concerned with the form he should use to understand and to speak than with the content of what he says and hears. Excessive care in the use of vocabulary is matched by an underlying fear of making mistakes, of misunderstanding or being misunderstood, rooted in the omnipotence of thought and word. Lying down and very still on the couch, he tends to lift his forearms while he speaks to prevent the analyst from entering his ambit and interrupting him (Liberman, 1970–72, Vol. 2, p. 516).

These patients make the greatest effort to separate themselves from the analyst, they speak most and express themselves best. If we transcribe one of their sessions, we find it fills several sheets. These are patients who make organized chronicles in time and space: "On Friday, when I left this place, I met so-and-so at the corner. And we arranged to see each other that night to have dinner together with our wives. And we did so." They order their speech and introduce it with an "I am going to tell you". In this way they control and disconcert us, or tire, irritate or bore us.

The patient with a narrative style continually clarifies his point. The characteristic of this style is that the message tends to concentrate on the context and the referential function: "The said function always leads the therapist to locate himself in a particular context. The patient tries to lead him there utilizing the characteristics of the narrative, to control the mental processes of the receptor, fixing the mind of the latter in a world known by the patient in which data are ordered exclusively by him" (ibid., p. 520).

As we know from the classic writers, obsessional neurosis has its point of fixation in the secondary (or retentive) anal phase. According to Freud, obsessional neurosis appears typically in the latency period; but, in fact, Klein (1932) has shown that obsessive techniques are established in the second year of life, during the period when sphincter control is attained.

The Style 4 individual has, at a given moment in his development, suffered a premature socialization process. This individual becomes an orderly and obedient child, who overadapts. He does errands for his mother and homework for his teacher; he is always a good student and receives a prize for being the best. Liberman concludes that the narrative style constitutes the empirical expression of the typical defence mechanisms of obsessional neurosis: reactive formation, undoing and isolation. As Victor H. Rosen (1967) has said, anal-retentive control allows the sequence of a narrative to be sustained and, when it fails, the discourse "becomes soiled".

By dint of being a good patient, the logical person becomes the caricature of a patient. If the analyst has to change or cancel a session, he chooses this type of patient, allowing himself to be led by the limits his control establishes. In fact, this is a serious error, because to alter the setting for a patient of this type can be catastrophic.

34.5.5 Style 5 (suspense)

The style of the fearful, fleeing person is suspense, which is characterized by a climate of astonishment, fear and searching. The characters are clearly outlined, and the signs are selected in order to postulate unknown quantities in which the individual is engaged and tries to get the analyst involved. The discourse shows the typical phobic avoidance at the level of words and turns of phrase without losing coherence and order. Sometimes the main discourse is interrupted, and, something like an "aside" in theatrical technique, an independent sequence is inserted, after which there is a return to the central theme.

The style of suspense shows a clear opposition between verbal language on the one hand, and paraverbal and non-verbal language on the other. The last two registers are the most revealing, because they show the patient's real attitudes, whereas the verbal register tends to hide them.

This discordance marks a deception, but while in the epic style the deception is aimed at the other (the victim), here the deceived is the emitter himself.

The thematics of this style always turn on risk, adventure and discovery and are opposed to routine, conformity and tranquillity. Competitiveness frequently appears between persons of the same sex for a heterosexual love object, as a typical expression of the positive Oedipus complex. These and other emotions surface clearly in this discourse, coloured by phobic techniques of approach and distance, which Mom (1956, etc.) described, and which circumscribe, at times, an attractive and dangerous pole and (at the other end) a calming but boring one.

Style 5 patients are those who best mobilize the anxiety signal described by Freud in 1926. When that anticipatory function of the ego fails, an object relation with anxiety that crystallizes in a phobia is established. Like the Style 1 patient, these patients are curious, but they try to create suspense, imprinting on the session the expectation that something is going to happen. Thus, these individuals transfer their phobia and state of alert to the atmosphere of the session. For this patient, the analyst can be a detective who is able to find the culprit, the phobigenous object.

As we just said in describing the discourse of these persons, the greatest alteration is found at the syntactic level when phobic avoidance operates on words and turns of phrase. Semantically there is no special disturbance, and pragmatically what is most characteristic of this style, as its name indicates, is the attempt to create suspense in the recipient, to whom the role of non-participant observer is always ascribed.

34.5.6 Style 6 (aesthetic)

The patient with a dramatic style that provokes an aesthetic impact is the demonstrative person, according to the communicative modes, who corresponds to the hysteric of clinical psychiatry. Here we can appreciate "an optimum synchronization of the verbal, paraverbal and non-verbal codes to transmit a message" (Liberman, 1976a, p. 58). As with the previous style, space, time, objects and characters appear clearly delimited. But the difference here is that there are no brusque changes in the discursive sequences, nor is there an attempt to create an atmosphere of suspense, "but an optimal degree of redundancy is sought, either because the three codes transmit isomorphically the same message, or because they articulate in a complementary fashion in relation to that same objective" (ibid., p. 58).

This type of patient tries to create an aesthetic impact in the recipient. He delights in emitting signals and in receiving them. Liberman (ibid. p. 59) says there is a type of functional pleasure that corresponds with agreeable themes of frequent erotic content, with many elements of beauty and fascination.

The Style 6 patients are those who most provoke in the analyst a feeling of comfort and agreeableness. The transference resistance is based here on exhibitionism. If the analyst remains fascinated by the patient's devices, the session will become a type of spectacle and, naturally, will fail. The feelings of shame and of ugliness, the fear of ridicule are acknowledged as hysterical traits derived from the exhibitionist instinct and are the root of the aesthetic style.

34.6 Complementary styles

The six types I have just described, trying to adjust myself faithfully to Liberman's thought, never arise in a pure state. The styles are mixed, superimposed and counterposed. If the person has as a base a reflective style and tries to solve his emotional isolation and non-communication employing hysterical techniques, then he will be a clumsy hysteric, never an elegant hysteric. In the same way, a patient with a basically obsessive structure and therefore a narrative style, but who can appeal to the dramatic techniques of hysteria, will narrate but interpose dialogues:

"We arrived at the corner and she said to me, 'Where do you want to go?' And I said, 'You always want me to be the one who decides. No, this time, you decide.' Then she turned around and at that moment the others came and said, 'Hey! Are you two fighting again?'"

This is a chronicle narrated in the form of a theatrical libretto, where the subject, in some way, is acting the roles he is describing. The hysterical element gives the narrative technique greater plasticity.

Thus the style is never simple. Other registers are added to it which, although they complicate it and make it lose its sharp outline, also enrich and diversify it.

A basic postulate of all Liberman's thinking is that the styles are not only superimposed on each other, they are also complementary. Each style has a complementary one and therefore, at a given moment, will be the most adequate in a receptor capacity. The narrative style is complemented by the epic, the reflective by the dramatic, which creates suspense.

Liberman expounded clearly his ideas on stylistic complementation in his contribution to the issue of *Revista de Psicoanálisis* that commemorated thirty years of the magazine (1974), and in a special article for *Revista Uruguaya* in homage to Pichon Rivière (1978b.)

Stylistic complementation, Liberman (1978b) says, derives from the lines of interaction in psychotherapy; he then adds, "We should understand that complementation signifies the differences of roles and characteristics of the messages, and which contrasts with symmetrical interaction, where similarities prevail" (ibid., p. 45, fn.). If the analyst reasons or discusses with his obsessional patient, a symmetrical interaction is established; if he can employ the epic style in interpreting, he can achieve complementation, giving the patient what he lacks. As a corollary to these reflections, Liberman even affirms that the analysand's changes during the psychoanalytic process depend on the degree to which the verbal organization of the interpretation is adjusted to the receptive conditions of the patient, and, therefore, "the greater the degree of adequacy between the structure of the phrase formulated by the interpretation and the state of the patient when he receives it, the smaller the distortion" (ibid., pp. 45–46). Liberman says this adjustment expresses *stylistic complementation* (p. 46). The interpretation should offer the analysand those models of verbal thought he could not construct in the course of his development, and therefore, "the ideal, most exact interpretation is the one that gathers up in one statement only, the stylistic components the patient lacks" (p. 48). The complementary action, Liberman concludes, leads the patient to insight.

In other words, Liberman tries to give a linguistic content to what in phenomenological terms we call empathy, through stylistic complementation. Such empathy as arises in the session appears afterwards, when the session is being studied, as stylistic complementation.

Although stylistic complementation implies taking up a theoretical position towards the analysand, the transference and the analytic process, Liberman does not neglect other determinants. He warns that if the idea of complementary styles is overvalued, one runs the risk of losing spontaneity by submitting oneself to a search for the ideal complementation. This is why, "when we reach an optimal level of work, we effect the stylistic complementation without premeditating it" (ibid., p. 48).

Note

1. Sara Zac de Filc (1983) makes an accurate study of the function of the phonic aspects of language in interpretation and considers them an important part of the holding the analyst offers the analysand, pointing out the importance of including them in interpretation.

CHAPTER THIRTY-FIVE

Epistemological aspects of psychoanalytic interpretation

Gregorio Klimovsky

35.1 *Introduction*

The problem posed by the logical structure of interpretation and its contrastibility is not at all easy, and there are few logicians interested in these themes up to the present. I have had the opportunity of discussing them for years with many psychoanalysts, and if I have managed finally to draw some promising conclusions, major credit is due to friends who have taken part in these discussions.

Seen by a logician or an epistemologist, interpretation in psychoanalysis poses problems similar to those that arise when support is sought for physical theories and the reasons for accepting or rejecting them, as well as those that arise in the social sciences, specifically in disciplines such as history, when one wants to apply the concept of explanation to them. (In the present translation we use "epistemology" as being synonymous with "philosophy of science"—which is more common in English. We also use gnoseology" for "theory of knowledge" and for the German *Erkenntnistheorie*.)

Perhaps some of the most interesting debates in contemporary epistemology arise here. There is also little agreement. Among the analogies we see in this mosaic of difficulties, there exist, instead of certain results, a diversity of variations and possibilities.

The first problem that arises is that of the logical nature of interpretation. What happens when an interpretation is made; what structures does a logician find in it? Of several aspects that are immediately found to be characteristics of the act of interpreting, three are noticeable and lead to different problems: the explanatory, the semantic and the instrumental aspects. I will refer more to the first, but we should not forget that all three are interesting.

I have tried on several occasions to specify the problem of interpretation from an epistemological point of view. This is not easy, because psychoanalysts themselves do not seem to offer a complete conceptual unanimity and a clear profile of what they mean by interpretation, so that at times one does not know what is being discussed. It is quite curious that throughout the long, extensive, rich works produced by Freud, the word interpretation does not appear often, despite being one of the central notions of his theory and one of his main contributions.

It is evident from *The Interpretation of Dreams* (1900a) that many of the uses he makes of interpretation are rather canonical, where "interpretation" means something like an explanatory key of what is happening in the psyche or in the conduct of the individual, and not something else. But there are other contexts in Freud's work where interpretation appears, rather, as an instrument of psychoanalytic therapy and of the clinical task—as something peculiar that is not merely of an epistemological type but also possesses the characteristics of an instrument of action. We are not going to refer, however, to the different conceptions that psychoanalysts themselves have about interpretation, because it seems that this is a task that belongs to them. Some of this can be seen in Louis Paul's book, *Psychoanalytic Clinical Interpretation* (1963), where the selection of articles shows an attractive variety of conceptions about interpretation.

We said that in psychoanalytic interpretation three phenomena that always exist in it are superimposed.

The first is epistemological and relates to the type of knowledge the interpretation offers. An interpretation is a kind of miniature theory about what underlies a manifest phenomenon, meaning that to interpret implies producing a model or a hypothesis, in a way similar to that of the physicist when he wants to indicate what lies behind an effect. We can call this the gnoseological aspect of interpretation, and it poses typical epistemological problems.

The second facet linked to the phenomenon of interpretation is semiotic; it has to do with meanings. What is done at this level is to grasp the meanings offered by the material to which the interpretation refers. Here the task is similar to that of a linguist or semiologist and is of a different order to the gnoseological one, although both have aspects in common.

The third aspect is instrumental and perhaps, in some sense, therapeutic. Here psychoanalytic interpretation is an action: the one who interprets is doing something in order to produce a modification or a particular effect in the patient.

35.2 *The gnoseological aspect*

What strikes us first on studying the phenomenon of interpretation is that it is an act of knowledge: we try to obtain knowledge through it. It is an affirmation the analyst makes in relation to the material offered by the patient, with the aim of reading, describing or explaining it. It will immediately become clear why we do not use just one term, "to explain". In any case, this is the theoretical aspect—of hypothetic–deductive knowledge—implied by the interpretation. The first thing I wish to point out is that in an interpretation the psychoanalyst formulates a proposition; he enunciates what logicians call a *declarative sentence*—that is, something the psychoanalyst can be right or wrong about. In most cases, the affirmation that constitutes the interpretation has a hypothetical character, because the truth or falsity of what is being said is not known. Of course, this is not directly so for the patient; but it is not known by the therapist either. The interpretation is characterized to a considerable extent by conjecture. As such, it is, rather, a type of adventure that will demand, as the prophet said, that it be judged by its fruits. Only by knowing what the effects of that declaration are can its exactness be weighed.

To discuss the explanatory aspect, we will begin by saying that from a logical point of view it is worth distinguishing two types of interpretations: those obtained *through reading* and those that arise as a hypothesis, *through explanation*.

To make this clear, let us first make some epistemic allusions. Firstly, let us mention a characteristic of the type of theory and discourse psychoanalysis employs. It relates to the evident difference between types of material we could epistemologically call direct or theoretical. The former is more or less close to description, to observation, to clinical practice, and corresponds to empirical material (in psychoanalysis it is usually called "manifest material"). The latter is not directly visible and observable; it must be reached indirectly. This constitutes the latent, unconscious material.

What we have just pointed out is a difference made in certain scientific disciplines between what we could call the empirical side and the theoretical side of the reality studied. Furthermore, this difference is not found in all disciplines. There are purely empirical theories, theories that construct grand and very ingenious hypotheses, but on detectable and observable material. Darwin's theory of evolution, as the writer expounds it in the first edition of *On the Origin of Species* in 1859, for example, is of this type. This is well founded, ingenious and enormously explanatory because it gives account of a great quantity of facts, it permits predictions and is in turn explained by genetics, but it does not allude to theoretical material. All its notions (characteristics, variety, determination, adaptation) can be defined perfectly in a manifest way, in an empirical way. This is not what occurs in genetics, nor in chemistry or in psychoanalysis.

It is true that a psychoanalyst knows that the unconscious material can also in some sense be observed, detected and described. But there is a very clear difference: it is one thing to speak of the patient's conduct, of manifest material, and a very different thing to speak of his psychic structure, his fantasies, his unconscious. Here there is really a gnoseological jump as great as the one the chemist makes when he ceases to speak of the colour of litmus paper and begins to speak of the orbit of electrons in the atomic structure, and of the displacement of electrons in those orbits. In this sense, what happens within the psychic apparatus, precisely what interests the psychoanalyst, the heart of what he, in this sense, "sees", is quite analogous to what interests a chemist as to the internal structure of molecules, atoms and electrons. From this point of view these are quite similar theoretical situations. A problem psychoanalysis shares with all these theories of natural science is how to found our knowledge, how to order, to systematize that part of the science which is not directly accessible, directly operable, empirically tangible.

The problem of interpretation is directly related to this question, because the one who interprets (in the traditional form in which psychoanalytic interpretation may be said to exist, from Freud onwards) is neither describing, nor correlating, nor even placing one descriptive fact in the context of others. Actually, in the ordinary sense of the word, an interpretation always goes beyond the patient's conduct, the empirical datum, and bears much more deeply on primitive structures that are in the unconscious, on repressed events, on instinctive impulses and many other elements that are in no way comparable gnoseologically to what the verbal material and the patient's conduct itself manifest. And here the second question arises: how can the interpretation reach the material that is considered relevant; what is the appropriate procedure?

35.3 The "reading interpretation"

In science there are many procedures for gaining access to what is not directly visible or epistemologically direct. Somewhat metaphorically, we could say that the microscope and the telescope are like this, in that they allow—technically—observation of what is not directly observable, what is not empirically given. However, to observe through a microscope or a telescope, it is necessary to have a theory. Without a theory, one might react as did many of Galileo's colleagues: not wishing to observe anything through that instrument, which for them—due to their prejudice—must be magical, enchanted and defective. If there were really no scientific theory to justify it, the telescope could be thought of as something bewitched. There would be no understanding as to why it has to guarantee knowledge. Fortunately, there exists a theory—independent of biology or astronomy—which is the theory of optics. Its laws correlate what is located in the area of daily life, of immediate use (and which, in the apparatus, is in the eyepiece), with what is located in the objective, which is precisely what we wish to know. Therefore, when someone has internalized optics, placing in it, in good faith, the guarantee that the instruments function, he will no longer discuss optical problems when discussing astronomy or biology. He really accepts that when he observes certain phenomena on this side of the optical apparatus, it is because there are certain things on the other side.

The laws that correlate one type of variable with another, the empirical with the non-empirical, are usually called in epistemological jargon the *rules of correspondence*. They are also hypotheses, laws provided by some scientific theory, which correlate the visible with what is not visible, manifest material with latent content, to use the classic psychoanalytic expressions that Freud introduced in studying the dream.

To understand each other in what follows, what we are calling manifest material is, from the epistemological point of view, observable material. It is what can be called empirical material, material one can have access to, one can know, even in the behaviourist sense of the word. That the patient said a particular thing, or failed to say it (this is sometimes important, and even more so for Lacanians), is a fact that can be registered. Even if there were cameras or hidden recording apparatus, the fact would be there and could not be denied. We also have what belongs to the unconscious part of the individual, everything that is latent material—unobservable, not empirical—which the epistemologists call, using a nomenclature we do not like but which is imposed, "theoretical" objects. These are the objects "one makes conjectures about with the help of the theory, but which are not directly observable". For psychoanalysis, behaviour is directly observable; the unconscious is not; it is only conjectural or indirect. But psychoanalysis wants to reach precisely the unconscious, because what is important is there, so that its problem is how to provide support for what is conjectured, on the basis of directly observable behaviour. In this sense, psychoanalysis is a much more daring discipline than behaviourism, because the latter does not wish to know the other side of the question, which, for the behaviourist, is not scientific. For behaviourism, to be scientific is to adhere only to what is directly observable. The psychoanalyst thinks, instead, that it will be scientific to provide support for what is said about the unconscious.

In this way, one will distinguish observable material, which we will call A, from type-B material, which is unobservable and conjecturable. And there is no doubt that interpretation is something that attempts to link material A to material B.

At times observable material A is linked with the conjectured, B, through a law that says: if A then B—or: if A occurs, then B occurs. If we have a round form, A, on this side of the eyepiece, then, by virtue of my having accepted the laws of optics, we will have B—a cell, for example—at the opposite end. In some way, when we are confronted by A, we can understand, if we have internalized the law in question—as we said earlier—that we are confronted by B, or it is as if we were seeing B, although in fact all we see is A.

An English epistemological empiricist would protest here, saying that, in fact, from the most serious point of view in the history of knowledge and its foundations, the only thing that can be said is that we know A. But we all know that the act of knowing, as also the act itself of perceiving, implies an inextricable and "gestaltic" mix of empirical and conceptual aspects. Even seeing the book we have on the table is something that is given to us as an empirical datum and in a totally immediate way, without being divided into a stage where there are data that we interpret afterwards. Evidently, in a naive way, we are confronted by a book, although, in fact, what happens is something more complex in that we perceive a "Gestalt" formed by sense elements and conceptual elements that correspond to the concept of book.

To conclude, if a scientist has internalized certain laws in his conception of the world, undoubtedly when confronted by the mark or image of the eyepiece, he will "gestaltically" be seeing what he says he sees, and which is, in actuality, in the objective—the cell or the micro-organism. When one internalizes such a law, one ends up by *seeing*, by having experiences that go beyond the pre-theoretical experience. Put in another way, the hypotheses of the type we mentioned, as in the case of eyeglasses, finally make one "see" what one could not really see without them.

There is something interesting here, because, with everything we have said, we could be suggesting that perhaps the psychoanalysts have, by analogy with biologists, a type of "private optics" which provides them with some kind of microscope that allows them to reach the latent material through the manifest material. This idea is completely accurate, although the difference is that, while the biologists were fortunate in having physicists provide them with the microscope and the law that says "if A then B" for its use, psychoanalysts have had to develop their own optics through their theories. In fact, it is psychoanalysis itself that arrives at the type of law "if A then B", which permits understanding—in an unequivocal way, through a behavioural trait and the rule of correspondence—of what is happening internally in the person studied.

The examples we can give are probably naive, as are all those that attempt to illustrate a field foreign to the specialist. If we take into consideration the way Freud explains the structure of pathological phenomena in *The Ego and the Id* (1923b) and in *Inhibitions, Symptoms and Anxiety* (1926d), we can formulate a law that, in simple terms, tells us something like this: if the right occasion arises for the person to develop an action he or she is interested in yet does not carry out, then it is the superego that has inhibited the action of the ego. It is understood that this is an affirmation of the type "if A then B", because we are saying that if an agent's action is lacking in circumstances that would be appropriate for it, then what occurs is that the superego exercises an inhibiting action. In fact, from the epistemological point of view, the superego and the inhibiting action are not manifest, empirical material. To provide an epistemological foundation for psychoanalysis, the superego is not a datum. What is a datum is the fact that an action favoured by the environment, and which the agent was manifestly interested in performing, has not been carried out. For example, the boy and the girl are together, in appropriate circumstances. She is desirous and approving; he likes the girl. Suddenly—and one does not know what has happened—he picks up a book and begins to read. These are the data, not the superego and its inhibiting action.

Nevertheless, psychoanalysis has arrived at a hypothesis such as the one in our example, based on Freud's studies. And this hypothesis can contrast well with, and be well supported by, previous empirical observation, so that a psychoanalyst no longer discusses it, because he has many reasons for thinking that he functions quite well with this conceptual theoretical apparatus. (Fortunately, no scientist poses epistemological questions continuously about everything he does. We believe that patients would flee in horror if the psychoanalyst were constantly to re-examine epistemologically the theory he employs to cure them.) Therefore, in the type of example we gave, there is always a law incorporated into the "theoretical automatism" of the psychoanalyst. But it is clear that if we have that law, we are in a similar position to the biologist who relies on the optics of the microscope. If we know that A is the case—which here is the lack of positive conduct I referred to—and since we know that this is related to B, what happens in the unconscious, we can make that "gestaltic", conceptual type of reading of the experience. In the same way that in daily life we all have the right to say we have a datum such as "what is on my table is a book", so the psychoanalyst would say he has as a datum the inhibition of the ego by the person's superego. In short, then, when we consider the logical form of the relation between one variable and another, we will effect the "reading" of B, which, as you have noted, is not visible, on the basis of A, which is what is visible.

Let us point out once again that if we apply the law, "if A then B", this is because we are supposing that the variables A and B are in a particular relationship, such that A implies B, a supposition it is assumed is supported by a particular psychoanalytic theory.

This relation between A and B that allows us to make a "reading interpretation" consists in that A is a *sufficient condition* for B, and also, as the logicians say, B is a *necessary condition* for A. This means A cannot occur without the presence of B. When a law such as this has been included in a theory, it allows us to "read" in the material what we would not see without the law—in our example, the inhibitory action of the superego through the peculiar behaviour of the boy. If we have a law that tells us that when this conduct is present, then perforce the inhibition must be present, we can say we are *reading* the inhibition through the manifest datum.

It is true that whoever does not have the theory at his disposal, or is simply not used to utilizing it, cannot do this. A layman would not see the superego inhibiting the ego. He would simply see an intriguing, incomprehensible conduct. In this sense, I repeat, the theory allows us to see what we could not see without it: it really has the same effect as a magnifying lens. Repetition does not make the metaphor less exact. In the same way, the semiotic rules tell us how to grasp the meaning in an analogous fashion: if we have a sign A (constituted by visible traits) and we want to *read* it, apprehending its meaning B, the rules that establish meaning will teach us that "if sign A occurs, meaning B is present". This is why we speak of *reading*, if this is to grasp meaning B through sign A .

If manifest material is linked to latent material through a type of lawful relation of the type we have just described—that is, through a hypothesis that says that if this manifest material is present then it is necessarily accompanied by particular latent material—we are then authorized to say, for this case alone, that the interpretation is a *reading*, that we are really grasping what occurs in the unconscious through what we observe, through the manifest material. Moreover, we insist that it can be said, naturally and without qualification, that we are *seeing* it. This, incidentally, scandalizes those who have not reflected on the problem of the epistemology of psychoanalysis—a reaction caused particularly by the fact that at times one speaks of communication "from unconscious to unconscious", of grasping the unconscious (of the other person) directly, and these ways of speaking seem very suspicious to the outsider, who is tempted to think of telepathy, magical relations, or some mysterious type of universal, subterranean channel that connects two different minds.

In fact, there seems to be no difficulty from the logical point of view. The problem is clear: if the psychoanalyst, through his theory (and his practice), has incorporated a type of law that relates manifest material to latent material on the lines of "if A then B", then he has legitimate access to the experience of the unconscious of the other person, in the same way that a biologist does not doubt for a moment that he is looking at the cell through his microscope. Just as the biologist has no gnoseological problem because of his way of speaking, so the psychoanalyst does not have this problem either.

From the logical point of view, then, the problem is clear, although we are aware that there can be technical difficulties implied by this type of interpretation. We will not discuss them, because we are not competent to do so. But we wish to indicate here that, although these reading interpretations can be objected to technically because they are not instrumental, or because they facilitate an excessive intellectualization, or whatever, they are irreproachable for the logician.

Our first conclusion, then, is that there is a type of interpretation that is a reading, in which the latent material is read through the manifest material, where *read* means detected through a law. When the law is of the type "if A then B", the manifest material is what is called a *sufficient condition*. Its presence is enough; it is sufficient to make a link with the presence of what must accompany it. The other, the latent material, is the *necessary condition* and is what is read.

For this to be possible, the interpreter must, of course, have internalized the laws, either through his study of psychoanalytic theory or, in a non-explicit way, through indirect reference from his teachers—meaning that although our teachers are not the science of optics in its entirety, they will at least be the eyeglasses we use. This is simply because directed practice teaches many laws, many regulations. Let this be a modest justification for the important role theory plays in learning—and this goes for historians, sociologists, clinical psychologists and psychoanalysts. Without incorporating the hypotheses that establish this type of correlation, there would be no possibility of effecting the type of reading that is in this case the psychoanalytic interpretation. But this is also the case for sociological interpretation, which would be the reading of a variable (or a fact) through indicators, as they say—and the indicators are assumed to be variables or manifest data.

35.4   The explanation–interpretation

In our opinion, however, the typical case of psychoanalytic interpretation is not the one we have just described but its inverse, where the manifest content is the necessary condition and the latent content is the sufficient condition. This means that what psychoanalysis offers us this time is that if B is present in the unconscious, then A has to occur in the behaviour. As can be appreciated here, this example is the reverse of the former, where we had "if A is present, A is accompanied by B". Now we say if B is present, B is accompanied by A, but A is what is visible. Consequently, to see A does not allow us to say with certainty that B is present. When this occurs, we can no longer say when confronted by manifest material—without further ado—that we are reading the latent content. This would be to commit a fundamental logical error. It is true that if someone drinks hemlock he will die, but it is not true that if someone is dead it is because he has drunk hemlock. There are many other ways of dying. (Let us remember that the statement "If B then A", as well as the previous one, "if A then B", are, as stated earlier, "rules of correspondence"—that is, they link "empirical" concepts and phenomena A with "theoretical" notions and events B. Their role in science is very important, as the present discussion shows.)

In the face of this configuration, what we can do is to suppose that the latent content is B, because we are confronted by material A, and the law says that if B is present in the unconscious, material A must appear in the manifest content. However, one should bear in mind that there could be another cause C that could be producing the presence of A, instead of B (perhaps a certain law "If C then A" is also true).

To give an example of this type we can begin with the classical oedipal configuration and establish, in the case of a male, a law that says that if the imago of the father is aggressive, then, according to the theory of transference, this man also tends to see an aggressive note in male figures with whom he has a dependent relation. However, with this law we cannot conclude that because the patient is describing someone as aggressive, it follows that he is transferring onto him the figure of the father. Everything we said could be true, but there could be another cause for seeing X (the manifest material) at this moment as aggressive. He could, for example, be expressing sibling rivalry, he could be projecting into X his own aggression towards his mother and, of course, he could be objectively observing the facts. We have to limit ourselves, then, in principle, to saying that the patient's tendency to see someone as aggressive is due to the hypothetical existence of the imago of the father, or for some other reason. We do not know exactly what is happening, and, in any case, we cannot say we are "reading", through his manifest material, the aggressive imago of the father.

Nevertheless, it is probable that the psychoanalyst, despite everything, would say: yes, but it is only the figure of the father. When he does this, the psychoanalyst has not read the latent material. What he has really done is to formulate a hypothesis: the very useful one of assuming the material is as described. To assume this is useful in an explanatory way for him, because he avails himself of a law that says that when this latent material is present, certain particular things have to occur in the manifest conduct. On the basis of the hypothesis that the aggressive imago of the father presses at that moment on the patient, plus the law that says that this unconscious imago is accompanied by certain references or particular material, the reason for the patient offering certain material is *explained* .

The model of what happens here is what is usually called an explanatory design, which is, in fact, quite complicated. We do not wish to develop further here what is called *Hempel's model* (1965) and its logical structure as an indication of what an explanation is. It is enough that in this type of interpretation first a hypothesis is proposed; then, on seeing that from the hypothesis, with the help of a law, what is already known (the manifest material) can be deduced, we say that we have explained it.

This is the most usual way of interpreting, because psychoanalysis is rather a modelistic theory: it offers a model of functioning of the psychic apparatus, from which certain consequences arise in relation to the manifest conduct of human beings, and patients in particular. In this sense, it seems that laws of the type we are studying operate more frequently, although not in obligatory fashion, in psychoanalysis: if internally something of type B occurs, something of type A will be seen. In the cases that concern us, therefore, to interpret will be to propose a hypothesis and see how from it is deduced, with the help of laws, what we wanted to explain.

In clinical practice a psychoanalyst does not take the steps we have described, of course. The psychoanalyst has internalized psychoanalytic theory, as he has also internalized the logic of practical and effective thought, the same as all of us. What we say is that, when a psychoanalyst is confronted by the manifest material, he employs a quick and automatic procedure to look at various models, various possibilities of what is occurring internally. He also examines, quickly and automatically, from which of those models he can best deduce the effective behaviour he is already acquainted with. Once he notices the right model, he grasps it immediately as the explanatory model. Consequently, interpretation is used as a hypothesis for what occurs internally.

As in the case of laws that allow "readings", the law applied in these cases comes from psychoanalysis and forms part of the training, the theoretical practice the psychoanalyst has incorporated during his learning. Although it is performed automatically, the operation we have just described can be carried out only by means of at least a minimal theoretical skill. It is required in order to be able to produce a great number of models and to see quickly which are the best ones for a deductive explanation of the material. The patient does many things; all human beings do many things, and all are in some sense interpretable. But psychoanalysis is concerned with grasping, in some way, those that are susceptible of a more significant and interesting interpretation. In order for the psychoanalyst to capture, from the almost infinite torrent of acts the patient performs as a human being, the one that interests him, he has to have a theoretical intuition that enables him to see, behind the material, the model that—logically connected—will finally be an interesting interpretation of the patient's behaviour.

After this near-apotheosis of the role of theory to demonstrate how it influences the act of interpreting, we have to say here, however, that there is a difference between what is interpretation now and what was interpretation in the first place. If psychoanalysis is not discussed, if psychoanalysis is incorporated as a theory, in the first case—the reading—then there is nothing to say. A reading has been carried out, and that is enough. When, through the manifest material, the latent material is reached on the basis of a reading relation of the microscope type, we know that necessarily if the manifest material we see is there, it is because the latent material has to be there, and this is enough. It is true that one can observe here that psychoanalysis, although it has a more deterministic than probabilistic model, sometimes accepts the said correlations as a tendency and a probability rather than rigorously. Therefore one should not say, even with the "if A then B" type of law, that one has read B inexorably through A. One should only say it is probable. We do not wish to concentrate deeply on this question now, since it is not essential to the problem we are discussing; moreover, having qualified our case, we can understand that this is so. What matters is that, along this path, a reading is a reading, and it is as if one had widened the empirical base: one sees the patient better, in a broader perspective.

The other type of interpretation, the explanatory one, in which the correlation is "if B then A", presents a different problem. The interpretation is a hypothesis about what happens with B, what happens from the internal side of the question. It is a hypothesis we make because we try to know the patient, we wish to know him better, just as scientists make hypotheses because they wish to know the nature of the universe. But hypotheses have to be contrasted, have to be falsified. How can an interpretative hypothesis—an interpretation—be evaluated?

The answer a naive epistemologist would give is that an interpretation, the same as any hypothesis, is validated or compared through its consequences and what can be deduced from them. When we make a hypothesis, practical, clinical, observable consequences can be deduced from it. If things occur as we affirmed, then the interpretation is good. If this is not the case, then the hypothesis (the interpretation) is bad. *Grosso modo* this is what would happen. It is good to remember here a type of *slogan* in scientific method that says that, however good the practical, clinical and observable consequences of a hypothesis, this does not demonstrate its truth. The reason is that logicians unfortunately know that, reasoning correctly, the false can be deduced from the true. What we are saying is a logical tragedy, but nothing can be done about it. Those who invented logic realized perfectly well that logical laws only guarantee that if one starts with truths, one must arrive at truths: this is certain, and here logic is well-behaved. On the other hand, if one starts with falsehoods, logic is indifferent to this matter. Let us say that, for logic, he who starts with falsehoods should face the consequences, as in the Spanish saying, "if you sleep with children, you wake up wet". In this sense, logic guarantees nothing in relation to what happens if one begins with false statements. Unfortunately, then, sometimes one begins with falsehoods and yet, through deduction, one arrives at truths. When one begins with a hypothesis, if it is false, it might allow one to deduce true consequences. Of course such a thing could be prohibited. But how does one know a hypothesis is false? This is precisely the difficulty. The point of formulating a hypothesis is that one does not know whether it is true or false. One assumes it is true, but it is not certain. The history of science shows this to be so continually. It is not impossible, then, for a false interpretation to permit true consequences or conclusions. Therefore it is perfectly possible for an interpretation to be supported by manifest material and nevertheless to be false. In any case, this is what a hypothetic–deductivist would think, because in the end, in this sense, an interpretation is not very different to any other hypothesis. If clinical practice goes well systematically after the psychoanalyst has made the interpretation, it is a good sign, in its favour; if not, then it is an unfavourable sign.

We will now consider some specific difficulties of the scientific method when applied to psychoanalysis. But first I wish to indicate that sometimes the two types of interpretations we have studied are conjoined, and the law is of the type "A if and only if B". In this case there is a "necessary and sufficient condition": if the latter is present, the former must be present; if the former is present, the latter must be present. When such a convenient situation presents itself, we have, simultaneously, an explanation and a reading. The laws are not always as good as this, but it can happen.

With this we can see that there are three gnoseological possibilities for interpretation: explanation, reading and simultaneous reading and explanation.

In his "On Narcissism", for example, Freud (1914c) seems to employ a type of law as follows: there is a type of connection of the type "if and only if", a necessary and sufficient condition, between the libido invested in the representation of an organ, of an external object, or of a personality structure on the one hand (and having an unconscious or latent character), and the behavioural affect directed towards an object, an organ or a structural part of our psychic apparatus. If the libido is thus, the behaviour will be thus; if not, not. The behaviour is "if and only if". In understanding this implicitly, Freud has a reading and an explanatory tool simultaneously. For example, as a reading tool, if he sees an individual who is very interested in himself, who overestimates and is excessively concerned with himself, Freud understands that the libido is being invested in the ego. The libido of the individual is placed in the ego because he overestimates himself. This is the reading part: to see what the individual is doing is to realize where the libido is.

In some circumstances, especially in relation to narcissistic behaviour, it is the other way round: if we suppose that the libido is narcissistic, we can deduce that this individual tends to overestimate himself. We would then be explaining his conduct.

35.5 Some specific difficulties

Is there something else to say against this? Unfortunately, the situation is much more complicated than what has been discussed so far. In the social sciences and in psychoanalysis, there really seems to be a special difference that complicates the question and produces the difficulties that define the very marrow of epistemology in the interpretative task. This is that interpretation, as in the case of the social sciences, has some fairly negative characteristics. They form part of what in the language of social sciences is called *autopredictive* hypotheses (or self-fulfilling prophecies), and also *suicidal* hypotheses, depending on what occurs.

Sociologists know well that a hypothesis, independently of its truth or falseness, by the fact of being stated, sets in motion a series of processes that can end in their apparent confirmation or their apparent refutation. The old and real example Nagel gives in *The Structure of Science* (1961) is quite clear. A New York newspaper said that the New York State Bank, a private bank despite its name, was in difficulties, and it would very probably become bankrupt. In the afternoon, fearful clients produced a run of such magnitude that the bank, in effect, went broke. Apparently, the newspaper was right; the hypothesis was corroborated. But one smells a trap in all this, because if the newspaper had not made those statements, the bank might not have gone broke. In this sense, the hypothesis is vitiated because it is auto-predictive; the fact of stating it provokes consequences that finally corroborate it.

There are also quite obvious cases where a hypothesis, by the fact of being stated, can in the end be refuted. If an Argentinian newspaper had said, in earlier times which luckily are no more, that there were rumours that General X and General Y would engage in a *coup d'état* the following day and imprison the entire government, it is very probable that by the afternoon the government would have locked up the generals in question, and then there would have been no *coup d'état*. However, this is not a refutation of what the newspaper said. The newspaper could maintain that had it not stated what it did, had it not been indiscreet, the *coup d'état* would have taken place.

From the methodological point of view, there is certainly a difficulty here—the value of the hypothesis seems incapable of being tested if this situation, of the hypothesis being stated, is produced. This touches interpretation, which almost by definition is a hypothesis that has to be stated, to which the patient is going to react precisely because it has been stated.

This is not an insoluble difficulty in itself, because, returning to the previous sociological example, we would consider that in this situation there was no contrastibility, since this possibility was frustrated by the fact that the hypothesis was stated. However, this does not mean that scientifically nothing is to be done here, because there are laws (the laws of the propagation of rumours, not the economic laws of how banks close) that state what happens when certain rumours circulate. In our example, the sociologist has seen how the law is corroborated that says that a bank can become insolvent through a fearful reaction on the part of the public when there are rumours that it is in difficulties.

The relation there is between a stated hypothesis and the empirical reaction that occurs when it is stated does not, then, remain outside scientific method. This is an interesting point worth indicating. Another is that, in any case, the primitive hypothesis has not been refuted, nor has anything pertinent been done with it, because it is understood that a scientific law obtains only in the absence of disturbance. No one would contrast a scientific law other than in adequate conditions. Someone who innocently wishes to prove the law that states that inflammable material will burst into flame if a match is used does not refute the law if he places the inflammable material in a hermetically sealed container, because the law says, in fact, that there should be no disturbance of this type when the match is near it. A law is fulfilled only in the absence of disturbances, and it is necessary to define what these disturbances are. It is understood that a sociological law of the type we are considering would say that when banks are in certain difficulties—for example when they have invested everything in real estate and have no liquidity—if a state of general lack of liquidity should occur, they will crash. Evidently, a law such as this could be contrasted by observing what happens with some banks when the newspapers have not yet reported their difficulties. Clearly, there is an enormous quantity of possibilities for economic investigation of this type.

The problems posed by interpretation are similar. In the meantime, the testing of interpretations sometimes has a perfectly possible and normal counterpart, and it is that the psychoanalyst can formulate in his mind the interpretative hypothesis, without at that point communicating it to his patient. There is no reason why one must tell the patient everything that one thinks of him. Thus there are conjectures about the patient's internal structure that could, in some sense, be called interpretative hypotheses, although they have not been expressed verbally. These can be compared in the normal way through the hypothetic-deductive method. If we propose a hypothesis with the data we have about the patient, certain predictions about his future conduct can be deduced, which would eventually be corroborated or refuted. Therefore we can begin by saying that, although we define interpretation as the concrete and explicit event of formulating an interpretative hypothesis—and admitting that this undoubtedly causes a disturbance—this does not prevent the psychoanalyst from formulating his hypotheses *internally* as to how (and who) the patient is, and trying to verify them through his future conduct. Interpretation in this sense is not an obstacle. On the contrary, it can be quite well supported from this angle of the problem. However, it is no less true, and it is worth pointing out, that the autopredictive and suicidal effects of an interpretation evidently exist, as Wisdom (1967) indicates.

If the patient is kind enough to corroborate our interpretative hypothesis before we have formulated it, and if there are already sufficient indicators to consider it corroborated, the interpretation is finally formulated with sufficient support. This is because, as we said at the beginning, interpretation not only has an affirmative, hypothetical character, but it is also an instrument, a weapon, not only a hypothesis. One does something to the patient to provoke a change. We can indicate here that to use an instrument to produce events also implies knowledge of the laws of correlation: one has to know that if certain things are done, they will produce certain changes. Let us insist once more that with insufficient theoretical preparation and lacking theoretical practice during training, one will not know that the instrumental use of certain things will cause certain effects.

But let us return to what we were considering. It is obvious, and this is what Wisdom indicates, that through certain defence mechanisms, or simply through suggestion, it is perfectly possible that the patient will not only reject an interpretation explicitly, but the emerging material that follows does not adapt to the interpretation. Conversely, if the patient liked the interpretation because it serves as a screen for more dangerous things, he may throw out empirical material to give the appearance of corroborating it. Freud studied this specifically in "Constructions in Analysis" (1937d), one of his last works, where he insists that neither "yes" nor "no" on the patient's part can be taken as corroboration or refutation as such.

The fact that the interpretation has the characteristics of "spoken (or stated) hypothesis" leads to the situation we have called autopredictive or suicidal hypothesis. This poses quite interesting problems for the epistemologist and the methodologist. How should we really proceed? We think many things can be done. There is no insoluble difficulty here, but rather a refinement. First, as we have said, there are occasions where our interpretative hypotheses do not form part of our explicit interpretations, and we keep them for our private understanding of the patient. We can test them through the usual methods of contrasting hypothesis. This is part of what we can call the "silent aspect" of the psychoanalyst's work. Secondly, it seems quite probable to many psychoanalysts (although totally false to others—and behind this lies a very complicated situation) that, in fact, the part that comprises adaptive behaviour to interpretations is quite narrow and is limited to manifest verbal and ostensible behaviour, to what is immediately given. It is probable that there are, in fact, many channels of communication as regards the patient, and a great quantity of verbal, non-verbal and behavioural elements that are sufficient indicators to examine what is really happening to the analysand (Benito M. López, personal communication).

In this sense it seems that, to a large extent, the testing of the interpretations is there in any case, in the empirical, clinical material that is really available. Additionally, there are often issues relating to historical data which can in some way be known later by the psychoanalyst and which also constitute a type of indicator.

Let me point out that this is a theme bristling with methodological obstacles. Although it is true that the patient's subsequent conduct can be particular and adaptive to the interpretation, yet the psychoanalyst can distinguish, according to the clinical picture, between internal structure and the latent problems of the analysand, and the mode of adaptation may be different when the interpretation is correct from when it is not. It could be said that the way to resist an accurate interpretation is not the way to resist an inaccurate interpretation. Finally, therefore, there is what we can call an interesting problem of semiotics and of channels of communication, which would show that the modes of resistance, the manoeuvres directed for or against the interpretation by the patient, and which make verification difficult, are, however, peculiar manoeuvres that could, in some way, be transformed into indicators of exactitude or inexactitude in its informative aspect.

Wisdom refers to this when he proposes to evaluate the interpretation by establishing the type of defence the patient adopts. The defence should be approached with the same theory used in formulating the first interpretative hypothesis, so that the analyst will not be able to utilize the associative (and defensive) material to formulate an interpretation foreign to the theory that originated the first one.

35.6   *The semantic and instrumental aspects of interpretation*

We said at the beginning that psychoanalytic interpretation should be viewed at least through a triple perspective. We have examined to some extent the gnoseological aspect of interpretation. We will now deal with the two remaining aspects—the semantic and the instrumental.

The *semantic aspect* has to do with the symbolic or sign function contained in the patient's activity. To interpret in the semantic sense implies an exercise of signification, an act of assigning meaning (significance). Let us say, as an aside, that contemporary semiotics is a multiple science that is split into many schools. Here we encounter an additional difficulty, because the very idea of sign, meaning, sense or symbol varies from theory to theory.

According to the point of view we are now considering, the manifest material not only has "lawful" relations with the latent material, but also relations of significance (meaning). These are not exactly the same as the "lawful" relations, which in my examples seem to be something similar to correlation, to cause and effect.

What in fact one wishes to state when it is affirmed that the manifest material symbolizes material of another order—unconscious or latent—is that it operates as an indicator, that the elements of the language have meaning with which to refer to objects.

What can all this mean? There is here a great disparity in the situations to be viewed. I will indicate two or three cases to present the problem. On some occasions the relation a sign has with what is signified is what is called a natural relation. It is, for example, the sense in which it can be asserted that thunder is a sign of the storm or that smoke signals fire. When this is meant, the sign is transformed into an indicator of what has been signified (indicated, meant), which does not introduce much novelty into our discussion. These are precisely the relations I referred to when I spoke of necessary and sufficient conditions. It would be the sense of affirming, for example, that if the impatient behaviour of an analysand symbolizes the avidity of the baby, this is because having undergone an emergency situation of deprivation during the oral phase is a necessary and sufficient condition for the presence of this material in the transference.

What introduces real novelty here is that there exist certain implied rules that enable something to symbolize something else, as a code does. However much we delve, the word "father" does not have any element similar to the father as objective reality. It cannot be connected to what it represents in the way in which smoke and fire are connected. There is no "lawful" character here from cause to effect. There will undoubtedly be historical and philological reasons that led certain communities to use that word and no other, but this is not exactly the same. There has been an adoption, as it were, of that relation of symbolization.

Why do these relations of symbolization occur? They can take many forms. There are also natural codes in this sense; in other words, human beings can adopt certain codes because they have a propensity to do so. It would be something similar to how certain animals tend to flee from shadows that move, because their genetic code has programmed them for that. These are what can be called "natural symbols". Psychoanalysis has not found many, but there are very interesting observations that show that the human being takes certain symbols as natural, in relation to a particular situation. They are not linguistic. Certain hypnotic experiments have been carried out in different cultures, and the reaction has been very similar with regard to what constitutes a phallic symbol, for example, without the mediation of any linguistic convention.

Another type of relation in symbolization is the one called "by isomorphism". In this case the structure of the sign corresponds to the form of what is symbolized. This is why structuralists think they have discovered a fruitful correspondence between the structure of a story or a dream and that of a myth or a profound belief.

The third case is that of conventional codes that are typical of the language. Here there is a structure symbolizing another through certain rules of convention.

The problem for psychoanalysis is, obviously, that language is not the only operator through which the human being realizes conventions according to which something starts to symbolize something else. There is a continuous quantity of imposed and aleatory codes through which man transforms objects into conventional symbols of other things. What must be grasped are these conventions. Again, this is a terrain where the psychoanalyst meets with a very serious epistemological problem, because he has to do two things: he has to become aware of the *ad hoc* code the patient has adopted at a given moment, and then he has to recognize it in the unfolding of the analytic process. All this constitutes a fairly complicated epistemological field about which much can be said.

Finally, let us look briefly at the *instrumental aspect* of psychoanalytic interpretation. It seems clear that an interpretation "does" something. To interpret is not merely to give an opinion about what is happening in or with the patient. It is not merely to form a structural picture about the patient in order to keep silent about it. One states it, and in stating it one is evidently doing something, one is effecting a mode of action, an operation. Therefore the idea of interpretation is indissolubly linked here to the fact that it is a mode of action, a way of articulating the relation with the patient. This is true not only for the psychotherapist who interprets, seeking to promote a change in the patient, but also for the analyst who only seeks insight, because this is in any case a way of operating on the patient, although it is, in fact, different from the previous one.

In this sense there arise, from the logical point of view, all the more or less ordinary and complicated difficulties jurists encounter when they try to define, for example, what an action is, what the consequence of an action is, what the responsibility of the action is, which is the inherent and which is the secondary effect of the action, what guilt and responsibility there is, and so forth. These problems are undoubtedly very interesting, but we are only going to refer to them tangentially.

Just as the main problem in the gnoseological area of interpretation is to separate the true from the false, in the instrumental aspect to define the good and the bad is decisive. With the true and false we refer to the patient's knowledge; with the good and bad, on the other hand, we take account of the aims of therapy. This objective (or aim) presupposes another theoretical reference, which complicates things considerably.

In the instrumental aspect there is what we could call a type of normative ethical code behind the therapeutic process, and this makes the issue clear. Interpretation always has instrumental, therapeutic motives, and the underlying value aspects have to do with the cure. Naturally, this implies, in turn, a value definition of the cure and of what is considered normal or pathological. As in the case of the informative aspect, in this area of the issue we will in any case find ourselves within the frame of an axiological theory that requires a series of initial understandings. Just as we will have to understand whether the patient is sitting down, whether he said a particular thing, whether he has a given symptom, it is assumed there must exist a prior understanding of whether a particular thing is desirable or not. However, this is no obstacle to the neutral attitude of psychoanalysis and of the psychoanalyst, in the cognitive aspect. Although we can disagree about ultimate values that must be obtained through analytic therapy, there is something logical and objective that is in any case independent of this—namely, that if we accept value $V1$ and wish to reach results that correspond to value $V1$, we have to make use of certain laws of cause and effect. These laws of psychoanalysis say that in order to produce $V1$, Cause a must be produced. If we have a change of mind and, rather than producing $V1$, we want to produce value $V1$, then we will have recourse to another law, which says that to obtain $V1$, first Cause b must be produced, of which $V1$ will be the effect. To conclude, there is an aspect of psychoanalysis independent of the value question, that of relations of causality or the semiotic relations there are between the variables that constitute the motive for psychoanalytic investigation.

Whatever our system of values is, the causal laws have a certain objective independence. We can discuss, as jurists do, whether or not it is good to shoot someone and kill him. But there is something neutral that transcends the different ethical positions, and this is that the shot was the cause of the death.

In considering the instrumental aspect of the interpretation we need to separate two things: first, what we might call the value background, which is implicit in the teaching of interpretation and its instrumental values; and, second, a series of causal rather than value problems, which are the "objective" property of everybody at the same time. This is the sense in which the non-value aspect of the sciences constitutes the common heritage of all points of view, although they may differ as to values. The laws of causality are at the service of everyone. Which causal relations we will use and to what purpose depends on ideological positions and other factors. Undoubtedly, to apply an interpretation, having assigned a value to it, we need to know the causal relations between the interpretation and the behaviour.

In accordance with the theory of action, then, therapy takes interpretation as an instrument, not to get to know the patient, but as an agent of change.

There is a series of interesting things here, which Freud discussed in 1937 in "Analysis Terminable and Interminable" and in "Constructions". What he finds first is the way in which a patient responds to the interpretation. It is not a case of complete fortuitousness in respect of what is said. Further, it is very curious that there is some connection between the instrumental effect of the interpretation and its gnoseological excellence. Freud asserts that a mistaken interpretation has little effect, compared with the type of behavioural change the accurate interpretation produces. The patient's reaction to the true interpretation or construction is much more notable and appropriate. It is a notable and not unavoidable discovery, because the instrumental efficacy of the act of interpreting does not have to be taken as being linked to the truth. In journalism and in marketing a product, it is known that the success of an information or publicity campaign is not linked to it being true. This is an unfortunate situation we are all acquainted with. It constitutes the basis for the theory of ideology.

Freud's thought on this point is that the patient's ideology (I use the word "ideology" in a very general and metaphorical sense, as everything the patient believes and thinks, as well as his defences, suggestibility and so forth) cannot be sufficient to avoid evident effects of the truth. Epistemologists have not yet pointed out the importance of this.

We think what has been said is enough to show the three zones in which the epistemology of psychoanalysis moves: the problem of theory (explanation and reading); the problem of rational action (with the theory that supports it) and the immense problem of how to come to know the (natural or conventional) symbolic quality that leads from the manifest to the latent material. These are the three problems—typical but of a different order—that confront the epistemologist with regard to this difficult issue.

We have tried to show that the interpretative instrument in psychoanalysis is not like the needle of a pressure gauge, which moves and takes different positions. Interpretation is not a simple and automatic sign. On the contrary, it requires—as does everything that is hypothesis and theory—creativity and talent. Because of this, freedom of thought favours an aptitude for interpretation. An individual who is prone to stereotyped reactions is not, in general, going to make good interpretations. The practice of interpretation is peculiar. It is an act of spiritual creation (from the logical point of view), and this explains why the personality of the psychoanalyst will be enriched by the fact of practising interpretation. But this is a hypothesis that will have to be examined.

35.7   Final reflections

As a theory of the psychic apparatus, psychoanalysis is situated among other psychiatric or psychological theories. It seems difficult to think of it as *one* theory, since very different themes are studied within psychoanalysis. The theory of instincts is not the same as the theory of defence mechanisms, economic theory, structural theory and others we can think of. Taking psychoanalysis as a whole, it is obvious that Lacan, Melanie Klein and Hartmann are quite different. Each one of these positions presents, in some way, a different theoretical picture, not only as a whole, but also as to the details of function of the psychic apparatus. Whoever produces interpretative hypotheses and contrasts them does so within a global theoretical framework. There is not what we could call an isolated interpretation. To make interpretations, one must not only count on quite a large arsenal of rules of correspondence of the type we have already indicated, but one must also be located within a theoretical conception of the functions of the psychic apparatus. If we cannot agree about what our position is, the discussion will become difficult and even impossible. There is no sense in talking of testing interpretations in a vacuum.

Let us take the opportunity of saying here that, when the interpretation is examined, in some sense one's whole theoretical framework is tested. Although this is absolutely true, it is appropriate to remember here that the psychoanalyst (and the scientist in general) is not immediately going to question his theory if the result of one experiment is a failure. There are all sorts of sociological and methodological reasons why the scientist does not throw out his great hypothesis in the face of an apparent contrast. He will say the interpretation is bad—and more so if he is judging the interpretation of another, of his colleague! However, if difficulties begin to come up with the answers to the interpretations, if one feels well prepared and expert yet begins to fail systematically, one must ask at a given moment where this type of difficulty originates, and whether it is one's theoretical framework that disturbs the efficiency of interpretation. At this moment the analyst can think that what is happening in his practice in some way shows him it is time to change something at the heart of the theory itself.

This can be seen in the history of Freud's thought. Some things failed for Freud at a given moment in relation to his patients (cathartic hypnosis, for example). However, he did not think then that he was a fool, and that he used the (cathartic) method badly. Interestingly, he never lost faith in his abilities as a scientist. Rather, he lost faith in some of his scientific hypotheses, although, basically, they could be readapted. The most typical example in this respect—and the most heroic one—was when he abandoned the theory of seduction around 1896, to go on then to construct the libido theory.

All the sciences have something in common and something different. They have in common what we could call "the great strategies of their problems". When we speak of sciences in which there is a factual aspect that is in some way related through logical laws with the theory, then the relations between one aspect and another rest on the general characteristics of corroboration and refutation. But we can also say that the type of material studied varies from one science to another, and this means first a change in the nature (of the material), and secondly a change in the empirical laws. The strategy does not change—it is the tactics and the methodology to be used that do. Clearly the study of isolated systems or semi-isolated bodies, for example, is not the same as that of a live organism with interrelated parts. The idea to be used cannot be the same one in both cases; it must change. Even if we were not studying the human body and had to compare the mechanics of billiard balls to the functioning of a computer, we would see there something qualitatively different. This does not mean that the logical problem of how to validate a model is different in either case. But the technique in relation to the material and the production of the hypothesis changes. In this sense, the general problems pertaining to psychoanalytic theory, to the construction of its concepts, to the delimitation of its empirical domain, to the formulation of parts of the theory, and so forth, are not very different to what happens in the epistemology of many other disciplines. As to the peculiarities of the material considered, the psychoanalyst has greater affinity with what can be found in sociology, for example, than in chemistry or physics.

However, despite this difference and the fact that the tactics, *modus operandi* and articulation of the theory change completely, we would venture to affirm that the difference is not ultimately as great as it would seem. In the end, how can the scientist advance without constructing models of what occurs? Since empirical data are complicated and include a great number of factors, some of which are hidden, if one were not to produce models then empirical data alone, or what is ostensible, would be insufficient for advancement. Here psychoanalysis provides the best justification for what we are saying, as a theory whose merit consists of underlining the greater weight of unconscious or latent material, in its application, as compared to manifest material. If this is so, if we are dealing with the production of models, we should not be scandalized at the great number of procedures required to gain access to the models. It will be a question of character modality. Those with a more Anglo-Saxon temperament will produce models with separate variables and will try to distinguish the variables, and will study correlations and conflicts between the variables. Others will tend towards biological models; still others will incline to the cybernetic model and—why not—to what we could call *sui generis* models for psychoanalysis. Because in the end, if psychoanalysis develops as a mature science, it will find that the successful models are those proper to it, and not those developed by analogy with other disciplines. Then, just as biology has its homeostatic models and sociology its structural models, psychoanalysis will have its *psychoanalytic models*. In this sense, we will say that in the final instance and similarly to other sciences, the peculiarity of the psychoanalytic material does not alter the deep logical structure of the problem of the validation of theories. But it does change the type of imagination, the creative act of the investigator to propose his hypotheses, to form his theorems and his theories. Here is where we find something *sui generis* in psychoanalysis. One who has not worked in psychoanalysis and who does not understand its methodology well will not realize how its models are produced, nor the difficulties inherent in the problems with which psychoanalysis deals.

Let us conclude by saying that psychoanalysis should integrate itself in other scientific disciplines, subordinating itself to the general requirements of the method without abdicating from that which is idiosyncratic.

After having posed this great problem, which arises continually when the epistemology of psychoanalysis is discussed, I would like to deal briefly with another problem that is rarely considered and is in some way symmetrical to the previous one. The opposite question is rarely asked— whether psychoanalysis has contributed to the understanding of general epistemology. Undoubtedly physics and mathematics have made contributions to epistemology which allowed an understanding of the logical structure of theories. Is there something in the psychoanalytic mode of thinking that influences the epistemologist's viewpoint of the course of science? Without being an expert on Bion or Money-Kyrle, I think these analysts, for example, have attempted to advance somewhat, systematically, along this path. It seems to me that it is precisely the peculiarity of its problems, and the particular model of psychoanalysis, of its thought, that can have an indirect and revolutionary effect on the study of how scientific models were formed in physics, in chemistry and in the other theories, by giving the underlying reasons. There are, of course, books giving a precise description of how paradigms and scientific theories were formed, and how they ceased to be that. But it may be that psychoanalysts will have something to say about how unconscious motivations influence in some way the appearance of certain models rather than others in scientific theories. In this sense, psychoanalysis can offer something of great value, intrinsic to it, towards the understanding of the other disciplines.

PART FOUR

ON THE NATURE
OF THE PSYCHOANALYTIC PROCESS

CHAPTER THIRTY-SIX

The analytic situation

We must now look into a complex and attractive theme, the *psychoanalytic process*. This is something that awakens the enthusiasm and even the impassioned interest of analysts, and so it should be. If the study of the technique has a fundamental objective, it can be none other than that of contributing to each analyst's acquisition of his style and his analytic being, of his identity. The latter depends on the congruence between what he thinks and what he does, which derives in good part from how the psychoanalytic process is understood. An analyst who thinks in a way that is coherent with what he does, although his scheme of reference may not be to my liking, will always be preferable to one who thinks as I do and not as he (in fact) does.

I refer to the analytic process in broad and intentionally imprecise terms in order to cover the totality of issues we will study. However, if we wish to be rigorous, what we must first do is to distinguish the process from the *analytic situation*.

36.1 An attempt at definition

The practical analyst uses these two terms, "situation" and "process", with sufficient precision. He rarely commits errors in using them, since they are sanctioned by ordinary language. We will say, for example, that the analytic situation has become stabilized or complicated, and that the process continues or has been arrested—never the other way around. Nevertheless, when we try to conceptualize what is easy for us to distinguish, we encounter difficulties.

According to the *Shorter Oxford Dictionary*, "situation" means "place or position of things in relation to surroundings". In this way, we could say, in principle, that when we speak of the analytic situation in ordinary language terms, we mean that the analytic treatment has a place, a location. We can say in very general terms, then, that the analysis (or the cure) takes "place" in the analytic situation.

Up to this point I think most analysts are in agreement, because I have tried to define the analytic situation in very broad, almost tautological terms, which are analytic in the Kantian sense. The difficulties appear when we wish to fill this first attempt at a definition with concrete contents.

The analytic situation has been defined as a particular relation between two persons who abide by certain rules of behaviour in order to carry out a particular task, which brings out two well-defined roles, those of analysand and of analyst. The task these two persons propose to carry out consists in the exploration of the unconscious of one of them, with the technical participation of the other. Gitelson proposed the following definition: "The analytic situation may be described as the total configuration of interpersonal relationships and interpersonal events which develop between the psychoanalyst and his patient" (1952, p. 1). Lagache's definition is very similar. He uses the word "ambience" for situation: "The analytic ambience is the totality and the sequence of the material and psychological conditions in which the psychoanalytic sessions develop" (Lagache, 1951, p. 130).

In defining the analytic situation as the totality of transactions that occur between analysand and analyst in virtue of the task that brings them together, we are implying that there are rules that must order that relation. What rules these are must, then, be established. These are norms that have been stipulated empirically in virtue of the best development of the analytic task. They continue to be, without any substantial modification, those that Freud proposed in his articles on technique around 1910, especially in his "Recommendations" in 1912 and 1913. Those proposals have not undergone basically any modification, and it is important to know that the most disparate schools respect and admit to them. There could be some exceptions, but in general everyone follows them. (In chapter 37 we discuss Lacan's open session or session of free time.)

36.2 Situation and field

When we begin to define the analytic situation as a relationship between two people who come together to carry out a particular task, we slide imperceptibly from the situation into the process. It could not be otherwise, because every task implies a development, an evolution in time, while the situation, if we are going to respect what the word tells us, is something that is in its place and does not move.

The difference between situation and process is basically, then, that the former has a spatial reference and the latter necessarily includes time.

Now if we were to leave aside time and define the analytic situation (as we already have done) as the totality of transactions between analysand and analyst in virtue of the roles each one fulfils and of the task that brings them together, we would say the analytic situation is a *field*.

We understand a field here as the zone of interaction between an organism and its environment, since these two factors cannot be separated. The qualities of the organism always derive from its relation with the totality of conditions it finds itself in. As Lagache (1955) says, "there is no organism which is not placed within a situation, nor a situation without an organism" (quoted in Zac, 1968, p. 28). Just as the psychological field is defined by the interaction of the organism and its ambience, in the same way "the analytic field results from the interaction of the patient and the ambience, which includes the person and the role of the analyst" (ibid.).

36.3   The analytic situation as a dynamic field

Following Pichon Rivière's footsteps, Argentinian and Uruguayan writers generally understand the analytic situation as a field that is simultaneously one of observation and one of interaction.

One of the first works on the theme, and perhaps the most complete, is that of Madeleine and Willy Baranger (1961–62). The Barangers' starting point is that the analytic situation can no longer be understood as the objective observation of an analysand in regression by an analyst-eye (1969, p. 129). Such a description is unilateral, since, beyond his undisputed neutrality, the analyst intervenes in fact and by right in the situation he himself has partly created.

The two members of the analytic couple are linked complementarily, and neither of the two can be understood without the other. On this basis the Barangers propose to apply the concept of field from Gestalt psychology and from Merleau-Ponty to the analytic situation. "The analytic situation has its spatial and temporal structure, is orientated by lines of force and particular dynamics, has its own evolutionary laws, its general objective and its momentary objectives" (ibid., p. 130). The analyst's observation, to the extent that it refers to the patient and to himself, "can only be defined as observation of this field" (ibid.).

The Barangers' basic idea is, then, that the analytic situation constitutes a field that must be explained by the lines of force arising from that special and new configuration between its two protagonists, each one in his role and with his own objectives. What distinguishes the psychoanalytic field, say the Barangers, is that it is configured as an *unconscious fantasy*. These two theories, the field and the unconscious fantasy, are connected when it is asserted that the unconscious fantasy that appears in the field is always a fantasy in which both its members participate.

Everyone who accepts the theory of countertransference expounded in chapter 21 and thereafter will accept in principle the Barangers' proposal, inasmuch as it maintains that the analyst participates in the analytic situation, although the degree of that participation can be argued. For the Barangers, this participation is considerable, since they argue that the fantasy not only *appears* in the field but *is* a field fantasy in which both protagonists are equally involved. Of course this is where the discussion can become livelier: how much is the analyst involved?

The difference between this position and that of Leo Rangell, among the ego psychologists, is wide. At the Latin-American Congresses of 1964 and 1966, Rangell (1966, 1968a) maintained that the psychoanalytic process takes place in the patient. On the other hand, for the Barangers and the Latin-Americans it takes place between the patient and the analyst. (At the Madrid Congress of 1983, however, I heard Rangell say that the process occurs between analyst and analysand.) Other ego psychologists, such as Weinshel (1984) and Loewald (1970), for example, conceive the analytic situation as an interaction between analyst and analysand. Loewald says that there is no room in psychoanalysis for the idea of an observer extraneous to the object of study, and he adds, "We become part and participant of and in the field as soon as we are present in our role as analysts" (1970, p. 278).

The Latin-American analysts maintain that the process takes place between analyst and analysand. The Barangers want to underline this point when they say that the psychoanalytic field is dynamic. But they conceive it as a shared fantasy. They affirm that when the analyst's fantasy about the analytic situation coincides with that of the analysand, a fantasy of the couple has been configured.

Psychoanalytic treatment is a structure, because its elements have to do with each other, and each defines the rest. This is why the Barangers affirm that the reaction of the analysand can be understood only by taking account of its occurrence as a function of the analyst. Further, in that structure both sides are engaged, and from this a fantasy arises that is common to both.

The concept of a shared fantasy can be understood in various ways. The coincidence can be reduced to the fact that analyst and analysand think the same. If they do not think the same, the process of communication might not exist either. In my view the Barangers wish to say something more, which is that the same configuration may arise at a given moment in analyst and analysand. One and the same fantasy may be created in both. Referring to the example of sneezing, the analyst sneezes and then interprets that the patient feels cold and abandoned. The patient accepts this interpretation, feels that it is so, and the analyst's urge to sneeze is gone. At that moment in the session analyst and analysand felt the same. Analytic work is fertile only when this phenomenon of resonance arises, where I feel what my patient feels, and through this shared fantasy insight will arise. Until this shared fantasy is achieved, the analyst will only theorize about the patient. What has been shared in this example is a traumatic situation of lack of affect. This fantasy is an effect of the field. "Field" here is not simply where the analytic situation takes place, but the place where the interaction occurs.

The psychoanalytic field has a spatial and a temporal structure, which delimit the analyst's consulting-room and the prior agreement on the duration and rhythm of the sessions. Within this framework the functional configuration of analysand and analyst arises, and it always assumes an irreducible ambiguity. What is essential about the analytic procedure, the Barangers say, is that every event that occurs in the field is at the same time something else (1969, p. 133).

"What structures the bipersonal field of the analytic situation is essentially an unconscious fantasy. But it would be a mistake to understand it as an unconscious fantasy of the analysand alone" (ibid., p. 140). The analyst, they assert, cannot be a mirror, because a mirror does not interpret. Therefore we can conceive of the basic fantasy of the session only as the fantasy of a couple, analogous to that which arises in analytic group therapy (ibid.). Therefore "it is not the same to discover the unconscious fantasy that underlies a dream, or a symptom, and to understand the unconscious fantasy of a psychoanalytic session" (ibid., p. 141). The field fantasy is, therefore, created *between* the two members of the analytic couple, "something radically different to what they are separately, each one of them" (ibid.). This unconscious bipersonal fantasy, the object of the analyst's interpretation, "is a structure constituted by the interplay of the processes of projective and introjective identification, and of the counter-identifications that act, with their limits, functions and characteristics, differently in the analysand and the analyst" (ibid., p. 145).

In sum, then, in applying the field theory to the analytic situation, the Barangers join the theories of Gestalt to the ideas of Merleau-Ponty in an explanation that rests on Susan Isaacs's concept of unconscious fantasy, Klein's two modalities of (introjective and projective) identification and Grinberg's theory of projective counteridentification.

Let us say, therefore, that on this point, also following Pichon, the Barangers explain the changes in the psychoanalytic field as the dialectics between stereotype and mobility of the field. (We will return to the fantasy of the couple in dealing with insight.)

36.4 On the concept of field

The Barangers' merit is to have understood the analytic situation as a field of interaction and observation where both analysand and analyst are present, a field where the analysand is not alone, since the analyst accompanies him as a participant observer, as Pichon said, following Sullivan.

To accept this idea does not, however, compel us to agree with the Barangers in their views on the way the analyst participates, nor to endorse their position on the fantasy of the couple.

Other writers hold that the analytic situation configures, in effect, a field of interaction and observation. But they maintain that what is distinctive of the psychoanalytic field is that the observation data come from the patient, while the analyst—who observes and participates—abstains rigorously from offering any data. The aim of the analytic situation is to create a field of observation where the data are offered exclusively by the analysand (Zac, 1968, p. 28).

The difference from the Barangers' view is noticeable because they do not take sufficiently into account the degree of participation by the two members. For them, the fantasy of the couple is equal in analysis and in group psychotherapy, although here the participation of the members is symmetrical.

Bleger thinks as Zac does when he deals with the interview (see chapter 4) and says that "the first fundamental rule in this respect is to try to obtain the configuration of the field specially and mainly by the variables which depend on the interviewee" (Bleger, 1971, p. 14). He nevertheless acknowledges that "everything that emerges is always relational, or in other words, derives from a field, but in the interview we try to ensure that this field be determined predominantly by the personality modalities of the interviewee" (ibid., p. 15).

The Barangers differ from Bleger and from Zac in that they do not believe that the analyst can maintain a position at that level.

* * *

In a work written in collaboration with Jorge Mom for the Madrid Congress, the Barangers (1983) again reflect on the field theory and on the other themes treated here, modifying some of the points that I have just questioned. The analytic situation is defined by them differently from the way it is defined in their aforementioned work and from that on insight in Mexico in 1964. In their report in Mexico the Barangers even say that "the analytic situation is essentially symbiotic; first, because it reproduces regressive repetitions of the symbiotic dependence on the parents, and secondly, because it is directed towards the production of projective identification" (Litman, 1966, p. 66). We will return to this theme further on.

In the more recent work, on the other hand, they say that "such a definition could only apply, and without great precision, to extremely pathological states of the field: a field characterized either by an invincible symbiosis between the two participants, or by the annihilating parasiting of the analyst by the analysand" (M. Baranger et al., 1983, p. 3). It is also worth pointing out that these writers do not refer to their own points of view as they appear in the works we are considering, but rather to Melanie Klein, who never conceived the analytic situation as symbiotic. The concept of symbiosis is Mahler's and Bleger's, but not Klein's.

36.5 *Analytic situation and therapeutic alliance*

Between 1950 and 1970, Elizabeth R. Zetzel developed an important piece of work, which we dealt with in studying the therapeutic alliance. In contemplating the analytic situation from that angle, she would say that what is essential in the analytic situation is precisely the therapeutic alliance. The analytic situation is what is stable and real and pertains to the task. What appears on this stable basis in the field of work is what is called transference neurosis. The concept of analytic situation remains, then, strongly linked to that of therapeutic alliance. Both turn out to be the same thing.

In defining the therapeutic alliance as the nucleus of the analytic situation, in counterposition to the analytic process, with its epicentre in the transference neurosis, Zetzel (1966; "El proceso analítico", presented at the Second Pan-American Congress of Psychoanalysis in Buenos Aires) takes account of the distinction David Rapaport makes in *The Structure of Psychoanalytic Theory* (1959) and in other works when he compared the id and the ego as two antagonistic systems with reference to the mobility of energy. What characterizes the id is mobile, fluid and changeable energy, while the energy changes of the ego are very slow. This cannot surprise us, in fact, because ultimately, from this point of view, the main function of the ego is precisely to control energy—to bind it (in more technical terms). What is manifested as a free current of energy in the id is transformed in the ego system into bound currents on the basis of anticathexes. It is precisely on the basis of these postulates that Rapaport insists that the introduction of ego psychology implies a qualitative change in psychoanalytic theory. The latter finally abandons what was especially criticized in early psychoanalysis—the fundamental concern with instincts—which has been called the theory of the ever-seething cauldron. In fact, as Rapaport says, the ever-seething cauldron theory is a model applicable to the id, not to the apparatus as a whole, in that the ego is just the opposite of a seething cauldron.

On the basis of this model, Zetzel says that the analytic situation has as its base the therapeutic alliance, where changes exist but are very slow. The analytic process, for its part, is much more rapid and mobile and corresponds to the energetic modality of the unconscious, of the id, which takes shape in the transference neurosis. It can also be said that from Zetzel's point of view analytic treatment consists in the gradual integration of certain areas, as they are analysed—and which originally belonged to the transference neurosis—into the ego structure, thus becoming part of the therapeutic alliance. The essence of analytic therapy is founded, in fact, on this change—if a particular conflict is analysed in the transference neurosis and made conscious, it becomes the property of the ego, a new facet of the ego that establishes a real relationship with the analyst, since if the therapeutic alliance can be defined at all, it is as a real type of relation with the analyst. What was subsumed in the vivacity of the transference neurosis becomes a stable aspect of the relation between the analyst and the analysand, and which now belongs to the working alliance.

In this way the nature of the therapeutic action of psychoanalysis is convincingly defined as a transposition from one sector to the other, which increases the integration of the ego and changes the energy processes.

I will offer a simple example so that this point of view can be understood. If the transference neurosis of an analysand consists in feeling a great sexual curiosity about his analyst's work, and the analyst can analyse this conflict successfully, the transformation of a scopophilic tendency into a capacity for observation will have been achieved. The scopophilic impulses will then remain in the service of adaptation, configuring a realistic, instrumental capacity for observation. The voyeuristic impulse is transformed, passing from the transference neurosis to the therapeutic alliance. Let us say here that this is always achieved through an identification of the patient's ego with the analyst's ego, as Sterba (1934) indicated. This is because the scopophilic conflict is resolved when the patient realizes that the analyst observes him without deriving from this event a direct libidinous satisfaction. When all these changes occur what has previously belonged to the transference neurosis passes to the working alliance. From that moment, the analysand will have a greater chance of observing his unconscious processes. His observing ego and his working alliance with the analyst will grow.

The dialectic postulated by Zetzel and the ego psychologists in general between the transference neurosis and the working alliance is clear and congruent with the basic lines of this doctrine. On the other hand, the proposed identification of the transference neurosis with the psychoanalytic process and the therapeutic alliance with the analytic situation are more debatable. If we accept that they are homologous, then there are only two concepts although we use four words. The therapeutic alliance and the transference neurosis, as they have been repeatedly defined, are an object relation and cannot be the same as the place that contains them.

When a moment ago we defined the nature of the therapeutic action of psychoanalysis according to ego psychology, we said it consists in the resolution of the transference neurosis and its transformation into the therapeutic alliance. Things are not so simple, however.

As understood by the ego psychologists, the essential function of the therapeutic alliance is to allow the regressive process that the transference neurosis institutes, so that what I said a moment ago is only partially true. The curative process consists in the transformation of the transference neurosis into the therapeutic alliance, and this continues to be valid. But the inverse situation is not wholly valid, because it is also necessary for certain stable elements, the automatic ego defences, to participate in the transference neurosis. This regression is, then, a desired effect of the therapeutic process. On this point it is clear that the relation between the analytic situation and the working alliance, and between the analytic process and the transference neurosis, cannot be homologous. Since a basic thesis of ego psychology is that the transference neurosis is formed through regression, one would then have to say that the situation becomes a process, which is inconsistent with Zetzel's ideas. I think Zetzel cannot escape this difficulty, because she does not distinguish the analytic situation from the setting. What the Boston analyst says about the analytic situation belongs, in my view, to the setting—to the fixity and stability of the setting, as we will see in chapter 37.

36.6 The primary narcissism of the analytic situation

In a report presented on 10 November 1956 to the Congress of Romance-Language Psychoanalysts (*Revue Française de Psychanalyse*, 1957; it is also the first essay ["The Analytic Situation and the Dynamic of the Healing Process"] in *Le narcissisme*, 1971), Béla Grunberger offered an original vision of the way the analytic situation is constituted and the process is developed. His starting point is that the analytic situation should be separated from the transference, which runs through the analytic process in its entirety. He delineates, following Baudouin (1959), the *analytic transference* [*le transfer de l'analyse*] from the *analytic rapport* [*le rapport de l'analyse*]. The formula Grunberger proposes, once he has defined these two concepts, is to analyse the transference—that is, the resistance—and let the *rapport* operate on its own account (*"Analyser le 'transfert d'analyse', c'est-à-dire la résistance et laisser agir le 'raport d'analyse', est certainement une bonne formula, encore faudrait-il reconnâitre ce second facteur et bien le séparer du premier"* [It is indeed a good formula to analyse analytic transference, resistance, and to leave analytic rapport to work, but one must recognize this second factor and carefully separate it from the first]—*Le narcissisme*, p. 56, no. 5). This difference assumes two theoretical areas and, simultaneously, two technical attitudes, since the transference is defined as an object relation, whereas the *rapport* is located in the field of narcissism.

In this way, the analyst's role as a mirror gains new meaning. The analyst should constitute himself strictly as the patient's *alter ego*, a mirror whose sole function is that of allowing the patient to see himself reflected there. To fulfil his mission, the analyst should be only a function, without material support, invisible and always behind the analysand, "for otherwise the presence of an object would drive the analysand from his narcissistic position" (1971, *Narcissism*, p. 40). Otherwise he expels the analysand from the narcissistic position proper to him. In the analytic situation the analysand is alone, without being so totally, since the analytic situation virtually contains the object relation, which is established gradually. The analysand is, for Grunberger, a Narcissus contemplating himself in the water, and behind him he has the analyst as his nymph, Echo.

With these theoretical tools, Grunberger can now give his own version of the process of regression during the analytic cure, limiting it to the transference neurosis as object relation (oedipal and pre-oedipal). It should be distinguished from the non-objectual and unconflicted narcissistic phenomena of the analytic relation, whose essential phenomenological expression is euphoria, elation (ibid., p. 43). To combine these two orders of phenomena in a sole concept makes the transference lose its specificity. It transforms it into a multiple-use term, a joker, which appears to ignore that the transference in fact implies a conflict that is carried from one object to another.

The narcissistic position (or state) just described appears from the beginning of analysis, while the transference is established slowly and much later on; and it operates, in fact, in a contrary direction. While the transference is the fount of resistances (the resistance of transference), the narcissistic state is revealed as the *primum movens* of the analytic process (ibid., p. 43). It is precisely the elation concomitant with the analytic situation that makes it possible for the oedipal elements gradually to become conscious.

The Freudian precept that the analysis should develop in frustration is adjusted to the oedipal desires, but not to narcissism. The narcissistic pleasure the patient derives from the fact of being in analysis is precisely the necessary condition for the analytic situation to establish itself firmly and for the therapy to be successful (ibid., p. 44).

Grunberger considers that the analyst's narcissistic cathexis at the beginning of the cure is due to the analysand projecting his ideal ego into the analyst [*Moi idéal*]. The originality of the Freudian procedure resides in not maintaining that narcissistic equilibrium, leading the analysand to a more evolved relation, the object relation.

When he presents his conclusions at the end of this original study, Grunberger again indicates that the narcissistic element (however difficult it may be to specify this concept) is the dynamic factor that fuels the psychoanalytic process with its strength.

In the analytic process the analysand finds himself face to face with himself through the analyst as intermediary and in special circumstances that stimulate a controlled narcissistic regression that offers the possibility of a specific development, the analytic process. The liberated narcissistic libido is the one that provides the analytic situation with the dynamic energy that will operate throughout the entire process (ibid., p. 87).

To conceive the analytic situation as narcissistic, Grunberger has to reconsider the problem of the instincts. For this writer there is a parallel process, where the analytic material discovered developed on a superficial level, while the underlying energetic process courses on a deep level. If Grunberger locates narcissism at the deep level, this is because he thinks that instinctive life in its multiple and varied manifestations is rooted in narcissism. The instinct expresses and is the instrument of action of narcissism. The latter, then, deploys the fundamental power. The search for an instinctual satisfaction always relies on the need to feel oneself able to obtain it, and at times it is enough to feel oneself capable of satisfying oneself without needing to fulfil the instinctual desire itself. " 'Being able to do' is what is essential, and 'doing' often serves merely to prove it" (ibid., p. 88).

If we begin with the concept of narcissism that Grunberger proposes, and we accept that transference and *rapport* are two different things, then Grunberger's investigation appears to us to be both clear and rigorous—almost impregnable. I have already indicated the convincing way in which situation and process are delineated and defined, the originality the Freudian metaphor of analyst as mirror acquires and the structural specifications with which Grunberger enables us to understand better the function of the ideal ego [*Idealich*] and of the ego ideal [*Ichideal*, superego] in the complexities and subtleties of the analytic situation. Let us add now that the differences proposed by Grunberger aim—and he does not ignore this—from a different point of view, at the dialectic between transference neurosis and therapeutic alliance, with a revision of Greenacre's (1954) concept of basic transference. The same revision also covers, I think, other concepts that attempt to give an account of the structure of the analytic situation, like Glover's (1955) floating transference and the dyadic relation Gitelson (1962) studied at the Edinburgh Congress of 1961, based on what Spitz (1956b) called the diatrophic attitude of the analyst in his essay on countertransference.

As opposed to all these, and certainly to those of us who reject the theory of primary narcissism, Grunberger—faithful to his ideas—considers this special type of relation between analysand and analyst as *by definition* non-objectual and unconflicted.

From this derives a practice that restricts criteria of analysability to neurotic patients who can derive a narcissistic satisfaction from the analytic situation (euphoria, elation), and which lends special (and I think excessive) consideration to the primitive mechanisms, the analytic atmosphere, where the silence of the analyst acquires great relevance. It practically occupies a strategic position in the design of the cure. Exceptional cases apart, the analyst's silence is not a traumatizing element. "By remaining silent, the analyst in effect remains in the narcissistic realm, which is *unconflicted by definition*" (Grunberger, 1971, *Narcissism*, p. 67).

The main inconvenience I perceive for this technical conception is that, even in the hands of the most experienced analysts such as Béla Grunberger, very dangerous areas of idealization can remain unanalysed. The analysand does not always succeed in realizing that the analyst's silence is a technical attitude and "is for his good".

CHAPTER THIRTY-SEVEN

Analytic situation
and analytic process

37.1 Brief review

In chapter 36 we provisionally defined the analytic situation as the place where the treatment develops, as a relation between two people who assume defined roles in order to carry out a particular task. We used as a basis for our discussion the works of the Barangers and those of Zetzel and Grunberger. In these writings the analytic situation is described from very different perspectives. For the Barangers, the analytic situation is a dynamic field where a shared fantasy arises, while for Zetzel the analytic situation is what is stable, what forms the therapeutic alliance and is opposed to the transference neurosis. Finally, for Grunberger the analytic situation is the narcissistic pool that fuels the process.

The Barangers affirm that the analytic situation should be defined as a field where the fantasy of the couple operates. It is a fantasy shared by analyst and analysand, which becomes mobile through a mutual process of projective identification. When analyst and patient become conscious of the fantasy they share, insight is born in the field. We offered the critique that this position seems extreme to us and we also indicated that in a recent work, written in collaboration with Mom for the Madrid Congress, our writers modified some of their viewpoints.

We also saw that Zetzel maintains that the same relation exists between situation and process as between therapeutic alliance and transference neurosis. Leaving aside the reduction from four concepts to two in this classification, we criticized it from within its own guidelines, recalling that this theory postulates that analysis consists in the gradual conversion of the transference neurosis into the therapeutic alliance. This would mean that the analytic process would become the analytic situation, which is inconsistent. Since the therapeutic alliance is postulated as a prerequisite for the onset of the process of regression that the transference neurosis requires, this means that we would have to conclude that the therapeutic alliance is at the same time cause and consequence of the transference neurosis.

Grunberger's theory is consistent, and its internal coherence is irreproachable, although inseparable from the writer's conception of narcissism, which infiltrates not only the theory of the process and its practice, but also the idea of transference, because in Grunberger's view a narcissistic transference cannot, by definition, exist.

37.2   Situation and process

Other Argentine writers, such as Bleger and Zac, propose that the analytic situation be defined on the basis of the process. Bleger (1967a) established that the psychoanalytic *process* needs, as does any other process, a *nonprocess* to be able to come into effect. He said that this fixed or stable part is the *setting*. The setting is thus defined as a group of constants thanks to which the psychoanalytic process can take place. On the basis of Bleger's stipulative definitions (indicated here) I hope my objections to Zetzel's proposal of the homologous relation between the analytic situation and the therapeutic alliance defined as what is stable, thus confusing the latter with the setting, will be better understood.

Following the line of thought initiated by Bleger, Joel Zac (1971) studies just these *constants* of psychoanalysis and defines them in principle as variable factors that Freud established (or fixed) according to certain prior hypotheses.

On the basis of impeccably recorded empirical observations and certain generalizations arising from those same observations, Freud was able to conceive how psychoanalytic treatment ought to develop, establishing in this way the defining hypotheses of psychoanalysis—that is, those postulates without which psychoanalysis cannot occur and outside which psychoanalysis could never be what it is. From these defining hypotheses derive the rules that constitute the setting and without which psychoanalytic treatment does not "take place". This is why Zac says that "defining the setting would be impossible without some prior hypotheses that state that, unless certain variable factors are fixed as constants in a definitive way, certain laws would intervene that would imply, in turn, a particular type of consequences" (1971, p. 593).

Freud's directing idea in fixing the constants of the setting—Zac continues—is to establish the most favourable conditions for the development of the cure. In this way, the setting consists in the set of stipulations that assure minimum interference with the analytic task and, equally, offer the maximum information the analyst can receive.

37.3 Zac's three constants

Zac maintains that in analytic treatment there are three types of constants. The first derive from the theories of psychoanalysis and are those we have just dealt with. Zac calls these constants *absolute*, because they appear in every psychoanalytic treatment, since they have a direct relation with the defining hypotheses of our discipline. As well as absolute constants, there are *relative* ones, of two types: those that depend on each analyst, and those that derive from the particular couple formed by each analyst and analysand. Although these constants are relative, once they have become established they are fixed constants.

Among the relative constants *that depend on the analyst*, we can mention some of his personality traits, his scientific ideology, and other more concrete ones such as the location of his consulting-room, the type and style of his furniture, the regulation of fees and holidays, and so forth. The length and timing of his holidays are constants that basically depend on the analyst. The stability of the rhythm of work, on the other hand, belongs to the absolute constants and the psychoanalyst could not, for example, change arbitrarily the time already fixed for his holidays. Certainly the already classic work by the Balints (1939) refers to these constants relative to the analyst. They are identified as expressive forms of the analyst. Alice and Michael Balint call these particular modalities of the analyst counter-transference. But, in fact, it is better to conceive of them as parts of his setting as a real support for the relation, without precluding that they could be invested with transferential and countertransferential significance.

Zac distinguishes, finally, a third type of constants, which are also relative and *which depend on the couple* and not on psychoanalysis or the psychoanalyst—that is, on the couple formed specifically by a particular analyst and his analysand. Let us say here that these constants are the ones that offer the greater support to countertransference conflicts. A constant of this type could be, for example, that the time of the session is fixed to be convenient for both parties, or that an analyst who takes his holiday in February takes account of a lawyer's holiday in January. (Note: in Argentina, lawyers and the judiciary in general all go on holiday in January.)

As we have just seen, Zac's reflection studies which constants determine the setting. In the beginning, as stated in Genesis, there was chaos. There were only variables. Freud arrives and establishes order: there will be six sessions per week, one a day; a particular hour belongs to a particular patient, and neither the patient nor Freud change it, and so forth. Freud, then, arbitrarily transformed some variables into constants: he could have fixed others. But those he fixed are the ones that make the analytic treatment possible, and this is why everyone says they express his genius yet again. Thanks to these stipulations, the cure can take place, because the place of the cure—that is, the analytic situation—is found precisely there, among those constants.

Once the variables were fixed so as to constitute the setting, the other variables initially contained in the analytic situation would generate the psychoanalytic process.

37.4   Contract and setting

The set of variables that remained fixed, let us repeat, constitutes what is called the *setting*, because they really are the framework within which the process is located. Some of these rules are explicitly formulated at the time the contract is made, as we saw in chapter 6. Others will be formulated at the appropriate time and yet others perhaps never, although all of them will have to be respected and preserved. The analysts who, for technical reasons, prefer not to receive gifts, for example, will not introduce this rule in the contract. It would be officious and even a way of encouraging them, because "no" does not exist in the unconscious. The rule will be made explicit when the patient's material justifies it and not otherwise.

The constants of the setting are, then, empirical rules dictated by Freud on the basis of his clinical experience, which led him to set up a definite and strict framework in his relation to the patient, so that the treatment could develop in the best way possible, with the least possible disturbance. Some of these rules are those that regulate any type of task between two people, such as the exchange of time and money, the place and time of the encounter, and so forth, because no task can be realized without stipulating some rules to carry it out. But these are not the ones that interest us the most—it is, rather, the others, those that derive specifically from the analytic treatment, from that singular relationship established between analyst and analysand; we will have to deal with these now.

At the time of his technical writings, Freud's discoveries were already clear and defined as to the importance of the development of a singular process in his relation with the patient, which from 1895 onwards he had called transference. It is precisely because Freud had discovered this phenomenon that the specific rules of analytic treatment are directed in essence to allowing the evolution of the transference phenomenon without obstacles. It is empirically known that every circumstance that reveals something pertaining to the personal ambit of the analyst can disturb this development. The aim of the setting is to protect the patient from those revelations and also the analyst from his own errors, which disturb the process and consequently damage the patient and the analyst himself. As to the rules of the setting, they are made to enable the cure to develop in the best possible way. They imply not only a technical but also an ethical position on the analyst's part.

The setting is, then, a *framework* that harbours a type of content, the *process*. Between the analytic process and the setting there arises a container/contained relation in Bion's terms (1963).

This content consists in the very singular relation of analyst and analysand that we studied in part 2; this relationship is composed of three elements: transference, countertransference and therapeutic alliance. We can also say that the content we are considering configures the *transference neurosis*, or, following Racker (1948), the transference and *countertransference neurosis*. This content is essentially variable, changing, never the same. This is why Freud compared analysis to a game of chess, where only the opening and end-game moves can be charted, but never the game in the middle. For this process to arise and develop, the existence of the most stable framework, the setting, is required.

37.5   On the rules of the setting

Freud's recommendations in the technical writings are grouped into two classes. Some are direct and specific recommendations, and there is little or nothing to argue about them. They can be accepted or rejected, but not discussed. They belong to the relative constants that depend on the analyst and figure among those that have to do with the regulation of timetables, fees, holidays. Some analysts prefer to give each patient the same time every day, wishing to simplify things. Others do not follow this rule and even consider that, in varying the times, different aspects of the personality can be detected, since people do not function the same way at different times of the day.

The frequency and duration of the sessions are absolute rather than relative constants. Most analysts think the most convenient rhythm for analysis is five sessions per week. Freud offered six. In Argentina, the great majority of analysts work with four sessions, generally giving economic reasons for this, which does not personally convince me very much. I have seen the Argentine economy vary *ad infinitum*, with no changes at all in the frequency of sessions per week. More precisely, I never saw the number of sessions *increased* in moments of bonanza.

The number five—beyond the many symbolisms that can be interpreted—seems to me the most adequate, because it establishes a substantial period of contact and a clear break at the weekend. It is very difficult for me to establish a real psychoanalytic process with a rhythm of three times a week, although I know many analysts manage it. A rhythm as inconsistent and alternating as an analysis every other day does not, in my opinion, enable the conflict of contact and separation to arise with sufficient strength. The treatments of one or two sessions per week do not generally constitute a psychoanalytic process, although it may be called that. I am inclined to believe that in these cases the analyst believes, undoubtedly in good faith, that he is carrying out an analysis. But the process exhibits the characteristics of psychotherapy—that is, dispersion or omission of the transference, manifest or latent reassurance formulated as interpretation, neglect of separation anxiety (which is conventionally interpreted or not interpreted at all) and so forth.

If the treatment consists of four sessions a week, it is better to make them consecutive, although the period of separation is thus prolonged. If the treatment consists of three sessions, there are analysts who make them consecutive so as to have a time during which full contact is established, although a considerable interval then follows. Others prefer three sessions on alternate days. I am inclined towards the latter procedure because, as I have already said, I think that three sessions on consecutive days do not manage to constitute a real psychoanalytic treatment, however much they may try to adapt to its form. Sessions on alternate days gives the treatment a definite flavour of psychotherapy, which I think accords more with reality.

A very special case arises with patients who have to travel long distances for their analysis and for whom there is no solution other than to give them the four or five sessions in a couple of days. This also happens with candidates who travel to get to their training analysis. It is possible that in these decidedly atypical cases, the training analyst's skill and the strong motivation of the candidate (when added to a not too severe pathology) can make up for the great disadvantages of this design.

As to the duration of the sessions, few analysts question the classic 50 minutes. In some centres where psychotherapy is practised the session lasts 30 minutes, and this marks a definite difference between one method and another. I do not accept the analysis *on demand* as in *The Piggle* (Winnicott, 1977) or Lacan's session of free time.

For reasons that pertain to his communication theory and to the way he conceives the structure of the analytic session, Lacan works with what is called free or open time. He thinks the session should not end routinely but as a significant act, either to mark out the closure of a structure or to reveal the analysand's empty word. This technical conduct has been fiercely combated by many analysts. Without ignoring the unquestionable coherence that exists on this point between Lacan's theory and technique, I think that its basis is inconsistent. This is because what we have to do is to interpret and not to sanction the analysand's conduct by means of an action that, however well thought out, carries within it the heavy burden of a training through rewards and punishments. Note also that in this critique I am conceding to the Lacanian analyst an objectivity that I would never recognize in myself. In fact, I do not trust the objectivity of my countertransference too much, and less than ever in this case, where the decision I may take will benefit me specifically, prolonging *my* free time. I consider, finally, that even if this were not the case, the analysand would have every right to think so, which would result, in effect, in an unanalysable situation. I do not base myself, in these reflections, on the fact that the sessions end almost always before and not after the 50 minutes, since it would be equally contrary to the analyst's art to convey specifically, through his conduct, that he is happy or displeased. One does not have to be very perceptive, however, to think that analysts who follow Lacan are as human as the others. A Lacanian analyst I know personally, and of whose intelligence and professional probity I have direct proof, once told me this very interesting anecdote. He arrived for his supervision with one of the most distinguished analysts of the *École*, a fervent defender of the open session or of free time, and he saw with dismay the large number of patients in the waiting-room. Between patients, at some point, the supervisor emerged and told him he would be ready in less than an hour, and so it was. How could he have known? And let it not be said that in this case the analyst was unfaithful to his theories, precisely because what I maintain is that with ideas such as these one is always at the mercy of the countertransference. One would then have to consider whether Lacan's insistence that resistance begins with the analyst does not have an initial explanation in this singular rule of his setting.

It is worth indicating, finally, that many of Lacan's disciples think that the session of free time is more part of the style of the master than of his technique, because they do not follow him on this point.

37.6   *On the analytic attitude*

Freud's recommendations refer not only to the constants of the setting but also to the *analysts' mental attitude*, which, in the final instance, gives them their sense and value. The analyst's mental attitude means his disposition to work with the patient, realizing in the best way possible the task to which he has committed himself, and which consists in exploring the patient's unconscious mental processes and enabling him to understand them. This task is difficult for the analysand because it provokes anxiety, awakening resistances, and because the exploration assumes a real and immediate character through the enigmatic and unavoidable transference phenomenon. The analyst's work is not simple either; he must be a serene and impartial observer and at the same time be committed. The analyst participates in the analytical situation (the field), but he must do it in such a way that the data of observation come from the analysand (see chapter 36).

Freud typified the analyst's mental attitude in two rules, the rule of abstinence and *analytic reserve*, condensed in the famous metaphor of the analyst as mirror. In his "Recommendations" of 1912 Freud's memorable words are, "The doctor should be opaque to his patients and, like a mirror, should show them nothing but what is shown to him" (1912e, p. 118). Following this beautiful metaphor, we could say today: the analyst should reflect and not project what the analysand puts into him; the analyst should be a flat mirror, allowing the countertransference the least possible curve of distortion. Analytic reserve is necessary, then, so that the analytic situation can be established. Otherwise the transference phenomena become so unperceivable and so incomprehensible that the analytic situation is damaged from the root upwards.

The *rule of abstinence* refers to the fact that the analyst should not gratify the patient's desires in general—and of course particularly his sexual desires. This rule, which in principle applies to the analysand, also applies inexorably to the analyst, and it could not be otherwise. When we indulge our own desires, the rule has ceased to be applied, not only for reasons of equanimity and ethics but also for psychological ones. If we allow the patient to gratify us, we are also gratifying him. If I ask my analysand a question in order to gratify my curiosity, he is already gratifying himself with his reply (or his refusal to reply, which is no different).

A good part of Leo Stone's (1961) commendable monograph is concerned with the rule of abstinence and with analytic reserve. He recommends an attitude of greater equanimity and less rigidity in the application of abstinence and reserve. Stone says the strict application, without nuances, of these rules does not always contribute to the stability of the analytic situation and can even be utilized by analysand and analyst to satisfy sadomasochistic desires and/or to fulfil obsessive ceremonies, the more dangerous when they are syntonic. Stone emphasizes the contrapuntal nature of the psychoanalytic relationship and maintains that "the psychoanalytic attitude . . . is best understood by *both* parties as a *technical* instrumentality, with which an interested physician can best help his patient" (1961, p. 33; italics in original).

On this point, as in many other areas of the practice, there are no fixed rules. What is adequate at one moment can be a grave error five minutes later. In each case we will have to listen to what the analysand says, what the theory stipulates and what the countertransference conveys to us.

* * *

There are two ways, then, of understanding the setting: as a behavioural event or as a mental attitude.

From a formal or behavioural viewpoint, the setting is certainly a behavioural act and even a rite in the best sense of the word. This aspect, however, although a necessary condition for analytic work, will never be, in my view, sufficient for the process to really develop.

The setting is substantially a mental attitude on the analyst's part, specifically the mental attitude of introducing the least number of variables in the development of the process. This should be called the setting in the final instance, and not only a particular conduct. If, at a given moment, when I greet the patient, he stumbles, I will try to do something, in the most discreet possible way, to keep him from falling. In this case I understand that I have not modified my setting; internally, my setting is the same, to make the patient come in without exposing him to any extemporaneous stimulus that would therefore be prejudicial to the process. This is why the setting should be conceived fundamentally as an ethical attitude.

I remember a woman who found it difficult to walk and to lie down after an orthopaedic intervention. In the immediate post-surgical period she telephoned to ask me whether I would agree to adding some cushions to my couch, so that she would be able to come to the sessions. The alternative was to lose a great many sessions, which she would not like. She seemed well disposed to accept whatever I might suggest. I immediately replied that I would make the necessary changes in my consulting-room, and she came the following day, accompanied by a nurse. I found her in the waiting-room holding on to the arm of the nurse, and I led her myself to the consulting-room and helped her to make herself comfortable on the couch. I preferred to lead her by the arm myself into the consulting-room, despite the physical contact this implied; to delegate this to the nurse would have been inconsistent with my setting, since no person other than my patient ever entered my consulting-room. It is evident that this decision is very debatable, and if another analyst had decided to do the opposite, I would never think him mistaken.

What I wish to indicate is that this major alteration (a formal or ritual one) of the setting, being aimed at interrupting the analytic process no more than was indispensable, did not provoke singular difficulties. The logical fantasies of dependence in the maternal transference, and of seduction by the father, appeared—without acquiring at all the typical characteristics the material assumes in the case of a countertransferential acting out. This is why I said that the setting is, above all, a mental attitude of the analyst. Incidentally, I have been able to observe that analysts who criticize the "rigidity" of the setting do so because in general they have not yet arrived at a clear concept of what the setting really is.

The difficulty I have just pointed out affects, of course, the analysand as well, as Olagaray (1980) points out; he maintains that the *establishment* of the setting occurs at the beginning of treatment, but its *internalization* is achieved only at the end. In that setting is the space in which psychoanalytic treatment "takes place", its introjection marks the possibility of defining a continent in the internal world where psychological activity can develop, where the subject and his objects can live and share their lives, where his conflicts can be located and solved.

The general attitude of the analysand towards the setting, and of course his dreams, show how the difficulties in understanding the value and function of the setting have to do with the course of the analytical process, and—I would add—with the slow process through which the analyst comes to understand his work and build his identity.

CHAPTER THIRTY-EIGHT

The analytic setting

38.1 Recapitulation

We stated at the beginning of part 4 that the concept of analytic situation is easier to understand intuitively than to conceptualize, and unfortunately we are demonstrating this. And it is certainly not easy to separate the analytic situation from the analytic process.

In chapter 37 we examined Zac's (1968, 1971) effort to distinguish situation from process, as well as the clear and concise way he studies the variables and constants that both configure and make possible the analytic process. In "Un enfoque metodológico del establecimiento del encuadre" [A Methodological Focus on the Establishment of the Setting] (1971), one of the most meticulous works I have read on the subject, Zac emphasizes that those constants are linked to a particular theoretical conception; we all recognize as a streak of genius in Freud his identification of those variables that must be transformed into constants for the process to assume an analytic character. In studying the constants, Zac distinguishes the absolute ones, which depend on psychoanalytic theory, and the relative ones, which have to do with the analyst and with the analyst/analysand couple.

38.2 Bleger's theses

We will now see how Bleger (1967a) tries to understand the analytic process with a dialectic of constants and variables.

Both Bleger and Zac, and generally all the Argentinian writers who studied this theme, including Liberman (1970–72, Vol. 1, especially chapter 1), are inclined to apply the term "analytic *situation*" to the group of relations that include the process and the setting.

As Bleger (1967a) says, no process can occur without something within which it can develop, and those tracks along which the process unfolds constitute the setting: for the process to develop there must be a setting that contains it. In other words, when we speak of an *analytic process*, we imply that it must be part of a whole whose span is greater and covers more ground: the *analytic situation*. A basic thesis of Bleger's article is, then, that the analytic situation constitutes a *process* and a *non-process*, called the *setting*.

According to this proposal, situation and process are perfectly delineated with a stipulative definition, but at the cost of taking autonomy away from the concept of analytic situation. At the end of the chapter we will return to this and propose another solution.

Bleger's other thesis is that the division between constants and variables is aleatory by definition, in that we fix as constants those variables that seem best to us. This is also the case in the practice, because sometimes the constants become variables; the framework becomes process.

The third thesis is that although the changes in the setting sometimes give us access to problems that go unnoticed until then, modifying the setting to achieve these aims is not in any way justified. This technical conduct is inconvenient, for two reasons: first, because what emerges is an artifice that will lack the force of proof and will never be straightforwardly analysable; and, second, because one can never be sure that the analysand will react in the way foreseen. The experiment can fail, and then we remain without provision in the face of changes we ourselves proposed. These two reasons lead Bleger to affirm that the analyst has no technical and ethical freedom to modify the setting in search of particular responses, in which he is against active techniques and corrective emotional experience.

Bleger's final postulate is that in the immobility of the setting predominantly psychotic anxieties are deposited. Up to this point Bleger's principles can be shared from diverse theoretical perspectives. But Bleger now takes a further step that is very consistent with his way of thinking, and it is that the mute part that deposits itself in the setting is symbiosis. Further on we will deal with the theory of development Bleger proposes, and with his concept of psychosis. Let us say now that it is possible not to share his ideas on this point, while his explanations on the dialectics of the psychoanalytic setting can still be fully accepted.

For now we can agree, then, that the muteness of the setting should be preferentially attended to and considered as a problem, in effect. The greatest risk of the setting is its muteness, because since we tend to set it as fixed and stable, we do not consider it and we do not interpret it adequately. The muteness of the setting is taken for granted and is therefore never discussed.

Bleger, of course, thinks—as do most writers—that any information the patient receives about the analyst has a disturbing character, and that it is often in these circumstances that the strongest and least visible anxieties are mobilized. But what he wishes to indicate is precisely the opposite case, which is rarely if ever studied.

38.3 The setting that becomes process

When the setting is disturbed, Bleger affirms, it becomes process, because what defines the setting is its stability. An experience we have all often had is that, when a rupture of the setting has occurred, new configurations—often very interesting ones—appear in the material. I definitely agree with Bleger that this does not authorize in any way our modifying the setting for experimental purposes.

I also wish to emphasize, because it is very important, that when I say the setting is stable, I mean, more specifically, that as opposed to variables that change continually, the setting tends to modify itself slowly and not in direct relation to the process but to general rules. In other words, the setting changes slowly, with autonomy and never as a function of the variables of the process.

Whenever we modify the setting in response to the characteristics of the process, we are employing the active technique. If a person, for example, is greedy, that greed should be analysed and not managed by increasing or diminishing the number of sessions. Another example could be the fees. An increase or decrease of fees should never occur on the basis of the material that is emerging. The material can show convincingly that the analysand desires that the fees be increased or decreased. But the decision to propose a change in the amount should never be based on that circumstance, but on the basis of objective facts that are fundamentally foreign to the material. What will make us increase or decrease the fees will not be the patient's desires but the factual data (however difficult it may be for us to evaluate them and however much we may be mistaken in our evaluation). It is worth indicating here that the error we may commit in evaluating the objective facts does not affect the method and does no more than reveal a personal mistake, which is always correctable and analysable. On the other hand, I firmly believe that if we modify the setting, responding to the material, we commit an error we will not be able to analyse, simply because we have abandoned the psychoanalytic method for a moment. The setting should not depend on the variables. (I remember that when I began my training analysis, it was often "interpreted" that the analysand wanted or needed the fees to be increased. These interpretations, prior to an increase, were directed to the guilt or the desire to repair, but never, as is natural, to the masochistic element. And, of course, they occurred uniformly at a particular time of the year—or of the economic cycle.) Jean Laplanche thinks the same in pronouncing himself against any manipulation of the setting. Every manipulation appears to be a way of communicating messages, but it only manages to destabilize the variables on which the interpretation should operate (1982, p. 139). "I think"—Laplanche says severely (and I agree with him), "that any action on the setting constitutes an acting out of the analyst" (ibid., p. 143).

It is also necessary to indicate that this type of error does not in any way depend on the content of what we may do, nor on the goodwill with which we proceed. What matters here is not that we have good intentions, but that we have altered the bases of the analytic situation. In this sense, and in clear opposition to what Nacht (1962, etc.) always says, it is not worth being a good person if that makes one a bad analyst. And one would still have to see what kind of good persons we are if we proceed in this way!

However, this rule is not absolute. Sometimes it is appropriate to take into account certain desires of the analysand and for diverse reasons, since the setting must be firm but also elastic. This allowance must always be minimal, conforming to reality no less than our countertransference; and it should never be made with the idea that on the basis of this type of modification we are going to obtain structural changes in the patient.

In short, I think that the process *inspires* the setting but should not determine it.

38.4 A clinical example

I remember a young, intelligent and likeable businessman, whose discreet psychopathic traits were not unnoticed by me. On the occasion of a readjustment of fees, already arranged for because of inflation, he affirmed that the proposed fee was more than he could pay. He described the difficulties he was in with his small business (and which I knew about), he reminded me that his wife was also in analysis and he ended by asking me for a reduction of at least ten percent. I accepted, not without pointing out that, as far as I could judge, he was able to pay the full fees. He felt very happy and relieved when I accepted his proposal and continued associating with general themes. A bit later he said he had been remembering in the last few days an anecdote from his childhood that provoked a singular feeling in him. When he was in the third year, he collected stickers, as did most of his schoolmates, and the teacher also had her album. To complete his, he lacked one of the rarer stickers and noticed with great excitement that his teacher had more than one of these. Taking for granted that she would not know the value of one of these stickers, he proposed an exchange and offered her any one of his. She accepted, and thus he completed his collection and was able to exchange it for a much-desired football, which accompanied him for a long time through his childhood, which was in fact quite desolate. I told him then that perhaps he misjudged his teacher. It is probable that she knew that the sticker he wanted was difficult to obtain but gave it to him generously, knowing how much he wanted that football. He suddenly changed his hypomanic tone and said with insight that perhaps I was right; he had never thought about it. But he had to acknowledge that his teacher was intelligent and generous. He then remembered various anecdotes in which she was revealed as helping her students, with goodwill. A couple of weeks later he said the situation in the factory had improved, and he could pay me the full fees. I accepted.

I think my conduct in this case was correct and strictly analytical. In deciding on it I took account of the intensity of his projective mechanisms. The patient had said, from the first session onwards and without shyness, that I had charged him unduly, that I took advantage of him and that my dishonesty was evident. When he asked me for a reduction of fees, he did so, however, with a respectful attitude, however reactive it may have been, and evincing real reasons: the financial difficulties of his business and the meagre family budget. After examining my countertransference, I decided to accept his proposal, fully conscious that the request compromised my setting but certain that in ensuring recognition of my rights (which, on the other hand, were not so threatened) or in interpreting his desire to pay less, I would only have encountered the wall of his recalcitrant projection. I think that what was done was justifiable in that the purpose was not to correct his fantasies, showing him that I was "good", but to adjust my setting to the rigidity of his defence mechanisms. I also took account of my inability to ascertain how accurate his appreciation of the state of his business was, and as the wise Latin maxim says, *in dubia pro reo*.

The analysand responded to my (minor) generosity with a much greater one: with the screen memory from his latency, which once again allowed me to confront him with his psychopathic mechanisms (deceit, mockery).

Although it is not relevant, I wish to mention in passing that, due to reasons of tact, I did not include myself in the interpretation of the generous teacher ("and this happens to you with me in connection with the reduction of fees"). I think, however, that the interpretation I formulated in historical terms had a latent content of genuine transference resonance. I did not think it appropriate to make it explicit at that moment. When he decided to pay the full fee shortly afterwards, I was able to interpret the transference conflict in detail.

38.5   *The muteness of the setting*

Bleger's idea about the muteness of the setting deserves fuller discussion. His work studies the dialectics of the psychoanalytic process when the constants of the setting become variables at a given moment and emphasizes that when that dialectic is not fulfilled, the analyst has to remain very attentive.

Bleger's essay asks what happens when the analysand *fulfils his role* in the setting. This is why he says he will study the setting when it is *not* a problem, precisely in order to demonstrate that it is one. As in the case of love and the child, Bleger says, the setting is felt only when it "cries"; and his investigation is directed precisely to the setting that does not cry, that is mute. He is quite right, because if the setting is altered, the analyst is on the alert, while when there is no alteration we tend to remain unconcerned.

Bleger refers, then, to the cases where the setting is not altered at all; where the analysand accepts it completely, totally and tacitly, without comment. There, he warns us, the most regressive situations can remain latent, and the most tenacious defences can take shelter.

Bleger does not doubt that the setting has to remain mute. On the contrary, it has acquired definition because it must remain so in order to carry out the session, in order for the process to take place. And he also says that altering it to influence the analysand and the process is never justified. But Bleger knows, as we all do, that the setting will not always remain inanimate. There has to be stability, but changes are inevitable: at some point the patient will arrive late, or the psychoanalyst will have a cold—to mention trivial things. As long as the psychoanalyst does not become ill, the hypochondriac fantasies may remain fixed in the setting, which lends "real" support to the idea of an analyst invulnerable to illness. We can now understand why Bleger is right in saying that there are aspects of the setting that remain mute, and that it is necessary to be careful, because that silence implies a risk; it can conceal an ambush, a trap.

38.6   Setting and symbiosis

It is well known that Bleger begins with the hypothesis that neurotic and psychotic aspects coexist in the subject. The neurotic part of the personality notes the presence of the setting and registers the experiences it provokes (the session was too long or too short, it began two minutes before or after the appointed time). This is the evaluation of the setting we all accept, and of course Bleger does, too. What he adds to this scheme belongs to the psychotic part of the personality—which he liked to call PPP—which takes advantage of the lack of change in the setting in order to project the indiscriminate relation with the therapist. There is therefore no incompatibility between the setting that speaks and corresponds to the neurotic aspects and the mute setting of the psychosis. The former is verbalized, while the latter remains immobilized and is recognized only when the setting is altered. In other words, the psychotic aspects of the personality take advantage of the immobility of the setting to remain mute. More precisely, the mute psychosis perforce has to fix itself to the setting, which is, by definition, the part of the analytic process that does not speak.

When Bleger states that the setting lends itself to receiving the psychotic aspects that remain mute and deposited there, he is thinking about his own theory of psychosis and development. Bleger thinks that at the beginning there is an amalgam (syncitium), a conjoining of I and not-I, formed by a social organism that is the mother–child dyad. The ego develops as a result of a process of differentiation. The fundamental requirement for development is the inclusion of the I (the ego) in a not-I from which it can gradually differentiate itself. This not-I, which functions as a container for the ego to distinguish itself, is precisely the one that is transferred to the setting.

For this theory, then, the non-differentiated part of the personality has its most natural correlate in the setting, which, by definition, is the container where the psychoanalytic process develops. According to Bleger's ideas, the setting lends itself exceedingly well to the transference (to it) and the repetition of the initial situation of the mother–child symbiosis. As we can see, his ideas are consistent with his own theories.

Although we may accept other ideas about development and psychosis, Bleger's specifications on the process and the setting are of permanent value.

38.7 Meaning and function of the setting

Bleger's idea about the mutism of the setting is, in my view, an original contribution to the study of the analytic process, and it becomes even more salient when it is explained as a function of psychosis. Almost two decades separate us from Bleger's death (on 20 June 1972, at an age when everything had led to the expectation that he would continue his vigorous work for many more years); in that time we have arrived at a better understanding of the mute language of psychosis, and we can now formulate his ideas with greater precision.

When Bleger warns us of the risk that the setting may remain mute, he refers to its meaning, but not to its function. We should distinguish these two factors. The setting has the *function* of being mute, so that against this background the process may speak; but to think that it does so entirely would amount to thinking that there is something that, by its nature, cannot be covered with meaning (significance). We can penetrate the *significance* of the setting without thereby touching its functions, and the more so if we think of it as a container of psychotic anxieties. Thus it must be borne in mind that there always exists a psychotic transference that takes advantage of the stability of the setting to go unnoticed, to remain immobilized and deposited. (This leads us to a deep and difficult discussion, the relation of the psychoanalytic situation and process to the beginnings of development, which I will deal with further on.)

In differentiating between function and meaning, it is clear that to res-cue the latter it is not necessary to modify the former. Obviously, when the function is modified, the meaning is sometimes brought out; but we can arrive at that meaning through the material about the function of the set-ting that the patient brings. In this sense we can conclude that no basically mute setting exists, and that the setting is always a signifier.

I remember what a student told me about the muteness of the setting: sometimes the setting is mute because the analyst is deaf. One would then have to speak of the deaf-muteness of the setting, to include the counter-transference and also the analyst's theories on psychosis. If the non-verbal language of psychosis is understood, the setting ceases to be mute, and it appears with its value as signifier.

Currently we know with considerable certainty that the most archaic part of the personality, which in fact corresponds to the pre-verbal period of the first months of life and is directly related to the psychotic phenom-enon, is expressed preferentially through non-verbal and paraverbal chan-nels of communication, as we explained in dealing with interpretation. (This theme is illustrated in my work on the reconstruction of early psy-chic development, which is included here as chapter 28.) It can appropri-ately be said that psychosis is really mute insofar as it is structured by mechanisms that go beyond the word. When the psychosis begins to speak, it ceases to be psychosis.

Let us look for a moment at the notion of the breach of the setting itself. If we wish to define it objectively, the breach of the setting consists in something that alters the rules of treatment noticeably and suddenly, and consequently changes the analytic situation. At times the alteration stems from the analysand, in the form of an acting out; or it stems from an error (or an acting out) of the analyst, or, at other times, from a fortuitous circumstance generally, non-pertinent information the analysand receives from third parties. In any case, the framework within which the process develops is shaken; a crack opens, through which the analysand can liter-ally intrude upon the analyst's private life and/or his way of functioning.

Together with this objective definition, in speaking of the breach of the setting, we should take the analysand's fantasies into account. The patient can deny that there has been a breach of the setting, just as he can think one occurred where none did. As always in our discipline, the analysand's response will be the decisive element. The setting is, then, an objective fact that the analyst proposes (in the contract) and that the analysand will progressively cover with his fantasies.

From an instrumental perspective, the setting is instituted because it offers the best conditions for the development of the analytic task, and, oddly, a good part of this task consists in ascertaining what the patient thinks of this situation we establish, what theories he has about it. The setting is the Rorschach sheet on which the patient will see things—things that reflect him.

38.8 *Other clinical material*

I remember a patient who relied on the fact that I always attended to him in the same way for an aristocratic and omnipotent fantasy that I was his valet, that I opened the door for him, entered behind him, cleaned his bottom, and so forth. This fantasy, linked to the setting, remained immobilized for a long time, completely mute. I was obviously not predisposed to analyse it, because I take it for granted that the way of receiving the patient should not vary much and is a part of my setting. It is true that the idea of the valet appeared in other contexts, but not with the strength and almost delusional conviction it assumed on the special occasions when I had to change my way of receiving him.

A female patient who had been in analysis for six years and was very wealthy broke off the analysis three days after a readjustment of fees that did not differ in any way from previous readjustments. Without saying anything, she left for Europe, and from there she wrote to her analyst, saying she had committed an act of folly and wished to renew her treatment. The patient had a son who was in analysis, and with this increase, for the first time in six years, she had exceeded the fees she paid for her son's treatment. At that moment a psychotic situation projected into the setting was mobilized: this was that she always had to spend less on her own treatment than on that of her son, because if she spent more, she became like her own parents, who had always been concerned with making money without taking an interest in her. This was never made explicit in the treatment, and she never had the slightest problem in paying. In fact, money meant little for her. The sum in itself had no significance; but a really infinitesimal difference was sufficient for her to become, through the influence of the increase, the mother who is concerned more with herself than with her son, and she abandoned the treatment.

As can be assumed, this type of conflict in respect of her relation to selfish parents and her maternal function externalized itself in diverse contexts. But it always corresponded to the neurotic levels of the relationship with the parents, with how they had managed money, the sensation that money mattered more to them than she did as a daughter, and that this was what produced in her a permanent sense of being devalued, and so forth. In the psychotic part, on the other hand, the payment operated as a concrete situation that demonstrated magically that she did not act with her son as her parents (so she thought) had acted with her. This aspect was totally split off and located in the sum she paid for her own and her son's analysis.

These two examples are sufficient to illustrate, I believe, the way in which the psychotic part remains immobilized in the setting. I also think it is noticeable that this happens because the psychosis does not speak with words, and at times we do not hear it. With respect to my (male) analysand, it was only after this episode that I was able to realize that I had often analysed his attitude of superiority towards me because he belonged to a higher social class than mine; but never that he really believed that this circumstance defined inevitably the roles of servant (valet) and master in the transference.

With respect to the woman who committed the "folly" of interrupting her analysis because a baseless equilibrium had been altered, the material seems to contain a querulous note towards the parents of childhood, which appeared totally embedded in the neurotic material of her understandable infantile frustrations.

In other words, I think that if we are able to listen to the psychosis, it will be less able to fit itself into the silence of the setting and go unnoticed.

38.9   Setting and meta-setting

We have studied at length the relations of the process with the setting, and we have subscribed to the opinion of most writers that the setting should not change according to the eventualities of the process.

The setting receives, on the other hand, influences from the social milieu in which the treatment develops. This is inevitable, and also convenient. Certain situations in the environment should be gathered up by the setting, which thus acquires its seat in the social milieu in which it finds itself. The setting should legitimately modify itself on the basis of elements of the reality to which, in the final instance, it belongs.

Liberman (1970–72, Vol. 1) calls the social milieu that encircles the setting and to some extent operates on it the *meta-setting*. It constitutes contingencies that the analytic contract does not always strictly envisage, but which weigh on the setting from without, and which the setting must take into account in the long or short term. A typical example is inflation. Another example could be respect for important holidays: on these days it is advisable not to work. Argentinian analysts who do not work on national holidays (but do so on less important holidays) faced a minor conflict years ago when October 12, the day America was discovered and which President Hipólito Yrigoyen had exalted as "The Day of the Race", ceased to be a national holiday. For a few years it no longer was considered as such; but after the Malvinas (Falkland Islands) conflict it became a major holiday again. This is a typical example of an "alteration" of the setting that comes from outside and corresponds to the meta-setting.

With the expressive name of *super-imposed* worlds, Janine Puget and Leonardo Wender study a phenomenon that is certainly common and almost always goes unnoticed: when analyst and analysand share information that is in principle extraneous to the analytic situation and yet is incorporated into the process in its own right. In these cases an external reality common to both emerges in the analytic field. "Its presence in the material is a fount of distortions and of a transformation in the analyst's listening, as well as a disturbance in the analytic function" (1982, p. 520). The analyst thus suddenly finds himself in a situation where he is, in effect, sharing something with his analysand, which makes him lose the protection the setting offers and exposes him to strong countertransference conflicts that particularly threaten his narcissism and his scopophilia.

Although the field of observation of Puget and Wender has broad limits that extend from the ethics to the technique, from the countertransference to the setting and from the theory to the method, I have decided to study it on this point as a privileged example of the ways in which the psychoanalytic setting depends on the social boundaries within which analyst and analysand inevitably find themselves.

38.10 Definition—a new attempt

Throughout these chapters we have been able to see that there are, in effect, various alternatives in defining the analytic situation and establishing its links with the analytic process.

As we said earlier, the term "situation" in ordinary language denotes the place where something is located, the place where something occurs. Depending on our theoretical perspective, that "place" can be understood as a structure or a Gestalt, as a field or an existential encounter.

If we conceive it as a *structure*, the analytic situation presents itself to us as a unity formed by diverse members—more precisely, two members—each of which only acquires meaning in relation to the others. With this perspective it is said that the transference cannot be understood separately from the countertransference, or that the analysand's instincts and feelings have to do with the presence of the psychoanalyst. This is why Rickman (1950, 1951) emphasizes that the fundamental characteristic of the Freudian method is to be a "two-person psychology".

The concept of Gestalt or structure does not differ much from that of field, and in fact those who define the analytic situation as a *field* rely on gestaltic and structural ideas. When we define it in this way, we mean that lines of force that stem from the analysand and the analyst, who in this way are located in a field of interaction, run through the analytic situation.

The analytic situation, finally, could be understood as an existential *encounter* between analyst and analysand. If we do not conceive it thus, that is because we do not enter into that line of thought; but all the existential analysts define it in this way, beyond the differences that may distinguish them. For all of them the psychotherapeutic session is a place of encounter, of being-in-the-world.

In the above three definitions I see a pair of decisive elements: (1) the analytic situation is recognized of itself, it has autonomy, and (2) it is ahistorical, atemporal, does not exist prior to the moment in which it is constituted.

There is another way of defining the analytic relation, which, in my view, is very different to the previous ones, although they may be confused sometimes. In this case the analytic situation is defined stipulatively on the basis of the process. To be realized, the process needs, by definition, a non-process, which is the setting; then the term "situation" covers both. The idea that there must be something fixed for the process to develop is logical, irreproachable. But we are not therefore going to redefine the analytic situation as the set of constants and variables. It is true that thanks to this expedient the vagueness of ordinary language is resolved, but at the expense of simplifying the facts, taking autonomy away from the analytic situation.

If we decide to maintain the conceptual currency of the analytic situation, we have to recognize it as atemporal and ahistorical, but then we are going to contrast and compare it with the notion of process, with which it re-enters history.

To close this discussion with a personal opinion, I will say that between situation and process there is the same relation as that between the *current state* and the *evolution* of the classic clinical case history—or, equally, between the synchronic and diachronic linguistics of Ferdinand de Saussure (1916). The *synchronic* perspective studies the language as a system, at a given moment and in a particular state, without reference to time. The *diachronic* study of the language, on the other hand, concerns itself with its evolution in time. This distinction was one of Saussure's great contributions, because it allowed him to distinguish two types of events: language as a system, and language in its historical evolution.

Applying these concepts, we can say that the analytic situation is synchronic, and the analytic process is diachronic, and to study them we should distinguish between them carefully, without avoiding the sometimes inextricable web of their relations.

CHAPTER THIRTY-NINE

The analytic process

39.1 General discussion

In the three previous chapters we studied the *analytic situation* in particular. After reviewing different ways of understanding it, we favoured the concept of a place, a *space* without time, where the singular relation is established, which involves the analysand and the analyst, who have formally shared, well-defined and objective roles with respect to the fulfilment of a particular task.

We also saw that the analytic situation requires a framework in order to establish itself, which is the *setting*, underpinned by the rules that make it possible. These rules find their justification in the theories of psychoanalysis and of the psychoanalyst and emerge from an agreement by the parties concerned, which constitutes the *analytic contract*.

In his *An Outline of Psycho-Analysis* written in 1938, shortly before his death, Freud called this agreement *Vertrag*, which can be translated as pact, contract. The analyst should ally himself with the weakened ego of the patient, against the instinctual demands of the id and the moral requirements of the superego, thus effecting a pact, where the ego promises us the most complete sincerity in providing information, and we offer in exchange our knowledge for the interpretation of the unconscious aspects of its material, together with the strictest reserve. "This pact constitutes the analytic situation" (Freud, 1940a [1938], p. 173).

On the basis of the analytic situation conceived in this way, the analytic task develops in *time*, configuring the psychoanalytic process, to which we will now direct our attention.

39.2 The concept of process

Before dealing specifically with the psychoanalytic process, we will consider the concept of process, following the article Gregorio Klimovsky (1982) wrote on this theme.

Perhaps the broadest and most general definition of *process*, Klimovsky says, is the one that defines it in virtue of time—that is, for each value of the time variable is fixed a certain state in the system being studied. What occurs in the system being studied (which for us is the psychoanalytic treatment) is given as a function of time, in the same way as the volume of a mass of gas is a function of the pressure and temperature in the Boyle and Mariotte Law. According to this very general definition, "a process is a function that correlates, for each instance of a given lapse, a certain state or configuration characteristic of the individual or community being investigated" (ibid., p. 7). When we order certain events in the analysand's life in a temporal order, we are defining a process in that we order the events in virtue of time. In considering the present illness in the context of the clinical history, for example, we are following this method, given that we note the symptoms and the moment of their appearance. Sometimes this chronological ordering of the symptoms is sufficient for an almost certain diagnosis of a particular illness—as in the case of the epigastric syndrome and of the pain of the right iliac zone in acute appendicitis, for example.

In a second definition of the term "process", everything that is occurring in time acquires a unity relative to a final determining state. The process courses towards an objective and ends when it has reached it. In this sense we could say that the cathartic method consisted in a process that, on the basis of hypnosis, aimed at the recovery of memories (the widened consciousness) and ended in abreaction.

The third definition of process that Klimovsky distinguishes has to do with the causal chain—that is, subsequent states are somehow determined by previous ones, in either a continuous or a discrete way. When we try to understand the analytic process in terms of progression or regression, when we divide it into stages that depend on particular configurations that lead, when they are resolved, to new ones that are foreseen, we are in fact giving explanations of this type. A good example here is Klein's theory of the positions in its genetic formulation in that it supposes an evolution of process from the paranoid–schizoid to the depressive position. (The theory of the positions should be understood from three points of view: as a psychopathological constellation, as phases of development—genetic explanation—and as a structure, expressed by Bion, 1963, with his equation of two members, P ↔ D, which for Meltzer, 1978, constitutes an economic principle.)

There is yet a fourth way of using the term "process": as a "succession of events with their causal connexions plus the actions the therapist applies at certain moments for the sequence to be that one and no other" (Klimovsky, 1982, p. 8). It is understandable that if we think that each state depends on what has occurred previously, then we will try to do something to achieve a change in the sequence. It seems to me that this is the model best adapted to the psychoanalytic process, and it offers us a convincing explanation of what we do. In the face of a particular configuration of the material and of the analytic relation, we can foresee what will happen afterwards (anxiety and/or resistance will increase, for example), and we will try to intervene with the interpretation for this not to happen.

As Klimovsky says, the therapeutic process, to be such, has to provoke *changes*, because otherwise it would not be a process in the sense of the second and third definitions; and these changes are those we try to encourage through interpretation. To operate in this way in the psychoanalytic process, we have to know, in the first place, which situations are possible when confronted by a particular configuration during the analytic session. Then we must decide which situation is preferable (which entails a complex axiological problem) and, finally, what course of action we must follow to achieve it. By course of action we mean here what is the most adequate interpretation or what we could do instead if we were to question the interpretation.

On the basis of Klimovsky's convincing scheme we will now review the principal theories that try to explain the psychoanalytic process, but before this I will deal with a somewhat academic problem—the nature of the analytic process—because I am convinced that our practice will always depend, sooner or later, on how we understand it.

39.3   On the nature of the psychoanalytic process

When we try to ascertain the nature of the psychoanalytic process—that is, its essence or root—we arrive at a point where two opposing and apparently irreconcilable conceptions appear. For one of these, the psychoanalytic process arises spontaneously and naturally from the analytic situation in which analysand and analyst are placed. For the other, on the other hand, the process is an artifice, an artefact or contrivance, of the rigorous conditions in which analysis develops and to which the patient must adapt (or "submit").

Characterized in this way, both positions seem extreme and intemperate, seemingly without a point of contact or convergence.

When it is maintained that the psychoanalytic process is *natural* and any type of artifice is denied it, it is thought that the transference is basically a spontaneous process, that all of us have a natural tendency to repeat in the present the old ways of our remote infantile past, that it is in no way necessary to pressurize or induce the analysand for this to happen, that our method, in the end, always operates *per via di levare* and not *di porre*. Certainly the fact is ignored that any process where the hand of man intervenes is artificial. According to the dictionary definition, "artifice" signifies both what human art and ingenuity produce and, figuratively, what is false. In this discussion, therefore, we should not allow ourselves to be influenced by the emotional content of the terms.

Those who defend the alternative conception, on the other hand, and affirm that the analytic process is an *artificial* product of our technique begin by saying that the relation the analytic setting imposes on the two participants in the cure is excessively rigid and conventional, it lacks any spontaneity, and it is acknowledged to be asymmetrical. What sort of dialogue can this be where one of the participants lies down and the other sits, where one speaks without being allowed to take refuge in any of the rules of normal conversation and the other remains impenetrable, responding through interpretation? No, it is asserted, the analytic process runs its course along paths so rarely frequented that it has an ineluctable seal of artifice. Were it not so, were the analytic process to run its course naturally, the past would have to repeat itself without changes, and there would really be no process.

The two positions as explained above rely on valid arguments, but they also have their weak points. To emerge from these extreme positions, which are not the best ones for a discussion, let us say, rather, that certain writers maintain that the analytic process is *natural* in that it seeks to set in motion the *mental growth* arrested by the illness. The human being has an inherent potential for growth, for development—as Bibring (1937) maintained—and our whole task, in fact a humble one, only consists in removing the obstacles for that Heraclitean river of life (or the mind) to follow its course. We have no push pump nor any other more modern apparatus to pump the water forward; neither do we need it.

Those not resigned to such unstimulating work maintain that, on the contrary, the analytic process is by definition *creative*, original, unrepeatable. The analyst participates actively and continuously, each interpretation impels the process and takes it along new paths, "y hace camino al andar" [and forges the road to walk on]. What the analyst may or may not say, what the analyst selects for interpretation, the way he interprets . . . everything gives the analytic process its seal. Therefore no two analyses are the same, and no analysand is the same for them.

The arguments could multiply and, as in all controversial themes, each side might find refuge in "what Freud says". Transference, Freud said in "Remembering, Repeating and Working-Through" (1914g), creates an intermediate zone between the illness and life, where the transition from one to the other becomes possible. As Loewald (1968) states, Freud thinks that this new illness, the transference neurosis, is not an artefact but derives instead from the libidinal nature of the human being (*Papers on Psychoanalysis*, p. 310). Thus the transference neurosis is a no-man's-land between artifice and reality.

In general, all analysts admit that analysis is a process of growth and also a creative experience. Everything depends, then, on which of these two aspects we give preference to. I favour the first alternative and think that the essence of the process consists in removing the obstacles, so the analysand can go his own way. The analyst's creation consists, for me, in the capacity to give the analysand the necessary instruments for him to orientate himself alone and become himself again. The analyst is creative more through what he reveals than by what he creates. This point is rigorously presented in Loewald's work previously quoted. It centres the discussion on the new significance the illness acquires in the transference neurosis. Loewald says that to give the transference neurosis a new meaning does not mean to invent a new meaning, but it is also not merely to reveal an archaic meaning to the analysand. Instead, a meaning is created through the interaction of analyst and patient which has new dynamic tensions and engenders new, autonomous and healthier motivations (ibid., p. 311). This position with three variants seems useful to me, but I continue to think, as I said in Helsinki (Etchegoyen, 1981b), that the psychoanalyst rescues rather than creates meanings that have been lost.

39.4 Review of the main theories

In accordance with Klimovsky's specifications detailed in section 39.2, we could now define the psychoanalytic process as a temporal unfolding of a chain of events that tend towards a final state with the intervention of the analyst. To be more precise, let us say that these events relate to each other through phenomena of regression and progression, that the state they tend towards is the cure (whatever it may be) and that the analyst's intervention consists basically (or exclusively) in the act of interpreting.

There are several theories that try to explain the development of the analytic process, and of these the most accepted is *the theory of therapeutic regression*. (I dealt with this theme at length in an earlier work, "Regresión y encuadre" [Regression and Setting], 1979a—see chapter 40 in this volume.)

While most of the ego psychologists decidedly favour the theory of regression in the setting, there are also those within that current of thought who do not accept it, such as Arlow and Brenner and Calef and Weinshel, among the main ones. Weinshel, as also other San Francisco analysts, understands the analytic process on the (certainly very Freudian) idea of resistance. For Weinshel the analytic process consists in resolving the repressions through the work in common of analysand and analyst, in the context of an object relation that involves processes of identification and transference. We will see that, in this context, the ideas of regression and therapeutic alliance do not find a theoretically valid place. The whole line of reasoning is based on an interesting and seldom read work by Bernfeld, "The Fact of Observation in Psychoanalysis" (1941), as we will see in what follows.

The Kleinian analysts never concerned themselves much with the theory of the regression in the setting, although it is true that this school's body of doctrine presents itself as basically incompatible with that explanation.

To give account of the dynamics of the analytic process, the proposal of the Kleinian school should be sought, in my view, in separation anxiety. It is evident that someone like Klein, who postulates without concessions the object relation at the outset, must sooner or later rely for an understanding of the process on the dialectics of contact and separation.

Meltzer's (1967) book on the analytic process is inspired precisely by the rhythm of contact and separation, which is convincingly explained on the basis of projective identification. We will examine this in due course.

Among the post-Kleinian writers, I think Winnicott concerned himself most with this theme. His ideas follow a different and original course. For him, the analytic setting facilitates and allows a process of regression that is indispensable to retrace a wrong path, to stanch the wounds of early emotional development.

In his work presented at the London Congress, André Green (1975) studies the development of the analytic process and indicates the presence of a double anxiety in order to explain it, especially in borderline cases— separation anxiety and intrusion anxiety. From the dialectic between the two arises the *psychose blanche*.

39.5   Weinshel's observations

Edward M. Weinshel proposed an interesting model of the analytic process on the basis of the analysis of resistance, which is undoubtedly a constant of Freudian thought, based on the ideas of Bernfeld, whose influence on the psychoanalytic groups of the West Coast of the United States was considerable in his final years. (Weinshel presented his work on 12 April 1983 in his country, and a few days later at the Psychoanalytic Association of Buenos Aires, at the invitation of President Polito. The definitive text was published in *The Psychoanalytic Quarterly*. Bernfeld [1892–1953] arrived in San Francisco in 1937.)

Weinshel takes as his starting point what Freud says in "On Beginning the Treatment": "The analyst . . . sets in motion a process, that of the resolving of existing repressions. He can supervise this process, further it, remove obstacles in its way, and he can undoubtedly vitiate much of it. But on the whole, once begun, it goes its own way, and does not allow either the direction it takes or the order in which it picks up its points to be prescribed for it." Comparing this with the process of gestation, Freud says that the psychoanalytic process is "determined by events in the remote past", which "ends with the severance of the child from its mother" (1913c, p. 130).

In this way, the psychoanalytic process is something that occurs between two people, analysand and analyst, who work together and where there will be object relations, identifications and transferences (Weinshel, 1984, p. 67).

Freud's position never varied, Weinshel points out, as to the basis of the analytic process, which consists in overcoming the resistances, that process being what leads to insight through interpretation. In this way, he articulates the process with the resistances, and these with interpretation and insight. Within this theoretical framework, which without doubt most analysts share, transference is, for Weinshel, the main vehicle for observation and management of the resistances. Analytic work varies in inverse relation to resistance, and therefore the patient's cooperation fluctuates continuously. It is on this basis that Weinshel questions the concept of therapeutic alliance (or working alliance), which is not something that is acquired once and for all. The working alliance appears as a relatively transitory rather than a constant structure and for this reason becomes a potentially confused concept of little usefulness, especially if it is thought of as a psychologically discrete entity (ibid., p. 75).

In Siegfried Bernfeld's seldom read work (published in the *Journal of Psychology* of 1941 and quoted previously), Weinshel finds those thoughts that allow a better understanding of the nature of the analytic process.

Bernfeld thinks that if we wish to discover the scientific method of psychoanalysis at root, we should begin with the model of *ordinary conversation*, since the scientific method in general is no more than the ordinary techniques made more refined and verifiable (Weinshel, 1984, p.75). For Bernfeld, psychoanalysis is a special conversation, where the patient has to free-associate. At a given moment in this sophisticated conversation, an obstacle will appear, which is what we conceptualize as resistance and Bernfeld calls *the state of hiding a secret*. It can yield and be followed by a *confession*, facilitated by an *interference*, an intervention of the other, which in our practice is the analyst's interpretation. After the confession of his secret, the analysand can continue his conversation. This is repeated many times, and this dialectic between secret and confession influenced by the analyst's interpretation is, for Bernfeld, the analytic process.

Bernfeld's viewpoint corresponds with and broadens his ideas on interpretation in his work of 1932 ("Der Begriff der 'Deutung' in der Psychoanalyse" [The Concept of "Interpretation" in Psychoanalysis], discussed earlier. Bernfeld defined psychoanalysis there as a science of tracks. The fundamental method of psychoanalysis is neither final nor functional interpretation, but genetic interpretation or reconstruction, which should seek out the origins through the tracks that still persist (1932, section 3). The process that must be reconstructed has left particular tracks, and the psychoanalyst launches himself into this search. This is why Bernfeld compares the analyst's work with that of the detective who tries to retrace the criminal's tracks. For this reason Ekstein (1966) says in his interesting study on interpretation that the detective, like the archaeologist, works from the present to the past and tries to reconstruct the events (Bernfeld, 1932).

It is worth pointing out that, for Bernfeld, verification in psychoanalysis does not have to do with the truth or reality of the confession, that is, with its content, but with the patient saying what he has been hiding. Without ignoring the possibility of a false confession, Bernfeld considers that the analyst is in an advantageous position to verify the correctness of the confession when he ponders adequately the facts of observation offered to him according to the resistance-free-association model. What really matters is that the patient has confessed his secret. This is why Weinshel thinks that the analytic process should be defined more by the work (of overcoming the resistances) than by its objectives.

* * *

As I had the opportunity of telling Weinshel in Buenos Aires, I agree with his concept of analytic process as work the analysand and the analyst carry out together to overcome the resistances, but not with Bernfeld's methodological scheme.

I think the distance between ordinary conversation and psychoanalytic dialogue is too great for us to place them in the same class. I also think that the secret-confession model is not the one best adapted to psychoanalytic technique. I think the word "secret" is applicable to what is conscious (or at most preconscious) but not to the systemic unconscious (Ucs), which is the strict area of our work.

Additionally, leaving aside Bernfeld's scheme and looking at Weinshel's conception, the emphasis on the resistances does not always seem to do justice to the complexity of the analytic process, where the resistance and the repressed configure an inextricable dialectic pair and should not be separated.

Finally, one must take into account that the very ideas of secret, confession and resistance acquire special meanings during the course of the process and we will then no longer be able to operate clearly with them. We will have to analyse the fantasies they are covering, abandoning in consequence—at least at that moment—the dialectic of Bernfeld and his disciples.

It is worth remembering here what Giovacchini (1972a) said about resistances. To analyse the resistances is not the same as to conquer or overcome them, since this attitude can create a restrictive and moralizing attitude that is not good for the analytic process and even less so for seriously ill patients.

Weinshel's ideas, finally, seem to be more applicable to neurotic than to more severe cases.

39.6 The Ulm process model

The psychoanalytic process depends on many factors, and among them we have to emphasise the process concept held by the analyst. Helmut Thomä and Horst Kächele, two meticulous investigators from Ulm, considered this a decisive factor, because the definition of the process already implies the model by which it operates. Through its great complexity and its infinite variations, the analytic process lends itself to the justification of any model whatsoever, and that incurs a double risk: theoretical because it confirms the presupposed theory (which in fact becomes irrefutable), and practical in that it denies the analysand the freedom of spontaneity.

Models are necessary, however, to put in order the multitude of clinical data, and no one can avoid using them, so that the question "is not whether the analyst derives his course of action from his model, but whether he follows this course of action in a strictly prescriptive way" (Thomä & Kächele, 1987, Vol. 1, p. 333). In other words, observation will not be stereotyped but heuristic, that is, always open to what is happening and what may happen. The model must serve to describe and not prescribe.

Just as there are two models of science, *that of nature* ["*Naturwissenschaften*"] and *that of the spirit* ["*Geisteswissenschaften*"], so there are also two types of model for the psychoanalytic process: natural–scientific and social–scientific. The analysts of the Department of Psychotherapy of the University of Ulm have a dyadic, bipersonal, social–scientific conception of the psychoanalytic process; they maintain that the models used in the natural sciences are not suitable for our discipline, since the analyst, as a participating observer, has a decided influence on the field of observation. Though Thomä and Kächele recognize that this epistemological criterion is increasingly questioned, they do not doubt that there is a qualitative difference between the physicist who observes particles and waves and the psychoanalyst who aspires to give an account of the therapeutic process to which he is committed.

The authors from Ulm oppose the idea that psychoanalytic treatment responds to a natural model that arises from inherent regularities, provided that the analyst does not disturb it. "On the contrary, we assign the analyst a central role in codetermining the structure of the therapeutic process. He fulfils this role in a dyad-specific way which depends on his own personality and on the patient. This view of the therapist's role cannot be reconciled with the conception of the psychoanalytic process as a natural event" (ibid., p. 337).

The models that assume a natural course for treatment conceive it in general as a replica of early infantile development. Thomä and Kächele do not question at all that man's psychic development takes place by definite stages—symbiosis, pre-oedipal and oedipal conflicts, for example—so that in broad outline they can provide a useful guide to evaluate the course of the process, but always provided that we do not forget that the therapeutic process differs from the original infantile experience on essential points: "early experiences *cannot* be re-experienced authentically" (ibid., p. 335), since the therapeutic process always involves a variety of overdetermined experiences. The principle of genetic continuity of Joan Riviere (1936b) and Susan Isaacs (1943), which draws on an undeniable Freudian tradition, must be counterbalanced by the concept, also very Freudian, of *après coup*

["*Nachträglichkeit*"], according to which the earlier event only assumes its meaning afterwards. As Baranger, Baranger and Mom (1983) point out, this principle emphasizes the difference between psychoanalysis and evolutional psychology.

Thomä and Kächele (1987) maintain that in models based on the idea that the psychoanalytic process follows a natural kind of growth, the patient's development occupies the centre of interest. If we consider that psychoanalytic treatment is dyadic, that is to say a process of interactional negotiation, then the therapist's contribution becomes very important.

On the basis of these general considerations, Thomä and Kächele expound the Ulm process model, which proposes to combine the analyst's free-floating attention with a focal strategy, which is directed towards the points on which the attention is to be centred. The *focus* has to be understood as a heuristic process the usefulness of which must be shown by the progress of the treatment, and nothing is further from the spirit of the authors than rigid focalization. Although the focus exists independently of the analyst's intervention, since the patient has formed it in fact in his own symptoms, it is also undeniable that it depends on the analyst's attention. "We consider the interactionally formed focus to be the axis of the analytic process, and thus conceptualize psychoanalytic therapy as an *ongoing, temporally unlimited focal therapy with a changing focus*" (ibid., p. 347, italics in original). In this way "we use 'focus' to refer to the major interactionally created theme of the therapeutic work, which results from the material offered by the patient and the analyst's efforts at understanding" (ibid., p. 350). At the end of their exposition Thomä and Kächele say clearly and forcefully: "We would like to contrast the conception of the process as an ongoing, temporally unlimited focal therapy with qualitative changing focus to the fictive notion of a puristic psychoanalytic process" (ibid., p. 352). It is obvious that the authors completely reject the possibility that the analyst can recover objectivity from the analysis of his countertransference and thus participate in the course of the process without being involved in it to an unhealthy extent.

The methodological warnings of the men of Ulm are correct, and I too believe that past experiences are never reproduced word for word. If it were so, the outcome of present experience would of necessity have to be identical with early experience; but it does not necessarily follow from this that in the analytic situation the analyst intervenes with his own personal conflicts. As they say themselves, the interaction of therapeutic work consists in the analysand *proposing* and the analyst *responding* with his (technical) capacity to understand, that is, to interpret. In this way the analyst's countertransferential involvement, however great it is, can be resolved cleanly, re-establishing the inescapable asymmetry of the analytic link, which enables us to work *per via di levare* and give back to the analysand what really belongs to him.

CHAPTER FORTY

Regression and setting

The purpose of this chapter is to study how regression and the setting are related in the psychoanalytic process. In my view this is a problem of great theoretical density to which not all investigators have accorded equal importance. Viewed from the point of view of everyday practice, it appears simple and without complications: moments of regression are inherent in the analytic process, and the analyst confronts them regularly. Thus we accept without further ado that the process has to do with regression, and we consider it an empirical fact that does not require great theoretical reflection. And yet, when the causal link between the regression and the setting is discussed, we suddenly find ourselves at the centre of the major currents of contemporary psychoanalytic thought.

Without doubt those who have attended most to this theme are the ego psychologists. They could never be criticized for not having fixed their position. Supported lucidly by their own ideas, and with great consistency between theory and practice, they define the problem and consider it as

This chapter represents, with minor modifications, a paper I presented to the Athenaeum of the Buenos Aires Psychoanalytical Association (APdeBA) on 9 October 1979; it appeared in *Psicoanálisis*, 1 (1979). Some quotes from the original have now been given in greater detail, and, making good an omission from the previous version, I have added a section commenting on Arlow and Brenner (1964), whose main ideas I share.

fundamental. However, other schools do not seem to have devoted sufficient attention to it.

Regression in the psychoanalytic process was the official theme of
the Seventh Latin-American Congress of Psychoanalysis in Bogotá in
1969. The Argentinian participants were Avenburg, Madeleine Baranger,
Giuliana Smolensky de Dellarossa, Rolla and Zac. Although they themselves identified at the outset the theoretical differences that divide them,
they did agree on the existence of a regression "that contributes to the
process, in part constitutes it and is an intrinsic and necessary part of it".
They distinguished two types of regression—the pathological regression
characteristic of the illness that brings the patient to the treatment, and the
useful, operative regression in the service of the ego, which facilitates the
therapeutic task.

After the presentation in Bogotá and inspired by it, Ricardo Avenburg
(1969) studied minutely the subject of regression in the analytic process in
Freud's work, to demonstrate that it does not appear to be explicitly developed.

Let us say here that, in Freudian thought, the concepts of fixation and
regression are the explanatory key of psychopathology. But they were
never carried over to the analytic situation. Freud applies the concept of
regression exclusively to the illness and not to the therapy. Let us remember, for example, his lively manner when he says in "The Dynamics of
Transference" (1912b) that an indispensable requirement for the appearance of a neurosis is that the libido take a regressive course, while analytic
treatment follows it, examines it and seeks to make it conscious so as to
put it in the service of reality. "The libido (whether wholly or in part) has
entered on a regressive course and has revived the subject's infantile
imagos. The analytic treatment now proceeds to follow it; it seeks to track
down the libido, to make it accessible to consciousness and, in the end,
serviceable for reality" (1912b, p. 102).

40.1   *Therapeutic regression*

It is well known that many ego psychologists state firmly that the analytic
process is of a regressive nature, that this regression is produced as a
response to the setting and is the necessary condition to constitute an
analysable transference neurosis. With other nuances this opinion is found
among most ego psychologists of Europe and the New World, as well as
among many other investigators.

To understand the theory of therapeutic regression of ego psychology,
we have to take into account mainly two factors: first (and I think fore-
most), Hartmann's (1939) concept of *secondary autonomy*; second, the function of the setting.

If we re-read attentively David Rapaport's "The Autonomy of the
Ego" (1951, especially section 4), we will see a clear exposition of the prin-

ciple of secondary autonomy. The defensive apparatuses that arise from the conflict can become independent of their source, and we know this because in our therapeutic task we find defences that we are unable to tear down despite prolonged analysis. Aside from this practical consideration, Rapaport insists that every counterphobic attitude and every reactive formation carries a concomitant *motivating value,* which, although it arose out of the conflict, is not lost in a successful analysis. In short, what is produced as a result of the conflict can sooner or later become independent of it, becoming relatively autonomous.

In section 5 of the same work Rapaport distinguishes, within one and the same psychic formation, the autonomous aspect of this motivating value from the defensive aspect. Rapaport's conclusion is that, since the secondary autonomy is always relative, the analyst should respect it so as not to provoke a regressive process, which may even lead to psychosis. The analyst cannot eschew treating the defence embedded in the conflict without attacking the autonomy of the motivating value. Thus a direct interpretation of the aggressive meaning of reactive independence set off in a borderline case a clinical picture of catatonic excitation (ibid., p. 366).

Rapaport concludes that "autonomy, particularly secondary autonomy, is always relative, and the onslaught of drive motivations, especially when unchecked by therapeutic help or when aided by overzealous therapeutic moves, may reverse autonomy and bring about a regressed, psychotic state in which the patient is, to a far-reaching extent, at the mercy of his drive impulses" (ibid., p. 366).

As I have tried to show in speaking of the therapeutic alliance (chapter 18) and also in the sections on interpretation (especially chapter 25), the interpretations Rapaport fears so much are not, in fact, interpretations, but, rather, disqualifying manoeuvres on the part of the analyst, due to ignorance or very strong countertransference conflicts, or, at other times, a negative therapeutic reaction on the part of the analysand who seeks to fault the analyst.

Elizabeth R. Zetzel is following the same line of thought when she says in her already classic work, "Current Concepts of Transference" (1956a), that the transference neurosis develops *after* the ego defences have been sufficiently stirred up to mobilize the instinctual conflicts hidden until then (p. 371). On the same page she says that the ego psychologists' hypothesis is that, in the course of development, the instinctual energy within reach of the mature ego has been neutralized and divorced, in relative or absolute form, from the meaning of the unconscious fantasies, and this is how the analysand appears at the beginning of analysis.

In "El proceso analítico" [The Analytic Process], presented at the Second Pan-American Congress of Psychoanalysis in Buenos Aires in 1966, Zetzel said that according to her point of view, transference neurosis depends on the regression and the concomitant modification of the unconscious automatic defences that opens up hitherto inaccessible areas (1966, p. 73).

The second factor that must be taken into account to understand ego psychology's theory of therapeutic regression is that the setting within which psychoanalytic treatment develops stirs up the phenomenon of regression. This new theory, which certainly seeks its support in clinical practice, matches the previous one and is its corollary. If the transference neurosis depends on regression, how could a patient be treated without the existence of some artifice that produces an imbalance in his secondary autonomy? I say this because I think that this necessity in the theory weighs in the appreciation of the clinical facts these writers rely on.

Psychoanalytic treatment as a task the analyst proposes to the patient demands, then, great effort, which is resolved through a specific defence mechanism, regression. The analytic atmosphere puts the analysand's entire psychological structure into a state of tension, and from this a regressive process results. (Freud has already shown us in chapter 22 of his *Introductory Lectures on Psycho-Analysis*, 1916–17, for example, that the current conflict arises from a deprivation that sets in motion a regressive process.) This process of regression, it is maintained, is different from those the individual may suffer in his relations in life; and this difference is rooted in the setting where it takes place.

The ego psychologists think that the setting was designed by Freud precisely to provoke the patient's regression and so that it can be regulated by the analyst.

Leaving aside personal differences that can sometimes become important, all of them think that the setting implies sensory deprivation, emotional frustration, limitation of the object world and infantile atmosphere.

To quote Dr. Zetzel again, in her presentation to the Second Congress she says that the analyst's silence, as we know already, is an important factor in this regression. She adds that the analyst's activity, on the other hand, "tends to minimize the regression due to its sensory impact", because it is possible that an active intervention from the outset, whatever its content, is meaningful mainly as sensory experience that limits the regression in the analytic situation.

Sensory deprivation refers not only to the auditory sphere but also to the visual one. Therefore, she says, the analyst's silence, like his temporary invisibility, continues to be for many analysts an indispensable feature of the analytic process (see 1966, p. 73).

Here again we find in Rapaport some theoretical grounds for these assertions. In "The Theory of Ego Autonomy: A Generalization" (1957), supported by experimental facts, he affirms that sensory deprivation (in perfectly dark rooms devoid of noise) sets in motion autistic fantasies and deep regressive phenomena in the subjects (section 3, p. 727).

These authors in general view the atmosphere of deprivation in which analysis is necessarily carried out, the analyst's reserve, the asymmetry of the relation and so forth as factors that condition the regressive process, in that they limit or annul the object relation.

Finally, many if not all of the writers we are considering think, as do Ida Macalpine (1950) and Menninger (1958), that regression is due to the setting *infantilizing* the patient.

Ida Macalpine maintains that (almost) all the elements of the setting lead inevitably to regression. I say *almost* because she asks herself why the permissive atmosphere of analysis does not *impede* regression. In effect, it is a point her theory cannot explain and on which Winnicott (1958) relied to develop his original viewpoint of regression as a *curative* process, which the setting makes possible, offering the analysand highly favourable conditions to face again and resolve the failures in his development.

Returning to Macalpine, I wish to emphasize that the regression she is thinking of is fundamentally a temporary, chronological regression, when she considers that the setting *infantilizes* the patient. It is worth reflecting on the 15 items the writer offers as support for her thesis: the limitation of the object world (agreeing with the other writers quoted); the constancy of the environment; the fixity of the analytic routines, a reminder of the strict routines of infancy (although they could also be a reminder of the no less strict routines of adult life); the fact that the analyst does not answer; the interpretations of the infantile level, which stimulate behaviour of the same type; the lessening of personal responsibility in the analytic session; the magical element of every doctor–patient relationship, which is in itself a strongly infantile factor; the free association that frees the fantasy of the conscious controller; the authority of the analyst as father; the atemporality of the unconscious; and so forth. It is hardly necessary to point out that some of these items pertain to the analysand and not to the setting, so that in fact they militate against the writer's thesis: I refer to the magical element of the doctor–patient relationship, the analyst's paternal authority, the atemporality of the unconscious.

Seduced and frustrated, Macalpine's patient is divorced more and more from the reality principle and allows himself to be led by the pleasure principle.

Ida Macalpine's position is extreme, and in my judgement quite refutable, but more moderate writers are basically of the same opinion. Joseph Sandler, a prominent disciple of Anna Freud, in the book written together with Dare and Holder, gives the term "regression" the specific sense of emergence of past, often infantile, experiences, which appear as a characteristic of the analytic process (1973, p. 25).

Another scientific leader of ego psychology, Hans W. Loewald, begins from different principles in his famous work of 1960 but reaches the same conclusions. Loewald affirms that the objective of the analytic process is for the ego to resume its development (arrested by the illness) in relation to the analyst as a new object. He immediately concludes, however, that this is achieved by stirring up and utilizing a controlled regression. "This regression is one important aspect under which the transference neurosis can be understood" (p. 17).

Lacan (1958a), despite his well-known disagreements with ego psychology, also accepts fully the theory of therapeutic regression. He agrees basically with Macalpine's study, which he thinks is exceptional due to its perspicacity (p. 603). He only differs in the idea that it is not the lack of object relation but the *demand* that creates regression (p. 617). The analyst is silent and with this frustrates the speaker, since a response is just what the latter asks of him. We know that, in effect, Lacan and his school are characterized by a rigorous silence in the analytic situation, which in my view operates as an artifice. If I do not misunderstand it, this is what Lacan asserts when he says that with the offer (of speaking) he has created the demand (ibid.).

With similar lines of reasoning, that is, the expectations awoken in the analysand by the analyst's silence, Menninger (1958) explains regression in the psychoanalytic process.

Reik's attitude is similar to that of Lacan and Menninger, according to which silence is a decisive factor in setting up the analytic situation, awakening in the analysand the obsession to confess (see, for example, "In the Beginning Is Silence" and "La significación psicológica del silencio"). What Reik adds without saying so is the function as artefact that the mute analyst fulfils.

Together with Dr. Zetzel, there were five Argentinian participants at the Pan-American Congress in Buenos Aires: Grinberg, Marie Langer, Liberman and Emilio and Geneviève Rodrigué (Grinberg et al., 1966a). With a different focus from that of the great analyst from Boston, these writers understand the analytic process in the dialectics of progress and regression (an idea that inspires my own thinking). They rely on Kris's (1936, 1938, 1950, 1956a) concept of regression in the service of the ego. But they firmly maintain that the setting *infantilizes* the patient (Grinberg et al., 1966a, p. 100), without taking the step I will attempt to take in a moment. (These writers also say that there is another aspect of the analytic situation that also induces regression, and this is the *holding*, which reproduces the good relation of the baby–analysand with the analyst who sustains and shelters him. And they add that the useful regression in the progress of the analytic process comes from this second aspect of the analytic situation.)

I wish first to mention that David Liberman (1976a) agrees with Ida Macalpine as to the importance of the analytic atmosphere in producing the transference regression. Liberman is close to Macalpine in his way of conceiving the development of the transference, although he emphasizes that she points out that the patient brings to analysis the disposition to transference (1976a, chapter 5, pp. 97–98). Liberman's focus on interaction is meant not so much to account for the nature of transference regression as to demonstrate that the patient's behaviour during the session "will depend on the analyst's behaviour towards him" (p. 114). However, this could also be explained by the transference–countertransference relation within the progression–regression parameters, without the support of Macalpine and the regression in the setting.

Finally, I wish to point out that in "El proceso didáctico en psicoanálisis" [The Didactic Process in Psychoanalysis], a work read at the Training Pre-Congress in Mexico (1978), Dr. Katz points out that the disposition to transference proper to anyone is observed in *every* didactic process, while the student of psychoanalysis—who certainly does not escape from this rule—"has the advantage of trying to discover the roots of his conduct and anxiety so as to modify them and facilitate his learning". I agree completely with this point of view.

40.2   *Discussion*

To begin the discussion of the theory I have just expounded, I will go resolutely to the point and say that regression in the psychoanalytic process has to do with the illness and not with the setting. The patient *comes* with his regression, his illness is the regression.

The setting does not cause it; the regression is already there. What the setting does is to detect and contain it. This is why I think Winnicott's concept of *holding* (1958, passim) or the *container* of the Kleinian writers is valid in explaining the dynamics of the analytic process.

I wish to be precise: psychoanalytic treatment does not stir up the regression beyond the coefficient between emotional balance and imbalance of the person concerned, in the way in which other significant and difficult life experiences could (marriage or divorce, examinations, achieving an important post, birth or death in the family).

Let us examine at greater length the factors of the setting that may condition regression, beginning with sensory deprivation. Every task that requires an effort and mental concentration tries to avoid stimuli that disturb it. These are the conditions we try to obtain when we read, listen to music or carry on a serious conversation. If in these instances a regression is produced, we are not going to attribute it to the sheltered atmosphere but to the individual's psychopathology. To understand it thus it is enough to think of the adolescent who masturbates in the silence of his study or the believer who has profane thoughts in the serene atmosphere of his church.

In addition, sensory deprivation is very difficult to quantify, and one must ask oneself whether in doing so one does not beg the question. I remember a pleasant moment afforded us by the healthy humour of a North American colleague at the Pan-American Congress of New York in 1969, when Dr. Zetzel and I related the *first analytic session*. I took a case (1969) among those I had recently begun, on arriving in Buenos Aires; she took material from a supervision. We were discussing sensory deprivation and interpretations in the first session when our colleague pointed out that the interventions of the Boston analyst were three times as numerous as mine!

Hand in hand with sensory deprivation goes deprivation of the object world, which comprises two cases: when the analyst is silent or when he speaks. The analyst is always present in the session, since he is listening when he is silent. The analysand can consider that silence as deprivation if he decides that the analyst's attention is not sufficient. But this is already a product of his fantasy. In extreme cases, as in Reik's, Lacan's or Menninger's technique, an artefact operates, as I have said: these writers are silent in order to *force* regression. If the analyst is mute so that the patient can regress, then the analysand does well to regress, that is, to seek another medium of communication upon seeing that the word is of no use to him. But then we will no longer be able to speak of transference regression but, conversely, of a real conduct that responds to the proposals of the non-interlocutor. (Racker said so, rightly, in criticizing Reik's mutism not only as an artefact but also as an acting out.) The analyst is "the dummy", as Lacan is never tired of saying, comparing the psychoanalytic process to the game of bridge.

In the other case, when the analyst speaks and interprets the transference neurosis, it is clear that the only real deprivation is that which arises from pregenital and oedipal desires. If we wished to speak in terms of the dissociation of the ego and the therapeutic alliance, as do Sterba (1934), Fenichel (1941), Bibring (1954), Zetzel (1956a), Stone (1961), Greenson (1965a) and others, we would say that the experiencing ego suffers from being deprived of its oedipal object, while the observing ego enjoys a full object relationship with the working analyst.

What can be said about emotional frustration and infantile (or *infantilizing*) atmosphere? Sometimes analysts forget that frustration can be defined only within a particular context, and it is, at the same time, an *opinion* on the part of the subject. The criteria we rely on to say that the setting frustrates are always located within the infantile context and entirely ruled by the patient's pleasure principle, while the reality principle is forgotten. Vice versa, analysts define frustration objectively, from outside. What the setting frustrates are certain infantile fantasies, that is, regressive ones, and in no way the real and basic desire, that of being analysed, which is the motive for seeking treatment. I remember the comment of a young female analysand, when I first began to practise, after she had accidentally encountered my wife. She became very jealous and declared openly that she wanted to be my wife, and to go to bed with me; then suddenly she added, "I suppose that you do not analyse your wife". The "frustration" of that young woman, then, arose from her oedipal desires, not from the reality of the analytic situation. (In the same way, any analyst's wife could "feel frustrated" at not being her husband's analysand.)

There is also much emphasis on the fact that the analytic couch, the asymmetrical dialogue and the analyst's reserve can only foment regression. Here objective reality is again confused with the patient's infantile desires and fantasies. The confusion between objective and psychic reality (fantasy) is perhaps the weakest point in Macalpine's argument. If I tell a person that she has to lie down on a couch in order that a particular task (analysis, auscultation, massage, etc.) can be accomplished, then if that person thinks of a rape scene, that is her affair.

It is worth indicating that the empirical facts continually confirm these general considerations.

Here are two examples from my practice. In the first instance, I was 30 years old; the second is a recent occasion. Among my first patients there was a woman a bit older than myself, who had the same names as one of my small daughters(!), with a marked Charcot-type hysteria. During some three months of face-to-face treatment twice a week she improved noticeably, and I was very satisfied. I interpreted the meaning of her symptoms, preferably in terms of sibling rivalry with her sisters (I seem to remember), with some cautious references to her Oedipus complex related to her parents. The transference was nowhere to be seen. At that time I bought my couch. In the following session I told her it would be better for her treatment for her to lie down and speak as usual. She lay down, was silent for a short time, and then a crisis of hysterical *grand mal* began, in a typical state of passionate movements: she sighed, she made erotic gestures and lifted her skirt. Suddenly she got up and like a shot she threw herself into my arms, wanting to kiss me. I got out of that difficulty as best I could, I managed to get her to sit down on my immaculate couch and, more composed, I asked her what had happened. She said she thought I had invited her into a sexual relationship. She said she had fallen in love with me a long time before but did not dare confess it. Seated face to face, looking into those eyes of mine [sic], how was she not going to fall in love! Here, then, it was the face-to-face position that set the transference love in motion. Now, forty years too late, I could interpret to her that if I had caused her to fall in love by looking at her, face to face, why did she not think my words were really true when I told her to lie down on the couch so that her treatment could develop under better conditions? But no, for her, to sit or to lie down was the same thing; it was not the setting but the Oedipus complex that fed her desire.

Some years ago a resident who had begun his training analysis but was not yet a candidate asked me urgently for a supervision. He was treating a homosexual face to face five times a week(!). This was psychotherapy, he made clear to me, and even his own analyst had suggested he should not use the couch. However, his patient had requested that the treatment continue on the couch because the face-to-face position awoke in him homosexual fantasies he was finding unbearable. The inexperienced colleague agreed and now came to me very worried, because his analyst had interpreted that decision as an acting out, as a desire to become an analyst before his time. The training analyst added that the only thing he would achieve was a homosexual regression on the part of his patient, which he would find impossible to manage. Thus we see how we analysts sometimes listen more to our theories than to our patients. (This anecdote was actually more convincing, but I can make it public only in this way.)

When Zetzel (1968) described the non-analysable hysteric at the Copenhagen Congress, she characterized her thus, among other things, because she presents regressive transference phenomena during the first interviews and before occupying the couch. In other words, the regression depends on the degree of illness, not on the setting.

Recently Pablo Grinfeld told me (personal communication) of a similar experience, although there one sees that it is precisely the analyst's behaviour in his setting that contains the regression. A female analysand, after improving appreciably with a few years of analysis, told him, "I am grateful for everything you do for me, your technique and the way you treat me; but I thank you even more for having made me lie down on the couch, preserving me in this way from the torture of the erotic desires that assailed me in two treatments face to face". This sincere patient, it seems, also attributed her erotic fantasies to being seated, without thinking that there was no repetition in this treatment of the insoluble transference love of previous treatments because the analyst interpreted it systematically and without hesitation from the beginning, until the homosexual aspects of the Oedipus complex were unmasked, which covered the erotic genital transference.

It is repeatedly asserted that free association is an invitation to regression. This depends on how it is introduced and especially on how the fundamental rule is conceived.

In chapter 2 of *The Ego and the Mechanisms of Defence*, Anna Freud (1936) says that while in the hypnosis of the cathartic method the ego was excluded, in the free association of psychoanalysis the ego is required to exclude itself, suspending all judgement about ideas that occur to it, ignoring the logical connection among them. At first sight, it seems that this invitation to associate freely foments regression. However, Anna Freud continues, "The warrant is valid only for their translation into word representations: it does not entitle them to take control of the motor apparatus, which is their real purpose in emerging" (p. 13). It is often forgotten that free association, as verbalization, implies the exercise of the secondary process. In addition, it is not entirely exact to claim that with free association the ego is asked to eliminate itself: it is asked, in the fashion of Husserl's eidetic reduction, to pay attention to everything that emerges in consciousness and to make a responsible and voluntary effort to communicate it. The fundamental rule is not only an invitation to free the primary process, but also a requirement, from the perspective of the therapeutic alliance. Whereas the obsessive will have doubts about what he has to communicate and how he should do it, the depressive will feel he faces a problem of conscience when hurtful things occur to him, and the psychopath will believe we have given him free reign to insult us. Not only the id, but also the ego and the superego are involved in free association.

Every analyst knows that the patient approaches the unreachable ideal of free association when he nears the end of the treatment and not when he begins. In other words, only the healthy ego can fulfil—and barely at that—the fundamental rule.

Following Kris's ideas closely, Hartmann says that only the adult ego can set aside at a given moment one of its high functions, and it is precisely because he cannot use this mechanism (among other reasons) that the child cannot free associate (Hartmann, 1952, p. 178).

To end this brief discussion of the factors of the setting invoked to explain regression, there is perhaps nothing better than to quote one of the best-known defenders of this theory, Ralph R. Greenson (1967). Macalpine and other writers, Greenson says, have indicated how certain elements of the setting and of the analytic procedure stir up regression and the transference neurosis. He says that "some of these same elements also help in the formation of the working alliance" (ibid., p. 208). Thus, for example, the frequency of the sessions and the duration of the analytic treatment not only stimulate regression but also indicate the range of objectives and the importance of an intimate and detailed communication. The couch and the silence offer opportunity for reflection and for introspection as well as for the production of fantasies.

If the same elements foment the transference neurosis and the therapeutic alliance, would it not be more logical to cease to invoke them?

* * *

We said that the theoretical basis for the theory of therapeutic regression is Hartmann's concept of secondary autonomy, and we will refer to it in what follows to see what bases it provides for the theory we are considering.

We have seen that Rapaport (1951) maintains that secondary autonomy is always relative and warns that it can be reversed, a point Hartmann always made. Rapaport divides the ego into two sectors and recommends that the analyst analyse the defence involved in the conflict without attacking the autonomy of the motivational value, if he does not want to cause regression. The main theoretical preoccupation in this work is to indicate two parts of the ego that offer themselves to the clinical task and to the interpretation, which, when it goes the wrong way, may cause an undesirable regression. In this way two questions are posed: what part of the ego should undertake the regressive path in the transference neurosis, and with what type of regression?

Elizabeth R. Zetzel answers these questions in her 1965 work, where she tries to reformulate the meaning of regression in the analytic situation in terms of the different functional units of the ego—of the intrasystemic conflict, as Hartmann suggested in his "Technical Implications of Ego Psychology" in 1951. Zetzel postulates a *closed system* where those fantasies, desires and memories lodge whose emergence determines an internal situation of danger (1965, p. 40). The therapeutic regression consists in reopening this closed system, accompanied by a gradual diminution of the unconscious and automatic ego defences. It would have to be demonstrated first that this system exists, and then that the key that opens it is regression. Why not think that interpretation is the best key to penetrate this type of defence?

On this point Zetzel is led to distinguish between the regression that involves the defensive ego and the corresponding instinctual contents and the regression that undermines the basic capacities of the ego (ibid., p. 41).

Everything makes me think that Dr. Zetzel is referring here to the two parts of the ego of Rapaport's work, since her thinking relies immediately on the concept of secondary autonomy. Throughout his *Essays on Ego Psychology* (1964), Hartmann maintains that the areas of the ego that reach secondary autonomy are more stable than the ego defences. However, he does not doubt that in particular circumstances they can dissolve; they can return, losing their principal quality, that of operating with bound, neutralized energy. This regressive damage of secondary autonomy in the face of situations of tension should be carefully separated from instinctive regression, an indispensable correlate of the analysis of transference (Zetzel, 1965, p. 46).

Once secondary autonomy has been differentiated from instinctive regression to explain (or justify) therapeutic regression, it is not surprising that the latter is called "regression in the service of the ego", following Kris (1936, 1950, 1956a).

However, the concept of regression in the service of the ego has nothing to do, in my view, with the theory of therapeutic regression. It is above all a formal regression, which goes from the secondary to the primary process and from the latter back to the former, and not the temporal regression that takes us from the psychoanalytic couch to the first years of life. The regression in the service of the ego assumes that the preconscious mental processes (which are the target of Kris's penetrating investigation) are continuously revitalized by returning for a moment to the source, that is, to the primary process. It is a formal and topographical regression, but by definition it has no temporality. The regression in the setting, on the other hand, has been defined implicitly as temporal and explicitly as defensive.

Dr. Zetzel concludes that it is necessary to differentiate the *defensive ego*, which must regress, from the *autonomous ego*, which must maintain its capacity for consistent object relations (ibid., p. 50; the structure of this sentence expresses the preceptive underpinning of this theory). In this way we have to postulate the existence of an intrasystemic conflict between the ego of secondary autonomy and the defensive ego.

On reaching this point, however, it can be appreciated that the whole theory loses consistency in that it has to renounce the concept of secondary autonomy and avail itself of the *ad hoc* hypothesis of the closed system. This is because the defensive ego that "must" regress (and I ask myself what we can do with our analytic technique to make the patient obey this order) does not need to do so at all because it is already in a state of regression: it operates with free (not bound) energy, it utilizes the primary process, it is linked to infantile oedipal or pre-oedipal objects, it employs archaic defence mechanisms and so forth. (We have also dealt with this theme in chapter 18.)

40.3   *Commentary*

As with vital processes studied in biology, psychology and sociology, analysis always develops with advances and retreats that alternate and oppose each other. This course is proper to it; the setting does not create it. In general terms, we can consider that it operates as the *current* conflict, while the patient's *disposition* will give account of the regressive phenomena that appear, according to the complemental series. On the other hand, the analyst's interpretative activity, if it is accurate, generally carries the process forward in terms of growth, integration or cure (unless the patient responds in a paradoxical way, as in the negative therapeutic reaction). This is specific to analysis, because the current conflict with the setting is no more significant than any other in real life. I do no more here than apply the Freudian concept of the primacy of the *infantile conflict* in the explanation of the neuroses.

The radical difference between the experience of analysis and others in daily life is that the patient's pathological conduct receives a different treatment. The patient repeats, the analyst does not. This emphatic assertion does not imply a special conception of the process. I believe it is acceptable for those who locate it in the patient, in the field, in the interaction and so forth. We can differ, even greatly, on the degree and type of participation by the analyst. But we all consider that the relation is asymmetrical, a point Liberman made throughout his work, and particularly in chapter 1 of *Lingüística, interacción comunicativa y proceso psicoanalítico* (1970–72, Vol. 1). No analyst doubts the need to be reserved, the need not to interject opinions, advice, admonitions and personal references.

Perhaps the greatest difficulty in the theory of therapeutic regression is not so much that it transforms a spontaneous process into an artefact, but that it can explain how an analysis begins, but never how it terminates. Ida Macalpine and Menninger pose this problem and recognize the difficulty. Macalpine, consequent with her rigorous points of view, is led to conclude that many of the achievements of analysis occur after termination. For his part, Menninger, with admirable honesty, says that he has not been able to integrate this point into his theory.

However, most of the defenders of therapeutic regression do not appear to consider this problem. They take for granted that, as the transference neurosis is resolved, the patient approaches the cure and the end of analysis. But then one must conclude that the regression was due to the illness (which is what diminished) and not to the setting, which remains constant.

At times we allow ourselves to be led by a type of optical illusion, and we say that a particular conflict (dependence on the mother, fear of castration *vis-à-vis* the father, sibling rivalry) acquired unusual intensity due to transference regression. If we observe well, we will see that the conflict already existed but was not recognized and was scattered in the varied relations of real life. Sibling rivalry, for example, will occur with the real brothers and sisters, with children, with friends, with colleagues, and so forth. If this rivalry were not active, its analysis would be unnecessary. It is the *gathering* of the transference, as Meltzer (1967, chapter 1) says with precision, that increases the sum of intensity of the transference phenomenon. In other words, as acting out diminishes thanks to our interpretative activity, the transference grows.

In straightforward opposition to those who believe the objective of the setting is to elicit regression, I think, as do many other writers, that the setting detects and reveals regression while it contains it. Furthermore, I maintain that Freud designed it thus in the second decade of the century, when he wrote his definitive essays on technique. It was the discovery of the transference, for example, that made Freud understand that he should be reserved. Therefore he suggests (1912e) that we should be impenetrable for the patient. If reciprocal confessions are established, Freud says, we abandon the psychoanalytic terrain and provoke an insatiable curiosity in the patient. In realizing the curiosity of the patient (which arises from infantile sexual investigation), Freud introduces the rule, and it is not that he shows himself to be reserved to awaken regressively the analysand's curiosity.

I agree with Zac when he asserts that "the setting is conceived so that the patient can achieve a therapeutic alliance with the analyst (once he has internalized the setting)" (1971, p. 600).

When in session 76a of little Richard's analysis in 1941 Melanie Klein arrives with a parcel for her grandchild and the patient discovers it, she realizes she has committed a technical error because, as she says, this arouses jealousy, envy and feelings of persecution in the patient (Klein, 1961, p. 387n). It is not that the analyst should not speak about his family so as not to awaken jealousy. Jealousy is there, and it is inadvisable to reactivate it artificially by speaking of children or grandchildren or, in this case, with revealing parcels. A "sensory deprivation" here would have saved little Richard from an inopportune attack of jealousy.

As far as possible, the setting, far from fomenting regressive phenomena, *avoids* them. Therefore the word *containment* is most adequate, due to its dual meaning.

It is not only the experience of Freud and his great followers that the setting becomes more rigorous on the basis of the hard lessons of clinical practice, but also that of each analyst in his individual development. Painfully we are learning to respect our setting, on seeing that when we ignore it we have to face intense regressive reactions in our patients.

To conclude, the setting was not designed to stir up regression but, on the contrary, to discover and contain it. It is not that the transference neurosis is a response to the setting, but that the setting is the most valid and rational response of our technique in the face of the phenomena of transference.

40.4   Arlow's and Brenner's ideas

In their account presented at the First Pan-American Congress, these distinguished investigators developed the theme, "The Analytic Situation", expounding very interesting ideas. We will study some of them in speaking of situation and process; others relate to the theme that occupies us here. Arlow and Brenner hold that the analytic situation has been designed with the intention of reaching the objectives of analytic therapy, that is, helping the patient to achieve a solution to his intrapsychic conflicts through understanding, which will allow him to manage them in a more mature way. In accordance with these postulates, a series of conditions is established in the analytic situation, thanks to which the functioning of the analysand's mind, his thoughts and the images that arise in his consciousness are determined endogenously to the limit as far as is humanly possible (1964, p. 32).

These writers doubt that the regression observed in the treatment derives from the setting (ibid., pp. 36–37), and they add that the analysand is not entirely passive, immature and dependent, as is frequently claimed; they end by insisting that the analytic situation is organized in accordance with the psychoanalytic theory of the functioning of the mind and responding to the objectives of psychoanalysis as therapy.

CHAPTER FORTY-ONE

Regression
as a curative process

In chapter 40 we discussed broadly an absorbing and difficult theme, the theory of *therapeutic* (or transference) *regression*, according to which the analytic setting stirs up a regressive process that institutes the transference neurosis and makes psychoanalytic treatment possible. We also said that this theory is not the only one that tries to explain the analytic process, nor the only one that proposes a relation between the setting (*holding*) and regression. For many writers the setting (*holding*) permits (more than promotes) a regression that is a *curative* (not a pathological) process. Among these, Donald W. Winnicott is the outstanding one, and we will concern ourselves particularly with his ideas.

41.1   On the concept of regression

To understand the complex discussion that follows, it is advisable to re-state the concept of regression itself, as Freud introduced it in *The Interpretation of Dreams* (1900a, chapter 7), where he distinguishes three types of regression: (1) *topographical* regression, which has to do with a forward–backward direction in the area of the Ψ systems; (2) *temporal* regression, which reverses the course of time and takes us to the past; and (3) *formal* regression, where there is a return from more mature to more primitive methods of expression (ibid., p. 548). The same ideas inform Freud's "A Metapsychological Supplement to the Theory of Dreams" (1917d).

Freud's classification is still extant, but it is indubitable that, since then, other writers have proposed different concepts or, at least, nuances that we should take into account if we are to discuss our theme with clarity. Thus, we would have to specify to what regression we are referring when we affirm that the psychoanalytic process is of a regressive nature or when we maintain the converse. Here and everywhere, if we follow a lax criterion, the concept will be more applicable but less rigorous.

Although it is true that, in introducing his classification in the book of dreams, Freud was not much in favour of separating the three types of regression—because in the end the three are actually one and the same I think that as the investigation discovered the forms, it also separated them. Freud said that what is oldest in time is most primitive in form, and topographically closest to the perceptual pole (1900a). But the most current concepts on the structure of the psychic apparatus allow the thought—without doing too much violence to the original concept—that regressive phenomena of a partial nature can occur, that regression does not have to operate necessarily as a totality. A regressive process can arise, then, at a chronological level, which does not entail the formal aspect. A formal regression may also take us from the secondary process to the primary process without our moving in time, as occurs in effect with jokes. When we make a joke or when we laugh at a joke told to us, we use the expressive forms of the primary process, but we are not thereby located in the past. I would even dare to say that the joke achieves its effect precisely because this dissociation is maintained between a formal regression and the adult who perceives and understands it (Freud, 1905c).

The concept of regression, then, should be used in a more rigorous way; it should be more restrictive, because sometimes a topographical regression that is not simultaneously formal or chronological can take shape. Many combinations can arise, although in practice most frequently the three types of regression appear together. An excellent example of these possible dissociations is Saura's technique in La prima Angélica [Cousin Angelica], where the chronological regression occurs without the formal and the topographical one. What most impresses the psychologist in Saura's original technique, I think, is that his artifice corresponds to a psychological reality, because when I remember the child I was, let us say, at the age of three, I do so from the perspective of the present, and I do not transfer myself completely to that situation. If I did so, I would have a disturbance in the localization of memory called ecmnesia.

41.2   Regression in the service of the ego

In dealing with insight, we will study in some detail the ideas that lead Kris from "The Psychology of Caricature" (1936) and "Ego Development and the Comic" (1938) to his substantial 1950 study of the preconscious mental process, on which he bases his concept of insight (1956a). Here we wish only to indicate that Kris compares the concept of pathological regression with that of *useful regression*, which he calls regression in the service of the ego. *Pathological* regression is something that overcomes the ego. The ego is dominated by it, and all it can do is to try to control it with its defence mechanisms. Regression *in the service of the ego*, on the other hand, is an active process. The ego makes use of it actively, stirs it up, directs it and employs it. It seems evident to me—and this evidence is ignored by most writers—that the regression Kris speaks of is always formal, sometimes topographical and never chronological. Without varying its temporal orientation, the ego directs itself to the id, and this sets in motion the primary process to re-establish its strength and creative capacity. This formal regression is accompanied more often than not by a topographical regression, which can be missing, however, if the recourse to the primary process occurs in the light of consciousness. Temporal regression, on the other hand, cannot occur, because it contradicts by definition what Kris says. Why revert to the primary process if there is no adult ego to put it in its service? If the regression were also chronological, there would be only an infantile (regressive) ego not competent to use it.

The key to an understanding of what Kris is saying is found in "On Preconscious Mental Process", which appeared in the *Psychoanalytic Quarterly* of 1950. In a series of interesting reflections, Kris explains there how the ego functions. Substantially, his basic theory is that the ego has, among its capacities or abilities, that of instrumental *regression* (returning) when it is convenient to do so. That is, there are types of regression. The first type overcomes the ego and is linked more to its defensive activities, which obliges it to retreat in the field of battle. As well as in this passive regression the ego is swept by when it cannot face a particular situation, there is another, in which the ego maintains all its potentialities while it regresses partially in a controlled way, with some strategic aim. An army does not always retreat because the other side is dominating it. At times retreat is a tactical manoeuvre so as to attack in another way or to confuse the other side. In the same sense, regression would be useful—a *regression in the service of the ego*—when the ego is itself able to stir up a regressive process to enrich itself through the contributions of the primary process. It is interesting that Kris speaks concretely—and he says so specifically in his article—of a formal regression, where the ego, which commands the secondary process, regresses towards the primary process and cathects it to incorporate it into its structure and to obtain greater scope, greater energy. In this way, the specific mobile energies of the primary process can be utilized by the ego, which transforms them into the bound energy of the secondary process. This point seems particularly important to me, because if we are going to accept a regression in the service of the ego, we will have to conceptualize it as formal in that the ego regresses or returns to the primary process, and eventually as topographical if there is a passage from the *Cs* or *Pcs* systems to the *Ucs*, but not as a chronological regression. Let us add that it is on the basis of the integrating function of the ego that this process can be realized, according to Kris (1950, p. 558).

Many writers go imperceptibly from therapeutic regression to regression in the service of the ego, with which, in my view, they fall into a conceptual error. The therapeutic regression the ego psychologists postulate is something that overcomes the ego in the difficult conditions of the analytic setting; it is not a useful regression, in Kris's sense, although it may be used by the analyst.

Among the attempts to apply Kris's ideas to the regressive phenomena proper to the analytic process, a work of note is that presented by Grinberg, Marie Langer, Liberman and the Rodrigués at the Pan-American Congress of Buenos Aires in 1966. For these writers the analytic process is seen in the light of phenomena of progression and regression, which is exact, although perhaps too wide a concept, since many processes, if not all, proceed in terms of advances and retreats. Within this wide framework, they try to specify the characteristics of the analytic process on the basis of *useful* and *pathological* regression. Specifying these concepts, they call pathological regression the one the patient *brings* to the treatment. Useful regression, on the other hand, refers to that tactical movement that goes backwards in order to leap forward, as Lenin would have said. "An analytic process implies *progress*, but we understand *progress* as a development where the useful regression on the couch serves as a primordial lever" (Grinberg et al., 1966a, p. 94). Grinberg et al. also postulate that there is a progression that damages the ego ("*progresión en perjuicio del yo*").

Winnicott's ideas approximate to Kris, somewhat, in that they assume that the process of regression is useful, but they rely on other theoretical supports and arise out of his practice with psychotic patients. Winnicott, a Freudian analyst, knew Freud well; Melanie Klein also had much influence on his work, although he parted from her at a given point, as we saw in discussing early transference. He has affinities with Anna Freud, whom he follows, for example, in the concept of primary narcissism. But he is not particularly interested in Hartmann's metapsychology. Also, to complete what I said earlier, the regression Winnicott studies is above all chronological; it has a projection in time. And it is basically the temporality of the analytic process that permits its development and establishment. This difference is fundamental for me, to the point where I would venture to assert that Kris's regression has to do with the analytic situation and Winnicott's with the analytic process.

41.3 *Brief review of Winnicott's ideas*

Let us recall briefly some of Winnicott's works, which we have already studied relating to early transference (chapter 16).

Winnicott arrived at psychoanalysis from paediatrics, and during World War II he analysed psychotics, from which he gained considerable experience. On the basis of this work, Winnicott distinguishes three types of patients in his valuable work "Primitive Emotional Development" (1945). This tripartite classification was maintained throughout his work and gradually became more precise.

The *first type* Winnicott distinguishes are the classic neurotics Freud described, understood and treated. They are able to relate to people as whole objects and present conscious and unconscious fantasies that enrich and create difficulties in this relation and are always linked to the Oedipus complex.

The *second type* are patients who are concerned with their internal world and organization; they are the ones Melanie Klein studied in her works on mourning, where depression and hypochondria occupy the salient place. (It must be borne in mind that this work by Winnicott antedates by a year that of Klein on schizoid mechanisms.) Although the structure of these patients differs from that of the others, the technique is still the same for Winnicott; it is not necessary to change anything.

Very different are the patients of the *third type*, where the object relations are pre-oedipal, prior to the depressive position defined by Melanie Klein (or Winnicott's *stage of concern*), and the classic technique is no longer appropriate. These are patients whose *primitive emotional development* has failed, and they have a basically psychotic structure.

While the first type of patient imagines that the analyst works for love of him (the patient), with which hate is deflected, the second imagines that the analyst's work arises from his (the analyst's) own depression, as a result of the destructive elements of his love in itself. But in the third case things change radically, and what the patient needs is for the analyst to be able to see his (the analyst's) love and hate converge on his object, the analysand. ("To progress further along these lines, the patient who is asking for help in regard to his primitive, predepressive relationship to objects needs his analyst to be able to see the analyst's undisplaced and co-incident love and hate of him"—1945, *Through Paediatrics*, p. 147.) For these patients, Winnicott continues, the end of the session and all the rules and regulations of analysis express the analyst's hate, just as good interpretations express his love.

In expounding Winnicott's ideas on countertransference, we saw that this writer attributes psychosis to environmental failure. Relying on Jones (1946) and on Clifford M. Scott (1949), Winnicott asserts in "Mind and Its Relation to the Psyche–Soma" (1949) that the mind is not in principle an entity for the individual who develops satisfactorily; it is, simply, a functional modality of his psyche–soma (corporal scheme).

In some individuals, however, the mind is differentiated as something apart, as an entity with a false localization. This deviant development supervenes as a result of mistaken behaviour on the mother's part, especially an erratic conduct that provokes excessive anxiety in the child.

An opposition develops then between the mind and the psyche–soma which leads to a false growth, a false self.

These original, suggestive and audacious ideas are again presented in "Psychosis and Child Care" (1952). ("Mind and Its Relation to the Psyche–Soma" was published in 1954, but it had been presented in 1949.) Here there is a clear exposition of the role of the environment (the mother) and its disturbances (*impingement*), which leads to the formation of the false self when the area of illusion fails.

41.4   *Regression according to Winnicott*

In the previous paragraph I expounded some of Winnicott's ideas without attempting to cover the range of his thought but only to see what his concept of regression stems from.

Given that psychosis is a failure of nurture, which leads the individual to configure a false self that protects the true self, it is logical to affirm that it will have a cure only when the primitive emotional development that was unsuccessful and deviated can be resumed through a singular experience that allows the individual to go back and begin again. The analytic setting, Winnicott says, offers the individual the adequate holding—the support—that makes that regression possible. The regression of the patient in the analytic setting signifies a return to early dependence, where the patient and the setting are fused in an experience of primary narcissism, on the basis of which the true self can finally resume development.

It seems, then, that what conditions regression for Winnicott is the positive aspect of the analytic holding. It is practically the opposite of what we previously discussed. It is precisely the permissive and gratifying element of the analytic holding that can stir up a regressive process that proceeds towards the cure via infantile dependence. The basic idea of transference regression did not, in fact, take account of this. The idea of transference regression takes account of the opposite, and Macalpine says so, limiting the circumstances, when she recognizes that, in fact, the permissive and gratifying aspects of the analytic situation should not condition a regression. What conditions regression, she says, are the frustrating aspects of the setting, which cause an adaptive response.

All these ideas achieve their most complete formulation in one of Winnicott's most famous works, "Metapsychological and Clinical Aspects of Regression Within the Psycho-Analytical Set-up", read at the British Psycho-Analytical Society in March of 1954 and published the following year.

In Type 3 patients, where primitive emotional development failed, where the mother was not able to contain the child, the analytical work applicable to Groups 1 and 2 should be set aside, at times for a long time.

The analyst will limit himself to allowing an intense regression of the patient in search of his true self and to observing the results.

It is necessary to underline that Winnicott understands the idea of regression within a highly organized defence mechanism of the ego, which involves the existence of a false self (1955, *Through Paediatrics*, p. 281).

Winnicott's conception stems from his ideas on primitive emotional development, which we have already explained, as well as from the postulate that the individual is able to defend his self against environmental faults, freezing the situation in the hope that a more favourable situation will occur. From this it is clear that, for Winnicott, regression is part of a healing process, a normal phenomenon that can be studied in the healthy person (ibid.).

When the individual freezes the situation that is preventing him from maturing so as to preserve his real self in development, the false self is organized. This *false self* appears as a "mental" process, already split off from the psychosomatic unity that had been maintained until then. The false self appears, then, as a very special defence to preserve the real self and can be modified only on the basis of a process of regression. However, Winnicott continues, the individual never completely loses hope and is always prepared to go back, in order to begin again the process of development from the point at which it was interrupted. This process of regression is a highly hierarchical and extremely complex defence mechanism, to which the individual is always prepared to have recourse when the environmental conditions give him some hope that now things can develop in another way.

41.5   Of Winnicott's theory and technique

When a serious developmental disturbance that has perturbed primitive emotional development with the formation of a false self has occurred, the only way to correct it is by giving the patient the opportunity to regress— this is not in the sense of a useful, momentary and formal regression in the service of the ego, but a temporal regression of whatever depth is necessary to arrive at the point where the situation was frozen, to begin again.

Just as for Group 1 patients the classic technique is appropriate where the setting serves as a support for the integrative process, and just as the Group 2 patients have sufficient integration for the classic technique to be applied to them (that of Freud), the situation is completely different for the third group. Winnicott postulates that the more serious the disturbance, the greater and more precocious was the fault in the milieu. Furthermore, these lesions, these injuries that occurred at the beginning of life, are cured only by being faced again and beginning anew. Here there is nothing for it but to repair the damage: one tries to offer the analysand conditions for the establishment of a healthy process of regression, always prepared to initiate itself, and for it to proceed as long as necessary and to the required depth. To succeed in ensuring this process, not to interfere with it, it is necessary to have skill, Winnicott says, because it is very difficult.

In these cases, the technique does not consist in interpreting but in accompanying, with understanding and without interfering, the inexorable process of regression the patient undertakes. The analyst should not interpret, nor should he support. He should allow the regressive process to continue, taking care of his patient. It is not always clear what Winnicott's technique consists of on this point. Are silence and company sufficient, or should there be some type of bodily contact?

It is also not easy to define the limits of the concept of environmental failure. Winnicott accepts a period of primary narcissism. When he broke from Melanie Klein in 1969 in the Symposium on Envy and Jealousy of the British Psycho-Analytical Society, he said that primitive emotional development can only be studied considering the mother–child dyad as an inseparable unity. Put in this way, and if we accept the concept of primary narcissism Winnicott maintains, then his methodological proposal should be accepted as an analytic and not a synthetic judgement in Kant's terms. But then it must be elucidated what role the two poles that compose that dyad play in it. This is because the methodological affirmation that the child cannot be studied separately from the mother also implies the opposite—that the environment, that is, the mother, should not be studied separately from the child. Since Winnicott never leaves out of consideration the genetic equipment of the newborn child, then inevitably the thought is that the child influences his environment (mother), with which we are already supporting the Freudian idea of complemental series that Klein utilizes, questioning at root the doctrine of environmental failure, which the child has nothing to do with.

Winnicott's theory of curative regression raises various objections, two of them fundamental, that refer to the technique and the theory.

With respect to the technique, in what way are we not to interfere with that process of regression the patient undertakes? It is difficult to say, and Winnicott never clarifies this completely. What does Winnicott mean when he says the patient does not need interpretations but, instead, certain specific care? As I have already said in my comments (and critique) of what Winnicott calls the real feelings in the countertransference, it seems evident to me that this writer supposes there are things that lie outside the analysand's (or the patient's) subjectivity.

With reference to the theory, the greatest issue pertains to the eternal dilemma of nature and culture. In his theory of development, Winnicott emphasizes the direct action of the milieu on the individual's development and does not make him as responsible as does Klein.

To discuss Winnicott on this point it is necessary to recall his ideas on primitive emotional development. Winnicott speaks of three processes—personalization, realization and integration—which arise in direct contact with the mother. Some patients have missed this, and the analyst's technique should then consist in allowing the patient to obtain from the analyst what he lacks—a notion of time, for example—that he did not initially obtain from his mother.

By *realization*, Winnicott means the process of adaptation to reality, which is effected in the area of illusion, where what the child hallucinates and the mother offers with her breast converge. Gradually the process enriches itself, so that, with each new experience, the child avails himself of what he obtained in the previous one and can now evoke. The contact with external reality is, then, frustrating in that it takes illusion away, but it is also highly gratifying in that it enriches and stimulates.

41.6   An example taken from Masud Khan

Khan (1960) presents the case of Mrs. X, a 40-year-old patient with a character neurosis and identity problems, in whom the transference neurosis took the form of an anaclitic regression in the analytic setting that made specific demands on the analyst personally. In the structure of this case it is evident that the characterological disturbance had the function of taking care of the self and, therefore, it distorted ego development and made its enrichment impossible, militating against genuine emotional experiences and object relations.

After nine months of treatment, Mrs. X began to withdraw from her social milieu and also from the analyst. She rejected transference interpretations but listened with much interest to the interpretations of her dreams and fantasies. A hypomanic state then developed in which the analysand felt herself to be in command of her life and her analysis, without the transference interpretations having any effect. This state shielded her from any feeling of dependence vis-à-vis her social milieu and her analysis: it was precisely the opposite of anaclitic regression (p. 136). Here I think there is a clear conceptual error, which permeates the whole theory of curative (healing) regression, in the idea that the manic defence that reverses the situation of dependence—on the basis of a return to early omnipotence—does not imply regression. (In the same way, Zetzel thinks that the excessive attachment of the obsessional neurotic to reality operates against the necessary process of regression in the setting, without understanding that this deceptive recourse to reality carries in itself the mark of regression.)

A few days before the first vacation, the analysand stole two books; the analyst offered to return them, which the analysand accepted gratefully.

In the second phase, which began after the holiday and lasted 18 months, a period of gradual and controlled regression supervened, which the analysand described as a state of being nothing, and from which she recuperated.

In this second year of analysis, the patient began to understand how her infantile conflicts were repeated in her marriage and her analysis. She made a decision to study, and the analyst also gave her specific help by suggesting reading material. After passing an examination without finding a favourable response in her husband, she began to regress. This period, which lasted for three months, was initiated with suicidal fantasies that were similar to those she had at the beginning of treatment, with an acute feeling of lack of self-esteem and a strong dependence on the analyst, who helped her in real matters every time she asked him to do so.

The emergence from the period of regression was produced after the patient again had suicidal fantasies, but now she herself considered them as an act of aggression towards her analyst. After this period, the analysand felt more real and was able to face her guilt feelings towards her mother, whom she had left in her native country, where she had died in the gas chambers.

The third part of the treatment lasted for six months; it began with a new conflict with the husband, who wanted the patient to look after their child before the time that had been agreed. The patient developed strong paranoid ideas against the husband and the analyst who connived against her. The analyst did not expect this reaction and found himself disarmed, while the analysand continued to attend the sessions and spoke but little. A battle was in progress, and the analyst began to feel she was compelling him to hate her, and interpreted this. He added later that if she felt threatened by husband and analyst conspiring against her with the idea that she should take care of her son, it was because she had murderous fantasies towards him. She then remembered some peculiarities of her period at the breast and the envy she felt against her younger brother and the feelings of murderous hate against him. This opened up the path to an analysis of oral sadism, with which the treatment approached its end.

This case, so well related by Khan, should be understood—as I see it—as a strong regression in the face of the separation of the first summer holiday and in terms of a strong negative transference. Had there been interpretation in that direction instead of the analyst offering himself as a good mother who returns books and takes specific care of her "daughter", the analysis could have developed along more regular channels, without recourse to the stage of regression. I also think that the paranoid experience of the analysand as to the analyst wanting her to take care of her child finds its nucleus of truth—as Freud would say—in this technique, which oscillates from the most profound regression to the most splendid adulthood.

41.7 The basic fault

On the basis of the active technique (Ferenczi, 1919b, 1920) and of the principles of relaxation and neocatharsis (Ferenczi, 1930) Michael Balint develops his lengthy and profound investigation which culminates in *The Basic Fault* (1968).

Like Winnicott and many others, Balint also divides analysands into two categories—those who reach the genital oedipal level and those who do not.

At the *oedipal level* of development both analyst and analysand have the same language at their disposal. The analyst's interpretation is an interpretation for the analysand, beyond the latter's acceptance or rejection, satisfaction or anger.

When the *basic fault* operates, a breach appears between analyst and analysand, which Ferenczi (1932) indicated clearly as a confusion of tongues between the adults and the child, in his presentation at the Wiesbaden Congress in September 1932. (Ferenczi died soon afterwards, aged 60, on 25 May 1933.)

At the oedipal level there is, then, a common language between the subject and the others, which has to do with a triangular, tripartite relation, with two persons and not one. In the Oedipus complex proper, this triangularity has its reference points in the father and the mother. But it is also found in the pregenital stages, where milk or faeces constitute this third element. A defining characteristic of this stage is that it is naturally bound to the conflict.

The principal characteristics of the other level, that of the basic fault, is that all the events that take place in it develop between two people; there is no third, and adult language is useless if not erroneous (Balint, 1968, pp. 16–17). "The chief characteristics of the level of the basic fault are (a) all the events that happen in it belong to an exclusively two-person relationship—there is no third person present; (b) this two-person relationship is of a particular nature, entirely different from the well-known human relationship of the Oedipal level; (c) the nature of the dynamic force operating at this level is not that of a conflict, and (d) adult language is often useless or misleading in describing events at this level, because words have not always an agreed conventional meaning" (Balint, 1968, pp. 16–17).

Balint thinks that analysis operates with two basic and equally important instruments, interpretation and the object relation. As can be deduced from his own argument, at the level of the basic fault the really operative factor is the object relation. The question then arises about what type of object relation the analyst should offer the analysand to repair the basic fault.

Balint thinks that, in order to reach the type of object relation the basic fault requires, the analyst should respond to the analysand's needs not with interpretations or words but, rather, with some type of enacted behaviour that respects, above all, the analysand's level of regression to a level where speech and words lack meaning. The analyst has to offer himself as an object that can be cathected by primary love. On this point, then, the analyst's greatest virtue is to be there without interfering. The analyst should renounce completely his omnipotence, to achieve a position of equality with his analysand, where interpretation, management and corrective emotional experience are equally extemporaneous. It should not be forgotten that in the area of the basic fault there is no conflict and, therefore, nothing to resolve.

Balint's technique, which I have just outlined briefly, differs in many aspects from that of Winnicott, in that it eludes all management of the regression, and even of that proposed in his works of the 1930s. (See, for example, "Early Development States of the Ego. Primary Object Love", 1937.) Here all the analyst "does" is to tolerate the regression of the analysand, without aspiring to overcome it with interpretations or manoeuvres that try to re-establish his omnipotence. If this attitude is to be understood as a moment of reflection and respect for the analysand and for our own labour, then Balint's proposal only adds a grain of philosophical modesty to our daily technique—which is no small thing!

41.8 The testimony of Margaret Little

It is difficult to be certain about the particularities of Winnicott's technique because his writings deal more with the strategy of inducing regression and dependence than with the tactics directed to that end. At the beginning of the decade of the 1990s—more precisely, in 1990—a book by Margaret Little appeared that is a valuable document that helps to dispel our ignorance in this respect. No one can doubt the author's truthfulness and courage, and we all respect her contributions on transference and countertransference theory (Little, 1981). Even if a single person's testimony cannot, of course, be definitive, this one makes a convincing impression, particularly as it is consistent with what can be inferred from a careful reading of Winnicott's works.

Little was in analysis with Ella Freeman Sharpe from 1940 until 1947. During those years, encouraged by her analyst, she decided to make a career in the British Psycho-Analytical Society, where she qualified first as an Associate Member and subsequently as a Member.

At the end of 1945 a distressing event occurred in Margaret Little's life. Her father became seriously ill and then died. In the week of the funeral, she was supposed to read the paper that would qualify her for full membership, but she did not want to do so in order not to disturb her mourning. Ella Sharpe insisted on her presenting it and interpreted that she was envious of her own ability to write papers. Little shows herself to be very critical of her analyst concerning that episode and even writes: "Between my immediate distress and my psychotic transference, I could not stand up to her, but I felt it as a massive interference with my mourning" (Little, 1990, p. 36). She offers this incident as an example of Sharpe's mistakes. At any rate, she did read her paper, and it was praised. If Ella Sharpe urged Margaret Little to present it and even resorted to threats, then that, to me, as an opponent of the active technique of analysis, was a mistake. I wonder, too, what Little would have made of it if Winnicott, on the basis of the theories of holding and regression to dependence, had done the same.

A year later analyst and patient agreed to terminate the analysis, and Margaret Little travelled to Amsterdam for a Congress. There she was able to enjoy the company of friends and colleagues and even became aware for the first time of a man's interest in her. To judge from these results, Sharpe's analysis must have been quite effective. Yet Little never tires of criticizing her for having interpreted only the Oedipus complex and infantile sexuality and not having touched upon her early anxieties.

On her return to London, Little received the unfortunate news that her analyst had died. She was helped by Sylvia Payne and Marion Milner, and ultimately opted to go to Donald Winnicott.

The analysis with Winnicott began in 1949 and was marked by many vicissitudes. A powerful resistance marked its commencement. In one of the early sessions Margaret Little was seized with despair and had an impulse to throw herself out of the window, but she rejected the idea because she felt that Winnicott would stop her. She then thought of flinging all the books in the library onto the floor and eventually smashed a vase filled with lilacs. Winnicott left the room, returning just before the end of the hour while the patient was attempting to clear up the mess she had made. At the next session, an exact replica of the vase and flowers had replaced the originals. A few days later Winnicott told her that he had greatly valued that object. Recalling this episode on one occasion after the analysis was over, both agreed that Winnicott had made a technical error because he had not been prepared to contain that fit of destruction; that is why he had left the consulting-room.

After the vase incident, the analysand started having spasms of terror that made her grab Winnicott's hands and cling to them; in this way he held her throughout her session. Little presents this as an illustration of Winnicott's containing attitude. Holding is, of course, a key concept in his technique. As Little points out, it must be understood both figuratively and literally. *Metaphorically*, "holding" means making contact with the analysand at every level and assuming the responsibility not accessible to his weak ego; *literally*, it entails an acceptance that the analyst will allow the analysand to cling to his hands, will hold his head, will offer him food, and so on. In the case in question, and given that Winnicott himself considered it a technical error to have left the consulting-room, his patient's subsequent terror spasms could also have been contained with an interpretation of what had passed: "You feel terror that I will leave the consulting-room again, leaving you at the mercy of your impulses"—or something along these lines.

A significant experience in Little's analysis was when she told Winnicott about the death of a childhood friend: tears came into his eyes, and this allowed Margaret to cry for that far-off loss as she had never done before. She recalled that her mother had never let her cry and had once said: "Cheer up, darling! You'll soon be dead." Winnicott grew angry and exclaimed: "I really *hate* your mother!"—thereby making the analysand's words a reality. For Margaret Little, these *direct* answers are an essential part of the holding offered her by Winnicott.

Winnicott's open, spontaneous gesture in saying "I really *hate* your mother" must surely have been a great help to Margaret Little in her constant struggle against her mother; however, it was also a departure from the sober neutrality of the method that protects us from seduction and idealization. This technique is justified by the analysand's level of regression, from which she can be rescued only by such a direct intervention, on the assumption that these experiences go beyond words. Yet this is a highly debatable idea—and Dr Little herself unwittingly calls it into question when she writes: "As he [the analysand] is not an infant he reacts to failures in an adult way, with an adult body, so that there is danger" (ibid., p. 90). This implies that there are two ways rather than one of resolving psychotic anxieties: either entering into the *direct* relationship in which transference and countertransference act on each other to abolish subject–object polarity, or establishing with the patient a communication that preserves asymmetry and discrimination.

In the Winnicottian conception, regression to dependence is the procedure of choice for acceding to and resolving psychotic anxieties. This is amply illustrated by Margaret Little's book: Winnicott, for example, gave her extended 90-minute daily sessions that ended with coffee and cakes.

Following the anguished summer holidays of 1952, Winnicott, afraid that she might commit suicide, suggested that the following year she should spend the corresponding period in hospital. After an initial violent protest, she eventually agreed. Once the 1953 London International Congress was over, Winnicott took Little to a psychiatric hospital, where she spent five weeks. Here she found the *facilitating environment* that allowed her to regress to dependence, while Winnicott, on holiday, remained constantly in touch with her. This illustration deserves some comment. In view of the eminently personal character of regression to dependence, which entails returning to the very source of life—going back to the mother in search of the true self—it becomes difficult for me to accept that this process could be delegated to a third party, let alone to an impersonal one like a hospital. Yet that is how Margaret Little understands it.

What is clear is that, after she left hospital, Margaret Little's analysis proceeded without problems. It soon aligned itself with the classical model, involving analysis of the Oedipus complex and of infantile sexuality, which were accessible once the psychotic anxieties had been analysed.

I agree with Grotstein in finding another technical aspect of regression to dependence hard to understand. Little tells us that patients sometimes had to queue up to begin the process of regression to dependence, because Winnicott could offer himself to only one patient at a time: "The timing of a full regression could not be mine alone; it depended to a large extent on his case load. He spoke of patients having to 'queue up' sometimes to go into such a state, one waiting until another had worked through it and no longer needed him in that way. But it was mine insofar as it could not be until I was ready" (ibid., p. 47f.).

We must, then, once again suppose here that the process of regression to dependence is not spontaneous, at least as regards its onset; it depends on the adult collaboration of the patient, who must wait his turn. Why should we not try to elicit the same collaboration from the patient for the analysis of his psychotic nuclei? Grotstein asks the same question in his introduction to Little's book: "How he was able to stave it off in those patients waiting their turn is incomprehensible" (Grotstein, 1990, p. 6).

* * *

In seeking to follow Margaret Little's book carefully so as to point out certain unclear aspects of Winnicott's technique, I had an opportunity to put his ideas to the test.

CHAPTER FORTY-TWO

Separation anxiety
and psychoanalytic process

42.1   Summary and introduction

In the previous discussion we tried to establish some relations between the psychoanalytic process and regression.

We began by explaining the theory that regression is a function of the process. We call this explanation of the ego psychologists *therapeutic regression*, according to which the analytic environment conditions a regressive process, which is a necessary condition for approaching the patient in psychoanalytic treatment. I indicated that this thesis is at least questionable and, in my view, erroneous. Many writers think, as I do, that the patient's psychopathology—and not the analytic setting—gives rise to regression, although they do not always bother to make this assertion or provide bases for it. The critique of the ego psychologists' theory of therapeutic regression can be made through a simple question: if interpretation is able to demolish the defences, why is it not also able to modify them? This critique, made on the basis of the ego psychologists' own argument, is difficult for them to answer. As far as I know, Rapaport never posed this question. If interpretation can do more, it should also be able to do less.

In counterposition to therapeutic regression (or regression in the setting, as it is also called) we mentioned the concept of regression conceived as a healing process. This conception is diametrically opposed to the previous one. In the former conception, the setting induces in the analysand a regressive process, which the treatment eventually cures him of, whereas in the latter the regressive process arises thanks to the setting and is essentially curative, like a spontaneous movement towards health. Among the writers who defend this idea we have studied Winnicott, but Balint, Bruno Bettelheim and others think the process of regression is very curative. One of Bettelheim's works is called "Regression as Progress" (1972) to emphasize that what we call regression is ultimately a progressive process. It is worth indicating here that what this article says is not identical to what Winnicott maintains, nor to Balint's proposals with his initial idea of *new beginning* (1937, 1952) and later (1968) of the basic fault. But in any case, the idea that the process of regression carries in itself the seed of the cure is common to all these writers. Consequently, the analyst has to respect and not interfere with this movement.

To distinguish these theories from the other one, we grouped them under the title of *healing regression*. We also said this is not an unassailable theory. Although no scientific theory is, the idea that it is necessary to regress to the sources in order to take a new and different path from there poses problems at the level of theory and practice, and perhaps at the ethical level. I discussed this in chapter 41 and fixed there my personal position, accepting that the theme should remain open because I believe the problem has not been decidedly resolved.

With reference to Winnicott, the writer who most brilliantly developed this theory, it is evident that he establishes a difference between those patients in whom primitive emotional development is affected (and for whom some type of management is required) and patients who arrive at the stage of *concern*, equivalent to Melanie Klein's depressive position, or those who reach the triangular situation, where the classic technique is perfectly applicable.

In all these works, then, Winnicott reduces management—whatever it may be—to a reduced group of patients. It is more difficult to decide what this management consists in. It is possible to respond in different ways, and I think I am not wholly mistaken if I affirm that Winnicott himself vacillates. Sometimes *management* suggests what would be common to all of us; at other times it resembles Sechehaye's (1951) symbolic realization and gives one the feeling that with this concept Winnicott departs considerably from the classic technique.

42.2   *The concept of holding*

In this chapter we discuss another theme, which is linked to the previous one but radically different from it, in studying the analytic process in virtue of what maintains it and what makes it possible. Although the theories may differ in many respects, the idea that analysis should offer the patient particular conditions so that he can be analysed is something contained in and accepted by all the theories, because, in effect, this is beyond question. At this point the concept of regression does not interest us any longer; we only need to know which elements of the setting offer the natural framework of containment to enable the process to develop.

The theme that concerns us now is linked to a modality of anxiety—
that is, *separation anxiety*, as Freud studies it in *Inhibitions, Symptoms and
Anxiety* (1962d) in relation to the absence of the object (mother). What
interests us is the way this anxiety leaves a deep mark in the analytic
process. As we conceive it, the analytic process tries to be isomorphic in
some way with reality. Therefore this separation anxiety is no more than a
special type of linking modality in which the subject needs someone at his
side. If separation anxiety exists and makes itself felt in the analytic situation, then the analyst has a twofold task—that of lending it a support and,
at the same time, that of analysing it.

This is the theme that will concern us in the following chapters, beginning with Meltzer's contributions following Klein's ideas on projective
identification. We will deal with another Meltzer—the one who begins
from Esther Bick's studies on the skin and on autistic children. Subsequently and elsewhere we shall try to see how Winnicott's theory of holding (or of separation anxiety in general) can acquire a greater level of
abstraction in Bion's ideas of container and contained. The moral of the
theme we initiate here is that the analyst's task consists largely in detecting, analysing and resolving separation anxiety. Let us say here that this
process arises in all the cycles of the analysis: from session to session, from
week to week (where we can perhaps grasp it most and to which Zac has
made relevant contributions), during the holidays and, of course, at the
end of treatment. Let us add that the interpretations that tend to resolve
these conflicts are decisive for the course of the analysis and not always
easy to formulate. The analyst sometimes does not understand this type of
anxiety in all its magnitude. The patient, for his part, is entirely set on not
understanding it, in that to recognize it leads him to a dangerous dependence on the object, the analyst. Therefore the possibility of interpreting
separation anxiety accurately is always reduced or limited. Patients often
tell us that interpretations of this type sound hackneyed and conventional.
They are often right, because if there is something which, in fact, cannot be
interpreted in a routine manner, it is separation anxiety: it is not something conventional, but full of life. A warning here, however—the best
interpretations of anxieties of separation are those the patients resist most
and vehemently object to as conventional.

This clinical phenomenon is more in evidence for the experienced analyst who has learned to interpret separation anxiety with accuracy and in
time. Those still in the process of learning do not always notice it, and at
times they are discouraged by the stubborn and challenging criticisms of
the analysand, as is observable in the process of supervision.

This phenomenon can be explained in various ways: through fear of
dependence and of repeating the traumas of infancy; or because it wounds
the narcissism and megalomania of someone who thought himself independent, or because of envy. I believe all these alternatives exist, and
among them the envy of the analyst as an object that accompanies and is
present carries a weight that cannot be set aside.

42.3   *Projective identification and separation anxiety*

Here we will deal with writers such as Meltzer and Resnik, who interpret separation anxiety from the point of view of the theory of projective identification and what underlies it—a theory of mental space, of the space of the internal world. Their works help to interpret separation anxiety more precisely and clearly. Interpretations in this area are not always made at the correct level. In general, the inexperienced analyst tends to locate himself on a level of greater integration than the patient has. He tells him, for example, that the patient missed him during the weekend. This interpretation is sometimes very optimistic, because it implies that the analysand is able to distinguish subject and object. Most frequently, especially at the beginning of treatment, separation anxiety is denied, reinforcing narcissism, which is the great solution to all problems. This is why Meltzer says in the first chapters of *The Psychoanalytical Process* (1967) that massive projective identification is the best defence against separation anxiety.

In severe cases—those Meltzer studied in his 1966 work on anal masturbation and projective identification—an almost delusional structure can be discerned, which has to do with pseudo-maturity and constitutes a serious psychopathological problem. (Meltzer calls *pseudomaturity* a group of phenomenological data that correspond clinically with Winnicott's *false self*, with Helene Deutsch's, 1942, as if personality and with what Karen Horney, 1950, calls the *idealized image of the self in Neurosis and Human Growth*.) In pseudo-maturity there is recourse to very energetic projective identifications, which disturb reality and the autonomy of internal objects to deny separation anxiety in an almost delusional type of functioning.

The efficacy of massive projective identification to account for separation anxiety resides precisely in that the anxious part of the self is resolutely, violently placed in an object (external or internal). In this way the analysand presents himself as free of anguish, and no interpretation will be operative while we are not able to reverse the process of projective identification. If we interpret without taking this into account, it is certain that we will hit our heads against a brick wall: the wall of projective identification where our effort is rejected. In fact, these interpretations are not only naive, but also imprudent and mistaken, because if the analysand put into me or into his wife that part of himself that is able to feel the link of dependence, my telling him that he missed me is completely false. He did not miss me, because he did something precisely so as not to have to do so.

What Meltzer teaches us is that these difficulties can be resolved only by attending to the great complexity of a process that sometimes acquires a delusional hue, where the subject–object confusion is very great and is in the service of denying separation anxiety.

* * *

To sum up: When it mobilizes primitive ego mechanisms, separation anxiety can utilize anal masturbation to carry out an act corresponding to a model of intrusion into the object, which, in the final instance, shields the subject from that threat. Once this type of defence has been consummated, we will have to "search for" our patient, as Resnik (1967) says, lost in a place of infinite space where we will find him inside the object where he placed himself. First we have to find the analysand and then bring him to the session. Only then will we be able to make an interpretation in the here and now, because, obviously, if the patient is not "here", there is no point making a *hic et nunc* interpretation.

It is interesting to note that these same mechanisms operate also in less severe cases, that is, in neurosis, where they should equally be interpreted. (We will return to this subject in a subsequent chapter, when we deal with geographical confusions.)

42.4   *The role of anal masturbation in separation anxiety*

That masturbation is the remedy most used to overcome solitude and jealousy in the face of the primal scene is something we all learned from the pioneer analysts. But on the basis of the work Meltzer presented at the Amsterdam Congress, "The Relation of Anal Masturbation to Projective Identification" (published in the *International Journal of Psycho-Analysis* in 1966), the link between solitude, separation anxiety and masturbation acquires another significance, a more profound and complex one. Meltzer maintains in that paper that anal masturbation has an intimate and intrinsic relation with projective identification: at the critical moment of separation, the baby who sees the mother retreat, turning her back on him, identifies the breast with the mother's buttocks, and these with his own. Then a masturbatory activity begins, in which he introduces his fingers into the rectum, and thus anal masturbation becomes the model for projective identification. In patients who are not excessively disturbed, not clearly psychotic, anal masturbation has a cryptic character. This is why, if the analyst wishes to integrate this body of theory into his interpretations on separation anxiety, he perforce has to detect it in the material from dreams or fantasies. Genital masturbation is generally more manifest than the anal variety, which does not imply we should neglect the latter in interpreting separation anxiety.

The theory of projective identification Meltzer uses naturally follows the tradition of Melanie Klein's early works, when the latter maintained the universality of the process of masturbation and emphasized that the guilt that accompanies it is always linked to aggressive impulses against the objects. In this way, in interpreting separation anxiety one must pay attention not only to what is projected, but also to the *consequences* of the projection. It is not merely due to the need to alleviate separation anxiety that a person gets inside an object, but also because of aggressive motives, to erase the difference between subject and object. Aggression, envy and jealousy always participate in the process.

I think that this concept of masturbation as an expression of jealousy and especially of envy is a distinctive feature of Kleinian analysts. The always lively polemics on whether negative transference should be interpreted at the outset refers in the final instance to how and when separation anxieties and their contents are installed.

42.5 Separation anxiety, time and space

Beyond the extreme cases Meltzer describes as pseudomaturity, it can be asserted that whenever one interprets on the basis of the mechanisms of projective identification, one is touching on the patient's omnipotence and narcissism, as well as on his pseudo-maturity. In consequence, it is possible that the patient responds by placing himself above the analyst, to deny the dependence. It is then necessary to tune the analytic instrument to detect in this response the sometimes subtle indicators that allow us to dismantle this defence.

Resnik tries to answer some of these issues with his emphasis on space in the analytic situation. It is one thing for me to talk about Russell Square to my analyst, and another to talk to him *from* there. If the latter occurs, my analyst's possibilities of communicating with me are as distant as this beautiful square near the British Museum is from Buenos Aires.

Resnik's contribution is therefore interesting, in that it warns us that, in cases such as this, if we wish to apply our technique better, the first thing we have to do is to tell the patient something that can "bring" him from the square to the consulting-room.

Projective identification implies by definition a conception of space; but it can also be said that it is through projective identification that this notion is acquired. This is a difficult problem, which Resnik tries to resolve by saying that one must not confuse projective identification, which already implies a recognition of space, with the narcissistic prolongations to extracorporeal space, which he considers a process *prior* to projective identification. That is, Resnik distinguishes two processes: that of projective identification proper, and a previous process, which he describes with the use of pseudopodia, in the sense that the pseudopodia do not imply the knowledge of space because they are inside the subject.

Resnik's theory, ingenious but questionable, seems to return to the classic concept of primary narcissism. Although Melanie Klein does not say so specifically, her theory of object relations is also a theory of space and, in this sense, to claim that at the beginning there is no space signifies that there is no object either. We will see further on that Bick and Meltzer face the same type of problem when they maintain that at first it is necessary to create a space so that projective identification can operate. On this point, I think that the theory of projective identification should be accepted just as Melanie Klein formulated it, as a theory that includes the concept of object relation that is inseparable from space; if not, it should be abandoned in favour of theories based on primary narcissism.

León and Rebecca Grinberg also pose this difficult problem in a more recent work, "Modalidades de relaciones objetales en el proceso analítico, [The Modalities of Object Relations in the Analytic Process] (1981), where the notions of time and space occupy a prominent place. The Grinbergs' reflections deserve a special mention with regard to the link Bion calls *"at-one-ment* with O", a state of unification with O which, as far as I can understand it, revives the hypothesis of primary narcissism.

42.6   *Adhesive identification*

The works we discussed in the previous sections are based essentially on the relation between separation anxiety and projective identification. Both Resnik and Meltzer are analysts who know Melanie Klein in depth, follow her teachings and operate with the concept of projective identification. However, we have already noted that Resnik thinks there is something *before* projective identification (mental pseudopodia), which we discussed briefly. Now we will see that Meltzer—at a given moment in his investigation—also feels that development does not begin with projective identification. I think the Grinbergs also incline towards this idea.

For many years the idea of projective identification has structured the thought of the Kleinian school and has influenced others, perhaps more than it seems. The one who has made most use of it among the ego psychologists in the United States is surely Otto Kernberg (1969), who may differ from Klein in many aspects but knows and respects her. In recent years, Joseph Sandler has paid much attention to this idea. As the Sigmund Freud Professor of Psychoanalysis in the Hebrew University of Jerusalem, he called, in 1986, the First Conference of the Sigmund Freud Centre, which dealt with projective identification. On that occasion the outstanding specialists Betty Joseph, Otto F. Kernberg, W. W. Meissner and Rafael Moses spoke on the subject. Sandler chaired the meeting and read a paper on the concept of projective identification, following its development from when Melanie Klein introduced it, up to the present time.

After the introduction of this concept in the work on schizoid mechanisms of 1946, the Kleinian school considers projective identification as a prototype that can be counterposed in a valid way to introjective identification. For some writers this discovery marks the zenith of Klein's creation and justifies considering her a genius, not simply a first-class investigator like others. It is advisable to emphasize that the idea of projective identification also proposes a revolutionary concept of narcissism, since it is parts of the self (together with impulses and internal objects) that are placed in the object. The self maintains a relation with this object, in that in some obscure way it recognizes the parts as its own. A confusion between subject and object is thus defined, or it can also be said that this is a type of relation where there is a strong narcissistic component. That is, once I have placed something of mine in the object, my relation with it refers in part to myself.

For many years, according to Meltzer (1975), for the Kleinian school the concept of projective identification was synonymous with narcissistic identification. In this way, the two types of identification Freud describes in *The Ego and the Id* (1923b)—primary identification and secondary identification (to a process of mourning)—are subsumed in introjective and projective identification. But with Esther Bick's brief, three-page article on "The Experience of the Skin in Early Object-Relations" (1968), a new panorama opens up.

Bick effectively proposes a new type of narcissistic identification and therefore of object relation, which implies a rupture with what, until then, was understood on the basis of the theory of projective identification.

The basic idea of Bick's work is that, beyond the object's corporeality (that is, postulating that the object has depth) there is another type of narcissistic identification—a *very* narcissistic one—in that the superimposition of subject and object is very great, and in which the idea of "getting in" is replaced by that of "getting in contact with". This process is very archaic and always appears linked to an object of psychic reality equivalent to the *skin*. Initially the self experiences itself as needy parts of an object that contains and unifies them, and this object is the skin as an object of psychic reality. This skin object must be incorporated early on, because if and only if this incorporation occurs can projective mechanisms function: while there is no space in the self, these mechanisms cannot function, by definition (Bick, 1968, p. 484).

As Esther Bick herself says in her enduring work, the containing aspect of the analytic situation resides particularly in the setting, and therefore in this area firmness in technique is crucial (ibid., p. 486).

This work raises the importance of the psychoanalytic setting and its firmness in the process of development which is the analytic cure, taking into account that analysis is a *relation*, and that this relation is not continuous but *discontinuous*. In the psychoanalytic process there are obviously many interruptions: holidays, weekends and, perhaps the worst of all, those that occur from day to day—a difference of 50 minutes as against 23 hours.

The innovative theory of adhesive identification, which begins with Bick, is developed and expanded afterwards in the book by Meltzer and his collaborators, John Bremner, Shirley Hoxter, Doreen Weddell and Isca Wittenberg (1975) on autism. It is full of suggestions and an audacious exploration of origins. Where these investigations are going and where they will take us—since, in effect, they pose the possibility of a new theory of development—is not something that has to be discussed in this book. It is more a problem of developmental psychology than specifically a problem of technique, although we cannot elude it with a methodological side-step.

These works of the English school correspond noticeably to the investigations of Didier Anzieu (1974) on *le moi-peau* [the skin ego]. With a different theoretical support, Anzieu indicates the basic importance of the skin in early development and relates it beautifully to the "bath of words" with which the mother envelops the infant. Although the theory is the same, the technical consequences vary noticeably, and where the Englishwoman derives the necessity for a firm skin-setting, the Frenchman favours a more tolerant and indulgent attitude.

In *Explorations in Autism* (Meltzer et al., 1975) Meltzer, in taking up again the problem of adhesive identification, speaks of four types of object relation, which are also various types of conception of space—of what he calls dimensionality, which has a history, a development. For Meltzer there is *one-dimensional* space, defined as and by the instinct that arrives, touches and leaves. Time and space are fused in a lineal dimension of self and object, in a radial world like that of the amoeba and its pseudopodia. The objects are attractive or repellent, and time is not distinguished from distance—a closed time, a mix of distance and velocity. The autistic world is, for Meltzer, of this type—one-directional and mindless, a series of events not at the disposal of memory or thought (compare this with what Resnik says about pseudopodia).

Bi-dimensional space, that of adhesive identification, is a space of contacts, of surfaces, perhaps what Freud has *in mind* when he says that the ego is a surface that contacts other surfaces (*The Ego and the Id*). The significance of the object depends on the sensual qualities that can be grasped on its surface, with which the self also experiences itself as a sensitive surface. Thought cannot develop when there is "a lack of an internal space within the mind in which fantasy as trial action, and therefore experimental thought, could take place" (*Explorations in Autism*, p. 225). Here Meltzer agrees with what Arnaldo Rascovsky maintains since he published in 1960 *El psiquismo fetal* [Foetal Psychism].

Then there is *tridimensional* space, where projective identification dominates. It arises once the object has been experienced as resistant to penetration, and the concept of orifices in the object and in the self is constituted. The object is thus transformed into a tridimensional and containing one, and the self also acquires the third dimension in identifying with it. Time is now oscillatory in that it is conceived through the fantasy of entering and leaving the object through projective identification. Meltzer says that "time which had been indistinguishable from distance in the one-dimensional mindlessness and had achieved a certain vague continuity or circularity from moving from point to point on the surface of a two-dimensional world, now begins to take on a directional tendency of its own, a relentless movement from inside to outside the object" (Meltzer et al., 1975, p. 226).

Adhesive identification offers a new explanation for a phenomenon described by many writers, such as Helene Deutsch (*as if personality*), Winnicott (*pseudo-self* or *false self*), Bleger (*factual personality*), Meltzer (*pseudomaturity*). When various writers whose ways of thinking are diverse describe the same phenomenon, this is because they are seeing something that exists, that is universal. What characterizes these patients is a note of inauthenticity, which makes one think that the process of identification occurs in a really superficial way. It is attractive to think that this superficiality corresponds to the dynamic process of adhesive identification; but it could not be so. We have already seen that Meltzer himself introduced the concept of pseudo-maturity in his 1966 work and makes it derive from projective identification with the internal parents.

In any case, all these theories point to a special type of reaction, which is characterized by its inauthenticity (falseness). The clinical value of this concept is very great, because it gives us precious elements for understanding a particular type of patient. Without these theories it is easier to react badly towards them—with contempt or rage, for example. If an analysand identifies with me through an unimportant detail of my attire, I may feel more bothered than if he does so through one of my character traits. But in fact in both cases he is expressing a form of identification, nothing more. The two processes should be understood and not judged axiologically.

It is necessary to indicate that we must always distinguish, with particular clinical material, the type—adhesive, projective, or introjective—of identification. On the other hand, as always, the manifest material will never be what is decisive. The same act, the same symbol can express different levels of the process. I remember a patient from many years ago who, on beginning his analysis, started to wear a waistcoat, as I do. Some years later, however, the waistcoat represented the breast for him, and then the process had another meaning. In this difficult task of discrimination, what perhaps helps us most is an experience of countertransference when one feels that the identification is very false or naive.

Finally, there is *tetra-dimensional* space, which includes the notion of time, linked to introjective identification, that is, to the idea that time does not return. At this level of development a new type of identification operates, which Freud discovered and described in *The Ego and the Id* (Klein's introjective identification?), which is no longer narcissistic in that it is founded on a conception of space and time that recognizes the existence and autonomy of the object.

The ideas of Bick and Meltzer are attractive and directly applicable to certain configurations of the analytic process. In this sense they are useful in practice in the consulting-room, as I have tried to show in a work I wrote with Norberto Bleichmar and Celia Leiberman de Bleichmar some years ago (Etchegoyen et al., "El sueño como superficie de contacto" [The Dream as a Contact Surface], 1979). At times the quality of the identification process seems to warn us that the analysand does not seek to enter the object but to be in contact with it through an imitative, naive and mimetic conduct. This was particularly clear in the case presented at the Symposium on Dreams in 1979. It was about a young woman of 22, afflicted with a severe dermatitis, and with important psychological problems. Her clinical history strongly suggested a period of infantile autism, and her object relations were always adhesive, superficial and fickle. This type of link appeared in analysis in various ways, but especially in the relating of dreams, which was used as an interface to contact the analyst, where the dream related represented exactly what Bick calls *second skin*—a phenomenon that replaces real contact by another false, artificial one. This form of contact provoked countertransference reactions of rejection, until the interpretative task centred on the analysand's efforts to link herself via adhesive identification, with which the (until then) erratic analytic situation changed considerably.

42.7   Improvisation on developmental theories

The ideas we have studied in the last two chapters constantly bring us back from the theories of the psychoanalytic process to those of development—that is to say, to developmental psychology, and more exactly to the developmental psychology of the first year of life.

Freud was able to elaborate a theory of infantile development (the Oedipus complex) on the basis of the analysis of adult men and women, through reconstructions and with his theory of transference. His hypotheses were subsequently strongly supported by child analysts.

On the basis of her play technique, Melanie Klein tried to reconstruct early development, showing that analytic instruments can give us information about the earliest period of human life. To follow or refute her, other investigators and other researches appeared. We have dealt with some, but not all of these, in these chapters and the corresponding ones on early transference.

We have explained some ideas on how the child's notions of space and time may be constructed. If we follow Bick and Meltzer, we would have to think of the notion of space as a representation of *sui generis* characteristics—as another thing or object where the rest of the representations are contained. This is what seems to emanate from these works on the basis of Bick's initial description. Would we then have to conclude that there is an evolution from the one-dimensional to the tetra-dimensional? There is no complete answer; these questions are being investigated.

Resnik, whose thinking, I believe, is close to Bion's, explains how things as such can enter the mind on condition that we conceive the mind as a space where things can be located. To the extent that I feel that "Russell Square is in my mind" or that "the sea is in my mind" (not that I have the image of the square or the sea), I am denying the distance— which is also to deny loss and absence. I can only have an image of the sea when the sea itself is not there, when I recognize its absence. On this point, Resnik's ideas relate to Bion's (1962a, 1962b) theory of thinking as well as Hanna Segal's (1957, 1978) works on symbolism. Bion would say that the Russell Square that is in the mind cannot be processed as an *alpha* element but simply as a *beta* element.

There is undoubtedly some difference between the existentialists' notion of space as categorical and almost ontological, and the space Meltzer, Resnik and, more recently, the Grinbergs, have studied. The space they refer to derives from a theory of object relations that is silent about the categories of space and time Kant thinks of as *a priori* forms of sensibility suitable for the ordering of experience.

The conception of space that Resnik's amoeba might have must be very much like that of Meltzer's one-dimensional space. If the experience consists in sending out a pseudopodium and retracting it, the idea of space must be lineal and that of time will be perforce subsumed in the other: time is how long I take to send out my pseudopodium and retract it.

To conclude, let us say that, in fact, the processes of the beginning of life are very difficult to elucidate and apprehend. As we approach the origins, the facts become more subordinate to the theories with which we are obliged to contemplate them. Currently the solution is being sought along other paths, such as baby observation and ethology. Among us, José A. Valeros (1981) has most resolutely made known the new studies on baby observation, while Terencio Gioia has lucidly applied the contributions of ethology to the theory of instincts (1977, 1983a) and to the explanation of early psychic development (1983b). I consider them entirely valid, but I do not think they will resolve by themselves the problems of psychoanalytic science, which are specifically our problems. We will have to apply them in our area cautiously, always keeping in mind that the problems of psychoanalysis should be resolved within analysis, naturally accepting modestly but with lucidity what comes to us from outside. What I see up to now is that we psychoanalysts use the new studies as grist for our mill. This is the point where the discussions end with an "I think thus".

I believe we are innately programmed to perceive space and time, and that the theme for investigation is how experience operates in the development of the notion of time and space that was potentially there in the genetic code. But I doubt that human development goes genetically from a one-dimensional world to one of four. (See the recently quoted work of the Bleichmars and the prologue to the Spanish edition of Meltzer et al., 1975.)

In general, when we want to give an account of origins, we easily fall into contradictions. Thus, for example, Bick maintains that if there is no containing skin, "the function of projective identification will necessarily continue unabated" (1968, p. 484); but she also says that projective identification requires the prior creation of a space in the self. That is, she says two different things: that if there is no space in the self, projective identification cannot function, and if that space in the self is not created, projective identification continues limitlessly. Meltzer tries to resolve this contradiction when he refers to this work in his book, but I am not sure he manages it. I think it is an insoluble contradiction, because if only the introjection of a skin-object makes the creation of an internal space possible, where does this first introjection lodge?

The idea of adhesive identification is valid; but to locate it in a theory of development is difficult.

For Melanie Klein, projective identification inaugurates development. In my view, this theory assumes that the child is programmed at the outset to grasp (the sense of) space and to relate to the mother; it comes into the world with a preconception of the mother, as Bion and Money-Kyrle say. I think this thesis has strong ethological support.

Similar difficulties, I believe, arise for Lacan and his dove. When he introduced his famous theory of the mirror stage to give an account of narcissism, Lacan (1949) relied on an ethological reference: that the dove sees its image in the mirror and ovulates. Then, he says, not without reason, that the ego is imaginary and eccentric, because my identity as ovulating dove is given by what I see outside—which, for the baby, is obviously the mother. The mirror stage, as far as I understand it, is linked to Freud's concept of primary identification as something prior to any object charge. Lacan uses the mirror model where I would use that of adhesive and projective identification. But, in any case, is the dove not programmed to ovulate if it sees an individual of the same species? Beyond doubt, the dove is programmed to ovulate when it sees and recognizes a member of its species. The dove does not ovulate when it sees Alain Delon, and even less Marlon Brando. The dove's ovulatory conduct is incorporated in its genome, its genetic information. But not all species ovulate when they see members of their own species—there are, in fact, many other ways of setting ovulation in motion. Is it necessary to add to this? I do not know whether it is possible, or necessary, for the psychoanalyst. I do not know whether it is necessary to see how things begin, because some are fixed phylogenetically to begin with. The other problem would be one of genetic information: determining when information has been incorporated in the DNA that would enable the dove (or what will be a dove—because perhaps it was this before becoming a dove) to ovulate in this way. The latter conditions the identity of the dove, because it also signifies that only if it ovulates can it have doves.

42.8 Separation anxiety and analytic cycles

Beyond theories and predilections, all analysts are consensual witnesses in affirming that the rhythm of contact and separation proper to the analytic process greatly influences the way the analysand behaves. This influence is more easily seen in connection with the holidays, then with the weekends, and lastly from session to session. These are the three circumstances provided for and foreseen by the setting where the alternatives of contact and separation come into play.

Zac (1968) studied at length the way separation anxiety appears at the weekend. He studied the fluctuations that are observed as the sessions take their course, as well as their consequences, and the way of, and opportunity for, interpreting.

Leonardo Wender, Jeannette Cvik, Natalio Cvik and Gerardo Stein (1966) studied the effects of the beginning and the end of the session in the transference and countertransference. For these writers the session has a "pre-beginning"—the time that elapses from the moment analyst and patient have some perception of each other (the ringing of the doorbell, for example) to the formal beginning of the session. And equally, the session has a "post-ending" (post-final) from the moment the analyst ends the session until all contact with the patient has ceased.

Wender et al. maintain that in the "pre-beginning" the analysand produces, and in some way expresses, the unconscious fantasy with which he comes to the session. This fantasy will be processed during the session, and the "post-ending" will gather it up to elaborate another fantasy, in which the original one and its development in the session will be contained. The analyst, for his part, will also produce some fantasies, which are the correlate of the others. These are moments, then, of tension and regression, where the analyst should pay attention to his fantasies (his countertransference thoughts, Racker would say), and to all the analysand's messages, which will generally reach him through non-verbal or para-verbal channels.

To sum up, the writers advise attention to these moments and warn of the dangers of making the setting more rigid to avoid anxiety.

I agree fully with these points of view. Clinical practice has taught me that to fix attention on the movements of contact and separation at the beginning and end of the session is very useful and sometimes more functional than to pay attention to the holidays or weekends. A female patient taught me this. Her material was a chorus of separation anxieties at the end of each week. However, during several years of analysis she never accepted from me an interpretation of this type. Since she was one of those quasi-colleagues Liberman (1976b) speaks of in his work at the London Congress, and she knew the great theories, she always disqualified me as a Kleinian. She asserted that I insisted too much on this point. Despite everything, I would again interpret, I think adequately, because the material clearly revealed it to me, until one day I interpreted the separation at the end of the session. I expected the patient's usual criticism, but she told me without hesitation that this was true. I then asked her, naively, why she accepted that she was anxious at that moment because she had to go, and she denied it whenever I interpreted the same with regard to the weekend. "No, don't be silly", she replied brusquely. Only then did I finally understand that the experience of the weekend was so overwhelming for her that she could neither work through nor accept it. Day-to-day working-through was feasible, but not from Friday to Monday. Here is a good example of a cliché interpretation of the weekend.

We therefore have to interpret separation anxiety as an important aspect of the process, day by day, week by week, during the holidays and, logically, at the end of analysis, when the theme again arises with unusual force. As Rickman (1950) said, at the end of analysis separation anxiety appears more linked to depressive anxieties, while at the beginning catastrophic, confusional or paranoid anxieties appear.

Needless to say, if the regular alternatives of contact and separation put the whole system into a state of tension, irregular alternatives will increase it even more. When the analytic rhythm is interrupted in an unforeseen way, the disturbance is always greater and the treatment is even at risk—and more so, the more sudden the absence or alteration.

The analytic setting, then, tends to make separation anxiety noticeable; it serves to detect it. An ego psychologist (such as Dr. Zetzel or Ida Macalpine) will say that the analytic setting, with its constant rhythm and regulated interruptions, reactivates separation anxiety through regression. For other analysts, on the other hand, the setting is only the magnifying lens that makes us see a phenomenon that is already there, which exists in its own right. What is called *management* by Alexander can be understood only on the basis of the former alternative—that if I change the rhythm of the sessions, I am going to quell separation anxiety. Those of us who think otherwise are convinced that, with Alexander's procedure, separation anxiety will appear elsewhere, and this can change only through interpretation.

I hold, with Romanowski and Vollmer (1968), that separation anxiety is reactivated through analysis due to the intolerance of frustration, which increases voracity, and because the analysand misunderstands the stability of the setting as an idealized breast, which reinforces his omnipotence and makes him more sensitive to absence.

If we know how to search for and detect it, separation anxiety appears in other circumstances, and therefore is not the patrimony of the conditions of the analytic setting, but an essential ingredient of every human relation. Ferenczi made this beautifully manifest in his work "Sunday Neurosis" (1919a), which merited a study by Abraham in the same year (1919c).

Separation anxiety is always part of a theory of object relations. But since this theory changes according to the writer, so does the focus of each person's understanding.

For Freud, separation anxiety is the counterpart of castration anxiety. In *Inhibitions, Symptoms and Anxiety* two fundamental types of anxiety are studied: *castration anxiety*, which comes from an attack on corporal integrity (the loss of the penis), linked by definition to a triadic or triangular relation—that is, an oedipal one—and *separation anxiety*, which flourishes during the pregenital stages and is linked to a situation where only a subject and an object intervene. The object is first the mother; but there is also a dyadic relation with the father. When a person has successfully traversed the long and thorny path that leads him to a realistic dyadic relation with his primitive love objects, he fulfils one of Zetzel's (1968) criteria of analysability, because only when that step has been taken can he validly deal with the management of triadic relations: the Oedipus complex.

The above-mentioned distinction Freud makes between castration anxiety and separation anxiety is accepted by all the schools, but the way of interpreting separation anxiety varies. If the Kleinian theory of separation anxiety is accepted, persecutory and depressive anxieties will be interpreted, assuming that, as the process advances, depressive anxieties will predominate. However, we should not forget that this school, or, at least, some of its members, also speak of catastrophic and confusional anxieties.

Winnicott thinks that when separation anxiety is linked to the dyadic relation, it demands *management* of the situation rather than an interpretative attitude. Because of their level of regression, these patients are not able to comprehend the verbal message. Consequently, only through certain modifications of the setting will the analyst be able to draw near to them and respond to their demands. These are problems linked to primitive emotional development, within which the essential needs of psychic development should be satisfied. In this way, management becomes the basis of our therapeutic conduct, and we deceive ourselves when we trust interpretation—the word—too much.

From a similar theoretical position, Balint also thinks that in the area of the basic fault the opportunity for a *new beginning* in development must be given to the patient, especially when the crucial moment of separation arises at the end of analysis. Balint's technique, however, continues to rely on interpretation, which should respect the level of regression of the patient.

Margaret Mahler thinks that separation anxiety arises when the symbiotic phase ends and the struggle for individuation begins, and there the dialectic of progression and regression becomes dramatic. Everything that provokes that development causes anxiety, the anxiety of growth. Consequently, the patient needs to be understood and to have the anxiety with which the painful process of separation and individuation begins interpreted.

Bleger uses a scheme similar to Mahler's, but what is decisive for him is to interpret the fear of the dissolution of the symbiosis as a relation to the agglutinated object, whose essential characteristic is that it has no discrimination. Bleger maintains that the mobilization of this link provokes a catastrophic anxiety and puts into operation the most primitive defences. There is a great fear of progressing towards independence, to the extent that progress represents the loss of the symbiotic object.

Finally, the theories of early development are manifold, and many are the ways of integrating them into analytic work. In practice, I think the major difference among the different writers centres on the place aggression occupies in early development and, in consequence, how far one should go in the analysis of negative transference. The hypothesis of primary envy implies a way of interpreting negative transference that is not supported by other major thinkers.

* * *

To sum up: There are strong and multiple resistances and counter-resistances to the analysis of separation anxiety in that it is linked to the fear of becoming conscious of the existence of a link and this link implies a dependence of each one on the other. At this point we touch on a problem for the analyst—his countertransference. The analyst will have to acknowledge that he is also implicated in the therapeutic link. The patient's separation also implies an anxiety for us, because we are left without our object, although we deny it at times, displacing it onto the professional or the economic plane. The truth is that the absence of just one patient alters—or ruins—our working day. If the analyst denies his link of dependence with the patient, he runs the risk of projecting into him his own dependence, which is one of the most frequent causes of the cliché interpretation.

A justified interpretation of separation anxiety brings out in its true colours perhaps man's most painful problem, his link with others, his dependence and his condition of orphan. We should know, therefore, that every time we interpret separation anxiety, we confront our analysand with solitude and we attack his omnipotence.

CHAPTER FORTY-THREE

The setting
and the container/contained theory

43.1 Summary

We are going to examine this theme not so much as a function of Bion's complex and highly suggestive work, but more along the lines of what we are studying, which is the psychoanalytic process. Let us remember that when we began this study, we established first the relation between the process and the setting. We studied how the setting influences the development of the process specifically—because, of course, every setting influences the development of the process to which it belongs and, vice versa, no process can arise other than within a setting. At this moment, for example, I am trying to provide the adequate setting in order to locate Bion within this chapter, so that we do not lose ourselves. If we do not keep in mind that our purpose is to give account of the theories that try to help us to understand the psychoanalytic process, we will take another path and may even learn much about Bion—but not about what we really ought to study.

We have seen, then, that the relation of the psychoanalytic process to the phenomena of regression and progression inherent in the very definition of process can be explained from two theoretical points of view: one that maintains that regression depends on the setting and one that, conversely, maintains that regression derives from the illness. The first theory understands regression as an artificial product of the setting, thanks to which analytic treatment can be effected, and we have therefore called it the theory of *therapeutic* regression. The opposite theory admits, on the other hand, a *psychopathological* regression, to which the analytic setting accommodates itself in the most rational way possible.

We then studied a third possibility, according to which there is a *curative regression*, which gives the patient the opportunity of starting again from scratch. The cure consists in providing the opportunity for the development of a process of regression on the basis of which the individual's natural tendency to grow healthily can re-establish itself, transforming itself from a potential into an actual reality. This theory necessarily relies on the *ad hoc* thesis that we are born with a disposition to growth that will inexorably be fulfilled if the environment does not interfere. Those of us who think, on the contrary, that growth is in itself a conflict will never accept this theory. (I think I remember from my diffuse ethological studies that certain pigeons continue to receive nourishment indefinitely from their solicitous, overprotective parents, since the expenditure of energy to open the beak is much less than that needed to fly, were it not for an opportune parental nip of the beak.)

The idea of holding belongs, in fairness, to Winnicott, but it is found in almost all the analysts of the English school and has also spread throughout the psychoanalytic world. I would say that all analysts who accept the decisive role of the mother (or surrogates) in the first year of life can only think that this maternal function is linked to some type of support, and Winnicott aptly called this *holding*. The concept is found in many thinkers, but Winnicott introduced the name, and with it a consistent theory of the role of the mother in development. Winnicott affirms vehemently that the development of the child cannot be explained without including the mother.

Finally, leaving behind the complex relations between process, regression and setting, we then used the concept of holding to present another way of understanding the psychoanalytic process, where the containing function of analysis and of the analyst facilitates first receiving and then giving back the anxieties of the individual who undertakes analysis. This is, then, a very different focus from the one that considers regression as a psychopathological phenomenon with which our technique must deal. On the basis of these premises we reviewed those writers who focus on the analysis of separation anxiety in the analytic setting. Now we propose to study another theory of this group, where the skin concept of Bick and Meltzer, Winnicott's holding concept and Resnik's space concept are conceptualized from a higher level of abstraction.

To clarify the issue, we might say that the concept of holding does not differ substantially in all the writers we are considering, but it is used with different therapeutic objectives. In the previous chapters we indicated that the analytic process—due to its structure and organization—confronts the patient with periods of contact and separation that condition a special type of anxiety, *separation anxiety*, which is fundamental in the early period of life. With this theoretical supposition, the setting should be designed to serve as a container for the hazards of contact and separation.

In chapter 42 we saw that the concepts of projective and adhesive identification serve to understand and manage separation anxiety when it operates through primitive mechanisms. The best device in the face of separation anxiety seems to be projective identification, because if one can get into the object there is no experience of separation anxiety. However, in the first stages of development, when tridimensional space has not yet been configured, the only device in the face of separation anxiety consists in making *contact* through adhesive identification. In both types of identification there exists a confusion of subject and object, and therefore the two are narcissistic, although the adhesive type does not have the "depth" of the projective type.

It will be understood that Bick's skin concept is different, but also coincident with that of holding. Winnicott does not emphasize the skin but, rather, the arms. In any case, both concepts correspond to a large extent, although they answer to different referential schemes. Didier Anzieu's investigation into what he calls the "ego-skin" also converges on this. Anzieu arrives along his own path at a theoretical position similar to those of Winnicott and Bick.

43.2   The container/contained theory

Following this line of thinking, we will now apply Bion's (1962b) *containing function* to the analytic process. The idea has affinity to Winnicott's concept of holding and Bick's skin concept, although there are some differences that are not really substantial. Formally, it seems that Bion's concepts of container and contained have a higher level of abstraction than that of holding (which always evokes somewhat an idea of diapers and the mother's arms), or than that of skin, which is so concrete. Bion tries to be abstract and even includes signs to express his ideas. The female and male signs represent the container and the contained, and he says—in a picaresque way—that these signs symbolize and at the same time denote the sexual organs and coitus. This is an idea drawn from Ferenczi's theory of genitality (1924), when he defines coitus as an attempt to return to the mother's womb. The male identifies his penis with the baby who gets inside. From this it follows, however much it may displease us, that coitus is strictly an operation of a high level of abstraction, and not at all concrete.

In fact, what Bion is concerned with via his container/contained theory is the very primitive—and, I think, very concrete—relation the child has with the breast. If he is hungry, the child seeks something that will alleviate his discomfort. The breast turns out to be the container that anxiety can direct itself to and from which the baby can receive milk and love, as well as meaning, in such a way as to change the situation. This idea of container and contained represented by the baby and the breast taken as signs of explanation is the starting point for a whole series of highly important developments in Bion's work, from which arises a theory of thinking no less than a theory of object relations. We will examine Bion's two theories, in order to articulate them through practice, because we are trying to study theories that will enable us to grasp separation anxiety and interpret it beyond the generalities, which are never very efficient or operative.

To explain how thoughts originate, Bion uses the concept of projective identification as Melanie Klein conceived it. Bion never speaks of adhesive identification, and it is possible that he made no contact with this idea. As opposed to Bick and Meltzer, Bion—when he speaks of container and contained—takes space (tridimensionality) as given.

After his paper at the Edinburgh Congress of 1961, "A Theory of Thinking" (1962a), and after having studied both schizophrenic psychosis and schizophrenic thought during the previous decade, Bion initiates a new stage in his relevant work, which takes him to the examination of thought and its origin.

Bion affirms that we are born with a *preconception* of the breast—something that links the hunger we can feel with the capacity of satiating it. The breast we speak of here—following Melanie Klein—although concretely the mother's breast, is also a global and abstract concept. Bion refers to this when he says that there is a preconception of the breast. When the real mother responds to the child's preconception, then the *conception* of the breast is constituted. In other words, the conception of the breast is reached when the real experience, the *realization* of the breast, is joined to the *a priori* preconception of it. This conception, in turn, evolves (see the scheme Bion proposes in his *Elements of Psycho-Analysis*, 1963).

However, there is another alternative, the one that, in fact, sets in motion the process of thinking. This is one of Bion's most beautiful contributions (see *Learning from Experience*, 1962b, especially chapters 11–12). Bion asks what happens when the breast is absent—when it fails to appear. There will always be an interval in which the need exists and is not satisfied. This is inevitable and, even were it not so, development would be impeded. Bion agrees here with Winnicott, who says the mother has to "disillusion" the baby gradually, frustrating him so that he gradually abandons the illusion that he commands the breast, that he creates the breast.

Bion says that, in principle, the baby does not feel that the breast is absent, but that there is a bad breast inside, a bad breast that is present and that he wants to expel. When the breast does come to him, the baby feels that, from outside, he has been helped to expel that bad breast. (This bad breast, which is present and which can only be expelled, is what is called a *beta element* in the theory of functions.)

In the face of this circumstance (and this is the key to Bion's reflection), the baby, the individual and all of us face a dramatic alternative, which is to ignore the frustration and "evacuate" or deny it. The other alternative is to acknowledge it and try to modify it. Bion soberly calls *thought* the attempt to modify frustration. "Sooner or later the 'wanted', breast is felt as an 'idea of a breast missing', and not as a bad breast present" (ibid., p. 34).

This explanation, where there is interaction between preconception and conception, innate tendencies and experience, fantasy and reality, frustration and satisfaction—all in very primitive terms—shows us a theory of object relations at the root of thinking. For Bion, perhaps even more than for Melanie Klein, projective identification is an object relation as much as a defence mechanism. It is undoubtedly the conjunction of the instinct or impulse and the mechanism, of anxiety with an object relation, that leads Klein to abandon the theory of primary narcissism and maintain that development centres on the object relation. That relation arises at the outset, and there is no psychology without object relation (Klein, 1952a). This theory, of course, is not accepted by Anna Freud, Margaret Mahler and all those who maintain the idea of primary narcissism.

43.3   Maternal "reverie"

Bion skilfully uses the theory of projective identification to give account of the early links. Perhaps more than Melanie Klein, he understands projective identification as an archaic type of communication. The concept of maternal reverie is linked precisely to the messages the baby directs to the mother, putting into her, via projective identification, parts of himself in distress. In emphasizing the communicative aspect of projective identification, Bion enhances its value in early object relations.

To respond to that primitive and archaic method of communication that is the baby's projective identification, Bion assumes that there is a special response in the mother he calls *reverie*. (I think that the baby's projective identification and the mother's reverie have a consistent relation with the *fixed action patterns* and *innate releasing mechanisms* described by the ethologists.) Bion has surely proposed this term because it evokes in us a penumbra of associations that paradoxically design its significance. *Reverie* in French comes from "dream" and means that state where the spirit allows itself to be led by its memories and imaginings. In Spanish, the word that most resembles it is *ensoñar*; in English, "enveloping in a dream" or "recreating through dreaming". The mother responds to the baby, enveloping it in her dreaming, recreating it, as if she were floating with her dreams (or more correctly, daydreams) above the objective events. Aside from scholastic disputes, Bion's reverie seems very similar to Winnicott's "area of illusion", as far as I understand it.

The reverie function considered thus has a strong similarity to the formation of a dream, with the passage from the primary process to the formation of oneiric images, which Bion assigns to the *alpha function* in his theory. This is certainly something quite different from the baby's emotional experience, because in any case the latter has to be signified by the mother: the mother has to give it significance. There has to be, then, a strong (introjective) identification that allows the mother to feel the baby within her, to feel what he feels. At least for me, this process strongly suggests the mechanism of primary dream-work: The child enters the mother, and the mother changes the primary process, through which the child enters into her, into a secondary process.

To conclude, I think if Bion prefers the term *reverie* to other more usual ones, such as maternal care, it is because he aspires to reach another level—perhaps a more abstract, more subjective, more psychological one. The expression "maternal care" has too much of a connotation of the factual aspects of child-care and lacks emotional resonance. What Bion wishes to emphasize is precisely this aspect of the issue: the inter-subjective emotional contact that gives the mother/child relationship significance.

43.4   Enforced splitting and static splitting

Bion not only studies the containing function of the mother's breast, which we later apply as a model to analytic treatment, making it isomorphic with the containing function of the setting, he also explains some psychopathological instances of this type of relation. One of them is the child who, for diverse reasons linked to endogenous or exogenous problems (such as the lack of maternal reverie or the child's envy of the breast, which is able to provide him with everything he needs), can find himself in a situation where the process of breast-feeding is interfered with. For Bion, the act of sucking is very complex. It is at least bifrontal in that it implies incorporating milk to satisfy a physical need, at the same time introjecting the breast in an emotional experience of vital importance. When this process is interfered with through a factor such as envy, whether it is the envy the child feels for the breast or one that comes from outside via the father, the siblings or the mother herself (because the mother can feel envy of the baby's well-being, just as the analyst can feel envy of his patient who improves), the child then faces an almost insuperable situation. To suck awakens in him so much unease that he cannot do it. He would thus be condemned to die of hunger, so he then appeals to what Bion calls *enforced splitting*: he accepts nourishment from the mother but denies the emotional experience. This enforced splitting later appears in those voracious and always unsatisfied adults who can never understand the symbolic (or spiritual) value of certain experiences. They are insatiable types, attached only to the material, without gratitude and always unsatisfied. If they buy paintings, this is not due to their aesthetic inclinations, but as an investment or to keep up with the neighbours. These people always have serious thought disturbances because they failed at root. They cannot understand the emotional experience that goes beyond instinctive satisfaction, conditioning the process of thought and love (1962b, chapter 5).

In these cases, ignoring his voracity, the individual feels himself tied to the breast or, better still, tied by the breast. He feels that the breast forces him, because he projects his voracity into it, and it then returns to him like a boomerang and makes him feel tied, although what really ties him is his avidity. A patient, some days after having asked to see me twice a day to end his analysis quickly, reproached me, saying I was one of those analysts who would never terminate analysis because I was such a perfectionist. I would never be satisfied with my analysand's progress. Let us say here that when he began analysis, his sole interests were money and sex.

We will refer to *static splitting* when we deal with the reversal of perspective. This phenomenon (see Bion, 1963) is a special form of resistance, where the patient reverses the analytic situation and the premises of analysis. Based on his own premises, which are, of course, unconscious, the analysand alters the process once and for all, so that each thing interpreted to him is automatically reversed. Bion called this process *static splitting*: it is a type of substantial change that paralyses the process of introjection and projection.

43.5 Applications

Bion's ideas are valuable in interpreting separation anxiety, taking into account the nuances it can present. After all the ground we have covered, we are, I believe, far from the cliché interpretation that is limited to the assertion that the patient felt badly because he missed the analyst during the weekend. There is an entire series of nuances available to us now, which go from the object relation to desire, from voracity and envy and the processes of splitting to loss, dependency and sorrow, with which we can tell the patient what is really happening to him, and not simply sentimental generalities.

I remember a supervision of a case of a patient who arrived one Monday and spoke anxiously and at length about a whole series of problems that had arisen since Friday's session: what had happened with her son, a stormy telephone call from her mother-in-law, a fight with her husband. The analyst's first interpretation was that she needed to tell her about all these situations of tension and anxiety she had undergone during the weekend, and which had become difficult to bear, so that the analyst could receive them, take charge of them and gradually give them back to her, so that she (the patient) could think about them. The aim of this interpretation was to make the patient conscious of the (certainly legitimate) way in which the patient uses her analyst, and in telling her, the analyst not only understands what is happening but, in effect, takes charge. Before becoming conscious of this situation, it was not worth entering into the content of the various problems.

An interpretation such as this seems simple, but, in fact, it is complicated and subtle. If we think of the theoretical background that supports the analyst, we will see it is not at all simplistic or conventional. The analyst made the interpretation supported by Bion's concept of the container and by the theories of the alpha function and maternal reverie.

The analysand's response was a dream she had that morning, just as she woke up: "*I dreamed I was waiting for the maid to come and clean the house, and I began to get desperate because she did not come. I knew I needed her, because if she is not here my time becomes disorganized.*" The dream confirms that the interpretation was correct and turned out to be functional, in that it alludes without much distortion to her need for the analyst to clean and organize her, to help her to think. It confirms that the point of urgency was the containing function of the analyst who, as is often the case in dreams, appears as the servant. The formulated interpretation, which made her remember the dream, was better than any other, which, attending to the contents, would leave aside the projective management of the anxiety (Celia Leiterman de Bleichmar, personal communication).

It can also be said that the analyst was able to *think* about what was happening to her and, in telling her, gave back to her analysand the alpha function she had projected into her during the weekend. The analysand was then able to think and remembered the dream that confirmed the hypothesis of the interpretation. Her apt and rapid response makes one suppose this patient was not seriously ill. She was able to respond well, and a good interpretation was sufficient for her to recover her capacity to think. However, I am convinced that if some of the conflicts offered by the material had been interpreted, she would not have understood, because she needed above all someone who would contain her anxiety and make her think.

Another important aspect of this material, and in general of this chapter, is that the idea of evacuation is different from the pejorative definition ordinary language commonly gives it. That she identifies her analyst with the servant expresses the positive transference, because for her the servant was very important. It had always been difficult for her to tolerate a servant who helped her.

If interpretations of separation anxiety are made adequately, as in this example, they open up the path to analytic dialogue, they reconstruct the relation between analyst and analysand on an equal footing, they re-establish the working alliance and then permit an interpretation of the contents of the material.

Lastly, I wish to assert that an interpretation such as this tries to make the patient conscious of his need to be contained, and it is superior to an understanding silence and to any manoeuvre or management that attempts to fulfil the holding function or reinforce the working alliance. It is better because what the analysand needs at that moment is not enacted but interpreted. I know very well, however, that many analysts will disagree with me on this point.

* * *

The clinical use of the container/contained theory entails quite complicated problems. How much does one receive, and at what point does one
give back? This is not easy to say. Only the analysand's material, experience and the countertransference can orientate us. In general, it is through
the patient's material and the countertransference that one decides when
one can or should intervene. The idea of a container obviously implies, by
definition, that not everything the patient says should be given back to
him in the form of an interpretation. In this sense I can say that the theory
of the containing function, which undoubtedly begins with Melanie Klein
but acquires greater stature in the thought of Winnicott, Bion, Esther Bick
or Meltzer, in some way justifies the ego psychologists who said Melanie
Klein interpreted too much. I think that, in fact, Melanie Klein at first
gave back the patient's projections too soon. Now we know the necessity
of interpreting, and even of interpreting in Klein's manner; but it is also
necessary to measure the dosage. We preserve, then, Klein's idea that the
problems must be resolved through—and only through—interpretation.
But the theory of a containing analyst implies greater complexity in the
interpretative task. As we have seen, the new focus is linked considerably
to the studies on countertransference.

Green, in his previously quoted work (1975), poses this problem on the
basis of his scheme of two types of anxiety: separation and intrusion. He
considers speaking too much or being too silent as equally bad, since
through excessive speaking we intrude, and through excessive silence we
increase separation anxiety. This is why Green thinks a technique such as
Winnicott's is the most advisable. At one end of the spectrum is Balint's
technique. He tries to intervene as little as possible to allow and to stimulate the *new beginning* under the analyst's benevolent protection. At the
opposite end, Kleinian technique, conversely, tries to organize experience
as much as possible through interpretation. Winnicott is situated between
these two extremes. He gives the setting its appropriate place and recommends a non-intrusive attitude. "If I feel in harmony with Winnicott's
technique, and if I aspire to it without being able to master it, it is because,
despite the risk of fostering dependency, it seems to me to be the only one
which gives the notion of absence its rightful place" (Green, 1975, p. 17).

Because of what I have just said, I think Green's reflections take the
problem to a different place from the one where I wished to locate it. I am
convinced that silence and the word should also be interpreted. In other
words, the concept of distance proposed by Green must not be transformed into a stable strategy of the analyst. It must vary constantly as a
concrete and immediate response to what is going on in the session, in
accordance with what arises from both the analysand's material and the
countertransference, including what they both think about the distance
itself.

PART FIVE

ON THE STAGES OF ANALYSIS

CHAPTER FORTY-FOUR

The initial stage

In part 4 of this book we studied in some detail the nature of the analytic process. We began by distinguishing situation and process. We then reviewed the principal theories that try to explain it, with which we had to consider multiple and sometimes divergent—if not opposing—points of view.

Now we have a less complex task, on a lower theoretical level, which is nonetheless interesting, and it is to typify the *stages of analysis*. As we examine them, the reader will verify their practical importance, no less than the support the previous arduous study provides in their understanding.

44.1   The three classic stages

To begin this chapter, we must pose a prior problem, and it is whether stages in analytic treatment really exist—because they may not exist. In fact, most writers think they do; I do not know whether some doubt this, but the discussion—however brief—is in any case pertinent. A stage in this context means that in the evolution of the psychoanalytic process there are characteristic, definite moments, different from the rest, with special dynamics that distinguish them.

Freud (1913c) compared psychoanalytic treatment to the noble game of chess, to indicate what I have just explained. He said there are three stages in chess and also in analysis. Due to their intrinsic characteristics, only the first and last of these lend themselves to study. The middle stage, on the other hand, lends itself to so many variations—to borrow a term from chess—that it is practically impossible to study it systematically. When Freud says the beginning and end of the analytic process can be systematized, he means that these stages (and by elimination also the middle stage) have specific mechanisms. This is true, to the point where the protocol of a psychoanalytic session can reveal the stage it belongs to: the experienced analyst can determine this at times with sufficient precision.

There is another circumstance that points to the specificity of these stages. Even in those cases where the progress of analysis has not been satisfactory enough to think of ending, if the ending is presented as a possibility, certain mechanisms that are proper to the last stage unfold, although other indicators reveal that that final stage has not really been reached.

The three stages Freud outlines are those classically admitted to be typical of psychoanalytic treatment—the same ones Glover studies in his well-known book on technique, published in 1955.

The *first stage*, the *opening stage* of analysis, begins with the first session and generally has a limited duration, at least in typical cases, which varies from two to three months, according to most writers. It is characterized by adjustments that emerge in the relationship between analyst and patient as each states his expectations and tries to understand those of the other.

The *second* or *middle stage* is the least typical, the longest and the most creative. It begins when the analysand has understood and accepted the rules of the game: free association, interpretation, a permissive and nondirective atmosphere, and so forth. Its duration varies. It lasts until the original illness (or its replica, the transference neurosis) disappears or is substantially modified. This stage is distinguished by continual fluctuations of the process, with its tides of regression and progression governed always by the level of the resistance.

Then the *third stage* begins, the *termination of analysis*, which for classic writers does not last long. In the first stage hope and mistrust appear as inevitable colourings, whereas now, in the final stage, without exception sorrow appears due to the parting, and the joy of reaching the final stage, and uncertainty about the future.

To conclude, we see that the three stages of psychoanalytic treatment exist in their own right, and each has distinctive characteristics. The total duration of the cure has been extended much more since Freud said, in "On Beginning the Treatment", that prolonged periods, from one semester to a year at least, are required: "To speak more plainly, psycho-analysis is always a matter of long periods of time, of half a year or whole years—of longer periods than the patient expects" (1913c, p. 129). However, the characteristics described here have always been the same. The conclusion is that the division of the treatment into stages is not purely phenomenological or morphological, in the sense that every task has a beginning, a middle and an end; on the contrary, it is justifiable, because it is possible to ascribe to each stage characteristics that are proper and essential to it.

44.2   Meltzer's division

The tripartite division that Freud, Glover and other classic writers followed is so natural to us that it is difficult to think of changing it. Does not every process have a beginning, a middle and an end? Nevertheless, in studying the psychoanalytic process in his book in 1967, Meltzer proposes a more complex and detailed division, which consists of five stages, the second and third stages being each divided into two. To formulate this proposal, Meltzer relies on two basic instruments of Kleinian doctrine, projective and introjective identification, which in this case are equivalent to the paranoid–schizoid and depressive positions. Obviously, if these concepts are not accepted, neither can the division be. Those who accept the reality of these mechanisms, however, will think that Meltzer's proposal permits a distinction the other theories cannot make.

Although I write for all analysts and not only for those of my school, I am going to follow Meltzer on this point, confident that the reader will be able to appreciate the advantages of this classification, although he may neither accept it nor apply it in practice.

The first stage of analysis, which Meltzer has called the *gathering of the transference*, corresponds to the opening stage of the tripartite division. Meltzer's descriptions correspond to Glover's, since in a typical case he assigns about two to three months to this stage. (It goes without saying that when I speak of phases in the treatment I always speak of averages and with a wide margin of variation.)

The middle stage is divided into two, according to the form and intensity of the projective identification. At the beginning of analysis, in *the stage of geographical confusions*, projective identification operates massively against separation anxiety, provoking a confusion of identity in which it is not clear who is the analyst and who is the patient. (Recall what was said about the use of projective identification to conquer separation anxiety in chapter 43.)

When separation anxiety abates sufficiently over time and as treatment progresses, problems of identity are overcome. But others appear which, following Erikson (1950), Meltzer calls the *stage of confusions of zones and modes*. Now the analyst and the patient are differentiated, each one in his place. There is no longer a confusion of identity, but there is a confusion of functioning. This stage, which for Meltzer is the longest in the cure, consists in the gradual clearing up of confusions in the erogenous zones, with which the relation with the breast and the triangular oedipal situation emerge more clearly.

When this is gradually being achieved, the introjective processes finally begin to predominate rather than the projective ones, and the analysand approaches the depressive position. Here Meltzer is closely following Klein, who said, in 1950, that the termination of analysis is linked to the resurgence of depressive anxieties, which she linked specifically to the loss of the breast.

Meltzer also distinguishes two moments in the third stage, or the ending of analysis. The first of these begins when the analyst is seen as a love object that can be lost, thanks to the predominance of introjective mechanisms. Omnipotence has clearly given way, and the analysand recognizes the value of his link with the analyst and depends on him. As Klein said in the work just quoted, depressive anxiety now occupies the centre of the stage. Since the predominance of depressive anxieties in the psychic apparatus is always precarious and unstable, Meltzer calls this fourth stage of analysis the *threshold of the depressive position.*

When the analysand has managed to enter this area sufficiently, the proximity of an inevitable, undesired situation begins to impose itself on him, with which he enters the final period of analysis, which, following the Kleinian model of development, Meltzer calls the *weaning process.*

Meltzer's last two stages are, then, covered by the process of mourning with which analysis ends, as conceived by many writers—not only Kleinians—so that they can be accepted without following strictly the writer's referential scheme. Let us say, to conclude, that these two stages are not always clearly distinguishable, although it is undeniable that there is a moment where the analysand confronts the possibility of concluding the analytic experience, and another at which the separation actually occurs.

44.3   The opening stage

As we have just seen, writers of diverse schools broadly agree as to the general characteristics and the duration of the initial stage of analysis. But the way it is conceived and the technique employed vary greatly, as we will see in what follows.

In general, a duration of no more than two or three months is assigned to this stage for a typical patient, that is, a neurotic. For very disturbed patients (psychotics, borderline patients, perverts, addicts and psychopaths) this period can present special problems and last much longer. I recall, for example, the case of a woman with a promiscuous sexual life and a strong latent homosexuality who in the initial interviews expressed great doubts about having analysis with me or with a female colleague with whom she had also had an interview. She finally chose me, but during a long year of analysis (long, at least, from the point of view of my countertransference!), she continually considered changing her analyst, because a woman would understand her better than I would. I thought that analysis had begun more than once, yet she would again pose the previous problem of the choice of analyst. Although it is true that I could analyse these fantasies and that she could accept my interpretations, recognizing implicitly that she was, in effect, being analysed by me, her reserve hung like the sword of Damocles over the relationship.

Those writers who consider analysis as a regressive process can make a clear-cut division between the first and second stages, saying simply that the transition occurs when the initial transference phenomena crystallize in the transference neurosis and when, in parallel, the therapeutic alliance is established. These writers conceptually distinguish, in a decisive manner, between transferences (in the plural) and transference neurosis.

The difference between the transference reactions of the beginning and the transference neurosis that is established afterwards goes back to Edward Glover's "Lectures on Technique in Psycho-Analysis" at the London Institute at the beginning of 1927. (They were published in the *International Journal of Psycho-Analysis* and are the basis of his book on technique.) In chapter 5 of this conference paper, entitled "The Transference Neurosis", Glover speaks of spontaneous transference reactions that are different from and arise prior to the transference neurosis, which begin when the patient's conflicts converge in the analytic situation: ". . . when the ground of the patient's conflict has been shifted, from the external situations or internal maladaptations of a symptomatic sort, to the analytic situation itself" (1928, p. 7).

In his book Glover called these phenomena *floating transference*—a very descriptive and fitting expression in that it captures the great mobility of the incipient transference phenomenon. Utilizing a model I find very beautiful, Glover compares the beginning of analysis to the compass, in the sense that when one places a compass on the table, the needle oscillates considerably, but then less and less, until it finally directs itself to the north, which analogously means to the analyst. The floating transference flows into the transference neurosis.

With these characterizations Glover does not depart from Freud's essay of 1913, which has been discussed. As everyone remembers, Freud advises: "*So long as the patient's communications and ideas run on without any obstruction, the theme of transference should be left untouched. One must wait until the transference, which is the most delicate of all procedures, has become a resistance*" (1913c, p. 139; italics in original).

Freud immediately asks himself when the analyst ought to begin his interpretative task, and his reply is clear: "Not until an effective transference has been established in the patient, a proper *rapport* with him. It remains the first aim of the treatment to attach him to it and to the person of the doctor. To ensure this, nothing need be done but to give him time" (ibid.).

I think it is not excessive to assume that the difference Freud establishes between *rapport* and transference resistance corresponds broadly to Glover's floating transference and transference neurosis. However, we will return to this when we examine Maxwell Gitelson's account in the Symposium on the Curative Factors in Psychoanalysis at the Edinburgh Congress of 1961.

* * *

Glover described some elements that enable one to detect the passage from the floating transference to the transference neurosis, that is, from the first to the second stage. The analytic atmosphere of the initial stage begins to change subtly and the analyst finds that, *"Instead of going backwards chronologically in the patient's history, we find ourselves pressed forward by the patient's increasing concern with the present day"* (Glover, 1955, p. 111; italics in original). The patient's libido is seen to be directed increasingly to the analyst and the analytic situation and, through a great number of subtle indicators, it becomes clearer each time that the analysand is reacting to the analytic situation. In directing himself to the session, the patient can now have an attack of anxiety, and the natural pauses between free associations lengthen, until the entire session is transformed into a great and tense pause. Among this group of indicators there is one to which Glover accords great importance, namely, when the analysand finally says that it is now time for the analyst to speak.

Glover's observations are interesting because they show the typical evolution of an analysis. Freud makes similar comments in "The Dynamics of Transference" (1912b), when he says that if the association ceases, this is because the patient is held by a thought that refers to the analyst. But in his essay of 1913, Freud says the resistance can be established from the first moment, and it is then better to tackle it directly—which is not completely consonant with his opinion that one must first achieve rapport with the patient and interpret afterwards. (Note what Klein thinks in this respect, as discussed in chapter 31.)

The nomenclature with which Meltzer defines this stage, the "gathering of the transference", corresponds to what has been described up to now, in that the transference phenomena are at first dispersed, and the analyst has to gather them up. But this task is more active for the Kleinians than for Freud or Glover. Nevertheless, Meltzer does not undervalue the conventional aspects of the analytic situation and the contact with what he calls the *adult part* of the patient's personality, child or adult. Meltzer favours combining—at the beginning of analysis—interpretations with the necessary clarifications about the setting and the analytic procedure. Anxiety should be not only *modified* through interpretation but also *modulated* through the setting.

Let us say, to conclude here, that during this first stage the analytic relation is very fluid, and conventional rules weigh strongly on it. When these rules are abandoned, it can be asserted that the first stage has been completed. Then a patient can tell me he does not like a particular object in the waiting-room, or a woman can tell me that she is menstruating, with the understanding that I will take those statements as free associations and as nothing else.

It is not always possible to move suddenly from a conventional situation of current social relations to the very singular analytic situation. Certain tolerance and much tact are necessary vis-à-vis a patient who begins analysis and does not realize what the rules of the game are, because he does not yet know them or because of his psychopathological problems. Without falling into demagogy and support, one can always be courteous without ceasing to be an analyst. At times, a new patient asks a direct or naive question that it is impossible to answer without serious diminution of analytic reserve. At these times something can be said in reply without leaving the patient stranded and offended and without answering the question directly.

44.4 The dyadic relation

It is difficult to do justice to the richness of the paper Gitelson (1962) presented in Edinburgh, not only because of the variety of concepts he employs, but also because of the writer's multiple objectives. Gitelson proposes partly to fix his position in relation to the curative factors in psychoanalysis, questioning severely some attitudes that, while seeming to humanize the procedure, abandon its technique. But he also investigates the origin of the transference neurosis and the therapeutic alliance, placing them within the framework of a theory of development.

Gitelson applies the model of the dyadic mother/child relation to the configuration observed at the beginning of analysis. Between the analyst as mother and the patient as infant, a dyadic relation is constructed, which is the necessary condition for the establishment of the therapeutic alliance and the transference neurosis. The latter is, for Gitelson—as for all ego psychologists generally—a triangular relation, the typical oedipal situation. What will later become the therapeutic alliance is, in the first stage of analysis, no more than the dyadic relation between an analysand who brings his most primitive needs and an analyst who responds adequately. Gitelson calls this attitude of the analyst who responds to the analysand's needs *diatrophic function*, following Spitz. Spitz (1956b) said that, in the face of the patient's initial needs, the analyst responds with a phenomenon of countertransference that constitutes his diatrophic response to the dyadic situation. Here, as can easily be understood, the countertransference is not conceived as a disturbing phenomenon but, on the contrary, as completely adequate to the patient's needs, similar to the parent's response to the child's requirements. (Spitz derives his adjective from the Greek verb signifying to maintain or support.) The child incorporates the diatrophic attitude of the parents at the end of the analytic relation through a process of secondary identification, which is located in the first six months of the second year of life and initiates, for Spitz, the path of socialization, which will lead the child to become a parent also at the appropriate time. Spitz follows here his well-known theory of the development of the child's object relations in three stages: (1) the *objectless stage*, which goes from birth to the smile in the third month; (2) the *stage of the precursor object* or first libidinal object, which lasts until the anxiety of the eighth month, and (3) the *object stage* properly speaking, which extends to two-and-a-half years, where the child reaches the symbolic level of thought with the semantic *no* (see *La première année de la vie de l'enfant*, 1958, and "Transference: the Analytical Setting and Its Prototype", 1956a). This adequately sublimated function is a necessary condition for analytic work, a point on which Spitz concurs with Money-Kyrle (1956) in his idea of normal countertransference.

Always following Spitz, Gitelson feels that the analyst's diatrophic attitude has its counterpart in the child's anaclitic relation with his mother in the stage of secondary identification. In these conditions, the patient feels the need for an *ego-support*, and the analyst has, as does the mother, the function of an auxiliary ego for the patient. This can properly be called *rapport*—the hopeful sense of a diatrophic response from the analyst. The rapport Freud said was a necessary condition of analysis derives from this first contact between analyst and analysand, which establishes the anaclitic–diatrophic equation. Rapport, Gitelson asserts, is the first representative of the floating transference (1962, p. 199). At a later moment, and thanks to the rapport, the floating transference becomes a transference neurosis, and the rapport remains as the therapeutic alliance. Defining his terms rigorously, Gitelson says the transference neurosis is anaclitic and the therapeutic alliance is diatrophic.

If the anaclitic–diatrophic equation does not occur spontaneously, Gitelson does not think it can be reconstructed. This is, for him, the necessary condition for analysis to begin. If this foundation is not there, this stage will not be fulfilled, and the moment when the therapeutic alliance and the transference neurosis will be delineated will not arrive. On this point, Gitelson agrees with his colleagues of the ego psychology school, and not with those who think that the original situation can be reconstructed (Winnicott, Balint) or interpreted (Klein). For Gitelson, the dyadic situation is not interpretable: if the patient is able to establish it (that is, if it is analysable) and if we know how not to interfere with it, it will develop spontaneously. On this point Gitelson follows Freud strictly when the latter says that if at the beginning of treatment the analyst does not disturb the course of the process, the patient will soon assign him to a benevolent figure from his past, and at that point the transference neurosis is initiated.

Gitelson operates throughout his essay with the idea that the human being is endowed with an impulse for development. This idea undoubtedly comes from Freud; but it was Edward Bibring (1937) who developed it theoretically in his contribution to the Symposium on the Theory of the Therapeutic Results of Psycho-Analysis in Marienbad in 1936.

Bibring speaks in his paper on how the curative factors operate from the id, the ego and the superego. When he speaks of the id, he says there is an impulse towards development that he considers fundamental.

44.5 *On the analyst's personality*

I said that a central proposal in Gitelson's account is to defend psychoanalytic method in the face of psychotherapies—whether analytic or not—and
also vis-à-vis analysts who make the course of the process depend on the
analyst's personality and advocate the humanization of the cure. The basis
of this discussion is the place we will accord in our theories to the analyst's humanity. That it operates as a *necessary* factor seems undeniable to
me, and I think no one can doubt it. What is being discussed is whether
the analyst's humanity can also be a *sufficient* factor in the results of our
method. If an analyst lacks objectivity or goodness, or even pity for the
defects of man (I do not say understanding, nor even respect, just pity), he
cannot be an analyst. No one doubts that all these factors, and uprightness
and honesty, are fundamental. If these conditions are not a given, it is
logically impossible for the analyst to arrive at an interpretation, because
the latter does not arise from an intellectual process. It arises, for example,
from the honesty with which I am able to confront what the analysand is
doing or telling me. If the analyst is not upright, if he is neither honest nor
just, he will never make the correct interpretation. I do not think this is
what is being discussed, but, rather, the idea of humanizing the analytic
relation so that it becomes a curative factor in itself. What Gitelson says,
which is also what this book maintains, is that these elements are not
curative factors but *requirements*.

The analyst's passivity is attacked, as is his silence, and the restriction
he himself imposes of only interpreting, and it is proposed that it is necessary to participate more. This point of view has been elevated to a theory
of practice by existential psychotherapy: what really counts is the existential encounter. These existential encounters may sometimes be encounters
and at other times fabulous non-encounters, as in the case of Medard Boss
when he stops his patient's hiccups by pressing his neck as if to strangle
him, so frightening his patient out of his hiccups. Gitelson reacts to all this
with a great deal of energy, which only confirms what everyone who
knew him affirmed: his own good nature, his immaculate intellectual probity. Gitelson does not want to fall into a reassurance situation, an existential encounter or one of simplistic humanization, nor does he wish to
approach the converse, the stance of the rigid and distant analyst who
thinks he is following the rules of his art when what he is really doing is
displaying his obsessive neurosis, if not his sadism or schizoid aspect.
With the theory of an anaclitic–diatrophic relation, Gitelson proposes to
clear the field without falling into a cheap humanization. We know we
sometimes fall into this in daily practice in the consulting-room, and that
there are also some in psychoanalysis who favour it. Perhaps the greatest
effort in Gitelson's work is that of not allowing suggestion to intervene in
the first stage of treatment, and this is why he criticizes the ideas of Radó
(1925) at the Salzburg Congress.

CHAPTER FORTY-FIVE

The middle stage of analysis

45.1 *The concept of transference neurosis*

As we saw in chapter 44, the classic way of understanding the middle stage of analysis is by following the concept of transference neurosis, which Freud introduced in "Remembering, Repeating and Working-Through" (1914g). Freud maintains in this essay that at the beginning of analysis a very peculiar phenomenon is established: the neurosis that the patient first brought to the consulting-room stabilizes. It does not produce new symptoms; it tends to diminish or even disappear, while other symptoms that are isomorphic with those of the original neurosis begin to appear. They reveal a connection with the analysis and/or with the analyst. Freud called these symptoms (no doubt fittingly) *transference neurosis*.

As I have said repeatedly, transference neurosis must be understood as a technical concept, in that it postulates that the conditions of the analytic treatment and the analytic process itself transform those symptoms that were grouped as a particular clinical entity into others. The new version always has direct or indirect reference to the treatment, and certainly to the analyst. It is precisely this new production of the illness that can really be tackled by the psychoanalytic method.

However, in Freud's work it is nowhere claimed that the only symptoms that can undergo this process of conversion are the neurotic ones. On the contrary, what Freud often said is that *all* the symptoms the patient presents are susceptible to this mutation, to this alchemy which transforms them into transference. In the work we are discussing, for example, Freud cites the case of an elderly woman who suffered twilight states during which she abandoned her husband and her home. She also "abandoned" Freud after a week of treatment in which the transference grew at a disturbing rate without giving him time to prevent such a catastrophic repetition (1914g, p. 154). Here, obviously, the clinical picture is not of a neurotic but of a psychotic (twilight) state, and the transference in any case still occurs, assuming the character of an incoercible resistance.

When the transference becomes essentially negative, as with paranoid patients, Freud said elsewhere, any possibility of psychoanalytic treatment ceases. The transference phenomenon exists, it presents itself, but we cannot resolve it. In his "On Narcissism: An Introduction" (1914c), however, Freud established a clear difference between transference neurosis and narcissistic neurosis, affirming that only in the former is there a capacity for object relations, that is, a transference of libido that makes psychoanalytic treatment possible. This classification belongs, in fact, to psychopathology and not to the technique. But what is in fact being discussed is whether these two classes are identical and whether they can be superimposed on each other, as some believe. When we speak of indications or contraindications for psychoanalytic treatment, we enter into this controversy; if we apply the psychopathological concept of transference neurosis to clinical practice, then in effect we are also taking a particular position with respect to the extent of the method. It will be remembered that on that occasion, and also in dealing with forms of transference in chapter 12, I distinguished between the two concepts. I defined transference neurosis as a phenomenon that occurs in practice, as a technical concept that covers the reconversion of the psychopathological process in virtue of the analyst as a person and of his setting, without judging the possibility of analysing the transference. Weinshel (1971) also established the difference between transference neurosis as a technical concept and as a psychopathological concept, although the development of his thought takes him, in my understanding, to superimpose transference neurosis on transference in general.

45.2   Variations on the same theme

To discuss what transference neurosis consists in, what its nature is and what its limits are, is the manifest content of an academic controversy. The latent ideas that determine it, however, have to do with different forms of understanding analysis and its practice, when it begins and how far the transference extends, how interpretation operates, how the setting works.

Gitelson's work views these problems strictly, in that it delineates and circumscribes the transference neurosis as a triangular and specifically oedipal situation, which can be reached and modified by interpretation.

The dyadic relation at the beginning of life between the child and the mother is always reproduced when analysis begins, but it will never be part of the transference neurosis, that is, interpretable or modifiable. Spitz (1956b) introduced the concept of diatrophic attitude to specify a particular spontaneous and unconscious conduct on the analyst's part (that is why, I think, he calls it countertransference), which responds to the patient's anaclitic position. But neither Spitz nor Gitelson think these phenomena can be analysed. Their thinking is similar to Elizabeth R. Zetzel's when she says that only the Oedipus complex can be analysed and that the necessary condition for this is that the future patient has already resolved his dyadic conflicts with the father and the mother.

It is, in fact, not always easy to decide within the immediate and complex relationship of the consulting-room whether a relation is dyadic or triadic, beyond the fact that if we were to follow such pristine rules as these we would incur a contradiction just by telling a patient that he identifies interpretation with the mother's milk. Patients such as the one who escaped from Freud in a twilight state—and even Dora—seem to show clearly that the cautious attitude of the classic analysts, of most French and other European analysts, of many ego psychologists and of the analysts of the Anna Freud Centre (formerly the Hampstead Clinic) has its drawbacks.

As competent a theoretician as Loewald (1968) seems to realize this in his work on the concept of the transference neurosis. He presents the case of a young woman of 19 whose transference neurosis had an intense and rapid development, which obliged him to interpret the transference early on, leaving the analysis of resistances to a better occasion. The major resistance in this case, Loewald says, was the transference itself.

The situation of a transference neurosis that establishes itself slowly while the relaxed analyst fulfils Freud's mandate to clear up the resistances while not touching the difficult theme of the transference is an ideal in our practice (and of our transference neurosis with Freud), which is only permitted to us when we face a case of neurosis that is not too severe. In other cases, which are now the most frequent ones, transference phenomena soon present themselves; and the same always happens with children and adolescents.

A singularly explanatory case is presented by Harold P. Blum (prepublished for the Madrid Congress of 1983). The case concerns a young man who before the first session telephoned to say that his mother had died, and he would contact Blum after the funeral. A year and a half later he saw Blum again and confessed that he had lied; his mother was still alive, and now he did want an analysis. Blum took him on, and he was able to analyse this colossal lie thoroughly and refer it to conflicts with the live (and ill) mother and the dead father, in the patient's vehement transferential version. Knowing Blum's theories and his enviable technical capacity, I ask myself what he would have done if this patient, instead of beginning analysis by telephoning to say that his mother had died, had come to the first session recounting a dream more or less as follows: "*Last night I dreamed my mother died. I was talking to you on the telephone to tell you I would contact you after the funeral, but in fact I only came back to see you a year and a half later.*" Blum's patient and the one I imagine are not the same one, I know, because pseudology and acting out are not the same as telling a dream. The dream I propose, however, would make Blitzsten and his disciples say the analysis would not be viable. We have already seen that when the analyst appears in person in the analysand's first dream it is because the latter is not analysable or the former committed an unforgivable error. Since Blum had committed no error, the patient of the dream would be unanalysable—yet in a more serious version than the one I imagined, he was not. Faithful to his theories, would Blum have remained silent in the face of that dream, hoping that rapport would be established and the transference neurosis would be installed via regression? I think (perhaps because I am a Kleinian), that silence in those circumstances would have been a mistake, if not a countertransferential acting out, and that the only possibility was to interpret the transference without hesitation—and I am sure that Blum, going beyond theoretical differences, would have done just that.

45.3 Transference and countertransference neurosis

In the two previous sections (and also, in Part 3, in the chapters on the forms of transference) I discussed the concept of transference neurosis. I proposed widening it, in effect, in that the new version of the illness that arises in the treatment comprises not only neurotic but other types of symptoms.

We will now consider another extension of the concept, the one Racker proposed in his work, "The Countertransference Neurosis" (1948 [1968]). Within the psychoanalytic process, the function of the analyst is both as interpreter and as object (1968, p. 105). The countertransference influences these two functions, facilitating or obstructing the course of the cure. The countertransference can indicate to the interpreter–analyst precisely what he should interpret, when and how, just as it can impede his understanding of the material with rationalizations and blind spots. His function as object will also depend at each moment, for good or ill, on the countertransference.

Racker says that it cannot be expected that the analyst will remain immune to the countertransference, because this would amount to saying that the analyst has no unconscious. But it is possible that if the analyst observes and analyses his countertransference, he can use it to advance the course of the cure.

In the same way that the analysand's entire personality vibrates in its relation to the analyst, so the analyst also vibrates in his relation to the analysand, without neglecting thereby the quantitative and qualitative differences (ibid., p. 105).

Racker maintains that the analyst continues to have conflicts, however much he may have been analysed—and well analysed—and his profession of itself provides them continuously. "Just as the whole of the patient's images, feelings, and impulses towards the analyst, insofar as they are determined by the past, is called 'transference' and its pathological expression 'transference neurosis', in the same way the whole of the analyst's images, feelings, and impulses towards the patient, insofar as they are determined by the past, are called 'countertransference' and its pathological expression may be called 'countertransference neurosis'" (ibid., p. 106).

Racker shows in his Study how the analyst's negative and positive Oedipus conflict, as well as his pre-oedipal oral and anal conflicts, are reproduced in the countertransference.

Following Racker, we will call the middle stages of analysis *transference and countertransference neurosis*, considering that the analyst's participation is inevitable. The analytic process involves both analyst and analysand, although the degree and quality of that participation are open to discussion; it is obviously not identical in both cases. The necessary condition to establish the psychoanalytic process is precisely that the interaction between those two people, analyst and analysand, be of a particular type, and not as in daily life. We stated earlier that the beginning stage of analysis consists in the analyst adopting an attitude that distinguishes him in that he does not respond in the expected way vis-à-vis the patient's conventional attitude, with its presuppositions and the expectation that the analyst will react as his peers habitually do. We also said that when the patient understands this difference, he begins a new relation, the properly analytic one, in which he no longer expects the responses he has been accustomed to, but a very special response, which emerges from two basic roots—the rule of abstinence and interpretation. As soon as the relation changes and ceases to be conventional to abide by this new code, the second stage of analysis begins.

While the development of the first stage varies according to the focus of each school and even of each analyst, in the one we are now considering the divergences are not so great. If there is a surprising degree of agreement on the duration of the first stage, the one we are now discussing—due to its nature—has no fixed duration. In this stage the process of transference and countertransference develops with its infinite hues, subtleties, contradictions and (why not say it) disagreements and contradictions, which we will never be able to calculate. The most we can say is that it will last years, never months, and that its evolution will depend on how the two protagonists participate in it. If in the first stage the analyst's ability is tested only by the most irregular patients, in the middle stage it will be tested at every moment. The fate of the cure will depend on it, as well as on the degree of illness and on the patient's cooperation.

45.4 Geographical confusions

In contradiction to Freud, to Glover and to all those who have dealt with the middle stage as a unitary one, Meltzer distinguishes two stages here. Perhaps it is unnecessary to say that, in establishing them, Meltzer does not propose a radical division, but a theoretical instrument, which, rather retrospectively, enables us to distinguish different moments when we study the process from without. There are no clear limits, just as there are none in the three classic stages.

As we have already said, Meltzer's two stages gravitate around *projective identification*. In the second stage, which concerns us now, the patient has recourse to *massive* projective identification. Therefore Meltzer designates it as the *stage of geographical confusions*, since the "geography" of unconscious fantasy is radically disturbed. In terms of identity, the difference between subject and object has not been reached or is lost, because massive projective identification implies a substantial confusion between subject and object. This confusion is precisely the patient's trump card in resolving the problems that arise for him in the analytic relation: so as not to acknowledge the difference with the analyst, the patient avails himself of that very intense process of projective identification. As we saw in studying the theories of the process, Meltzer's perspective (as Zac's) is based on separation anxiety. This theory is linked to the idea of early object relations because it implies that there is an object relation as soon as the analytic relation is established.

Meltzer, then, is among those who understand the psychoanalytic process in terms of separation anxiety. For him, the repeated experience of contact and separation that establishes the rhythm of the psychoanalytic sessions is a predominant influence on the process—simultaneously, of course, with the expectations the patient brings. Therefore the regularity of the sessions, their rhythm and number, are important. The stability of the analytic situation is the basis for the actual development of the process. This is a specifically Kleinian idea in that it relies on a theory of early object relations, although no analyst ignores the importance of contact and separation. Whatever the theoretical support, the analyst will always have to interpret these elements; he will have to integrate them into his theories, because they arise repeatedly in clinical practice. We have seen the importance of accurate interpretation of separation anxiety and how difficult it is to do so without engaging in mechanical and often flat interpretations, which patients rightly reject. I have also stated that the patient resists these interpretations strongly because he fears the link we are trying, with difficulty, to establish, and he does so for the most part by cancelling us out.

The patient is not a very trustworthy judge, but he is the only one we have. His criticisms can be true, just as they can be tendentious: the more the patient seeks to attack the analytic link, the more severe his criticisms will be of our (good) interpretations about the weekend.

45.5 The toilet–breast

In the stage of geographical confusions, the analyst should function and should show that he functions as a *container* of the analysand's anxieties. The fundamental analytic task at this stage is the analyst's containment and interpretation of the patient's anxiety. To the extent that this process is carried out, if the patient deposits—or, rather, *evacuates*—his anxiety (the term here has a literal sense) and the analyst is able to bear it, a type of relationship is established in which the patient feels the analyst as an object whose function is to contain him. Meltzer calls this object, whose function is to receive what the patient evacuates or projects, the *toilet–breast*, because it is obviously linked to the oral stage of development. In this way, the massive projective identification of the patient has its correlate in an attitude of the analyst which reproduces the archaic type of relation that occurred between the baby and the mother as container of his anxiety. This object is partial because it represents neither the mother as a whole nor the totality of the breast, but only its containing function—hence its name, *toilet–breast*.

As this process repeats itself, the analysand develops a growing confidence in the toilet–breast and gradually introjects it. It can be said, theoretically, that from the moment this toilet–breast has been sufficiently introjected, the patient has within him an object where he can deposit his anxieties, and at that moment the second stage of the analytic process ends.

For Meltzer it is a key moment, the crossing of the border between madness and mental health, between psychosis and sanity. This concept is evidently similar to the dividing line Abraham (1924) drew between the first and second anal stage to separate psychosis and neurosis. Abraham and Meltzer, at different historical moments and with different theoretical supports, concur in indicating a clinically significant point: when the individual can contain his anxieties and has no need to project them, he has crossed the limit between psychosis to neurosis, between mental health and illness in psychiatric terms.

According to Meltzer, if the analyst is not too clumsy and the patient is not too ill, this process can be reached in a year of work—a period I consider somewhat brief. Everything naturally depends on the ability of the analyst to detect the mechanism of massive projective identification and to interpret it, which always increases with clinical experience, and on the degree and frequency with which the analysand uses it. A factor that lengthens the time is the envy with which the analysand may respond to the (good) interpretations of his massive projective identification. The period of time can then vary, but I dare say that the usual patient can achieve this in a couple of years or a little longer. In addition, it is easy to understand that this period lasts noticeably longer, and sometimes can never be completed, in the case of psychotics, perverts, drug addicts or psychopaths.

I remember the dream of a homosexual patient at the end of her first year of analysis (Etchegoyen, 1970). She dreamt she was visiting the greatest homosexual organization in the world, which was beneath a city. In descending, she felt the need to go to the bathroom; she asked permission to do so and was shown where it was. She entered the bathroom and saw a small staircase there; she descended and saw another bathroom and another staircase. Thus she descended five times, until she woke up. I think the functioning of the analytic setting for this patient can be appreciated in this dream: the five sessions protect her from a massive return to homosexuality, as subsequently happened, in effect. In this dream the idea that the five analytic sessions really represent the toilet-breast appears clearly.

During the stage of geographical confusions the interpretative task, according to Meltzer, can be defined as going from the mechanism to the anxiety. This is often at the root of the difference between an adequate interpretation and an inadequate one. This is why we said in chapter 44 that when the analysand has massively projected his anxious part into an object, the only thing we can do like a detective—is to find out where the anxious child is hidden, to put him again in his (appropriate) place within the patient. When the analyst does this, the patient begins to feel anxiety; the interpretation has gone from the mechanism to the anxiety. In this stage, then, to the extent that the analyst interprets adequately, the analysand's anxiety increases.

Therefore what is essential at this stage is to interpret the mechanism—massive projective identification—to re-establish the object relation and the anxiety, because what the mechanism did was precisely to annul the object relation to avoid anxiety.

45.6 The skin

When Meltzer wrote *The Psychoanalytic Process* in 1967, Esther Bick was just beginning her investigation on the skin as an object of psychic reality. The concept of a toilet–breast is conceived in terms of the functioning of projective identification and is not applicable, in my opinion, to that of adhesive identification as developed by Bick and Meltzer. To account for the new phenomena, perhaps Meltzer would have to develop a new concept or broaden the previous one. I believe Winnicott's concept of holding to be best adapted to Meltzer's two modalities of narcissistic identification, since "holding" (support) fits both the skin and the arms, the breast or the body of the mother.

What we have just described is clearly a special type of process. The toilet–breast is a space in which projective identification "takes place", As long as the latter does not exist, there can be no real processes of projective identification.

After Esther Bick's (1968) work, which we have already commented on, the skin appears as a fundamental object in the psychic domain. Before there can be a container/contained relation (within and without) there has to be a bipersonal relation of contact. What is characteristic of projective identification is a concept of space: projective identification presupposes a three-dimensional object. The relation Bick studied in psychotic and autistic children, the one she saw when observing babies, and what Meltzer and his study group investigated in parallel in autistic and psychotic children, is a type of relation that does not seem to be linked to a three-dimensional process, but merely to one of contact. It is a narcissistic identification in that it erases the difference between subject and object; but it does not enter into anything; it makes contact; it does no more than touch the surface of the other. The process of identification is superficial, it has no consistency—without giving these words the pejorative sense usually assigned to them. These people are individuals who depend greatly on the opinion of others and in which the process of identification is mimetic, imitative, and has no density. They are very concerned with *status*, the social *role*; they would rather have a title than practice their profession.

David Rosenfeld (1975) also thinks that the skin plays an important role in the constitution of the corporal scheme and in the first object relations. On the one hand, the skin provides the experiences of softness and heat that spring from the earliest relation with the mother; on the other, the skin fulfils a function of support and organization for the dispersed parts of the self, which maintains a relation with the penis within the breast.

In clinical practice the phenomenon of adhesive identification is noted as a special modality for the management of separation anxiety. The analysand seeks contact, is interested in hearing the analyst's voice or in being heard, without the content of the discourse counting for him. He tends to crumble, and at times the desperate search for company and contact appears very clearly in dreams. As with Kanner's (1943, 1953) autistic children, this type of analysand does not seem to listen; the words go in one ear and out the other, as if there were no space in the head to contain them.

Following these investigations, then, one would have to think that the third dimension belongs to a subsequent stage of development, which is initiated at a bidimensional level, as has been maintained by Arnaldo Rascovsky ever since he wrote his book on fetal psychism (*El psiquismo fetal*, 1960). This implies, then, that adhesive identification comes prior to projective identification and that there is (or should be) a stage *prior* to Melanie Klein's paranoid–schizoid position, as Rascovsky (fetal psychism) and Bleger ("glischrocaric" position) maintain. (For a more detailed discussion see my introduction to the Spanish edition of Meltzer et al., *Explorations in Autism*, 1975.)

45.7 The confusions of zones and modes

The development of analysis in its intermediate, most prolonged and perhaps most complex stage, during which the neurosis of transference and countertransference develops, cannot be systematized, but does admit comments on how this lengthy period can be understood. We have noted Racker's specifications on the transference neurosis, and we are now looking at Meltzer's contributions. As the toilet–breast takes shape in the internal world, another configuration appears, which Meltzer calls the *stage of confusions of zones and modes*. Projective identification has (by then) noticeably diminished and will no longer direct the dynamic of the psychoanalytic process substantially. Although in the variations of contact and separation there will always be recourse to massive projective identification, in the rest of the process the task will be centred much more in the arrangement and reordering of zonal confusions and not in the problems of identity.

If in the first stage one goes from the mechanism to the anxiety; in the second, conversely, one passes from the anxiety to the mechanism. In the first stage there is an attempt to consolidate the analyst's containing function, to allow the patient to introject the analyst as a toilet–breast. The interpretation goes from the mechanism to the anxiety precisely because massive projective identification, when it erases the differences between subject and object, shields the one who employs it from the anxiety. As we correct the geographical confusion and render to Caesar the things that are Caesar's and to God the things that are God's, the patient begins to feel anxiety, because it is only on the basis of differentiation between subject and object that all the vicissitudes of the link (which was not there previously) can be felt.

In the following stage the situation is different, not to say diametrically opposed. The individual shows himself to be anguished, and when we elucidate his zonal confusions we reveal to him the mechanism that explains his anxiety. In this stage the link is there; it exists; and we can operate with it and its vicissitudes, making the patient see that invariably the consequence of his zonal confusions is anxiety. For example, a patient comes to the session in an anxious state and begins to talk in a continuous and excessive manner. The interpretation indicates that he confuses his tongue with his urethra to urinate the analyst (expel him). The interpretation gives the patient the reasons for his anxiety and naturally has to alleviate it.

There is always a basic premise for Meltzer behind all these confusions: that of denying the difference between the adult and the child. All the interpretations at this stage are directed to correcting this confusion, in the final instance. The interpretation always refers to the difference between adult and infantile functioning—a theme that Janine Chasseguet-Smirgel (1975) has studied in depth.

This aspect of interpretation is both unavoidable and always painful. It is unavoidable because if we do not take it into account, these interpretations could be decoded by the patient as if they sanctioned an equality where an asymmetry should exist. It is at this moment in analysis, perhaps, that the concept of asymmetry in the transference neurosis acquires its fullest expression, and our task consists in enabling the patient to accept it, however painful it may be. There are many ways of interpreting the differences between adult and infantile functioning, as well as of undermining the idealization that is precisely the basic mechanism through which infantile sexuality equates itself with adult sexuality. It is not enough to tell a patient, at this stage, that he (or she) wants to give me a baby with his (or her) feminine infantile part, but also that only by idealizing faecal material can he think that his baby is equal to the one made by the parents. This last aspect of the interpretation is unavoidable, beyond the tact with which it is formulated. An interpretation that limits itself to indicating the production of faecal babies without modifying the idealization that presupposes the confusion of excrements and babies will only reinforce the idealization of infantile sexuality. It could be said, in fact, that in general the fact alone of interpreting in that direction already implies the indication of the differences. But it is not always so. When the manic mechanisms are most in evidence, the attempt to erase the difference between the adult and the child is stronger, and then we will have to integrate this aspect more firmly in the interpretation.

Because of everything that has been stated, it can be understood that a configuration appearing at this stage of analysis is what Meltzer calls diffuse genitalization, with its concomitant problems of excitement. The purpose of this is to indicate that one of the most characteristic zonal confusions is that different bodily organs can function as genitals. The child utilizes his organs as effectors of his sexuality, confused with his genitals, because, in effect, the special quality of the orgasm, a typical acquisition of adult sexual life, has not been reached by him. Consequently, it is only on the basis of erasing this difference that the sensual activity of the child can be equated with the adult's.

Another aspect Meltzer indicates in this stage is the attempt to take possession of the object. It is a primitive form of love, very selfish and jealous, whose logical corollary is to think that one is endowed with the virtues with which to conquer the object. Here again the idea of confusions of zones and modes evidently reveals itself.

Lastly, the most frequent and difficult configuration to manage in this stage and one in which all defences seem to converge is a persistent attempt to establish, through seduction, a link of mutual idealization. As far as this is achieved, the patient can sustain the idea that he is equal to the analyst, that everything unites them and nothing separates them. Thus access to the depressive position is obliterated, because as this situation is consolidated, the analysand will never arrive at true dependence and the loss of the object, the two features that define the depressive position. The analyst will have to demonstrate here his capacity to undo the patient's persistent, monotonous, multiform attempt that results from this type of idealization. It is really difficult to overcome this continual attack by the patient in search of the idealized link, which, if established, leads the analysis into an impasse, often disguised as a "happy ending".

In Meltzer's third stage (which is the second part of the middle stage of analysis), projective identification continues to function in the face of the problems of separation at the beginning and the end of the hour, the week or the holidays. During the rest of the time it no longer operates massively and is linked to the ordering of the operative erogenous zones and the modes of infantile sexuality. The need to erase the differences between the child and the adult then appears, mediated by envy and jealousy, when the child confuses, for example, his tongue with the nipple or his anal product with the parents' generative capacity. Now we interpret from the anxiety to the mechanism, trying to show that the former is the unavoidable corollary of the latter. We try to make the analysand see that he feels anxiety because he is utilizing a defence mechanism that attacks, undermines and disturbs the functioning of the object.

Let us say, to conclude, that Meltzer assigns to this stage a duration of three or four years in the adult and two or three in the child.

CHAPTER FORTY-SIX

Theories of termination

46.1 General panorama

The problems posed by the termination of analysis are so many and so varied that they must be confronted with a certain systematization. We are going to explain them by attempting to group them from three viewpoints: theoretical, clinical and technical. These areas frequently overlap, of course, and they cannot be delineated in an absolute way although it is pertinent to establish them for the purposes of explanation. We are going to add post-analysis to this (the post-analytic period) as a stage of singular importance whose study, recently begun, deserves extension.

The *theoretical* problem consists in deciding what determines the end of analysis, which is equivalent to saying what should be our criteria of the cure, what assumptions will we refer to in the face of the always difficult solution to the problem of an individual's mental health, and what differences will we establish between illness and health. Freud deals lucidly with this in his article, "Analysis Terminable and Interminable" (1937c), which we will recall more than once in this chapter. It is interesting to point out that the criteria for a cure will be different depending on the theoretical supports from which we attempt to approach them. Hartmann's psychology of adaptation, for example, leads to the idea that the termination of analysis implies reinforcing the area free of conflict and a sufficiently adaptive ego functioning, whereas the Kleinian school will emphasize working through the depressive anxieties. Lacan will say, acidly undervaluing the psychology of adaptation, that a good ending sanctions the subject's submission to the symbolic order, and Winnicott will maintain that the analysand will have acquired his true self and in accepting disillusionment sufficiently will now know how much he owes his mother.

Apart from this theoretical focus of the termination of analysis there is a clinical one, which basically has to do with the subject of *indicators*. To be able to speak of a termination of analysis, obviously we have to find clinically those signs that allow us to assert with reasonable confidence that the analysand is about to enter or has entered the stage of termination. Again, these clinical indicators depend very much on the previously mentioned theoretical supports. But, leaving this aside, all analysts understand that these indicators exist and that they allow us to detect the state of the analytic process at a given moment. There are, in effect, many indicators— which we will discuss—but let us say now that John Rickman defines them accurately in his short, clear work of 1950. There are also other indicators that appear *as a result* of termination being suggested: the decision to end the treatment is always accompanied, in effect, by depressive anxieties and/or phobic or paranoid fears of being without the analyst, even in the case where the process has not reached the stage of termination. Therefore from the clinical point of view we must distinguish the indicators that *signal* to us that the process has reached its end from those that *result* from this phase of the process.

Finally, we should consider the *technical* aspects of termination—that is, how and when to effect it. Here we will have to study the moment when the patient perceives that his analysis has entered the final stage and we agree with that appreciation. Generally we are speaking here of two different moments, because that the analysand should make an assumption is one thing, and that the analyst should share it is another. The analyst's opinion matters, because it is introduced as something *real*, something that is added to the original contract. This happens only when we agree that the new dialect moment we can properly call the stage of termination has been set in motion. This part of the process will last for a variable but never a brief period of time—in my opinion always more than two years—during which there will be moments of progress and integration and others of "inexplicable" regression. It is what Meltzer calls the threshold of the depressive position, which culminates in the weaning process; at this point there arises in the analysand an urgent need to reach the end. This new phase culminates when a date for ending is agreed upon. This must never be either too near or too distant—the time measured in months, not in weeks or years, because if it were in weeks, we would have to conclude that we had delayed too long before announcing it, and if it were in years, we would be reaching out to a too distant future, where the idea of separation could not take shape.

Another paradox—and perhaps the most unbearable—of our impossible profession is that psychoanalytic treatment ends only *afterwards*, that

628 ON THE STAGES OF ANALYSIS

is, when the analysand, now alone and free, decides it in the *post-analytic* period.

46.2 Is analysis terminable?

Among the numerous theoretical problems that the termination of analysis can cause, two are in my opinion the most important: whether a termination of analysis really exists, and which are the curative factors.

Whether analysis can and should end has always been discussed, both before and after the famous article of 1937. Everything makes one suppose that the discussion will continue forever.

Freud's main arguments in "Analysis Terminable and Interminable" (1937c) still stand. Beyond the formal aspects with which an analysis ends—in effect, when analyst and analysand end their interviews—there are also some theoretical reasons for affirming that analysis has to have a termination. Analysis, Freud says, began with certain objectives and should end when these have been reached.

Freud also thinks that a good analysis should protect the individual from recurrences, giving him sufficient tools to resolve his conflicts, within certain limits. When life goes beyond them, with its severity and injustices, this must not simply be attributed to the analysis. The fact that a process ends does not mean it cannot be initiated anew. On the other hand, Freud does not say what we should do if those objectives are *not* achieved. This theme is rarely brought up, perhaps because we would then have to re-solve a no less thorny problem: when are we going to say that analysis has failed? This question is difficult to answer precisely because the limits of analysis are never clear, just as its objectives are not perfectly clear and immovable.

Freud also says that analysts should reanalyse themselves every five years, which makes one think that he has doubts at least about the termination of a training analysis. However, it must be remembered that this wise warning is made in view of the highly unhealthy work the analyst carries out; here therefore the previous principle applies as to the circumstances of the future life of the ex-analysand.

Perhaps this is the moment to state that Freud's 1937 opinions on the efficacy and limits of analytic treatment are balanced and do not differ too much from those he maintained throughout his life, from the *Studies on Hysteria* up to the Budapest Congress and via the articles of 1905—a point Wallerstein (1965) also makes.

On the other hand, it must be remembered that "Analysis Terminable and Interminable" speaks of treatments of very brief duration, different from present-day analyses, especially in the case of training analyses, which Freud conceived almost as a rite of initiation. He even says that, when the learner has a firm conviction of the existence of the unconscious and has taken charge of the strange phenomenon of the emergence of the repressed material, what one can aspire to in a training analysis has already been achieved (1937c, p. 248). Currently it is evident that we do not think in this way; we think a training analysis should be undertaken just like any other analysis and should be deep and prolonged.

Freud's article, known and acknowledged by all analysts, should be read together with the one Sándor Ferenczi presented at the Innsbruck Congress in September, 1927. Freud refers to it continuously, not only because towards the end of his life he must often have remembered Ferenczi, but also because of the great merit of the Hungarian analyst's paper.

In his article Ferenczi (1927) insists that analysis can reach the point of termination, so long as the analyst is courageous and patient in allowing the process to develop without a preconceived time limit and knows how to deal with both symptoms and character. I also do not think the comparison should be made between an acid pessimism on Freud's part and a radiant optimism on Ferenczi's part. I think these two great works are balanced, although they may have more than one discrepancy. Freud, for example, was sceptical about being able to reactivate the analysand's potential conflicts, because he saw only two equally impracticable alternatives: to talk about them or to provoke them artificially in the transference. But Ferenczi thinks they can be reached because he operates with a theory of character that was not in Freud's mind at the time.

Ferenczi roundly asserts in his article that analysis can and should terminate, and he adds that a correct termination cannot be abrupt but must be gradual and spontaneous instead: "The proper ending of an analysis is when neither the physician nor the patient puts an end to it, but when it dies of exhaustion..." (1927, *Final Contributions*, p. 85). He then adds: "A truly cured patient frees himself from analysis slowly but surely; so long as he wishes to come to analysis, he should continue to do so" (ibid., p. 85). Ferenczi describes this final stage as a real mourning: the analysand realizes he continues in analysis due to the gratification of his infantile desires, but that the analysis does not produce effects any longer in reality. At that moment, with sorrow, he ceases to attend the sessions, seeking in his surroundings sources of gratification that are more real. Ferenczi concludes with these wise words: "The renunciation of analysis is thus the final winding-up of the infantile situation of frustration which lay at the basis of the symptom-formation" (ibid., p. 85).

It is possible that we now have different proposals about the formation of symptoms, but Ferenczi's idea that the termination of analysis means that infantile models of gratification are taken as having terminated in order to direct oneself, sorrowfully but resolutely, to more realistic satisfactions is fully relevant today.

In manifest disagreement with his teacher (and with his analyst!) Ferenczi maintains that the objective of the training analysis is not to inform the future analyst about the mechanisms of his unconscious but to equip him with the best instruments for his future work, and that it is inconceivable that the training analysis will be shorter than the therapeutic one. On this point time has favoured Ferenczi—because Freud is not always right! (For a more detailed discussion see Etchegoyen & Catri, *Freud, Ferenczi y el análisis didáctico*, 1978.)

The conviction Freud and Ferenczi share with many analysts who emerged after them that analysis should end is based on clinical data that are well proven, although other data point to the contrary.

The insoluble problem should perhaps be transferred to another area, where we begin by asking ourselves what we understand by termination of analysis, and which are the objectives we take account of when we think of termination. But this leads us to the other theme of the theory of termination, that of the curative factors.

As a process, psychoanalysis should have a terminating-point *by definition*, because when we initiate it we fix contractually an objective, and we never say that we now begin a task from here to eternity. If this discussion has become interminable, it is because, among other things, the analytic process that analyst and analysand take on is not demarcated from the self-analysis, as a personal tool, which will be applied throughout life. Studies at university or at the Institute of Psychoanalysis end; learning continues thereafter forever.

46.3   The aims of the cure

Most analysts hold today that analysis as a procedure that seeks to reach certain objectives should be differentiated from analysis as a program of personal development that lasts throughout life and is, in fact, interminable. These are two different things, although they tend to converge in practice, since the initial objectives can vary—and this is legitimate—as the analysand begins to understand better both his difficulties and what help analysis can really offer. This broad approach should always be circumscribed by the initial objectives of the process, and the analyst would do well to recall them when the analysand, carried by the intellectual enthusiasm of discovery and also, let us not forget, by his transference conflicts, wishes to leave them aside.

The difference just established will continue to be in force even when we think that psychoanalysis should not be constrained by the medical model of cure or treatment. We can maintain that psychoanalysis aims at mental growth, a change of character or the expansion of the personality, without thereby altering the objectives of the process, and that it ought to end when the analysand has sufficiently approximated to those goals, having acquired the necessary tools to carry on by himself.

An analysis postulated as interminable—based on the certain fact that mental growth, integration, mental health or whatever are never wholly achieved and that a legitimate search can always go further—would lead to a radical contradiction, because none of these objectives is compatible with an interminable relation with one who helps to achieve them. There can be no mental growth, nor integration, nor mental health if these are achieved only on the basis of the other and not through oneself. There is therefore an incompatibility here that is not only tactical but also logical; in order to be independent, one cannot depend on the other eternally.

This line of reasoning is obvious, but it is not always taken into account when the question of the termination of analysis arises, nor when the difficult decision has to be made of an ending forced by the sometimes unavoidable exigencies of life, such as a job offer, a scholarship or marriage, when the analysand is obliged to choose between continuing the treatment or following another path. Here the evaluation of the analyst in the terms just presented can be decisive. For the analyst to accept that the analysand should leave, while saying, like Pontius Pilate, that the treatment has been interrupted, is not the same as for him to terminate the analysis while allowing for the possibility that the termination would have been otherwise, had the circumstances been different.

46.4   The curative factors

The other problem linked to the theory of the termination of analysis—and one that is no less important than the previous one—is that of the curative factors. Logically, if we think that analysis is a task that ends when it has been fulfilled, then the issue of what we mean by the fulfilment of that task immediately arises, and this leads us to the curative factors.

Obviously no discussion of curative factors can take place without taking account of the theory of illness and cure with which we operate. But it is also true that when scholastic differences are examined, one finds they pertain more to form than to substance, which therefore shows that psychoanalysis is sound enough as a scientific doctrine.

We thus find ourselves confronted with a series of problems that refer to the phenomena of personal integration and development, and which will weigh strongly on what we decide in respect of termination.

As I have just said, although the consideration of curative factors varies according to the school of thought, one must not be swayed too much by this type of discussion, which is at times less valuable than it seems. In fact, the diverse criteria of the cure proposed do not differ too much when they are examined calmly and dispassionately. The theoretical supports and the methods for their attainment vary; but if they are compared, one immediately realizes where they correspond.

Let us take as an example Hartmann's criteria of cure—that is, the reinforcement of the area free of conflicts and, consequently, a better adaptation to reality—and let us compare them with what Klein proposes when she affirms that paranoid and depressive anxieties have to be worked through. Put thus, the difference is evident and irreducible. Klein always said, however—following Freud in "Mourning and Melancholia" (1917e

[1915])—that one of the fundamental elements of the depressive position is the contact with the object—that is, with reality. Mourning, Freud says, consists in that reality painfully reveals to us that the object is no longer there. And mourning, for Klein, consists in being able to accept psychic reality and external reality just as they are. Although Hartmann does not speak of mourning, his concept of adaptation to reality comes from Freud. Hartmann and Klein, then, have to agree that an analysand should end his analysis better in contact with reality than he was before he began.

Let us take another criterion, such as Lacan's access to the symbolic order. Lacan always becomes angry with Hartmann; he has his reasons, but I do not know if they are justified. Considered in a pedestrian manner, Hartmann's criterion of adaptation sounds sociological and is repugnant to Lacan. Personally, I have many points of disagreement with Hartmann, but I do not believe he is superficial or a simple (simplistic) representative of "the American way of life". If one judges dispassionately what Lacan says, one realizes that it is necessary to abandon the imaginary order, which is the order of dual and narcissistic relations, to elaborate a conceptual or abstract type of thought, which he rightly calls symbolic. This thought is what allows access to the order of the real. Clearly, what is real for Lacan must be different to what is real for Hartmann; but it is also undeniable that they use the same word.

These are only examples to show that, always keeping in mind the diversity of the theories, we must see where and how far we differ. As lucid a follower of Lacan as Jacques-Alain Miller considers Lacan's ideas on access to the symbolic order as similar to those of Klein on the depressive position. This is because the analyst's function, Miller says, consists in disappearing, in not allowing the imaginary situation to dominate the picture: the psychoanalyst should always be in the place of the great Other. For Miller—and I think he is right—all this has to do with Melanie Klein's depressive position and the loss of the object.

In sum, then, even though the subject of curative factors leads us inexorably to the most complicated theoretical problems of our discipline and to the point of possibly a major confrontation of the schools, it is also true that in the practice of the consulting-room there is a broad-enough agreement, which is surprising, as to the evaluation of the analysand's progress.

46.5   *The point of irreversibility*

The two great articles by Freud and Ferenczi that we commented on instigated a great theoretical discussion on the termination of analysis, which has lasted until today. Ferenczi said that if the analyst is patient and skilful, he can take analysis, like a ship, into a safe port, and Freud asserted with his habitual intellectual rigour (at the end of section 7 in "Analysis Terminable and Interminable", 1937c) that "the business of the analysis is to secure the best possible psychological conditions for the functions of the ego; with that it has discharged its task" (p. 250).

Among the many congresses and meetings where the subject of termination of analysis has been discussed, I wish to recall those of 1949. At the British Psycho-Analytical Society there was a Symposium on the Criteria for Termination of Psychoanalytic Treatment on 2 March 1949, in which Michael Balint, Marion Milner and Willy Hoffer participated; Melanie Klein spoke about this theme at the Zurich Congress in August, and Annie Reich and Edith Buxbaum did likewise in the United States. On 6 April of that same year John Rickman, H. Bridger, Klein and Sylvia Payne presented many brief communications on the subject. I will now discuss Rickman's contribution (1950), which holds within its two pages an entire theory of the criteria and indicators for termination.

In order to terminate an analysis, Rickman looks for the *point of irreversibility*, where the process of integration of the personality and of adaptation have reached a level that will be maintained after treatment has terminated—with the exception, naturally, of circumstances of enormous stress. On this basis, Rickman proposes a list of six items: (1) the capacity to move with freedom from the present to the past and vice versa, that is, having removed infantile amnesia, which includes working through the Oedipus complex; (2) the capacity for heterosexual genital satisfaction; (3) the capacity to tolerate libidinal frustration and deprivation without regressive defences or anxiety; (4) the capacity for work and also the ability to bear not working; (5) the capacity to tolerate aggressive impulses in oneself and in others without losing object love and without feeling guilt; and (6) the capacity for mourning.

These criteria should be valued as a group, in combination and counter-position, in order to decide in each particular personal case whether they have reached the point of irreversibility.

In considering all these factors in terms of the transference relation, Rickman asserts categorically that "The weekend break, because it is an event repeated throughout the analysis, which is also punctuated by the longer holiday breaks, can be used by the analyst when making the integrative pattern before referred to in order to assess the development of the patient" (1950, p. 201).

This is why Rickman says that the way in which the analysand thinks of his analyst during the weekend can be a very sensitive and certain indicator that the point of irreversibility has been reached: to imagine the analyst tied like a slave to his consulting-room, studying for the entire weekend, is not the same as imagining him in the theatre or enjoying his family life.

Willy Hoffer (1950), at the above-mentioned symposium, established three criteria for termination: (1) the degree of awareness of unconscious conflicts; (2) the modification of the mental structure by removing resistances; and (3) the transmutation of acting out and of the transference (primary process) into memory (secondary process).

The criterion for termination, Hoffer says, can be defined as the capacity of auto-analysis, which comes from an identification with the analyst in his function, that is, the identification with the analyst's skill in interpretation, in analysing resistances and transforming acting out into memories of infantile conflicts and traumas through the medium of transference acutely experienced and interpreted (ibid., p. 195).

46.6 The new beginning

At the same symposium, Balint (1949) spoke of the termination of psychoanalysis as a *new beginning*. The analysand gradually abandons his suspicious attitude towards the external world and particularly towards the analyst, and, in parallel, there emerges a very peculiar type of relation with the object, which can be called *primary object love* (archaic, passive). Its characteristic feature is the unconditional expectation of being loved without having the obligation to give anything in return, of obtaining the desired gratification without taking account of the object's interests. This gratification is demanded with vehemence and never goes beyond the level of the preliminary pleasure. These desires, Balint continues, can never be fully satisfied within the strict framework of the analytic situation but should be well understood and also satisfied to a considerable degree (ibid., p. 196). If this is achieved, then the analysand will make the new beginning from primary object love to *mature genital love*, where he will be able to attend to his own demands no less than to those of his love object.

Once this process has been successfully completed, the analysand feels he is undergoing a type of renaissance (re-birth), with a great feeling of liberty. He feels that he is parting for ever from something precious and loved, with the ensuing feelings of sorrow and mourning. This pain is alleviated, however, thanks to the feeling of security that emerges from the new possibilities of a happy life.

Balint's ideas can be traced to the Twelfth International Congress held in Wiesbaden in 1932, where he read his "Charakteranalyse und Neubeginn" (1932). Two years later, at the Lucerne Congress, Balint read "The Final Goal of Psycho-Analytic Treatment" (1934).

Balint considers the new beginning to be a phenomenon that appears regularly at the end of analysis and constitutes an essential mechanism in the process of the cure.

One of the characteristics of the instincts that are mobilized in the new beginning, and which, in fact, designate Balint's theoretical position, is that they are always directed without exception towards the object, that is, the analyst, and they are not, therefore, auto-erotic or narcissistic instincts. The new beginning is, then, a new attempt to establish an object relation, to try to find the love object that was absent in childhood. The patient is cured, Balint says, when it becomes possible for him to attempt to love anew (1934, p. 216).

The following year (1937), in Volume 23 of *Imago*, Balint published a new contribution on the subject. (It appeared several years later in 1949 in the *International Journal of Psycho-Analysis*.) Here Balint explains in greater detail the result of his investigations on the final stage of psychoanalytic treatment. He observes that when the analysis has advanced significantly, the patient expects and often demands certain kinds of gratification from the analyst and also from his milieu. If in the face of these demands the analyst fulfils strictly the rules of analysis, then the analysand will respond with frustration, rage and sadism, which will precipitate him into the world of paranoid and depressive anxieties described by Melanie Klein. If, conversely, in order to prevent this catastrophe, these modest desires are satisfied, one jumps from the frying pan into the fire, and an almost manic state is instituted, which borders on addiction or perversion. It is not difficult to foresee that, if this desired type of satisfaction is suspended or delayed, the uncontainable reaction just described occurs.

The desires the analysand in fact wishes to satisfy—Balint continues—are in effect innocent and even naive: to receive some special word from the analyst, to call him by his first name or to receive similar treatment, to see him outside the analytic situation, to acquire something, however insignificant, from the analyst as a gift or a loan. Often these desires go no further than wishing to touch the analyst or to be touched or caressed by him.

These desires have two special qualities: they refer to objects (and therefore the theory of primary narcissism is rejected), and they never go beyond the level of preliminary pleasure. It follows from this, in consequence, that if the satisfaction arrives opportunely and with adequate intensity, the response is also adequate and quiet. Balint says that "properly this feeling of pleasure could be described as a *tranquil, quiet sense of well-being*" (1937, p. 269; italics in original).

All this has a history for Balint. These are reactions to frustration, and they allow a better-adjusted and more equal psychoanalytic conduct, which permits a "new beginning"; conversely, a new frustration of primary object love will lead again to the bad solution of childhood, the recourse to narcissism and the manifestation of sadistic impulses. He says that the narcissism that is observable in clinical practice is, therefore, "always a protection against the bad or only reluctant object" (ibid.).

When, in 1952, the *International Journal of Psycho-Analysis* commemorated the 70th birthday of Melanie Klein, Michael Balint contributed an article, "New Beginning and the Paranoid and the Depressive Syndromes"; in it he fixes his position vis-à-vis the Kleinian school and explains clearly his ideas on the new beginning.

As opposed to Klein and her students, Balint (1952) maintains that psychological development begins with a stage of primary object love where aggression, and its correlate, persecutory anxiety, do not intervene. Balint feels that sadism and persecutory anxiety are not inherent in development but (undesired) consequences of faults in upbringing. He also thinks that those initial faults are reproduced in the treatment in search of a new beginning, a new point of departure that can repair them.

Balint finds that some patients can resolve their conflicts about the desires of the new beginning simply by analysing them, but others return to an infantile state in which they are completely defenceless [*Hilflosigkeit*], in which they do not seem able to understand the intellectual considerations that interpretation can transmit to them. In these cases, says Balint, "my patients and I agreed that some of the primitive wishes belonging to such a state should be satisfied in so far as they were compatible with the analytic situation" (ibid., p. 215).

* * *

These works by Balint already contain his theory of the basic fault, which we discussed in dealing with regression as a curative process in chapter 41. The theory is deeply influenced by the theory of trauma expounded by Ferenczi in the last years of his life (in "The Principles of Relaxation and Neocatharsis", 1929; "Child-Analysis in the Analysis of Adults", 1931; "Confusion of Tongues Between Adults and the Child", 1932). In 1968 the idea of a necessary regression was decisively formulated; but Balint seems less disposed to satisfy it than in the writings we are considering. Although he is actually very sober in the way in which he satisfied primary object love, it cannot be ignored that this drastic departure from the technique can have a symbolic value of great magnitude and complexity for the analysand, which could be sufficient to set in train a process of dissociation and idealization of parallel intensity. I know this is a very Kleinian objection, but it should not be set aside for this reason. Balint's technique will always operate at the concrete level of a corrective emotional experience, since it is admitted by definition that the analysand does not understand on this point the symbolic value of the word. In this way an inevitable dissociation is sanctioned between the traumas of the past and the blessing of the present, between the ununderstanding objects and the analyst who was able to understand. Nothing can guarantee that in other human relations the ex-analysand will again carry forward his "new beginning", sure of being satisfied again, as he was by his analyst. In this sense, the experience Balint recommends does not seem to me the best one with which to face difficulties in life.

On the other hand, if Balint can agree with his analysand on the gratification that will be met (see quote) and, consequently, acknowledges the analysand's capacity for abstraction and symbolic thought, why does he not utilize it to make him continue the analysis as the art is practised?

* * *

In his paper to the 48ème Congrès de la Langue Française des Pays Romans, which took place in Geneva in May 1988, Jean-Michel Quinodoz amply developed the subject of separation anxiety in psychoanalytical treatment. He considers that separation anxiety comprises two types of clinical phenomena, according to the degree of distance that exists between subject and object. When the relationship with the object is narcissistic (Fairbairn's infantile dependence, 1941) separation has to do with differentiating one from the other; when this is achieved (mature dependence), then the subject can really feel the separation.

The end-result of completely working through the separation anxiety gives rise to a special feeling in the analysand, which Quinodoz calls *portance*, which means *se porter* [feel] in oneself and also *supporter* [bear] the anxiety of seeing the object go away without resorting to primitive defence mechanisms (splitting, projective identification). *Portance* often appears clearly in dreams of flying or of journeys at the end of analysis and is a valuable indicator that the analysand has reached an important point in development, similar in my view to Rickman's point of irreversibility.

CHAPTER FORTY-SEVEN

Clinical aspects of termination

In chapter 46 we made a quick study of the theoretical problems posed by the termination of analysis, asking ourselves whether analysis was really terminable and then reviewing the objectives of the cure. In this chapter we discuss the clinical aspects of the end of analysis, leaving for chapter 48 the technique of termination.

47.1 Types of termination

Not all analyses end in the same way; therefore one could speak of the clinical forms of termination, as in internal medicine.

Freud said in "Analysis Terminable and Interminable" (1937c), not without a certain irony, that an analysis terminates when the patient ceases to attend the sessions. It is difficult to deny this, although we could say, conversely—and Freud, in fact, did not ignore this—that an analysis ends, not when a patient ceases to attend, but much later, or perhaps earlier. If it ends before, this is a bad situation; it should therefore end long after the actual date of ending, that is, in post-analysis. The Freudian *boutade* that analysis ends when the analyst no longer sees his client is true, then, only from the descriptive point of view, not from the dynamic one, because an analysis that really ends is prolonged for an appreciable time beyond the last session.

After this digression, let us return to the *types* of termination. Again we find ourselves with a paradox here, and it is that there is only one *termination*—the one achieved through agreement between analyst and analysand. In other cases, if the decision is unilateral or is imposed by circumstances outside the intentions of both parties, one does not generally speak of termination, but of *interruption* of the analysis, or of *irregular termination*.

There can be a few cases in which external factors prevent an analysand from attending or an analyst from continuing to take charge of the analytic process already begun. In our country (Argentina) this happened unfortunately more than once during the years of Videla's dictatorship; but apart from such exceptional circumstances, external factors are not the most important ones, or at least they assist internal ones.

If the interruption comes from internal factors, we speak of resistance. Frequently the resistance comes from the analysand, and the analyst has not been able to resolve it. But it can also come from the analyst. Sometimes the analyst decides not to continue an analysis because it seems to him that the patient will not be cured and he is wasting time, or because he cannot tolerate the emotional burden he experiences in relation to that patient. If these motives are conscious, then it would be better to say so to the analysand, recognizing thereby one's limitations and leaving him free to try a new analysis, another treatment or whatever. To tell the truth can be very painful for oneself and for the other; but it is only bad to lie, and it is also bad not to realize what our desires are and to act them out. Let us also say, to be more precise, that if the analyst decides not to continue the analysis for rational motives, whether it is because he thinks the analysand cannot be treated or because he gives priority to other circumstances in the patient's life, resistance does not apply here.

The most frequent of the causes of interruption we are considering comes from the analysand and is called *incoercible resistance*. In fact, all resistances are analysable up to the point where they cease to be so, and then we say they are incoercible. They come from the analysand, but this does not mean they do not influence the analyst. Any incoercible resistance influences the analyst, either because he contributed to provoking it or because he was not able to manage it.

The other case where the analysis ends irregularly is the *impasse*, where the treatment does not really end but is prolonged indefinitely. We discuss this in chapter 60, but let us say here that both parties are responsible for this situation, and generally both admit it. Given its insidious nature, the impasse always lasts a long time and can go unnoticed until either the patient or the analyst, and sometimes both by common agreement, understand that the situation can yield nothing more, and in this way the treatment is interrupted.

It is said that the impasse at the end of analysis does not exist and that what occurs is that there is nothing more to analyse. Perhaps this is what Ferenczi thought when he said analysis should end by exhaustion. I think this idea is erroneous, since there are always conflicts to analyse. In fact, to reiterate something I have already said in discussing the theory of termination, analysis as a process of development does not end. What ends is the relation with the analyst, precisely when the analysand believes (and the analyst supports him) that he can continue his journey alone, when the objectives initially posed have been fulfilled. Among these the idea that the task will continue to be carried out by the patient should be included. Nobody "graduates as an analysand", believing he no longer has to think about his unconscious.

47.2   The indicators

An important aspect of the practice of termination is precisely how it is diagnosed, how the course of the analytic process is evaluated, how to judge whether termination approaches. This is the interesting subject of the *indicators*.

As can be assumed, the analyst's theories influence detection and evaluation, especially if the indicators are highly abstract. However, I am going to deal with this theme without reference to the theories—at least to the great theories. High-level indicators are not the most useful ones from the point of view of clinical practice, and therefore at this point in the exposition they are not of interest.

Freud said, for example, that the therapeutic objective of psychoanalysis is to make the unconscious conscious and also to erase the amnesia of the first flowering of infantile sexuality, of the Oedipus complex. He also said: "where the id was, there the ego shall be", in the sense of an evolution from the primary to the secondary process. These objectives are shared by all analysts. We would also subscribe to what Ferenczi proposed in 1927 as to the analysand modifying his character and abandoning the fantasy and the lie for a submission to reality. Hartmann states that what is decisive is that the analysand consolidate his area of primary autonomy and expand secondary autonomy, which is always relative but not therefore less important for the individual, in order to function well. Lacan favours the passage from the imaginary order to the symbolic order. Melanie Klein, finally, demands that an analysis should end when the paranoid and depressive anxieties of the first year of life have been worked through.

The objectives of the cure I have just recorded, as others that have also been proposed, are naturally connected with the various high-level abstract theories that their various exponents maintain. But they should not be confused with the indicators. It is true that on the basis of the theories, the indicators are fixed and defined. No patient is going to tell us, I think, that he wishes to end his analysis because his depressive anxieties have been sufficiently worked through, or because he has noticeably extended the area of secondary autonomy. It is the concrete clinical indicators that appear spontaneously that are of relevance here.

One of them, the most obvious and common one—but not to be dismissed—is that the *symptoms* the patient brought with him to the treatment have been modified. We can also understand characteropathic traits as symptoms here. Perhaps this is not the best criterion, because there are other finer ones. But it is, on the other hand, an ineluctable one. If it is absent, there is no sense in thinking about other factors: before considering that an analysis can be terminated it is necessary to verify that the symptoms that were the reason the patient entered into treatment, and others that might have arisen during its development, have been sufficiently modified. I do not say that they have been rooted out, because in an anxious emergency the symptom may reappear. What analysis aims for is to modify the continual presence, to lessen the difficulty and the suffering, that those symptoms signified. It is one thing to hold obsessional ceremonies that contain a death clause, and another to check two or three times that a stamp is in its place. The intensity and frequency of the symptoms, as well as the attitude towards them, will guide us on this point.

The modification of the symptoms, as I have just explained, is an important criterion, but it is certainly not the only one. There are other criteria: for example, the normalization of sexual life. The classic authors from Freud onwards, and no one more than Reich, always insisted that an analysis should end when genital primacy has been attained. This criterion continues to be valid as long as genital primacy does not become a sort of myth or unreachable ideal. It is a valid and accessible ideal for an individual to have, at the end of his analysis, a regular, satisfying and not too contentious sexual life. It is certainly not the case that the patient should "do his homework, and have the good sexual life that his analyst prescribes for him, directly or indirectly, but, rather, that he enjoy it freely, that the fantasies and dreams that accompany it reveal the libido expressing itself affirmatively, always attending to the pleasure of the other as well (the object relation). There is nothing more autonomous and creative than the adult sexual life of the ordinary adult. Meltzer (1973) says the adult's sexual life is introjective (reflective) and polymorphous, continuing and perfecting Reich's classic works on orgastic impotence.

Family relations should also have been modified, and this is another important indicator. As with the previous one, it is worth more if it arises out of the material than if it is stated directly. If a person speaks very well of his sexual life or says that he gets on marvellously well with his relations, we have the right to doubt this. The indicators are valid when they are not proclaimed. It is more important for the individual to say in passing that he had a good encounter with his wife and tell the analyst in the same session a dream that confirms this, or to say that the relationship is better now, or that his adolescent son, who has always been so rebellious, has begun to get on better with his siblings. A pathognomonic sign that ejaculatio praecox is giving way is found in the analysand's comment that his wife is now more interested in sex and it seems to him she is not so frigid any more. These data will always be important, especially because the statements are not made to gain approval.

With respect to *social relations*, indirect data are more interesting than the person's direct statements. In principle, it must be considered that if a person has an unmanageable level of conflict with his milieu, it is because he is not well. If he were, he would find a way of resolving those difficulties, or he would simply seek a less conflictive atmosphere.

At times, as a product of the analysis or because life is like that, one loses friends (sorrowfully, if we have been analysed well) because one realizes the relationship is not what it was. In the same way, and also without proposing it, one may gain others who are perhaps more in harmony with our internal changes and our external reality. Then, as long as there is a manifest conflict, difficult to manage, with the environment, one would have to think, in principle, that analysis has not ended. The opposite circumstance is not at all certain, however, since the lack of conflict can express simply masochism or submission. We have here, incidentally, a valid indicator that can be explained in terms of various different theories. An ego psychologist would say that the conflict-free ego sphere has widened, and the individual's adaptation has improved. I would prefer to say that the amount of projective identification has diminished. The theories change; the indicator remains.

The indicators that register family relations are always sensitive and very illustrative. Sometimes, thanks to analysis, one divorces or does *not* divorce but, rather, changes the partner who still is there, because one sees him (or her) from a different perspective and his or her defects become more tolerable. As Martin Fierro wisely said, *"Aquel que defectos tenga / disimule los ajenos"* ["He who has defects, let him not look upon those of others"]. We must also keep in mind that our changes always influence others, making them progress or making their difficulties manifest. When a woman with promiscuous fantasies is cured of agoraphobia, the husband may feel more sexually attracted to her, or he may feel jealous every time she goes out. The husband's increased paranoia is not necessarily a bad thing; it may serve to make him conscious of illness, so that he enters treatment. The possibilities are really infinite. Many years ago I employed Sackel's method to treat the brother of a colleague suffering from schizophrenia simplex that had gone unnoticed for many years. He remained in bed most of the time, cared for solicitously by his mother. Insulin and my presence rapidly modified that sad emotional devastation. The patient's eyes began to shine, he got out of bed and began to think of returning to his studies, or at least to work in his father's business. The mother then told me that it was advisable to suspend treatment for a few days because her son had a cold. I continued nevertheless, thinking that schizophrenia is much more serious than a seasonal catarrh. The mother then fell ill, the patient began to become delusional, and my friend asked me to interrupt the cure. Thus I learned, painfully, how strong family ties are.

The diminution of *anxiety* and *guilt* are, of course, important indicators, although the aim is not that they should be entirely absent, but that they can be faced and managed. A patient once told Mrs. Bick that he did not know why he felt so anxious driving his car, and she "interpreted" that it was because he did not know how to drive. The analysand very reluctantly took some lessons, and the anxiety disappeared. It is not bad to feel anxiety if it warns us of a real danger (a crash) or even a subjective one. It is a bad thing to deny, project or act out anxiety. The same applies to guilt feelings if they enable us to notice our errors and improve our consideration for others.

In his work presented at Innsbruck, Ferenczi (1927) accords great importance to *the truth* and the lie. His account begins with a man who deceived him about his economic situation and affirms that "a neurotic cannot be regarded as cured if he has not given up pleasure in unconscious fantasy, i.e., unconscious mendacity" (p. 79). Later Bion, who so often seems to go the way of Ferenczi although he never makes a point of this, would take up the same problem in *Attention and Interpretation* (1970, chapter 11).

When we spoke of the irreversible point in chapter 46, we saw that Rickman took *the weekend* as an important indicator, in that it measures the way the analysand faces separation anxiety. Let us remember that Rickman attends not only to the analysand's behaviour in the situation of separation but also to the fantasies he has about the other, the analyst.

Rickman's ideas were later taken up by other authors, especially in London and Buenos Aires, to underline the importance of separation anxiety in the course and the outcome of the psychoanalytic process. We saw, for example, that Meltzer constructs his theory of process in good part on the basis of the strategies the analysand uses to elaborate or elude separation anxiety. At about the same time, Grinberg (1968) studied the importance of separation anxiety in the genesis of acting out, as did Zac (1968). The weekend separation, Zac says, leaves the analysand without the container of his anxiety, which amounts to saying that the analyst inoculates him with anxiety and madness, to which he responds by acting out to re-establish the previous precarious equilibrium.

Most, if not all, analysts support what Freud said in his splendid work, "Moral Responsibility for the Content of Dreams" (1925i): in that *dreams* are part of ourselves, we are always responsible for them. For some, such as Meltzer (1967), not only the latent ideas but also the manifest content can be an important indicator, since the latter can express graphically what Meltzer likes to call the geography of unconscious fantasy.

If, as Freud asks of us in his short essay, we can accept that the censurable desires that appear in our dreams belong to us, this is because we are able to observe without distortion our psychic reality, and we are then closer to ending analysis. What Meltzer says follows the same track, although it is different in that he deals with the manifest content. If the dreamer appears represented by different characters who are all similar to him, in his opinion, this means he has achieved an integration of different facets of the personality, so that the analysis is considered to be at a very advanced stage. For example, I dream that I am walking, holding a child's hand, and I say that it is my grandchild or that he has one of my infantile characteristics, something I had as a child, something that I feel represents me directly. It can be assumed that this infantile part is incorporated into (my) self; on the other hand, if I were to say that it is an unknown child or that it runs away, one would have to think that this cannot be the case.

As we saw in dealing with styles in chapter 34, Liberman has elaborated a theory of *linguistic indicators*. He postulates as a basic achievement of psychoanalytic treatment an ideally plastic ego—an ego that has been able to incorporate qualities or functions that he lacked and to moderate those he has to excess. There are complementary styles and, as we become able to use them in counterpoint, we come closer to a state of health, that is, the termination of analysis.

Liberman expounded some of these ideas in his communication at the first symposium of the Buenos Aires Association, "Analysis Terminable and Interminable" Forty Years On, in 1978. Just as Melanie Klein observed that as a child progresses in analysis, new ways of playing appear, in the same way changes in the adult appear through his linguistic behaviour. "We observe this each time our patients increase their linguistic capacity and effort (see Chomsky, 1965) in moments of insight, which arise as an epiphenomenon from a process of working-through that occurs inside and outside the session" ("What Subsists or Does Not, from 'Analysis Terminable and Interminable'?", Liberman, 1978a). An indicator that may be particularly sensitive, and which in principle appears spontaneously, is the *musical component of the language*, of which Fernando Guiard (1977) gave a penetrating account. The references to intonation and rhythm can indicate significant changes, which speak of a deep melodic line in the interaction of communication. Through indicators of this type we can divine, as Guiard shows us, a range of feelings that not only serve as indicators of the termination but also point to the subject's possibilities of sublimation and to his adequate grasp of the analyst's feelings.

* * *

Keeping in mind that there can be other indicators I have omitted or forgotten, I wish to point out that the indicators expounded here are useful and reliable if they are adequately evaluated. One of them is certainly never enough; but if several indicators appear, if they arise spontaneously and in different contexts, we can think with assurance that we are on the right path.

I wish to underline once again that the indicators are valid if and only if they are gathered from the material spontaneously and indirectly— never if they are introduced subliminally in the analysand as an ideology of the analyst. When I began my training analysis in Buenos Aires at the end of the 1940s, *Character Analysis* was highly valued. The idea of genital primacy operated for us, the candidates, as a superego exigency, which really had little or nothing to do with the exercise of sexuality. Thus a precise and valuable indicator such as this was entirely denaturalized.

47.3   *The post-psychoanalytic process*

Of the many who have dealt with the post-psychoanalytic process, none, perhaps, have done so with as much thoroughness as Fernando E. Guiard (1979), whom we will follow in our exposition.

It is not enough to include auto-analysis in the post-analysis. "We should be interested in the subsequent fate of our analysands and try to share with our colleagues, whenever possible, the data obtained", Guiard proposes (ibid., p. 173).

To obtain data from the post-analytic period, we count on three possibilities: *spontaneous* contact, if the ex-analysand writes or visits us; *accidental* contact, if we find out something about the analysand coincidentally; and *programmed* contact, proposed by the analyst when his aim is a *follow-up*.

In recent years there has been a growing tendency to accord real importance to the post-analytic period. Leo Rangell (1966) holds that it should be considered as another phase of the psychoanalytic process—that is, it should be included in and considered as part of the cure. Guiard goes further in maintaining that it should be accorded full autonomy and considered as a new and different event, which he proposes to call the *post-psychoanalytic process*. At first sight it seems to me too great a rupture. According to Guiard, this is a process of mourning, on the outcome of which will depend the future of the analysis, and he affirms that "it is not only a continuation of the analytic process, but it is also a new process set in train by the perceptual absence of the analyst" (Guiard, 1979, p. 195).

Following the general lines of the theory of therapeutic regression, Rangell feels that post-analysis is the cure of the transference neurosis, and he compares it with the surgical post-operative period in which the patient has to recover not only from the original illness but also from the surgery itself. Guiard shares this criterion when he says that the post-analytic process is like a convalescence both of the transference neurosis, that intermediate zone between illness and life, as Freud called it (1914g) and, at the same time, from a new illness occasioned by the separation that must be faced in solitude. Whoever does not accept the theory of regression in the setting—as in my case—will not perceive post-analysis as an iatrogenic illness and a convalescence of the process, but as a natural and painful stage in which analysis culminates. Guiard's idea of convalescence does not support his proposal to consider post-analysis as a new and different process.

For Guiard, the post-analytic process evolves in three stages: the *initial* stage, in which the analyst is missed and his return is yearned for; then a stage of *working through*, in which the ex-analysand fights for his autonomy and accepts solitude; and finally the *outcome*, in which autonomy is achieved and the analyst's *imago* becomes more abstract (Guiard, 1979, p. 197).

According to this perspective, Guiard recommends caution and patience during the period in which the post-psychoanalytic process occurs. It must be interrupted with a new analysis only if one is certain that this process will not develop appropriately.

47.4   The follow-up

If we attempt to study the psychoanalytic process and also to evaluate the results of an analysis, then we have to decide to establish with the analysand, prior to ending analysis, some type of future contact. In general, the most logical method is that of periodic interviews.

Personally, I am in favour of establishing in the best way possible an agreement to carry out the *follow-up*, but this is not simple. For one thing, it depends completely on the patient, since to demand that he appear would be not to end the analysis, but to maintain the link. Furthermore inasmuch as we cannot use the analytic instruments of observation, the follow-up interviews are neither convincing nor trustworthy.

I propose to patients that they come to see me three and six months after ending analysis, and then once or twice a year, for a variable period. Some fulfil the suggested programme, others do not. One must not lose sight of the fact that the analyst is important during the analysis because there is a process of concentration of the transference (or of transference neurosis) which is resolved, and what remains is irremediably lost. The analyst finally becomes a person who is in his place—an important place in the memory of the patient, but no longer in his life. The destiny of a good analyst (in the patient's mind) is nostalgia, absence and, in the long run, oblivion.

In post-analytic interviews, whether spontaneous or agreed, I adopt an affectionate and conventional attitude, seated face-to-face with my ex-analysand, and I only interpret occasionally. I agree with Rangell that if the interpretation is necessary and expected, the ex-analysand will receive it well.

I leave the direction of the interview to the ex-analysand, and I accept that he may or may not pay me, as he wishes. A serious and responsible female patient who adjusted strictly to the programme of interviews we had agreed on never paid me. In one case, however, she consulted me because she was very anxious about becoming a grandmother. She realized by herself in the interview that the event had reactivated her conflict with her mother. On this occasion she paid me and left calmly, not without saying that my fee was low. (During her treatment she had always said the contrary.)

She then attended the last interview we had agreed on and said goodbye with much affection and sincere gratitude. Shortly afterwards I saw her in a shop, and I was very glad to see her. I think the same happened to her. Setting my analytic reserve aside, I asked her to telephone me so that we could meet again. She promised to do so but did not; I do not know whether to attribute this to her condition as ex-analysand or simply to the fact that she is from Buenos Aires.

Some analysts accept that an ex-analysand, especially a colleague, will consult them occasionally to be helped to resolve some problem of their self-analysis. To my mind, a request of this sort can be complied with on occasion but never systematically, because it would then be a covert way of carrying on the analysis or beginning it again. At any rate, there are very experienced analysts who supervise systematically (once a week, once a fortnight, once a month and even more sporadically) the self-analysis of their ex-analysands or other colleagues, especially starting from dream-analysis.

The experience of termination should be concrete and unambiguous, leaving the analysand free to return, if he wishes, beyond the agreed follow-up interviews. Freud said that the affective link of intimacy analysis leaves is valid, and it is logical that an ex-analysand, if confronted by a particular emergency, might wish to talk to the one who had been his analyst.

Any analytic termination is a trial, which does not mean it is effected lightly; it means, rather, that the analyst may have made a mistake, or the patient may have problems that make him regress. We cannot compare analytic termination to the one the surgeon carries out after an appendectomy, certain that his patient will never again have appendicitis, not even if he has Meckel's diverticulum! Since one never knows whether the ex-patient will need more analysis, it is fitting to maintain a certain reserve. But these precautions will vary over the years and with the preferences of each ex-analysand. We will always have the right to preserve our intimacy, but not to impose our idea of distance on others.

In principle I am not in favour of exchanging the analytic relationship for a friendly one, which in my opinion is inappropriate. I understand that there can be a natural tendency in this direction and that on occasion, in the course of time, a friendship can develop spontaneously, but I do not believe that all my patients have to become my friends. It could be that this friendship is a remainder of the transference, and even if it is not, it leaves the patient unprotected, in that he no longer has an analyst should he wish to return to analysis.

CHAPTER FORTY-EIGHT

The technique
of termination of analysis

48.1 *Introduction*

We said in the previous chapters that each stage of analysis has its particular dynamics, which results in clinical indicators that allow us to approach it. We also said that the indicators for termination appear gradually and spontaneously until they acquire enough clarity. We studied the basic ones: the morphology of dreams, the type of communication and the stylistic modalities, the behaviour with the spouse or partner, the family and the social milieu, the management of anxiety (separation) and guilt and, of course, the alleviation of symptoms. Love and work, it has always been said, are the two great areas where the degree of mental health of human beings can be measured.

We will now examine the third point of view from which the process of termination should be studied: the technical aspect—that is, the *modus operandi* of terminating the analysis.

In the course of the analytic process we will see, without intending to (because it is spontaneous), that the analysand has been changing. He will also observe this himself, in his own way. We will note that his symptoms are no longer there or that they have diminished considerably, that he has recovered his genital capacity, that he works well and can also enjoy his leisure, and so forth. This is accompanied by the emergence of the indicators studied, and, once these indicators have presented themselves, the problem arises of how the process of termination is to be accomplished.

There are many ways of bringing an analytic process to an end, depending on the analyst's theories and style, on the patient's predilections and even on his social milieu and the circumstances of his life.

48.2   The models of termination

We have said that clinical indicators of the termination of analysis are explicable in terms of certain theories; nevertheless, they exist in their own right and should not be superimposed on the hypotheses that can be applied to them. Let us say here that termination takes shape in *models*. Although these models vary infinitely, as do the cases in clinical practice they are ascribed to, they converge in the long run into two fundamental forms that seem to include the others: birth and weaning. Again we should warn that these models should not be superimposed here on the theories they refer us to; we can accept a particular model without having to subscribe to the theory that has given rise to it.

The birth model was studied by Balint and Abadi, among others; they hold that the termination of analysis is isomorphic with the experience of birth. In chapter 46 we saw that Balint (1949) compares analytic termination to the passage from primary object love to mature genital love, which represents a *new beginning*: the analysand feels that he is being born into a new life, where feelings of sorrow due to loss are mixed with hope and happiness.

Abadi (1960) also uses the model of birth to give account of the termination of analysis according to his own theory of development. The basic situation of the human being turns on birth: the life of man develops from intrauterine captivity to life in freedom outside. The dynamics of this situation depend on the prohibition of the mother, who impedes birth, in conflict with the child's desire for liberty and the guilt that accompanies him for the crime committed in being born and therefore going against maternal prohibition. This conflict crystallizes in the trauma of birth. The analyst's principal task is, then, to accompany his analysand in his natural process of liberation. This perspective converts psychoanalysis, as a conception of man, into an ideology of freedom (ibid., p. 167).

Melanie Klein firmly believes that the experience of terminating a successful analysis is an exact replica of weaning: to end the analysis is literally to be weaned from the analyst–breast—to repeat that basic, fundamental experience. In the Kleinian school no one argues about this viewpoint; as it is accepted that the infantile depressive position is organized basically around the experience of the loss of the breast. Following this line of thought, Meltzer calls the last stage of the psychoanalytic process *weaning*.

It is advisable to point out here that Klein considers that this first experience of mourning for the breast will be reactivated later at other crises of growth, such as bowel training, the loss of oedipal objects and all the subsequent situations of mourning in the course of life. For Klein any mourning is a mourning for all (situations of) mourning.

Arminda Aberastury rightly said that deep mourning, which is prolonged through adolescence, is occasioned by the loss of bi-sexuality, the hermaphroditic psychic dream that is difficult for us to abandon in order to turn out tediously as men or women.

Those who believe, like Rangell, that the experiences of the first year of life are not recoverable can accept that the termination of analysis may adopt the models of birth or weaning but never as the out-and-out repetition of those distant and inaccessible episodes.

The models of termination should not be confused, then, with abstract theories that try to explain by means of these models the deep dynamics of the last stage of analysis. I can have the model that ending my analysis is like graduating from school or as a doctor or like learning to dance or swim, but this does not mean that the promotion (in the former case) or the learning (in the latter case) was the starting-point of my mental life, my character, my neurosis.

The distinction I have just proposed has, in my opinion, methodological value, but it should not be thought of as clear and distinct. In a concise and elegant work, Janine Chasseguet-Smirgel (1967) showed convincingly that dreams of examinations have to do with processes of maturation, and it is not entirely coincidental that high-school examinations in Germany are called *Matura*. In this case, then, to graduate from high school can be a model for the process of ending analysis, inasmuch as it refers to a concrete and singular life experience.

Sylvia Payne, in a brief article (1950), points out that analytic termination is similar at times to the fear of growing up or of becoming an adult, of leaving school or university, of being born again, of being weaned or of fulfilling a process of mourning—that is, critical moments in development that require a reorganization of the ego and the libidinal interests of the individual.

In a brief and enduring work on teething, walking and language in relation to the depressive position, Arminda Aberastury (1958; originally published when Arminda was married to Pichon Rivière, but here included in the List of References under Aberastury) articulated the theory of the infantile depressive position via language, teething and walking, which distance the child from the breast and protect it from oral sadism. When I analysed a man who was late in walking due to a congenital hip luxation (dislocation), the model of learning to walk imposed itself perforce as a model of the termination of the analysis.

* * *

Otto Rank (1924) was certainly the first to consider birth as the model for analytic termination. Later on he developed a complete theory of deep psychology (will psychotherapy), quite far removed from orthodox psychoanalysis, where all therapeutic efforts would centre on the birth trauma. *Das Trauma der Geburt* was published in Vienna in 1924, and it is evident that he counted in principle on Freud's scientific interest; the latter did not, in fact, concur with Rank in his subsequent postulations.

Rank starts out from the frequently observed fact which I have already pointed out—that all patients symbolize the end of analysis as a birth. This fantasy soon became for Rank not only a symbol but also, and strictly, a repetition of the birth in the course of the analysis. From this Rank deduces that birth configures the primordial anxiety of the human being, all other anxieties being organized from it, a point of view adopted by Freud in *Inhibitions, Symptoms and Anxiety* (1926d [1925]).

Although doubts exist about the influence of Rank's ideas on Freud's second theory of anxiety, as Strachey (1959) says in his introductory note to the book in 1926, in my opinion Rank's theory on the birth trauma probably influenced Freud at that time. Rank, of course, derived from it an explanation of neurosis and of cultures where the birth trauma came to occupy the place of the Oedipus complex.

48.3   The termination of analysis and mourning

It is widely held that the end of analysis stirs up a process of mourning, without thinking thereby that it is isomorphic with the child at the breast at the moment of weaning, as Klein postulates.

In this context, Annie Reich (1950) points out, for example, that the termination of analysis carries with it a double loss, transferential and real. The former is inevitable since, even in the most successful analysis, elements of transference remain, and it never ends by becoming exhausted, as Ferenczi wanted it to be. And, together with this loss of objects transferred from childhood, the analysand loses the analyst himself, the analyst in person. A relationship that has lasted for a long time and achieved a high degree of intimacy and confidence cannot be abandoned without sorrow. Having in mind the magnitude of this double loss, Annie Reich advises fixing the date in advance, several months previously.

We have already seen that Klein (1950) established a direct relationship between the infantile depressive position, which is decisive for her in the structure of the mind, and the termination of analysis. An analysis that has taken a satisfactory course should lead to a situation of mourning because it reactivates and revises all the mourning situations of life, from the first and main one, the mourning for the breast. The criteria for analytic termination always refer, then, to an adequate elaboration of the paranoid and depressive anxieties of the first year of life. Abraham had also postulated—as a necessary point in adult depression—the existence of a primary depression (protodepression) before the Oedipus wishes have been overcome (1924, p. 459). Klein follows this same line of thought, but her proposal is much more audacious and rigorous in that she locates that protodepression much earlier (in the second trimester of life) and structures it as an ineluctable phase of normal development.

Since depressive anxieties are by definition fluid and changeable, Meltzer calls the one we are studying *the threshold of the depressive position*, in his classification of the stages of the analytic process. Nobody, in fact, *arrives* at the depressive position, which, rather than being an achievement, is an aspiration—not a place or a thing but a complex constellation of fantasy and reality organized around the object relation and strongly inspired by the urgency of reparation.

As the confusions of zones and modes of the third stage are resolved, the feeding breast appears as the principal object of psychic reality, and its confluence with the hitherto dissociated toilet–breast confronts the child with the strongest depressive anxiety in the realization that his aggression has been directed in the final instance to the object that gave it life. The correlate of this basic moment of development is the analysand's recognition of the autonomy and function of the analyst. When this is achieved, Meltzer says, the fourth stage of the analytic process begins, and from that moment the idea of termination hangs like the sword of Damocles over the analysand.

Meltzer says that what draws our attention and weighs on the countertransference of the unprepared analyst is the fact that the analysand acknowledges the method before acknowledging the analyst himself. He will say that he needs analysis but will doubt that his analyst is the one best suited to offer him the treatment. Money-Kyrle (1968) also describes the same configuration, as we shall see, in saying that a classification of "good analyst" may not be applied to one's own analyst.

This is a stage of struggle in which the impulse towards integration clashes constantly with the regressive withdrawal to the comfortable terrain of the confusion of zones and modes. The psychoanalyst has to make a great effort to accompany his analysand through the difficult course of maturation that involves acknowledging and at the same time losing the breast, simultaneously with the pain and jealousy vis-à-vis the pregenital and genital primal scene, which will lead to the recognition of coitus as the supreme act of creation and pleasure and, finally, of the creative and reparatory function of the father's penis and testicles.

As we have already said, in the best of cases the threshold of the depressive position is reached, according to Meltzer, in two or three years of analysis in the case of children and in four or five with adults, a stage that—in my own experience—analysands reach somewhat later.

As to the duration of that stage itself, this varies greatly according to the particular case: the agonizing fluctuations between integration and regression may be prolonged for varying periods of time. But I think that from the first appearance of the idea that the analysis is in the process of termination until the ending itself is confronted, a period of more than two years elapses.

48.4   *Improvement-phobia*

The termination of analysis is generally considered as a process of mourning, a moment when the phobic fear of remaining alone, abandoned and without protection, is reactivated. Garma (1974) gives the phobic fears of the end of analysis an original meaning.

For Garma, mourning during termination is always accidental and usually conceals a subtle defensive strategy. What really counts is the analysand's need to liberate himself from bad, persecuting objects that impede his progress. A phobic situation thus takes shape, in which the analysand does not wish to improve for fear of the damaging internal objects. It is clear that the phobia Garma describes is not the phobia we all see in the very natural expression of the fear of remaining without the analyst and having to face a potentially hostile world. This common phobia is a mixture of not only persecutory but also depressive anxieties, which everyone accepts. Garma is saying something else.

If a psychoanalytic treatment has a successful outcome, then the analysand has the logical desire of improving further in order to behave in an adult and capable manner when the moment of separation from his analyst arrives. However, this positive desire is opposed by the internal persecutory objects, which are projected in turn into the analyst, allowing only a limited improvement. This configuration crystallizes in the three basic resistances Garma describes: the phobia of improvement, the intensification of the process of mourning and the undermining of the analyst's capacity.

Once the dynamics proposed by Garma are understood, it becomes clear that the phobia of termination expresses the fear of being cured in the face of the attack of the internal persecuting objects: the analysand flees the cure so as not to confront them. The phobia sanctions in this way, for Garma, the submission to the internal persecutors and also, of course, to the analyst, who through projection represents them.

The best strategy for consolidating these phobic defences is the intensification of mourning reactions in the face of future separation. What the analyst must then do is to unveil such a placating strategy instead of accepting the false feelings of mourning. Garma, like most, believes that there are feelings of loss and sorrow at the end of analysis. But when the false defensive mourning is cleared away, the ending of analysis is accompanied essentially by an experience of affirmation and satisfaction.

The third defence the analysand avails himself of to avoid the conflict with his persecuting objects at the moment of analytic termination is the denigration of the analyst. In degrading the analyst, the patient achieves two great defensive advantages: if the analyst is incompetent, then he can hardly help him to improve, and, at the same time, the tendency to denigrate himself, to consider himself incapable of any progress, is projected into the analyst. The objective of these attempts to undermine is not "to free himself of self-denigration through projection (projective identification) into his analyst, but, rather, they attempt to make the analyst inferior in some way, just as the analysand unconsciously thinks he himself is" (Garma, 1974, pp. 686–687).

I agree with Garma that the mourning for persecutory objects that impede growth is a false mourning and that what can best be done is to expel them in order to liberate oneself. But, as opposed to Garma, I believe that the matter does not end there, but it is precisely at that point that the true ending begins. Let us recall that Meltzer indicates at the beginning of the threshold of the depressive position a curious splitting, which offers a different theoretical explanation for Garma's good clinical observations: the patient acknowledges the virtues of analysis but does not believe in his analyst. If the analyst refers the denigration to the persecutory objects that impede the patient's progress or growth, he leaves the dissociation intact, and the difficulties remain projected in the objects of childhood. The dangerous corollary of this dissociation is that the analyst who allows growth remains idealized.

The major objection to Garma's theory is that if the internal persecutors are so malevolent that mourning their loss is only a defence, then the conclusion would have to be that the internal world has not changed sufficiently. Garma's theory, to conclude, may reinforce the paranoid and manic mechanisms—what Racker (1954) called *recriminatory mania*.

48.5   Detachment

There is, without doubt, a moment during the course of analytic termination when the idea imposes itself on analyst and analysand that the objectives with which the treatment began have been sufficiently fulfilled and that the time to say goodbye has arrived.

From the technical viewpoint various courses of action can be followed, according to the analysand's predilections, the analyst's style and the real circumstances. A definite date can be fixed, or this can be carried out in two steps, affirming first that the analysis will not be prolonged beyond a certain date, and then fixing the precise date of the last session.

As we have said, Meltzer calls this stage *weaning*, but I have preferred to call it *detachment* in order not to tie myself to a particular model, however significant it seems. Personally I have no doubt that the depressive position is a pivotal moment in development and turns on mourning the loss of the breast; but I also think that the richness of clinical material obliges us to consider each case as particular and unique, disposing us always to discover what is unrepeatable.

Arlow and Brenner (1964), to refute the idea that the analytic process reproduces the early stages of development, cite the case of a man for whom the termination of analysis represented the loss of the foreskin rather than the breast. In this, as in all cases, to apply a theoretical scheme to the material of the patient would have made us lose what was specific in his feeling of loss. However, I in no way believe that an experience such as this should be counterposed to the other by asserting that for this man it was the foreskin and *not* the breast that constituted the lost object. This, for me, is no more than a negation. Primary objects are interchangeable, and whoever experiences sorrow for the loss of his foreskin will also feel it for the breast, which has also been lost.

The great paradox, the great tragedy of the ending of analysis, is that it should end when it has become advantageous and creative. But a fundamental achievement of maturation is precisely that one takes charge of the passage of time, and with it of the urgency of completing the task at hand, being needed for others in the future.

In the stage of detachment, analyst and patient are pressed by the idea of time. Time is running out, it passes inexorably, one cannot go back; and in fact any experience acquires its sense when one envisages that it must end. In this, existential philosophy is right when it enables us to understand that being is only at the end of existence. If there were no end to it, no experience would make sense, as Borges shows us beautifully in "El inmortal".

The recognition that time passes marks the necessity of ending the analytic process. This arises not only from the depressive experience of the children about to be born—"who are more needy than I am", as patients often say—or from the reparatory desire to give the analyst back his free time, but also from a concern for the task that one must take on for oneself, as an independent person who is able to complete what one has begun. This is not motivated by a search for triumph, but by a feeling of unavoidable loss and nostalgia. If I do not take this step, I will never achieve my real being, and this is a fundamental responsibility, not only in respect of third parties but also towards oneself. This conviction arises from depressive anxiety and is always accompanied by a deep feeling of nostalgia and loss.

48.6   *On the forms of termination*

It is generally thought that it should never be the analyst who proposes termination. The only thing the analyst can do with validity is to interpret that the patient is thinking of ending, that he desires it or fears it, when he notices that these desires exist and the patient represses them; but in principle he should not give opinions. In this case, as in all others, the analyst should try to see what the patient thinks and reserve what he himself thinks. Here, however, an exceptional circumstance intervenes, an unavoidable step, which engages the analyst's opinion. Often in the course of an analysis we may have interpreted a fantasy of termination, for example when the patient makes a flight into health; but now it is different, because once the patient accepts that he thinks he is in the phase of termination, he will ask our opinion, and then we will naturally have to give it. At first sight it seems that we deviate from our technique here; but in fact this is not so. Our technique says that in all those situations where we are committed via the analytic contract, we will have to give an opinion, for example when we speak of fees, holidays, the use of the couch or free association. Here also we will have to say something, conscious that in doing so the conditions of the analysis change, and the ending, formally and strictly, is initiated.

I think the analyst should offer his opinion as and when necessary and without anticipating what is coming. Now we are referring to the special moment when the analyst confirms that the analysis is entering the period of termination, without saying in advance how and when it will end. The decision to end has been taken by both parties, but nothing has yet been said about the termination itself. This last part of the process always lasts a long time, which depends on when the analyst has given his agreement and, of course, on many other variables. Ordinarily this stage of detachment goes on for months, not weeks or years.

In general, the agreements the analyst gives respond to the analysand's conscious or unconscious ideas, and thus periods that become more definite are agreed on, and in principle these will be irrevocable. That is, the analyst will take three decisive steps, saying first that he agrees that the analysis should end, then that it could be this year or the next, and later on, if all goes well, a date for termination can be fixed. As Annie Reich (1960) said, I believe the date should be fixed two or three months in advance, which is a sensible period of time. A longer period is not very realistic, and we would be at the stage where the detachment is still being worked through; less would not be convenient, because if the analysis has gone well, the anxiety that will necessarily arise will be great, and time is needed to work through it. Once fixed, this period should be irreversible; otherwise we will fall into a trap: the next date that we might agree on could also be changed. Freud was right on this point when he said in "Analysis Terminable and Interminable" (1937c) that a lion only springs once. If we err in this matter, the analytic contract is vitiated. To prolong the date of termination once it has been agreed amounts to beginning all over again. It will always be preferable to keep the date and leave open the possibility of a new analysis, with the same analyst or another, which would perhaps be better in this case. An error on this point, whether we like it or not, poses the whole situation again. Of course there may be some exceptions, when in the face of a traumatic incident in real life—the death of a loved one, for example—a brief postponement of the date can be considered. Although it is true that a completed analysis has to enable the person to face misfortune, it is also sensible not to stretch the cord of mental health too much. Anyway, in this type of case the analyst can offer postponement, and the analysand can decide.

I agree with Leo Rangell that the last stage of analysis reveals special aspects of the analysand that should be carefully analysed and worked through before the true ending is reached: "Just as there are typical individual reactions to the beginning phase and to work during the middle segments of analysis [the patient's own rate, rhythm and style] so the end-work also reveals crucial aspects of the patient's psychic functioning and is to be worked through to completion before the actual ending" (Rangell, 1966, p. 151).

The analysis of the subject of termination, of what this means for the patient and of what his reactions are, will take a variable amount of time. At this stage, Rangell says, problems of countertransference are experienced which can lead the analyst to shorten or lengthen this period. Guiard (1974, 1976) looked at these.

It is during the period of termination that the permanent evaluation of the course of the process becomes most necessary, as Polito (1979) states when he advises stepping back at a given moment and comparing what is happening now with past situations, in the way cross-sections are taken. The privileged moment for this type of evaluations is, without doubt, the final stage of analysis, after the date for ending has been fixed, because it is then that vivid images appear which reveal the changes that have occurred.

There are some analysts, like Edith Buxbaum (1950), who respect the infantile patterns of the patient, his style or his history, in relation to the way the analysis should end. Thus, for example, if the patient had an overprotective mother and wishes to end, this will have to be conceded in order to correct that bad childhood experience. I disagree with this technical attitude, which in my opinion appears to be an active technique.

Finally, one must take into account that if the detachment phase is not effected in time, a "hyper-maturation" occurs. The problem arises when the moment of definitive separation arrives, when the patient has the idea that he has achieved his objectives, that others have not been and will not be achieved because of his limitations, yet he does not dare to go. A specific impasse can take shape here in the face of the possibility of continuing the analysis and neglecting other vital possibilities. A moment comes when all this—the debit and credit of termination—hangs in the balance. At that moment, as the fear of the risks of continuing alone or the desire of avoiding the inevitable experience of loss begin to dominate the rational motives for termination, a hypermaturation is produced. Then the patient begins to attend sessions not because he really needs analysis, but for other reasons. A courageous decision must be taken at this point. Perhaps this is why Ferenczi said that analysis should end through exhaustion. In fact, it would seem there is no termination through exhaustion in the sense that the relationship becomes exhausted. But there is a termination through exhaustion in the sense that the morbid process exhausts itself, while the process of human contact grows. However, one must not forget that every working relationship tends to perpetuate itself in terms of human relationship, which is legitimate. But inasmuch as this aim displaces and undermines the initial one, we are in fact faced with a perverse situation. Then lacunae are created that may soon become more important than continuing the relationship.

PART SIX

ON THE VICISSITUDES OF THE PSYCHOANALYTIC PROCESS

CHAPTER FORTY-NINE

Insight
and its defining characteristics

49.1 General considerations

I f the psychoanalytic process aims to achieve insight, then insight constitutes by definition the backbone of the psychoanalytic process.

This idea is not polemical in itself, because most analysts accept it; on the other hand, there is controversy about whether there are other factors that, together with insight, determine the course of the process. Here there is certainly a basic problem that we will not study at this point; but it is necessary to note that, at times, discrepancies arise from the scope accorded to the terms in question.

Nacht (1962, 1971; Nacht et al., 1958) can question the neutral attitude of classic technique and contrast it with what he calls the analyst's *presence*, but he does not doubt the function of insight, as can be seen in his account at the Edinburgh Congress of 1961. In any case, and as opposed to Nacht, it is generally thought that insight is achieved basically through psychoanalytic interpretation, although some argue that it can also be achieved through other methods. A man as meticulous as Bibring (1954), for example, says that insight is achieved not only through interpretation but also through clarification, although this is again a problem of definition. As Wallerstein (1979) says, it is easier to state it than to distinguish it in practice.

* * *

This chapter, along with chapters 50 and 51, appeared under the title "Insight", in *Trabajo del Psicoanálisis*, 2 (1983).

To sum up: it is generally agreed that insight is the principal mover of the progressive changes analysis (the cure) promotes; but there are some who take other elements into account and/or question the conditions in which insight operates.

On the other hand, no one doubts that there are other factors that can remove the symptoms and even promote changes in the personality, but these belong to suggestive or suppressive therapies, which are not like psychoanalysis but act *per via di porre*.

49.2   *The Freudian version of insight*

"Insight" is not, in fact, a Freudian term. It comes from the English language, not only as a word but also as a concept, since English-speaking analysts in Europe and America coined it. However, I think that those who employed this word did not do so with the idea of introducing a new concept; they thought, rather, that they had found an elegant and precise word to express something that belongs entirely to Freud. Analysis aims to offer the analysand a better knowledge of himself; what is meant by insight is that privileged moment of awareness. However, let us make it clear that the word *Einsicht*, corresponding to the English word *insight*, rarely appears in Freud's work, and certainly not with the theoretical significance currently accorded to it.

Throughout his determined investigation Freud affirms that what is fundamental in his method is knowledge. At one time it will be focused on memories, at another on the instinctual drives, but the aim is always knowledge, the search for truth.

As we all know, in the 1915 metapsychology knowledge consists in *making conscious the unconscious*. At first this famous aphothegm had the topical significance of a passage from the unconscious (*Ucs*) to the preconscious (*Pcs*) system, but to this was soon added the dynamic point of view, in that it is on the basis of conquering resistances that something becomes conscious. In this way the idea is enriched and acquires a meta-psychological content, without its essence changing.

The third point of view of metapsychology, the economic one, is that the acquisition of consciousness occurs in relation to the amount of excitation (cathexis) that arises in the process. The importance of the quantitative factor in relation to the efficacy of interpretation was studied by Reich (1933) and by Fenichel (1941), although it is already present, in effect, in the cathartic method, when Freud and Breuer (1895d) indicate that the pathogenic memory is efficacious in modifying neurotic symptoms only when it reaches a sufficient affective charge.

The economic concept is, then, simultaneous with (or prior to) the topographical one; the dynamic one, on the other hand, cannot be established before the theory of repression is formulated.

In short, the rule of making conscious what is unconscious gradually acquires the diverse meanings that Freud unfolds in his first metapsychology, which are applied naturally and without violence when the concept of insight appears. The term "insight" moulds itself perfectly to the methodology of the works of 1915. Freud could well have said: the psychoanalytic method has as its aim to make conscious what is unconscious, and we call that acquisition of consciousness insight.

Years later, when the structural point of view was introduced, Freud employed another model, saying that the basis of psychoanalytic treatment was that the ideational processes went from an unorganized to a highly organized system, from the id to the ego: *Where id was, there shall ego be*; and this passage from one system to another implied, in effect, a change from primary to secondary process. In his *Écrits*, Lacan (1966) gives the Freudian text, *Wo Es war, soll Ich werden*, a different translation and scope: "Where that was, my advent must be" to express a central idea of his theory, that is, the radical eccentricity (off-centredness) of one's being in relation to oneself which man is confronted with [*"l'excentricité radicale de soi à lui-même a quoi l'homme est affronté"*] (Lacan, "L'Instance de la lettre dans l'inconscient", 1966, p. 524. Maci—personal communication—translates the Freudian expression in this way: "my being is to relocate myself with respect to the Other"). These reflections are important, certainly; but I do not think they affect the argument I am developing.

49.3   Transformations of the term "insight"

The word "insight" has gained ground until it has transformed itself from a word in ordinary speech into a technical expression. No one currently doubts, when he uses it, that he is employing a theoretical term. If we examine psychoanalytic writings, we can see that it appears in the 1920s, but not in the sense that it has now acquired.

In his work on tic, Ferenczi (1921) quotes a "very intelligent catatonic patient who possessed insight to a remarkable degree" (p. 51). When he had presented the same case in a previous work he did not use *Einsicht* but *Selbstbeobachtung* [self-observation] ("Einige klinische Beobachtungen bei der Paranoia und Paraphrenie", 1914). (In *First Contributions*, 1916, p. 295, both "self-observation" and "auto-observation" are used.)

A particularly modern use of this word can be found in Hermine von Hug-Hellmuth's classic work on the technique of child analysis (1921), read at the Sixth International Congress, at the Hague, in 1920. She says that the aim of analysis is to promote the fullest insight into unconscious instincts and feelings: "Whereas in the analysis of the adult, we aim at bringing about full insight into unconscious impulses and feelings, in the case of a child, this kind of avowal expressed, without words, in a symbolic act, is quite sufficient" (1921, p. 296). In this section and in others in this work the term "insight" seems to be employed with the same rigour as it is today.

It is always difficult to decide when a word in ordinary language acquires theoretical significance. But in the case of "insight", we have two important reference-points. At the Fourteenth International Congress in Marienbad in August of 1936 the Symposium on the Theory of the Therapeutic Results of Psychoanalysis took place. Six of the great analysts of the day took part: Edward Glover, Fenichel, Strachey, Bergler, Nunberg and Bibring (see *International Journal of Psycho-Analysis*, *18*, parts 2 and 3). Diverse hypotheses were considered in relation to the nature of therapeutic action in psychoanalysis, but the word "insight" does not appear anywhere. Strachey (1934) mentions it when he says that the second stage of mutative interpretation fails if the patient has no insight and cannot discriminate between what is happening to him with his analyst and what comes from the past. But he did not use it in Marienbad, undoubtedly because he did not consider it necessary. (As stated in chapter 33, however, Strachey's work on mutative interpretation is, perhaps, the one that best specifies the concept of insight.)

A quarter-century later, in 1961, the theme was again taken up at the Twenty-second International Congress in Edinburgh. The symposium was called "The Curative Factors in Psycho-Analysis", and Maxwell Gitelson, Sacha Nacht and Hanna Segal participated, together with Kuiper, Garma, Pearl King and Paula Heimann, who joined the discussion (see *International Journal of Psycho-Analysis*, *18*, parts 4 and 5). All the interest of the exponents centred on insight, and no one questioned that it is a predominant (and perhaps sole) factor to explain the curative factors. Thus, the lapse between the two symposia represents the span of time in which the word "insight" became a strictly technical term.

49.4 The meanings of the noun "insight"

The English word "insight" is composed of the prefix *in-* ["internal", "inward"] and *-sight* ["view", "vision"]. Literally, then, "insight" means internal vision, inward vision, of things beyond the surface, discernment. The dictionary says that it is "the capacity of understanding hidden truths etc., esp. of character or situations" (*The Concise Oxford Dictionary of Current English*). "Insight", then, signifies new and penetrating knowledge.

This leads us to ask what scope we should give the word "insight" in psychoanalysis, since it can be taken in a broader or narrower sense.

Broadly, it means new knowledge, knowledge that, as Rapaport (1942, p. 100) says, goes beyond appearances. Insight always implies access to a knowledge that until then was unavailable. This (broad) definition can refer, however, both to external or internal events. As in the case of Köhler's monkey, I realize that if I put one stick into another, I invent a new instrument; it can be said that I have had insight in that I have created something, because I was able to go beyond the given, the manifest. Insight would be that moment of novelty, of creation.

If the word "insight" is applied in this way to define the instant in which we accede to new knowledge, it still belongs, in my opinion, to ordinary language. This is how Rapaport (1942) uses it, and this is how it appears in much psychoanalytic writing. In 1931, in the preface to the third English edition of *Die Traumdeutung*, in referring to his discoveries on dreams, Freud says: "Insight such as this falls to one's lot but once in a lifetime" (1900a, p. xxxii). No doubt he refers to the act of creation implied by understanding the difference between the manifest and latent content of dreams, if this is how we wish to understand that brilliant, unparalleled discovery. Melanie Klein (1955a), in her work on play technique, also says that the analysis of Rita and Trude, and even more of other children whose analysis lasted longer, gave her insight into the role of orality in development (1975, Vol. 3, pp. 13–135).

It is evident to me that, in these excerpts, Rapaport, Freud and Klein refer to the moment when scientific knowledge is acquired—knowledge that belongs to the world and not the subject.

However, I believe the word "insight" only becomes a theoretical term in psychoanalysis when it is employed in a restricted sense. It is in the Freudian spirit (and is the basis of our clinical work) that, when we apply the word "insight" to the new knowledge the patient acquires in psychoanalysis, we refer to personal knowledge. To make conscious what is unconscious means that *I* (in myself) make the unconscious conscious. The process is not transferable and does not refer to what is external. Not all new knowledge, therefore, is insight, only that which fulfils the Freudian principle of making conscious what is unconscious. In this sense, we should not say that when the analyst realizes what is happening to the analysand, he has insight. Strictly speaking, what he acquires at that moment is knowledge pertaining to the analysand. The analyst can have insight only into his countertransference. In the understanding I have of my patient, there is always a passage through my internal life, where I become conscious of my similarity to or difference from the analysand through my countertransference. That moment I would certainly call insight.

Insight is, then, a process through which we reach a new and different vision of ourselves. When the word "insight" is used in psychoanalysis, it is necessary to do justice to the prefix *in-*, because insight is not just any kind of knowledge, but specifically self-knowledge.

49.5 *Insight and the Gestalt theory*

Although I am inclined to think, as do Sandler et al. (1973, pp. 115–116), that insight is a word from ordinary language which gradually became more technical, I must admit that others think that it reached psychoanalysis via learning psychology and the Gestalt theory.

It is known that *Gestalttheorie* arises as a reaction to the psychology of elements, and it fixes its attention on structure, on wholes, on configurations. Associationism does not permit apprehension of the internal organization and.the objective of the psychological event. The *Gestalt* (form) is something more than the sum of its parts; the whole has more preeminence than the elements that compose it; the prime datum is the structure.

The theory of form, which surely gave a satisfactory explanation of the phenomenon of perception, was applied also to other areas of psychology, although not always with the same success. It was stated, for example, that memory or thought can also be understood as *Gestalten*, without having recourse to the explanations of analysis and synthesis that the theory of trial and error implies.

In studying chimpanzees, Köhler (1917) was able to observe some singular events. When faced with a problem such as reaching a banana with a stick not long enough for the task, the animal is disconcerted—as if it were thinking—and suddenly, in an act of intuition that Köhler specifically calls *insight*, he realizes that by placing one stick within another he lengthens his tool sufficiently to reach the fruit, and he does so. Köhler wants to demonstrate here that thought is not achieved through trial and error, and it is better to explain it through a Gestalt.

The word "insight" used by Köhler was then transferred from form psychology to learning theory (one does not learn by trial and error but by grasping totalities) and from there finally reached psychoanalysis. (A clear exposition of this development can be found in the monograph by Sara Zac de Filc, 1979.)

Thomas French wrote an article in 1939 entitled "Insight and Distortion in Dreams", in which he uses the word "insight, in a way similar to that of Köhler. French holds that the difference between Köhler's chimpanzee and his patient on the couch is not as great as one may think. Despite the theory of desire being different, because the chimpanzee knows that he desires the banana and the patient does not know what he desires, once the patient achieves insight into his unconscious wish, then he is faced with a similar problem to that of the pongid (ape): that of resolving the conflict between his internal desire and the rest of his personality, which rejects or accepts it only under certain circumstances. This process of integration is similar, then, to the activity Köhler's chimpanzee has to carry out. The idea of insight in relation to the *gestaltic* capacity of tying loose ends can be used, French concludes, both in psychoanalysis and in learning psychology.

Although French is interested in the adaptive behaviour of the ego faced with the conflict caused by his desire, it does not seem advisable to me to understand insight as a problem of sheer behaviour. It is better to think that there is insight when the patient becomes conscious of his desire. How he then proceeds if he comes into conflict with that wish is not a problem of insight but, in every case, of working-through. It is unlikely that when the chimpanzee eats his banana he is simultaneously satisfying an unconscious desire of *fellatio!*

49.6   Insight as a field phenomenon

For Madeleine and Willy Baranger (1961–62, 1964), insight is a field phenomenon. The analytic situation is defined as a bipersonal field around three basic configurations: the structure determined by the analytic contract, the structure of the manifest material and the unconscious fantasy. The point of urgency of the interpretation, where these three configurations meet, depends not only on the patient, but also on the analyst: "The point of urgency is an unconscious fantasy, but a fantasy of *the couple.* Despite the 'passivity' of the analyst, he is involved in the fantasy of his patient. His unconscious responds to it, and *contributes to its emergence and its structuring*" (Baranger & Baranger, 1969, p. 166).

The dynamics of the analytic situation are thus defined as a situation of the couple, which "depends as much on the analyst, with his personality, his technical modality, his tools, his theoretical frame of reference, as on the analysand, with his conflicts and resistances, on his whole personality" (ibid., p. 167).

The field functions on the basis of the identifications of analyst and analysand, although "it is necessary to distinguish the nature of the processes of projective and introjective identification in the analyst and in the analysand. It is this difference which testifies to the asymmetrical character of the field" (ibid., p. 169).

Despite the Barangers' assertion that the analytic situation is asymmetrical, all their thinking is organized on the basis of the fantasy of the couple, which I can only understand as symmetrical. In "La situación analítica como campo dinámico" ["The Analytic Situation as a Dynamic Field"] (1961–62) one reads: "What structures the bipersonal field of the analytic situation is essentially an unconscious fantasy. But it would be mistaken to understand it as an unconscious fantasy of the analysand alone. The recognition that the field of the analytic situation is a field of the couple is familiar. But it is accepted that the structuring of this field depends on the analysand, and one tries to act in consequence of this (preserving the analysand's freedom)" (1969, p. 140). This is a praiseworthy aim, they comment ironically, and immediately add: "These restrictions having been made, we cannot conceive the basic fantasy of the session—or the point of urgency—other than as a fantasy of the couple (as in analytic group therapy, where one speaks, and quite rightly, of 'group fantasy'). The basic fantasy of a session is not the mere understanding of the analysand's fantasy by the analyst, but something that is constructed in the relation of the couple" (pp. 140–141). Immediately toning down these assertions, the Barangers add that there is no doubt that the two members of the couple have different roles and that the analyst should not impose his own fantasy, "but we have to acknowledge that for a 'good' session [to take place], the basic fantasy of the analyst and the analysand have to correspond in the structuring of the analytic session" (p. 141).

On these bases, the Barangers conclude that insight is a phenomenon of the bipersonal field, it is the work of two people (1969, p. 173). They therefore differentiate it sharply from insight as a personal quality, as a moment of self-discovery. The word is the same, but the phenomena are radically different (ibid., p. 173)

49.7 Insight and the mental process

The Barangers' investigation has, among other merits, that of underlining the importance of the analytic couple in the development of insight, showing in turn that the analyst participates in this process. We can concur with them in that to give the patient insight we have to have insight into ourselves, without thereby agreeing with their idea that insight is a field phenomenon, a light that goes on, in a place from which it simultaneously illuminates the two members of the analytic couple. In my opinion, the field phenomenon the Barangers describe lays the basis for insight but is not insight itself.

Insight should be considered conceptually as non-transferable: I can only have insight into myself. The analytic process constitutes a special situation, but it does not alter what I have just said, and in general interpretation as an agent of insight is constructed not only on the basis of our knowledge (of psychoanalytic theory, of the patient) but also on the basis of a moment of insight into our countertransference.

Blum (1979) comes very near to what is held here, I feel (without being as restrictive as I am, since he thinks the analyst should have insight into the defences of the patient, of his conflicts and character), when he affirms that analytic insight is necessary for the conduct of clinical analysis and the resolution of countertransference. "The analyst's insight, often enriched and advanced by creative patients, should be distinguished from the patient's insight. The analyst must have insight into the patient's defences, conflicts and character. The analyst's insight is neither symmetrical nor synchronous with that of the patient, and both precedes and permits proper interpretation and reconstruction. Analytic insight is necessary for the conduct of clinical analysis and resolution of counter-transference" (Blum, 1980b, p. 44).

Insight should be considered, then, as the fundamental personal act of seeing oneself (Paula Heimann, 1962, p. 231). Insight is a *reflection* in the double sense of meditating and of "bending" something inwards. Insight belongs to processual and not to personalistic psychology (Guntrip, 1961). As the Barangers say, the relation with the object is very important in achieving insight; but beyond what can arise in the field, insight is always a reflection. For the (personalistic) field phenomenon to become insight, the introjective identification still needs to provoke a moment of reflection in the strictest sense of the word.

What I have just stated should be considered a defining characteristic of insight. It is not an academic specification; it has to do with the way this concept links up with the idea of making conscious the unconscious, which obviously refers to oneself. And, more importantly, it defines a form of practice that inclines the patient to take charge of his own problems.

This conceptual difference is also supported by the facts: Experience shows that a field situation can be clarified without insight arising, and that understanding is not simultaneous in analyst and analysand. I agree on this point with Liberman when he says that insight can occur in the analyst outside the session (1970–72, Vol. 1, especially chapter 2, "Investigación durante las sesiones con el paciente y las sesiones como objeto de investigación").

According to the Barangers, the fantasy of the field is a dual one: analyst and analysand both participate. To defend this position the argument of group therapy is sometimes evinced, where the fantasy (or the dream) that appears in one of the members is really a group one. But there is a difference: in the group all the members participate with specific contributions. Analysis is nevertheless a radically asymmetrical situation. It is precisely because of this that we can reach the patient's desires or fantasies and operate *per via di levare*: what we offer is the adequate framework for the analysand to express himself, never elements that come from ourselves. The idea of a shared fantasy, a fantasy of the field, is no doubt applicable to the theory of analytical psychology, because the Jungians believe the analyst should communicate his thoughts and dreams to the patient. Then there will be a configuration of a field fantasy. But our method is not based on that type of provision. As Grande (personal communication, 1978) says, the field is what the patient uses up in us; and, theoretically, on this point the best analyst will be the one who possesses an optimally malleable structure, where the field is sculpted, if possible, one hundred percent by the patient. That this ideal is never reached does not alter our theoretical presuppositions, nor should it modify our technique.

49.8   *The analyst's insight: a clinical example*

I remember a patient who, over a long period of time, told me very interesting dreams, which I interpreted with real pleasure and "accuracy" without the process developing. Then I dreamed that I had an anal situation with her. This provoked a painful surprise in me and a strong depression, but it led me to understand what was happening. A few days later, the patient dreamed that she was lying on the couch face down and moved her buttocks in an exciting way. She recounted this dream without much distress and with an almost amused tone; it seemed odd to her, and she wished to know how I would interpret it. With these associations, and on the basis of the insight I had had on my countertransference, I interpreted that the dream she was telling me was, in concrete terms, her bottom; she wanted to excite me with the account of her dream more than finding out what it meant.

In this case, as in many others, the moment of insight in the countertransference preceded the possibility of interpreting. I acknowledge that it was an extreme case, but it is illustrative for this reason. There is no doubt that in this case I went further than usual in my countertransference conflict, and in this way arose the dream. Had I grasped my conflict earlier and used it to understand my patient, I would have been able to tell her much earlier the meaning that telling me her "beautiful" dreams had for her. Perhaps this would have been sufficient, with which I would have avoided having to dream it and suffer the emotional shock it occasioned. It goes without saying that the analysand resisted in principle my interpretation; but later, in another context, she confirmed it, indicating that she had the idea that her voice was very agreeable to me. Only at that moment did *she* have insight into the situation.

This example serves to differentiate between two orders of phenomena: understanding and insight. To enable the patient to achieve insight, the analyst has to begin on the basis of a process of insight into himself, which always amounts to resolving a countertransference conflict.

* * *

To sum up: we understand by insight a special type of knowledge, new, clear and different, which suddenly illuminates consciousness and always refers to the person who experiences it. It is a theoretical term of psychoanalysis which belongs to processual psychology, not to personalistic psychology, in that it points to the mental process of making conscious what is unconscious, which was always, for Freud, the operative key of his method.

CHAPTER FIFTY

Insight
and working-through

50.1 *Insight as knowledge*

In chapter 49 we defined insight as a special type of knowledge that includes among its characteristics that of being new and non-transferable. Let us say now that, as with all knowledge, insight implies a relation between two terms or members that can be of a diverse nature. At times it implies the perception of a special type of link, that is, of how two terms are related in a causal explanation: for example, the way the intake of alcohol is related to inebriation. It can also be about an instrumental relation between means and ends, such as the appetitive behaviour of a bird and its finding food. Finally, at other times, the relation is between the symbol and what is symbolized, between signifier and signified. In each of these cases the subject suddenly grasps a relationship that had not been intelligible for him until then and changes the meaning of his experience.

It has always seemed to me that, in this sense, insight occupies a polar place with *primary delusional* experience. Jaspers (1913) defined primary delusional experience [*primäres Wahnerlebnis*] as a *new connection of meaning*, which imposes itself suddenly on the patient and is unintelligible to the observer. It cannot be empathized with. We can, of course, accept Jaspers' phenomenological definition, although as psychoanalysts we may have empathy with the unconscious elements that lead to that new rela-

---

This chapter, along with chapters 49 and 51, appeared under the title "Insight", in *Trabajo del Psicoanálisis*, 2 (1983).

tion of meaning. A patient with paranoia taught me this. I saw him many years ago in Mendoza. He had gone hunting to San Rafael, in the south of the province, with a friend; the two of them were in a truck. Suddenly his friend, while changing gears, touched his leg: "and at that moment", said the patient, "I felt a strange excitement and realized my friend was my wife's lover". From the phenomenological viewpoint this new connection of meaning can leave the great Jaspers without empathy—but not so the meanest of Freud's disciples. At that moment I understood the projective mechanisms of my patient, and I felt really moved by that laboratory-like demonstration.

What I wish to say is that insight is a phenomenon that is in the same category as the primary delusional experience, except that it is located at the other end of the scale. In insight, the new connection of meaning serves precisely to perceive a reality to which there had until then been no access. If my patient had said to himself: "Then it means that my friendship with X has an erotic component, that I have some type of homosexual feeling for him, as proven by the fact that when he touched my leg in the truck I felt a shiver", that man would have had a moment of insight instead of the primary delusional experience that set his irreversible paranoia of jealousy in train.

As in the case of the primary delusional experience, insight is a new connection of meaning, which changes the subject's idea of himself and of reality. It is difficult to establish in what the difference between the two phenomena consists, but let us say provisionally that the primary delusional experience *constructs* a theory and insight *destroys* it. But this is only an approximation which we will have to return to further on.

To end this section, I wish to recall that, on several occasions, Freud established a relation between his theories and delusion. It is enough to remember what he wrote at the end of his work on Schreber (1911c): "It remains for the future to decide whether there is more delusion in my theory than I should like to admit, or whether there is more truth in Schreber's delusion than other people are as yet prepared to believe" (p. 79).

50.2 Dynamic insight

On the basis of these general ideas we will now see how insight is classified, because important clarifications will arise from this. The most typical classification, which is found everywhere, divides *intellectual* from *emotional* insight. Zilboorg (1950), for example, adopts it. And he energetically emphasizes that true insight is emotional, which, as we will see, can be questioned.

From the 1950s onwards, for various reasons we cannot consider here, the study of insight came to the fore. This process, as we have said, culminated in the Edinburgh Congress and has continued unabated. At that time several important studies were carried out. After Zilboorg, there was a study by Reid and Finesinger (1952), then that of Richfield (1954) and one by Kris (1956a) two years later.

Reid and Finesinger, who joined forces in Maryland to carry out an interesting investigation, criticized the classification of insight into intellectual and emotional using arguments that are worth recalling. The classification fails basically because, in fact, the concept of insight itself implies a cognitive, intellectual process. Therefore all insight is essentially intellectual, and there can be no insight devoid of this. There is a difference, however, and they find it in the relation of insight to emotion: sometimes the emotion is not substantial; it does not go beyond the affective component of any intellectual process. At other times, on the other hand, insight is closely linked to emotion, and in two ways that might be called "input" or "output": as content or consequence. The first of these possibilities is not very significant: Insight refers here to an emotion; its *content* is an emotion, one of the terms of the relation grasped at the moment of insight is an emotion. If at a given moment a patient takes responsibility for the hate he feels towards his father, in his insight the emotion appears as content. This category is not very significant, because it could equally be said that an insight is infantile when it refers to something that happened in childhood. This error is similar to that of classifying delusions according to content rather than structure. It is different if insight liberates certain emotions. Insight, in this case, consists in the subject taking charge of a psychological event that provokes in him an emotional response.

Having clarified in this way the twofold relation between insight and affect, Reid and Finesinger propose to call both of these "*emotional insight*", contrasting them with the intellectual insight they call *neutral* to avoid the pleonasm of calling a process intellectual when it is, by definition, just that.

Interested in the role of insight in psychotherapy, Reid and Finesinger say that neither of these two types of insight (neutral or emotional) accounts for the main problem: why insight is operative in some instances and not in others. They then propose a third type that they call *dynamic* insight, which has to do with the theory of repression. At the moment when the repression is lifted, the insight is *dynamic* and is the only really efficient one.

We can now sum up in a simple synoptic graph the investigation done at Maryland University:

$$\text{insight} \begin{cases} \text{neutral} \\ \text{emotional} \\ \text{dynamic} \end{cases} \begin{cases} \text{emotion as content} \\ \text{emotion as result} \end{cases}$$

As its name indicates, dynamic insight occurs when knowledge penetrates the barrier of repression in the strictest Freudian sense and enables the ego to take charge of a desire that was unconscious until then (Reid & Finesinger, 1952, p. 731).

50.3   *Ostensive and descriptive insight*

When Richfield again took up the theme, two years later, he offered a valid criticism of the work just quoted. Reid and Finesinger's classification begs the question, since insight is called dynamic if it promotes change, whereas, if change is not achieved, we will say retroactively that the insight was only neutral or emotional. This creates a vicious circle. I agree with Richfield, and I would add that the idea of insight being effective does not belong properly to our theme, but, rather, to that of curative factors, which is not the same thing. In this chapter I do not propose, in principle, to elucidate why insight is operative (or curative), but to define its categories, which may later permit a firmer formulation of a theory of cure.

Reid and Finesinger's classification can also be objected to in another way, and it is that of the two types of emotional insight mentioned, the second—the one that mobilizes an emotion—is always dynamic, because it is only when the repression is lifted that the emotion that has been repressed until then arises. Therefore, in fact, there are not three types of insight, as assumed by the Maryland investigators, but only two. In other words, the insight they call emotional is always either neutral or dynamic.

To avoid the risk of falling into circular reasoning, but following closely Reid and Finesinger's specifications, Richfield proposes a new classification of insight, which is, I think, the best.

Richfield starts from Bertrand Russell's (1929) theory of definitions, separating these into two types: from word to word, and from word to thing. Sometimes we define something with words—with other words—and these are *verbal* definitions. Had we only word-to-word definitions, however, we would be sailing in a sea of abstractions. We must also have definitions that correlate word and thing. These are called *ostensive* because they indicate, they point to the object. The blind man cannot make an ostensive definition of colour, and in this sense he will always be radically deficient. It does not matter if he knows better than I do which are the Ångstrom units of the spectrum of each colour, nor whether he knows how Picasso used blue or Van Gogh yellow. He may know a great deal about all this, but if I ask him, "what is yellow?, he will never be able to say, standing in front of a Van Gogh painting: "*this* is yellow", because he obviously lacks the facility for an ostensive definition. (For a thorough discussion of this theme, see chapter 1, "Meaning and Definition", in John Hospers, *An Introduction to Philosophical Analysis*, 1953.)

There are, then, two types of definition and, consequently, two types of knowledge. With verbal definitions we obtain knowledge *by description*, always indirectly; ostensive definitions, on the other hand, give us direct knowledge, *by familiarity*.

Applying Russell's concepts to insight, we can say that when unconscious psychological phenomena are described and understood with words, there is *descriptive*, or verbal, *insight*, which goes from word to word. But there is also an *ostensive insight* when the person suddenly feels he is in direct contact with a particular psychological situation. This is so true that often, when we interpret in the belief that we are really transmitting an ostensive insight, we tell the patient: "See, there you have it, this is what I was telling you", or something similar. And often we point (with our hand) from our chair.

These two types of definitions (and of knowledge), which come from Russell and which all the modern analytic philosophers accept, are absolutely necessary. Applied to insight, they sanction a clear difference, but not a supremacy, because these two types of knowledge are not mutually exclusive: things must be known word to word and also ostensively.

50.4   *The concept of working-through*

Richfield's two types of insight—descriptive and ostensive—enable us to propose an explanation that articulates insight and working-through (elaboration). But for now our intention is more direct: to see what is understood by working-through.

As we all know, Freud introduced the concept of working-through [*Durcharbeiten*] in an essay (1914g) called, precisely, "Remembering, Repeating and Working-Through". Towards the end of his article, Freud says, on the basis of an example, that analysts often consult him, complaining that they had pointed out their resistances to the patient and that nevertheless nothing has changed or, worse, that the resistance has strengthened and the whole situation has become more obscure than ever. Freud replies that the patient must be given time to *work through* his resistance, continuing his treatment in accordance with the fundamental rules of the analysis until that impulse, which has been pointed out to him and which he has accepted intellectually, imposes itself on his consciousness, "and it is this kind of experience which convinces the patient of the existence and power of such impulses" (1914g, p. 155). According to his original definition, then, *working-through* consists in mobilizing the resistances for the intellectual knowledge to recover the affect that belongs to it. The training analyst can tell his candidate that he feels rivalry towards his fellow students as siblings, and he can reply that it is so; but from this to the moment when he really feels the hostile instinct and can refer it to the infantile conflict with the newborn sibling there is a long journey full of the obstacles of elaboration.

The reader will no doubt remember Freud telling "The Rat Man" in the sixth session of analysis that his desire for his father's death comes from his childhood, and so forth. In a footnote Freud states: "It is never the aim of discussions like this to create conviction. They are only intended to bring the repressed complexes into consciousness, to set the conflict going in the field of conscious mental activity, and to facilitate the emergence of fresh material from the unconscious. A sense of conviction is attained only after the patient has himself worked over the reclaimed material, and so long as he is not fully convinced the material must be considered as unexhausted" (1909d, p. 181n). Through the process of working-through these *Erwartungsvorstellungen* [anticipatory ideas], as Freud once called them, carry conviction to the patient. Although we do not currently have recourse to that somewhat artificial technical expedient, at least when we make the first interpretation in connection with an important theme, we do not expect the analysand to respond with emotional insight, that is, with full affect. It would even be a bad thing to think thus: psychoanalysis would be very easy and boring. A long time elapses from our first interpretation to the patient's recognition of the impulse within. As an analysand who was able to make contact with his oedipal desires told Fenichel: "I knew psychoanalysis was true, but I never knew *how* true."

At the end of his marvellous 1914 essay, Freud says that working-through is the inheritor of the abreaction of the cathartic method (1914g). In effect, it is so, since within the theoretical frame of the cathartic method working-through is inconceivable. The cathartic therapy assumes that a particular memory strongly charged with affect has been excluded from normal consciousness. This memory is something like a psychic hernia; and, when we reach it, unleash it, a discharge of affect occurs, and it becomes as manageable as other memories that were not segregated from the flow of consciousness, suffering there the inexorable usage of time. When the cathartic method is abandoned for the theory of resistance, the concept of abreaction is no longer operable.

Some think that between abreaction and working-through there are only differences of degree and that the moments of elaboration, as a summation, represent the total discharge of affect of the cathartic method. I do not believe this to be the case, precisely because the concept has changed. Between the cathartic method and psychoanalysis there is an essential difference, a change of paradigm, as Kuhn (1962) would say. (We discussed this point in greater detail in chapter 33, in dealing with mutative interpretation and abreaction.)

50.5   *The relations between insight and working-through*

The idea that the aim of psychoanalysis is to give the patient a special knowledge of himself has been part of the method since the beginning and even earlier, with the cathartic method. The word "insight" condenses this project of knowledge, and now we will study the metapsychology of the process that culminates in that singular moment of insight, which will lead us straight to the great problem of working-through.

The relation of insight to working-through is stated, in effect, when Freud (1914g) introduces the second of these concepts. In this work Freud describes working-through as the interval between the moment when the patient becomes aware of something the analyst has told him and the point when, overcoming his resistances, he accepts it with conviction. I think that in this description the concepts of descriptive insight (what the analyst says) and ostensive insight (the result of the work on resistances) are implied, although Freud certainly does not use these terms. What Freud called *working-through* in 1914 is nothing other than that steep slope the analysand must climb from descriptive to ostensive insight.

Strachey's (1934) investigation can be articulated precisely on this point. Considered from this perspective, the second step in mutative interpretation shapes a moment of ostensive insight in which the analysand contacts directly, not through words, the instinctual drive and its original target. This is why I said that mutative interpretation contains the best explanatory theory of how insight is achieved through interpretation, and also the best example of what is called ostensive insight. From this viewpoint it can be asserted that, by definition, only transference interpretation can promote direct, ostensive knowledge.

I repeat, then, that the process of working-through Freud describes in his work of 1914 leads from intellectual, verbal or descriptive insight to ostensive insight, which we can now say is also always emotional. When I take charge of my instinct, my desire, I feel the consequent affect, and this in the double sense of Reid and Finesinger: I relive the emotion, and at the same time I take on those feelings that that awareness ineluctably awakens—feelings which, beyond emotion as content, arise from insight as promoter of a state of consciousness. (In Kleinian theory, as we will see further on, these feelings are linked to the infantile depressive position.)

50.6 *The other phase of working-through*

The movement that leads from descriptive to ostensive insight, which Freud described in 1914 in introducing the concept of working-through, is only the first part of a cycle. Working-through has, in my opinion, a second phase, which we will now study and in which is rooted a radical difference in relation to abreaction.

In what we have just described as the first phase of the process of working-through, one goes from descriptive to ostensive insight. Through slow work on the resistances we attempt to refer the words to the facts or events. After the critical moment when insight arises, we take the opposite path, trying to give meaning to our emotions and putting them into words. This is one instance of working-through where events turn into words, in which we *think* our emotions; we realize their scope and their consequences. This is why García Lorca said, "*las mejores emociones son los grandes pensamientos*" [great thoughts are the best emotions].

The moment of ostensive insight is surely fundamental. But for it to endure, it must be carefully cast into words. I dare say that if this process is not fulfilled, ostensive insight, however emotional and authentic it may be, remains an abreactive process that does not lead to integration.

The moment of ostensive insight has to do with the primary process, with the experience. On that basis, the experience begins to clothe itself in words. The experience is certainly basic; if it is not there, nothing else is valid. But alone it is not sufficient; it is necessary to integrate it into the ego and the secondary process, clothing it with words and seeing what consequences follow from it.

With this I hope to have clarified somewhat the relation of insight to working-through, in showing how the two phenomena are indissolubly linked and, most importantly, trying to specify the nature of the link between the two, which is complex, or twofold, going and returning. There is, then, a continuous process of working-through, with crises great or small, which can be called insight. The name is arbitrary, because where working-through ends and insight begins is a question of taste, of definition. Working-through is a diachronic process, with a duration in time, a magnitude spanned by the abscissa. Insight, on the other hand, is a point that cuts vertically, like the ordinate; it is synchronic.

If one waits to obtain a precise and accurate interpretation, what is obtained is a crisis, as when Freud told Elisabeth von R that she wanted her sister to die so she would be able to marry her brother-in-law. There is then a moment of critical and typical insight (1895d, pp. 156–157). With the current technique, we try to avoid too acute a crisis, through a more assiduous method which shelters the analysand from excessive anxiety (and us from his excessive envy) and which makes the process more gentle. However, despite the course of analysis becoming less rough, there will always be these two situations—diachronic and synchronic—which define insight and working-through, respectively.

In short, then, relying on the existence of two types of insight, I have been able to establish a two-way relation between insight and working-through, which permits a clearer perception of both concepts, without avoiding the complexities of their subtle interplay.

We can lay the foundation more convincingly now for the essential difference between abreaction and elaboration. As opposed to the cathartic method, psychoanalysis does not depend on the discharge of a quantum of excitation, but on the dynamic and structural change that goes from words to deeds—that is, from descriptive to ostensive insight and, most importantly on this point, from ostensive to descriptive insight. This last step is decisive, in my opinion, in understanding where the failure lies in cathartic theory and also in those neocathartic theories that have been developing, from Ferenczi's (1919b, etc.) work onwards. Abreactive techniques fail because, once there is a discharge of affect, the subject tends to repeat it without having assimilated the process that provoked it. I maintain that this process is linked to a new moment of working through, which goes (or returns from) ostensive to descriptive insight.

In this way the divergence that arises in the attempt to locate insight in relation to working-through is resolved. Some say that insight comes first and sets in train the process of working-through; others say that the process of working-through must develop first, crystallizing in insight.

We have characterized Freud's 1914 position (with good arguments, I believe) as maintaining the first point of view. Most of those who studied this subject—as did Klein (1950), Lewin (1950), Kris (1956a, 1956b) and Phyllis Greenacre (1956)—are aligned in this position. Greenson (1965b), on the other hand, holds decidedly to the second, which seems to be that of Freud himself after 1920.

For Greenson, analysis has two moments, before and after insight, and only the latter is called working-through. Let us see how the Los Angeles analyst expresses himself: "We do not regard the analytic work as working through before the patient has insight, only after. It is the goal of working through to make insight effective, i.e., to make significant and lasting changes in the patient. By making insight the pivotal issue we can distinguish between those resistances which prevent insight and those resistances which prevent insight from leading to change. The analytic work on the first set of resistances is analytic work proper; it has no special designation" (Greenson, 1965b, p. 282). In this way, Greenson approaches Freud's 1926 working-through concept.

As I think I have shown, this problem is not well formulated, since it does not account for there being *two* types of insight and not one, just as there are two phases in the working-through cycle.

50.7 Two concepts of working-through

Until now, we have worked with the concept of working-through introduced by Freud in 1914, which has to do with resistance in terms of the theory of the two principles. As we all know, however, this concept changed radically after *Beyond the Pleasure Principle* (1920g) introduced the hypothesis of a death instinct. When the structural theory culminates in *Inhibitions, Symptoms and Anxiety* (1926d), Freud delineates a new version of resistance separated into five types, one of which is *the resistance of the id.*

The concept of working-through that emerges in 1914 as the necessary pair to compulsion repetition becomes in 1926 that which opposes the death instinct.

In a brief work called "On the Existence of Two Levels in the Process of Working-Through" (Etchegoyen et al., 1982a), we indicated the risks of not differentiating clearly between these two concepts of working-through.

Freud's 1914 conception relies on the idea that the laws of the pleasure principle provoke a compulsion to repeat, which constitutes the field of transference. The concept of transference neurosis is linked from its birth to the compulsion to repeat, whose counterpart is working-through. Working-through is the therapeutic instrument that, "by delving deeply into resistance (here those belonging to the ego) ends up by making conscious and resolving the impulses that generate them" (Etchegoyen et al., 1982a, p. 32).

When Freud reviews the concept of working-through twelve years later, after the theoretical change produced in the interval, "the repetition compulsion has been set up as an explanatory principle and, owing to its link with the death instinct, from being the consequence it has been transformed into the *cause* of the conflict" (ibid., p. 33). The concept of working-through is ascribed to the fight against the resistances of the id. Working-through changes in tune with the concept of repetition and goes beyond the pleasure principle.

As the work I am discussing indicates, the most significant consequence of this theoretical change is that Freud has to separate repression from resistance and ascribe to the ego a teleological attitude in reference to abandoning his resistances: "For we find that even after the ego has decided to relinquish its resistances it still has difficulty in undoing the repressions, and we have called the period of strenuous effort which follows after its praiseworthy decision, the phase of 'working-through'" (1926d, p. 159). Following this dichotomy, Meltzer says in chapter 8 of *The Psycho-Analytic Process* (1967) that the function of deciding to abandon the resistances corresponds to insight and to the acceptance of responsibility, which belongs to the adult part of the personality; equally, ending the repressions corresponds to changes operating at the infantile levels of the personality.

Returning to Freud, it is evident that the intention of abandoning the resistances belongs to the ego—and, it could be asserted, to the conscious ego—while the process of working-through has to do with the id. The way Freud expresses himself seems to imply that the decision to abandon the resistances leads us to the conscious ego: "If the resistance is itself unconscious, as so often happens owing to its connection with the repressed material, we make it conscious. If it is conscious, or when it has become conscious, we bring forward logical arguments against it; we promise the ego rewards and advantages if it will give up its resistance" (1914g, p. 159).

This text strongly suggests that one must avail oneself of psychotherapeutic manoeuvres to win the ego's collaboration, while the conflict and its elaboration (working-through) remain located in the id.

The conclusion that emerges from our 1982 study is that if we keep the process of working-through within the area of the id, we have to modify the ego with rational arguments that are nothing other than psychotherapy and, more precisely, existential psychotherapy.

Coderch (1995) too considers that working-through has two phases, one of which involves interpretation and the other insight. The *working-through of interpretations* allows the patient to overcome his defences and acquire consciousness of—that is, insight into—his conflicts. Insight is always accompanied by depressive anxieties, and these mark the beginning of a second phase of working-through, the *working-through of insight*, which presupposes the working-through of the depressive position, because "insight gives rise to change only if followed by the working-through of the depressive position and by reparation" (p. 481). Coderch is here recalling Melanie Klein's comment in the conclusions to *Envy and Gratitude* (1957), to the effect that repeated analysis of the anxieties and defences related to envy and destructive impulses permits progress in integration, as well as her emphasis on the importance of working-through in the psychoanalytic process. According to Klein, when the analysis reaches these deep layers of the mind, envy diminishes, object relations are improved, and the perception of internal and external reality is heightened; she then notes that the insight obtained in the integration process enables the patient to acknowledge the destructive parts of his personality. Coderch surely has this in mind when he writes of a working-through of insight, although it seems more logical to assume that Klein is emphasizing the importance of working-through in the processes of integration, which envy impedes in a very special way. Of course, for Klein, insight implies a mourning situation, and it therefore seems to me more consistent to speak of the working-through of the mourning resulting from insight than of the working-through of insight itself.

In defence of his classification, Coderch asserts that, if we suppose that insight inevitably gives rise to psychic change, we make the patient the prisoner of his own insight. This would result in the paradox that the patient finds himself compelled to suffer the psychic changes imposed by insight. I understand Coderch's ingenious argument but do not agree with it, precisely because I believe that insight does not *impose* change but only makes it possible. Insight is the moment of orphanhood, uncertainty and pain that accompanies integration; it presupposes the abandonment of a *theory* that the analysand had about himself, about others and about his history. Insight gives the analysand the freedom to construct new theories and to travel along new roads; it does not bind him, nor does it lead him anywhere. Insight is but the beginning of a path which the person who has achieved it (and suffers from it) must negotiate.

50.8 *"Verarbeitung"* [working out] and *"Durcharbeiten"* [working-through]

Other authors (Laplanche & Pontalis, Joyce McDougall) prefer to differentiate psychic working out from working through, taking into account the fact that Freud uses the concept of work [*Arbeit*] in various contexts to refer to functions of the mind between which it seems appropriate to distinguish.

In *The Language of Psychoanalysis* (Laplanche & Pontalis, 1968), *psychic working out* [*psychische Verarbeitung*] is understood as the application of the idea of work to psychic function. It is a general notion rooted in the Freudian paradigm of a psychic apparatus that transforms instinctual energy, controlling, directing and binding it. In "actual" neuroses, which Freud (1895b) introduced at the start of his work and to which he returned in the Schreber case (1911c) and in "On Narcissism: An Introduction" (1914c), there is a defect of psychic working out that conditions the stasis of sexual energy and is directly shown in symptoms entirely without psychological content. *Working-through* [*Durcharbeiten*] has a more restricted scope than psychic working out, since it is applied exclusively to processes inherent in psychoanalytical treatment. As we have already seen, according to the point reached by Freudian research, *Durcharbeiten* means working on the resistances that operate in subjection to the pleasure principle (1914), or overcoming the resistance of the id, which always goes beyond the resistances of the ego and even its functions (1926). Although in "Remembering, Repeating and Working-through" the ego works by resisting the libidinal impulse that is repeated in search of primal pleasure, in "Inhibitions, Symptoms and Anxiety" the ego mobilizes the pleasure principle to oppose the blind repetition of the mute death-instinct that arises from the id.

Joyce McDougall (1985) also favours the distinction between *Verarbeitung* ["working out"] and *Durcharbeiten* ["working-through"] and applies both concepts not only to the analysand but also to the analyst, who must always be aware of his own conflicts during and after the session. "The analyst's work does not end when the session is over" (1985, p. 22) and the thoughts that sometimes assail him when he least expects it, when he is not working, will be most useful to him if he works them out properly. They will at least help him to understand his countertransference conflicts, and he will thus have an unsuspectedly valid way of understanding his analysand; and, on the other hand, they may be a sound jumping-off point for questioning the psychoanalytical theories with which he is dealing, and even for creating new concepts. In McDougall's view the two forms of working-through that she accepts also correspond to two ways of thinking in analytical work, clinical and theoretical, which must be carefully distinguished. Thus the analyst can, in a creative way, follow two paths that open to him spontaneously. One leads him to clinical work with his analysands; the other leads him better to understand his theories, to revise them, and, in the most favourable case, to create new ones.

50.9   *Insight and the infantile depressive position*

There is almost total agreement in comparing working-through to the process of mourning. This idea is clear in Fenichel (1941), but it can perhaps be found in previous works and later in others such as Bertrand D. Lewin, Ernest Kris, Phyllis Greenacre and Ralph R. Greenson. All of them think working-through is carried out, as in the case of mourning, through a process, through *work*. This is also accepted by Klein, who goes further, maintaining that insight itself implies a process of mourning.

Klein's works on the infantile depressive position (1935, 1940) describe what is for her the foundation stone of development: the child recognizes a total object in which good and bad converge. Up to this point, these elements had been separated by schizoid mechanisms. This process of synthesis of the object has its correlate in the integration of the ego, which endures vivid painful feelings in taking charge of the fact that its aggressive impulses are really directed to its love-object. With great (depressive) anxiety over the fate of the loved object, the ego thus makes contact with its hate and aggressive impulses. Within this theoretical framework, insight is defined as the capacity to accept psychic reality, with its hate and love impulses directed to the same object.

Like Freud (1917e [1915]) and Abraham (1924), Klein (1950) thinks that mourning follows the loss of the object; but this loss is a consequence not only of the external object's behaviour but also of the subject's ambivalence towards the internal object that represents the primary objects (1975, Vol. 3, p. 44). The recognition that the good internal object has been (and can be) attacked and destroyed sets in train the mourning process, with its cortège of depressive anxieties and guilt feelings, which awaken in turn the tendency to repair, which entails hope.

For Klein, then, insight results in the introjection of the object and the integration of the ego, which characterize the depressive position. As she says, depressive pain "is bound up with an increasing insight into psychic reality which in turn contributes to a better understanding of the external world" (ibid.). When insight changes the individual's attitude towards the object, his love and responsibility increase. Meneghini (1976) notes that many of Klein's ideas on the relationship between insight, working-through and mourning can be traced to her first work, "The Development of a Child" (1921), where, following Ferenczi (1913), she describes the struggle between the feeling of omnipotence and the reality principle.

In her classic work at the Edinburgh Congress, Hanna Segal (1962) makes the role of insight prominent in the psychoanalytic process. For her, too, insight becomes concentrated in the mourning situation that arises when the mechanisms of projective identification and splitting that operate in the paranoid–schizoid position are corrected.

Insight, which for Segal consists in acquiring knowledge of one's own unconscious, operates therapeutically for two reasons: (1) because it produces the process of integration of the split-off parts of the ego, and (2) because it turns omnipotence into knowledge. For Segal, insight is not only knowledge of the parts of the self (which had been lost through projective identification) but also incorporation of past experiences, which reinforce the feeling of identity and the power of the ego.

In recovering the lost parts of the self and the forgotten and/or distorted experiences through insight, the individual can restructure and fortify his ego and trust in the good objects that can help him and diminish his omnipotence and omniscience.

50.10   The developmental lines of insight

Following Anna Freud's (1963) fertile concept of *developmental lines*, some of her disciples, such as Clifford Yorke and colleagues (1989), have studied insight in relation to the growth of the mind of the child.

At the Anna Freud Centre (formerly the Hampstead Clinic), analysts establish a clear difference between insight proper, self-observation and still more primitive stages, which the mental apparatus registers as it matures. Self-observation is a prerequisite for insight but does not always lead to it. Self-observation can remain in the service of the gratification of the id, as of the superego's severe criticism and even of the defence mechanisms, sanctioning a pathological dissociation in the ego.

In this school of thought it is understood that the baby, subject to the more immediate movements of the primary process, cannot have insight. According to the rule of the pleasure principle, the most primitive form of experiential discrimination must consist in the alternation of the pleasurable and the unpleasurable. (As we saw in the previous section, Klein dates the development of the infant much earlier and does not seem disposed to recognize stages in the acquisition of insight.) From the inevitable interaction of the child's instinctual drives and the limitations of reality, and in accordance with the constitutional lines along which the ego matures, the world of representations becomes organized so the limits between ego and not-ego can be established. In this way the child achieves an initial classification of his experiences that is certainly highly subjective, where pleasant experiences are ascribed to the ego and the others to the not-ego. Perhaps we face here a very primitive form of self-observation, although the child still lacks that internal eye that makes self-observation possible. This type of functioning spans the whole preverbal stage, while the gradual acquisition of language accelerates cognitive development considerably. At this point the child acquires a sufficient degree of structure in his mental apparatus to be able to exercise a rudimentary capacity for self-observation, making him accessible to psychoanalytic treatment, although he is still far from achieving complete object constancy, which requires the recognition that the object has its own needs and desires. Following Rees (1978), Hansi Kennedy asserts that at six or seven years of age the child is egocentric from the cognitive point of view, and his comprehension of others is limited to subjective experiences (1978, p. 13). If one bears in mind that insight depends on the integrative function of the ego, as Kris (1956a) maintains, then one must conclude that in early infancy and in latency the child is far from being able to utilize the experience of insight, as the adult does. During early infancy the child's capacity for self-observation is limited and comes from the internalization of the parents' demands and approval. This capacity for self-observation strengthens gradually, although it always goes hand in hand with the child's tendency to "externalize" his conflicts. For the rest, it is rare to find a child under five with real insight into how the past affects present experience.

In latency the child has a capacity for insight because the superego is already formed, and the conflicts are internalized. At this point in development repression and other defence mechanisms operate to contain the unacceptable instinctive derivatives. Here, then, self-observation and reflection are ensured. But in any case the child fights insight and tends to distance himself from his internal world, externalizing his conflicts. The child attributes his problems to external causes and seeks to solve them also in the external world and not through understanding.

The adolescent, on the other hand, is by definition very introspective and reflective, but the intensity of his sexual and aggressive desires terrifies him, so that he struggles energetically with the recognition of his internal conflicts and their reappearance in the present.

Only in the adult is self-observation confirmed as an autonomous function, with which an optimal degree of self-observation is achieved and with it a desire to know oneself.

* * *

To sum up: in *early infancy* children have a limited capacity for self-observation, which leads to the perception of desires and feelings and to recognizing difficulties, which are precisely the mark of objective insight. During *latency* the child has the instruments for insight, but the capacity to cooperate with the analyst will fluctuate intensely, and the resistances to introspection and insight will be very strong. Finally, in *adolescence*, there is a natural introspective attitude, together with a capacity for understanding the unconscious motives of behaviour, with which the conditions are fully given for real insight, although at this stage they still tend to see always what is immediate and present, to the detriment of interest in the past and the influence it can exert on the present, which seems to be a feature only of the adult spirit.

50.11 Insight as the ostensive, counterinductive resolution of a pragmatic paradox

According to Ahumada (1991, 1994, 1997a, 1997b), genuine psychoanalytic insight evolves in individuals through access to, and an ostensive resolution of, a pragmatic paradox. He thus follows Richfield (1954) in the idea that only a "knowledge by acquaintance" becoming conscious leads to ostensive insight and to structural psychic change, and Bateson (1973) in the overall primacy of pragmatics over semantics. Ostension—pointing to events, saying "this"—takes place in both perceptual and mnemic screens.

Inductive generalization extends to a class as a whole that which has been observed in individual instances of the class; counter-induction involves the observational refutation of a given class (clinically, of a given concept, emotion, or impulse) in individual instances: ostensive distinction of particulars leads to the elucidation of an until then unknown theory-in-use. The analyst purveys descriptions from new angles on the analysand's own experiences, which will allow the latter then an ostensive recovery in perceptual or mnemic screens of heretofore indiscernible events; comparison then makes possible an experiential test of the analyst's own implicit theories.

Psychic reality is seen to operate as an unconscious deductive matrix of theories about relationships—that is, as pragmatic–emotional categories structuring how the analysand acts and misperceives his links to significant others. Conscious inferential thought that can be mapped verbally is, on the other hand, organized in terms of individuals and their characteristics. Access, in individual, concrete events, to a knowledge by acquaintance of the unconscious classes ruling his pragmatic and semantic forms of colligating facts amounts to an experiential reality-testing of his unconscious frames or theories resulting from early inductive generalizations, on which his relations are structured: it is thus a precondition for conscious refutation. Interpretations are subordinate to such a task: they posit a tentative "knowledge by description", a provisional mapping by way of interpretive conjectures, which, if adequate, will help the analysand attain a *multiple description* from new standpoints of his psychic reality. This leads, in turn, to conscious ostensive refutation or reformulation of his heretofore unconscious ways of colligating facts of relationship. Ahumada thinks— and he is entirely correct—that a substantive degree of pragmatic (and semantic) neutrality on the part of the analyst will serve as a backcloth against which the analysand can delineate and articulate what he observes in and out of the session.

The analysis of a post-autistic adolescent affected by pseudo-stupidity, brought to treatment by his parents mainly because of his terror of his grandfather, affords Ahumada (1997a) the opportunity to illustrate in detail how, after substantial clinical progress, some weekend material of incipient genital sexuality evinces the equation within a frame or class (marked by terror ruling how he acts and feels) comprising three consciously quite different individuals: the coast-guard in the role of sexual policeman, his grandfather (with whom by this time he already had a very affectionate relationship), and his analyst. Multiple observation of how a single unconscious form evolves through such unlike individuals permits the analysand to single this out and attain a leap from mere knowledge by description to a knowledge by acquaintance, ostensively acknowledging in a vivid way what had often enough been interpreted to him: that unconsciously he felt his analyst as a sexual policeman—that is, his ever-present fears of his analyst as a sexual rival, ready to attack his amorous feelings.

CHAPTER FIFTY-ONE

The metapsychology of insight

51.1 Insight and preconscious mental process

Following the main lines of ego psychology, Kris (1956a) explains some of the vicissitudes of insight on the basis of the concept of free and bound energy—that is, of the conceptual differences between primary and secondary process. The purest Hartmannian psychology shines in this work, together with Kris's own contributions on preconscious thought based on his studies of caricature (1936) and the comical (1938), which culminate in 1950 with his work "On Preconscious Mental Process".

To be more exact, in order to explain insight Kris uses not only the dialectic of the primary and secondary process but also the model of the psychic apparatus Freud proposed in 1923. From the structural point of view, Kris thinks of insight as a bifrontal phenomenon that is located simultaneously in the ego and in the id: there is an incorporative (oral) form and an anal mode of insight (gift, treasure), which are clearly instinctive models, that is, of the id.

What is most distinctive about Kris's contribution is surely his explanation of the process of working-through. Working-through consists in the modification and re-ordering of the free charges of the primary process in such a way that, organized as a preconscious mental process, they are

---

This chapter, along with chapters 49 and 50, appeared under the title "Insight", in *Trabajo del Psicoanálisis*, 2 (1983).

deposited in the *Pcs* system until, at a given moment, they suddenly arise as insight.

Kris's reasoning originates in what he calls "the good analytic hour". (I think all analysts count one or two of these in their experience!) They are sessions that really do not begin favourably, nor do they proceed smoothly, but, rather, in a tense and heavy atmosphere. The transference is predominantly hostile, the atmosphere one of pessimism, if not of defeat. Suddenly, however, and frequently towards the end, everything seems to settle, and things are pieced together like a jigsaw. A brief interpretation from the analyst is sufficient to make things clear. Sometimes that interpretation fits in a simple question, or the patient makes it obvious by arriving at conclusions himself. (This description by Kris reminds me of what Freud says in his "Remarks on the Theory and Practice of Dream-Interpretation", 1923c: there is first a period in which the material expands, until it suddenly becomes concentrated and structured like a puzzle which clearly reveals the latent ideas of the dream.)

These sessions come out so well—Kris continues—that they seem prepared beforehand. In fact, one cannot think that this elaborated configuration comes from the trend of what is repressed to reach the level of consciousness, but, rather, from the integrative functions of the ego, from the preconscious mind. All the work of the previous sessions has been organized in the preconscious and suddenly emerges. Kris calls working-through the process that reorganizes, at the level of the *Pcs* system, the charges of the *Ucs*. The insight in which the good analytic hour culminates is the product of analytic work that has liberated the countercathectic energies linked to the repressed material, making them available to the bound energy of the secondary process.

Together with the good analytic hour, Kris also describes the deceptively good hour, which appears to be authentic but can be recognized because the insight emerges too quickly, without the previous arduous, difficult work we have just discussed. The associations spring up easily, and insight arrives almost magically, as a gift of the gods (or of the analyst). This insight does not result from a process of working-through: the integrative functions of the ego operate only in the service of seducing the analyst, of winning his love. It is easy to predict that this spurious insight will not last beyond the positive phase of the transference. It can also be added that if an analysand seeks to please the analyst, it is because the fear exists that things that one does not wish to reveal will appear. To please is then to placate. (From my point of view, the desire to please the analyst has only one legitimate place in genuine insight, and it is when it appears as a consequence of the achievement of insight, arising from the impulse to repair.)

In a second case of the deceptively good hour insight is in the service of a desire to become independent of the analyst, of competing via the resource of self-analysis. If one has insight only as a consequence of contradicting the analyst, the understanding obtained will not be worth much. This type of insight will never be efficient, because what really matters is to show the other that one knows more, interprets better, than he does. The intrinsic truth there can be in what the analysand says does not in the final analysis reach him, because he is not interested in the truth of what is happening, but in demonstrating that he knows more than his analyst. On this point, the context of discovery operates as a suicidal hypothesis in the context of justification. The epistemology of psychoanalysis is as complex as this.

There is still a third type of deceptively good hour, where the integrative functions of the ego seem to proliferate and the entire life of the patient is seen from a simplistic and unilateral perspective. Everything derives from a particular model, from an early cataclysm in infancy. When this tendency operates, one soon notices a certain stretching of the data and easy transformations of what should be a difficult achievement of the understanding. To account for this phenomenon, which is understood without difficulty via Bion's idea of the −K link, Kris appeals to a difference between the ego's synthetic and integrative functions. The synthetic function has to do with the primary process; the integrative function is proper to the secondary process. This *ad hoc* hypothesis, which is easier to explain than to prove, reveals by counterposition a difficulty in Hartmannian metapsychology.

There are, therefore, three types of deceptively good sessions, as well as a type of false insight corresponding to each: one that has to do with positive transference and tries to please the analyst, and a second with the negative transference of contradiction; the third is a way of applying the psychoanalytic method mechanically, when on the basis of one event alone (which can be real) one tries to account for all problems. In the three cases the desire to understand is not authentic; it is subordinate to the affects that dominate the transference. Bion (1962b) would say the link is L, H or −K.

Kris's three types of false insight are valid and must be taken account of in clinical practice; one should distinguish in each case what is authentic from what is spurious. In the most authentic of insights there will always be a desire to please the analyst, and, in the same way, even in the most envious of impulses to self-analysis there will always exist a nuance of legitimate independence. Mental acts are never simple, as Wälder (1936) warned us, and in all cases one will have to consider one aspect, then another. The difference between genuine and spurious insight, then, is not always easy to establish. To make things still more complicated, sometimes real insight can be used as defence or gratification.

A great part of analytic work takes place in darkness, Kris says pithily. The path is illuminated here and there by some spark of insight, after which new zones of anxiety emerge, other conflicts arise in the material, and the process continues. In this way, the long-term changes that analysis promotes can be achieved without the patient becoming fully conscious of the path traversed.

If insight is real and genuine, it is recognized by its fruits: the tendency to act out decreases, and the conflict-free ego sphere is broadened thanks to the increase of secondary autonomy. Insight mobilizes new repertories of behaviour, with a tendency to produce adapted responses of a varied type. The ability to offer these responses constitutes, according to Kris, a valid criterion with which to evaluate the course of analytic work and, eventually, its termination.

Insight is part of a circular process: without the dynamic and structural changes already described insight could never arise. But, reciprocally, once established, insight promotes changes in the structure of the mind. Blum (1979) also emphasizes as a characteristic the circular interaction between the development of insight and the analytic work that conditions structural changes that facilitate insight.

There are some points wherein Kris's investigation resembles Klein's— for example, in what refers to archaic models, the prototypes of the id in insight. In the oral type of fantasy Kris outlines, knowledge compares in the id to food that can be incorporated and metabolized. In this way, the oral prototype of insight is very similar to the relation of the child to the breast, just as Klein describes it. Another zone of contact between the two theories can be found in the theme of integration. Kris conceives the structural changes that insight promotes as a change in the ego's integrative function. The explanations of the Kleinian school also accord the greatest importance to the integration of the ego, but in this theory integration depends on the achievement of the depressive position.

Although no one doubts that insight has to do with the secondary process and with verbal engrams, the value of Kris's investigation lies therefore in the fact that he proposes an explanation of these facts that is consistent with his own theoretical framework. In this way, the relationship between insight and verbalization is part of a particular theory on the organization of preconscious mental thought. When repression lifts, and as one passes from the primary to the secondary process, the charges liberated from their fixations can be utilized in the service of the integrative function.

Following in the footsteps of Kris, who was his teacher, Edward Joseph (1984) has published a very comprehensive work on insight, which he considers as the result of an extremely complex process involving not only the patient who, in the course of the analysis, is re-organizing his preconscious mental processes, but also the analyst, who plays his part by transmitting his understanding with his interpretations and also with his empathic response and the information that comes to him from his countertransference.

In Joseph's view the emotional element is indispensable to the attainment of insight, which is nevertheless a cognitive phenomenon and an uncompromising search for truth. In this sense insight always involves the quality of consciousness and of words.

51.2 Regression/progression dialectics

Grinberg, Langer, Liberman and the Rodrigués (1966b) wrote a brief essay for the *Revista Uruguaya*, explaining the process of working-through "as the dynamics which result from a dialectic movement between regression and progression" (p. 255). When in the same year these authors presented their point of view on the analytic process at the Second Pan-American Congress of Psychoanalysis, they returned to these ideas, filling them in and completing them (1966a). These works are interesting because, in assembling a great number of psychoanalytic theories, they manage to establish a clear relationship between insight and working-through.

A central thesis of these authors is that there is no sharp division between insight and working-through. Insight is a specific moment of the process of working-through; insight and working-through are inseparable.

They define working-through, as we have said, as the dynamics resulting from a movement of progression and regression. The progressive aspect of this dialectic arises from overcoming the reiterative and stereotyped defences, from the gradual abandonment of the compulsion to repeat archaic models of instinctive discharge.

The regressive element of working-through is not attributed (as could be expected) to the reiterative defences just described, to those models of instinctive discharge that repetition compulsion imposes, but to the curative process itself. The concept of regression used is the one Winnicott postulated in 1955 as a complex system of defences, a latent capacity awaiting favourable conditions that permit a return to the past to reinitiate a new process of development. The psychoanalytic process is a state of moratorium, Erikson (1962) says, which makes regression possible in order to begin anew.

In their attempt at synthesis, Grinberg and his colleagues combine Winnicott's and Kris's (1936, 1938, 1950) ideas on regression in the service of the ego. This approach does not seem completely convincing, however, because Winnicott speaks of a temporal regression and Kris's useful regression is, above all, formal—from primary to secondary process.

In their presentation at the Congress, they define the analytic process through the use of the same conceptual instruments they applied to working-through: "Analytic process implies *progress*, but we understand *progress* as a development where the useful regression on the couch serves as a prime lever" (1966a, p. 94).

As in the work of mourning to which it is compared, working-through requires time; it is necessarily a slow and painful process. The Argentinian authors agree in this with Melanie Klein, who located insight at the centre of the depressive position—that is, when pain arises because of the damaged object, to which is added pain due to the damaged parts of the self (Grinberg, 1964).

51.3   Insight and scientific knowledge

With the conceptual instruments that we have been developing, we can now try to establish a relationship between insight and scientific knowledge. As far as the investigation of the unconscious is concerned, the psychoanalytic method is part of the scientific method. When the analyst works thoroughly, he does nothing other than apply the scientific method: that is what the search for insight is.

Scientific investigation consists in applying and contrasting theories. The essence of the scientific method, Popper (1953) says, resides in the fact that theories are tested and refuted. There can be no irrefutable theory, because it would cease to be scientific if it were.

We can conceive the analytic process in the same terms and assert that, basically, it consists in analyst and patient investigating the patient's theories about himself and testing them. If these theories are reliably refuted, the analysand, in general, exchanges them for others better adapted to reality. If the analysand has many resistances, preventing him from abandoning his theories, it is because the new ones almost always favour him somewhat less, to the detriment of his omnipotence. By "theories" I mean here all the explanations one has about oneself, one's family and society; the explanations with which each one of us gives account of his conduct or disturbance; and also, of course, the theories one has about one's personal history (as I tried to show in chapter 28).

As in scientific investigation, the analytic process continually tests the theories the analysand has about himself and leads him to confront these with the content of reality. In the face of facts, the theory the patient has about himself is confirmed (and this is always temporary because no theory is definitive) or refuted.

While the facts confirm the patient's theory, there is no insight; but as soon as the theory is refuted, insight appears and new knowledge emerges. Insight, let us not forget, is always a discovery, a new connection of meaning. This is why I said earlier that insight destroys a theory and the primary delusional experience constructs it.

That is inevitably a moment of inescapable orphanhood, and for various reasons. To lose a theory is to remain without weapons with which to confront the facts, and, of course, it is a weakening of omnipotence. We have also said that the new theory is always less favourable to the subject than the previous one—which was there for that reason. In this way, and on the basis of other elements, we have come to describe the moment of integration of the depressive position where insight flowers.

As we have just defined it, insight as gaining awareness implies the abandonment of particular explanatory hypotheses that had until then been useful to us, or at least comforting and satisfying. This is necessarily accompanied by lesser or greater mourning, by a conception of life, with its logical effect of pain. From this point of view we could say that insight triggers mourning in the K link (Bion) no less than in the L and H links (Melanie Klein). To this Rabih rightly adds (in a personal communication), the loss of the analyst as an object of transference, which is the corollary of mutative interpretation.

From the point of view from which we are considering it, the mourning that precipitates insight is linked to the loss of a theory. From that moment on, one begins to ask oneself questions about the meaning things now have and to construct a new theory. As this process is fulfilled, one goes (or returns) from ostensive to descriptive insight, the new facts are integrated into the personality, and the new theory begins to be tested. Richfield (1954) says something similar when he affirms that this is a necessary part of working-through, if we do not wish to live continually from emotion to emotion.

For the ideas I am developing it is not important that one theory be created as soon as another is abandoned. There can be a certain distance between the loss of one theory and the construction of another. What I am really interested in pointing out is that, on the basis of that moment of ostensive insight, a conceptual instrument is created, which is the new theory.

51.4   Some specifications on insight and affect

The moment of ostensive insight is by definition—as is now understood—an affective moment, not only due to the feelings of depression I mentioned earlier but also because of what may ensue: gratitude, hope, joy, the desire to repair, worry. . . . When insight becomes the new theory, it is already devoid of affect. I believe this point has not been understood by those who value emotional more than intellectual insight. In fact, both have their moment and their efficacy. What is now intellectual had not been intellectual when it was acquired. We should not, therefore, belittle intellectual insight; on the contrary, we should think that one type of insight is no more valid than another. As in the case of scientific theories, each moment of insight brings us closer to the truth; but the fact that a scientific theory refutes another does not mean that the first did not have value.

When we place emotional above intellectual insight, we are in fact tracing a dividing line which is not the best. In some way, we are affirming that what is already known has no value; that only what is known from that point onwards is valuable. This is neither just nor true. Spurred by practice, we go in search of an insight that lies ahead; but we forget that the insight we now have was a dynamic process at a given moment. Instead of counterposing them, it is preferable to think that ostensive (affective, dynamic) insight and descriptive (intellectual, verbal) insight form part of the same process, and what differentiates them is only their moment of expression in the process. Pablo Grinfeld (1984), in a well-researched paper, recovered the value of the intellectual aspects of psychoanalytic interpretation on the basis of this nucleus of ideas.

51.5   Spontaneous insight

Considerations such as the one just stated lead me to reconsider the value of spontaneous insight. Segal (1962) affirms that insight is a specifically analytic phenomenon. Many others, such as the Barangers (1964), are of the same opinion. To evaluate *spontaneous* insight as being of a lower quality than *analytic* insight is no more than an ideological position, in my opinion. I would even add that the insight one acquires with difficulty prior to starting analysis is perhaps the most decisive of all, because without it life would have been so distorted that even approaching an analyst would never have been thought of.

What no one doubts is that the analytic setting offers the best conditions for insight to occur. It gives us the possibility of seeing and reviewing our past in the present. It enables us to understand how what we took into account only theoretically is operating at this precise moment and how, through interpretation, the analysand can introject this process in an act of real transcendence. Analysis offers all this evidently to a much greater extent than does any other human relation, and this is not a great feat: the analytic setting is designed to offer the best conditions for acquiring insight through that singular experience where the patient repeats and the analyst interprets. In this way, the original experience can again be examined with greater objectivity, and the theories of the analysand are tested and eventually modified. All this, however, can also occur outside the analytic framework. It would be more hazardous and less elegant, but not impossible. As Guiard said in the first Symposium of the Buenos Aires Association in 1978, there are wise men who, without having been analysed, have a knowledge of life and of themselves that we, as analysts, would like to have.

When Bion (1962b) maintains that there exists in every individual a psychoanalytic function of the personality, is he not stating in precise terms what I have just said? Psychoanalysis only develops a function that was already there. What the analyst does when he interprets is the same as what the mother or father did (through *reverie*) when they understood the child. Analysis proposes the best way to reach insight—but not the only way. I think that Hansi Kennedy (1978) is of the same opinion in that she thinks the parents can influence the child's capacity for self-observation and insight according to how they teach him to manage his instincts and feelings (p. 26).

I think, then, that there are no fundamental differences between analytic and spontaneous insight. Even the *idea* of a fundamental difference seems suspect to me. Were we really to accept it, we would have to conclude that analysis makes us different and superior to other mortals, which is obviously untrue. In my experience I have seen how this type of idea occurs in newly formed psychoanalytic groups and disturbs their development. It is even believed that an analyst can only talk to analysts, or at least to analysands, which transforms the group into a lodge. The truth is that we do not have qualities different from those who have not been analysed; we have had the opportunity to undergo an experience that offers us an advantage, nothing more. After a good analytic treatment we are certainly always better persons than we were previously, but not necessarily better than others.

51.6   A clinical vignette

A female patient I analysed for many years had a bad relationship with her only sister, who was born when she was 15 months old. She came to analysis with a "theory" of her relationship with this sister: she maintained that they got on badly because her sister was selfish. After some time in analysis I proposed, based on what I observed in the transference, a new theory: her hostility towards her sister, beyond the latter's possible selfishness, was due to her inopportune birth. This interpretation, that is, my theory, was at first totally rejected. She was neither jealous, nor did she remember jealousy in childhood.

However, as she began to feel jealous of my other analysands, of my relatives and friends, even without knowing them, my theory was finally accepted. Then a new theory came to replace the old. Her problems were explained by her mother's abandonment of her in favour of her sister, obliging her to grow up prematurely, since she was unable to attend to two daughters simultaneously. At times the new theory fed parasitically on the analysis, as in Kris's third type of pseudo-insight. It was the whole truth, the only truth. The one who three years earlier had laughed at what I had told her, affirming good-humouredly (and sometimes with bad humour) that only an orthodox and fanatical analyst such as I was could think that an infant of 15 months could feel jealous of her newborn sister, now told me that I refused to believe that that experience had marked her forever, since she did not have the good fortune to have an understanding mother.

This person does not belong to the analytic milieu, but she lives in the city, has many interests and knows what is happening. When I was appointed to a particular post, she found out somehow, and she took it for granted that I was going to neglect her if not interrupt the treatment.

Happily I was able to continue seeing her as usual. She then began to feel envious of my ability to attend both to her and to new occupations. Now the transference conflict could be referred to the past: I told her that as a child she must have felt similarly towards her mother. She had said more than once that her mother was very efficient. But she never thought that efficiency could have bothered her. I concluded that if she really felt so much hatred for her mother, it was not only because she could not forgive her for having given her a sister prematurely, but also because she had not been able to tolerate her ability to manage with two small children. As expected, this theory was also totally rejected by the analysand. But she finally had to acknowledge that, in fact, my capacity to attend to her properly despite my other occupations bothered her. Thus she gradually accepted the conclusion that she had had a good mother after all, beyond all her mistakes and adverse circumstances in life. When she was able to accept that, she was already at the end of her analysis. (For a more detailed study see Etchegoyen, 1981c.)

This brief clinical history also serves to illustrate that the difference between intellectual and emotional insight is based on an error of perspective in time. We tend to see the process proceeding from present to future, and it could not be otherwise; but this can lead us astray. When I propose to make the patient see that in her infancy her mother was not as bad as she thinks (and I propose to do this when I see it arise from the transference) then I, as an analyst, think that what is most important is that she should see this situation. However, four years earlier, it seemed to me that it was really important for her to see that the birth of her sister truly disturbed her, while she denied this, saying I was ridiculous. When I am at a given stage of the analytic process, the only thing I value is the point towards which I direct myself. However, this is because I make an arbitrary division. Had she not had insight as to her infantile jealousy of her newborn sister and the real maternal deprivation she suffered, the latter insight would have been impossible.

This point of view clarifies why I do not share the assertions of Reid and Finesinger on the role of insight in psychotherapy. It is not true that some insights are curative and others are not; all were curative in their time. Let us take the case Reid and Finesinger give: that of the hypothetical patient who had dyspepsia after fighting with his wife at the table. They say that when the patient thinks that fighting with his wife at the table gives him a stomach-ache, he has only intellectual insight, and that the really valid insight is the *dynamic* one of his oral passivity, his envy or avidity, of his Oedipus complex. I think that the two moments of insight are equally valid. When this patient arrives, his insight into the effect on his dyspepsia of the battles at the table is already intellectual; but when he first had this insight, it surely was not so. I would even affirm that, without that first insight, he would probably have developed a paranoia and would have come to the first session saying his wife wished to poison him. It is only the urgency of our task, the necessity of resolving the problem at hand, that makes us think that the emotional insight lies ahead and that the intellectual variety has been left behind. It is part of the inexorable advance of the process of working-through that insight, when it reaches its ostensive climax, then becomes intellectual, because one is not tearing one's hair out all day, like Freud's hysterics who suffered from reminiscences.

At times intellectual insight is confused with intellectualization, which is not the same thing. Once an analyst has interpreted castration anxiety and it has been accepted, this knowledge can be raised as a banner in order not to see, for example, homosexual tendencies and a negative Oedipus complex. That a theory can be utilized in column 2 of Bion's Grid (or as a minus K link) does not take away from it the value it originally had. The analysand has the right to use his theories badly; we, as analysts, are obliged to perceive (and reveal) how a theory that has been valid can be transformed into an obstacle to knowledge. Following Bion's theory of knowledge, Grinberg (1976c) indicated that even the Oedipus complex can serve as a defence against the Oedipus complex itself.

As we have described it, the moment of ostensive insight can only be accompanied by a situation of mourning, of loss, of orphanhood: the object is not there, the theory has failed, one's omnipotence is reduced, one is guiltier than one had thought. But at the same moment in which I consciously mourn, I realize that analysis can give me a knowledge I did not have and a better life; then hope springs forth.

Depressive pain is, then, a necessary condition for insight, a point Gregorio Garfinkel (1979) has insisted on. There can be no insight without pain. Once that moment of pain has passed, however, a feeling of internal peace will arise, where joy and hope will germinate—a handsome repayment for the pain that existed.

This passage through pain is unavoidable even in the case where a moment of historical truth is recovered that alleviates some unjustified guilt. If the process is authentic and has not been carried out in terms of manic revindication, other determinants will be seen via this special altruism: if someone takes on guilt that is not his, it is because in some way it suits his resistances. (This applies exactly to the concept of borrowed guilt, which Freud introduces in chapter 5 of *The Ego and the Id*, 1923b, when he studies the negative therapeutic reaction.)

51.7   Insight and internal objects

When we discussed insight as a field phenomenon, I said that in my opinion insight is not transferable and that it is advisable to consider it as a part of processual psychology and not of personalistic psychology. Now we must reopen this discussion, but on the basis of the theory of internal objects and, more precisely, of the qualities of the objects of the self.

When we studied the place of insight in the preconscious mental process, we saw that, through interpretation, the free charges of energy of the primary process are liberated from their fixations and reorganized into the *Pcs* system. It then goes without saying that verbalization is inherent in insight, because as long as there is no verbal representation, there is no secondary process, and the principle that insight arises when what was in the unconscious system passes into the preconscious is not fulfilled. Insight, then, implies verbalization, which is equivalent to saying that insight is inherently linked to the process of symbolization, because what we do during a moment of insight is to symbolize or conceptualize experience in a certain way. If this process does not occur, neither does insight. Klein (1932) is therefore very categorical in saying that the analysis of a child has to end with the verbalization of the conflicts and that, while this is not achieved, analysis has not ended. Liberman (1981) also indicates the importance of what he calls *verbalized insight*. In sum, word, secondary process and symbolization are the indispensable ingredients of the act of insight. Insight sanctions access to the symbolic order, if we wish to put it in Lacan's (1966) terms.

This implies giving the internal objects new equipment, as Meltzer (1967) says. By "equipment", Meltzer means a particular quality of the internal object. I think equipment and qualities of the object are synonymous here, but the word "equipment" has plasticity. While the infantile self projectively identifies his hostile tendencies into the internal parents and tries to damage them, control them and impede their creative union, his (masturbatory) attacks are linked to omnipotent fantasies. But as the attacks decrease—and they obviously decrease because one acquires more awareness of the damage to the object and the desire to repair it—the internal objects achieve a greater freedom of action. Then they can carry out the tasks the individual requires and which the objects of external reality had previously carried out. This is accompanied by a process of introjective identification, on the basis of which the individual feels that it receives from those objects their good qualities. (On this point I believe there is a certain theoretical consonance between the internal parents of Kleinian theory and Lacan's Great Other.) From this point of view, insight consists in a process of assimilation of the internal objects. In order to understand insight, it is important to emphasize the introjective process. When the analyst interprets, he gives the patient new elements of judgement to correct a particular conception he had of himself; he allows him to refute an earlier theory. But at the same time the patient introjects this action of having interpreted and thus gradually incorporates an analyst with certain qualities, an analyst who is able to remember, to contain, and so forth. Consequently, insight means not only changing the conception we had of ourselves, but also incorporating the object that has made the change possible. And it is on the basis of the introjection of this object that we will function with growing autonomy. Equipment and qualities of the object are practically the same thing.

The idea that through the process of introjection the individual incorporates the qualities of the object who is the bearer of insight raises again a basic problem of the theory of the cure—that is, how much comes from insight and how much from the analytic relation. This disjunction appears clearly in Wallerstein's (1979) work already quoted. He draws a strict distinction between the specifically analytical area of insight and other forms of the cure, such as Alexander's corrective emotional experience. Wallerstein, like Loewald (1960), holds that analytic treatment gives the patient the possibility of rediscovering the guidelines of his past in his new relation with the analyst. For the Kleinian theory of the internal objects it is also the case that the introjective process implies a moment of mourning in which the object is introjected as a function of a new relation with it. Thus in neither theory does this process bear any trace of suggestion or education.

CHAPTER FIFTY-TWO

Acting out
[1]

52.1 General panorama

Having studied at length the analytic process and its stages, we are now concerning ourselves with the vicissitudes offered by the course of the cure—the factors that facilitate its progress or impede it. In chapters 49, 50 and 51 we studied insight and working-through as propellers of psychoanalytic treatment, and we will now look at the *pathology of the process*—what can detain it or make it fail.

If the essential proposal of analysis is to obtain insight, then we can say by definition that we will call everything that impedes it pathology of the process. I believe there are three areas in which the process finds obstacles: acting out, negative therapeutic reaction and reversible perspective. The first two are better known and were studied initially by Freud; the third is a contribution we owe to Bion, although a specific reference can be found in Klein, as we shall see further on.

The entire pathology of the process is summed up, in my opinion, in these three mechanisms or, as I prefer to call them, *strategies*. What is common to all three is that they prevent insight from crystallizing. What distinguishes them is that each operates in its own special way. *Acting out* disturbs the analytic task, which is also the task of achieving insight. The *negative therapeutic reaction*, as its name indicates, does not impede the task, but it disturbs the achievements of insight, which are lost or not consolidated. In the *reversible perspective*, finally, insight is not achieved because the patient does not wish it so and in fact is looking for something else. In sum, acting out operates on the *task*, the negative therapeutic reaction on the *achievements* and the reversal of perspective on the *contract*; at least, this is how I see things and how I have tried to systematize them.

I also think that every time one of these processes is sustained and it becomes impossible to resolve it, one arrives at the dead end of the *impasse*. In this sense, the impasse is not in the same class as the other three— it is different (Etchegoyen, 1976).

52.2   Acting out:
an imprecise concept

Of all the concepts with which Freud constructed psychoanalysis, probably none was more discussed over time than acting out. Some attribute these discrepancies to the fact that the notion of acting out became unduly broadened, others to it being unclear at the outset. But no one doubts that there are few subjects where there is greater disagreement. It would seem that the only possible accord on this point is that there is no agreement.

In initiating their study, Sandler and colleagues (1973) say that "Of all the clinical concepts considered in this book, *acting out* has probably suffered the greatest extension and change of meaning since it was first introduced by Freud" (p. 94). In his classic 1945 article, Fenichel also gives a provisional definition, which he himself considers insufficient; he adds that it is better for a rigorous definition to be the result of an investigation and not its starting-point. His article, however, does not carry out that program. At the Thom Clinic Symposium, Peter Blos (1962) complained that the concept of acting out was overburdened with references and meanings; he yearned for the clarity it had thirty years earlier, when it was considered a legitimate and analysable defence. At the Copenhagen Congress, Anna Freud (1968) also indicated the expansion of the concept and tried to make it more precise, and Grinberg (1968) began his presentation by indicating the penumbra of associations that surrounds the concept of acting out, revealing the pejorative connotation it sometimes carries.

Although all analysts may have different ideas about acting out, very few consider it unimportant. The general opinion is that acting out is an idea that carries weight in psychoanalytic theory and practice. As Greenacre says, "Not very much has been written about the problems of acting out in the course of analysis, although they are most difficult to deal with, frequently interfere with analysis and sometimes escape detection unless and until they become flagrant" (1950, p. 455).

Something that distinguishes the analyst from other psychotherapists is that he operates with the concept of acting out—that is, he understands, as belonging to the treatment, aspects of the analysand's behaviour that seem to have nothing to do with it. No other therapist proceeds in this way. Hence, to detect acting out and distinguish it from situations that are not acting out gives us a sense of analytic identity. For it is obvious that not *everything* a patient *does* is acting out.

In chapters 52, 53 and 54 we will try to contribute to the clarification of the concept of acting out—a task that is by no means easy but certainly a very interesting one. We do not aspire to solve this vast problem; we would, however, like to demonstrate why it is difficult to define it, indicating how it is understood according to the perspective taken. In other words, it is necessary to ask what we are going to call acting out, trying at the same time to provide a basis for our opinions. In principle I think much dissent arises from the fact that we do not all mean the same thing when we speak of acting out.

52.3   Introduction of the term

In acting out, everything is debatable—even when it appears in Freud's work! The concept is often traced to Freud's *Psychopathology of Everyday Life* (1901b); others, on the other hand, think it originates in the "Postscript" to the "Fragment of an Analysis of a Case of Hysteria" ("Dora", 1905e) .

In order to understand acting out, Phyllis Greenacre (1950) and Eveoleen N. Rexford (1962), among others, begin with erroneous motor conduct (parapraxes, slips in speech and in mental operations) which Freud studied in his *Psychopathology*, where he describes mistaken acts or actions as a product of a psychic conflict that results in a struggle of tendencies. These acts have a psychological meaning, which can be uncovered through the psychoanalytic method. It is, above all, those he studies in chapter 9 ("Symptomatic and Chance Actions") that would be called acting out later on. As will be remembered, in this class of parapraxes no objective is suspected, and this distinguishes them from those that have one that is not attained due to an impeded execution. In these casual actions Freud always discovers an unconscious purpose that converts them into symptomatic ones.

It is advisable to specify that to describe this type of conduct in the *Psychopathology* Freud uses the word *handeln* [to act], while in the "Postscript" he uses *agieren*, which also means to act. It is evident that only if we think that Freud used another word without a specific theoretical intention that we can maintain that the concept of acting out is already present in 1901. If, on the other hand, we prefer to think that Freud used a different word in order to differentiate between the two concepts, parapraxis and acting out, we are forced to conclude that the *handeln* of 1901 is different from the *agieren* of 1905. This apparently futile discussion already contains the basic problem: whether acting out is nothing more than a neurotic act, or more than that.

52.4   *Neurotic act and acting out*

The difference between neurotic act and acting out rightly worries
Fenichel in his essay of 1945b, to which we all return to calibrate our
theoretical instrument. Fenichel emphasizes the action as the defining feature (as already contained in the name): this action is not merely a simple
movement or an imitative (mimicking) expression; it is a complex action, a
mode of behaviour. Symptoms (and Fenichel is evidently already thinking
here of compulsive acts) can also involve actions, but they are in general of
limited extent and always ego-dystonic. If they are of great complexity and
are rationalized to the point of being ego-syntonic, then it is fitting simply
to call them "acting out".

As we can see, what differentiates—for Fenichel—acting out from
compulsive symptom (or in general from parapraxes), beyond the purely
quantitative factor of its complexity, is only its syntony with the ego. Perhaps this is why the authors quoted earlier think that symptomatic and
casual actions, which are syntonic, are closer to acting out than parapraxes
(slips) properly speaking, where the dystony is so evident and clumsy.

Certainly in this way one is not able to distinguish acting out from
neurotic act. Were we to be satisfied with what Fenichel says, acting out
would cease to belong as a concept to the theoretical corpus of psycho-
analysis, which is undoubtedly the legitimate aspiration of those who
think that this concept is indissolubly linked to moral and ideological pre-
cepts that make it irreconcilable with psychoanalysis as a scientific discipline and as a technique. Others think, however, that the concept of acting
out should be preserved as a fundamental part of psychoanalysis, without
withdrawing from the difficulties that confront us in according it a theoretical location and the real danger of misusing it in practice.

Those who define acting out phenomenologically, whether manifestly
or cryptically, have not decided to give up its use in scientific terminology.
This lack of consequence cannot, in fact, be attributed to Gioia, who says
clearly: "Its defining characteristic, which differentiates it particularly from
other manifestations of transference and/or resistance, is purely phenomenological" (1974, p. 977).

What I wish to indicate here is that the theoretical posture of all those
who define acting out phenomenologically (and it is certainly legitimate)
should necessarily lead to the statement that the concept of acting out has
no autonomy and does not strictly belong to psychoanalytic theory. This is
very difficult to do, however, because ordinary language on this point is a
strong determinant. During my thirty years and more as an analyst I have
never heard of a colleague who would not use the term "acting out" to
describe the neurotic conduct, for example, of a patient who suddenly
breaks off treatment and leaves without paying. I think—without irony—
that the ordinary language of analysts sanctions here the reality of a theoretical distinction.

What this means is that acting out is neurotic conduct, but not all neurotic conduct is acting out. In other words, acting out should be defined metapsychologically as a theoretical concept of psychoanalysis, and not only as a phenomenon of the psychology of conscience. If we reduce acting out solely to the phenomenal appearance of resistance and/or transference, we greatly restrict the possibility of apprehending the psychological act in its full complexity.

52.5   A simple clinical example

A woman came to her session on a Friday, the first day of the month, worried because she left the money to pay for the sessions on the table in her house, which she left hurriedly so as not to arrive late and keep me waiting. She apologized sincerely, regretting that she could not pay me until the following Monday. I told her that in principle the agreed date of payment was neither that Friday nor even the following Monday. She knew this; but in any case she did not like to keep me waiting. I repeated then the well-known interpretation about the weekend, which she always rejected, telling her that, with her forgetfulness, she had inverted the situation and this time *I* was the one who waited over the weekend. She said that this was in fact the case; she noticed that her discomfort had disappeared as if by magic, and she added that, for the first time, she understood "about the weekend".

This is a trivial example, and all analysts will have had similar experiences. The patient forgot the money: this is undoubtedly a slip, a neurotic act expressing an unconscious conflict. She preferred to explain it by her haste to arrive on time and not to make me wait. Her rationalization, however, contains the basis of her conflict: to make me wait; and the next association was about the weekend. In forgetting her money, she tried not to become conscious of the anxiety about the weekend, placing it in me. When I interpreted, I was almost certain that this time the interpretation would be accepted, because she spoke of having forgotten, of anger, of irritation, about waiting, about the weekend.

With all these elements it was difficult to think about an acting out. Further, there were other convincing elements of judgement. The analysand remembered and recorded her forgetfulness, although formally she had no need to apologize. She had ample time to pay. In addition, my countertransference informed me that I could trust the patient's associations and that there were no great obstacles in the communication process.

To confuse this slip with acting out would therefore be a big mistake and an injustice. This act of forgetfulness basically had a communicative attitude and was in service of the process. It is not worth calling it "acting out"—not even partial acting out, as Rosenfeld (1964a) would have called it. However, if the analysand had omitted to communicate her act of forgetfulness to me and, despite this, I had rescued it from the material, I would have been inclined to think, in principle, that it could be acting out, and in this case surely an interpretation about the weekend would not have been operative.

52.6   Freud's "agieren"

Freud uses the verb *agieren* for the first time to characterize the neurotic conduct of the analysand in the "Postscript" to "Dora", where he says that "Thus she *acted out* an essential part of her recollections and phantasies instead of reproducing it in the treatment" (1905e, p. 119; italics in original). In this first definition, Freud clearly contrasts acting out [*agieren*] with the memories and fantasies that are reproduced in the cure. Foreshadowing the broad discussion the subject will require of us, I will say here that this definition is perfectly adjusted to what I consider as acting out.

As a working hypothesis we will consider, then, that only neurotic conduct that has the specific sense of not reproducing itself in the treatment, as Freud says in the "Postscript", should be considered as acting out. If this difference (or another one) is not maintained, any justification to continue to speak of acting out disappears because it becomes synonymous with neurotic acts.

I believe I am not mistaken in asserting that in "Dora" Freud distinguishes the transference from acting out. For one thing, Freud did not interpret Dora's transference in time (since he had not read the "Postscript", as we have!). There is, also, the solution Dora finds via acting out.

I personally understand Dora's acting out as I believe Freud does when he says she acted a fragment of her fantasies and memories *instead* of reproducing them in the treatment. I emphasize "instead of" because this is, for me, the main characteristic of acting out. The transference is a way of remembering; acting out is a way of *not* remembering.

52.7   Acting out, remembering, repetition

The sharp difference I have just proposed undeniably becomes less clear if we follow closely how the Freudian investigation on transference and acting out unfolds.

Freud develops these concepts in his essay "Remembering, Repeating and Working-Through" (1914g), where he introduces the idea of repetition to account for the transference phenomenon. Although the model of the clichés of 1912, and that of new editions and reimpressions of 1905, had already distanced him from the associationist theory of the false link of 1895, he now introduced the concept of *compulsion to repeat*, which came to play an important role in his new theories.

The relation between memory and repetition becomes much more subtle and complex. With the new technique (the analysis of resistances), "the patient does not *remember* anything of what he has forgotten and repressed but *acts* it out. He reproduces it not as a memory but as an action; he *repeats* it, without, of course, knowing that he is repeating it" (1914g, p. 150; italics in original). During the entire course of analysis the patient continues to have this compulsion to repeat, and the analyst finally understands that this is his way of remembering (ibid., p. 150). This clear Freudian assertion is validly relied on by those who maintain that, as to a special form of memory, acting out is no more than a resistance like any other and should be evaluated and analysed as such.

However, there are also valid reasons for thinking that the relation between repetition, transference and acting out is not satisfactorily defined in the 1914 essay, nor in Freud's subsequent writings.

As we have just seen, Freud sometimes equates acting out and transference; at other times he seems to distinguish between them, as when he suggests that thanks to the transference link the possible achievement is that the analysand does not carry out repetitive acts, utilizing as material his intention of doing so *in statu nascendi*. Undoubtedly the relation between acting out and transference is not clear for Freud: sometimes he superimposes the two concepts, sometimes not (see Guillermo Lancelle, 1974).

To understand Freud's hesitation it is necessary to indicate, in the first place, that the change of technique (in the sense of analysing the resistances) does not question at that moment the objective of the treatment, which continues to be the recovery of memories. In the second place, the newly formulated principle of compulsion to repeat can be applied equally to acting out and to the transference, without it necessarily implying that these two processes are identical. Acting out and transference are undoubtedly the same genetically, because the two derive from the compulsion to repeat; but they could be different in structure and significance. Acting out could be something special and with a particular structure, although it arises out of repetition.

52.8   *Another clinical example*

Let us look now at an example which—for me—clearly configures an acting out and which is diametrically opposed to the recently mentioned parapraxis.

A woman in a very good economic position said she was going to Europe for two months and was not going to pay the fees during her absence because her husband refused categorically to do so. She was not in agreement with her husband on this point; but she could do nothing about it. Because of the total structure of the situation, which at that point presented itself as a *fait accompli* that the analysand in no way felt responsible for, an acting out could be assumed. During the following month the analyst interpreted in diverse contexts that the husband was a part of herself (projective identification), without anything appearing to change. The analysand completely rejected this type of interpretation and others formulated to her, while the analyst firmly maintained his interpretative line and never failed to interpret each time the occasion presented itself. The analysand complained about the analyst's rigidity, despite never in fact having posed any problem and having limited herself to announcing that her husband would not pay the analyst. If the analyst would not consider the situation, she threatened that she would have to interrupt the treatment.

Close to the day of departure, one of those difficult, agitated sessions ensued, and she recounted what had happened in her gymnastics class. She paid regularly there, on a monthly basis. When she told the secretary she would be away and the secretary told her she would nevertheless have to pay for the classes in her absence, she went crazy. She shouted and said, violently, that she would certainly not pay for the two months when she would be away. This time it was easy for the analyst to make her see how much this anecdote confirmed the interpretations on payment of fees.

When the (very competent) analyst of this patient consulted me, he felt worried. He considered that the situation was extremely difficult and realized that he was sustaining a special burden in his countertransference. He thought that if he did not yield in some way, the analysand could carry out her threat of not continuing the analysis. He also knew that to please her without further ado was clearly to abandon the method. Note that the countertransference warned the analyst of the danger the patient's treatment and his own technique were in. The analysand, on the other hand, was manifestly preoccupied only about money.

This example shows that the structure of acting out is always complex. Analysis of the situation before and after the incident at the gymnasium revealed that the analysand's neurotic conduct had many determinants. The analyst was able to discover the patient's various motives while not losing sight of the fact that, in announcing ahead of time what she was going to do, the patient was cooperating as best she could. The analyst remained firm, that is, without acting, until his interpretations took effect, and finally, the analysand recovered the possibility of cooperation. To be precise, what we call acting out in this clinical material is the decision—placed in the husband—not to pay for sessions lost during the trip. The incident at the gym, on the other hand, is a neurotic action but not an acting out in that it assists the process of working-through *instead* of obstructing it.

While the situation was totally projected into the husband and the patient presented it as a *fait accompli*, the problem was difficult to resolve. In this case, as in many others, projective identification is the instrument employed in acting out, as Grinberg (1968) and Zac (1968, 1970) say. But neither projective identification nor its consequences amount to acting out. To further the main thesis of these chapters, I wish to state that the patient's acting out does not consist in projecting her desire not to pay into the husband. Acting out begins precisely when the patient rejects the possibility of analysing that situation (which, once projected, no longer belongs to her) and demands, on the contrary, that the analyst adjust to that "reality" rather than trying to analyse it with his lamentable rigidity.

What arose clearly after her return (from her trip) was that she wanted the analyst to err in order for her to leave treatment, accusing him because of the mistake committed. Since this appeared at that time in convincing dream material, the error she awaited was that the analyst should charge her (rigidity) or the opposite, because this would demonstrate what she already knew; that he was capable of anything in order to keep her. This last intention of the analysand can arouse some scepticism, because in general we prefer to think that analysands do not fully understand the rules of the game—that is, our technique—rather than recognizing that they can judge us with exactitude and implacable justice. However, had the analyst in our example yielded and, accepting as fact the husband's opinion, had he agreed not to charge for missed sessions, and had the traveller not returned, all analysts would think that the patient was right and that the analyst was to blame for the interruption. Via a *reductio ad absurdum*, I think this proves the analysand unconsciously wanted the analyst to err. At the same time—oh paradox!—we would also think she had acted out. However, the contradiction is resolved if we consider that the decision not to return would have been logical and rational taking the analyst's mistake into account, but that this mistake had been precipitated by the woman's acting out.

I recall an episode that occurred some years ago that can illustrate this. It was the beginning of an analysis of a middle-aged woman, more melancholy than beautiful, who in the middle of a session got up to get her cigarettes. With the proverbial psychoanalytic mentality I saw her take four or five steps from the couch to the desk where her bag was before she returned to lie down on the couch. Episodes such as these are more than frequent in the practice of all analysts, and generally they are extinguished in some conventional interpretation. The unexpected in this case was the very vivid fantasy I had: I stood up, went to meet her and hugged and kissed her without circumspection. Having returned to the couch, the patient resumed one of her favourite themes: I was unbearable due to my coldness, my severity and my technique. I was a machine, a robot who cared only about meeting who knows what absurd postulates.

She preferred her previous analyst a thousand times to me; although incompetent, as least he was human. And she added something that made a profound impression on me: "When I arose from the couch I thought fleetingly that you were going to try to touch and kiss me, and then I really would have left you flat then and there and would not have come back."

A person can get up from the couch to look for cigarettes simply because he wishes to smoke, and this can be a rational action (leaving aside the neurotic or psychotic impulses of the smoking habit). If a desire to alleviate his anxiety or distract his attention impels him, then we can say this is a neurotic act. But if the unconscious fantasy is to remove the analyst from his place literally, then and only then is this an acting out. And the patient in this case continued complaining about my coldness and demanding direct proof of my affection until, fed up with me, she left the treatment some months later.

Note that the analysand's acting out is, according to my criterion, an attempt to make me err—an attack on my task, which she understands very well. What she does not want is for me to be a competent analyst, and when she succeeds in her attempt, she will rightly cease to attend. She preferred the inconsistency of her previous analyst a thousand times to my unbearable and dehumanized technique, although at the same time she was attributing feelings—and, moreover, passionate feelings—to me.

What gives acting out its specific quality is, in my opinion, the (naturally unconscious) intention to attack the task, to make it impossible. I think that in these two cases all the characteristics that distinguish acting out from neurotic conduct can be noted. Acting out characteristically places the analyst in a compromising situation, which always creates strong countertransference conflicts. As we have seen, in our first case the situation was virtually insoluble: if the analyst had distanced himself from the contract, he would have ceased to be an analyst; if he did not, the conclusion was the same, since the analysand would then have left because his rigidity would have prevented him from understanding that she could not bend her stubborn husband's will. A defining feature of acting out is that it confronts the analyst with events that compel him to act.

In this way we return to the first Freudian characterization: that Dora *acted* a portion of her memories and fantasies *instead* of reproducing them in the cure. This is why I say that acting out is fundamentally an attack on the task, something that is done *instead* of the analytic task, or the task (without qualification). It is an action that is the opposite to the one supposedly expected. Zac (1968) considers that it is characteristic for acting out to constitute an attack on the setting. I agree with this opinion, although I think the setting is attacked as guarantor of the analytic task.

In other words, to define acting out in metapsychological terms, it is necessary to refer it to the analytic process and to the setting. As in the case of perversion, the diagnosis of acting out cannot be done phenomenologically but only in metapsychological terms.

52.9   *Acting out and transference*

Perhaps all controversies converge in the relation between acting out and transference. The two concepts always appear together in Freud's works, from the "Postscript" (in 1905e) to the *Outline of Psychoanalysis* (1940a).

Sometimes Freud seems to counterpose them, sometimes he makes them homologous, and at times, perhaps, he confuses them.

To avoid ambiguities, a first step would be to compare the terms "acting out" and "transference". Transference is broader; it takes in more. Everything the analysand thinks, says or does impelled by the compulsion to repeat is transference, and in principle there is no doubt that acting out remains within the scope of this definition. What is repeated in acting out is, however, precisely an intention to ignore the object, to distance oneself from it, and this is one of its defining characteristics. The transference repeats in order to remember, acting out repeats in order not to. Transference communicates; acting out does not. The fact that the analyst may discover the meaning of an acting out does not imply that this was the analysand's intention. The transference goes towards the object; the acting out distances itself from the object.

* * *

To sum up: we can now establish some conclusions: (1) both transference and acting out derive from the compulsion to repeat; (2) transference is a more inclusive concept, and therefore all acting out is a transference, but not vice-versa; and (3) acting out responds to special intentions, which make it advisable to maintain it as a special type of repetitive conduct.

In chapter 53 we try to see how far these specifications can be justified.

CHAPTER FIFTY-THREE

Acting out
[2]

In chapter 52 we attempted to explain how the concept of acting out arose in Freud's writings, taking as a reference-point symptomatic and chance actions (1901b, chapter 9), the "Postscript" to "Dora" (1905e) and "Remembering, Repeating and Working-Through" (1914g). We also saw that the remembering/repeating antinomy seems to feed simultaneously the concepts of acting out and transference, which sometimes are superimposed and sometimes are separated in Freudian thought. We also reviewed the 1945 essay in which Fenichel makes an effort to delineate the concepts of transference, acting out and neurotic act without fully achieving this. Finally, I proposed some arguable and provisional specifications to orientate us in our discussion.

53.1 Anna Freud's first contributions

Some years before Fenichel's essay, Anna Freud dealt with the theme of acting out and transference in "The Application of Analytic Technique to the Study of the Psychic Institutions" (chapter 2 of *The Ego and the Mechanisms of Defence*, 1936). In this case, as in her entire book, Anna Freud lucidly applies the structural doctrine, trying to order the concepts in relation to theory and practice.

I have earlier indicated Anna Freud's decisive contribution to the theme of transference in distinguishing between the transference of libidinal impulses and the transference of defence as counterposed expressions of the id and the ego. I must now add that, in addition to these two categories, she identifies a third type, *acting in the transference*. This is a third type of transference, which Anna Freud distinguishes from the other two: "Now an intensification of the transference may occur, during which for the time being the patient ceases to observe the strict rules of analytic treatment and begins to act out in the behaviour of his daily life both the instinctual impulses and the defensive reactions which are embodied in his transferred affects. This is what is known as acting in the transference—a process in which, strictly speaking, the bounds of analysis have already been overstepped" (1965–71, Vol. 2, p. 23).

Acting out can offer the analyst valuable knowledge about the patient, but it is not very useful for the course of the cure and "is even more difficult for the analyst to deal with than the transference of the various modes of defence" (ibid., p. 24). Thus, Anna Freud concludes: "It is natural that he [the analyst] should try to restrict it as far as possible by means of the analytic interpretations which he gives and the non-analytic prohibitions which he imposes" (ibid.).

Anna Freud separates acting out as a special form of transference for two reasons: it is outside the framework of the cure and it is difficult to manage, to the point where it is necessary to use prohibitions to halt it. Although Anna Freud accords importance to acting out occurring outside the analytic ambit, her criterion is not merely spatial or geographical, since she links that condition to a maximum of resistance and a minimum of insight. Although this is perhaps a way of furnishing extra proof for myself, I would say that Anna Freud indicates, as a characteristic of acting out, its intention of not offering information.

53.2 Freud's last opinions

I think Anna Freud's reflections could have influenced her father's thinking when he returned to the theme in the final years of his life. It is worth studying thoroughly what Freud says in the *An Outline of Psychoanalysis* (1940a), not only because his final written references to the subject are certainly there, but also because this essay, which Freud wrote in 1938 and did not finish, is considered a valid exposition and almost a testament of the creator of psychoanalysis. (It is not known whether Freud had begun his work on this before leaving Vienna; it is certain, however, that most of it was written down after his arrival in London.)

Part 2 of the work deals with psychoanalytic practice, and in chapter 6, "The Technique of Psycho-Analysis", he speaks of the analytic situation, transference and acting out. These last two concepts are explained simultaneously, and Freud certainly does not clear up this time the obscurities we indicated in his previous writings.

Freud says, "We think it most undesirable if the patient *acts* outside the transference instead of remembering. The ideal conduct for our purposes would be that he should behave as normally as possible outside the

treatment and express his abnormal reactions only in the transference"
(1940a [1938], p. 177; italics in original).

In this text I believe I see Anna Freud's influence when Freud draws a
distinction between acting within the transference and acting outside it,
which he calls undesirable.

The section is obscure and can be read in various ways; but there is no
doubt of Freud's inconsistency when he says that it is undesirable for the
analysand to act outside the transference instead of limiting himself to
remembering. He should have said, instead of limiting himself to acting in
the transference: outside the treatment the analysand is not asked to remember, but he is asked not to act out.

On the previous page Freud says: "Another advantage of transference,
too, is that in it the patient produces before us with plastic clarity an
important part of his life-story, of which he would otherwise have probably given us only an insufficient account. He acts it before us, as it were,
instead of reporting it to us" (ibid., pp. 175–176).

Here Freud clearly thinks now that transference repetition, which in
this context he calls *agieren*, is superior to remembering (that is, to what
the patient relates), given that it provides us with a scene from his past
with vivid clarity. *Agieren*, which is "undesirable outside the transference"
in the quotation on p. 177, had not been so on pp. 175–176, where it even
ceases to be a resistance and turns out to be superior to remembering,
which is always insufficient. On this point, the fact that the 1914 aphothegm has been inverted can go unnoticed: resistance consists in the analysand referring (remembering) *instead of acting in the transference*.

I have paused at these two complex excerpts and indicated their lack
of continuity because to ignore this leads to fruitless discussions. In emphasizing certain sections in the text and leaving aside others, our personal opinion will be backed by Freud's authority. The same goes for the
1914 essay and the "Postscript" of 1905.

I am inclined to think that transference and acting out are two indispensable theoretical terms, which Freud formulated without managing to
solve all their enigmas. What matters is that—conscious of our limitations—we try to continue without trying to make our imaginary Freud
resolve the problems in a sort of *après coup*.

53.3 Acting out, communication and language

Some time after Fenichel's (1945b) essay, Phyllis Greenacre's brilliant contribution (1950) appeared in the *Psychoanalytic Quarterly*. Following
Fenichel's exposition, she defines acting out as "a special form of remembering, in which the old memory is re-enacted in a more or less organized
and often only slightly disguised form" (1950, p. 456). Without being in
any way aware that his conduct is motivated by memories, the subject
finds it plausible and appropriate, while to others it appears maladjusted.

Fenichel separated acting out from transference because in the former it is action that predominates, and in the latter it is feelings. He maintained that acting out rests on three conditions: "(a) A (perhaps constitutional) 'alloplastic readiness'; (b) fixations on orality, high narcissistic need, and intolerance toward tensions; (c) early traumata" (1945b, pp. 300–301). Early traumas condition a repetitive conduct in which acting out operates as an abreactive mechanism similar to that of the traumatic neuroses.

Greenacre follows Fenichel's steps and adds to these three conditions another two: a tendency to dramatize through great visual sensitization and a marked unconscious belief in magical acts (1950, p. 458). This type believes that it is sufficient to dramatize something for it to become true. If I pass myself off as a millionaire, I am one. In individuals with a tendency to act out, the sense of reality is revealed to be particularly deficient.

Greenacre locates in the second year of life the moment when the tendency to act out can be organized, in that at this moment three deeply significant circumstances converge: speech, walking and sphincter control.

When the disturbances of the early months of life, which increase the oral instincts, diminish tolerance to frustration and augment narcissism, are joined to the conflicts of the second year, the conditions arise for the appearance of the acting-out tendency. The development of language is inhibited, and, in parallel, the alloplastic tendency to discharge increases. Greenacre says that "the capacity to verbalize and to think in verbal terms seems to represent an enormous advance not only in the economy of communication, but also in the focusing of the emotions which are associated with the content of thought" (ibid., pp. 461–462). These circumstances, Greenacre concludes, are of major importance in understanding the problems of acting out, where there is always a disproportion between verbalization and motor activity. It is worth indicating here that this line of investigation concurs with that of Liberman in the study of the action-oriented personality and the epic style, as we saw in chapter 34.

53.4 Acting out and primal objects

Acting out is not a subject that particularly concerned Melanie Klein, although her disciples, especially Rosenfeld, studied it later.

When she analysed Felix because of his tic during the beginning of the 1920s, before having developed the play technique, Klein imposed on him certain prohibitions to ensure the continuity of analysis, since the boy's object choices were aimed at fleeing from the fantasies and desires directed at that moment to the analyst in the transference (see "A Contribution to the Psychogenesis of Tics", 1925, p. 115). On this point Klein implicitly explained her conception of acting out, to which she returned so fleetingly in "The Origins of Transference" (1952a). When she asserts that transference is rooted in the earliest stages of development and in the deepest layers of the unconscious, Melanie Klein maintains that the patient tends to manage the conflicts reactivated in the transference with the same methods he used in the past. One of the theses of this concise and vigorous article is that transference should not be understood only in terms of the direct references to the analyst in the material. In that it is rooted in the earliest stages of development and springs from deep layers of the unconscious, transference is more ubiquitous than is generally believed and can be extracted from what the analysand says, from the events of his daily life and from all his relationships. These relationships, Melanie Klein asserts, have to do with the transference; and it is here that she specifically refers to acting out, when she says: "For the patient is bound to deal with conflicts and anxieties re-experienced towards the analyst by the same methods he used in the past. That is to say, he turns away from the analyst as he attempted to turn away from his primal objects; he tries to split the relations to him, keeping him either as a good or as a bad figure: he deflects some of the feelings and attitudes experienced towards the analyst on to other people in his current life, and this is part of 'acting out'" (1975, Vol. 3, pp. 55–56).

These references are too succinct to know what Klein thinks about acting out, but it can be asserted that she sees it as a special form of transference, which leads the analysand to withdraw from the analyst as he withdrew from the primal objects.

53.5   Partial and excessive (total) acting out

With his usual erudition but with less precision than at other times, Herbert Rosenfeld (1964a) approaches the theme of acting out basing himself on Freud and Klein.

Reading Freud in a particular way, as we all do, Rosenfeld does not doubt that repetition, transference and acting out are the same thing. Having resolved this problem drastically, another problem arises for Rosenfeld (as a sort of return of the repressed), which leads him to classify acting out as partial and excessive. Thus in *Psychotic States* (1965) he affirms: "... some acting out occurs in every analysis, and that one might well be justified in saying that partial acting out is not only inevitable but is in fact an essential part of an effective analysis. It is only when this partial acting out increases and becomes excessive, that both the analysis and the patient are endangered" (p. 200). To maintain his classification, Rosenfeld says that when Freud declared himself in favour of restricting acting out he meant excessive acting out, "... since we regard some acting out as an important and necessary part of any analysis ..." (ibid., p. 201).

Rosenfeld thinks that differentiating between major and minor acting out resolves the difficulties, but in fact it does not. The weak point in his argument is that it unifies in a sole concept two diametrically opposed processes: partial acting out, which expresses the patient's cooperation, and excessive acting out, which endangers analysis. To refer to excessive acting out Rosenfeld uses the adjective *"disastrous"*, which is highly expressive. The words "partial" and "excessive" imply quantitative differences; but Rosenfeld's concepts are qualitative and, even more, diametrically opposed.

I see another, and I believe not insignificant, difficulty in Rosenfeld's classifications: when to classify acting out as partial and when as excessive. Are we going to say that if a patient arrives two minutes late, his acting out is partial, and if he arrives twenty minutes late, it is excessive? I think that what we have to understand is the structure of this situation and not the phenomenological aspect of lateness; twenty minutes and two minutes can have the same metapsychological value, although perhaps in the former case the result, for the session, is "disastrous" and not so in the latter case, although we all gain more from a case in which a short session due to extreme lateness has brought out some important conflict and turned out to be very useful. Because of the nature of his classification, Rosenfeld is more exposed than he believes to subjective and ideological judgements.

Based on what Klein said in 1952, Rosenfeld considers that the patient repeats with the analyst the way he distanced himself from his primal object and adds that acting out will be partial or excessive according to the degree of hostility with which the patient initially withdrew from the breast.

Here Rosenfeld makes an interesting contribution by indicating that on the degree of hostility with which the child withdraws from the breast will depend the destiny of his future relations. But I believe that he again errs in thinking that every moving away is an acting out. Within Kleinian theory, moving away from the breast marks a culminating moment in child development—the passage from the breast to the penis. And, as a necessary process of maturation, it is a normal (and rational) act, never a neurotic act or an acting out. What Klein said in 1952 is that withdrawal from the analyst reproduces the withdrawal from the primal object, and this special type of transference is a part of acting out. When the depressive position is reached, the subject does not "withdraw" from the object but loses and mourns it. Klein refers to an aggressive withdrawal that is premature and pathological and implies abandoning the object due to hate, omnipotence and contempt. I believe, therefore, that it is only when the normal mourning process for the loss of the breast is not carried out, that turning away can be regarded as acting out.

53.6 *Papers read at the Copenhagen Congress*

In a Symposium on Acting Out and Its Role in the Psychoanalytic Process at the Twenty-fifth International Congress in Copenhagen in July 1967, Anna Freud and León Grinberg were speakers, and other important analysts participated. In Anna Freud's communication the main concern was outlining the concept; Grinberg's account contributed rich clinical material as the starting-point for a theoretical discussion where separation anxiety would be understood as a decisive factor, in the light of the theory of projective identification.

In her attempt at clarification, Anna Freud starts from a historical fact: that the theoretical terms of psychoanalysis vary with the extension of the theories themselves, which we do not always notice in employing them. She mentions two concepts with opposite outcomes: "transference" gradually expanded until it came to signify *everything* that occurs between analyst and analysand, whereas "complex", which initially included a very wide range of events, came to be restricted just to the Oedipus and castration.

In "Remembering, Repeating and Working-Through" (Freud, 1914g) acting out is defined in opposition to remembering as a compelling urgency to repeat the forgotten past, not only re-living the emotional experiences transferred to the analyst but also in the entire ambit of the situation in the present. Acting out was understood as replacing the capacity or the desire to remember as a function of resistance, so that "the greater the resistance, the more extensively will acting out (repetition) replace remembering" (Freud, 1914g, p. 151).

Anna Freud considers that this definition is clear if it is understood within the framework of the theories of the time, where recovering memories still occupied an important place, together with the dynamic conflict of the struggle of tendencies. At times, the forgotten past or the derivatives of impulses can be obtained through interpretation, so that they enter consciousness, reaching the level of the secondary process.

On the other hand, at other times the repressed psychic contents can be obtained only "in the form of being re-lived" in the transference (A. Freud, 1968, p. 166). Anna Freud says that the result will be a repetition from the past in the conduct to which, nevertheless, analytic rules will apply (ibid.). In this case, acting out is limited to re-experiencing impulses and affects and to re-establishing infantile demands and attitudes; but it is arrested just before motor action appears, leaving the working alliance intact. "Acting out in the transference within these limitations was recognized in earliest times as an indispensable addition to remembering" (ibid.). As in the previous case, the analyst's aim here also is to grasp the "revivals" when they emerge, now as behaviour, in order to interpret them, incorporating the material that comes from the id within the range of the ego.

There is a third possibility, which concerns the failure of the analyst's efforts, when the power of the forgotten past—or, rather, of the force of the repressed impulses—overcomes the limits imposed on motor action. In the transference, this can signify the rupture of the treatment alliance and the end of analysis. The other inconvenience in this type of acting out is that it is not limited to the analytic situation and invades the patient's ordinary life, which can be very dangerous.

* * *

To sum up: in locating the concept of acting out within the framework of the classic theories at the beginning of the First World War, Anna Freud distinguishes three types or degrees, which have to do with the intensity of the resistance and the stability of the treatment alliance, trying to give coherence to Freud's thought in those years. Although she does not equate transference with acting out, as do Rosenfeld or Gioia, she has to establish two (or three) different categories of acting out, where the first helps the treatment and the second damages it.

After her detailed reflections on the origins of the term, Anna Freud asserts that the concept of acting out had to expand in tune with the new theories. As the technical principle that the analysis of the transference is the fundamental field of analytic therapy became more firmly established, the dialectic of remembering versus repeating was imperceptibly abandoned, because the thought prevailed that repeating in the transference is the best way of remembering. In the same way, the growing importance acquired in contemporary analysis of the relationships of the child with the mother in the pre-oedipal stage of development reinforces the importance of motor conduct, since those events were not verbal and can be communicated only through re-enactment.

Another factor that has contributed to broadening the concept of acting out is that the new theories of the instincts accord greater importance than hitherto to aggression, which by definition is channelled especially through the muscular system, that is, through action. Also, the development of ego psychology and the growing attention on the functioning of the ego has led to closer observation of the conduct and character of our analysands; similarly, in the case of the analysis of children, adolescents and psychotics, where the conflicts are frequently channelled through action.

53.7 Grinberg's contributions

Grinberg's contributions, undoubtedly the newest of the symposium, try to explain acting out and account for its specific mechanisms.

Grinberg begins by indicating that beyond the pejorative connotations of the term, which tend to equate it with the analysand's bad behaviour, in fact some indicate the malignant character of acting out, whereas others emphasize its communicative and adaptive nature. He was particularly concerned with massive acting out, which provokes strong countertransference reactions.

Separation anxiety as the origin of acting out was indicated by Bion (1962b), Greenacre (1962), Zac (1968) and several others. Grinberg resolutely follows the view on separation anxiety and asserts that one of the essential roots of acting out stems from experiences of separation and loss, which determined, at a given moment, primitive mourning that was not worked through. When this type of conflict is re-enacted in the transference, the analysand utilizes the analyst as an object (container) into which he pours the pain of separation and loss. But when the analyst is not there, this is transformed into a beta element,[1] which has to be evacuated into another object, with which acting out takes shape. (Zac, 1968, reaches the same conclusion in the above-mentioned work, which has very illustrative clinical material.) At times the container object is represented by the person's own body, and then psychosomatic symptoms or hypochondria appear as *acting out equivalents*. When the dream functions as a container, we have what Grinberg calls *evacuative dreams*, which are very different from elaborative dreams (Grinberg et al., 1967).

As can be deduced from this, Grinberg considers that projective identification is the basic acting out mechanism, in that it allows evacuation into the object of the parts of the self that cannot be tolerated and contained. If the analyst is able to contain within himself the projections of the analysand and if he returns them adequately, then the analytic process continues its course, with the consequent development of insight and working-through. In other circumstances, however, the outcome is different, and then acting out is maintained and aggravated by a special deficit in the transference–countertransference interplay. Various motives can explain the analyst's fault, from his lack of reverie and his unconscious complicity to a severity that leads him to prohibit instead of understanding and interpreting; but in all cases the mechanism of projective counteridentification operates, as described by Grinberg himself (1956, 1957, etc.).

Grinberg remembers what Phyllis Greenacre said in her paper, "Problems of Acting Out in the Transference Relationship", which she presented at the Boston Symposium of 1962. She had reached similar conclusions on the basis of a very different referential scheme: "There is a trying out of the analyst in a wearing-down effort to see where the limit of tolerance really is. The whole performance has a tantrum form, but of a special kind in which there is a relentless demand for reciprocation and discharge through or with the *other*, the analyst. One understands here a special significance of the term *projective identification*. Sometimes there is clearly a beating fantasy behind this provocativeness" (1962, p. 223; italics in original).

From Fenichel onwards, many, from Bird (1957) to Rosenfeld (1964a), have indicated the analyst's participation in acting out, and Grinberg concludes that the modes of functioning of projective identification and projective counteridentification configure essential mechanisms in the particular type of object relation established in the acting out phenomena. To underline the peculiarity of this phenomenon, Zac (1968, 1970) says concretely that acting out *inoculates* the receptor.

In summing up the dynamics of massive acting out, Grinberg indicates the tolerance to psychic pain in the face of the experience of loss, which seeks discharge through projective identification in an object that can respond in turn with an action. These are narcissistic patients who maintain idealized links where admiration, avidity and envy alternate. They com-

bine in their defence mechanisms manic denigrating attitudes with a dissociation between the omnipotent aspect of the self and the self that is more
adapted to reality, which can also be called the psychotic and neurotic
parts, respectively, following Bion (1957). This particular type of object
relation is very labile and enters into a crisis at the first experience of loss
and frustration, which leads to evacuation into the object of the part of the
self that carries the painful feelings (neurotic part). While acting out prof-
fers information, if the message of the neurotic part is annulled by the
attack of the psychotic part, acting out configures a specially tenacious
type of resistance.

Acting out, Grinberg concludes, is constructed like a dream in which
certain elements of reality are transformed regressively into primary process. In this sense, acting out is like a dream dramatized and enacted during waking consciousness—a dream that could not be dreamt.

Note

1. Bion's beta elements serve only for evacuation through projective identification and
   the production of acting out.

CHAPTER FIFTY-FOUR

Acting out [3]

In chapters 52 and 53 I tried to explain the concept of acting out within a historical perspective that took us from the "Postscript" to the "Fragment of an Analysis of a Case of Hysteria, and "Remembering, Repeating and Working-Through" to the Copenhagen Symposium. I included in that review a series of major contributions, but I could not integrate others that are no less important.

I shall begin this chapter by referring to the opinions of Laplanche and Pontalis, whose contributions I consider significant when approaching this complex concept, and I shall then propose a synthesis of the current views—at least, what I believe to be the current views—on acting out.

54.1   The concept of acting out in the "The Language of Psychoanalysis"

In *The Language of Psychoanalysis*, Laplanche and Pontalis (1968) devote two entries to acting out, attempting to indicate the great theoretical problems posed by this concept and the ambiguities noticeable in all writing that dealt with it, not excluding Freud's. Aiming to delineate the concept, Laplanche and Pontalis propose this definition: "Such action generally displays an impulsive aspect relatively out of harmony with the subject's usual motivational patterns, and fairly easy to isolate from the overall trends of his activity. Acting out often takes the form of aggressive behaviour directed either at the self or at others. When it occurs in the course of analysis—whether during the actual session or not—acting out should be understood in its relationship to the transference, and often as a basic refusal to acknowledge this transference" (*The Language of Psychoanalysis*, p. 4).

According to this definition, acting out can exist independently of psychoanalytic treatment and, when it appears in the course of the analysis, it can be within or outside the session. Further, during the analysis, acting out is linked to the transference and sometimes constitutes an attempt to ignore it radically. English and English, in their *Dictionary* (1958), consider that transference and acting out are the same thing. In their *Glossary*, Moore and Fine (1968) define acting out as the tendency of certain people to reproduce their forgotten memories, attitudes and conflicts through action rather than words, without being conscious of this. They distinguish acting out *in the transference*, directed to the analyst, from acting out *outside the transference*, directed to other persons but permanently linked to the analytic situation.)

The *Language of Psychoanalysis* reminds us that Freud asserts, in the *Outline* (1940a), that it is undesirable for the analysand to act outside the transference—and this, incidentally, is why Freud recommended that no important decisions be taken during treatment.

The quotation continues: "One of the outstanding tasks of psychoanalysis is to ground the distinction between transference and acting out on criteria other than purely technical ones—or even mere considerations of locale (does something happen within the consulting-room or not?). This task presupposes a reformulation of the concepts of *action* and *actualization* and a fresh definition of the different modalities of *communication*.

"Only when the relations between acting out and the analytic transference have been theoretically clarified will it be possible to see whether the structures thus exposed can be extrapolated from the frame of reference of the treatment—to decide, in other words, whether light can be shed on the impulsive acts of everyday life by linking them to relationships of the transference type" (Laplanche & Pontalis, 1968, *The Language of Psychoanalysis*, p. 6).

I have repeated these ideas here because Laplanche and Pontalis propose, I believe, a program for conceptually reordering acting out, acknowledging that it is a very difficult task in which the complexities of the theory and the subtleties of clinical practice are conjoined with not a few prejudices.

54.2 Acting out and action

The relations between acting out and action are not at all simple. Hartmann (1947) was right in affirming at the beginning of "On Rational and Irrational Action" that we did not have then—and probably do not have now—a systematic psychoanalytic theory of action. Hartmann indicated in his essay that all actions—even those that respond to instinctive and affective demands—arise from the ego, and they always have an aim. Therefore the replacement of the motor response by organized actions is an essential part of ego development—the replacement of the pleasure principle by the reality principle. Although every action has its starting-point in the ego, an action can be defined as rational if it takes into account objectives and the reality context within which they should be reached, simultaneously weighing the consequences, whether at a conscious or at a preconscious level, and including a balanced judgement on the means available. Rational action belongs to the area of the secondary process, and the more conduct is rational, the more it is syntonic not only with objective, but also with subjective reality. "For the sake of clarification it might also be useful to introduce here a distinction between two forms of reality-syntonic behaviour. Behaviour may fit into the reality conditions in the sense that it actually furthers the attainment of a certain aim though it might not have been calculated to do so; in this case we may call it *objectively reality syntonic*. Or behaviour may attain a given aim as a consequence of being calculated to reach it, we call this form *subjectively reality syntonic*" (1947, pp. 49–50; italics in original).

After the Copenhagen Congress, Daniel Lagache (1968) dealt with the complex relations between acting out and action indicating that acting out cannot be characterized as an action that tends to discharge impulses because every action implies a discharge of impulses. Acting out refers to concrete and particular actions that respond to a particular latent model, because acting out is not a psychological, but a metapsychological model.

The metapsychological model of acting out for Lagache is the *parade*, that is, a representation of unconscious fantasies or memories through acts that allow what they hide to be revealed. With the term *parade* Lagache denotes the intentions of showing and representing, as in the military parade or in the theatrical representation, and I could even say that he employs the word as we do when we allude in popular language to someone who pretends to have what he does not, in fact, have. In opposition to the *parade* of acting out, Lagache proposes the *true action*, which realizes the objective and rational intentions that mark the relation between the agent and his action.

Lagache's specifications are valid in that they reveal acting out as a metapsychological concept; but to refer it to an unconscious parade fantasy seems infelicitous to me. The parade is applicable to hysteria and not to acting out. What differentiates them is, in my opinion, that the communicative intention of hysteria does not belong to acting out. If we follow Lagache, hysteria and acting out are superimposed. I think the metapsychological specificity of acting out should be sought in the *intentions* with which that action is carried out—and therefore the objectives that are being pursued. Acting out, then, should not be confused with theatrical display, which always has a communicative intention.

Leopold Bellak (1965) also bases the definition of acting out in motor conduct, in action, when he says that acting out is a somatic statement of non-verbal content, although he blurs completely, I think, the distinction between neurotic act, motor·symptom and acting out.

54.3   The intentions of acting out

To delineate the concept, I have started from a simple premise—that all acting out is an (irrational) neurotic act but not every neurotic act is an acting out. It can certainly be asserted that there is no difference between neurotic conduct and acting out—but then why continue to speak of acting out? If we accept instead that the two concepts are different, the question logically arises: what transforms a neurotic act into acting out?

To answer this question, which is also to define acting out, I emphasize the phrase "instead of", which Freud uses in the "Postscript" (in 1905e) and also later, in 1914, when he says that the patient acts instead of remembering. It is true that Freud says (a few lines later) that acting out is the way the patient has of remembering, with which acting out and transference are superimposed on each other. Trying to resolve this dilemma, I stated earlier that transference and acting out originate in the same phenomenon, repetition; but they are differentiated by *intention* (meaning unconscious desire or unconscious fantasy). Transference repeats *in order* to remember—acting out *instead of*. If this difference is not accepted, acting out is left hanging in the air; it becomes a phenomenological concept, a special type of transference made through action, but one that has no specificity and remains outside metapsychology. I will refer later on to the difficulties posed by my suggestion.

In defining acting out as something that is done *instead of*, I am naturally not referring exclusively to remembering, because as Anna Freud (1968) says, we have changed on this point since 1914, and we accord greater importance than we did to the transference conflict (without neglecting history and memories). Thus acting out also takes place *instead of* insight and working through. I understand "instead of" as what is opposed to the *task* of analysis, be it to recover memories, to gain insight or (as I believe) both.

As we have seen, the attack on the task or on the setting has been recognized by many as a defining characteristic of acting out, but few indicated it with greater precision than Leo Rangell (1968b) at the Copenhagen Symposium. Rangell's starting-point is that acting out must be distinguished from neurotic actions—a concept that is certainly more inclusive—and he proposes to define it as "action undertaken by the patient to resist the movement of the therapeutic process" (ibid., p. 195). Rangell holds (as I certainly do) that this definition is consistent with Freud's first formulation in 1905, when he says that Dora acted her memories and fantasies instead of reproducing them in the cure. After distinguishing acting out from other neurotic conduct (as we have just done), Rangell defines acting out in these terms: "Acting out is thus a specific type of neurotic action, directed towards interrupting the process achieving effective insight, thereby seen mostly in the course of psychoanalysis but also elsewhere" (ibid., p. 197).

Rangell believes that whenever there exists the possibility of insight outside the analytic situation, a response analogous to acting out in analysis can occur. But I believe the process to be broader and more frequent: whenever we do something *instead of* the task at hand, we are acting out. Sandler and colleagues (1973) are also disposed to extend the concept of acting out to situations that are different from analytic treatment, as long as the changes of meaning such an extension can entail are recognized. On the other hand, others, Moore and Fine among them, think that the term loses precision outside the context of the analytic situation.

If we accept that acting out is a neurotic act performed "instead of" a particular task, then any conduct that is "instead of" what should be done will be an acting out. If the same conduct fulfils what has been proposed, then it is not an acting out. Just as perversion can be diagnosed only metapsychologically, the same applies to acting out: beyond the neurotic conduct it always implies, it can be called acting out only if the intention is to oppose the task proposed (remembering, gaining insight, communicating etc.).

In this way, the concept of acting out is maintained, without subsuming it under that of neurotic conduct or of transference, which is located in another position and belongs to another class. It is a special form of transference a special class of ego strategy. The negative therapeutic reaction is also a part of the transference; but it is studied at another level and with another methodology.

54.4   Acting out and communication

We know as analysts that every conduct is an expression of ourselves, and everything said or done can be validly interpreted. As we can always interpret something to our analysands (and we are sometimes right!), we tend to forget that at times the patient has the intention of not communicating anything to us. Elsa Garzoli (personal communication) rightly says that acting out informs but does not communicate. When we stated that acting out opposes the work of analysis, be it insight, working through and/or the recovery of forgotten memories, we should have added that it is also opposed to the task of communicating.

This is why I tend to separate conceptually acting out from hysteria. Acting in the sense of theatrical display (or parade) should not be confused with acting out, which differs from it. The hysteria tends to dramatize, which implies communication—so much so that when a hysteric acts, we say he wants to call attention to himself, that he is "showing off". Hysterical theatricality is not authentic because it only has the pretension of trying to impress us, but it does not lack communicative intention. Acting out, on the other hand, does not pursue communication as an aim, but discharge and inoculation instead.

54.5 An amusing clinical example

Years ago, when I was very inexperienced although I was sometimes able to interpret a simple dream, a young man who was having sexual difficulties attended his Monday session. He came with the idea that he ought to tell me that he had masturbated, but the idea of talking about it was disagreeable to him. He finally decided to ignore the thorny theme and told me a dream. I told him the dream had to do with masturbation and, as the manifest content and some of its sparse associations referred to the weekend, I suggested that perhaps he had felt lonely during the last few days and had masturbated. I diagnosed then, through the dream, that he had masturbated and when he had done so. He answered then, with humour, that had he known how I was going to interpret his dream, he would not have had so many qualms when he arrived; he had thought of telling me he had masturbated but had lacked the courage to do so.

In what sense can it be said that telling this dream is an acting out? I say it is because *he* (not I) had felt he should tell me he had masturbated and told me the dream *instead*. To say he told me the dream simply to cooperate with me would be naive: he did not think that I would find him out. This is why I think *repeating instead of remembering* (or communicating) is what defines acting out.

The example seems valid to me, and for various reasons, especially because if we link conceptually acting out to an attack on the task, we can diagnose and interpret it with precision. Because it is simple and amusing, this example shields us from ideological deviations, from superego admonitions and, also, from being too unimaginative and traditional in our work. As long as we know that the dream is the most direct route to the unconscious (and the example confirms this once more), to tell it in this case is clearly an acting out if we take the analysand's intentions into account. Intentions are what count for us and not results, because we are not behaviourists.

The example also shows that it is not the extent but the sense (meaning) that defines acting out. However small and insignificant it may be, this is a case of acting out, because the patient planned it thus—despite the fact that it backfired and in telling the dream allowed the analyst to speak not only of masturbation but of the acting out.

Interpreting acting out in this case is saying simply that the patient tells the dream so as not to speak of masturbation. This interpretation was not offered by the analyst but by the patient himself, without this altering the argument in any way. The interpretation of acting out generally precedes other interpretations, because it seeks to reveal the analysand's lack of cooperation and re-establish, by analytic means, the working alliance.

As analysts we should be very tolerant, but never naive. Once this basic situation has been cleared up, the way is open for other interpretations, since the analytic situation is always complex and is ruled by Wälder's (1936) principle of multiple function.

When the analysand acknowledged he had told the dream in order to avoid speaking of masturbation, I was able to interpret to him not only the need to hide the masturbation in terms of the paternal (or it could have been maternal) transference, but also the desire to deceive me, which appeared linked to his conviction that with a dream he always made me content and ran no risks. Only then was I able to tell him that there also existed in him a desire to speak of masturbation, and this was why he told the dream. A correct and complete interpretative task could never limit itself to interpreting the acting out without also seeing this other aspect. Nevertheless, it would be a serious error to tell him, for example, that "at heart" the dream was a desire to cooperate. This interpretation is incorrect in every sense and, for me, matters as much as presenting oneself as the idealized father who permits and stimulates masturbation. In other words, interpreting acting out is basically attending to a fragment of the negative transference. One must bear in mind that if the young executive in my example had thought I would discover the masturbation through the dream, he could have said nothing about either the dream or the masturbation. Let us say, finally, that not being able to speak about the masturbation was not only the expression of his fear of castration vis-à-vis the analyst as father in the direct oedipal situation, but also of a deeper conflict with his young wife, who wished to become pregnant. The dream clearly showed that he did not wish to assume the role of father in order to deprive his wife of her maternity, and that this conflict was also reproduced in the transference in that he did not tell me about the masturbation in order to sterilize me as an analyst. In this specific case—and insofar as masturbation takes place *instead* of coitus—it is appropriate to call it acting out, with which I can demonstrate that the concept can also be employed outside analysis without losing its precision.

To conclude, our example attempts to show that the concept of acting out can be used without succumbing to ideological or moralistic deviations, which those who combat it (rightly) fear. A theory, however, cannot be invalidated because it exposes ideological deviations, since these are inherent in our prejudices and not in the theory itself.

54.6   Acting out, language and thought

When Phyllis Greenacre (1950) indicates that in acting out there is a disturbance that compromises both action and word simultaneously, she takes a decisive step in the understanding of this phenomenon. In acting out, Greenacre says, there exists "a distortion in the relation of action to speech and verbalized thought" (ibid., p. 458). The action replaces language, and the discharge occupies the place of communication and thought (ibid., p. 458). Speech serves to discharge more than to communicate, and its function is degraded in the service of exhibitionistic tendencies (ibid., p. 461). Here one could add that it is not only for exhibitionistic reasons that the communicative function of language is exchanged for action, but also for other motives such as attacking or inoculating the object.

This also applies to the relation between acting out and thinking. Acting out can be explained as a special form of the pathology of thought. I will follow on this point Bion's (1962a, 1962b) theory on the nature and origin of thought, to which I referred earlier.

Bion maintains that the baby is born with a *preconception* of the breast, and when he encounters the breast itself (*realization*), he constructs a *conception* of the breast. For Bion, what will determine the first thought is the absence of the breast. (On this point Bion concurs with Lacan, for whom the absence of the object also sets in motion the chain of metonymic displacements which will structure the symbolic order—see, for example, Lacan, 1957.) In the face of this decisive emergency the baby has two alternatives, to tolerate or avoid frustration (absence). If the baby *avoids* frustration, he transforms the absent breast into a bad breast that is present and expels it as a beta element. On the other hand, when he is able to hold back the action and *tolerates* frustration, recognizing the breast as absent, he has constructed his first thought.

The act by which, *instead of* thinking of the good breast as absent, he expels it as a bad breast that is present in the form of a beta element, is, for me, *the prototype of acting out*. In this way, thanks to Bion's ideas, I have been able to propose an explanation of acting out in accordance with what I have been expounding in these chapters. Acting out is thus linked to a way of behaving in relation to reality which has recourse to action instead of thinking. This also agrees with Freud's two principles (1911b), where thought arises out of retaining the charge—a deferred action. Acting out represents the inverse process—a regressive movement, which goes from thought to action (and not from action to thought).

Acting out arises from a regressive attempt to convert thought into action—into non-thought. Acting out represents, then, a special form of action that does not allow thought to develop, an idea that has to do with learning from experience and mental growth (Bion) and objective knowledge in Popper's sense (1972), that is, how action can be used to test reality and not to impose on it our (omnipotent) "theories".

In this way what Melanie Klein said in 1952 becomes clear: when the baby withdraws from the primal object, it is part of acting out. I understand this affirmation now in the sense that, in withdrawing, the baby does not fulfil his task, because the task of sucking is the task *par excellence*, the *prototype* of growth, not only in man but in all mammals. That the child should turn away from the breast may not in itself be acting out because there may be many reasons for this; we can only classify this behaviour as acting out if the child turns away in order not to suck. This is why precocious genitalization configures an acting out in development, whereas the normal passage from the breast to the penis does not. I agree here with Herbert Rosenfeld (1964a) when he underlines the importance of hostility in the withdrawal from the object in cases he calls excessive acting out.

Finally, I would like to engage in a speculation. Melanie Klein applied her theory of primary envy to the negative therapeutic reaction (as shown in the next few chapters). Bion made it play a big part in the reversible perspective. No one has yet tried to understand acting out from this point of view, but I am convinced that, when we do so, we will understand better the relations of acting out to confusional states, which Rosenfeld indicated in 1964 with the negative transference and with the undeniable difficulties that acting out poses for the development of the analytic process.

When Melanie Klein explains the defences against envy in chapter 6 of *Envy and Gratitude* (1957), she recalls what was said earlier about the withdrawal from the primal object and links envy to acting out more clearly, saying that, in her view, "*acting out*" insofar as it is used to avoid integration, becomes a defence against the anxieties aroused by accepting the envious part of the self" (p. 219; italics in original).

54.7   Acting out and play

Serge Lebovici took part in the Copenhagen Congress with a concise and convincing exposition, in which he declared himself in favour of distinguishing acting out as a special form of the repetition compulsion, reminding us of what Freud (1940a) says in the *Outline* and taking as a starting-point for his reflections the suggestive field of child analysis.

When the child's play expresses acting out, Lebovici says, it should be understood as a phenomenon of resistance, which is different in essence from playing as an infantile method of elaborating fantasies. The difference between play in the strict sense and acting out can be difficult, and more difficult still when the analyst participates subtly with a problem of countertransference. At times an interpretation in which the child is told, "you are afraid", and which he misunderstands as "you do not dare to", leads to acting out, as happens more than once, in Lebovici's opinion, with Kleinian technique. Given that this type of misunderstanding has to do with the immaturity of the child's psychic apparatus, Lebovici favours a technical variation in which the analyst assumes the superego function of introducing certain restrictions, since "the child psychoanalyst must consider that he is an adult faced with a still impotent child, in order to lead the latter to the constructive possibilities of secondary elaboration" (1968, p. 203).

Leaving aside the basic problem posed by Lebovici discussed since the 1927 Symposium on Child Analysis (as dealt with in chapter 31), the advisability of distinguishing playing properly speaking from acting out is in every sense a methodological specification I support decisively.

Lebovici is inclined to think that acting out tends only to repeat, whereas playing possesses a symbolic and elaborative component. On the basis of the process of splitting described by Klein, the child projects into his playing his painful experiences and, consequently, his bad object relations. In this way, acting out is related to projection and can be corrected only through the analyst's interpretative work, which offers the opportunity of setting in motion the process of working through. Thanks to this process, acting out is subject to counter-cathexis and gradually is transformed into secondary process.

To conclude, for Lebovici, in the field of metapsychology, acting out is "a bridge between simple going into action, and fantasy elaboration" (ibid., p. 204).

Acting out "is, first of all, a form of defence against his impulses, and, secondly, an insufficiently elaborated defence, for it does not lead to the production of fantasies, and, thirdly, a situation which justifies this interpretation, for it implies an elementary organization of the ego" (ibid., pp. 204–205).

* * *

Lebovici's specifications are really useful in distinguishing two different levels of the child's play activity, which can be characterized clinically and metapsychologically without ideological deviations being incurred in any way. These are two areas that exist and must be distinguished not only in our theory, but also in our practice.

54.8   Acting out and early development

In the previous section I suggested that acting out is rooted in the early stages of development, and I related it to the task *par excellence* of all mammals—sucking at the breast. Perhaps the prerogative (and the *pesadumbre* [sorrow], according to Rubén Darío) of *Homo sapiens* is to suck and think the breast. To withdraw from the breast in order not to think of and feel the pain of absence is the prototype of acting out. I proposed to differentiate in this way, at the outset, *acting* from *acting out* as two polar and antithetical processes, as the two ways in which reality and absence can be confronted.

In this way the concept of acting out is restricted to a mental attitude, that of not fulfilling the task undertaken, whereas neurotic action is characterized, rather, by the versatility that leads it from one object to another, naturally to the detriment of mental functioning and object relations.

In relation to these ideas it is understood that preverbal means of communication should not be considered as acting out. In speaking of early constructions in chapter 28, I expounded clinical material that attempts to show how the significant events of the first year of life are reproduced in the transference, and I compared them with the forms assumed by infantile conflict. I said then that the early conflict is channelled through action, and I counterposed it as transference psychosis against the transference neurosis of the infantile conflict.

The greatest obstacle I see to my proposal is that at times it requires very subtle distinctions, and the more so if one takes into account that, given that a psychic act is always overdetermined, in the consulting-room the concrete case obliges us to a very careful evaluation—in the face of what the patient does—in order to distinguish how much there is of a neurotic act, of acting out and, finally, of non-verbal communication. I can say, in my defence, that evaluations that are as difficult as these arise constantly in our practice.

* * *

Eugenio Gaddini, in the paper he presented at the 1981 Helsinki Congress, also seeks the explanation of acting out in the earliest stages of development, without underestimating the influence of subsequent experiences. Gaddini uses the term "acting out" broadly and does not believe it necessary to distinguish between action and acting out, although he rigorously distinguishes acting out that facilitates and promotes the analytic process from acting out that goes against the process—the latter being the one I propose to call acting out in its strict sense.

In the beginning was the act, Freud said in *Totem and Taboo* (1912–13); paraphrasing him, Gaddini says that in the beginning was acting out. Both in early development and in the psychoanalytic process acting out can be in the service of development regulating tensions, or it can function as a defence against development and against the psychoanalytic process, eliminating the tensions instead of regulating them, maintaining a state of non-integration that arrests the process of integration and impedes, finally, the objective recognition of oneself. Defensive acting out "tends to counter-act recognition of one's autonomy and one's real dependence. Acting out leaves out reality, it is magic and omnipotent" (Gaddini, 1981, p. 57).

Gaddini says that acting out is more in the service of needs than of desires and refers it to the basic experience of separation of the child from his mother. "This experience has less to do with the moment mother stops breast-feeding the baby, and much more with the overwhelming time when the child has to realize its being separate, and with the capacity to deal with this change" (ibid., pp. 57–58). The strongest anxieties arise at this point, because the child tries to re-establish the lost situation magically, and the anxiety arises of a possible loss of the self. If the self is organized pathologically, the ego can suffer a coercion of such magnitude that it submits to the omnipotent needs of the self. On the basis of this scheme of early psychic development, Gaddini can distinguish acting out in the service of the analytic process from the acting out that interrupts it, which he defines in the following terms: "Acting out, stabilized as a de-

fence, is used to put the entire executive apparatus, consciousness included, in the service of the magic and omnipotent autarchy of the self,
instead of serving autonomy" (ibid., p. 58).

Gaddini maintains that there is a *crucial phase* in analysis, when the
analysand becomes aware that the analyst is someone different and separate, which marks the crumbling of omnipotence, with great anxiety over
the loss of the self. At this moment, Gaddini continues, acting out can
increase dangerously, and the possibility of the analysand deciding to interrupt the treatment increases with it.

Without having to discuss Gaddini's theory of development, I wish to
indicate the agreement between his concept of the two types of acting out
and mine in distinguishing acting and acting out in the early stages of life.

54.9   In favour of acting out

Throughout my exposition, we have had the opportunity of examining the
most varied lines of thought on acting out. Having cleared up my own
position in these last sections, I can now say that many analysts have
rightly indicated, and with good reason, the positive aspects of acting out.

For Ekstein and Friedman (1957), acting out is a form of experimental
remembering. They view acting out as a precursor of thought, a primitive
way of resolving problems; playing contains the seeds of acting out and of
thought. Playing, however, requires a certain degree of ego maturation
and is only possible, therefore, when a sufficient integration of the ego has
been achieved. Before play can be structured, precursors exist, which
Ekstein and Friedman call *play action* and *play acting*.

At the beginning of life, adaptation consists in immediate instinctive
discharge. These impulsive actions at the beginning of life are gradually
transformed into *play action*, which is deferred action in relation to reality,
so that it combines the quasi-gratification of playing with a first attempt to
resolve the conflict. As the child develops, he replaces *play action* with
fantasy, and with higher forms of thought, as he approaches the realm of
the secondary process.

In this way Ekstein and Friedman propose an interesting gradation of
the stages of mental development, beginning with immediate action, following with *play action*, passing through fantasy and play acting and arriving at deferred action and adaptive direction.

On the basis of this scheme they propose that acting out has two components: (1) experimental memory, which is directed to the past and inappropriate to reality, and (2) elemental thought and reality test, which is
directed to the future.

In the clinical case that serves as the basis for this work, Ekstein and
Friedman (1957) remark: "In this case, the assumption was made that the
acting out, play action, and *play acting,* rather than being merely a substitute
for recollection, *represented experimental recollection,* a primitive mode of the

ego to bring about reconstruction, which is in the service of adaptation" (pp. 627–628; italics in original).

At the Amsterdam Congress of 1965, Limentani (1966) presented a concise and coherent paper in which he proposes "A Re-evaluation of Acting Out in Relation to Working-Through". Limentani emphasizes the analysand's wish to communicate with the analyst in a non-verbal way. Without ignoring the negative aspects of acting out, Limentani holds that the acting out that appears during the process of working through can have a helping function for the course of the analytic process. Limentani also considers that acting out can sometimes avoid a serious psychosomatic illness, and then it becomes necessary to tolerate it, allowing it time to decrease gradually, without this implying complacency or complicity.

Limentani concludes that acting out is a complex phenomenon, for which there may be more than one explanation; but, as opposed to the proposal in this book, he is not inclined to establish metapsychological categories within this complex phenomenon.

Zac (1968, 1970) believes that acting out operates as a security valve that shields from danger, although he also holds that the main function of acting out is to attack the setting.

54.10   Acting out and acting in

The German word *agieren* was translated into English as *acting out*; it fared well and was adopted by analysts in Latin languages.

The verb *to act* has various meanings in English: to perform, to function, to simulate, to behave. The adverb *out* is used to signify different things according to the verb it modifies.

These multiple meanings of the compound verb *to act out* undoubtedly contributed to the fact that mistakes are frequent when this expression is used in psychoanalysis, although I am inclined to think that the difficulty is more profound and has to do with the ambiguity of the concept itself, as maintained also by Laplanche and Pontalis and more recently by Dale Boesky (1982) in his well-documented study for the Helsinki Congress.

A typical mistake in this sense is when the concept of *acting in* is counterposed to that of acting out, in an attempt to imply in this way what happens within or outside the session. In this turn of phrase the weight of the adverb *out* is noticeable, as there is an attempt to distinguish between what happens *in* the session and *out* of the session. The difference has only a phenomenological, or, rather, a spatial value. No dynamic or metapsychological specifications are discernible. It does not seem to make much difference whether a candidate asks his training analyst's permission to borrow a book as he is leaving the consulting-room or when he meets him at the Association. At most it can be argued that, in the first case, the analyst is in a better situation to interpret the candidate's behaviour, but this is relative: it is likely that, in both cases, the analyst will interpret in the session that follows the request. (It is understood that this example is schematic and presupposes that the request is effectively an acting out—which can be asserted only on the basis of unconscious material—and that the other variables are identical.)

This mistake cannot, however, be attributed to Meyer A. Zeligs, who in 1957 introduced the term *acting in* to distinguish certain attitudes of posture of the analysand during the session, which he locates halfway between acting out and conversion symptoms. What the analysand does with his body and with his postural attitudes in the session is something midway between acting out and memory (or verbalization), in that it is a way of not verbalizing or remembering, but, rather, closer to symbolization, to verbal thought. Halfway between the primary process (acting out) and the secondary process (thought), acting in would be a moment of transit, an evolutionary step.

Zeligs's proposal has been taken up by only a few analysts. In general, it is not accepted, perhaps because of the linguistic ambiguities I mentioned at the beginning, and probably also because the metapsychological characterization he proposes is not very convincing. In effect, the need to pay attention to the patient's behaviour and to analyse it comes to us from the classic writers and occupied a central place in Reich's technique.

A different position to that of Zeligs is Rosen's (1963, 1965), for whom acting in characterizes the psychotic phenomenon, where external actions arise as a response to desires and dreams, without contact with reality. For Rosen the proposition "in" means what comes from within and ignores reality. According to this proposal acting out should be reserved for the neurotic phenomenon. Rosen says that acting in is coordinated with acting out in the same way as the primary process is with the secondary process, or the unconscious with the conscious (Rosen, 1965, p. 20). In this way, the neurotic phenomenon of acting out is superimposed on rational and conscious action.

Rosen compares psychosis with a nightmare and understands by acting in a peculiar type of conduct in which the subject is preoccupied with the events of his internal world, which is a dreamlike world, without receiving any influence from the events of the external world. This is what Rosen calls acting in. Acting in is acting as if in a dream, with reference to an internal milieu, splitting reality off completely. Rosen asserts that this milieu is the mother, and this leads to his special way of treating the psychotic, that of *direct analysis*, where the doctor assumes the role of a *foster mother*.

54.11   A suggested synthesis

Having run the arduous course of the controversies surrounding acting out, I would like to propose a final synthesis of this absorbing theme.

Despite the imprecision that surrounds it, despite its contradictions and burden of prejudices and ideological connotations, the term "acting out" continues to be present in the ordinary language of all analysts, and the concept is regularly discussed in scientific meetings at every level. This real and enduring presence supports the idea that acting out is a basic concept for psychoanalytic theory and should be maintained, for which it is necessary to redefine it in metapsychological terms, not simply in terms of behaviour.

The name and concept of acting out are indissolubly linked to action, even for the particular case in which acting out can consist in *not* doing something specifically. It should therefore be included in the broader category of neurotic acts. Every action that, as a result of the conflict, deviates from the proposed aims and declared objectives is a neurotic act. Naturally, acting out shares these characteristics, but it has others that restrict and differentiate it: every acting out is a neurotic act, but not every neurotic act is an acting out.

As a neurotic act, acting out is dependent on the conflict, but this conflict assumes specific features in that it consists basically in replacing thought and memory, communication and the word by action.

A major controversy arises on this point, since the replacement of the word by the act can be a means of expressing oneself or the opposite. If we apply to these two objectives the term "acting out", as seems to be the preferred inclination of most analysts, then we must perforce distinguish two types of acting out: one that favours communication, recognizes the object relations and is in the service of integration and development, and one that opposes these ends, seeking to perpetuate omnipotence, omniscience and narcissism.

If we include both alternatives in the concept of acting out, we do greater justice, it seems, to the undeniable complexity of the phenomena; at the same time we shield ourselves from ideological evaluations that can lead us to qualifying the analysand's conduct as good or bad. However, this qualification is ideological only if we sanction it from the egocentrism of our *furor curandis*, of our narcissistic need to have a "good" analysand. On the other hand, if we acknowledge two objective modalities in our patients and in our practice, in the face of which we should apply with rectitude the impartial instruments of our work, then the classification of good and bad is scientific, it refers to the facts, and it confronts us with our daily task. When the haematologist says, in the globular count, "this is bad", he does not refer to the bad behaviour of the patient or of his erythrocytes, but simply to the objective fact that the number of red corpuscles deviates from the norm.

However many discussions there may be on early development, all of us are agreed that at this stage there is no articulate verbal language, and we are not going to find it when it is reproduced in the transference either. If this is so, then to expect the analysand to communicate to us something that is ineffable would by definition be both capricious and cruel. To operate as analysts, then, we will have to understand this type of message and give it back in some way to the analysand, knowing that he is communicating in the only and therefore best way possible.

A polar opposite is the other type of acting out, or acting out *tout court*, where action appears *instead of* communication, thought and/or memory. Here there is an intention (in the sense of unconscious fantasy) that goes *against* what has been agreed on. From this point of view, acting out is defined as an action effected "instead of" the task that must be carried out. This task, in the case of analysis, would be to achieve insight, but it can also be affirmed that acting out is opposed to memory, to thought, to communication, or that it attacks the setting or the therapeutic alliance, according to our theoretical predilections. In this sense acting out is a regressive device that operates to interfere with the task. The regressive movement that goes from thought to act, from word to non-thought, is omnipotent and omniscient; it serves narcissism and not the object relation and wants to go back instead of seeking development or growth. According to various points of view, this operative modality could be explained by the bad relation with the breast, where primal envy plays an important role, by difficulties in the process of individuation or other doctrinal schemes; but what always remains is that this is a regressive movement that leads from thought back to the act.

Finally, acting out should be considered as a special form of transference in that it confuses the past with the present and operates at the level of a primary process. But, as opposed to other modalities of the same phenomenon, this form seeks to ignore the relation, to take it along other paths and towards another destiny. The certain fact that acting out is nothing other than another aspect of the transference should not lead us to forget its specificity, in the same way that no one doubts that the negative therapeutic reaction is a modality of the transference link, but we all consider that it is worth respecting its autonomy.

CHAPTER FIFTY-FIVE

Negative therapeutic reaction [1]

55.1   Negative therapeutic reaction and guilt feelings

The *negative therapeutic reaction* (NTR) is a clearer and less controversial concept than acting out. Acting out is, as we have seen, a difficult concept to grasp, to delineate; that of NTR, on the other hand, thanks to the mastery of Freud's exposition in 1923, is clear, which allows for a firm starting-point in the discussion.

In "The Dependent Relationships of the Ego", chapter 5 of *The Ego and the Id* (1923b), Freud says that certain patients cannot tolerate the progress of the treatment or the words of stimulus that, at a given moment, the analyst believes it is appropriate to offer, and they react in a way that is contrary to what is expected. This reaction arises not only when they are told something positive about the course of the treatment, but also when some progress has been realized in the treatment. When a problem has been resolved or a resistance has been conquered, the analysand's response, instead of being an experience of progress and relief, is the contrary. Freud says that these are people who cannot tolerate any type of praise or appreciation and respond inversely to all progress in the cure.

Freud introduces the concept we are studying to explain the action of the superego, and he states that this type of reaction is indissolubly linked to the sense of guilt, which operates on the basis of the action of the superego. What leads to this contradictory response in the patient, which worsens when it ought to have the right to improve (to say it in superego terms), is, then, the superego, which does not assign this right to him. The idea that the negative therapeutic reaction is linked to the sense of guilt is basic, then, to Freud's thought.

Thanks to the newly constructed structural theory, Freud was able to explain the strange attitude of people who behave in a very peculiar manner in treatment, so that they become worse when the conditions for progress are there. Something in them opposes improvement and leads them to perceive the cure as a danger, and this attitude does not change after having analysed rebelliousness in the transference, narcissism and the secondary gain of the illness. Freud then concludes that the explanation is found in a "moral" factor, in the sense of guilt that finds satisfaction in the illness and that—as heir to the relationship with the father—comes from castration anxiety, although also from the anxieties of birth and separation from the protective mother.

Progress in the study of the superego and, in addition, the increasing attention NTR has been receiving, are facts that lead one to think that the sense of guilt and NTR are not interchangeable as Freud at first defined them. Now we know, in effect, that NTR can assume diverse forms and has multiple causes. Sandler and colleagues (1973) and others, however, prefer to reserve the term "NTR" for the clinical phenomenon initially described in *The Ego and the Id*—that is, the reappearance of symptoms that come from the guilt generated by an atmosphere of encouragement, optimism or approval (ibid., pp. 92–93).

55.2   The masochism of the ego

NTR was incorporated into the corpus of psychoanalytic theories in 1923, but the idea can be traced in other writings before this date, and subsequently in the writings of Freud and other psychoanalysts.

A year later, in "The Economic Problem of Masochism" (1924c), Freud specified some of his points of view. He indicates that to speak of an unconscious sense of guilt offers some difficulties, since patients do not readily admit they can hide internally guilt that they do not perceive, and, in addition, speaking with propriety, there are no feelings in the Ucs. For these reasons, Freud is inclined to change the earlier nomenclature and refers, not to a sense of guilt, but to a *need for punishment*.

These two concepts, Freud continues, are not totally identical, because the sense of guilt has to do with the superego's severity or sadism, whereas the need for punishment alludes to the masochism of the ego; nevertheless it is obvious that these two characteristics always go together in some measure.

When Freud emphasizes that NTR is linked to the ego's masochism, he opens up another perspective, because the sense of guilt and the need for punishment can then be distinguished from each other. As Freud had already observed in "Some Character-Types Met with in Psycho-Analytic Work" (1916d), the need for punishment is precisely a way to defend oneself from the sense of guilt: one prefers punishment in order not to have a sense of guilt. Therefore an exaggerated guilty conscience can lead the individual to crime: "Paradoxical as it may sound, I must maintain that the sense of guilt was present before the misdeed, that it did not rise from it, but conversely—the misdeed arose from the sense of guilt" (chapter 3, "Criminals from a Sense of Guilt", 1916d, p. 332). And Freud adds that analytic work shows repeatedly that the sense of guilt springs from the Oedipus complex. In the face of this twofold and terrible crime of killing the father and possessing the mother, Freud concludes, the crime actually committed will always be less serious.

In "Some Character-Types" (1916d), Freud not only offers this Copernican turn from the guilt to the crime but also establishes a connection between failure and sense of guilt, illustrating his thesis with Shakespeare's Macbeth and with Rebecca Gamvik from Ibsen's drama. The relationship between triumph and guilt is also implicit in the 1923(b) work and subsequently, because NTR always carries the mark of triumph and defeat.

55.3   The first references

Freud described NTR in 1923(b) but he had discovered it earlier, and it is easy to notice, in addition, that psychoanalysts of the previous decade clearly perceived in some of their patients the singular conduct that would be specified only in the subsequent decade.

In "Remembering, Repeating and Working-Through" (1914g), for example, Freud refers to the inevitable worsening during the cure and warns that the patient's resistance can use this for its own ends. In these comments there is certainly a reference to the concept, but it is not clear as it appears in chapter 6, "The Obsessional Neurosis", of the "Wolf Man" (1918b [1914]). Freud indicates there that at ten years of age, thanks to the influence of his German tutor, the patient abandoned his acts of cruelty with small animals, not without reinforcing this tendency for a time. Freud adds that "he still behaved in just the same way during analytic treatment, for he showed a habit of producing transitory 'negative reactions'; every time something had been conclusively cleared up, he attempted to contradict the effect for a short while by aggravation of the symptom which had been cleared up" (Freud, 1918 [1914], p. 69).

In 1919 Abraham referred to the same type of problems in an admirable article on "A Particular Form of Neurotic Resistance Against the Psychoanalytic Method" (1919a). His reflection centres on the particular difficulty of some patients who cannot assume their role as such and who permanently question and undermine the analyst's function. Abraham declares graphically that these people cannot understand that the aim of the treatment is the cure of their neurosis, and he points out that narcissism (and pride as an aspect of narcissism), competitive rivalry and envy are important impelling forces in the development of this type of reaction, which make analysis very difficult.

Simultaneously with others of that period, such as Ferenczi, Jones, Glover and Alexander, Abraham initiates with this essay the theory of character subsequently developed by Wilhelm Reich, and at the same time sows the seed for the studies of NTR that Freud would later develop.

55.4 Death instinct and NTR

From chapter 5 of *The Ego and the Id* (1923b) to "The Economic Problem of Masochism" (1924c) there is no decisive theoretical change, but, rather, specifications within the newly forged structural theory: NTR is due as much to the sadism of the superego as to the masochism of the ego. If the former has to do mainly with the (unconscious) feeling of guilt, the latter refers to the moral masochism that is ultimately the ego version of guilt. In his later writings, Freud returned to the theme on various occasions.

In *Civilization and Its Discontents* (1930a), Freud understands civilization from the perspective of *Eros* and *Thanatos*. Aggression, he says at the end of chapter 6, is an original instinctive disposition in the human being and constitutes the major obstacle to the development of civilization. Civilization is a process in the service of Eros, whose tendency is to unite men into families, peoples and nations; but the aggressive instinct proper to human nature is opposed to the civilizing program, setting man against all men and all men against the individual.

In the following chapter Freud explains the method he feels is the most important one to inhibit innate human aggression, and it is to introject it, internalize it, send it back to its point of origin, that is, to the ego. A part of the ego takes charge of it and, converted into the superego, faces the ego and threatens it with the same hostility the ego directed towards others. The tension between the severe superego and the ego it submits to is called sense of guilt, which is externalized as a need for punishment.

Chapter 32 in the *New Introductory Lectures on Psycho-Analysis* (1933a), which deals with anxiety, confirms the 1923 definition and adds that those people in whom the sense of guilt is extremely strong exhibit NTR in analytic treatment at each progressive step in the cure.

When Freud wrote "Analysis Terminable and Interminable" (1937c) at the end of his lengthy investigation, he again indicated the importance of the sense of guilt and the need for punishment among the factors that impede a successful outcome for analysis and can make it interminable. He again mentions masochism, NTR and the sense of guilt, to conclude that it is no longer possible to continue to assert that psychic phenomena are dominated exclusively by the pleasure tendency. In section 6 Freud says: "These phenomena are unmistakable indications of the presence of a power in mental life which we call the instinct of aggression or of destruction according to its aims, and which we trace back to the original death instinct of living matter" (Freud, 1937c, p. 243).

We see, then, that Freud maintained his early ideas throughout his work, but he was increasingly inclined to understand NTR as an expression of the death instinct.

55.5   The two 1936 works

In 1936 Karen Horney's and Joan Riviere's works on NTR appeared, containing significant contributions.

In "The Problem of the Negative Therapeutic Reaction", Horney indicates, in the first place, that NTR must not be confused with any setback in the psychoanalytic cure. I think this is an important specification. If we forget it, the concept is diluted, and the clear Freudian postulation is forgotten. By definition, psychoanalytic treatment advances and recedes; it is always located in the dialectic of progression and regression; it could not be said, then, if we decide that the analytic process requires progression and regression, that every regression is a NTR. We cannot base the concept of NTR on the analysand becoming worse. Karen Horney, following Freud (and taken up by Melanie Klein later on), indicates as a characteristic the *paradoxical* worsening that occurs when there should be progress or even, as she emphasizes, when progress *has occurred*.

Another of Horney's contributions is that she centres her study on the patient's response to interpretation. This has to do with the way I personally characterize NTR: something that depends on achievements. NTR is possible only if the task has been completed, if there is an achievement. It is important to point out that this achievement is generally acknowledged by both sides. But what is decisive is that the *patient* recognizes it as such in some way—explicitly, by saying that the interpretation is correct, or implicitly, because he has a sensation of relief or registers some positive change. It is precisely from that moment of relief and change onwards that the patient's destructive criticism begins, which sometimes leads almost instantaneously to a paradoxical situation: what had relieved him a moment earlier is now rubbish; and this must be stated in not very academic terms because, in fact, as Abraham (1919a) indicated, anal sadism is closely linked to this type of destructive criticism. The instrument that transforms the achievement into disaster is principally, then, anal sadism, although surely no one denies that oral sadism is also in play, as Abraham himself said in other works of that period.

Horney defines, then, two fundamental characteristics: (1) that NTR must be studied with reference to the development of analytic work and in particular to how the patient responds to interpretation, and (2) that the concept should be restricted to unjustified and unexpected worsening.

Perhaps the most precise qualification for this phenomenon is *paradoxical*.

It is surely not always easy to decide whether the patient's response is logical or paradoxical. In clinical practice things are never schematic, but in any case, what is substantially essential to NTR is that it transforms the good into the bad. In the face of a particular deterioration, then, one must distinguish what is logical from what is paradoxical in that regression. It is logical that when the analyst reveals something disagreeable to the analysand, the latter increases his resistance and his hostility. This reaction, however, is not unexpected either for the analyst or for the analysand. In addition, the advance persists, it is not annulled, although the resistance may have increased temporarily. The patient can reject the interpretation or consider it erroneous or aggressive, without it necessarily negating what has been interpreted. In NTR, on the other hand, the interpretation is recognizably efficacious to begin with but then operates in a contrary sense. The difference is evident, which does not mean that it is easy to establish it in the face of the clinical material. Sometimes the two types of reaction correspond, are superimposed. Then the percentage of each must be weighed. If the analysand feels hurt because his homosexuality has been interpreted, or his tendency to theft or his incestuous desires, then his negative reaction is comprehensible, and the analyst's task will not be so difficult. It will consist in some way in giving him time to work through his resistance, as Freud said in 1914. In the other case the interpretative activity has to be more defined and precise, because we face a greater problem. In other words, NTR has to do not with the content of the interpretation but with its effect. This difference is decisive in my opinion.

55.6   *The aggressive drives in the negative therapeutic reaction*

We saw that Freud's thinking gradually approached a more instinctive conception of NTR, without jettisoning his initial structural conception (sense of guilt). Horney takes the same approach when she studies the instinctive roots of NTR.

Horney holds that NTR germinates in a certain type of person, not in everyone, and it is one in whom narcissism and sado-masochistic features predominate, which conditions a distorted reaction to interpretation, leading to competition with the analyst. Such patients have a pronounced rivalry, and it operates in relation to the analyst—a characterological feature studied by Abraham in his 1919a essay, which led him to examine envy and anal sadism.

In addition to their intense rivalry, and depending largely on it, these patients are very sensitive to everything that can damage their self-esteem and increase their sense of guilt. This is why they tend to experience interpretation as something that diminishes or accuses them. In them the general rule, according to which the lack of self-esteem and the sense of guilt potentiate each other, is fulfilled. There is therefore only one step to feeling rejected and misunderstood.

The corollary to this complex characterological structure is that progress and triumph imply too great a risk. The patient fears awakening rivalry in others if he makes progress, and he feels scorned if he fails.

55.7 Negative therapeutic reaction and depressive position

The other great work of 1936, Joan Riviere's "A Contribution to the Analysis of the Negative Therapeutic Reaction", which is firmly based on the theory of the depressive position formulated by Melanie Klein at the Lucerne Congress in 1934, was read by Riviere to the British Society on 1 October 1935. Riviere feels that Klein's theoretical proposals help in understanding these patients and allow more optimism in approaching them, to the extent that it is possible for us to understand what this ominous severity of the superego consists in.

Riviere's proposal is to refer to particularly refractory cases for analysis, which for her are the serious character neuroses, and on this point she relies on the Abraham's (1919a) essay. These are narcissistic patients who are very sensitive and easily hurt, who, beneath a mask of friendly cooperation plagued with rationalizations—*a mask of compliance* (Riviere, 1936a, p. 306)—constantly oppose and challenge the analyst and his method.

Joan Riviere's entire essay deals with narcissistic resistances as defined by Abraham or Freud's concept of the superego's resistance, that is, the sense of guilt, on the basis of the theory of internal objects and of the depressive position. NTR thus loses some of its clinical specificity; but in the long or short run, what Joan Riviere says is applicable to it.

Joan Riviere's starting-point for her investigation is that in those patients who manifest NTR, the depressive position is particularly intense, and this leads them to display maximally the manic defence with its denial of psychic reality (and consequently of external reality), contempt and control of the object. The concept that unites all these instruments of manic defence is omnipotence, with its inevitable corollary, the denial of dependence.

With these conceptual instruments, Riviere can say, with reason, that all the characteristics Abraham described refer to manic defence: the omnipotent control of the analyst and the analysis, the refusal to free-associate, the rejection of interpretations, the attitude of defiant and obstinate challenge, the attempt to supersede the analyst and even to analyse him. The manic defence thoroughly explains the selfishness, the lack of gratitude and the pettiness of these personalities.

Riviere thinks that manic defence and omnipotent control of the object try to avoid the depressive catastrophe and that, beyond their activity of defiance and hostility, these patients seek to cure not themselves but their internal objects, damaged by their egoism, their greed and their envy. In offering to cure them, the analysis becomes a seduction, inviting them to a betrayal, to allowing themselves to be led once more by selfishness and lack of concern for the objects of their internal world. Riviere explains the incongruence of NTR by the paradoxical contradiction between manifest egoism and unconscious altruism (ibid., p. 316).

* * *

To sum up: we can synthesize Joan Riviere's contribution, saying that NTR operates as a form of control to avoid the catastrophe of the depressive position, and we have to understand this control as the basic instrument of manic defence to maintain a particular *status quo*, whose rupture would precipitate the feared eruption of depressive feelings.

55.8   The role of envy

Following the two seminal works of 1936, the theme of NTR was recognized and taken into consideration by analysts. It frequently appears in papers on theory and technique, although studies of great stature did not appear until Klein's *Envy and Gratitude* (1957).

In chapter 2 of her book, Klein says that envy and defences against it play an important role in NTR (1975, Vol. 3, p. 185). Referring strictly to Freud's first definition, as had Karen Horney, Klein clearly indicates that NTR should be studied as a function of the patient's response to interpretation. What is distinctive in NTR is first a moment of relief, then immediately or soon afterwards an attitude that negates the achievement obtained. A patient who kept on praising a mistake I had once made would, whenever I made a good interpretation (which sometimes happened!) and she felt relief, immediately say, "You have finally said something worth while! It is the first time you have opened your mouth to say something important! Because you stay silent all the time and you should have given me this interpretation years ago, I have been waiting for it. And you have only come to this realization now." It was noticeable and even pathetic to see her repeat this over and over again, in a stereotyped way, in nearly identical words and with the same commentary; and it was painful to see how the insight just achieved faded. Also, the repetition of her criticism did not serve as a warning to her in any way, and she always expressed herself as if it were the first time.

For Klein, responses to interpretation such as these, when there has been relief, are typical of NTR. Patients criticize us for various reasons and, it goes without saying, sometimes with reason; but when they feel the need to devalue analytic work that in their own opinion has relieved them, it is because envy is present (ibid., p. 184).

In this way, Klein describes the field of action of envy in NTR precisely, distinguishing the envious attack from the constructive criticism of the analysand. This difference is fundamental and not always easy to establish. In fact, when a person responds to an interpretation, accepting it fully and complaining that the analyst has only just realized this, the latter tends to agree, thinking he really should have realized it earlier, which is always absolutely true. A thorough analyst should always be prepared to accept the criticisms of his patient. Patients rarely criticize us and always find it difficult to do so; so any criticism by the patient should be attended to and, without masochism, encouraged. However, this creates a very special situation, because in fact criticism in NTR is not constructive; by definition, it hides an envious attack. It is not always easy to rescue ourselves from this criticism without suffocating healthy rebelliousness or the just criticism of the patient; but it is not impossible either. This is a delicate theme of analytic ethics and technique, to which Melanie Klein refers in *Envy and Gratitude* (1957).

Klein's investigation on NTR follows, as she herself says, Freud's discoveries as subsequently developed by Joan Riviere; and, although it is true that in concentrating on envy she seems to favour (as did Freud in 1937) a merely instinctive explanation, it is obvious that the object relation occupies a decisive place in her explanation, as it does as a rule in her work. This is important because, in fact, if one takes only envy into consideration, envy as a drive, and tries to interpret baldly in these terms, the NTR deepens instead of receding. Joan Riviere rightly advises that an emphasis on negative transference will certainly lead to a deadlock: "Nothing will lead more surely to a negative therapeutic reaction in the patient than failure to recognize anything but the aggression in his material" (1936a, p. 311). In fact, what must be interpreted is the subtle conjunction of narcissistic object relations, the erosive action of envy and the sense of guilt all this provokes. If one can combine all three factors (and others we study further on) in one interpretation, an avenue can be opened up in this difficult situation, which always moves very slowly.

55.9   Negative therapeutic reaction and lethargy

Contemporaneous with Klein's works on envy are those on the NTR by Fidias R. Cesio in Buenos Aires. In 1956, Cesio presented a case of NTR where the analyst noticed the cold the patient felt during sessions. This was sometimes followed by lethargy and sleepiness, literally paralysing the analyst's therapeutic efforts. The (female) patient died after an attack of eclampsia in which her baby was saved, thus fulfilling her frequently expressed desire to give her life for her child. In the clinical history of this patient her father's suicide when she was five years old had been decisive, and Cesio understood the lethargy as an identification with the corpse her unconscious contained. In that same period Cesio (1957) had studied lethargy in the transference and its projection into the analyst, who is invaded by drowsiness and somnolence.

When he returned to the theme in 1960, Cesio formulated his main thesis, the existence of *lethargic* (literally, "lethargized") *objects* [*objetos aletargados*] in the unconscious of patients who present NTR. He considers this "lethargized" object as equivalent to the psychotic nucleus and also to the prenatal ego of the patient. For him, lethargy is a state of apparent death in a destroyed and poisonous internal world.

The ego in such patients tries to maintain the lethargy of its objects, and it operates in the same way on the analyst. Permanently controlled, as Joan Riviere (1936a) said, the analyst ends up by feeling as if he were lethargic and dead. This also explains that these patients literally cling to the analyst, who now represents for them their primal objects.

In that the lethargic object contains the individual's most destructive impulses and represents his psychotic nucleus, it follows that every time the analysis mobilizes that structure, the destructive components pressure the ego and place it in grave danger (Cesio, 1960, p. 14). Cesio holds, as did Freud in his final years, that the death instinct plays a significant role in these patients: one part of the death instinct is contained in the lethargic object, the other in the ego that "lethargizes" the objects (and the analyst)—a theme he develops more thoroughly in the second part of this work, pointing out the connection between death instinct and anality.

CHAPTER FIFTY-SIX

Negative therapeutic reaction [2]

56.1 Historical perspective

In chapter 55 we began to study the negative therapeutic reaction, following the path from *The Ego and the Id* (Freud, 1923b) to Melanie Klein's contributions. We also included Freud's first references in *From the History of an Infantile Neurosis* (Freud, 1918b [1914]), and we looked at Abraham's essay, which was to become a major influence.

Following the integrating approach of an article by Limentani (1981), it is interesting to note that in this account of the NTR a singular phenomenon is present, which does not always occur in the development of psychoanalytic knowledge: it is that knowledge about it has been increasing without controversy. Freud's first explanation, that the negative therapeutic reaction has to do with a sense of guilt that arises from a very severe superego, has been maintained from 1923 onwards. To this is added what Freud said a year later, already imbued with the idea of the death instinct in respect of primary masochism. The new idea is not opposed to the previous one; instead it complements it, since, in general, when one has an excessively severe superego, one also has a masochistic ego that submits to it and seeks to pacify it. Failure is always rooted in masochism, as Ángel Garma (1962, etc.) has taught us so often.

If we consider the two 1936 articles, we see that they broaden the issue without rejecting what Freud had already noted. Freud himself specifically mentioned rebelliousness, narcissism and secondary gain from illness in 1923. But, consistent with his line of investigation in this context, he asserted that the sense of guilt is the most important factor. Horney again indicated the strong rivalry of these patients and their fear that progress would cause envy in others, and Riviere linked the sense of guilt with unconscious altruism and great lability in the face of the depressive position (described by Klein), which increases the manic defences excessively.

Just as Freud used the NTR to lay the foundation for the idea of the superego and structural theory, Klein later employed it to illustrate the action of envy. This work is also not opposed to earlier ones; it adds to those factors discovered by Freud and then developed by Riviere, and it complements Freud's thinking in 1937 when it links the theory of envy to the death instinct (see Etchegoyen & Rabih, "Las teorías psicoanalíticas de la envidia", 1981).

56.2   Some methodological specifications

Before continuing with studies carried out after Klein, it is worth pausing to remember that we are studying the vicissitudes of the analytic process, after having dealt with the process itself. We said that there are factors that spur the process, such as insight and working-through, and others that impede it; acting out; the negative therapeutic reaction, with which we are at present concerned; and the reversible perspective, which will be our next theme.

From the methodological point of view, it is important to classify these three defensive modalities as *technical* and not psychopathological concepts, because if we do not establish this distinction we can make mistakes or become confused. An excellent work such as Joan Riviere's, for example, makes this mistake on occasion, in that it superimposes the study of the NTR on the severe characteropathies, which are not the same thing. The latter pertain to psychopathology, the former to technique. There is certainly a connection between them, because NTR arises predominantly in patients with severe characterological disturbances; but it can also be found in other nosographic forms. When Hanna Segal (1956) studied depression in the schizophrenic, she showed convincingly that intolerance to depressive pain can set in train a negative therapeutic reaction linked to the patient's experience of progress. The patient regresses (NTR), in such a way that she projects her pain into the analyst and makes her feel very discouraged: "She is mad again", and so forth. This case illustrates that although the negative therapeutic reaction predominates in the serious character neuroses, it is also found in other illnesses.

Acting out, NTR and the reversible perspective configure a class of phenomena that form a complete set of responses, which can be called *strategies of the ego* (Etchegoyen, 1976), in that they are much more complicated than the defensive tactics or techniques; they are operations whose objective is not immediate, but ultimate.

Whereas acting out impedes the development of the task to avoid the painful experience of insight and the reversible perspective challenges the analytic contract, in NTR the task is realized and insight is effected, but then a response that negates these achievements occurs. Further on we compare the NTR with acting out, but let us indicate here that in acting out the analysand withdraws from the object (breast, analyst), seeking something to replace it, and in NTR the presence of the object is recognized in principle. This recognition implies an achievement—something has been received, and then it is attacked. The NTR is constituted at the moment of recognition when the manoeuvre to reverse the situation begins. Therefore the negative therapeutic reaction is linked to a sense of guilt. In acting out, on the other hand, one cannot feel guilt if one claims to have operated on the basis of frustration, of absence of the object. This is why the psychopath who tends to defend himself by acting out does not recognize his guilt.

56.3   Diagnostic elements

In the diagnosis of the NTR the indicators are important, especially because the nature of NTR is such that it can go unnoticed. At times it is necessary to be very attentive in order to detect exactly when the analysand recognizes the help received and begins to undermine it. Melanie Klein emphasizes that criticisms of an interpretation that produced relief should make us assume the presence of the negative therapeutic reaction, even in the case where this criticism contains an element of truth. One does not look a gift horse in the mouth, as the saying goes. If the analyst has managed to relieve the patient's anxiety or to resolve his conflict, then to ask him why he did not do so earlier, why he delayed, or to criticize the way he expressed himself, however justified these reflections may be, is probably an expression of the negative therapeutic reaction, an envious attack, or whatever. This does not mean that a simple interpretation of the patient's envious attack is in order. The great danger in employing the concept of NTR too generously is of reinforcing our omnipotence. In any case, Melanie Klein insists on this phenomenological event, the experience of relief, the feeling that the interpretation has relieved and clarified something. (The same can apply to the patient's opinion about the course of analysis.) What comes later as criticism of the interpretation must be taken as an indication of a negative therapeutic reaction. Although for ethical or strategic reasons we can attend to these objections or criticisms without arguing against them, we should not allow ourselves to be deceived by their apparent rationality.

Another important indicator for me is confusion. Melanie Klein indicates in her 1957 book that envy produces confusion because it does not permit a distinction between the good and bad object—a significant contribution. I refer to confusion as an indicator. Here, once again, one will have to take the precautions already mentioned. If I offer an interpretation that I feel hits home and the patient says he does not understand it, I initially think I have not been clear, because I am not so vain as to think I always express myself well. But in this sense I also try not to be naive, because commonly in these cases an attempt at a clearer interpretation is not accepted by the patient for other reasons.

Another factor is conviction. I do not say that if a patient has no conviction about what has been interpreted he is expressing his negative therapeutic reaction, because this would again place me at the epicentre of omnipotence. What I am saying is that often this type of patient acknowledges that the interpretation is true but remains somewhat unconvinced. When the patient says he is not convinced by the interpretation, this already implies some conflict, because what the analyst says is not to convince him but to inform him. If the patient says the interpretation does not convince him, that is something to attract our attention, because he could say he disagrees, that the interpretation seems mistaken or the logic is faulty. The idea that the analyst wishes to convince him usually implies a strong conflict: the patient is attributing to the analyst an intention that is inadvisable for our technique.

56.4   Function of the internal objects

I think that currently we understand better not only the struggle between the life and death tendencies in NTR, but also the function of the objects of the self.

In this sense Herbert Rosenfeld's (1971, 1975a, 1975b, 1987) investigation is most valuable. Its starting-point is a dissociation of the self into omnipotent-narcissistic and dependent-infantile. On the basis of this scheme, similar to Fairbairn's (1944) of the libidinal ego and the internal saboteur (anti-libidinal ego), and which also pertains to Meltzer's (1968) ideas on the tyrant, a drama arises between the infantile self and the narcissistic self.

At the Helsinki Congress, Gaddini (1981), in studying acting out, proposed a similar division of the psychic apparatus between the omnipotent self and the ego. If suddenly progress becomes visible, "the ego tends to show its powerful inner enemies that what has emerged is not true, that nothing has happened", with which a typical NTR has been set in motion (1981, p. 60).

For Herbert Rosenfeld, the capacity for love is located in the *infantile self*, as is dependence, because when we recognize the existence of a love object we are immediately in a situation of dependence in relation to it, whatever the relationship may be between that object and ourselves. In the other part, the *narcissistic self*, are located envy and destructiveness.

This dual structure of the individual crystallizes in the analytic process in a permanent struggle between the analyst's repeated attempts to make contact with the infantile part which is capable of dependence (and therefore of cooperation) and the specific attacks that the narcissistic self directs towards the analyst and the infantile self.

In his presentation at the Vienna Congress of 1971, Rosenfeld follows the line which, from Abraham (1919a) and Reich (1933) onwards, connects narcissism, aggression and resistance, as well as Klein's (1946) ideas on the original dissociation of the object and the self, and the role of primary envy. The latter, as we know, begins for Klein from the earliest phase of life and the relationship of the baby with the mother's breast. This envy of the good, giving object appears in the transference through the most disparate manifestations and very typically—we have already seen—in NTR. Beyond other, more subtle motives that are complex and indirect, it is evident that the theory of primary envy offers a consistent explanation of the paradoxical response of a person who acknowledges he has benefited yet responds negatively.

For Rosenfeld, the narcissistic self appears highly organized as a delinquent and powerful gang who, with threats and propaganda, keeps the infantile self enslaved. Each time the latter wishes to express himself or tries to liberate himself, the gang that dominates and squashes him appears again. This is how the dramatics of NTR take shape, and how the relationship of dependence and love of the infantile self with the analyst is checked. In this way, as Meltzer says in the first pages of *The Psychoanalytical Process* (1967), the cure really consists in a difficult and risky salvage operation. This is why Rosenfeld says that "it is essential to help the patient to find and rescue the dependent sane part of the self from its trapped position inside the psychotic narcissistic structure as it is this part which is the essential link with the positive object relationship to the analyst and the world" (1971, p. 175).

In this way, Rosenfeld's personalistic explanation not only integrates validly the diverse investigations on NTR, but it also allows us greater equanimity in interpreting: we can see not only envy, masochism and narcissism, but also love, jealousy and guilt, until unconscious altruism is reached and finally that love and guilt "so deeply buried" that Joan Riviere searched for with so much passion and patience. One of the artifices employed by the narcissistic self to make an ally of the infantile self is precisely to make it feel jealous, because by definition jealousy is an attribute of the infantile self; envy, on the other hand, belongs above all to the narcissistic self. When the narcissistic self and the infantile self are joined in a perverse couple that excludes the analyst, the latter meets with serious obstacles in his work.

56.5 Manic defences and manic attacks

When Herbert Rosenfeld (1975a) takes up Riviere's investigation, he establishes an important specification as to the value of the manic defences of NTR. Riviere conceives mania only as a method of defence, mobilized energetically by the patient to avoid depressive catastrophe, guilt and isolation. But it is also a means of attacking the object; this is why Rosenfeld speaks of manic *defences* and *attacks*, as do Betty Joseph (1971, 1975) and other post-Kleinian writers. In this sense, the sense of guilt is explained not only by the subsequent attacks on the oedipal and pre-oedipal objects of early childhood, but also by those that take place in the present against the analyst as represented in the transference, and even against the real analyst who is helping the subject. Let us say, also, that this sense of guilt is based substantially on the infantile libidinous self and comes from two sources: from the predominantly envious attack of the destructive, omnipotent and narcissistic self, and also from the infantile self in that, through fear or jealousy, it allows itself to be seduced by the former and supports it. In other words, the sense of guilt and the need for punishment are better understood from the perspective of this dual structure of the self.

It is neither envy (or aggression in general), nor the sense of guilt, alternatively or exclusively, that explains the NTR, but the joint action of both, in that the sense of guilt arises from the attacks on the object through envy, jealousy, rivalry or whatever. Jealousy, envy and rivalry germinate, for their part, in the narcissistic structure and the lack of self-esteem, which potentiate each other.

* * *

To sum up: narcissism, envy and the sense of guilt form a union in which each factor arises as a function of the others. Joan Riviere rightly stresses the patient's fear of becoming dependent; but she does not realize that the guilt is linked precisely to rejection of dependence with a permanent envious attack on the object. This is surprising if one takes account of the fact that four years earlier, in "Jealousy as a Mechanism of Defence" (1932), Riviere had unmasked with admirable precision the envy that can lie behind jealousy.

56.6   Narcissistic self and superego

Rosenfeld revises Freud's explanations of 1923 and 1924, trying to unlink from the superego the attacks of the narcissistic self against the infantile self and the object, which seems somewhat artificial to me and, of course, open to argument. In fact, it is difficult to define the attack on the good interpretation because of injury to the ego's narcissism or because the superego tells the ego it does not deserve it, that it should not receive the good given to it. This is related to Freud's alternative of the masochistic ego and the sadistic superego, and with what Bion calls, in the final chapters of *Learning from Experience* (1962b), the *"super"-ego* or *super-super-ego*, an instance that does not wish to know the truth and denies knowledge and science on the basis of a morality based on nothing. Bion's supersuperego is very close, in my opinion, to the narcissistic self: when the narcissistic self fallaciously assumes a moral character to attack the ego, we have that condition. In other words, when we say the narcissistic self attacks the infantile self, we have the impression of being far from super-ego functioning, from a moral instance. But this attack is almost always clothed in an ethical moral character (delusional ethics), with which we are already within the range of superego function. Divergence, then, depends on our emphasis on one factor or another.

56.7   Criticism, idealization and countertransference

We have already said that an adequate analysis of the patient's criticisms opens up an approach to latent envy. Let us say here that this approach is difficult, because it presents us with two dangers instead of one: ignoring what may be true in those criticisms and, inversely, in order to accept and tolerate them, placating the patient. Both errors have the same conse-quence, the establishment of an idealized link, where the negative transfer-ence is once again dissociated. The situation is not always resolved through acknowledgement of the "objective" part of the patient's criti-cism—and I use quotes to recall that our task is not to establish the objec-tivity of the facts but to try to discover the analysand's fantasies, so that he can decide on the facts himself.

It is always necessary to take into account very carefully how the theory of envy can be used by the analyst to foment idealization in the analysand and deny the analyst's own limitations and faults. A good tech-nique should recognize the patient's reasons, not only due to the unavoid-able requirements of ethics, but precisely so that envy can appear as it should appear, that is, in the face of the analyst's *accuracy*. If the analyst does not recognize his faults, he may interpret as envy what is really his own error. It is worth pointing out here as a self-evident truth that if the analyst does not work with sufficient accuracy envy does not appear and has no reason to appear!

For all these reasons, it is understood that the analysis of envy is never easy and that of the NTR even less so, where a great number of factors that influence and potentiate each other are involved. At the same time, I am certain envy is a necessary factor for NTR and can therefore never be set aside entirely in our interpretative strategy. An absorbing polemic opens up here, which has to do not only with technique but also with the theories of early development, which we discuss with reference to the works of Limentani and Ursula Grunert.

56.8   The dangers of being healthy

The line of thought we have been following starts with the principle that progress, health and relief are a benefit that the analysand rejects. It is appropriate to ask, however, whether these benefits might be bad for the one who receives them. Limentani (1981), among others, poses this question. He had already indicated the good side of acting out. Limentani's work is guided by a beautiful phrase from T. S. Eliot in *The Family Reunion*: "Restoration of health is only the incubation of another malady." And do not we sceptical Argentinians say that sometimes the remedy is worse than the malady?

Limentani, then, proposes to investigate those aspects of NTR that serve to reveal the deep fears that health can arouse in certain patients. NTR undoubtedly indicates that something is going badly in the analytic situation, but it is also undeniable that this is a complex syndrome, among whose multiple causes are the sense of guilt, the need for punishment, narcissism, depression, rivalry and envy, the death instinct, the regressive tendency towards symbiotic fusion with an absorbing mother, and so forth.

Limentani presents two clinical cases, which register the entire above-mentioned list although he thinks that, finally, the dominant fantasy in the transference was the fusion with the mother, with a feeling of being abruptly separated from the analyst (1981, p. 387).

Based on his clinical experience, Limentani holds that the patient defends himself with the NTR from a danger or a threat and that if he attacks us, it is because this attack is his best defence. Agreeing entirely with Pontalis (1979), Limentani thinks that the NTR is a special form of acting out by means of which a very early traumatic experience such as separation from the mother or weaning is repeated. In conclusion, Limentani maintains that "in the more chronic forms the [negative therapeutic] reaction is a special kind of acting out of the transference in the psychoanalytic situation, when it is also a particular stubborn defence against the re-experience of pain and psychic suffering associated with early trauma" (1981, p. 389).

56.9 Symbiosis and negative therapeutic reaction

Ursula Grunert, Jean and Florence Bégoin and Janice de Saussure contributed to a discussion on "New Perspectives on the Negative Therapeutic Reaction" at the Third Conference of the European Federation in 1979.

Ursula Grunert (1981) begins from Margaret Mahler's theory of development in terms of separation–individuation. If the diverse subphases of the process of separation during the early years of infancy have been safeguarded, there will be no real NTR during analysis. But if the process of separation was not fulfilled until a certain degree of object constancy had been reached, then this feared obstacle can arise.

For Grunert, the NTR "represents the gesture of distancing, of the 'no' which corresponds to the various phases of the process of separation as activated in the transference. It can either give expression to the wish for autonomy and separation or hide the wish for merging" (1981, p. 5). We should see NTR as the pathological separation of the dyadic relation, which finds in the transference the most appropriate place for the production of its new edition, and it can be resolved only there.

I do not find Ursula Grunert's clinical example with her patient A very convincing; I agree with the patient that the analyst does not do what is most adequate. The analyst cites an interpretation in which, gathering up the patient's associations, she tells her: "You feel as though you are betraying your mother if you want to make yourself independent" (ibid., p. 6). In the following session the patient brings a dream: "*I want to go away and am packing. My mother is baking a cake but it is unpalatable. I get furious and do it myself.*" Through her associations the patient is aware of how much her mother had kept her dependent through spoiling her. As the dream shows, the mother wishes to hold on to her with the indigestible cake and only by becoming furious can the patient take the road to independence. In the ensuing session (the one where the NTR is present), the analysand arrives very depressed, saying that no one can help her, least of all the analyst, since with her she had exchanged an old dependence for a new one.

I do not really think that a disturbed symbiosis that marks a child deeply can be resolved with interpretations that make the mother responsible and leave the transference situation to one side, exchanging one form of dependence for another, as the analysand says. I also think that the dream refers to the transference and that the analysand criticizes (as I do) Dr Grunert's extratransference interpretations (the unpalatable cake).

In any case, as she says, the analysand was able to accept that the analyst herself could be an object she could become dependent on; with this an intense and prolonged negative transference unfolded, which was worked through adequately, thanks to the latent positive transference.

Grunert concludes that the multiple experiences of separation that accompany analysis allow the reactivation of the disturbed process of separation in infancy and set in motion the process of working through. In this way, the NTR should be considered not only as an obstacle but also as an opportunity to experience emotionally the faults of development in the transference and arrive at their solution through the elucidation of the well-disposed analyst (ibid., p. 19).

The ideas of Limentani, Gaddini and Ursula Grunert are based on Winnicott's and Margaret Mahler's theories of development, in which the rupture of the primitive mother–child relation is considered a decisive moment in development. It is worth emphasizing (because it is a historical fact) that José Bleger had simultaneously arrived at similar conclusions when he published "Symbiosis" in 1961 (in Bleger, 1967b). In this work Bleger characterizes symbiosis as the link with what he calls the *agglutinated object* at a point of development prior to Klein's paranoid–schizoid position, which he calls *the glischrocaric stage*. This very primitive link can be the origin, among other phenomena, of the negative therapeutic reaction, which would then be a (desperate) attempt to re-establish the indiscriminate state between I and not-I.

Cesio's studies in the 1950s also point in the same direction, in that they understand the negative therapeutic reaction as a way of avoiding catastrophic anxiety and psychosis linked to fetal psychism.

56.10   Negative therapeutic reaction and negative transference

At times the tendency is to superimpose the negative transference and the negative therapeutic reaction, which is a mistake that can serve, in fact, to locate them in a different class of phenomena. Negative transference has to do with the ego's defensive tactics or techniques; the NTR, with ego strategies. The negative transference *per se* is not concerned with the negative therapeutic reaction; it can even be, and often is, a form of cooperation with the analysis. The question arises if and only if the analysand feels relief with an interpretation of the negative transference and then attacks it: "Your interpretation is correct and now I don't feel anxiety; but I ask myself why you always interpret my negative feelings. I feel humiliated. It seems you can never see anything good in me." As is obvious, this reaction can also arise when the positive transference is interpreted. An analysand always protested haughtily because I interpreted only the negative transference, which he explained as being due to my being a low Kleinian (he used other words); but once I interpreted—I think correctly—his good feelings towards me, and to this his rejoinder was, "Hey! You are treating me like a . . . homosexual!" (He did not in fact use this precise word.)

There is no doubt that behind the negative therapeutic reaction there is always a negative transference; it is also true that there is always much more than this. It is not simply envy or the death instinct that are at play, but also the sense of guilt and the need for punishment, the need to control the object and to repair it, the need to maintain union against all odds, the need to liberate oneself in order to be independent and a thousand other things we have to interpret. The negative therapeutic reaction is not fed exclusively by negative feelings. I would say that if the only thing I feel is envy, I am not going to have a negative therapeutic reaction but a negative transference. There must also be a capacity for dependence, libido, guilt feelings, altruism and other elements for the negative therapeutic reaction to be constituted. Joan Riviere rightly said that if only negative feelings are interpreted to these patients, this type of reaction is encouraged rather than diminished. This is logical, because this attitude tends to reproduce in the analytic process the dangerous internal configuration of a sadistic superego (the analyst) and a masochistic ego-patient.

The negative transference is not bad in itself when it appears in the analysis. As a part of the conflict, it must be expressed, to enable the analyst to interpret it as he does all the other desires and feelings that appear in the session. If I attack my analyst and simultaneously I have the idea that I am giving him material, in fact what I expect is for him to understand the motives for my aggression and to interpret them. As I said in speaking of the classification of the transference, the adjectives "posi-tive" and "negative" are applied to separate emotions and pulsions not with a normative and even less an ideological criterion!

Nor should the "negative" therapeutic reaction denote an axiological position, however much the analyst's always disturbing countertransfer-ence indicates the analysand's reaction as being bad. The analysand reacts however he can, and we have to interpret what happened with all possible equanimity. I think that the zeal of those who point out that the negative therapeutic reaction is not so *negative* tends to avoid this equivocation, indicating the error of qualifying ideologically what is happening. The term certainly describes a response by the analysand, but it does not clas-sify it as good or bad.

56.11   Negativism and the negative therapeutic reaction

From a similar point of view, Olinick (1964) understands NTR as a special case of negativism, which expresses the analysand's rebellious *no* at times through action or acting out. This negativism should be explained on the basis of Freud's work on negation (1925h) and also of Spitz's (1957) *seman-tic no*. As we know, the "no" that appears at around 15 months of age is, for Spitz, one of the indicators of development, together with the smile in the third month and anxiety in the eighth month. The semantic no of the child is an identification with the object that frustrates him and, at the same time, the first symbolic communication.

Anna Freud (1952) demonstrated convincingly that negativism can be an extreme defence when the subject feels he runs the risk of becoming emotionally dominated or enslaved. (Anna Freud's original term was *Hörigkeit*, which was translated into English as "emotional surrender".)

Olinick holds that patients who tend to react with NTR are those who link their strong negativism to a structure where masochism and depres-sion come together. Depression and rage are generally projected into others, who then react with depression. The countertransference reaction to these patients is therefore boredom and somnolence.

I agree with Olinick's observations; however, I think they are specific not to the NTR but, rather, to the serious character neurosis described by Abraham (1919a), which was also the basis for Joan Riviere's (1936a) point of view. This clinical picture can, in fact, lead to a sado-masochistic trans-ference–countertransference link, which corresponds to Kernberg's (1965) "chronic countertransference fixation".

56.12   *Negative therapeutic reaction and acting out*

Throughout this chapter and chapter 55 I have maintained that NTR is a very useful tool for psychoanalytic practice, since it brings out a particular attitude of the analysand and marks out the path for our effort. I also said that the concept of NTR, as opposed to that of acting out, was clearly defined by Freud from the beginning, and investigations referring to his work are profitable.

Some recent works, however, tend to superimpose NTR on acting out. As we have seen, Limentani (1981) says that the most chronic forms of NTR are a special type of acting out in the transference. Pontalis (1979) is even more categorical in his attempts to dismantle the NTR.

Pontalis emphasizes the word *reaction* and indicates that, by definition, this term responds to a previous action. This leads Pontalis (1979) to the area of action, to *agieren*, where the action of a negative mother can only condition a similar response in the child. Hence the title of his work: "*Non, deux fois non. Tentative de définition et de demantèlement de la 'réaction thérapeutique négative'*" [No, Twice No. An Attempt at the Definition and Dismantlement of the "Negative Therapeutic Reaction"]. At the end of his work, Pontalis says that there are mothers—and analysts—of whom one needs to believe, and they also need to believe, that they are irresistible. Therefore it follows that there will be resistance, with all of one's strength, to an analysis that, from the moment one is committed to it, gives only the illusion of re-encountering the object, of its non-temporal possession, but institutes separation (1979).

In locating the analytic situation along the coordinates of action and reaction, Pontalis slides from NTR to acting out; this is why he considers the analytic situation as tense, and there is no way the analyst can get bored with these patients, although he may suffer. Pontalis is describing, in effect, the typical analytic situation of acting out. I then ask myself whether his characterization of NTR as a form of *agieren* does not lead to the proposal to run the two concepts together, in full agreement with the last section of his work, where he says that to dismantle NTR it is better to fail in defining it.

Perhaps this is the time to clarify that in delineating the concepts of acting out and NTR I do not wish to suggest that they always appear clearly outlined in clinical practice. At times both phenomena appear simultaneously in a patient; at other times—I think more commonly—it can be observed that acting out is in the service of NTR. Sometimes the patient "erases with his elbow what he writes with his hand", as the saying goes: he *acts* in order to negate the progress recently achieved. Thus I think two illustrative cases Limentani presents in his work are clear examples of acting out in the transference being used instrumentally to establish or maintain the NTR.

However, I think that generally patients who adopt one do not often avail themselves of the other. The patient who develops a negative therapeutic reaction will always continue along that line, from first to last in his analysis, and the same goes for acting out. The patient who employs acting out to control his anxiety in the face of the unknown at the beginning of analysis will use it five or ten years later to avoid anxiety arising from the ending of analysis. What changes is the degree and the plasticity. Generally I think that ego strategies, as characterological structures, maintain their stability, although analysis makes them more fluid and versatile. If I undergo analysis because of my obsessive neurosis, analysis is not going to transform me into a type of action, but it will facilitate my incorporating some new repertoires and my response through acts, if circumstances dictate this, leaving reasoning aside.

In common with most analysts, I think that the analysand who acts charges the countertransference more than the patient with a negative therapeutic reaction. The countertransference response to the patient who acts out is vivid and painful. On the other hand, as Cesio indicates, when the NTR dominates the picture, the analyst tends to decrease his concentration on the patient and to react with tiredness, boredom and lethargy. Despite what Pontalis says, these are not the patients who have us on edge.

It should not be thought that the strongest countertransference reactions are the most disturbing because, in fact, the analyst has a countertransference conflict if he becomes angry or frightened as much as if he is bored. The countertransference conflict is measured more by its intensity than by its characteristics.

The same goes for the analysand. The prognosis depends on the intensity of the conflicts and on how the analysand responds to interpretation. Many assert that the NTR is more serious than acting out, but this is because they redefine it as something insuperable. I do not think it is; NTR can be severe or mild, easy to modify or irreversible, just as acting out can. One might think here, as does Freud, that God favours the strongest battalions.

56.13   *Paradoxical thinking*

When Laplanche and Pontalis (1968) define NTR in *The Language of Psycho-Analysis*, they indicate its paradoxical nature. This idea is also found elsewhere, and when I spoke of impasse and NTR in 1976, I indicated that these patients function subtly in the area of logical paradoxes. These same thoughts inspire Didier Anzieu in his work, "The Paradoxical Transference" (1975). Anzieu starts out from the studies of the Palo Alto school on paradoxical communication and invalidating transactions. When this distorted type of communication between parents and children is reproduced in the analysis, a paradoxical transference is configured, which may also entrap the analyst in a paradoxical countertransference, leading the analysis along the ominous path of the NTR. As the communication specialists of the Palo Alto school say, one can only get out of a paradoxical communication by "metacommunicating" the situation itself, so that the principal interpretative task in these cases turns on how messages become distorted in the analytic situation.

In his attempt to understand paradoxical thinking in terms of psychoanalytic theories and not only communicational ones, Anzieu maintains that the factors most in play are narcissism and the death instinct, which he also links to the studies of the Kleinian school on envy.

On this point it is appropriate to point out a phenomenon that is identical to NTR, although it bears a contrary sign. I refer to the backing this type of analysand can give to the analyst's errors. This curious phenomenon, which is frequent but is rarely studied, can be called *iatrogenic positive reaction*. In these cases the analyst's error promotes the agreement, if not the applause and even the improvement, of the analysand. Liberman also deals with this phenomenon, indicating that the patient can decode the interpretations in terms of negative or positive feedback: a patient cooperates when he gives the analyst a feedback that allows him to reinforce his accurate hits and correct his errors (negative feedback). On the other hand, in the negative therapeutic reaction the opposite occurs: the patient gives negative feedback to what is accurate and positive feedback to what is mistaken. I have already mentioned the patient who always congratulated me for something I had said at the beginning of her treatment, and which was a clear mistake on my part. This type of response must be taken into account, because it can be very dangerous: "I like the fact that you keep me waiting because you seem more human to me." In this way negative feedback is given to the error, and it increases each time. If I think the patient is satisfied with my tardiness, I will tend to be even more late.

56.14   *Final comment*

If we are faithful to the definition of 1923, the negative therapeutic reaction appears to us as one of the hazards of analytic work, characterized by a paradoxical response in which the analysand becomes worse when he should be improving (and after having improved).

Initially, Freud attributed NTR to a sense of guilt (severe, sadistic superego), then to moral masochism (masochistic ego) and finally to the death instinct, without these explanations being mutually exclusive—nor are those given subsequently by Karen Horney (rivalry, fear of envy), Joan Riviere (fear of depressive catastrophe, unconscious altruism) and Melanie Klein (envy). The latest explanations proposed tend to be based on conflicts of integration (Gaddini, Limentani) and the mother–child symbiosis (Ursula Grunert).

Although some of these points of view can be irreconcilable at the level of the theories that support them, I think all the factors appear in clinical practice, and all should be interpreted at the appropriate moment. With only one or two of these we are not going to respond to the splendid complexity of analytic practice. What separates us here into schools is that, when the moment arrives to convert our clinical experience into concepts, we say that "ultimately the decisive factor is . . ."; but, in fact, when faced by NTR, we have to interpret it in many ways and from different points of view.

Finally, everything seems to indicate that early conflicts play an important role in the negative therapeutic reaction (the same goes for acting out and reversible perspective), but it would be a mistake to confront it with a preconceived scheme of development in the hope of finding confirmation through the clinical material. As analysts the only thing we can do is to gather up that clinical material just as it appears in the transference, and to be prepared with equal modesty for it to support or to refute our ideas.

CHAPTER FIFTY-SEVEN

Reversible perspective
[1]

57.1 Brief recapitulation

In studying the vicissitudes of the analytic process, we have separated the factors that influence it into good and bad ones, according to a somewhat Manichaean criterion. This separation can be useful to us, however, provided that we take it as an orientation that does not absolve us from recognizing the formidable complexity of clinical events. We have thus placed insight and working-through into a column of worthy and unique phenomena; into the other column we placed the negative therapeutic reaction, acting out, and the one we are about to consider: reversible perspective. These three phenomena go together because they belong to the same class; they all try to impede the development of insight, or they try to avoid the mental pain that insight invariably provokes, which is the same thing. As we have seen, insight is always accompanied by pain.

The study of acting out, the negative therapeutic reaction and reversible perspective allows us to understand and roughly locate the behaviour of patients during the analytic process. There are those who develop their analysis (and their life) using acting out as a principal instrument of adaptation or, better still, maladaptation; others employ the negative therapeutic reaction; still others use reversible perspective. I think this grouping is valid and useful if we know how to recognize its limitations; and I also think these clinical pictures are interrelated, in the sense that acting out can be used as a way of establishing the negative therapeutic reaction, and the latter can lead, in turn, to reversible perspective. This path, it appears, can only be crossed in this direction and not vice-versa; it is a path upwards. When Abraham (1919a) says that his narcissistic patients have great difficulty in recognizing the analyst's role and continually discuss his interpretations, and so forth, we are in an imprecise range, and we do not really know whether Abraham's genius is detecting what will later be called negative therapeutic reaction or reversible perspective.

57.2   First approximations

Reversible perspective will give us the opportunity of studying a singular aspect of the analytic process and will also be a reason for approaching Bion's original ideas. By *reversible perspective* we mean processes of thought linked to a drastic attempt to destabilize the analytic situation and turn it on its head.

Bion introduces this concept in *Elements of Psycho-Analysis* (1963) when he studies the psychotic part of the personality, not the analytic process. In considering reversible perspective from a technical point of view I present it, in fact, in a context other than that initially proposed by Bion, but I do not violate his thought in any way, in that he thought these ideas have to do with the practice in the consulting-room.

Bion discovers, then, reversible perspective in studying the psychotic part of the personality, alongside attacks on linking, transformations in hallucinosis and other phenomena. (For a more detailed study see "Psychosis", in Grinberg, Sor & Bianchedi, 1972, chapter 2; Sor & Gazzano, *Cambio catastrófico*, 1989.)

Bion describes *attacks on linking* in a work with the same title (1959), and in "On Arrogance" (1958). The psychotic part of the personality makes destructive attacks upon everything it feels has the function of joining one object with another, and which in principle are the emotions. Bion holds that the prototypes of any link are the breast and the penis, which suffer the violent sadism of the child in the first months of life, as Melanie Klein postulated from her first works onwards.

When a triad formed by arrogance, stupidity and curiosity is found in clinical practice, this is because the attack on the link has operated devastatingly; it is, therefore, an indication of a psychotic catastrophe in which primal objects were severely damaged. Bion's triad is difficult to manage clinically, because on one side lies peremptory and intrusive curiosity, and on the other an insulting arrogance that renourishes itself in the stupidity projected into the object. This leads the patient into a continued and despised devaluation of others, and among them, of course, the analyst and his interpretations. All this implies a surcharge in the countertransference, which is difficult to bear.

Transformations in hallucinosis are always linked to an original disaster where the emotional contents of the baby did not find the maternal reverie sufficient to be converted into alpha elements. Hallucination is always, in the final instance, the expulsion of beta elements from the psychic apparatus. Transformations in hallucinosis arise basically from intolerance of the absent object or from frustration and pain, which are the same thing. (In this I follow "Transformation in Hallucinosis", in Grinberg et al., 1972, chapter 5, and, of course, Bion, *Transformations*, 1965.) It must be borne in mind that, for Bion, hallucination is not only a clinical symptom of psychosis but a particularity of its functioning, which consists in evacuating split-off parts of the personality and reversing the function of the sensory organs, which, having been receptors, become effectors.

The other function of the psychotic part, the reversible perspective, is precisely the opposite of the changing perspective of insight. In this type of mental functioning, the desire to know (K link) becomes a desire to ignore (minus-K link). In the same way, the alternating and complementary functioning between the paranoid–schizoid and the depressive positions (Ps ↔ D) and the container–contained relation ($\venus\mars$), which in Bion's view are the pillars on which the apparatus for thinking thoughts is constructed, present a negative sign.

57.3 The psychotic part of the personality

As we have just seen, Bion discovers and studies reversible perspective from the dual angle of his theory of thought and his concept of the *psychotic part of the personality* (PPP), not from the point of view of the technique, as we are going to do.

For Bion, as for Bleger (1967b), although with other theoretical suppositions, PPP is fundamentally a mode of mental functioning that is counterposed to another, the so-called neurotic part of the personality. To speak of psychotic personality (or psychotic part of the personality) does not imply a psychiatric diagnosis, which depends on which part, the psychotic or the neurotic one, predominates or leads the personality. On the mixture of the two, on their algebraic sum and also on their interaction depends the functioning of the individual. Consequently, the idea of the psychotic part does not in any way imply a psychiatric diagnosis.

There are several elements that serve to define the psychotic personality, and one of those that best characterize it is the hatred of internal and external reality and, consequently, of all instruments that enable the individual to contact it. This is because a hatred of reality leads necessarily to an attack on the mental apparatus as the instrument with which to grasp it. Searles (1963) says, however, and with good reason, that the psychotic's hatred of reality may also express a very justified hatred of his first object relations, which were very negative (a psychotic mother, for example).

Another way of defining PPP that is different only in appearance is to say that the psychotic part has a great intolerance of frustration. If intolerance of frustration is high, it is immediately understood that the above-mentioned hatred of reality exists, because reality, which is frustration for everyone, is even more so for this type of person; the PPP always measures reality by what it does not offer, by the limits it imposes.

To define the psychotic personality as one with a hatred of reality or an intolerance of frustration can imply two different approaches, however, because the former attempts to impose a qualitative difference that is not there in the latter. When I say that the psychotic part of the personality is characterized by a hatred of reality, I assume this does not happen with the neurotic personality. The second way of conceptualizing the difference is purely quantitative, because we say that the psychotic personality is the one with a *great* intolerance of frustration—that the *degree* of intolerance is greater. The difference in degree should not lead us to ignore that there is a basic difference: it is probable that a characteristic of PPP is precisely to conceptualize reality as frustration, since reality is not *only* frustration. Sometimes this error infiltrates our scientific theories.

Another way of defining the psychotic personality is in terms of instincts. The death instinct predominates in the psychotic personality, a formula that would be acceptable to Melanie Klein and perhaps to Freud at the time when he wrote "Analysis Terminable and Interminable". We could also say that the psychotic personality basically employs envy to develop its object relations, in opposition to the neurotic part, which uses libido. Here it is advisable to re-establish that the difference is quantitative because, if we take literally what I have just said, the difference would be radical and unsalvageable. It is better to say, then, that there is a predominance of life or death instinct, of libido or envy, of love or hate. In the PPP the destructive instincts dominate clearly, to the point where love is transformed into sadism. This idea of Bion's reminds us of Fairbairn (1941) when he says that the problem of the schizoid personality is how to love without destroying with his love (whereas that of the depressive is how to love without destroying with his hate). Hate of internal and external reality is in my opinion related to Garma's (1931, 1962) enduring ideas; he maintains that the psychotic withdraws from external reality, not to satisfy his instinctive libidinal desires, but, on the contrary, to reject them.

An outstanding feature of PPP on which Bion insists is that projective identification is pathological and very destructive: this is how thought is attacked and bizarre objects are formed.

The features indicated explain amply another characteristic of PPP, the fear of imminent annihilation, which leaves its mark on the nature of the object link.

57.4   *Relations between the neurotic and psychotic part*

Bion's observations in respect of the type of object relation structured by the PPP form a brilliant page in the history of psychoanalysis. We have already referred to this theme with regard to transference, and the reader will undoubtedly remember the "Development of Schizophrenic Thought", in which Bion (1956) describes the fundamental features of the schizophrenic personality, and which is a forerunner of "Differentiation of the Psychotic from the Non-psychotic Personalities" (1957). The object relations of the psychotic part are at the same time premature and precipitate, fragile and tenacious.

Bion's investigation has been able to clarify, then, two forms of mental functioning that reveal the enormous complexity of the psychic structure and that extend as a continuum from the neurotic to the psychotic pole. Bion's work is the culmination of a sustained effort by Freud to integrate and delineate psychosis and neurosis, which then reappears in Klein's theory of the positions without the excesses of German psychiatry at the beginning of the century. In his attempt to draw a radical distinction between neurosis and psychosis, Jaspers (1913), for example, creates an abyss between them with his concepts of *process* and *development* in terms of empathy. (*Development* can be understood empathetically and consists in a response to a conflict; *process* is neither situational nor understandable, so we cannot reach it with the phenomenological instrument of empathy.) In this way, Bion's ideas represent a substantial contribution in the development of psychoanalytic thought.

Bion affirms that the gap between the neurotic and the psychotic personality is not great initially; but as the individual develops, and as a result of various circumstances (that are due to that individual and to his milieu), this gap can widen.

We have just said that, in studying the functioning of the personality, Bion emphasizes the relationship between *container* and *contained*. To define them he utilizes two symbols that not only allude to functions but also, in some way, represent them concretely. For Bion there is a *positive form* of the container–contained relation and a *negative form* of the same: $+\female\male$ and $-\female\male$.

The $\female\male$ relationship is necessary for mental growth. The contained has to find something that receives and is able to modify it; the container needs something to fill it. The child projects his fears into the mother, and the mother tolerates them within herself and assimilates them; and she gives back to the child less anxious, less painful, more tolerable contents (the contained) through her voice, her milk, her warmth.

In the psychotic part of the personality the container–contained relation does not occur in positive terms but in terms of stripping and denudation. What the individual feels in these conditions is that the contained enters the container in order to destroy it; conversely, the container receives the contained to take things from it, to strip it.

These concepts have considerable clinical reality. The analysand can feel that the interpretation is a destructive content that erupts in his mind to damage and disintegrate him; and vice versa, he can receive the interpretation to strip it of its significance, transforming it into something bad.

Another important aspect of the psychotic personality has to do with the structure of the superego. In the psychotic personality there is a *super-*

ego that raises the moral flag simply to externalize its envy, destructiveness and malice. For this super-superego the moral norm is no more than an affirmation of superiority born of omnipotence and, without any rational base, is opposed to science.

There is a relationship between Bion's ideas here and those Herbert Rosenfeld proposed in 1971, at the Vienna Congress, when he characterized an infantile and a narcissistic self. The narcissistic self, impelled by voracity and envy, is very similar to the PPP; the infantile self, which is capable of love and dependence, corresponds to the neurotic part. The difference between Bion and Rosenfeld lies more in the method than in the content. Rosenfeld's concepts emphasize the object relation more, and Bion emphasizes mental functioning. This conception is process-oriented; the former is personalistic, in Guntrip's (1961) sense.

57.5   *Thought and reversible perspective*

We have said that reversible perspective is one of the PPP's modes of functioning. I will now attempt to indicate its principal features. Let us begin by saying that reversible perspective is a special form of thought that tries to avoid mental pain at any cost. Thought is painful from its earliest origins because, as we have seen, the first thought arises when the pain of absence is accepted, when it is recognized that the breast is not there, instead of expelling it as a bad-breast-present-need-for-a-breast, that is, as a beta element.

To negate psychic pain, reversible perspective relies on a permanent modification of the mental structure, which Bion calls *static splitting*, and which is a type of permanent hallucination. Instead of this defence mechanism (or another) being used in the face of each situation of anxiety, splitting occurs here once and for all: to locate oneself along a particular perspective and not to move from it is precisely what results in every experience being understood from a position already taken and which we can define as tendentious; then the splitting is practically always the same. Bion calls this static splitting, which obviously corresponds to the views of the semiologists of classic psychiatry, who indicated rigidity of thought as a typical symptom of schizophrenia. In terms of the theory of transformations expounded by Bion in 1965, these would fall within the category of transformations in hallucinosis.

Once static splitting has been established, any information coming from the outside, from others, will only confirm what the individual thinks. If we could catch them in this process, these individuals would surprise us by their ability to turn things around, to accommodate things to what they think, to what is convenient for them—all is grist for their mill. In this way, the interaction remains static and it is as if the individual continually hallucinates a situation that does not exist.

The mental disposition that underlies static splitting rests entirely on the *premises* of thought. The individual holds fixedly to his premises, without expounding them and without even knowing them, because they are unconscious. He is continuously reinterpreting the analyst's interpretations so that they can blend with his own premises, which is also a way of saying that the analyst's premises have to be silently rejected—silently, because between analyst and analysand there is manifest accord and latent discord, of which the analyst usually becomes aware only when he realizes that the process is completely stagnant.

This explains, then, that at critical moments, when static splitting cannot be maintained, the patient, in order to re-establish equilibrium, has recourse to hallucinations, which, according to Bion, are often fleeting and evanescent, or to delusional thoughts, which are also volatile and cannot be grasped.

To explain what manifest accord and latent discord consist in, Bion gives the classic Gestalt-psychology example of the vase and the two profiles. They are opposite perspectives (*either* a "vase" or two "profiles"); both are legitimate as long as we do not define what we are going to call content or form in the lines we are perceiving.

Analyst and analysand see the same thing, but based on different premises. At the level of the events or facts there is accord; at the level of the premises, which are never made explicit, discord is permanent and total. This is what is singular about reversible perspective and what distinguishes it from acting out and NTR, where discord is visible and the premises are not substantially in question.

The premises the analyst proposes and which the analysand formally accepts are those that establish the psychoanalytic contract. This is why I say that reversible perspective questions the contract. The analysand who reverses the perspective denounces the analytic contract once and for all and holds to another he establishes himself, without, in fact, making it explicit. This explains why reversible perspective appears at the outset, which is also maintained by Sheila Navarro de López (1980).

57.6   A clinical case

A homeopathic doctor came to analysis because of various neurotic symptoms and anxiety crises, which had led him to depersonalized states bordering on madness. He began treatment in good faith, accepting all my norms. However, with a subtlety beyond my reach, he introduced his "parallel contract". It took me years to discover and reveal his premises.

In the initial interviews this intelligent colleague told me that he suffered from bronchial asthma. He added that he was a homeopath, and he had a long list of asthmatic patients, who had all been cured. In fact, if homeopathic treatment had failed in his case, it was because the drug indicated for him set severe anxiety crises in motion. This was why he had opted for analysis: his anxiety was intolerable, and he feared he was going mad. What he apparently sought, and what I thought he was seeking, was a resolution through analysis of his anxiety and his crises of depersonalization, and at the same time a modification of the psychological factors contributing to his bronchial asthma. His premises, however, were different: he wanted me to take charge of the anxiety that accompanied homeopathic treatment. Analysis had to allow him to carry out the homeopathic treatment without leaving him exposed to psychosis. In this way, analysis became an instrument of the homeopathic treatment and this was the situation I had to accept. Of course he did not present it in this way. At the outset he only asked me simply whether I thought it pertinent for him to undergo, in addition, a homeopathic treatment, which I did not oppose even in principle, because as a general rule I do not think there is a radical incompatibility between analysis and other types of treatments. If the other treatment is in the service of resistance, it must be analysed. Despite my seeing no decisive incompatibility, he himself created it, because in fact he came in order to demonstrate that homeopathy was better than psychoanalysis. What he was really asking me to do was to moderate, "with my psychoanalysis", the anxiety his infallible homeopathic treatment would produce, in order that he would be able to cure himself.

In this case there was clearly a parallel contract, one that was different from and incompatible with analysis. Analysis could include a medical or surgical treatment in conjunction with it if the latter is complementary or independent; but it can never be subordinated to it, because analytic treatment requires autonomy. Were I to accept the patient's premises, I would lose the freedom to analyse the homeopathic treatment as resistance, in case it existed as such. This point illustrates what static splitting consists in: insofar as the patient answers to his own premises, the concept of resistance is in abeyance. In other words, the patient asked me to analyse him so he could cure himself. The similarity to Bion's example of the brilliant patient is obvious (1963, p. 49). As a surgical assistant, what I was supposed to do was to hand him the forceps and hold the separators while he operated.

This situation was insuperable for me. All I could do was to tell him, after several years of analysis, that he should opt for one treatment or the other, and he finally opted for homeopathic treatment. I will add that this option, which I tried to offer to enable him to choose freely, was experienced by him as a challenge. And he took it up!

This was an illustrative and dramatic case, because the patient cooperated, had insight and was truly deserving of help and respect. He himself finally recognized that he was in a dilemma, because if he cured his asthma through psychoanalysis, he would have to opt for a complete change of his professional perspective. That is, the conflict began when he thought that analysis could modify his asthma.

This man's asthma had a clear seasonal component, which led him to repeated iterative crises at the beginning of spring. This did not occur in the third year of analysis, and then he secretly began to take pulsatilla, the homeopathic treatment he had prescribed for himself. In this way he could attribute his improvement *also* to his treatment and not only to mine. This episode made it clear to me, although not to him, that what guided him was professional rivalry and not his desire to be cured. His reasoning went from ingenuity to delusion. He said, for example, that he had administered pulsatilla so that homeopathy could participate in the cure of his asthma, and he considered me selfish because I wanted psychoanalysis to take all the credit. He even said, and his tone was pathetic: "What do I do if it turns out that it is the analysis and not the pulsatilla that cures my asthma? . . . What do I do with my patients? . . . Would I be deceiving them?" In other words, he had to adjust his medical practice to the day-dream that he, with his homeopathy, cured asthma. He wanted at all costs to maintain the omnipotence of this diurnal dream.

At another point, after a remission of the asthma over several months, during which he was convinced (as I was!) of the efficacy of analysis for his illness, he said that he wanted to become an analyst. I naturally adopted a neutral position in relation to this idea, neither encouraging nor discouraging him. When I interpreted, among other things, that he wanted to change professions in order to feel himself the owner of the "good" treatment, he felt I was denigrating his vocation, and he abandoned his project. From this moment on he became very obstinate; he began to sleep during the sessions, and some time later he decided to leave analysis and avail himself again of the homeopathic treatment. I will add, as an aside, to show to what extent these mechanisms operate outside analysis, that he had the same attitude to homeopathic treatment. He wished to treat himself, and when he went to the man he considered the best Argentinian homeopath, he silently questioned everything the latter did or indicated.

As Bion says, what is most characteristic in such cases is the manifest accord and the latent discord. Once he had formulated that implicit contract I had to adhere to, everything else could be viewed from that perspective. For example, every interpretation I offered to correct the asthmatic condition from the psychological point of view was a proof of rivalry on my part—a way for me to say that "my" interpretation was better than his pulsatilla. And, of course, when I employed the word "pulsatilla" to interpret masturbation, it was the same to him as telling Erlich that *salvarsán* cures because it contains the word "save" [Spanish: *salvar*] and not because of the arsenic. He felt that I interpreted thus simply because I wanted to discredit pulsatilla, comparing it with masturbation—obviously because I did not believe in homeopathy.

In fact, if we examine the patient's position from a strictly psychiatric point of view, we should conclude that, in effect, he had a delusion. For what other reason would he have taken the trouble to come and demonstrate to me that homeopathic treatment is better than analytic treatment? I had never told him the contrary. This is why Bion says that reversible perspective implies a delusion and, vice versa, that the patient uses delusion to maintain reversible perspective.

I can understand Bion's assertions completely with regard to my patient. At times he misunderstood me, but eventually I understood that these misunderstandings were brief delusional and hallucinatory moments. For example, on one occasion I was able to establish that he had heard that I had said, "This time I did put the lid on", after formulating an interpretation. At other times the pseudoperceptive phenomenon was less apparent, and he would limit himself to asserting that there was a buzzing tone or a soft, contemptuous little laugh in my voice. Illusions and hallucinations of memory were frequent and sometimes provoked a great uncertainty in me.

The mnemonic and perceptual phenomena, as well as the delusional interpretations, appeared when the interpretation threatened to shake the patient's entire structure; then he would hallucinate, or delusional ideas would appear in order to maintain the reversible perspective.

Bion says that these patients use reality in order to give expression to a daydream—in this case that of curing himself and showing me he could do so. I think the expression "daydream" is fitting: the patient is not delusional in principle, but he wants to maintain his daydreams at all costs, with which he ends up being delusional. What from the point of view of semiology begins by being an overvalued idea becomes a delusional one.

In patients with reversible perspective we see most clearly that the relation among the three phenomena we are studying is not a two-way relation, because the other two phenomena are subordinate to reversible perspective. With regard to the NTR this is very evident during those moments when the achievements become more unbearable for the analysand. Let us recall my homeopathic colleague's strong response when he experienced the first spring without asthma. Acting out also operated at this point, when he began to take pulsatilla without telling me.

The use of acting out as an instrument to maintain reversible perspective is very frequent. At times we do not notice it, unfortunately, and only interpret the acting out and not what nourishes it. In the homeopath I was often able to note this situation. This patient had had a previous analysis, in which his homosexual tendencies were interpreted—and adequately, I am sure. He immediately annulled these interpretations with an acting out that transformed him from a model husband into a Don Juan of imposing promiscuity. He went to bed with patients, friends and even his wife's sister-in-law. This conduct was interpreted by his competent previous analyst as an attempt to reaffirm his masculinity and overcome castration anxiety via acting out. These interpretations were certainly correct; but, due to the material gathered in his analysis with me, the impression was that acting out also fulfilled the function of maintaining the perspective through which he saw things, and that no one could teach him anything.

CHAPTER FIFTY-EIGHT

Reversible perspective
[2]

58.1 *Reintroduction of the theme*

Reversible perspective is an extreme case of rigidity of thought which constitutes static splitting. It is an attitude that, by changing *premises*, promotes a definitely dissociative situation. In this way, reversible perspective is at the extremes of a series of phenomena of distortion that can be studied at the level of communication or of thought. What Bion and Money-Kyrle both point to (as we will see in chapter 59) is the will to misunderstand as an attitude of spirit and not just as a failure of communication. This is, precisely, what places reversible perspective into the same class of phenomena as acting out and the negative therapeutic reaction, because the three try to impede that special form of thought that is insight: acting out achieves this through a regression from thought to action; the negative therapeutic reaction, by undermining the insight achieved; and reversible perspective, via an attitude that is the opposite of insight (minus-K link). It is no accident, in my opinion, that Bion takes as an example the patient who dazzles the analyst with his insight.

Another element that unifies the three strategies is that when they persist, they lead to the impasse.

Let us remember, finally, that in general it is the borderline states that employ reversible perspective and not the overt psychosis, where delusion is evident.

58.2   Klein's concept of "reversal"

An important antecedent to Bion's works on reversible perspective can be found in Melanie Klein's (1961) analysis of Richard, after the analyst's journey to London. This refers to a week where work began on Tuesday, and to material that was used for "The Oedipus Complex in the Light of Early Anxieties" (1945).

In Session 42, on Thursday, in reference to a drawing, Klein interprets that Richard has placed the father in the baby's place, transforming him into a gratified baby; then she makes a comment, which is Note 2 of the session. She says: "Reversal is a very important mechanism in mental life. The young child, feeling frustrated, deprived, envious or jealous, expresses hate and a feeling of envy by omnipotently reversing the situation so that he will be adult and the parents neglected. In Richard's material in this session reversal is used in a different way. Richard puts himself into his father's place; but in order to avoid destroying the father, he changes him into a child and even into a gratified child. This form of reversal is more influenced by loving feelings" (1975, Vol. 4, p. 201n). Here are found the seeds of the theory of reversible perspective, as Bion would develop it in *Elements of Psycho-Analysis* (1963, chapters 11, 12, 13).

It is also worth pointing out that Klein distinguishes two polar situations in the mechanism of *reversal*, according to the predominance of either loving or destructive (jealous, envious) feelings. In the first case, evidently, reversal has to do with the natural processes of identification that promote mental growth and which, in terms of social psychology, configure the so-called *role play*. In my opinion, only in the second case, when destructive instincts predominate, can one properly speak of reversible perspective.

These two situations should therefore not be confused. Role play has a clear, positive sense in that it carries an intention of working through the conflict and repairing the objects, which by definition do not exist in reversible perspective. I think what is decisive is the type of underlying fantasies: in role play the difference between subject and object—the sensation that I am putting myself in the other's place—is not entirely erased. The mechanism is more plastic, whereas in reversible perspective the mechanism is rigid and the tone delusional.

58.3   Other clinical cases

One patient invariably arrived late, always by a quarter of an hour or more. Whatever the timetable, her session always began 16 or 17 minutes after the agreed time. The conventional interpretations—rivalry, rebelliousness, control, and so forth—did not affect this situation in any way. Once, however, the patient spoke about her favourite childhood game, and on this basis another line of interpretation could begin, inspired by a reversible perspective. There was a path of stone tiles between her house and the nearby swimming pool, which people used on the way to the pool. According to which tiles these people stepped on, she would establish what role they would have as characters in her fantasy. No one ever knew, of course, the roles assigned to them. But every day upon rising in the morning she established the rules of the game, which could be different although they always meant that she would know, depending on whether they stepped on the tile on the right or on the left, what character that person would represent. The model of this extravagant game served to make it clear that, in coming late, she made her analyst step on the tile that would convert him into a character of her fantasy. She did something similar at the beginning of each session: the analyst had to say something, to ask, interpret or move, before she would begin to speak.

When this was interpreted to her, the analysand associated something that facilitated an understanding of what was happening: "Last night I finished a novel. I regretted leaving those characters! Well, it doesn't matter, I will begin another straight away, and I will be with other characters." Therefore analysis was also, for her, a novel where she installed characters, created actors. While her premise was that the analyst is a character acting his role, the role she has assigned to him, everything that could be interpreted to her was already included in the story line of her novel (static splitting). With her initial silence she waited for her character, the analyst, to begin to act his role, be it by speaking or by moving. The novel into which she transformed the analysis—and her whole life—was a way of maintaining a circular time where everything could be foreseen: since everything was repeated, everything was the same. The analysand once recalled some verses by Horace, on sacrilegious knowledge, which is to attempt to know the hour of death, one's own death.

This example shows convincingly that to interpret at the level of defence mechanisms is not enough. Because as long as one interprets lateness or silence in terms of fear, frustration, revenge, envy, Oedipus complex, castration anxiety, omnipotent control or whatever, one has not reached the level at which the conflict is rooted. The interpretative task should aim for a more substantial change, which reaches the analysand's occult premises. The present example has an additional interest; it shows that the hidden premises can configure a type of material that leads us to simple, correct and conventional interpretations, such as those about a late arrival. Only if we are very alert can we think that arriving late to the sessions may imply something as complex as what the analyst discovered in this case. The reversal of perspective is usually detected when the analyst notes that "everything is going well" but the analysand is still the same. We have to be very alert, because apparently simple and egosyntonic attitudes that are susceptible to rational explanation can be covering a conflict of that nature, with a background of delusion.

Recently another colleague, Dr Myriam Schmer, told me of a very interesting case. It was that of a young man who went through a long period of impasse. When he began to mobilize himself, thought disturbance appeared clearly, and the patient remembered in a dramatic way that he had been left-handed but was forced to use his right hand. The material clearly showed that this infantile experience had much to do with reversible perspective. I would not hold to the simple idea that reversible perspective occurs in such left-handed people, but it is probable that in the life of such patients there were experiences that tried to force his nature. He also remembered that when he had begun to write he did so in a way no one understood, until a neurologist, who had diagnosed dyslexia, put a mirror in front of his writing and demonstrated that he wrote symmetrically: in the mirror the writing was completely legible.

I think it would be very interesting to investigate whether, as I believe, a relation exists between reversible perspective and S– (space) answers in Rorschach tests, where the background is taken as the figure. It is known that these blank-space answers measure oppositionism, and it is considered necessary to have a number of S-replies, since they imply autonomy—that one is not dominated by the milieu. The S-answer expresses oppositionism in all its degrees and levels, normal and pathological. It is not, in fact, among the rules of the test that one should see what is printed as a figure and the blank space as a background, just as it is not among the rules of psychoanalysis that the future patient should pronounce himself in favour of analysis and against any other type of treatment. Returning to the homeopath I had treated, the difficulty arises not in his thinking that homeopathy works better than psychoanalysis, but in the fact that he came to analysis to demonstrate this. The comparison between the two treatments is logical, and my patient had a right to do it. But he did something more, because he internally rejected the premise that he had come to me for analysis and not to obtain my support for effecting a homeopathic cure. On this point he ignored my premises. On the other hand, had he said that analytic treatment was of no use and that he was going to discontinue it and look for something better, he would have upheld the premise that he was in analysis and did not wish to go on.

There is no doubt that as we become accustomed to discovering these cases, which on account of their nature often go unnoticed, we will see that they become more frequent. At the London Congress, Liberman (1976b) spoke of a special type of patient: the quasi-colleague who offers special difficulties. He makes an emblematic use of psychoanalysis, is in analysis as a matter of prestige and seeks through analysis to augment his self-esteem through the nourishment of his narcissism. I consider that some, though not all, such patients can be included in the category we are studying.

Finally, it is worth indicating that the training analysis, which really has *two* objectives, lends itself considerably, due to its essential ambiguity, to this class of phenomena.

Because of all this, it is probable that reversible perspective appears more frequently than we think. However, we should not think that every patient who distorts analysis or has secondary intentions should be included in this category. The psychopath, for example, has secondary intentions but does not abandon the "primary" ones: he comes to analysis, although he certainly will not know for a long time what analysis means for him. Many cases of perversion would be better understood if we studied them from this point of view. I refer not to the homosexual who both wishes and does not wish to cure himself, but to the one whose intention is to demonstrate to me that he is homosexual, with the clear unconscious design of making me, as an analyst, recognize this fact, and consequently of making me accept that my desire to treat him was a mistake and, by definition, a prejudice.

58.4   Reversible perspective and insight

When we studied insight we compared it (and of course contrasted it) with Jaspers's primary delusional experience, because in both a new connection of meaning arises. Let us now say that, for Bion, insight is conceptually linked to reversible perspective: it is its opposite. Insight can be defined precisely as the capacity to assume the other's point of view, of grasping something with a *different perspective* (reversal of perspective), which is equivalent to binocular vision. The reversible perspective is the opposite— a psychotic mechanism that prevents me from changing and reversing my point of view to accept that of the others. (It is known that Bion prefers to speak of *vertex* and not viewpoint, in order not to be imprisoned by the eye, the visual sense.) With the notion of reversible perspective, which he contrasts with the reversal of perspective, Bion convincingly defines the role of interpretation and insight. In fact, when we interpret, what we do is give the patient another perspective on the facts he is describing and judging. We offer him the possibility of reviewing and eventually reversing his original perspective. This capacity of seeing from another point of view is precisely what characterizes insight. In sum, then, reversible perspective is an antagonistic process but at the same time linked to reversal of perspective—the capacity for insight.

Now that we have contrasted the reversal of perspective with reversible perspective, let us add that although these phenomena are opposed, they belong to the same class. And so as not to elude the complexity of the clinical facts, let us add that the patient who uses reversible perspective comes to analysis not only to carry out this phenomenon but also to be cured—that is, so that we can lift the cross from his shoulders. The outcome will depend, as always, on how much each of these desires weighs on him, as well as on our ability to understand him without falling into the trap.

The desire to be cured, which for the patient will mean not turning things around any more, can vary in degree, but it will always be possible to contact the part that wishes to emerge from hell. I think Bion indicates the same thing when he says that the analyst's tactics are rooted in destabilizing the defence, in transforming the static situation again into a dynamic one. Nunberg's (1926) pathological will to recovery expresses, on the one hand, the reversal of perspective, but also, on the other, the desire for a cure.

It may also be said that the two polar experiences of insight and reversible perspective correspond to the K and minus-K links and must be understood as examples of *catastrophic change*. This concept, which emerged in Bion's thinking when he wrote *Transformations* in 1965, occupied an increasingly central place in his thinking. In *Cambio catastrófico* [Catastrophic Change], a profound and stimulating book, Darío Sor and María Rosa Senet de Gazzano consider that "insight, as understood in psychoanalytical processes, represents a catastrophic change" (1988, p. 36) in that it disorganizes the system that preceded it and assumes the crossing of a breach, or caesura, with all the risks that that implies.

58.5   Narcissism and reversible perspective

We have just consoled ourselves with the idea that we can always find in the patient a part (infantile self, neurotic part, cooperative, rational ego or whatever) that will not reverse the perspective and which could then be the lever for our efforts. I will now deal with the part that does reverse perspective, and in principle we can affirm that it pursues narcissistic ends.

The reversible perspective consists, by definition, in that the subject begins analysis not in order to know himself, to be cured, to grow or to resolve his problems, but with a different idea, which can even be to show his analyst that he does not need analysis. He wishes to impose his premises and ignore those of the other in an extraordinary display of narcissism. Yet there is an Achilles' heel in this tenacious system, because it requires the other to demonstrate (and to demonstrate to the other) that what is asserted is true.

Analysis is possible if the basic premise is that the analyst is the analyst and the patient is the patient. I think that ultimately it is this premise that is always called into question. Essentially it is the subject–object polarity that falls victim to the fascination of narcissism. The difficulty of accepting the existence of the other is equivalent to the inability to accept a reality other than that of our dreams.

The reversible perspective includes the object only for the latter to confirm what the subject thinks, so that the object can substantiate the reality of the subject's dreams. In Bion's example, the analysand recounts an experience that was as real to him as if it were a dream, so that the analyst, in analysing it as a dream, can confirm that it was a dream and nothing more. Thus the object (the analyst) exists only to confirm what the subject thought or to deny what, for him, is real.

As Dr. Navarro de López (1980) indicates, the conspicuous subject–object confusion of the reversible perspective depends on an excessive use of projective identification in the service of an intense and aggressive scopophilia. The analysand does not look at the interpretation with his own eyes but with those of the analyst he has put himself into.

I think that on this point Bion leads us to one of the most acute problems of psychoanalytic investigation in our time: narcissism.

Even in this exquisitely narcissistic relation in which the subject seeks me out in order to demonstrate that he does not need me, I exist for him—even if it is only so that I can help him maintain his narcissism! If it were so, one would have to think that we come programmed for the object relation and that it is not true that our aim is to conserve narcissism.

Bion, in fact, maintains that we are born with a capacity for understanding what the sexual life of parents consists in—that is, with a preconception of the oedipal myth. The neurotic tries not to take charge of this knowledge, but he does not attempt not to have it, to destroy it. Psychosis seeks a more radical solution, and it is that if one attacks the preconception of the parents' coitus, then there will be no more parental coitus. The hatred of reality is of such magnitude that it leads to an attack on the mental apparatus capable of perceiving it. This is why Bion says that, evidently, to fix the premises satisfies the narcissism of the one who proposes them.

Bion states that in the reversible perspective the conflict is between Oedipus and Tiresias, not between Oedipus and Laius. The Oedipus/Laius conflict turns on the L (love) link and the H (hate) link, whereas Tiresias/Oedipus conflict pertains to the K (knowledge) link. The problem between Oedipus and Laius is who is Jocasta's owner; between Oedipus and Tiresias, who possesses knowledge.

Let us say, in comparison, and only in passing because it merits a more thorough reflection, that for Lacan narcissism is called into question by castration. The imaginary order is supported by the non-recognition of castration, which provokes a specular structure in which the child feels that he is the mother's penis and the mother feels that the child is her own penis. There is no difference between subject/object, and a third entity, the father, is required in order to break that specular relation and to allow, for the first time, the recognition of differences, which is also the insertion of man into the cultural milieu.

We all ask ourselves, in the final analysis, how we can recognize the other, so as to accept the asymmetry that creates or recognizes the subject/object polarity.

CHAPTER FIFTY-NINE

The theory of misunderstanding

59.1 Bion and Money-Kyrle

The reversible perspective fits in with Roger Money-Kyrle's (1968, 1971, etc.) works on the construction of the concept, the misunderstanding and the spurious object. These studies cover a wide spectrum, but we will approach them only from the technical viewpoint, that is, in their practical application.

Summing up chapters 57 and 58, the phenomenon of the reversible perspective accounts for cases where a manifest accord between analyst and analysand hides a truly radical discrepancy. The analysand does not question; on the contrary, he accepts what the analyst says, agrees with him and even differs (on occasion), as anyone might, while all along he views everything on the basis of different premises. What is really in play, then, are the suppositions of the relation and the task. A parallel contract is configured, and while we have no access to that hidden contract we will never grasp the reason for the reversal of events.

In locating this phenomenon with his Grid, Bion (1963) says that the conflict is not between Oedipus and Laius but between Oedipus and Tiresias, because what is in question is knowledge.

Following the rows of the grid, there is a slide; when the analyst functions at the level of concrete thought, the patient operates with a high level of abstraction, and vice versa. Thus, for example, when the analyst speaks of the Oedipus myth (Row C), the patient decodes in terms of the theory of the Oedipus complex (Rows F or G), which is equivalent to saying that he is intellectualizing. Conversely, when the analyst tries to abstract on the basis of experience, the analysand descends in the scale of abstraction and consequently denies the interpretation its symbolic value: castration anxiety is interpreted to him and he feels the interpretation as a concrete attack on his penis, like castration itself. Thus analyst and analysand can never understand each other—they never meet. Bleger (1967b) explained this phenomenon by saying that the analysand *rotates*, that is, he listens with the NPP when we speak to the PPP and vice versa. Thus he invalidates our interpretations and disorients us.

The reversible perspective operates through static splitting modifying the premises. The patient prevents the fertilization of his preconceptions by the events of reality, the *realizations*, so that conception and then concept cannot arise, and mental growth is arrested. It is an extreme way to avoid the pain provoked precisely by the incapacity for understanding or the perception of madness. If one is adept at understanding things from another perspective, this is because one is radically incapable of seeing them as others do. This obstinate attitude could not be observed better than in the patient who, after an excellent interpretation by his doctor, said, "This interpretation reached me; it made me do a 360-degree turn".

As a necessary and extreme mechanism to avoid pain and achieve equilibrium in some way, the reversible perspective is tenacious. From it arise evanescent hallucinations, fleeting delusions, acting out, and so forth. Sometimes, as an extreme device, an incoercible resistance appears, and the patient abandons treatment.

All these phenomena are quite frequent; in fact, they appear in order to maintain the reversible perspective, no less than to express it. They are, in the end, symptoms, constitutive elements of the situation itself, because the reversible perspective is, finally, a great misunderstanding, of which the others, the minor misunderstandings, are only symptoms. When we understand it we realize that the study of the reversible perspective leads us imperceptibly—it could be no other way—to the area of thought disturbance, the key to Bion's investigation.

From our point of view, which is that of psychoanalytic technique, thought disturbance is interesting when it constitutes a problem in the practice, and the theme arises both in Bion's and in Money-Kyrle's work.

The intellectual relationship between these two investigators is evident, more than their differences. The first of these is that while Bion studies the more serious cases, where psychosis is involved or at least where the psychotic part of the personality plays the major role, Money-Kyrle interests himself in the less serious. Bion is concerned with psychosis and Money-Kyrle with neurosis, although this is not an absolute.

I think a more consistent difference is that Bion studies *thought* above all, and Money-Kyrle studies *knowledge*—without, of course, being unaware of how much the two areas have in common.

Finally, I think Money-Kyrle bases himself more than does Bion on evolutionist and biological (ethological) considerations.

59.2 *Money-Kyrle's intellectual development*

Although Money-Kyrle, who is upright and modest, underlines his intellectual debt to Bion, we should keep in view that his first works appeared at the end of the 1920s and he has concerned himself with these themes ever since.

Money-Kyrle says that as a psychoanalyst he passed through three great stages that mark the evolution of psychoanalysis itself as a science. First mental illness was conceived as an inhibition of sexual life; then this vision changed in favour of a more structural one, in the sense of a conflict between instinctual drives and defence, which is also a conflict between the ego and the superego, a conflict of an ethical nature. In recent years, finally, special value is placed on the disturbance of thinking, the conceptual error that feeds and provides the basis for mental illness.

Naturally these three points of view are not in opposition: rather, they are complementary—on the one hand, the sexual inhibitions that so concerned Freud in the first years of his investigation are linked to the structural conflict he himself described and Melanie Klein subsequently explored; and, in turn, this conflict of structures can also be understood as errors in conceptualizing particular objects, impulses or experiences.

Another way of defining Money-Kyrle's point of view is that he does not study instinct as impulse, or as charge, but as knowledge. In fact, instinct implies these two things—pulsion and knowledge. Freud had already said this in his *Three Essays* (1905d), when he defined instinct no less through its charge than via its source and its *object*. The instinctual drive has to be accompanied by some type of representation of the object where it applies. Although pulsion and object can be separated methodologically, the instinct in its totality is a unitary structure. At times one forgets this, but it is so. And Money-Kyrle reminds us of this.

The cognitive aspect of the instinct (instinctive knowledge, innate knowledge) is studied more by ethologists than by psychoanalysts. Money-Kyrle, who knows this, ends his 1971 article with these words: "Perhaps I can claim some theoretical advantage if they [his ideas] help to bridge the gap between psychoanalysis and ethology" (1971, *Collected Papers*, p. 448).

It can be said in conclusion that Money-Kyrle, in an investigation that endured throughout his long life, joins psychoanalysis at either end with biology and philosophy and traces an arc that goes from Plato and Aristotle to Lorenz and Tinbergen, passing through the work of Schlick and logical positivism.

59.3 *Concept building*

There are two areas in which Money-Kyrle's inquiry develops: the construction of the concept and the location of experience in a space-time system. In fact, these two areas are not substantially different, because to localize experiences implies the construction of the concepts of space and time. But evidently Money-Kyrle proposes greater autonomy for these two categories where the experiential factors are, for him, a more decisive influence. It will be seen, however, that poor orientation towards the object, towards the *base*, as he calls it, can be linked to a mistaken concept of the base; this means that the two are not easily separable. Money-Kyrle's investigation can be condensed at this point into two words: *misconception* and *disorientation*. Misconception has to do with concept building; disorientation refers to the categories of space and time. One of Money-Kyrle's strong and original theses is that when the interplay of genetic information and the milieu is not adequate, this does not remain as a gap in knowledge; it proliferates as inadequate knowledge: he calls this *misconception*.

For Money-Kyrle, the concept is constructed at the point of encounter between experience and what is innate. He follows here Bion's idea of a preconception that joins with a fact of experience (*realization*) to form a conception.

Money-Kyrle's other source of support is the well-known philosopher Moritz Schlick, a logical positivist and head of the famous Vienna Circle. For Schlick, knowledge is not acquired by becoming conscious of the sensory-emotional experience but by *recognizing* what that experience is (ibid., p. 418). Money-Kyrle holds that this recognition is equivalent to locating something as a member of a class. We are born, then, with a capacity for recognizing certain objects as members of a class.

Without reopening the ancient debate between nominalism and realism—that is, whether there are really universals or only words that name groups of qualities we subtract from reality—let us say simply that to maintain that there are classes does not imply ontological realism, but, rather, that we have a particular capacity for distinguishing, within the continuum of experience, certain qualities that go together, which we call *classes*. We can assume that there are classes without supporting Plato's Ideas or Aristotle's universals. Instead, we can postulate a gradual approach to reality, establishing classes that become increasingly rational, modifying them as our understanding of the nature of the processes increases. To give an example, the class of congenital malformations was divided into the class of genetic cerebropathies and the class of embryopathies or viral embryonitis when the effect of German measles in the mother was discovered. That is, we are approaching more rational, more realistic classes. I think this does not diminish Money-Kyrle's idea of class, which is based on very specific knowledge of the genome.

In any case, Money-Kyrle says that we are born with the possibility of recognizing, of distinguishing, from experience, some classes or, equivalently, of locating the facts of experience within certain classes. This is why the child can assign the class "breast" to the maternal breast or to the bottle and distinguish what does not belong to this class. "A class represented by a memory image functioning as a name is a concept" (ibid., p. 419).

Everything leads one to assume that in the newborn infant the first innate preconception is that of the breast (or nipple), or better still that of a good or bad breast (or nipple), given that the emotions of love and hate colour preconception from the beginning. On the basis of the first experience with an object that can be classified as a breast, the class is considerably reduced, and the conception is linked to a particular breast (or bottle) given in a certain way, and so forth.

In parallel with the concept of breast (or nipple), something that contains it, the mouth, is constructed as a concept. From this moment on, other concepts are constructed by division and combination—by splitting and integration, to use more psychoanalytic terms.

We are born programmed and prepared to classify "the things of life"; but this development is never easy, because in us operates a powerful force for ignorance, for forgetfulness, for self-deception.

We possess adequate instruments for the perception of reality, for *classifying* the facts of experience; however, we have to learn anew what we already know through arduous and persistent effort. Just as we are born with an inherent love of truth (epistemophilic instinct, K link), we also bring with us the tendency to distort it when it opposes us. Therefore, and this is Money-Kyrle's other strong thesis, when we do not construct the right concept it is not only because the milieu deprived us of the adequate *realizations*, but also because we have a strong tendency to distort. The human spirit has a very strong disposition not to know, to misunderstand, to ignore. Money-Kyrle is in agreement here with the benevolent scepticism that permeates Freud's work and becomes theory in "Formulations on the Two Principles of Mental Functioning" (1911b).

For Money-Kyrle, the basic conflict of the human being is perhaps that between a powerful impulse to know and the no less powerful one not to know, to distort the facts of life. (At the end of the first part of her inaugural work, "The Development of a Child", 1921, Melanie Klein describes the struggle between the pleasure principle and the reality principle in terms of an impulse to know versus the feeling of omnipotence of the child, which Ferenczi, 1913, studied in "Stages in the Development of the Sense of Reality": see M. Klein, 1975, Vol. 1, p. 16.) Money-Kyrle explains this tendency to distort with two theoretical instruments: the pleasure principle and envy.

In accordance with the pleasure principle, pairs of concepts rather than single concepts are constructed, because each concept formed, in that it implies pleasurable or unpleasurable experiences, is automatically linked to the good and the bad.

If envy operates strongly, the bad concept will always be formed, but the good concept may not be formed. Its replacement will then be a *misconception*.

Knowledge is painful because it is always linked to absence, to a lack. If the breast were not lacking at a given moment, if the breast were always in my mouth, I would have no misconceptions with respect to it. It is the emptiness of the absence that is filled with misconceptions. But absence is indispensable because if the breast were always in the baby's mouth, he could never understand that the breast and the mouth are different.

59.4   Stages in the development of the concept

Whereas Bion's sophisticated Grid goes from beta elements to the deductive scientific method and algebraic calculus, Money-Kyrle postulates only three phases: (1) concrete identification, (2) unconscious ideographic representation and (3) conscious, predominantly verbal representation.

The first stage, *concrete representation*, is not strictly speaking representational, since the representation is not distinguished from the object represented. As far as I understand it, this idea corresponds to what Freud (1915e) calls thing representation in the unconscious. Money-Kyrle quotes the case of a patient who had a series of light icteroid (jaundiced) episodes due to constriction of the bile ducts, which, through the evolution of the clinical material, seemed to correspond to the first stage of his classification, which were then clearly expressed as oneiric ideograms. Money-Kyrle seems to think that these episodes were the physiological expression of what Hanna Segal (1957) called symbolic equation (Money-Kyrle, 1978, p. 422), but I am inclined to think that both thing representation and symbolic equation correspond better to the second stage, which we will now examine.

Then the *unconscious ideographic representation* follows, in which there is already an initial distance between thing and symbol, as is observed in dreams.

The final stage of cognitive development corresponds to the *verbal representation* of conscious thought.

59.5   The space–time system

We have explained the origin and construction of the concept, and now we will deal briefly with Money-Kyrle's theory of how the concepts of space and time are reached.

Money-Kyrle holds that we are born with a disposition to orientate ourselves towards reality. In "Cognitive Development", the work that we are discussing, he deals with the spatial orientation that directs us towards a base. It is interesting to indicate, because it clearly defines Money-Kyrle's position, that *base* does not pertain to the person but specifically to the object. Psychologically, the base is the point of intersection of the Cartesian coordinates to which the subject always has recourse in order to orientate himself. The base all the others derive from is the first object outlined in the sensory confusion of the newborn, that is, the breast, or perhaps specifically the nipple.

The development of the system starting from the base is from the breast to the mother, then to both parents (Oedipus complex), siblings, family and society.

The orientation towards the good base can be lost in various ways of *disorientation*. Sometimes the child gets into the base with a total projective identification, either through envy or seeking protection in the face of danger—a theme treated in a paper by Jorge Ahumada (1982). In these cases, the confusion of identity is very great, and the process can be chronic and syntonic if the circumstances of life and the individual's capabilities permit it. In a previous work, Money-Kyrle (1965) attributed megalomania to this mechanism and maintained that man began to use clothing in order to consummate the projective identification with his totemic animal, that is, the parents. In a recent work, Ahumada (1982) studies the importance of detecting in the analysand's material whether the analyst is recognized as the base, which can go unnoticed, since the analysand cannot express this, and the analyst takes it for granted that he exists for the other. Often the lack of a base—that is, of a breast capable of introjecting the painful states—appears in the material as the idea that the analyst is cold or insensitive. Following what Money-Kyrle said in his last work (1977), Ahumada emphasizes the need to distinguish destructive projective identification from desperate projective identification, which is an attempt to connect (or reconnect) with the base.

Another eventuality where the good base is lost is when it is confused or exchanged for the bad one. The wrong base represents, simply, the one that is inconvenient for the subject in those circumstances.

As a third possibility, Money-Kyrle studies the orientation towards a confused base and takes Meltzer's (1966) paradigm, when the child confuses the mother's breast with the bottom that goes away and then with his own bottom, which he enters in a masturbatory act.

It is worth indicating that the ideas of misconception and disorientation have immediate and current application in practice. At times no interpretation is more precise than that of indicating to the patient his disorientation—how he seeks what is really not advisable or fitting for him. Until we interpret this mistaken search as the analysand's basic error, the disorientation will probably persist, and the analysand will continue to err; and we will also err, accompanying him with interpretations that only reach what is contingent and inessential.

Many interpretations on the transference love are, for example, better formulated if the mistaken search is made evident—that a man is sought when an analyst is needed, a penis instead of a breast, a father instead of a husband. At the beginning of her transference love a married woman of middle age roundly affirmed that all she needed to become healthy was to fall in love. The same could be said for the acting out of a man who, during the first weekend break from analysis, went to bed with his maid-servant and gave her the equivalent of what he paid for a session.

The same can be said for the *misconception*. Ultimately our work is based in large part on rectifying what the patient misunderstands in what we tell him. We have a tendency to ignore that the patient does not always understand us, that sometimes his understanding is impeded at the level of ideas, of concepts. To take a very clear example from everyday practice: the classic interpretations of the weekend, sometimes rightly criticized as clichés, will always be such if we begin from the mistaken supposition that the patient knows what waiting is or has the concept of what the absence of the object is. If one of these concepts fails and another, mistaken one replaces it, then these interpretations are irremediably inoperative, how-ever true they may be, because the patient cannot understand them. An intelligent patient who always criticized the flatness of my interpretations about the weekend changed dramatically when I began to point out that, for her, the word absence had no significance, that she did not know what absence meant. And it was really so, so that everything I had interpreted to date had been useless or, in the best of cases, just a vague preparation for being able to understand that she lacked a concept, the concept of absence. As long as she lacked this concept I could not interpret the week-end absence properly.

If the analyst perceives where the misconception is and what concept it replaces, he sets in motion a process that restores to the patient, if it ends happily, the concept that is lacking. I have seen in my practice that when I interpret in this way, I can reach a level of precision and singular effi-ciency that is not without elegance. In a recalcitrant case of ejaculatio prae-cox, for example, I achieved some progress when I began to interpret to my analysand that he did not have a clear concept of what waiting means. It is obvious that if this concrete point is not dealt with, it will be difficult to correct the symptom.

The surest point of departure for the proper application of these ideas in clinical practice is to take them seriously and also to take the analysand seriously when he says that he does not understand us. In the example of the intelligent woman who denied the validity of my interpretations of the weekend, the situation began to change once I took account of her re-peated affirmations that she did not understand me. Until that moment I would explain again and again, and when she insisted that she did not understand me, I would interpret that she doubted me (which was also true) or mocked me (which again was also true).

59.6   Basic types of knowledge

"The Aim of Psycho-Analysis" (1971), one of Money-Kyrle's last works, considered what types of knowledge come with the genome, and he pro-posed three: recognition of the breast as a supremely good object, recognition of the parents, coitus as an insuperable act of creation and the recognition of the inevitable passage of time and finally, death (1978, p. 443).

Money-Kyrle's proposal is highly speculative, and he is aware of this. Perhaps the development of future investigations will lead us to accept that innate knowledge is of another kind; but, in any case, the types mentioned find sufficient support in psychoanalytic investigation as a whole.

In addition, the thesis that we come into the world with certain elemental types of knowledge seems to be currently considerably supported by ethological investigation, and in the end it does no more than align Homo sapiens with all the species of the animal kingdom. The animal is capable of recognizing certain stimuli as a signal that sets *fixed action patterns* in motion.

As can be seen in Konrad Lorenz's The Evolution and Modification of Behaviour (1971) and in many current works on ethology, the signal that acts as a stimulus and sets in motion a particular type of behaviour can be contingent but well determined. Lorenz cites the female turkey's behaviour of attention to her young as very specific (and, for me, dramatic). The turkey responds initially to the gobbling of her chicks with maternal care behaviour. Whatever object in the nest fails to emit these signals is ejected by the diligent mother with repeated thrusts of her beak. If an artificial object endowed with a mechanism that emits the signal of the chick is placed into the nest, it will be recognized as a chick. If the turkey's cochlea is damaged, she will expel the chicks from her nest as soon as they are hatched. However, a few days later this rigid instinctive behaviour is modified through learning, and the mother will continue to care for her chicks even if they do not emit the signal.

Returning to Money-Kyrle's three innate kinds of knowledge, we saw that they are supported by the general body of the theory of psychoanalysis, but it is worth pointing out that they are also the subject of some of our great controversies—in the first place, the issue of the object relation existing at the outset and the claim that there can be no stage of primary narcissism. It is also affirmed that first there is a dyadic relation with the breast and then a triangular oedipal relation. For Money-Kyrle the sexual instinct is not only genetic but also the object of the instinct and the relation of the three objects among themselves (primal scene). He neither ignores nor has reason to ignore the great weight of the Oedipus complex in man's access to culture (society), but he postulates it as innate knowledge, which the culture only reinforces, inhibits or deviates from.

59.7 Mourning and memory

Returning to the three acts of recognition already studied, it can be said that the point of departure for a healthy development is to be able to recognize the breast as a good object, since on that basis all other relations come into being. This is difficult because we cannot enjoy the breast indefinitely.

Money-Kyrle believes that the concept of a good breast is always formed and maternal care is sufficient for this, however insufficient it may be, if it enables the child to stay alive. Naturally, the worse the maternal care, the less firmly will the concept of the good breast be established and the more vulnerable it will be during the absence (of the breast). If development is more or less normal, then the memory of the good breast subsists through the alternations of contact and separation; it is recognized when it returns, and when it goes definitively, it precipitates the process of mourning that Melanie Klein (1935, 1940) called the *depressive position*, during which the lost good breast is internalized.

Money-Kyrle is inclined to think that the internalization of the lost good object in the process of mourning is equivalent to establishing a concept (perhaps at the level of ideographic representation). But what he does not doubt is that the possibility of facing mourning and the capacity for remembering are inseparable, because "without the memory there can be no mourning and without the mourning there can be no memory" (Money-Kyrle, 1978, p. 444).

59.8   The spurious object

When memory and loss become intolerable, then the good object is no longer recognized as such, and it is exchanged for another to which the virtues of the original are mistakenly attributed. The prototype of this pathological model of development takes us once more to the confused and excited feelings of the child, as described by Meltzer in 1966, and to which we referred when speaking of the base. When the child exchanges the breast for his bottom, we can affirm that a fundamental misconception has occurred. I should point out that in this basic misconception there is certainly, in Money-Kyrle's view, also an obscure memory of intrauterine life. If that were so, then we should have to add another piece of innate knowledge to Money-Kyrle's list, which would lead us to take up once more the idea of primal narcissism.

From the faults in the behaviour of the object to endogenous envy, many factors can explain why an individual seeks a spurious object to replace the real one. At any rate, without a discussion of its development, the idea serves in practice because it permits interpretation—with greater precision and less charge in the countertransference—when it is understood that the patient seeks a spurious object because he has forgotten the authentic one, because he has not been able to wait for it and is not able to recognize it. This reasoning is applicable to acting out over the weekend and also in large measure to the transference love in which the spurious object for the female is the penis. I remember a male patient who told me in a challenging tone that what he needed, to be cured, was a woman.

Analysis was of no use. What I had to do was to help him to find a woman, the ideal woman, an infallible recipe for all his problems. He sought a spurious object; he thought that the vagina of a woman would resolve all his problems; but in fact what he needed was an analyst and not a *Celestina* to resolve his problems. And in this patient, the idealized vagina was confused with the rectum, while the much-disdained psychoanalytic function represented the breast, on the basis of a horizontal splitting of the mother's body (or, if we prefer, of a displacement from top to bottom). In this brief example it is clear that operating with the idea of a spurious object, one can interpret with precision, and I would even say with serenity, better shielded from the countertransference tension that is inevitably felt when the patient literally hands us the sword and goes in search of other solutions, which are sometimes dangerous and always miss the mark.

Just as Bion says that one has to see the patient every time as if it were the first, meaning that one must not be tied to the prejudices one already has about the patient, Money-Kyrle tells us that the patient also sees us in each session as if it were the first time, because he does not always recognize us when he arrives—and that we do not realize this because it is obvious and very painful. If one operates by taking this scheme into account, and if it is sensitive to what the patient says, then this type of problem will appear frequently and concretely. I remember, for example, a patient who used to tell me on Mondays, "I don't know who you are". I interpreted these associations as hostility arising from the weekend. But, in fact, the problem was more serious, and she had forgotten me; she had lost contact totally. In interpreting that she was angry because of the weekend, I did not touch the essential—that is, that the interruption on Friday led her to forget the object totally, and therefore she did not recognize me. I interpreted that she did not know me in order to express her anger, taking as contempt at almost a social level what was more profound and dramatic. She really did not remember. And when the situation was correctly interpreted, the analysand responded with an association that had an allegorical value for her, but which showed me an essential aspect of her conflict, despite the intellectualized aspect that covered it. She said a baby can only remember the nipple when it has it in its mouth.

59.9 *Nature and culture*

I think Money-Kyrle's central idea is that knowledge has a development, in the sense that there are endogenous and exogenous factors, genetic and acquired ones, that determine and propel it. Knowledge does not arise at the outset and once and for all—rather, it is a process. And the most important function of psychism (mental functioning) is, perhaps, to approach the genetic sources of knowledge. It also seems that, unfortunately, a fundamental mental function is to distort that initial and basic knowledge, which may be a way of saying, by way of complaint, simply that man is an animal capable of creating symbols.

In this way the works of Money-Kyrle present, from a new, strictly' psychoanalytic point of view, the old problem of nature and nurture, in that they affirm that these interact, as the new sociobiological currents also assert. This was expounded some years ago by Lionel Tiger and Robin Fox and more recently in the studies of Edward D. Wilson (1978). In *The Imperial Animal* (Tiger & Fox, 1971) there is much emphasis on the value of hierarchical structures in the behaviour of primates in general and especially in hominids. The general thesis of this book is that there is no radical opposition between nature and culture, because we are *by nature* cultural animals. In this sense, there appears a strong refutation of Freud's idea when in 1930, and in fact throughout his work, he sets instinct against culture. (As we know, Anna Freud maintained this line of thought decisively in *The Ego and the Mechanisms of Defence*, 1936.)

With his delicate psychoanalytic instruments, Money-Kyrle tries to find out what is genetic, what is acquired and what is the relationship between the two.

Money-Kyrle takes as a basis that we are born with particular *preconceptions*, in Bion's sense (and also in the ethological sense of genetic knowledge), and that these preconceptions have to come together with particular experiences, which Bion calls *realizations*. That is, given a particular preconception I have, when I find an example in the milieu, I "realize" that this is what I was looking for. Schlick comes in at this point when he says that to know is always to recognize the object as a member of a class.

The concept of classes is exceedingly interesting, and Money-Kyrle examines it with regard to Plato and Aristotle. Plato says that there are *Ideas* of which the things of reality are mere imitations. All the things and beings of this world, everything our senses perceive, are only appearances. We live as prisoners in a cave, and we see only shadows, which we take as reality. Reality can only be formed by Ideas, which are perfect, eternal and incorruptible. Real knowledge is based on the reality of Ideas, hence the name "realism" for this philosophical position, to which is opposed the nominalism of William of Occam and that of others. It is on the basis of Ideas that we recognize the facts or events of reality, which are always inferior to them. If this doctrine is stripped of all the ideological *Anlage* of a man like Plato, who lived during the period of Athenian decadence when the Peloponnesian Wars had just ended with the surrender of his city in 404 BC (see Sarton, 1952, chapter 16), we find that what Plato means is that we have some type of knowledge prior to experience which allows us to take up a position in relation to it. Kant was later to say something similar when he opposed the English idealists and told Locke that the brain is not a *tabula rasa* because when one is born *a priori* conditions already exist. Schlick, for his part, refers to a capacity to locate things within classes.

The concept of class is complex. But it is enough to say that it can be admitted that in nature some characteristics go together, and this is what enables us to make classifications. The classifications change as we acquire greater knowledge, because knowledge brings us closer to the so-called natural classes. Take, for example, the classification of Linnaeus. Although his work preceded any evolutionist commitment, he was nevertheless able to devise a classification that has stood the test of time, even if it later underwent modifications, because he was an observer of genius, rigour and lucidity. Despite their name, the "natural" classes are continuously modified because, as we understand better what is essential in a class, we can improve its definition or characterization. No one would place lions and camels in the same class because they are the same colour; there are other characteristics, such as herbivorous or carnivorous, which seem more significant to us. In classifying butterflies, on the other hand, colour may be important, because it can decide the survival of a species if it facilitates its adaptation. Money-Kyrle operates with this concept of class when he asserts that man is born with an innate knowledge of some classes of objects.

Money-Kyrle studies concept building, and one of his basic theses is that it can fail for various reasons, which depend on the individual himself or on the milieu. If the *realizations* are not very efficient (exogenous factor) or if tolerance to pain is very low (endogenous factor), a specific will to ignore appears, and for this reason concepts that should be formed are transformed into misconceptions.

This part of the theory of misconceptions is closely linked to the theory of memory and of recognition—here in the dual sense of gratitude, of being recognized, and of memory, since if I do not remember something, I cannot recognize it. Recognition is linked to the depressive position because it conditions depression, as depression also conditions memory. How can I be depressed other than by remembering what I had and do not have? And, vice versa, how can there be memory other than on the basis of mourning for what is not there? Thus the three concepts—memory, mourning and time—are fundamental and indispensable to this doctrine.

CHAPTER SIXTY

Impasse

60.1 *Summary*

It is easy to define the *psychoanalytic impasse* in general terms. But it is difficult to discover it and complicated to resolve it. This chapter attempts to define the concept, to locate it in the appropriate field (technique) and to indicate its principal sources (psychopathology).

On the definition there are few doubts. The French word is, of itself, clear and universal. It means a *blocked road*, and it is used when something that has been developing normally is suddenly blocked and delayed. We often see it used in newspapers to indicate an initiative that has stalled, and it is used in the same sense in psychoanalysis, in my opinion. However, the current usage of the term requires that the arrest occur while the general conditions of the analytic situation are maintained. The specification of Mostardeiro, Pechansky et al. (1974) is then very pertinent, indicating, as it does, that one can speak of impasse in psychoanalysis only when the formal conditions of treatment are fulfilled: if the setting is noticeably altered, it is not appropriate to speak of it. In the impasse, analytic work is carried out, the patient associates, the analyst interprets, the setting is maintained in its fundamental constants; but the process neither advances nor retreats. This certainly does not imply that there are no faults in the

---

Reprinted with some modifications from "Psychoanalytic 'Impasse' and the Strategies of the Ego", *Revista de Psicoanálisis*, 1976; this chapter is a recapitulation of Part 6.

setting and in the analyst's work. They always exist, as in every analysis; but their presence is not decisive. The analyst's engagement is so complete (and complex) in the impasse that there is a tendency to classify it via the patient and via the analyst. However, there are many reasons for not accepting this criterion, and the first is that in the true impasse both causals always appear as superimposed on each other and indefinite: the impasse is neither incoercible resistance nor technical error.

It is worth pausing for a moment to discuss these terms. *Incoercible resistance* erupts in the process *from* the analysand, and always brusquely. Generally it presents itself at the outset; if it does so later, it will be easy to determine the moment and the circumstances of its appearance, which is sudden and stormy. It is something obvious and belongs to the patient. He himself considers it so, and the analyst, for his part, does not feel personally involved beyond his ineluctable professional responsibility. Sooner or later, if this disturbing situation is not resolved, the patient interrupts the treatment on his own account or with our consent.

The *technical error* bears on the process also in a particular direction: it arises from the analyst, and both participants consider it thus or, in any case, and also at first sight, from a third party whose opinion has been requested—the supervisor. (The technical error includes the analyst's theoretical limitations but not those of psychoanalysis, since otherwise any obstacle could be attributed to our ignorance—which is laudable from an ethical viewpoint and legitimate epistemologically but lacking significance in practice.)

In separating (the patient's) incoercible resistance and (the analyst's) technico–theoretical error, impasse is better defined and more specific, without thereby ignoring the forms of the transactions, nor pretending that this conceptual distinction is easily applicable to the clinical case. For example, sometimes an apparent incoercible resistance may be a response to something the analyst did, and, vice versa, the technical error may come from the patient, as in the phenomenon of projective counteridentification as described by Grinberg (1956, 1963). It is also possible, as is seen in clinical practice, that the analysand who abandoned treatment as a result of resistance or technical error meets with an impasse in a second attempt. In short, the three processes are superimposed on each other and related, but nevertheless there is no need to confuse them. For the sake of precision, impasse should be reserved for cases where the failure is not visible and the treatment continues.

Giovacchini and Bryce Boyer (1975) define "impasse" as a situation in which the therapist, who feels uncomfortable and frustrated, tends to introduce a parameter, that is, a non-analytic procedure, or else to interrupt therapy (p. 144). This definition does not seem entirely satisfactory to me, for various reasons. The impasse can exist without the analyst finding himself obliged to act. The analyst's acting out, if it is produced, would be a consequence of the impasse, but not one of its defining features. And, further, Eissler's (1953) parameter has to do with a technical attitude, which, beyond the accord we give it, does not necessarily imply acting out.

Giovacchini and Bryce Boyer argue that the impasse is the transferential correlate of a crisis of early development and, as such, is intrinsic to the psychopathology of the patient, with which the (psychopathological) cause is confused with the technical consequence, the impasse. In any case, their *clinical* observation is accurate, in that the crises of early development have their "inevitable" correlate in the transference (as shown in chapter 28). But it does not seem *inevitable* to me that transference repetition leads to the impasse.

Laertes Moura Ferrão (1974) questions the very concept of impasse and maintains that it is permeated by an erroneous conception of psychoanalysis. Due to its origins and its nature, psychoanalysis resembles (and is confused with) a medical treatment and even a moral and religious treatment. The idea of medical or moral cure influences our conception of the psychoanalytic process and has repercussions in the omnipotence of patient and analyst. Following Bion in *Second Thoughts* (1967b), Moura Ferrão maintains that psychoanalysis is not a curative procedure but a method of knowledge to facilitate the growth of the individual. Without entering into a discussion on the essence of this issue and even from the perspective of the author, the impasse would exist equally as an obstacle to the growth of the individual.

Maldonado, who had carried out a sustained study of the impasse (1975, 1979, 1983), is inclined to think that the impasse "is not merely a secondary result of the patient's resistance; on the contrary, it is an objective towards which the patient directs himself, and it answers to an unconscious fantasy which tends to achieve the paralysis of the object in its autonomy and its link with him" (see Maldonado, 1983, p. 206). He rightly asserts that in the analysand's unconscious there exists a representation of the analytic process, which gives account of its unfolding. Therefore one can often detect in the material the fantasy of a process that has been arrested.

To conclude, I think I do not stray from the general use of this term if I give an elucidative definition of the impasse in terms of the following essential features: psychoanalytic impasse is a technical concept; it comprises an insidious arrest of the process; it tends to perpetuate itself; the setting is preserved in its basic constants; its existence is not obvious as incoercible resistance or technical error; it is rooted in the patient's psychopathology; and it involves the analyst's countertransference. (Rudolph Carnap, in *Logical Foundation of Probability*, 1950, chapter 1, distinguishes three types of definitions: *analytic*, which includes the common uses of the term; *stipulative*, which suggests a specific use; and *elucidative*, which proposes a normalized use on the basis of how the term is used in current speech and writing.)

Even a layman can think that a long and painful procedure such as the psychoanalytic cure, which by definition is understood as a sustained effort to overcome a *resistance*, must be particularly exposed to the impasse, and so it is. However, the problem is rarely mentioned and studied. (In Edward Glover's classic book, 1955, however, many valuable references to the subject can be found throughout under the designations *analytic stagnation* and *stalemate analysis*.)

When we study it seriously, we are obliged to confront ultimate questions on the value of our method and the efficacy of our technique. The impasse of just one treatment leads the authentic analyst invariably to a review of his profession and his discipline. The same does not occur with the failure or the interruption of the treatment, which generally only evoke more personal, immediate and recognizable faults. This is another—almost hygienic—reason for defining the term and not confusing it with the other cases, which are always more justifiable and less disturbing to our conscience. (If we wished to utilize the concepts of the epistemologist Thomas S. Kuhn, 1962, on the structure of scientific revolutions, we could say that therapeutic failures in general are perceived as an internal difficulty of the theory, and they do not endanger the *psychoanalytic paradigm*; the impasse, on the other hand, constitutes a real *anomaly* and is equivalent to a threat of crisis. The internal difficulties Kuhn says, do not alter normal science, whose fundamental task is the resolution of enigmas. But anomalies lead to crisis, which compels reconstruction of the discipline on the basis of a new paradigm. As can be seen in what follows, the phenomenon of impasse has repeatedly had this effect. It is worth emphasizing that Giovacchini and Bryce Boyer, 1975, p. 161, lucidly link—albeit in another context—the impasse to an existential crisis of the analyst, to an attack on his values.)

The analysts who questioned Freud in the 1930s and created neopsychoanalysis did so because the dead end of their practice led them to seek out other theories. It is enough to re-read Karen Horney's *New Ways in Psychoanalysis* (1939) to see that this is the case. *Daseinanalyse*, which Binswanger initiated soon afterwards, would proclaim on the same basis that a revision was required of Freud's theoretical suppositions and those of his followers inasmuch as they operate against the immediate perception of the patient as existent [*Dasein*]. The contradictions and shortcomings of the culturalists of existential analysis are well known; but this does not detract from the fact that the repeated confirmation that a treatment does not progress and is stalled leads to new paths.

The same types of difficulties had contributed ten years earlier to Freud radically modifying his theories. The concept of *repetition*, which was imposed in 1914 and led him six years later to postulate the death instinct, is surely rooted in the clinical difficulty of making certain patients progress. The analysis of the "Wolf Man" had reached its impasse in 1913, and we already know the drastic way (surely not exempt from a strong countertransference tonality) in which Freud resolved it (or thought he had resolved it).

Reading the Freud of the 1920s—a Freud who enunciates the structural theory—from this point of view, one has no difficulty in following the thread that goes from the repetition compulsion to the death instinct and the (cruel) superego in *The Ego and the Id* (1923b, chapter 5). There Freud describes in a masterly way the negative therapeutic reaction, whose relationship to the impasse is so evident that they are sometimes considered synonymous.

It is also a frank recognition that the analysis practised towards the end of the 1920s often led to stagnation, which impelled Wilhelm Reich's investigations, culminating in 1933 in his enduring *Character Analysis*, and others concerned with this problem (and with narcissism), such as Herbert Rosenfeld (1971, 1987), have studied this problem more recently. Reich gives us a clear and concrete vision of the impasse in the noisiest of its expressions when he describes the *chaotic situation* in chapter 3, "On the Technique of Interpretation and the Analysis of Resistance". His method of attack on the characteromuscular armour through vigorous and systematic analysis of the transference resistance was basically an effort to prevent the impasse. (Reich maintained that the chaotic situation was always a consequence of a technical error: the neglect of the characterological defences [economic point of view]. Despite this extreme assertion—which Fenichel, 1935, 1941, rightly refuted, affirming that there are spontaneous chaotic situations, that is, attributable mainly to the patient himself—Reich's concept of narcissistic defence opened up the path of investigation.) No one doubts that narcissism is a necessary factor in the impasse; but in my opinion what really matters is to unravel the defensive and offensive strategies the ego uses (and in particular the narcissistic ego as described by Rosenfeld, 1971), which lead to the impasse. Therefore in this work the relationship between impasse and narcissism is not considered (it is repeatedly referred to in the bibliography), although it always exists, because it is not specific enough. The subject was dealt with by the participants in a discussion on "Narcissistic Resistance" of the *American Psychoanalytic Association* in 1968, especially by Edith Jacobson and Paul Sloane (Segel, 1969).

Lately, however, Maldonado (1983) has proposed a more specific relationship between impasse and narcissism, maintaining that the impasse responds to the patient's concrete fantasy: Armoured in his narcissism, he literally does not give the analyst anything. The *sine qua non* condition for communication is for the other to exist, and narcissism radically ignores this. Therefore, for Maldonado, the typical material of the impasse does not communicate anything; it has no symbolic value; it is not significant. The correlate of this psychopathological situation is that the patient's material during the impasse is characterized by a marked diminution or absence of representations that form visual images.

The subject offers many difficulties, not just because the study of the impasse leads us immediately to the basic review of our science. By its very nature, the impasse is very similar to, and is even confused with, the natural course of analysis.

It is significant that the idea of the impasse appears implicitly in Freud in 1914, when he introduces the concept of working-through. He says then, specifically, that the newly qualified analyst, by not taking this process (working-through) into account, can think that the treatment is failing and stalling. Having made an adequate interpretation, he observes that there is no immediate change in a particular configuration of resistance (see "Remembering, Repeating and Working-Through", 1914g). In my opinion, impasse is precisely *the opposite of working-through*: when the latter process is arrested, the impasse appears. Mostardeiro et al., coincidentally, say (1974, p. 18) that the concept of impasse should apply to the way the analytic *process* develops, not to the cure or the removal of symptoms. (It is advisable to clarify here, following an observation by Benito López, that I use the concept of working-through in the sense it has in "Remembering, Repeating and Working-Through", 1914g—that is, as a process that modifies resistance in general, and not the resistance of the id, which, in *Inhibitions, Symptoms and Anxiety*, 1926d, is linked to the biological stereotypes and to the death instinct. I follow, then, the suggestion made by Sandler et al., 1973, when they propose to keep the term "working-through, as an essentially clinical and descriptive term, without ascribing to it a special dynamic explanation. The broad meaning of the term was maintained by Fenichel at the Marienbad Symposium of 1936—and later in 1941 and 1945a—in opposition to Bibring's viewpoint [modifications of the id] and above all to that of Nunberg, 1937. Meltzer, 1967, chapter 8, in discussing the concept of working-through, operates at the same time with the two conceptions, trying to integrate them; for more details, see chapter 50.)

If what I have just explained is true, then a serious obstacle for the satisfactory understanding of the impasse is immediately noticed. In considering that the psychoanalytic cure relies on working-through, we see how much the impasse is intrinsically linked to it. When are we going to decide that the incessant return of the same problems can no longer be considered working-through, but constitutes an impasse? This decision belongs entirely to the analyst, and we never know whether he takes it objectively or under the influence of the countertransference engagement, which always exists in these cases. Would Freud decide today that the "Wolf Man" is in an impasse? The experience we now have would surely have made him more cautious and persevering, because three (or four) years of analysis are insufficient to resolve a neurosis as serious as the one that led to a psychotic crisis in 1926, and to his re-analysis with Ruth Mack Brunswick between October 1926 and February 1927, an analysis that he had to take up again years later (Mack Brunswick, 1928a). (And even before this, in 1919–20, the patient had had a second analysis with Freud of four months' duration.)

* * *

To sum up: the methodological (and/or) technical difficulties of psychoanalysis, the complex (or confused) relationship of the impasse to the process of working-through and the countertransference engagement, make us doubt when we formulate the diagnosis of the impasse.

From Racker's studies (1960) it is clear that the countertransference neurosis (and particularly what he calls countertransference positions) is a factor of prime importance in the establishment of the impasse. The same consequences can be derived from the works of Paula Heimann (1950, 1960) and from the copious current bibliography on countertransference. Betty Joseph in her valuable work on fetishism (1971), and Herbert Rosenfeld in his lectures at the Argentine Psychoanalytic Association (1975b) and, of course, in his posthumous book (1987), emphasize the subtle interaction between analyst and patient in the impasse, especially through the erotization of the transference link, a point to which I will return later.

The diagnostic problem becomes even more complex because we cannot rely on the patient's opinions. More than once, the one who suffers the impasse does not mention it, and he will deny it resolutely if we mention it. A very intelligent analysand, for example, in a rebellious period of impasse at the end of a long and fruitful analysis, received my interpretations by saying that this time I had indeed managed to reach the heart of the matter, that I had completely disarmed him, that I had finally hit home. Now there really would be the possibility of analysing such-and-such!— and so on, indefinitely. He raised the banner of progress to deny stagnation. The analysand's opinion in the opposite case is not reliable either, since it is common for him to deny any real progress, saying he is still the same, that he is stuck (or worse).

In other words, before raising the possibility of an impasse, the analyst should see it appear not only in his mind (countertransference) and in that of the patient (transference), but also in the material.

However, the diagnosis is not impossible and even becomes clear if attention is paid to the patient's material, to the general course of the process and even to the analysand's views about what is happening. The dream of Meltzer's (1973) patient, lying lazily on the bed at a summer hotel when the time for departure had already passed, is, for example, a convincing indicator that the process is stalled (or at least that the patient thinks so). Meltzer points out another important clinical indicator: a type of denial referred to by Freud: "I cannot avoid it, and it is not my fault; and anyway, what is wrong with it?" Willy and Madeleine Baranger (1961–62; 1964, p. 171) rightly point out that the *bulwark* described by them (and which explains many cases of impasse) is almost always accompanied by the complaint of going round and round in circles, as on a merry-go-round (see, for example, Maldonado's, 1975, convincing example about the merry-go-round, p. 124). Certainly there are frequent dreams or allusions to cars that are stalled, vehicles that do not run, watches that are broken, and so forth. No one can describe the impasse better than

Maldonado's (1983) patient, who saw himself as a hamster who turned the wheel of his cage with great velocity but always in the same place.

In all these cases, however, adequate interpretation of what is—or, better still, of what is *not*—happening can change the picture. The impasse is then resolved, as is any other difficulty, and it ceases to be one. The fact that things cannot usually be resolved so easily, and that we therefore speak of an impasse precisely when something is not immediately resolved, does not clear up what is unreliable in the diagnosis. The temporal factor, the evidence that identical phases repeat themselves, without any confidence that time may change them (working-through), is what, in my opinion, best reveals the impasse. I have repeatedly seen that in the course of a particular temporal cycle (a session, a week, even a year) a problem is convincingly resolved through interpretation, only to arise again intact at the end of the period, and this permits a fairly certain diagnosis, even a presumptive one, of impasse.

In his original but controversial work, "A Technique of Interruption of the Analytic Impasse" (1977), Meltzer demands that the impasse be present for a year before his technique becomes applicable. This is undoubtedly a very prudent estimate, but it is nevertheless arbitrary. He adds that another year will elapse before the patient accepts his proposal, without ever agreeing that the technique of interruption was adequate.

All roads lead to Rome, and all the eventualities of our technique can lead to the dead end of the impasse; but three deserve emphasis: acting out (Freud, 1905e, 1914g), the negative therapeutic reaction (Freud, 1923b, 1924c, 1937c) and the reversible perspective (Bion, 1963). Very different in their clinical phenomenology and in their psychodynamics, the three are members of the same class, which is evident if we take them as *technical* and not psychopathological concepts. This distinction matters, because the link between the technical and the psychopathological is not univocal—although, for example, psychopathy is sometimes confused with acting out and serious characteropathy with the negative therapeutic reaction.

This difference enables us to notice that, although the three processes mentioned form defensive modalities and belong therefore in the broad category of defence mechanisms, they should be assigned to another category, a different and higher entity. Defence mechanisms are *techniques of the ego*, while acting out, the negative therapeutic reaction and the reversible perspective, due to their complex nature in which various offensive and defensive modalities coexist, form instead tactics or *strategies* of the ego. They are more global, specific and highly complicated forms of behaviour of the patient during treatment—strategies to attack and impede the development of the cure and not simply to protect himself. When they achieve this, they produce the impasse.

What most distinguishes the three strategies we are considering, what differentiates them from each other, is their place of influence in the psychoanalytic process, although differences can also be established according to the type of transference conflict that gives rise to them and the countertransference responses they provoke; or according to the type of thought disturbance that feeds them and the form of adaptation they follow; or, finally, according to the clinical picture they most frequently form part of.

Acting out acts fundamentally on the *task*. If we begin with Freud's 1914 concepts, we could say that transference is a special form of remembering, whereas acting out arises so as not to remember, and this permits its definition as *anti-task* except that currently we replace the word "remember" with "communicate" (Greenacre, 1950; Liberman, 1970–72, Vol. 2, p. 537: the patient with an epic style), or *thinking* (Bion, 1962a, 1962b; Money-Kyrle, 1968). Equally, it can be said that acting out attacks the analytic setting, as Zac (1968, 1970) prefers, because the setting is established precisely in order to carry out the task.

Its influence on the (analytic) work and a special type of thought disturbance are the coordinates that permit recognition of a particular type of behaviour as acting out. These two factors are intrinsically related, as we saw in chapter 54. The lack of the breast, according to Bion, sets in motion the process of thought, in that it determines that frustration (lack, absence) is either tolerated and modified or negated and evaded. For the absent breast to be transformed into thought, the baby has to carry out a painful task: to *think* instead of feeling that there is a bad breast that must be evacuated. This basic situation, this *proto-task*, is the one that is in play in all acting out. Therefore acting out is always linked to separation anxiety (Grinberg, Zac) and to conflicts of dependence, which has constant repercussions of alarm or disquiet in the countertransference. Liberman (1970–72, Vol. 2) says that this is the type of patient we think about after the session.

In the negative therapeutic reaction, on the other hand, the point of action of ego strategy does not touch on the task but on the *achievements*. The negative therapeutic reaction, as its name indicates, only supervenes when something positive has been carried out, and the ego defence is directed precisely against this achievement of analysis. As Freud indicates in his inaugural work of 1923 and Melanie Klein in *Envy and Gratitude* (1957), the negative therapeutic reaction supervenes after a moment of relief and progress, a moment of insight in which the patient understands and values the work of the analyst. A contradictory and paradoxical response then unfolds, which was pointed out earlier in the valuable works of Karen Horney (1936) and Joan Riviere (1936a), and which Melanie Klein linked twenty years later to the envy of primal objects. The paradoxical attitude is always evident in these patients. One of them always remembered with admiration Groucho Marx's famous anecdote: he resigned from a club, saying that he was not going to belong to a club that was willing to accept him as a member. When I interpreted to this patient that he did not want to get cured in order to see me fail as an analyst, he rightly answered that I had to cure him precisely of that desire not to be cured so as to see me fail; and he added triumphantly that if I were to achieve this, then my interpretation would be demonstrably wrong. The paradox leads here to a dead end.

The adaptation of acting out is typically alloplastic, in Ferenczi's (1913) sense, while in the negative therapeutic reaction (and, of course, in the reversible perspective) the adaptive process arises in thought and in character structure. It is auto-plastic, with ideational rumination in the first case; with rigidity and a special type of dissociation in the second case— the *static splitting* described by Bion (1963). This also explains why acting out is typical of psychopathy, although not exclusive to it, while the negative therapeutic reaction germinates in the serious characteropathies, which Abraham studied with admirable lucidity in 1919. Joan Riviere's investigation is based on this work when she asserts that it is in serious characteropathies where (manic) defences operate with greater energy against the depressive position, which is particularly intense in patients who exhibit the negative therapeutic reaction.

Just as acting out constantly provokes alarm and surprise in the analyst, so the negative therapeutic reaction infiltrates a peculiar feeling of boredom, deception and fatalism, which Cesio (1960) defined as lethargy. Although chronic acting out can lead to a dead end, where many things happen without anything really happening, it more often leads to a sudden and surprising interruption; on the other hand, patients with the negative therapeutic reaction, because of its persevering and adhesive nature, are more vulnerable to the impasse (a reason why these two conditions are confused).

The reversible perspective described by Bion (1963) consists in a manifest accord and a latent and radical disagreement, according to which the patient sees everything that passes in the analytic process from a different perspective, based on other premises. He is in analysis not in order to understand his problems, but so as to demonstrate, to himself and to the analyst, some other thing—for example, that he is more intelligent, has more insight, has a greater capacity for love. This attitude is, in my opinion, a fundamental influence on the *contract*. The patient makes a type of parallel and hidden contract to which all his experiences during analysis will refer, from which all the analyst's interpretations will be reinterpreted and to which they will be accommodated.

In extreme cases, Bion says, the reversible perspective occurs in latent and borderline psychotics; but it is also possible to discover it in less serious cases, where it then adopts a less extreme modality, and the rigidity of thought (proper to these personalities) is not so absolute.

A colleague who was in treatment with me for several years came not for treatment of his asthma and neurosis, but for me to enable him, by moderating his anxiety, to carry out a homeopathic treatment, which would be the really curative one. The inconvenience of this infallible treatment, which he himself applied as a homeopath to many asthmatics, was that it sometimes mobilized excessive, intolerable anxiety. The function of analysis was to contain that anxiety. Obviously this singular therapeutic contract was discovered after a long and arduous analytic process, and it had little or nothing to do with what we had agreed at first, despite some ambiguous proposals the patient offered with a skill he was not conscious of. Clearly by him all my interpretations were seen as an *attack* or (rarely) as a *support* for the homeopathic treatment. It was clear that, from his point of view, the psychoanalytic treatment was proof of my rivalry, if not of my envy and arrogance. Each time the analysis progressed, the idea of the homeopathic treatment reappeared. At times his insistence on administering it to himself bordered on infantile caprice, at others on dishonesty. Thus when after the third winter of analysis spring came and he had none of his usual asthmatic crises, he secretly began to take the homeopathic medicine he regarded as indicated in his case so as to attribute his improvement to it. (See the details of this case in section 57.6.)

After this brief exposition of the principal characteristics of acting out, the negative therapeutic reaction and the reversible perspective as causes of the impasse, we can offer some provisional conclusions. (It will not escape the reader's attention that I do not in any way view acting out, the negative therapeutic reaction and the reversible perspective as defining features of the impasse. These characteristics were indicated at the outset. Our thesis should be interpreted as maintaining that the three phenomena are concomitant notes, necessarily related as causal agents to the impasse, which would be the effect of one of these causes or eventually of others. On the distinction between essential and concomitant features, see Hospers, 1953.)

I think the situation of impasse can occur at any moment in analysis, and this is probably the opinion of W. and M. Baranger (1961–62, 1964), whose studies on the bulwark are an original contribution to the subject. (I think the *bulwark* can be reduced, always, to one of the three phenomena mentioned, especially acting out via erotization of the transference link. The same conclusion applies to bad faith—M. Baranger, 1959—which Maldonado emphasizes in his 1975 study. According to Maldonado, bad faith operates as verbal acting out in his patient. I am inclined to think, however, that in this illustrative clinical case verbal acting out is used to maintain—in "bad faith"—a reversal of perspective.) It is improbable, however, that the impasse appears at the outset, other than in the most energetic cases of reversible perspective, when the analysand arrives with an unconscious, rigid, parallel contract, which is to be applied without concessions. If so, then a certain time will necessarily elapse before its discovery. As we have already said, at the beginning of analysis incoercible resistance is usually observed, not the impasse. Sometimes the clinical situation is complex, as in Herbert Rosenfeld's (1975a) case: analysis begins with an incoercible resistance (for whose production, according to him, certain technical errors were also responsible) and, after a very difficult and rough course, a situation of impasse occurs, which the analyst resolves with mastery.

Meltzer (1967) maintains, on the other hand, that the impasse super-venes at the threshold of the depressive position, when the patient has to take charge of his moral pain, his guilt and his badness. Following the line of least resistance, he prefers to use the analyst indefinitely as a toilet breast while he maintains the nourishing breast dissociated in an external object, thanks to acting out—or, less frequently, in my opinion—reinforc-ing the negative therapeutic reaction with the closed system of manic de-fences Joan Riviere described in her memorable paper. It must be borne in mind that at this juncture of analysis the patient, already free from symp-toms and inhibitions and with a good social and sexual adaptation, is probably feeling cured; and from the psychiatric point of view, he is. However, he continues to be very egocentric and he is preoccupied more by his personal well-being than by his objects. His feelings of gratitude for the analyst (as what he is and what he represents) continue to be skin-deep and conventional, while his guilt is more proclaimed than felt. This is a crucial moment, which confronts him with a real option, and it is not surprising that he employs an existential trick to elude the full weight of his responsibilities. The pressure to arrive at a *happy ending* of mutual idealization with the analyst through subtle forms of acting out within (erotization) or outside the transference (progress) is always very strong, and no analyst is immune to this subtle and persistent call.

The massive and uncontrolled acting out of the first stages of analysis generally leads to interruption, not to impasse. Acting out leads to the impasse only when it is insidiously mobilized against depressive anxieties and becomes less violent but more pertinacious and astute. Many analyses end with an acting out of this type. At times acting out is so egosyntonic and so acceptable socially that it convinces the analyst. A countertransfer-ence conflict always participates here, as Zac suggests (personal communi-cation), because the analyst also wishes to see his patient well and to spare himself the painful effort of concluding the treatment. Thus, the impasse leads finally to marriage or divorce, a change of job, the constitution or the break-up of a commercial institution, and so on. If the analysand is a can-didate, then the acting out consists in his becoming a member of the asso-ciation, with the approval of the analyst. (In this way a normative requirement—the termination of a training analysis—is confused with the substantive termination of an analysis. There are, unfortunately, many of these cases, and no one can be sure of avoiding them.)

The impasse resulting from the negative therapeutic reaction can be installed halfway through analysis, when the zonal or geographical confu-sions are resolved (Meltzer, 1967), but it is manifested more usually when the depressive anxieties become acute. At this moment the manic defences are more energetic, and the early envy of the feeding breast is reactivated. However, I think—as does Herbert Rosenfeld (1975a)—that the negative therapeutic reaction has to do not only with the manic defences, as Joan Riviere maintained, but also with manic attacks (or offences). It can then provoke the impasse. The same can be deduced from the Barangers' studies, since the bulwark often constitutes a perverse activity that is jealously guarded by the analysand and, as such, is closely linked to persecutory anxieties. In these cases one frequently finds that analysis is transformed into the fetish of the pervert or the drug of the addict.

On the other hand, there is no doubt that the impasse of the reversible perspective, due to its nature and characteristics, is *d'emblée*, although much time can elapse before it is detected. It is worth remembering here Bion's (1963) precise words when he says that the accord is manifest while the discord is latent, hidden and ignored, despite being radical.

60.2   Discussion and commentary

A psychoanalytic treatment can fail for many reasons, and the impasse is only one of them; but it is so singular that it merits preferential attention. Stealthy and silent, the difficulty of detecting and resolving it is intrinsic in its nature, as is studying it and reflecting on it. It is perhaps the worst risk in our hazardous occupation and the most certain threat to our instrument of work. Just one of these cases is sufficient to shake our scientific ideology, because impasse is not simply an internal difficulty of the theory but a real anomaly, which brings into question the psychoanalytic paradigm and threatens with a crisis. And in general it does not present itself to the newly trained analyst but to one who already has sufficient experience to remove more visible obstacles.

This chapter proposes to locate the impasse in the context of the psychoanalytic process, tries to define it, indicates its particulars and seeks its causes. My reflections arose in principle from a double experience—the teaching of technique and the task of the consulting-room. Both converge in an essential event, where the psychoanalytic process appears as a permanent effort towards insight (and working-through), with defined and specific obstacles, which can be systematized and understood only as ego strategies.

As for its conceptual location, the impasse belongs to the field of technique, not to that of psychopathology. A point of convergence for the most diverse circumstances, it always presents itself as a complex and multidetermined phenomenon; it should be distinguished from incoercible resistance and technical error, which are always simpler in structure and noisier in their presentation. Keeping in mind that among the three there are forms of circulation in which the distinctive features are superimposed, and even taking account of evolutionary modalities that undeniably bring them closer together, the impasse has a high profile precisely because it never reveals it; it is never evident. It does not select the guilty party either, since it reaches both analyst and patient. Both perceive it thus; both feel it and even recognize it. Since the countertransference is always deeply and subtly involved, it is not worth distinguishing an impasse of the analyst from an impasse of the patient: it belongs to both.

Narcissism, the early crises of development, traumatic situations and the severe deprivations of the early years are predisposing factors. But no psychopathological situation is sufficient in itself for the impasse to appear. When the impasse is constituted, we are no longer in the field of psychopathology, but in that of practice, of technique.

I think I do not deviate from the general use of this term if I define it in an elucidative manner through the following essential features: the impasse is a technical concept; it constitutes an insidious arrest of the psychoanalytic process; it tends to perpetuate itself; the setting is preserved in its constant fundamentals; its existence is not evident; it is rooted in the patient's psychopathology and involves the analyst's countertransference.

* * *

Due to its nature, the impasse resembles and is confused with the natural course of analysis. Therefore I consider it *the opposite of working-through*, and I underline this idea as the epicentre of my reflections. When working-through is arrested, the impasse appears. The diagnosis is thus difficult, because the dividing line is blurred (between working-through and impasse), and because it is traced in principle by an analyst who is involved in the process itself. To arrive at a diagnosis, then, the analyst should attend to the indications that come from both the transference and the countertransference; but it can find support only when he sees the impasse appear objectively and repeatedly in the analysand's material, which implies that the diagnosis will be made more frequently by examining the material of the sessions than in the sessions themselves.

The *ego strategies* can assume different forms, but in the current state of psychoanalytic investigation they can be said to comprise three fundamentals: acting out, the negative therapeutic reaction and the reversible perspective. The three can function jointly or alternatively and, in my opinion, the three trace arcs of different diameters. That is, acting out can operate in the service of the negative therapeutic reaction, and the latter can be a modality of the reversible perspective, but not vice versa, which follows from the area each one operates in. Acting out acts on the *psychoanalytic task*, the negative therapeutic reaction on its *achievements* and the reversible perspective silently calls into question the *contract*, the basic agreement between analyst and patient.

* * *

Although the three processes mentioned form defensive modalities and are therefore part of the defence mechanisms, another category—a different and higher entity—should be assigned to them because of their complex nature where diverse defensive and offensive manoeuvres are in play. More global, they are specific and highly complicated forms the patient uses during treatment—*strategies* to attack and impede the development of the cure and not simple techniques to protect himself. I also think they belong to the psychotic part of the personality, as Dario Sor suggested to me a long time ago.

The strategies of the ego maintain an obvious relation with certain nosological pictures: acting out with psychopathy; negative therapeutic reaction with the serious characteropathies; the reversible perspective with the borderline personality—but in this work they are studied independently of psychopathology, since the relation is not univocal.

In studying the impasse as to its moment of appearance and according to the strategies mentioned, the clinical experience induces me to think that it can appear at any moment of the analytic process, although it is possible to establish some specifications.

Perhaps the most frequent—and the most difficult—impasse to solve is the one Meltzer describes at the threshold of the depressive position, when the patient has to take charge of his moral pain, his guilt and his badness. Following the line of least resistance, he prefers to use the analyst indefinitely as a toilet–breast, while he maintains a dissociation of the feeding breast in an external object, due to acting out or the negative therapeutic reaction. At this moment an erotization of the transference–countertransference link frequently occurs.

The impasse by negative therapeutic reaction may occur around the halfway-point in the analysis, when paranoid anxieties still predominate, but it is more probable that this happens when depressive anxieties, and with them primal envy, are growing. Unlike other Kleinian analysts, I believe that envy operates throughout the development of the personality (and of the psychoanalytical process), and does not belong exclusively to the paranoid–schizoid stage.

The impasse of the reversible perspective, due to its nature and characteristics, is *d'emblée*, although much time can elapse before it is discovered, especially if the patient's secret contract manages to establish a false therapeutic alliance with the unwary analyst.

* * *

To sum up: the impasse is a technical concept (not a psychopathological one), which consists in an insidious arrest of the psychoanalytic process; it tends to perpetuate itself; the setting is preserved; it is rooted in the patient's psychopathology, and it involves the analyst. Different from other forms of failure of the psychoanalytic treatment, such as (the analysand's) incoercible resistance or (the analyst's) technical error, the impasse belongs to both, because the countertransference is always involved. Stealthy and silent, the difficulty of detecting and resolving it is intrinsic to its nature, as are studying and reflecting on it. It is a real anomaly that shakes our scientific ideology. Due to its nature, the impasse resembles and is confused with the natural course of analysis, because it is *the reverse of working-through*: when working-through ceases, the impasse is established.

The psychoanalytic process should be understood as a permanent effort towards insight, with defined and specific obstacles I propose to call *ego strategies.* The ego strategies can assume different forms, but currently they can be said to comprise three: acting out, the NTR and the reversible perspective, which act on the task, the achievements and the contract, respectively. These ego strategies, although they form part of the defence mechanisms, are more complex and global because they include defensive and offensive modalities. They are the forms the patient deals with in treatment—strategies to attack and impede the development of the cure, which, if achieved, leads to the impasse.

* * *

Experience acquired during the past 15 years has shown me conclusively that it is as dangerous not to diagnose the impasse as to see it where it does not exist. Many young, intelligent and meticulous analysts consult me about cases in which the impasse is simply the slow arduous process of working-through, a natural attribute of difficult cases. On the other hand, we must not lose sight of the fact that the impasse is a difficulty like so many others of our day-to-day work; we must tackle it with the instruments we always use, without abandoning the method nor losing patience.

Epilogue

I said in the introduction that it is very difficult to write a book on psycho-analytic technique, but I put all my efforts into the enterprise so as not to make the reader's task difficult. I also tried to be lively, but unfortunately the colloquial tone of the original untidy notes from the seminars, which I dictated throughout the years, was gradually lost, while the quantity of bibliographical data and of the direct excerpts from the authors being dis-cussed increased heavily. This had to be an even stricter procedure where I was in dissent—I recall what José Gabriel, one of my great teachers at the Colegio Nacional, said: one can praise something one has not read; but when one wishes to criticize, one must read attentively. What most bothers me in my few readings and many re-readings of psychoanalytic texts is when words that an author has never said are put into his mouth so that he can then be refuted. With Freud, on the other hand, one searches for what he said that appears to confirm what we are saying. Obscurity also bothers me, but less so, since it is a lack of courtesy to-wards the reader; I think, however, that clarity is not always attained, and in any case the creator can be led to write what he can express, however he can express it. Given that I am not among the creators, I easily avoided that inclination, always or almost always, to the point where I prefer not to include something I cannot understand or cannot render correctly. I prefer Lope de Vega to Góngora. I am not trying to state the obvious, that every-one must be clear; I simply describe my style and the type of superego it adjusts to.

I like neither polemics nor eclecticism—the former, because passion generally makes it lose its way; the latter, because if we assume that our

choice will always be right, we commit, by implication, the sin of omniscience. I try to maintain an attitude of respect towards others, and I think I
sometimes achieve it—"*pero yo canto opinando / que es mi modo de cantar*"
["but I give voice to my opinion / which is my way of singing"]—as
Martin Fierro does. I try to explain the theories faithfully—that is, in good
faith. When I discuss them, I do so first within their own frame of reference before comparing them with others, which is legitimate only as a
subsequent reflection.

I noticed in teaching, and also while writing, that if the technique is
studied deeply and seriously, sooner or later one arrives at the theory;
hence the title of this work, where—more than the rule or norm—the object of study is the basis for it—its reason for being. The complexity of the
analytic situation is such that fixed rules are few. In analytic practice the
only valid prescription in the face of a given situation is to combine and
contrast all the available elements of judgement and then choose a path
that seems suitable to us, knowing that each moment is unrepeatable and
incomparable. Certainly there can be no practice that is not founded on
theory, and no psychoanalyst doubts that there is a path that comes and
goes between theory and practice, and that the one renourishes, enriches
and purifies the other. But I also have the vivid impression—although I
may be mistaken—that if we start from the practice, we can approach the
theoretical problems better than if we just study and compare the theories.
Hence this book arrives at the theory always along that path, without
deliberate intent.

Something I learned throughout the years, perhaps more in re-reading
than in reading, is how difficult it is to recognize the limitations of the
theories one defends and maintains, to see where their Achilles' heel is—
and it is always there. We all have a strong tendency to deny the faults of
our theories and, at the same time, a type of greed in not abandoning
whatever we like about those theories that are not our own; this is, perhaps, the bedrock of eclecticism. No author, Freud included, is free of that
fault, and the only thing we can do is to notice it and be very conscious of
it so that it does not dominate us. I realize that here, with what I am
saying, I come very close to Kuhn, except that I add to the very evident
pressure of the scientific community on each person—which the great
epistemologist from Berkeley outlined so well—the psychological dispositions. It is absolutely necessary to pay the price of uncertainty and of
incompleteness entailed in the theories we defend, because otherwise we
leave science and begin to operate with infallible theories.

Together with the above, there is a difficulty specific to investigation in
our discipline, and it is that sometimes the needs of the psychoanalytic
movement are confused with the bare requirements of truth. I am not going
to make the simple claim that psychoanalytic science should have no
policy, because everything, everyone has one—but it is advisable to distinguish between these two areas. If we confuse them, we are immediately

exposed to obscurantism and dogma. As for the rest, if we really thought that our theories are better given that we have a reason for our supporting them, then we would not have to try to impose them. It would be enough for us to discuss them and, in the best of cases, to defend them, thinking that in the long run they will outlast the others. And if this is not the case, then let the truth always be welcome, whatever its origin.

One of the methodological proposals of this work has been to separate technique from psychopathology. Both are, in fact, superimposed on each other in clinical practice; but when this also occurs in the mind of the scholar, as often happens, sterile confusions result. The clinical phenomenon is certainly unitary (and complex!), but the areas of study should be clearly defined.

In addition, I am convinced—and I have attempted to indicate it repeatedly—that many discussions come from semantic not to say spurious motives, among which I have already mentioned the needs of the psychoanalytic movement and the impassioned defence of particular theories or authors, the lack of precision with which we use words, and the frequency with which we forget that psychic acts are overdetermined. There is another, very important factor: the tendency to take discussions out of their context. I will not say that if we do not follow a historical trail we are at fault or that this path is unavoidable, but I will say that some dissent can be overcome if we view problems from a historical perspective. And further, when we do so, we realize that what we see as originality is sometimes only forgetfulness of what has already been written. "What can I plagiarize in order to be original?" Arturo Marasso used to ask in his unforgettable classes of introduction to literature. This is why this work studies many themes on the basis of their chronological development, in order to insert them into their rightful context; for others, on the other hand, this approach is not practical.

The most persistent purpose of this work has been, I think, in conclusion, to draw a clear distinction between psychoanalysis and any hidden or overt way of psychotherapy, through a model that respects the internal life of the analysand and abstains rigorously from suggestion and direct action, however beneficial it may appear to us.

REFERENCES

Abadi, M. (1960). Complejo de Edipo. Replanteo de su estructura originaria. Proto-anhelo y protoculpa del nacimiento impedido. *Revista de Psicoanálisis*, 17: 165–189.

Aberastury, A. (1950). Fobia a los globos en una niña de 11 meses. *Revista de Psicoanálisis*, 7: 541–554.

Aberastury, A. (1958). La dentición, la marcha y el lenguaje en relación con la posición depresiva. *Revista de Psicoanálisis*, 15: 41–48.

Abraham, K. (1908a). The psycho-sexual differences between hysteria and dementia praecox. In: *Selected Papers* (Chap. 2), 1973.

Abraham, K. (1908b). The psychological relations between sexuality and alcoholism. In: *Selected Papers* (Chap. 3), 1973.

Abraham, K. (1910). Remarks on the psycho-analysis of a case of foot and corset fetishism. In: *Selected Papers* (Chap. 5), 1973.

Abraham, K. (1919a). A particular form of neurotic resistance against the psycho-analytic method. In: *Selected Papers* (Chap. 15), 1973.

Abraham, K. (1919b). The applicability of psycho-analytic treatment to patients at an advanced age. In: *Selected Papers* (Chap. 16), 1973.

Abraham, K. (1919c). Some remarks on Ferenczi's papers on "Sunday neurosis". In: *Clinical Papers and Essays on Psycho-Analysis* (Chap. 12). London: Hogarth, 1955. [Reprinted London: Karnac Books, 1979.]

Abraham, K. (1920). The narcissistic evaluation of excretory processes in dreams and neurosis. In: *Selected Papers* (Chap. 17), 1973.

Abraham, K. (1924). A short study of the development of the libido, viewed in the light of mental disorders. In: *Selected Papers* (Chap. 26), 1973.

Abraham, K. (1925). Character-formation on the genital level of libido-development. In: *Selected Papers* (Chap. 25), 1973.

Abraham, K. (1973). *Selected Papers on Psychoanalysis*. London: Hogarth. [Reprinted London: Karnac Books, 1979.]

Abt, L. E., & Weissman, S. L. (Eds.) (1965). *Acting Out. Theoretical and Clinical Aspects*. New York: Grune & Stratton.

Adler, A. (1912). *The Neurotic Constitution*. New York: Dodd Mead, 1926.

Adler, A. (1918). *The Practice and Theory of Individual Psychology*. New York: Harcourt, Brace, 1929.

Ahumada, J. L. (1982). Sobre la vivencia inconciente del analista como "base". *Psicoanálisis, 6*: 585–605.

Ahumada, J. L. (1991). Logical types of ostensive insight. *International Journal of Psycho-Analysis, 72*: 683–691.

Ahumada, J. L. (1992). De l'ange déchu et du sujet: une critique des bases de la pensée de Jacques Lacan et de se technique [On the fallen angel and the subject: A critique of Jacques Lacan's starting points and technique]. *Revue française de Psychanalyse*.

Ahumada, J. L. (1994). What is a clinical fact? Clinical psychoanalysis as inductive method. *International Journal of Psycho-Analysis, 75*: 949.

Ahumada, J. L. (1997a). Counter-induction in psychoanalytic practice: epistemic and technical aspects. In: J. L. Ahumada et al. (Eds.), *The Perverse Transference and Other Matters: Essays in Honor of R. Horacio Etchegoyen* (pp. 181–202). Northvale, NJ: Jason Aronson.

Ahumada, J. L. (1997b). Disclosures and refutations. Clinical psychoanalysis as a logic of enquiry. *International Journal of Psycho-Analysis, 78*: 1105–1118.

Alexander, F. (1923). The castration complex in the formation of character. *International Journal of Psycho-Analysis, 4*: 11–42.

Alexander, F. (1925). A metapsychological description of the process of cure. *International Journal of Psycho-Analysis, 6*: 13–34.

Alexander, F. (1927). The neurotic character. *International Journal of Psycho-Analysis, 11* (1930): 292–311.

Alexander, F., & French, Th. (1946). *Psychoanalytic Therapy*. New York: Ronald Press.

Alvarez, B. (1974). Acerca de la interpretación como una proposición científica. *Revista de Psicoanálisis, 31*: 794–807.

Alvarez de Toledo, L. G. de (1954). El análisis del asociar, del interpretar y de las palabras. *Revista de Psicoanálisis, 11*: 267–313.

Annes, S. P., et al. (1974). *Estudios psicoanalíticos*. Porto Alegre: Private publication.

Anzieu, A. (1969). L'interpretation: son écoute et sa comprehension pour le patient. *Bulletin de l'Association Psychanalytique de France, 5* (April): 33–44.

Anzieu, A., & Anzieu, D. (1977). La interpretación en primera persona. In: L. Grinberg (Ed.), *Prácticas psicoanalíticas comparadas en las neurosis* (pp. 17–26). Buenos Aires: Paidós.

Anzieu, D. (1959). *L'auto-analyse de Freud et la découverte de la psychanalyse, Vols. 1–2*. Paris: Presses Universitaires de France, 1954–1975. [*Freud's Self-Analysis*. London: Hogarth, 1986.]

Anzieu, D. (1969). Dificulté d'une étude psychanalitique de l'interpretation. *Bulletin de l'Association Psychanalytique de France, 5* (April): 12–33.

Anzieu, D. (1970). Elements d'une théorie de l'interpretation. *Revue française de psychanalyse, 34*.

Anzieu, D. (1974). Le moi-peau. *Nouvelle Revue de Psychanalyse, 9*: 195–208. [Skin ego.

In: S. Lebovici & D. Widlocher, *Psychoanalysis in France* (Chap. 2). New York: International Universities Press, 1980.]

Anzieu, D. (1975). Le transfert paradoxal. *Nouvelle Revue de Psychanalyse, 12*: 49–73.

Arlow, J. A., & Brenner, Ch. (1964). The psychoanalytic situation. Discussed by A. Aberastury, F. R. Cesio, D. Liberman, J. M. Mom, & A. Rascovsky. In: R. E. Litman (Ed.), *Psychoanalysis in the Americas* (pp. 23–55). New York: International Universities Press, 1966.

Avenburg, R. (1969). La regresión en el proceso analítico en la obra de Freud. *Revista de Psicoanálisis, 26*: 669–677.

Avenburg, R. (1974). La interpretación. Comments by M. Abadi, H. Rosenfeld, & J. Zac. *Revista de Psicoanálisis, 31*: 541–566.

Avenburg, R. (1983). Desarrollo acerca de sus ideas sobre Psicoanálisis. Unpublished.

Avenburg, R., & Guiter, M. (1976). The concept of truth in psychoanalysis. *International Journal of Psycho-Analysis, 57*: 11–18.

Avenburg, R., et al. (1969). La regresión en el proceso psicoanalítico. VII Latin-American Psychoanalytic Congress, Bogota. *Actas*.

Balint, A., & Balint, M. (1939). On transference and counter-transference. *International Journal of Psycho-Analysis, 20*: 223–230. [Also in: *Primary Love and Psycho-Analytic Technique*. London: Hogarth. Reprinted London: Karnac Books, 1985.]

Balint, M. (1932). Charakteranalyse und Neubeginn. *Internationale Zeitschrift für Psychoanalyse, 20*, 1934.

Balint, M. (1934). The final goal of psycho-analytic treatment. *International Journal of Psycho-Analysis, 17* (1936): 206–216.

Balint, M. (1937). Early developmental states of the ego. Primary object love. *International Journal of Psycho-Analysis, 30* (1949): 265–273. [Original edition: *Imago, 23*: 270–288, 1937.]

Balint, M. (1949). On the termination of analysis. *International Journal of Psycho-Analysis, 31* (1950): 196–199.

Balint, M. (1952). New beginning and the paranoid and the depressive syndromes. *International Journal of Psycho-Analysis, 33*: 214–224.

Balint, M. (1954). Analytic training and training analysis. *International Journal of Psycho-Analysis, 35*: 157–168.

Balint, M. (1968). *The Basic Fault. Therapeutic Aspects of Regression*. London: Tavistock.

Baranger, M. (1959). Mala fe, identidad y omnipotencia. In: W. Baranger & M. Baranger, *Problemas del campo psicoanalítico* (Chap. 6), 1969.

Baranger, M., & Baranger, W. (1961–62). La situación analítica como campo dinámico. *Revista Uruguaya de Psicoanálisis, 4*: 3–54. [Also in: *Problemas del campo psicoanalítico* (Chap. 7), 1969.]

Baranger, M., & Baranger, W. (1964). Insight in the analytic situation. In: R. E. Litman (Ed.), *Psycho-Analysis in the Americas* (Part 2, Chap. 5). New York: International Universities Press, 1966.

Baranger, M., Baranger, W., & Mom, J. (1983). Process and non-process in analytic work. *International Journal of Psycho-Analysis, 64*: 1–15.

Baranger, W. (1976). El "Edipo temprano" y el "complejo de Edipo". *Revista de Psicoanálisis, 33*: 303–314.

Baranger, W., & Baranger, M. (1969). *Problemas del campo psicoanalítico*. Buenos Aires: Kargieman.

Barugel, N. (1984). El papel de la identificación con el objeto atacado en el desarrollo del yo. VI Simposio de la Asociación Psicoanalítica de Buenos Aires, 1984. *Actas*, 120–133.

Bateson, G. (1973). *Steps to an Ecology of Mind*. Hertfordshire: Paladin.

Baudouin, Ch. (1950). La reactivation du passé. *Revue française de Psychanalyse, 14*: 2–18.

Bellak, L. (1965). The concept of acting out: theoretical considerations. In: L. E. Abt & S. L. Weissman (Eds.), *Acting Out. Theoretical and Clinical Aspects* (Chap. 1). New York: Grune & Stratton.

Berenstein, I. (1972). Comentario al trabajo de David Liberman "Evaluación de las entrevistas diagnósticas previas a la iniciación de los tratamientos analíticos. Criterios diagnósticos y esquemas referenciales". *Revista de Psicoanálisis, 29*: 484–488.

Berenstein, I. (1976). *El complejo de Edipo. Estructura y significación*. Buenos Aires: Paidós.

Berenstein, I. (1984). La estructura de los gemelos. Una formación psíquica temprana. *Psicoanálisis, 6*: 243–259.

Beres, D. (1970). The concept of mental representation in psychoanalysis. *International Journal of Psycho-Analysis, 51* (1): 1–9.

Bergeret, J. (1972). Les états-limites et leurs aménagements. In: J. Bergeret, A. Achainre, A. Bécache, et al., *Psychologie pathologique*, 4th ed. (pp. 192–210). Paris: Masson, 1986.

Bergeret, J., et al. (1980). *La cure psychanalytique sur le divan*. Paris: Tchou.

Bermann, C. (1962). La psicoterapia en el ambiente sanatorial. In: G. Bermann (Ed.), *Las psicoterapias y el psicoterapeuta*. Buenos Aires: Paidós, 1964.

Bernfeld, S. (1932). Der Begriff der "Deutung" in der Psychoanalyse. *Zeitschrift für angewandte Psychologie, 42*: 448–497.

Bernfeld, S. (1941). The fact of observation in psychoanalysis. *Journal of Psychology, 12*: 289–305.

Bettelheim, B. (1972). Regression as progress. In: P. L. Giovacchini (Ed.), *Tactics and Techniques in Psychoanalytic Therapy* (Chap. 9). New York: Jason Aronson.

Bianchedi, E. T. de, & Sor, D. (1967). Revertir la perspectiva. *Revista de Psicoanálisis, 24*: 143–150.

Bibring, E. (1936). The development and problems of the theory of the instincts. *International Journal of Psycho-Analysis, 22* (1941): 102–131.

Bibring, E. (1937). Symposium of the theory of the therapeutic results of psychoanalysis. *International Journal of Psycho-Analysis, 18*: 170–189.

Bibring, E. (1954). Psychoanalytic and dynamic psychotherapies. *Journal of the American Psychoanalytic Association, 2*: 745–770.

Bick, E. (1968). The experience of the skin in early object-relations. *International Journal of Psycho-Analysis, 49*: 484–486.

Binswanger, L. (1922). *Einführung in die Probleme der Allgemeinen Psychologie*. Heidelberg: Springer Verlag.

Bion, W. R. (1950). The imaginary twin. In: *Second Thoughts* (Chap. 2), 1967b.

Bion, W. R. (1954). Notes on the theory of schizophrenia. *International Journal of Psycho-Analysis, 35*: 113–118. [Also in: *Second Thoughts* (Chap. 3), 1967b.]

Bion, W. R. (1956). Development of schizophrenic thought. *International Journal of Psycho-Analysis, 37*: 344–346. [Also in: *Second Thoughts* (Chap. 4), 1967b.]

Bion, W. R. (1957). Differentiation of the psychotic from the non-psychotic personalities. *International Journal of Psycho-Analysis, 38*: 266–275. [Also in: *Second Thoughts* (Chap. 5), 1967b.]

Bion, W. R. (1958). On arrogance. *International Journal of Psycho-Analysis, 39*: 144–146. [Also in: *Second Thoughts* (Chap. 7), 1967b.]

Bion, W. R. (1959). Attacks on linking. *International Journal of Psycho-Analysis, 40*: 308–315. [Also in: *Second Thoughts* (Chap. 8), 1967b.]

Bion, W. R. (1961). *Experiences in Groups and Other Papers*. London: Tavistock Publications.

Bion, W. R. (1962a). A theory of thinking. *International Journal of Psycho-Analysis, 43*: 306–310. [Also in: *Second Thoughts* (Chap. 9), 1967b.]

Bion, W. R. (1962b). *Learning from Experience*. London: Heinemann. [Reprinted London: Karnac Books, 1984.]

Bion, W. R. (1963). *Elements of Psycho-Analysis*. London: Heinemann. [Reprinted London: Karnac Books, 1984.]

Bion, W. R. (1965). *Transformations: Change from Learning to Growth*. London: Heinemann. [Reprinted London: Karnac Books, 1984.]

Bion, W. R. (1967a). Notes on memory and desire. *Psychoanalytic Forum, 2* (3). [Also in: *Cogitations* (extended edition). London: Karnac Books, 1994.]

Bion, W. R. (1967b). *Second Thoughts. Selected Papers on Psycho-Analysis*. London: Heinemann. [Reprinted London: Karnac Books, 1984.]

Bion, W. R. (1970). *Attention and Interpretation*. London: Tavistock [Reprinted London: Karnac Books, 1984.]

Bird, B. (1957). A specific peculiarity of acting out. *Journal of the American Psychoanalytic Association, 5*: 630–647.

Bleger, J. (1961). La simbiosis. *Revista de Psicoanálisis, 18*: 361–369.

Bleger, J. (1967a). Psicoanálisis del encuadre psicoanalítico. *Revista de Psicoanálisis, 24*: 241–258. [Also in: *Simbiosis y ambigüedad* (Chap. 6), 1967b.]

Bleger, J. (1967b). *Simbiosis y ambigüedad. Estudio psicoanalítico*. Buenos Aires: Paidós.

Bleger, J. (1971). La entrevista psicológica: su empleo en el diagnóstico y la investigación. In: *Temas de psicología. Entrevistas y grupos*. Buenos Aires: Nueva Visión.

Bleichmar, C. L. de (1989). El problema naturaleza–cultura en Psicoanálisis. In: N. M. Bleichmar & C. Leiberman de Bleichmar, *El Psicoanálisis despues de Freud* (pp. 507–525). Mexico: Eleia, 1989.

Bleichmar, N. M. (1988). Transference love: on the analysis of the Oedipus complex at the beginning and at the end of the treatment. *The Journal of the Melanie Klein Society, 6*: 83–107.

Bleichmar, N. M., & Bleichmar, C. L. de (1989). *El Psicoanálisis despues de Freud. Teoría y clinica* (with the collaboration of S. Wikinski). Mexico: Eleia.

Bleuler, E. (1911). *Dementia Praecoz., oder Gruppe der Schizophrenien*. In: G. Aschaffenburg, *Handbuch der Psychiatrie*. Leipzig/Vienna: Deuticke. [*Dementia Praecox, or the Group of Schizophrenics*. New York: International Universities Press, 1950.]

Blos, P. (1962). The concept of acting out in relation to the adolescent process. In: E. N. Rexford (Ed.), *A Developmental Approach to Problems of Acting Out* (pp. 153–182). New York: International Universities Press, 1978.

Blum, H. P. (1977). The prototype of preoedipal reconstruction. *Journal of the American Psychoanalytic Association, 25*: 757–785.

Blum, H. P. (1979). The curative and creative aspects of insight. *Journal of the American Psychoanalytic Association*, 27: 41. [Also in: *Psychoanalytic Explorations* (pp. 41–69), 1980a.]

Blum, H. P. (Ed.) (1980a). *Psychoanalytic Explorations of Technique. Discourse on the Theory of Therapy.* New York: International Universities Press.

Blum, H. P. (1980b). The value of reconstruction in adult psychoanalysis. *International Journal of Psycho-Analysis*, 61: 39–52.

Blum, H. P. (1983). The psychoanalytic process and analytic inference: a clinical study of a lie and loss. *International Journal of Psycho-Analysis*, 64: 17–33.

Boesky, D. (1982). Acting out: a reconsideration of the concept. *International Journal of Psycho-Analysis*, 63: 39–55.

Borges, J. L. (1944). Funes el Memorioso. In: *Obras Completas.* Buenos Aires: Emece, 1974.

Borges, J. L. (1949). El inmortal. In: *Obras Completas.* Buenos Aires: Emece, 1974.

Boss, M. (1957). *Psychoanalyse und Daseinsanalytik.* Berlin: Hans Huber.

Brenman, E. (1980). The value of reconstruction in adult psychoanalysis. *International Journal of Psycho-Analysis*, 61: 53–60.

Bryce Boyer, L. (1969). La técnica psicoanalítica en el tratamiento de ciertos trastornos caracterológicos y esquizofrenicos. *Revista de Psicoanálisis*, 26: 765–839.

Buxbaum, E. (1950). Technique of terminating analysis. *International Journal of Psycho-Analysis*, 31: 184–190.

Bychowski, G. (1956). Homosexuality and psychosis. In: S. Lorand & M. Balint (Eds.), *Perversions: Psychodynamics and Therapy* (pp. 97–130). New York: Random House.

Carloni, G. (1984). Tatto, contatto e tattica. *Rivista di Psicoanalisi*, 30: 191–205.

Carnap, R. (1950). *Logical Foundation of Probability.* London: Routledge & Kegan Paul.

Carpinacci, J. A. (1975). Algunas consideraciones sobre la "construcción" en Psicoanálisis. Comments by I. Berenstein, E. T. de Bianchedi, & B. Winograd. *Revista de Psicoanálisis*, 32: 227–269.

Cassirer, E. (1923–1929). *Philosophie der simbolischen Formen, Vols. 1–3.* Darmstadt: Wissenschaftliche Buchgesellschaft. [*Filosofía de las formas simbólicas, Vols. 1–3.* Mexico: Fondo de la Cultura Económica, 1971, 1972, 1976.]

Cesio, F. R. (1956). Un caso de "reacción terapéutica negativa". *Revista de Psicoanálisis*, 13: 522–526.

Cesio, F. R. (1957). El lenguaje no-verbal. Su interpretación. *Revista de Psicoanálisis*, 14: 110–120.

Cesio, F. R. (1960). El letargo. Una contribución al estudio de la reacción terapéutica negativa. *Revista de Psicoanálisis*, 17: 10–24, 289–298.

Cesio, F. R. (1976). La transferencia en el sueno y en el tratamiento psicoanalítico. *Revista de Psicoanálisis*, 24: 809–815.

Chasseguet-Smirgel, J. (1967). Note clinique sur les rèves d'examen. *Revue française de Psychanalyse, 1.* [Also in: *Pour une psychanalyse de l'art et de la creativité* (Chap. 6). Paris: Payot, 1971.]

Chasseguet-Smirgel, J. (1975). *L'idéal de Moi: Essai psychanalytique sur la "maladie d'idealité".* Paris: Tchou. [*The Ego Ideal.* London: Free Association, 1985.]

Chomsky, N. (1965). *Aspects of the Theory of Syntax.* Cambridge, MA: MIT Press.

Clavreul, J. (1963). Notas sobre la cuestión de la realidad en las perversiones. Lecture. *Societé Psychanalytique de France*, May 7. Universidad Nacional de Buenos Aires, card 508.

Clavreul, J. (1966). Le couple pervers. In: P. Aulagnier-Spairani et al., *Le désir et la perversion*. Paris: Ed. du Seuil, 1967.

Coderch, J. (1995). *La interpretación en psicoanálisis. Fundamentos y teoría de la técnica*. Barcelona: Editorial Herder.

Darwin, Ch. (1859). *On the Origin of Species*. London: John Murray.

Dayan, M. (1982). La señora K interpreta. *Trabajo de Psicoanálisis*, 1: 267–303.

Del Valle, E. (1979). *La obra de Melanie Klein, Vol. 1*. Buenos Aires: Kargieman.

Del Valle, E. (1986). *La obra de Melanie Klein, Vol. 2*. Buenos Aires: Lugar Editorial.

Deutsch, H. (1926). Okkulte Vorgänge während der Psychoanalyse. *Imago, 12*. [*Occult Practices Occurring during Psychoanalysis*. New York: International Universities Press.]

Deutsch, H. (1942). Some forms of emotional disturbances and their relationship to schizophrenia. *Psychoanalytic Quarterly, 11*: 301–321. [Also in: *Neurosis and Character Types. Clinical Psychoanalytic Studies* (Chap. 20). New York: International Universities Press, 1965.]

Dubcovsky, S. (1979). La inflación. Algunas consecuencias de las crisis económicas sobre la práctica psicoanalítica. *Revista Argentina de Psicología*: 25–51.

Dupetit, S. (1982). *La addicción y las drogas*. Buenos Aires: Ed. Futuro.

Dupetit, S. (1988). La mirada del tigre: acerca de la transferencia en pacientes adictos. I Argentine Congress of Psychoanalysis (pp. 57–75). Buenos Aires: Grafitt.

Eagle, M. N. (1984). *Recent Developments in Psycho-Analysis. A Critical Evaluation*. New York: McGraw-Hill.

Eissler, K. R. (1953). The effect of the structure of the ego on psychoanalytic technique. *Journal of the American Psychoanalytic Association, 1*: 104–143.

Eissler, K. R. (1958). Remarks on some variations in psychoanalytical technique. *International Journal of Psycho-Analysis, 39*: 222–229.

Ekstein, R. (1966). *Children of Time and Space, of Action and Impulse*. New York: Appleton-Century-Crofts.

Ekstein, R., & Friedman, S. W. (1957). The function of acting out, play action and play acting in the psychotherapeutic process. *Journal of the American Psychoanalytic Association, 5*: 581–629.

Ellenberger, H. F. (1970). *The Discovery of the Unconscious. The History and Evolution of Dynamic Psychiatry*. New York: Basic Books.

English, H. B., & English, A. C. (1958). *A Comprehensive Dictionary of Psychological and Psychoanalytic Terms*. New York: Longmans Green.

Erikson, E. (1950). *Childhood and Society*. New York: W. W. Norton.

Erikson, E. (1962). Reality and actuality: an address. *Journal of the American Psychoanalytic Association, 10*: 415–474.

Etchegoyen, R. H. (1960). Comentarios sobre el análisis de un psicópata. Unpublished.

Etchegoyen, R. H. (1969). La primera sesión de análisis. Comments by L. Alcantara de Amaral, J. Naiman, & L. Rangell. *Revista de Psicoanálisis, 28* (1971): 501–535.

Etchegoyen, R. H. (1970). Homosexualidad femenina: aspectos dinámicos de la recuperación. *Revista Uruguaya de Psicoanálisis, 12*: 431–477.

Etchegoyen, R. H. (1973). A note on ideology and psychoanalytic technique. *International Journal of Psycho-Analysis, 54*: 485–486.

Etchegoyen, R. H. (1976). El "Impasse" psicoanalítico y las estrategias del yo. *Revista de Psicoanálisis, 33*: 613–636.

Etchegoyen, R. H. (1977). Perversión de transferencia. Aspectos teóricos y técnicos. In: L. Grinberg (Ed.), *Prácticas psicoanalíticas comparadas en las psicosis* (Chap. 2, pp. 58–83). Buenos Aires: Paidós.

Etchegoyen, R. H. (1978a). Some thoughts on transference perversion. *International Journal of Psycho-Analysis, 59*: 45–53.

Etchegoyen, R. H. (1978b). Las formas de transferencia. *Psicoanálisis, 2*: 1065–1089.

Etchegoyen, R. H. (1979a). Regresión y encuadre. *Psicoanálisis, 1*: 479–503.

Etchegoyen, R. H. (1979b). Introduction to the Spanish edition of Donald Meltzer et al., *Exploración del autismo* (pp. 11–16). Buenos Aires: Paidós.

Etchegoyen, R. H. (1981a). Notas para una historia de la escuela inglesa de Psicoanálisis. *Revista de la Asociación Escuela Argentina de Psicoterapia para Graduados, 6*: 13–30.

Etchegoyen, R. H. (1981b). The relevance of the "here and now" transference interpretation, for the reconstruction of early psychic development. *International Journal of Psycho-Analysis, 63* (1982): 65–75.

Etchegoyen, R. H. (1981c). Instances and alternatives of the interpretative work. *International Review of Psycho-Analysis, 8*: 401–421.

Etchegoyen, R. H. (1982). Fifty years after the mutative interpretation. *International Journal of Psycho-Analysis, 64* (1983): 445–459. [First published in *Revista Chilena de Psicoanálisis.*]

Etchegoyen, R. H. (1983). Insight. *Trabajo del Psicoanálisis, 2*: 253–287.

Etchegoyen, R. H. (1985). Los estilos interpretativos. *Psicoanálisis, 7*: 111–138.

Etchegoyen, R. H. (1988). Reflexiones sobre la transferencia. I Congreso Argentino de Psicoanálisis. *Actas* (pp. 77–101). Buenos Aires: Grafitt.

Etchegoyen, R. H., Bleichmar, N. M., & Bleichmar, C. L. de (1979). El sueno como superficie de contacto. Second Symposium, Buenos Aires Psychoanalytic Association (APdeBA). *Actas*: 40–48.

Etchegoyen, R. H., & Catri, J. (1978). Freud, Ferenczi y el análisis didáctico. In: First Symposium, Buenos Aires Psychoanalytic Association (APdeBA). *Actas*.

Etchegoyen, R. H., López, B. M., & Rabih, M. (1985). On envy and how to interpret it. *International Journal of Psycho-Analysis, 68* (1987): 49–61.

Etchegoyen, R. H., & Rabih, M. (1981). The psychoanalytic theories of envy. *The Journal of the Melanie Klein Society, 3* (1) (1985): 50–80.

Etchegoyen, R. H., et al. (1982a). On the existence of two levels in the process of working-through. *The Journal of Melanie Klein Society, 3* (1985): 31–39.

Etchegoyen, R. H., et al. (1982c). El complejo de Edipo y los precursores del superyó. XIV Latin-American Psychoanalytic Congress. *Actas, 2*: 143–148.

Etchegoyen, R. H., et al. (1982b). De los comienzos del complejo de Edipo. XIV Latin-American Psychoanalytic Congress. *Actas, 2*: 137–141.

Fairbairn, W. R. D. (1941). A revised psychopathology of the psychosis and psychoneurosis. *International Journal of Psycho-Analysis, 22*: 250–279. [Also in: *Psychoanalytic Studies of the Personality*. London: Tavistock, 1952.]

Fairbairn, W. R. D. (1944). Endopsychic structure considered in terms of object-relationships. *International Journal of Psycho-Analysis, 25*: 70–93.

Fairbairn, W. R. D. (1958). On the nature and aims of psycho-analytical treatment. *International Journal of Psycho-Analysis, 39*: 374–385.

Federn, P. (1943). Psychoanalysis of psychosis. In: *Ego Psychology and the Psychoses* (Chap. 6). London: Imago, 1953. [First published in *Psychiatric Quarterly*. Reprinted London: Karnac Books, 1977.]

Federn, P. (1947). Principles of psycho-therapy in latent schizophrenia. In: *Ego Psychology and the Psychoses* (Chap. 7). London: Imago, 1953. [Reprinted London: Karnac Books, 1977.]

Fenichel, O. (1935). Concerning the theory of psychoanalytic technique. In: *Collected Papers* (first series, Chap. 30), 1953. [Also in: P. Louis (Ed.), *Psychoanalytic Clinical Interpretation* (pp. 42–64). London: Collier-Macmillan, 1963. First published in *Internationale Zeitschrift für Psychoanalyse, 21*: 78–95.]

Fenichel, O. (1937). Symposium on the theory of the therapeutic results of psychoanalysis. *International Journal of Psycho-Analysis, 18*: 133–138.

Fenichel, O. (1941). *Problems of Psychoanalytic Technique*. New York: Psychoanalytic Quarterly Inc.

Fenichel, O. (1945a). *The Psycho-Analytic Theory of Neurosis*. London: Kegan Paul.

Fenichel, O. (1945b). Neurotic acting out. In: *Collected Papers* (second series, Chap. 22), 1953.

Fenichel, O. (1953). *Collected Papers*. New York: David Lewis.

Ferenczi, S. (1909). Introjection and transference. In: *First Contributions* (Chap. 2), 1916.

Ferenczi, S. (1911). On the part played by homosexuality in the pathogenesis of paranoia. In: *First Contributions* (Chap. 5), 1916.

Ferenczi, S. (1913). Stages in the development of the sense of reality. In: *First Contributions* (Chap. 8), 1916.

Ferenczi, S. (1914). Some clinical observations on paranoia and paraphrenia. In: *First Contributions* (Chap. 11), 1916. [First published as "Einige klinische Beobachtungen bei der Paranoia und Paraphrenie". *Internationale Zeitschrift für Psychoanalyse, 2*: 2–17.]

Ferenczi, S. (1916). *First Contributions to Psycho-Analysis*. London: Hogarth, 1952. [Reprinted London: Karnac Books, 1980.]

Ferenczi, S. (1919a). Sunday neurosis. In: *Further Contributions* (Chap. 13), 1926.

Ferenczi, S. (1919b). Technical difficulties in the analysis of a case of hysteria. In: *Further Contributions* (Chap. 15), 1926.

Ferenczi, S. (1920). The further development of an active therapy in psycho-analysis. In: *Further Contributions* (Chap. 16), 1926.

Ferenczi, S. (1921). Psycho-analytical observations on tic. In: *Further Contributions* (Chap. 12), 1926.

Ferenczi, S. (1924). *Thalassa. A Theory of Genitality*. New York: Psychoanalytic Quarterly Inc., 1938. [Reprinted London: Karnac Books, 1989.]

Ferenczi, S. (1926). *Further Contributions to the Theory and Technique of Psycho-Analysis*. London: Hogarth. [Reprinted London: Karnac Books, 1980.]

Ferenczi, S. (1927). The problem of the termination of the analysis. In: *Final Contributions* (Chap. 7), 1955.

Ferenczi, S. (1928). The elasticity of psycho-analytic technique. In: *Final Contributions* (Chap. 8), 1955.

Ferenczi, S. (1930). The principles of relaxation and neocatharsis. In: *Final Contributions* (Chap. 10), 1955.

Ferenczi, S. (1931). Child-analysis in the analysis of adults. In: *Final Contributions* (Chap. 11), 1955.

Ferenczi, S. (1932). Confusion of tongues between adults and the child. The language of tenderness and of passion. In: *Final Contributions* (Chap. 13), 1955.

Ferenczi, S. (1955). *Final Contributions to the Problems and Methods of Psycho-Analysis.* New York: Brunner/Mazel, 1980. [Reprinted London: Karnac Books, 1994.]

Ferenczi, S., & Rank, O. (1923). *The Development of Psycho-Analysis.* New York: Nervous and Mental Disease Monograph Series, 1925.

Filc, S. Z. de (1979). Insight. Unpublished.

Filc, S. Z. de (1983). El rol continente de los elementos sonoros de la interpretación. Unpublished.

Fliess, R. (Ed.) (1948). *The Psycho-Analytic Reader.* New York: International Universities Press.

Fornari, F. (1981). Il *codice vivente.* Turin: Boringhieri. [Quoted by R. Speziale-Bagliacca, 1982.]

Forsyth, D. (1922). *The Technique of Psychoanalysis.* London: Paul, Trench, Trubner. [Quoted by R. Menninger, 1958.]

Frankl, V. E. (1955). *Homo patients.* Vienna: Franz Deuticke.

French, Th. M. (1939). Insight and distortion in dreams. *International Journal of Psycho-Analysis, 20*: 287–298.

Freud, A. (1927). Four lectures on child analysis. In: *Writings, Vol. 1* (pp. 3–69), 1965–71. [*Einführung in die Technik der Kinderanalyse.* Vienna: Internationaler Psychoanalytischer Verlag.]

Freud, A. (1936). *The Ego and the Mechanisms of Defence.* In: *Writings, Vol. 2,* 1965–71. [Reprinted London: Karnac Books, 1993.]

Freud, A. (1946). The psycho-analytical treatment of children. In: *Writings, Vol. 1,* 1965–71.

Freud, A. (1952 [1949–51]). Studies in passivity. In: *Writings, Vol. 4* (Chap. 10, pp. 245–259), 1965–71. [Abstract in *International Journal of Psycho-Analysis, 33* (1952): 265.]

Freud, A. (1954). The widening scope indication for psychoanalysis. Discussion. *Journal of the American Psychoanalytical Association, 2*: 607–620. [Also in: *Writings, Vol. 4,* Chap. 17), 1965–71.]

Freud, A. (1963). The concept of developmental lines. In: *Psychoanalytical Study of the Child, 18*: 245–265.

Freud, A. (1965). The therapeutic possibilities. *Normality and Pathology in Childhood: Assessments of Development,* 1965. In: *Writings, Vol. 6* (Chap. 6, pp. 213–235), 1965–71. [Reprinted London: Karnac Books, 1989.]

Freud, A. (1965–71). *The Writings of Anna Freud, Vols. 1–7.* London: Hogarth.

Freud, A. (1966). The ideal psychoanalytic institute: a utopia. In: *Writings, Vol. 7* (pp. 73–93), 1965–71.

Freud, A. (1968). Acting out. *International Journal of Psycho-Analysis, 49*: 165–170. [Also in: *Writings, Vol. 7* (Chap. 7, pp. 94–109), 1965–71.]

Freud, S. (1890a) formerly (1905b [1890]). Psychical (or mental) treatment. *S.E., 7*: 281–302. [For the actual date of this work, see the *Editor's Introduction* to "Papers on Hypnotism and Suggestion", by James Strachey. *S.E., 1.*]

Freud, S. (1894a). The neuro-psychoses of defence. *S.E., 3.*

Freud, S. (1895b). On the grounds for detaching a particular syndrome from neurasthenia under the description "anxiety neurosis". *S.E., 3.*

Freud, S. (1895d), with Breuer, J. *Studies on Hysteria. S.E., 2.*

Freud, S. (1898a). Sexuality in the aetiology of the neuroses. *S.E., 3.*

Freud, S. (1899a). Screen memories. *S.E., 3.*

Freud, S. (1900a). *The Interpretation of Dreams. S.E., 4–5.*

Freud, S. (1901a). On dreams. *S.E., 5.*

Freud, S. (1901b). *The Psychopathology of Everyday Life. S.E., 6.*

Freud, S. (1904a). Freud's psycho-analytic procedure. *S.E., 7.*

Freud, S. (1905a). On psychotherapy. *S.E., 7.*

Freud, S. (1905c). *Jokes and Their Relation to the Unconscious. S.E., 8.*

Freud, S. (1905d). Three essays on the theory of sexuality. *S.E., 7.*

Freud, S. (1905e [1901]). Fragment of an analysis of a case of hysteria. *S.E., 7.*

Freud, S. (1909b). Analysis of a phobia in a five-year-old boy. *S.E., 10.*

Freud, S. (1909d). Notes upon a case of obsessional neurosis. *S.E., 10.*

Freud, S. (1910a). Five lectures on psycho-analysis. *S.E., 11.*

Freud, S. (1910c). *Leonardo da Vinci and a Memory of His Childhood. S.E., 11.*

Freud, S. (1910d). The future prospects of psycho-analytic therapy. *S.E., 11.*

Freud, S. (1910k). "Wild" psycho-analysis. *S.E., 11.*

Freud, S. (1911b). Formulations on the two principles of mental functioning. *S.E., 12.*

Freud, S. (1911c). Psycho-analytic notes on an autobiographical account of a case of paranoia (Dementia Paranoides). *S.E., 12.*

Freud, S. (1911e). The handling of dream-interpretation in psycho-analysis. *S.E., 12.*

Freud, S. (1912b). The dynamics of transference. *S.E., 12.*

Freud, S. (1912e). Recommendations to physicians practising psycho-analysis. *S.E., 12.*

Freud, S. (1912–13). *Totem and Taboo. S.E., 13.*

Freud, S. (1913c). On beginning the treatment (Further recommendations on the technique of psycho-analysis, I). *S.E., 12.*

Freud, S. (1914c). On narcissism: an introduction. *S.E., 14.*

Freud, S. (1914g). Remembering, repeating and working-through (Further recommendations on the technique of psycho-analysis, II). *S.E., 12.*

Freud, S. (1915a). Observations on transference-love (Further recommendations on the technique of psycho-analysis, III). *S.E., 12.*

Freud, S. (1915c). Instincts and their vicissitudes. *S.E., 14.*

Freud, S. (1915d). Repression. *S.E., 14.*

Freud, S. (1915e). The unconscious. *S.E., 14.*

Freud, S. (1916d). Some character-types met with in psycho-analytic work. *S.E., 14.*

Freud, S. (1916–17). *Introductory Lectures on Psycho-Analysis. S.E., 15–16.*

Freud, S. (1917c). On transformation of instinct as exemplified in anal erotism. *S.E., 17.*

Freud, S. (1917d). A metapsychological supplement to the theory of dreams. *S.E., 14.*

Freud, S. (1917e [1915]). Mourning and melancholia. *S.E., 14.*

Freud, S. (1918b [1914]). From the history of an infantile neurosis. *S.E., 17.*

Freud, S. (1919a). Lines of advance in psycho-analytic therapy. *S.E., 17.*

Freud, S. (1919e). A child is being beaten. A contribution to the study of the origin of sexual perversions. S.E., 17.

Freud, S. (1920a). The psychogenesis of a case of female homosexuality. S.E., 18.

Freud, S. (1920g). Beyond the Pleasure Principle. S.E., 18.

Freud, S. (1921c). Group Psychology and the Analysis of the Ego. S.E., 18.

Freud, S. (1922b). Some neurotic mechanisms in jealousy, paranoia and homosexuality. S.E., 18.

Freud, S. (1923a [1922]). Two encyclopaedia articles. S.E., 18.

Freud, S. (1923b). The Ego and the Id. S.E., 19.

Freud, S. (1923c). Remarks on the theory and practice of dream-interpretation. S.E., 19.

Freud, S. (1923e). The infantile genital organization: an interpolation into the theory of sexuality. S.E., 19.

Freud, S. (1924b). Neurosis and psychosis. S.E., 19.

Freud, S. (1924c). The economic problem of masochism. S.E., 19.

Freud, S. (1924d). The dissolution of the Oedipus complex. S.E., 19.

Freud, S. (1924e). The loss of reality in neurosis and psychosis. S.E., 19.

Freud, S. (1925d). An Autobiographical Study. S.E., 20.

Freud, S. (1925h). Negation. S.E., 19.

Freud, S. (1925i). Some additional notes on dream-interpretation as a whole. (B) Moral responsibility for the content of dreams. S.E., 19.

Freud, S. (1925j). Some psychical consequences of the anatomical distinction between the sexes. S.E., 19.

Freud, S. (1926d). Inhibitions, Symptoms and Anxiety. S.E., 20.

Freud, S. (1926e). The Question of Lay Analysis. S.E., 20.

Freud, S. (1927d). Humour. S.E., 21.

Freud, S. (1927e). Fetishism. S.E., 21.

Freud, S. (1930a). Civilization and Its Discontents. S.E., 21.

Freud, S. (1931b). Female sexuality. S.E., 21.

Freud, S. (1933a). New Introductory Lectures on Psycho-Analysis. S.E., 22.

Freud, S. (1937c). Analysis terminable and interminable. S.E., 23.

Freud, S. (1937d). Constructions in analysis. S.E., 23.

Freud, S. (1939a). Moses and Monotheism. S.E., 23.

Freud, S. (1940a [1938]). An Outline of Psycho-Analysis. S.E., 23.

Freud, S. (1940e [1938]). Splitting of the ego in the process of defence. S.E., 23.

Freud, S. (1950a [1887–1902]). The Origins of Psycho-Analysis. S.E., 1.

Freud, S. (1951–74). The Standard Edition of the Complete Psychological Works of Sigmund Freud. Translated from German by James Strachey. London: Hogarth.

Fromm-Reichmann, F. (1939). Transference problems in schizophrenics. Psychoanalytic Quarterly, 8: 412–426. [Also in: Psychoanalysis and Psychotherapy. Chicago/London: University of Chicago Press, 1959.]

Fromm-Reichmann, F. (1950). Principles of Intensive Psychotherapy. Chicago: University of Chicago Press, 1960.

Frosch, J. (1988a). Psychotic character versus borderline, part 1. International Journal of Psycho-Analysis, 69: 347–357.

Frosch, J. (1988b). Psychotic character versus borderline, part 2. International Journal of Psycho-Analysis, 69: 445–456.

Gaddini, E. (1981). Acting out in the psychoanalytic session. *International Journal of Psycho-Analysis, 63* (1982): 57–64.

Gálvez, M., et al. (1979). Suenos con el analista. Second Symposium, Buenos Aires Psychoanalytic Association (APdeBA). *Actas.*

Garbarino, H. (1972). Comment to David Liberman's paper, Evaluación de las entrevistas diagnósticas previas a la iniciación de los tratamientos analíticos. Criterio diagnósticos y esquemas referenciales. *Revista de Psicoanálisis, 29:* 488–490.

Garfinkel, G. (1979). Interpretación onirica e insight. Tolerancia al aprendizaje de la distorsión perceptual. Second Symposium, Buenos Aires Psychoanalytic Association (APdeBA). *Actas.*

Garma, A. (1931). Realität und Es in der Schizophrenie. *International Zeitschrift für Psychoanalyse, 18* (1932): 183–199.

Garma, A. (1950). On the pathogenesis of peptic ulcer. *International Journal of Psycho-Analysis, 31:* 53–72.

Garma, A. (1954). *Genesis psicosomática y tratamiento de las ulceras gastricas y duodenales.* Buenos Aires: Nova.

Garma, A. (1962). *El Psicoanálisis. Teoría, clinica y técnica.* Buenos Aires: Paidós.

Garma, A. (1974). Tres aspectos basicos de las resistencias transferenciales en las etapas finales del tratamiento psicoanalítico. *Revista de Psicoanálisis, 31:* 681–708.

Garzoli, E. H. (1981). Sobre la adicción de transferencia. *Psicoanálisis, 3:* 193–229.

Gear, M. C., & Liendo, E. C. (1972). Estrategia psicoanalítica: fichaje clinico y programmación terapéutica. *Revista de Psicoanálisis, 29:* 531–588.

Gear, M. C., & Liendo, E. C. (1974). *Semiologia psicoanalítica.* Buenos Aires: Nueva Visión.

Gear, M. C., Hill, M. A., & Liendo, E. C. (1981). *Working through Narcissism. Treating Its Sadomasochistic Structure.* New York: Jason Aronson.

Gear, M. C., Liendo, E. C., & Lee Scott, L. (1989). *Changing Mind-Sets. The Potential Unconscious.* New York/London: New York University Press.

Gill, M. (1954). Psychoanalysis and exploratory psychotherapy. *Journal of the American Psychoanalytic Association, 2:* 771–797.

Gill, M. (1979). The analysis of transference. *International Journal of Psycho-Analysis, 8:* 45–56, 1980–1981.

Gill, M. (1982). *Analysis of Transference, Vol. 1: Theory and Technique.* New York: International Universities Press.

Gill, M., & Hoffman, I. Z. (1983). *Analysis of Transference, Vol. 2: Studies of Seven Audio-Recorded Psychoanalytic Sessions.* New York: International Universities Press.

Gill, M., & Rapaport, D. (1962). *Aportaciones a la tear y técnica psicoanalítica.* Mexico: Pax-Mexico.

Gillespie, W. H. (1956). The general theory of sexual perversion. *International Journal of Psycho-Analysis, 37:* 398–403.

Gillespie, W. H. (1964). The psycho-analytic theory of sexual deviation with special reference to fetishism. In: I. Rosen (Ed.), *The Pathology and Treatment of Sexual Deviation,* 2nd ed. London: Oxford University Press, 1979.

Gioia, T. (1974). El concepto de acting out. *Revista de Psicoanálisis, 31:* 969–984.

Gioia, T. (1977). Ensayo critico acerca de la hipótesis psicoanalítica del instinto de muerte. *Revista de Psicoanálisis, 34:* 269–356.

Gioia, T. (1983a). Consideraciones acerca de la hipótesis del instinto de muerte, desde un punto de vista epistemológico. *Psicoanálisis, 5*: 19–27.

Gioia, T. (1983b). El miedo y la angüstia. *Psicoanálisis, 5*: 417–448.

Giovacchini, P. L. (1972a). Interpretation and definition of the analytic setting. In: *Tactics and Techniques in Psychoanalytic Therapy, Vol. 1* (Chap. 14, pp. 291–304), 1972c.

Giovacchini, P. L. (1972b). The symbiotic phase. In: *Tactics and Techniques in Psychoanalytic Therapy, Vol. 1* (Chap. 7, pp. 137–169), 1972c.

Giovacchini, P. L. (1972c). *Tactics and Techniques in Psychoanalytic Therapy, Vols. 1 & 2*. New York: Jason Aronson.

Giovacchini, P. L., & Bryce Boyer, L. (1975). The psychoanalytic impasse. *International Journal of Psychoanalytic Psychotherapy, 4*: 25–47.

Gitelson, M. (1952). The emotional position of the analyst in the psychoanalytic situation. *International Journal of Psycho-Analysis, 33*: 1–10.

Gitelson, M. (1962). The curative factors in psycho-analysis. The first phase of psycho-analysis. *International Journal of Psycho-Analysis, 43*: 194–206.

Glover, E. (1926). The neurotic character. *International Journal of Psycho-Analysis, 7*: 11–30.

Glover, E. (1927). Lectures on technique in psycho-analysis. *International Journal of Psycho-Analysis, 8*: 311–338, 486–520.

Glover, E. (1928). Lectures on technique in psycho-analysis. *International Journal of Psycho-Analysis, 9*: 7–46, 181–218.

Glover, E. (1931). The therapeutic effect on inexact interpretation: a contribution to the theory of suggestion. *International Journal of Psycho-Analysis, 12*: 397–411.

Glover, E. (1933). The relation of perversion formation to the development of reality sense. *International Journal of Psycho-Analysis, 24*: 486–503.

Glover, E. (1955). *The Technique of Psycho-Analysis*. New York: International Universities Press.

Glover, E., Fenichel, O., et al. (1937). Symposium on the theory of the therapeutic results of psychoanalysis. *International Journal of Psycho-Analysis, 18*: 125–189.

Goodman, L., & Gilman, A. (1945). *The Pharmacological Bases of Therapeutics, Vols. 1 & 2*. New York: Macmillan.

Green, A. (1975). The analyst, symbolization and absence in the analytic setting (on changes in analytic practice and analytic experience). *International Journal of Psycho-Analysis, 56*: 1–22. [In: *On Private Madness* (pp. 30–59). London: Hogarth Press, 1986; reprinted London: Karnac Books, 1997.]

Greenacre, P. (1950). General problems of acting-out. *Psychoanalytic Quarterly, 19*: 455–467. [Also in: *Trauma, Growth and Personality* (Chap. 11), 1953.]

Greenacre, P. (1953). *Trauma, Growth and Personality*. London: Hogarth. [Reprinted London: Karnac Books, 1987.]

Greenacre, P. (1954). The role of transference. Practical considerations in relation to psychoanalytic therapy. *Journal of the American Psychoanalytic Association, 2*: 671–684.

Greenacre, P. (1956). Re-evaluation of the process of working through. *International Journal of Psycho-Analysis, 37*: 439–444.

Greenacre, P. (1962). Problems of acting out in the transference relationship. In: E. N. Rexford (Ed.), *A Developmental Approach to the Problem of Acting Out*, 2nd ed. (pp. 215–234). New York: International Universities Press, 1978.

Greenacre, P. (1975). On reconstruction. *Journal of the American Psychoanalytic Association, 23*: 693–771.

Greenson, R. R. (1960). Empathy and its vicissitudes. *International Journal of Psycho-Analysis, 41*: 418–424.

Greenson, R. R. (1965a). The working alliance and the transference neurosis. *Psychoanalytic Quarterly, 34*: 155–181.

Greenson, R. R. (1965b). The problem of working through. In: M. Schur (Ed.), *Drives, Affects, Behavior. Essays in Memory of Marie Bonaparte, Vol. 2* (pp. 277–314). New York: International Universities Press.

Greenson, R. R. (1967). *The Technique and Practice of Psychoanalysis, Vol. 1*. London: Hogarth Press.

Greenson, R. R., & Wexler, M. (1969). The non-transference relationship in the psycho-analytic situation. *International Journal of Psycho-Analysis, 50*: 27–39.

Greenson, R. R., & Wexler, M. (1970). Discussion of "The non-transference relationship in the psycho-analytic situation". *International Journal of Psycho-Analysis, 51*: 143–150.

Grinberg, L. (1956). Sobre algunos problemas de técnica psicoanalítica determinados por la identificación y contraidentificación proyectivas. *Revista de Psicoanálisis, 13*: 507–511.

Grinberg, L. (1957). Perturbaciones en la interpretación por la contraidentificación proyectiva. *Revista de Psicoanálisis, 14*: 23–30.

Grinberg, L. (1958). Aspectos mágicos en la transferencia y en la contratransferencia. Sus implicaciones técnicas. Identificación y "contraidentificación" proyectivas. *Revista de Psicoanálisis, 15*: 341–368.

Grinberg, L. (1959). Aspectos mágicos en las ansiedades paranoides y depresivas. *Revista de Psicoanálisis, 16*: 15–26. [Also in: *Guilt and Depression*, 1993.]

Grinberg, L. (1962). On a specific aspect of countertransference due to the patient's projective identification. *International Journal of Psycho-Analysis, 43*: 436.

Grinberg, L. (1963). Psicopatología de la identificación y contraidentificación proyectivas y de la contratransferencia. *Revista de Psicoanálisis, 20*: 113–123.

Grinberg, L. (1964). *Culpa y depresión. Estudio psicoanalítico*, 2nd ed. Buenos Aires: Paidós, 1971. [*Guilt and Depression*, 1993.]

Grinberg, L. (1968). On acting out and its role in the psychoanalytic process. *International Journal of Psycho-Analysis, 49*: 171–178.

Grinberg, L. (1974). Pasado, presente y futuro de una trayectoria psicoanalítica. *Revista de Psicoanálisis, 31*: 177–199.

Grinberg, L. (1976a). *Teoría de la identificación*. Buenos Aires: Paidós. [Also in: *The Goals of Psychoanalysis*, 1992.]

Grinberg, L. (1976b). *Psicoanálisis: aspectos teóricos y clinicos*, 1st ed. Buenos Aires: Alex Editor. [2nd ed. Barcelona: Paidós, 1981.]

Grinberg, L. (1976c). El Edipo como resistencia contra el Edipo en la práctica psicoanalítica. *Revista de Psicoanálisis, 33*: 549–562. [Also in: *Goals of Psychoanalysis*, 1992.]

Grinberg, L. (1977a). Afectos dolorosos en los pacientes fronterizos. Su abordaje técnico. In: L. Grinberg (Ed.), *Prácticas psicoanalíticas comparadas en las psicosis* (Chap. 4). Buenos Aires: Paidós.

Grinberg, L. (Ed.) (1977b). *Prácticas psicoanalíticas comparadas en las neurosis*. Buenos Aires: Paidós.

Grinberg, L. (Ed.) (1977c). *Prácticas psicoanalíticas comparadas en las psicosis*. Buenos Aires: Paidós.

Grinberg, L. (1982). Los afectos en la contratransferencia. Más allá de la contraidentificación proyectiva. Introduction to the panel *Los afectos en la contratransferencia*. XIV Latin-American Psychoanalytic Congress, FEPAL, Garamond. *Actas*, 205–209.

Grinberg, L. (1992). *The Goals of Psychoanalysis: Identification, Identity, and Supervision* London: Karnac Books.

Grinberg, L. (1993). *Guilt and Depression*. London: Karnac Books.

Grinberg, L., & Grinberg, R. (1981). Modalidades de relaciones objetales en el proceso analítico. *Psicoanálisis*, 3: 431–470.

Grinberg, L., Langer, M., & Rodrigué, E. (Eds.) (1982). *Psicoanálisis en las Americas*. Buenos Aires: Paidós.

Grinberg, L., Sor, D., & Bianchedi, E. T. de (1972). *Introducción a las ideas de Bion*. Buenos Aires: Nueva Visión. [*Introduction to the Work of Bion*. London: Karnac Books.]

Grinberg, L., et al. (1966a). El proceso analítico. In: L. Grinberg, M. Langer, & E. Rodrigué (Eds.), *Psicoanálisis en las Americas* (pp. 93–106), 1982.

Grinberg, L., et al. (1966b). Elaboración en el proceso analítico. *Revista Uruguaya de Psicoanálisis*, 8: 255–263.

Grinberg, L., et al. (1967). Función del sonar y clasificación clinica de los suenos en el proceso analítico. Commentary by E. Rodrigué, A. Rascovsky, & J. Zac. *Revista de Psicoanálisis*, 24: 749–789.

Grinberg, L., et al. (1973). Utilización de los mitos como modelos para la comprensión del concepto interpretación-construcción. In: L. Grinberg, *Psicoanálisis: aspectos teóricos y clinicos* (Chap. 15), 1976b.

Grinberg de Ekboir, J. (1976). Doctor Sigmund Freud, psicoanalista. Su actualidad y vigencia. *Revista de Psicoanálisis*, 33: 719–734.

Grinfeld, P. (1984). Sobre los aspectos intelectuales de la interpretación psicoanalítica. *Psicoanálisis*, 6: 143–175.

Grinstein, A. (1968). *On Sigmund Freud's Dreams*. Detroit: Wayne State University Press.

Grotstein, J. S. (1990). Introduction. In M. I. Little, *Psychotic Anxieties and Containment: A Personal Record of an Analysis with Winnicott*. Northvale, NJ: Jason Aronson, 1990.

Grubrich-Simitis, I. (1986). Six letters of Sigmund Freud and Sandor Ferenczi on the interrelationship of psychoanalytic theory and technique. *International Review of Psycho-Analysis*, 13: 259–277.

Grunberger, B. (1956). Essai sur la situation analytique et le processus de guérison (La dynamique). *Revue française de Psychanalyse*, 21 (1957): 373–458. [In: *Narcissism. Psychoanalytic Essays*. New York: International Universities Press, 1979.]

Grunberger, B. (1957). Regression narcissistique et situation analytique. In: J. Bergeret et al., *Le cure psychanalytique sur le divan* (pp. 47–71). Paris: Tchou, 1980.

Grunberger, B. (1971). *Le narcissisme. Essai de psychanalyse*. Paris: Payot. *Narcissism: Psychoanalytic Studies*. New York: International Universities Press, 1979.]

Grunert, U. (1981). The negative therapeutic reaction as a reactivation of a disturbed process of separation in the transference. In: *Psycho-Analysis in Europe*. European Psycho-Analytic Federation, Bull. 16. Barcelona: Talleres Graficos L and E.

Guiard, F. (1974). El analista frente a su tarea y a si mismo. Reflexiones ante la evaluación retrospectiva de un tratamiento. *Revista de Psicoanálisis, 31*: 627–680.

Guiard, F. (1976). Una dificultad del final del análisis relacionada con la erotización del vinculo transferencia–contratransferencia. *Revista de Psicoanálisis, 33*: 337–345.

Guiard, F. (1977). Sobre el componente musical del lenguaje en etapas avanzada y finales del análisis. Consideraciones técnico–clinicas y metapsicológicas. Commentary by I. Barpal de Katz, S. Dupetit, D. Liberman, & G. Sabsay de Foks. *Revista de Psicoanálisis, 34*: 25–76.

Guiard, F. (1979). Aportes al conocimiento del proceso post-analítico. *Psicoanálisis, 1*: 171–204.

Guntrip, H. (1961). *Personality Structure and Human Interaction.* London: Hogarth Press. [Reprinted London: Karnac Books, 1995.]

Guttman, S. (1968). Indications and contraindications for psychoanalytic treatment. *International Journal of Psycho-Analysis, 49*: 254–255.

Habermas, J. (1968). Erkenntnis und Interesse. Frankfurt: Suhrkamp Verlag. [*Knowledge and Human Interests.* Boston: Beacon Press, 1971.]

Hartmann, H. (1939). *Ego Psychology and the Problem of Adaptation* (trans. David Rapaport). New York: International Universities Press, 1958.

Hartmann, H. (1947). On rational and irrational action. In: *Essays on Ego Psychology* (Chap. 3, pp. 37–68), 1964.

Hartmann, H. (1950). Comments on the psychoanalytic theory of the ego. In: *Essays on Ego Psychology* (Chap. 7), 1964.

Hartmann, H. (1951). Technical implications of ego psychology. *Psychoanalytic Quarterly, 20*: 31–43. [Also in: *Essays on Ego Psychology* (Chap. 8), 1964.]

Hartmann, H. (1952). The mutual influences in the development of ego and id. *Psycho-Analytic Study of the Child, 7.* [Also in: *Essays on Ego Psychology* (Chap. 9), 1964.]

Hartmann, H. (1964). *Essays on Ego Psychology.* New York: International Universities Press.

Hartmann, H., & Loewenstein, R. M. (1962). Notes on the superego. *Psychoanalytic Study of the Child, 17.*

Hautmann, G. (1983). Del disegno degli imperi al gemello imaginario. *Revista di Psicoanalisi, 29*: 166–195.

Heimann, P. (1950). On countertransference. *International Journal of Psycho-Analysis, 31*: 81–84. [Also in: M. Tonnesmann (Ed.), *About Children and Children-No-Longer.* London: Routledge, 1989.]

Heimann, P. (1956). Dynamics of transference interpretations. *International Journal of Psycho-Analysis, 37*: 303–310. [Also in: M. Tonnesmann (Ed.), *About Children and Children-No-Longer.* London: Routledge, 1989.]

Heimann, P. (1960). Countertransference. *British Journal of Medical Psychology, 33*: 9–15. [Also in: M. Tonnesmann (Ed.), *About Children and Children-No-Longer.* London: Routledge, 1989.]

Heimann, P. (1962). The curative factors in psycho-analysis. *International Journal of Psycho-Analysis, 43*: 218–220. [Also in: M. Tonnesmann (Ed.), *About Children and Children-No-Longer.* London: Routledge, 1989.]

Heimann, P. (1969). Post-script. In: M. Tonnesmann (Ed.), *About Children and Children-No-Longer.* London: Routledge, 1989.

Heimann, P. (1970). Remarks of the moderator to: The non-transference relationship in the psychoanalytic situation. *International Journal of Psycho-Analysis*, 51: 145–147. [Also in: M. Tonnesmann (Ed.), *About Children and Children-No-Longer*. London: Routledge, 1989.]

Hempel, C. G. (1965). *Aspects of Scientific Explanation and Other Essays in the Philosophy of the Science*. New York: Free Press.

Hoffer, W. (1950). Three psychological criteria for the termination of treatment. *International Journal of Psycho-Analysis*, 31: 194–195.

Hornby, A. S., et al. (1963). *The Advanced Learner's Dictionary of Current English*. London: Oxford University Press.

Horney, K. (1936). The problem of the negative therapeutic reaction. *Psychoanalytic Quarterly*, 5: 29–44.

Horney, K. (1939). *New Ways in Psychoanalysis*. New York: W. W. Norton.

Horney, K. (1950). *Neurosis and Human Growth. The Struggle Toward Self-realization*. New York: W. W. Norton.

Hospers, J. (1953). *An Introduction to Philosophical Analysis*, 2nd ed. Englewood Cliffs, NJ: Prentice-Hall, 1967.

Hug-Hellmuth, H. von (1921). On the technique of child-analysis. *International Journal of Psycho-Analysis*, 2: 287–305.

Isaacs, S. (1939). Criteria for interpretation. *International Journal of Psycho-Analysis*, 20: 148–160.

Isaacs, S. (1943). The nature and function of phantasy. *International Journal of Psycho-Analysis*, 29 (1948): 73–97. [Also in: M. Klein et al., *Developments in Psycho-Analysis* (Chap. 3). London: Hogarth, 1952. Reprinted London: Karnac Books, 1989.]

Jacobson, E. (1954a). Transference problems in the psycho-analytic treatment of severely depressive patients. *Journal of the American Psychoanalytic Association*, 2: 595–606.

Jacobson, E. (1954b). The self and the object world. *Psychoanalytic Study of the Child*, 9: 75–127.

Jacobson, E. (1964). *The Self and the Object World*. New York: International Universities Press.

Jaspers, K. (1913). *General Psychopathology*. Manchester: Manchester University Press, 1963.

Jelliffe, S. E. (1914). *The Technique of Psycho-Analysis*. New York/Washington: Nervous and Mental Disease Publishing Company.

Jellinek, E. M. (1953). Las fases de la alcoholomania. In: *La etiologia y tratamiento del alcoholismo* (pp. 89–106). Buenos Aires: Ministerio de Asistencia Social y Salud Pública, 1957.

Jinkis, J. (1974). La derivación de un termino como construcción de un concepto. El significante. *Imago*, 2: 76–88.

Jones, E. (1908). Rationalisation in everyday life. In: *Papers on Psycho-Analysis*, 2nd ed. (Chap. 2, pp. 8–15.), 1918.

Jones, E. (1918). *Papers on Psycho-Analysis*. 2nd ed. London: Baillière, Tindal & Cox, 1948. 5th ed. [Reprinted London: Karnac Books, 1977.]

Jones, E. (1933). The phallic phase. *International Journal of Psycho-Analysis*, 14: 1–33. [Also in: *Papers on Psychoanalysis*, 5th ed. (Chap. 26), 1918.]

Jones, E. (1946). A valedictory address. *International Journal of Psycho-Analysis, 27*: 7–12.

Jones, E. (1953–57). *Sigmund Freud: Life and Work*. London: Hogarth Press, Vols. 1–3.

Joseph, B. (1971). A clinical contribution to the analysis of a perversion. *International Journal of Psycho-Analysis, 5* : 441–449. [Also in: *Psychic Equilibrium and Psychic Change*. London: Routledge, 1989.]

Joseph, B. (1975). The patient who is difficult to reach. In: P. L. Giovacchini (Ed.), *Tactics and Techniques in Psychoanalytic Therapy, Vol. 2* (Chap. 6, pp. 205–216). New York: Jason Aronson. [Also in: *Psychic Equilibrium and Psychic Change*. London: Routledge, 1989.]

Joseph, E. (1984). Insight. In: A. Richards & M. Willick (Eds.), *Psychoanalysis: The Science of Mental Conflict* (pp. 263–282). Hillsdale, NJ: Analytic Press, 1986.

Jung, C. G. (1907). The psychology of dementia praecox. In: *The Collected Works, Vol. 3* (p. 151). London: Routledge & Kegan Paul, 1960.

Jung, C. G. (1910). Über Konflikte der kindlichen Seele. *Jahrbuch der psychoanalytischen u. psychopathologischen Forschung, 2*: 33.

Kaiser, H. (1934). Problems of technique. In: M. S. Bergmann & F. R. Hartman (Eds.), *The Evolution of Psychoanalytic Technique* (Chap. 27). New York: Basic Books, 1976.

Kanner, L. (1943). Autistic disturbances of affective contact. *The Nervous Child, 2*: 217–250.

Kanner, L. (1944). Early infantile autism. *Journal of Pedriatics, 25*: 211–217.

Kanner, L. (1953). *Child Psychiatry*. Baltimore, MD: Springfield.

Kanzer, M. (1968). Ego alteration and acting out. Comment by Samuel Ritvo. *International Journal of Psycho-Analysis, 49*: 431–437.

Katan, M. (1959). Comments on "ego distortion". *International Journal of Psycho-Analysis, 40*: 297–303.

Katz, I. Barpal de (1978). El proceso didáctico en Psicoanálisis. Pre-Congreso Didáctico de Mexico. *Actas.*

Kennedy, H. (1978). The role of insight in child analysis: a developmental viewpoint. In: H. P. Blum (Ed.), *Psychoanalytic Explorations of Technique* (pp. 9–28). New York: International Universities Press, 1980.

Kernberg, O. (1965). Notes on countertransference. *Journal of the American Psychoanalytic Association, 13*: 38–56.

Kernberg, O. (1966). Structural derivatives of object relationships. *International Journal of Psycho-Analysis, 47*: 236–253.

Kernberg, O. (1967). Borderline personality organization. *Journal of the American Psychoanalytic Association, 15*: 641–685. [Also in: *Borderline Conditions*, 1975.]

Kernberg, O. (1968). The treatment of patients with borderline personality organization. *International Journal of Psycho-Analysis, 49*: 600–619.

Kernberg, O. (1969). A contribution to the ego-psychological critique of the Kleinian school. *International Journal of Psycho-Analysis, 50*: 317–333. [Also in: P. L. Giovacchini (Ed.), *Tactics and Technique in Psychoanalytic Therapy, Vol. 1* (Chap. 4). New York: Jason Aronson, 1972.]

Kernberg, O. (1975). *Borderline Conditions and Pathological Narcissism*. North Vale, NJ: Jason Aronson, 1985.

Kernberg, O. (1976a). *Object Relations Theory and Clinical Psychoanalysis*. New York: Jason Aronson.

Kernberg, O. (1976b). Technical considerations in the treatment of borderline personality organization. *Journal of the American Psychoanalytic Association, 24*: 795–829.

Kernberg, O. (1980). *Internal World and External Reality*. New York: Jason Aronson.

Kernberg, O. (1982). The diagnosis of borderline states in adolescence. In: S. C. Feinstein (Ed.), *Adolescent Psychiatry*. Chicago, IL: University of Chicago Press.

Kernberg, O. (1984). *Severe Personality Disorders: Psychotherapeutic Strategies*. New Haven/London: Yale University Press.

Khan, M. M. R. (1960). Regression and integration in the analytic setting. *International Journal of Psycho-Analysis, 41*: 130–146. [Also in: *The Privacy of the Self* (Chap. 11). London: Hogarth Press, 1974; reprinted London: Karnac Books, 1996.]

King, P. (1980). The life cycle as indicated by the nature of the transference in the psychoanalysis of the middle-aged and elderly. *International Journal of Psycho-Analysis, 61*: 153–160.

King, P., & Steiner, R. (Eds.) (1991). *The Freud–Klein Controversies, 1941–1945*. London: Routledge.

Klauber, J. (1972). On the relationship of transference and interpretation in psychoanalytic therapy. *International Journal of Psycho-Analysis, 53*: 385–391. [Also in: *Difficulties in the Analytic Encounter* (Chap. 2), 1981.]

Klauber, J. (1981). *Difficulties in the Analytic Encounter*. New York: Jason Aronson. [Reprinted London: Karnac Books, 1986.]

Klein, G. S. (1966). Two theories or one? In: *Psychoanalytic Theory. An Exploration of Essentials* (Chap. 2). New York: International Universities Press, 1976.

Klein, M. (1921). The development of a child. In: *Love, Guilt and Reparation and Other Works (Writings, Vol. 1*, Chap. 1), 1975.

Klein, M. (1923a). The role of the school in the libidinal development of the child. In: *Love, Guilt and Reparation and Other Works (Writings, Vol. 1*, Chap. 3), 1975.

Klein, M. (1923b). Early analysis. In: *Love, Guilt and Reparation and Other Works (Writings, Vol. 1*, Chap. 4), 1975.

Klein, M. (1925). A contribution to the psychogenesis of tics. In: *Love, Guilt and Reparation and Other Works (Writings, Vol. 1*, Chap. 5), 1975.

Klein, M. (1926). The psychological principles of early analysis. In: *Love, Guilt and Reparation and Other Works (Writings, Vol. 1*, Chap. 6), 1975.

Klein, M. (1927). Symposium on child analysis. In: *Love, Guilt and Reparation and Other Works (Writings, Vol. 1*, Chap. 7), 1975.

Klein, M. (1928). Early stages of the Oedipus conflict. In: *Love, Guilt and Reparation and Other Works (Writings, Vol. 1*, Chap. 9), 1975.

Klein, M. (1929). Personification in the play of children. In: *Love, Guilt and Reparation and Other Works (Writings, Vol. 1*, Chap. 10), 1975.

Klein, M. (1930). The importance of symbol-formation and in the development of the ego. In: *Love, Guilt and Reparation and Other Works (Writings, Vol. 1*, Chap. 12), 1975.

Klein, M. (1932). *The Psycho-Analysis of Children. The Writings of Melanie Klein, Vol. 2*. London: Hogarth Press, 1975. [Reprinted London: Karnac Books, 1998.]

Klein, M. (1935). A contribution to the psychogenesis of manic-depressive states. In: *Love, Guilt and Reparation and Other Works (Writings, Vol. 1*, Chap. 17), 1975.

Klein, M. (1940). Mourning and its relation to manic-depressive states. In: *Love, Guilt and Reparation and Other Works (Writings, Vol. 1*, Chap. 20), 1975.

Klein, M. (1945). The Oedipus complex in the light of early anxieties. In: *Love, Guilt and Reparation and Other Works (Writings, Vol. 1*, Chap. 21), 1975.

Klein, M. (1946). Notes on some schizoid mechanisms. In: *Envy and Gratitude and Other Works (Writings, Vol. 3*, Chap. 1), 1975.

Klein, M. (1948). On the theory of anxiety and guilt. In: *Envy and Gratitude and Other Works (Writings, Vol. 3*, Chap. 2), 1975.

Klein, M. (1950). On the criteria for the termination of a psycho-analysis. In: *Envy and Gratitude and Other Works (Writings, Vol. 3*, Chap. 3), 1975.

Klein, M. (1952a). The origins of transference. In: *Envy and Gratitude and Other Works (Writings, Vol. 3*, Chap. 4), 1975.

Klein, M. (1952b). Some theoretical conclusions regarding the emotional life of the infant. In: *Envy and Gratitude and Other Works (Writings, Vol. 3*, Chap. 6), 1975.

Klein, M. (1955a). The psycho-analytic play technique: its history and significance. In: *Envy and Gratitude and Other Works (Writings, Vol. 3*, Chap. 8), 1975.

Klein, M. (1955b). On identification. In: *Envy and Gratitude and Other Works (Writings, Vol. 3*, Chap. 9), 1975.

Klein, M. (1957). Envy and gratitude. A study of unconscious sources. In: *Envy and Gratitude and Other Works (Writings, Vol. 3*, Chap. 10), 1975.

Klein, M. (1958). On the development of mental functioning. In: *Envy and Gratitude and Other Works (Writings, Vol. 3*, Chap. 11), 1975.

Klein, M. (1959). Our adult world and its roots in infancy. In: *Envy and Gratitude and Other Works (Writings, Vol. 3*, Chap. 12), 1975.

Klein, M. (1961). *Narrative of a Child Analysis. The Writings of Melanie Klein, Vol. 4*. London: Hogarth Press, 1975 [reprinted London: Karnac Books, 1996].

Klein, M. (1975). *Love, Guilt and Reparation and Other Works 1921-1945. The Writings of Melanie Klein, Vol. 1* (ed. R. Money-Kyrle with B. Joseph, E. O'Shaughnessy & H. Segal). London: Hogarth Press [reprinted London: Karnac Books, 1992].

Klein, M. (1975). *Envy and Gratitude and Other Works. The Writings of Melanie Klein, Vol. 3* (ed. R. Money-Kyrle with B. Joseph, E. O'Shaughnessy & H. Segal). London: Hogarth Press [reprinted London: Karnac Books, 1993].

Klein, M., Heimann, P., Isaacs, S., & Riviere, J. (1952). *Developments in Psycho-Analysis*. London: Hogarth Press. [Reprinted London: Karnac Books, 1989.]

Klimovsky, G. (n.d.). La estructura lógica de las teorías psicoanalíticas. Unpublished.

Klimovsky, G. (1982). Concepto de proceso. *Revista del Hospital Italiano de Buenos Aires (suplemento psicopatológico)*: 7–10.

Klimovsky, G. (1984). Significación, lenguaje y metalenguaje. *Psicoanálisis, 6*: 45–55.

Klimovsky, G. (1989). La epistemologia de Sigmund Freud. XXXVI International Psychoanalytic Congress, Rome, 1989. Unpublished.

Knight, R. P. (1952). An evaluation of psychotherapeutic techniques. *Bulletin of the Menninger Clinic, 16* (1963): 113–124. [Also in: *Selected Papers* (pp. 193–207), 1972.]

Knight, R. P. (1953a). Borderline states. *Bulletin of the Menninger Clinic, 17*: 1–12. [Also in: *Selected Papers* (pp. 208–223), 1972; and in R. P. Knight & C. R. Friedman, comps., *Psychoanalytic Psychiatry and Psychology* (pp. 97–109), 1954.]

Knight, R. P. (1953b). Management and psychotherapy of the borderline schizophrenic patient. *Bulletin of the Menninger Clinic, 17*: 139–150. [Also in: R. P. Knight & C. R. Friedman, comps., *Psychoanalytic Psychiatry and Psychology* (pp. 110–122), 1954.]

Knight, R. P., & Friedman, C. R., comps. (1954). *Psychoanalytic Psychiatry and Psychology*. New York: International Universities Press.

Kohler, W. (1917). *The Mentality of Apes* (trans. E. Winter). London: Kegan Paul, 1931.

Kohut, H. (1959). Introspection, empathy and psychoanalysis. An examination of the relationship between mode of observation and theory. *Journal of the American Psychoanalytic Association, 7*: 459–483.

Kohut, H. (1966). Transferencia y contratransferencia en el análisis de personalidades narcisisticas. In: L. Grinberg, M. Langer, & E. Rodrigué (Eds.), *Psicoanálisis en las Americas*: 174–185. Buenos Aires: Paidós, 1968.

Kohut, H. (1971). *The Analysis of the Self. A Systematic Approach to the Psychoanalytic Treatment of Narcissistic Personality Disorders*. New York: International Universities Press.

Kohut, H. (1977). *The Restoration of the Self.* New York: International Universities Press.

Kohut, H. (1982). Introspection, empathy and the semi-circle of mental health. *International Journal of Psycho-Analysis, 63*: 395–407.

Kohut, H. (1984). *How Does Analysis Cure?* Chicago: University of Chicago Press.

Kohut, H., & Wolf, E. S. (1978). The disorders of the self and their treatment: an outline. *International Journal of Psycho-Analysis, 59*: 413–425.

Kris, E. (1936). The psychology of caricature. *International Journal of Psycho-Analysis, 1 7*: 285–303. [Also in: *Psychoanalytic Explorations in Art* (Chap. 6), 1955.]

Kris, E. (1938). Ego development and the comic. *International Journal of Psycho-Analysis, 19*: 77–90. [Also in: *Psychoanalytic Explorations in Art* (Chap. 8), 1955.]

Kris, E. (1950). On preconscious mental process. *Psychoanalytic Quarterly, 19*: 540–560. [Also in: *Psychoanalytic Explorations in Art* (Chap. 14), 1955.]

Kris, E. (1951). Ego psychology and interpretation in psychoanalytic therapy. *Psychoanalytic Quarterly, 20*: 15–30.

Kris, E. (1955). *Psychoanalytic Explorations in Art*. New York: International Universities Press.

Kris, E. (1956a). On some vicissitudes of insight in psychoanalysis. *International Journal of Psycho-Analysis, 37*: 445–455.

Kris, E. (1956b). The recovery of childhood memories in psychoanalysis. *Psychoanalytic Study of the Child, Vol. 11* (pp. 54–88). New York: International Universities Press.

Kuhn, T. S. (1962). *The Structure of Scientific Revolutions*. Chicago: University of Chicago Press. 2nd ed., 1970.

Kuiper, P. C. (1968). Indications and contraindications for psychoanalytic treatment. *International Journal of Psycho-Analysis, 49*: 261–264.

Lacan, J. (1949). Le stade du miroir comme formateur de la fonction du Je telle qu'elle nous est revélée dans l'expérience psychanalytique. In: *Écrits* (pp. 93–100), 1966.

REFERENCES 835

Lacan, J. (1951). Intervention sur le transfert. In: *Écrits* (pp. 215–226), 1966.
Lacan, J. (1953a). Some reflections on the ego. *International Journal of Psycho-Analysis*, 34: 11–17.
Lacan, J. (1953b). Fonction et champ de la parole et du langage en psychanalyse. In: *Écrits* (pp. 237–322), 1966.
Lacan, J. (1953–54). *Le Seminaire de Jacques Lacan, Vol. I: Les écrits techniques de Freud, 1953–1954*. Paris: Editions du Seuil, 1975. [*The Seminar of Jacques Lacan, Book 1: 1953–54*. Cambridge: Cambridge University Press, 1988.]
Lacan, J. (1954–55). *Le Seminaire de Jacques Lacan, Vol. II: Le moi dans la théorie de Freud et dans la technique de la psychanalyse, 1954–1955*. Paris: Editions du Seuil, 1978. [*The Seminar of Jacques Lacan, Book 2: 1954–55*. Cambridge: Cambridge University Press, 1988.]
Lacan, J. (1955). Le seminaire sur "La lettre volée". In: *Écrits* (pp. 11–61), 1966.
Lacan, J. (1956). Object relation. Unpublished.
Lacan, J. (1957). L'instance de la lettre dans l'inconscient ou la raison depuis Freud. In: *Écrits* (pp. 493–528), 1966.
Lacan, J. (1957–58). *Les formations de l'inconscient. Bulletin de Psychologie*, 12: 182–192, 250–256.
Lacan, J. (1958a). La direction de la cure et les principes de son pouvoir. In: *Écrits* (pp. 585–645), 1966.
Lacan, J. (1958b). La signification du phallus. "Die Bedeutung des Phallus". In: *Écrits* (pp. 685–695), 1966.
Lacan, J. (1964a). *Le Seminaire de Jacques Lacan. Vol. XI: Les quatre concepts fondamentaux de la psychanalyse*. Paris: Editions du Seuil. [*The Seminar of Jacques Lacan, Book 2: The Four Fundamental Concepts of Psycho-Analysis*. Cambridge: Cambridge University Press, 1988.]
Lacan, J. (1964b). Du "Trieb" de Freud et du désir du psychanalyste. In: *Écrits* (pp. 851–854), 1966.
Lacan, J. (1966). *Écrits*. Paris: Editions du Seuil. [*Écrits: A Selection*. London: Hogarth, 1977. Reprinted London: Routledge, 1989.]
Lagache, D. (1951). Le problème du transfert. XIV Conference des psychanalystes de la langue française, Paris, November, 1951. *Revue Française de Psychanalyse*, 16 (1–2), 1952. [Also in: *Oeuvres, Vol. 3*. Paris: Presses Universitaires de France, 1980.]
Lagache, D. (1953). Some aspects of transference. *International Journal of Psycho-Analysis*, 34: 1–10. [Also in: *The Work of Daniel Lagache: Selected Writings* (pp. 109–128). London: Karnac Books, 1993.]
Lagache, D. (1955). *Elements de psychologie médicale*. In: *Oeuvres, Vol. 3*. Paris: Presses Universitaires de France, 1980.
Lagache, D. (1964). Symposium on fantasy. Fantasy, reality and truth. *International Journal of Psycho-Analysis*, 45: 180–189. [Also in: *The Work of Daniel Lagache: Selected Writings* (pp. 109–128). London: Karnac Books, 1993.]
Lagache, D. (1968). Acting out et action. Difficultés terminologiques. *Revue française de Psychanalyse*, 32: 1055–1066.
Lancelle, G. (1974). Acting out y transferencia. *Revista de Psicoanálisis*, 31: 985–1004.
Langer, S. (1942). *Philosophy in a New Key: A Study in the Symbolism of Reason, Rite, and Art*. Cambridge, MA: Harvard University Press.

Laplanche, J. (1987). *Problematiques 5. Le Baquet. Transcendence du transfert.* Paris: Presses Universitaires de France.

Laplanche, J., & Pontalis, J. B. (1968). *Vocabulaire de la psychanalyse.* Paris: Presses Universitaires de France. [*The Language of Psychoanalysis.* London: Hogarth Press, 1973. Reprinted London: Karnac Books, 1988.]

Lebovici, S. (1968). Contribution to the Symposium on Acting Out. *International Journal of Psycho-Analysis, 49*: 202–205.

Lerner, H., & Nemirovsky, C. (1989). La empatia en el psicoanalizar. *Psicoanálisis, 11*: 129–143.

Lévi-Strauss, C. (1977). *Structural Anthropology.* London: Penguin.

Levy, S. T. (1985). Empathy and psychoanalytic technique. *Journal of the American Psychoanalytic Association, 33*: 353–378.

Lewin, B. D. (1950). *The Psychoanalysis of Elation.* New York: W. W. Norton.

Lewin, K. (1935). *A Dynamic Theory of Personality: Selected Papers.* New York: McGraw-Hill.

Liberman, D. (1956). Identificación proyectiva y conflicto matrimonial. *Revista de Psicoanálisis, 13*: 1–20.

Liberman, D. (1957). Interpretación correlativa entre relato y repetición: su aplicación en una paciente con personalidad esquizoide. *Revista de Psicoanálisis, 14*: 55–62.

Liberman, D. (1958). Autismo transferencial. Narcisismo, el mito de Eco y Narciso. *Revista de Psicoanálisis, 15*: 369–385.

Liberman, D. (1962). *La comunicación en terapéutica psicoanalítica*, 2nd ed. Buenos Aires: EUDEBA, 1966.

Liberman, D. (1970–72). *Lingüistica, interacción comunicativa y proceso psicoanalítico, Vols. 1–3.* Buenos Aires: Galerna.

Liberman, D. (1972). Evaluación de las entrevistas diagnósticas previas a la iniciación de los tratamientos analíticos. Criterios diagnósticos y esquemas referenciales. Commented by I. Berenstein, H. Garbarino, A. L. A. Perrotta & R. J. Usandivaras. *Revista de Psicoanálisis, 29*: 461–509.

Liberman, D. (1974). Complementariedad estilistica entre el material del paciente y la interpretación. *Revista de Psicoanálisis, 31*: 201–224.

Liberman, D. (1976a). *Lenguaje y técnica psicoanalítica.* Buenos Aires: Kargieman.

Liberman, D. (1976b). Changes in the theory and practice of psychoanalysis. *International Journal of Psycho-Analysis, 57*: 101–107.

Liberman, D. (1978a). Qué es lo que subsiste y lo que no de "Análisis terminable e interminable"? First Symposium, Buenos Aires Psychoanalytic Association (APdeBA). *Actas.*

Liberman, D. (1978b). El diálogo psicoanalítico y la complementariedad estilistica entre analizando y analista. *Revista Uruguaya de Psicoanálisis, 58*: 37–48. [Also in: *International Journal of Psychoanalytic Psychotherapy, 8.*]

Liberman, D. (1981). La verbalización del insight en la sesión analítica. XXXII International Psychoanalytical Congress, Helsinki, July, 1981. Unpublished.

Liberman, D., Achával, J., Espiro, N., et al. (1969). Modos de reparación y desenlaces de procesos terapéuticos psicoanalíticos. *Revista de Psicoanálisis, 26*: 123–139.

Liberman, D., Ferschtut, G., & Sor, D. (1960). El contrato psicoanalítico. *Revista de Psicoanálisis, 18* (1961), special issue: 85–98.

Liberman, D., Piccolo, E.G. de, Dimant, S. N. de, et al. (1982). *Del cuerpo al simbolo. Sobre adaptación y enfermedad psicosomática.* Buenos Aires: Kargieman.

Limentani, A. (1966). A re-evaluation of acting out in relation to working-through. Commented by R. R. Greenson. *International Journal of Psycho-Analysis, 47*: 274–285. [Also in: *Between Freud and Klein* (pp. 35–49), 1989.]

Limentani, A. (1972). The assessment of analysability: a major hazard in selection for psychoanalysis. *International Journal of Psycho-Analysis, 53*: 351–361. [Also in: *Between Freud and Klein* (pp. 50–72), 1989.]

Limentani, A. (1981). On some positive aspects of the negative therapeutic reaction. *International Journal of Psycho-Analysis, 62*: 379–390. [Also in: *Between Freud and Klein* (pp. 155–172), 1989.]

Limentani, A. (1989). *Between Freud and Klein: The Psychoanalytic Quest for Knowledge and Truth.* London: Free Association Books. [Reprinted London: Karnac Books, 1999.]

Lindon, J. A. (1967). On regression: A workshop. *Psychoanalytic Forum, 2* (4): 295–316.

Lipps, T. (1898). *Komic und Humor.* Hamburg/Leipzig.

Litman, R. E. (Ed.) (1966). *Psychoanalysis in the Americas.* Original contributions from the First Pan-American Congress for Psychoanalysis. New York: International Universities Press.

Little, M. (1951). Counter-transference and the patient's response to it. *International Journal of Psycho-Analysis, 32*: 32–40.

Little, M. (1958). On delusional transference (transference psychosis). *International Journal of Psycho-Analysis, 39*: 134–138.

Little, M. (1966). Transference in borderline states. *International Journal of Psycho-Analysis, 47*: 476–485.

Little, M. (1981). *Transference Neurosis and Transference Psychosis.* New York: Jason Aronson.

Little, M. (1990). *Psychotic Anxieties and Containment: A Personal Record of an Analysis with Winnicott.* Northvale, NJ: Aronson.

Loewald, H. W. (1960). On the therapeutic action of psycho-analysis. *International Journal of Psycho-Analysis, 41*: 16–33. [Also in: *Papers on Psycho-Analysis* (Chap. 14), 1980.]

Loewald, H. W. (1968). The transference neurosis: comments on the concept and the phenomenon. *Journal of the American Psychoanalytic Association, 19* (1971): 54–66. [Also in: *Papers on Psychoanalysis* (Chap. 17), 1980.]

Loewald, H. W. (1970). Psychoanalytic theory and the psychoanalytic process. In: *Papers on Psychoanalysis* (Chap. 16, pp. 277–301), 1980.

Loewald, H. W. (1980). *Papers on Psychoanalysis.* New Haven, CT: Yale University Press.

López, B. (1972). Descubrimiento de la fantasia e invención de la interpretación en el abordaje técnico de los trastornos de caracter. *Revista de Psicoanálisis, 29*: 189–215.

López, B. (1987). Sindrome fronterizo: cuerpo, encuadre y discurso. *Psicoanálisis, 9*: 75–98.

López, B., & Navarro de López, S. (1981). Voyeurismo y tarea interpretiva. *Psicoanálisis, 3*: 623–647.

López, B., & Rabih, M. (1966). Entrevista inicial y contraidentificación proyectiva.

Symposium on *El proceso analítico. Transferencia y contratransferencia*. Argentine Psychoanalytic Association (APA). *Actas*.

Lorand, S. (1946). *Technique of Psychoanalytic Therapy*. New York: International University Press.

Lorenz, K. (1965). *Evolution and the Modification of Behaviour*. Chicago, IL: Chicago University Press.

Lorenzer, A. (1970). *Sprachzerstörung und Rekonstruktion. Vorarbeiten zu einer Metatheorie der Psychoanalyse*. Frankfurt: Suhrkamp Verlag.

Lorenzer, A. (1972). *Zur Begründung einer materialistischen Sozialisationstheorie*. Frankfurt: Suhrkamp Verlag.

Lorenzer, A. (1973). *Über den Gegenstand der Psychoanalyse oder: Sprache und Interaktion*. Frankfurt: Suhrkamp Verlag.

Löwenstein, R. M. (1951). The problem of interpretation. *Psychoanalytic Quarterly, 20*: 1–14.

Löwenstein, R. M. (1954). Some remarks on defences, autonomous ego and psychoanalytic technique. *International Journal of Psycho-Analysis, 35*: 188–193.

Löwenstein, R. M. (1957). Some thoughts on interpretation in the theory and practice of psychoanalysis. *Psychoanalytic Study of the Child, 12* (pp. 127–150). New York: International Universities Press. [Also in: L. Paul (Ed.), *Psychoanalytic Clinical Interpretation*. London: Collier-Macmillan, 1963.]

Löwenstein, R. M. (1958). Remarks on some variations in psycho-analytic technique. *International Journal of Psycho-Analysis, 39*: 202–210.

Macalpine, I. (1950). The development of the transference. *Psychoanalytic Quarterly, 19*: 501–539.

Maci, G. A. (1979). *La otra escena de lo real. Topologia del significante y espacios del sujeto*. Buenos Aires: Nueva Visión.

Maci, G. A. (1983). *La repetición significante. Objeto y marca*. Buenos Aires: Candil.

Mack Brunswick, R. (1928a). A supplement to Freud's "History of an infantile neurosis". *International Journal of Psycho-Analysis, 9*: 439–476. [Also in: R. Fliess (Ed.), *The Psycho-Analytic Reader*. New York: International Universities Press, 1948.]

Mack Brunswick, R. (1928b). The analysis of a case of paranoia. Delusion of jealousy. *Journal of Nervous and Mental Diseases, 70* (1929): 1–22. [First published in *Internationale Zeitschrift fur Psychoanalyse, 14*: 458.]

Mack Brunswick, R. (1940). The preoedipal phase of the libido development. *Psychoanalytic Quarterly, 9*: 293–319. [Also in: R. Fliess (Ed.), *The Psycho-Analytic Reader* (p. 231). New York: International Universities Press, 1948.]

Mahler, M. S. (1952). On child psychosis and schizophrenia: autistic and symbiotic infantile psychoses. In: *Selected Papers, Vol. 1* (Chap. 7, pp. 131–153), 1979.

Mahler, M. S. (1958). Autism and symbiosis, two extreme disturbances of identity. *International Journal of Psycho-Analysis, 39*: 77–83. [Also in: *Selected Papers, Vol. 1* (Chap. 9), 1979.]

Mahler, M. S. (1967). On human symbiosis and the vicissitudes of individuation. In: *Selected Papers, Vol. 2* (Chap. 6, pp. 77–97), 1979.

Mahler, M. S. (1972a). On the first three subphases of the separation–individuation process. In: *Selected Papers, Vol. 2* (Chap. 8, pp. 119–130), 1979.

Mahler, M. S. (1972b). Rapprochement subphase of the separation–individuation process. In: *Selected Papers, Vol. 2* (Chap. 9, pp. 131–148), 1979.

Mahler, M. S. (1979). *Selected Papers, Vols. 1 & 2.* New York: Jason Aronson.
Mahler, M. S., Pine, F., & Bergman, A. (1975). *The Psychological Birth of the Human Infant.* New York: Basic Books. [Reprinted London: Karnac Books, 1985.]
Mahony, P. J. (1986). *Freud and the Rat Man.* New Haven & London: Yale Universities Press.
Maldavsky, D. (1985). El trabajo de construcción en el análisis. Problemas teóricos y clinicos. *Actualidad Psicológica, 11* (109): 18–24.
Maldavsky, D. (1986). *Estructuras narcisistas: constitución y trasformaciones.* Buenos Aires: Amorrortu Editores.
Maldavsky, D. (1988). Clinica psicoanalítica: las modalidades trasgresoras. *Gaceta Psicológica, 16:* 27–29.
Maldonado, J. L. (1975). "Impasse" y "mala fe" en el análisis de un paciente. *Revista de Psicoanálisis, 32:* 115–141.
Maldonado, J. L. (1979). Impasse y pseudoproceso psicoanalítico. *Psicoanálisis, 1:* 569–602.
Maldonado, J. L. (1983). Compromiso del analista en el impasse psicoanalítico. *Revista de Psicoanálisis, 40:* 205–218.
Mandler, G., & Kaplan, W. K. (1956). Subjective evaluation and reinforcing effect of a verbal stimulus. *Science, 124:* 582.
Masotta, O. (1969). Psicoanálisis y estructuralismo. In: *Introducción a la lectura de Jacques Lacan* (pp. 13–144). Buenos Aires: Proteo, 1970.
Masotta, O. (1977). Prólogo a Jacques Lacan. *Los cuatro principios fundamentales del Psicoanálisis.* Barcelona: Barral, 1977.
Matte Blanco, I. (1988). *Thinking, Feeling, and Being. Clinical Reflections on the Fundamental Antinomy of Human Beings and World.* London: Routledge.
McDougall, J. (1985). *Theatres of the Mind. Illusion and Truth on the Psychoanalytic Stage.* New York: Basic Books.
McDougall, J. (1989). *Theatres of the Body. A Psychoanalytic Approach to Psychosomatic Illness.* London: Free Association Books.
Mead, G. H. (1934). *Mind, Self and Society.* Chicago, IL: University of Chicago Press.
Meltzer, D. (1966). The relation of anal masturbation to projective identification. *International Journal of Psycho-Analysis, 47:* 335–342.
Meltzer, D. (1967). *The Psychoanalytical Process.* London: Heinemann. [Reprinted Perthshire: Clunie Press.]
Meltzer, D. (1968). Tyranny. British Psychoanalytic Society. *Scientific Bulletin, 24.* [Also in: *Sexual States of Mind* (Chap. 20), 1973.]
Meltzer, D. (1973). *Sexual States of Mind.* Perthshire: Clunie Press.
Meltzer, D. (1975). Adhesive identification. *Contemporary Psycho-Analysis, 2:* 289–310.
Meltzer, D. (1977). Una técnica de interrupción de la impasse analítica. In: L. Grinberg (Ed.), *Prácticas psicoanalíticas comparadas en las neurosis* (Chap. 8, pp. 165–176). Buenos Aires: Paidós, 1977.
Meltzer, D. (1978). *The Kleinian Development, Vols. 1–3.* Perthshire: Clunie Press.
Meltzer, D. (1981). The Kleinian expansion of Freud's metapsychology. *International Journal of Psycho-Analysis, 62:* 177–185. [Also in: *Dream Life* (Chap. 3), 1983.]
Meltzer, D. (1983). *Dream Life. A Re-examination of the Psychoanalytical Theory and Technique.* Perthshire: Clunie Press.
Meltzer, D., Bremner, J., Hoxter, S., Weddell, D., & Wittenberg, I. (1975). *Explorations in Autism. A Psychoanalytical Study.* Perthshire: Clunie Press.

Meneghini, L. C. (1976). Algunas consideraçoes sobre elaboraçao, "working through" e luto. Unpublished.

Menninger, K. (1952). A *Manual for Psychiatric Case Study.* New York: Grune & Stratton.

Menninger, K. (1958). *Theory of Psychoanalytic Technique.* New York: Basic Books.

Miller, J.-A. (1969). La suture. (Elements de la logique du signifiant). *Cahiers pour l'analyse, 1:* 39–51.

Miller, J.-A. (1979). *Cinco conferencias caraqueñas sobre Lacan.* Caracas: Ateneo de Caracas.

Mirsky, I. A., et al. (1950). Pepsinogen (uropepsin) excretion as an index of the influence of various life situations on gastric secretion. *Proceeding A. Research Nervous & Mental Diseases, 29:* 638.

Mirsky, I. A., et al. (1952). Blood plasma pepsinogen, I & II. *Journal of Laboratory and Clinical Medicine, 40* (1–2.)

Mom, J. (1956). Algunas consideraciones sobre el concepto de distancia en las fobias. *Revista de Psicoanálisis, 13:* 430–435.

Money-Kyrle, R. E. (1956). Normal counter-transference and some of its deviations. *International Journal of Psycho-Analysis, 37:* 360–366. [Also in: *Collected Papers* (Chap. 21), 1978.]

Money-Kyrle, R. E. (1965). Megalomania. In: *Collected Papers* (Chap. 26, pp. 378–388), 1978.

Money-Kyrle, R. E. (1968). Cognitive development. *International Journal of Psycho-Analysis, 49:* 691–698. [Also in: *Collected Papers* (Chap. 31), 1978.]

Money-Kyrle, R. E. (1971). The aim of psycho-analysis. *International Journal of Psycho-Analysis, 52:* 103–107. [Also in: *Collected Papers* (Chap. 33), 1978.]

Money-Kyrle, R. E. (1977). On being a psycho-analyst. In: *Collected Papers* (Chap. 35, pp. 457–465), 1978.

Money-Kyrle, R. E. (1978). *Collected Papers.* Ed. D. Meltzer. Perthshire: Clunie Press.

Moore, B. E. (1968). Contribution to Symposium on acting out. *International Journal of Psycho-Analysis, 49:* 182–184.

Moore, B. E., & Fine, B. D. (1968). *A Glossary of Psychoanalytic Terms and Concepts,* 2nd ed. New York: The American Psychoanalytic Association.

Morris, C. W. (1938). Foundations of the theory of signs. In: O. Neurath (Ed.), *International Encyclopedia of Unified Science.* Chicago, IL: University of Chicago Press.

Mostardeiro, A. L. B., Pechansky, I., et al. (1974). O impasse psicoanalítico. *Revista Latino Americana de Psicoanálisis, 1* (1).

Moura Ferrao, L. (1974). O impasse analítico. *Revista Latino Americana de Psicoanálisis, 1* (1).

Nacht, S. (1962). The curative factors in psychoanalysis. *International Journal of Psycho-Analysis, 43:* 206–211.

Nacht, S. (1971). *Guérir avec Freud.* Paris: Payot.

Nacht, S., & Lebovici, S. (1958). Indications and contraindications for psychoanalysis of adults. In: S. Nacht et al., *Psychoanalysis of Today.* New York/ London: Grune & Stratton, 1959.

Nacht, S., et al. (Eds.) (1958). *Psychoanalysis of Today.* New York/London: Grune & Stratton, 1959.]

Nagel, E. (1961). *The Structure of Science.* London: Routledge & Kegan Paul.

Nasio, J. D. (1984). Lo inconciente, la transferencia y la interpretación del psico-analista: una visión lacaniana. In: J. D. Nasio (Ed.), *En los limites de la trans-ferencia*. Buenos Aires: Nueva Visión, 1987.

Navarro de López, S. (1980). Tres formas de resistencias iniciales: pseudo-identidad, reversión de la perspectiva y relación adictiva. *Psicoanálisis*, 2: 1137–1165.

Nunberg, H. (1920). On the catatonic attack. In: *The Practice and Theory of Psycho-analysis*. New York: Nervous & Mental Diseases Company, 1948.

Nunberg, H. (1926). The will to recovery. *International Journal of Psycho-Analysis, 7*: 64–78.

Nunberg, H. (1932). *Principles of Psychoanalysis. Their Application to the Neuroses*. Prologue by Sigmund Freud. New York: International Universities Press, 1955.

Nunberg, H. (1937). Symposium on the theory of the therapeutic results of psycho-analysis. *International Journal of Psycho-Analysis, 18*: 161–169.

Nunberg, H. (1951). Transference and reality. *International Journal of Psycho-Analysis, 32: 1–9*.

Olagaray, J. (1980). Encuadre, espacio interno y fase final de análisis. Presented to the Mendoza Psychoanalytic Society. Unpublished.

Olinick, S. L. (1954). Some considerations of the use of questioning as a psycho-analytic technique. *Journal of the American Psychoanalytic Association, 2*: 57–66.

Olinick, S. L. (1964). The negative therapeutic reaction. *International Journal of Psycho-Analysis, 45*: 540–548.

Orr, D. W. (1954). Transference and countertransference: a historical survey. *Journal of the American Psychoanalytic Association, 2:* 621–669.

Painceira, A. J. (1979). Problemas técnicos en el análisis de pacientes esquizoides. *Psicoanálisis, 1*: 407–434.

Painceira, A. J. (1987). La patologia narcisista: una revisión a la luz de los aportes de Donald Winnicott acerca del self verdadero y falso. *Neuropsiquiatria Inter-nacional, 10*: 5–17.

Painceira, A. J. (1989). Nacimiento y desarrollo del self a partir de la obra de Winni-cott. *Psicoanálisis, 11*: 257–280.

Paul, L. (Ed.) (1963). *Psychoanalytic Clinical Interpretation*. London: Collier-Macmillan

Payne, S. (1950). Short communication on criteria for terminating analysis. *Interna-tional Journal of Psycho-Analysis, 31*: 205.

Paz, C. A. (1964). Actualización: el paciente fronterizo en la psicopatología actual y su importancia en Psicoanálisis. *Revista de Psicoanálisis, 21*: 239–258.

Paz, C. A. (1969). Reflexiones técnicas sobre el proceso analítico en los pacientes fronterizos. *Revista de Psicoanálisis, 26*: 571–630.

Paz, C. A., Pelento, M. L., & Olmos de Paz, T. (1976–77). *Estructuras y estados fronterizos en los niños, adolescentes y adultos, Vols. 1–2*. Buenos Aires: Nueva Visión.

Paz, C. A., et al. (1980). *Analizabilidad y momentos vitales*. Valencia: Naullibres.

Perrota, A. L. A. (1974). Las intervenciones no interpretativas. *Revista de Psicoanálisis, 31*: 567–625.

Petot, J. M. (1979). *Melanie Klein. Premières découvertes et premier système*. Paris: Dunod. [*Melanie Klein, Vol. 1: First Discoveries and First System, 1919–1932* (trans-lated by Christine Trollope). New York: International Universities Press, 1990.]

Pichon Rivière, E. J. (1946). Contribución a la teoría psicoanalítica de la esquizo-frenia. *Revista de Psicoanálisis, 4*: 1–22.

Pichon Rivière, E. J. (1951). Algunas observaciones sobre la transferencia en los pacientes psicóticos. *Revista de Psicoanálisis, 18* (1961): 131–138.

Pichon Rivière, E. J., et al. (1960). Técnica de los grupos operativos. *Acta Neuropsiquiatrica Argentina, 6*: 32–38.

Poland, W. S. (1975). Tact as a psychoanalytic function. *International Journal of Psycho-Analysis, 56*: 155–162.

Polito, R. C. (1979). Evaluación del proceso analítico. *Psicoanálisis, 1*: 205–220.

Pontalis, J. B. (1979). Non, deux fois non. Tentative de définition et de demantèlement de la "réaction thérapeutique négative". *Nouvelle Revue de Psychanalyse, 24* (1981).

Popper, K. R. (1953). Science: conjectures and refutations. In: *Conjectures and Refutations, 1963*.

Popper, K. R. (1958). *The Logic of Scientific Discovery*. London: Hutchinson.

Popper, K. R. (1963). *Conjectures and Refutations. The Growth of Scientific Knowledge*. London: Routledge & Kegan Paul.

Popper, K. R. (1972). *Objective Knowledge: An Evolutionary Approach*. Oxford: Clarendon Press.

Puget, J., & Wender, L. (1982). Analista y paciente en mundos superpuestos. Commentary by M. I. Siquier & R. Serebriany. *Psicoanálisis, 4*: 503–536.

Quinodoz, J. M. (1988). Les interpretations de l'angoisse de separation dans la cure psychanalytique. XLVIII Congrès des psychanalystes de la langue française des pays Romans. Geneva, 12–15 May, 1988. Geneva: Private publication.

Rabih, M. (1981). La seudoalianza terapéutica. Algunas de sus manifestaciones clinicas. *Psicoanálisis, 3*: 169–191.

Racker, H. (1948). A contribution to the problem of counter-transference. *International Journal of Psycho-Analysis, 34* (1953): 313–324. [Also as "The countertransference neurosis", in *Transference and Countertransference, 1968*.]

Racker, H. (1952). Considerations on the theory of transference. In: *Transference and Countertransference, 1968*.

Racker, H. (1953). The meanings and uses of countertransference. In: *Transference and Countertransference, 1968*.

Racker, H. (1954). Psycho-analytic technique and the analyst's unconscious mania. In: *Transference and Countertransference, 1968*.

Racker, H. (1956). Counterresistance and interpretation. In: *Transference and Countertransference, 1968*.]

Racker, H. (1958a). Psycho-analytic technique. In: *Transference and Countertransference, 1968*.

Racker, H. (1958b). Classical and present techniques in psycho-analysis. In: *Transference and Countertransference, 1968*.

Racker, H. (1958c). Analysis of transference through the patient's relations with the interpretation. In: *Transference and Countertransference, 1968*.

Racker, H. (1960). *Estudios sobre técnica psicoanalítica*. Buenos Aires: Paidós. [*Transference and Countertransference, 1968*.]

Racker, H. (1968). *Transference and Countertransference*. London: Hogarth. [Reprinted London: Karnac Books, 1982.]

Radó, S. (1925). The economic principle in psycho-analytic technique. *International Journal of Psycho-Analysis, 6*: 35–44.

Radó, S. (1926). The psychic effects of intoxicants: an attempt to evolve a psychoanalytical theory of morbid cravings. *International Journal of Psycho-Analysis, 7*: 396–413.

Rangell, L. (1954). Similarities and differences between psychoanalysis and dynamic psychotherapy. *Journal of the American Psychoanalytic Association, 2*: 734–744.

Rangell, L. (1966). An overview of the ending of an analysis. In: R. E. Litman (Ed.), *Psychoanalysis in the Americas.* New York: International Universities Press (Chap. 7, pp. 141–173), 1966.

Rangell, L. (1968a). The psychoanalytic process. *International Journal of Psycho-Analysis, 49*: 19–26.

Rangell, L. (1968b). A point of view on acting out. *International Journal of Psycho-Analysis, 49*: 195–201.

Rangell, L. (1985). On the theory of theory in psychoanalysis and the relation of theory to psychoanalytic therapy. *Journal of the American Psychoanalytic Association, 33*: 59–92.

Rank, O. (1924). *The Trauma of Birth.* London: Routledge & Kegan Paul.

Rapaport, D. (1942). The history of the awakening of insight. In: *Collected Papers* (Chap. 8, pp. 100–112), 1967.

Rapaport, D. (1951). The autonomy of the ego. In: *Collected Papers* (Chap. 31, pp. 357–367), 1967. [First published in *Bulletin of the Menninger Clinic, 15* (1951): 113–123.]

Rapaport, D. (1957). The theory of ego autonomy: a generalization. In: *Collected Papers* (Chap. 57, pp. 722–744), 1967.

Rapaport, D. (1959). *The Structure of Psychoanalytic Theory: A Systematizing Attempt.* New York: Psychological Issues (Chap. 6), 1960.

Rapaport, D. (1967). *Collected Papers.* Merton M. Gill (Ed.). New York: Basic Books.

Rapela, D. J. (1982). Relación transferencia–contratransferencia. *Revista Chilena de Psicoanálisis, 4*: 41–45.

Rappaport, E. A. (1956). The first dream in an erotized transference. *International Journal of Psycho-Analysis, 40* (1959): 240–245.

Rascovsky, A. (1960). *El psiquismo fetal.* Buenos Aires: Paidós.

Rees, K. (1978). The child understanding of his past. *Psychoanalytic Study of the Child, 33* (pp. 237–259). New York: International Universities Press.

Reich, A. (1950). On the termination of analysis. *International Journal of Psycho-Analysis. 31*: 179–183.

Reich, A. (1951). On counter-transference. *International Journal of Psycho-Analysis, 32*: 25–31.

Reich, A. (1966). Empathy and countertransference. In: *Psychoanalytic Contributions.* New York: International Universities Press, 1973. [Quoted by Levy, 1985.]

Reich, W. (1926). Zur Technik der Deutung und der Widerstandsanalyse. *Internationale Zeitschrift fur Psychoanalyse, 13* (1927). [Also in *Character Analysis* (Chap. 3, pp. 36–49), 1933.]

Reich, W. (1927). Über Charakter Analyse. *Internationale Zeitschrift fur Psychoanalyse, 14* (1928): 180. [Also in R. Fliess (Ed.), *The Psycho-Analytic Reader* (pp. 106–123). New York: International Universities Press, 1948. Also in *Character Analysis* (Chap. 4, pp. 50–105), 1933.]

Reich, W. (1933). *Character Analysis.* New York: Orgone Institute Press, 1945.

Reichenbach, H. (1938). *Experience and Prediction.* Chicago, IL: Chicago University Press.

Reid, J. R., & Finesinger, J. E. (1952). The role of insight in psycho-therapy. *American Journal of Psychiatry, 108*: 726–734.

Reider, N. (1957). Transference psychosis. *Journal of the Hillside Hospital, 6*: 131–149.

Reik, T. (n.d.). The psychological meaning of silence. *Psychoanalytical Review, 55* (2) (1968): 172–186.

Reik, T. (1924). Some remarks on the study of resistances. *International Journal of Psycho-Analysis, 5*: 141–154.

Reik, T. (1933). New ways in psycho-analytic technique. *International Journal of Psycho-Analysis, 14*: 321–334.

Reik, T. (1937). *Surprise and the Psycho-Analyst.* New York: Dutton.

Reik, T. (1949a). *The Inner Experience of a Psychoanalyst.* London: Allen & Unwin.

Reik, T. (1949b). In the beginning is silence. In: *The Inner Experience of a Psychoanalyst* (Chap. 12, pp. 121–126), 1949a.

Resnik, S. (1967). La experiencia del espacio en el "setting" analítico. *Revista Uruguaya de Psicoanálisis, 9*: 293–308.

Resnik, S. (1969). Teoría y técnica psicoanalítica de la psicosis. In: L. Grinberg (Ed.), *Prácticas psicoanalíticas comparadas en las psicosis* (Chap. 7, pp. 167–200). Buenos Aires: Paidós, 1977.

Resnik, S. (1978). *Personne et psychose. Études sur le langage du corps.* Paris: Payot.

Resnik, S. (1986). *L'esperienza psicótica.* Turin: Boringhieri.

Rexford, E. N. (1962). *A Developmental Approach to Problems of Acting Out,* 2nd ed. New York: International Universities Press, 1978.

Richfield, J. (1954). An analysis of the concept of insight. *Psychoanalytic Quarterly, 23*: 398–408. [Also in L. Paul (Ed.), *Psychoanalytic Clinical Interpretation* (pp. 93–111), London: Collier: Macmillan, 1963.]

Rickman, J. (1950). On the criteria for the termination of an analysis. *International Journal of Psycho-Analysis, 31*: 200–201. [Also in *Selected Contributions* (Chap. 16), 1957.]

Rickman, J. (1951). Number and the human sciences. In: *Selected Contributions* (Chap. 22, pp. 218–223), 1957.

Rickman, J. (1957). *Selected Contributions to Psycho-Analysis.* London: Hogarth Press.

Riesenberg, R. (1970). The mirror: a perverse sexual fantasy in a woman, seen as a defence against psychotic breakdown. *British Psycho-Analytical Society Scientific Bulletin, 37.* [*Revista de Psicoanálisis, 27*: 793–826.]

Riesenberg Malcolm, R. (1986). Interpretation: the past in the present. *International Review of Psycho-Analysis, 13*: 433–443.

Ríos, C. (1984). Origenes y alcances de la teoría significante. *Psicoanálisis, 6*: 111–130.

Riviere, J. (1932). Jealousy as a mechanism of defence. *International Journal of Psycho-Analysis, 13*: 414–424. [Also in A. Hughes (Ed.), *The Inner World and Joan Riviere: Collected Papers 1920–1958.* London: Karnac Books, 1991.]

Riviere, J. (1936a). A contribution to the analysis of the negative therapeutic reaction. *International Journal of Psycho-Analysis, 17*: 304–320. [Also in A. Hughes (Ed.), *The Inner World and Joan Riviere: Collected Papers 1920–1958.* London: Karnac Books, 1991.]

Riviere, J. (1936b). On the genesis of psychical conflict in earliest infancy. *International Journal of Psycho-Analysis, 17*: 395–422. [Also in A. Hughes (Ed.), *The Inner World and Joan Riviere: Collected Papers 1920–1958.* London: Karnac Books, 1991.]

Rodrigué, G. T. de (1966). Sobre la formulación de la interpretación. In: E. Rodrigué

& G. T. de Rodrigué, *El contexto del proceso analítico* (Chap. 5, pp. 108–119). Buenos Aires: Paidós.

Rolla, E. H. (1972). La entrevista clinica. *Revista de Psicoanálisis, 29:* 603–643.

Romanowski, R., & Vollmer, G. (1968). A regressao no processo analítico. Regressao e angüstia de separaçao. In: S. P. Annes et al. (1974), *Estudios psicoanalíticos* (pp. 76–74). Porto Alegre: private publication.

Rosen, J. N. (1963). "Acting-out" and "acting-in". *American Journal of Psychotherapy, 17:* 390–403.

Rosen, J. N. (1965). The concept of "acting in". In: L. A. Abt & S. L. Weissman (Eds.), *Acting Out. Theoretical and Clinical Aspects* (Chap. 2, pp. 20–29). New York: Grune & Stratton, 1965.

Rosen, V. H. (1967). Disorders of communication in psycho-analysis. *Journal of the American Psychoanalytic Association, 15:* 467–490.

Rosenfeld, D. (1972). El paciente drogadicto: guia clinica y evolución psicopatológica en el tratamiento psicoanalítico. *Revista de Psicoanálisis, 29:* 99–135. [In: *The Psychotic. Aspects of the Personality.* London: Karnac Books, 1991.]

Rosenfeld, D. (1975). Trastornos en la piel y el esquema corporal. Identificación proyectiva y el cuento infantil "Piel de Asno". *Revista de Psicoanálisis, 32:* 309–348.

Rosenfeld, D. (1980). The handling of resistances in adult patients. *International Journal of Psycho-Analysis, 61:* 71–83. [Also in *The Psychotic. Aspects of the Personality.* London: Karnac Books, 1991.]

Rosenfeld, H. A. (1952a). Notes on the psycho-analysis of the superego conflict in an acute schizophrenic patient. *International Journal of Psycho-Analysis, 33:* 111–131. [Also in *Psychotic States* (Chap. 4), 1965.]

Rosenfeld, H. A. (1952b). Transference-phenomena and transference-analysis in an acute catatonic schizophrenic patient. *International Journal of Psycho-Analysis, 33:* 452–464. [Also in *Psychotic States* (Chap. 5), 1965.]

Rosenfeld, H. A. (1960). On drug addiction. *International Journal of Psycho-Analysis, 41:* 467–475. [Also in *Psychotic States* (Chap. 7), 1965.]

Rosenfeld, H. A. (1964a). An investigation into need of neurotic and psychotic patients to act out during analysis. In: *Psychotic States* (Chap. 12), 1965.

Rosenfeld, H. A. (1964b). On the psychopathology of narcissism: a clinical approach. *International Journal of Psycho-Analysis, 45:* 332–337. [Also in *Psychotic States* (Chap. 10), 1965.]

Rosenfeld, H. A. (1965). *Psychotic States.* London: Hogarth. [Reprinted London: Karnac Books, 1985.]

Rosenfeld, H. A. (1971). A clinical approach to the psychoanalytic theory of the life and death instincts: an investigation into the aggressive aspects of narcissism. *International Journal of Psycho-Analysis, 52:* 169–178.

Rosenfeld, H. A. (1972). A critical appreciation of James Strachey's paper on the nature of the therapeutic action of psychoanalysis. *International Journal of Psycho-Analysis, 53:* 455–461.

Rosenfeld, H. A. (1975a). Negative therapeutic reaction. In: P. L. Giovacchini (Ed.), *Tactics and Techniques in Psycho-Analytic Therapy, Vol. 2* (Chap. 7, pp. 217–228). New York: Jason Aronson, 1972.

Rosenfeld, H. A. (1975b). Notas sobre algunos factores terapéuticos en Psicoanálisis. Lecture at Argentine Psychoanalytic Association (APA). Unpublished.

Rosenfeld, H. A. (1978). Notes on the psychopathology and psychoanalytic treatment of some borderline patients. *International Journal of Psycho-Analysis, 59*: 215–221.

Rosenfeld, H. A. (1987). *Impasse and Interpretation*. London/New York: Tavistock Publications.

Rosolato, G. (1966). Étude des perversions sexuelles à partir du fetichisme. In: P. Aulagnier-Spairani et al., *Le désir et la perversion*. Paris: Ed. du Seuil, 1967.

Ruesch, J. (1957). *Disturbed Communication*. New York: W. W. Norton.

Ruesch, J. (1961). *Therapeutic Communication*. New York: W. W. Norton.

Rycroft, C. (1956). The nature and function of the analyst's communication to the patient. *International Journal of Psycho-Analysis, 37*: 469–472. [Also in: *Imagination and Reality: Psycho-Analytical Essays*. London: Hogarth; reprinted London: Karnac Books, 1987.]

Sachs, H. (1923). Zur Genese der Perversionen. *Internationale Zeitschrift fur Psychoanalyse, 9*: 172. [Also in: *Psychoanalytic Quarterly, 55* (1986): 477–488.]

Sachs, H. (1925). Metapsychological points of view in technique and theory. *International Journal of Psycho-Analysis, 6*: 5–12.

Sandler, J. (1988a). The concept of projective identification. In: *Projection, Identification, Projective Identification* (Chap. 2, pp. 12–26), 1988b.

Sandler, J. (Ed.) (1988b). *Projection, Identification, Projective Identification*. London: Karnac Books.

Sandler, J., Dare, C., & Holder, A. (1973). *The Patient and the Analyst. The Clinical Framework of Psychoanalysis*. London: Allen & Unwin. [Reprinted London: Karnac Books, 1979.]

Sandler, J., & Sandler, A.-M. (1983). The "second censorship", the "three box model" and some technical implications. *International Journal of Psycho-Analysis, 64*: 413–425.

Sandler, J., & Sandler, A.-M. (1984). The past unconscious, the present unconscious, and interpretation of the transference. *Psychoanalytic Inquiry, 4*: 367–399.

Sandler, J., & Sandler, A.-M. (1987). The past unconscious, the present unconscious and the vicissitudes of guilt. *International Journal of Psycho-Analysis, 68*: 331–341.

Sandler, J., Kennedy, H., & Tyson, R. L. (1980). *The Technique of Child Psychoanalysis. Discussions with Anna Freud*. London: Hogarth Press. [Reprinted London: Karnac Books, 1990.]

Sarton, G. (1952). *Ancient Science Through the Golden Age of Greece*. Cambridge, MA: Harvard University Press.

Saussure, F. de (1916). *Cours de linguistique générale*. Published by C. Bally & A. Sechehaye, with the collaboration of A. Riedlinger. Paris: Payot, 1931. [*Course in General Linguistics*. New York, Philosophical Library, 1959.]

Schenquerman, N. (1978). Análisis interminable por iatrogenia en el uso de la interpretación y su efecto placebo. First Symposium, Buenos Aires Psychoanalytic Association (APdeBA). *Actas*.

Schmideberg, M. (1935). Reassurance as a means of analytic technique. *International Journal of Psycho-Analysis, 16*: 307–324.

Schur, M. (1972). *Freud: Living and Dying*. London: Hogarth Press.

Schust, J. P. (1970). Mesa redonda sobre "Construcciones en el análisis", de Sigmund Freud. M. Abadi, A. Aberastury, R. Avenburg, G. Roger Garcia Reinoso, D. Liberman & L. Wender, participants. *Revista de Psicoanálisis, 27*: 723–761.

Scott, W. C. M. (1949). The body scheme in psychotherapy. *British Journal of Medical Psychology*, 22.

Searle, J. R. (1969). *Speech Acts. An Essay in the Philosophy of Language.* Cambridge: Cambridge University Press.

Searles, H. F. (1961). Phases of patient–therapist interaction in the psycho-therapy of chronic schizophrenia. *British Journal of Medical Psychology*, 3: 169. [Also in: *Collected Papers on Schizophrenia*, 1965.]

Searles, H. F. (1963). Transference psychosis in the psychotherapy of chronic schizophrenia. *International Journal of Psycho-Analysis*, 44: 249–281. [Also in: *Collected Papers on Schizophrenia*, 1965.]

Searles, H. F. (1965). *Collected Papers on Schizophrenia and Related Subjects.* London: Hogarth. [Reprinted London: Karnac Books, 1986.]

Sechehaye, M. A. (1951). *Symbolic Realization.* New York: International Universities Press.

Segal, H. (1950). Some aspects of the analysis of a schizophrenia. *International Journal of Psycho-Analysis*, 31: 268–278. [Also in: *The Work of Hanna Segal*, 1981.]

Segal, H. (1954). A note on schizoid mechanisms underlying phobia formation. *International Journal of Psycho-Analysis*, 35: 238–241. [Also in: *The Work of Hanna Segal* (Chap. 11), 1981.]

Segal, H. (1956). Depression in the schizophrenic. *International Journal of Psycho-Analysis*, 37: 339–343. [Also in: *The Work of Hanna Segal* (Chap. 9), 1981.]

Segal, H. (1957). Notes on symbol-formation. *International Journal of Psycho-Analysis*, 38: 391–397. [Also in: *The Work of Hanna Segal* (Chap. 4), 1981.]

Segal, H. (1958). Fear of death. Notes on the analysis of an old man. *International Journal of Psycho-Analysis*, 39: 178–181. [Also in: *The Work of Hanna Segal* (Chap. 15), 1981.]

Segal, H. (1962). The curative factors in psycho-analysis. *International Journal of Psycho-Analysis*, 43: 212–217. [Also in: *The Work of Hanna Segal* (Chap. 5), 1981.]

Segal, H. (1964a). Symposium on fantasy. Fantasy and other mental process. *International Journal of Psycho-Analysis*, 45: 191–194. [Also in: *The Work of Hanna Segal* (Chap. 3), 1981.]

Segal, H. (1964b). *Introduction to the Work of Melanie Klein.* London: Heinemann. [2nd ed., London: Hogarth Press, 1975. Reprinted London: Karnac Books, 1988.]

Segal, H. (1978). On symbolism. *International Journal of Psycho-Analysis*, 59: 315–319.

Segal, H. (1979). *Klein.* Glasgow: William Collins Sons. [Reprinted London: Karnac Books, 1989.]

Segal, H. (1981). *The Work of Hanna Segal. A Kleinian Approach to Clinical Practice.* New York: Jason Aronson. [Reprinted London: Karnac Books, 1986.]

Segel, N. P. (1969). Narcissistic resistance. Panel reports. *Journal of the American Psychoanalytic Association*, 17: 941–954.

Sharpe, E. F. (1927). Symposium on child-analysis. *International Journal of Psycho-Analysis*, 8: 380–384.

Sharpe, E. F. (1930–31). The technique of psychoanalysis. *International Journal of Psycho-Analysis*, 11: 251–277 & 361–386; 12: 24–60. [Also in: *Collected Papers on Psycho-Analysis* (pp. 9–106). London: Hogarth Press, 1950.]

Silvestre, M. (1987a). El saber del psicoanalista. (Un comentario de "Variantes de la cura tipo"). In: E. Lorent, G. Miller, J.-A. Miller, et al., *El significante de la transferencia* (pp. 33–44). Buenos Aires: Manantial.

Silvestre, M. (1987b). *Demain la psychanalyse*. Paris: Novarin.

Simmel, E. (1948). Alcoholism and addiction. *Psychoanalytic Quarterly, 17*: 6–31.

Sor, D., & Gazzano, M. R. S. de (1988). *Cambio catastrófico. Psicoanálisis del darse cuenta*. Buenos Aires: Kargieman.

Speziale-Bagliacca, R. (1982). *Sulle spalle di Freud. Psicoanalisi e ideologia fallica*. Rome: Astrolabio-Ubaldini.

Spitz, R. A. (1956a). Transference: the analytical setting and its prototype. *International Journal of Psycho-Analysis, 37*: 380–385.

Spitz, R. A. (1956b). Countertransference comments on its varying role in the analytic situation. *Journal of the American Psychoanalytic Association, 4*: 256–265.

Spitz, R. A. (1957). *No and Yes. On the Genesis of Human Communication*. New York: International Universities Press.

Spitz, R. A. (1958). *La premiere année de la vie de l'enfant)*. Paris: Presses Universitaires de France. [*The First Years of Life*. New York: International Universities Press, 1966.]

Steiner, R. (1985). Some thoughts about tradition and change arising from an examination of the British Psychoanalytical Society's Controversial Discussions (1943–1944). *International Review of Psycho-Analysis, 12*: 27–71.

Steiner, R. (1989). Some introductory notes concerning the "Opening remarks" by James Strachey. British Psycho-Analytical Society. *Bulletin* (July).

Sterba, R. (1929). The dynamics of the dissolution of the transference resistance. *Psychoanalytic Quarterly, 9* (1940): 363–379. [First published in *Internationale Zeitschrift fur Psychoanalyse*.]

Sterba, R. (1934). The fate of the ego in analytic therapy. *International Journal of Psycho-Analysis, 15*: 117–126.

Sterba, R. (1975). The formative activity of the analyst. In: P. L. Giovacchini (Ed.), *Tactics and Techniques in Psychoanalytic Therapy, Vol. 2* (Chap. 8, pp. 229–238). New York: Jason Aronson, 1972.

Stern, A. (1938). Psychoanalytic investigation of and therapy in the borderline group of neurosis. *Psychoanalytic Quarterly, 7*: 467–489.

Stevenson, I. (1959). The psychiatric interview. In: S. Arieti (Ed.), *American Handbook of Psychiatry, Vol. 1* (pp. 197–214). New York: Basic Books.

Stone, L. (1954). The widening scope of indications for psycho-analysis. *Journal of the American Psychoanalytic Association, 2*: 567–594.

Stone, L. (1961). *The Psychoanalytic Situation*. New York: International Universities Press.

Strachey, J. (1934). The nature of the therapeutic action of psycho-analysis. *International Journal of Psycho-Analysis, 15*: 127–159.

Strachey, J. (1937). Symposium on the theory of the therapeutic results of psychoanalysis. *International Journal of Psycho-Analysis, 18*: 139–145.

Strachey, J. (1953). Footnote to *The Interpretation of Dreams* (Freud, 1900a). *S.E., 5*: 562.

Strachey, J. (1955). Editor's introduction to *Studies on Hysteria* (Freud, 1895d). *S.E., 2*: ix–xxviii.

Strachey, J. (1958). A comment to "The dynamics of transference" (Freud, 1912b). *S.E., 12*: 98.

Strachey, J. (1959). Editor's introduction to *Inhibitions, Symptoms and Anxiety* (Freud, 1926d). *S.E., 20*: 77–86.

Strachey, J. (1960). Editor's preface in *Jokes and Their Relation to the Unconscious* (Freud, 1905c). *S.E., 8:* 3–8.

Strachey, J. (1966a). Editor's introduction to "Papers on hypnotism and suggestion (1888–1892)". *S.E., 1:* 63–69.

Strachey, J. (1966b). Footnote to "A project for a scientific psychology", 1895 (Freud, 1950a [1887–1902]). *S.E., 1:* 373.

Strachey, J. (1989 [1941]). Opening remarks at a practical seminar. British Psycho-Analytical Society. *Bulletin* (July).

Suarez, J. C. (1977). El amor transferencia. Unpublished.

Sullivan, H. S. (1944–45). *The Psychiatric Interview.* New York: W. W. Norton.

Sulloway, F. J. (1979). *Freud, Biologist of the Mind. Beyond the Psychoanalytic Legend.* London: Burnett Books.

Szasz, T. S. (1963). The concept of transference. *International Journal of Psycho-Analysis, 44:* 432–443.

Thomä, H., & Kächele, H. (1987). *Psychoanalytic Practice.* Berlin: Springer-Verlag. [Reprinted London: Karnac Books, 1994.]

Tiger, L., & Fox, R. (1971). *The Imperial Animal.* New York: Dell, 1974.

Urtubey, L. (1971–72). El fetishismo como "solución" al Edipo temprano. *Revista Uruguaya de Psicoanálisis, 13:* 385–432.

Valeros, J. A. (1981). Hay una "microscopia" en psicología humana. Fourth Symposium, Buenos Aires Psychoanalytic Association (APdeBA). *Actas:* 126–138.

Wälder, R. (1936). The principle of multiple function. Observations on over-determination. *Psychoanalytic Quarterly, 5:* 45–62.

Wälder, R. (1937). The problem of the genesis of psychical conflict in earliest infancy. *International Journal of Psycho-Analysis, 18:* 406–473.

Wallerstein, R. S. (1965). The goals of psychoanalysis. A survey of analytic viewpoints. *Journal of the American Psychoanalytic Association, 13:* 748–770.

Wallerstein, R. S. (1967). Reconstruction and mastery in the transference psychosis. *Journal of the American Psychoanalytic Association, 15:* 551–583.

Wallerstein, R. S. (1979). Some thoughts about insight and psychoanalysis. Delivered to the Hampstead Clinic, London, November 1979. Unpublished.

Wallerstein, R. S. (1985). How does self psychology differ in practice? *International Journal of Psycho-Analysis, 66:* 391–404.

Wallerstein, R. S. (1986). *Forty-Two Lives in Treatment. A Study of Psychoanalysis and Psychotherapy.* New York/London: Guilford Press.

Wallerstein, R. S. (1988). One psychoanalysis or many? *International Journal of Psycho-Analysis, 69:* 5–21.

Weinshel, E. M. (1966). Severe regressive states during analysis. Panel report. *Journal of the American Psychoanalytic Association, 14:* 538–568.

Weinshel, E. M. (1971). The transference neurosis: a survey of the literature. *Journal of the American Psychoanalytic Association, 19:* 67–88.

Weinshel, E. M. (1984). Some observations of the psychoanalytic process. *Psychoanalytic Quarterly, 53:* 63–92.

Wender, L., Cvik, J., Cvik, N., & Stein, G. (1966). Comienzo y final de sesión. Dinámica de ciertos aspectos transferenciales y contratransferenciales. Argentine Psychoanalytic Association, (APA), X Symposium. *Actas.*

Widlocher, D. (1970). *Freud et le problème du changement.* Paris: Presses Universitaires de France.

Wilson, E. D. (1978). *On Human Nature*. London: Harvard University Press.

Winnicott, D. W. (1945). Primitive emotional development. *International Journal of Psycho-Analysis, 26*: 137–143. [Also in: *Through Paediatrics* (Chap. 12, pp. 145–156), 1958.]

Winnicott, D. W. (1947). Hate in the countertransference. *International Journal of Psycho-Analysis, 30* (1949): 69–74. [Also in: *Through Paediatrics* (Chap. 15, pp. 194–203), 1958.]

Winnicott, D. W. (1949). Mind and its relation to the psyche–soma. *British Journal of Medical Psychology, 27* (1954). [Also in: *Through Paediatrics* (Chap. 19, pp. 243–254), 1958.]

Winnicott, D. W. (1950). Aggression in relation to emotional development. In: *Through Paediatrics* (Chap. 16, pp. 204–218), 1958.

Winnicott, D. W. (1952). Psychosis and child care. *British Journal of Medical Psychology, 26* (1953). [Also in: *Through Paediatrics* (Chap. 17, pp. 219–228), 1958.]

Winnicott, D. W. (1953). Transitional objects and transitional phenomena. *International Journal of Psycho-Analysis, 34*: 89–97. [Also in: *Through Paediatrics* (Chap. 18, pp. 229–242), 1958.]

Winnicott, D. W. (1955). Metapsychological and clinical aspects of regression within the psycho-analytical set-up. *International Journal of Psycho-Analysis, 36*: 16–26. [Also in: *Through Paediatrics* (Chap. 22, pp. 278–294), 1958.]

Winnicott, D. W. (1956). On transference. *International Journal of Psycho-Analysis, 37*: 386–388. ["Clinical varieties of transference", in *Through Paediatrics* (Chap. 23, pp. 295–299), 1958. Also in R. Langs (Ed.), *Classics in Psychoanalytic Technique*. New York: Jason Aronson, 1981 (revised ed., 1990).]

Winnicott, D. W. (1958). *Through Paediatrics to Psycho-Analysis*. London: Hogarth Press, 1977. [Reprinted London: Karnac Books, 1991.]

Winnicott, D. W. (1960a). Ego distortion and the true and false self. In: *The Maturational Process* (Part 2, Chap. 4), 1965.

Winnicott, D. W. (1960b). Countertransference. *British Journal of Medical Psychology, 33*: 17–21. [Also in: *The Maturational Processes* (Part 2, Chap. 6), 1965.]

Winnicott, D. W. (1965). *The Maturational Processes and the Facilitating Environment*. London: Hogarth Press. [Barcelona: Ed. Laia, 1975. Reprinted London: Karnac Books, 1990.]

Winnicott, D. W. (1977). *The Piggle. An Account of the Psychoanalytic Treatment of a Little Girl*. New York: International Universities Press.

Wisdom, J. O. (1967). Testing an interpretation within a session. *International Journal of Psycho-Analysis, 48*: 44–52.

Wolmann, B. B. (1967). *Psychoanalytic Techniques*. New York: Basic Books.

Yampey, N. (1985). Sobre la comprensión psicoanalítica. *Revista de Psicoanálisis, 42*: 347–359.

Yorke, C. (1965). Some metapsychological aspects of interpretation. *British Journal of Medical Psychology, 38*: 27–42.

Yorke, C., Wiseberg, S., & Freeman, T. (1989). *Development and Psychopathology. Studies in Psychoanalytic Psychiatry*. New Haven, CT: Yale University Press.

Zac, J. (1968). Relación semana/fin de semana. Encuadre y acting-out. *Revista de Psicoanálisis, 25*: 27–91.

Zac, J. (1970). Consideraciones sobre el acting out y aspectos técnicos de su tratamiento. *Revista de Psicoanálisis, 27*: 307–364.

Zac, J. (1971). Un enfoque metodológico del establecimiento del encuadre. *Revista de Psicoanálisis, 28*: 593–610.

Zac, J. (1973). *Psicopatia.* Buenos Aires: Kargieman.

Zeligs, M. A. (1957). Acting in. A contribution to the meaning of some postural attitudes observed during analysis. *Journal of the American Psychoanalytic Association, 5*: 685–706.

Zetzel, E. R. (1956a). Current concepts of transference. *International Journal of Psycho-Analysis, 37*: 369–376.

Zetzel, E. R. (1956b). An approach to the relation between concept and content in psychoanalytic theory. *Psychoanalytic Study of the Child, 11.*

Zetzel, E. R. (1964). The analytic situation. In: R. E. Litman (Ed.), *Psychoanalysis in the Americas* (pp. 86–106). New York: International Universities Press, 1966.

Zetzel, E. R. (1965). The theory of therapy in relation to a developmental model of the psychic apparatus. *International Journal of Psycho-Analysis, 46*: 39–52.

Zetzel, E. R. (1966). El proceso analítico. In L. Grinberg et al. (Eds.), *Psicoanálisis en las Americas* (pp. 69–80). Buenos Aires: Paidós, 1982.

Zetzel, E. R. (1968) . The so-called good hysteric. *International Journal of Psycho-Analysis, 49*: 250–260.

Zetzel, E. R. (1969). The first psychoanalytic session. Unpublished.

Zetzel, E. R., & Meissner, W. W. (1974). *Basic Concepts of Psycho-Analytic Psychiatry.* New York: Basic Books.

Zilboorg, G. (1950). The emotional problem and the therapeutic role of insight. *Psychoanalytic Quarterly, 21* (1952): 1–24.

Zilboorg, G., & Henry, G. W. (1941). *A History of Medical Psychology.* New York: W. W. Norton.

INDEX

Abadi, M., on termination of analysis, 649
Aberastury, A., 650
  on child analysis, 27
Abraham, K., 151, 163, 198, 214, 372, 388,
      399, 400, 411, 423–424, 465–467,
      592, 620, 682, 741–743, 747, 751,
      758, 763, 801
  on age, 16, 17
  classification of, 466–467
  on fundamental rule, 391
  on hysteria and dementia praecox, 169
  on negative therapeutic reaction, 739–
     740
  on neurosis, 84–85
  on primary depression, 651–652
  treatment of manic-depressive patients
     by, 18
abreaction, 444
  and mutative interpretation, 454
abstinence, rule of, 12, 522–523
  and pertinence of information, 13
  and professional confidentiality, 12
accessibility, concept of, 33–35
Achaval, J., 468
act, neurotic, and acting out, 703–704
acting out, 700–737, 803–804
  and acting in, 733–735
  and action, 722–724
  and communication, 725–726
  and language, 713–714
  concept of, 701–702, 734–737
  and early development, 730–732
  equivalents, 719
  excessive, 715–716
  and impasse, 799, 800
  intentions of, 724–725
  and language, 713–714, 727–729
  and negative therapeutic reaction, 758–
    759
  and neurotic act, 703–704
  partial, 715–716
  and play, 729–730

  and primal objects, 714
  prototype of, 728
  and remembering, 705–706
  and repetition, 705–706
  and thought, 727–729
  and transference, 709–710
  verbal, 309
addiction, 202
  countertransference, 200–201
  transference, 198–201
  treatment of 198–201
adhesive identification, 583
Adler, A., 63, 333, 334, 398, 400
  on character, 400
  on masculine protest, 143
affect, and insight, 693–694
age:
  and analysability, 20
  role of in selection of patients, 15
agieren, 758
  [to act], 94
  [acting out], 733
  Freud's use of, 705
  vs. *handeln* [to act], 702
Agrippa, 3, 4
Ahumada, J. L., 143, 272, 685
  on projective identification, 785
Aichhorn, A., 18, 466
alcoholics, treatment of, 18, 200
Alexander, F., 279, 309, 391, 392, 445, 446,
    460, 591, 699, 740
  on superego, modification of, 442–443
alliance:
  pseudo-therapeutic, 249–250
  therapeutic, *see* therapeutic alliance
alter ego, transference, 166–168
altruistic surrender, 24
Álvarez, B., 326
Alvarez de Toledo, L., 424
  on interpretation, 464
ambivalence, 104
anaclitic–diatrophic relation, 613

negative therapeutic reaction (*continued*):
    and envy, 744–745, 753
    and guilt feeling, 737–738
    historical perspective, 747–748
    and idealization, 753
    and impasse, 799, 800–801
    indicators of, 749–750
    and internal objects, 750–751
    and lethargy, 745–746
    and masochism of ego, 738–739
    and need for punishment, 738–739
    and negative transference, 756–757
    and negativism, 757–758
    and symbiosis, 754–756
negativism, and negative therapeutic
        reaction, 757–758
Nemirovsky, C., 271
neopsychoanalysis, 7
neurosis, 218
    countertransference, *see*
            countertransference neurosis
    definition, 381
    infantile, 203–204
    and indications for analysis, 16
    narcissistic, 160
    obsessional, 466, 475
    and repetition, 95
    transference, *see* transference neurosis
    traumatic, 99, 116
    types of, 392
neurotic act, and acting out, 703–704
neurotic part of personality, vs. psychotic
        part of personality, 765–767
Nietzsche, F., 332–333
Non vixit dream, 381–385
normal person, analysis of, 22–23
notation, 315–316
NTR, *see* negative therapeutic reaction
Nunberg, H., 59, 170, 212, 394–395, 441, 664,
        789
    on desire for cure, 23–24
    on reversible perspective, 777
nymphomania:
    definition, 158–159
    transference, 158

object:
    internal, and insight, 697–699
    libido, 162
    love, primary, 209
    primal, 714–715
    relations:
        and countertransference, 281–292

development of, stages of, 611–612
    early, 211–212
    and narcissism, 208–210
    spurious, 788–789
    subjective, 184
obsessive, analysable, 31–32
Occam, W. of, 790
Oedipus complex, 26, 115, 120–122, 125, 370,
        574–575, 592, 739
    and depressive position, 212
    discovery of, 9
    stages of, 122–123
    early, 202–212
Olagaray, J., on setting, 524
Olinick, S. L., 314, 458
    on negative therapeutic reaction, 757–
        758
ontopsychoanalysis, 7

pact, analytic, *see* analytic contract
Painceira, A. J., 178, 180
    on schizoid and borderline, 185
    on transference psychosis, 151
Palo Alto school, 759, 760
Paneth, J., 381–385
Paracelsus, 3
paradoxical thinking, 759–760
parameter, pseudo-, 346
parent imago, idealized, 160
participant observer, 44–45
paternal metaphor, 123
Paul, L., 480
Pavlov, I. P., 362
payment, methods of, and psychoanalytic
        contract, 68–70
Payne, S., 410, 574, 633
    on termination of analysis, 650
Paz, C. A. O. de, 177, 178, 180
    on borderline:
        psychosis, 183–184
        structures and states, 177
    Pechansky, I., on impasse, 792–793
Pelento, M. L., 177
Penisneid [penis envy], 142
perception:
    vs. conception, 111–112
    and ego, 430
    microscopic, 470
    telescopic, 472
Perrotta, A. L. A., 407
personality:
    and analysability, 20
    of analyst, 613